1 MONTH OF
FREE
READING

at
www.ForgottenBooks.com

By purchasing this book you are eligible for one month membership to ForgottenBooks.com, giving you unlimited access to our entire collection of over 1,000,000 titles via our web site and mobile apps.

To claim your free month visit:
www.forgottenbooks.com/free921726

ISBN 978-0-260-00666-0
PIBN 10921726

CONTENTS.

GRAND ARMY OF THE REPUBLIC.

Department of Massachusetts. Headquarters, 167 Tremont St., Boston.

The Department of Massachusetts comprises seventy-eight (78) Posts, with over seven thousand (7,000) members. These Posts have all been organized and chartered since October, 1866, and the members are soldiers and sailors who served honorably in the army or navy during the late War of the Rebellion. This is strictly a charitable organization, and it does not take part in politics, nor in any questions of a partisan character.

OFFICERS FOR 1869.

Grand Commander, FRANCIS A. OSBORN, of Boston.
Senior Vice-Grand Commander, JOSIAH PICKETT, of Worcester.
Junior Vice-Grand Commander, HORACE C. LEE, of Springfield.
Assistant Adjutant-General, THOMAS SHERWIN, jun., of Boston.
Assistant Inspector General, ORSON MOULTON, of Boston.
Assistant Quartermaster-General, WM. S. GREENOUGH, of Boston.
Assistant Surgeon-General, SAMUEL A. GREEN, of Boston.
Chaplain, WM. G. SCANDLIN, of Grafton.

Council of Administration.

A. B. R. SPRAGUE ... of Worcester.
WILLIAM S. COBB ... of New Bedford.
HENRY R. SIBLEY ... of Charlestown.
GEORGE H. PEIRSON ... of Salem.
LUKE LYMAN ... of Northampton.

Delegates to the National Encampment.

A. B. R SPRAGUE, of Worcester, Delegate at Large.

J. A. TITUS ... of Worcester.
C. B. KENFIELD ... of Boston.
A. M. WILLIAMS ... of Taunton.
S. E. CHAMBERLAIN ... of Cambridge.
J. W. DENNY ... of Boston.
WM. F. DRAPER ... of Milford.

Acting Assistant Inspectors General.

W. H. LAWRENCE	of East Boston.
C. W. C. RHOADES	of Boston Highlands.
J. W. HOLMES	of Springfield.
CHAS. H. CLEVELAND	of Worcester.
T. L. BARKER	of Fitchburg.
W. F. DRAPER	of Milford.
G. S. MERRILL	of Lawrence.
O. L. WILBUR	of New Bedford.
GEO. H. LONG	of Charlestown.

Posts of the Department of Mass., Grand Army of the Republic.

ROSTER OF OFFICERS ELECTED DECEMBER, 1868.

Post.	Commander.	Location.
1.	Wm. S. Cobb	New Bedford
2.	Francis B. Smith	Nantucket
3.	Alfred M. Williams	Taunton
4.	J. S. Drayton	Melrose
5.	J. G. B. Adams	Lynn
6.	Geo. O. Wilder	Holliston
7.	E. M. Chamberlin	Boston
8.	Lewis Finney	Middleboro'
9.	C. H. Williams	Hudson
10.	R. E. Blake	Worcester
11.	Geo. R. Kelso	Charlestown
12.	Geo. E. Tibbetts	Wakefield
13.	A. B. Holmes	No. Bridgewater
14.	Oscar L. Brown	Hopkinton
15.	C. G. Attwood	Boston
16.	H. M. Phillips	Springfield
17.	B. R. Davis	Orange
18.	A. G. Forbush	Ashland
19.	Thaddeus L. Barker	Fitchburg
20.	A. S. Graton	Paxton
21.	John W. Fairbanks	Westboro'
22.	James H. Barker	Milford
23.	Geo. A. Butler	East Boston
24.	A. J. Hall	Grafton
25.	L. B. Willard	Uxbridge
26.	Joel Seaverns	Boston Highlands
27.	A. B. Clarke	Oxford
28.	S. A. Lawrence	West Boylston
29.	G. F. Frost	Waltham
30.	W. H. Cary	Cambridgeport
31.	Charles H. White	Ashburnham
32.	F. C. Choate	South Boston
33.	Edwin F. Wyer	Woburn
34.	John R. Lakeman	Salem
35.	C. A. Blanchard	Chelsea
36.	Edwin Baltwood	Amherst
37.	Henry Bemis	Spencer
38.	Artemas D. Ward	Brookfield
39.	J. B. Wildes	Lawrence
40.	Francis A. Bicknell	No. Weymouth
41.	Phineas Solomon	Westfield
42.	W. O. Fiske	Lowell
43.	H. J. Batchelder	Marlboro'
44.	Luke Lyman	Northampton
45.	F. W. Perkins	Gloucester
46.	Edward T. Marvel	Fall River
47.	W. Frank Holt	Haverhill
48.	Geo. V. Barrett	Groton
49.	Luther Dame	Newburyport
50.	James R. Browne	Barre
51.	Chas. H. Deyo	No. Brookfield
52.	J. W. Allen	No. Easton
53.	Wm. A. Burrage	Leominster
54.	S. C. Chamberlain	Berlin
55.	S. C. Hartwell	Southbridge
56.	Lemuel Pope	Cambridge
57.	Robert L. Sawin	East Cambridge
58.	James L. Bates	Weymouth
59.	Geo. W. Rockwood	Sterling
60.	R. R. Clarke	Whitinsville
61.	E. P. Morton	Webster
62.	J. Cushing Edmands	Newton
63.	Chas. E. Gerrald	Natick
64.	A. S. Davidson	Clinton
65.	E. H. Hammond, S. V. C.	Warren
66.	Godfrey Rider, Jr.	Medford
67.	Wm. A. Stone	Manchester
68.	Chas. B. Fox	Dorchester
69.	Amos B. Holden	Westminster
70.	Lewis R. Whitaker	Franklin
71.	D. E. King-bury	Holyoke
72.	A. St. J. Chambre	Stoughton
73.	E. P. Reed	Abington
74.	Chas. L. Rice	East Abington
75.	W. Syming Brown	Stoneham
76.	Samuel H. Doten	Plymouth
77.	S. W. Armington	Holden
78.	F. P. Harlow	So. Abington

N. B. — Posts 3, 4, 20, 24, 26, 28, 31, 36, meet on Monday evening.
Posts 1, 6, 7, 11, 14, 17, 18, 19, 23, 29, 33, 34, 39, 41 — Tuesday.
Posts 9, 12, 15, 21, 22, 25, 30, 32, 38, 45 — Wednesday.
Posts 5, 10, 27, 42, 43, 46, 48, 51 — Thursday.
Posts 2, 8, 16, 35, 37, 40, 44 — Friday.
Posts 49, 50 — Saturday.

GOVERNMENT OF THE
COMMONWEALTH OF MASSACHUSETTS,

And Officers immediately connected therewith — with places of residence.

1869.

EXECUTIVE DEPARTMENT.

HIS EXCELLENCY, WILLIAM CLAFLIN, of Newton.........................Governor.
HIS HONOR, JOSEPH TUCKER, of Lenox,.....................Lieutenant Governor

COUNCIL.

District 1. — Marshall S. Underwood ....of Dennis.
    "   2. — Charles Endicott ....of Canton.
    "   3. — Thomas Rice, Jr..................................of Newton.
    "   4. — Otis Norcross ....of Boston.
    "   5. — Roland G. Usher.................................of Lynn.
    "   6. — Thomas Talbot ....of Billerica.
    "   7. — Charles Adams, Jr...........................of North Brookfield.
    "   8. — Horatio G. Knight..............................of Easthampton.
Private Secretary of the Governor, Charles H. Taylor.................of Boston.
Messenger to the Governor and Council, Wm. H. D. Eaton........of Cambridge.

SECRETARY OF THE COMMONWEALTH.

Oliver Warner...of Northampton.
1st Clerk, Charles W. Lovett, of Boston. | *2d Clerk*, Benj. C. Piper, of Boston.

TREASURER AND RECEIVER-GENERAL.

Jacob H. Loud..of Plymouth.
1st Clerk, Daniel H. Rogers, of Brookline. | *2d Clerk*, Artemas Harmon, of Malden.

PAYMASTER.

William H. Porter...of Salem.

DEPUTY TAX COMMISSIONER.

D. A. Gleason ....of Medford.

AUDITOR OF ACCOUNTS.

Henry S. Briggs..of Pittsfield.
1st Clerk, Edward S. Davis, of Lynn. | *2d Clerk*, Augustus Brown, of Salem.

ATTORNEY-GENERAL.

Charles Allen..of Boston.

ASSISTANT ATTORNEY-GENERAL.

James C. Davis..of Greenfield.

Governor's Staff.

ADJUTANT AND INSPECTOR-GENERAL. (Rank, Major-General.)
James A. Cunningham...of Gloucester.
QUARTERMASTER-GENERAL. (Rank, Brigadier-General.)
John H. Reed...of Boston.
SURGEON-GENERAL. (Rank, Brigadier-General.)
William J. Dale...of North Andover
ASSISTANT ADJUTANT-GENERAL. (Rank, Colonel.)
Nehemiah Brown...of Boston.
ASSISTANT ADJUTANT-GENERAL. (Rank, Lieutenant-Colonel.)
Henry Ware..of Cambridge.
DEPUTY QUARTERMASTER-GENERAL. (Rank, Colonel.)
Samuel E. Chamberlain ....of Cambridge.
ASSISTANT SURGEON-GENERAL. (Rank, Colonel.)
Anson P. Hooker...of Cambridge.
SURGEON-GENERAL'S DEPARTMENT. (Rank, Colonel.)
William C. Capelle...of Boston.
ASSISTANT INSPECTOR-GENERAL. (Rank, Captain.)
William E. Wilson..of Boston.
AIDS TO THE COMMANDER-IN-CHIEF. (Rank, Colonel.)
Adin B. Underwood..of Newton.
James L. Bates..of Weymouth.
Edward N. Hallowell..of Boston.
J. Cushing Edmunds...of Newton.

2

SENATE.

Robert C. Pitman, of New Bedford, . . . *President.*

Suffolk County.

1st District. —	Charles R. McLean,	. . .	of Boston
2d "	Alonzo M. Giles,	. . .	" "
3d "	Ellis W. Morton,	. . .	" "
4th "	Horace H. Coolidge,	. . .	" "
5th "	Samuel D. Crane, .	. . .	" "
6th.. "	Benjamin Dean, .	. . .	" "

Essex County.

1st District. —	George H. Sweetser,	. . .	of Saugus
2d "	Nathaniel J. Holden,	. . .	of Salem
3d "	Julius A. Palmer,	. . .	of Boxford
4th "	Richard Plumer, .	. . .	of Newburyport
5th "	J. Scott Todd, .	. . .	of Rowley

Middlesex County.

1st District. —	O. H. P. Smith,	. . .	of Charlestown
2d "	George O. Brastow,	. . .	of Somerville
3d "	Estes Howe, .	. . .	of Cambridge
4th "	Edmund Dowse	. . .	of Sherborn
5th "	Daniel Needham,	. . .	of Groton
6th "	Joseph G. Pollard,	. . .	of Woburn
7th "	Joshua N. Marshall,	. . .	of Lowell

Worcester County.

1st District. —	Francis H. Dewey,	. . .	of Worcester
2d "	Charles A. Wheelock,	. . .	of Uxbridge
3d "	Lucius J. Knowles,	. . .	of Warren
4th "	George M. Buttrick,	. . .	of Barre
5th "	John H. Lockey,	. . .	of Leominster

Hampden County.

1st District. —	Charles R. Ladd,	. . .	of Springfield
2d. "	George S. Taylor,	. . .	of Chicopee

Hampshire, Franklin, and Berkshire Counties.

Hampshire District. —	Edward A. Thomas,	. .	of Prescott
Franklin "	Whiting Griswold,	. .	of Greenfield
Berkshire and Hampshire,	Richmond Kingman,	.	of Cummington
Berkshire. —	C. J. Kittridge,	. . .	of Hinsdale

Norfolk and Plymouth Counties.

1st Norfolk District. —	George H. Monroe,	.	of Boston
2d Norfolk "	Charles Marsh, .	. .	of Quincy
3d Norfolk "	Joseph G. Ray, .	. .	of Franklin
1st Plymouth "	Gershom B. Weston,	.	of Duxbury
2d Plymouth "	Jonathan White, .	.	of N. Bridgewater
Norfolk and Plymouth. —	Francis A. Hobart,	.	of Braintree

Bristol County.

1st District. —	Harrison Tweed,	. .	' of Taunton
2d "	Robert C. Pitman,	. .	'. of New Bedford
3d "	John B. Hathaway,	. .	of Fall River

Barnstable, Nantucket, and Dukes Counties.

Cape District. —	Nathaniel E. Atwood,	.	. of Provincetown
Island "	George A. King	. .	of Barnstable

OFFICERS OF THE SENATE.

Stephen N. Gifford, *Clerk.*
Rev. Edward N. Kirk, D.D., *Chaplain.*
John Morrissey, *Sergeant-at-Arms to both branches of the General Court.*

HOUSE OF REPRESENTATIVES.

HARVEY JEWELL, of Boston, ... *Speaker.*

Suffolk County.

1. Wesley A. Gove, of Boston.
   Luther A. Wright, of Boston.
   Francis A. Perry, of Boston,
2. Dennis Cawley, Jr., of Boston.
   Murdock Matheson, of Boston.
   Michael Carney, of Boston.
3. Avery Plumer, of Boston.
   Lyman S. Hapgood, of Boston.
   John H. Roberts, of Boston.
4. Dexter S. King, of Boston.
   John Brown, of Boston.
   John P. Ober, of Boston.
5. Otis Rich, of Boston.
   William G. Brooks, of Boston.
   Dennis J. Gorman, of Boston.
6. Harvey Jewell, of Boston.
   Linus M. Child, of Boston.
   John J. Smith, of Boston.
7. Patrick A. Collins, of Boston.
   Hugh A Madden, of Boston.
   William P. Tyler, of Boston.
8. Moses Kimball, of Boston.
   P. Ambrose Young, of Boston.
   Nathaniel C. Nash, of Boston.
9. L. Miles Standish, of Boston.
   Jeremiah L. Newton, of Boston.
10. Samuel G. Bow dlear, of Boston.
    Alvah A. Burrage, of Boston.
11. James Horswell, of Boston.
    Solomon Carter, of Boston.
    Lansing Millis, of Boston.
12. Robert Johnson, of Boston.
    William W. Nichols, of Boston.
13. Andrew L. Haskell, of Chelsea.
    Rufus S. Owen, of Chelsea.
    Caleb Lombard, of Chelsea.

Essex County.

1. Joseph N. Clark, of Salisbury.
   William H. Haskell, of Amesbury.
2. S. K. Towle, of Haverhill.
   Eben Mitchell, of Haverhill.
   Thorndike D. Hodges, of Haverhill.
3. W. A. Russell, of Lawrence.
   Frederick Butler, of Lawrence.
   Kimball C. Gleason, of Methuen.
4. Augustine K. Russell, of Andover.
5. Oliver S. Butler, of Georgetown.
6. David T. Woodwell, of Newburyport.
   Horace Choate, of Newburyport.
   Joseph N. Rolfe, Newbury.
7. Josiah Lord, Jr., of Ipswich.
8. Benjamin F. Cook, of Gloucester.
   Josiah O. Friend, Jr., of Gloucester.
   J. Franklin Dyer, of Gloucester.
9. Ambrous Hodgkins, of Rockport.
10. John I. Baker, of Beverly.
    Freeborn W. Cressey, of Beverly.
11. Edwin Mudge, of Danvers.
12. Robert S. Daniels, of Peabody.
13. John Barlow, of Salem.
    Moses H. Hale, of Salem.
14. Thomas S. Waters, of Salem.
15. Joseph S. Knight, of Marblehead.
    R. P. A. Harris, of Marblehead.
16. William W. Kellogg, of Lynn.
17. William R. Melden, of Lynn.
18. Benjamin Dupar, of Lynn.
19. William H. Merritt, of Lynn.
20. James Hewes, of Lynnfield.

Middlesex County.

1. Samuel S. Willson, of Charlestown.
2. William W. Davis, of Charleston.
   William Hichborn, of Charlestown.
3. Caleb Rand, of Charlestown.
   Samuel D. Sawin, Charlestown.
4. George P. Cox, of Malden.
   John Runey, of Somerville.
   Charles H. Guild, of Somerville.
5. James A. Hervey, of Medford.
6. Salem Wilder, of Winchester.
7. James R. Morse, of Cambridge.
8. Asa P. Morse, of Cambridge.
   Martin L. Smith, of Cambridge.
   Charles A. Fiske, of Cambridge.
9. Charles J. McIntire, of Cambridge.
10. John B. Goodrich, of Newton.
    Life Baldwin, of Brighton.
11. Henry Chase, of Watertown.
12. Royal S. Warren, of Waltham.
13. Newton Morse, of Natick.
14. Benjamin A. Bridges, of Holliston.
15. M. C. Phipps, of Hopkinton.
16. Theodore C. Hurd, of Framingham.
17. F. H. Morse, of Marlborough.
18. Joseph A. Priest, of Littleton.
19. John N. Sherman, of Wayland.
20. Addison G. Fay, of Concord.
21. Richard D. Blinn, of Lexington.
22. William T. Grammar, of Woburn.
23. Levi S. Gould, of Melrose.
    Samuel Cloon, of Stoneham.
24. Samuel P. Breed, of No. Reading.
25. William Fletcher, of Chelmsford.
26. James B. Francis, of Lowell.
    Joseph L. Sargent, of Lowell.
27. Asahel D. Puffer, of Lowell.
28. David Lane, of Lowell.
29. William H. Parker, of Lowell.
30. Asa Clement, of Dracut.
31. William Livermore, of Groton.
32. A. A. Plimpton, of Shirley.

Worcester County.

1. George H. Barrett, of Ashburnham.
2. Thomas H. Goodspeed, of Athol.
3. C. S. Greenwood, of Gardner.
4. Stephen D. Goddard, of Petersham.
   Charles Wilcox, of New Braintree.
5. F. Foster Bailey, of Fitchburg.
   Elnathan Davis, of Lunenburg.
   Charles H. Merriam, of Leominster.
6. Jacob Fisher, of Lancaster.
7. Edward H. Hartshorn, of Berlin.
8. Henry White, of Boylston.
9. Willis Smith, of Rutland.
10. Warren Williams, of Worcester.
    Thomas L. Nelson, of Worcester.
    Walcome W. Sprague, of Worcester.
11. Anry G. Coes, of Worcester.
    John Dean, of Worcester.
    George M. Woodward, of Worcester.
12. George K. Nichols, of Grafton.
13. William M. Child, of Westboro'.
14. George L. Gibbs, of Northbridge.
15. Alfred A. Burrill, of Milford.
    Thomas G. Kent, of Milford.
    Alexander H. Allen, of Mendon.
16. George J. Sanger, of Webster.
    James M. Cudlift, of Sutton.
    Marcus M. Luther, of Douglas.

Worcester County — continued.
17. Ezra Rice, of Auburn.
     Manning Leonard, of Southbridge.
18. Ezra Batcheller, of N. Brookfield.
     Daniel W. Knight, of Brookfield.

Hampshire County.

1. Haynes K. Starkweather, of North-
     ampton.
     William I. Edwards, of Westhampton.
2. Marcus A. Bates, of Worthington.
3. Stephen M. Crosby, of Williamsburg.
4. Elliott Montague, of South Hadley.
5. Henry B. Blake, of Belchertown.
6. Edward Smith, of Enfield.

Hampden County.

1. Ferdinand L. Burley, of Wales.
2. Joseph Vaill, of Palmer.
3. Tilly Haynes, of Springfield.
     Emerson Wight, of Springfield.
4. Horace Smith, of Springfield.
5. William W. Amadon, of Springfield.
6. S. H. Walker, of Holyoke.
     Jerome Wells, of Chicopee.
7. William Melcher, of W. Springfield.
     Edwin Gilbert, of Southwick.
8. Samuel Horton, of Westfield.
9. Franklin C. Knox, of Blandford.

Franklin County.

1. Lyman F. Moore, of New Salem.
2. D. Dwight Whitmore, of Sunderland.
3. Daniel H. Newton, of Greenfield.
     Avery J. Denison, of Leyden.
4. Alfred Belden, of Whately.
     Clark Sears, of Hawley.
5. Roger H. Leavitt, of Charlemont.

Berkshire County.

1. Justus Tower, of Lanesboro'.
2. Shepherd Thayer, of Adams.
     Werden R. Brown, of Cheshire.
3. Thomas F. Plunkett, of Pittsfield.
     James Wilson, of Dalton.
4. Thomas K. Plunkett, of Hinsdale.
5. Albert Langdon, of Lenox.
6. Alanson Crittenden, of Otis.
7. Herbert C. Joyner, of Gt. Barrington.
8. Orlow Wolcott, of Sandisfield.

Norfolk County.

1. Eliphalet Stone, of Dedham.
2. Charles A. Howins, of W. Roxbury.
3. James Ritchie, of Boston.
     Moody Merrill, of Boston.
     Charles H. Hovey, of Boston.
4. Benjamin Franklin, of Boston.
5. Henry J. Nazro, of Dorchester.
     William T. Adams, of Dorchester.
6. Henry Barker, of Quincy.
7. Levi W. Hobart, of Braintree.

8. James Humphrey, of Weymouth.
     Elmer Hewett, of Weymouth.
9. Samuel Clark, of Randolph.
10. Henri L. Johnson, of Stoughton.
11. Francis W. Bird, of Walpole.
     Frank M. Ames, of Canton.
12. Chauncy G. Fuller, of Wrentham.
     John M. Merrick, of Foxborough.
13. Ruel F. Thayer, of Bellingham.
14. Abner L. Smith, of Dover.
15. Abijah W. Goddard, of Brookline.

Bristol County.

1. Joseph D. Peirce, of Attleboro'.
2. William D. Witherell, of Norton.
3. Enoch King, of Raynham.
4. Edgar H. Reed, of Taunton.
     Alfred M. Williams, of Taunton.
     LeBaron B. Church, of Tau :ton.
5. Ebenezer Dawes, of Dighton.
6. Rufus S. Slade, of Swansea.
7. Abraham G. Hart, of Fall River.
     Weaver Osborn, of Fall River.
     Iram Smith, of Fall River.
8. Isaac A. Anthony, of Westport.
9. George F. Howland, of Dartmouth.
10. Rodney French, of New Bedford.
     Samuel S. Paine, of New Bedford.
11. John A. P. Allen, of New Bedford.
     Jethro C. Brock, of New Bedford.
12. Lewis S. Judd, of Fairhaven.

Plymouth County.

1. Loring Bates, of Cohasset.
2. Charles N. Marsh, of Hingham.
3. Edward Stowell, of So. Scituate.
4. Charles P. Lyon, of Halifax.
5. Joseph A. Stranger, of Kingston.
6. William Bartlett, of Plymouth.
     William E. Barnes, of Plymouth.
7. Ezra C. Brett, of Wareham.
8. Thomas Ellis, of Rochester.
9. Augustus Pratt, of Middleboro'.
10. Nahum Leonard, Jr., of W. Bridgew'r.
11. Jacob Bates, of E. Bridgewater.
     Welcome H. Wales, of N. Bridgew'r.
12. Charles W. Soule, of Abington.
     Albert Chamberlin, of Abington.

Barnstable County.

1. Lemuel B. Simmons, of Barnstable.
     Alvah Holway, of Sandwich.
     Francis A. Nye, of Falmouth.
2. Samuel H. Gould, of Brewster.
     Shubael B. Kelley, of Harwich.
3. Ensign B. Rogers, of Orleans.
4. John C. Peak, of Wellfleet.
     Obadiah S. Brown, of Truro.

Dukes County.

1. Charles Bradley, of Tisbury.

Nantucket County.

1. Isaiah F. Robinson, of Nantucket.

OFFICERS OF THE HOUSE.

Wm. S. Robinson, *Clerk.*
Rev. Orin T. Walker, *Chaplain.*
John Morissey, *Sergeant-at-Arms.*

COMMITTEES.

STANDING COMMITTEES OF THE SENATE.

Judiciary. — Messrs. Dewey, Dean, Holden, White, and Coolidge.

Probate and Chancery. — Messrs. Marshall, Morton, and King.

Treasury. — Messrs. Lockey, Palmer, and Thayer.

Printing. — Messrs. Monroe, Hathaway, and Knowles.

Bills in Third Reading. — Messrs. Holden, Coolidge, White, King, and Morton.

Engrossed Bills. — Messrs. Ladd, Pollard, and Wheelock.

Leaves of Absence. — Messrs. Giles, Hathaway, and Ray.

STANDING COMMITTEES OF THE HOUSE.

Judiciary. — Messrs. Nelson of Worcester, Child of Boston, Kent of Milford, Hurd of Framingham, Newton of Boston, McIntire of Cambridge, Goodrich of Newton.

Probate and Chancery. — Messrs. Humphrey of Weymouth, Perry of Boston, Joyner of Great Barrington, Merrill of Boston, Merriam of Leominster, Willson of Charlestown, Woodward of Worcester.

Finance. — Messrs. Kimball of Boston, Rich of Boston, Crosby of Williamsburg, Nazro of Dorchester, Newton of Greenfield, Waters of Salem, Leonard of Southbridge.

Elections. — Messrs. Child of Boston, Collins of Boston, Anthony of Westport, Madden of Boston, Horton of Westfield, Rolfe of Newbury, and Barnes of Plymouth.

Bills in the Third Reading. — Messrs. Newton of Boston, Hodges of Haverhill, Nichols of Boston, Langdon of Lenox, Melden of Lynn, Witherell of Norton, Child of Westboro'.

Engrossed Bills. — Messrs. Rand of Charlestown, Harris of Marblehead, Melcher of West Springfield, Johnson of Stoughton, Brown of Cheshire, Phipps of Hopkinton, Stranger of Kingston.

County Estimates. — Messrs. Holway of Sandwich, Dennison of Leyden, Wilcox of New Braintree, Sears of Hawley, Robinson of Nantucket.

Pay Roll. — Messrs. Marsh of Hingham, Sherman of Wayland, Gibbs of Northbridge, Brown of Truro, White of Boylston.

Leave of Absence. — Messrs. Fuller of Wrentham, Smith of Rutland, Slade of Swansea, Priest of Littleton, and Fiske of Cambridge.

Public Buildings. — Messrs. Breed of North Reading, Wilson of Dalton, Rogers of Orleans, Smith of Cambridge, Choate of Newburyport.

Printing. — Messrs. Kellogg of Lynn, Owen of Chelsea, Walker of Holyoke, Carney of Boston, Davis of Charlestown.

JOINT STANDING COMMITTEES.

Agriculture. — Messrs. Needham and Thomas, *of the Senate.* Messrs. Stone of Dedham, Tower of Lanesboro', Clement of Dracut, Starkweather of Northampton, Pratt of Middleboro', *of the House.*

Banks and Banking. — Messrs. Lockey and Kingman, *of the Senate.* Messrs. Wells of Chicopee, Fisher of Lancaster, Hapgood of Boston, Baldwin of Brighton, Haskell of Amesbury, *of the House.*

Claims. — Messrs. Coolidge and Thomas, *of the Senate.* Messrs. Crosby of Williamsburg, Brooks of Boston, Allen of Mendon, Barker of Quincy, Goddard of Petersham, *of the House.*

Education. — Messrs. Marshall and Morton, *of the Senate.* Messrs. Merrick of Foxboro', King of Boston, Blake of Belchertown, Adams of Dorchester, Chase of Watertown, *of the House.*

Federal Relations. — Messrs. Brastow and Weston, *of the Senate.* Messrs. Hervey of Medford, Collins of Boston, Williams of Taunton, Smith of Boston, Lane of Lowell, *of the House.*

Fisheries. — Messrs. Weston and Atwood, *of the Senate.* Messrs. Simmons of Barnstable, Bradley of Tisbury, Coes of Worcester, Brett of Wareham, Hewes of Lynnfield, *of the House.*

Harbors. — Messrs. McLean, Coolidge, and Plumer, *of the Senate.* Messrs. Francis of Lowell, Bird of Walpole, Cox of Malden, Allen of New Bedford, Nelson of Worcester, Fay of Concord, Smith of Springfield, Johnson of Boston, *of the House.*

Library. — Messrs. Dean, Dowse, and Buttrick, *of the Senate.* Messrs. Sanger of Webster, Davis of Lunenburg, Hewitt of Weymouth, *of the House.*

Manufactures. — Messrs. Knowles and Kittredge, *of the Senate.* Messrs. Plunkett of Pittsfield, Butler of Lawrence, Guild of Somerville, Dean of Worcester, Cunliff of Sutton, *of the House.*

Mercantile Affairs. — Messrs. Crane and Pollard, *of the Senate.* Messrs. Nash of Boston, Gould of Melrose, Burrage of Boston, Montague of South Hadley, Church of Taunton, *of the House.*

Insurance. — Messrs. Crane and Ladd, *of the Senate.* Messrs. Ober of Boston, Horswell of Boston, Hewins of West Roxbury, Warren of Waltham, Parker of Lowell, *of the House.*

Military Affairs. — Messrs. Todd and Smith, *of the Senate.* Messrs. Grammar of Woburn, Gove of Boston, Barrett of Ashburnham, Daniels of Peabody, Lyon of Halifax, *of the House.*

Parishes and Religious Societies. — Messrs. Dowse and Palmer, *of the Senate.* Messrs. Vaill of Palmer, Smith of Fall River, Edwards of Westhampton, Reed of Taunton, Goddard of Brookline, *of the House.*

Prisons. — Messrs. Todd and Smith, *of the Senate.* Messrs. Hart of Fall River, Crittenden of Otis, Nichols of Grafton, Carter of Boston, Hichborn of Charlestown, *of the House.*

Public Charitable Institutions. — Messrs. Howe and Kittredge, *of the Senate.* Messrs. Bird of Walpole, Leavitt of Charlemont, Towle of Haverhill, Gould of Brewster, Cawley of Boston, *of the House.*

Public Lands. — Messrs. Weston and Wheelock, *of the Senate.* Messrs. Mudge of Danvers, Standish of Boston, Friend of Gloucester, Batcheller of North Brookfield, J. R. Morse of Cambridge, *of the House.*

Railways. — Messrs. Griswold, Tweed, and Hobart, *of the Senate.* Messrs. Baker of Beverly, Plumer of Boston, Ritchie of Boston, Judd of Fairhaven, Thayer of Adams, Haynes of Springfield, Russell of Lawrence, Ames of Canton, *of the House.*

Horse Railways. — Messrs. Needham, Sweetser, and Ladd, *of the Senate.* Messrs. Hurd of Framingham, Bowdlear of Boston, Sargent of Lowell, Millis of Boston, Blinn of Lexington, Barlow of Salem, Wales of North Bridgewater, Amadon of Springfield, *of the House.*

Roads and Bridges. — Messrs. Marsh and Plumer, *of the Senate.* Messrs. Humphrey of Weymouth, Brown of Boston, Smith of Boston, Leonard of West Bridgewater, Fletcher of Chelmsford, *of the House.*

State House. — Messrs. Giles and McLean, *of the Senate.* Messrs. Bowdlear of Boston, Osborne of Fall River, Bates of Cohasset, Howland of Dartmouth, Matheson of Boston, *of the House.*

Towns. — Messrs. Sweetser and Ray, *of the Senate.* Messrs. Kent of Milford, Bailey of Fitchburg, Bates of East Bridgewater, Goodspeed of Athol, Sawin of Charlestown, *of the House.*

Hoosac Tunnel and Troy and Greenfield Railroad. — Messrs. Brastow, Tweed, and Griswold, *of the Senate.* Messrs. Kimball of Boston, Francis of Lowell, Williams of Worcester, Young of Boston, Cook of Gloucester, Runey of Somerville, Lombard of Chelsea, Hale of Salem, *of the House.*

JOINT SPECIAL COMMITTEES.

Indians. — Messrs. Holden, King, and Kingman, *of the Senate.* French of New Bedford, Bird of Walpole, Pierce of Attleboro', Ellis of Rochester, Puffer of Lowell, Roberts of Boston, Dupar of Lynn, Soule of Abington, *of the House.*

License Law. — Messrs. White, Tweed, Dean, Todd, and Buttrick, *of the Senate.* Messrs. Baker of Beverly, Vaill of Palmer, Plunkett of Pittsfield, Burrage of Boston, Johnson of Boston, Nelson of Worcester, Plumer of Boston, Crosby of Williamsburg, Child of Boston, Davis of Lunenburg, Hurd of Framingham, Ritchie of Boston, *of the House.*

Compensation of the Governor, Lieutenant Governor, &c.

The salary of the Governor is $5,000; of the Lieutenant-Governor, $10.00 per day during the session of the Council. The pay of the Councillors is $5.00 per day for each day's attendance during the year. The pay of Senators and Representatives is $5.00 per day for each day's attendance during the session.

The salary of the Secretary of the Commonwealth is $2,500; Treasurer, $3,500; Auditor, $2,500; Attorney General, $3,500; Adjutant General, $2,500.

UNITED-STATES SENATORS FROM MASSACHUSETTS.

Charles Sumner, of Boston,.................term expires March 3, 1875.
Henry Wilson, of Natick,..................term expires March 3, 1871.

REPRESENTATIVES TO THE 41st CONGRESS FROM MASSACHUSETTS.

[Terms expire March 3, 1871.]

District 1. James Buffinton,............................of Fall River.
"   2. Oakes Ames.................................of Easton.
"   3. Ginery Twichell,...........................of Brookline.
"   4. Samuel Hooper, ...of Boston.
"   5. Benjamin F. Butler,........................of Gloucester.
"   6. Nathaniel P. Banks,........................of Waltham.
"   7. George S. Boutwell,........................of Groton.
"   8. George F. Hoar,............................of Worcester.
"   9. William B. Washburn,.......................of Greenfield.
"   10. Henry L. Dawes,............................of Pittsfield.

COUNCILLOR DISTRICTS,

As established by Chap. 221, Acts of 1866.

Dist.

1. — The Island, the Cape, the First Plymouth, and the Second and Third Bristol Senatorial Districts.
2 — The Second Plymouth, the First Bristol, the Norfolk and Plymouth, and the Second and Third Norfolk Senatorial Districts.
3. — The Sixth Suffolk, the Frst Norfolk, the Third and Fourth Middlesex, and the Second Worcester Senatorial Districts.
4. — The First, Second, Third, Fourth, and Fifth Suffolk Senatorial Districts.
5 — The five Senatorial Districts in the County of Essex.
6. — The First, Second, Fifth, Sixth, and Seventh Middlesex Senatorial Districts.
7. — The First, Third, Fourth, and Fifth Worcester, and the Franklin Senatorial Districts.
8. — The Hampshire, the First and Second Hampden, the Berkshire, and the Berkshire and Hampshire Senatorial Districts.

SENATORIAL DISTRICTS,

As established by Chap. 120, Acts of 1866, with the number of legal voters in each district.

[Whole number of legal voters in the State on the 1st of May, 1865, 216,282. Average ratio for each district in the State, 6,157.]

Suffolk County. — Six Senators. [Average ratio, 6,133.]

First District. — Chelsea, North Chelsea, Winthrop, and Ward No. 1, Boston. Legal voters, 6,360.
Second District. — Wards Nos. 2, 3, and 6, Boston. Legal voters, 8,795.
Third District. — Wards Nos. 4 and 5, Boston. Legal voters, 6,195.
Fourth District. — Wards Nos. 8 and 9, Boston. Legal voters, 5,137.
Fifth District. — Wards Nos. 10 and 11, Boston. Legal voters, 5,109.
Sixth District. — Wards Nos. 7 and 12, Boston. Legal voters, 5,224.

Essex County. — Five Senators—[Average ratio, 6,618.]

First District. — Lynn, Lynnfield, Marblehead, Nahant, Saugus, and Swampscott. Legal voters, 6,855.
Second District. — Danvers, Hamilton, Middleton, Salem, §South Danvers, Topsfield, and Wenham. Legal voters, 6,215.
Third District. — Andover, Boxford, Haverhill, Lawrence, Methuen, and North Andover. Legal voters, 7,111.
Fourth District. — Amesbury, Bradford, Georgetown, Groveland, Newbury, Newburyport, Salisbury, and West Newbury. Legal voters, 6,267.
Fifth District. — Beverly, Essex, Gloucester, Ipswich, Manchester, Rockport, and Rowley. Legal voters, 6,624.

Middlesex County — Seven Senators. [Average ratio, 5,991.]

First District. — Charlestown. Legal voters, 5,596.
Second District. — Belmont, Malden, Medford, Somerville, Waltham, Watertown, and * West Cambridge. Legal voters, 6,462.
Third District. — Cambridge and Brighton. Legal voters, 5,810.
Fourth District. — Ashland, Framingham, Holliston, Hopkinton, Natick, Newton, Sherborn, Wayland, and Weston. Legal voters, 6,259.
Fifth District. — Acton, Ashby, Boxborough, Carlisle, Concord, Dunstable, Groton, Hudson, Lincoln, Littleton, Marlborough, Pepperell, Shirley, Stow, Sudbury, Townsend, Tyngsborough, and Westford. Legal voters. 5,828.
Sixth District. — Bedford, Billerica, Burlington, Lexington, Melrose, North Reading, Reading, †South Reading, Stoneham, Tewksbury, Wilmington, Winchester, and Woburn. Legal voters, 6,014.
Seventh District. — Chelmsford, Dracut, and Lowell. Legal voters, 5,967.

Worcester County — Five Senators. [Average ratio, 6,451.]

First District. — Worcester. Legal voters, 5,889.
Second District. — Blackstone, Douglas, Grafton, Mendon, Milford, Northborough, Northbridge, Shewsbury, Southborough, Upton, Uxbridge, and Westborough. Legal voters, 6,683.
Third District. — Auburn, Brookfield, Charlton, Dudley, Leicester, Milbury, Oxford, Southbridge, Spencer Sturbridge, Sutton, Warren, Webster, and West Brookfield. Legal voters, 6,535.
Fourth District. — Athol, Barre, Dana, Gardner, Hardwick, Holden, Hubbardston, New Braintree, North Brookfield, Oakham, Paxton, Petersham, Phillipston, Royalston, Rutland, Templeton, and Winchenden. Legal voters, 6,383.

* Changed to Arlington, April 30, 1867.   † Changed to Wakefield, June 30, 1868.
§ Changed to Peabody, 1868.

Fifth District. — Ashburnham, Berlin, Bolton, Boylston, Clinton, Fitchburg, Harvard, Lancaster, Leominster, Lunenburg, Princeton, Sterling, West Boylston, and Westminster. Legal voters, 6,574.

H. mpden County — Two Senators. [Average ratio, 6,165.]

First District. — Brimfield, Holland, Monson, Palmer, Springfield, Wales, and Wilbraham. Legal voters, 6,306.

Second District. — Agawam, Blandford, Chester, Chicopee, Granville, Holyoke, Longmeadow, Ludlow, Montgomery, Russell, Southwick, Tolland, Westfield, and West Springfield. Legal voters, 6,024.

Hampshire County — One Senator. [Average ratio, 6,347]

Hampshire District. — Amherst, Belchertown, Easthampton, Enfield, Granby, Greenwich, Hadley, Hatfield, Northampton, Pelham, Prescott, South Hadley, Southampton, Ware, Westhampton, and Williamsburg. Legal voters, 6,347.

Berkshire and Hampshire Counties — One Senator. [Average ratio, 6,149.]

Berkshire and Hampshire Districts. — Alford, Becket, Egremont, Great Barrington, Lee, Lenox, Monterey, Mount Washington, New Marlborough, Otis, Sandisfield, Sheffield, Stockbridge, Tyringham, West Stockbridge, Chesterfield, Cummington, Goshen, Huntington, Middlefield, Plainfield, and Worthington. Legal voters, 6,149.

Berkshire and Franklin Counties — One Senator. [Average ratio, 6,013.]

Berkshire District. — Adams, Cheshire, Clarksburg, Dalton, Florida, Hancock, Hinsdale, Lanesborough, New Ashford, Peru, Pittsfield, Richmond, Savoy, Washington, Williamstown, Windsor, Hawley, and Monroe. Legal voters, 6,013.

Franklin County — One Senator. [Average ratio, 6,987.]

Franklin District. — Ashfield, Bernardston, Buckland, Charlemont, Coleraine, Conway, Deerfield, Erving, Gill, Greenfield, Heath, Leverett, Leyden, Montague, New Salem, Northfield, Orange, Rowe, Shelburne, Shutesbury, Sunderland, Warwick, Wendell, and Whately. Legal voters, 6,987.

Norfolk County — Three Senators. [Average ratio, 6,134.]

First District. — Brookline, * Roxbury, and West Roxbury. Legal voters, 6,235.

Second District. — Canton, Dedham, Dorchester, Dover, Milton, Needham, and Quincy. Legal voters, 6,004.

Third District. — Bellingham, Foxborough, Franklin, Medfield, Medway, Randolph, Sharon, Stoughton, Walpole, and Wrentham. Legal voters, 6,084.

Bristol County — Three Senators. [Average ratio, 6,192.]

First District. — Attleborough, Easton, Mansfield, Norton, Raynham, and Taunton. Legal voters, 6,058.

Second District. — Acushnet, Dartmouth, Fairhaven, and New Bedford. Legal voters, 6,272.

Third District. — Berkley, Dighton, Fall River, Freetown, Rehoboth, Seekonk, Somerset, Swanzey, and Westport. Legal voters, 6,246.

Plymouth County — Two Senators. [Average ratio, 5,925.]

First District. — Carver, Duxbury, Kingston, Lakeville, Marion, Mattapoisett, Middleborough, Plymouth, Plympton, Rochester, and Wareham. Legal voters, 5,973.

Second District. — Abington, Bridgewater, East Bridgewater, Halifax, Hanson, North Bridgewater, Pembroke, and West Bridgewater. Legal voters, 5,878.

Norfolk and Plymouth Counties — One Senator. [Average ratio, 5,904.]

Norfolk and Plymouth District. — Cohasset, Hanover, Hingham, Hull, Marshfield, Scituate, South Scituate, Braintree, and Weymouth. Legal voters, 5,904.

Barnstable, Dukes, and Nantucket Counties — Two Senators.
[Average ratio, 5,123.]

Island District. — Barnstable, Falmouth, Sandwich, Chilmark, Edgartown, Gosnold, Tisbury, and Nantucket. Legal voters, 4,562.

Cape District. — Brewster, Chatham, Dennis, Eastham, Harwich, Orleans, Provincetown, Truro, Wellfleet, and Yarmouth. Legal voters, 5,684.

* Annexed to Boston, January, 1868.

REPRESENTATIVE DISTRICTS,

As established by the County Commissioners of the several Counties other than Suffolk. and the Mayor and Aldermen of the City of Boston, for the County of Suffolk, pursuant to the 21st Art. of Amendments of the Constitution and Chap. 103 of the Acts of 1866; with the number of Legal voters in each District (according to the census of 1865), and the number of Representatives to which said districts are respectively entitled. Number of Representatives, 240. Number of voters to each Representative, 1,026.

Suffolk County.

Dist.		Voters.	Rep.
1. Boston 1st Ward.		3,530	3
2. Boston 2d Ward.		3,085	3
3. Boston 3d Ward.		3,050	3
4. Boston 4th Ward.		3,076	3
5. Boston 5th Ward.		3,119	3
6. Boston 6th Ward.		2,660	3
7. Boston 7th Ward.		2,857	3
8. Boston 8th Ward.		2,877	3
9. Boston 9th Ward.		2,260	2
10. Boston 10th Ward.		2,546	2
11. Boston 11th Ward.		2,563	3
12. Boston 12th Ward.		2,367	2
13. Chelsea, North Chelsea, Winthrop.		2,830	3
	Total,	36,820	36

Essex County.

1. Salisbury, Amesbury, West Newbury.		2,116	2
2. Haverhill, Bradford.		2,802	3
3. Lawrence, Methuen.		3,247	3
4. Andover, North Andover.		1,240	1
5. Georgetown, Groveland, Boxford.		994	1
6. Newburyport, Newbury.		2,979	3
7. Ipswich, Rowley.		1,002	1
8. Gloucester, Essex.		2,902	3
9. Rockport.		915	1
10. Beverly, Manchester, Hamilton.		1,992	2
11. Danvers, Wenham.		1,092	1
12. South Danvers.		961	1
13. Salem 1st Ward, 2d Ward, 3d Ward.		2,035	2
14. Salem 4th Ward, 6th Ward.		1,036	1
15. Marblehead, Salem 5th Ward.		2,105	2
16. Lynn 4th Ward, Nahant.		1,079	1
17. Lynn 2d Ward, 5th Ward.		1,220	1
18. Lynn 3d Ward, Swampscott.		1,133	1
19. Lynn 1st Ward, 6th Ward, 7th Ward.		1,146	1
20. Saugus, Lynnfield, Middleton, Topsfield.		1,076	1
	Total,	33,072	32

Middlesex County.

	Voters	Rep
1. Charlestown 1st Ward.	1,421	1
2. Charlestown 2d Ward.	2,015	2
3. Charlestown 3d Ward.	2,160	2
4. Somerville, Malden.	3,020	3
5. Medford.	1,031	1
6. West Cambridge, Winchester.	822	1
7. Cambridge 1st Ward, 5th Ward.	1,247	1
8. Cambridge 2d Ward, 4th Ward.	2,661	3
9. Cambridge 3d Ward.	1,244	1
10. Newton, Brighton.	2,249	2
11. Watertown, Belmont.	908	1
12. Waltham.	1,032	1
13. Natick.	1,099	1
14. Holliston, Sherborn.	939	1

15. Hopkinton, Ashland.		1,187	1
16. Framingham.		857	1
17. Marlborough.		849	1
18. Hudson, Stow, Boxborough, Littleton.		904	1
19. Acton, Sudbury, Wayland.		986	1
20. Concord, Lincoln, Weston.		910	1
21. Lexington, Bedford, Burlington, Carlisle.		803	1
22. Woburn.		1,385	1
23. Stoneham, South Reading, Melrose.		1,947	2
24. Reading, North Reading, Wilmington.		1,012	1
25. Chelmsford, Billerica, Tewksbury.		1,054	1
26. Lowell 1st Ward, 2d Ward, 6th Ward.		2,072	2
27. Lowell 3d Ward.		836	1
28. Lowell 4th Ward.		1,174	1
29. Lowell 5th Ward.		1,068	1
30. Dracut, Tyngsborough, Dunstable, Westford.		986	1
31. Groton, Pepperell.		998	1
32. Townsend, Ashby, Shirley.		1,029	1
	Total,	41,935	41

Worcester County.

1. Ashburnham, Winchendon.		1,119	1
2. Royalston, Athol.		1,031	1
3. Gardner, Templeton.		1,114	1
4. Petersham, Dana, Phillipston, Hubbardston, Barre, Hardwick, New Braintree.		2,152	2
5. Westminster, Fitchburg, Lunenburg, Leominster.		3,034	3
6. Lancaster, Bolton, Harvard.		996	1
7. Clinton, Berlin, Northboro'.		1,058	1
8. Sterling, West Boylston, Boylston.		1,020	1
9. Rutland, Holden, Princeton, Oakham.		1,088	1
10. Worcester 1st Ward, 2d Ward, 3d Ward, 8th Ward, Paxton.		2,983	3
11. Worcester 4th Ward, 5th Ward, 6th Ward, 7th Ward.		3,053	3
12. Grafton, Shrewsbury.		1,104	1
13. Westborough, Southborough.		882	1
14. Northbridge, Upton.		993	1
15. Milford, Mendon, Blackstone, Uxbridge.		3,180	3
16. Douglas, Webster, Dudley, Oxford, Sutton, Millbury.		3,164	3
17. Auburn, Leicester, Spencer, Charlton, Southbridge.		2,127	2
18. Sturbridge, Brookfield, North Brookfield, W. Brookfield, Warren.		2,157	2
	Total,	31,780	31

Hampshire County.

1. Easthampton, Hunting- ton, Northampton, Southampton, West- hampton.	2,318	2
2. Chesterfield, Cumming- ton, Goshen, Middle- field, Plainfield, Wor- thington.	1,086	1
3. Hadley, Hatfield, Wil- liamsburg.	1,092	1
4. Amherst, So. Hadley.	1,090	1
5. Belchertown, Granby, Pelham.	1,022	1
6. Enfield, Greenwich, Prescott, Ware.	1,060	1
Total, 7,668		**7**

Hampden County.

1. Monson, Brimfield, Hol- land, Wales.	1,102	1
2. Palmer, Wilbraham.	966	1
3. Springfield, 1st Ward, 2d Ward, 3d Ward.	2,039	2
4. Springfield, 4th Ward, 6th Ward.	858	1
5. Springfield, 5th Ward, 7th Ward, 8th Ward.	1,281	1
6. Holyoke, Chicopee, Ludlow.	2,105	2
7. Granville, Southwick, Agawam, W. Spring- field, Longmeadow.	1,676	2
8. Westfield.	1,326	1
9. Chester, Blandford, Montgomery, Rus- sell, Tolland.	917	1
Total, 12,330		**12**

Franklin County.

1. Warwick, Orange, New Salem.	1,003	1
2. Montague, Sunderland, Leverett, Shutes- bury, Wendell.	1,071	1
3. Greenfield, Coleraine, Leyden, Bernardston, Gill, Northfield, Er- ving.	2,098	2
4. Deerfield, Shelburne, Whately, Conway, Ashfield, Hawley.	2,059	2
5. Buckland, Charlemont, Heath, Rowe, Monroe	979	1
Total, 7,117		**7**

Berkshire County.

1. Hancock, Lanesboro', New Ashford, Wil- liamstown	971	1
2. Adams, Cheshire, Clarksburg, Flor- ida, Savoy.	2,243	2
3. Dalton, Pittsfield, Richmond.	1,923	2
4. Becket, Hinsdale, Peru, Washington, Wind- sor.	902	1
5. Lenox, Stockbridge, West Stockbridge.	1,003	1
6. Lee, Monterey, Otis, Tyringham.	1,318	1
7. Alford, Egremont, Gt. Barrington, Mount Washington.	1,111	1
8. New Marlborough, San- disfield, Sheffield.	1,095	1
Total, 10,566		**10**

Norfolk County.

1. Dedham.	1,263	1
2. West Roxbury.	991	1
3. Roxbury, 2d Ward, 3d Ward, 4th Ward, 5th Ward.	3,435	3
4. Roxbury 1st Ward.	998	1
5. Dorchester.	1,860	2
6. Quincy.	1,276	1
7. Braintree.	777	1
8. Weymouth.	1,843	2
9. Randolph.	1,261	1
10. Stoughton.	1,020	1
11. Canton, Milton, Wal- pole, Sharon.	1,812	2
12. Foxborough, Wren- tham, Medway.	2,007	2
13. Franklin, Bellingham.	819	1
14. Needham, Medfield, Dover.	855	1
15. Brookline.	761	1
Total, 21,525		**21**

Bristol County.

1. Attleborough.	1,112	1
2. Mansfield, Norton.	873	1
3. Easton, Raynham.	987	1
4. Taunton.	3,086	3
5. Seekonk, Rehoboth, Dighton, Berkley.	1,215	1
6. Somerset, Swansea, Freetown.	1,055	1
7. Fall River.	3,297	3
8. Westport.	769	1
9. Dartmouth.	777	1
10. New Bedford 1st Ward, 2d Ward, 3d Ward.	2,463	2
11. New Bedford, 4th Ward, 5th Ward, 6th Ward.	2,082	2
12. Fairhaven, Acushnet.	950	1
Total, 18,576		**18**

Plymouth County.

1. Cohasset, Scituate.	1,064	1
2. Hingham, Hull.	931	1
3. South Scituate, Hano- ver, Hanson.	1,166	1
4. Marshfield, Pembroke, Halifax.	1,029	1
5. Duxbury, Kingston.	985	1
6. Plymouth, Carver, Plympton.	2,034	2
7. Wareham, Marion.	855	1
8. Mattapoisett, Roches- ter, Lakeville.	987	1
9. Middleborough.	1,112	1
10. Bridgewater, West Bridgewater.	1,019	1
11. East Bridgewater, No. Bridgewater.	2,120	2
12. Abington.	1,883	2
Total, 14,643		**15**

Barnstable County.

1. Barnstable, Sandwich, Falmouth. Yarmouth	3,238	3
2. Dennis, Harwich, Brewster.	2,013	2
3. Chatham, Orleans.	1,075	1
4. Eastham, Wellfleet, Tru- ro, Provincetown.	2,006	2
Total, 8,364		**8**

Dukes County.

1. Edgartown, Tisbury, Chilmark, Gosnold.	1,107	1

Nantucket County.

1. Nantucket.	809	

CONGRESSIONAL DISTRICTS.

A ESTABLISHED BY CHAP. 226 OF THE ACTS OF 1862.

District 1.

The several towns in the counties of Barnstable, Dukes, and Nantucket, together with the cities of New Bedford and Fall River, and the towns of Acushnet, Dartmouth, Fairhaven, Freetown, and Westport, in the county of Bristol; and the towns of Carver, Duxbury, Halifax, Kingston, Lakeville, Marion, Mattapoisett, Middleborough, Pembroke, Plymouth, Plympton, Rochester, and Wareham, in the county of Plymouth.

District 2.

The towns of Attleborough, Berkley, Dighton, Easton, Mansfield, Norton, Raynham, Rehoboth, Seekonk, Somerset, Swansea, and the city of Taunton, in the county of Bristol; and the towns of Abington, Bridgewater, East Bridgewater, Hingham, Hanover, Hanson, Hull, Marshfield, Scituate, South Scituate, North Bridgewater, and West Bridgewater, in the county of Plymouth; and the towns of Braintree, Canton, Cohasset, Dorchester, Milton, Quincy, Randolph, Sharon, Stoughton, and Weymouth, in the county of Norfolk.

District 3.

The * city of Roxbury and the town of Brookline, in the county of Norfolk; and the territory comprised in the wards numbered four, seven, eight, ten, eleven, and twelve, in the city of Boston, in the County of Suffolk.

District 4.

The territory comprised in the wards numbered one, two, three, five, six, and nine, in the city of Boston, the city of Chelsea, and the towns of North Chelsea and Winthrop, in the County of Suffolk; and the city of Cambridge, in the county of Middlesex.

District 5.

The cities of Lynn, Newburyport, and Salem, and the towns of Amesbury, Beverly, Danvers, Essex, Georgetown, Gloucester, Groveland, Hamilton, Ipswich, Lynnfield, Manchester, Marblehead, Middleton, Nahant, Newbury, Rockport, Rowley, Salisbury, † South Danvers, Swampscott, Topsfield, Wenham, and West Newbury, in the county of Essex.

    * Annexed to Boston.
    † Changed to Peabody.

District 6.

The city of Lawrence, and the towns of Andover, Boxford, Bradford, Haverhill, Methuen, North Andover, and Saugus, in the county of Essex; and the city of Charlestown, and the towns of Belmont, Billerica, Burlington, Lexington, Malden, Medford, Melrose, North Reading, Reading, Somerville, † South Reading, Stoneham, Tewksbury, Waltham, § West Cambridge, Wilmington, Winchester, and Woburn, in the county of Middlesex.

District 7.

The city of Lowell, and the towns of Acton, Ashby, Ashland, Bedford, Boxborough, Brighton, Carlisle, Chelmsford, Concord, Dracut, Dunstable, Framingham, Groton, Holliston, Hopkinton, Lincoln, Littleton, Marlborough, Natick, Newton, Pepperell, Sherborn, Shirley, Stow, Sudbury, Townsend, Tyngsborough, Watertown, Wayland, Westford, and Weston, in the county of Middlesex; and the towns of Dedham, Dover, Medfield, Needham, and West Roxbury, in the county of Norfolk.

District 8.

The city of Worcester, and the towns of Auburn, Blackstone, Boylston, Brookfield, Charlton, Douglas, Dudley, Grafton, Holden, Leicester, Mendon, Milford, Millbury, New Braintree, Northborough, Northbridge, North Brookfield, Oakham, Oxford, Paxton, Rutland, Shrewsbury, Southborough, Southbridge, Spencer, Sturbridge, Sutton, Upton, Uxbridge, Warren, Webster, Westborough, West Boylston, and West Brookfield, in the county of Worcester; and the towns of Bellingham, Foxborough, Franklin, Medway, Walpole, and Wrentham, in the county of Norfolk.

District 9.

The several towns in the counties of Hampshire and Franklin, and the towns of Ashburnham, Athol, Barre, Berlin, Bolton, Clinton, Dana, Fitchburg, Gardner, Hardwick, Harvard, Hubbardston, Lancaster, Leominster, Lunenburg, Petersham, Phillipston, Princeton, Royalston, Sterling, Templeton, Westminster, and Winchendon, in the county of Worcester.

District 10.

The city of Springfield, and the several towns in Hampden county, together with the several towns in Berkshire county.

    ‡ Changed to Wakefield.
    § Changed to Arlington.

JUDICIARY OF MASSACHUSETTS.

UNITED STATES COURTS.

Nathan Clifford, *Circuit Judge.*
John Lowell, *District Judge.*
George S. Hillard, *District Attorney.*
Walb'ge A. Field, *Asst. Dis. Attorney.*
M. F. Dickinson, Jr., *2d Asst. Dis. Attorney.*
Edward P. Nettleton, *3d Asst. Dis. Attorney.*
Geo. L. Andrews, *Marshal.*
Joseph B. Keyes, *Deputy Marshal.*
Samuel W. Richardson, *Deputy Marshal.*
John G. Stetson, *Clerk Circuit Court.*
Seth E. Sprague, *Clerk District Court.*

[Offices of all the above are at the United States Court House, 140 Tremont Street, Boston.]

Commissioners of the Circuit Court of the United States, for the first Circuit, and District of Massachusetts : Chas. Levi Woodbury, Elias Merwin, Charles P. Curtis, Jr., Caleb Wm. Loring, Wm. S. Dexter, Henry L. Hallett, Charles W. Tuttle, Chas. Demond and W. W. Warren of Boston ; William L. Smith, of Springfield ; Austin S. Cushman, Oliver Prescott, of New Bedford ; and Thornton Davis, of Greenfield.

Circuit Courts, holden 15th of May and 15th of October, in each year.

District Courts, holden at Boston, 3d Tuesday in March ; 4th Tuesday in June ; 2d Tuesday in Sept. ; and 1st Tuesday in Dec. ; and Special Courts are holden usually on each Friday, and on other days at the discretion of the Judge.

SUPREME JUDICIAL COURT.

Reuben A. Chapman, Monson, *Chief Justice.*
Ebenezer R. Hoar, Concord,
Horace Gray, Jr., Boston,
John Wells. Chicopee,
James D. Colt, Pittsfield,
Seth Ames, Boston, *Associate Justices.*
Salary of the Chief Justice. $5,500, and of each Associate, $5,000.
Charles Allen, Boston, *Attorney General.* Salary, $3,500, and $1,000 Clerk hire.

George C. Wilde, Boston, *Clerk for the Commonwealth.*
Geo. W. Nichols, Boston, *Asst. Clerk.*
Albert G. Browne, Jr., Boston, *Reporter.*

LAW TERMS.

At Boston, 1st Wed. Jan. of each year, which term may be adjourned from time to time to such places and times as may be most conductive to the dispatch of business and the interest of the public ; and all questions of law, whether arising upon appeal, exception, or otherwise, and from whichever court, shall be therein entered and determined, if the same arise in either of the following counties : Essex, Suffolk, Middlesex, Norfolk, Plymouth, Bristol, Barnstable, Dukes, or Nantucket.

For Berkshire County, at Pittsfield, 2d Tues. Sept.

For Bristol County, at Taunton, 4th Tues. Oct.

For the Counties of Hampshire and Franklin, at Greenfield, Mon. af. 2d Tues. Sept.

For Hampden County, at Springfield, 4th Mon. Sept.

For Plymouth County, at Plymouth, 3d Tues. Oct.

For Worcester County, at Worcester, 1st Mon. of Oct.

For Essex County, at Salem, 1st Tues. of Nov.

TERMS FOR THE TRIAL OF JURY CASES.

For the Counties of Barnstable and Dukes, at Barnstable, 1st Tues. May.

Berkshire Co., at Pittsfield, 2d Tues. May.

Bristol Co., at Taunton, 3d Tues. Ap. ; at New Bedford, 2d Tues. Nov.

Essex Co., at Salem, 3d Tues. Ap., and 1st Tues. Nov.

Franklin Co., at Greenfield, 2d Tues. April.

Hampden Co., at Springfield, 4th Tues. April.

Hampshire Co., at Northampton, 3d Tues. April.

Middlesex Co., at Lowell, 3d Tues. April; and Cambridge, 3d Tues. Oct.
Nantucket Co., at Nantucket, 1st Tues. July.
Norfolk Co., at Dedham, 3d Tues. Feb.
Plymouth Co., at Plymouth, 2d Tues. May.
Suffolk Co., at Boston, 1st Tues. Oct. and April.
Worcester Co., at Worcester, 2d Tues. April.

SUPERIOR COURT.

——, *Chief Justice.* Sal. $4,440. Julius Rockwell, Pittsfield; Otis P. Lord, Salem; Marcus Morton, Andover; Ezra Wilkinson, Wrentham; John P. Putnam, Boston; Lincoln F. Brigham, Salem; Chester I. Reed, Dedham; Charles Devens, Jr., Worcester, *Associate Justices.* Salary, $4,200 each.

Jos. A. Willard, Boston, *Clerk.*
Edwin A. Wadleigh, Boston, *Asst. Clerk.*
F. H. Underwood, *Clerk (Criminal Business).*

TERMS OF THE COURT.

Barnstable Co., at Barnstable, on Tues. next after 1st Mon. April, and 1st Tues. Sept.
Berkshire Co., at Pittsfield, 4th Mon. Feb., June and Oct. (*Civil*), 1st Mon. Jan. and July (*Criminal*).
Bristol Co., at Taunton, 2d Mon. March and Sept.; at New Bedford, 2d Mon. June and Dec.
Dukes Co., at Edgartown, on last Mon. May and Sept.
Essex Co. at Salem, 1st Mon. June and Dec. (*Civil*), 4th Mon. Jan. (*Criminal*); at Lawrence, 1st Mon. March (*Civil*), 2d Mon. Oct. (*Criminal*); at Newburyport, 1st Mon. Sept. (*Civil*), 2d Mon. May (*Criminal*).
Franklin Co., at Greenfield, 3d Mon. March and 2d Mon. Aug. and Nov.
Hampden Co., at Springfield, 2d Mon. March and June, and 4th Mon. Oct. (*Civil*), 3d Mon. May and 1st Mon. Dec. (*Criminal*).
Hampshire Co., at Northampton, 3d Mon. Feb., 1st Mon. June. 3d Mon. Oct. (*Civil*); 2d Mon. June, and 3d Mon. Dec. (*Criminal*).
Middlesex Co., at Lowell, 2d Mon. Mar. and 1st Mon. Sept. (*Civil*), and 3d Mon. Oct. (*Criminal*); at Cambridge, 1st Mon. June, 2d Mon. Dec. (*Civil*), and 2d Mon. Feb. and 4th Mon. June (*Criminal*).

Norfolk Co., at Dedham, 4th Mon. Ap., Sept., and Dec. (*Civil*). 1st Mon. Apr., Sept., and Dec. (*Criminal*).
Nantucket Co., at Nantucket, 1st Mon. June and Oct.
Plymouth Co., at Plymouth, 2d Mon. Feb. and June, and 4th Mon. Oct.
Suffolk Co., at Boston, 1st Tues. Jan., Ap., July, and Oct. (*Civil*), and 1st Mon. every month (*Criminal*.)
Worcester Co., at Worcester, 1st Mon. March, Mon. next af. 4th Mon. Aug. and 2d Mon. Dec. (*Civil*), 3d Mon. Jan., 2d Mon. May, and 3d Mon. Oct. (*Criminal*); at Fitchburg, 2d Mon. June and Nov. (*Civil*), and 2d Mon. Aug. (*Criminal.*)

DISTRICT ATTORNEYS.

[Elected by the several districts for terms of three years, ending January, 1872.]

Northern District. — Middlesex County, Isaac S. Morse, of Cambridge.
Eastern District. — Essex County, Edgar J. Sherman, of Lawrence.
Southern District. — Bristol, Barnstable, Dukes, and Nantucket Counties, George Marston, of Barnstable.
South-Eastern District. — Norfolk and Plymouth Counties, Edward L. Pierce, of Milton.
Middle District. — Worcester County, Wm. W. Rice, of Worcester.
Western District. — Hampden and Berkshire Counties, Edward B. Gillett, of Westfield.
North-Western District. — Hampshire and Franklin Counties, Samuel T. Spaulding, of Northampton.
Suffolk County. — J. Wilder May, of Boston. P. R. Guiney, of Boston (appointed by Governor and Council), Assistant Attorney.

MUNICIPAL COURTS.

MUNICIPAL COURT OF BOSTON.

John W. Bacon, *Chief Justice.* Mellen Chamberlain and Francis W. Hurd, *Associate Justices.* John C. Leighton, *Clerk,* criminal business. Wm. T. Connolly, *Clerk,* civil business.

MUNICIPAL COURT OF THE SOUTHERN DISTRICT OF BOSTON.

Peter S. Wheelock, *Justice.* Ira Allen and Solomon A. Bolster, *Special Justices.* Alfred Williams, *Clerk.*

MUNICIPAL COURT OF TAUNTON.

William Henry Fox, *Prin. Justice.*
William E. Fuller, *Associate Justice.*
James P. Ellis, *Clerk.*

MUNICIPAL COURT OF WORCESTER.

Hartley Williams, *Standing Justice.* J. A. Titus, *Special Justice.*
Clark Jillson, *Clerk.*

POLICE COURTS.

POLICE COURT OF ADAMS.

Joel Bacon, *Standing Justice.*
Charles Marsh, Henry P. Phillips, *Special Justices.*

POLICE COURT OF CAMBRIDGE.

John S. Ladd, *Standing Justice.*
George W. Livermore, Henry W. Mussey, *Special Justices.* Thomas McIntire, Jr. *Clerk.*
Court sits for trial of criminal cases daily at 9, A. M.; for civil business every Thursday at 10, A. M.

POLICE COURT OF CHARLESTOWN.

George Washington Warren, *Standing Justice.* Charles D. Dunton, *Special Justice.* Andrew J. Bailey, *Clerk.*

POLICE COURT OF CHELSEA.

Hamlett Bates, *Standing Justice.*
Erastus Rugg, Hosea Ilsley, *Special Justices.*

POLICE COURT OF CHICOPEE.

Edwin O. Carter, *Standing Justice.*
Charles Sherman, *Special Justice.*

POLICE COURT OF FALL RIVER.

Louis Lapham, *Standing Justice.*
James Ford, *Special Justice.* Augustus B. Leonard, *Clerk.*

POLICE COURT OF FITCHBURG.

Thornton K. Ware. *Standing Justice.* David H. Merriam, Edward P. Loring, *Special Justices.* F. G. Fessenden, *Clerk.*

POLICE COURT OF GLOUCESTER.

James Davis, *Standing Justice.*
Elbridge G. Friend, *Special Justice.*

POLICE COURT OF HAVERHILL.

Henry Carter. *Standing Justice.*
Thorndike D. Hodges, Wm E. Blunt, *Special Justices.* Joseph K. Jenness, *Clerk.*

POLICE COURT OF LAWRENCE.

Wm. Stevens, *Standing Justice.*
Wm. H. P. Wright, Gilbert E. Hood, *Special Justices.* Chas. E. Briggs, *Clerk.*

POLICE COURT OF LEE.

Isaac C. Ives, *Standing Justice.*
James Bullard, Franklin W. Gibbs, *Special Justices.*

POLICE COURT OF LOWELL.

Nathan Crosby, *Standing Justice.*
George Stevens, John Davis, *Special Justices.* Samuel P. Hadley, *Clerk.*

POLICE COURT OF LYNN.

James R. Newhall, *Standing Justice.* N. Mortimer Hawkes, *Special Justice.* Henry C. Oliver, *Clerk.*

POLICE COURT OF MILFORD.

Charles A. Dewey, *Standing Justice.* Abraham Mead, Elias Whitney, *Special Justices.*

POLICE COURT OF NEW BEDFORD.

Alanson Borden, *Standing Justice.*
Edmund Anthony, Wm. W. Crapo, *Special Justices.* Francis L. Porter, *Clerk.*

POLICE COURT OF NEWBURYPORT.

Wm. E. Currier, *Standing Justice.* John N. Pike, Henry W. Chapman, *Special Justices.* Edward W. Rand, *Clerk.*

POLICE COURT OF PITTSFIELD.

Phineas L. Page, *Standing Justice.*
Geo. S. Willis, James H. Dunham. *Special Justices.*

POLICE COURT OF SALEM.

Jos. G. Waters, *Standing Justice.*
Stephen P. Webb, Joseph B. F. Osgood, *Special Justices.* Samuel P. Andrews, *Clerk.*

POLICE COURT OF SPRINGFIELD.

Jas. H. Morton, *Standing Justice.*
Chas. A. Winchester, Edward Morris, *Special Justices.*

POLICE COURT OF WILLIAMSTOWN.

John R. Buckley, *Standing Justice.*
Andrew M. Smith, Henry L. Sabin, *Special Justices.*

BARNSTABLE COUNTY.

Incorporated, June 2, 1685.

SHIRE TOWN,················ ···············BARNSTABLE.

COUNTY OFFICERS.

Judge of Probate and Insolvency,··· Joseph M. Day,··········*Barnstable.*
Register of Probate and Insolvency,· Jonathan Higgins,···········*Orleans.*
Clerk of the Courts,··············· James B. Crocker,········*Yarmouth.*
Register of Deeds, ···············: Frederick Scudder,··········*Barnstable.*
County Treasurer,·············· Samuel Higgins,··········*Chatham.*

Overseers of House of Correction, Barnstable,···············
- Josiah Hinckley,·········*Barnstable.*
- George A. King,·········*Barnstable.*
- Ebenezer Smith,·········*Barnstable.*

Overseers of House of Correction, Provincetown,···············
- James Gifford,·········*Provincetown.*
- Robert Knowles,·······*Provincetown.*

Sheriff,···················· David Bursley,···········*Barnstable.*

Deputy Sheriffs.

Barnstable, Thomas Harris.
Brewster, S. Clark.
Dennis Port, Isaiah C. Inman.
Falmouth, Isaac S. Lawrence.
Harwich Port, Elbridge G. Doane.
Provincetown, Robert Knowles.
Sandwich, Ezra T. Pope.
Wellfleet, Reuben C. Sparrow.
Yarmouth, Benjamin H. Matthews.

Jailers.

Barnstable, George H. Whelden.
Provincetown, Joshua Cook.

Sessions of Probate Court.

At *Barnstable,* 2d Tuesday of Jan., Feb., Mar., Aug., and Dec., and 3d Tuesday of April, June, and Sept.
At *Falmouth,* 3d Tuesday of Nov.
At *Harwich,* 2d Monday after 1st Tuesday of May, and on 2d Mon. of October.
At *Provincetown,* Wednesday next after 3d Tuesday of May, and on Wednesday next after 2d Monday of October.
At *Wellfleet,* Tuesday next after the 2d Monday of Oct.

County Commissioners.

E. Stowell Whittemore, *Sandwich.* Dec., 1869. James S. Howes, *Dennis.* Term expires, Dec. 1870. Daniel Paine, *Truro,* Dec., 1871.
Special Commissioners, Isaac Bea, *Chatham,* Dec., 1871. Wm. H. Underwood, *Harwich,* Dec., 1871.
Times of Meeting.—At *Barnstable,* 2d Tuesday of April and 2d Tuesday of Oct.

Commissioners of Wrecks.

Barnstable, Thomas Harris.
Chatham, Josiah Hardy.
Eastham, Abijah Mayo.
Hyannis, Alvan S. Hallett.
North Eastham, Isaiah H. Horton.
Orleans, George W. Coming.
Sandwich, Azariah Wing.
Truro, Asa Sellew.
Wellfleet, William Cleverly, Isaiah Hatch, Robert H. Libby, Robert Holbrook, Mulford Rich, John Newcomb.

Commissioners of Insolvency.

Falmouth, Erasmus Gould.
Wellfleet, Robert H. Libby.
Yarmouth, John W. Sears.

Public Administrator.

Truro (North), Smith K. Hopkins.

Commissioners to Qualify Civil Officers.

Barnstable, Joseph M. Day, George Marston, Frederick Scudder.
Brewster, George Copeland, Winslow L. Knowles.
Dennis (West Dennis), Obed Baker, 2d, Zadoc Crowell.
Falmouth, Samuel P. Bourne, Wm. Nye, Jr.
Harwich, Nathaniel Doane, Jr.
West Harwich, Nehemiah D. Kelley.
Orleans, Jonathan Higgins.
Provincetown, Nathan D. Freeman, Jeremiah Stone.
Sandwich, E. Stowell Whittemore, Chas. B. Hall.
Wellfleet, Simeon Atwood, Jr. Thomas Holbrook.
Yarmouth, James B. Crocker.

32 MASSACHUSETTS DIRECTORY.

Justices of the Peace.

[Including Justices of the Peace and Quorum, designated by the star*, and Justices of the Peace and Quorum throughout the Commonwealth, designated by a †].

Barnstable, Chas. C. Bearse, Walter Chipman, †Joseph M. Day, Joseph R. Hall, Alvan S. Hallett. James H. Hallett, †Nathaniel Hinckley, Ferdinand G. Kelley, *Geo. A. King, Elijah Lewis, 2d, Asa E. Lovell, *George Marston, Charles H. Nye, Sylvanus B. Phinney, Frederick Scudder, Nathaniel Sears, John P. Washburn, Asa Young.

Cotuit Port, Andrew Lovell.
West Barnstable, Frederick Parker.
Hyannis, Theodore F. Basset.
Osterville, Geo. H. Hinckley.

Brewster, Freeman Cobb, *George Copeland, Tully Crosby, Solomon Freeman, Samuel H. Gould.

West Brewster, Anthony Smalley.

Chatham, Samuel Higgins, Josiah Mayo, David Mayo, Warren Rogers, Nathaniel Snow, Ephraim Taylor.
Chatham Port, Isaac Bea.
North Chatham, Benj. T. Freeman.
South Chatham, Levi Eldridge.

Dennis, Joshua C. Howes, James S. Howes, Obed Howes.
Dennis Port, Joseph K. Baker, Jr., *James Berry, Shubael B. Howes, Joshua Wixon.
East Dennis, Seth Crowell, Stephen Homer.
South Dennis, Jona. Bangs, Miller W. Nickerson, Marshall S. Underwood.
West Dennis, Obed Baker, 2d, Edward E. Crowell, Nehemiah Crowell, Zadoc Crowell, Alvan Small.

Eastham, Myrick Clark, Mich'l Collins, Elijah E. Knowles.

Falmouth, Samuel P. Bourne, Jabez Davis, Erasmus Gould, Thomas Lewis, Jr., Joshua C. Robinson, George W. Swift, Oliver C. Swift, Richard S. Wood.
North Falmouth, Francis A. Nye.
West Falmouth, Gilbert R. Boyce.

Harwich, Joseph C. Berry, Obed Brooks, Cyrus Cahoon, Frederick Hebard, James S. Paine, Danforth S. Steele, Nathan Underwood.
Harwich Port, Nathaniel Doane, Valentine Doane, jr., Shubael B. Kelley, Ozias Long.
South Harwich, Cyrus Weeks.
West Harwich, Isaiah Chase, Davis Lothrop.

Orleans, John Doane, † Jonathan Higgins, Ensign B. Rogers.
South Orleans, † John Kenrick.

Provincetown, Jonathan Cook,

Nathaniel H. Dill, Nathan D. Freeman, James Gifford, Simeon S. Gifford, Benj. F. Hutchinson, Godfrey Rider, Jeremiah Stone.

Sandwich, Benjamin F. Bourne, Edward W. Ewer, Hiram T. Gray, Charles B. Hall, Ebenezer Nye, Frederick S. Pope, Asa Raymond, † E. Stowell Whittemore.
South Sandwich, Solomon C. Howland.

Truro, Daniel Paine.
North Truro, Smith K. Hopkins.

Wellfleet, Ebenezer T. Atwood, Simeon Atwood, Ebenezer Freeman, Thomas Holbrook, Robert H. Libby, Nathaniel P. Wiley.

Yarmouth, Chas. Thacher.
Yarmouthport, James B. Crocker, Amos Otis, * Charles F. Swift.
South Yarmouth, Russell D. Farris, Elisha Taylor.
West Yarmouth, Theodore Drew.

Trial Justices.

Barnstable (Hyannis), Theodore F. Basset.
Chatham (Port), Isaac Bea.
Dennis (South), Marshall S. Underwood.
Falmouth, Richard S. Wood.
Provincetown, Benjamin, F. Hutchinson.
Sandwich, E. Stowell Whittemore.
Yarmouth (Port), James B. Crocker.

Notaries Public.

Barnstable, George A. King, George Marston.
Hyannis, Alvan S. Hallett.
Brewster, Tully Crosby.
Chatham, Isaiah Harding, Warren Rogers.
Dennis, Obed Baker, 2d.
Dennisport, Joseph K. Baker. jr.
West Dennis, Edward E. Crowell.
Falmouth, Richard S. Wood.
Harwich, William H. Underwood.
West Harwich, Nehemiah D. Kelley, Anthony Kelley.
Provincetown, Thomas Hillard, Benjamin F. Hutchinson, Godfrey Rider.
Sandwich, Charles B. Hall, E. Stowell Whittemore.
Truro (North), Smith K. Hopkins.
Wellfleet, Thomas Holbrook.
Yarmouth (Port), Wm. P. Davis.

Coroners.

Barnstable, Special, Thos. Harris.
Provincetown, Jeremiah Stone.
Sandwich, Isaac K. Chipman.
Truro, Daniel Paine.

Agent Province Lands.

Provincetown, Joshua E. Bowley.

BERKSHIRE COUNTY.
Incorporated, April 21, 1761.
SHIRE TOWN......................PITTSFIELD.
COUNTY OFFICERS.

Judge of Probate and Insolvency,.... James T. Robinson,....North Adams.
Register of Probate and Insolvency,... Andrew J. Waterman,... ...Lenox.
Clerk of the Courts,................ Henry W. Taft,............Lenox.
Register of Deeds (North District),.. Richard Whitney,......... Adams.
Register of Deeds (Middle District),.. George J. Tucker,... ....Lenox.
Register of Deeds (South District),... Isaac Seeley,......Great Barrington.
County Treasurer,......·......... George J. Tucker,...........Lenox.
Overseers of House of Correction,.. { Henry W. Taft,............Lenox.
George J. Tucker, ...Lenox.
Sheriff,........................ Graham A. Root,..........Sheffield.

Deputy Sheriffs.
Adams, William G. Farnsworth; —
Adams (North), Wm. Hodskin, Josiah Q. Robinson.
Becket, Timothy F. Snow.
Great Barrington, Harvey Holmes, F. G. Abbey.
Hinsdale, J. M. Tuttle.
Lanesborough, J. W. Newton, Henry H. Newton.
Lee, A. H. Pease, Moses H. Pease, Otis S. Lyman.
Lenox. Phineas Cone, Hiram R. Wellington.
Otis, Edward L. Day.
Peru, George Wells.
Pittsfield, John Crosby, jr.
Sheffield, George B. Cook.
Stockbridge, Horace P. Streeter.
Tyringham, Lucien B. Moore.
West Stockbridge. George H. Cobb.
Williamstown, John R. Bulkley, Samuel B. Kellogg.

Jailer.
Lenox, Phineas Cone.

Sessions of Probate Courts.
At Great Barrington, Wed. next after 1st Tu. in Feb., Apr., June, Oct., and Dec.
At Lee, Wed. next after 1st Tu. of Jan., Mar., May, July, and Sept.
At Pittsfield, 1st Tu. of Jan., Feb., March, Ap., May, June, Sept., Oct., and Dec., and 3d Tu. in July, and 2d Tu. of Nov.

Sessions of Court of Insolvency.
At Pittsfield, 1st Wed. of every month.

County Commissioners.
Henry Noble, Pittsfield, term expires Dec. 1869 ; William Hill. Lenox, term expires Dec. 1870 ; William T. Filley, Lanesborough, term expires Dec. 1871.

Special Commissioners, Emmons Arnold, Sheffield ; John B. Wells, Cheshire.
Times of Meetings. — At Pittsfield, 1st Tu in April, July, and Sept., and last Tu. in Dec.

Commissioners of Insolvency.
Adams (North), Arnold G. Potter.
Lenox, Andrew J. Waterman.
Pittsfield, Edgar M. Wood.

Public Administrator.
Stockbridge, Henry J. Dunham.

Masters in Chancery.
Lee, John Branning.

Commissioners to Qualify Civil Officers.
Adams (North), Henry P. Phillips Benjamin F. Robinson.
Dalton, Zenas M. Crane.
Great Barrington, Billings Palmer, Increase Sumner, Ralph Taylor.
Lanesboro', William T. Filley.
Lenox, Henry W. Taft, George J. Tucker, William S. Tucker.
New Marlboro', Noah Gibson.
Pittsfield, Robert W. Adam, James M. Barker, J. N. Dunham.
Sandisfield (New Boston), Orlo Burt.
Stockbridge, Henry J. Dunham, Charles M. Owen.
Williamstown, Henry L. Sabin, John Tatlock.

Justices of the Peace.
(Including Justices of the Peace and Quorum, designated by a *, and Justices throughout the Commonwealth, designate by a t.)
Adams, Oscar A. Archer, John F. Arnold, Frederick P. Brown, Daniel F. Burlingame, Henry J. Bliss, Hiram T. Crandall, William G. Farnsworth, Franklin O. Sayles, Daniel Upton; —
North Adams, Nathan S. Babbitt, Joel Bacon, Salmon Burlingame,

William McKay, Henry S. Millard, George W. Nottingham, Henry P. Phillips, *William P. Porter, Andrew Potter, Arnold G. Potter, Abiathar W. Preston, *Benj. F. Robinson, †James T. Robinson, Jarvis Rockwell, Shepard Thayer, Ezra D. Whitaker, Ashley B. Wright.

Alford, Reuben C. Fitch, Ezra C. Ticknor.

Becket, Mark P. Carter, William S. Huntington, Charles O. Perkins; — *West Becket*, Stephen W. Carter.

Charlemont, Bernard N. Farren.

Cheshire, Henry J. Brown, Stephen Chapman, Edmund D. Foster, James N. Richmond.

Clarksburg, Waterman Brown, Fred. H. Brunson.

Dalton, † Zenas M. Crane, Henry Ferre, Alvin B. Hayes, William H. Wharfield.

Egremont (South), Joseph A. Benjamin, Henry E. Codding, John M. Joyner; —*North Egremont*. *James H. Rowley, William W. Stillman.

Florida, Nahum P. Brown, Israel Whitcomb.

Great Barrington, R. N. Couch, Justin Dewey, Jr., William Dewey, Julius Dresser, Augustine Giddings, Walter W. Hollenbeck, Herbert C. Joyner, Seth Norton, Billings Palmer, Isaac Seeley, John M. Seeley, *Increase Sumner, Charles J. Taylor, Joseph Tucker, Merritt I. Wheeler.

Hancock, Lyman Eldridge, Lester Gorton, Calvin P. Lapham, Rufus L. Mason.

Hinsdale, Theodore Barrows, *Milo Stowell, Amory E. Taylor, Charles K. Tracy, John M. Tuttle.

Lanesborough, Wm. T. Filley, Wm. A. Fuller, Wm. B. McLaughlin, Jedediah W Newton, Ezra H. Sherman, Justus Tower, Richard Whitney.

Lee, Alonzo Bradley, John Branning, Harrison Garfield, Wm. H. Harding, Albert M. Howk, John M. Howk, Edward A. Langdon, Samuel S. Rogers, Norman W. Shores, Edwin Sturges, Marshall Wilcox; —*South Lee*, Amos B. Manley.

Lenox, †Julius Rockwell, Henry W. Tait, *George J. Tucker, *William S. Tucker, Andrew J. Waterman, Hiram B. Wellington ; —*Lenox Furnace*, Robert G. Averill, Henry Sedgwick, Thomas Sedgwick.

Monterey, Marshall S. Bidwell, Album J. Fargo, Egbert B. Garfield, Milton Judd, Wilber C. Langdon, Wm. S. Langdon, William Wallace

Langdon, Oscar L. Mansir, Lyman Thompson, Albert Tryon.

Mount Washington, Orrin C. Whitbeck.

New Ashford, Phinehas Harmon, George W. Phelps, Noble F. Roys.

New Marlborough, Harvey Sheldon, Augustus Turner, Elias Wright, Sheldon W. Wright ; —*Hartsville*, Harlow S. Underwood; —*Mill River*, Edwin Adam.

Otis, Alanson Crittenden, Elam P. Norton, Samuel H. Norton. *East Otis*, Henry G. Mather.

Peru, Benjamin F. Pierce, George Wells.

Pittsfield, Robert W. Adam, James M. Barker, Samuel W. Bowerman, † Henry S. Briggs, Benjamin Chickering, †Henry Chickering, Henry Colt, †James D. Colt, † Thomas Colt, John Crosby, jr., Daniel Day, James H. Dunham, Charles N. Emerson, Lorenzo H. Gamwell, Jacob L. Greene, Samuel E. Howe, Jared Ingersoll, Matthias R. Lanckton, Phineas L. Page, Thomas P. Pingree, * Thos. F. Plunkett, † Wm. R. Plunkett, Wesley L. Shepardson, William M. Walker, John C. West, Edgar M. Wood.

Richmond, William Bacon.

Sandisfield, Franklin G. Abby, Joshua M. Sears, Edward C. Wolcott. *Montville*, Thos. M. Judd, Wm. W. Langdon, George A. Shepard, Orlo Wolcott.—*New Boston*, *Orlo Burt, Samuel C. Parsons.

Savoy, Jos. B. Ingraham, Leonard McCulloch, Harmon Snow.

Sheffield, James Bradford, John D. Burtch. Bela N. Clark, Edward Ensign, Oliver Peck, Gilbert Smith.— *East Sheffield*, Roscoe C. Taft.—*Ashley Falls*, Robert E. Hedden.

Stockbridge, Henry J. Dunham, Daniel B. Fenn, Joseph R. French, †John Z. Goodrich, John B. Hull, Marshall Warner.

Curtisville, Henry M. Burrall.

Tyringham, Eli G. Hale.

Washington, Simpson Bell, Philip Eames.

West Stockbridge, George H. Cobb, Geo. W. Kniffin, Wm. M. Kniffin, Wm. C. Spaulding.

Williamstown, John R. Bulkley, Keyes Danforth, *Daniel Dewey, Benjamin F. Mills, Henry T. Tallmadge, John Tatlock, †Joseph White.

Windsor, Norman Miner, Ahimaz W. Warren, James L. White.—*East Windsor*, George Hathaway, Reuben

Pierce. Philo Wright.—*Savoy*, Andrew J. Babbitt.

Trial Justices.

Becket (North), William S. Huntington.
Great Barrington, Billings Palmer.
Hinsdale, Charles J. Kittridge.
Lenox, William S. Tucker.
New Marlborough, Harlow S. Underwood.
. Sandisfield, Joshua M. Sears.
Sheffield, Oliver Peck.
Stockbridge, Henry J. Dunham.
West Stockbridge, Wm. C. Spaulding.

Notaries Public.

Adams (North), Wm. P. Porter, Arnold G. Potter, Edward S. Wilkinson.—*(South)*, Henry J. Bliss, Franklin O. Sayles, Harvey H. Wellington.

Great Barrington, Isaac Seeley, Isaac B. Prindle.
Lee, John Branning, Norman W. Shores, Wm. Taylor, Marshall Wilcox.
Pittsfield, Robert W. Adam, James M. Barker, James Buel, Charles N. Emerson.
Stockbridge, Henry J. Dunham, Jonathan E. Field, Daniel R. Williams.
West Stockbridge, Henry F. Fitch.

Coroners.

Dalton, Joseph W. Russell.
Lee, Abial H. Pease.
Lenox (special), Hiram B. Wellington.
Pittsfield, Oliver E. Brewster, Henry M. Peirson, Walter Tracy.
Sheffield, George B. Cooke.
Williamstown, John R. Bulkley.

1755052

BRISTOL COUNTY.

Incorporated, June 2, 1685.

COUNTY TOWNS.........TAUNTON AND NEW BEDFORD.

COUNTY OFFICERS.

Judge of Probate and Insolvency.... Edmund H. Bennett.......*Taunton.*
Register of Probate and Insolvency... W. E. Fuller............*Taunton.*
Clerk of Courts................... Simeon Borden..........*Taunton.*
Registers of ⎱ *North District*....... Joseph Wilbar...........*Taunton.*
. Deeds ⎰ *South District*......... Charles C. Sayer......*New Bedford.*
County Treasurer................ Thomas J. Lothrop........*Taunton.*
Overseers of House of Correction.. ⎰ James D. Thompson ⎱ *New Bedford.*
                                    ⎱ John B. Baylies ⎰
Sheriff........................ Chas. B. H. Fessenden..*New Bedford.*
Jailers................ .... ⎰ Isaac G. Carrier.........*Taunton.*
                                  ⎱ Charles D. Burt.......*New Bedford.*

Deputy Sheriffs.

Attleborough, James W. Riley, Quincy A. Hooper.
Dartmouth, Wm. Barker, Jun.
Easton, Rufus H. Willis.
Fall River, James Wixon, Joseph Healy, Franklin Gray.
Fairhaven, Albert G. Liscomb.
Freetown, Guilford Hathaway.
Mansfield, Alson W. Cobb.
Norton, George H. Arnold.
New Bedford, Charles D. Burt, H. N. Kimball, Wm. S. Cobb, Philip H. Howland.
Raynham, S. W. Robinson.
Somerset, Edmund Buffinton.
Swansea, James Barney.
Taunton, Isaac G. Carrier, Henry

F. Cobb, Orrin M. Ingalls, Sylvester Makepeace, Geo. H. Babbitt, jun., Peter C. Thayer.

Sessions of Probate Courts.

At *Fall River*, 1st Fr. of Jan., Apr., Oct., and 2d Fr. of July.

At *New Bedford*, 1st Fr. of Feb., May, Aug., and Nov.; also, by adjournment, on the third Wednesday of each month.

At *Taunton*, 1st Fr. of March, June, Sept., and Dec.; also, by adjournment, on the 3d Fr. of every month, at the Registry Office, from 10 to 11 o'clock, A. M.

Sessions of Court of Insolvency.

At *New Bedford*, 3d Wednesday of every month.

At *Fall River;* at such times as business may require.

County Commissioners.

E. B. Towne, *Raynham,* term expires 1869; Elisha Thornton, jr., *New Bedford,* term expires 1870; Guilford H. Hathaway. *Fall River,* term expires 1871.

Special Commissioners, Leonard Hodges, *Norton,* term expires Dec., 1871; Abraham Dyer, *Westport,* term expires Dec. 1871.

Times of Meeting.—At *Taunton,* on the 4th Tuesdays in March and Sept.

Commissioners of Insolvency.

Mansfield. E. Maltby Reed.
New Bedford, Chas. W. Clifford.
Taunton. Geo. Edgar Williams.

Commissioners of Wrecks.

New Bedford, Job Almy.
Westport, Abraham Dyer, Edward Akin.

Public Administrators.

New Bedford, Edwin L. Barney, Charles T. Bonney, Wm. W. Crapo, Richard A. Pierce.

Master in Chancery.

New Bedford, Edwin L. Barney.

Commissioners to Qualify Civil Officers.

Easton (North), Anson Gilmore.
Easton (South), Seba Howard.
Fall River, Hezekiah Battelle, Josiah C. Blaisdell, Simeon Borden, John S. Brayton, James Ford, Foster Hooper, Phineas W. Leland.
Freetown, Ebenezer W. Peirce.
New Bedford, Eli Haskell, Thomas M. James, Wm. H. Taylor, James D. Thompson, Jos. S. Tillinghast.
Taunton, George H. Babbitt, Samuel L. Crocker, James P. Ellis, Horatio Pratt, Joseph Wilbar, George M. Woodward, Thomas J. Lothrop.

Justices of the Peace.

(Including Justices of the Peace, and Quorum designated by a *, and Justices throughout the Commonwealth, designated by a †.)

Acushnet, Cyrus E. Clark, Benjamin White, — *Long Plain,* Abial P. Robinson.

Attleborough, Henry K. W. Allen, John T. Bates, N. H. Bliss, Simeon Bowen, *Elkanah Briggs, Joseph W. Capron, John Daggett, Lyman W. Dean, *Hartford Ide, † Elisha G. May, Joseph A. Perry, *Henry Rice, Horatio N. Richardson, Lyman M. Stanley, Gardner C. Wright. — *North Attleborough,* Thomas A. Barden, Homer M. Daggett, Thomas G. Sandland, Timothy A. Stanley. — *South Attleboro',* Wm. P. Shaw.

Berkley, Wm. Bobbitt, Abiel B. Crane, Oliver E. French, Giles L. Leach, Walter D. Nichols.

Dartmouth, Elisha S. Crapo, Francis W. Mason. — *North Dartmouth,* Wm. Barker, jun., Albert F. Chase, Calvin K. Turner, 2d, Hiram Whalon. — *South Dartmouth,* Benjamin S. Anthony, Samuel M. Davis, John Grey.

Dighton. Geo. C. Burgess, William Cobb, Noah Chace, Oliver Eaton, Jeremiah P. Edson. Geo. E. Gooding, Alfred W. Paul, Joseph Pitts, Jervis Shove.

Easton, †Oliver Ames, Tisdale Harlow, George W. Kennedy, Albert A. Rotch. — *North Easton,* Joseph Barrows, Alson Gilmore, Charles H. Reed, John H. Swain, Daniel B. Wheaton. George G. Withington. — *South Easton.* †Guilford White, Seba Howard, Harrison T. Mitchell.

Fairhaven, Henry T. Aiken. Lemuel S. Aiken, Edwin R. Almy, Chas. Bryant, James V. Cox, Charles Drew, John A. Howes, Albert Sawin, Geo. H. Taber, Job C. Tripp.

Fall River, Job B. Ashley, Geo. A. Ballard, *Hezekiah Battelle, Josiah C. Blaisdell, Frederick A. Boomer. †Simeon Borden, †John S. Brayton, Robert C. Brown, Edward P. Buffinton, Samuel A. Chace, Oliver Chace, John Collins, Prelet D. Conant, William M. Connelly, Henry Dinan, Charles C. Dillingham, †Walter C. Durfee, Benjamin Earl, Alexander D. Easton, Morton Eddy, George O. Fairbanks, †James Ford, Stephen B. Gifford, William R. Gordon, Horatio N. Guam, Abraham G. Hart, Guilford H. Hathaway, John B. Hathaway, Charles J. Holmes, *Foster Hooper, Wm. H. Jennings, *Phineas W. Leland, Aug. B. Leonard, Benjamin K. Lovatt, Jas. M. Morton, James M. Morton, jun., William H. Peirce, Thomas T. Potter, Clinton V. S. Remington, John P. Slade, Isaac Smith jr., Charles P. Stickney, Benjamin F. Winslow, *Eliab Williams, Jona. M. Wood, Jas. Wixon, †Stephen C. Wrightington.

Freetown, Alden Hatheway, Thomas G. Nichols, Ebenezer W. Peirce. — *East Freetown,* Charles A. Morton. Reuel Washburn.

Mansfield, Moses H. Baker, William B. Bates, Jacob A. Blake, Darwin Deane, Ellis Fairbanks, Thomas M. George, William Graves, Thomas E. Grover, Herman Hall, Elijah Hodges, Artemas C. King, Wm. Robinson, Seth C. Shepard, Isaac Stearns, Charles P. White.

New Bedford, †Charles Almy, Edmund Anthony, †Edwin L. Barney, Joseph A Beauvais, Charles T. Bonney, Alanson Borden, George A. Bourne. T. Frank Brownell, James M. Bunker. Charles D. Burt, *Edward N. Burt, Samuel P. Burt, Chas. W. Clifford, †John H. Clifford, Wendell H. Cobb, William S. Cobb, Thomas Coggeshall, David B. Coleman, †James B. Congdon, Timothy D. Cook, William Cook, †William W. Crapo, Austin S. Cushman, John Davis, Ezra K. Delano, Tilson B. Denham, Tristram R. Dennison, *Thomas D. Eliot, †Rodney French, Nathaniel Gilbert, George C. Hatch, Moses E. Hatch, Luther G. Hewins, James C. Hitch, *Joshua C. Hitch, Abraham H. Howland, Cornelius Howland, jun., †George Howland, jun., Thos. M. James, Wm. H. Johnson, David B. Kempton, Manasseh Kempton, Horatio N. Kimball, Warren Ladd. George R. Long, Adam Mackie, Albert K. Paulding, †Richard A. Peirce. John H. Perry, George R. Phillips, William Phillips, Andrew G. Pierce, Philip A. Pierce, †Robert C. Pitman, *Francis L. Porter, Thos. T. Potter, *Oliver Prescott, Isaiah C. Ray, Benj. T. Rickerson, James Robinson, Morrill Robinson, jr, Charles C. Sayer, Otis Seabury, Thos. M. Stetson, Joshua C. Stone, William H. Taylor, Elias Terry, William C. Thomas, *James D. Thompson, *John T. Tillinghast, *Joseph S. Tillinghast, Charles W. Underwood, Hiram Van Campen, Lemuel T. Wilcox. Allred Wilson, Borden Wood, James B. Wood.

Norton, Horatio Bates, Daniel S. Cobb, George B. Crane. John Crane, Leonard Hodges, Harrison T. Lincoln, Austin Messenger, John R. Rogerson, Wm. D. Witherell, Elkanah Wood.

Raynham, Braddock Field, Samuel Jones. Sylvanus Makepeace, Joseph R. Presho, Godfrey Robinson. Nathan W. Shaw, Seth D. Wilbur. —*Taunton*, Enoch King.—*East Taunton*, Chauncey G. Washburn.

Rehoboth, George W. Bliss, Danforth G. Horton, Cyrus M. Wheaton. —*North Rehoboth*, Lemuel Morse.

Seekonk, Raymond H. Burr, Davis Carpenter, Viall Medbury.

Somerset, George F. M. Forrester, William P. Hood, Job M. Leonard, Joseph Marble, Avery P. Slade, Jonathan B. Slade.

Swansea, Joseph G. Luther, Allen Mason, Wm. Mitchell.—*North Swansea*, Mason Barney, jr.

Taunton. Charles H. Atwood, Geo. B. Atwood, Geo. H. Babbitt, †Edmund H. Bennett, Zebina Blake. Wm. Brewster. James Brown, William H. Brown, †Samuel L. Crocker, Robert Crossman 2nd, Jas. H. Dean, James M. Cushman. *Jas. P. Ellis, Charles Foster, William H. Fox, Henry J. Fuller, William E. Fuller, Henry N. Harvey, Andrew H. Hall, John Holland, James R. Husband, Abijah M. Ide, Charles F. Johnson, †Thomas J. Lothrop, Chas. L. Lovering, Willard Lovering, Steph. Peirce, *Horatio Pratt, Allen Presbrey. John Radley, Charles A. Reed, Erastus M. Reed, John E. Sanford, Albert E. Swasey, Peter C. Thayer, Samuel M. Tinkham. Geo. A. Washburn, Isaac Washburn, Jos R. Wheeler. †Henry B. Wheelwright, Joseph Wilbar. Jos. E. Wilbar, G. Edgar Williams, Henry Williams, George M. Woodward, Solomon Woodward, jr.—*East Taunton*, David Dean.

Westport, George H. Gifford. Isaac Howland.—*South Westport*, Zelotes L. Almy, Charles Fisher.—*Central Village*, Ezra P. Brownell.

Trial Justices.

Easton, Albert A. Rotch.

Freetown, Ebenezer W. Peirce.

Mansfield, Erastus M Reed.

North Attleborough, Henry Rice.

Somerset, Jonathan B. Slade.

Swansea (North), Mason Barney, jr.

Taunton. James P. Ellis.

Westport, Geo. H. Gifford.

Notaries Public.

Attleborough, John Daggett, Lyman W. Dean, George B. Richards. *North Attleborough*, Simeon Bowen.

Easton, George W. Kennedy, John H. Swain.

Fairhaven. Edwin R. Almy, Chas. Drew.

Fall River. Josiah C. Blaisdell, Fred. A. Boomer, Simeon Borden, John S. Brayton, Robert C. Brown, Benjamin Earl, Morton Eddy, Chas. J. Holmes, James M. Morton. jr. Charles P. Stickney, Eliab Williams, Benjamin F. Winslow.

New Bedford. †Joseph A. Beauvais. Charles T. Bonney, Alanson Borden, James M. Bunker, Samuel P. Burt, Christopher A. Church, Charles W. Clifford, Wendell H. Cobb, Wm.

W. Crapo, Austin S. Cushman, Thomas Dawes Elliot, Geo. C. Hatch. Isaac Howland, Elisha C. Leonard, Edward Munro, Albert R. Paulding, Robert C. Pitman, Isaiah C. Ray, Joseph L. Silva, Henry F. Shearman, Thomas M. Stetson, Joshua C. Stone, James Taylor, Wm. H. Taylor, Frederic A. Washburn, William H. Watkins, Augustus L. West, Borden Wood. *Taunton,* James P. Ellis, Wm. E. Fuller, Charles A. Reed, George M. Woodward.

Coroners.

Attleborough, John T. Bates, Elijah R. Read, Lyman M. Stanley.
Dighton, Alfred W. Paul.
Fall River. Chas. C. Dillingham.
Freetown. Ebenezer W. Peirce.
New Bedford, Horatio N. Kimball, William O. Russell.
Raynham, Seth D. Wilbur.
Somerset. Philip Bowers, Geo. F. M. Forrester.
Taunton, special, George H. Babbitt, jr.

DUKES COUNTY.

Incorporated, 1683.

SHIRE TOWN, ... EDGARTOWN.

COUNTY OFFICERS.

Judge of Probate and Insolvency, ...	Theodore G. Mayhew, ... *Edgartown.*
Register of Probate and Insolvency, ..	Hebron Vincent, ... *Edgartown.*
Clerk of Courts, ...	Richard L. Pease, ... *Edgartown.*
Register of Deeds, ...	John S. Smith, ... *Edgartown.*
County Treasurer, ...	Barnard C. Marchant, ... *Edgartown.*
Sheriff, ...	Samuel Keniston, ... *Edgartown.*
Deputy Sheriffs, ... {	Thomas H. Lambert, ... *Chilmark.* Jonathan Luce, ... *Tisbury.*
Jailer, ...	Samuel S. Daggett, ... *Edgartown.*

Sessions of Probate Court.

At *Edgartown,* 3d Mon. of Jan. and July, and 1st Mon. of March and Dec.
At *Tisbury,* 3d Mon. of April, and 1st Mon. of Sept.
At *West Tisbury,* 1st Mon. of June and 3d Mon. of Oct.

County Commissioners.

John W. Mayhew, *Chilmark,* term expires Dec., 1869 ; James Mayhew, *Tisbury,* Dec., 1870; Charles J. Barney, *Edgartown,* Dec., 1871.
Special Commissioners. — Abraham C. White, *Gosnold,* Dec. 1871; Archibald Mellen, *Edgartown,* Dec., 1871.
Times of Meeting. — At *Edgartown,* Wed. next after 3d Mon. in May, and Wed. next after 2d Mon. in Nov.

Commissioners of Insolvency.

Chilmark, James O. Lambert.
Edgartown, Archibald Mellen.
Tisbury, Frederick W. Manter.

Public Administrator.

Edgartown, Samuel G. Vincent.

Commissioners of Wrecks.

Edgartown, William P. Chadwick, Charles F. Dunham, Thomas J. Dunham, Rufus F. Pease.

Commissioners to Qualify Civil Officers.

Edgartown, Theo. G. Mayhew, Joseph T. Pease.
Tisbury, Thomas Bradley.

Justices of the Peace,

*[Including Justices of the Peace and Quorum, designated by a * and Justices throughout the Commonwealth, designated by a t]*

Chilmark, Smith Mayhew, John W. Mayhew.
Edgartown, Sirson P. Coffin, Joseph Dunham, Ichabod N. Luce, Barnard C. Marchant, †Theodore G. Mayhew, Archibald Mellen, †Samuel Osborne, Jr., Jeremiah Pease, *Joseph T. Pease, *Richard L. Pease, Rodolphus Pease, Hebron Vincent.
Gosnold, John W. Gifford.
Tisbury, Henry Bradley, Moses Brown, Matthew P. Butler, Samuel Flanders, William B. Mayhew, Eliakim Norton.— *W. Tisbury,* John D. Rotch.

Trial Justices.

Edgartown, Jeremiah Pease.
Tisbury, Eliakim Norton.

Notaries Public.

Edgartown, Wm. Bradley, Wm. P. Chadwick, Sirson P. Coffin, David Davis. Charles F. Dunham, Tarlton C. Luce, Shaw Norris, Joseph T. Pease, Richard L. Pease.

Gosnold, John W. Gifford.
Tisbury, Henry W. Beetle. Henry Bradley. Chas. Holmes, John Holmes, John Holmes, Jr.

Coroner.

Tisbury (Holmes's Hole), John Holmes, Jr.

ESSEX COUNTY.

Incorporated May 10, 1643.

SHIRE TOWNS .... SALEM, NEWBURYPORT, AND LAWRENCE.

COUNTY OFFICERS.

Judge of Probate and Insolvency,.... George F. Choate ....Salem.
Register of Probate and Insolvency,.. Abner C. Goodell, Jr.........Salem.
Clerk of Courts, ... Asahel Huntington..........Salem.
Register of Deeds,................. Ephraim Brown..............Salem.
County Treasurer, ... Allen W. Dodge. ....Hamilton.

Overseers of House of Correction at Lawrence,
{ Ebenezer B. Currier..... Lawrence.
  John Keeley.............Haverhill.
  Sherman Nelson. ......Georgetown.

Overseers of House of Correction at Ipswich,
{ Henry Hobbs ....Wenham.
  S. P. Cummings ....Danvers.
  Aaron Sawyer...........Amesbury.

Sheriff,......................... Horatio G. Herrick.......Lawrence.

Deputy Sheriffs.

Amesbury, Joseph T. Clarkson.
Andover, E. Kendall Jenkins.
Danvers, Charles H. Adams.
Essex, Ezra Perkins, Jr.
Georgetown, Otis Thompson, Geo. W. Boynton.
Gloucester, George Lane.
Haverhill, Phineas E. Davis, David Boynton.
Ipswich, Joseph Spiller.
Lawrence, Alanson Briggs, James M. Currier.
Lynn, Charles Merritt.
Methuen, Charles E. Goss.
Newburyport, John Akerman, Jas. W. Cheney.
Peabody, Stephen Upton.
Salem, Dan'l Potter, John D. Cross.

Jailers.

Newburyport, John Akerman.
Salem, John D. Cross.
Lawrence, Horatio G. Herrick.

Masters of House of Correction.

Ipswich, Yorick G. Hurd.
Lawrence, Horatio G. Herrick.

Sessions of Probate Court.

At *Gloucester*, 2d Tu. in April and Oct.
At *Haverhill*, 3d Tu. in May and Nov.
At *Ipswich*, 3d Tu. in March and Sept.
At *Lawrence*, 2d Tu. in Jan., Feb , March, June, Sept., Nov.. and Dec.
At *Newburyport*, 3d Tu. in Jan., Feb., April, June, Jy., Oct., and Dec.
At *Salem*, 1st Tu. in every month.

Sessions of Court of Insolvency.

At *Salem*, on the 2d and 4th Mon. of each month.
At *Lawrence*, on Probate Court days in afternoon.
At *Newburyport*, on Probate Court days in afternoon.

County Commissioners.

James Kimball, *Salem*. term exp. 1869; Jackson B. Swett, *Haverhill*, term exp. 1870; Charles P. Preston, *Danvers*. term exp. 1871.
Special Commissioners — Amos Poor, *West Newbury*. Daniel W. Bartlett, *Essex*; terms expire 1871.

Times and Places of Meeting — At *Ipswich*, on the 2d Tu. of April. *Salem*, on the 2d Tu. of July. *Newburyport*, on the 2d Tu. of Oct. On the 4th Tu. of Dec., at *Salem*, *Ipswich*, or *Newburyport*, as the Court may determine at the term next preceding. At *Lawrence*, on the last Tu. of Aug.

Commissioners of Insolvency.
Lawrence, William L. Thompson. *Newburyport*, Wm. E. Currier. *Salem*, Wm. P. Upham.

Public Administrators.
Andover, George Foster. *Gloucester*, David W. Low. *Newburyport*, Edmund Smith. *Salem*, Wm. P. Upham. *Saugus*, Elijah P. Robinson.

Masters in Chancery.
Hamilton. Daniel E. Safford. *Lawrence*, Nathan W. Harmon, Edgar J. Sherman. *Salem*, Geo. F. Choate, Jonathan C. Perkins.

Commissioners of Wrecks.
Gloucester, John Ayars, Jr., Dan. Robinson. *Ipswich*, Theodore Andrews. *Lynn*, Nathaniel Lear. *Newburyport*, Edmund Smith. *Swampscott*, John Chapman.

Commissioners to Qualify Civil Officers.
Andover, George Foster, Nathan W. Hazen. *Beverly*, Fred. W. Choate, James Hill. *Gloucester*, Charles P. Thompson, John S. Webber. *Haverhill*, David Boynton, James H. Duncan, Jas. Gale, William Taggart. *Ipswich*, Charles Kimball, Geo. R. Lord. *Lawrence*, James H. Eaton, George R. Rowe. *Lynn*, Wm. Bassett, Amos Rhodes, Jeremiah C. Stickney. *Marblehead*, Joseph P. Turner. *Newbury*, Daniel Lunt. *Newburyport*, John T. Brown, Moses Pettingell, John Porter, Edward W. Rand. *Salem*, John Chapman, Asa'l Huntington, Charles Kimball, George R. Lord, Joseph B. F. Osgood, George Wheatland, Henry Whipple.

Justices of the Peace.
(*Including Justices of the Peace and Quorum, designated by a *; and Justices throughout the Commonwealth designated by a †.*)

Amesbury, Wm. C. Binney, Jones Frankle, Joseph Gale, Joseph Merrill, *Jonathan Nayson, Orlando S Patten. — *South Amesbury*, Charles E. Rowell, Geo. Turner. — *West Amesbury*, †Joshua Colby, John S. Morse, Frederick Sargent, Patten Sargent, David M. Tukesbury.

Andover, Asa A. Abbott, Isaac O. Blunt, William Chickering, †Francis Cogswell, Samuel T. Cooper, John Flint, †George Foster, George W. Foster, Moses Foster, Samuel Gray, *Nathan W. Hazen, John B. Jenkins, *Samuel Merrill, †Marcus Morton, Willard Pike.

Beverly, Hooper A. Appleton, †John I. Baker, Stephens Baker, †Frederick W. Choate, Francis J. Crowell, Chas. Davis Robert R. Endicott, Josiah A. Haskill, James Hill, John B. Hill, Abraham B. Lord, Elijah E. Lummus, Nathan P. Meldrum, Francis Norwood, Joseph E. Ober, Samuel Porter, George Roundy, Joseph D. Tuck, Richard P. Waters, Elisha Woodberry.

Boxford. Benj. S. Barnes, Moses Dorman, John F. Kimball, George Perley.

Bradford, Henry Carter, Harrison E. Chadwick, †George Cogswell, Charles B. Emerson, Walter Goodell, Nathaniel Hatch, Wm. Hazletine, Samuel W. Hopkinson, *George Johnson, Horatio Pearl.

Danvers, I. W. Andrews, Francis Dodge, Samuel P. Fowler, Horace L. Hadley, Andrew Nichols, John W. Porter, John A. Putnam, George Tapley, William L. Weston. — *Danversport*, Ebenezer Hunt, Rufus Putnam.

Essex, Daniel W. Bartlett, Aaron L. Burnham, Ebenezer Burnham, Hervey Burnham, *Nehemiah Burnham, *David Choate, Ezra Perkins, Jr. Ebenezer Stanwood.

Georgetown, Charles E. Jewett, †Jeremiah P. Jones, Caleb Tenney, Gorham D. Tenney, Orlando B. Tenney, Richard Tenney.

Gloucester, John J. Babson, Edward E. Burnham, Henry A. Burnham, Benj. H. Corliss, John Corliss, James Davis, Elbridge G Friend, Charles E. Grover, David W. Low, George J. Marsh, Aaron Parsons, Alfred Presson, Joseph O. Procter, Benjamin H. Smith, Cyrus Story, Chas. P. Thompson. — *East Gloucester*, Humphrey L. Calder. — *Annisquam*, John N. Davis. — *Lanesville*, Joseph Blood.

Groveland, Wm. S. Balch, Nathan-

iel H. Griffith, Charles W. Hopkinson, Gardner P. Ladd, Nathaniel Ludd, Amos Parker, *Jacob W. Reed, *Charles G. Savary, Jeremiah Spofford.

Hamilton, William A. Brown, Jos. P. Lovering, Daniel E. Safford.

Haverhill, John A. Appleton, Wm. E. Blunt, Franklin Brickett, David Boynton, Calvin Buttrick, Jesse Clement, Henry Cummings, Alpheus Currier, James T. Davis, Phineas E. Davis, †James H. Duncan, Wm. B. Eaton, Orenzo T. Emerson, Edward G. Frothingham, Edward G. Frothingham, jr., James Gale, James E. Gale, Charles E. Hall, Andrew W. Hammond, Thorndike D. Hodges, †Nathaniel S. Howe, †Caleb D. Hunking, *Elias T. Ingalls, Addison B. Jaques, Wm. Jeffers, Joseph K. Jenness, John Keeley, *Alfred Kittredge, Nathan S. Kimball, John Jas. Marsh, Henry N. Merrill, John B. Merrill, Chas. J. Noyes, John M. Poor, Oliver H. Roberts, William Taggart, Samuel White, Elbridge G. Wood.—*East Haverhill*, Ensign S. Hunkins.

Ipswich, Theodore Andrews, Stephen Baker, Wesley K. Bell, *Aaron Cogswell, Gilbert Conant, Joseph Farley, Wm. H. Graves, George Haskell, †Chas. Kimball, Charles A. Kimball, Edward P. Kimball, George R. Lord, Joseph Ross, Charles A. Sayward, Joseph Spiller, *Abram D. Wait.

Lawrence, Nathaniel Ambrose, Pardon Armington, Clark L. Austin, Horace C. Bacon, James L. Barker, Jonathan C. Bowker, Charles E. Briggs, Elbridge T. Burley, Geo. D. Cabot, Alonzo C. Chadwick, Benj. Coolidge, Ebenezer B. Currier, James H. Eaton, Alfred J. French, George A. Fuller, John S. Gile, W. Fisk Gile, Henry H. Hall, *Nathan W. Harmon, Rollin E. Harmon, Michael D. Hart, Gilbert E. Hood, William H. Jaquith, William D. Joplin, Wm. S. Knox, George S. Merrill, William Morse, Christopher G. Newton, E. B. Osgood, Thomas A. Parsons, Joseph L. Partridge, Robert W. Pearson, William R. Pedrick, George H. Poor, John R. Rollins, George R. Rowe, Aretes R. Sanborn, John C. Sanborn, †George W. Sargent, Caleb Saunders, Daniel Saunders, Daniel Saunders, Jr , Edgar J. Sherman, Henry L. Sherman, James H. Stannard, Artemas W. Stearns, Ivan Stevens, William Stevens, Andrew C. Stone, David S.

Swan, John K. Tarbox, Wm. L. Thompson, Nathaniel G. White, Geo. P. Wilson, William H. P. Wright.

Lynn, Daniel Alley, Gustavus Andrews, David Austin, Charles C. Aver, William Bassett, Jacob Batchelder, John Batchelder, John W. Berry, Samuel J Berry, Abijah E. Blood, Andrews Breed, Hiram N. Breed, Jos. Breed, 2d. Geo. H. Chase, Charles B. Clough, *Oliver B. Coolidge, *Edward S. Davis, Thomas Driver, Benjamin V. French, John E. Gray, *Joseph Haines, N. Mortimer Hawkes, William Howland, Ephraim A. Ingalls, Nathaniel Ingalls, William F. Johnson, Benj. H. Jones, Charles E. Kimball, Rufus Kimball, James S. Lewis, Valentine Meader, Edwin J. Medbury, Charles Merritt, Henry Moore, Benjamin Mudge, Ezra W. Mudge, Peter M. Neal, Asa T. Newhall, George T. Newhall, James R. Newhall, Joseph P. Newhall, *Thomas B. Newhall, Henry C. Oliver, Isaiah H. Parrott, Eben Parsons, Ira J. Patch, †Dean Peabody, Daniel Perley, Edward K. Phillips, Charles J. Pickford, Wm. D. Pool, Amos Rhodes, Simon J. Roney, George D. Sargeant, James M. Sargent, Joseph N. Saunderson, †Wm Schouler, John L. Shorey, N. Everett Silsbee, Herbert A. Smith, Charles H. Stickney, *Jeremiah C. Stickney, Amos P. Tapley, Waldo Thompson, Wilder S. Thurston, Minot Tirrell, Jr., Cyrus M. Tracy, Geo. B. Tucker, †Gardiner Tufts, †Roland G. Usher, Jabez Wood, John P. Woodbury.

Lynnfield, Andrew Mansfield, Josiah Newhall. — *Lynnfield Centre*, Jacob Hood, John Perkins.

Manchester, David B. Kimball, John Lee, John Price.

Marblehead, Sam. Bowden, Glover Broughton, Wm. B. Brown, William H. Coates, *William Fabens, William C. Fabens, Thomas Foss, William Gilley, Jr., Jas. Gregory, William G. Haskell, Andrew Lackey, Wm. W. Pratt, John Sparhawk, Samuel S. Trefry, Joseph P. Turner.

Methuen, Chas. F. Abbott, Stephen Barker, †Gerry W. Cochrane, John Davis, Jacob J. Emerson, Jr., John W. Frederick, George W. Gage, Charles E. Goss, Joseph Howe, †Jos. S. Howe, Joseph F. Ingalls, John Low, Ebenezer Sawyer, Chas. Shed.

Middleton, Amos Batchelder, Eben S. Phelps.

Nahant, Washington H. Johnson.

Newbury, David S. Caldwell, William Little, Daniel Lunt, Henry E. Pearson, Hermon D. Rogers — *Byfield*, Martin Root.

Newburyport, David J. Adams, *John Akerman, Josiah Atkinson, Michael Atkinson, Isaac. H. Boardman, William H. Brewster, Jacob G. Brown, John T. Brown, John Burrill, Henry W. Chapman, Frederick J. Coffin, Stephen Collins, Charles Cook. Moody D. Cook, Albert Currier, William E. Currier, †Caleb Cushing, William Cushing, Charles C. Dame, Benjamin Davis, Jr., Nathaniel Foster, B. Gardner Gerrish, Joseph G. Gerrish, Major Goodwin. Thomas C. Goodwin, William Graves, Nathaniel Greeley, Joshua Hale, Josiah L. Hale, Moses E. Hale, George W. Hill, Nathaniel Hills, Philip K. Hills, Jacob Horton, Francis A. Howe, George W. Jackman, Jr., Harrison G. Johnson, Colby Lamb, *Caleb Lamson, Micajah Lunt. *Stephen W. Marston, David J. Merrill, Amos W. Mooney, *Edward S. Moseley, C. Osgood Norse, Nathan A. Moulton, Henry W. Moulton, Amos Noyes. Thomas Pearson, *Moses Pettingell, †Samuel Phillips, Nathaniel Pierce, †Daniel P. Pike, John N. Pike, Richard Plumer, *Edward W. Rand, Moses D. Randall, David Smith, *Edmund Smith, John H. Smith. Wooster Smith, †Eben P. Stone, Jacob Stone, William Thurston, David Wood.

North Andover, Daniel Carleton, George L. Davis, James M. Hubbard, Theron Johnson, Horace N. Stevens, Moses T. Stevens.

Peabody, †Alfred A. Abbott, Lewis Allen, Francis Baker, Sidney C. Bancroft, James P. King, George A. Osborn, Benjamin C. Perkins, Fitch Poole, †Eben S. Poor, Nathan H. Poor, Moses Preston, *John W. Proctor, Thomas E. Proctor, Thomas A. Stimpson, †William Sutton, Stephen Upton, William Walcott, Hiram O. Wiley, Daniel Woodbury.

Rockport, Zeno A. Appleton, Eben Blatchford, Henry Dennis, Henry Dennis, Jr., Ezra Eames, Newell Giles, John W. Marshall, Alfred Parsons, William Pool, George H. Vibbert, William Whipple, Nathaniel F. S. York.

Rowley, Edward Smith, J. Scott Todd.

Salem, Nathaniel K. Allen, *Samuel P. Andrews, Wm. Archer, Eleazer Austin, John A. Bassett, Ephraim Brown, †Albert G. Browne, John T. Burnham, Samuel B. Buttrick, *Joseph S. Cabot, John Carlton, Oliver Carlton, †John Chapman, †George F. Choate, William S. Cleveland, William Cogswell, Humphrey Cook, Francis Cox. George R. Curwen, William H. Dalrymple, Henry Derby, John H. Derby, *George H. Devereux, John D. Eaton, William C. Endicott, John G. Felt, George F. Flint, †Caleb Foote. Wm. H. Foster, Charles B. Fowler, James A. Gillis, Abner C. Goodell, Jr., Benj. A. Gray, Mark Haskell, Nathaniel J. Holden, George Holman, Thomas F. Hunt, †Asahel Huntington, *Stephen B. Ives, Jr., John Jewett, Daniel H. Johnson, Thomas H. Johnson, James Kimball, John Kinsman, William W. Lander, Solomon Lincoln, Jr.. Thos. Looby, †Otis P. Lord, George B. Loring, *Micajah B. Mansfield, William Maynes, Henry P.. Moulton, Ezra F. Newhall, †William D. Northend, William Northey, †Henry K. Oliver, Charles S. Osgood, †Joseph B. F. Osgood, Robert Osgood, John Brooks Parker, Edward F. Payson, Robert Peele, George F. Peirson, Aaron Perkins, †Jonathan C. Perkins, Jairus W. Perry, Chas. A. Phillips. Stephen H. Phillips, Willard P. Phillips. Geo. D. Phippen, Chas. H. Price, Robert S. Rantoul, Charles A. Richardson, Joseph J. Rider, David Roberts, James Ropes, Charles Sewall, James Shatswell, Henry B. Smith, James C. Stimpson. Augustus Story, Gilbert L. Streeter, Charles E. Symonds. Nathaniel G. Symonds. J. Hardy Towne, *Charles W. Upham, William P. Upham, George Upton, Benjamin E. Valentine, *Eben N. Walton. *Joseph G. Waters, *Stephen P. Webb. Nath'l Weston, *George Wheatland, Stephen G. Wheatland, Jonathan F. Worcester.

Salisbury, George W. Cate. Thomas J. Clark, Benjamin Evans, *Josiah B. Gale, Benjamin E. Fifield, Aaron Morrill, jr., John Rowell, Azor O. Webster, Daniel Webster.—*East Salisbury*, Cyrus Dearborn, jr.

Saugus, Augustus B. Davis. Geo. W. Fairbanks, Harmon Hall. Wilbur F. Newhall, William H. Newhall. Elijah P. Robinson, George H. Sweetser.

Swampscott, William H. Fletcher, Philander Holden. Samuel C. Pitman.

Topsfield. Joseph W. Batchelder, Nehemiah Cleaveland. Nathaniel Conant, Charles H. Holmes, Salmon D.

Hood, Samuel S. McKenzie, *Richard Phillips. jr., Benjamin Poole.

Wenham, Andrew Dodge, Rufus A. Dodge.

West Newbury. *David L. Ambrose, John C. Carr, Nehemiah F. Emery, Edmund Little. William Merrill, Joseph Newell, Thomas : S. Ordway, Samuel Rogers.

Trial Justices.

Amesbury, Geo. Turner.
Andover, George H. Poor.
Beverly. James Hill.
Essex. David Choate.
Georgetown, Orlando B. Tenney.
Ipswich, Joseph Farley.
Marblehead, William Fabens.
Methuen, William M. Rogers.
Peabody, Benjamin C. Perkins.
Rockport, Henry Dennis.
Rowley, J. Scott Todd.
Salisbury, George W. Cate.
Saugus, Augustus B. Davis.

Notaries Public.

Amesbury, George Turner.
Andover, George Foster, George H. Poor.
Beverly, Fred'k W. Choate, Samuel Porter, Joseph D. Tuck.
Danvers, Samuel Preston.
Gloucester, James Davis, John B. Dennis, David W. Low, Benjamin H. Smith. -- *East Gloucester*, Humphrey L. Calder.

Haverhill, David Boynton, Moses E. Emerson, John L. Hobson, John J. Marsh, William Taggart.
Lawrence, John F. Cogswell, W. Fisk Gile, Nath'l G. White.
Lynn, Edward S. Davis, William Howland. James R. Newhall, Amos Rhodes, Cyrus M. Tracy.
Marblehead, Samuel Bowden, William Fabens, James Gregory.
Newburyport, Isaac H. Boardman, John T. Brown, Henry W. Chapman, John Porter, Edward W. Rand.
Peabody, Alfred A. Abbott, Benjamin C. Perkins, Fitch Poole.
Salem, Samuel P. Andrews, Wm. C. Endicott, James A. Gillis, Henry P. Guilford, Micajah B. Mansfield, Joseph B. F. Osgood, Joseph G. Waters, Stephen P. Webb, Jonathan F. Worcester.
Salisbury, Thomas J. Clark.

Coroners.

Amesbury, George Turner.
Andover, Stephen Tracy.
Danvers, Richard Hood.
Georgetown, Joseph P. Stickney.
Lawrence, John Stowe, — special, William D. Lamb.
Lynn, Hiram N. Breed.
Newburyport, Wooster Smith, Edward W. Rand.
Salem, Eben N. Walton.
West Newbury, Nehemiah F. Emery.

FRANKLIN COUNTY.

Incorporated, June 24, 1811.

SHIRE TOWN,............... ....GREENFIELD.

COUNTY OFFICERS.

Judge of Probate and Insolvency.... Charles Mattoon,.........*Greenfield*.
Register of Probate and Insolvency.. Chester C. Conant,......*Greenfield*.
Clerk of Courts,................... Edward E. Lyman,......*Greenfield*.
Register of Deeds,............... Humphrey Stevens,......*Greenfield*.
County Treasurer,.............. Bela Kellogg,...........*Greenfield*.
Overseers of House of Correction,.. { Lewis Merriam, ...*Greenfield*.
Rufus Howland, ...*Greenfield*.
Sheriff, ... Solomon C. Wells,........*Greenfield*.

Deputy Sheriffs.

Ashfield, Job Lilly.
Buckland, Justus B. Frost.
Charlemont, Charles Peck.
Coleraine, Shubael B. Buck.
Conway, George C. Kaulback.
Deerfield (South), Austin Ware.

Greenfield. Lorenzo D. Joslyn, Geo. A. Kimball. Chauncey Bryant.
Montague, William W. Thayer.
Northfield. Elisha Alexander.
Orange, Wilson Wheeler.
Shutesbury, John H. Forbes.

Deputy in Hampshire County.

Amherst, Frederick A. Palmer.

Northampton, Ansel Wright, Jr.

Jailer and Master of House of Correction.

Solomon C. Wells, *Greenfield.*

Sessions of Probate Court.

At *Conway.* 3d Tu. in May.

At *Greenfield*, 1st Tu. of every month except November.

At *Northfield*, on the 2d Tu. in May and September.

At *Orange*, 2d Tu. in March and Dec., and 3d Tu. in June.

At *Shelburne Falls*, on the 21 Tu. in Feb. and 4th Tu. in October.

Sessions of Court of Insolvency.

At *Greenfield*, on the 1st Monday in each month.

County Commissioners.

Davis Goddard. *Orange;* Richard C. Arms, *Deerfield;* Geo D. Crittenden, *Buckland.*

Special Commissioners, William C. Campbell. *Conway*; Albert Montague, *Sunderland.*

Times of Meeting. — At *Greenfield*, 1st Tu. in March and Sept., and 2d Tu. in June and Dec.

Commissioners of Insolvency.

Greenfield, Geo W. Bartlett.

Orange, Hiram Woodward.

Shelburne, H. M. Puffer.

Public Administrator.

Greenfield, Humphrey Stevens.

Masters in Chancery.

Greenfield, Chester C. Conant, Samuel O. Lamb.

Commissioners to Qualify Civil Officers.

Charlemont, Stephen Bates; *East Charlemont*, Roger H. Leavitt.

Greenfield, Daniel W. Alvord. Almon Brainard, Chester C. Conant, Wendell T. Davis, George Grennell, Whiting Griswold, Edward E. Lyman, Charles Mattoon, Humphrey Stevens.

Orange, Davis Goddard, Edwin Stone, Hiram Woodward.

Justices of the Peace.

[Including Justices of the Peace and Quorum, designated by a *, and Justices throughout the Commonwealth, designated by a †.]

Ashfield, Lott Bassett, Silas Blake. Alvin Perry, Henry S. Ranney. *South Ashfield*, Wait Bement, Charles H. Day.

Bernardston, Silas N. Brooks, Bryant S. Burrows. William Dwight, Aretas Ferry, Ebenezer S. Hulbert.

Buckland, Ezekiel D. Bement, Josiah Trow. — *Shelburne Falls*, Jas. S. Halligan.

Charlemont, Richard E. Field, Isaac D. Hawkes, Horace H. Mayhew, Joseph H. Sears, Ansel L. Tyler. — *East Charlemont*, B. Parsons Mansfield, Ashmun H. Taylor, Roger H. Leavitt.

Coleraine, Orson R. Curtis, Hugh B. Miller, David L. Smith, Hezekiah Smith, Ephraim H. Thompson.

Conway, Henry W. Billings, Horace B. Childs, *Asa Howland, Austin Rice, John D. Todd.

Deerfield, Wm. D. Bates, Dexter Childs, David W. Childs, Henry S. Childs, Austin DeWolf, Virgil M. Howard, Robert M. Pease, Ransom N. Porter, George Sheldon, Christopher A. Stebbins, Moses Stebbins. — *South Deerfield*, Charles Stowell, Nath'l G. Trow, Artemas Williams.

Erving, Newton J. Benjamin, Noah Rankin.

Florida, Nahum P. Brown.

Gill, Nelson Burrows, Josiah D. Canning, Roswell Field, Jonathan S. Purple.

Greenfield, *David Aiken, George W. Bartlett, Joseph Beals, Edward Benton, *Almon Brainard, Henry A. Buddington. Chester C. Conant, *Wendell T. Davis, *Austin DeWolf, Wm. Elliott, Bernard N. Farren, Alfred R. Field, Charles K. Grennell, †George Grennell, *Whiting Griswold, Wm. S. B. Hopkins, Rufus Howland, Samuel O. Lamb, Theo. Leonard, Edward E. Lyman, Samuel J. Lyons, †Charles Mattoon, Lewis Merriam, Daniel H. Newton, *Sam'l H. Reed, Fred. G. Smith, Humphrey Stevens, Anson K. Warner, *Wm. B. Washburn, Alfred Wells, Noah S. Wells, Gorham D. Williams.

Hawley, William O. Bassett.

Heath, Aaron Dickinson.

Leverett, Luther Dudley, Alden C. Field, Humphrey S. Leach.

Leyden, George Childs.

Monroe, David Goodell.

Montague, Philander Boutwell, Isaac Cheney, Sandford Goddard, Erastus F. Gunn, Seymour Rockwell, Harrison F. Root, Joseph H. Root, William W. Thayer, Charles P. Wright.

New Salem, Samuel Giles, Elijah F. Porter, Willard Putnam, Jabez Sawyer. — *Millington*, Lyman E. Moore. — *North New Salem*, Beriah W. Fay.

Northfield, Elisha Alexander, Sam'l W. Dutton, Charles Osgood, Albert C. Parsons, Charles Pomeroy.

Northfield Farms, Simeon A. Field.
Orange, Edward Barton, Rufus D. Chase, Damon E. Cheney, Andrew J. Clark, Levi Gage. Jr., Davis Goddard, George A. Maynard, †Edwin Stone, John W. Wheeler, Geo. A. Whipple, Hiram Woodward. — *North Orange*, Hillel Baker.
Rowe, Samuel P. Everett, James M. Ford.
Shelburne, Orsamus O. Bardwell, Charles M. Duncan, Pliny Fisk, Elam Kellogg.
Shelburne Falls, Samuel D. Bardwell, Samuel T. Field, Zebulon W. Field, James S. Halligan, Alanson K. Hawks, Arthur Maxwell.
Shutesbury, Hardin Hemenway, Samuel H. Stowell.
Sunderland, Henry J. Graves, Avery D. Hubbard, †Horace Lyman, Albert Montague, John M. Smith, Levi P. Warner, D. Dwight Whitmore. — *South Deerfield*, Nathaniel G. Trow.
Warwick, James Goldsbury, Clark Stearns. James Stockwell.
Wendell, Thomas D. Brooks.

Wendell Depot, John C. Holston.
Whately, James M. Crafts, Samuel Lesure, Justin R. Smith, Samuel B. White.

Trial Justices.

Charlemont, Richard E. Field.
Coleraine, Hugh B. Miller.
Greenfield, Almon Brainard, Wendell T. Davis.
Leverett (North), Luther Dudley.
Montague, Sanford Goddard.
Orange, Hiram Woodward.
Shelburne Falls, Samuel D. Bardwell.

Notaries Public.

Conway, Henry W. Billings.
Greenfield, William H. Allen, Wendell T. Davis, Charles K. Greenell.
Orange, Rufus D. Chase.
Shelburne Falls, Samuel T. Field, Alanson K. Hawks, Arthur Maxwell.

Coroners.

Deerfield, Moses Stebbins.
Gill, Roswell Purple.
Greenfield, Rufus Howland. Sam'l J. Lyons; *Special*, Alfred Wells.

HAMPDEN COUNTY.

Incorporated, February 20, 1812.

COUNTY OFFICERS.

Judge of Probate and Insolvency,.... William S. Shurtleff,.... *Springfield*.
Register of Probate and Insolvency,... Samuel B. Spooner,...,...*Springfield*.
Clerk of Courts,................. George B. Morris,.......*Springfield*.
Register of Deeds,................. James E. Russell,.......*Springfield*.
County Treasurer,................. M. Wells Bridge,.......*Springfield*.
Overseers of House of Correction,.. { George Dwight,..... ....*Springfield*.
Gideon Wells,......... *Springfield*.
E. V. B. Holcomb ....*Chicopee*.
Sheriff,......................... Addison M. Bradley,.....*Springfield*.

Deputy Sheriffs.

Blandford, W. H. H. Blair.
Chicopee, N. Cutler.
Chicopee (Falls), Morris Morton.
Granville, Ethan D. Dickinson.
Huntington, G. S. Lewis.
Holyoke, Thomas H. Wellington.
Ludlow, Davenport L. Fuller.
Monson, Edward P. Newton.
Palmer, James S. Loomis.
Palmer (Thorndike), Geo. Moores.
Springfield, David A. Adams, A. H. G. Lewis.

Tolland, Philip L. C. Slocum.
Westfield, L. B. Walkly, Timothy M. Cooley.
E. Wilbraham, E. C. Colton.
South Wilbraham, F. K. Lathrop.

Jailer.

Addison M. Bradley, *Springfield*.

Sessions of Probate Court.

At *Monson*, 2d Tu. of June.
At *Palmer*, 2d Tu. of Sept.
Springfield, 1st Tu. of Jan., Feb., Mar., April, May, June, July, Sept.,

Nov., Dec., and 4th Tu. of April, Aug., and Sept.

At *Westfield*, 3d Tu. Mar. June, Sept. and Dec.

Sessions Court of Insolvency.

At *Springfield*, 2d and 4th Sat., of each month.

County Commissioners.

Randolph Stebbins, *Longmeadow*, Term expires Dec. 1871. Phinehas Stedman, *Chicopee*. Term expires Dec. 1870. Wm. M. Lewis, *Blandford*, Term expires, Dec. 1869.

Special Commissioners.

Albert D. Bagg, *W. Springfield*. Term expires Dec. 1871. Newton S. Hubbard, *Brimfield*, Term expires Dec. 1871.

Times of Meeting. — At *Springfield*, 2d Tu. of April, and 1st Tu. of Oct. and 4th Tu. of June and Dec.

Commissioners of Insolvency.

Palmer, James G. Allen. *Agawam*, Charles C. Wright. *Westfield*, Henry B. Lewis.

Public Administrator.

Palmer, James G. Allen.

Commissioners to Qualify Civil Officers.

Palmer, James G. Allen, Gordon M. Fisk.

Springfield, George Bliss, George B Morris, Oliver B. Morris, Samuel B. Spooner, William S. Shurtleff.

Westfield, William G. Bates, Jas. Fowler, Norman T. Leonard, Henry B. Lewis, Milton B. Whitney.

Wilbraham (*South*), Solomon C Spelman.

Justices of the Peace.

[*Including Justices of the Peace and Quorum, designated by a* *; *and Justices throughout the Commonwealth designated by a* §]

Agawam,. Joseph Bedortha, James H. Ferre. *Feeding Hills*, Charles C. Wright.

Blandford, Wm. M. Lewis, Elisha W. Shephard. — *North Blandford*, Samuel A. Bartholomew.

Brimfield, *Henry F. Brown, Jas. B. Brown, Samuel W. Brown. — *East Brimfield*, Parsons Allen.

Chester, Joel Haskins, Elisha C. Pease. — *Chester Centre*, Benjamin B. Eastman, Thad. K. Dewolf. *North Chester*, William M. Bemis, Herman Powers.

Chicopee, Ezekiel Blake, Edwin O. Carter, Edward W. Chapin, Nath'l

Cutler, Lester Dickinson, Amory Doolittle, Enoch V. B. Holcomb, George H. Knapp, George D. Robinson, *George M. Stearns, Warren Smith, Phineas Stedman, †John Wells. — *Chicopee Falls*, Andrew Hubbard, George S. Taylor.

Granville (*Corners*), Rufus H. Barlow, Ralph S. Brown, William Wells. *East Granville*, Daniel H. Drake. *West Granville*, James M. Goodwin.

Holland, William A Webber.

Holyoke, Joseph P. Buckland, S. Stewart Chase, Chester Crafts, Chas. H. Heywood, Robert Mitchell, Jos. Murray, William B. C. Pearsons, *Porter Underwood.

Longmeadow, Gad O. Bliss, Dimon Chandler, Stephen T. Colton. *East Longmeadow*, George W. Converse, Oliver Wolcott.

Ludlow, Chauncy L. Buell, John P. Hubbard, Eli M. Smith, Henry K. Wight.

Monson, †John M. Brewster, Jr., Joseph H. Brewster, George A. Convers, †William N. Flynt, *Austin Fuller, Edward F. Morris, Hiram Newton, George H. Newton, John Newton, Calvin S. Pease, Daniel G. Potter, Joseph L. Reynolds, Joshua Tracey, Joel B. Williams.

Montgomery, Horace Bartholomew, Berijah H. Kagwin.

Palmer, Braman B. Adams, James G. Allen, Alonzo V. Blanchard, Samuel M. Bliss, Enos Calkins, *Gordon M. Fisk. — *Thorndike*, Joseph H. Blair, *Gamaliel Collins, Gamaliel Collins, Jr., Charles L. Gardner, Abraham R. Murdock, Samuel Shaw, †Horace P. Wakefield. — *Three Rivers*, George W. Randall, Dwight M. Stebbins.

Russell, Nelson D. Parks.

Southwick, Sardis Gillett, Seymour L. Granger, Amasa Holcomb, Ransford W. Kellog, Joseph W. Rockwell, Carmi Shurtleff.

Springfield, Waitstill H. Allis, †Henry Alexander, Jr., Charles A. Beach, Stephen C. Bemis, Augustine Bent, †George Bliss, Ephraim W. Bond, Henry W. Bosworth, Melville W. Bridge, Albert D. Briggs, Timothy M. Brown, Horatio N. Case, Wm. G. Chamberlain, Horace J. Chapin, Samuel Chapin, Benjamin Davis, Timothy M. Dewey, Elijah W. Dickinson, Hugh Donnelly, Albert T. Folsom, Edmund Freeman, Joseph B. Gardiner, Homer N. Gilmore, William S. Greene, Sanford J. Hall, Erastus Hayes, Roger B. Hildreth, Henry S.

Hyde, *Joseph Ingraham, James Kirkham, Marcus P. Knowlton, Henry S. Lee, Charles R. Ladd, Nehemiah A. Leonard, Charles Marsh, James E. McIntire, William E. Montague, Roger S. Moore. Edward Morris, *Henry Morris, George B. Morris. *James H. Morton, Simeon Newell, William Patton, Smith R. Phillips, Samuel W. Porter, Joseph C. Pynchon, *Caleb Rice, Charles W. Rice, James A. Rumrill, James E. Russell, Sidney Sanders, Stephen E. Seymour, Charles L. Shaw, William S. Shurtleff, Heman Smith, *William L. Smith, Augustus L. Soule, Samuel B. Spooner, John M. Stebbens, †William Stowe, †James M. Thompson, Lewis A. Tifft, †Eliphalet Trask, †George Walker, Gideon Wells, Charles A. Winchester.

Tolland, Aurelius Fowler, Geo. W. Granger, Fowler T. Moore, Philander F. Twining.

Wales, Ferdinand L. Burley, Absalom, Gardner, Elijah Shaw.

Westfield, †William G. Bates, Phineas L. Buell, †James Fowler. Samuel Fowler, *Henry Fuller. James C. Greenough, *Norman T. Leonard, *Henry B. Lewis, Leicester Loomis, David Moseley, Asa P. Rand, Millard L. Robinson, Homer B. Stephens, Asa B. Whitman, Milton B. Whitney.

West Springfield, Richard Beebe, John W. Harmon, Edward Parsons, Justin L. Worthy.

Wilbraham, A. Jackson Blanchard, Luther B. Bliss, John M. Merrick, William W. Merrick, Ira G. Potter, Francis J. Warner.—*South Wilbra*ham, Gilbert Rockwood, Solomon C. Spellman, William P. Spellman.

Trial Justices.

Holyoke, William B. C. Pearsons, Porter Underwood.

Monson, Austin Fuller.

Palmer, Gamaliel Collins ; *special*, Chas. L. Gardner.

Russell, Nelson D. Parks.

Westfield, Samuel Fowler, Henry B. Lewis.

Wilbraham (South), Solomon C. Spellman.

Notaries Public.

Chicopee, Edward P. Nettleton, Edward H. Lathrop, George D. Robinson. George M. Stearns.

Holyoke, Charles W. Ranlet, Porter Underwood.

Monson, John Newton, Joel B. Williams.

Palmer, James G. Allen.

Springfield, Ephraim W. Bond, T. Alden Curtis. William S. Greene, Frederic H. Harris, Edward H. Hyde, Henry S. Lee, Chas. Marsh, James E. McIntire, Edward Morris, James A. Rumrill, Stephen E. Seymour, Augustus L. Soule, John M. Stebbins, Jas. M. Thompson. Geo. Walker.

Westfield, Henry Fuller, Henry B. Lewis, Asa P. Rand, Homer B. Stevens, Milton B. Whitney.

Coroners.

Holyoke, Charles Blodgett.

Springfield, Joseph Ingraham, Wm. E. Montague. Eliphalet Trask.

Westfield. Jehiel Abbott. *Special*, James H. Waterman.

HAMPSHIRE COUNTY.

Incorporated, May 7, 1662.

SHIRE TOWN,................NORTHAMPTON.

COUNTY OFFICERS.

Judge of Probate and Insolvency,.... Samuel F· Lyman,.....*Northampton*.
Register of Probate and Insolvency,.. Luke Lyman, ...*Northampton*.
Clerk of Courts,................. William P. Strickland,..*Northampton*.
Register of Deeds,................ Harvey Kirkland,.....*Northampton*.
County Treasurer,................ Henry S. Gere,......*Northampton*.
Overseers of House of Correction,.. { William P. Strickland,.*Northampton*.
  Luke Lyman,........*Northampton*.
  Daniel Kingsley,......*Northampton*.
Sheriff,................ Henry A. Longley,....*Northampton*.

Deputy Sheriffs.

Amherst, Frederick A. Palmer.
Belchertown, Samuel W. Longley.
Easthampton, J. Lyman Campbell.
Enfield, Henry M. Potter.
Hadley, Enos E. Cook.
Huntington, Gilbert S. Lewis.
Northampton, Ansel Wright, Ansel Wright, Jr.
Plainfield, Leonard Campbell.
South Hadley, Samuel N. Miller.
Ware, Samuel H. Phelps.
Worthington, Edward C. Porter.

Deputies in Hampden County.

Holyoke; Thomas H. Wellington.
Westfield, L. B. Walkley.

Deputies in Franklin County.

Greenfield, Lorenzo D. Joslyn, Chauncey Bryant.

Jailer and Master of House of Correction.

Henry A. Longley, *Northampton*.

Sessions of Probate Court.

At *Amherst*, 2d Tu. in Jan. and Aug.
At *Belchertown*, 2d Tu. in May and Oct.
At *Northampton*, 1st Tu. of every month.
At *Williamsburg*, 3d Tu. in May and Oct.

Sessions of Court of Insolvency.

At *Northampton*, 2d Wednesday of every month.

County Commissioners.

P. Smith Williams, *Hadley*, term expires 1869; Elisha A. Edwards, *Southampton*, 1870; Justin Thayer, *Northampton*, 1871.
Special Commissioners.—L. Nathan Graves, *Williamsburgh*, 1871; Austin Eastman, *Amherst*, 1871.
Times of Meeting.—At *Northampton*, 1st Tu. in March, Sept., and Dec., and Tu. next after 2d Monday of June, annually.

Commissioners of Insolvency.

Belchertown, Franklin Dickinson.
Enfield, Charles S. Richards.
Northampton, Wm. P. Strickland.

Public Administrators.

Northampton, Samuel L. Parsons.
Ware, Otis Lane.

Commissioners to Qualify Civil Officers.

Amherst, Ithamar F. Conkey,
Belchertown, Calvin Bridgman.
Enfield, Josiah B. Woods.
Northampton, Haynes H. Chilson, Harvey Kirkland, Henry A. Longley,

William P. Strickland, Oliver Warner, Eliphalet Williams.
Ware, George H. Gilbert, Franklin D. Richards.

Justices of the Peace.

(Including Justices of the Peace and Quorum, designated by a *, and Justices throughout the Commonwealth, designated by a †).

Amherst, Simeon Clark, William S. Clark, † Ithamar F. Conkey, Edward P. Cushman, John E. Cushman, George Cutler, † Edward Dickinson, Wm. A. Dickinson, Henry A. Marsh, Abner G. Mosman, Frederick A. Palmer, Oliver Pease. — *North Amherst*, Marshall B. Cushman, Horace Cutler.
Belchertown, Leonard Barrett, Phineas Bridgman, Franklin Dickinson, Thos. R. Greene, Asahel Goodell, Joshua G. Longley, * Samuel W. Longley.
Chesterfield, Oliver Edwards, Albert Nichols, Orson M. Pearl.
Cummington Francis H. Dawes, Darius W. Lovell, Nathan Orcutt, William Richards — *West Cummington*, Fordyce Whitmarsh.
Dana, Daniel Stone.
Easthampton, William G. Bassett, Lafayette Clapp, William N. Clapp, George S. Clark, Chas. B. Johnson, † Horatio G. Knight, Lauren D. Lyman, Edmund H. Sawyer, Alfred L. Strong, Seth Warner, Charles E. Williams, Joseph W. Winslow, Samuel Williston.
Enfield, Ezra Cary, * Charles Richards.
Goshen, Alvan Barrus, Calvin A. Packard.
Granby, Philo Chapin, Charles S. Ferry.
Greenwich, Stephen Douglas. — *Greenwich Village*, David Allen, Jabez B. Root, Cullen Warner, Jno. Warner.
Hadley, George Allen, Simon F. Cooley, David S. Cowles, Royal M. Montague, † Eleazer Porter, James B. Porter, Rodney Smith, Levi Stockbridge, Samuel C. Wilder, * Perez S. Williams.
Hatfield, Samuel P. Billings, William H. Dickinson, Horace W. Field, John T. Fitch, George W. Hubbard, Silas G. Hubbard, Henry S. Porter.
Huntington, † Alfred M. Copeland, Josiah H. Goddard, Garry Munson, John Parks, Elijah N. Woods.
Middlefield, *John L. Bell, Sumner U. Church,
Northampton, William Allen, William F. Arnold, † Osmyn Baker,

Haynes H. Chilson, * Charles Delano, Pliny Earle, Eugene C. Gardner, William B. Hale, John C. Hammond, Henry R. Hinckley, Benjamin S. Johnson, Harvey Kirkland, Joshua Knowlton, Henry A. Longley, Caleb Load, Luke Lyman, † Samuel F. Lyman, Enos Parsons, * A. Perry Peck, Milo J. Smith, *Samuel T. Spaulding, Haynes K. Starkweather, Hiram Stebbins, William H. Stoddard, Wm. P. Strickland, Justin Thayer, † Oliver Warner, James L. Warriner, Eliphalet Williams, Lucien B. Williams. —*Florence*, Daniel W. Bond.

Pelham, David Abercrombie, John Jones.

Plainfield, Albert Dyer, Jason Richards.

Prescott, Liberty Crosett. — *North Prescott*, Edward A. Thomas.

Southampton, Elisha A. Edwards, Isaac Parsons.

South Hadley, Elliot Montague, G. Morgan Smith.

South Hadley Falls, Joseph Bardwell, R. Ogden Dwight, Hiram Smith jr., Henry W. Taylor.

Ware, Henry C. Davis, William C. Eaton, George H. Gilbert, Lewis N. Gilbert, Joseph Hartwell, † William Hyde, † Otis Lane, Milton Lewis, Samuel H. Phelps, Franklin D. Richards, Addison Sandford, † Charles A. Stevens, Charles E. Stevens, Philo D. Willis.

Westhampton, Anson Chapman,

Thomas C. Davenport, George B. Drury.

Williamsburg, Luther Bodman jr., Thos. M. Carter, * Salmon H. Clapp, † Stephen M. Crosby, John B. Gleason, Hiram Nash, Addison H. White.

Worthington, John Adams, Elisha H. Brewster, Ethan Clark, Daniel F. Hewitt, Edward C. Porter.

Trial Justices.

Amherst, Oliver Pease.

Belchertown, Franklin Dickinson.

Easthamp'on, Seth Warner.

Enfield, Charles Richards.

Northampton, Wm. P. Strickland.

Palmer, Charles L. Gardner.

South Hadley Falls, R. Ogden Dwight.

Ware, Franklin D. Richards.

Worthington, Elisha H. Brewster.

Notaries Public.

Amherst, Ithamar F. Conkey, Edward Dickinson.

Belchertown, Franklin Dickinson.

Easthampton, Edmund H. Sawyer.

Northampton, Henry H. Bond, Charles Delano, Harvey Kirkland, A. Perry Peck, C Edgar Smith, Samuel T. Spaulding, William E. Turner.

Ware, William S. Hyde, Otis Lane.

Coroners.

Greenwich, Stephen Douglas.

Hadley, Eleazer Porter.

Northampton, Ansel Wright. —*Special*, Ansel Wright jr.

MIDDLESEX COUNTY.

Incorporated May 10, 1843.

SHIRE TOWNS,........CAMBRIDGE AND LOWELL.

COUNTY OFFICERS.

Judge of Probate and Insolvency,.... Wm. A. Richardson,......*Cambridge*.

Register of Probate and Insolvency,... Joseph H. Tyler,..*(East) Cambridge*.

Assistant,   "   ... Isaac F. Jones,....*(East) Cambridge*.

Clerk of the Courts,.............. Benj. F. Ham,..........*Winchester*.

Assistant,   "   .... John J. Sawyer,..........*Somerville*.

Register of Deeds (South District),.. Chas. B. Stevens,..*(East) Cambridge*.

Register of Deeds (North District),.. Ithamar W. Beard,..........*Lowell*.

County Treasurer,................ Amos Stone, ...*Charlestown*.

Overseers of House of Correction,... { G. D. B. Blanchard,........*Malden*. James M. Usher,........*Medford*. Thomas Rice, Jr.,..........*Newton*.

Sheriff, ... Charles Kimball,..........*Lowell*.

Deputy Sheriffs.

Cambridge (East), Luther L. Parker.

Charlestown, Lowell W. Chamberlin.

Concord, John B. Moore.

Framingham, Joseph G. Bannister.

Groton, Andrew Robbins.

Groton Junction, Benj. L. Howe.

Hopkinton, Jonathan Whittemore.

Hudson, Charles H. Robinson.

Lowell, James Hopkins, Jefferson Bancroft, William H. Clemence.

Melrose, John H. Clark.

Medford, John T. White.

Reading, Daniel B. Lovejoy.

Townsend, B. F. Lewis.

Waltham, Eben W. Fiske.

Woburn, Horace Callamore.

Jailers.

Cambridge, Charles J. Adams.

Lowell, Charles Kimball.

Master of House of Correction.

Cambridge (East), Chas. J. Adams.

Sessions of Probate Court.

At *Cambridge*, 1st, 2d, and 4th Tu. of each month, except August.

At *Lowell*, 3d Tu. of Jan., March, May, July, Sept. and Nov.

Sessions of the Court of Insolvency.

At *Lowell*, 3d Tu. of Jan., March, May, July, Sept. and Nov.

At *Cambridge*, 2d and 4th Wed. of each month, except August and on other days by special assignment and adjournment.

County Commissioners.

Leonard Huntress, *Tewksbury*, term expires Jan. 1870; Joseph H. Waitt, *Malden*, Jan. 1871; Edward J. Collins, *Newton*, Jan. 1872.

Special Commissioners. — William F. Ellis, *Ashland*, Jan. 1872; Samuel Staples, *Concord*, Jan. 1872.

Times and Places of Meeting. — At *Cambridge*, 1st Tu. of Jan.; at *Lowell*, 1st Tu. of Sept.

Commissioners of Insolvency.

Cambridge, John W. Hammond.

Lowell, George Stevens.

Marlborough, Wm. B. Gale.

Public Administrators.

Charlestown, Duncan Bradford.

Lowell, Jonathan Ladd, George Stevens.

Masters in Chancery.

Cambridge (East), Joseph H. Tyler.

Charlestown, Charles Robinson, Jr., Wm. S. Stearns.

Lowell, Arthur P. Bonney, Wm. S. Gardner, Chas. F. Howe.

Commissioners to Qualify Civil Officers.

Cambridge (East), Isaac F. Jones.

Charlestown, John W. Pettengill, Bickford Pulsifer, Amos Stone, Phinehas J. Stone, Charles Thompson, Geo. Washington Warren.

Concord, Geo. M. Brooks, George Heywood.

Framingham, Colman S. Adams, Moses Edgell.

Groton, Benj. P. Dix.

Hopkinton, Silas Mirick.

Lowell, Alpheus R. Brown, Nathan Crosby, Geo. Stevens, S. W. Stickney, John F. Rogers.

Newton (Corner), Horace R. Wetherell.

Pepperell, Christopher W. Bellows.

Reading, Alfred A. Prescott.

Shirley, James O. Parker, James C. Parsons.

Stoneham, Dexter Buckman, Geo. W. Dike, Alonzo V. Lynde.

Justices of the Peace.

[Including Justices of the Peace and Quorum, designated by a *, and Justices throughout the Commonwealth, designated by a †.]

Acton, Luther Conant, Ebenezer Davis, Samuel Hosmer, Henry M. Smith, *Moses Taylor, William D. Tuttle, Daniel Wetherbee. — *S. Acton*, W. E. Faulkner, Jona. K. W. Wetherbee. — *West Acton*, Nath'l. E. Cutter, Alden Fuller, Andrew Hapgood.

Arlington, John F. Allen, Ira O. Carter, Samuel S. Davis, Addison Hill, John Osborn, William E. Parmenter, Benjamin Poland, Abel R. Proctor.

Ashby, Dennis Fay, James M. J. Jefts, Francis W. Wright.

Ashland, William F. Ellis, Elias Grout, William Seaver, Samuel W. Wiggins.

Bedford, *Phineas W. Chamberlin, Amos B. Cutler, Thos. Stiles.

Belmont, George S. Adams, John L. Alexander, Wm. A. Blodgett, Henry M. Clarke, William H. Locke, Francis E. Yates.

Billerica, Leander Crosby, Dudley Foster, Geo. C. Gilman, Charles H. Parker, Gardner Parker, James Stott, †Thomas Talbot, Geo. H. Whitman.

Boxboro', Cephas Hartwell, Amos Holbrook, Oliver Wetherbee.

Brighton, Henry Baldwin, Isaac G. Braman, Joseph B. Braman, Joseph Duncklee, *Chas. Heard, George H. Howe, Daniel Kingsley, Augustus Mason, James M. Murdock, Edmund Rice, Albert T. Sinclair, Webster F. Warren, William Warren, William W. Warren, F. Lyman Winship.

Burlington, Nathan Blanchard, Silas Cutler, William Winn.

Cambridge, John N. Barbour, James E. Bates, John H. Bentley, Marshall T. Bigelow, Daniel A. Buckley, John Cahill, Francis L. Chapman, Joseph Cutler, Curtis Davis, Henderson J. Edwards, John C. Farnham, Stephen T. Farwell, John J. Fatal, Benj. A. Gould, *James D. Green, Hamlin R. Harding, J. Watson Harris, Chas. W. Hawkes, Joseph G. Holt, Varnum S. Holt, Henry O. Houghton, Peter M. Howard, Joseph W. Kinsley, Rufus Lamson, Chas. C. Little, John Livermore, Chas. R. Metcalf, †Isaac S. Morse, James R. Morse, Henry W. Mazzey, Daniel W. Niles, John H. Partridge, George F. Pinkham, J. Stacey Read, †Chas. Theo. Russell, Edwd. G. Russell, Chas. H. Saunders, Geo. S. Saunders, Wm. A. Saunders, John A. Smith, Joshua B. Smith, †Wm. B. Stearns, Atherton H. Stevens, Fordyce M. Stimpson, Richard Stone, Jr., Henry Thayer, Henry B. Ward, †Henry Ware, †Emory Washburn, †Albion K. P. Welch, John W. Wellman, Benj. W. Whitney, Wm. L. Whitney.

Cambridgeport, Sumner Albee, George P. Carter, Josiah G. Chase, Josiah W. Cook, Jas. Cox, Watson G. Cutter, Abraham Edwards, Wm. F. Engley, Joel W. Flotcher, Geo. H. Folger, Hamlin R. Harding, Jos. A. Holmes, Jos. G. Holt, John D. Howe, Bela F. Jacobs, Justin A. Jacobs, Wm. F. Knowles, George C. Little, * Isaac Livermore, John Livermore, John S. March, John McDuffee, *Lucius R. Page, Zebina L. Raymond, Edward Richardson, †William A. Richardson, †John Sargent, James M. Thresher, Enoch H. Wakefield, Benj. Welsh.

East Cambridge, John W. Hammond, *Isaac F. Jones, Eli C. Kinsley, *John S. Ladd, Lorenzo Marrett, Wm. W. Mason, Thomas McIntire, Jr., Luther L. Parker, Benj. R. Rand, Charles B. Stevens, George Stevens, *Joseph Whitney, John T. Wilson, William Wyman.

North Cambridge, William Frost, Chester W. Kingsley, Jabez A. Sawyer.

Carlisle, George F. Duren, Selar Simonds.

Charlestown, Edwin F. Adams, Jas. Adams, Simeon P. Adams, Andrew J. Bailey, Ebenezer Barker, Duncan Bradford, Alfred Bridge, Philander S. Briggs, Benjamin F. Brown, Henry C. Burgess, John H. Butler, Cornelius

S. Carter, Abram Chamberlin, Lowell W. Chamberlin, *Francis Childs, Bradley M. Clark, Gilbert D. Cooper, *James Dana, Thomas M. Devens, Thomas Doane, Thomas J. Eliott, †John H. Ellis, Henry K. Frothingham, Richard Frotningham, John Gardner, Nathan B. Gifford, Gustavus V. Hall, Albert O. Hart, Joseph S. Hart, Charles H. Hildreth, Walter Howe, *Liverus Hull, †Horace G. Hutchins, George H. Jacobs, William H. Keith, George P. Kettrell, Seth W. Lewis, William B. Long, Rufus Mason, Anthony S. Morss, James W. O'Brien, William Peirce, William W. Peirce, John W. Pettingill, George W. Prescott, *Bickford Pulsifer, Olvin F. Raymond, †Charles Robinson, Jr., Trueworthy S. G. Robinson, Timothy T. Sawyer, William Sherburn, James W. Simpson, *William S. Stearns, Amos Stone, †Jas. M. Stone, †Phineas J. Stone, Charles E. Sweney, *Erdix T. Swift, Charles S. Tenney, †Chas. Thompson, Francis Thompson, Ewd. Thorndike, Everett Torrey, *Edwin G. Walker, *George Washington Warren, David B. Weston, Rufus A. White, *Sidney A. Willard, Daniel Williams, Samuel S. Willson, Edwin Woodman.

Chelmsford, Ziba Gay, Jos. Reed, Eli F. Webster.—*North Chelmsford*, Benj. Adams, Nathan B. Edwards, *Henry W. B. Wightman. — *West Chelmsford*, Jonathan J. Hoyt, Dawson Pollard, Christopher Roby.— *Middlesex Village*, Samuel Parker.

Concord, Richard Barrett, *George M. Brooks, Lorenzo Eaton, *George Heywood, †John S. Keyes, D. Goodwin Lang, Joseph Reynolds.

Dracut, Orford R. Blood, George W. Coburn, Ira Hall, Henry Richardson, Atkinson C. Barnum.

Dunstable, James T. Burnap, Allen Cummings, Benjamin French, Gilman Roby, James M. Swallow.

Framingham, Colman S. Adams, Joseph G. Bannister, Jas. W. Brown, Jas. W. Clark, Moses Edgell, *Alexr. R. Esty, †Constantine C. Esty, David Fisk, Charles J. Frost, Robt. Gordon, Jonathan Greenwood, William Hastings, Benjamin K. Haven, *Franklin F. Heard, Theodore C. Hurd, *Wm. G. Lewis, Warren Nixon, Francis C. Stearns, Ebenezer Stone, Charles S. Whitmore. — *S. Framingham*, Alex. Clark, Newell Clark. — *Saxonville*, Charles Fiske, Henry Richardson, Ebenezer Stone.

Groton, Josiah K. Bennett, †Geo.

S. Boutwell, Geo. D. Brigham, John J. Graves, *Asa F. Lawrence, Asa S. Lawrence, Daniel Needham, *Samuel W. Rowe, Andrew Spaulding, Willard Torrey, Alden Warren. — *Groton Junction*, E. Dana Bancroft, Benj. L. Howe, John Q. A. McCollister, Abel Prescott, John F. Robbins, Levi Sherwin, John Spaulding, Jr., Benj. F. Taft.

Holliston, John M. Batchelder, Luther Bellows, Elias Bullard, Andrew J. Cass, Festus C. Currier, Geo. B. Fiske, George E. Johnson. *Alden Leland, Orrin Thomson, Edwin F. Whiting.

Hopkinton. Charles W. Claflin, Daniel Eames, John A. Fitch, Clement Meserve, *Silas Mirick. Augustus Phipps, Lucius H. Wakefield, J. A. Woodbury. — *Hayden Row*, Uriah Bowker, Martin V. Phipps. — *Woodville*, Albert Wood.

Hudson, Francis Brigham, James T. Joslin, George S. Rawson, Charles H. Robinson, Silas H. Stuart.

Lexington, Joseph N. Brown, Asa Cottrell, Isaac N. Damon, George O. Davis, Howland Holmes, †Charles Hudson, Hammon Reed, *Aug. E. Scott.

Lincoln, James L. Chapin, S. Benton Thompson.

Littleton, John W. Adams, Peter C. Edwards, Shattuck Hartwell, Jos. A. Harwood, James Kimball, William Kimball, Joseph A. Priest, Samuel Smith.

Lowell, Julian Abbot, Jas. C. Abbott, *Edwin A. Alger, Wm. H. Anderson, Nathan Allen, Otis Allen, Jas. Bailey, Squire L. Bailey, *Jefferson Bancroft, Jacob Baron, Frank F. Battles, Ithamar W. Beard, Wm. S. Bennett, Wm. H. Bent Amos A. Blanchard, Wm D. Blanchard, Charles R. Blaisdell, Morrill M. Bohonan, †Arthur P. Bonney, Gerit J. Bradt, Geo Bragdon, *Alpheus R. Brown, *Samuel A. Brown, Thomas F. Burgess, †Benjamin F. Butler, Abner W. Buttrick, John A. Buttrick, Geo. J. Carney, Enoch B. Carter, *Robert B. Caverly, Alfred H. Chase, Jeremiah Clark, Charles B. Coburn, Lorenzo D. Cogswell, Wm. T. Connolly, James Cook, Isaac Cooper, Horatio G. F. Curliss, Charles Cowley, John E. Crane, Caleb Crosby, *Nathan Crosby, Jeremiah Crowley, Joshua W. Daniels, John Davis, Benj. C Dean, Luke C. Dodge, Luther J. Eames, Patrick Egan, Alpha B. Farr, David C. G. Field, Horatio R. Fletcher, Jonathan P. Folsom,

James B. Francis, Abram French, Josiah B. French, John F. Frye, Geo. Gardner, *William S. Gardner, Thos. G. Gerrish, Alfred Gilman, Silas F. Gladwin, †John A. Goodwin, Benj. Goddard, Francis Goward, George A. Griffin, Fred. T. Greenhalgh, *Sam'l P. Hadley, Jr., Amos B. Heywood, Epapheas A. Hill, Joseph S Holt, James Hopkins, *Hocum Hosford, Charles F. Howe, Lorenzo G. Howe, John Q. A. Hubbard, Elihu S. Hunt, John B. Hunt, Lucius W. Huntington, George L. Huntoon, *Andrew F. Jewett, Francis Jewett, Jeremiah P. Jewett, Jonathan Johnson. Moses A. Johnson, J. Judson Junkins, *Joseph B. Keyes, †Charles Kimball, J. Chelis Kimball, John F. Kimball, *John A. Knowles, David Lane, Cyrus Latham, Cyrus H. Latham, Alvin Lawrence, Ambrose Lawrence, George P. Lawrence, Samuel Lawrence, †Peter Lawson, John T. Lee, Wm. E. Livingston, James Loughran, *Sewall G. Mack, John F. Manahan, Joshua N. Marshall, John H. McAlvin, John F. McEvoy, Geo. F. Morey, Samuel A. McPhetres, Albert M. Moore, Horace E. Morse, †John Nesmith, Alanson Nichols, Frank A. Nichols, William North, Wm. L. North, Francis H. Nourse; William F. Osgood, Geo. W. Partridge, *Ephraim B. Patch, †Josiah G. Peabody, John Pearson, John N. Peirce, Jr., Henry P. Perkins, Major G. Perkins, Abiel Pevey, Geo. E. Pevey, †Abner J. Phipps, Joseph D. Pinder, Joel Powers, Asahel D. Puffer, *Thos. W. Pressey, John W. Reed, Edward C. Rice, †Daniel S. Richardson, Geo. F. Richardson, Geo. Ripley, Jacob Rogers, John F. Rogers, Chester W. Rugg, *William F. Salmon, *Benjamin C. Sargeant, Joseph L. Sargent, Alfred Scott, George F. Scribner, Luther E. Shepard. Wm. Shepard, *Edward F. Sherman. Harrison G. Sleeper, John W. Smith, William S. Southworth, *Andrew J. Stackpole, *George Stevens, †Sam'l W. Stickney, Holland Streeter, *Theo' H. Sweetser, Wilfred P. Taylor, Edw. Tuck, Artemas S. Tyler, Jonas P. Varnum, Aldis L. Waite, Benjamin Walker, Dan'l R. Wallace. Edw. F. Watson, Jas. Watson. *Wm. P. Webster, Chas. A. Welch, †Tappan Wentworth, Wm. T. Whitten, Henry H. Wilder, Benj. J. Williams, Chas. M. Williams, Andrew C. Wright, Asabel B. Wright, Hapgood Wright, Samuel N. Wood, *George D. Woodman.

Malden, David Ayers, Benj. Bordman, Elisha S. Converse, *Geo. W. Copeland, Geo. P. Cox, †William J. Eames, Loren L. Fuller, Joseph Gerrish, William Hardy, Walter Harmon, Benjamin G. Hill, Charles H. Hill, William Johnson, Azro D. Lamson, Erastus W. Leavens, Charles Merrill, Manson L. Mills, Horatio G. Pope, William H. Richardson, †William S. Robinson, Joseph M. Russell, Albert F. Sargent, *Wm. S. Stearns, Francis C. Swett, Joseph H. Waitt, Joseph H. Whitman, Samuel Woods.— *South Malden*, Eustace J. Cooper, James G. Foster, George Shattuck. — *Maplewood*, Joshua Webster.

Marlborough, Jacob M. Baker, Edward L. Bigelow, Levi Bigelow, John Chipman, *Wm. B. Gale, John Goodale, Chas. M. Howe, Elbridge Howe, Edward F. Johnson, Samuel B. Maynard, Stephen Morse, Daniel F. Murphy, Edmund C. Whitney, Lewis Wilkins, Nahum Witherbee.

Medford, Almarin F. Badger, †Elihu C. Baker, Eleazer Boynton, Jr., Albert H. Butters. James O. Curtis, Mark H. Durgin. Daniel A. Gleason, Joseph P. Hall, Thomas S. Harlow, Benj. F. Hayes, Asa Law, Samuel C. Lawrence, Parker R. Litchfield, Lewis W. Osgood, Baxter E. Perry, Charles Russell, *John Sparrell, James F. Usher, *James M. Usher. — *West Medford*, Luther Farwell, Nehemiah T. Merritt.

Melrose, William Bogle, Andrew H. Briggs, Jonathan Cochran, Nelson Cochran, David Fairbanks, Joseph A. Fairbanks, George W. Farnsworth, William C. Farnsworth, William J. Farnsworth, †Daniel W. Gouch, Levi S. Gould, *Alonzo V. Lynde, Henry A. Norris, Horatio N. Perkins, Wm. F. Poole, Joseph B. Sanford, Emory B. Smith.

Natick, †John W. Bacon, George Beard, Alex. Blaney, Henry Coggin, Moses Eames, John M. Farwell, Stedman Hartwell, Charles L. Hosmer, Walter N. Mason, Edwin C. Morse, William Nutt, Asher Parlin, Emmons Partridge, Elijah Perry, George L. Sleeper, Edward P. Travis.

Newton (*Corner*), Joseph N. Bacon, George E. Bridges, Samuel Chism, †Alfred B. Ely, John M. Fisk, Henry Fuller, John B. Goodrich, †George N. Hitchcock, Horatio N. Hyde, Florentine W. Pelton, Stephen W. Trowbridge, †Adin B. Underwood, Horace B. Wetherell, Ebenezer Woodward — *Newton Centre*, Ezra C. Hutchins,

†James F. C. Hyde, Charles E. Lane, †David H. Mason, William Morton, George C. Rand, Marshall S. Rice, John D. Towle, John Ward, Andrew H. Ward.— *Newtonville*. Horatio F. Allen, †William Claflin, Cornelius P. Harkins, Dustin Lancey, Andrew H. Ward.—*Auburndale*, Cephas Brigham, †Jas. B. F. Marshall, Henry H. Matteer, Henry B. Williams. — *Newton Lower Falls*, Isaac Hagar. Luther E. Leland, †Thomas Rice, Jr. — *Newton, Upper Falls*, Joseph Barney, Charles Ellis, Hosea C. Hoyt, Otis Pettee. — *West Newton*, George E. Allen, †Julius L. Clarke. †Edward J. Collins, †Seth Davis, Thomas Drew, William P. Houghton, Adolphus Smith, Elisha F. Thayer, Ira D. Van Duzee, Nathan Weston, Jr.

North Reading, Samuel P. Breed, Samuel Flint, Charles P. Howard.

Pepperell, *Christopher W. Bellows, Summer Carter, Putnam Shattuck, Samuel P. Shattuck, Levi Wallace, Abel B. Winn.

Reading, Solon Bancroft, Hiram Barnes. George Batchelder, John Batchelder, Stephen Foster, Chauncy P. Judd, John B. Leathe, Stillman E. Parker, Nathan P. Pratt, *Alfred A. Prescott, Wm J. Wightman, Carroll D. Wright.

Sherborn, Henry W. Bullard, Jeremiah Butler, Joseph Dowse, Jr., James H. Leland.

Shirley, Stephen J. Ballou, Jerome Gardner, Moses T. Gardner, James Gerrish, John K. Going. Abel L. Lawton, James P. Longley, David Porter, (*Groton Junction*), Peter Tarbell.

Somerville, Albion H. Bailey, Clark Bennett, Gilman F. Besent, Samuel J. Bradlee, †George O. Brastow, John H. Brookhouse, Thomas Cunningham, George H. Dickerman, Charles E. Gilman, John K. Hall, Francis Houghton, Charles H. Hudson, George W. Ireland, Oren S. Knapp, Chas. S. Lincoln, John C. Magoun, William H. Pierce, Edward C. Purdy, Aaron Sargent, †James M. Shute, Thomas G. Temple, Francis Tufts, *Columbus Tyler, John E. Tyler, Robert A. Vinal, William H. Weston, Geo. W. Whittle.

Stoneham, *Dexter Bucknam, *Edward Bucknam, Silas Dean, †George W. Dike, *Lyman Dike, Amasa Farrier, Ira Gerry, Amos Hill, 2d, Moses L. Morse, William B. Stevens, Samuel Tidd.

Stow, Ephraim Stone, Chas. Tower, Edwin Whitney.

Sudbury, Jonas S. Hunt, James Moore. Charles Thompson.—*So. Sudbury*, B. H. Richardson.—*Assabet*, Asahel Balcom.

Tewksbury, †Arthur P. Bonney, Oren Frost, Leonard Huntress, †Thomas J. Marsh, George Pillsbury, Elijah M. Read, *Benjamin F. Spaulding, Frank M. Spaulding, Richard Tolman.

Townsend, Samuel S. Haynes, Albert Howe, Asa S. Lawton, Henry Seeva, Frederic A. Worcester.— *W. Townsend*, Levi Stearns, George Taft, Jas. N. Tucker.

Tyngsboro', Luther Butterfield, Reuben S. Coburn.

Wakefield, Lucius Beebe, *Henry D Austin, Jas. O. Boswell, George W. Cutter, Chester W. Eaton, Lilley Eaton, Daniel P. Emerson, Abel F. Hutchinson, Edward Mansfield, Daniel Norcross, Byron A. Osgood, Edward A. Upton, Philip C. Wheeler, Adam Wiley. — *Greenwood*, Paul H. Sweetser.

Waltham, Josiah Beard, *Frank W. Bigelow, Henry A. Brown, Lorenzo Burge, Thomas W. Farnsworth, *Eben W. Fiske, Daniel French, †Henry F. French, Edward L. Hill, Charles H. Houghton. Jarvis Lewis, Josiah Rutter, Sylvanus W. Smith, William G. Sprague, Fred. M. Stone, Augustus Townsend, Samuel O. Upham, Samuel B. Whitney.

Watertown, Joel Barnard. Jr. Chas J. Barry, Charles Bemis, Isaac V. Bemis, Elijah Clark, Joseph Crafts, Geo. Frazar, David T. Huckins, Wm. H. Ingraham, Jesse A. Locke, George N. March, Samuel Richardson, Isaac Robbins, William White, Leonard Whitney, Jr., B. Osgood Wilson. — (*Wakefield*). Cyrus Wakefield.

Wayland, Richard F. Fuller, David Heard, Lewis Jones, †Edward Mellen, Jonas A. Morse, Henry Wight.

Westford, John W. P. Abbot, Geo. T. Day, Asa Hildreth, Edward Prescott, Luther Prescott.

Weston Frederick T. Bush, George W. Cutting, Jr., Alonzo S. Fiske, Horace Hews, Edwin Hobbs.

Wilmington, Cyrus L. Carter, Wm. H. Carter, Lemuel C. Eames. Samuel B. Nichols.

Winchester, George P. Brown, *Oliver R. Clark, Abraham B. Coffin, †William Everett, *Benjamin F. Ham, Frederick O. Prince, Andrew N. Shepard, †Edwin A. Wadleigh.

Woburn, Edward W. Champney, Horace Collamore, George H. Conn, *Joshua P. Converse, Parker L. Converse, *John Cummings, John W. Day, Marcus Eaton, David D Hart, Edward D. Hayden, Sparrow Horton, Josiah Hovey, John Johnson, True L. Norris, John L. Parker, Thomas J. Porter, Lemuel G. Richardson, Lewis L. Whitney. — *East Woburn*, Albert L Richardson. — *North Woburn*, Albert Thompson, Cyrus Thompson, *Leonard Thompson, Samuel F. Thompson, Edward E. Thompson, Moses F. Winn.

Trial Justices.

Ashland, William Seaver.
Concord. Joseph Reynolds.
Framingham, Colman S. Adams.
Groton, Samuel W. Rowe.
Holliston. Alden Leland.
Hopkinton. John A. Woodbury.
Hudson, James T. Joslin.
Lexington. Augustus E. Scott.
Malden, John W. Pettengill.
Medford, Benj. F. Hayes.
Melrose, Andrew H. Briggs.
Natick, George L. Sleeper.
Newton (*Corner*), Stephen W. Trowbridge.
Auburndale, Cephas Brigham.
Shirley. David Porter.
Somerville. Francis Tufts.
Sudbury, Asahel Balcom.
Tewksbury. Richard Tolman.
Townsend, Henry Seeva.
Wakefield. Edward A. Upton.
Waltham. Josiah Rutter.
Wayland, David Heard.
Westford, Luther Prescott.
Woburn, Parker L. Converse.

Notaries Public.

Brighton, Bela S. Fiske, Edward P. Wright.
Cambridge, Levi L. Cushing. Jr., Joseph G. Holt, Benj. W. Whitney. — *Cambridgeport*, John N. Barbour. — *East Cambridge*, Lorenzo Marrett.
Charlestown, Duncan Bradford, William Peirce, Lucius H. Warren.
Concord, George M. Brooks.
Framingham, Constantine C. Esty, John M. Farwell.
Groton Junction. J. K. Bennett.
Holliston. Elias Bullard.
Hopkinton, Silas Mirick.
Lowell, Edwin A. Alger, Joseph H. Ely, Geo. D. Hills, John A. Knowles, Samuel W. Stickney, Abel Whitney, Charles M. Williams.
Malden. Albert F. Sargent.
Marlborough, Edmund C. Whitney.
Medford, Benj. F. Hayes, Charles Russell.
Newton Corner, Andrew B. Cobb.
Newtonville, Dustin Lancey.

Shirley, David Porter.
Somerville, Samuel J. Bradlee.
Townsend, Edward Ordway.
Wakefield, James O. Boswell, Chester W. Eaton, Byron A. Osgood.
Waltham, Byron B. Johnson, Frederick M Stone.
Woburn, Alpha E. Thompson.

Coroners.

Brighton, Isaac G. Brainan, Augustus Mason.
Cambridge, Francis H. Brown.
Cambridge (Port), William W. Wellington. ,
Cambridge (East), Luther L. Parker, Edward H. Weston.
Charlestown, Duncan Bradford, Seth W. Lewis.
Framingham, Colman S. Adams.

Groton, Asa S. Lawrence, John Q. A. McCollester.
Hopkinton, Silas Mirick.
Lowell,—*Special*, Jefferson Bancroft, Thomas W. Pressey, Jeremiah P. Jewett.
Malden, Francis C. Swett.
Marlborough, Nahum Witherbee.
Medford, John T. White.
Melrose, William J. Farnsworth.
Natick, Alexander Coolidge.
Newton (West), Wm. P. Houghton.
Newton (Corner), John M. Fisk.
Reading, Horace P. Wakefield.
Somerville, John C. Magoun.
Sudbury, Webster Moore.
Tewksbury, Benj. F. Spaulding.
Waltham, Ebenezer W. Fiske.
Westford, Edward Prescott.
Winchester. Alonzo Chapin.
Woburn, Thomas J. Porter.

NANTUCKET COUNTY.

Incorporated, June 20, 1695.

COUNTY OFFICERS.

Judge of Probate and Insolvency,... Edward M. Gardner,......*Nantucket*.
Register of Probate and Insolvency,. Thaddeus C. Defriez.......*Nantucket*.
Town and County Treasurer,...... Samuel Swain,..........*Nantucket*.
Clerk of the Courts,.............. George Cobb, ...*Nantucket*.
Register of Deeds, ... William H. Waitt..........*Nantucket*.
Sheriff,...................... Joseph M'Cleave..........*Nantucket*.
Jailer and Master of House of Correction. } Roland Folger,...........*Nantucket*.

Sessions of Probate Court.
Holden on Thursday next after 2d Tuesday in each month.

Commissioners of Wrecks.
Nantucket, George W. Coffin, Alexander B. Dunham, Peter Folger.

Public Administrator.
Nantucket, Geo. Cobb.

Commissioners of Insolvency.
Nantucket, George Cobb, William Cobb.

Commissioners to Qualify Civil Officers.
Nantucket, George Cobb, William B. Mitchell.

Notaries Public.

Geo. Cobb, Philip H. Folger, Edward M. Gardner, Alfred Macy.

Justices of the Peace.

[Including Justices of the Peace and Quorum, designated by a *, and Justices of the Peace throughout the Commonwealth, designated by a †].

Nantucket, Asa G. Bunker, *Geo. Cobb, Wm. Cobb, Thaddeus C. Defriez, Philip H. Folger, Wm. C. Folger, †Edward M. Gardner, Alfred Macy, George W. Macy, Thomas Macy, *Joseph Mitchell. William B. Mitchell. Alexander B. Robinson, Andrew Whitney.

NORFOLK COUNTY.

Incorporated, March 26, 1793.

SHIRE TOWN,...........................DEDHAM.

COUNTY OFFICERS.

Judges of Probate and Insolvency.... George White............*Needham.*
Register of Probate and Insolvency... Jonathan H. Cobb,.........*Dedham.*
Ass't Register of Probate and Insol.,. Jonathan Cobb,...........*Dedham.*
Clerk of Courts,.................... Erastus Worthington,......*Dedham.*
Register of Deeds,.............. ... James Foord,..............*Dedham.*
County Treasurer,.................. Chauncey C. Churchill,....*Dedham·*
Overseers of House of Correction,... { H. O. Hildreth,...........*Dedham·* C. C. Churchill,..........*Dedham.*
Sheriff,........................... John W. Thomas,..........*Dedham.*

Deputy Sheriffs.
Canton, Rufus C. Wood.
Dedham, Augustus B. Endicott.
Dorchester. John Robie.
Foxborough, Alfred Fales.
Medway, Alexander Fairbanks.
Medway (West), Valentine R. Coombs.
Milton. John D. Bradlee.
Quincy, Washington M. French.
Randolph, William H. Warren.
Stoughton. Hiram Gay.
Weymouth, Geo. W. White Jr.

Sessions of Probate Court.
At *Dedham,* 1st Tu. of each month except August.
At *Dorchester (Harrison square),* every Wed. except during the month of August.

County Commissioners.
Milton M. Fisher, *Medway,* term expires Dec. 1869; Joseph M. Churchill, *Milton,* term expires Dec. 1870; David H. Bates, *Braintree,* term expires Dec. 1871.
Special Commissioners. — Galen Orr, *Needham,* term expires Dec. 1871; Amos H. Holbrook, *Bellingham,* term expires Dec. 1871.
Times of Meeting. — At *Dedham,* 3d Tu. of April. 4th Tu. of June and Sept., and last Wed. of Dec.

Commissioners of Insolvency.
Dedham, Frederick D. Ely.
Dorchester, Thomas F. Temple.
Randolph, Wm. E. Jewell.

Public Administrator.
Dedham, Ira Cleveland.

Masters in Chancery.
Dedham, Thomas L. Wakefield, Erastus Worthington.
Dorchester, Richard T. Lombard.

Commissioners of Wrecks.
Cohasset. Loring Bates, Warren Bates Jr., Joseph H. Smith.

Commissioners to Qualify Civil Officers.
Braintree, Naaman L. White.
Dedham, Chauncy C. Churchill, Jonathan H. Cobb, Edmund Thomas.
West Roxbury. William Harris.
Weymouth (South), Appleton Howe.
Wrentham, Daniel A. Cook.

Justices of the Peace.
*(Including Justices of the Peace and Quorum, designated by a *, and Justices throughout the Commonwealth, designated by a †.)*

Bellingham, Andrew A. Bates, Nathan A. Cook. *North Bellingham,* Savel Metcalf.
Braintree, John B Arnold, Edward Avery. James M. Cutting, Chas. H. Dow, Asa French, Jonathan French, Elias Hayward. John Kimball, Ebenezer F. E. Thayer. *Naaman L. White.— South Braintree,* David H. Bates, Joseph R. Frasier, Elias Hayward, Albert H. Gould. Francis A. Hobart, Newell A. Langley, Noah Torrey.
Brookline, Wm. Aspinwall, Benj. F. Baker, William I. Bowditch, Charles Burrill. John W. Candler, †William L. Candler, †Theophilus P. Chandler, Nathaniel G. Chapin, David H. Daniels, William Dearborn, Francis P. Denny, Gustavus M. Finotti, George Griggs, George E. Hersey, George F. Homer, Bradford Kingman, *Amos A. Lawrence, Francis W. Lawrence, †Henry Lee, Jr., Augustus Lowell, Thomas Parsons, Charles Pope, Augustine Shurtleff, Lewis Slack, William B. Towne, †Ginery Twitchell, Otis Withington.
Longwood. John Ruggles.

Canton. *Ellis Ames, Frank M. Ames, †Charles Endicott, Charles H. French, Daniel T. V. Huntoon, Wm. Mansfield, *Samuel B. Noyes, James T. Sumner, Rufus C. Wood.

Cohasset, Solomon J. Beal, Martin Lincoln, John Q. A. Lothrop, Aaron Pratt, Andrew J. Souther, Edward Tower.

Dedham, James M. Battles, Charles J. Capen, *Chauncey C. Churchill, *Ira Cleveland, John D. Cobb, Jonathan Cobb, *Jonathan H. Cobb, *Waldo Colburn, John Cox, Jr, Merrill D. Ellis, Fred. D Ely, Augustus B. Endicott, James Foord, Calvin Guild, Henry O. Hildreth, Lewis H. Kingsbury, Anson Morse, Henry W. Richards, *Ezra W. Sampson, John N. Stevens, Mirick P. Sumner, Ezra W. Taft, *Edmund Thomas, John W. Thomas, †Ezra Wilkinson, †Erastus Worthington. — *South Dedham,* Jos. Day, Ebenezer F. Gay, Willard Gay, William S. Gay, Curtis G. Morse. *Readville,* Enoch P. Davis.

Dorchester, †Thomas J. Allen, Samuel Atherton, *Edmund J. Baker, Eleazer J. Bispham, Samuel A. Bradbury, Thomas W. Capen, William T. Carlton, William L. Clark, Ebenezer Clapp, Albe C. Clark, Henry G. Denny, S. Parkman Dexter, Ebenezer Eaton, Isaac Field, George A. Fisher, Charles F. Gerry, Oliver Hall, Wm. A. Hayes, Dan'l Harwood, Chs. Howe, Henry Humphreys, Edward Jarvis, Edward King, Wm. P. Leavitt, Richard T. Lombard, †Samuel P. Loud, John J. May, John Mears, Jr., †John H. W. Page, Sam'l B. Pierce, *Nathaniel F. Safford, Joseph P. Silsby, J. M. R. Story, Thomas F. Temple, Wm. F. Temple, †Edmund P. Tileston, Franklin L. Tileston, Nath'l Tolman, †Thomas Tolman, Jas. H. Upham, Geo. H. Vincent, *Robt. Vose, Robert Vose, Jr., Charles V. Whitten, †Marshall P. Wilder, William Withington. — *Neponset,* Luther Briggs. — *Harrison Square,* Josiah H. Carter, William Pope. — *Milton,* †Asaph Churchill, Sylvester H. Hebard, John Robie.

Dover, Linus Bliss, Calvin Richards.

Foxborough, James Capen, *James E. Carpenter, Edmund Carroll, Julius Carroll, Otis Cary, Edwin W. Clarke, John M. Everett, Alfred Fales, Edward D. Hewins, Alfred Hodges, Charles W. Hodges, Isaac Smith, Wm. H. Thomas.

Franklin, Paul B. Clark, Adams

Daniels, Albert E. Daniels, Waldo Daniels, Edmund Davis, James M. Freeman, George W. Nason, Jesse L. Nason, Stephen W. Richardson, Wm. Rockwood, Alpheus A. Russegue, Adin D. Sargeant, Saul B. Scott, Charles W. Stewart, Horatio Stockbridge, Hiram W. Jones.

Hyde Park, Robt. S. Capen, Henry B. Terry, Isaiah W. Thayer, Roswell Turner.

Medfield, Charles Hamant, Charles C. Sewall.

Medway, Wm. H. Cary, †Milton M. Fisher, †Warren Lovering, *Luther Metcalf, Clark Partridge. — *East Medway,* Amos H. Bullen. — *West Medway,* Charles H. Deans, Asa M. B. Fuller, John S. Smith, William H. Temple, Addison P. Thayer, Marcellus A. Woodward. — *Rockville,* Amos H. Boyd, Willard P. Clark.

Milton, Samuel Babcock, Gideon Beck, John D. Bradlee, Chas. Breck, Chas. M. S. Churchill, †Joseph McK. Churchill, Fredk. A. Eustis, †Thornton K. Lothrop, George Penniman, Edward L. Pierce, Jason Reed, Jas. M. Robbins, *Henry S. Russell, Jas. B. Thayer, Roswell W. Turner, George Vose, Josiah Webb, Seth D. Whitney. — *Hyde Park,* Willard F. Estey.

Needham, Solomon Flagg, Charles C. Greenwood, Emery Grover, †Artemas Newell. — *Charles River Village,* Wilson J. Welch. — *Newton Upper Falls,* Richard Boynton. — *Newton Lower Falls,* Joshua J. Gould, Ellsworth Torrey. †Geo. White. — *Grantville,* Geo. K. Daniell. — *Wellesley,* Henry F. Durant, George Jennings, Moses Winch.

Quincy, Wyman. Abercrombie, Ebenezer Adams. †John Q. Adams, Seth Adams, Henry Barker, John Chamberlin, Noah Cummings, †Wm. B. Duggan, Washington M. French, Geo. L. Gill, John Hardwick, Edwin A. Hill, Charles A. Howland, George H. Locke, Charles Marsh, *William S. Morton, William S. Pattee, Whitcomb Porter, E. Granville Pratt, Josiah P. Quincy, Joseph W. Robertson, Jas. E. Tirrell, Isaiah G. Whiton.

Randolph, John Adams, Hiram C. Alden, Eleazer Beal, J. White Belcher, Abel B. Berry, Ezra S. Conant, Joseph N. DuBois, Zenas French, Daniel Howard, Frederick Howard, Nathaniel Howard, William E. Jewell, Seth Mann, 2d, John G. Poole, Jas. Augustus Tower, Royal W. Turner, †Seth Turner, George W. Wales

William H. Warren, Oramel White, Thomas White. — *East Randolph.* Jacob Whitcomb. — *South Randolph,* Thomas West.

Sharon, Sanford W. Billings, Lewis W. Morse, Josiah Johnson, Otis Johnson, William R. Mann.

Stoughton, Halsey J. Boardman, Lucius Clapp, Jesse Holmes, Clifford Keith, Luther S. Leach, Albert T. Pierce, Isaac H. Stearns, Amasa Southworth, George Talbot, Jabez Talbot, Jr. — *East Stoughton,* Christopher Dyer, Jr.

Walpole, Samuel Allen, Jr., Nathaniel Bird, Smith Gray, James G. Hartshorn, James H. Leland, Charles S. Mason, George P. Morey, James G. Scott, Joshua Stetson, William S. Tilton, Horatio Wood. — *East Walpole,* †Francis W. Bird, Samuel Bird. — *South Walpole,* Truman Clarke.

West Roxbury, †Jonathan Amory, Francis V. Balch, Joseph H. Billings, Benjamin H. Currier, Abijah W. Draper, Ephraim M. Dudley, John M. Fessenden, James Hewins, Leonard P. Holden, Edward H. Kettell, Joseph Lyman, William H. Mackintosh, Theodore B. Moses, Thos. Motley, Alexis Poole, Frank W. Reynolds, †B. F. Thomas, Ebenezer W. Tolman, Christopher M. Weld. — *Jamaica Plain,* David S. Greenough, Jr., Robert M. Morse, Jr., Thomas P. Proctor, Robert Seaver, William Maccarty.

Weymouth, Francis Ambler, Everett C. Bumpus, Ebenezer A. Hunt, Richard A. Hunt, John W. Loud, Elias Richards, Asa B. Wales, Saml. Webb, Amos S. White, George W. White, Jr. — *East Weymouth,* Warren W. Barker, Francis B. Bates, Lovell Bicknell, Zachariah L. Bicknell, Thomas J. Burrill, Abner Holbrook, *Alvah Raymond, Joseph Totman. — *North Weymouth,* Elias S. Beals, James Humphrey, N. Quincy Tirrell, Jas. Torrey, Franklin Woodside. — *South Weymouth,* George H. Bates, Appleton Howe, Jacob Loud, John A. E. Loud, Quincy L. Reed, Noah Vining, B. F. White, Oran White.

Wrentham, William W. Cowell, Nathan Ely, Jr., Calvin Fisher, Jr., Charles J. Randall, Samuel Warner. — *North Wrentham,* James T. Ford, Daniel J. Holbrook. — *Sheldonville,* George Sheldon.

Trial Justices.

Canton, Charles Endicott. *Cohasset,* Solomon J. Beal. *Dedham,* Frederick D. Ely. *Dorchester,* Thomas F. Temple. *Foxborough,* Alfred Fales. *Franklin,* Alpheus A. Russegue. *Hyde Park,* Willard F. Estey. *Medway (West),* Chas. H. Deans. *Milton,* Charles M. S. Churchill. *Needham,* Emory Grover. *Quincy,* John Quincy Adams, Wm. S. Morton. *Randolph,* J. White Belcher. *Stoughton,* Halsey J. Boardman. *West Roxbury (Jamaica Plain),* James Hewins. *Weymouth,* Everett C. Bumpus. *Wrentham,* Samuel Warner.

Notaries Public.

Canton, Francis W. Deane, Charles Endicott. *Cohasset,* James C. Doane. *Dedham,* Lewis H. Kingsbury. *Dorchester,* Isaac Swan, Thos. F. Temple. *Franklin,* Alpheus A. Russegue. *Medway,* Milton M. Fisher. *Quincy,* Henry F. Barker. *Randolph,* Royal W. Turner. *Roxbury,* Morrill P. Berry, George B. Faunce, James Ritchie, William Whiting. *Weymouth,* Everett C. Bumpus, Amos S. White. — *South Weymouth,* Quincy L. Reed. *Wrentham,* Samuel Warner.

Coroners.

Braintree, Jonathan French. *Cohasset,* John Q. A. Lothrop. *Canton, Special,* Rufus C. Wood. *Dorchester, Special,* Robert Vose. *Medway,* Valentine R. Coombs. *Milton,* John D. Bradlee. *Needham,* George K. Daniell. *Quincy,* Lewis Bass. *Randolph,* Ralph Houghton. *Stoughton,* Nathaniel Wales. *Weymouth,* George W. White, Jr.

PLYMOUTH COUNTY.

Incorporated June 2, 1685.

SHIRE TOWN,.........................PLYMOUTH.

COUNTY OFFICERS.

Judge of Probate and Insolvency.... Wm. H. Wood,......*Middleborough.*
Register of Probate and Insolvency... Daniel E. Damon,.... ...*Plymouth.*
Clerk of Courts................... William H. Whitman,.....*Plymouth.*
Register of Deeds................ William S. Danforth,.....*Plymouth.*
County Treasurer................ William R. Sever,........*Plymouth.*

Overseers of House of Correction.. { William H. Whitman,.....*Plymouth.*
J. D. Robbins, ...*Plymouth.*
Daniel E. Damon,.......*Plymouth.*

Sheriff......................... James Bates,............*Plymouth.*

Deputy Sheriffs.

Abington, Josiah Cushman.
Bridgewater, P. D. Kingman.
Duxbury, Wm. J. Alden.
Hingham, G. F. Hersey.
Marion, Daniel Hall.
Marshfield, John Baker.
Middleborough, James Cole.
N. Bridgewater, Otis Hayward.
N. Carver, Benj. Ransom.
Plymouth, John Perkins.
    "   John Atwood,
Rochester, R. C. Randall.
S. Scituate, Willard Torrey.
Scituate, J. O. Cole.

Jailer and Master of House of Correction.

Plymouth, James Bates.

Sessions of Probate Courts.

At *Abington*, 4th Mon. of May, Aug., and Nov.
At *Bridgewater*, 4th Mon. of Sept.
At *East Bridgewater*, 4th Mon. of Feb. and Dec.
At *Hingham*, 4th Mon. in March.
At *Middleborough*, 4th Mon. of Jan., April, and 2d Mon. in July.
At *North Bridgewater*, 3d Mon. of April and Oct.
At *Plymouth*, 2d Mon. of Jan., Feb., March, April, May, June, Sept., Oct., Nov., and Dec.
At *South Scituate*, 4th Mon. of June.
At *Wareham*, 4th Mon. of Oct.

Sessions of Insolvency Court.

At *Plymouth*, 2nd Mon. in every month.

County Commissioners.

Harrison Staples, *Lakeville*, term expires Dec. 1869; Wm. P. Corthell, *Abington*, 1870; Charles H. Paine, *Halifax*, 1871.

Special Commissioners.—Alden S. Bradford, *Kingston*, term expires 1871; Jedediah Dwelley, *Hanover*, 1871.

Times of Meeting.—At *Plymouth*, 3d Tu. in March, 1st Tu. in Aug. and Jan.

Commissioners of Insolvency.

Abington. Jacob B. Harris.
North Bridgewater, Jonas R. Perkins.
Plymouth, John J. Russell.

Commissioners of Wrecks.

Duxbury, Elisha Holmes.
Hull Nehemiah Ripley, Jr.
Marshfield, John Baker. Otis Baker, Curtis B. Goodsil, Geo. H. Hall.
East Marshfield, Chas. L. Tilden.
Plymouth, Josiah D. Baxter, Barnabas H. Holmes.
Scituate, Perry L. Parker, John Tilden.—*North Scituate*, John Damon, Wm. J. Newcomb.

Public Administrator.

Duxbury, Samuel Stetson.

Master in Chancery.

Plymouth, William H. Whitman.

Commissioners to Qualify Civil Officers.

Abington, Isaac Hersey, Jesse E. Keith.
Bridgewater, Josh. E. Crane, Abraham Washburn, 2d.
Duxbury, Samuel Stetson, Gershom B. Weston.
Hingham, Amos Bates, Solomon Lincoln.
Middleborough, Everett Robinson, Eliab Ward.
North Bridgewater, Franklin Ames, Geo. W. Bryant, Jonas R. Perkins.

Plymouth, Wm. S. Danforth, Jacob H. Loud, John J. Russell, William H. Whitman.

Rochester, Joseph Haskell, Theophilus King, James Ruggles.

Scituate, John Beal, Elijah Jenkins.

South Scituate, Anson Robbins, Samuel A. Turner.

Wareham, Seth Miller.

West Bridgewater, Austin Packard.

Justices of the Peace.

(Including Justices of the Peace and Quorum designated by a *; and Justices throughout the Commonwealth designated by a †.)

Abington, Nathan'l A. Faunce, Isaac Hersey. Charles W. Howland, Freeman P. Howland, Jesse E. Keith, Micah Nash, James Noyes, Otis W. Soule, Bela Thaxter, Samuel B. Thaxter, John D. Wormell. — *East Abington*, Nathaniel Beal, Charles Bearse, †Jacob B. Harris, Zenas Jenkins, Levi Reed, Franklin Smith, Horace C. Totman. — *North Abington*, Samuel Dyer, David Ford, James Ford, George W. Pratt, Edward P. Reed.— *South Abington*, William P. Corthell, Benj. Hobart, Wm. L. Reed, Jared Whitman.

Bridgewater, Horace Ames, Samuel Breck, Frederick Crafts, †Joshua E. Crane, †Levi L. Goodspeed, Philip E. Hill, * Lewis Holmes. Mitchell Hooper, Lafayette Keith, Hosea Kingman, Philip D. Kingman, *Williams Latham, Franklin Leach, Elisha G. Leach, Spencer Leonard, †Asa Millett, Jeremiah Tucker, Eli Washburn.

Carver, †Jesse Murdock, Benjamin Ransom, William Savery, Thomas Southworth, Thomas Vaughan.

Duxbury, Benjamin Alden, Nathaniel Ford, John Holmes, John S. Loring, Samuel Loring, Samuel Stetson, Joshua W. Swift, † Gershom B. Weston. — *West Duxbury*, Elbridge Chandler, Henry B. Maglathlin, Geo. B. Standish. — *South Marshfield*, Benjamin Boylton.

East Bridgewater, Jacob Bates, *Moses Bates, Joseph Chamberlain, Aaron Hobart, Jr., Henry Hobart, Benjamin W. Keith, Thomas Keith, Ezra Kingman, †James H. Mitchell, Wm. H. Osborne, Calvin Reed, John Reed.

Halifax, Edwin Inglee, Charles H. Paine, Ira L. Sturtevant, Dexter C. Thompson, Ephraim B. Thompson.

Hanover, Robert S. Curtis, Jedediah Dwelley, David B. Ford, Lemuel C. Waterman.

Hanson, Geo F. Stetson, Joseph Smith. — *South Hanson*, Isaiah Bearce, Eben B. K. Gurney. — *South Hanover*, Edward Y. Perry.

Hingham, Quincy Bicknell, Henry Hersey, James S. Lewis, †Solomon Lincoln, Charles N. Marsh, Charles W. Seymour, Elijah Shute. — *South Hingham*, Joseph B. Thaxter, Jr., Israel Whitcomb.

Hull, Lewis P. Loring.

Kingston, Joseph S. Beal, Alden S. Bradford, Philander Cobb, Samuel E. Cushman, Walter H. Faunce, Jas. Foster, Edward Gray, Noah Prince, Edwin Reed, Joseph Stetson.

Lakeville, Reuben Hafford, Abiezer T. Harvey, Eleazer Richmond, Churchill T. Westgate, Henry L. Williams, Asa T. Winslow.

Marion, Daniel Hall, Barnabas Hiller, Joseph S. Luce. Charles Sturtevant, Moses H. Swift.

Marshfield, John Baker, John Ford, *Luther Hatch. — *North Marshfield*, †Hiram A. Oakman.

Mattapoisett, Wilson Barstow, Amittai B. Hammond, Noah Hammond, Thomas Nelson, Noah C. Sturtevant.

Middleborough, Ichabod F. Atwood, John Bennett, Stillman Benson, Sylvanus Hinckley, Noah C. Perkins, Andrew J. Pickins, Stillman B. Pratt, Zebulon Pratt, Everett Robinson, Augustus H. Soule, Andrew L. Tinkham, Sidney Tucker, Eliab Ward, Benjamin P. Wood, Cornelius B. Wood, George W. Wood, †William H. Wood. — *North Middleborough*, Andrew L. Alden, Wm. B. White. — *East Middleborough*, Joshua M. Eddy.

North Bridgewater, †Franklin Ames, George W. Bryant, David L. Cowell, Daniel Crocker, Francis M. French, Sumner A. Hayward, Augustus T. Jones, Edwin H. Kingman, Isaac Kingman, Charles Lincoln, *Jones R. Perkins, Wm. Perry, Loring W. Puffer, Isaac E. Snell, Edward Southworth, Jr., Chandler Sprague, †Jonathan White, Wm. F. Winship. — *Campello*, Nelson J. Foss, Arga B. Keith, Josiah W. Kingman, Galen E. Pratt.

Pembroke, John Oldham, 2d, Jas. H. Whitman. — *East Pembroke*, Geo. F. Hatch, Andrew E. Poole.— *North Pembroke*, Francis Collamore. — *South Hanson*, *Martin Bryant, William H. H. Bryant.

Plymouth, Amasa Bartlett, Gustavus D Bates, Jas. Bates, *Josh D. Baxter, Lemuel Bradford, Chas. O. Churchill, James Cox, Daniel E. Damon, Allen

Danforth, †William S. Danforth, †Chas G. Davis, William T. Davis, George G. Dyer, Timothy Gordon, John T. Hall, John Harlow, Benj. Hathaway, Barnabas H. Holmes, Thomas Loring, † Jacob H. Loud, Leander Lovell, Albert Mason, John Perkins, Thomas Pierce, Daniel J. Robbins, Edmund Robbins, †John J. Russell, Thomas B. Sears, †Eleazer C. Sherman, Charles W. Spooner, Isaac N. Stoddard, *William Thomas, Ezekiel C. Turner, *William H. Whitman, Oliver T. Wood. — *Chiltonville*, George Bramhall.

Plympton. James C. Ellis, Josiah S. Hammond, Zaccheus Parker, Wm. Perkins, William H. Soule. — *North Plympton.* Zenas Cushman.

Rochester. John Blackmer, Thomas Ellis, Theophilus King, James H. Look, George Pierce, James Ruggles. — *North Rochester,* Israel F. Nickerson.

Scituate, George M. Allen, *John Beal, Elijah Jenkins, Ezekiel Jones, Caleb W. Prouty. — *North Scituate,* Joseph O Cole, Geo. C. Lee, George W. Merritt, Shadrach B. Merritt.

South Scituate, Ebenezer T. Fogg, Charles A. Litchfield, Samuel Tolman, Jr., George H. Torrey, *Samuel A. Turner. — *West Scituate,* Elisha Jacobs, Perez Simmons.

Wareham, William Bates, Joseph P. Hayden, Darius Miller, Seth Miller, Jr., Adolphus Savery, James G. Sproat. — *East Wareham,* John M. Kinney, Nathaniel Sherman.

West Bridgewater, Dwelley Fobes, James Howard, Austin Packard.

Trial Justices.

Abington, Otis W. Soule.
Bridgewater, Lewis Holmes, Elisha G. Leach.
East Bridgewater, William H. Osborne.
Hingham, James S. Lewis.
Middleborough, Cornelius B. Wood.
North Bridgewater, Jonas R. Perkins, Rufus L. Thatcher.
Plymouth, Albert Mason.
Scituate. Caleb W. Prouty.
Wareham, William Bates.
West Bridgewater, Austin Packard.

Notaries Public.

Abington, Jesse E. Keith.
East Bridgewater, Moses Bates.
Hingham, Henry C. Harding.
Mattapoisett, Thomas Nelson.
North Bridgewater, Jonas R. Perkins.
Plymouth, William S. Danforth, Jacob H. Loud, John J. Russell.
Scituate, John Beal.
Wareham, William Bates.

Coroners.

Bridgewater, Philip D. Kingman.
Marshfield (East), Charles L. Tilden, Eliot K. Tilden.
Middleborough, Eben. W. Drake.
North Bridgewater, Benjamin A. Packard.
Scituate, John Beal.
Wareham, Levi A. Runnells.

SUFFOLK COUNTY.

Incorporated, May 10, 1843.

SHIRE TOWN,..BOSTON.

COUNTY OFFICERS.

Judge of Probate and Insolvency,....	Isaac Ames,.................	Boston.
Register of Probate and Insolvency...	William C. Brown,...........	Boston.
As't Register of Probate and Insolvency	James L. Crombie,...........	Boston.
Clerk of Supreme Court............	George C. Wilde,............	Boston.
Assistant Clerk Supreme Court, ...	George W. Nichols,.........	Boston.
Clerk of Superior Court,...........	Joseph A. Willard,..........	Boston.
Assistant Clerk Superior Court, ...	Edwin A. Wadleigh,........	Boston.
Clerk of Superior Court, crim'l business,	Francis H. Underwood,......	Boston.
Register of Deeds,................	James Rice,................	Boston
County Treasurer, ...	Frederick U. Tracy,........	Boston.
Commonwealth's Attorney, ...	J. Wilder May,.............	Boston.
Assistant " "	P. R. Guiney,.............	Boston.
Sheriff,........................	John M. Clark, *office Ct. House,Boston.*

Deputy Sheriffs.

Benj. F. Bayley, *Court House.*
John B. Dearborn, "   "
Bradford S. Farrington, "
William D. Martin, "   "
Harum Merrill,   "   "

Master of House of Correction.
Charles Robbins, *South Boston.*

Sessions of Probate Courts.

At the Probate Office in *Boston,* every Monday in each month except July.

Masters in Chancery.

Boston, Robert I. Burbank, John Codman, Horace H. Coolidge, Chas. C. Nutter, Giles H. Rich, James B. Richardson, James B. Thayer.

Commissioners of Insolvency.

Boston, Augustus O. Allen, David H. Coolidge, Joseph Willard.

Public Administrators.

Boston, Francis E. Parker. Joseph F. Clark, Lorenzo S. Cragin, James Schouler.

Commissioners to Qualify Civil Officers.

Boston, John P. Bigelow, Nehemiah Brown, Charles B. Hall, William G. Harris, Charles W. Lovett, Benjamin C. Piper, David Pulsifer.
Chelsea, Henry J. Coolidge, Hosea Ilsley, Jacob Mitchell.

JUSTICES OF THE PEACE IN BOSTON.

(Including Justices of the Peace and Quorum, designated by a *; and Justices throughout the Commonwealth, designated by †.)

Abbot Edwin H.
Abbott Abiel
Abbott Curtis
†Abbott Josiah G.
Abbott Samuel A. B.
Abell Chas. R.
Adams Albert W.
Adams Chas. B. F.
Adams Chas. F., Jr.
Adams Francis M.
Adams George E.
Adams George Z.
Adams J. Gedney
Adams Joseph H.
Adams Nathaniel
Adams Paul
*Adams Simeon P.
Adams Thomas
Ager George B.
Ager Solomon
Aibee Sumner
Alexander John L.
Alger Edwin A.
Allen Augustus O.
†Allen Charles
*Allen Charles E.
Allen Ira
Allen James W.
Allen Stephen M.
Allen Stillman B.
Ames Fisher
Ames George
†Ames Isaac
Ames P. Adams
†Ames Seth
Amidon Philip R.
†Amory Charles
†Amory Jonathan
Amory Thomas C.
Anderson Wm. S.
Andrews Frank W.
Andrews John L.
Andrews Samuel
Andrews William
Andrews Wm. T.
Angell Geo. T.
Apollonio Nich. A.
Appleton John
Archibald Geo. F.
Aspinwall William

Atherton Samuel
Atkins Ebenezer
Attwood Corn'is. G.
Atwood Charles
*Austin Ivers J.
Austin Milton
Avery Edward
Aver Dulious
Babcock John R.
Bacon Charles H.
Bacon Francis
Ball Geo. W.
Bailey Adrian F.
Bailey Wm. H.
Baker Amos
Baker John R.
Baker William P.
Baker William W.
Balch Francis V.
Baldwin Elizur
Baldwin Geo. W.
Baldwin Henry
Ball Jonas
Ball Joshua D.
Ballard James M.
Bancroft George
Barnard Charles A.
Barnard Geo. M., Jr.
Barnes Edwin C.
Barnes Francis G.
Barrows Horace G.
Barry H. Storer
Bartlett Francis
*Bartlett Homer
*Bartlett Sidney
Bartlett Sidney, Jr.
Bassett Edgar
Batchelder Sam'l, Jr.
†Bates Lucas G.
Bates Moses
Bates Samuel W.
Baxter Francis J.
Baxter Thompson
Bayley Benj. F.
Bayley James C.
Beal Alexander
Beal Jairus
Beal James H.
Beal William L.
Beals William

Beebe James M.
Bell James B.
Bell Theodore H.
Bellows Josiah G.
Bemis George
Bennett Joseph
Bent S. Arthur
Benton Austin W.
Berry Abraham H.
Berry Morrill P.
Berry Nehemiah C.
Bicknell William E.
Bigelow Abraham O.
Bigelow Edwin M.
Bigelow George B.
Bigelow Geo. F.
†Bigelow Geo. T.
Bigelow Timothy
Bird George W.
Bishop Robert R.
Blackmar Witha'd W.
Blake Alpheus P.
Blake Edward
Blake John H.
Blanchard Charles
Blaney David H.
Blaney Henry
†Bloch Abraham F.
Blodgett Caleb, Jr.
Blodgett Luther
Blodgett Geo. B.
Blood Charles S.
Blume Andreas
Boardman Alon. W.
Boardman Halsey J.
*Boit Edward D.
Bolles Matthew
Bolster Solomon A.
Bond Pelham
Borrowscale John
Botume John, Jr.
Bowditch Wm. I.
Bowen Stephen
Bowker Albert
Bowman Selwin Z.
Boyden Joseph A.
Bradbury Horace D.
Bradbury Samuel A.
Bradford J. Russell
Bradish Levi J.

Bradlee John T.
*Bradlee J. Putnam
Bradlee Nathaniel J.
Bradlee Samuel J.
Bradley Joseph
†Brailey Joseph H.
*Bragdon Joseph H.
Bragg Henry W.
Braman Edward H.
Braman G. T. W.
Braman Jarvis D.
Bramhall William
Breed George F.
Brewer Gardner
Brewer Nathaniel
Brewer Thomas M.
Brewster Aug. O.
Brewster John
Bridge Abel E.
Briggs Andrew H.
Briggs Harrison O.
Briggs Lloyd
†Brigman William
Brigham Wm. T.
*Brimmer Martin
Brooks Benj. F.
Brooks Francis A.
Brooks Henry C.
Brooks Wm. G.
Brown Alpheus R.
Brown Charles H.
†Brown Edward
Brown Jeremiah
Brown John
Brown John Murray
†Brown Nehemiah
Brown Richard S.
Brown William B.
Brown William C.
Browne C. Allen
Browne Edward I.
Browne Geo. M.
Bruce George A.
Bryant Charles B.
Bryant David
Bryant G. J. F.
Bryant John D.
Bryant Napoleon B.
Buck Edward
Buck Robert H.

Bugbee James M.
Bullard Daniel W.
Bullens Geo. S.
†Burbank Robert I.
Burge Lorenzo
Burgess Charles S.
Burnett Lysander
Burrage Alvah A.
Burt William L.
Butler John Henry
Butterfield John W.
Byam George A.
Cadazan John D.
Callender Benjamin
Calrow William H.
Campbell Isaac T.
Capelle Wm. C.
Capen John
Capen Robert S.
Capen Samuel C.
Carpenter Geo. O.
Carpenter James E.
Carruth Francis S.
Cary A. Claxton
Cary Nathan C.
Caverly Charles, Jr.
Cazneau Andrew
Chadwick Chris. C.
Chamberlin Edw. M.
Chamberlin David
Champney Edw. W.
†Chandler Peleg W.
Chapin George H.
Chapin Nath. G.
Chapman Geo. R.
Chapman John W.
Chase Geo. W.
Chase Henry S.
Cheever Tracy P.
Child Dudley R.
Child George H.
Child Linus
Child Linus M.
Chipman Geo. W.
Chute Chas. F.
Church Henry A.
Churchill Henry P.
Clapp Charles W.
Clapp George H.
Clapp Henry A.
Clapp Joshua W.
Clapp Otis
Clapp Wm. W.
Clark Albe C.
Clark Benj. G.
*Clark John M.
Clark Joseph C.
Clark Robert F.
Clarke Henry M.
Clarke Thomas W.
Cary Henry D.
Cleaves Nathaniel
Cleaves N. Porter
Cleland William
Cobb Samuel C.
Cobb Samuel A.
Codman Charles R.
Codman Edward W.
Coffman John
Colla Charles H.
Collin G. Winthrop
Collin Henry A.
Cogswell William
Colborn Jeremiah
Colborn Wm. G.
Colt John F.
Colt Charles D.
Collins Dennis J.
Collins James H.
Collins John H.
Collins Patrick A.
Comer George N.
Connolly Wm. T.
Connor James W.
Converse Joseph H.
Converse Joshua P.
Cook Charles E.
Cook Edward
Cook Rufus R.
Cook William

Cook William H.
*Cooke Josiah P.
Coolidge Austin J.
Coolidge David H.
Coolidge Horace H.
Coolidge John T., Jr.
Coolidge Joseph R.
Cooper Samuel
Coting Chas. U.
Cottrell Asa
Cowdin John
Cowdin Robert
Cowles Wm. W.
Cowley Charles
Cragin L. S. Jr.
Cram Geo. W.
Crandall H. Burr
Crane David F.
Crane Horatio N.
Crane John E.
*Crane Samuel D.
Creech Sam'l W., Jr.
Crocker George G.
†Crocker Henry
Crocker Samuel R.
Crocker Uriel
Crocker Uriel H.
Cromble James L.
Crosby Joseph B.
Crosby Sumner
Crowley John C.
†Crowninshield F. B.
Culver Wm. C.
Cumings Charles B.
Cumings Bradley N.
Cummings John A.
*Currier Benj. H.
Currier T. Florian
†Curtis Benj. R.
Curtis Charles P.
Curtis Frederick
Curtis George J.
Curtis James F.
Curtis James W.
Curtis Samuel S.
Curtis Walter
Cushing Benjamin
Cushing Hayward P.
Cushing Henry W.
Cutler Eben
Cutler Edmund F.
Cutler Joseph
Cutler Lucius A.
Cutter Isaac J.
Cutter John A. B.
Cutter Leonard H.
*Dabney Lewis S.
*Dale Theron J.
†Dale William J.
Dall William
Dalton Henry L.
*Dame Abraham A.
Dame Charles C.
Dame Theodore S.
Damrell John S.
Dana Richard H.
Dana Rich'd H., Jr.
Dana Samuel T.
Daniels Joshua W.
Daniels Nathan H.
Darling Samuel C.
Davenport Henry
Davenport Orl do H.
Daviez Daniel
Davis Adolphus
Davis Barnabas
Davis Charles
Davis Charles E., Jr.
Davis Edward S.
Davis Henry
†Davis James C.
*Davis Jerome
Davis Joshua T.
Davis Joshua W.
Davis Samuel C., Jr.
Davis Thomas W.
Davis Wm. F.
Davis William F.
Day Moses H.

Dean Benj.
Dean Thomas
Dearborn Edmn'd B.
Dehnois Stephen G.
Delano Frank H.
Denton Charles
Dento Sylvanus A.
Denny Daniel
Denny Henry G.
Denny J. Wild o
Derby George S.
Derby Isaac W.
Dewey S. W., Jr.
Dewson Francis A.
Dexter George S.
Dexter William S.
Dickinson M. F., Jr.
Dillaway Charles K.
Dimmock Wm. R.
Dingley Edward H.
Dingley John T.
Dixon Oliver
Dixon Francis B.
Dockray Jas. R. Jr.
Dodge John C.
Doherty Wm W.
Donahoe Patrick
Donnelly Chas. F.
Doolittle Oscar E.
Dorr Wm B.
Dow James B
Dow James B., Jr.
Dowling Martin
Drake Jeremy
Draper Moses
Drew Charles H.
Dudley Dean
Dunham Charles E.
Dunham Josiah
Dunklee Benj. W.
Dunlap John S.
Dupee James A.
Durant Henry F.
*Durgin Samuel H.
Dalton Henry W.
Dyer B. Franklin
Dyer Frank B.
Dyer Micah, Jr.
Eager George R.
Eastburn John H.
Eastman Ambrose
Eddy Robert H.
Edmunds Charles
Edson William
Edwards Hend'n J.
Edwards Henry
Egan James
Eldridge Charles W.
Eldridge John L.
Ellicott Joseph P.
Elliott James R.
Ellis Abijah
Ellis Charles M.
Ellis George W.
†Ellis John H.
Ellis John T.
Ellis Rowland
Ellison William P.
Emery Caleb S.
Emery George F.
English James L.
Estabrook G. Wm.
Estey Willard F.
Eustis William T.
Evans Alonzo H.
Evans George E.
Everett H. Sidney
Everett J. Mason
Everett Otis
Fallon Joseph D.
Farmer Jesse
Farnsworth Ezra
Farnsworth Isaac D.
Faunce George B.
Fay Frank B.
Felton Alexander C.
Fennelly Richard J.
Fessenden Benjamin
Field Benj. F.
Field George G.

Field Walbridge A.
Firth Abraham
Fisher George A.
Fisher Theo. W.
Fisk Asa
Fiske Chas. H.
Fiske Francis S.
†Fiske John M.
Fitch Henry H.
Fitch Jonas
Fitz Daniel F.
Flatley Michael J.
Fleming Chas. H.
Fletcher Joel W.
†Flint Charles L.
Flood Hugh
Floyd Edward E.
Floyd Samuel E.
Flynn Daniel F.
Flynn James J.
Folger George H.
Folger John B.
Folsom Albert A.
Forsaith Wm. J.
†Foster Dwight
Foster Eben R.
Foster Nathan'l, Jr.
Fowle Wm. B.
*Fox James A.
Francis Nathaniel
Freeman William
French Abram
French Francis O.
French George P.
French James
Frost Eben R.
Frost Henry W.
Frothingham S., Jr.
Frothingham T. B.
*Fuller Henry Ward
Fuller Henry Wm.
Fuller Richard F.
Fuller Samuel D.
Fuller Stephen P.
Furber William H.
Gaffiel Thomas
Galloupe Chas. W.
†Gardner Henry J.
Gardner Wm. S.
*Gaston William
*Gay Ebenezer
Gay Eben F.
Gibbens Joseph M.
Gibbs Amory T.
Gibbs Franklin
Gilbert Benj N.
Gilchrist Daniel S.
Giles Alfred F.
Gilley John E. M.
Gillingham Csp'r S.
Gilman Joan E.
Glaney John
Gleason Daniel A.
Gleason Horace
Glidden Daniel A.
Goddard Maurice
†Goddard Thomas A.
Goldsbury John
Goo rich Elijah D.
Goodrich John B.
Goodwin Albert G.
Goodwin Frank
Gore Henry W.
Gorr Theodore W.
Gould Francis
Goul Frederick
Gould Jesse
Gove John
Grafton Daniel G.
Granger David
Grantham Fred. W.
Graves Wm. E.
Gray Hollis R.
†Gray John C.
Gray John C., Jr.
*Gray William
Gray William R.
Green Nicholas St. J.
Greenleaf Rich'd C.
Greenough Wm. W.

Griggs George
Groves Henry B.
Guild Charles E.
Guild James
Guild Josiah F.
Guild William H.
Hackett Frank W.
Hale Cyrus K.
†Hale George S.
Hale Moses L.
Hale Theodore P.
Haley John J.
Hall Andrew T.
†Hall Charles B.
Hall Edward F.
Hall Edwin H.
Hall Francis A.
Hall John K.
Hallett Henry I.
Hamblin Howard M.
Hanson Hadley P.
Hapgood Lyman S.
Harding Wm. B.
Harding Wm. P.
Harlow Thomas S.
Harman Thomas L.
Harrington John C.
Harrington John C.
Harris Edward D.
Harris J. Watson
Hart S. Rowland
Hartwell Alfred S.
†Harvey Peter
Harwood Irving I.
Haskell Daniel N.
Hassam John
Hastings John T.
Hastings Andrew J.
Hastings John W.
Hatch Albert D.
Hatch Samuel
Hatch Windsor 2d
Hathaway Simon W.
*Haven Franklin
†Haven Franklin, Jr.
Hawkes Chas. W.
Hawkes Thomas B.
Hayden Charles J.
Hayden William
†Hayes Francis B.
Hayes Francis L.
Hayes William A.
Hayward James
Hazelton Horace L.
†Healy John P.
Hedge William
Hemenway Alfred
Henshaw Joseph L.
Hersey Alfred C.
Hewes Jabez F.
Hewins James
Hibbard Wm. C.
Hichborn Geo. B.
Higginson Stephen
Hildreth Edwin A.
Hill Cement H.
Hill Hamilton A.
Hill Hamilton A.
Hill Noble H.
Hill Thomas
Hill Thomas H.
Hill Wm. H.
Hillard George S.
Hilliard William
Hills William S.
Hinckley Samuel
Hinds Calvin P.
Hobart Aaron
Hobbs George M.
*Hobbs William, Jr.
Hodgman Job H.
Holbrook Horatio N.
Holden Artemas R.
Holland Henry W.
Hollis Thomas
Holman Ralph W.
Holmes George
Holmes Jabez S.
Holmes John S.
Holmes O. W., Jr.

Holmes Richard
Holway Merrill S.
Homer George
Homer George F.
†Homer Peter T.
Hooper Robert, Jr.
†Hooper Samuel
Houghton Charles
Hovey Joseph F.
Hovey Solomon
Howard James M. F.
Howard Martin
Howe Charles
Howe John D.
Howe Moses G.
*Howes Lewis W.
Howland Ichabod
Hoyt Henry
Hubbard Charles
Hubbard Chas. E.
Hubbard Josiah W.
Hudson Charles H.
Hudson John E.
Hudson John W.
Humphrey Francis J.
Hunnewell Francis
Haut Henry C.
Hunt Moses
Hunting Edward A.
Hunting Geo. F.
Huntington C. W.
Hurd Charles H.
Hurd Francis W.
Hurd Theo. C.
Hutchins Ezra C.
Hutchins Henry C.
Hutchinson Chas. C.
Hutchinson Wm. H.
Hyde Henry D.
Ingalls Melville E.
Ireson S. Edwin
*Ives Stephen B, Jr.
Jackson Abraham
Jackson Charles E.
Jackson John G.
Jackson Patrick T.
Jackson Samuel S.
Jacobs Asa, Jr.
Jacobs Francis W.
Jacobs Geo H., Jr.
James E. Worthen
Jaques Francis
Jaques Samuel
Jeffries John, Jr.
Jenks Lemuel P.
Jennison Samuel
†Jewell Harvey
Johnson Henry A.
Johnson Henry W.
Johnson Robert
Johnson Samuel, Jr.
Johnson J. Albert
Jones Augustine
†Jones Edward J.
Jones George S.
Jones Jerome
Jones Leonard A.
Jordan Wm. H. S.
Josselyn F. M.
Joy Alton K. P.
Kelly W. F. A.
Kemp H. N. D., Jr.
Kent James D.
Kent Barker B., Jr.
Kent Wm. H.
Kern Francis V. B.
Kettell Edward H.
Kettell John B.
Keyes Charles G.
Keyes Eben W.
Keyes Joseph B.
Kidder Gardiner G.
Kidder Henry P.
Kilton John F.
Kimball David
Kimball David P.
Kimball Edgar L.
Kimball Henry H.
Kimball J. Chellis
Kimball John H.

Kimball M. Day
Kimball Otis
King Dexter S.
King John G.
Kingsbury Aaron
Kingsbury Geo. H.
Kingsbury Wm. B.
Kingsbury Wm. S.
Kinsley Edw. W.
Kittredge Chas. F.
Kittredge Francis W.
Knapp Oren S.
*Knight Henry T.
Kuhn George H.
Kuhn John
Kurtz John
Kyle Winslow S.
Lamb Thomas
Lamson Artemas W.
Lamson Nathan P.
Lane Charles E.
Lappen Owen
Lathrop John
Lathrop Wm. M.
Lawrence Abbott
*Lawrence Amos A.
Lawrence Francis W.
Lawrence Gard. W.
Lawrence James
Leach George C.
Leary Michael
Leary Timothy J.
Leavitt Thos. H.
Lee James W.
Lee James Howard
*Leighton John C.
Leighton John W.
Leland Emerson
Leonard Geo. B.
Leonard Joseph
Leonard Nahum
Lewis Weston
Lewis Winslow
Lincoln Arthur
Lincoln Chas. D.
Lincoln Chas. E.
*Lincoln F. W. Jr.
Lincoln Lowell
Lincoln Robert B.
Litchfield Ira
Little Charles H.
Little Lemuel
Little Samuel
Littlefield Walter
Livermore Isaac
Lloyd Edward S.
Locke Jesse A.
*Locke John O.
Lombard Richard T.
Long John D.
Long William H.
Lord J. Brown
Lord Thomas H.
Loring Caleb W.
Loring Francis C.
Loring John A.
Lothrop Eben W.
Lothrop Loring
†Lothrop T. K.
Loud Andrew J.
Loud Samuel C.
Lovejoy Samuel M.
Lovejoy William B.
Lovett Charles W.
Lovett Chas. W. Jr.
Lovett Joshua
Low William
Lowe Abraham T.
Lowell Augustus
Lowell John
Lucas Winslow B.
Lunt Henry
Lynch Patrick
Lynde Alonzo V.
Lyndon Patrick F.
Mackintosh H. B.
Macy George N.
Mason Herbert
Maguire Thomas F.
Mahan John W.

Mahoney James S.
Muir George H.
Mandell Moses J.
Manley John R.
Mann Nehemiah P.
Mansfield Gideon T.
Marble William
March George N.
March John S.
Marsh Henry A.
Marsh Lucius B.
Marsh Robert
Martin William D.
Mason Osman
Mason Walter N.
Mason William H.
Mather Henry H.
Matthews Nathan
Matthews Richard
May John
Maynadier James E.
McCarthy William
McCartney Wm. H.
McCleary Samuel F.
McClellan John
McGilvray David P.
McIntire Charles J.
McKim John W.
McPhail A. M. Jr.
Mead Michael
Means William G.
Mears Granville
Merriam Adolphus
Merriam Otis W.
Merrill Amos B.
Merrill James C.
Merrill Moody
Merrill Franklin S.
Merritt Nehemiah P.
Merwin Elias
Meserve Isaac H.
Messinger Geo. W.
Meston Lyman B.
Metcalf Henry B.
Meliken Eben C.
Mills Dexter T.
Mills John F.
Milton George W.
Minot John O. B.
†Minot William
Minot William Jr.
Mollneux Robert W.
*Moore Charles W.
Moore Edward B.
Moore Fredk. H.
Moore H.
Morrill George
Morris Robert
Morse Bushrod
Morse George A.
Morse Horace E.
Morse James C.
Morse John E., Jr.
Morse Nathan
Morse Rob't. M., Jr.
Morton Andrew J.
Morton Ellis W.
Moseley Edward A.
Motte Ellis L.
Moulton Baxton C.
Moulton Chas. J. B.
Mowry Oscar B.
Munro Peter G.
Munroe Francis J.
Munroe William
Murdock Joseph
Murdock Judson
†Nash Stephen G.
Nason J. Byron
Nazro Charles G.
Neale Alonzo F.
Needham Daniel
Nettleton Edward P.
Newell John
Newhall Ezra F.
Newmarch Samuel
Newton Jeremiah L.
Nichols Oscar B.
Nichols Geo. W.
Nichols John P.

Nichols Lyman
Nichols Wm., Jr.
Nichols Wm. F.
Nichols Win. W.
Nicholson James L.
Nickerson Joseph
Nickerson Pliny
Nickerson Sereno D.
Noble John
Noble John
Noble William
Norcross Oris
Norris Arthur F. L.
Norris George W.
Norton Michael
Nowell John A.
Noyes George D.
Nutter Charles C.
Nutter Thomas F.
Ober John P.
Osborne James C.
O'Leary James
Olney Richard
Ordway John P.
Osborn Francis A.
Osgood Byron A.
Osgood Lewis W.
Otis Edmund B.
Otis William C.
Owen Roscoe P.
Page Calvin G.
Page Edward
Page Timothy R.
Paige James W.
Paine Robert Treat
Paine Rob. Treat, Jr.
Palfrey Francis W.
Palmer Julius A.
Palmer William H.
Park Daniel
Park George W.
Park John C.
Park William D.
*Parker Aurelius D.
Parker Chas. Ham.
Parker Chas. Henry
Parker Henry G.
Parker Horatio G.
Parker John R.
Parker John D.
†Parker Samuel E.
*Parker William
Parker William M.
Parkman William
Parks Nathl. Austin
Parmenter Wm. E.
Parsons Solomon
Persons Thomas
Patten Chauncs B.
Paul Joseph F.
Payne Charles F.
*Payson Thomas E.
Peabody William S.
Peabody W. B. O.
Peirce William
Peirce William H.
Pearson Charles L.
Perkins Charles B.
Perkins H. W. Jr.
Perkins Thomas H.
Perkins William
Perkins Wm. E.
Perry Baxter E.
Perry Francis A.
Perry George A.
Peters Edward D.
Peterson Reuben, Jr.
Phillips Charles A.
*Phillips Geo. Wm.
Pickering Edward
Pickering Henry
Pickering John
Pierce Edward H.
Pierce Edward L.
Pierce Jacob W.
Pike Charles E.
Pike Ezekiel W.
Pingry Samuel H.
Pinkerton John M.
Pitcher James W.

Plumer Avery
Plummer Chas. G. C.
†Plummer Farnham
Pond Benjamin
Poor Franklin N.
Poor John O.
Porter Edward F.
Porter Jerome B.
Porter John L.
Potter Andrew B.
Potter Asa P.
Potter Robert K.
Powell J. D. N. R.
Powers Charles E.
Pratt Albert S.
Pratt Eleazer F.
Pratt George A.
Pratt George L.
Pratt George W.
Pratt Isaac, Jr.
Pratt Jerahmeel C.
Pratt William H.
Pray Benj. S.
Prescott Levi T.
Preston George H.
Preston Jonathan
*Price E. Sewall
Prince Frederick O.
Prince Thomas
Proctor Darwin A.
Proctor George B.
Proctor Thomas P.
†Pulsifer David
Pulsifer Eben
Putnam Edwin M.
Putnam George, Jr.
Putnam John P.
Quincy George H.
†Quincy Josiah
Quina James
†Rand Edward S.
Rand Edw. S., Jr.
Rand Franklin
Rand George C.
Randall Otis G.
Rabney Ambrose A.
Ray Edwin
Read Charles C.
Read James
*Redfield Isaac F.
Reed Edward
Reed George M.
Reed James H.
Reed John
†Reed John H.
Reed Sampson
Reynolds Henry R.
Rhodes John B.
†Rice Alexander H.
Rice Freeman
Rice Henry A.
Rice James
Rice Samuel
Rich Giles H.
Rich Otis
Rich Thomas P.
Richards Edward
Richards George H.
Richards J. Avery
Richardson Abijah
Richardson G. P., Jr.
Richardson Ivory N.
Richardson Ivory W.
Richardson Jackson
Richardson Jas. B.
Richardson Jedrey
Richardson John
Richardson John D.
Richardson Thos. F.
*Riley Patrick
Riley Thomas
Ripley Ebed L.
Risley John E
†Ritchie Harrison
Robb James B.
Roberts George L.
Robert Joseph D.
Robinson A. J.
Robinson Edwin A.
Robinson George I.

Robinson Thomas
Robinson Thos. W.
Robley Robert C.
Rogers Benjamin F.
Rogers Charles O.
Rogers Daniel H.
Rogers Henry M.
Rogers Joseph P.
Rogers Shubael G.
Rollins James W.
Ropes John C.
Ross Samuel J.
Rowean Thomas
Royce Burnham
Ruffin George L.
Rumrill James A.
Russ Augustus
Russell Benj. F.
Russell Daniel W.
Russell George
Russell Samuel H.
†Russell Thomas
Russell Thomas H.
Russell William G.
Salisbury Daniel W.
Sampson Oscar H.
Samuels Edward A
Sanborn Edward W.
Sanford Joseph B.
Sanford Oliver S.
†Sanger George P.
Saunders Daniel, Jr.
Savage Edward H.
†Savage James
Sawyer Fred. W.
Sawyer Jabez A.
Sayer James F.
Sayles Henry
Scanlan Michael
Schouler James
Scott Augustus E.
Scudder Henry A.
Searle George W.
Sears Philip H.
Sears Willard T.
Seaver Nathaniel
Seaver William
Sedgwick Arthur G.
Sever James W.
Sewall Samuel E.
Shapleigh Richu. W.
Sharp Daniel
Shattuck Geo. O.
Shaw Benjamin S.
Shaw Joseph H.
Shaw George S.
Shaw Lemuel
Shaw Roland C.
Shaw Samuel P.
Shaw Samuel S.
Shaw Southworth
Sheldon Henry N.
Shepard Chas. A. B.
Shepard Edward O.
Sherman Edward L.
Sherman George
Sherman J. Edwin
Sherwin Edward
Sherwin Thomas, Jr.
Shimmin Chas. F.
Shirley Daniel H.
Shiverick George
Shurtleff Hiram S.
†Shurtleff Nathl. B.
Siders Charles
Sisby Joseph P.
Simonds Alvan
Simonds John H.
Simpson Daniel P.
Sinclair Albert T.
Skews Chas. W.
Slade Lucius
Sleeper Herbert
*Sleeper Jacob
Slocum William F.
Smith Amos
Smith Benjamin
Smith Charles
Smith Chauncey
Smith Emory B.

Smith Francis M.
Smith Franklin W.
Smith Henry Hyde
Smith Horace
Smith H. Farnham
*Smith Joshua B.
Smith Phineas B. Jr.
Smith Robert D.
Smith Thos. C.
Smith Thomas M.
Snelling Samuel G.
Snow Samuel
Snow Samuel T.
*Sohier Edward D.
*Sohier William
Somerby Gusta's A.
Soren John J.
Spaulding Ira D.
Speare Alden
Spinney Samuel R.
Sprague Charles J.
Sprague Henry H.
Spurr Oliver H.
Stackpole Andrew J.
Stackpole J. Lewis
Stafford Chas. F.
Standish L. Miles
Standish William
Stansbury Chas. F.
Stanwood Charles
*Staples Hamilton B.
Starkweather Geo. C.
Stearns Edward
Stearns Nath'l C.
Stebbins Solomon B.
Stedman Daniel B.
Stedman Francis W.
Stetson Sidney A.
†Stetson Wm. J.
Stevens Benj. F.
Stevens Chas. E.
Stevens Henry J.
Stevens Hiram A.
Stevens James M.
Stevens Munroe
Stevens Oliver
Stevens William B.
Stevenson J. Thos.
Stiles I. Augustus
Stinson Aug. G.
Stoddard Charles
Stodder John W. T.
Stone Anson J.
Stone Richard, Jr.
Storey Charles W.
Storrow Charles S.
Storrow James J.
Story Isaac
Stratton T. Wilson
Stubbe Wm. H.
Sturtevant Thos. L.
Sullivan Edward
Sullivan Geo. S.
Sullivan Richard
†Sumner Charles
Suter Hales W.
Swan Chas. A. F.
Swan William W.
Sweeney Daniel A.
Sweet Samuel W.
Swinson William
Tallon James H.
Tarbell John P.
Tasker Ebenezer
Taylor George H.
Taylor T. Albert
Teele John O.
Tenney Alonzo C.
Tenney Benj. F.
Teschemaker P. E.
Thacher Isaac
Thacher Thomas
Thaxter David
Thaxter Danl. McB.
Thaxter Joseph B.
Thayer Chas. F.
Thayer Isaiah W.
Thayer James B.
Thayer Nathaniel
Thomas Charles G.

6

Thomas James B, F.
Thomas Seth J.
Thomas William
Thompson Chas. W.
†Thompson N. A.
Thompson N. W.
Thompson Wm. V.
Thomson James D.
†Thorndike John H.
Thorndike Sam'l L.
Thornton J. Wingate
Thwing Supply C.
Tighe John
Tilton Warren
Titus John W.
Tobey Gerald C.
Tobey Seth
Todd Jacob
Todd Paul P.
Tolman Eben'r W.
Tompkins Dexter A.
Tompson Samuel
Torrey Benj. B.
Torrey Calvin
Torrey Charles
Torrey Geo. W.
Torrey Joseph G.
Towne Geo. G.
Towne William B.
Towne William H.
Tracy Frederick U.
†Train Charles K.
Treadwell John P.
†Trumbull Geo. C.
Tucker Horace G.
Tucker James C.
Tucker John C.
Tucker Joseph W.
Tucker Payson E.
Tucker William W.
Turner Alfred T.
Turner Charles W.
Turner Henry C.
Turner Job A.
Tuttle Charles W.
Tuttle Samuel J.
Tuxbury Geo. W.
Tyler Charles H.
Tyler Columbus
Tyler John
Tyler John S.
Tyler J. Kendall
Tyler Wm. C.
Tyrdale Theo. H.
Underwood Geo. L.
Underwood Guy C.
Upham Henry
Upham William
†Upton Geo. B.
Urbino Samson R.
Usher James F.
Van Campen Savill-
lin
Veazie Joseph A.
†Vincent George H.
Vincent Wm. B.
Wade Joseph M.
Wadsworth Alex.
Wadsworth Alex. F.
Wakefield Cyrus
Wakefield Enoch H.
Wakefield Thos. L.
Walbridge Fred. G.
Walcott Henry P.
Walker Clement A.
Walker Henry W.
Walker Samuel A.
†Walley Samuel H.
Walley William F.
Wallis Elbridge G.
Ward Frantis J.
Ward Joseph H.
Ward Joseph W.
Ward Michael J.
Ward Samuel E.
Ware Darwin E.
Ware Geo. W, Jr.
†Ware Henry
Warner Aaron E.
Warner John

Warren Alfred B.
†Warren Charles H.
Warren Daniel
Warren George W.
Warren Henry
Warren Wm. W.
Warren Wm. W.
Warren Winsl'w, Jr.
Washburn Alex. C.
Washburn Chas. R.
Washburn John M.
Waters Edwin F.
Watson John C.
Way John M.
Way Samuel A.
Webb Charles H.
Welch Jonathan W.
Wellington Ambrose
Wellington Asa
Wellington Hiram
Wellman John W.
Wellman Wm. A.
Wells Benj. T.
Wells Michael F.
Wells Samuel, Jr.
Wentworth Alou. B.
Wentworth Sam. H.
Wesson Leonard
†West Benj. H.
Weston Nathan, Jr.
Weston Thomas, Jr.
Wheeler Charles
Wheeler Samuel L.
Wheeler Willard D.
Wheelock Ford'ec F.
Wheelock John
Wheelwright A. C.
Whipple John L.
White Benj. F.
White Charles J.
White Edwar't A.
White Horace H.
White Luther L.
White Rufus A.
Whitman Jos. H.
Whitman Wm. D. A.
Whittemore Benj. F.
Whittemore Henry
Whitten Chas. V.
Whitwell Wm. S.
Wiggin Charles E.
Wiggins John H.
Wightman Jos. M.
Wilbur Asa
Wilbur Horace B.
†Wilber James H.
Wilkins Fred'k. A.
Willard Joseph
†Willard Joseph A.
Willcut Levi C.
Willcut Sam'l D. G.
Willett William
Willey Tolman
Williams Alfred
William- Elijah
Williams H. Bigelow
Williams Horace
Williams Horace P.
Williams Jas. M. W.
Williams Moses, Jr.
Williams Robert B
Williams W. Roscoe
Williamson E. E.
Williamson Wm. C.
Willis Clement
Wilson Clement A.
Wilson Henry W.
Wilson John T.
Winnett Jason
Winship F. Lyman
Winslow Edward
Winslow Frank
Winslow John B.
Winslow J. Ambrose
Wise Edward
Wolcott Edmund
Woodbury Jesse P.
Woodman Horatio
Woolson James A.
Worthington Roland

†Wright Albert J.
Wright Carroll D.
Wright Edwin
*Wright Isaac H.
Wright John S.
Wright Smith

Wyman Asa, Jr.
Wyman Isaac C.
Wyman Oliver C.
Young Hiram C.
Young P. Ambrose

The following residents of Boston Highlands hold commissions as Justices for Norfolk County: —

Ira Allen, Wm. Bacon, Jr., Morrill P. Berry, Solomon A. Bolster, John J. Clarke, James H. Collins, Wm. A. Crafts, Sereno E. D. Currier, Geo. Curtis, Henry Davenport, Chas. K. Dillaway, Caleb S. Emery, George B. Faunce, George Frost, *William Gaston, Daniel A. Glidden, Alden Graham, Charles E. Grant, James Guild, Patrick R. Guiney, Peter Higgins, †James M. Keith, †Wm. S. King, Wm. B. Kingsbury, †Wm. S. Leland, Samuel Little, †Theo Otis, Jeremiah Plimpton, Jerahmeel C. Pratt, †Chandler R. Ransom, Giles H. Rich, †James Ritchie, Alvin M. Robbins, Geo. Simpson, William Seaver, Charles A. B. Shepard, Phineas B. Smith, Jr., Geo. C. Starkweather, Thomas Thacher, Supply C. Thwing, Joseph W. Tucker, Francis J. Ward, Chas. R. Washburn, Moses H. Webber, †Peter S. Wheelock, Wm. Whiting, Charles Whittier, Franklin Williams.

Justices of the Peace.

[Including Justices of the Peace and Quorum, designated by a *, and Justices throughout the Commonwealth, designated by a †.]

Chelsea, Isaiah M. Atkins, Edwin C. Barnes, James E. Barrell, Samuel Bassett, †Hamlett Bates, Ralph Beatley, John Bell, Caleb Blodgett, Jr., George C. Bossom, Wm. P. B. Brooks, Wm. C. Brown, Simeon Butterfield, Thomas H. Carruth, Mellen Chamberlain, Henry L. Champlin, Ira Cheever, Tracy P. Cheever, Albert Dwight, James P. Farley, Frank B. Fay, Orin W. Fiske, Eustace C. Fitz, John W. Fletcher, James B. Forsyth, Rufus S. Frost, Benjamin J. Gerrish, John E. M. Gilley, Jesse Gould, *John W. Graves, John T. Hadaway, Andrew L. Haskell, William O. Haskell, Charles Hubbard, *Henry T. Knight, Samuel S. Jackson, William H. Long, Eben W. Lothrop, John Low, Stillman P. Marsh, Henry Mason, Samuel W. Mason, Otis Merriam, Otis W. Merriam, Levi B. Miller, Jacob Mitchell, Robert Morris, Samuel Orcutt, John P. Payson, Wm. R. Pearmain, †Israel Perkins, James T. Phelps, Benj. Phipps, Jr., Allen Pratt, John M. Prince, Harvey Rogers, Erastus

Rugg. Alonzo C. Tenney, Jonn Warner, Charles J. White, Jos. Wyeth.

North Chelsea, Benj. H. Dewing, Daniel T. Fuller, Jonathan Harrington. Ivory N. Richardson.

Winthrop, David Belcher, *Edw'd Floyd.

Coroners.

Boston, Frederic S. Ainsworth, Ira Allen, Horace G. Barrows. George E Evans, Vine H. Fitch, John S. H. Fogg. John W. Foye, Paschal P. Ingalls, Richard M. Ingalls, Edward B. Moore. Aaron P. Richardson, Duncan McB. Thaxter, David Thayer, Wm. E. Underwood, Arthur H. Wilson; *Special*, Erastus W. Sanborn, Chas. Smith.

Chelsea, James B. Forsyth, Jacob Mitchell, Erastus Rugg.

Notaries Public.

Boston, Albert W. Adams, Chas. B. F. Adams, Edwin A. Alger, P. Adams Ames, Jona. Amory, Sam'l Andrews, Geo. T. Angell, Herman Askensay, John R. Baker, Elisha Bassett, Adolphus Bates, James B. Bell, Morrill P. Berry, Charles Blanchard, Abraham F. Bloch, Luther Blodgett, Jos. R. Bradford, Samuel J. Bradlee, Lloyd Briggs, Charles H. Brown, Robert H. Buck, Robert L. Burbank, Benjamin F. Burnham, Wm. W. Burrage, Henry D. Clary, Henry A. Coffin, Wm. W. Cowles, Benj. H. Currier, Samuel S. Curtis, George H. Cutter, Timothy Davis, Thomas A. Dexter, Chas. E. W. Dimmock, Charles H. Drew, Francis S. Dyer, George W. Estabrook, George B. Faunce, Henry H. Fitch, George H. Folger, John B. Folger, William H. Foster, Benjamin

W. Gilbert. John E. M. Gilley. Theo. W. Gore, J. Brainerd Hall. Richard S. Haven, Joseph L. Henshaw, Calvin P. Hinds, George M. Hobbs, William Hobbs. Jr., Job H. Hodgman, John S. Holmes, Willis Howes, John W. Hudson, Francis W. Jacobs, Samuel Jennison, Freeman M. Joselyn, John H. Kimball, Nathan P Lamson, William M. Lathrop, Thomas H. Leavitt, Wm. H. Lewis, Walter Littlefield, John D. Long, Samuel C. Loud, Samuel M. Lovejoy. Ebenr. M. McPherson, John Otis Mills, James C. Morse, Andrew J. Morton, Ellis L. Motte, Edward P. Nettleton, Curtis C. Nichols, Byron A. Osgood, N. Austin Parks, Claudius B. Patten, Asa P. Potter, Christopher Prince, Otis G. Randall, Henry Rice, J. Avery Richards, James Ritchie, Edward Russell, Daniel Sharp, Geo. S. Shaw, George Sherman, J. Edwin Sherman, H. Farnam Smith, David D. Stackpole, George C. Stearns, Joseph L. Stone, William H. Stubbe, Hales W. Suter, J. Watson Taylor, Duncan McBean Thaxter, Charles F. Thayer, Newell A. Thompson, William H. Thompson, Paul P. Todd, Joseph W. Tucker, John S. Tyler, Chas. F. Walcott, Aaron E. Warner, Oliver Warner, Alfred B. Warren, John C. Watson, Ambrose Wellington, Frank G. Webster, William C. Williamson, W. Roscoe Williams, F. Lyman Winship, J. P. Cushing Winship.

Chelsea, Hamlett Bates, John E. M. Gilley, Jason B. Loomis.

Commissioners of Wrecks.

Boston, Moses B. Tower.
Winthrop, Edward Floyd.

STATE LIBRARY.

In the State House, for the use of the Governor, Lieutenant-Governor, the Council, the Senate, the House of Representatives, and such other officers of the government and other persons as may from time to time be permitted to use the same.

The Library is open during the Session of the Legislature, each day, without intermission, from 9, A.M., to 5, P.M., except on Saturday P.M. when it is closed at 1 o'clock.

All persons whatsoever may use the Library for consultation or reference.

TRUSTEES.

Edwin P. Whipple, Jacob M. Manning, George O. Shattuck, of Boston.
Joseph White, Librarian, *Ex. officio*.
Samuel C. Jackson, acting Librarian.
C. R. Jackson, E. M. Sawyer, Assistants.

WORCESTER COUNTY.

Incorporated, April 2, 1731.

SHIRE TOWNS,................ .....WORCESTER AND FITCHBURG.

COUNTY OFFICERS.

Judge of Probate and Insolvency,.... Henry Chapin,.......... *Worcester.*
Register of Probate and Insolvency,.. Charles E. Stevens,...... *Worcester.*
Ass't Register of Probate and Insolvency Frederick W. Southwick,. *Worcester.*
Clerk of Courts, ... Joseph Mason, ... *Worcester.*
Assistant Clerk,........ .... John A. Dana, ... *Worces'er.*
Register of Deeds,....:.............. Alexander H. Wilder,.... *Worcester.*
County Treasurer, ... Charles A. Chase, ... *Worcester.*

Overseers of Houses of Correction,.. { Julius E. Tucker, / Saml. A. Porter, / Joseph D. Daniels, } ..... *Worcester.* / Alvah Crocker, / William Baker, } ......*Fitchburg.*

Sheriff,.........................John S. C. Knowlton,...... *Worcester.*

Deputy Sheriffs.

Athol, Gardiner Lord, Jr.
Barre, Daniel Cummings.
Blackstone, Edmund O. Bacon.
Clinton, Enoch K. Gibbs.
Fitchburg, Francis Buttrick.
Grafton, S. Davis Hall.
Leominster, Emery Tilton.
Milford, Samuel W Hayward.
North Brookfield, Luther P. De Land.
Oxford, Orrin W. Chaffee.
Southbridge, Solomon Thayer.
Spencer, Nathan Hersey.
Uxbridge, Merrill Greene.
Webster, Solomon Shumway.
Winchendon, Joseph S. Watson.
Worcester, Daniel F. Newton; Jonathan B. Sibley, Frank A. Newton.

Jailers.

Rufus Carter, *Worcester.*
Edwin Upton, *Fitchburg.*

Sessions of Probate Courts.

At *Barre,* Fri. next after 3d Tu. of May and Oct.
At *Clinton,* 3d Tu of May and Oct.
At *Fitchburg,* Wed. next after 3d Tu. of May and Oct.
At *Milford,* 4th Tu. of May, and Wed. next after 4th Tu. in Oct.
At *Templeton,* Thurs. next after 3d Tu. of May and Oct.
At *Uxbridge,* 4th Tu. of Oct.
At *West Brookfield,* 2d Tu. of May and Oct.
At *Worcester,* 1st Tu. of every month.

County Commissioners.

Velorous Taft, *Upton,* term expires Dec. 1869; J. Warren Bigelow, *Rutland,* term expires Dec. 1870; William O. Brown, *Fitchburg,* term expires Dec. 1871.
Special Commissioners, John McLellan, *Grafton;* Silas Holman, *Bolton.*
Times of Meeting. — At *Worcester,* 4th Tu. in Mar., 3d Tu. in June, 2d Tu. in Sept., and 4th Tu. of Dec.

Commissioners of Insolvency.

Athol. Farwell F. Fay.
Fitchburg, David H. Merriam.
Westborough, Arthur G. Biscoe.
Worcester, Frank P. Goulding.

Public Administrators.

Lunenbury, Thomas Billings.
Shrewsbury, Adam Harrington.

Masters in Chancery.

Milford, Hamilton B. Staples.
Worcester, J. Henry Hill, Joseph Mason, Henry C. Rice, Hartley Williams.

Commissioners to Qualify Civil Officers.

Athol (Depot), Charles Field, Nathaniel Richardson.
Barre, Lyman Sibley, Edwin Woods.
Fitchburg, Ebenezer Torrey, Geo. A. Torrey, Nathaniel Wood.
Milford, Thos. G. Kent, Hamilton B. Staples.
Oxford, Emery Sanford, Jasper Brown.

Worcester, Henry Chapin, John A. Dana, Charles W. Hartshorn, John Mason, Joseph Mason, George W. Richardson, William A. Smith, Chas. E. Stevens.

Justices of the Peace.

[*Including Justices of the Peace and Quorum; designated by a *, and Justices throughout the Commonwealth, designated by a †.*]

Ashburnham, John L. Cummings, Daniel Ellis, Jr., William P. Ellis, Jerome W. Foster, Ohio Whitney, Jr. — *Ashburnham Depot,* Wilbur F. Whitney. — *North Ashburnham,* Alfred Whitmore.

Athol, Benjamin Estabrook, Farwell F. Fay, Thomas H. Good-peed, Lyman W. Hapgood, Joseph M. Harrington, Franklin R. Haskell. — *Athol Depot,* † Charles Field, George W. Horr, Howard B. Hunt, Nathaniel Richardson, Walter Thorpe.

Auburn, John Mellish, Eugene H. Newton, Isaac Sawin, Demosthenes Tiffany.

Barre, Pliny H. Babbitt, Chas. Brimblecom, Humphrey F. Brooks, †Edward Denny, J. Martin Gorham, *James W. Jenkins, Henry E. Rice, Henry J Shattuck, Edwin Woods, John F. Woods.

Berlin, Albert Babcock, William Bassett, Rufus S. Hastings, Josiah E. Sawyer.

Blackstone, Albert Babcock, Sylvanus H. Benson, Estes Burdon, Silas A. Burgess, Arthur Cook, Moses Farnum, Theo. S. Johnson, Francis Kelly, Arthur B. Putman, Moses D. Southwick, Preserved S. Thayer, Chas. A. Wight, Willard Wilson.

Bolton, Roswell Barrett, Amery Holman, Silas Holman, Solomon H. Howe, Edwin A. Whitcomb.

Boylston (Centre), Charles Andrews, Henry H. Brigham, Jos. M. Wright.

Brookfield, George S. Duell, Geo. Forbes, *Dwight Hyde, George W. Johnson, Hiram Pierce, Emmons Twichell.

Charlton, Rufus B. Dodge, Alfred E. Fiske, Levi Hammond, *Salem Towne. — *Charlton City,* Lewis E. Capen, Simeon Lamb, *William P. Marble.

Clinton, Daniel H. Bemis, Artemas E. Bigelow, Everett W. Bigelow, Henry N. Bigelow, Elisha Brimhall, *John T. Dame, Franklin Forbes, Enoch K. Gibbs, Henry C. Greeley, Charles F. W. Parkhurst, Wellington E. Parkhurst, Ezra Sawyer, Charles G. Stevens, Joshua Thissell, Charles W. Worcester.

Dana, Nathaniel L. Johnson, Daniel Stone.

Douglas, Enoch Brown, Wm. D. Jones. — *East Douglas,* Fenner Batcheller, Adolphus F. Brown, Samuel W. Heath, Lyman Parsons.

Dudley, Moses Barnes, Amasa Davis, William L. Davis, Ira F. Jacobs, Charles C. Wood.

Fitchburg, Chas. J. Billings, Hiram A. Blood, Thomas R. Boutelle, Lewis H. Bradford, William E. Brown, Thomas C. Caldwell, George D. Colony, Alvah Crocker, *Oliver Ellis, *Sewall Goodrich, *Stillman Haynes, †Alfred Hitchcock, Henry Jackson, George Jewett, Alpheus P. Kimball, John W. Kimball, Edward P. Loring, Moses G. Lyon, *Charles Mason, David H. Merriam, William J. Merriam, Alfred Miller, †Amasa Norcross, Hale W. Page, John J. Piper, George Raymond, Otis T. Ruggles, Alvin M. Sawyer, Abel Simonds, Charles H. B. Snow, Cyrus Thurston, George E. Towne, †Ebenezer Torrey, Geo. A. Torrey, William H. Vose, Thornton K. Ware, Joseph Willard, Henry A. Willis, *Nathaniel Wood, James M. Woodbury, William Woodbury, Jr.

Gardner, John Edgell, Thomas E. Glazier, Charles Heywood, John M. Moore, Francis Richardson, Edward J. Sawyer, Simeon W. A. Stevens, Asaph Wood.

Grafton, Joseph B. Adams, Seth J. Axtell, *Abraham M. Bigelow, Edw'd B. Bigelow, Thomas T. Griggs, S. Davis Hall, Samuel Harrington, Lewis Holbrook, Samuel A. Knox, John McClellan, Jasper S. Nelson, George K. Nichols, James G. Putnam, Ashley W. Rice, George F. Slocomb, Jesse H. Smith, Rufus E. Warren, †Jona D. Wheeler, Willard D. Wheeler, Jas. W. White, Stephen R. White, Henry F. Wing, Charles C. Wood, Jonathan H. Wood. — *Saundersville.* Gilbert C. Taft.

Hardwick, Daniel S. Collins, James P. Fay, Albert E. Knight. — *Gilbertville,* William H. Tucker.

Harvard, Samuel G. Clarke, Edwin A. Hildreth, Augustus G. Hill. Eliakim A. Holman, Augustus J. Sawyer, Samuel F. Whitney, Wm. B. Willard.

Holden, Israel M. Ball, Charles Chaflin, Charles Flagg, Joseph H. Gleason, Joab S. Holt, David F. Parmenter.

Hubbardston, Wm. Bennett, Benjamin D. Phelps, Levi Pierce, Lyman Woodward.

Lancaster, Francis B. Fay, Jacob
Fisher, George W. Howe, John L. S.
Thompson, Solon Whiting.

Leicester, John D. Cogswell, Chas.
A. Denny, Joseph A. Denny, Silas
Gleason, Cheney Hatch, John N.
Murdock, Henry O. Smith, Luke G.
Sturtevant. *Clappville,* Elbridge G.
Carlton.

Leominster, James Bennett, Alfred
L. Burditt, Geo. S. Burrage, Leonard
Burrage, Chauncey W. Carter, Caleb
C. Field, John H. Lockey, Chas. H.
Merriam, Samuel Putnam, Merritt
Wood.

Lunenburg, William Baker, Thomas
Billings, George A. Cunningham,
Chas. A. Goodrich, *Cyrus Kilburn,
James Putnam.

Mendon, Nathan George, John G.
Metcalf, Samuel H. Taft, Gustavus B.
Williams.

Milford, Charles F. Chapin, James
R. Davis, William F. Draper, Lewis
Fales, Zibeon C. Fields, Leander Hol-
brook, †Thomas G. Kent, †Aaron C.
Mayhew, Abraham Mead, Geo. G.
Parker, John S. Scammel, Hamilton
B. Staples, Andrew J. Sumner, Alvin
G. Underwood, Orison Underwood,
Alexander T. Wilkinson, D. Lucien
Wilkinson.

Millbury, David Atwood, Henry L.
Bancroft, George A. Flagg, John
Hopkins, *Samuel D. Torrey.— *West
Millbury,* Ephraim Goulding.

New Braintree, Josiah P. Gleason,
William A. Mixter.

Northborough, Wilder Bush, Samuel
Clark, George C. Davis, Walter Gale,
Milo Hildreth, Anson Rice, Abraham
W. Seaver.

Northbridge, Joel Bachelor, P.
Whitin Dudley, Wm. D. Maseroft,
Hiram Wing. — *Whitinsville,* Robert
G. Adams, H. Aug. Goodell, †Charles
E. Whitin.

North Brookfield, †Charles Adams,
Jr., Robert E. Beecher, George
Harwood, Erastus Hill, John Hill,
Hiram Knight, Bonum Nye, Joshua
Porter, Augustus Smith, †Amasa
Walker.

Oakham, Moses O. Ayres, James
Allen, Mark Haskell.

Oxford, Charles A. Angell, Jasper
Brown, Jonathan P. Dana, George F.
Daniels, Alexander De Witt, Wm.
E. Pease, John B. Pratt, Samuel W.
Smith, John Wetherell. — *North Ox-
ford,* E. Harris Howland.

Paxton, David G. Davis, Silas D.
Harrington, William Milligan, Geo.
W. Partridge.

Petersham, Collins Andrews, Steph.
D. Goddard, John G. Mudge, Josiah
White, Lewis Whitney.

Phillipston, Jason Goulding, Edw'd
Powers.

Princeton, Asa H. Goddard, David
H. Gregory, Albert C. Howe, Eph-
raim Osgood, Joseph A. Reed, †Chas.
Russell.

Royalston, Barnet Bullock, Jervis
Davis, Nahum Longley.

Rutland, Alonzo Davis, Abram H.
Temple, J. Warren Bigelow.

Shrewsbury, Frederick A. Brigham,
Charles O. Green, Wm. H. Knowl-
ton, George Leonard, Jonathan H.
Nelson, Thomas W. Ward.

Southboro', Franklin Esre, Jonas
Fay, Richardson Goddard, Stephen J.
Metcalf, Curtis Newton, Dexter
Newton, Henry S. Wheeler. — *Cor-
daville,* Hubbard Wilson.

Southbridge, Andrew J. Bartholo-
mew, *Frederick W. Bothman, Henry
Clarke, Sylvester Dresser, Samuel M.
Lane, Manning Leonard, John O.
McKinstry.

Spencer, David Bemis, John N.
Grout, Nathan Hersey, *Luther Hill,
William Pope, Theodore C. Prouty,
Thomas A. Prouty, William Sampson,
Richard Sugden. — *Leicester,* George
A. Craig.

Sterling, Eli Kilburn, William D.
Peck.

Sturbridge, Henry Haynes, Benja-
min D. Hyde. — *Fiskdale,* E. L.
Bates, Avery P. Taylor, David
Wight.

Sutton, Harvey Dodge, William R.
Hill, Horace Leland, Edmund J.
Mills, Solomon Severy, James Taylor,
Russell Titus, *John W. Whipple. —
Manchaug, William Abbott. — *West
Sutton,* Nathan Waters — *Wilkinson-
ville,* Isaac B. Hartwell.

Templeton, Edwin G. Adams, John
M. Brown, Gerard Bushnell, Stilman
Cady, Gilman Day, Elisha C. Farns-
worth, Dexter Gilbert, Joshua B.
Gould, George P. Hawkes, Hosea F.
Lane, *Artemas Lee, Veranus P.
Parkhurst, Henry Smith, Wm. Smith,
E. Wyman Stone, Wm. N. Walker,
John W. Work.

Upton, George S. Ball, Elisha B.
Fiske, Nahum W. Holbrook, Henry
D. Johnson, Levi W. Taft, Velorous
Taft.

Uxbridge, Valentine M. Aldrich,
Henry Capron, Alvin Cook, Francis
Deane, Frederic B. Deane, Merrill
Greene, George W. Hobbs, Zadok
A. Taft, Charles Wing.

Warren, James S. Davis. †Joseph F. Hitchcock, Joseph B. Lombard, D. Warren Shepard, Wm. L. Powers. John Tyler. — *West Warren*, Amos F. Howard.

Webster, Hiram Allen, Frederic D. Brown, Chester C. Corbin, †Wm. H. Davis, Rufus C. Hall, John F. Hinds, Edwin May, John B. Hasler, Albert Morton, John H. Stockwell, Seymour A. Tingier.

Westboro', Arthur G. Biscoe. John A. Faverweather, Jabez G. Fisher, Samuel M. Griggs, Daniel F. Newton, Benjamin B. Nourse.

West Boylston, Albert Hinds, Geo. F. Howe, David C. Murdock, David P. Waite. Aaron E. Winter. — *Oakdale*, Ebenezer M. Hosmer, Harrison E. Morton.

West Brookfield, Lemuel Fullam, Alanson Hamilton, Avery Keep, Horace G. Rawson, Edwin B. Tainter.

Westminster, Joel Merriam, Jr., Daniel C. Miles, Harrison G. Whitney, James B. Wood, Benjamin Wyman.

Winchendon, Amos W. Buttrick, Bethuel Ellis. *Edwin S. Merrill, Lafayette W. Pierce, Charles J. Rice, Ira Russell, Joseph S. Watson, Windsor N. White, *Giles H. Whitney.

Worcester, Frederick E. Abbott, †P. Emory Aldrich, Lucius S. Allen, James G. Arnold, Henry Bacon, Peter C. Bacon, Phineas Ball, Richard Ball, Chas. Ballard, James H. Bancroft, Frederick J. Barnard, Wm. S. Barton, Daniel W. Bemis. Merrick Bemis, James H. Benchley, Francis T. Blackmer, James B. Blake, Harrison Bliss, Charles E. Briggs, Horace E. Brooks, John H. Brooks. Frederick P. Brown, †Alexander H. Bullock, †Augustus G. Bullock, Asa L. Burbank, Charles W. Burbank, Albert C. Buttrick, Jona. Cary, †Henry Chapin, †Anthony Chase, Charles A. Chase, Samuel H. Colton, Edwin Conant, Wm. Cross, Augustus N. Currier, Appleton Dadmun, Caleb Dana, *John A. Dana, Edward L. Davis, †Isaac Davis, William S. Davis, Jonathan Day, William S. Denny, †Francis H. Dewy, Thomas H. Dodge, †John Milton Earle, A. Jones Eaton, Geo. H. Estabrook, Samuel B. L. Goddard, Milton B. Goodell. John B. Gough, Ransom M. Gould, Frank P. Goulding, James Green Jr., *William N. Green, John R. Greene, *William Greenleaf. Emine P. Halsted, Theron E. Hall, Timothy W. Hammond, William B. Harding, Adam Harrington, Clarenden Harris, *Charles W. Hartshorn, Dan'l W. Haskins, Sam'l F. Haven, Daniel A. Hawkins, Jr., Charles Hersey. *J. Henry Hill, Geo. F. Hoar. George Hobbs, Charles A. Holbrook, Clark Jilson, George A. Kimball, Francis L. King, Francis H. Kinnicutt. †John S. C. Knowlton, Thomas Magennis, Jerome F. Manning, Henry A. Marsh, John Mason, *Joseph Mason, *William B. Maxwell, Matthew J. McCafferty, Isaac S. Merriam, Henry K. Merrifield, Chas. M. Miles, Thomas L. Nelson, John C. Otis, Nathaniel Paine. Henry L. Parker, Loren C. Parks, Frank W. Perry, Ivers Phillips, Charles B. Pratt, Charles L. Putnam. Charles W. Rice, Henry C. Rice, †William W. Rice, *Geo. W. Richardson, Stephen Salisbury, Stephen Salisbury, Jr., Charles E. Simmons, Samuel Smith, Sidney Smith, Charles E. Stevens, †Elijah B. Stoddard, Samuel V. Stone, George Swan, Putnam W. Taft, Adin Thayer, Lewis Thayer, Josiah A. Thompson, Joseph A. Titus, Julius E. Tucker, Samuel Utley, Edward W. Vaill, Gill Valentine, George F. Verry, Horace B. Verry, Justin A. Ware. *Charles Washburn, †John D. Washburn, Wm. Ansel Washburn, †John W. Wetherell, Timothy W. Wellington, Hen. M. Wheeler, Franklin Whipple, Harvey B. Wilder, And'w A. Willams, †Hartley Williams, William A. Williams, Chas. Wood, George M. Woodward, Henry Woodward.

Trial Justices.

Athol (Depot), Franklin R. Haskell.
Barre, Edwin Woods.
Blackstone, Theodore S. Johnson.
Brookfield, George S. Duell.
Clinton, Daniel H. Bemis.
Douglas (East), Samuel W. Heath.
Grafton, James W. White.
Holden, David F Parmenter.
Leominster, Charles H. Merriam.
Millbury, George A. Flagg.
Northborough, Samuel Clark.
Southbridge, Sylvester Dresser.
Spencer, Luther Hill.
Sutton, Edmund J. Mills.
Templeton, E. Wyman Stone.
Uxbridge. Zadok A. Taft.
Warren, Joseph F. Hitchcock.
Webster. John H. Stockwell.
Westborough, Samuel M. Griggs.
West Boylston (Oakdale), Ebenezer M. Hosmer.
Winchendon, Bethuel Ellis.
Worcester, Henry C. Rice.

Notaries Public.

Ashburnham, Jerome W. Foster.
Athol, Farwell F. Fay.
Athol (Depot), Chas. Field, Nathaniel Richardson.
Barre, Charles Brimblecom.
Blackstone, Silas A. Burgess.
Brookfield, George W. Johnson.
Clinton, Charles G. Stevens.
Douglas (East), Lyman Parsons.
Fitchburg, Hiland C. Hitchcock, Geo. A. Torrey, Thornton K. Ware, Nathaniel Wood, James M. Woodbury.
Gardner, Francis Richardson.
Grafton, James W. White.
Lancaster, John L. S. Thompson.
Leicester, Charles A. Denny, Cheney Hatch.
Leominster, Jas. Bennett, Chauncey W. Carter.
Milford, Napoleon B. Johnson, Thomas G. Kent.
Millbury, Ira N. Goddard.
Northborough, Samuel Clark.
Northbridge, (Whitinsville), Edward Whitin.
Oxford, Emory Sanford.

Southbridge, Manning Leonard' Calvin A. Paige.
Spencer, Luther Hill.
Uxbridge, John W. Capron.
Webster, John H. Stockwell, Royal Storrs.
Westborough, Arthur G. Biscoe, Benjamin Boynton.
Winchendon, Edwin S. Merrill, Giles H. Whitney.
Worcester. Wm. S. Barton, Charles M. Bent, John Boyden, John A. Dana, William T. Harlow, J. Henry Hill, Henry L. Parker, Henry C. Rice, Samuel Smith, Elijah B. Stoddard, Joseph Trumbull, Hartley Williams.

Coroners.

Clinton, Lucius Field.
Fitchburg, Alfred Miller.
Southboro', (Special) Curtis Newton.
Sturbridge, David Wight.
Sutton, (Special) John W. Whipple.
Warren, Nelson Carpenter.
Winchendon, Joseph S. Watson.
Worcester, Frank H. Rice, J. Marcus Rice. Special, Jonathan B. Sibley.

CONSTABLE OF THE COMMONWEALTH.

EDWARD J. JONES, Office, 50 Bromfield St., Boston.

DEPUTY STATE CONSTABLES.

Barnstable County.
Yarmouth Port, Benjamin H. Mathews.

Berkshire County.
No. Adams, Wm. McKay.
"　　　Lester M. Hayden.

Bristol County.
New Bedford, W. C. Thomas.
"　　　Charles H. Morton.
Taunton, Robert Crossman, 2d.

Dukes County.
Edgartown, Jason L. Dexter.

Essex County.
Georgetown, Geo. P. Boynton.
Lawrence, Melvin Beal.
Gloucester, Joseph A. Moore.
Lynn, John F. Broan.
Rowley, Richard C. Hale.

Franklin County.
Coleraine, H. B. Miller.
Northfield, George H. Phelps.

Hampden County.
Springfield, Samuel Chapin.
"　　　Harvey H. Billings.

Hampshire County.
Goshen, T. P. Lyman.
Ware, Wm. E. Lewis.

Middlesex County.
Charlestown, Jonathan Oldham.
East Cambridge, A. H. Stevens, Jr.

Lowell, N. W. Norcross.
Woburn, John E. Tidd.
Marlboro', Micah B. Priest.

Norfolk County.
East Weymouth, A. J. Gary.
Neponset, Benjamin P. Eldridge.
Randolph, Isaac Porter.

Plymouth County.
North Abington, Geo. C. Pratt.
No. Bridgewater, Uriah Macoy.
Plymouth, Joshua D. Baxter.
"　　　James B. Collingwood.

Suffolk County.
BOSTON.
Names and Residences.

Gustavus Andrews, at Lynn.
Richard F. Andrews, at Lynn.
John J. Brown, 43 Spring.
Sidney M. Copeland, 1624 Washington.
Chauncey C. Dean, 91 Winthrop.
Charles E. Dodge, 125 Chelsea.
J. Waldo Denny, 20 Oak.
John E. Gilman, 59 South Margin.
John Green, at Chelsea.
John B. Hollis, 1 Madison Place.
Levi Hutchins, at Chelsea.
Daniel C. Jones, 24 Bennet.
H. D. Littlefield, 58 Harrison ave.
B. H. Liliscott, Boston Highlands.
James H. Maguire, 32 Spring.
F. A. Marsh, 1590 Washington.
William Mooney, 124 Purchase.
George Munroe, Boston Highlands.

William C. Murphy, 1 Providence.
Daniel Noonan, 12 Tyler.
Edward L. Noyes, 277 Eustis.
Holli- C. Pinkham, 219 Chelsea, E. B.
C. R. M. Pratt, Boston Highlands.
Francis M. Smith, 122 Harrison ave.
Lebbeus Stetson, Somerville.
John W. T. Stodder, 33 Bradford.
George P. Stone, at Lynn.
John Tewksbury, 101 Brighton.

Charles W. Thompson, 30 Eliot.
James A. Vialle, at Hyde Park.
Chelsea, James P. Wade, at Chelsea.

Worcester County.

Worcester, Charles N. Hair.
Fitchburg, John W. Kimball.
Milford, A. W. Keene.
North Brookfield, E. J. Russell.

POST-OFFICES & POST-MASTERS IN MASSACHUSETTS.

Towns are also given which are not Post-offices; but their Post-offices immediately follow.
For Money Order Offices, see page 78.

Abington,	Benj. L. Nash
East Abington,	James M. Underwood
North "	Emery Burgess
South "	Albert Davis
Acton,	John E. Cutter
South Acton,	James E. Harris
West "	Charles Hastings
Acushnet,	Cyrus E. Clark
Adams,	John E. Mole
North Adams,	Edwin Rogers
Blackinton,	Edward W. Blackinton
Adainsville, see Coleraine	
Agawam,	Lyman Allen
Feeding Hills,	Ezra G. Gaylord
Alford,	Asa L. Landon
Allston, see Brighton	
Amesbury,	David Batchelder
South Amesbury,	Chas. E. Rowell
West "	Joseph W. Sargent
Amherst,	Jairus L. Skinner
North Amherst,	Horace Cutler
South "	Waltstill Dickinson
Andover,	Samuel Raymond
Ballard Vale,	Isaac O. Blunt
Annisquam, see Gloucester	
Arlington,	Frederick E. Fowle
Ashburnham,	Geo. C. Winchester
Ashburnham Depot,	David E. Poland
Burrageville,	Jonas W. Dwinnell
Ashby,	Charles O. Green
Ashfield,	Moses G. Cook
South Ashfield,	Chandler A. Ward
Ashland,	James B. Jones
Ashley Falls, see Sheffield	
Ashleyville, see West Springfield	
Assabet, see Sudbury	
Athol,	Thomas H. Goodspeed
Athol, Depot,	Howard B. Hunt
Attleborough,	Nathan C. Luther
North Attleborough,	Thos R. Jones
South "	James S. Day
Hebronville,	Emory A. Perrin
Auburn,	Elisha S. Knowles
Auburndale, see Newton	
Baldwinsville, see Templeton	
Ballard Vale, see Andover	
Bancroft, see Middlefield	
Barnstable,	James Clagg
West Barnstable,	Shadrack N. Howland
Hyannis,	Rufus S. Pope
Cotuit Port,	Mrs. Charlotte P. Kelley
Marston's Mills,	Chas. Bassett
Centreville,	Ferdinand G. Kelley
Osterville,	George H. Hinckley
Barre,	Aspasio T. Wilson
Barre Plains,	Edward Denny
Smithville,	J. Edwin Smith
Becket,	Jonathan W. Wheeler
Becket Centre	Charles O. Perkins
West Becket,	Miss Emily A. Sowle
Bedford,	Marcus B. Webber
Belchertown,	Samuel W. Longley
Bellingham,	Ruel F. Thayer
N. Bellingham,	Sylvanus J. Lawrence
Caryville,	Calvin Fairbanks

Belmont,	John L. Alexander
Waverley,	Seromus Gates
Berkley,	Daniel S. Briggs
Berkshire, see Lanesborough	
Berlin,	Rufus S. Hastings
West Berlin,	Silas R. Carter
Bernardston,	William Dwight
Beverly,	Thos. A. Morgan
North Beverly,	Stephen F. Hathaway
Beverly Farms,	Isaac S. Day
Billerica,	Franklin Jaquith, jr.
North Billerica,	James Whittemore
Blackinton, see Adams	
Blackstone,	Jeremiah Getchell
North Blackstone,	Emanuel N. Paine
Millville,	Preserved S. Thayer
Blandford,	Lucius B. Shepard
North Blandford,	Edwin Ely
Bolton,	Ezra S. Moore
Bond's Village, see Palmer	
Boston,	William L. Burt
Boxborough,	James E. Hayden
Boxford,	Roscoe W. Gage
West Boxford,	Philneas P. Tyler
Boylston,	James A. Weeks
Boylston Centre,	Henry White
Bradford,	James Kimball, jr.
Braggville, see Holliston	
Braintree,	E. Watson Arnold
South Braintree,	Joseph Dyer. jr.
Brewster,	Martha B. Huckins
West Brewster,	Mrs. Mercy Ryder
East "	Joseph Foster
South "	Nathaniel Myrick
Bridgewater,	Lewis Holmes
Scotland,	Miss Hasadiah K. Chipman
Brighton,	Mrs. Sibbyl S. Day
Allston,	John Parkhurst
Brimfield,	Henry F. Brown
East Brimfield,	Charles Varney
Parksville,	Rufus Foskit
Brookfield,	Francis Howe
East Brookfield,	George Forbes
Brookline,	Cyrus W. Ruggles
Buckland,	& John Porter
Burlington,	Silas Cutler
Burrageville, see Ashburnham	
Byfield, see Newbury.	
Cambridge,	George M. Osgood
East Cambridge,	Nathan K. Noble
North "	James B. Nason
Cambridgeport,	John McDuffie
Campello, see No. Bridgewater	
Canton,	Rufus C. Wood
Carlisle,	Charles T. Worthy
Carver,	Eli Southworth
North Carver,	Benj. Ransom. jr.
South "	Thomas B. Griffith
Caryville, see Bellingham	
Centreville, see Barnstable	
Central Village, see Westport	
Charlemont,	Ansel L. Tyler
East Charlemont,	Lorin Merriam
Charles River Village, see Dover	
Charlestown,	Wm. H. DeCosta

Charlton, Alfred F. Fiske
Charlton City, Mrs. Julia A. McIntire
Charlton Depot, Almon Sampson
Chatham, Ziba Nickerson
Chatham Port, Enos Kent
North Chatham, Benj. T. Freeman
South " Levi Eldridge, jr.
West " Samuel Doane
Chelmsford, Eli F. Webster
North Chelmsford, Joseph W. Smith
West " Christopher Ruby
Middlesex Village, John W. Damon
Chelsea, Hadley P. Burrill
Cherry Valley, see Leicester
Cheshire, Peter A. Trotter
Chester, William Fay
North Chester, Herman Powers
Chester Centre, Thaddeus K. DeWolf
Chesterfield, Joel Engram, jr.
West Chesterfield, Joseph W. Tirrell
Chicopee, Andrew S. Hunter
Chicopee Falls, Wm. H. Gilbert
Willimansett, Pascal J. Newell
Chilmark, John Dunham
Chiltonville, see Plymouth
Clappville, see Leicester
Clarksburg, no P. O.; address N. Adams
Cliftondale, see Saugus
Clinton, Enoch K. Gibbs
Cochesett, see West Bridgewater
Cochituate, see Wayland
Cohasset, Edward Tower
North Cohasset, Welcome Beal
Cold Brook Spring, see Oakham
Cold Spring, see Otis
Coleraine, Horace Smith
Adamsville, John Wilson
Elm Grove, Albert H. Temple
Griswoldville, Joseph Griswold, jr.
Shattuckville, Calvin W. Shattuck
College Hill, see Medford
Collins's Depot, see Wilbraham
Concord, Henry L. Whitcomb
Conway, Richard Tucker
Cordaville, see Southborough
Cotuit Port, see Barnstable
Cummington, Darius W. Lovell
Cummington W. Village, Chas. Harlow
Curtisville, see Stockbridge
Dalton, Thomas G. Carson
Dana, William H. Balcom
North Dana, Nelson Bosworth
Danvers, Joseph E. Hood
Danvers Centre, Albert H. Mudge
Danvers Port, David Mead
West Danvers, Samuel Walcott
Dartmouth, Francis W. Mason
North Dartmouth, Wm. C. Vickery
South " Thomas E. Sanford
Dedham, Ambrose B. Galucia
West Dedham, Theodore Gay, 2d
South " Willard Gay
Readville Station, Enoch P. Davis
Deerfield, Charles Williams
South Deerfield, Obed S. Arms
Dennis, Howes Chapman
Dennis Port, Thos. Howes, jr.
South Dennis, Marshall S. Underwood
East " Lothrop Howes, jr.
West " Zadock Crowell
Dighton, William B. Whitmarsh
North Dighton, Edward Almy
Dorchester, Robert Vose, jr.
Harrison Square, Jeremiah Sanborn, jr.
Mattapan, Charles E. Stevenson
Neponset Village, Amory C. Southworth
Douglas, Miss Mary Ann Holman
East Douglas, Fenner Batchelder
Dover, Isaac Howe
Charles River Village, Marshall Newell
Dracut, James H. Wilson
Dudley, William L. Davis
West Dudley, Wm. H. Parsons
Dunstable, Henry J. Tolles
Duxbury, Henry L. Sampson
West Duxbury, George B. Standish
East Bridgewater, Benj. W. Keith
Joppa Village, Warren K. Churchill
Eastham, Micah S. Paine
North Eastham, David C. Atwood

East Hampton, Jeremiah H. Bardwell
Easton, John Kimball
North Easton, George B. Cogswell
South " George Copeland
Edgartown, William Bradley
Egremont:
North Egremont, Seymour B. Dewey
South " Joseph A. Benjamin
Elm Grove, see Coleraine
Enfield, Gilbert E. Walker
Erving, Noah Rankin
Essex, Daniel W. Bartlett
Fairhaven, Jonathan T. Buttrick
Long Plain, John Manter, Jr.
Fall River, Edwin Shaw
Falmouth, Thomas H. Lawrence
East Falmouth, Joshua W. Davis
North " Ferdinand G. Nye
West " Stephen Dillingham
Hatchville, Silas Hatch, 2d
Wood's Hole, Owen Eldridge
Waquoit, Crocker H. Bearse
Farnumsville, see Grafton
Fayville, see Southborough
Feeding Hills, see Agawam
Feltonville, now Hudson
Fiskdale, see Sturbridge
Fitchburg, George E. Goodrich
West Fitchburg, Wm. Baldwin
Florence, see Northampton
Florida, Nathan White
Hoosac Tunnel, Hiram G. Phelps
Forge Village, see Westford
Foxborough, Joseph F. Hodges
East Foxborough, David Wyman
West " Miss Fanny S. Everett
Framingham, Mrs. Julia H. S. Wilde
South Framingham, Willard Howe
Saxonville, Luther F. Fuller
Franklin, Smith Fisher
Franklin City, Saul B. Scott
South Franklin, Joseph H. Wadsworth
Freetown, Joshua Shove
East Freetown, Reuel Washburn
Gardner, Charles W. Bush
South Gardner, Simeon W. A. Stevens
Georgetown, Charles W. Tenney
Gilbertville, see Hardwick
Gill, Josiah D. Canning
Glendale, see Stockbridge
Globe Village, see Southbridge
Gloucester, Charles E. Grover
Annisquam, John D. Davis
Lanesville, Albert Young
East Gloucester, Joseph W. Wonson
West Gloucester, Henry C. L. Haskell
Goshen, Joseph Hawks
Grafton, J. Frank Searle
Farnumsville, Alfred Morse
New England Village, Wm. T. Barker
Saundersville, Gilbert C. Taft
Granby, Philo Chapin
Graniteville, see Westford
Grantville, see Needham
Granville :
Granville Corners, Rufus H. Barlow
East Granville, Ralph S. Brown
West Granville, Lyman W. Shepard
Great Barrington, Isaac Seeley
Housatonic, John M. Seeley
VanDeusenville, Miss Jane Van Deusen
Greenfield, Lewis Merriam
Greenwich, Geo. R. Dickinson
Greenwich Village, Sylvester F. Root
Greenwood, see Wakefield
Griswoldville, see Coleraine
Groton, Henry Woodcock
Groton Junction, William H. Harlow
West Groton, Edmund Blood
Grout's Corner, see Montague
Groveland, Chas. H. Hopkinson
South Groveland, Eustis P. Parker
Hadley, William S. Shipman
North Hadley, Simon F. Cooley
Halifax, Caleb Poole, jr.
Hamilton, Francis C. Morton
Hancock, Wm. H. Lapham
Hanover, Robert S. Curtis
South Hanover, Isaac G. Stetson
West Hanover, Horatio B. Magoun

Hanson, Andrew Bowker
South Hanson, Cyrus A. Bates
Hardwick, Albert E. Knight
Gilbertville, Lewis N. Gilbert
Harrison Square, see Dorchester
Hartsville, see New Marlborough
Harvard, Zophar Wetherbee
Still River, William F. Bateman
Harwich, William H. Underwood
East Harwich, Joshua H Chase
North " Elijah B. Sears
South " William M. Eldridge
West. " Erastus Chase
Harwich Port, Shubael B. Kelley
Hatchville, see Falmouth
Hatfield, Joseph S. Wells
North Hatfield, Reuben H. Belden
Haverhill, Edwin P. Hill
East Haverhill, Augustus S. Chase
Hawley, Edwin Scott
West Hawley, Mark H. Vincent
Hayden Row, see Hopkinton
Haydenville, see Williamsburg
Heath, Horace McGee
Hebronville, see Attleborough
Hingham, Edwin Wilder, 2d
South Hingham, Josiah Lane
Hinsdale, John Cady
Holden, Samuel W. Armington
Holland, Francis E. Kinney
Holliston, George B. Fiske
East Holliston, Edward C. Parker
Braggville, Dennis Hartshorn
Holmes's Hole, see Tisbury
Holyoke, Charles B. Presco
Ireland, Chester Crafts
Hoosac Tunnel, see Florida
Hopedale, See Milford
Hopkinton, John A. Fitch
Hayden Row, Benjamin Phipps
Woodville, Albert Wood
Housatonic, see Great Barrington
Hubbardston, Lyman Woodward
Hudson, Silas F. Mauson
Hull, Joseph Pope
Huntington, Samuel T. Lyman
Norwich, Osman E. Knight
Hyannis, see Barnstable
Hyde Park, Thomas Hammond
Indian Orchard, see Springfield
Ipswich, John H. Cogswell
Ireland, see Holyoke
Jamaica Plain, see West Roxbury
Joppa Village, see East Bridgewater
Kingston, Azel H. Sampson
Lakeville, Cephas Haskins
Lancaster, Humphrey Barrett
South Lancaster, Daniel M. Howard
Lanesborough, Charles L. Wood
Berkshire, William G. Harding
Lanesville, see Gloucester
Lawrence, Geo. S. Merrill
Lee, Eliphalet Wright
East Lee, Wm. P. Hamblin
South Lee, William G. Merrell
Leeds, see Northampton
Leicester, Lyman D. Thurston
Cherry Valley, Joseph Bottomly
Clappville, John Hill Rouse
Lenox, Thomas Post
Lenox Furnace, Andrew T. Servin
New Lenox, Oscar S. Hutchinson
Leominster, Charles H. Coburn
North Leominster, William F. Howe
Leverett, Bradford M. Field
North Leverett, Otis Chittenden
Lexington, Leonard G. Babcock
East Lexington, Augustus Childs
Leyden, Mrs. Nancy J. Vining
Lincoln, James L. Chapin
Littleton, Joseph A. Harwood
Lock's Village, see Wendell
Longmeadow, Lester Noble
East Longmeadow, Cortez F. Russell
Long Plain, see Fairhaven
Lowell, John A. Goodwin
Ludlow, Eli M. Smith
Lunenburg, Daniel Putnam
Lynn, Geo. H. Chase
Lynnfield, Henry W. Swasey

Lynnfield Centre, Jonathan Bryant
Malden, Temple Dodge
South Malden, Joseph Gerrish
Maplewood, Elkanah A. Cummings
Manchaug, see Sutton
Manchester, Julius F. Rabardy
Mansfield, Francis Drake
West Mansfield, Albert Perry
Maplewood, see Malden
Marblehead, Stephen P. Hathaway, jr.
Marion, Sylvanus W. Hall
Marlborough, John S Fay
Marshfield, George M. Baker
East Marshfield, Mrs. Almira L. Damon
North Marshfield, Benjamin Hatch
Marston's Mills, see Barnstable
Mattapan, see Dorchester
Mattapoisett, William E. Sparrow
Medfield, Isaac Fiske
Medford, George C. Hervey
West Medford, William C. Frederick
College Hill, John A. Whitney
Medway, Henry E. Mason
East Medway, Milton Daniels
West Medway, Lewis Clark
Rockville, Erastus H. Tyler
Melrose, Caleb Howard
Mendon, Henry A. Aldrich
Methuen, Charles Shed
Middleborough, Andrew L. Tinkham
East Middleborough, Joshua M. Eddy
North " Solomon White
South " Simeon D. Wilbur
Rock, Israel Smith
Middlefield, Oliver Church
Bancroft, Chester W. Merrifield
Middlesex Village, see Chelmsford
Middleton, Amos Batchelder
Milford, George P. Woodbury
South Milford, Hamblet B. Fisk
Hopedale, Geo. Draper
Millbury, Roland E. Bowen
West Millbury, Ephraim Goulding
Mill River, see New Marlborough
Millville, see Blackstone
Millington, see New Salem
Milton, Henry Pope
Mirickville, see Taunton
Mittineague, see West Springfield
Monroe, Stillman Whitcomb
Monson, Daniel G. Potter
Montague, Isaac Cheney
Grout's Corners, John G. Creagh
Montague City, Rector L. Goss
Monterey, Wilbur C. Langdon
Montgomery, Henry S. Stiles
Montville, see Sandisfield
Monument, see Sandwich
Mount Auburn, see Watertown
Mount Washington, no P. O.; address So. Egremont
Nahant, Welcome W. Johnson
Nantucket, Andrew Whitney
Natick, John B. Fairbanks
South Natick, Isaac B. Sanger
Needham, Obed C. Parker
Grantville, Alvin Fuller, 2d
Wellesley, Francis W. Fuller
Neponset, see Dorchester
New Ashford, Miss Caroline Dewey
New Bedford, Cyrus W. Chapman
New Boston, see Sandisfield
New Braintree, George K. Tufts
Newbury:
Byfield, Miss Harriet L. Moody
Newburyport, George J. L. Colby
New England Village, see Grafton
New Lenox, see Lenox
New Marlborough, Sheldon W. Wright
Hartsville, Austin Brett
Mill River, John S. Wolfe
Southfield, Augustus Turner
New Salem, Frederick A. Haskell
North New Salem, Coolidge A. Ballard
Millington, Lyman E. Moore
Newton, Edwin Holman
Newton Centre, Stillman C. Spaulding
Newton Lower Falls, William Mills
Newton Upper Falls, James H. Grant
Newtonville, Jeremiah B. Lovett

West Newton,	John Mead
Auburndale,	George I. Bourne
Northampton,	Lorenzo W. Joy
Florence,	Henry F. Cutler
Leeds,	Alfred P. Critchlow
North Andover,	John Foster
North Andover Depot,	Andrew Smith
Northborough,	John B. Crawford
Northbridge,	Leander F. Smith
Northbridge Centre,	Wm. B. Fuller
Whitinsville,	Jas. F. Whitin
North Bridgewater,	Henry French
Campello,	Nelson J. Foss.
North-West Bridgewater.	Levi French
North Brookfield,	Wm. H Beecher
North Chelsea,	James L. Wiggin
Northfield,	George Hastings
Northfield Farms,	Moses Fifield
West Northfield,	Elijah E. Belding
North Reading,	Alonzo E. Damon
Norton,	Mrs. Harriet Hodges
Norwich, see Huntington	
Oakdale, see West Boylston	
Oakham,	Alanson Prouty
Cold Brook Springs,	Geo. L. Ripley
Orange,	Davis Goddard
North Orange,	Nathan L. Johnson
Orleans,	Miss Amelia Snow
South Orleans,	John Henrick
East Orleans,	Lot Higgins
Osterville, see Barnstable	
Otis,	Joseph L. Waters
East Otis,	Lorenzo E. Perkins
West Otis,	Lyman H. Thomson
Cold Spring,	Wm. J. Canfield
Otter River, see Templeton	
Oxford,	William E. Pease
North Oxford,	Miss M. E. Stone
Palmer,	Cyrus Knox
Thorndike,	Gamaliel Collins
Three Rivers,	George W. Randall
Bond's Village,	Nathan D. Wight
Parksville, see Brimfield	
Paxton,	Nathaniel Clark
Peabody,	David Woodbury
Pelham,	Myret E. Boynton
Pembroke,	James H. Whitman
East Pembroke,	Miss L. A. Hatch
Pepperell,	John Loring
East Pepperell,	James A. Elliott
Peru,	Sylvester S. Bowea
Petersham,	Samson Wetherell
Phillipston,	Jason Goulding
Pigeon Cove, see Rockport	
Pittsfield,	Henry Chickering
West Pittsfield,	Augustus W. Williams
Plainfield,	Leonard Campbell
Plainville, see Wrentham	
Plymouth,	George F. Weston
South Plymouth,	Josiah C. Hovey
Chiltonville,	Geo. Bramhall, jr.
Plympton,	Zaccheus Parker
Plympton Station,	Cephas Washburn
North Plympton,	James M. Harrub
Pocasset, see Sandwich	
Pratt's Junction, see Sterling	
Prescott,	Liberty Cosette
North Prescott,	Edward A. Thomas
Princeton,	David H. Gregory
East Princeton,	Joseph Whitcomb
Provincetown,	Benj. F. Hutchinson
Quincy,	John B. Bass
Quincy Point,	Zenas H. Sidelinger
Randolph,	John G. Poole
East Randolph,	Ephraim W. Lincoln
South "	Daniel Faxon
Raynham,	Richard A. Leonard
Reading,	Lewis E. Gleason
Readville Station, see Dedham	
Rehoboth,	John C. Marvel
North Rehoboth,	Greenville Stevens
Richmond,	Miss Jennie E. Williams
Ringville, see Worthington	
Rochester,	John W. Sherman
North Rochester,	John B. Deruin
Rock, see Middleborough	
Rockbottom, see Stow	
Rockport,	William W. Marshall
Pigeon Cove,	Austin W. Story
Rockville, see Medway	

Rowe,	Edward Wright
Rowley,	Thomas R. Cressey
Royalston,	Charles H. Newton
South Royalston,	Benj. B. Murdock
Russell,	Justin D. Parks
Rutland,	Alonzo Davis
North Rutland,	Guilford Welch
West "	Andrew J. Pierce
Salem,	
Salisbury,	Ezra Merrill, jr.
East Salisbury,	Cyrus Dearborn
Sandisfield,	Miss Caroline A. Balch
Montville,	Eliud Taylor
New Boston,	Samuel C. Parsons
South Sandisfield,	Rollin A. Webster
Sandwich,	Frederic S. Pope
East Sandwich,	Joseph Ewer, jr.
North "	Charles Bourne
South "	Solomon C. Howland
West "	Isaac Keith
Monument,	Abram F. Swift
Pocasset,	Asa Raymond
Spring Hill,	Paul Wing
Saugus,	Miss Charlotte M. Hawkes
Saugus Centre,	Julian D. Lawrence
Cliftondale,	George H. Sweetser
Saundersville, see Grafton	
Savoy,	Calvin Bowker
Saxonville, see Framingham	
Scituate,	Ezekiel Jones, jr.
North Scituate,	Benjamin Brown, jr.
Scotland, see Bridgewater	
Seekonk:	
South Seekonk,	Nathan Monroe
Sharon,	Charles F. Bryant
East Sharon,	Warren Cobb
Shattuckville, see Coleraine	
Sheffield,	Mrs. Abigail R. Ensign
East Sheffield,	Robt. L. Taft
Ashley Falls,	Albert Le Roy
Shelburne,	John A. Franklin
East Shelburne,	Henry M. Fisk
Shelburne Falls,	Alfred Bowen
Sheldonville, see Wrentham	
Sherborn,	Henry W. Bullard
Shirley,	Jonas Longley
Shirley Village,	William W. Edgerton
Shrewsbury,	Samuel J. Howe
Shutesbury,	Abel P. Brown
Smithville, see Barre	
Somerset,	Nathan S. Davis
Somerville,	William H. Weston
East Somerville,	Francis G. Hartshorn
North Somerville,	Thomas G. Temple
Southampton,	Ard G. Judd
Southborough,	Miss Sally W. Esty
Cordaville,	Curtis Wood
Fayville,	Miss A. E. Newton
Southbridge,	Mrs. Sophronia F. Bacon
Globe Village,	William J. Keith
South Danvers, changed to Peabody	
Southfield, see New Marlborough	
South Hadley,	Gilbert M. Smith
South Hadley Falls,	Hiram Smith, jr.
South Reading, changed to Wakefield	
South Scituate,	Eben T. Fogg, jr.
West Scituate,	Benjamin N. Curtis
Southwick,	Orrin A. Granger
Southwick,	Horace A. Grout
North Spencer,	Sheldon C. Tyrrell
Springfield,	William Snowe
Indian Orchard,	Calvin J. Eaton
Spring Hill, see Sandwich	
State Line, see West Stockbridge	
Sterling,	Perley Bartlett
West Sterling,	Julius Fitts
Pratt's Junction,	Isaac H. Currier
Still River, see Harvard	
Stockbridge,	Nathaniel A. Waters
Curtisville,	Henry M. Burrall
Glendale,	Cha. les Goodrich
Stoneham,	Edward T. Whittier
Stoughton,	Charles S. Richardson
East Stoughton,	Abraham Holmes
North "	Henry M. Gill
Stow,	John S. Fletcher
Rock Bottom,	Augustus Rice
Sturbridge,	Henry Haynes
Fiskdale,	Emory L. Bates
Sudbury,	B. Allen Burbeck

Assabet,	Abel G. Haynes	Oakdale,	Joseph E. Waite
North Sudbury,	James P. Stone	West Bridgewater,	Jarvis D. Burrell
South "	Emory Hunt	Cochesett,	Charles Perkins
Sunderland,	Horace Lyman	West Brookfield,	Ezra H. Blair
Sutton,	Wilder S. Holbrook	Westfield,	Edwin B. Smith
West Sutton,	Samuel N. Waters	Westford,	John B. Fletcher
Manchaug,	William Abbott	Forge Village,	Luther Prescott
Wilkinsonville,	David T. Dudley	Graniteville.	Isaac P. Woods
Swampscott,	Jacob P. Porter	West Gloucester, see Gloucester	
Swansea,	Henry O. Wood	West Hampton,	Thomas C. Davenport
North Swansea,	Mason Barney, jr.	Westminster,	Samuel G. Kendall
Taunton,	Abijah M. Ide	Wachusett Village,	Benjamin Wyman
East Taunton,	Chauncy G. Washburn	West Newbury,	Michael W. Bartlett
Mirickville,	William Simins	Weston,	George W. Cutting
Templeton,	Julius A. Jones	Westport,	Nathaniel W. Winchester
Baldwinsville,	Edwin Sawyer	South Westport,	Frederick Brownell
East Templeton,	Fitch L. Sargeant	Central Village,	Stephen A. Brownell
Otter River,	Francis Leland	Westport Point,	Alexander H. Cory
Tewksbury,	Henry E. Preston	West Roxbury,	William S. Keith
Thorndike, see Palmer		Jamaica Plain,	Mrs. Maria A Robinson
Three Rivers, see Palmer		West Scituate, see South Scituate	
Tisbury:		West Springfield,	Henry A. Phelon
West Tisbury,	Joseph B. Nickerson	Ashleyville,	Edward Kneeland
Holmes's Hole,	James D. Peakes	Mittineague,	Luke Biliss
Tolland,	Miss Jane E. Harrison	West Stockbridge,	William C. Spaulding
Topsfield,	Benjamin P. Adams	West Stockbridge Centre,	Jas. B. Munn
Townsend,	Charles Osgood	State Line,	George Arnold
Townsend Harbor,	Charles Emery	Weymouth,	George W. White jr.
West Townsend,	Augustus G. Stickney	East Weymouth,	Henry Loud
Truro,	Samuel C. Paine	South "	Eleazer S. Wright
North Truro,	John Grozer	North "	John W. Bartlett
Tyngsborough,	J. H. D. Littlehale	Whately,	Samuel Lesure
Tyringham,	Orson Webster	East Whately,	Caleb L. Thayer
Upton,	Horace Forbush	Whitinsville, see Northbridge	
West Upton,	Eli W. Batchelor	Wilbraham,	Mrs. Hannah E. Hempstead
Uxbridge,	Charles A. Taft	South Wilbraham,	Sol. C. Spellman
North Uxbridge,	Arnold S. Sweet	Collins's Depot,	Warren Collins
Van Deusenville, see Great Barrington		Wilkinsonville, see Sutton	
Wachusett Village, see Westminster		Williamsburg,	Henry L. James
Wakefield,	Samuel Kingman	Haydenville,	Joel Hayden, jr.
Greenwood,	Charles M. Oliver	Willimansett, see Chicopee	
Wales,	Absalom Gardner	Williamstown,	Calvin R. Taft
Walpole,	George H. Gill	South Williamstown,	Wm. E. Johnson
East Walpole,	George W. Johnson	Wilmington,	Joseph A. Ames
South "	Naaman B. Wilmouth	North Wilmington,	Silas Buck
Waltham,	Newell Sherman	Winchendon,	Edwin S. Merrill
Waquoit, see Falmouth		Winchester,	George P. Brown
Ware,	John W. Cummings	Windsor,	L, Emerson Bicknell
Wareham,	Miss Ann C. Churchill	East Windsor,	Reuben Pierce
East Wareham,	Washington Bassett	Winthrop,	Warren Belcher
West "	Moses S. F. Tobey	Woburn,	Nathan Wyman
Warwick,	Abner Albee	North Woburn,	Edward E. Thompson
Warren,	Joseph F Hitchcock	East "	Albert L. Richardson
West Warren,	Lewis Elwell	Wood's Hole, see Falmouth	
Washington,	Frederick W. Manley	Woodville, see Hopkinton	
Watertown,	Arch'd McMaster	Worcester,	Josiah Picket
Mt. Auburn,	Robert B. Safford	Worthington,	Horace Cole
Waverly, see Belmont		West Worthington,	Russell Bartlett
Wayland,	John M. Seward, jr.	Ringville,	Wm. D. Sanderson
Cochituate,	Daniel C. Atwood	South Worthington,	Elisha R. Converse
Webster,	Augustus E. Day	Wrentham,	Alfred Barnard
Wellesley, see Needham		North Wrentham,	Henry Trowbridge
Wellfleet,	George T. Wyer	West "	Philander P. Cook
South Wellfleet,	Stephen A. Hatch	Plainville,	John P. Cheever
Wendell,	Joseph Forbes	Sheldonville,	Homer A. Follett
Wendell Depot,	Danforth Putnam	Yarmouth,	Isaac Ryder
Lock's Village,	William K. Haskell	Yarmouth Port,	Benjamin H. Matthews
Wenham,	William W. Fowler	West Yarmouth,	Freeman H. Crowell
Westborough,	Josiah Childs	South "	Peleg P. Akin
West Boylston,	Albert Hinds		

U. S. ENGINEERS.

U. S. Engineers' office for Fort and Sea Walls, 75 State street.

Maj.-Gen. H. W. Benham, senior Engineer in charge of Forts Warren, Independence, and Winthrop, and the Sea Walls of Boston Harbor; Brevt.-Major Geo. Burroughs, and Lieut. W. S. Stanton, assistants.

U. S. Engineers' office for improvements in Boston and Provincetown Harbors, City Hall. Major-Gen. John G. Foster, Engineer in charge, Col. G. L. Gillespie, Asst.

LIST OF MONEY-ORDER OFFICES

IN NEW ENGLAND. Corrected October 5, 1868.

RATES OF COMMISSION CHARGED FOR MONEY ORDERS:

On Orders not exceeding $20 .... 10 cents
Over $20 and not exceeding $30 .... 15 cents
Over $30 and not exceeding $40 .... 20 cents
Over $40 and not exceeding $50 .... 25 cents

No single order issued for more than $50.

Maine.

Alfred.
Augusta.
Bangor.
Bath.
Belfast.
Bethel.
Biddeford.
Brunswick.
Bucksport.
Calais.
Camden.
Dexter.
Eastport.
Ellsworth.
Farmington.
Fort Fairfield.
Foxcroft.
Gardiner.
Houlton.
Lewiston.
Machias.
Mechanics' Falls.
Norway.
Pembroke.
Phillips.
Portland.
Presque Isle.
Richmond.
Rockland.
Searsport.
Skowhegan.
South Berwick.
Waterville.
Winterport.
Wiscasset.
Yarmouth.

New Hampshire.

Bristol.
Charlestown.
Claremont.
Concord.
Dover.
Exeter.
Fisherville.
Franklin.
Gorham.
Great Falls.
Hanover.
Hinsdale.
Keene.
Laconia.
Lancaster.
Lebanon.
Littleton.
Manchester.
Milford.
Nashua.
New Ipswich.
Newport.
Peterborough.
Plymouth.
Portsmouth.
Suncook.

Vermont.

Bellows Falls.
Bennington.
Bradford.
Brandon.
Brattleborough.
Burlington.
Castleton.
Derby Line.
East Alburgh.
Fair Haven.
Island Pond.
Ludlow.
Manchester.
Middlebury.
Montpelier.
Newbury.
Northfield.
Rutland.
St. Albans.
St. Johnsbury.
Sheldon.
Springfield.
Vergennes.
Waterbury.
West Randolph.
Windsor.
Woodstock.

Massachusetts.

Amherst.
Andover.
Boston.
Bridgewater.
Cambridge.
Cambridgeport.
Charlestown.
Chelsea.
Chicopee.
Clinton.
Dedham.
East Hampton.
Edgartown.
Fall River.
Fitchburg.
Foxborough.
Gloucester.
Great Barrington.
Greenfield.
Groton Junction.
Haverhill.
Holliston.
Holyoke.
Lawrence.
Lee.
Lowell.
Lynn.
Marblehead.
Marlborough.
Milford.
Nantucket.
Natick.
New Bedford.
Newburyport.
Newton.
North Adams.
Northampton.
Orleans.
Palmer.
Pittsfield.
Plymouth.
Provincetown.
Roxbury.
Salem.
Sandwich.
Springfield.
Taunton.
Waltham.
Ware.
Webster.
Wellfleet.
Westfield.
Williamstown.
Worcester.
Yarmouth Port.

Rhode Island.

Bristol.
East Greenwich.
Newport.
Pawtucket.
Providence.
Wakefield.
Warren.
Westerly.
Wickford.
Woonsocket Falls.

Connecticut.

Bridgeport.
Bristol.
Cheshire.
Collinsville.
Colchester.
Danbury.
Derby.
Essex.
Falls Village.
Guilford.
Hartford.
Litchfield.
Middletown.
Milford.
Mystic Bridge.
Naugatuck.
New Britain.
New London.
New Milford.
New Haven.
Norwalk.
Norwich.
Putnam.
Rockville.
Stafford Springs.
Stamford.
Thompsonville.
Waterbury.
West Killingly.
West Meriden.
West Winsted.
Willimantic.
Wolcottville.

TOWN AND CITY CLERKS, 1868.

Barnstable County.

Barnstable, F. G. Kelly, Centreville
Brewster, Chas. S. Foster
Chatham, Josiah Mayo
Dennis, Jonathan Bangs, South Dennis
Eastham, Joshua Paine
Falmouth, Thos. Lewis, Jr.
Harwich, B. G. Phillips
Orleans, Freeman Mayo
Provincetown, Paron C. Young
Sandwich, David C. Percival
Truro, Samuel C. Paine
Wellfleet, James T. Atwood
Yarmouth, Wm. P. Davis

Berkshire County.

Adams, A. B. Wright
Alford, William B. Fenn
Becket, Mark P. Carter
Cheshire, Edwin F. Nickerson
Clarksburg, Eli T. Clark, North Adams
Dalton, Henry Ferre
Egremont, Joseph A. Benjamin, South Egremont
Florida, A. D. Tower
Great Barrington, Isaac Seeley
Hancock, Chas. B. Wells
Hinsdale, John Cady
Lanesborough, Chas. B. Whitney
Lee, J. F. Cook
Lenox, David E. Bangs
Monterey, A. Garfield
Mount Washington, Orrin C. Whitbeck, South Egremont
New Ashford, E. Ingraham
New Marlborough, Seth Pease, Mill River
Otis, Isaac J. Norton
Peru, H. A. Messenger
Pittsfield, James M. Barker
Richmond, H. B. Stevens
Sandisfield, Eliud Taylor
Savoy, Eusibius McCullock
Sheffield, John D. Burtch
Stockbridge, E. Seymour
Tyringham, Geo. W. Garfield
Washington, Simpson Bell
W. Stockbridge, Wm. C. Spaulding
Williamstown, B. F. Mather, Jr.
Windsor, L. E. Bicknell

Bristol County.

Acushnet, Benjamin White
Attleborough, N. C. Luther
Berkley, T. P. Burt
Dartmouth, John W. Howland.
Dighton, Wm. Wood
Easton, John Kimball
Fairhaven, Tucker Damon, Jr.
Fall River, George A. Ballard
Freetown, D. C. H. Hatheway
Mansfield, E. M. Reed
New Bedford, Henry T. Leonard
Norton, Austin Messenger
Raynham, A. A. Leach
Rehoboth, Cyrus M. Wheaton
Seekonk, Willard C. Ormsbee
Somerset, J. B. Slade
Swansea, J. G. Luther
Taunton, James M. Cushman
Westport, Albert C. Kirby, Central Village.

Dukes County.

Chilmark, James M. Tilton
Edgartown, B. C. Marchant
Gosnold, Samuel E. Skiff
Tisbury, Lot Luce

Essex County.

Amesbury, Jos. Merrill
Andover, E. K. Jenkins
Beverly, James Hill
Boxford, Roscoe W. Gage
Bradford, Nathaniel Hatch
Danvers, A. S. Howard
Essex, John C. Choate
Georgetown, Chas. E. Jewett
Gloucester, David W. Low
Groveland, Chas. H. Hopkinson
Hamilton, I. F. Knowlton
Haverhill, William B. Eaton
Ipswich, Wesley K. Bell
Lawrence, Geo. R. Rowe
Lynn, Benj. H. Jones
Lynnfield, J. Danforth, Lynnfield Centre
Manchester, John Lee
Marblehead, Glover Broughton
Methuen, Charles Shed
Middleton, J. A. Batchelder
Nahant, Alfred D. Johnson
Newbury, Wm. Little
Newburyport, Eleazer Johnson
North Andover, A. D. Carlton

Peabody, Nathan H. Poor
Rockport, William Pool
Rowley, John S. Prime
Salem, Stephen P. Webb
Salisbury, Samuel J. Brown
Saugus, Wm. H. Newhall
Swampscott, Wm. D. Brackett, Jr.
Topsfield, J. P. Towne
Wenham, Joseph Cook
West Newbury, John C. Carr

Franklin County.

Ashfield, Henry S. Rancey
Bernardston, Silas N. Brooks
Buckland, Samuel Tobey, Shelburne
    Falls
Charlemont, H. H. Mayhew
Coleraine, A. C. Smith
Conway, H. W. Billings
Deerfield, Charles Williams
Erving, Noah Rankin
Gill, Josiah D. Canning
Greenfield, Noah S. Wells
Hawley, T. H. Sears, West Hawley
Heath, Ephraim Scott
Leverett, E. M. Ingram
Leyden, David Mowry
Monroe, Joseph H. Hicks
Montague. J. H. Root
New Salem, Royal Whitaker
Northfield, Samuel W. Dutton
Orange, R. D. Chase
Rowe, James M. Ford
Shelburne, A. K. Hawkes
Shutesbury, Joseph A. Haskins
Sunderland, J. M. Smith
Warwick, A. S. Atherton
Wendell, Marcus M. Stebbins
Whately, Samuel Lesure

Hampden County.

Agawam, S. H. Bodurtha
Blandford, Elisha W. Shepard
Brimfield, Henry F. Brown
Chester, Timothy Keeffe
Chicopee, Lester Dickinson
Granville, J. M. Gibbons, Granville
    Corners
Holland, F. E. Kinney
Holyoke, E. H. Flagg
Longmeadow, Oliver Wolcott, East
    Longmeadow
Ludlow, Benjamin F. Burr
Monson, George H. Newton
Montgomery, L. T. Allyn
Palmer, James B. Shaw
Russell, Horace Parks

Southwick, Goodman B. Palmer
Springfield, Albert T. Folsom
Tolland, Wm. W. Harrison
Wales, G. S. Rogers
Westfield, George H. Douglas
W. Springfield, J. M. Harmon
Wilbraham, Frank Clark

Hampshire County.

Amherst, Samuel C. Carter
Belchertown, E. R. Bridgman
Chesterfield, Albert Nichols
Cummington, Almon Mitchell
East Hampton, Charles B. Johnson
Enfield, Augustus Moody
Goshen, Elijah Billings
Granby, Philo Chapin
Greenwich, David Allen, Greenwich
    Village
Hadley, Wm. S. Shipman
Hatfield, Wm. D. Billings
Huntington, Wm. S. Tinker
Middlefield, J. McElwain
Northampton, W. F. Arnold
Pelham, Calvin D. Eaton
Plainfield, Freeman Hamlen
Prescott, H. B. Hodgkin
South Hadley, Joseph Bardwell
Southampton, Lyman C. Tiffany
Ware, Lewis P. Edwards
Westhampton, P. N. Loud
Williamsburg, Thomas M. Carter
Worthington, Edward C. Porter

Middlesex County.

Acton, William D. Tuttle
Arlington, John F. Allen
Ashby, A. A. Carr
Ashland, William A. Tilton
Bedford, Wm. A. Stearns
Belmont, Francis E Yates
Billerica, Dudley Foster
Boxborough, Oliver Wetherbee
Brighton, Webster F. Warren
Burlington, Samuel Sewall
Cambridge, Justin A. Jacobs
Carlisle, George F. Duren
Charlestown, Daniel Williams
Chelmsford, E. F. Webster
Concord, George Heywood
Dracut, Henry Richardson
Dunstable, James C. Woodward
Framingham, Charles S. Whitmore
Groton, George D. Brigham
Holliston, John M. Batchelder
Hopkinton, J. H. Palmer
Hudson, Edwin Amsden

Lexington, L. A. Saville
Lincoln, Henry C. Chapin
Littleton, Wm. Kimball
Lowell, John H. McAlvin
Malden, Albert F. Sargent
Marlborough, Edward L. Bigelow
Medford, Parker R. Litchfield
Melrose, Stinson Sewell
Natick, George L. Sleeper
Newton, Marshall S. Rice
North Reading, Charles P. Howard
Pepperell, David W. Jewett
Reading, Wm. J. Wightman
Sherborn, Jos. Dowse, Jr.
Shirley, Hermon S. Hazen
Somerville, C. E. Gilman
Stoneham, Silas Dean
Stow, Henry Gates
Sudbury, Jonas S. Hunt
Tewksbury, Samuel L. Allen
Townsend, Daniel Adams
Tyngsborough, W. A. Cummings
Wakefield, Benjamin F. Packard
Waltham, Daniel French
Watertown, Joseph Crafts
Wayland, Henry Wight
Westford, Rev. Leonard Luce
Weston, George W. Cutting, Jr.
Wilmington, W. H. Carter, North
  Wilmington
Winchester, George P. Brown
Woburn, Nathan Wyman

Nantucket County.

Nantucket, William Cobb.

Norfolk County.

Bellingham, R. F. Thayer
Braintree, E. Watson Arnold
Brookline, Benjamin F. Baker
Canton, Charles Endicott
Cohasset, Edward Tower
Dedham, Jonathan H. Cobb
Dorchester, Thomas F. Temple
Dover, Abner L. Smith
Foxborough, William H. Thomas
Franklin, Alpheus A. Russegue
Hyde Park, C. W. Turner
Medfield, H. J. Everett
Medway, George P. Metcalf
Milton, Jason Reed
Needham, Solomon Flagg, Wellesley
Quincy, George L. Gill
Randolph, Hiram C. Alden
Sharon, Otis Johnson
Stoughton, Luther S. Leach
Walpole, George P. Morey

West Roxbury, William Maccarty
Weymouth, Francis Ambler
Wrentham, Samuel Warner

Plymouth County.

Abington, Nathaniel T. Hunt
Bridgewater, Lewis Holmes
Carver, William Hammond
Duxbury, Josiah Peterson
East Bridgewater, Jacob A. Rogers
Halifax, Edwin Inglee
Hanover, Albert Stetson
Hanson, Josephus Bryant
Hingham, Charles N. Marsh
Hull, Orlando D. Cook
Kingston, Nathan Brooks
Lakeville, C. T. Westgate, Middle-
  borough
Marion, Jordan B. Barden
Marshfield, Daniel Stevens
Mattapoisett, Thomas Nelson
Middleborough, Cornelius B. Wood
North Bridgewater, W. H. Wales
Pembroke, Francis Collamore, North
  Pembroke
Plymouth, Leander Lovell
Plympton, William Perkins
Rochester, John S. Ryder
Scituate, J. L. Merritt, North Scituate
South Scituate, Ebenezer T. Fogg
Wareham, Alvan Gibbs
West Bridgewater, Austin Packard

Suffolk County.

Boston, Samuel F. McCleary
Chelsea, Samuel Bassett
North Chelsea, William T. Hall
Winthrop, Edward Floyd

Worcester County.

Ashburnham, Jerome W. Foster
Athol, Thomas H. Goodspeed
Auburn, Emory Stone
Barre, H. F. Brooks
Berlin, Josiah E. Sawyer
Blackstone, James K. Comstock
Bolton, Richard S. Edes
Boylston, H. H. Brigham, Boylston
  Centre
Brookfield, H. V. Crosby
Charlton, George H. Taft
Clinton, H. C. Greeley
Dana, D. L. Richards, North Dana
Douglas, Aaron M. Hill, East Doug-
  las
Dudley, Moses Barnes, Jr.
Fitchburg, Henry Jackson
Gardner, Francis Richardson

6

Grafton, James W. White
Hardwick, Albert E. Knight
Harvard, Hiram Whitney
Holden, S. K. Armington
Hubbardston, Lyman Woodward
Lancaster, J. L. S. Thompson
Leicester, Joseph A. Denny
Leominster, Joel C. Allen
Lunenburg, James Putnam
Mendon, David Adams
Milford, Lewis Fales
Millbury, Ira N. Goddard
New Braintree, George K. Tufts
Northborough. J. L. Stone
Northbridge, Hiram Wing
North Brookfield, Hiram Knights
Oakham, James Allen
Oxford, John B. Pratt
Paxton, John C. Bigelow
Petersham, Lewis Whitney
Phillipston, Lyman White

Princeton, D. H. Gregory
Royalston, George F. Miller
Rutland, George A. Putnam
Shrewsbury, Charles O. Green, Jr.
Southborough, Franklin Este
Southbridge, S. S. Perry
Spencer, John N. Grout
Sterling, William D. Peck
Sturbridge, Emory L. Bates, Fiskdale
Sutton, Wilder S. Holbrook
Templeton, Gerard Bushnell
Upton, W. B. Fay
Uxbridge. Henry Capron
Warren, Samuel E. Blair
Webster, S. A. Tingier
Westborough, Samuel M. Griggs
West Boylston, Edward Howe
West Brookfield, E. H. Blair
Westminster, William Mayo
Winchendon, Webster Whitney
Worcester, Samuel Smith

U. S. ASSESSORS AND COLLECTORS OF INTERNAL REVENUE IN THE STATE OF MASSACHUSETTS.

ASSESSORS.

District.
1st. Charles G. Davis, *Plymouth.*
2nd. Nathaniel Waly, *Stoughton.*
3rd. W. R. Lee, *Boston.*
4th. Otis Clapp. *Boston.*
5th. Eben. F. Stone, *Newburyport.*
6th. P. J. Stone, *Charlestown.*
7th. C. C. Esty, *Framingham.*
8th. Ivers Phillips, *Worcester.*
9th. Amasa Norcross, *Fitchburg.*
10th. C. N. Emerson, *Pittsfield.*

COLLECTORS.

District.
1st. James Buffinton, *Fall River.*
2nd. Benj. W. Harris, *Boston.*
3rd. Wm. H. McCartney, *Boston.*
4th. John Sargent, *Boston.*
5th. C. C. Dame, *Newburyport.*
6th. Nathaniel S. Howe, *Haverhill.*
7th. John Nesmith, *Lowell.*
8th. A. B. R. Sprague, *Worcester.*
9th. Daniel W. Alvord, *Greenfield.*
10th. E. R. Tinker, *North Adams.*

Supervisor, State of Massachusetts, John N. Barbour, *Boston.*

REGISTERS IN BANKRUPTCY,

IN MASSACHUSETTS.

District 1. — James M. Bunker, *New Bedford.*
"   2. — Samuel B. Noyes, *Canton.*
"   3. — William Rogers, *Boston.*
"   4. — Samuel L. Thorndike, *Boston.*
"   5. — Benjamin C. Perkins, *Salem.*
"   6. — Edgar J. Sherman, *Lawrence.*
"   7. — Andrew F. Jewett, *Lowell.*
"   8. — Peter C. Bacon, *Worcester.*
"   9. — Ithamar F. Conkey, *Amherst.*
"   10. — Joseph Tucker, *Lenox.*

MASSACHUSETTS VOLUNTEER MILITIA.

The number of Enrolled Militia in the Commonwealth for the year 1868 is one hundred and sixty-nine thousand one hundred and sixty-seven (169,167), an increase of six thousand six hundred and eighty-two (6,682) over the year 1867.

Agreeably to the provisions of Chap. 219, Acts of 1866, the number of companies of the Volunteer Militia were apportioned as follows: of Infantry, one hundred companies; of Cavalry, eight companies, and of Light Artillery, five companies. These were exclusive of the two companies of Cadets. There are at the present time ninety-four companies of Infantry, six companies of Cavalry, and four Batteries of Light Artillery. These are divided among counties as follows: Suffolk County, forty-one companies of Infantry, three companies of Cavalry, and two companies of Light Artillery. Middlesex County, eighteen companies of Infantry, two companies of Cavalry, and one company of Artillery. Essex County, fourteen companies of Infantry, and one company of Artillery. Bristol County, six companies of Infantry, and one company of Cavalry. Worcester County, seven companies of Infantry. Norfolk County, two companies of Infantry. Hampshire County, three companies of Infantry. Plymouth County, two companies of Infantry. Hampden County, one company of Infantry.

Commander in Chief and Staff.

Commander-in-Chief, His Excellency William Claflin, of Newton.
Adjutant-General (with rank of Major-Gen'l), James A. Cunningham, Boston.
Quartermaster-General (with rank of Brig.-Gen'l), John H. Reed, of Boston.
Surgeon-General (with rank of Brig.-Gen'l), Wm. J. Dale, of North Andover.
Aide-de-Camp (with rank of Col.), Adin B. Underwood, of Newton.
Aide-de-Camp (with rank of Col.), James L. Bates, of Weymouth.
Aide-de-Camp (with rank of Col.), Edward N. Hallowell, of Boston.
Aide-de-Camp (with rank of Col.), J. Cushing Edmands, of Newton.
Assist. Adjutant-General (with rank of Col.), Nehemiah Brown, of Boston.
Assist. Surgeon-General (with rank of Col.), Anson P. Hooker, of Cambridge.
Deputy Quartermaster-General (rank of Col.), S. E. Chamberlain, Cambridge.
Assist. Adjutant-General (with rank of Lt.-Col.), Henry Ware, of Cambridge.
Surgeon-General's Department (rank Major), William C. Capelle, of Boston.
Assist. Inspector-General (rank of Capt.), William E. Wilson, of Boston.

Division Commander and Staff.

Major-General, Benjamin F. Butler, of Lowell.
Assist. Adjutant-General (rank Col.), Elgar J. Sherman, of Lawrence.
Medical Director (rank Col.), Yorick G. Hurd, of Ipswich.
Assist. Inspector-General (rank Lt.-Col.) Wm. H. Lawrence, of Boston.
Assist. Quartermaster (with rank of Lt.-Col.), George J. Carney, of Lowell.
Aide-de-Camp (with rank of Major), Roland G. Usher, of Lynn.
Aide-de-Camp (rank of Major), Edward J. Jones, of Boston.
Judge Advocate (with rank of Major), Edwin L. Barney, of New Bedford.

First Brigade.

Brigadier-General, Isaac S. Burrill, of Boston.
Assist. Adjutant-General (rank of Lt.-Col.), Charles W. Wilder, of Boston.
Medical Director (rank of Lt.-Col.) Joseph Stedman, of West Roxbury.
Assist. Quartermaster (with rank of Captain), Samuel Talbot, Jr., of Boston.
Assist. Inspector-General (rank of Major), Charles A. Davis, of Boston.
Engineer (with rank of Captain), John Quincy Adams, of Chelsea.
Aide-de-Camp (rank Captain), Moses E. Bigelow, of Boston.
Judge Advocate (rank Captain), Solomon A. Bolster, of Boston.

First Regiment of Infantry.
Colonel, Geo. H. Johnston, of Boston.
Lieut.-Colonel, Alfred A. Proctor, of Boston.
Major, John McDonough, of Boston.
Adjutant, Henry W. Wilson, of Boston.

Quartermaster, Alfred E. Proctor, Boston.
Surgeon (rank of Major), Geo. J. Arnold, Boston.
Assist. Surgeon, Robert White, Jr., Boston.
Chaplain, Warren H. Cudworth, of Boston.

COMPANIES.

A. — Boston, *Capt.* Nathaniel H. Kemp.
1st *Lieut.*, Geo. A. J. Colgan.
2d *Lieut.*, Jas. F. McKenzie.

B. — Boston, *Capt.*, George H. Smith.
1st *Lieut.*, George R. Battis.
2d *Lieut.*, Shadrach K. Morris.

C. — Boston, *Capt.*, Henry Parkinson.
1st *Lieut.*, William H. Alexander.
2d *Lieut.*, James L. Martin.

D. — Boston, *Capt.*, Charles E. Burgess.
1st *Lieut.*, William G. Fish.
2d *Lieut.*, Henry A. Thomas.

E. — Boston, *Capt.*, Paul M. Foss.
1st *Lieut.*, George W. Carter.
2d *Lieut.*, George W. Westcott.

F. — Boston, *Capt.*, William Evans.
1st *Lieut.*, Matthew Walsh.
2d *Lieut.*, John Coullahan.

G. — Boston, *Capt.*, —— ——.
1st *Lieut.*, John W. W. Marjoram.
2d *Lieut.*, Charles H. Lambert.

H. — Chelsea, *Capt.*, John H. Perry.
1st *Lieut.*, Edwin H. Butts.
2d *Lieut.*, Henry Wilson, Jr.

I. — Dorchester, *Capt.*, Joseph T. Paget.
1st *Lieut.*, John E. E. Goward.
2d *Lieut.*, Edmund B. Smith.

K. — Boston, *Capt.*, James S. Kingman.
1st *Lieut.*, H. Floyd Faulkner.
2d *Lieut.*, Amos Cummings.

Third Regiment of Infantry.

Colonel, Thomas J. Borden, Fall River.
Lieut.-Colonel, G. Hurbert Bates, Scituate.
Major, Bradford D. Davol, Fall River.
Adjutant, Nathan Taylor, Fall River.
Quartermaster, Earl P. Bowen, Fall River.
Surgeon, Joseph W. Hayward, Taunton.
Assist. Surgeon. Robert E. Jameson, Abington.
Chaplain, Lewis B. Bates, New Bedford.

COMPANIES.

A. — Halifax, *Capt.*, —— ——.
1st *Lieut.*, Norton V. Bonney.
2d *Lieut.*, Lysander M. Thompson.

B. — Fall River, *Capt.*, Edward I. Marvel.
1st *Lieut.*, Joseph Bowers Jr.
2d *Lieut.*, Ferdinand S. Read.

C. — Scituate, *Capt.* John E. O. Prouty.
1st *Lieut.*, Henry H. Chubbuck.
2d *Lieut.*, James L. Prouty, 2d.

D. — Fall River, *Capt.*, Sierra L. Braley.
1st *Lieut.*, Frank McGraw.
2d *Lieut.*, Josiah A. Hunt.

E. — New Bedford, *Capt.*, Wm. E. Mason.
1st *Lieut.*, Thomas J. Gifford.
2d *Lieut.*, Sylvester C. Spooner.

F. — Taunton, *Capt.*, William Watts.
1st *Lieut.*, —— ——.
2d *Lieut.*, David B. Lincoln.

G. — Taunton, *Capt.*, Frederick Mason.
1st *Lieut.*, Francis L. Morse.
2d *Lieut.*, Frank Bosworth.

H. — Quincy, *Capt.*, William Boyd.
1st *Lieut.*, Henry Talbot.
2d *Lieut.*, Michael M. Leahy.

I. — Stoughton, *Capt.*, Jas. F. McGonigle.
1st *Lieut.*, Michael Conly.
2d *Lieut.*, Daniel Sullivan.

K. — Abington, *Capt.*, Joshua F. Winslow.
1st *Lieut.*, Morton E. Harding.
2d *Lieut.*, Timothy S. Atwood.

L. — Carver, *Capt.*, Thomas B. Griffith.
1st *Lieut.*, Linus A. Shaw.
2d *Lieut.*, Henry White.

M. — Plymouth, *Capt.*, Josiah R. Drew.
1st *Lieut.*, Edwin F. Phinney.
2d *Lieut.*, Sylvester R. Swett.

Seventh Regiment of Infantry.

Col., Chas. F. Harrington, Dorchester.
Lieut.-Col., Chas. H. Porter, Quincy.
Major, Charles E. Spanlding.
Adjutant, David C. Sisson, Boston.
Quartermaster, Jas. C. Laughton, Boston.
Surgeon, William H. Page, of Boston.
Ass't Surgeon, Charles W. Heaton, Boston.
Chaplain, —— ——.

COMPANIES.

A. — Boston, *Capt.*, Eben W. Fiske.
1st *Lieut.*, Watson Gore, Jr.
2d *Lieut.*, —— ——.

B. — Boston, *Capt.*, Walter S. Sampson.
1st *Lieut.*, Luther W. Bixby.
2d *Lieut.*, —— ——.

C. — Boston, *Capt.*, John W. Martin.
1st *Lieut.*, Daniel F. French,
2d *Lieut.*, Samuel B. Turner

D. — Boston, *Capt.*, —— ——.
1st *Lieut.*, —— ——.
2d *Lieut.*, Frank B. Bowers.

E. — Boston, *Capt.*, Henry J. Hallgreen.
1st *Lieut.*, Henry C. Dimond.
2d *Lieut.*, Frank E. Tufts.

F — Boston, *Capt.*, Samuel H. Robinson.
1st *Lieut.*, Geo. M. Lovering.
2d *Lieut.*, Francis W. Holmes.

G. — Disbanded.

H. — Disbanded.

I. — Boston, *Capt.*, Gurdon S. Brown.
1st *Lieut.*, Martin A. Munroe.
2d *Lieut.*, Albert P. Sanborn.

K. — Boston, *Capt.*, M. James Dunn.
1st *Lieut.*, Jefferson Hayes.
2d *Lieut.*, —— ——

Ninth Regiment of Infantry.

Col., Patrick A. O'Connell, Boston.
Lieut.-Col., James McArdle, Boston.
Major, Patrick E. Murphy, Boston.
Adjutant, Daniel G. McNamara, Boston.
Quartermaster, James J. Flynn.
Surgeon, John G. Blake, Boston.
Ass't Surgeon, James E. McDonough, Boston.
Chaplain, Henry M. Smyth, Boston.

COMPANIES.

A. — Boston, *Capt.*, Timothy Teaffe.
1st *Lieut.*, John McGrath.
2d *Lieut.*, Thomas J. McLaughlin.

B. — Boston, *Capt.*, John M. Tobin.
1st *Lieut.*, —— ——.
2d *Lieut.*, Timothy W. Murray.

C. — Chelsea, *Capt.*, —— ——.
1st *Lieut.*, Michael O'Donnell.
2d *Lieut.*, James A. Dinning.

D. — Boston, *Capt.*, Michael Scanlan.
  1st Lieut., Lawrence Logan.
  2d Lieut., Hugh McGunigle.

E. — Boston, *Capt.*, —— ——.
  1st Lieut., —— ——.
  2d Lieut., Charles R. Warren.

F. — Boston, *Capt.*, Henry P. Kelley.
  1st Lieut., Dennis J. Callahan.
  2d Lieut., John B. Reardon.

G. — Charlestown. *Capt.*, Matthew Walsh.
  1st Lieut., William G. McElroy.
  2d Lieut., —— ——.

H. — Boston, *Capt.*, Michael McDonough.
  1st Lieut., Peter F. Rourke.
  2d Lieut., John J. Weston.

I. — Boston, *Capt.*, Bernard F. Finan.
  1st Lieut., Hugh A. Madden.
  2d Lieut., —— ——.

K. — Boston, *Capt.*, Robert A. Miller.
  1st Lieut., —— ——.
  2d Lieut., Edward F. Myers.

Second Battalion of Infant

Major, Lewis Gaul, of Boston.
Adjutant, Burrill Smith. Jr., of Boston.
Quartermaster, Jacob E. Chase, Salem.

COMPANIES.

A. — Boston, *Capt.*, James B. Watkins.
  1st Lieut., Peter E. Hawkins.
  2d Lieut., James J. Gardner.

B. — New Bedford, *Capt.*, Wesley Furlong.
  1st Lieut., John T. Tolliver.
  2d Lieut., —— ——.

First Battalion of Cavalry.

Major, Lucius Slade, of Boston.
Adjutant, Charles B. Barrett, of Boston.
Quartermaster, Jas. H. Pushee, of Boston.
Asst. Surgeon, Benj. H. Mann, of Boston.

COMPANIES.

A. — Boston, *Capt.*, Barney Hull.
  1st Lieut., Geo. E. Richardson.
  2d Lieut., O. H. P. Smith.

B. — Boston, *Capt.*, Albert Freeman.
  1st Lieut., Murdock Matheson.
  2d Lieut., David Scott.

C. — Charlestown, *Capt.*, Freeman L. Gilman.
  1st Lieut., Wm. H. Roberts.
  2d Lieut., Kelsey M. Gilmore.

D. — Boston, *Capt.*, George Curtis.
  1st Lieut., Thomas Decatur.
  2d Lieut., Augustus P. Cabler.

First Battery of Light Artillery (Boston).

Capt., Butler Libby.
Adjutant, Benj. F. White, Cambridge.
1st Lieut., —— ——.
1st Lieut., —— ——.
2d Lieut., Ira C. Foster.
2d Lieut., Harry O. Simonds.
Asst. Surgeon, J. Russell Little.

Second Battery of Light Artillery (Boston).

Captain, Charles W. Baxter.
Adjutant, Nicholas T. Appolonio.
1st Lieut. Joseph M. Thomas.
1st Lieut., Charles W Beal.
2d Lieut., Horace J. Hooton.
2d Lieut., Thomas J. Tute.
Asst. Surgeon, William A. Browne.

Company E, Unattached Cavalry (New Bedford).

Captain, Geo. R. Hurlburt.
Adjutant, Charles S. Cummings.
1st Lieut., Joseph H. Burgess.
2d Lieut., Bradford Kinsley.
Ass't Surgeon, —— ——.

Second Brigade of Infantry.

Brigadier General, George H. Peirson, of Salem.
Asst. Adj.-Gen'l. (rank Lt. Col.), Robert S. Daniels, of South Danvers.
Medical Director, " " William Ingalls, of Boston.
Asst. Inspector Gen'l. (with rank of Major), Eben Sutton, North Andover.
Aide-de-Camp (with rank of Captain), John Kent, of Charlestown.
Asst. Quartermaster (with rank of Captain), Jos. A. Ingalls, Swampscott.
Engineer (with rank of Captain), Loring W. Muzzey, Lexington.
Judge Advocate (rank Captain), John W. Hudson, Lexington.

Fifth Regiment of Infantry.

Colonel, Geo. A. Meacham, Cambridge.
Lieut. Col., Walter Everett, Charlestown.
Major, Andrew A. Powers, Hudson.
Adjutant, Henry L. Swords, Charlestown.
Quartermaster, Daniel W. Lawrence, of Medford.
Surgeon, Joshua B. Treadwell, of Boston.
Asst. Surgeon, Amos H. Johnson. Salem.
Chaplain, Edward S. Atwood, Salem.

COMPANIES.

A. — Charlestown, *Capt.*, —— ——.
  1st Lieut. Thomas H. Haskell.
  2d Lieut., Frank Todd.

B. — Somerville, *Capt.*, G. W. Daniels.
  1st Lieut., William E. Dickson.
  2d Lieut., —— ——.

C. — Cambridge, *Capt.*, Robt. L. B. Fox.
  1st Lieut., Michael Dalton.
  2d Lieut., Albert C. Berry.

D. — Charlestown, *Capt.*, Alex. E. Hewes.
  1st Lieut., Richard R. Farmer.
  2d Lieut., Maurice F. Quinn.

E. — Medford, *Capt.*, Isaac F. R. Hosea.
  1st Lieut., Albert F. Dow.
  2d Lieut., Joshamus H. Whitney.

F. — Medford. *Capt.*, William H. Dane.
  1st Lieut., —— ——.
  2d Lieut., Charles O. Burbank.

G. — Woburn, *Capt.*, Cyrus Fay.
  1st Lieut., Edwin F. Wyer.
  2d Lieut., —— ——.

H. — Charlestown, *Capt.*, Edward F. Everett.
 2d Lieut., Albion P. Pease.
 1st Lieut., ——— ———.

I. — Hudson, *Capt.*, ——— ———.
 1st Lieut., Joseph W. Pedrick.
 2d Lieut., David B. Whitcomb.

K. — Peabody, *Capt.*, Benj. Beckett, Jr.
 1st Lieut., Frank C. Poor.
 2d Lieut., John A Messer.

Sixth Regiment of Infantry.

Colonel, Melvin Beal, of Lawrence.
Lieut.-Col. Benj. F. Goddard, of Lowell.
Major, James W. Hart, of Lowell.
Adjutant, George S. Merrill, of Lawrence.
Quartermaster, John W. Locke, of Lawrence.
Surgeon, Walter Burnham, of Lowell.
Ass't. Surgeon, George W. Sargent, of Lawrence.
Chaplain, George S. Weaver, of Lawrence.

COMPANIES.

A. — Wakefield, *Capt.*, James F. Emerson.
 1st Lieut., James F. Mansfield.
 2d Lieut., ——— ———.

B. — Groton, *Capt.*, Wm. T. Childs.
 1st Lieut., Charles F. Williamson.
 2d Lieut., Francis W. Cragie.

C. — Lowell, *Capt.*, Isaac B. Pendergast.
 1st Lieut., Lyman B. Manning.
 2d Lieut., Irving W. Mason.*

D. — Lowell, *Capt.*, James M. Torsey.
 1st Lieut., Alfred J. Hall.
 2d Lieut. Edwin W. Bartlett.

E. — Acton., *Capt.*, James Moulton.
 1st Lieut., James E. Harris.
 2d Lieut., Lucius S. Hosmer.

F. — Concord, *Capt.*, Caleb H. Wheeler.
 1st Lieut., James W. Carter.
 2d Lieut., George F. Wheeler.

G. — Lowell, *Capt.*, Albert Pinder.
 1st Lieut., George O. Tarbell.
 2d Lieut., Charles H. Richardson.

H. — Lowell, *Capt.*, Matthew Donnavan.
 1st Lieut., John O. Grady.
 2d Lieut., ——— ———.

I. — Lawrence, *Capt.*, Chas. O. Varnum.
 1st Lieut., Daniel A. Barr.
 2d Lieut., Richard Sullivan.

K. — Lawrence, *Capt.*, Smith Decker.
 1st Lieut., George N. Archer.
 2d Lieut., ——— ———.

Eighth Regiment of Infantry.

Colonel, Benjamin F. Peach, Jr. of Lynn.
Lieut. Col., Francis E. Porter, of Beverly.
Major, David W. Low, of Gloucester.
Adjutant, Abram. H. Berry, of Lynn.
Quartermaster, Charles E. Kimball, of Lynn.
Surgeon, John L. Robinson, of Wenham.

Ass't Surgeon, Ebenezer Hunt, of Danvers.
Ass't Surgeon, Amos H. Johnson, of Middleton.
Chaplain, John R. Thurston, of Newburyport.

COMPANIES.

A. — Newburyport, *Capt.*, Eben P. Cutter.
 1st Lieut., Andrew P. Lewis, Jr.
 2d Lieut., John A Beau.

B. — Newburyport, *Capt.*, Chas. L. Ayers.
 1st Lieut., George W. Clark.
 2d Lieut., George H. Stevens.

C. — Marblehead, *Capt.*, Philip T. Woodfin, Jr.
 1st Lieut., Benjamin Pitman.
 2d Lieut., Francis A. Osgood.

D. — Lynn, *Capt.*, Thomas H. Berry.
 1st Lieut., George E. Palmer.
 2d Lieut., John G. Warner.

E. — Beverly, *Capt.*, Hugh J. Munsey.
 1st Lieut., Benjamin F. Herrick.
 2d Lieut., Charles L. Dodge.

F. — Lynn, *Capt.*, John T. Whittier.
 1st Lieut., Josiah F. Kimball.
 2d Lieut., William H. Gale.

G. — Gloucester, *Capt.*, Benj. F. Cook.
 1st Lieut., John B. Dennis.
 2d Lieut., Fitz W. Perkins.

H — Salem, *Capt.*, John P. Reynolds.
 1st Lieut., Benjamin R. Symonds.
 2d Lieut., Edward A. Hall.

I. — Lynn, *Capt.*, Jeremiah C. Bacheller.
 1st Lieut., Charles C. Fry.
 2d Lieut., Philip Smith.

K. — Salem, *Capt.*, Sidney B. Rowell.
 1st. Lieut., George L. Goss.
 2d Lieut., Charles H. Phippen.

Company F. Unattached Cavalry (Chelmsford).

Captain, Christopher Roby.
Adjutant, H. Herbert Emerson.
1st Lieut., Allen Cameron.
2d Lieut., James A Davis.
Ass't Surgeon, Levi Howard.

Third Battery of Light Artillery (Malden).

Captain, Edward E. Currier.
1st Lieut., George H. Johnson.
1st Lieut., William H. Howe.
2d Lieut., George W. Barrett.
2d Lieut., ——— ———.
Adjutant, Edwin A. Yale.

Fourth Battery of Light Artillery (Lawrence.)

Captain, Henry M. McIntire.
1st Lieut., George G. Durrell.
1st Lieut., Joseph W. Gardner.
2d Lieut., Wallace M. Priest.
Ass't. Surgeon, John G. McAllister.

Third Brigade.

Brigadier-General. Robert H. Chamberlain, of Worcester.
Ass't Adj.-General, (rank *Lieut.-Col.*), ——— ———.
Medical Director (rank *Lieut.-Col.*) ——— ———.
Ass't-Inspector General (rank *Major*), ——— ———.
Ass't-Quartermaster (rank *Captain*), ——— ———.
Engineer (rank *Captain*), ——— ———.
Aide-de-Camp (rank *Captain*), ——— ———.
Judge Advocate (rank *Captain*), ——— ———.

Second Regiment of Infantry.

Colonel, Joseph B. Parsons, of Northampton.

Lieut. Colonel, John W. Trafton, of Springfield.

Major, Israel C. Weller, of Pittsfield.

Adjutant, (rank of 1st Lieut.)

Quartermaster, (rank of 1st Lieut.)

Surgeon, (rank of Major).

Chaplain, ——

Ass't. Surgeon, (rank of 1st Lieut.)

COMPANIES.

A. — Enfield, *Capt.,* Erskine E. Butler.
  1st Lieut., Albert F. Johnson.
  2d Lieut , Joseph R. Hunt.

B. — Springfield, *Capt.,* Hosea C. Lombard.
  1st Lieut.. John L. Knight.
  2d Lieut., Stephen A. Sargent.

C. — Worthington, *Capt.,* Anson F. Stevens.
  1st Lieut., Charles Underwood.
  2d Lieut., Stephen Hayward.

D. — Windsor, *Capt.,* Elisha C. Tower.
  1st Lieut.. Wilbur F. Wilde.
  2d Lieut., Charles W. Leonard.

E. — Pittsfield, *Capt.,* ——— ——.
  1st Lieut., Frederick A. Francis.
  2d Lieut., William F. Harrington.

F. — Northampton, *Capt.,* ——, ——.
  1st Lieut., Hubbard M. Abbott.
  2d Lieut., Edwin A. Ramsay.

G. — Springfield, *Capt.,* Sam'l B. Spooner.
  1st. Lieut., Homer G. Gilmore.
  2d Lieut., Henry M. Phillips.

H. — Northampton, *Capt.,* Marcus T. Moody.
  1st Lieut., Edward F. Hamlin.
  2d Lieut., George M. Fuller.

I. — Chicopee, *Capt.,* George H. Knapp.
  1st Lieut., David M. Donaldson.
  2d Lieut., Chester H. Ballard.

K. — Holyoke, *Capt.,* Oscar S. Tuttle.
  1st Lieut. James G. Smith.
  2d Lieut., Robert T. Prentis.

Tenth Regiment of Infantry.

Colonel, ——— ——.

Lieut-Colonel, James May, of Fitchburg.

Major, Willard Clark, of Milford. .

Adjutant, (rank of 1st Lieut.), Frank A. Leland, of Worcester.

Quartermaster, (rank of 1st Lieut.), Chas. S. Chapin, of Worcester.

Surgeon, (rank of Major), Samuel Flagg, of Worcester.

Chaplain, George S. Ball, of Upton.

Ass't Surgeon, (rank of 1st Lieut.), Isaac H. Stearns, of Milford.

COMPANIES.

A. — Worcester, *Capt.,* Joseph A. Titus.
  1st Lieut., William H. King.
  2d Lieut., Frank E. Hall.

B. — Fitchburg, *Capt,* Geo. E. Goodrich.
  1st Lieut , George L. Lawrence.
  2d Lieut., Harrison C. Cheney.

C. — Worcester, *Capt.,* Jas. M. Drennan.
  1st Lieut., George H. Conklin.
  2d Lieut., Joel H. Prouty.

D. — Fitchburg. *Capt.,* Hiram P. Minot.
  1st Lieut., George B. Proctor.
  2d Lieut., Thomas Marsh.

E. — Ashburnham, *Capt.,* Geo. E. Davis.
  1st Lieut., William H. Lindley.
  2d Lieut., Leander W Libby.

F. — Milford, *Capt ,* John G. McCarter.
  1st Lieut., Dexter P. Vant.
  2d Lieut., Paran C. H. Belcher.

G. — Grafton, *Capt.* John F. Searle.
  1st. Lieut., Albion L. Vining.
  2d Lieut., James W. McKenzie.

H. — Westminster, *Capt.,* Abner E. Drury.
  1st Lieut., Ethan W. Holder.
  2d Lieut., James H. Miller.

I. — Westboro', *Capt.,* Oliver M. Maser.
  1st Lieut., ——
  2d Lieut., Daniel McCarthy.

K. — Leominster, *Capt.,* Lucien A. Cook.
  1st Lieut., Eugene A. Bennett.
  2d Lieut., Thomas A. Hills.

First Company of Cadets (Boston).

Capt: (with rank of Lieutenant Colonel), John Jeffries, Jr.

Lieut. (with rank of Major), Stephen M. Weld.

Ensign (with rank of Major), Jeremiah Abbott.

Surgeon (with rank of Major), B. Joy Jeffries.

Adjutant (with rank of Captain), Thomas F. Edmands.

Quartermaster (with rank of First Lieutenant), Charles E. Stevens.

1st Lieut., William F. Lawrence.

1st Lieut., Otis E. Weld.

1st Lieut., ——.

1st Lieut., James H. Ellison.

1st Lieut., William S. Appleton.

1st Lieut., ——.

Second Company of Cadets (Salem).

Major, A. Parker Browne.

Capt., Samuel Dalton.

Adjutant, John P. Browning.

Quartermaster, Edward A. Simonds.

Surgeon, Charles Haddock.

1st Lieut., Joseph C. Foster.

1st Lieut., Philip G. Skinner.

2d Lieut., Edw. Hobbs.

2d Lieut., Charles E. Getchell.

2d Lieut., James Pope.

The following Military Company consists mainly of Officers of other corps of Militia.

ANCIENT AND HONORABLE ARTILLERY COMPANY.

OFFICERS FOR 1868-69. .

Captain, Major George O. Carpenter. *First Lieutenant,* Brev. Brigadier-General Wm. H. Lawrence. *Second Lieutenant,* George H. Allen. *Adjutant,* Brigadier-General Horace C. Lee. *First Sergeant,* Captain A. A. Folsom. *Second Sergeant,* Captain Caleb E. Neibuhr. *Third Sergeant,* John C. Farnham. *Fourth Sergeant,* Sergeant H. K. W. Hibbard. *Fifth Sergeant,* Sergeant David F. McGilvray. *Sixth Sergeant,* Captain William H Cundy. *Seventh Sergeant,* Lieut. Isaac Watts. *Eighth Sergeant,* Sergeant John Bottume, Jr. *Ninth Sergeant,* Captain Caleb Drew. *Tenth Sergeant,* Major John W. Mahan. *Treasurer and Paymaster,* Captain John G. Roberts. *Clerk and Assistant Paymaster,* George H. Allen. *Quartermaster,* Captain Charles S. Lambert. *Armorer,* Captain Richard M. Barker.

STATE BOARD OF AGRICULTURE, 1869.

Members ex-officiis. His Excellency William Claflin, His Hon. Joseph Tucker, Hon. Oliver Warner, *Secretary of the Commonwealth.* William S. Clark, *Pres. Mass. Agricultural College.*

Appointed by the Governor and Council.
Ephraim W. Bull, of Concord ; Louis Agassiz, of Cambridge ; Marshall P. Wilder, of Dorchester.

Chosen by the County Societies. — Massachusetts. Leverett Saltonstall, of Newton ; *Essex,* George B. Loring, of Salem ; *Middlesex,* John B. Moore, of Concord ; *Middlesex (North),* Asa Clement, of Dracut ; *Middlesex (South),* John Johnson, Jr., of Framingham ; *Worcester,* Thomas W. Ward, of Shrewsbury ; *Worcester (West),* Courtland Sanderson, of Phillipston ; *Worcester (North),* Thomas Billings, of Lunenburg ; *Worcester (Northwest),* Charles C. Bassett, of Athol ; *Worcester (South),* Newton S. Hubbard, of Brimfield ; *Worcester (Southeast),* William Knowlton, of Upton ; *Hampshire, Franklin and Hampden,* H. S. Porter, of Hatfield ; *Hampshire,* John A. Morton, of Hadley ; *Highland,* Monroe F. Watkins, of Hinsdale ; *Hampden,* William Birnie, of Springfield ; *Hampden (East),* J. S. Blair, of Brimfield ; *Union,* E. W. Boise, of Blandford ; *Franklin,* Imla K. Brown, of Bernardston ; *Berkshire,* Alexander Hyde, of Lee ; *Hoosac Valley,* John L. Cole, of Williamstown ; *Housatonic,* T. D. Thatcher, of Lee ; *Norfolk,* Eliphalet Stone, of Dedham ; *Hingham,* Albert Fearing, of Hingham ; *Brisol,* Avery P. Slade, of Somerset ; *Bristol (Central),* Nathan Durfee, of Fall River ; *Plymouth,* Charles G. Davis, of Plymouth ; *Marshfield,* George M. Baker, of Marshfield ; *Barnstable.* George A. King, of Barnstable ; *Nantucket,* James Thompson, of Nantucket ; *Martha's Vineyard,* John Pierce, of Edgartown ; Charles L. Flint, *Secretary.*

BOARD OF STATE CHARITIES.

Edward Earle, Worcester ; Nathan Allen, Lowell ; Samuel G. Howe, Boston ; Moses Kimball, Boston ; Josiah C. Blaisdell, Fall River ; S. C. Wrightington, Fall River, *General Agent ;* Julius L. Clarke, Newton, *Secretary.*

STATE ALMSHOUSES.

State Almshouse at Tewksbury.

Francis H. Nourse, Lowell ; Benj. C. Perkins, Peabody ; George P. Elliot, Billerica, *Inspectors.* Thos. J. Marsh, *Superintendent.*

State Almshouse at Bridgewater.

James Ford, Fall River ; James H. Mitchell, East Bridgewater ; Joseph B. Thaxter, Hingham, *Inspectors.* Levi L. Goodspeed, *Supt.*

State Almshouse at Monson.

Eleazer Porter, Hadley ; Gordon M. Fisk, Palmer ; Thomas Rice, Shrewsbury, *Inspectors.* Horace P. Wakefield, *Supt.*

State Hospital on Rainsford's Island.

Joseph McK. Churchill, Milton ; Jona. D. Wheeler, Grafton ; Chas. H. Warren, Boston, *Inspectors.* Marcus M. Nye, *Superintendent and Physician.*

HOSPITALS.

The Worcester Lunatic Hospital.

Was founded by the State. and was first opened for patients Jan. 18, 1833. It has of late been sustained by the price of board of patients. The charge is $3.50 and $5.00 per week. Patients are committed by order of Judges of Probate, by Overseers of the Poor, by warrant from the Governor, and by private bonds, with sworn certificates of insanity from two physicians. *Trustees*, R. W. Hooper, M.D., Boston; Hon. Charles Mattoon, Greenfield; Hon. Henry Chapin, Worcester; Wm. Workman M.D., Worcester; and Hon. S. E. Sewall, of Boston. *Resident Officers*, Merrick Bemis, M.D., *Superintendent;* Joseph Draper, M.D., *Assistant Physician;* Caroline A. Bemis, *Matron;* Janette W. Wright, *Clerk;* Daniel W. Bemis, *Steward and Treasurer.*

State Lunatic Hospital, Taunton.

Trustees, Le Baron Russell, Boston; Chas. R. Atwood, Taunton; George Howland, New Bedford: Oliver Ames, No. Easton; Chas. Edward Cook, Boston. *Resident Officers*, Geo. C. S. Choate, M.D., *Superintendent and Treasurer;* Norton Folsom, M.D., *Assistant Physician;* John Kittredge, *Clerk.*

Northampton Lunatic Hospital, at Northampton.

Silas M. Smith, of Northampton, Eliphalet Trask, of Springfield, Henry L. Sabin, M.D., of Williamstown, Edmund H. Sawyer, of East Hampton, Edward Hitchcock, M.D., of Amherst, *Trustees;* Pliny Earle, A.M., M.D., *Physician and Superintendent;* C. K. Bartlett, M.D., *Assistant Physician.*

Massachusetts General Hospital, McLean Street, Boston.

Incorporated 1811.

——— ———, *President.* Edward Wigglesworth, *Vice-President.* J. Thomas Stevenson, *Treasurer.* Henry B. Rogers, James M. Beebe, William S. Bullard, Charles H. Dalton, Samuel Eliot, George Higginson, Samuel G. Howe, James L. Little, John Lowell, Charles S. Storrow, Edmund Dwight, Ezra Farnsworth, *Trustees.* OFFICERS OF THE HOSPITAL.— Benjamin S. Shaw, M.D., *Resident Physician and Superintendent.* Geo. C. Shattuck, M.D., Francis Minot, M.D., Calvin Ellis, M.D., Samuel L. Abbot, M.D., James C. White, M.D., Henry K. Oliver, jr., M.D., *Visiting Physicians.* Henry J. Bigelow, M.D., Henry G. Clark, M.D., Samuel Cabot, M.D., George H. Gay, M.D., Richard M. Hodges, M.D., Algernon Coolidge, M.D., *Visiting Surgeons.* Hall Curtis, M.D., George E. Tarbell, M.D., *Physicians to Out-patients.* J. Theodore Heard, M.D., Charles B. Porter, M.D., *Surgeons to Out-patients.* Calvin Ellis, M.D., *Microscopist and Curator of the Pathological Cabinet.*

Officers of McLean Asylum for Insane Somerville.

John E. Tyler, *Superintendent.* James H. Whittemore, M.D., James H. Denny, M.D. *Assistant Physicians and apothecaries.* George W. Whittle, *Steward.* Mrs. Abby M. Whittle, *Matron.*

City Hospital, Boston.

Harrison Avenue, opposite Worcester square. Established for the reception of those only who require temporary relief during sickness; other persons are admitted temporarily when necessity requires. *Consulting Physicians and Surgeons*, S. D. Townsend, M.D.; Edward Reynolds, M.D.; Winslow Lewis, M.D; John Jeffries, M.D.; Silas Durkee, M.D.; Benjamin E. Cotting. M.D. *Visiting Physicians*, Fitch Edward Oliver, M D.; John N. Borland, M.D.; John G. Blake, M.D.; John P. Reynolds, M.D.; Henry I. Bowditch, M.D.; Alexander D. Sinclair. M.D. *Visiting Surgeons*, D. McB. Thaxter. Jr., M.D; Charles D. Homans, M.D.; David W. Cheever. M.D.; W. H. Thorndike. M.D.; George Derby, M.D.; F. C. Ropes, M.D. *Ophthalmic Surgeon*, Henry W. Williams, M.D. *Admitting Physician*, Howard F. Damon. M.D. *Pathologist*, Charles W. Swan, M. D. *Physicians to Out-Patients*, Charles W. Swan, M.D.; William B. Mackie, M.D. *Department for Skin Diseases, Out-Patients*, H. F. Damon, M.D. *Surgeon to Out-Patients.* M. F. Gavin, M.D. *House Physicians.* O. W. Doe, H. F. Borden, F. W. Goss. *House Surgeons*, F. W. Draper, George B. Shattuck, J. H. McCollom. *Ophthalmic Externe*, George E. Hatten. *Trustees for 1869.* [Elected by

concurrent vote in January.] *Alderman,* Newton Talbot. *Councilmen,* L. T. Snow, —— ——. *At Large,* John T. Bradley. *Pres.,* James Guild, N. C. Nash, Jeremiah Ricards, Theo. Metcalf, Jonas Ball. *Superintendent,* Lucius A. Cutler, residence and office in the Hospital. [Chosen by Trustees.] Salary, $1800.

Applications for admission of patients may be made to the Superintendent at the Hospital before 11 o'clock, A.M. The applicant will be visited the same afternoon by the Admitting Physician, and on his permit may be sent at once to the Hospital. Persons accidentally wounded, or otherwise disabled or injured, will be received at all hours.

Mass. Homœopathic Hospital.

Incorporated, 1855.

Charles B. Hall, *President.* Simon G. Cheever, *Treasurer.* George Bancroft, *Secretary.* Isaac Rich, Julius A. Palmer, Geo. S. Hillard, Alex. Strong, Samuel Gregg, Geo. Russell, L. McFarland, David Thayer, O. S. Sanders, F. H. Krebs, I. T. Talbot, Peter C. Brooks, Alpheus Hardy, Horatio Harris, Edward G. Tileston, Geo. F. Emery, Alexander H. Rice, R. L. Robbins, Joseph Story, Jacob S. Albee, *Trustees.*

Boston Lying-in Hospital.

Annual meeting in May. John Homans, M.D., *President.* Charles H. Parker, *Vice-President.* Thornton K. Lothrop, *Treasurer.* Francis A. Hall, *Secretary.*

The Society has not now any hospital, but dispenses its charities in private families.

Boston Lunatic Hospital, South Boston.

Clement A. Walker, M.D., *Superintendent.* Theodore W. Fisher, M.D., *Assistant Superintendent.*

STATE PRISON.

Located at Charlestown.

Gideon Haynes, *Warden.* Oliver Whitcomb, *Deputy-Warden.* William Peirce, *Clerk.* Amos B. Bancroft, *Physician.* George J. Carleton, of Newton, *Chaplain.* Everett Torrey, Charlestown; James Pierce, Malden; Joseph D. Pinder, Lowell, *Inspectors.*

Agent for Discharged Convicts, Daniel Russell, Boston.

THE PERKINS INSTITUTION AND MASS. ASYLUM FOR THE BLIND.

INSTITUTED, 1831. LOCATED AT SOUTH BOSTON.

Depository and Office, 20 Bromfield Street.

Edward Brooks, *President.* Joseph Lyman, *Vice-President.* William Claflin, *Treasurer.* Samuel G. Howe, M.D., *Director and Secretary.* Thos. T. Bouvé, Samuel Eliot, Josiah Quincy, James Sturgis, William B. Rogers, Augustus Lowell, George S Hale, of Boston; E. R. Mudge, Swampscott; Francis Brooks, Medford; Edward N. Perkins, Brookline; Joseph Lyman, Benjamin S. Rotch, Jamaica Plain, *Trustees.*

MASSACHUSETTS SCHOOL FOR IDIOTIC AND FEEBLE-MINDED YOUTH.

Eighth, between M and N streets, South Boston.

Samuel G. Howe, *President.* Emory Washburn, *Vice-President.* F. W. G. May, *Treasurer.* Edward Jarvis, *Secretary.* Samuel G. Howe, Samuel Eliot, Robert B. Storer, of Boston; Edward Jarvis, F. W. G. May, Daniel Denny, Jr., of Dorchester; Emory Washburn, of Cambridge; and Francis W. Bird, Walpole, *Trustees appointed by the Corporation.* John Flint, Boston; Josiah Bartlett, Concord; James B. Congdon, New Bedford; Lewis Allen, South Danvers; Henry G. Denny, Dorchester; James M. Barnard, Edwin Morton, Boston, *Trustees appointed by the Governor and Council.*

STATE REFORM SCHOOL FOR BOYS.

Congregate and Family Asylum combined.

WESTBORO'. ESTABLISHED 1848.

Henry Chickering, Pittsfield ; Levi L. Goodspeed, Bridgewater; Stephen G. Deblois, Boston ; Harmon Hall, Saugus ; John Ayres, Medford ; Edward A. Goodnow, Worcester; Geo. C. Davis, Northborough, *Trustees*. George C. Davis, Northborough, *Treasurer*. Joseph A. Allen, *Superintendent*. Orville K. Hutchinson, *Assistant Superintendent*. Henry H. Rising, *Physician*.

NAUTICAL BRANCH STATE REFORM SCHOOL.

Matthew Howland, New Bedford ; Thomas Russell, Boston ; William T. Davis, Plymouth ; William Fabens, Marblehead ; Alfred C. Hersey, Boston, *Trustees*. Charles W. Reed, Boston, *Treasurer*.

STATE INDUSTRIAL SCHOOL FOR GIRLS.

LANCASTER. ESTABLISHED 1855.

Frank B. Fay, of Chelsea ; George Cummings, Lancaster ; George B. Emerson, Boston ; Daniel Denny, of Dorchester ; R. Sturgis, Jr., of Boston ; John L. S. Thompson, Lancaster; Albert Tolman, of Worcester ; *Trustees*. Frank B. Fay, *Treasurer*. Russell Sturgis, Jr., *Secretary*.

Marcus Ames, *Superintendent and Chaplain*. Lucy A. Proctor, *Superintendent's Assistant*. A. E. Boynton, *Farmer*. J. L. S. Thompson, M. D., *Physician*. Mrs. Susan A. Byers, Mrs. Harriet P. Abbott, Mrs. Harriet F. Perry, Miss Eliza G. Longfellow, Miss Isabella C. Spaulding, *Matrons*.

The intention of this institution is to secure a *home* and a *school* for such girls as may be presented to the magistrates of the State appointed for that purpose, as vagrants, perversely obstinate, deprived of the control and culture of their natural guardians, or guilty of petty offences, and exposed to a life of crime and wretchedness.

There are now, January, 1869, five separate families, accommodating about 150 children.

Commissioners on admission to Industrial School. — Joseph A. Denny, Leicester; Luther Hatch, Marshfield ; Lewis E. Caswell, Boston ; William Willett, Boston ; Frank B. Fay, Chelsea ; Benjamin C. Perkins, Peabody ; Chas. H. Merriam, Leominster; Benj. F. White, Weymouth ; John L. S. Thompson, Lancaster ; Thorley Collester, Gardner; George D. Porter, Medford ; Loring Wheeler, Newton ; Samuel D. Davenport, Hopkinton ; Luther Hill, Spencer; William E. Currier, Stephen W. Marston, Newburyport; Franklin Dickinson, Belchertown ; Thornton K. Ware, Fitchburg; Elijah C. Shattuck, Berlin ; Dwight Hyde, Brookfield ; Abel F. Hutchinson, South Reading ; Benjamin G. Hill, Malden ; Dexter Bucknam, Stoneham ; Charles Robinson, Jr., Charlestown ; Ebenr. M. Hosmer, West Boylston ; John T. Dame, Clinton ; Warren Lovering, Medway ; William Taggart, Haverhill; Joseph F. Hitchcock, Warren ; Nathan W. Harmon, Lawrence ; Wendall T. Davis, Greenfield ; Alanson Borden, New Bedford ; Josiah Rutter, Waltham ; Orrin Thomson, Holliston ; E. Stowell Whittemore, Sandwich ; George Andrews, Henry J. Dunham, Stockbridge ; Samuel P. Andrews, Michael Carlton, Salem ; Wm. W. Blodgett, Pawtucket.

TRUSTEES OF THE SMITH CHARITIES.

NORTHAMPTON. INCORPORATED 1849.

For the benefit of Indigent Widows and Children.

Osmyn Baker, *President*.

Osmyn Baker, J. D. Billings, H. Stevens, *Trustees*.

CUSTOM-HOUSE OFFICERS.

District of Boston and Charlestown.

The Custom House opens at 9 o'clock, A. M., and closes at 3 o'clock, P.M.

Collector, Thomas Russell.

Deputy Collector and Auditor, John M. Fiske.

Deputy Collectors, George H. Kingsbury, James Baxter, Jr.

Cashier, Ephm. L. Frothingham, Jr.

Naval Officer, Francis A. Osborn.

Deputy Naval Officer, T. B. Dix.

Surveyor, A. B. Underwood.

Deputy Surveyor, Thos. Sherwin, Jr.

Assistant Deputy Surveyor, Augustus Sanderson.

Superintendent of Warehouses, Asa M. Cook.

General Appraiser, O. B. Dorrance.

Appraisers, Thos. G. Rice, Wm. E. Webster.

Assistant Appraisers, Francis Blake, Chas. D. Lincoln.

Boarding Officer, R. Torrey, Jr.

REVENUE CUTTER, "VIGILANT."

Captain, Jas. D. Usher; 1st Lieut., Wm. C. Piggott; 2d Lieut., H. W. Harwood; 3d Lieut., William McKendry; Pilot, Samuel N. Miller.

STEAM TUG, "H. HAMLIN."

Lieut. Com., Edward C. Gardner; 1st Asst. Engineer, James M. McDougal; Pilot, E. N. Thatcher.

SUB-TREASURY.

Assistant Treasurer, Franklin Haven, Jr.

District of Barnstable.

Port of Barnstable,—Chas. F. Swift, Collector; Walter Chipman, Deputy Collector.

Port of Falmouth. — Benj. P. Swift, Deputy Collector.

Port of Hyannis. — Alvan S. Hallett, Deputy Collector.

Port of Chatham. — Nath'l Snow, Deputy Collector.

Port of South Dennis. — Joseph K. Baker, Jr., Deputy Collector.

Port of Wellfleet. — Simeon Atwood, Deputy Collector.

Port of Provincetown. — Simeon S. Gifford, Deputy Collector; Nathaniel E. Atwood, Aid to the Revenue.

District of Edgartown.

Port of Edgartown. — John Vinson, Collector; Jeremiah Peace, Deputy Collector and Inspector.

Port of Holmes's Hole. — Henry W. Beetle, Deputy collector and Inspector.

District of Fall River.

Port of Fall River. — James Brady, jr., Collector; Isaac Borden, Deputy Collector and Inspector; Earl P. Bowen, Inspector, Weigher, &c.

District of Gloucester.

Port of Gloucester. — William A. Pew, Collector; Addison Center, Deputy Collector; B. H. Smith, Surveyor; F. J. Babson, B. F. Cook, Inspectors.

Port of Rockport. — T. F. Parsons, Jr., Inspector.

District of Marblehead.

Port of Marblehead. — William Standly, Collector; Wm. H. Coates, Deputy Collector; John Cross, Inspector, Weigher, &c.

Port of Lynn. — Lord Harris, Deputy Collector and Inspector.

District of Nantucket.

Port of Nantucket. — Isaac H. Folger, Collector; A. B. Robinson, Deputy Collector; Peter Folger, Inspector.

District of New Bedford.

Port of New Bedford. — Lawrence Grinnell, Collector; James Taylor, Deputy Collector; Geo. B. Richmond, Inspector; James V. Cox, Inspector and Boarding Officer; James C. Hitch, Clerk.

Port of Fairhaven. — Joseph Taber, Inspector.

Port of Mattapoisett. — Jonathan H. Holmes, Inspector.

Port of Sippican. — George H. Kelley, Inspector.

Port of Wareham. — Stephen Ellis, Deputy Collector and Inspector.

Port of Dartmouth. — Edward Howland, Inspector.

Port of Westport. — Russell Gifford, Inspector.

District of Newburyport.

Port of Newburyport. — Enoch G. Currier, Collector; Daniel P. Pike, Deputy Collector; John H. Smith, Inspector; Hervey Kimball, Weigher and Measurer; Henry Stover, Surveyor.

Port of Ipswich. — Reuben Daniels, Surveyor.

District of Plymouth.

Port of Plymouth. —Thomas Loring, Collector ; Charles O. Churchill, *Deputy Collector and Inspector.*

Port of Duxbury. — Harvey Soule, *Deputy Collector and Inspector.*

Port of Kingston. -- Steph. Holmes, *Deputy Collector and Inspector.*

Port of Scituate. — Joseph S. Drew, *Deputy Collector and Inspector.*

District of Salem and Beverly.

Port of Salem.— Robert S. Rantoul,

Collector ; Charles S. Osgood, *Deputy Collector ;* Joseph Moseley, *Surveyor ;* Wm. C. Waters, *Storekeeper;* Ephraim F. Miller, Nathaniel M. Hooper, Wm. P. Buffum, Samuel R. Hathaway, G. Parker Bray, Ephraim Felt, *Inspector ;* Simon O. Dalrymple, *Weigher and Gauger.*

Port of Beverly. — Gustavus Ober, *Inspector.*

Port of Danvers. — William Endicott, *Inspector.*

BOARD OF EDUCATION.

ESTABLISHED BY AN ACT OF THE LEGISLATURE, APRIL 20, 1837.

OFFICE AT THE STATE HOUSE.

The Governor, Lieutenant-Governor, and Secretary of the Commonwealth, *ex-officiis*, and eight members, one to be appointed annually by the Governor and Council ; David H. Mason. *Newton.* term expires, 1875 ; James Freeman Clarke, *West Roxbury*, 1876 ; John P. Marshall, *Somerville*, 1869 ; Gardner G. Hubbard, *Cambridge*, 1870 ; William Rice, *Springfield*, 1871 ; Emory Washburn, *Cambridge*, 1872 ; Samuel T. Seelye, *Easthampton*, 1873 ; John D. Philbrick, *Boston*, 1874.

Joseph White, *Secretary and Treasurer;* Samuel C. Jackson, *Assistant Secretary ;* Abner J. Phipps, *Agent.*

STATE NORMAL SCHOOLS.

ESTABLISHED BY LAW, 1838.

The State Normal Schools are designed for those *only* who purpose to teach, and especially for those who purpose to teach in the Common Schools. Of those who avail themselves of the advantages of these Schools, and who afterwards become teachers in the Common Schools of Massachusetts, no tuition fee is required.

There are at present four in the Commonwealth, as follows : —

STATE NORMAL SCHOOL, FRAMINGHAM.

FOR FEMALES ONLY.

Annie E. Johnson, *Principal.*

Originally established at Lexington, July 3, 1839. Transferred in May, 1844, to West Newton; from thence, in 1853, to Framingham.

BRIDGEWATER STATE NORMAL SCHOOL.

(Established, 1840.)

FOR BOTH SEXES.

Albert G. Boyden, A.M., *Principal.* George H. Martin.

Male applicants for admission must be at least 17 years of age. Female applicants, 16. Tuition free.

STATE NORMAL SCHOOL AT WESTFIELD.

(Incorporated, 1844.)

FOR BOTH SEXES.

John W. Dickinson, A.M , *Principal.*

J. C. Greenough, A.B., J. G. Scott, A.M.

This school first went into operation at Barre, September 4, 1839. In 1841 it was suspended, and in September, 1844, was re-commenced at Westfield.

SALEM STATE NORMAL SCHOOL.

FOR FEMALES ONLY. TUITION FREE.

Opened, September 13, 1854.

Daniel B. Hagar, A.M., *Principal.*

COLLEGES, ACADEMIES, ETC.

Harvard College, Cambridge.

(Incorporated, 1636.)

PRESIDENT,

_____

FELLOWS.

John A. Lowell, LL.D., George Putnam, D.D., George T. Bigelow, LL.D., Francis B. Crownins ield, A.M., Nathaniel Thayer, A.M., Nathaniel Silsbee, A.M., *Treasurer.*

OVERSEERS.

The President and Treasurer of the University, *ex officio,* and the following persons by election: —

Edward E. Hale, A.M., William Adams Richardson, A.M., Nathaniel B. Shurtleff, M.D., *Secretary*; Lorenzo R. Thayer, A.M., Reuben Totman, Robinson, A.M., John Codman Ropes, LL.B., David H. Mason, A.B., Francis Cogswell, A.M., James Walker, D.D., LL.D., Benjamin Smith Rotch, A.B., Richard H. Dana, LL.D., Geo. M. Brooks, LL.B., John W. Bacon, A.M., James Lawrence, A.M., Thomas B. Thayer, D.D., George W. C. Noble, A.B., William Gray, A.M., James Freeman Clarke, D.D., Darwin E. Ware, LL.B., Samuel Eliot, LL.D., Ralph Waldo Emerson, L.L.D., Seth Sweetser, D.D., Francis Edward Parker, LL.B., Henry Lee, A.M., Jonathan Ingersoll Bowditch, A.M., E. Rockwood Hoar, L.L.D., John H. Clifford, LL.D., *President* ; Francis Parkman, LL.B., Theodore Lyman, S.B., Charles William Eliot, A.M.

COLLEGE FACULTY.

Andrew P. Peabody, D.D., LL.D., Benj. Peirce, LL.D., Francis Bowen, A.M., Joseph Lovering, A.M., Henry W. Torrey, A.M., Evangelinus A. Sophocles, LL.D., James R. Lowell, A.M., Frances J. Child, Ph.D., Geo. M. Lane, Ph.D., James Jennison, A.M., Josiah P. Cooke, A.M., William W. Goodwin, Ph.D., Ephraim W. Gurney, A.B., Elbridge J. Cutler, A.B., *Registrar*; James M. Peirce, A.M., James B. Greenough, A.B., William Hyde Appleton, A.M., Prentiss Cummings, A.B., Isaac Flagg, A.M., Edwin P. Seaver, A.B., George A. Hill, A.B., Louis C. Lewis, A.B., Thomas Sergeant Perry, A.B.

Williams College, Williamstown.

(Incorporated, 1793.)

PRESIDENT,

MARK HOPKINS, D.D.

TREASURER AND SECRETARY,

JOSEPH WHITE.

TRUSTEES.

Henry L. Sabin, Charles Stoddard, William Hyde, John Todd, Absalom Peters, Henry W. Bishop, Adam Reid, Nahum Gale, Joseph White, Homer Bartlett, Erastus C. Benedict, James D. Colt, John Z. Goodrich, Robert R. Booth, William E. Dodge, Giles B. Kellogg.

FACULTY.

Rev. Mark Hopkins, D.D., LL.D., *President.* Albert Hopkins, LL.D., Rev. John Bascom, A.M., Arthur L. Perry, A.M., Charles F. Gilson, A.M., Sanborn Tenny, A.M., Rev. James M. Anderson, A.M., William R. Dimmock, A.M., Arthur W. Wright, Ph. D. Franklin Carter, A.M., Charles R. Treat, A.M., Rev. N. H. Griffin, D.D., *Librarian.*

Amherst College, Amherst.

(Incorporated, 1825.)

PRESIDENT,

Rev. WILLIAM A. STEARNS, D.D., LL.D.,

Rev. Joseph Vaill, D.D., Ebenezer Alden, M.D., Hon. Samuel Williston, Henry Edwards, Esq , Hon. Jonathan C. Perkins, Hon. Alexander H. Bullock, LL.D., Rev. William P. Paine, D.D., Hon. Henry Morris, Rev. Edward S. Dwight, Hon. Alpheus Hardy, Nathan Allen, M.D., Hon. Edward B. Gillett, Rev. Lewis Sabin, D.D., Rev. Richard S. Storrs, Jr., D.D., Samuel Bowles, Esq., Rev. Henry Ward Beecher, Rev. Edward S. Dwight, *Secretary.* Hon. Edward Dickinson, LL.D., *Treasurer.*

MEMBERS OF THE FACULTY.

Rev. William A. Stearns, D.D., LL.D., *President.* Ebenezer S. Snell, LL.D., Charles U. Shepard, M.D., LL.D., Rev. William S. Tyler, D.D., Rev. Julius H. Seelye, Edward P.

White, *Secretary of the Board of Education.*

FACULTY.

William S. Clark, Ph.D., Hon. Levi Stockbridge. Henry H. Goodell, A.M., Samuel F. Miller, Chas. A. Goessmann.

New-England Female Medical College, Boston.

TRUSTEES.

William Cumston, *Pres.* Amariah Storrs, *Treas.* Samuel Gregory, M.D., *Sec.* John S. Tyler, John Batchelder. Jonas Fitch, Osborn Howes, Benjamin Smith, Alden Speare, Curtis C. Nichols, Franklin Snow, Henry Hutchinson, Edward W. Kinsley, John Souther, Henry D. Hyde, Joshua Merrill.

FACULTY.

William Cumston, *Pres.* Stephen Tracy, M.D., *Dean of the Faculty.* Frances S. Cooke, M.D., Edward Aiken, M.D., Wm. H. Campbell, M.D., Anna Monroe, M.D. Annual term begins 1st Wednesday in November.

Andover Theological Seminary, Andover.

(Incorporated 1807.)

Rev. Seth Sweetser, D.D., *President.* Rev. Edwards A. Park, D.D., Austin Phelps, D.D., Rev. Egbert Smyth Rev. Wm. H. Thayer, Rev. Chas. M. Mead, Rev. John L. Taylor, D.D., *Professors.*

Phillips Academy, Andover.

(Incorporated, 1780.)

TRUSTEES.

Rev. Seth Sweetser, D.D., *President.* Samuel H. Taylor, LL.D., *Clerk.* Edward Taylor, Esq., *Treasurer.* Rev. Samuel C. Jackson, D.D.; Hon. Linus Child, M.A., Rev. Wm. A. Stearns, D.D., Hon. Reuben A. Chapman, LL.D., Hon. Alpheus Hardy, Rev. Amos Blanchard, D.D., Rev. Daniel T. Fiske, D.D., Hon. John Kingsbury, LL.D., Rev. Edmund K. Alden, D.D.

INSTRUCTORS.

Samuel H. Taylor, LL.D, *Principal.* William B. Graves, M.A., George C. Merrill, B.A., George H. Taylor, B.A., Wm. H. Hawkes, B.A., Prof. J. Wesley Churchill.

ACADEMIES.

Abbott Female, Andover. Inc. 1828. Principal, Miss Philena McKeen.

Auburndale Select Boys' School, Auburndale. Principal, Rev. Chas. W. Cushing. A.M.

Boston Dental College. President, I. J. Wetherbee, D.D.S.

BOSTON HIGHLANDS — Young Ladies' Private School. Principal, John Kneeland (see page 98).

Bradford Academy, Bradford. Inc. 1804. Principal, Abby H. Johnson.

Bridgewater, Bridgewater. Inc. 1799. Principal Horace M. Willard.

Bristol, Taunton. Incorporated, 1792. Principal, Henry Leonard.

Brookside Seminary, Stockbridge. Principal, George P. Bradley.

Carter's Commercial Academy, Pittsfield. Incorporated, 1864. Principal, Emerson F. Carter, A.M.

Charlestown Female Seminary, Charlestown. Incorporated, 1832. Principal, Catharine Badger.

Clark Institute, for Instruction of Deaf and Dumb, Northampton. Principal, Miss Harriet B. Rogers.

CODMAN HILL SCHOOL, for Young Ladies, Dorchester. Principal, Mrs. S. M. Cochrane.

Cotting Academy, Arlington. Principal, Henry C. Ide.

Day's Academy, Wrentham. Inc. 1806. Principal, —— Wiggin.

Dean Academy, Franklin. Inc. 1865. Prin., Timothy G. Senter, A. M.

Deerfield Academy. Deerfield. Inc. 1797. Prin., Virgil M. Howard.

Derby, Hingham. Incorporated 1797, Principal, —— Dupee.

Drury Academy, North Adams. Inc. 1843. Principal, A. D. Miner.

Dukes County Academy, West Tisbury. Prin., Moses Mitchell.

Dummer Academy, Byfield, Newburyport P. O. Prin., Levi W. Stanton.

Edwards Place School, Stockbridge. Prin., Jared Reid, jr.

Elm Wood Institute, Lanesborough. Principal, Alfred A. Gilbert.

Friends' Academy, New Bedford. Edward A. H. Allen.

Hanover Academy, Hanover. Inc. 1828. Prin., J. Prince Thorndike.

Highland Institute, Petersham. Principals, Rev J. Shepardson, and W. T. Leonard.

Highland Military School, Worcester. Principal, Caleb B. Metcalf.

Hitchcock Free Grammar School, Brimfield. Prin., Elias Brookings.

Holmes's Business Colleges, Taunton and Fall River. Principal, F. A. Holmes.

Hopkins's, Hadley. Principal, Charles H. Chandler.

Houghton School, Bolton. Incorporated, 1849. Principal, Sidney A. Phillips.

Howe School, Billerica. Principal, Samuel Tucker.

Howes' Business College, Worcester. Principal B. G. Howes.

Lancaster, Lancaster. Incorporated 1847. Prin., Wm. A. Kilbourn.

Lasell Female Seminary, Auburndale. Principal, Rev. Chas. W. Cushing, A. M.

Lawrence, Falmouth. Inc. 1835. Principal, Lucian Hunt, A. M.

Leicester, Leicester. Incorporated, 1784. Prin., D. P. Sackett.

Maplewood Young Ladies' Institute, Pittsfield. Founded, 1841. Principal, Rev. C. V. Spear.

Mendelssohn Musical Institute, Boston. Principal, Edward B. Oliver.

Middleboro' Commercial College, Middleboro'. Prin., J. B. Hambly.

Monson, Monson. Inc. 1804. Prin., Rev. Charles Hammond.

Mount Holyoke Female Seminary, South Hadley. Incorporated 1836. Principal, Helen M. French.

Mount Pleasant Institute for Boys, Amherst. Principal, H. C. Nash.
New England Conservatory of Music, Boston. Director, E. Tourjee.
New Salem, New Salem. Incor. 1795. Principal, F. F. Foster.
Newton Theological Institute, Newton Centre. Incorporated, 1826.
    President, Rev. Alvah Hovey, D.D.
Nichols, Dudley. Incorporated, 1819. Principal, Isaiah Trufant.
Oakland Institute, Needham.
Orchard Hill Family Boarding School for Young Ladies, Belmont. Prin-
    cipal, D. Mack.
Oread Collegiate Institute for Young Ladies, Worcester. Prin., Harris
    R. Greene, A. M.
Oread High and Grammar School for Boys, Worcester. Principal, H. M.
    Greene, A. M.
Partridge, Duxbury. Incorporated 1629. Principal, Rev. J. Moore.
PEIRCE ACADEMY, Middleboro'. Incorporated, 1808. Principal,
    J. W. P. Jenks, A.M.
Pepperell Academy, Pepperell. Principal, Lorenzo P. Blood.
Powers Institute, Bernardston. Incor. 1857. Prin., L. F. Ward.
Pratt Free School, North Middleborough. Prin., C. G. M. Dunham.
Rochester, Rochester. Incorporated 1854. Prin., Susan Partridge.
Round Hill Classical School, Northampton. Principals, Jonah Clark and
    J. F. Spalding.
Sanderson Academy, Ashfield. Principal, Miss Stone.
Sandwich Academy, Sandwich. Principal, Wm. C. Spring.
Sedgwick Institute, Great Barrington. Prin., S. Parsons Pratt.
Shelburne Falls, Shelburne Falls. Inc. 1847. Prin., J. N. Burnham.
Sheldon, Southampton. Incor. 1829. Prin., Chas. E. Harrington.
South Berkshire Institute, New Marlboro'. Incorporated 1856. Prin-
    cipal, B. F. Parsons.
South Egremont, South Egremont. Inc. 1830, Prin., James Shead.
Southwick Academy, Southwick. Principal, A. F. Egleston.
St. Mark's School, Southboro'. Principal, G. H. Patterson.
STOUGHTONHAM INSTITUTE, Sharon. Prin., Sanford Waters
    Billings.
UNION MERCANTILE SCHOOL, Chelsea. Prin., H. T. Wheeler.
Warren Academy, Woburn. Inc. 1830. Prin., William A. Stone.
Watatic Academy, Ashby.
Wesleyan Academy, Wilbraham. Com. 1824. Prin., Edward Cooke.
Westford Academy, Westford. Inc. 1793. Prin., M. Whitman.
Westminster Academy, Westminster. Prin., George Benton.
West Newton English and Classical School, West Newton: Incorporated
    1855. Principal, Nathaniel T. Allen.
Wheaton Female Seminary, Norton. Principal, Mrs. C. C. Metcalf.
Williams Academy, Stockbridge. Inc. 1828. Prin., E. W. B. Canning.
Williston Seminary, East Hampton. Incorporated, 1842. Principal,
    Marshall Henshaw, LL.D.
Willow Park Female Institute, Westborough. Prin., Emily A. Rice.
Worcester Academy, Worcester. Inc. 1834. Prin., Wm. C. Poland.
Worcester Co. Free Institute of Industrial Science, Worcester. Principal,
    C. O. Thompson.
Young Ladies' Institute, Charlestown. Prin., Leander A. Darling.
YOUNG LADIES' PRIVATE SCHOOL, Boston Highlands. Prin-
    cipal, John Kneeland (see page 98).
(see page 98).
    7

COMMISSIONERS, ETC.

Harbor Commissioners.

William Mixter, *Hardwick;* Samuel E. Sewall, *Melrose;* Josiah Quincy, *Boston;* Wm. W. Clapp, *Boston;* Fred. W. Lincoln, Jr., *Boston;* Darwin E. Ware, *Marblehead.*

Pilot Commissioners.

Elias E. Davison, *Boston;* John Williams, *Chelsea.* Office in Boston, 39 Lewis Wharf.

Commissioners on Troy and Greenfield R. R. and Hoosac Tunnel.

Alvah Crocker, *Fitchburg;* Tappan Wentworth, *Lowell;* Samuel W. Bowerman, *Pittsfield;* Benjamin H. Latrobe, *Consulting Engineer.*

Commissioners on Hours of Labor.

Henry I. Bowditch, *Boston;* Franklin B. Sanborn, *Concord;* Wm. B. Tilden, *Boston;* Elizur Wright, *Boston;* Geo. H. Snelling, *Boston;* Edwd. H. Rogers, *Chelsea;* William Hyde, *Ware;* Amasa Walker, *N. Brookfield.*

Commissioners of Fisheries in Merrimac and Conn. Rivers.

Theodore Lyman, *Brookline*, Alfred R. Field, *Greenfield.*

Commissioners Obstruction to Passage of Fish in Conn. and Merr. Rivers.

Theodore Lyman, *Brookline.;* Alfred A. Reed, *Boston.*

Superintendents of Alien Passengers.

James V. Cox, *of Fairhaven,* for New Bedford, Fairhaven, Dartmouth, Westport, Mattapoisett, Marion, and Wareham; Ephraim Burr, *Salem;* John Gilley, *Marblehead;* Parker Borden, *Fall River;* Samuel Haskell, *Gloucester.*

Guardians of Indians.

Charles Brigham, Jr., *Grafton;* Benj. F. Winslow, *Fall River;* John W. Bacon, *Natick;* Charles Endicott, *Canton;* E. Stowell Whittemore, *Sandwich;* Barnard C. Marchant, *Edgartown;* Erastus Alton, *Webster.*

Insurance Commissioner.

John E. Sanford, of *Taunton.* Office in Boston, at State House.

Agent of Province Lands.

Joshua E. Bowley, *Provincetown.*

Commissioner of Savings Banks.

Frederick M. Stone, of *Waltham.* Office in Boston, at State House.

Trustees Discharged Soldiers' Home.

Henry S. Briggs, *Pittsfield;* Julius L. Clarke, *Newton.*

Commissioners Street Railways.

Isaac F. Redfield, *Boston.;* Edwin L. Barney, *New Bedford;* Alfred R. Field, *Greenfield.*

COMMISSIONERS,

Resident in Massachusetts, appointed by other States to take testimony to be used, and Acknowledgments of Deeds to be recorded, in said States.

ALABAMA.

Boston, A. W. & C. B. F. Adams; Angell & Jennison, 46 Washington St, James B. Bell, B. H. Currier; A^{ll'}e^l E. Giles, John P. Healy, Abraham Jackson, Otis G. Randall·

Lawrence, John K. Tarbox ; *Stockbridge,* Jonathan F. Field; *Westfield,* N. T. Leonard; *Worcester,* J. Henry Hill.

ARIZONA TERRITORY.

Boston, A. W. & C. B. F. Adams, Angell & Jennison, 46 Washington St., James B. Bell.

ARKANSAS.

Boston, A. W. & C. B. F. Adams, Angell & Jennison, 46 Washington St., J. B. Bell, B. H. Currier, M. Dyer, Jr., John S. Holmes, John C. Park, Otis G. Randall, Paul P. Todd.

CALIFORNIA.

Boston, A. W. & C. B. F. Adams, Angell & Jennison, 46 Washington St., J. B. Bell, R. I. Burbank, Samuel R. Crocker, Benjamin H. Currier, Sam'l S. Curtis, John W. Draper, Edward Fiske, J. M. Fiske, George S. Hale, Benjamin Pond, Otis G. Randall, Daniel Sharp, Hales W. Suter, Charles A. F. Swan, Paul P. Todd.

Amesbury, William C. Binney; *Lowell,* Charles A. F. Swan; *New Bedford,* James M. Bunker ; *Worcester,* J. Henry Hill.

COLORADO TERRITORY.

Boston, A. W. & C. B. F. Adams, Angell & Jennison, 46 Washington St., James B. Bell, Samuel S. Curtis, O. G. Randall, I. H. Wright.

CONNECTICUT.

Boston, A. W. & C. B. F. Adams, Angell & Jennison, 46 Washington St., Edwin A. Alger, S. B. Allen, Ivers J. Austin, J. B. Bell, S. A. Bent, G. M. Browne, Edw. Buck, R. I. Burbank, T. P. Cheever, L. M. Child, D. H. Coolidge, Benjamin H. Currier, S. S. Curtis, Charles Demon, Thomas A. Dexter, Micah Dyer, Jr., Alfred B. Ely, George S. Hale, George R. Hastings, William Hobbs, Jr., David P. Kimball, Joseph Nickerson, Charles C. Nutter, Silas F. Plympton, John P. Putman, Otis G. Randall, Daniel

Sharp, Hales W. Suter, James B. Thayer, J. Wingate Thornton, Paul P. Todd, Edwin Wright.

Lowell, Jonathan Ladd; *Pittsfield,* C. N. Emerson ; *Worcester,* J. Henry Hill.

DAKOTAH TERRITORY.

Boston, A. W. & C. B. F. Adams, Angell & Jennison, 46 Washington St. James B. Bell.

DELAWARE.

Boston, A. W. & C. B. F. Adams, Angell & Jennison, 46 Washington St., S. B. Allen, J. B. Bell, B. H. Currier, Otis G. Randall.

Westfield, N. T. Leonard; *Worcester,* J. Henry Hill.

FLORIDA.

Boston, A. W. & C. B. F. Adams, Angell & Jennison 46 Washington, St., I. J. Austin, J. B. Bell, C. Browne, Benjamin H. Currier, Thomas A. Dexter, Francis E. Parker, Otis G. Randall.

Westfield, N. T. Leonard ; *Worcester,* J. Henry Hill.

GEORGIA.

Boston, A. W. & C. B. F. Adams, Angell, & Jennison, 46 Washington St., J. B. Bell, Edw. Buck, B. H. Currier, S. S. Curtis, Thomas A. Dexter, Otis G. Randall.

Westfield, N. T. Leonard.

IDAHO TERRITORY.

Boston, A. W. & C. B. F. Adams, Angell & Jennison, 46 Washington St., James B. Bell.

ILLINOIS.

Boston, A. W. & C. B. F. Adams, Charles Francis Adams, jr., Angell & Jennison, 46 Washington St. S. B. Allen, Ivers J. Austin, H. Baldwin, J. B. Bell, F. A. Brooks, D. H. Coolidge, Benjamin H. Currier, A. B. Ely, William Hobbs, Jr., Abraham Jackson, Alonzo V. Lynde, George H. Kingsbury, John T. Paine, Francis W. Palfrey, Benj. Pond, Otis G. Randall, A.E. Scott, Paul P. Todd, I. H. Wright. *Worcester,* J. Henry Hill.

INDIANA.

Boston, A. W. & C. B. F. Adams, Angell & Jennison, 46 Washington St.

Ivers J. Austin, Henry Baldwin, J. B. Bell, Edw. Buck, B. H. Currier, Samuel S. Curtis, Alfred B. Ely, William Hobbs, Jr., Nathan Morse, Benjamin Pond, Otis G. Randall, J. Wingate Thornton, Paul P. Todd.

IOWA.

Boston, A. W. & C. B. F. Adams, C. F. Adams, jr., Angell & Jennison, 46 Washington St. S. B. Allen, Ivers J. Austin, Joshua D. Ball, S. W. Bates, J. B. Bell, C. Browne, Robert I. Burbank, David H. Coolidge, Benjamin H. Currier, Samuel S. Curtis, William Hobbs, Jr., D. P. Kimball, Edward K. Phillips, Benjamin Pond, Otis G. Randall, Daniel Sharp, Augustus Russ, Hales W. Suter, James B. Thayer, Warren Tilton, Paul P. Todd, Ambrose Wellington.
Lowell, Robert B. Caverly; *Salem*, Robert S. Rantoul; *Westfield*, N. T. Leonard; *Worcester*, J. Henry Hill.

KANSAS.

Boston, A. W. & C. B. F. Adams, Angell & Jennison, 46 Washington St. James B. Bell, David H. Coolidge, Benjamin H. Currier, Samuel S. Curtis, H. B. Crandall, Otis G. Randall, A. E. Scott, J. Wingate Thornton, Paul P. Todd, Ambrose Wellington.
Cambridge, William A. Richardson.
Worcester, J. Henry Hill.

KENTUCKY.

Boston, A. W. & C. B. F. Adams, Angell & Jennison, 46 Washington St. J. B. Bell, Edw. Buck, Benjamin H. Currier, S. S. Curtis, Alfred B. Ely, Thomas S. Harlow, Otis G. Randall, Daniel Sharp, J. Wingate Thornton, John M. Way.

LOUISIANA.

Boston, A. W. & C. B. F. Adams, Angell & Jennison, 46 Washington St. J. L. Andrews, J. B. Bell, G. E. Betton, Benjamin H. Currier, Samuel S. Curtis, William Dehon, Alfred B. Ely, William Hilliard, Nathan Morse, Charles C. Nutter, Frederick O. Prince, Otis G. Randall, David Roberts, Geo. P. Sanger, J. Wingate Thornton.
Westfield, N. T. Leonard; *Worcester*, J. Henry Hill.

MAINE.

Boston, A. W. & C. B. F. Adams, Angell & Jennison, 46 Washington St. John S. Abbott, William A. Abbott, Edwin A. Alger, Augustus O. Allen,

Charles E. Allen, S. B. Allen, F. H. Appleton, Ivers J. Austin, Henry Baldwin, J. B. Bell, E. Blake, A. F. Bloch, Francis A. Brooks, Edward Buck, Robert I. Burbank, William L. Burt, Peleg W. Chandler, A. B. Collin, D. H. Coolidge, Asa Cottrell, Sam'l R. Crocker, Benj. H. Currier, Samuel S. Curtis, Edward A. Dann, Charles Demond, Thomas A. Dexter, John C. Dodge, A. Eastman, Alfred B. Ely, W. A. Field, John M. Fiske, William J. Forsaith, Alfred E. Giles, John E. M. Gilley, Geo. S. Hale, Franklin Hall, Thomas S. Harlow, S. Rowland Hart, Francis B. Hayes, Henry W. Haynes, H. L. Hazelton, Edw'd F. Hodges, Abraham Jackson, Harvey Jewell, Albion K. P. Joy, Chauncy P. Judd, D. P. Kimball, George H. Kingsbury, Alonzo V. Lynde, Sebeus C. Maine, Jeremiah L. Newton, Joseph Nickerson, Chas. C. Nutter, Thomas F. Nutter, Edmund B. Otis, William E. Parmenter, Edward K. Phillips, Benjamin Pond, F. O. Prince, Otis G. Randall, W. A. Richardson, David Roberts, James W. Rollins, Augustus Russ, George P. Sanger, Daniel Sharp, Robert D. Smith, Oliver Stevens, George S. Sullivan, Hales W. Suter, Charles A. F. Swan, James B. Thayer, James D. Thomson, Sam'l L. Thorndike, J. Wingate Thornton, Paul P. Todd, Samuel Tompson, Charles W. Tuttle, Alexander C. Washburn, Ambrose Wellington, Hiram Wellington, Samuel Wells, Jr., Paul Willard, Wm. C. Williamson.
Abington, F. P. Howland; *Cambridge*, Wm. A. Richardson; *Charlestown*, A. B. Shedd; *Edgarotun*, T. G. Mayhew; *Lowell*, Robert B. Caverly, Samuel Lawrence, Charles A. F. Swan; *New Bedford*, E. L. Barney; *North Bridgewater*, Jonas R. Perkins; *Springfield*, James H. Morton; *Westfield*, N. T. Leonard; *Worcester*, J. Henry Hill.

MARYLAND.

Boston, A. W. & C. B. F. Adams, Angell & Jennison, 46 Washington St., S. B. Allen, James B. Bell, B. H. Currier, Alfred B. Ely, Geo. Griggs, William Hobbs, Jr., Abraham Jackson, Francis E. Parker, Edward K. Phillips, Otis G. Randall.
New Bedford, E. L. Barney; *Worcester*, J. Henry Hill.

MICHIGAN.

Boston, A. W. & C. B. F. Adams,

Angell & Jennison, 46 Washington St., S. B. Allen, I. J. Austin, J. B. Bell, A. W. Boardman, Francis A. Brooks, Edward Buck, David H. Coolidge, Benjamin H. Currier, Saml. S. Curtis, Alfred B. Ely, H. L. Hazelton, William Hobbs, Jr., Henry A. Johnson, D. P. Kimball, George H. Kingsbury, Marcus Morton, Benj. Pond, Otis G. Randall, W. A. Richardson, A. E. Scott, Daniel Sharp, Hales W. Suter, James B. Thayer, Paul P. Todd.
Cambridge, Wm. A. Richardson; *New Bedford*, Wendell H. Cobb, William W. Crapo, Oliver Prescott; *Pittsfield*, C. N. Emerson; *Stowe*, Edwin Whitney; *Westfield*, N. T. Leonard; *Worcester*, J. Henry Hill.

MINNESOTA.

Boston, A. W. & C. B. F. Adams, Angell & Jennison, 46 Washington St., S. B. Allen, I. J. Austin, J. D. Ball, J. B. Bell, Benjamin H. Currier, Samuel S. Curtis, Dean Dudley, Edmund B. Otis, Benjamin Pond, Otis G. Randall, Paul P. Todd, J. H. Ward, Ambrose Wellington.
Cambridge, Wm. A. Richardson; *Worcester*, J. Henry Hill.

MISSISSIPPI.

Boston, A. W. & C. B. F. Adams, Angell & Jennison, 46 Washington St., James B. Bell, Benjamin H. Currier, Abraham Jackson, J. H. Ward.

MISSOURI.

Boston, A. W. & C. B. F. Adams, Angell & Jennison, 46 Washington St., J. B. Bell, B. H. Currier, Saml. S. Curtis, Alfred E. Giles, Abraham Jackson, Henry A. Johnson, Edmund B. Otis, Otis G. Randall, Daniel Sharp, Chauncy Smith, J. Wingate Thornton.
Worcester, J. Henry Hill.

MONTANA TERRITORY.

Boston, A. W. & C. B. F. Adams, Angell & Jennison, 46 Washington St., James B. Bell.

NEBRASKA.

Boston, A. W. & C. B. F. Adams, Angell & Jennison, 46 Washington St., James B. Bell, Benjamin H. Currier, Otis G. Randall.

NEVADA.

Boston, A. W. & C. B. F. Adams, Angell & Jennison, 46 Washington St., James B. Bell, Otis G. Randall, Chas. A. F. Swan.

Lowell, Chas. A. F. Swan; *Northampton*, A. P. Peck.

NEW HAMPSHIRE.

Boston, A. W. & C. B. F. Adams, Angell & Jennison, 46 Washington St., E. A. Alger, Ivers J. Austin, Phineas Ayer, Sumner Albee, S. B. Allen, John L. Andrews, James B. Bell, S. Arthur Bent, A. F. Blotch, George E. Betton, Caleb Blodgett, Jr., George A. Bruce, David Bryant, Robert I. Burbank, A. C. Clark, Joseph M. Churchill, A. B. Coffin, David H. Coolidge, Asa Cottrell, Samuel R. Crocker, Uriel H. Crocker, Benj. H. Currier, Samuel S. Curtis, Isaac J. Cutter, Charles C. Dane, Edward A. Dana, George S. Derby, Thomas A. Dexter, Mark F. Duncklee, Micah Dyer, Jr., Alfred B. Ely, W. A. Field, Daniel F. Fitz, Wm. J. Forsaith, H. F. French, J. E. M. Gilley, George S. Hale, Francis B. Hayes, Horace L. Hazelton, A. C. Hersey, William Hilliard, William Hobbs, Jr., Henry C. Hutchins, Horace G. Hutchins, Harvey Jewell, Albion K. P. Joy, D. P. Kimball, Alonzo V. Lynde, B. C. Moulton, Henry W. Muzzey, Stephen G. Nash, Jos. Nickerson, John Noble, A. F. L. Norris, Thomas F. Nutter, Benjamin Pond, Otis G. Randall, S. H. Randall, A. A. Ranney, J. B. Richardson, W. A. Richardson, William Rogers, James W. Rollins, Daniel Sharp, George S. Sullivan, Charles A. F. Swan, James B. Thayer Jas. D. Thomson, Samuel Tompson, S. L. Thorndike, J. Wingate Thornton, J. W. Titus, Paul P. Todd, Charles W. Tuttle, Ambrose Wellington, Samuel Wells, Jr., Alex. S. Wheeler, Charles Wheeler, Paul Willard, G. D. Woodman.
Amesbury, William C. Binney, G. W. Cate, George Turner: *Lawrence*, H. C. Bacon; *Lowell*, John Davis, Charles A. F. Swan, G. D. Woodman; *New Bedford*, E. L. Barney; *Winchendon*, L. W. Pierce; *Worcester*, J. H. Hill.

NEW JERSEY.

Boston, A. W. & C. B. F. Adams, Angell & Jennison, 46 Washington St., J. B. Bell, B. H. Currier, D. P. Kimball, George W. Phillips, Benjamin Pond, Otis G. Randall, Gerard C. Tobey, Paul P. Todd; *Northampton*, A. Percy Peck; *Worcester*, J. Henry Hill.

NEW MEXICO.

Boston, A. W. & C. B. F. Adams, Angell & Jennison, 46 Washington St., James B. Bell, B. H. Currier, Otis G. Randall.

NEW YORK.

Boston, A. W. & C. B. F. Adams, Angell & Jennison, 46 Washington St., S. B. Allen, E. A. Alger, E. Avery, J. B. Bell, A. F. Bloch, E. H. Currier, S. S. Curtis, Charles Demond, G. S. Derby, A. French, George S. Hale, Thornton K. Lothrop, Francis W. Palfrey. Benjamin Pond, Otis G. Randall, W. A. Richardson, David Roberts, George W. Searle, Daniel Sharp, Charles A. F. Swan, Samuel Tompson, I. H Wright.

Amherst, W. A. Dickinson ; *Lowell*, Robert B. Caverly, Charles A. F. Swan ; *Lynn*, Wm. Howland ; *New Bedford*, James M. Bunker, W. H. Cobb ; *Northampton*, A. P. Peck ; *Pittsfield*, C. N. Emerson ; *Springfield*, E. W. Bond, Wm. S. Donnelly, S. R. Phillips, Wm. S. Shurtleff, Augustus L. Soule ; *Westfield*, N. T. Leonard ; *Worcester*, J. Henry Hill.

NORTH CAROLINA.

Boston, A. W. & C. B. F. Adams, Angell & Jennison, 46 Washington St., James B. Bell, David H. Coolidge, Benjamin H. Currier, Samuel S. Curtis, Otis G. Randall, J. Wingate Thornton.

Worcester, J. Henry Hill.

OHIO.

Boston, A. W. & C. B. F. Adams, Chas. F. Adams, Jr., Angell & Jennison, 46 Washington St., S. B. Allen. Ivers J. Austin, Henry Baldwin, J. B. Bell. E. Buck, Robert I. Burbank, Fred. W. Choate, Joseph M. Churchill, Benj. H. Currier, Samuel S. Curtis, Charles Demond, Elbridge G. Dudley, Alfred B. Ely, Clement H. Hill, Wm. Hobbs, Jr., Edward F. Hodges. Henry A. Johnson, D. P. Kimball, Alonzo V. Lynde, Henry W. Muzzey, Edmund B. Otis, Francis W. Palfrey, Francis E. Parker, Benj. Pond, Otis G. Randall, Daniel Sharp, Hales W. Suter, James B. Thayer, Paul P. Todd, Calvin Torrey, Ambrose Wellington.

Northampton, A. P. Peck ; *Worcester*, J. H. Hill.

OREGON.

Boston. A. W. & C. B. F. Adams, Angell & Jennison, 46 Washington St., James B. Bell, Benjamin H.

Currier, Samuel S. Curtis, Otis G. Randall, Paul P. Todd.

PENNSYLVANIA.

Boston, A. W. & C. B. F. Adams, Angell & Jennison, 46 Washington St., S. B. Allen, Ivers J. Austin, J. D. Ball, J. B. Bell, Edward Buck, R. I. Burbank, Asa Cottrell, Benjamin H. Currier, Samuel S. Curtis, Charles F. Dana, Thomas A. Dexter, Charles Demond, Frank W. Hackett, Edward F. Hodges, Marcus Morton, Charles C. Nutter, Fred. O. Prince, Otis G. Randall, James W. Rollins, Hales W. Suter, J. Wingate Thornton, Paul P. Todd.

New Bedford, Alanson Borden ; *Westfield*, N. T. Leonard ; *Worcester*, J. Henry Hill.

RHODE ISLAND.

Boston, A. W. & C. B. F. Adams, Angell & Jennison, 46 Washington St., S. B. Allen, Isaac Ames, I. J. Austin, E. C. Baker, H. Baldwin, J. B. Bell, A. F. Bloch, C. Browne, E. Buck, J. P. Converse, B. H. Currier, Samuel S. Curtis, Wm. S. Dexter, George Griggs, Thomas S. Harlow, William Hilliard, William Hobbs, Jr., Abraham Jackson, James M. Keith, D. P. Kimball, Edward S. Rand, Otis G. Randall, David Roberts, Joseph B. Sanford, A. E. Scott, Dan'l Sharp. Lemuel Shaw, Hales W. Suter, Charles A. F. Swan, James B. Thayer, Paul P. Todd.

Amesbury, William C. Binney ; *Lowell*, Charles A. F. Swan ; *New Bedford*, E. L. Barney, R. C. Pitman ; *Springfield*, James H. Morton ; *Westfield*, N. T. Leonard ; *Worcester*, J. Henry Hill.

SOUTH CAROLINA.

Boston, A. W. & C. B. F. Adams, Angell & Jennison, 46 Washington St., J. B. Bell, B. H. Currier, Samuel S. Curtis, Thomas A. Dexter, Alfred B. Ely, George Griggs, Wm. Hilliard, Otis G. Randall.

Springfield, James H. Morton, Wm. S. Shurtleff ; *Westfield*, N. T. Leonard ; *Worcester*, J. Henry Hill.

TENNESSEE.

Boston, A. W. & C. B. F. Adams, Angell & Jennison, 46 Washington St., I. J. Austin, J. B. Bell, G. T. Bigelow, Causten Browne, Benjamin H. Currier, Benjamin Pond, Edmund B. Otis, Otis G. Randall, J. Wingate Thornton.

Westfield, N. T. Leonard ; *Worcester*, J. Henry Hill.

TEXAS.

Boston, A. W. & C. B. F. Adams, Angell & Jennison, 46 Washington St., Wm. Aspinwall, J. B. Bell, B. H. Currier, Samuel S. Curtis, Edward Fiske, George S. Hale, Edward F. Hodges, Otis G. Randall. *Westfield,* N. T. Leonard.

UTAH.

Boston, A. W. & C. B. F. Adams, Angell & Jennison, 46 Washington St., S. B. Allen, J. B. Bell, C. F. Blake, B. H. Currier, Otis G. Randall.

VERMONT.

Boston, A. W. & C. B. F. Adams, Angell & Jennison, 46 Washington St., S. B. Allen, Sumner Albee, Ivers J. Austin, J. B, Bell, H. J. Boardman, A. R. Brown, Robert I. Burbank, J. H. Butler, A. B. Coffin, Benj. H. Currier, Samuel S. Curtis, Charles F. Dana, Alfred B. Ely, W. A. Field, Geo. S. Hale, Francis H. Hayes, Wm. Hobbs, Jr., Edward F. Hodges, Josiah W. Hubbard, Henry C. Hutchins, Harvey Jewell, James M. Keith, D. P. Kimball, Lyman Mason, Nathan Morse, Benjamin Pond, Otis G. Randall, A. A. Ranney, B. F. Rice, Nathaniel Richardson, A. E. Scott, Chauncey Smith, Hales W. Suter, Charles A. F. Swan, D. M. B. Thaxter, J. Wingate Thornton, Paul P. Todd, Thomas L. Wakefield, Hiram Wellington, Paul Willard. *Lowell,* Jonathan Ladd, Charles A. F. Swan, William P. Webster; *Worcester,* J. Henry Hill.

VIRGINIA.

Boston, A. W. & C. B. F. Adams, Angell & Jennison, 46 Washington St., E. C. Baker, J. B. Bell, J. M. Churchill, J. R. Coolidge, B. H. Currier, Samuel S. Curtis, Geo. S. Hale, W. Hobbs, Jr., A. Jackson, E. B. Otis, Otis G. Randall.

WASHINGTON TERRITORY.

Boston, A. W. & C. B. F. Adams, Angell & Jennison, 46 Washington St., James B. Bell, B. H. Currier, Otis G. Randall, Oliver Stevens.

WEST VIRGINIA.

Boston, A. W. & C. B. F. Adams, Angell & Jennison, 46 Washington St., James B. Bell.

WISCONSIN.

Boston, A. W. & C. B. F. Adams, Angell & Jennison, 46 Washington St., S. B. Allen, Ivers J. Austin, Joshua D. Ball, J. B. Bell, F. A. Brooks, Causten Browne, Robert I. Burbank, Robert Codman, Benjamin H. Currier, Samuel S. Curtis, Francis B. Hayes, D. P. Kimball, Alonzo V. Lynde, F. E. Parker, Silas F. Plimpton, Benjamin Pond, Otis G. Randall, W. A. Richardson, Augustus Russ, Daniel Sharp, J. Wingate Thornton, Paul P. Todd, James B. Thayer, Alexander C. Washburn, Ambrose Wellington. *Lynn,* Wm. Howland. *Westfield,* N. T. Leonard. *Worcester,* J. Henry Hill.

COMMISSIONERS UNITED STATES COURT OF CLAIMS.

Boston, D. S. Gilchrist; *New Bedford,* Thomas M. Stetson; *Salem,* Joseph B. F. Osgood; *Worcester,* J. Henry Hill.

DIRECTORY.—CAUTION.

The public are cautioned against ever paying money in advance to any persons claiming to be connected with us or our publications, as our Agents never take any sum, however small, in advance.

SAMPSON, DAVENPORT, & CO.,

DIRECTORY PUBLISHERS,

47 CONGRESS STREET, - - - - - - BOSTON.

COMMISSIONERS,

Resident in other States, who have been appointed by the Governor of Massachusetts to take testimony and depositions to be read in the Courts of Massachusetts; also to administer oaths, and to take the Acknowledgement of Deeds, Powers of Attorney, and all instruments under seal, to be recorded in said Commonwealth.
[NOTE.—The term for which these Commissioners hold their office is restricted to three years.]

ARKANSAS.
Little Rock, Charles P. Redmond

CALIFORNIA.
Sacramento, Edward Cadwalader
"   SAMUEL CROSS
San Francisco, Wm. O. Andrews
"   John S. Bugbee
"   Otis V. Sawyer
"   N. Proctor Smith
"   Emile V. Sutter
"   Fred. I. Thibault
"   John White

CONNECTICUT.
Hartford, Charles E. Fellowes
"   Edward Goodman
"   Wm. Hammersley
"   Chas. J. Hoadley
Meriden (West), John H. Bario
Norwich, Ebenezer Learned

DISTRICT OF COLUMBIA.
Washington, Edmund F. Brown
"   JOHN F. CALLAN,
72 Louisiana av.
"   Nicholas Callan
"   Geo. F. McLellan
"   Joseph Peck

FLORIDA.
Jacksonville, Edward M. Cheney
"   Wm. P. Dockray
"   Oscar Hart

GEORGIA.
Augusta, Ellery M. Brayton,
"   Joseph P. Carr
Macon, WM. P. GOODALL
Savannah, Frank S. Hesseltine

ILLINOIS.
Chicago, William E. Furness
"   PHILIP A. HOYNE
"   Simeon W. King
"   Oliver R. W. Lull
"   CHAS. McDONNELL

INDIANA.
Indianapolis, Luther R. Martin

LOUISIANA.
New Orleans, Justin Castanie
"   P. Chas. Ouvellier

New Orleans, THOS. M. GILL,
attorney at law,
6 Carondelet st.
"   Andrew Hero, Jr.
"   Alanson B. Long

MAINE.
Auburn, John W. May
Bangor, John E. Godfrey
Bath, John H. Kimball
Eastport, WINSLOW BATES
Portland, JAS. O'DONNELL

MARYLAND.
Baltimore, Joseph T. Atkinson
"   Isaac Brooks
"   Hermon L. Emmons, Jr.
"   Wm. W. Latimer
"   William B. Hill

MICHIGAN.
Detroit, William J. Waterman

MINNESOTA.
Minneapolis, CYRUS ALDRICH

MISSISSIPPI.
Jackson, Hinds Co., G. A. Smythe

MISSOURI.
St. Louis, Edmund T. Allen
"   Joel G. Harper
"   Rudolph Mackwitz
"   Theodore Papin

NEVADA.
Austin, ALFRED E. SHANNON
Virginia, Wm. A. M. Van Bok-
kelen
"   Joseph L. King

NEW HAMPSHIRE.
Dover, Charles W. Woodman
Exeter, Charles G. Conner
Mason Village, John K. Mills
Keene, Francis A. Faulkner
Portsmouth, William H. Hackett

NEW JERSEY.
Jersey City, George W. Cassedy
Newark, James F. Bond
"   Staats S. Morris

NEW YORK.

Albany, Worthington Frothingham
" . Edward Wade
Buffalo, James S. Gibbs
Brooklyn, Gordon L. Ford
" William F. Goodwin
" Theodore Hinsdale
Hudson, Stephen L. Magoun
Lockport, John Hodge
" William A. Abbott
New York, John Adriance
" Frederick R. Anderson
" Francis C. Bowman
" Edmund B. Barnum
" Fisher A. Baker
" William H. Barker
" HENRY C. BANKS, 3 John, cor. Broadway
" James B. Bullock
" John Bissell
" John Butcher
" Edwin F. Cory
" Jedd P. C. Cotterill
" Frederick N. Dodge
" Matthew H. Ellis
" James H. Fay
" WM. FURNISS, 35 Wall
" Peter I. Gage
" Horace Graves
" NATHL. GILL, 117 Broadway (room 15)
" William A. Gardner
" James W. Hale
" Henry B. Hammond
" Charles P. Hartt
" Theodore Hinsdale
" Clarence M. Hyde
" Frederick I. King
" Horatio C. King
" Sylvester Lay
" Sigismond Lasar
" William F. Lett
" Moses B. Maclay
" Robert Maclay
" Rufus K. McHarg
" Montgomery M. Livingston
" Francis A. Marden
" George B. Morris, Jr.
" CHARLES NETTLETON, 117 Broadway
" Joseph B. Nones
" Alexander Ostrander
" Josiah Porter
" Michael Phillips
" Nath'l A. Prentiss

New York, Bushrod F. Rice
" Thomas Sadler,
" Henry D. Sedgwick
" Edward F. de Selding
" Isaac S. Smith
" Samuel Swan
" Frederick B. Swift
" Thomas L. Thornell
" Christian Von Hesse
" Joseph W. Wildey
Troy, Charles L. Alden

NORTH CAROLINA.

Wilmington, Robert S. French

OHIO.

Cincinnati, Samuel S. Carpenter
" ALEX. H. M'GUFFEY, 6 East Third St.
" Hiram D. Peck
" Reuben Tyler
Cleveland, George L. Ingersoll
" *Toledo,* Wm. H. Gorrill

PENNSYLVANIA.

Philadelphia, Arthur M. Burton
" J. Edward Carpenter
" Charles Chauncey
" Robert P. Dechert
" Edward Hopper
" Samuel B. Huey
" Sm'l W. Pennypacker
" Edward L. Perkins
" Theodore D. Rand
" Edward Shippen
" Joshua Spering
" Samuel L. Taylor
" Kinley J. Tener
Pittsburg, John McClaren
" William F. Robb

RHODE ISLAND.

Newport, Francis Brinley
Providence, Henry Martin

SOUTH CAROLINA.

Beaufort, Reuben G. Holmes
Charleston, Asher D. Cohen
" Virginius J. Tobias

TENNESSEE.

Knoxville, Charles Seymour
Memphis, C. Canning Smith

TEXAS.

Houston, Emile Simmler

VIRGINIA.

Richmond, Charles S. Bundy

WISCONSIN.

Milwaukie, Francis Bloodgood

JUDGES AND REGISTERS OF PROBATE, SHERIFFS, &c., IN MAINE.

ANDROSCOGGIN COUNTY.

Judge of Probate, Enos T. Luce, Auburn.
Register of Probate, George S. Woodman, Minot.
Register of Deeds, Silas Sprague, Greene.
County Treasurer, Alexander F. Merrill, Lewiston.
Clerk of Courts, Daniel P. Atwood, Auburn.
Sheriff, Isaac N. Parker, Lewiston.
Deputy Sheriffs, Thos. Littlefield, *Auburn.* Prescott R. Strout, *Durham.* George W. Coombs, *Lisbon Falls.* James Hervey, *Webster.* Noah G. Cofren, *Livermore Falls.* Daniel H. Teague, *Turner.* Wm. Keene, *Mechanic Falls.*

AROOSTOOK COUNTY.

Judge of Probate, Henry R. Downes, Presque Isle.
Register of Probate, Lyman S. Strickland, Houlton.
Register of Deeds, Hadley Fairfield, Houlton.
County Treasurer, Charles P. Tenny, Houlton.
Clerk of Courts, Ransom Norton, Houlton.
Sheriff, Daniel Randall, Island Falls.
Deputy Sheriffs, Geo. G. Bickford, *Houlton.* G. A. Hayden, *Presque Isle.* Michael Farrell, *Van Buren.* Osgood Pringry, *Island Falls.* Daniel Foster, *Fort Fairfield.* Ira B. Gardner, *Patten.* Wm. J. Nye, *Houlton.* Hiram R. Forbes, *Houlton.* Milton D. Teague, *Linden.* Baptiste Fornier, *Madawaska.* N. M. Bartlett, *Fort Kent.*

CUMBERLAND COUNTY.

Judge of Probate, John A. Waterman, Gorham.
Register of Probate, Edward R. Staples, Bridgton.
County Treasurer, Peter R. Hall, Windham.
Clerk of Courts, Daniel W. Fessenden, Portland.
Register of Deeds, Eben Leach, Raymond.
Sheriff, George W. Parker, Gorham.
Deputy Sheriffs, William Paine, *Standish.* Rufus Berry, *Gray.* Daniel L. Mitchell, *Yarmouth.* B. H. Hall, *Windham.* Eben N. Perry, *Cape Elizabeth.* Russell Lamson, *Bridgton.* Lyman Hall, *Naples.* Charles Crosman, *Brunswick.*

FRANKLIN COUNTY.

Judge of Probate, O. L. Currier, *New Sharon.*
Register of Deeds, J. S. Gould, *Wilton.*
County Treasurer, I. Warren Merrill, *Farmington.*
Clerk of Courts, Simeon H. Lowell, Farmington.
Sheriff, A. T. Tuck, Farmington.
Deputy Sheriffs, Wm. Lancaster, Cyrus G. Brown, *New Sharon.* J. E. Thompson, *Phillips.* George L. Riggs, *Chesterville.* John N. Foster, *Wilton.* Isaiah Mitchell, *Strong.* John Jackson, *Dixfield, Oxford County,* A. V. Hinds, *Kingfield.* Morrill F. Smith, *Weld.*
Coroner, Seward Dill, *Phillips.*

HANCOCK COUNTY.

Judge of Probate, P. Tuck, Bucksport.
Register of Probate, George H. Dyer, Franklin.
County Treasurer, Charles W. Tilden, Castine.
Clerk of Courts, H. B. Saunders, Ellsworth.
Register of Deeds, John O. Sargent, Brooklin.
Sheriff, Andrew B. Spurling, Orland.

KENNEBEC COUNTY.

Judge of Probate, Henry K. Baker, Hallowell.
Register of Probate, J. Burton, Augusta.
Register of Deeds, Archibald Clark, Wayne.
County Treasurer, Alanson Starks.
Clerk of Courts, William M. Stratton, Augusta.
Sheriff, Charles Hewins, Augusta.
Deputy Sheriffs, William H. Siddy, *Augusta.* George R. Stevens, *Belgrade.* Charles G. Thwing, *China.* Thomas B. Stinchfield, *Clinton.* George Wheeler, *Gardiner.* I. F. Thompson, *Hallowell.* James F. Blunt, *Mt. Vernon.* E. G. Fuller, *Readfield.* Charles R. McFadden, *Waterville.* Josephus Stevens, *Winthrop,* A. H. Barton, *Benton.*

KNOX COUNTY.

Judge of Probate, John C. Levenseller, Thomaston.
Reg. of Probate, Edwin C. Fletcher, Camden.
County Treasurer, Chas. A. Libby, Rockland.
Register of Deeds, George W. White, Rockland.
Clerk of Courts, Edwin Rose, Thomaston.
Sheriff, Thomas B. Grose, Rockport.
Deputy Sheriffs, Joseph E. Brown, *Camden.* Isaac Carkin, *McLain's Mills.* James Burns, *Washington.*

LINCOLN COUNTY.

Judge of Probate, John H. Converse, New Castle.
Register of Probate, Joseph J. Kennedy, Wiscasset.
Reg. of Deeds, Calvin R. Harraden, Wiscasset.
County Treas., William P. Lennox, "
Clerk of Courts, Geo. B. Sawyer, "
Sheriff, Frederick Kent, Bremen.
Deputy Sheriffs, Alvin Piper, *Wiscasset.* Thomas Boyd, *Boothbay.* Jas. E. Morse, *Whitefield.* Joseph Ford, *Jefferson.* Peabody Simmons, *Damariscotta.*

OXFORD COUNTY.

Judge of Probate, Aug. H. Walker, Lovell.
Register of Probate, Josiah S. Hobbs, Paris.
Register of Deeds, (eastern district), Sumner R. Newell, Paris, (western district), Asa Charles, Fryeburg.
County Treasurer, Horatio Austin, Paris.
Clerk of Courts, Wm. K. Kimball, Paris.
Sheriff, Cyrus Wormell, Bethel.
Deputy Sheriffs, C. M. Wormell, A. B. Goodwin, *Bethel.* Russell Lamson, *Bridgton.* Eben E. Rice, *Brownfield.* Thomas R. Day, *Bryant Pond.* Josiah W. Whitten, *Buckfield.* Oakes T. Bosworth, *Canton.* Jacob Thompson, *Cornish.* John Jackson, *Dixfield.* Andrew Buzzell, *Fryeburg.* Charles H. George, *Hebron.* Lorenzo D. Stacy, *Kezer Falls.* Benjamin Hartford, *Lovell.* Henry A. Jewett, *North Waterford.* Winthrop Stevens, *Norway.* Samuel T. Beale, *Oxford.* Sullivan R. Hutchins, *Paris.* Daniel H. Teague, *Turner.*

PENOBSCOT COUNTY.

Judge of Probate, J. E. Godfrey, Bangor.
Register of Probate, Jos. Bartlett, "
County Treasurer, A. C. Flint, "
Clerk of Courts, Ezra C. Brett, Oldtown.
Register of Deeds, Amos E. Hardy, Hampden.
Sheriff, John H. Wilson, Bangor.
Deputy Sheriffs, Elisha W. Shaw, *Newport.* Nathaniel Barker, *East Exeter.* Gustavus S. Bean, *Bangor.* Hartwell Lancaster, *Upper Stillwater.* Joshua M. Herrick,

East Corinth. Joseph Shepherd, *Dexter*.
Samuel Phipps, *Hampden*. Ira B. Gardner,
Patten. Leonard L. Buswell, *Lincoln*.
George P. Brown, *Newburgh*. Wm. L.
Scribner, *Springfield*. Thomas R. Gardner,
Corinna.
Jailer, George W. Whitney, *Bangor*.

PISCATAQUIS COUNTY.

Judge of Probate, Joseph S. Monroe, *Abbot*.
Register of Probate, Asa Getchell, Dover.
County Treasurer, Mark Pitman,   "
Clerk of Courts, Russell Kittredge,   "
Register of Deeds, Marcell W. Hall,   "
Sheriff, Edward Jewett, *Sangerville*.
Deputy Sheriffs, Dennis Sprague, *Milo*. El-
bridge G. Thompson, *Foxcroft*.

SAGADAHOC COUNTY.

Judge of Probate, Amos Nourse, Bath.
Register of Probate. Elijah Upton,   "
Register of Deeds, Henry M. Bovey,   "
County Treasurer, Henry M. Bovey,   "
Clerk of Courts, Joseph M. Hayes,   "
Sheriff, Patrick K. Millay, Bowdoinham.
Deputy Sheriffs, Albion J. Potter, Nathan
Coombs, Geo. W. Smith, *Richmond*. Seth
H. Leonard, *Bowdoin*. Ephraim Griffin,
Topsham.

SOMERSET COUNTY.

Judge of Probate, James B. Dascomb.
Register of Probate, George A. Fletcher.
Register of Deeds, Frank B. Ward, Brighton.
County Treasurer, John M. Wood.
Clerk of Courts, Albert G. Emery.
Sheriff, Joseph F. Nye. Kendall's Mills.
Deputy Sheriffs, M. D. Ward, *Skowhegan*.
S. T. Williams, *Athens*. Max. Foster,
Canaan. H. S. Nickerson, *Pittsfield*. J.
H. Chapman, *Hartland*. Levi Leighton,
Harmony. Jonah McIntire. *Solon*. Sam-
uel Bunker, *North Anson*. J. D. Bartlett,
No. New Portland. Levi Young, *Starks*.
Josiah Tilton, *Cornville*. A. D. Murray,
The Forks.
Deputy and Jailer, Isaiah Cook, *Norridge-
wock*.

WALDO COUNTY.

Judge of Probate, Asa Thurlough, Monroe.
Register of Probate. B. P. Field, Belfast.
County Treasurer, Geo. McDonald,   "
Register of Deeds, Marshall Davis,   "
Clerk of Courts, S. L. Milliken,   "
Sheriff, Irving Calderwood, Searsport.
Deputy Sheriffs, Loring Rose, *Brooks*.
Samuel Norton. *Palermo*. John Snow,
Winterport. W. P. Sprague, *Islesboro'*.
Alfred Berry, *Unity*. Samuel Richards,
Liberty.

WASHINGTON COUNTY.

Judge of Probate, Jotham Lippincott, Co-
lumbia.
Register of Probate, Mason H. Wilder,
Machias.
Register of Deeds, James C. Adams, Ma-
chias.
County Treasurer, I. Sargent, Machias.
Clerk of Courts, Phineas H. Longfellow,
Machias.
Sheriff, Benjamin W. Farrar, Machias.
Deputy Sheriffs, Manning Dunbar, *Cherry-
field*. Harrison T. Smith, *Machias*. James
Thompson, *Eastport*. E. E. Stoddard,
Pembroke.

YORK COUNTY.

Judge of Probate, Edward E. Bourne, Ken-
nebunk.
Register of Probate, Horace H. Burbank,
Limerick.
County Treasurer, John Hall, North Ber-
wick.   "
Clerk of Courts, Hampden Fairfield, Kenne-
bunkport.
Register of Deeds, Samuel Tripp, Alfred.
Sheriff, Richard H. Godding. Alfred.
Deputy Sheriffs. Abner Mitchell, *Alfred*.
David A. Hurd, *North Berwick*. Ebenz.
F. Nealley, *South Berwick*. Chas. H. Bart-
lett, *Kittery*. Joseph G. Harmon. *Limer-
ick*. D. W. C. Merrill, *Parsonsfield*. Oba-
diah Durgin, *Saco*. Thomas Tarbox. *Bux-
ton*. James M. Nowell, *Sanford*. Frank
N. Butler, *Lebanon*. Geo. P. Thompson,
York. Jacob Thompson, *Cornish*.

JUDGES AND REGISTERS OF PROBATE, SHERIFFS, &c., IN NEW HAMPSHIRE.

BELKNAP COUNTY.

Judge of Probate, Warren Lovell, Laconia.
Register of Probate, Woodbury L. Melcher,
Laconia.
County Treas., James M. Paine.
Sheriff, Hanson Beede, Meredith.
Deputy Sheriffs, Geo. D. Savage, *Alton*.
David C. Batchelder, *Laconia*. Warren
H. Smith, *Sanbornton*. Daniel S. Beede,
Meredith.
*Deputy Sheriffs in other counties deputized
to serve in this county*, A. J. Scruton,
Farmington. J. P. Sanborn. *Franklin*.
J. L. Pickering, *Concord*. Francis B. Ber-
ry, *Pittsfield*. D. P. Prescott, *Bristol*.

CARROLL COUNTY.

Judge of Probate, Larkin D. Mason, *Tam-
worth*.
Reg. of Probate, D. G. Beede, Sandwich.
County Treas., Thomas Nute, *Ossipee*.
Sheriff, Leavitt H. Eastman, *Conway*.
Deputy Sheriffs, Hugh M. Norton, *Conway*.
John Demeritt, *Effingham*. Luther Young,
Ossipee. Gilman Moulton, *Sandwich*. Hi-
ram Paul, *Wakefield*. Samuel E. Remick,
Tamworth. Alonzo Alley, *Madison*. Geo.
W. Hersey, *Wolfborough*. J. F. Cotton,
Moultonborough.
*Deputy Sheriff in Belknap county deputized
to serve in this county*, Hanson Beede,
Meredith.

CHESHIRE COUNTY.

Judge of Probate, Silas Hardy, Keene.
Register of Probate, Allen Giffin.   "
County Treas. George W. Tilden,   "
Sheriff, George W. Holbrook,   "
Deputy Sheriffs, Lockhart Davenport, *Hins-
dale*. Ralph J. Holt, Elisha F. Lane. Isaac
Aldrich, *Keene*. Geo. Rust, *Walpole*.
Daniel A. Hawkins, *Winchester*. Henry
Fletcher, *Chesterfield*. George L. Stearns,
Fitzwilliam.
*Deputy Sheriffs in Hillsborough county dep-
utized to serve in this county*. Charles
Scott, *Peterborough*. Rufus P. Claggett,
Newport.

COOS COUNTY.

Judge of Probate, Benjamin F. Whidden,
Lancaster.
Register of Probate, John M. Whipple, Lan-
caster.
County Treas. Edwin W. Drew, Stewarts-
town.
Sheriff, Benjamin H. Corning, Northumber-
land.
Deputy Sheriffs, Enoch L. Colby, Charles F.
Colby, *Lancaster*. Lucius Hartshorn,
Stratford. Samuel M. Harvey, *Columbia*.
Albert S. Eustis, *Colebrook*.

GRAFTON COUNTY.

Judge of Probate, Nathaniel W. Westgate,
Haverhill.

Register of Probate, Luther C. Morse, Haverhill.

County Treasurer, George T. Crawford, Alexandria.

Sheriff, Grove S. Stevens, Haverhill.

Deputy Sheriffs, George Morrison, *Bath*. David P. Prescott, *Bristol*. William W. George, *Canaan*. Curtis C. Bowman, *Littleton*. Dudley L. Clark, *Plymouth*. James G. Ticknor, *Lebanon*. Ephraim B. Strong, *Orford*. J. D. Osgood, *Wentworth*.

Deputy Sheriffs in other counties deputized to serve in this county, Jonathan P. Sanborn, *Franklin*. Albert Sanborn, *Wilmot*.

HILLSBOROUGH COUNTY.

Judge of Probate, David Cross, Manchester.

Register of Probate, Cornelius V. Dearborn, Nashua.

Register of Deeds, Dana W. King, Nashua.

County Treasurer, Henry B. Atherton, Nashua.

Sheriff, Charles Scott, Peterborough.

Deputy Sheriffs, William Wetherbee, *Amherst*; Isaac W. Farmer, Daniel L. Stevens, A. Spear, A. G. Fairbanks, *Manchester*; T. K. Ames, *Peterborough*; David Pattee, *Goffstown*; John G. Dickey, *Hillsborough*; John Taylor, Paris H. Hill, *Nashua*; Moses Clark, *East Wilton*; Daniel K. Marvell, *Milford*; Alfred S. Smith, *Pelham*; John B. Perkins, *Hollis*; John K. Mills, *Mason Village*.

Deputy Sheriffs in other counties deputized to serve in this county. Jonathan L. Pickering, *Concord*; D. Warren Cogswell, *Henniker*; Sylvanus Clogston, *East Washington*; David A. Wood, *East Jaffrey*; Albert P. Davis, *Warner*.

MERRIMACK COUNTY.

Judge of Probate, Hamilton E. Perkins, Concord.

Register of Probate, Isaac A. Hill, Concord.

County Treasurer, Andrew Gault, Bow.

Sheriff, Henry L. Burnham, Dunbarton.

Deputy Sheriffs, Newton C. Everett, *Andover*; John D. Wadleigh, *Bradford*; William H. Currier, *Canterbury*; Jonathan L. Pickering, Joshua B. Merrill, Charles C. Davis, *Concord*; Albert H. Drown, *Fisherville*; Albert Little, *New London*; Francis B. Berry, Jonathan Towle, *Pittsfield*; D. Warren Cogswell, *Henniker*; George B. Hardy, *Contoocookville*; Clifton B. Hildreth, *Pembroke*; Alpheus G. How, *Boscawen*; Jonathan P. Sanborn, *Franklin*; Eli Dodge, *South Newbury*; Albert P. Davis, *Warner*; Albert Sanborn, *Wilmot*.

Deputy Sheriffs in other counties deputized to serve in this county. David C. Batchelder, *Laconia* (Belknap Co.); Richard J. Sanborn, *Deerfield* (Rockingham Co.); Carr B. Haynes, *Concord* (Merrimack Co.); Daniel L. Stevens, Isaac W. Farmer, Alfred G. Fairbanks, *Manchester* (Hillsboro' Co.); Rufus P. Claggett, *Newport* (Sullivan Co.)

ROCKINGHAM COUNTY.

Judge of Probate, William W. Stickney, Exeter.

Register of Probate, Thomas Leavitt, Exeter.

County Treasurer, George E. Lawrence, Epping.

Sheriff, Joseph P. Morse, Portsmouth.

Deputy Sheriffs, George E. Eaton, *Candia*; Isaiah A. Dustin, *Derry*; Nathaniel H. Leavitt, George M. Perkins, *Exeter*; Benjamin S. Clifford, James M. Godfrey, *Epping*; Caleb Moulton, *Hampstead*; Miles Durgin, *Northwood*; Chas. H. Joy, *Newmarket*; Geo. P. Dearborn, *Nottingham*; Amos C. Clement, *Plaistow*; Amos Kimball, *Kingston*; Ezra A. J. Sawyer, Richard J. Sanborn, *Deerfield*; John N. Brown, *Seabrook*; James M. Platts, *Londonderry*.

Deputy Sheriffs in other counties deputized to serve in this county. Isaac W. Farmer, Daniel L. Stevens, Justin Spear, *Manchester*; Alfred S. Smith, *Pelham* (Hillsborough Co.); Francis B. Berry, *Pittsfield* (Merrimack Co.); Nathaniel Wiggin, *Dover* (Strafford Co.)

STRAFFORD COUNTY.

Judge of Probate, James H. Edgerly, Rochester.

Register of Probate, Amasa Roberts, Dover.

County Treasurer, Asa A. Tufts, Dover.

Sheriff, Luther Hayes, Milton.

Deputy Sheriffs, Wm. K. A. Hoitt, Jasper G. Wallace, *Dover*; Charles Joy, *Durham*; Andrew J. Scruton, *Farmington*; Joseph Jones, *Lee*; Henry Drew, *Strafford*; Stephen S. Chick, Wm. L. Bracey, *Somersworth*; Ebenezer S. Nowell, *Rollingsford*; Jonathan Wentworth, *Rochester*.

Deputy Sheriffs in other counties deputized to serve in this county. George D. Savage, *Alton* (Belknap Co.); Hiram Paul, *Wakefield* (Carroll Co.); John W. Smart, *Newmarket*; Geo. P. Dearborn, *Nottingham*, (Rockingham Co.)

SULLIVAN COUNTY.

Judge of Probate, W. H. H. Allen, Newport.

Register of Probate, Shepherd L. Bowers, Newport.

County Treasurer, Benj. Whipple, Charlestown.

Sheriff, John P. Chellis, Meriden.

Deputy Sheriffs, Abraham D. Hull, *Charlestown*; Henry L. Hubbard, James W. Bradley, *Claremont*; Lemuel Martindale, S. Alden Tracy, *Cornish*; Martin A. Barton, *Croydon*; Rufus P. Claggett, James L. Riley, *Newport*; Sylvanus Clogston, *Washington*.

Deputy Sheriffs in other counties deputized to serve in this county. Albert Little, *New London*; Eli Dodge, *South Newbury*; John Fellows, *Andover*; James G. Ticknor, *Lebanon*; William W. George, *Canaan*; Oscar F. Beckwith, *Alstead*; John G. Dickey, *Hillsborough*; Albert P. Davis, *Warner*.

JUDGES OF PROBATE, SHERIFFS, &c., IN VERMONT.

ADDISON COUNTY.

Judges of Probate, Samuel E. Cook, Weybridge (Addison District); Harvey Munsill, Bristol (New Haven District).

Clerk of Courts, D. Stewart, Middlebury.

State's Attorney, George W. Grandey, Vergennes.

Sheriff, Isaac M. Tripp, Middlebury.

High Bailiff, Edward Gorham, Addison.

BENNINGTON COUNTY.

Judges of Probate, Thomas White, Bennington (Bennington District); E. B. Burton, Manchester (for District of Manchester).

Clerk of Courts, J. V. Hall, Bennington.

State's Attorney, Ranney Howard, Manchester.

Sheriff, Leander Powers, Bennington.

High Bailiff, James McCall, Rupert.

CALEDONIA COUNTY.
Judge of Probate, Asa L·French, St. Johnsbury.
Clerk of Courts, A. E. Rankin, St. Johnsbury.
State's Attorney, H. C. Belden, Lyndon.
Sheriff, Nathan J. Pike, St Johnsbury.
High Bailiff, Wm. L. Pearl, Sheffield.

CHITTENDEN COUNTY.
Judge of Probate, Torrey E. Wales, Burlington.
State's Attorney, Daniel Roberts, Burlington.
Clerk of Courts, Andrew J. Howard, Burlington.
Sheriff, John C. Griffin, Williston.
High Bailiff, Joseph Barton, Charlotte.

ESSEX COUNTY.
Judge of Probate, William H. Hartshorn, Guildhall.
Clerk of Courts, Charles E. Benton, Guildhall.
State's Attorney, O. F. Harvey, Concord.
Sheriff, Joseph A. Mansur, Brighton.
High Bailiff, Daniel G. May, Concord.

FRANKLIN COUNTY.
Judge of Probate, Myron W. Bailey, St. Albans.
Clerk of Courts, J. H. Brainerd, St. Albans.
State's Attorney, Willard Farrington, St. Albans.
Sheriff, J. P. Place, Highgate.
High Bailiff, Julius Halbert, Fairfax.

GRAND ISLE COUNTY.
Judge of Probate, H. W. Allen, No. Hero.
State's Attorney, John M. Haurican, North Hero.
County Clerk, S. R. Goodsell, North Hero.
Sheriff, R. L. Clark, North Hero.
High Bailiff, Luther Pixley, South Hero.

LAMOILLE COUNTY.
Judge of Probate, Christopher C. Chadwick, Johnson.
State's Attorney, Charles J. Lewis, Morristown.
Clerk of Courts, E. B. Sawyer, Hyde Park.
Sheriff, Wm. C. Doane, Johnson.
High Bailiff, James T. Parish, Stowe.

ORANGE COUNTY.
Judges of Probate, John R. Cleaveland, Brookfield (for district of Randolph);
Henry W. Bailey, Newbury (for district of Bradford.
Clerk of Courts, L. G. Hinckley, Chelsea.
State's Attorney, Sam. M. Gleason, Thetford.
Sheriff, James P. Cleveland, jr., Braintree.
High Bailiff, Charles Crocker, Brookfield.

ORLEANS COUNTY.
Judge of Probate, E. A. Stewart, Derby.
Clerk of Courts, Isaac N. Cushman, Irasburgh.
State's Attorney, J. R. Robinson, Barton,
Sheriff, James Buswell, Barton.
High Bailiff, Lucian P. Gallup, No. Troy.

RUTLAND COUNTY.
Judges of Probate, Walter C. Dunton, Rutland (Rutland district); C. M. Willard. Castleton (Fairhaven district).
Clerk of Courts, H. H. Smith, Rutland.
State's Attorney, H. G. Wood Fairhaven.
Sheriff, William M. Field, Rutland.
High Bailiff, Alonzo Hyde, Middletown.

WASHINGTON COUNTY.
Judge of Probate, T. R. Merrill, Montpelier.
Clerk of Courts, L. Newcomb, Montpelier.
State's Attorney, Melville E. Smilie, Waterbury.
Sheriff, Clark King, East Montpelier.
High Bailiff, Sidney Brown, Waterbury.

WINDHAM COUNTY.
Judges of Probate, Abisha Stoddard, Townshend (for district of Westminster); Royal Tyler, Brattleborough (for district of Marlborough).
Clerk of Courts, Royal Tyler, Brattleborough.
State's Attorney, Chas. E. Arnold, Rockingham.
Sheriff, Seth N. Herrick, Brattleborough.
High Bailiff, Chas. C. Lynde, Guilford.

WINDSOR COUNTY.
Judges of Probate, John Porter, Hartford (for district of Hartford); Wm. Rounds, Chester (for district of Windsor).
Clerk of Courts, George B. French, Woodstock.
State's Attorney, Sam. E. Pingree, Hartford.
Sheriff, W. L. Stimpson, Ludlow.
High Bailiff, Granville P. Spaulding, Chester.

CLERKS OF COURTS, SHERIFFS, &c., IN RHODE ISLAND.

BRISTOL COUNTY.
Clerk of Supreme Court, C. A. Greene, Bristol.
Clerk of Court of Common Pleas, C. A. Greene, Bristol.
Sheriff, John B. Pearce, Bristol.

KENT COUNTY.
Clerk of Courts, Samuel L. Tillinghast, East Greenwich.
Sheriff, John Holden, Old Warwick.
Deputy Sheriff, Peleg Brown, Warwick.

NEWPORT COUNTY.
Clerk of Supreme Court and Court of Common Pleas, Thomas W. Wood.
Clerk of Court of Justices, Henry N. Ward.
Sheriff, William D. Lake, Newport.
Deputy Sheriffs, P. F. Little, *Little,* Comp.; Samuel Allen, *New Shoreham;* Wm. G. Peckham, 2d, Newport.

PROVIDENCE COUNTY.
Clerk of Supreme Court, Charles Blake.
Clerk of Court of Common Pleas, Daniel R. Ballou.
Sheriff, Christopher Holden.
Deputy Sheriffs, Roger W. Potter, Alfred B. Church, Nehemiah Kimball, Phineas Fairbrother, J. A. Gardiner, Lyman Upham, Isaac W. D. Pike, Ansel Carpenter, B. A. Slocomb, George A. Atwood. F. A. Goff.

WASHINGTON COUNTY.
Clerk of Supreme Court, John G. Clarke Kingston.
Clerk of Court of Common Pleas, J. Henry Wells, Kingston.
Sheriff, Weeden H. Berry, Westerly.
Deputy Sheriffs, Edmund S. Babcock, Kingston; Joseph James, jr., Wyoming.

CLERKS OF COURTS, SHERIFFS, &c., IN CONNECTICUT.

FAIRFIELD COUNTY.

State's Attorney, Nelson L. White, Danbury.
County Treasurer, W. S. Quintard, Norwalk.
Clerk of Courts, Elisha S. Abernethy, Bridgeport.
Sheriff, Matthew Bulkley, Weston.
Deputy Sheriffs, George W. Lewis, *Bridgeport*; Alfred A. Heath, *Danbury*; S. N. Osborne, *Easton*; David Lewis, *Huntington*; Aaron Sanford, jr. *Newtown*; Harvey Fitch, *Norwalk*; Edward A. Leeds, *Stamford*; E. Sherwood, *Fairfield*; Rufus D. Cable, *Westport*.

HARTFORD COUNTY.

State's Attorney, William Hamersley, Hartford.
Clerk of Courts, Chauncey Howard, Hartford.
Assistant Clerk, C. W. Johnson, Hartford.
County Treasurer, John R. Buck, Hartford.
Sheriff, Westell Russell, Hartford.
Deputy Sheriffs, William Dibble, *Hartford*; S. V. Woodbridge, *Collinsville*; Harvey Prior, *East Windsor*; Sanford Sheffield, *South Glastenbury*; A. W. Spaulding, *New Britain*; LaFayette Parks, *Suffield*; P. G. Parsons, *West Hartford*; E. N. Phelps, *Windsor*; Charles Annis, *Manchester*.

LITCHFIELD COUNTY.

State's Attorney, Charles F. Sedgwick, Sharon.
Clerk of Courts, William L. Ransom, Litchfield.
County Treasurer, Geo. A. Hickox, Litchfield.
Sheriff, Henry A. Botsford, Litchfield.
Deputy Sheriffs, Edward O. Peck, *Litchfield*; Edwin W. Spurr, *Canaan*; C. E. Baldwin, *Cornwall*; Julius Catlin, *Harwinton*; E. M. Howland, *Kent*; Hezekiah H. Stone, *New Hartford*; Gad N. Smith, *New Milford*; Robert Vandusen, *North Cannan*; Henry Miner, Marcus DeForest, *Woodbury*; Samuel B. Horne, *Winchester*.

MIDDLESEX COUNTY.

State's Attorney, William T. Elmer, Middletown.
Clerk of Courts, Charles G. R. Vinal, Middletown.
County Treasurer, George W. Harris, Middletown.
Sheriff, John I. Hutchinson, Essex.
Deputy Sheriffs, Arba Hyde, *Middletown*; Bazaleel Shailer, *Haddam*; Alfred M.

Wright, *Clinton*; Elizur Goodrich, *Portland*; Hosford B. Niles, *East Haddam*; Ansel D. Platt, *Saybrook*; Rufus C. Shepard, *Old Saybrook*; A. S. Bugbee, *Chatham*.

NEW HAVEN COUNTY.

State's Attorney, Eleazer K. Foster, New Haven.
Clerk of Courts, Arthur D. Osborne, New Haven.
County Treasurer, Stephen D. Pardee, New Haven.
Sheriff, Gideon O. Hotchkiss, Naugatuck.
Deputy Sheriffs, Jonathan W. Pond, *New Haven*; Wm. S. Hull, *Madison*; Edwin Birdsey, John C. Byxbee, *Meriden*; David Tucker, *Seymour*; George Blakeslee, *Waterbury*; William Platt, 2d, *Milford*.

NEW LONDON COUNTY.

State's Attorney, Daniel Chadwick, Lyme.
Clerk of Courts, William L. Brewer, Norwich.
County Treasurer, Leonard Hempsted, New London.
Sheriff, Richard A. Wheeler, Stonington.
Deputy Sheriffs, D. H. Chappell, *New London*; Jared B. Fillmore, *Norwich*; Isaac Johnson, *Bozrah*; Roswell Brown, *Groton*; L. L. Huntington, *Lebanon*; R. W. Chadwick, *Lyme*; Gilbert Billings, *North Stonington*; Edward De Wolf, *Salem*.

TOLLAND COUNTY.

State's Attorney, Dwight Marcey, Tolland.
Clerk of Courts, Joseph Bishop, Tolland.
County Treasurer, Clark Holt, Vernon.
Sheriff, Amos Pease, Somers.
Deputy Sheriffs, Wm. Cummings, *Coventry*; George Paulk, *Rockville*; Lorenzo D. Winters, *Stafford*; C. B. Pomeroy, *Tolland*; Harvey R. Crane, *Hebron*; Milton H. Keeney, *Union*.

WINDHAM COUNTY.

State's Attorney, Edward L. Cundall, West Killingly.
Clerk of Courts, Uriel Fuller, Brooklyn.
County Treasurer, John Gallup, 2d, Brooklyn.
Sheriff, Prescott May, Putnam.
Deputy Sheriffs, Charles H. Osgood, *Abington*; Joseph Snow, *Killingly*; Joseph W. Cutler, *Central Village*; Roderick Davison, *Willimantic*; Jeremiah Church, *West Woodstock*; Caleb A. Bosworth, *Westford*.

DIRECTORY.--- CAUTION.

The public are cautioned against ever paying money in advance to any persons claiming to be connected with us or our publications, as our Agents never take any sum, however small, in advance.

SAMPSON, DAVENPORT, & CO., Directory Publishers,

47 CONGRESS STREET, BOSTON.

POPULATION OF MASSACHUSETTS, 1865.

Total . . . . 1,267,320.

BARNSTABLE COUNTY.

Barnstable	4,913
Brewster	1,459
Chatham	2,637
Dennis	3,512
Eastham	757
Falmouth	2,294
Harwich	3,540
Orleans	1,560
Provincetown	3,475
Sandwich	4,105
Truro	1,448
Wellfleet	2,298
Yarmouth	2,465
	34,489

BERKSHIRE COUNTY.

Adams	8,298
Alford	461
Becket	1,393
Cheshire	1,650
Clarksburg	530
Dalton	1,127
Egremont	928
Florida	1,173
Great Barrington	3,920
Hancock	967
Hinsdale	1,517
Lanesborough	1,296
Lee	4,034
Lenox	1,687
Monterey	737
Mount Washington	233
New Ashford	178
New Marlborough	1,649
Otis	962
Peru	434
Pittsfield	9,679
Richmond	913
Sandisfield	1,411
Savoy	866
Sheffield	2,461
Stockbridge	1,967
Tyringham	650
Washington	859
West Stockbridge	1,621
Williamstown	2,568
Windsor	753
	56,966

BRISTOL COUNTY.

Acushnet	1,251
Attleborough	6,200
Berkley	888
Dartmouth	3,434
Dighton	1,815
Easton	3,084
Fairhaven	2,548
Fall River	17,525
Freetown	1,484
Mansfield	2,131
New Bedford	20,863
Norton	1,709

Raynham	1,868
Rehoboth	1,834
Seekonk	929
Somerset	1,791
Swanzey	1,335
Taunton	16,005
Westport	2,802
	89,505

DUKES COUNTY.

Chilmark	547
Edgartown	1,846
Gosnold	108
Tisbury	1,699
	4,200

ESSEX COUNTY.

Amesbury	4,210
Andover	5,309
Beverly	5,944
Boxford	808
Bradford	1,567
Danvers	5,144
Essex	1,680
Georgetown	1,926
Gloucester	11,938
Groveland	1,620
Hamilton	800
Haverhill	10,660
Ipswich	3,311
Lawrence	21,788
Lynn	20,800
Lynnfield	725
Manchester	1,643
Marblehead	7,320
Methuen	2,575
Middleton	922
Nahant	312
Newbury	1,363
Newburyport	12,980
North Andover	2,622
Rockport	3,367
Rowley	1,196
Salem	21,197
Salisbury	3,609
Saugus	2,006
South Danvers	6,050
Swampscott	1,619
Topsfield	1,212
Wenham	915
West Newbury	2,088
	171,192

FRANKLIN COUNTY.

Ashfield	1,221
Bernardston	992
Buckland	1,522
Charlemont	994
Colerain	1,726
Conway	1,538
Deerfield	3,040
Erving	576

Gill	635
Greenfield	3,211
Hawley	687
Heath	642
Leverett	914
Leyden	592
Monroe	192
Montague	1,575
New Salem	1,115
Northfield	1,600
Orange	1,909
Rowe	563
Shelburne	1,563
Shutesbury	788
Sunderland	861
Warwick	903
Wendell	602
Whately	1,012
	31,342

HAMPDEN COUNTY.

Agawam	1,665
Blandford	1,087
Brimfield	1,310
Chester	1,266
Chicopee	7,581
Granville	1,363
Holland	368
Holyoke	5,648
Longmeadow	1,480
Ludlow	1,233
Monson	3,132
Montgomery	354
Palmer	3,081
Russell	619
Southwick	1,155
Springfield	22,038
Tolland	611
Wales	606
Westfield	5,634
West Springfield	2,100
Wilbraham	2,111
	64,438

HAMPSHIRE COUNTY.

Amherst	3,413
Belchertown	2,636
Chesterfield	802
Cummington	960
Easthampton	2,869
Enfield	939
Goshen	412
Granby	908
Greenwich	647
Hadley	2,246
Hatfield	1,495
Huntington	1,163
Middlefield	723
Northampton	7,927
Pelham	739
Plainfield	579
Prescott	593
South Hadley	2,029

Southampton	1,216	Canton	3,318	Clinton	4,021
Ware	8,307	Cohasset	2,048	Dana	789
Westhampton	637	Dedham	7,158	Douglas	2,157
Williamsburg	1,972	Dorchester	10,729	Dudley	2,077
Worthington	925	Dover	616	Fitchburg	8,119
		Foxborough	2,778	Gardner	2,533
	39,199	Franklin	2,510	Grafton	3,962
MIDDLESEX COUNTY.		Medfield	1,011	Hardwick	1,968
		Medway	3,223	Harvard	1,653
Acton	1,680	Milton	2,769	Holden	1,846
Ashby	1,080	Needham	2,793	Hubbardston	1,646
Ashland	1,702	Quincy	6,718	Lancaster	1,767
Bedford	820	Randolph	5,734	Leicester	2,528
Belmont	1,278	Roxbury	28,426	Leominster	3,318
Billerica	1,808	Sharon	1,394	Lunenburg	1,167
Boxborough	454	Stoughton	4,850	Mendon	1,297
Brighton	3,859	Walpole	2,018	Milford	9,162
Burlington	594	West Roxbury	6,012	Millbury	3,780
Cambridge	29,111	Weymouth	7,981	New Braintree	752
Carlisle	629	Wrentham	3,072	Northborough	1,023
Charlestown	26,398			Northbridge	2,642
Chelmsford	2,296		116,334	North Brookfield	2,514
Concord	2,231	PLYMOUTH COUNTY.		Oakham	925
Dracut	1,905			Oxford	2,713
Dunstable	533	Abington	8,576	Paxton	626
Framingham	4,681	Bridgewater	4,196	Petersham	1,386
Groton	3,176	Carver	1,039	Phillipston	729
Holliston	3,125	Duxbury	2,377	Princeton	1,238
Hopkinton	4,140	East Bridgewater	2,977	Royalston	1,441
Lexington	2,223	Halifax	739	Rutland	1,011
Lincoln	710	Hanover	1,545	Shrewsbury	1,571
Littleton	967	Hanson	1,193	Southborough	1,750
Lowell	31,004	Hingham	4,176	Southbridge	4,151
Malden	6,871	Hull	280	Spencer	3,026
Marlborough	7,200	Kingston	1,626	Sterling	1,668
Medford	4,860	Lakeville	1,110	Sturbridge	1,993
Melrose	2,866	Marion	960	Sutton	2,238
Natick	5,220	Marshfield	1,810	Templeton	2,890
Newton	8,978	Mattapoisett	1,451	Upton	2,017
North Reading	991	Middleborough	4,525	Uxbridge	2,895
Pepperell	1,709	North Bridgewater	6,335	Warren	2,205
Reading	2,436	Pembroke	1,488	Webster	3,608
Sherborn	1,049	Plymouth	6,075	Westborough	3,141
Shirley	1,217	Plympton	924	West Boylston	2,293
Somerville	9,366	Rochester	1,156	West Brookfield	1,548
South Reading	3,245	Scituate	2,269	Westminster	1,689
Stoneham	3,299	South Scituate	1,578	Winchendon	2,802
Stowe	1,537	Wareham	2,842	Worcester	30,058
Sudbury	1,703	West Bridgewater	1,625		
Tewksbury	1,801				162,923
Townsend	2,056		63,074		
Tyngsborough	624	SUFFOLK COUNTY.		RECAPITULATION.	
Waltham	6,897			*By Counties.*	
Watertown	3,779	Boston	192,324		
Wayland	1,138	Chelsea	14,403	Barnstable	34,489
West Cambridge	2,760	North Chelsea	838	Berkshire	56,066
Westford	1,508	Winthrop	634	Bristol	89,505
Weston	1,231			Dukes	4,200
Wilmington	850		208,219	Essex	171,192
Winchester	1,969			Franklin	31,642
Woburn	7,002	WORCESTER COUNTY.		Hampden	64,436
		Ashburnham	2,153	Hampshire	39,190
	220,618	Athol	2,813	Middlesex	220,618
		Auburn	959	Nantucket	4,830
NANTUCKET COUNTY.		Barre	2,856	Norfolk	116,334
Nantucket	4,830	Berlin	1,062	Plymouth	63,074
		Blackstone	4,557	Suffolk	208,219
NORFOLK COUNTY.		Bolton	1,504	Worcester	162,923
Bellingham	1,240	Boylston	792		
Braintree	3,725	Brookfield	2,100		
Brookline	5,262	Charlton	1,925		1,267,329

MASSACHUSETTS
BUSINESS DIRECTORY,

Arranged Alphabetically by Business and Towns. When the Post Office address differs from the Town, it is given immediately after the name, and preceding the Town.

(Business Directory of Boston will be given by itself; for page, see Contents.)

Accountants.
Potter Southward, 2d,   New Bedford
Webb Hiram,   "
Holmes F. A.   Taunton

Acid Manufacturers.
Wells Orson & Sons, North Adams, Adams

Adjustable Circular Saw Bench Manufacturers.
GROSVENOR J. P., Mt. Vernon St.
(see page 737)   Lowell

Advertising Agents.
Burbank & Howland, 209 Main, Worcester

Ageing Boxes.
(For Print Works.)
KILBURN, LINCOLN, & CO. (see page 756)   Fall River

Agricultural Implement Manufacturers.
Harrington S. E. (seed sowers),
    N. Amherst,
Oliver Jas. (rakes and fish spears), Amherst
Houghton D. W. (plows and cultivators),   Athol
Sibley & Young, (scythes), "   "
HEALD S. & SONS (Bullard patent hay tedders, rakes, plows, cultivators, hay cutters, corn shellers, cheese presses, &c. &c, see pages 796 and 797)   Barre
Hulbert E. S. (hoes and corn knives), Bernardston
Edwards S. F.   "
Merritt L. (rakes),   Bolton
REED FRANKLIN, (rakes, hoes, &c. see page 793),   Brookfield
Mayhew H. H. (scythe snaths), Canton
Shedd John S. (plows),   Charlemont
Belcher & Taylor Agricultural Tool Co., Chicopee Falls,   Chelmsford
Whittemore, Belcher, & Co. Chicopee Falls,   Chicopee
    "
Briggs Albert, (stub hoes and picks), Dighton
Briggs Franklin, " " " "
AMES O. & SONS (shovels, spades, &c.)   "
    North Easton, Easton
Richardson Edwin (scythes), Fitchburg
SIMONDS BROTHERS & CO. (mowing, reaping, and planing knives, see page 658),   "

Buckeye Mowing Machine Co.   Fitchburg
    West Fitchburg,   "
Whitman & Miles Manufacturing Co. (mowing and reaping machine knives, &c.), West Fitchburg,   "
Simonds S. (hand rakes),   Greenfield
Felt & Co. (plows, harrows, &c.)   "
Ames Plow Co. Groton Junction, Groton
Bingham Silas (supplies),   Hinsdale
Brown Wm. & Bro. (hay forks),   "
Bates Caleb (revolving harrows and cultivators),   Kingston
Pope F. W. (forks),   Leominster
Graves S. S. (scythe snath irons), North Leverett,   Leverett
Colson Owen D.   Mattapoisett
Eddy W. S. & Son (shovels), East Middleborough,   Middleborough
Carpenter S. P. (pruning shears), Milford
Rugg Amos (rakes),   Montague
    Monterey
Heath Francis & De Witt, (rakes),
Sheldon G. L. (rock lifters and plows), Hartsville, New Marlboro'
Bay State Hardware Co.   Northampton
Clapp Wm. R. (mowing machines), "
Clement & Hawkes Manuf. Co. (hoes), "
Lyman A. E. & Son (garden rakes), "
Johnson W. H. (horse rakes), Northboro'
    No. Bridgewater
Reynolds E. D. & O. B. (seed sowers), "
Ross A. H. (horse hoes),   Northfield
Hunt, Waite, & Flint, (plows and harrows,)   Orange
BLANCHARD A. V. & CO. (plow handles and scythes),   Palmer
King George W. (shovels),   Raynham
Claflin Alfred (rakes),   Sandisfield
Phelps Newton, "   "
Stratton T. A. "   "
Whitney E. A. "   "
Weeks & Watson,   Sharon
Crassmon William (rakes), Shutesbury
OLD COLONY IRON CO. (shovels, &c.,)   Taunton
King J. S., East Taunton,   "
PERKINS S. & CO. (plow castings, see page 729), Weir,   "
Johnson Pembroke (fan mills), Templeton
Moore Bennett E. (rock puller), Tolland
Breaknedge James L. (rakes), Tyringham
Garfield John & Son,   "
Steadman William,   "
Reed David (fan mills), West Boylston
Tucker Ebenezer (picks &c.), Weston

8

Agricultural Implements — continued.
Behee Marcus (plows), South Wilbraham, Wilbraham
Jordan John (rakes,) East Windsor, Windsor
Ames Plow Co. (all kinds), Worcester
Kniffen Mowing Machine Co. (mowing machines, horse rakes, &c.,) "
RICHARDSON A. P. & CO. (mowing machines) 9 Central, "

Agricultural Warehouses.

(*See also Country Stores.*)

Sprague L. K., Athol Depot, Athol
HIGGINS SAMUEL, Chatham
Conant P. D. Fall River
Stillwell Daniel, "
Westgate James F. "
Fairbanks J. H. Fitchburg
Baldwin Joseph, "
Wright, Woodward, & Co. "
Plummer David, Gloucester
Norton S. & Co. Great Barrington
Allen's S. Sons, Greenfield
Arms Geo. A. & Co. "
Farrington & Burditt, Holyoke
Kimball W. A. & Co. Lawrence
Mason C. R. & Co. "
Dresser & Co. Lee
Chase, Sargent, & Shattuck, Lowell
Fielding & Bartlett, "
Rogers Jacob, "
Bowers & Jenks, Milford
Bartlett & Heywood, "
Almy John E. New Bedford
SULLINGS & KINGMAN, 128 Union, "
Vincent Ambrose, "
Woodworth D. T. Newburyport
Stockwell & Spaulding, Northampton
Todd Wm. H. "
Brown Ebenezer, Palmer
Chapin Henry W. Pittsfield
Adams, Richardson & Co. Salem
Hale Henry, "
NEWELL BROTHERS, Shelburne, Falls. "
Ferre Henry, Shelburne
NEWCOMB W. L. & CO. (see page Springfield
728), Taunton
Washburn Isaac, "
Spaulding Cyrus, Webster
Lovell J. D. Worcester

Album Manufacturers.

Simonds & Co. (tintype), New Bedford

Ale, Porter, and Cider.

Sawle Resolved, Fall River
Hurley & Co. Gloucester
Winn & Parker, "
Lawrence
SMITH ROBERT H. 479 Common, "
CASEY JOHN, 475 Common, "
Corcoran James, "
RAFFERTY HUGH, 37 Broadway, (see page 741), "
Robinson John, "
Corner John, Lowell
Lennon John, "
HEALD M. C. 114 S. Common, (see page 714), Lynn
Gould & Cummings, Newburyport
Perley Renton M. (agent), "
Thayer & Dodge, Palmer
FURNALD & BROOK (champagne cider), Quincy
Carey Hugh (agent), Salem
Devine P. H. "

Mudgett Samuel A. Salem
Robinson B. F. "
WINN S. B., Front, cor. Washington, "
BROOKS F. A. (see page 778), Springfield
Tripp William C. Taunton
Taylor L. C. Waltham
Hewitt G. F. Worcester

Anchor Manufacturers:

Cape Ann Anchor Works, Gloucester
Holmes Alex. Kingston
Dean Theodore, East Taunton, Raynham

Anti-Friction Lining Metal.

DODGE L. C. 55 Dutton (see page 741), Lowell

Apothecaries.

Nash Sylvanus, Abington
Dyer N. N., South Abington, "
ESTES J. J. East " "
Davis John R. Acushnet
DUNHAM GEO. Adams
Wilkinson & Mols, "
Burlingame & Darbys, No. Adams, "
Clark & Olds, " "
Norman Edward, "
Pettis N. C. & Co. " "
Rice G. L. & Brother, " "
Merrill F. W. Amesbury
Nayson Jonathan & Son, "
Barrows & Hubbard, Amherst
Deuel C. "
Orr Samuel K. Andover
Brown John J. "
Swift Jonathan, "
Parker Geo. H. "
Dodge Davies, Arlington
Green Charles O. Ashby
Tilton & Greenwood, Ashland
Williams John H. Athol
Fay Sereno E. Athol Depot, "
Harris John S. " "
Hardin N. H. Attleboro'
Hinckley O. M. Barnstable
Jaggar S. & Co. Centreville, "
Doane Geo. W. Hyannis, "
Shattuck Henry J. Barre
Wadsworth Joseph D. "
Stearns Elijah W. Bedford
Chapin & Reynolds, Belchertown
Hartshorn Edward, Berlin
Endicott Robert R. Beverly
Prince Asa, "
Woodbury Charles, "
Smith & Tullock, Blackstone
Stockbridge Horatio, "
Bigelow W. H. Bolton
Hayward Elias, So. Braintree, Braintree
Crocker Benjamin T. Bridgewater
Leach & Harris, Brighton
WARREN G. WM. Washington st. "
Carpenter C. B. Brookfield
BIRD GEO. W. Harvard st. Brookline
CURRIER WARREN G. "
Hubbard John H. Cambridge
Contri L. G. "
Ramsey Alexander H. "
Appleton H. K. jr. E. Cambridge, "
Ham Abner, (estate), " "
Jones Mark A. " "
Nichols H. C. "
Stevens Charles E. " "
Studley & Webber, " "
Bailey A. E. North Cambridge, "
Nason James B. " "
Bayley Augustus R. Cambridgeport, "
Orne Joel S. " "

Southworth G. M.   Cambridge
Southworth G. M.   Cambridgeport, "
Weston & Co. "
Woodward James B. "
Brooks W. W.   Canton
Adams William W.   Charlestown
Bailey Kendall Jr. "
Bond Wm. L. "
Dodge Levi G. "
Downs H. P. & Co. "
Faulkner A. D. "
Gibbs W. H. "
Harris J. A. "
Holden Wm. & Co. "
Hovey William, "
Kettell Geo. P. "
Kidder Samuel & Co. "
McLeod Angus, "
Melzar Aug. P. "
Morse Wm. B. "
Sanborn J. G. "
Stacy Benjamin F. "
Stowell J. & Co. "
Toppan Nathaniel D. "
Tower Walter S. "
NEWTON & SIMMONS,   Chatham
Jenks H. H.   Cheshire
Buck John,   Chelsea
Churchill George W. "
Freeman & Ilsley, "
Martin A. C. "
Mead Geo. M. "
Sullivan John A. "
White Joseph W. "
White & Ely,   Chester
JOHNSON WM. W.   Chicopee
KENT CYRUS F. (see page 774) "
SMITH WARREN, "
Smith Warren, Col. "
Paige Edgar T., Chicopee Falls, "
Boynton L. W. & Co.   Clinton
Burditt A. A. "
Ellms Edward E.   Cohasset
Smith Horace,   Coleraine
Reynolds Joseph,   Concord
MERRILL L. & SON,   Danvers
Marsh Geo.   Dedham
Smith Henry, "
Tinker Francis, South Dedham, "
Lord William E., East Dennis,   Dennis
FRAZAR GEORGE L., Washington,
   cor. Harvard,   Dorchester
Sanborn Jeremiah, "
Noble M. E.   Hyde Park, "
Southworth A. C.   Neponset, "
Hill Aaron M., East Douglas, Douglas
Conant John A. Mrs. East Bridgewater
Fay C. R. & Co.   East Hampton
Thompson A. W. North Easton, Easton
Maberry Edwin,   Edgartown
Pierce John, "
Church James I.   Fairhaven
Richmond Horatio W. "
Everett James B.   Falmouth
Baker Chas. A.   Fall River
Bennett Wm. G. & Co. "
Brown P. S. "
Chace J. E. & Son, "
Dailey & Gibbs, "
Kreis J. A. "
Pollard D. W. "
WHITAKER J. W., Ferry, cor. Canal, "
Cheate John,   Fitchburg
Greene Henry G. & Co. "
Lane James B. "
Macurda W. A. & Co. "
Phelps Eli "
THOMSON W. A.   Foxborough
Howe Willard, South Framingham, Framingham

Goodnow H. J., Saxonville, Framingham
Nolen William B.   Franklin
Peabody John W.   Freetown
Conant Francis,   Gardner
Emerson J. "
Bateman Lewis H.   Georgetown
Dorman William B. "
Price Augustus L.   Gloucester
Ware Wm. H. "
Wetherell Monson L. "
Hale C. A.   Grafton
White David, "
Morgan & Pixley, Great Barrington
Whiting Frederick T. "
Hovey Daniel,   Greenfield
Hovey George H. "
HOWLAND & LOWELL, "
Gerrish Charles,   Groton
Brock J. C. Groton Junction, "
Atwood Moses P.   Groveland
Porter Wm. P.   Hadley
Wilder Isaac M.   Hanover
Dodge Franklin,   Harwich
Mansell Geo. N. "
Emerson & Howe,   Haverhill
Frothingham & Howe, "
Kimball Geo. A. "
Priest M L. (bot), "
Fearing Wm. 2d,   Hingham
Hunt J. L. "
Andrews T. E.   Holliston
Bassett A. G.   Holyoke
Browning Bros. "
Goodall & Fitch, "
Morrill J. E. "
O'Connor J. J. "
Woodbury J. A.   Hopkinton
Manson S. F.   Hudson
Safford W. Augustus, "
Everett W. S.   Hyde Park
Geyer Andrew,   Ipswich
Thompson & Stevens, Lancaster
Brigham W. C.   Lawrence
Clarke Charles, "
Chickering Geo. E. "
Gilpatrick J. F. "
Graves F. E. "
Ordway Aaron, "
Sargent G. W. "
Talbot Geo. F. "
Whitney Henry M. "
Wood James E. "
Callender Brothers, "
Pease Francis M.   Lee
Brown P. R. "
Fuller & Jacobs,   Lenox
Wheelock & Whittier, Leominster
Babcock A. G. "
Allen H. W.   Lexington
Bailey F. & D.   Lowell
Butler F. H. & Co. "
Carleton & Hovey, "
Dows Amos W. "
Duncan Wm. H. "
French Wm. H. "
Gordon L. M. "
Hayes Joseph R. "
Hoyt Eli W., "
Kimball Chas. R. "
Lane Louisa C. "
Leighton W. H. "
PLUNKETT JOSEPH, Dutton, cor.
   Lowell, "
Thompson M. E. "
Brown Charles W.   Lynn
Bulfinch Jeremiah, "
Hodges Chauncy A. "
Holder & Co. "
Ladd William M. "

116 MASSACHUSETTS DIRECTORY.

Apothecaries — continued.

Murray James W.	Lynn
Proctor Benjamin,	"
Snow & Messinger,	"
Tapley Warren,	"
Woods S. H.	"
Cox Wm. W. N.	Malden
Josselyn C. B.	"
Lee & Co.	"
Lee Andrew,	Manchester
Borden C. T.	Mansfield
Goodwin William, 5th,	Marblehead
Graves Franklin,	"
Burdett William R.	Marlborough
Hunter Clifton D.	"
Marshall Frank A.	"
Sparrow William E.	Mattapoisett
Hooper Brothers,	Medford
Tufts James W.	"
Tourtelotte J. N. West Medway,	Medway
Larrabee John,	Melrose
Hartis Samuel H. jr.	Methuen
Shaw J. B. & J.	Middleborough
Bailey T. B.	"
Parker W. M.	Milford
Morgan H. E.	"
Wilson L. J.	"
Sears N. H.	"
Nye F. W. K.	Millbury
Mitchell Edward,	Milton
Jaggar Charles H.	Nantucket
Cummings F. E.	"
Daniels S. O.	Natick
Howe Elbridge,	"
	New Bedford
BLAKE JAMES E. 64 No. Second,	"
Bunker Elihu,	"
CADWELL WM. P. S. 49 Purchase,	"
Chisholm E. H.	"
Church C. M.	"
Clark Walter G.	"
Cornish A.	"
Holmes E. & Co.	"
Lawton C. H.	"
Otis Thomas,	"
Pease W. A.	"
Spencer C. L.	"
Thornton Elisha, jr.	"
WINSLOW EDWARD D. 105 S. Water,	"
Caldwell W. W.	Newburyport
Dickens Job T. (ecl.)	"
Hodge Charles M.	"
Nolcini C. A.	"
Smith Saml. A.	"
Noble John J., Newton Centre,	Newton
Billings E. T., Newton Corner,	"
Lowe C. H.	"
Snow I. H. West Newton,	"
WEBSTER J. F., Newton Upper Falls,	"
Perkins G. T. Newton Lower Falls,	"
Clark & Parsons,	Northampton
Edwards Oscar,	"
Kingsley Charles D.	"
Parsons Sidney C.	"
Low C. H.	North Andover
Bixby C. C.	North Bridgewater
Cobb Tyler,	"
Goldthwaite E.	"
Whipple J. J. & Co.	"
DeLand B. K.	North Brookfield
Andrews Robert,	Orange
Barton Edward,	"
Kenrick Alexander, East Orleans,	Orleans
Rawson Charles,	Oxford
Holbrook William,	Palmer
WOOD & ALLEN (see page 774),	"
Grosvenor D. P. jr.	Peabody
Meacom Geo. E.	"

Sweetser Thos. A.	Peabody
Brewster & Rice,	Pittsfield
Manning Mary S.	"
Spalding W. A.	"
WHELDEN CHARLES M. & CO., 65 North,	"
Hall John T.	Plymouth
Hubbard Benjamin,	"
Warren Winslow,	"
Wood Geo. F.	"
Baxter J. B.	Provincetown
Crocker J. M.	"
Hopkins Joshua F.	"
Hough Henry C.	"
Newton Horatio G.	"
Paine S. A.	"
Stone Jeremiah,	"
Hayden E. Mrs.	Quincy
Johnson Cotton C.	"
Pattee William S.	"
Veazie John H.	"
Allen E. A. (botanic),	Randolph
PORTER F.	"
Willis Wm. H.	Reading
Blatchford Eben,	Rockport
Barton Gardner,	Salem
Brooks William A.	"
Chamberlain Joseph W.	"
Emerton James,	"
Farrington George P.	"
Farrington Geo. P. jr.	"
Nichols Thos. B.	"
Pinkham C. H.	"
Pratt Henry J. & Co.	"
Price C. H. & J.	"
Webb William, jr.	"
Bartlett D. L. Amesbury,	Salisbury
HALL CHARLES B.	Sandwich
Bidwell M. S.	Sheffield
Baker Edwin, Shelburne Falls,	Shelburne
Taylor A. H.	"
Root M. N. & Co.	Somerville
Weston William H.	"
Judd A. G.	Southampton
Hartwell George H.	Southbridge
Keith Wm. J. Globe Village,	"
Sanderson Wm. T., So. Hadley Falls,	South Hadley
Sumner L. F.	Spencer
ALDEN & BREWSTER,	Springfield
Bigelow E.	"
Brewer H. & J.	"
BURDETT C. C. & CO.	"
Dickinson F. S.	"
Hooker John,	"
Merritt & Hall,	"
Stebbins E. C.	"
Webber J. T.	"
Stevens D. Indian Orchard,	"
Clarke W. B.	Stockbridge
Durkee T. G.	Stoneham
Goodrich Horace,	"
Wilkins H. E.	Stoughton
Porter Jacob P.	Swampscott
Barker A. J.	Taunton
Dunbar Samuel O. & Son,	"
Mitchell D. L.	"
Monroe Charles E.	"
Whitney & Forbush,	"
Willard A. L.	"
Woodward W. P.	"
Brown Moses, West Tisbury,	Tisbury
Leach William, Holmes's Hole,	"
Paine Samuel C.	Truro
Ward George W.	Upton
Mellor Godfrey K.	Uxbridge
Boardman E. E.	Wakefield
Mansfield J. D.	"
Emmons S. B.	Waltham

Hall Henry C.   Waltham
LEWIS JARVIS,   "
Rogers George H.   "
MINER D. W.   Ware
Pepper J. H. & Co.   "
Sawyer Frederick A.   Wareham
Blair & Keys,   Warren
Harwood Lucian,   "
Page Charles F.   Watertown
Sullivan J. Albert,   "
Bigelow Elisha M.   "
Dresser Horace M.   Webster
Paine Amasa E.   "
Johnson Benj. F.   Wellfleet
Henry S. G. & Co.   Wenham
Flagg John O.   Westborough
Baker & Williams,   West Boylston
Andrews J.   West Bridgewater
Colton John W.   Westfield
Holland Henry,   "
Eames & Giles,   Westminster
     West Roxbury
Barrett George N., Jamaica Plain,   "
Howard John C.   "
Boynton Henry B.   West Stockbridge
Moore James S.   "
White Amos S. & Co.   Weymouth
Brown L. T.   S. Weymouth,
Smith Nathan F.   Williamstown
Harris Brothers,   Winchendon
Skinner O. E. & Co.   "
Brown George P.   Winchester
Grosvenor J. M. & Co.   Woburn
Trull Elbridge,   "
Bush & Co.   Worcester
Buffington E. D.   "
Dinsmore Silas,   "
Fairbanks & Piper,   "
Green James & Co.   "
Green M. B. & Co.   "
Howland A. H. & Co. (hom. med.),   "
McConville M. S.   "
Scott David & Co.   "
Scott Nelson R.   "
Sibley, Ward, & Co.   "
Spaulding R.   "
Spurr George R.   "
Wetherbee E. D.   "
Warren E A.   "
Williams Aug.   "
Hale John,   Yarmouth Port, Yarmouth

Apple-Paring Machines.

Monroe Brothers,   "
Lockey J. H. & Co. (turn-table   Fitchburg
   apple-parers),   Leominster
Whittemore D. H.   Worcester

Architects.

Webber J. H.   Cambridgeport
Brown Josiah,   Fall River
Francis Henry M.   Fitchburg
CORSON H. W. (see page 753),   Franklin
WATSON D. S.   Gloucester
Newhall Wilbur F.   Lynn
Eaton Solomon K.   Mattapoisett
PINKHAM R. G.   Medford
Fales Lewis,   Milford
Hammond Caleb,   New Bedford
Eaton Solomon K.   "
Bailey John & Son,   Newburyport
Coffin Frederick J.   "
SARGENT RUFUS (see page 751),   "
Pratt Wm. F.   Northampton
Gardner E. C.   Florence,   "
Rathbun Charles T.   Pittsfield

Weissbein L.   Pittsfield
LORD & FULLER, 243½ Essex,
   (see page 747),   Salem
Foster J. C.   "
CHAPIN A. L.   Springfield
Washburn Jason,   "
Green George,   Westfield
Phelps Enoch, jr.   "
Towne & Dickinson,   "
Boyden E. & Son,   Worcester
Cutting A. P.,   "
Earle Stephen C.   "
Earle & Fuller,   "

Artesian Wells.

Fuller Waldo,   Kingston

Artificial Limb Manufs.

Salem Leg Co.   Salem
Douglass D. DeForrest,   Springfield

Artists.

Dunning Robert S.   Fall River
Grouard John E.   "
Gay William A.   Hingham
Hudson Wm. jr.   "
Sheldon J.   Lynn
Wilson A.   Malden
Gifford Charles H.   New Bedford
Cole Lyman E.   Newburyport
Hotchkiss W.   Northampton
Upham O. W. H.   Salem
Greeley J. A.   Amesbury, Salisbury
Gladwin George E.   Worcester
Greene C. G.   "
Willard W.   "

Auctioneers.

Cook Joshua,   Abington
Whitmarsh A.   "
Gilson Lorenzo C.   E. Abington,   "
Whitmarsh John F. E., N.   "   "
Hobart E. A.   S.   "
Blodgett Jonas,   Acton
Fuller Alden,   West Acton,   "
Hutchinson C. E.   Amherst
Whitney S. W.   "
Foster George,   Andover
Poland Benjamin,   Arlington
Wetherbee Marshall,   Ashburnham
Cummings J. L.   "
Wright F. W.   Ashby
Morse Ezra,   Ashland
Brown Jesse,   Athol
Lewis E. T.   "
Stratton A. G.   Athol Depot.   "
STARKEY, L. T. (see page 713) Attleboro'
Bearse Charles C., Cotuitport, Barnstable
Crosby Gorham,   Centreville,   "
Phinney Nelson,   "   "
Fassett Theo. F.   Hyannis,   "
Babbitt P. H.   Barre
Norcott Jarvis,   Becket
Lane Wm. A.   Bedford
Longley S. W.   Belchertown
Owen W. C.   "
Metcalf Savel,   Bellingham
PORTER SAMUEL,   Beverly
Bartholmn S. H., N. Blandford, Blandford
Barnes Benjamin S.   Boxford
Kendall Horace, Boylston Centre, Boylston
Pearl Horatio,   Bradford
Farnsworth Jonas,   Braintree
Potter Edward,   "

Auctioneers — continued.

Thayer E. F. E.	
Vinton Thomas P.	Braintree
French Jonathan,	S. Braintree, "
Frasier J. R.	" "
Swift Van R.	Bridgewater
Howe A. & G. H.	Brighton
Forbes George,	E. Brookfield, Brookfield
Ward Samuel,	Buckland
Winn William,	Burlington
Knights S. R.,	Cambridgeport, Cambridge
Monroe W. A.	E. Cambridge, "
Leavitt Joseph,	"
Ransom Benjamin,	Canton
Mahew Charles B.	North Carver, Carver
Carter A. J.	Charlemont
Chamberlin Lowell W.	Charlestown
Cooper G. D.	"
Dix & Simonds,	"
Hart Joseph S.	"
Robinson T. S. G.	"
Jones Joseph D.	"
Rogers Warren,	Chatham
Harding Isaiah,	"
Mullows Seth N.	"
Smith Charles H.	"
MERRIAM OTIS, 5 Gerrish block,	
Broadway (see page 714)	Chelsea
SAUNDERS & LOGAN, 67 Park,	"
(see page 712),	"
Wyeth Joseph,	"
Ingals H. J.	
Knox C. W.	Cheshire
Gove S. P.	Chester
Lothrop J. Q. A.	Cohasset
Moody & Day,	
McGee T. R.	Clinton
Staples Samuel,	Coleraine
Rhoades Aransford,	Concord
Barker Wm. jr., N. Dartmouth,	Cummington
Trefrey James,	East Dedham, Dartmouth
Ellis Jason, jr.	West " Dedham
Mansfield Allen B.,	S. Deerfield, Deerfield
Anderson William,	"
Howes James S.	East Dennis, Dennis
Sears Nathan,	" "
Nickerson Coleman,	West Dennis, "
Small Alvan,	" "
Lewis John A.	
Capen Aaron,	Dighton
Vose Robert, jr.	Milton, Dorchester
Brown A. F.	"
Tisdale William & J. P.	Douglas
Alden Benjamin,	Dover
Swift J. W.	Duxbury
Wadsworth Henry,	"
Alden S. G.	"
Clapp Lewis,	East Bridgewater
Knowles E. E.	East Hampton
Shute Charles H. & Son,	Eastham
Rowley James H., S. Egremont,	Edgartown
Potter Henry M.	Egremont
Story Norman,	Enfield
Stoddard Alden D.	Essex
GREENE & SON, 12 Pleasant,	Fairhaven
Gunn H. N. & Co.	Fall River
Bearse Crocker H.	"
Wood Richard S.	Falmouth
Eager William L. & Co.	"
McIntire David F.	Fitchburg
Clark John,	
Bateman L. H.	Framingham
Purple Roswell,	Georgetown
Lloyd John,	Gill
King A. D., Granville Corners,	Gloucester
Haskell L. W. P., East Granville,	Granville
Holmes Harvey,	"
Guinin William,	Great Barrington
	Greenfield

Ross H. P. Groton Junction,	Groton
Robbins Andrew,	"
Howe B. L.	"
Hopkinson Charles W.	Groveland
Wales James L. Jr.	"
Kellogg C. A.	Hadley
Inglee Edwin,	Halifax
Whiting Gilman C.	Hanover
Cox William,	Hanson
Gurney E. B. K.,	So. Hanson, "
Paige Frazier,	Hardwick
Farnsworth A. J.	Harvard
Puffer Josiah,	"
Brooks Obed,	Harwich
Cahoon Cyrus,	"
Nickerson Zenas,	"
Steele Danforth S.	"
Mayo Elisha, West Harwich,	"
Warner James W.	Hatfield
Bartlett J. C.	Haverhill
DAVIS PHINEAS E.	"
Marsh Geo. E.	"
Seymour C. W.	Hingham
Tuttle John M.	Hinsdale
Abbott Cheney,	Holden
Phipps Amos,	Holliston
Pond George N.	
Burnham P. H.	Holyoke
Quint Nathaniel W.	
Whittemore J.	Hopkinton
Hallock Isaac,	Hubbardston
Pope Abel H.	Hudson
Rawson & Sawyer,	
Baker Stephen,	Ipswich
Randall Theodore,	
Sampson Azel H.	Kingston
Bugbee A. V.	Lawrence
Howe M. N.	"
Jewett F. S. & Co.	"
Pedrick & Closson,	"
Rooney M. T.	"
Stanchfield Benj'n S.	"
Barnes John S.	Lee
Couch Charles M.	"
Whittemore Otis,	Leicester
Sears Samuel H.	Lenox
Shepardson L. S.	"
Brown Hamilton,	Leominster
Robinson J. D.	"
Damon I. N.	Lexington
Pierce P. P.	"
Kimball William,	Littleton
Warren J. D.	"
Abbott Joel A.	Lowell
Balch J. D. & Co.	"
PATCH E. B. & CO. 1 and 2 Coml. sq. "
Smith Eli M.	Ludlow
Mansfield Jonathan,	Lynn
Patten Wm. A.	"
Hill Benj. J.	Malden
Brown Wm. B.	Marblehead
Conway John jr.	"
Lovell Austin,	Marion
Ames Edward,	Marshfield
Baker John,	"
Ford John,	"
Bowles R. W.	Mattapoisett
Carr J. P.	"
Hamant Charles,	Medfield
White John T.	Medford
Johnson Abner, jr. E. Medway,	Medway
Low John,	Methuen
Alden Milton,	Middleboro'
Batchelder Francis E.	Middleton
Hixon Alfred,	Milford
Ryan William,	Millbury
Beck Gideon.	Milton
Bradley John D.	"

Newton George H. Monson
Cheeery Isaac, Montague
Thomas Lyman, Monterey
MYRICK ANDREW M. Nantucket
Liddell Timothy W. "
Burks A. W. Natick
Chamberlain W. "
Perry E. South Natick, "
Eaton George E. "
Jennings George. Wellesley, "
Baylies J. B. New Bedford
BOURNE GEO. A. 27 No. Water, "
Wady John G. "
Waterman N. "
White Jonathan P. & Co. "
Collins Stephen, Newburyport
Greenleaf George, "
Greenleaf Rufus L. "
Smith Edmund, '
- New Marlboro'
Underwood H. S. Hartsville, "
Kasson Wm. C. Southfield, "
Guild N. H. New Salem
Longley H. A. Northampton
Parsons E. "
Allen & Carlton, North Andover
Clapp B. R. North Bridgewater
Gifford H. A. "
Tinkham O. G. "
Thompson Hiram, North Brookfield
Harrington Jonathan, North Chelsea
Alexander Elisha, Northfield
Austin Henry P. Oakham
Murdock Ephraim, Orange
Woodward Hiram, "
Higgins Abner, Orleans
Chafee Orrin W. Oxford
Murdock A. R. Palmer
Harrington Silas D. Paxton
Trask Thomas, Peabody
Oldham John 2d, Pembroke
Boynton Alfred, Pepperell
Winn Abel B. "
Gay George, Pittsfield
Hall Timothy, "
Campbell Leonard, Plainfield
Holmes B. H. Plymouth
Peirce Clisson, North Prescott, Prescott
Goodnow William B. Princeton
BOWLY J. E. & G. Provincetown
Adams Ebenezer, Quincy
Faxen Henry H. "
French Joseph T. "
Roel E. M. Randolph
Wilbur Seth D. Raynham
Temple William H. Reading
Goff Enoch, Rehoboth
Horton D. G. "
Rowley J. S. Richmond
Ruggles James, Rochester
Smith Benjamin H. Rowley
Todd J. Scott, "
ARCHER WILLIAM, 34 Front and
18 Washington, Salem
Colman Benjamin, "
Fifield Benjamin E., Amesbury, Salisbury
Langdon W. W. Montville, Sandisfield
HALL CHARLES B. Sandwich
Prouty Caleb W. Scituate
Vinal Thomas, North Scituate, "
Foze Ebenezer T., South " "
Field Joel H. Sheffield
Gordon Harvey, "
Shelburne
Bardwell Jarvis B., Shelburne Falls, "
Hapgood Joab, Shrewsbury
Rufinton Edmund, Somerset
Hood William P. "

Newton Curtis, Southborough
Clemence Daniel D. Southbridge
South Hadley
Kellogg John E., S. Hadley Falls, "
Fogg Ebenezer T. South Scituate
Lee Lathrop, Southwick
Boyden John, Spencer
Eldredge J. & Co. Springfield
Beach T. D. "
Priest L. W. "
Rice Levi, Sterling
Dean Silas, Stoneham
Hunt J. S. Sudbury
Hoard N. S. & Brother, "
Moore Webster, "
Richardson B. H. South Sudbury, "
Hastings George, Sutton
Babbitt Geo. H. jr. Taunton
King William, "
Seekell John & Son, "
Tamplin T J. Baldwinville, Templeton
Goldsmith J. G., Otter River, "
Smith David, Holmes's Hole, Tisbury
Hood S. D. Topsfield
Lewis B. F. Townsend
Leseur Harvey, Upton
Barton A. Uxbridge
Morse Nahum, "
Fisk L. A. Wales
Tisdale Brothers, Walpole
Fiske Eben W. Waltham
Phelps Samuel H. Ware
HITCHCOCK C. S. Warren
Shumway Solomon, Webster
Wiley F. A. Wellfleet
Plummer Samuel T. Wenham
Newton Daniel F. Westboro'
Hildreth John H. West Boylston
Cutting John S. Oakdale, "
Smith George J. "
Smith A. W. West Brookfield
Mosley George H. Westfield
Morand Frederick, "
Rand Asa P. "
Gifford George H. Westport
West Roxbury
Bartlett Alden, Jamaica Plain, "
Duell James, West Stockbridge
Curtis Samuel, Weymouth
Richard S. Elias, "
Rogers Charles, South Weymouth, "
White Samuel B. 2d, Whately
Bliss Luther B. Wilbraham
Spellman W. P. South Wilbraham, "
Prince J. H. Winchester
Hovey Josiah, Woburn
Abbott B. W. Worcester
LAMSON & GLAZIER, 68 Main, "
Parker A. M. "
Putnam Brothers, "
Brewster Elisha H. Worthington
Ely Nathan, Wrentham
Yarmouth
Drew Theodore, West Yarmouth, "
Thacher Charles, Yarmouth Port, "

Auger, Bit, and Gimlet Makers.

Harlow C. C. Bridgewater
MILLER'S FALLS MANUF. CO.
(bit, brace, wrenches, and drill
chucks, see page 721), Greenfield
Drew C. & Co. (calking tools), Kingston
Moody H. T. (bung borers), Newburyport
Shepardson H. S. & Co., Shelburne
Falls, Shelburne
SNELL MANUF. CO. (see page
763), Fiskdale, Sturbridge

Awl Manufacturers.

(See also Boot and Shoe Tools.)

REED FRANKLIN. (brad and peg-
  ging, see page 788),
King William,   Canton
Foster & Whitten,   N. Easton,   Easton
Fulton Robert, (pegging),   Lynn
BUCK BROTHERS, (scratch awls,   Mansfield
  see page 761),   Millbury
            New England Village
PACKARD SUMNER, (machine peg-
  ging, see page 762),   "
                               Medway
FENN & DANIELS, West Medway,   "
Faxon William,   No. Bridgewater
Kingman L. A.   "
O'NEILL WM. H. (pegging and ma-
  chine, see page 769),   "
PACKARD J. W. (pegging and ma-
  chine, see page 769),   "
Woodward James F. & Co.   Wakefield

Axe Helve Manufacturers.

(See Handles.)]

Axe Manufacturers.

(See Edge Tools.)

Axletree Manufacturers.

LAZELL, PERKINS, & CO. Bridgewater
KINSLEY IRON & MACHINE CO.
  (see page 730),   Canton
DALZELL DAVID & SONS, (see
  page 799), South Egremont, Egremont
HALE PATENT WASHER CO.,
  Chas. H. Gifford, Treas., 82 Elm,
  (see page 759),   New Bedford
Linden Iron & Steel Manuf. Co, Walpole

Babbitt's Metal.

WILDER CHARLES, agent, 40
  Union (see page 783),   Worcester

Bacon Works.

                        Cambridge
Teele, Howe, & Co., Cambridgeport,   "
Thurlow B. F.   Newburyport

Bags and Bagging.

Dean George H.   Ludlow

Bait.

(Clam and Porgie.)

DODD A. W. & CO., Dodd's wharf,
  (see page 731),   Gloucester

Bait and Fruit Mills.

Richardson Mill Co., D. W. Low,
  agent,
Howard Waters,   Gloucester
                           Hingham

Bakers.

Brokey James,   North Adams,
Wilbur Jeremiah & Son,   "   Adams
Biddle Brothers,
DUTTON W. P.   Amesbury
Wood & Sawyer,   Arlington
Stickney George W.   Athol
Durrach James,   Beverly
White Brothers,   Brookline
Wright William,   Cambridge
                              "

Doyle M. J.   Cambridge
Gardner J. W.   East Cambridge, "
Gould William,   "   "
Stratton C. M.   "   "
Ball Joseph G.   Cambridgeport, "
Barbey J. A.   "
Fyfe Wm. E.   "
Foster Charles,   "
Kennedy Frank A.   "
Newmarch Joseph,   "
Thurston, Hall, & Co. "   "
Staples C. M. & J. N.   Canton
Bean D. L. & J. C.   Charlestown
Bemis Orlando,   "
Berry C.   "
Boardman Joseph L.   "
Davis William,   "
Downer & Sanderson,   "
Gilmore Orrin,   "
Goodrich Charles B. (crackers), ..
Knights & Co.   "
Lang John P.   "
Lewis S. W.   "
Moody Benjamin,   "
O'Flanagan David,   "
Parker Thomas,   "
Pendergast George S.
Stetson Emri B.   "
Willard J. H.   "
Austin C. F. & Co. (ship &c.),   Chelsea
Bassett Edward,   "
Beckert & Stoddard,   "
Moran P. & M.   "
Wakefield Horace,   "
Wedge Warren C.   Chicopee
Plaisted, Gardner, & Hunt,   Clinton
O'Leary S.   Dedham
Macomber Stearns, East Dedham, "
Waldron Francis, North Dighton, Dighton
Shephard James,   Dorchester
RUSSELL THOMAS,   Mattapan,   "
Walker William,   "
Buttrick J. T. (ship),   Fairhaven
Boutelle & Cushing,   Fall River
Barnaby & Gregory,   "
Christmas & Corcoran,   "
Fisher Mason & Co.   "
Pride William M.   Fitchburg
Green H. D. & Co.   "
Grier George,   Gloucester
Parsons Isaac W.   "
                          Great Barrington
MILLER BROS. (crackers, see p. 718) "
Savage George G.   "
Jones & Guillow,   Greenfield
Stevens T. K.   Groton Centre, Groton
Boynton & Brown (crackers), "   "
Downes John,   Haverhill
Pearson Bros.   z   "
Pearson H. C. & Co.   "
PERKINS WILLIAM, Winter st.   "
Hunt George,   Hingham
Wedge & Ward,   Holyoke
Lord Daniel P.   Hudson
Goodnow J. W.   Hyde Park
Estes James,   Ipswich
White William,   "
Sproul Frank,   Kingston
Kent J. P.   Lawrence
Gould W. E. & Co.   "
Sims & Malloy,   "
Wilson Allen,   "
Mitchell S. G.   "
Houghton & Burt   Lee
Bradt G. J. & D.   Leominster
Cornock James Mrs.   Lowell
Jeffries & Simpson,   "
Morris Martin,   "

Scripture Stephen A. Lowell
Somes William E. "
Breed Allen B. "
Crawford George P. Lynn
Dustin B. Clement, "
Holder Nathaniel; "
Peckham Alexander, "
Randloph Brewer F. "
Heercloss·Wm. & Co. Malden
Bailey George E. Mansfield
Allen Ambrose, Marblehead
Boardman Thomas, "
Dennis Benjamin. "
Lindsey Nathaniel B. "
Balch Albert B. Medfield
KIPPENBERGER & ROHDE, Medford
WITHINGTON &·Co., Salem st.
Hastings & Matthewson, Milford
Adams Samuel, Milton
Chase & Cook, Nantucket
Bartlett Oliver, Natick
New Bedford
FISHER·HENRY H. 134 Purchase, "
(fancy bread & cake, see page 730) "
Libby John & Co. "
Richmond Saml. P. "
Smith Horatio (ship), "
Snell D. A. (ship), "
Watson Samuel & Son (ship), "
Cole Benjamin W. Newburyport
Austin Geo. W. "
Butler J. W. & T. (ship bread), "
Greenleaf D. D. "
Pearson John, Jr. "
Bain Wm. Newton Corner, Newton
Carr Smith, Northampton
Hunt & Wilder. North Bridgewater
Washburn & Grover, "
Pratt Leonard Peabody
Roberts M. H. "
Stimpson Thos. "
Andier Fred. Pittsfield
PHELPS & CROSSMAN, 43 North, "
Teeling E. (cracker) "
Whiting George A. & Co. Plymouth
Terry John C. Plympton
Dill Nathaniel H. Provincetown
Hodges Wm. A. Quincy
Knowlton Eben, Rockport
Allen & Symonds, Salem
Eaton N. J. "
Frye Geo. H. "
Gardner Simon, "
Hathaway E. "
Hathaway John, "
Jelly Charles H. "
Pease & Price, "
Preston John, "
Stowe V. C. "
Thompson George J. "
Tibbetts A. J. "
Turell Benj. F. & Co. "
Watts Charles, "
Barbey J. Somerville
Shedd T. A. "
Olney M. K. Southbridge
Bond Albert, South Reading
Carr J. S. & Co. Springfield
Leibsitz & Lane, "
Lyman Harvey, "
McNALLY J. R. 254 Main, "
Towne E. H. "
Brown Andrew, Stoneham
Hatch Benj. C. Taunton
Lane Elias· N. "
Ormsby R. H. Myricks,
Marcy Leonard, Holmes's Hole, Tisbury
Levermore J. D. Waltham

Munster J. & A. Waltham
BYRNS JEREMIAH (see page 771), Ware
Bright C. H. Watertown
Flint John, Jr. Webster
Hall Wm. Wenham
Trowbridge J. A. Westborough
Pittsinger John A. Westfield
Whitney Harrison G. Westminster
West Roxbury
Goodnow Joseph W. Jamaica Plain, "
Howe A. S., South Weymouth, Weymouth
Carter & Converse, Woburn
Goddard John, Wash. sq. Worcester
Eddy Levi, 86 Southbridge, "
Plaisted Brothers, 115 Main, "
Stearns C. A. 88 Pleasant, "

Ball Manufacturers.

Harwood H. & Sons, Natick
Manning J. K. "

Band Sawing Machine.

ROLLSTONE MACHINE WORKS,
(see page 789), Fitchburg

Banding and Cordage.

CLARK JEREMIAH, 96 Middle,
(see page 738), Lowell

Banks.

(In Miscellaneous Department ; see Index.)

Bankers.

EASTON & MILNE, 14·No. Main, Fall River
Fletcher & Norton, Westfield

Bark Mills.

Frye Joseph S. Salem

Barrel Dealers.

SISSON OTIS A. 20 Middle, New Bedford

Barrel Head Manuf.

HARLOW I. H. & CO. (see page
768), Middleboro'

Barrel Manufacturers.

(See also Coopers.)
Coffin William S. Newburyport

Basket Manufacturers.

Ashburnham
Pratt John M., Ashburnham Depot, "
Higgins & Sibley, No. Blandford, Blandford
Williams T. A. & Co. Greenfield
Lincoln Jacob, Hingham
TOWER E. C. & BROTHER (see
page 705), Hinsdale
Leominster
Maynard Edmund, North Leominster. "
Kelley F. P. Lynn
Blake J. A. Mansfield
Corey Charles, "
Fisher Daniel, "
Hodges J. L. & I. G. "
Hodges V. B. "
Paine J. E. "
Folger Rowland, Nantucket
WILLIAMS MANUFACTURING CO.
(see page 772). Northampton
Brooks R. J. jr. & Brothers, Rutland
Pierce C. & A. J., West Rutland, "
Neis Martin, Swampscott
Brigham Edmund F. West Boylston
Goodell Norman H. "

Basket Makers — continued.

Pierce Ezra B.   West Boylston
Pierce J. Edward,   "
Burton Epraim (farm),   Worthington
Tower H. E. (factory),   "
Higgins Lyman, South Worthington,   "

Bed Comforter Manufacturer.

Fiske William,   Lowell

Bed Springs Manufacturers.

Cooke Henry A.   Charlestown
Crane J. H.   "

Bedstead Manufacturers.

(See also Furniture Manufacturers.)

Tucker Manufacturing Co. (iron),
   Cambridgeport,   Cambridge
Fay Wm.   Chester
Wright F. G. (cribs),   "
Elder H. S.   Cummington
Bingham Silas (cribs),   Hinsdale
Parish Elisha H.   "
Lee Charles,   Manchester
Glentz T. R. & Co.   Pittsfield
Marshall A. & Son;   Tolland
    Worthington
Bartlett & Jones, W. Worthington,   "

Beer Fauçet Manuf. (patent).

HARTLEY GEO. R., 20 Washington,   Taunton

Beer Manufacturers.

(See also Brewers.)

Fowler Samuel,   Chelsea
Richardson Israel,   "
Allen G. S. & Co.   Fall River
Kay James,   "
Sowle Resolved,   "
Longley Luther,   Leominster
Heald Martin C. (spruce),   Lynn
Hurley John,   "
Wood D. B.   (root),   North Bridgewater
Hall Henry,   (root),   North-west   "
Hurley John,   Salem
Tripp Wm. O.   Taunton
CARYL HENRY,   Ware

Bell Founders.

Holbrook & Son,   E. Medway,   Medway

Bell Hangers.

(See also Locksmiths.)

Hoyt R. J.   "
Junio Jacob,   Cambridgeport
Webster Geo. H.   Charlestown
Pierce E. M.   "
Southworth Spaulding,   Fall River
Thatcher Geo.   "
Trumbel J. W.   Lowell
Sears H. G. O.   "
SHERMAN & GIFFORD, 24 William,   New Bedford
Sargent C. R.   "
Alden Winslow,   Newburyport
Moody Geo. Z.   Randolph
Cummings C. A., 294 Main,   Springfield
    Worcester

Belting.

Carle Wm. & Co. (leather), So. Attle-
   borough,
Plimpton Joseph D. (leather),   Attleborough
FOSTER GEO. H. (leather, see page   Chicopee
   754),   Clinton
FRENCH J. B. & SON, 26 No. Main,   Fall River

Nichols J. F.   Fall River
Chase Edmund,
Russell & Houston   (leather),   Holyoke
    Lawrence
Colcord Elihu W. (leather), 272 Essex,   "
FOSTER E. E.   Methuen, cor. Frank-
   lin,   "
Page Edward & Co. (leather), Turn-
   pike, cor. Essex,   "
Gates Josiah & Sons, 4 and 6 Dutton,   Lowell
Whiting & Co., Shattuck, cor. Middle,   "
Stevens Solon, Fletcher, cor. Western
   avenue,   "
DRAPER GEORGE & SON (leather,
   see page 753), Hopedale,   Milford
Crockett William E.   Newburyport
BASSETT DANIEL H.   Pittsfield
COLT & POWER (see page 707),   "
RICE, ROBBINS, & CO.   "
FOSTER E. E., 196 Derby,   Salem
FOOT HOMER & CO., Main, cor.
   State,   Springfield
Goulding Peter, 45 Front,   Worcester
Graton & Knight, 37 Front,   "

Billiard Ball Manufacturers.

KNOWLTON GEO. K. & CO. 13
  Union (see page 751),   Lynn

Billiard Halls.

Nash J. S. & E. M.   Abington
Douglas William, East Abington,   "
Chamberlin J. N., North Abington,   "
Gilman Geo. H.,   "   "
Edmunds Joseph,   Adams
Kyser Hiram B., North Adams,   "
Richmond A. E. & W. J., No. Adams,   "
Clark D. O.   Amesbury
Averell & Holden,   Amherst
Drake B. B.   Athol
Andrews Warren, Athol Depot,   "
Briggs Crawford C.   Attleborough
Jones Samuel,   Barre
Rice C. E.   "
Bearse Orrin B.,   Hyannis,   Barnstable
French C. A., So. Braintree,   Braintree
Daly James B.   Brighton
Beach F. C.   Cambridge
Belcher & Richardson,   "
Lyon G. H.,   Harvard sq.,   "
Robinson A. W.   "   "
Morse Kendall,   Cambridgeport,   "
Phillips Chas. W.   "   "
Cunningham F. H.   Charlestown
Cutter M.   "
Damon Henry H.   "
Gahm Joseph,   "
Paine Thomas,   "
Waverley House,   "
Carter E.   Chelsea
Ireland George H.   "
Wilmarth R. E.   "
Daboll B. M.   Clinton
Berry James D.   Concord
Fell C. B.,   So. Deerfield,   Deerfield
Thayer Minot,   Milton,   Dorchester
Dean Frank,   Neponset,   "
Francis E. P.   Fall River
Wilbur Darius,   "
Hancock T. E.   Foxborough
Beaman Charles A.   Gloucester
Collins Tisdale D.   "
Elwell Kilby W.   "
WEBSTER NATHANIEL, Webster
   House,

Briggs George W.   Great Barrington
Simons S.   Greenfield
Taft Orin,   "
Reed Samuel,   Groton Junction,   Groton
Patch Wm.   Haverhill
Shute Joseph,   "
Perkins Jacob,   Holyoke
Wolcott D. P.   "
Barnard Henry L.   Hudson
Dow G. N.   Lawrence
Fremmer George,   "
Rollins D. C.   "
Peck Hiram A.   Lee
Armstrong C.   Lowell
Barnard J. & D.   "
Emery Henry,   "
Smith Kilburn,   "
Hoyt Joseph M.   Lynn
McMurphy William,   "
Oliver George S.   "
Tasco Nathan T.   "
Bates Caleb E.   Milford
Brown J. Frank,   Nantucket
Fisher Peter R.   "
Mulligan Simon,   Natick
Parker Jacob F.   New Bedford
Shore Matthew,   "
Sylvester David,   "
Week Michael,   "
Gallagher Thomas,   Newburyport
Hannah John,   Northampton
Wentworth S. C. & Co.   "
Gooch Edwin,   Florence,   "
Hayden S. E.   Palmer
Weeks J. W.   "
Roche E. L.   Peabody
Tibbetts J. H.   "
Angell Nathan,   Pittsfield
Eichelser Philip,   "
Willis F. B.   "
Fuller Chas.   Plymouth
Reed Allen,   Provincetown
Rogers Otis,   Quincy
Shaw S. B.   Randolph
Harris Isaac B.   Rockport
Hall Edward,   Salem
Ladd D. W.   "
Newall Thos. P.   "
Thompson Thomas,   Salisbury
Keenan James,   Sandwich
Colton E. B.   Springfield
FRASIER J. B.   Hampden House,   "
Gilmore D. O.   "
Hawks & Brother,   "
MADDEN JOHN,   Sanford st.   "
Winkler Berthold,   "
Pilling Benjamin,   Stockbridge
Richardson O.   Stoneham
Drake Augustus L.   Stoughton
Dean Wm. F.   Taunton
Evans H. H.   Wakefield
Lee Charles H.   Waltham
Sullivan Timothy,   "
Goodman O.   Ware
White L. C.   "
Briggs Ebenezer,   Wareham
Birge S.   Westfield
Fairfield Allen,   "
Tobey Elisha,   "
Treat John A.   "
  Weymouth
Lufkin James M.,   East Weymouth,   "
Richards Chas.   South   "   "
Crocker H. A.   Winchendon
Bay State House,   Worcester
Cork & Hewitt,   "
Perry Henry,   "
Wrigley & West,   "

Billiard Table Leg Manufs.

STIMPSON & CO.   Westfield

Bill Posters.

Sleeper G. F.   Lynn
Noyes Samuel,   20 Middle,   Newburyport
Vogel Charles L.   Pittsfield

Bit and Gimlet Manufs.

(See Auger, Bit, & Gimlet Manuf.)

Bit Brace Manufacturers.

  Greenfield
MILLER'S FALLS MANUF. CO.
  (patent adjustable, see page 721),   "
THOMPSON F. M. (see page 770),   "
Streeter A. W., Shelburne Falls, Shelburne

Bitters Manufacturers.

PLUMSTEAD DAVID C., King of
  health, 11 and 13 Winnisimmet, Chelsea
  Worcester
WORCESTER M. A. 6 Bridge, .
  (Greeley's Bourbon, see page 783),   "

Black Ball Manuf.

Hastings George W.   Grafton
HAUTHAWAY C. L. & SONS, (see
  page 799),   North Bridgewater
POPE T. W.   (see page 769),   "
WASHBURN ELISHA (dealer; see
  page 792),

Black Lead Crucibles.

PHŒNIX MANUFACTURING CO.
  Chas. R. Atwood, agt. (see page
  725),   Taunton
Taunton Crucible Co. Joseph L.
  Presbrey, agt.   "

Black Lead or Plumbago Dealers.

  Canton
MORSE BROTHERS (see page 764),   "

Blacking Manufacturers.

(See also Ink Manufacturers.)

Lyon N. U.   Fall River
Leonard T.   Grafton
FARRAR G. H.   Union, corner
  Washington (shoe, see page 706),   Lynn
Churchill J. S. & Co. (dressing for
  boots),   Natick
HAUTHAWAY C. L. & SONS
  (dressing for boots, see page
  799),   North Bridgewater
POPE T. W. (see page 769),   "
WASHBURN ELISHA (see
  page 792),   "
Whittemore David (dressing for boots), "
Packard E. & Co.   Quincy
Pike Martin P.   Randolph
Barker Reuben,   West Rutland,   Rutland
Little & Hurlburt,   Sheffield
American Manuf. Co.   Springfield

Blacksmiths.

(See also Carriage Smiths; also Ship Smiths.)

Lean W. M.   Abington
McNally Daniel,   "
Ahearn John,   East Abington,   "
Baker Horatio,   "   "
Baker Paul,   "   "
Bass Robert,   "   "
Denley W. D.   "   "

Blacksmiths — continued.

Kendrigan John,   E. Abington,   Abington
Varney George,   North Abington,   "
Williamson Geo. H.,   South   "   "
Harris Daniel,   Acton
Davis & Hosmer,   "
Dutton Solomon L.   "
Hall Enoch & Son,   West Acton,   "
Wooster W. Wallace,   South   "   "
Chamberlain James E.   Acushnet
Pierce David,   "
Pope Elihu,   "
Carpenter Lucius,   Adams
Kelly & Surell,   North Adams,   "
Vadner & La Mer,   "   "
Wells Walter R.   "   "
Witherell Edward J.   "   "
Adams Jesse,   Agawam
Worthington Ransford,   "
Bliss Wm.   Feeding Hills,   "
McCurdy Robert & Son,   "Alford
Currier John.   Amesbury
Kelly Michael,   "
Lane J. N.   "
Cooke David S.   "
Sabin W. C. & E. T.   Amherst
Spear Lucius   "
Barnard Alvin,   North Amherst,   "
Shattuck Alexander,   "   "
Cochran James H.   Andover
Poor Wm.   "
Smith J. H.   "
Poland David,   Ballard Vale,   "
Caldwell Joshua,   "
Higgins Thomas,   Arlington
Kimball William,   "
Richardson William H.   "
Libby G. L.   Ashburnham
Adams Daniel,   Ashburnham Depot,   "
Small Joseph,   Burrageville,   "
Gibson Elbridge,   Ashby
Osgood & Sawin,   "
Smith Alpha,   "
Stevens Edward D.   "
Gibbs L. J.   Ashfield
Greenwood Abner,   Ashland
Lamb Daniel,   "
Piper Harvey,   "
Foster & Conant,   "
Wheeler W. L.   Athol
Babbit Sewell,   Athol Depot,   "
Briggs T. M.   "   "
Fish & Nash,   "   "
Bullock J. D.   Attleborough
Hicks H. A. & Co.   "
Wales Atherton,   "
Witherell J. D.   "
Bruce Sam'l H.   North Attleborough,   "
Fisher E. T.   "   "
King & Brother,   "   "
Stanley John   "   "
Fuller Gustavus,   So. Attleborough,   "
Cummings John S.   "
Hallet Gorham,   Auburn
Sears H. B.   Barnstable
Blagden James,   Centerville,   "
Jones F.   Hyannis,   "
Crocker Isaiah,   "
Leonard S. L.   Osterville,   "
Gray Charles,   West Barnstable,   "
Gilbert H. M.   "
HEALD S. & SONS (light and heavy   Barre
  forgings; see pp. 796 and 797),   "
Shaw E. & S.   "
Frisbie Lester,   Becket
Laramie Joseph,   "
Bacon Elijah,   Bedford
Chellies Elbridge,   "

Skinner Joseph,   Bedford
Bridgeman Porter,   Belchertown
Curtis Alanson,   "
Hill John C.   "
Reed Sam'l L.   Belmont
Crane W. H. S.   "
Smith Riley,   Berkley
Day Josiah,   Berlin
Dewey Fred. A.   Bernardston
Dewey Joel N.   "
Moore Enoch.   "
Woodbury Wm. G.   "
Dutton Alexander,   Beverley
Eastman L. T.   Billerica
Lund Mark,   "
Fuller M. & O. W.   "
Taft Caleb,   Blackstone
Deagan John,   Millville,   "
Wyman Horatio,   Blandford
Bliss Alvin,   North Blandford,   "
Dwinells Asa P.   Bolton
Hildreth J. S.   "
Hoar Silas H.   Boxborough
Newhall Henry W.   Boxford
Anderson Robert B.,   West Boxford,   "
Henley Alonzo J.   "
Goodall R. B. T.   Boylston
Walton Chas. F.   Boylston Centre,   "
Hill & Hall,   "
Thayer & Phipps,   S. Braintree,   Bradford
Wild Elisha,   Braintree
Gillespie R.   "
South Thomas A.   Weymouth,   "
Crocker Benjamin,   Brewster
Wiles Moses E.   "
Harlow Southwork,   Bridgewater
Lazell, Perkins, & Co.   "
Maguire J.   "
Callahan John,   Brighton
Merrifield H. F.   "
White Charles,   "
Dawley Charles C.   Brimfield
Potter Edward W.   "
Bixby Johnson,   East Brimfield,   "
Brigham Alexander,   Brookfield
Johnson J. N.   "
Rice Parker A.   "
Willard C. K.   East Brookfield,   "
Madore Joseph,   Brookline
Woodward Royal,   "
Weller Henry,   Buckland
Innis George,   Shelburne Falls,   "
Alley R. J.   Burlington
Harkness Geo.   Cambridge
Nutting & Prescott,   "
Day Stephen,   East Cambridge,   "
Felt Geo. W.   "
Lehan D. H.   "   "
Robinson Joel,   "
Blake Darius,   North Cambridge,   "
Easter R. S. & Co.   "
Henderson Robert,   "
McAvoy Charles,   Cambridgeport,   "
McCarty Timothy,   "
McIntosh Geo.   "
McKenzie James K.   "
Spellman & Grady,   "
Thomson J. B.   "
Waugh Wm. A.   "
Woods & Whalen,   "
Worthen J. R. & Co.   "   "
Blackman Winthrop,   Canton
Hall John,   "
Hunt Geo.   "
Parkhurst Wm. M.   Carlisle
Lee Marshall,   "
Shaw Charles. S.   North Carver,   Carver
Carter Ashton,   Charlemont

Fuller Matthew R.	Charlemont
Graves Lucius H.	"
Guerin Eri,	"
Rice Hart A.	"
Cobine J.	Charlestown
Emery James, (carriage)	"
Fowler E. & Son,	"
Garland Albert S.	"
Gifford G. & E. H.	"
Ham Joseph,	"
Ham Philip,	"
Harmon E. S.	"
Hattie Wm.	"
Heath Thomas V.	"
Larkin Caleb,	"
Lilley Thomas,	"
Louer John,	"
Pleadwell John,	"
Robinson E. R.	"
Strand Thomas D.	"
Heredeen Henry,	Charlton
Ward John A.	Charlton City, "
HIGGINS SAMUEL,	Chatham
Mayo David,	"
Dadman N. P.	Chelmsford
Durant George,	"
Marshall E. H.	"
Wilkins W. L.	"
	Chelsea
DENNING PHILIP A. 56 Hawthorn, "
Hanstom Willis,	"
Malloy John,	"
Searle Walter,	"
Tyzzer J. jr.	"
Fairfield Peter,	Cheshire
Glover & Dawley,	"
Pease M.	Chester
Temple Edwin,	"
Litchfield Amon,	Chesterfield
Eddy Samuel E.	W. Chesterfield, "
Fitz George W.	Chicopee
Gates Henry,	"
Dame Peter,	Chicopee Falls, "
Cullen Peter,	North Adams, Clarksburg
Hosmer & Groby,	Clinton
Damon F. J.	Cohasset
Tilden A. & Son,	"
Dewey Robert,	Coleraine
Sheerer T.	"
Stratton Leonard,	"
Wilson David,	"
Webster Nelson,	"
Bigelow F. E.	Concord
Hall Edward,	"
Ames E. & E.	Conway
Gunn & Perry,	"
Bartlett Charles,	Cummington
Bishop Jubal,	"
Stevens Darius,	"
Bartlett Samuel F., W. Cummington, "
Bentley Alonzo F.	Dalton
Flerity J.	Dana
Mathews Edwin C.	North Dana, "
Doherty D.	Danvers
Pearly D. A.	"
Peart W. B.	"
Hilton & Brown,	Danvers Port, "
Marshall Simeon,	"
Manley Clark D.	Dartmouth
King Leander C.	North Dartmouth, "
Nickerson John H., South " "
Collins John,	Dedham
Dencef Michael,	"
Raymond Artemus,	East Dedham, "
Cobbett David & Bro., South " "
Adams Geo. W.	West " "
Soule Francis,	" " "
Childs Lemuel,	Deerfield

	Deerfield
Phillips Charles E.,	South Deerfield, "
Reardon Daniel,	" "
Sears Eldridge C.	Dennis
Rogers Wm. M.,	Dennis Port, "
Snow Heman,	" "
Sears Heman,	East Dennis, "
Bangs Jonathan, South Dennis, "
Baker Browning K., West " "
Thacher Benjamin,	" "
Briggs Matthew,	Dighton
Bushee Samuel,	"
Ingalls Allen H.	"
Perry Geo. B.	"
Reed Sandford,	"
Stubbings Thomas,	North Dighton, "
Porter Thomas,	" "
Cunningham Robert,	Dorchester
Daniels John,	"
Davenport O.	"
Haggerty John,	"
Hewins J. C.	"
Maclean Edward,	"
McIntosh J. F.	"
O'Callahan John C.	"
Thomas Nathan J., Harrison sq. "
Scannell D. M.,	Mattapan, "
Weeman M. F.	"
Berry Geo. W.	Neponset, "
Jordan W. I.	" "
Pratt J.	" "
Crane Henry,	Milton, "
Logee Sewall,	East Douglas, Douglas
Rivers Siplin,	"
Orcutt Henry,	Dover
Drew Jesse,	Dracut
Parker Benjamin,	"
Sawyer R. W.	"
Lindley George,	Dudley
Cutler George,	West Dudley, "
Woodward J. C. & Co.	Dunstable
Wright George P.	"
Delano Nathaniel,	Duxbury
Faunce Zenas,	"
Vinal Henry G.	"
Siddell Chas. W.	East Bridgewater
Sturtevant Joshua,	"
Paine Micah S.	Eastham
Senbury George,	"
Connell J. O.	East Hampton
Holcomb N. A.	"
Britton James,	Easton
Phelan Charles,	"
Lake J.	North Easton, "
Simpson Samuel,	South " "
Chadwick William,	Edgartown
Decker Peter,	S. Egremont, Egremont
Kline George,	"
Hall David,	North Egremont, "
Hallenbeck Norman, " "
Ramsey Daniel,	"
Hunt Joseph R.	Enfield
Snow E. F.	"
Burnett Henry F.	Erving
Gilbert Noah,	Essex
Haskell Francis,	"
Pierce Oliver,	"
Story Abel, jr.	"
Damon John,	Fairhaven
Babbitt Isaac N.	"
Lawton George,	"
Terry Isaac,	"
Ambler Newell,	Fall River
Angell Wm. R.	"
Blake & Macomber,	"
Durfee Oscar F.	"
Field Henry,	
Hinckley Nathaniel,	

Blacksmiths — continued.

Osborn W. & J. M.	Fall River
Packard W. H.	"
Thompson Asa,	"
White Geo.	"
Cahoon ——	Falmouth
Robinson William H.	"
Swift Seth, West Falmouth,	"
Brigham & Houghton,	Fitchburg
Davis Jonathan D.	"
Dole A. S.	"
Hawkins Gardner P.	"
Holt John T.	"
Pool Edward G.	"
Story & Weston,	"
Waters S. C. West Fitchburg,	"
Averill O. E.	Florida
Davis Patrick,	"
Tower Dennis,	"
Warren Paul,	"
Fales Alvin,	Foxborough
Fisher Leonard,	"
Igo William,	"
Warren Samuel,	"
Fennessey James,	Framingham
Strout Charles	"
White Frederick,	"
Easter Josiah, Saxonville,	"
Trowbridge Geo., South Framingham,	"
Hood & Murdock,	Franklin
Lawrence Leonard P.	"
Miller H. B.	"
Maguire & Hanley,	Freetown
Braley H. A. East Freetown,	"
Learned F. P.	Gardner
Lovell A. & Co.	"
May Patrick,	"
Learned W. H. So. Gardner,	"
Dean Jesse,	Georgetown
Holmes Charles,	"
Ilsley J. A.	"
Pettengill Henry	"
Bates George A.	Gill
Clark John,	"
Davis Stephen L.	Gloucester
Durland Charles H.	"
Harvey George,	"
Hilton William F.	"
Ireland & Frazier,	"
Lufkin Eben H.	"
Marion Joseph,	"
Procter Eben C.	"
Richardson Nathan,	"
Griffin Willard P. Annisquam,	"
Harvey Fitz O., East Gloucester,	"
McCaleb & McCusky,	"
Voss Adolph & Brother, "	"
Roberts Geo. H. Lanesville,	"
Billings Elijah,	Goshen
Casey Michael,	Grafton
Dwyer J. G.	"
McNutt George, N. E. Village,	"
Jones W. H. Saundersville,	"
Sibley Simeon, Farnumsville,	"
Smith Samuel C.	Granby
Stanley Henry F. & Son,	"
Esop F. W. Granville Cors.	Granville
Holcomb A. " " "	"
King S. " " "	"
Munn L. East Granville,	"
Colby Charles, Great Barrington	
Cone William 2d,	"
O'Brien John,	"
Reareuer Edward,	"
Church Charles, Housatonic,	"
Vandeusen Gilbert, Vandeusenville,	"
Cook R. W.	Greenfield
Ewers Benjamin,	"

Moore & Withey,	Greenfield
Morgan Jeremiah P.	"
Stafford ——	Greenwich
Russell Milo,	Groton
Childs Calvin & Son,	"
Warren Alden,	"
Parsons J. C. Groton Junction,	"
Strout Ebenezer,	Groveland
Cook Rufus,	Hadley
Shaw James,	"
Smith F. H.	"
Dickinson C. D. N. Hadley,	"
Mitchell George W.	Halifax
Appleton Joshua,	Hamilton
Grant Alexander A.	Hancock
Palmer Asa L.	"
Foster Otis,	Hanover
Wright Warren,	"
Pool Elias C.	Hanson
Hutchinson Albion, So. Hanson,	"
Amsden Nelson,	Hardwick
Giffin James,	"
White Josiah,	"
Harrod George E.	Harvard
Harrod William K. Still River,	"
Freeman Thomas,	Harwich
Thacher Solomon,	"
Young Simeon,	"
Hallett Josiah B. Harwichport,	"
Kingsley S. W.	Hatfield
Ayer William M.	Haverhill
Johnson Washington,	"
Houston Joseph U.	Hawley
Carley Cyrus W.	Heath
Damon Isaac N.	Hingham
Merritt Henry jr.	"
Murray Thomas,	"
Stoddar Caleb, South Hingham,	"
Cook Charles R. "	"
Jones Thomas, "	"
Demarse Peter,	Hinsdale
Macken Patrick,	"
Reanard Napoleon,	"
Buscom A. D.	Holden
Bassett James S.	"
Howe Amasa,	"
Roper Charles,	Holland
Blodgett William H.	Holliston
Kett John W.	"
Hunter D. R.	Holyoke
Newton E. A. & Brother,	"
Shilley E. D.	"
Hutchinson Louis,	Hopkinton
Morse Willard,	"
Rice & Fairbanks,	"
Staples A. H.	"
Mullen James, Hayden row,	"
Rice George, Woodville,	"
May P. C.	Hubbardston
Willard E.	"
Wilson A. H.	"
Brett Otis,	Hudson
Danforth Alfred,	"
Knight Rufus,	"
Lee J.	"
Thomas George H.	"
Donahue Michael,	Huntington
Howland Abner,	Hyde Park
Whittier N. B. & A. J.	"
Chapman Chas. W.	Ipswich
Goodhue Manassa C.	"
Poor Melzard,	"
Smith W. & B. H.	"
Bailey Caleb E.	Kingston
Chandler John S.	"
Delano Lewis S.	"
Perkins Ezra,	"
Southworth Enoch,	Lakeville

Rugg Sewal T.   Lancaster
Wellington George W.   "
Dewey William B.   Lauesborough
Dow Samuel W. jr.   "
Zinck William,   "

    Lawrence
BRYANT A. & SON, 250 Lowell,
Cochran W. N & B.   "
Emerson Albert,   "
Farrell Henry,   "
Holt Amos,   "
Lathrop E. & Co.   "
Brooks Anson,   Lee
Hinckley, Bradford, & Co.   "
Phinney L.   "
Thatcher Elile,   "
Dupar Oliver S.   East Lee,
Melius Edward L.   "   "
Livingston Wm. D., South Lee,
Brophy William,   Leicester
Usher Edward,   "
Barton Cheney, Cherry Valley,   "
Barnes Benj. F.   Clappville,   "
Servin Andrew T., agent Lenox Fur-
    nace,   Lenox
Washburn Franklin,   "
Arnold Samuel,   Leominster
Durant Charles W.   "
Wilder George,   "
Archibald Leander, N. Leominster,   "
Hill A.   Leverett
Marsh J. C.   "
Morgan W.   "
Whitney Collins, North Leverett,   "
Ham William,   Lexington
Russell J. A.   East Lexington,   "
Smith Josiah, 2d,   "   "
Upton William,   Leyden
Page Davio,   Lincoln
Hosley S. W.   Littleton
Johnson N. K.   "
Dion Basil,   Longmeadow
Mills Frederic, E. Lougmeadow,   "
Abbott A. H. & J. H.   Lowell
Blackington Daniel,   "
Coward Jacob B.   "
Crawford James,   "
Drew J. H. & Co.   "
Furbish & Sanborn,   "
Hill G. F.   "
Holt & Bergeron,   "
Jenkins Joel,   "
Lee John T.   "
LOVEJOY DANIEL, Rock, cor. Cush-
    ing (see page 744),   "
Meadowcrnft Jas. (horse shoer),   "
Nichols Converse,   "
Ordway J. C.   "
Stevens Joseph (shoer),   "
Stinson & Tighe,   "
Banister John,   Ludlow
Hayes Elizur,   "
Green Asahel,   Lunenburg
McIntire Moses,   "
Brown S. D. & Co.   Lynn
Clapp S. D.   "
Cushing Alonzo P.   "
Cutts Richard A.   "
McGlue John,   "
Nichols Henry S.   "
Otis George W.   "
Payne G. H. & G. S.   "
Smith D. B. & Co.   "
Welch Thomas,   "
Bent Stephen E.   Lynnfield
Benfield Geo. W., Lynnfield Centre,   "
Lonergan John,   "   "
Putnam H. L.   Malden

Young George E.   Malden
Cheever L. L.   South Malden,   "
Richardson Asa,   Manchester
Tobey J. A.   Mansfield
Kingman Ambrose, West Mansfield,   "
Forsyth Henry,   Marblehead
Graves George,   "
Randall & Murchison,   "
Ryan William,   "
Briggs Rufus F.   Marion
Brigham W. E.   Marlborough
Hale John,   "
KEANE JAMES,   "
Moulton William H.
S owe Emerson,
Taylor Levi,   "
Brown David,   Marshfield
Ewell Judson,   East Marshfield,   "
Rogers M. W.   "   "
Bowlin Josiah,   Mattapoisett
Bowlin W. F.   "
Durfee Edward,   "
Chenery William,   Medfield
Curry Patrick,   "
Hathaway J. D.   Medford
Moore Henry F.   "
Smith Charles A.   "
Symmes Alexander S.   "
Farrington Alfred,   Medway
Richardson Richard, East Medway,   "
Everett William,   West   "   "
Williams Wm. L.   "   "   "
Richards Wm. F.   Rockville,   "
McCoubry Thomas,   Melrose
Reidy & Barker,   "
Daniels Cyrus,   Mendon
Grow Lysander,   "
Foss & Barteaux,   Methuen
Woodman E.   "
Beals Eber,   Middleborough
Lane Benj. F.   "
Lincoln Lewis & Son,   "
Littlejohn O.   "
Wales Abijah T.   "
Soule James, East Middleborough,   "
Southard Calvin,   Rock,   "
Stiles David,   Middleton
Church & Wilkinson,   Milford
Itle Ira,   "
Masterson B.   "
Menkin Thomas S.   "
Supple Adam,   "
Feehan William,   Millbury
Harrington John E.   "
Parker S. R.   "
Sawyer Samuel,   "
Savory S. A.   West Millbury,   "
Crossman Lemuel,   Milton
Chapman & Strangman,   "
Scannel Dennis O.   "
Aldrich Henry E.   Monson
Aldrich Hiram,   "
Burdick George W.   "
Tucker J. M.   "
Hunter Warren,   Montague
Morse J. H.   "
Shepard H. H.   "
Goewey Erastus,   Monterey
Quermoroy Jonathan,   Mt. Washington
Dow J. R.   Nahant
Gardner Frederic C.   Nantucket
Mitchell David,   "
Parker Elisha,   "
Simmons Burgess T.   "
Smith Allen,   "
Swain George,   "
Donovan T.   Natick
McGlone M.   "

Blacksmiths — continued.

Parker & Allen,   Natick
Peters Patrick,   "
Hancock Henry,   South Natick,   "
Robbins John,   "
Greenwood Isaac,   Needham
Marshall John,   Wellesley,   "
Allen Benjamin W.   New Bedford
Brownell, Ashley, & Co.   "
Lee & Tripp,   "
Sherman Wm. D.   "
Skiff S. B. & Co.   "
Snow James M.   "
Springer Andrew R.   "
Swift George D.   "
Tripp J. M.   "
Johnson C. D.   New Braintree
Frost Austin N.   Newbury
Jordan Charles F.   "
Kent John N.   "
Adams Joseph C.   Newburyport
Donnahoe Edward,   "
George E. H. & G. J.   "
Haskell Luther,   "
Manning George W.   "
McGlew Hugh,   "
Moody H. T.   "
Moynihan Patrick,   "
Page John T.   "
Pettigrew Chas. D.   "
Wheeler Lemuel D.   "
Woods James M.   "
Church J. N.   New Marlborough
Potter Leonard,   "
Fowler Robert,   Hartsville,   "
Flow Peter,   Mill River,   "
Peters Thomas,   "   "
Chamberlin Cyrus,   New Salem
Powers Orrison,   "
Haskins Elan,   North Prescott,   "
Ellis S. S.,   North New Salem,   "
Cole Charles,   West Newton,   Newton
Peters Andrew,   "   "
Keegan Patrick,   "   "
Farrar J. C.   Newton Centre,   "
Mosher E. M.   Newton Corner,   "
Rooney D.   Newtonville,   "
Cunningham L. T.   Upper Falls,   "
McGlew Thomas,   Lower Falls,   "
Pulsifer John,   "
Clark Levi (shoeing),   Northampton
Francis V.   "
Kingsley Edwin L.   "
Phelps George S.   "
Weller S.   "
Dean Thomas,   Florence,   Northampton
Hartwell W. S.   "
Kennedy Martin,   Leeds,   "
Carr John V.   North Andover
Faulkner John,   "
Urry U.   "
Adams Sylvanus,   Northborough
Haven William T.   "
Flynn Daniel,   Northbridge
Flynn Thomas,   Whitinsville,   "
Bradford & Crocker,   North Bridgewater
Tyler A. D., & Sons,   "
Peck Hiram F.   "
Wade Albert R.   "
Hobbs Albert,   North Brookfield
Tucker John E.   "
Donelon Patrick,   North Chelsea
Moran Thomas L.   "
Somes Kink J.   "
Weeman J. E.   "
Alexander Charles,   Northfield
Alexander George & Son,   "
Mattoon Joseph,   "

Eaton George,   North Reading
Briggs Ebenezer,   Norton
Macomber James O.   "
Babbitt James,   Oakham
Briggs Albert,   "
Blodgett Nathaniel F.   Orange
Coolidge Henry H.   "
Goddard Elisha,   "
Spear Erastus,   "
Goodnow W.   North Orange,   "
Cole William W.   Orleans
Shattuck Abel,   "
Mayo Joseph,   East Orleans,   "
Champlain Albert,   Otis
Perkins L. E.   "
Whitney Miles F.   "
Davis Barney,   Oxford
Putnam H. W.   "
Rich George,   "
Walker Solomon,   North Oxford,   "
Davis Joseph C.   "   "
Clough J. M.   Palmer
Simonds H. B.   "
Stone George,   "
Barber John,   Thorndike,   "
Squires D. N.   Bondsville,   "
Comins William,   Paxton
Muzzy Charles A.   "
Annable Nathaniel,   Peabody
Dodge C. H.   "
Dole & Osgood,   "
Jones A. W.   "
Jones Thomas,   "
PIKE & WHIPPLE, (see page 748),   "
Smith William,   "
Dodge Lewis,   Pelham
Whitney James,   "
Flynn John,   Pembroke
Lewis Martin J.,   North Pembroke,   "
Gray Lewis T.   South Hanson,   "
Merritt Francis,   West Duxbury,   "
Lawrence Sumner P.   Pepperell
Horton Joseph S.,   East Pepperell,   "
Shattuck Silas P.,   "
Mongeon Bruno,   Peru
Borman Samuel,   Petersham
Martin Thomas,   "
White Josiah,   "
Bolton A. A.   Phillipston
Doane Ebenezer,   "
Barnes William,   Pittsfield
Barrett Justin S.   "
Bridges James A.   "
Drake Sandford, jr.   "
Hayden John,   "
Himes Daniel R.   "
Penner Dennis,   "
Robinson William,   "
Shay Martin,   "
Stapleton John,   "
Tracy Nelson,   "
Coty Romeo,   West Pittsfield,   "
Jackson Henry S.   "   "
Spearman J. & E.   Plainfield
Sweet A. H.   "
Fuller George,   Plymouth
Harvey Sylvanus,   "
Holmes N. H.   "
Raymond E. S.   "
Morton Henry,   Chiltonville,   "
Sherman Charles,   Plympton
Sturtevant Henry,   "
Churchill Spencer,   North Plympton,   "
Gardner Ira,   Prescott
Haskins Joseph H.,   North Prescott,   "
Davis Charles,   Princeton
Muzzy Benjamin F.   "
Wood John P.   East Princeton,   "

TAYLOR AMASA, Provincetown
Carter Thomas W. Quincy
Feltis Alexander, "
Feltis Horace, "
Ripley William, "
Tirrell Sons, "
Wild John Q. A. "
Campbell William, Randolph
Desmond Michael, "
Fardy Thomas, "
Young Edmund, East Randolph, "
Lincoln Russell, Raynham
Makepeace Sylvanus, "
Pettee Benjamin, "
Blunt John A. Reading
Eames Emery B. "
Parker Cephas, "
Totten Robert C. "
Davis Jas. M., North Rehoboth, Rehoboth
Fuller Hiram D. " " "
Ingram William, Richmond
Church Charles H. F. Rochester
Perkins Elbridge G. "
Smelie William, "
Cole & Cogswell, Rockport
Moore Ira F. "
Selig Thomas W. "
Pool Story D. Pigeon Cove, "
Sibley Peter P. Rowe
Sibley Joseph, "
Sibley Tyler, "
Swaney William, Rowley
Stockwell Winfield S. Royalston
Wheeler Leonard, "
Steel Summer S. Russell
Brancroft Leonard, Rutland
Fisher Alvin B. "
Fletcher David W. "
Richardson Billings F. "
Agge Jacob, Salem
Andrews Gilman, "
Cox Francis R. "
Cutts Benjamin, "
Hartigan Patrick, "
Murray & Carroll, "
Nichols John, "
Nichols J. Henry, "
Peirson George H. "
Perry F. L. "
PHILLIPS H. B. 194 & 196 Derby, "
Shoales C. J. "
Walton Josiah, "
Weir Daniel P. "
Wilkins Charles, "
Lane E. S. Amesbury, Salisbury
Pike Caleb, East Salisbury, "
Whitney J. H. & Son, Sandisfield
King Levi, Montville, "
Pease Levi, "
Pratt Frank, New Boston, "
Ellis John C. C. Sandwich
Ellis Freeman C. Monument, "
Burgess Aaron, Pocasset, "
Raymond Ebenezer, " "
Benson Hiram, W. Sandwich, "
Holway Seth, N. " "
Waterhouse Geo. H. East Saugus, Saugus
Neal James M. Saugus Centre, "
Bias Henry F. Savoy
Tinney Benjamin, "
Clapp Elijah, Scituate
Clapp Elijah T. "
Litchfield Isaac, "
Litchfield Seth, "
Merritt J. H. North Scituate, "
Bourn Z. W. Seekonk
Challice Ira, "
French Geo. "

Knapp Daniel S. Sharon
Stone Cyrus, "
Graham Jonathan, Sheffield
Dunbar William H. Ashley Falls, "
Griffith Grove D. "
Russell Henry R. East Sheffield, "
Smith Henry, " " "
Powers R. M. Shelburne
Miles Nathaniel, "
Poland S. "
Innis George, Shelburne Falls, "
Bickford Elbridge M. Sherborn
Ware Vorestus, "
Blood S. K. Shirley
Giddings William J. "
Holden Charles N. "
Harrod James, Shirley Village, "
Hyde Amasa, Shrewsbury
Newton Adam H. "
Whitney Charles L. "
Gray Wm. A. "
Haskins Joseph H. Shutesbury
Hayden Josiah T. "
Southwick Gilbert, "
Allen Richard, Somerset
DeCosta F. O. "
Wilson James, "
Dodge Sewall, Somerville
Gray S. N. North Somerville, "
Ewin John D. Southampton
Spiller George, Southborough
Walker Francis W. "
Webster Horace F "
Chamberlain Merrill, Southbridge
Stone George S. "
Clark Isaac, Globe Village, "
Ryan Francis, " " "
Cook Shubael, South Hadley
Judd E. B., South Hadley Falls, "
Sessions H. T. " " " "
Wetmore L. D. " " " "
Merritt Henry, South Scituate
Merritt Joseph, 2d, "
Merritt Wm. H. "
Gardner Horatio N., W. Scituate, "
Granger Heaton, Southwick
Goddard Joseph, Spencer
Belcher Gilbert, "
Kenely Edward, "
Richards Austin, "
Avery John, Springfield
Burke P. J. "
Hood John, "
Weeks J. L. "
Flynn John, Indian Orchard, "
Carter Asaph, Sterling
Welcome Charles, "
Bowen John W. Stockbridge
Stalker Peter, Curtisville, "
Boyce Charles M. Stoneham
Leads Joseph, "
Morse Isaac D. "
Richardson O. "
Haley S. W. East Stoughton, Stoughton
Waite & Son, " " "
Glven John, Stow
Nelson A. W. "
Soper Jacob, "
Watson Chas. E. Assabet, "
Barrows Joel E., Rock Bottom, "
Haynes Henry, Starbridge
Purdy James E. "
Rice Jonas, "
Knights Wheaton, Fishdale, "
Powers Abijah, Sudbury
Allen John P. South Sudbury, "
Chamberlain C. W. Sunderland
Newton Asahel, Sutton

Blacksmiths — continued.

Cullen Patrick,	Swampscott
Cowen William H.	Swansea
Lansing John W.	"
Pierce Isaiah W.	"
Puffer Chas.	"
Carey Daniel,	Taunton
Coe Jerome W. (carriage),	"
Chace Samuel B.	"
Conefy & McDonald,	"
Davis Geo. W.	"
Goff T. P.	"
McDonald Wm.	"
Morse Jason,	"
PECK & WHITE,	"
Porter Thomas,	"
Pierie & Dean,	"
Thayer Peter C.	"
Woods Job N.	"
Parris Lewis W.	Myricksville, "
Wade James & Son,	" "
Phelps Jonas,	Templeton
Winchester Harris,	"
Armitage B. F.	East Templeton, "
Shores William,	Baldwinville, "
Whitney E.	Otter River, "
Eaton Henry,	Tewksbury
Hill Amos,	"
Look Charles C.	Holmes's Hole, Tisbury
Luce Benjamin,	" " "
Bodfish N. P.	West Tisbury, "
Lovell & Baxter,	" " "
Ives Truman,	Tolland
Munn Dennis L.	"
Hobbs D. C.	Topsfield
Long Henry,	"
Maynard L.	Townsend
Wallace Bryant,	"
Hodgman Benjamin, West Townsend, "
Ranger Benjamin, Townsend Harbor, "
Eastman Samuel,	North Truro, Truro
Smith Samuel H.	" " "
Bryant Aaron,	Tyngsborough
Cummings Willard B.	"
McCarty John,	Tyringham
Haley John,	Upton
Ide Ira,	"
Lesure S. G.	"
Sadler Edwin,	"
Hill Reuben,	Uxbridge
King Luke,	"
Willard G. E.	"
Barry L. M.	North Uxbridge; "
Eames Joshua N.	Wakefield
Hart Abner,	"
Walton Joshua,	"
Haradon Hiram,	Wales
Parker Luther,	"
Ellis Billings,	Walpole
Hartshorn Warren,	"
Rogers James B.	"
Polleys Edmund,	East Walpole, "
Boyden Phineas,	South " "
Daniels Chas. H.	Waltham
McDonald H.	"
Smith Edwin,	"
Price J. E.	Ware
Stanton George A.	"
Winslow Daniel R.	"
Bolles Israel B.	Wareham
Cushman Jacob,	"
Hamlin Elkanah,	"
Brodys Luther,	Warren
Butterworth W. G.	"
Reed C. F.	West Warren, "
Batchelder Ira F.	"
Fisher Barnard,	Warwick
Ellis Abraham,	Washington

Hall James,	Watertown
Jackson A.	"
McDonnell P.	"
Nolan M. J.	"
TAYLOR J. MASON,	"
Mullin Jeremiah,	Wayland
Putnam C. & Son,	Webster
Warren William H.	"
Grant M. W.	Wellfleet
Higgins N. C.	"
Harrington Timothy,	Wendell
Bradbury Daniel,	Wenham
Kavanaugh Patrick,	"
Hardy C. S.	Westborough
Jackson Josiah,	"
Duclett Lewis,	West Boylston
Morse Charles,	"
Sturtevant Levi,	"
Lesure L. A.	Oakdale, "
Atwell Charles,	West Bridgewater
Dunbar Reuel,	Cochesett, "
Allen Frank,	West Brookfield
Bliss Geo. W.	"
Richards H.	"
Bryant Wm.	Westfield
Cornwell William B.	"
Gamache F. D.	"
Hathaway Joel,	"
Phelps Wm.	"
Chamberlin J. M.	Westford
Lanktree John,	"
Reed A. S.	"
Chapman Linus,	Westhampton
King Sylvester,	"
Adams G. & A. F.	Westminster
Bathrick Stephen,	"
Lamb Greenleaf,	"
Learned John K.	"
Carr Horatio F.	West Newbury
Dawkins Wm.	"
Johnson John,	"
Boyce Park,	Weston
Garfield Daniel,	"
Garfield Hiram,	"
Upham Joel,	"
Upham George,	"
Briggs Christopher,	Westport
Briggs Joseph A.	"
Gammons Matthias E.	"
Manly Sylvester,	Central Village, "
Mosher Sherman,	" "
Little Nathaniel,	South Westport, "
Cain Patrick,	West Roxbury
Hartshorn Charles P.	"
Lindall Horace,	"
Bruce Brainard T.,	Jamaica Plain, "
Dickson Alexander,	" " "
Starr William H.	"
Bliss H.,	Ashleyville, West Springfield
Harmon & Reynolds,	"
Diekie Robert,	"
Thompson & Degroff,	"
Crofoot Comfort B., West Stockbridge
Centre,	West Stockbridge
Thompson & DeGroff,	"
Scribner Smith,	State Line, "
	Weymouth
Healey Samuel,	East Weymouth, "
Ready John,	" " "
Blanchard James,	North " "
Prentiss J. F.	" " "
Reidy John,	South " "
Ripley J. G.	" " "
Roche John,	" " "
Fox Horace B.	Whately
Fox Selah W.	"
Train Roswell,	"
Streeter W. B.	Wilbraham

Twing Rufus, Wilbraham
Twing William B. "
Cunningham J. F., South Wilbraham, "
Bartlett Geo. O. Williamsburg
Culver Madison, "
Noble James, Williamstown
Welch Michael, "
Cole Albert D., South Williamstown, "
Ames J. A. Wilmington
Adams Oliver, Winchendon
Have Luke, "
Scott D. M. & S. M. "
Gross Frank, Winchester
McNally Peter, "
Orne E. H. "
Burlingame A. V. Windsor
Nichols Abial, "
O'Connell William, East Windsor, "
EASTER & CAMERON, Woburn
Ellis R. F. "
Hood Thomas R. P. "
Jones Charles, "
Pollard Charles P. "
Bemis A. J. Worcester
Brigham S. C. "
Chamberlain Lyman, "
Corbett Henry M. "
Cosgrove Francis, "
Fellows D. F. "
Fish H. C. "
Fish Rufus A. "
Hyde Charles, "
Jordan A. P. "
O'Leary & Bro. "
Melaven Morris, "
Noone & Coan, "
Wellington H. B. "
Whitney H. S. "
Wright Chas. "
Quinn Michael H. New Worcester, "
Mercer Frederick, Worthington
Butler Nathan C. South Worthington, "
Palmer Platt B. West Worthington, "
Willard Leonard, Wrentham
Colman B. S. Centre, "
Kendall C. P. "
Blake Levi, North Wrentham, "
Pettee William C., South "
Mason James B., Sheldonville. "
Mullen Robert, West Wrentham, "
Thacher Samuel, jr. Yarmouth
Homer Joseph B., South Yarmouth, "
Hallet Benjamin, 2d, Yarmouth Port, "
Hallet Edward B. " "

Blank Book Manufacturers.

(See also Book Binders.)

REMICK JOHN & SON, Cambridge-
  port,
Earl Newton R. Cambridge
SHEPLEY STEPHEN & CO. Fall River
  149 Main,
PROCTER BROS., 121 Front, Fitchburg
Dorr John C. Gloucester
Morris B. G. Lawrence
WHITCOMB I. A. 93 Essex (see
  page 793), "
WEBSTER W. T. 8 Exchange, Lynn
Parsons & Co. New Bedford
Bridgman & Child, Northampton
Cornwell Enos J. "
Keen Henry R. Pittsfield
Ives Henry P. Salem
Perley J. "
Bowles Samuel & Co. Springfield
Grout & Bigelow, Worcester
Sanford Wm. H. & Son, "

Blanket Manufacturers.

(See Woolen Goods.)

Bleacheries.

(See also Bonnet Bleacheries.)

WOLFENDEN ROBERT (bleacher
  and dyer of cotton and woolen
  yarn, braids, &c.) Attleboro'
LOWELL BLEACHERY, F. P.
  Appleton, agt. Lowell
  Mansfield
MOWRY G. W. & C. H. (bonnet) "
Hutchinson A. & Co. Rockville, Medway
Morris Thomas, Northampton
Williston & Arms Manufacturing Co. "
DANVERS BLEACHERY, James
  Dempsey, supt. Peabody
Middlesex Bleachery, Somerville
Waltham Bleachery, I. R. Scott,
  agent, Waltham
Worcester Bleach & Dye Works, Worcester

Blind Hinges and Fastenings.

Morris Geo. L. Taunton
Strange Elias W. & Co. 20 Washington, "

Blocks and Oars.

Fears Robert R. & Bro. Gloucester
JONES WILLIAM, "
Merchant S. Jr. & Co. "

Block Manufacturers.

*(See Bonnet and Hat Block Manufacturers;
Print Block Manufacturers; and Ship
Block Manufacturers.)*

Boat Builders.

Leonard Ebenezer, Long Plain, Acushnet
Eldredge Simeon, Chatham
Nye Asa, "
Frahm Frank, Chelsea
Horgan Thomas, "
Pettee James, Cohasset
Chandler Hiram W. Duxbury
Peterson Samuel S. "
Morse Uriah, Edgartown
Tilton P. A. "
Burnham Samuel, Essex
Allen James, Fairhaven
Delano Joshua, "
Hersell Wm. H. "
Grew Marshall, Falmouth
Marble John W. Freetown
Andrews H. N. & Co. Gloucester
Chapin John A. "
Davis Brothers, "
Turner Samuel S. Hanover
Jenkins & Small, Harwich Port, Harwich
Knights Edward G. Hull
Blankinship Walter, Marion
Blankinship Warren, "
Handy Noah, "
Jenney Alonzo, Mattapoisett
Robinson Jos. H. "
Burdett Barzilla R. Nantucket
Allen Bartlett, New Bedford
Allen Thomas N. "
Beetle James, "
Butler Wm. F. "
Cranston John, "
Gifford & Beetle, "
Lewis & Sheehy, "
Smith John B. "
Smith Levi W. "
Smith Wm. H. "
Tripp Theodore, "

Boat Builders — continued.
Warren John C. — New Bedford
Orne & Rolfe, — Newburyport
Ghen Samuel H. — Provincetown
Keiley David S. — "
McKensie Alexander, — "
SMITH WM. W. (see page 770), "
Maybury W. F. — Quincy Pt. — Quincy
Beck-tt & Fellows, — Salem
Keniston and Lowell, — Salisbury
Keniston G. & F. — "
Lowell D. M. & Co. — "
Lowell Hiram, — "
Lowell Wm. D. — "
Morrill Ezra C. — "
Morrill G. H. & Co. — "
Morrill Wm. C. — "
Lawley Geo. — Scituate
Brooks John W. — Swampscott
Knowlton J. A. — "
Lowell Hiram, — "
Cleveland William, Holmes's Hole, Tisbury
Smith Alphonzo, — "
Hopkins Hiram, — Wellfleet
Snow N. — "
Sheldon George, Sheldonville, Wrentham

Bobbin and Spool Manufs.

Clark Joseph D. (yarn beams), North Adams, — Adams
SWIFT RIVER BOBBIN & SPOOL WORKS. Hills, Westcott, & Co. (see page 774), — Amherst
JENISON R. F. & CO. (see page 762), — Blackstone
Leavitt Benning, — Chicopee
— East Hampton
BASSETT JOEL L. (see page 761), "
POTTER R. N. & BROS. Davol St. (see page 756), — Fall River
SPRAGUE L. & CO. Lowell St., near the Depot, — Lawrence
Parker & Cheney, Wamesit Steam Mills, — Lowell
Watson E. F. Mechanic Mills, "
Norton J. D. & Son, — West Hampton
Murdock Wm. — Winchendon
Parks Martin H. & Brothers, "

Boiler Makers.

(*See also Machinists.*)

Kendall & Roberts, — Cambridge
Allen & Endicott, — Cambridgeport
Cunningham T. — Charlestown
Robinson Steam Boiler Co. — Clinton
— Fall River
FALL RIVER IRON WORKS CO. Richard Borden, agent, "
McCabe & Co. — Lawrence
DOBBINS & CRAWFORD (proprietors of Lowell Steam Boiler Works, Dutton, near Mechanics Mills, see page 737), — Lowell
— New Bedford
Union Boiler Co. (Jas. C. Bradford, agent, 19 School), "
CLARY & RUSSELL, McKay, cor. Depot, (see page 708), — Pittsfield
Lang Alexander, "
— Salem
SALEM BOILER WORKS, (J. Hassam), Ward, opp. Union, "
Grimes & Ellison, — Springfield
ROCHE BROTHERS, (see page 780), "
Worcester Steam Boiler Works, Stewart & Dillon, — Worcester

Bolts.

(*Yellow Metal and Copper.*)
NEW BEDFORD COPPER CO. (see page 757), — New Bedford

Bolts, Nuts, and Washers.

HEALD S. & SONS, (see pages 796 and 797), — Barre
Foster Walter K. (washers), Cambridgeport, — Cambridge
American Bolt Co., Whipple's Mills, — Lowell
SMITH S. C., Mt. Vernon, near Broadway, "
American Screw Co. (Branch), — Taunton

Bone Setter.

SWEET JOB, Kempton, cor. Summer (see page 712), — New Bedford

Bones and Bone Dust.

Hargraves C. — Fall River
Littlefield Hiram, — Newburyport
WALTON TIMOTHY foot of Ord, (see page 748), — Salem
Olney D. K. — Southbridge

Bonnet and Hat Bleacheries.

(*See also Bleacheries.*)

Dickinson Richard, — Fall River
Borden Peleg Mrs. "
Drake Lavinia. "
Newell Frank A. "
Rockwood Ezra B. — Fitchburg
Carpenter S. A. — Haverhill
Wentworth John, — Gloucester
Gilmore Wm. S. — Lawrence
Fay R. Mrs. — Lowell
Flanders C. R. "
Fletcher S. R. "
White George A. — Lynn
MOWRY G. W. & C. H. — Mansfield
Leonard N. W. & J. M. — Middleborough
Scribner David, — Newburyport
Ayres Austin W. — Northampton
Bacon W. H. — New Bedford
Knapp A. B. "
Taber William H. "
Hills Sanford, — Pittsfield
Ghen Emily J. — Provincetown
Clapp & Wetherell, — Salem
Carter W. & J. — Springfield
Southlands Bleachery, "
Kendall Francis, — Worcester
Wheaton H. C. 205 Main, "

Bonnet and Hat Block Manuf.

Hemenway Josiah (plaster), South Framingham, — Framingham
Force E. (plaster) — Medway
Howard N. F. (plaster), — Foxborough
Robinson & Briggs, — Franklin
Stanley O. A. "
WILLIAMSON M. W. & CO. 5 Central Exchange, — Worcester

Bonnet and Hood Machinery.

HEALD S. & SONS, dies, pressing, and rolling machines, &c., &c., (see pages 796 and 797), — Barre
Thayer A. P. (pressing), — West Medway

Bonnet Frame Manufacturers.

WILLIAMSON M. W. & CO. 5 Central Exchange, — Worcester

Bonnet Manufacturers.

(See Straw Goods.)

Bonnet Trimming Manuf.

Attleborough
Blackinton V. H., Attleboro' Falls, "

Bonnet Wire Manufacturers.

Scott Saul B., Franklin City, Franklin
Hale B. S. & Son, Lowell
Cady Geo. L, "
Cooper & Southworth, Stoughton

Bookbinders.

(See also Blank Book Manufacturers.)

Hutchins J. O. . Amesbury
Morris Benjamin G. Andover
McDonald & Sons, Cambridge
Welch & Co., Cambridgeport, "
Houghton H. O. & Co. "
RIVERSIDE BINDERY, A. F.
Lemon (see page 711), " "
Wilson Joshua, " "
Cormerais Charles, ... Chelsea
Fletcher Otis, ...Clinton
Kent S. Davies, Concord
Earle Newton R. Fall River
Fraprie Geo. W. "
Johnson Charles, Fitchburg
Rice Levi W. Greenfield
Whitney H. O. Haverhill
Fenerty Joseph B. Lawrence
Morris B. G. "
WHITCOMB I. A. 93 Essex, "
(see page 793),
MERRILL JOSHUA & SON,
37 Merrimac, Lowell
Bacheller N. J. & Co. "
Sargeant B. C. "
Simonds S. B. "
Breare Thomas, Lynn
Gilley William jr. Marblehead
Blunt M. A. Milford
Howe William, New Bedford
Parsons & Co. "
Taber Brothers, "
Crofoot H. T. Newburyport
Bridgman & Childs, Northampton
Cornwell Enos J. "
Childs C. C. & Co. "
Koon Henry R. Pittsfield
Brooks Horace A. "
Perley Jonathan, Salem
Hutchins J. O., Amesbury, Salisbury
Bowles Samuel & Co. Springfield
Bridgman J. C. & Co. "
Hathaway William G. "
Brackett Charles A. Taunton
McLauthlin C. C. Waltham
Grout & Bigelow, Watertown
Sanford Wm. H. & Co. Worcester
Wesby Joseph S. "

Bookbinders' Shears.

Toulmin John, Worcester

Book Clasp Manufacturers.

Attleborough
Blackinton R. & Co., Attleborough
Falls, "
MERRITT & DRAPER (and orna-
ments), Mansfield

Booksellers and Stationers.

Nash Sylvanus, Abington
ESTES J. J. East Abington, "
Mole John E. Adams

Dalrymple Orson, North Adams, Adams
Phillips Harlon L. "
Merrill F. W. "
Adams J. S. & C. Amesbury
Spear M. N. Amherst
Draper Warren F. Andover
Dodge Davies, Arlington
Green Charles O. Ashby
HUNT & LORD, Athol Depot, Athol
Thompson C. J. Attleborough
Jones Thos. R., N. Attleborough. "
Hinckley O. M. Barnstable
Brooks Humphrey F. Barre
SIBLEY SIDNEY, "
Morgan T. A. Beverly
Stanley John W. "
Kimball James, jr. Bradford
SEVER, FRANCIS, & CO., Har-
vard sq., Cambridge
Richardson Benjamin H. "
Niles Daniel W Cambridgeport, "
Ellis D. F. C. Canton
Wood Rufus C. "
Cutter A. E. Charlestown
Hobbs G. W. "
Fiske & Cummins, Charlton
Boyden George C. Chelsea
Hayward Fanny C. "
Orcutt Samuel, "
Keefe T. Chester
Ballard E. Clinton
Burdett T. E. "
Whitcomb Henry L. Concord
Townsend Harvey, Conway
Carson Paper Co. Dalton
Hood J. E. Danvers
Allwright Alfred, Dedham
Doherty Edward, "
Nutter I. N. & E. W. East Bridgewater
Putnam F. H. East Hampton
Pease Silvanus L. Edgartown
Adams Robert, Fall River
Earl Benjamin, "
Pope I. P. (periodicals), "
Noros L. J. " "
Boutelle W. S. Fitchburg
SHEPLEY STEPHEN & CO., 149
Main, "
Whitney E. A. "
Phelps Eli, Foxborough
Coolidge Charles E. Gloucester
PROCTER BROS., 121 Front, "
ROGERS JOHN S. E., Low's blk. "
Morgan William, Great Barrington
Prindle & Tobey, "
Merriam Lewis, Greenfield
Sherwin Levi, Groton Junction, Groton
Curtis Henry J. Hanover
Nickerson Obed, Harwich
Morse Charles E. Haverhill
SMILEY JAMES V., 8 Main, "
Barnard John, Hingham
Baker John R. Holyoke
Cragin Harvey H. "
Loomis & Pomeroy, "
McCabe Felix, "
Underwood James J. Hudson
Geyer Andrew, Ipswich
Dow John C. & Co. Lawrence
Dyer & Co. "
Marston & Prince, "
Stratton Lewis, "
WHITCOMB I. A., 93 Essex, (see
page 793), "
Lyman & Chaffee, Lee
Northrop L. "
Stanly John G. Lenox
Colburn Charles H. Leominster

Booksellers and Stationers — continued.

Dayton L. N.	Leominster
Coggeshall F. P.	Lowell
Edwards George C.	"
Gordon & Co.	"
Judkins J. J.	"
MERRILL JOSHUA & SON, 37	"
Merrimac,	"
Ryerson H. J.	"
Sargent B. C.	"
Sheehan Edward,	"
Stanton Albert D.	"
Thwing J.	"
Whitney Abel,	"
Green Otis H.	Lynn
Merrill P. M. Miss,	"
Munroe James M. &. Son,	"
Putnam James F.	"
WEBSTER W. T., 8 Exchange,	"
PICKETT CHARLES,	Marlborough
Wood Horace F.	"
Le Baron Lemuel,	Mattapoisett
Richardson Alpheus,	Methuen
Shaw J. B. & J.	Middleborough
Emery William,	Milford
READE LAWRENCE, 72 Main,	
(Catholic, see page 782),	"
Stacy G. W.	"
Packard T. F.	Monson
Jaggar Charles H.	Nantucket
Mitchell Edward,	"
Hutchinson S.	New Bedford
Parsons & Co.	"
Taber Brothers,	"
Clark George W.	Newburyport
Hale L. C.	"
Moulton N. A.	"
Woodman H. A.	"
Bridgman & Childs,	Northampton
Marsh Joseph,	"
Bixby C. C.	North Bridgewater
Copeland C. F.	"
Goldthwaite E.	"
Thomas H. O.	"
Pease W. E. & Co.	Oxford
WOOD & ALLEN, (see page 774),	Palmer
Stevens B. F.	Peabody
Allen Phinehas & Son,	Pittsfield
Childs C. C. & Co.	"
Cowan James,	"
Doten Charles C.	Plymouth
HALL JOHN T.	"
PUTNAM A. L.	Provincetown
Pattee Wm. S.	Quincy
Follett Chas. A.	"
PORTER F.	Randolph
Rosenfield Nathaniel,	"
Clark Henry,	Rockport
Thurston William H.	"
Brooks D. B. & Brother,	Salem
Beckford Chas. A.	"
Chandler & Co.	"
Grindal Stover,	"
Ives Henry P.	"
Ives J. S.	"
MOODY L. B., 24 Washington,	"
WHIPPLE G. M. & A. A. SMITH,	
243 Essex,	"
Whipple Henry (charts),	"
Bartlett D. L., Amesbury,	Salisbury
HALL CHAS. B.	Sandwich
POPE FREDERIC S.	"
Bowen Alfred, Shelburne Falls,	Shelburne
Sawyer Susan H.	"
BARNES WM. C.	Southbridge
King J. A.	"
Granger Brothers,	Southwick
Hill Gurdon & Co.	Springfield

Bradley Milton & Co.	Springfield
Bridgman J. C. & Co.	"
Burt Augustine & Co.	"
Burt Roderick (wholesale & retail),	"
Clark Chas. W.	"
Holland W. I.	"
Fisk D. E. & Co.	"
Rude H.	
Ryan P. J.	"
Barker A. J.	Taunton
Dunbar Samuel O. & Son,	"
Mitchell D. L.	"
Monroe Chas. E.	"
Seaver Wm. P.	"
Smith John (Catholic),	"
Brown Moses, Holmes's Hole,	Tisbury
Crocker Wendal,	"
Sawyer Henry C.	Waltham
Wooley George,	
Cutler G. K.	Ware
McLauthlin C. C.	Watertown
Connor S. S.	Westfield
Fletcher J M.	Westford
White Amos S. & Co.	Weymouth
Lesure Samuel,	Whately
Metcalf J. H.	Williamsburgh
Smith Nathan F.	Williamstown
Merrill E. S.	Winchendon
Brown George B.	Winchester
Horton Sparrow,	Woburn
Dorman J. A. Mrs.	Worcester
Grout & Bigelow,	"
Hall C. C. & J. K.	"
Howes B. G.	"
Howland H. J. (publisher Worcester	
Directory),	"
Sanford Wm. H. & Son,	"

Boot and Shoe Blacking Manufacturers.

FARRAR G. H. Union, cor. Wash.	
(see page 706),	Lynn
HAUTHAWAY C. L. & SONS,	
(see page 799),	North Bridgewater
POPE T. W. (see page 769),	"
WASHBURN ELISHA (see page 792),	"

Boot and Shoe Bottomers.

George T. Q.	Danvers
Holmes A. L.	East Bridgewater
Churchill A. S Joppa,	"
Foster & Smith,	Haverhill
Harris Joseph,	"
Pinknam Bros.	"
Roberts Geo. A.	"
Bradley & Harrington,	Lynn
Cheney & Fields,	"
Cottle H. W.	"
Leavitt Mark,	"
Miles S. P.	"
Norton William,	"
Sanborn B. F. & J. R.	"
Willey Geo. A.	"
Gardner L. A.	Marshfield
Keith D. N. Campello,	No. Bridgewater
Mitchell T	"
Palmer Charles,	Randolph
Linton P. H.	Weymouth

Boot and Shoe Counters.

Penniman Ansel,	Braintree
KEITH & PACKARD,	No. Bridgewater
Phinney S. C. & J. G.	Stoughton

Boot and Shoe Dealers.

(See also *Boot and Shoe Manufacturers,*
also *Country Stores.*)

Wheeler Edw. A., E. Abington,	Abington
Gilbert J. C. & Co., So.	"

Fletcher John & Sons,   Acton
Robinson Charles,   West Acton,   "
Wilde Charles M.   Acushnet
Richmond Daniel C. & Son,   Adams
Doane & Rav,   North Adams,   "
Holmes & Searle,   "   "   "
Ingraham Harvey & Co.
   (jobbers),   "   "   "
Jewett & Rand,   "   "   "
Smith Dexter,   "   "   "
Clarkson J. T.   Amesbury
TRUE ALFRED M. (see page 800),   "
Whittier Isaac,   "
CARTER S. C.   Amherst
Kellogg D. H.   "
Sloan T. W.   "
Stratton R. W.   "
Cutler Horace,   North Amherst,   "
Barnard J. W.   Andover
Brown Benj.   "
Corse & Son,   "
JOHNSON JAMES,   Central st.   "
Smith J. R.   Ballard Vale,   "
Ramsdell Thomas,   Arlington
Speatman Robert,   "
Morse C. B.   Athol
Stratton H. M.   "
Adams & Stratton,   Athol Depot,   "
Carpenter D. W. & Co.   Attleboro'
COOPER JOHN, (ladies'), Attleborough
Barden T. A.   N. Attleborough,   "
Hawes A. Z.   "   "
HAWES JOHN A.   "   "
Coleman Bacon,   Hyannis, Barnstable.
Crowell Daniel,   "   "
RICE JOHN W.
Barnes Wright,   Barre
Hayes C. B. & E. K.   Becket
Burnham Charles L.   Belchertown
Dike Samuel,   Beverly
Wallis Jeremiah,   "
Parker Charles H.   Billerica
Bartlett Varnum,   Blackstone
Shephard L. B. & Son,   Blandford
Rogers Zoeth H.   Brewster
Cushman Darius,   Bridgewater
Wilber Richard W.   "
Rooney James,   Brookline
Weinstein Rupert,   "
Dollard James,   Cambridge
Mann Rufus,   "
Hayes Alvin,   Cambridgeport,   "
Mason James N.   "   "
Rohde Joseph,   "   "
Sampson William P.   "   "
Wilder Cyrus D.   "   "
Dwyer Timothy,   East Cambridge,   "
Guyer Lewis B. & Co. "   "   "
Hunnewell W. & Co.   "   "   "
Reed Enos,   "   "   "
Clark Thomas,   North   "
Ellis D. C. F.   Canton
Fuller E. O. & H.   "
Alden Charles W.   Charlestown
Atwood John O.   "
Byam Charles F.   "
Clayton William E.   "
Hale Apollos,   "
Martin Newhall & Co.   "
Poor George,   "
Pratt Elbridge S.   "
Quirk D. G. & Co.   "
Suddard J. C.   "
Sullivan John C. Mrs.   "
Tuck & Goodwin,   "
White Ebenezer,   "
Spalding A. F.   Chelmsford
Dammerall John,   Chelsea

Elbridge J. S. & Son,   Chelsea
Higgins Josiah,   "
Higgins Patrick,   "
Libby John A.
Richards C. E. & Co.
Ware Frank W.
Williams Thomas A. jr.   "
Allen C.   Chester
Chadwick J.   "
Beals W. P.   Chicopee
Chapman & Folsom,   "
Hitchcock J. M. & Co.
Parshley S. W.
Chapin Bell,   Chicopee Falls,   "
Donovan Daniel,   "   "   "
Barry John,   Clinton
Luthe G. W.   "
Lyon L. D.   "
Winter Waldo,   "
Bates Philander, .   Cohasset
Stacy & Davis   Coleraine
Davis George B.   Concord
Hastings Jonas,   "
Pierce Cyrus,   "
Adams Rawson,   Conway
DRAYTON CHARLES,   Danvers
Patch Abraham,   "
Allwright Alfred,   Dedham
Wiggin Andrew & Co.   "
Norris S. M.   East Dedham,   "
White Robert,   "   "   "
Bigelow S. Waldo   South   "   "
Tisdale Josiah,   "   "   "
Pratt Joshua G.   Deerfield
Arms Obed S.   South Deerfield,   "
Howe John,   Dorchester
Wendemuth E. R.,   Milton,   "
Twombly J. W. & Co.   "   "   "
Emerson Horace, East Douglas, Douglas
Hutchinson B. W.   East Hampton
Waite Joseph,   "
Lewis William,   Edgartown
Coffin Jared W.   "
Burnham D. B.   "
Howes Charles,   "
Pierce A. T.   Fairhaven
Breen Nelson   Fall River
Coburn J. C.   "
Conley John,   "
Dodge & Sears,   "
Duckworth R.   "
Eddy & Milne,   "
Emery B. & Co.   "
FRENCH J. B. & SON, 26 N. Main,   "
French Stephen L.   "
Gengan Nicholas,   "
Groves & Nichols,
Howarth Bros.
Houghton Geo. A.
O'Connell Michael,
Sanford Thos.
Smith Thomas B.
Sullivan J.
Waters George,
Whiting Lewis,   "
Alexander F. W.   Fitchburg
Balcom Frank S.   "
Boutwell E.   "
Eville John B.   "
Hogan Walter W.   "
Jennison Daniel,   "
Partridge A. & Bro.   "
Proctor George B.   "
Tenney Jonathan L.   "
Whitney E. A.   "
Alexander Jerry W., West Fitchburg, "
Butterworth Geo. H.   Foxborough
Lowe Joseph G.   "

Boot and Shoe Dealers — continued.

Stiff James,	Foxborough
Brown Matthew,	Franklin
Caswell A. W.	Gardner
Jewett Charles E.	Georgetown
CORLISS B. H. jr. 129 Front,	Gloucester
Griffin G. Frank,	"
Haskell J. W.	"
PARSONS W. FRANK & BRO. 86	
Front,	"
Pettingill Charles W.	"
Richardson J. H.	"
Staten Edward & Co.	"
York & Gott,	"
Barry James W.	Great Barrington
Burghardt Lonson N.	"
Mellen G. W. & Co.	"
Williams Elihu,	"
Fellows M. S.	Greenfield
Forbes J. N. & Co.	"
Ford H. L.	"
McFarland J.	"
Fuller Dexter,	Groton
Tenney J. C.,	Groton Junction, "
Curtis & Co.	Hanover
Brett Charles E.	Harwich
Buck Jonathan,	"
Small Philip N.	Harwich Port "
Bartlett J. C.	Haverhill
Bennett R. P.	"
Brown John,	"
Winn J. W.	"
Marsh Willam F.	Heath
Whiton E. L.	Hingham
Whiting E. F.	Holliston
Fiske George B.	"
Butler Joseph,	Holyoke
Clark Chandler,	"
Corser Charles A.	"
Cragin H. H.	"
Hart James,	"
Sackett L.	"
Wolcott George M.	"
Johnson David L.	Hubbardston
Hutchins & Co.	Hudson
Priest Samuel E.	"
Woods Elijah N.	Huntington
Adler L.	Hyde Park
Estey Chas. H.	"
Luce & Ingersoll,	"
Ellis George N.	Ipswich
TOZER WILLIAM H.	"
Blaisdell & Moore,	Lawrence
Chard Samuel,	"
Allard Henry D.	"
Brown C. W.	"
Clay H. T.	"
Cusack John,	"
Duncklee & Danforth,	"
French J. Y. & Co.	"
Heermann Lewis,	"
Mahony Daniel D.	"
Pearsons James,	"
Robinson H. G.	"
Robinson P. B.	"
Sanders J. L.	"
Warburton Peter,	"
Whittredge Alfred A.	"
Whithredge T. J.	"
Mecum A. R.	Lee
Davis Frank W.	Leominster
Kendall A. D.	"
Polley A. M. & Son,	"
Adams Bros.	"
Benson J. W.	Lowell
Boardman L. H.	"
Byam S. A.	"
Chase Lorenzo,	"

Collins J. B.	Lowell
Crane George & Son,	"
Dearborn E.	"
Donnolly John,	
Flanders H. R.	
Harvey & Burrill,	
Grant J. E.	
Huntoon M. C.	
Kittredge Daniel,	
Knowles Bros.	"
Lamb & Nichols,	"
Lovett Stephen,	"
McElholm William,	
McLaughlin James,	
McLees Thomas,	
Merrill A. A. & Co.	
Plummer J. W.	
Robbins A. F.	
Swan Daniel,	
Tackrah Henry,	"
Weeks Samuel D.	"
Wright C. & H. C.	"
Wright George,	
Wright Hapgood,	
Wright Nathan M.	"
Allard M. J. Mrs.	Lynn
Barry John,	"
Blake Edmond C.	"
Boynton Silas P.	"
Dunbar E. H.	"
Flagg Daniel,	"
Flagg Francis,	"
Goodridge Micajah N.	"
Herbert Thomas,	"
Hodgkins Joseph E.	"
Johnson H. H.	"
Lovering Richard,	"
Newhall Perry,	"
Osborne Wellman,	"
Webster E. W.	"
West Hiram,	"
Cox Henry J.	Malden
Mann J. T.	"
Richardson James C.	
Bessom W. C.	Mansfield
Foss Thomas,	Marblehead
Graves Joseph, 4th,	"
Hiller Joseph E.	"
LeMaster George,	"
PIERCE B. F.	"
Rogers William,	"
Watson Osgood H.	Marlborough
Jacobs & Cushing,	Medford
Gage Lewis,	Methuen
Law John,	"
Foss Edward S.	Middleborough
Washburn & Andrews,	"
Colburn F. A.	Milford
Darling R. L.	"
Folsom H.	"
Keane John,	"
Mott C. A.	"
Mott M. O.	"
Gerry Elbridge,	Millbury
Goddard N. & Son,	"
Blackman Elbridge,	Milton
Chapman & Strangman,	"
Crossman Lemuel,	"
Johnson Spencer W.	"
McKay Patrick,	"
Scannell Dennis O.	"
Allen E. W.	Monson
Bennett William H.	Nantucket
Lovell Charles,	"
MOWRY ALMON T.	"
Starbuck Charles H.	"
SIMONDS FRANK P.	Natick
Watson O. H.	"

New Bedford
DEVOLL PARDON, 26 Purchase, "
Donaghy Thomas E. (wholesale), "
Ellis T. H. & Co. "
Freeman Edward P. "
Lothrop Asa, "
Lucas A. E. & Co. "
Palmer A. R. "
Union Boot & Shoe Co. "
YOUNG & ELDER, 69 Union st. "
Bartlett G. W. & Co. Newburyport
Batchelder D. T. "
Daniels Charles H. "
Horton William F. "
Jordan Simon, "
Little William A. "
Morss William B. "
Peabody Charles, "
Tebbitts Henry, "
Witin J. M. "
Gammons J. E., West Newton, Newton
Spaulding S. C., Newton Centre, "
Holman Edward, Newton Corner, "
Robbins George, "
Jackson W. M. Lower Falls, "
Wheeling Loring, Upper " "
Clarke Charles E. Northampton
Bridgman & Graves, "
Hamlin & Smith, "
Slate & Baker, "
Montague R. Northborough
Carr Samuel A., Whitinsville, Northbridge
Brigham Charles D. North Bridgewater
Bryant G. E. & H. L. "
CUSHMAN N. & CO. (ladies'), "
Davis Benjamin P. "
Packard J. T. (ladies'), "
Whiting Daniel, North Brookfield
Fenno Joseph H. North Chelsea
Bridge Thomas E. Orange
Goddard Abner, "
Vose George, Orleans
Sparrow Alphonso, East Orleans, "
Dimock Lyman, Palmer
Eager F. M. "
Moore Dennison, Peabody
Morrison Joseph, "
Trask T. S. "
Teague C. E. "
Chapman Samuel H. Pepperell
Shattuck Putnam, "
Breakey John, Pittsfield
Brown John, "
Burbank & Enright, "
Childs F. L. "
Crafts Edward C. "
Fairfield David, "
Kerby & Abbott, "
Leonard & Burk, "
Pierce L. M. "
Prelizer & Kahl, "
Root Oliver & Co. "
Stevens Liberty, "
Bramhall Benjamin, "
Bartlett Ephraim, Plymouth
Holmes Ephraim B. "
Howland Jacob, jr. "
Knowles Joseph P. "
Mayo Richard, Provincetown
Sweetser Albert, "
Tanner Joshua, "
Turner Isaiah, "
Parker James, "
Reed C. T. "
Stetson D. B. Quincy
Allen E. A. "
Bassett Edwin, Randolph
Reed L., jr. Reading

Lurvey Samuel N. Rockport
Parsons & Kuntsford, "
York N. F. S. "
Story Henry L. Pigeon Cove, "
Bosson & Glover, Salem
Bott Thomas, "
Buswell Eben & Co. "
Cressey W. B. "
Flint Harrison O. "
Lake H. H. "
Low Aaron T. "
Martin & Cunningham, "
Morton H. & C. "
Moulton J. W. L. "
O'Connell Timothy, "
Palmer Theron, "
Perley John, "
Sweetser E. & Co. "
Symonds J. W. & Co. "
Burpee John, Amesbury, Salisbury
Osgood M. C. "
Whittier Isaac " "
Duffy A. A. Sandwich
Hunt Samuel W. "
Moroney William P. "
Sherman T. C. "
Shelburne
Bates George A. jr., Shelburne Falls, "
Jenks G. W. " " "
Bullard Henry W. Sherborn
Chace Joseph & Co. Somerset
Marble Joseph, "
Eberle Philip, Somerville
Comstock & Perry, Southbridge
Edwards & Co. "
McKinstry J. O., Globe Village, "
South Hadley
Gaylord John, South Hadley Falls, "
COMINS & CLARK, Spencer
Bradley & Fay, Springfield
Burke James, "
Childs James R. "
Cutler, McIntosh, & Co. "
Gibbs J. W. & N. G. "
Hixon, Birnie, & Shaw (wholesale), "
Kendall Joel, "
Larned Amos, "
Marsh W. P. & Co. "
Morse O. D. (wholesale and retail), "
Robbins J. S. "
Shaw H. A. 5 State Street, "
Tibbets & Dearden, "
Warner & Smith, "
Wright F. "
Heath J. B. Stoneham
Rowe Henry, "
Potter Benjamin, Swampscott
Curtis Heman F. Taunton
MASON DANIEL H. 39 Main, "
Hoys John, "
King A. F. "
Monroe & Andrews, "
Perry Henry C. "
Seaver N. B. "
Washburn & Elliott, "
Winch J. O. Templeton
Tisbury
Branscomb Stephen, Holmes's Hole, "
Luce Timothy, " "
Norton Leavitt T. "
Hudson S. Uxbridge
Sweet & Harwood, "
Whitmore H. & Co. "
Gage Benjamin, Wakefield
Merrill Greeley, "
Webster B. G. Wales
Warren Rufus, Waltham
Guild V. Ware

Boot and Shoe Dealers — continued.

Kennedy J.	Ware
Sagendorph P. H.	"
Moroney M. C.	Wareham
Powers William L.	Warren
Albee Abner.	Warwick
Coombs S. H.	Watertown
Otis Brothers,	"
Bates George D.	"
Stockwell C. B.	Webster
Tracy George,	"
Mildram Moses,	Wenham
Higgins Reuben, 2d,	Wellfleet
Rich Snow,	"
Whorf & Higgins,	"
Eaton William J.	Westborough
Winter Aaron E.	West Boylston
Knapp Isaac,	Westfield
Lewis B. F.	"
Shurtleff George & Co.	"
Williams Sylvester,	"
Judd F. H.	West Hampton
Vogle L.	West Roxbury
BUCHANAN JOHN, Jamaica Plain,	"
Fallmac Casper,	" " "
Kolb Peter C.	" " "
Leonard L., Mittineague, West Springfield	
Sabin C. H.	West Stockbridge
Shaw Nathan,	"
Crane John & Son,	Weymouth
White Derick,	"
Bates John W., East Weymouth,	"
Crafts C. W.	"
Thayer Caleb L.	Whately
Rice Chauncy,	Williamsburg
Mann Almon,	Winchendon
DUNN J. J.	"
Tarbell C. H.	"
Davis S. H.	Winchester
Buckman Alvah,	Woburn
Wood Artemas,	"
Wyman William R.	"
Allen & Reed,	Worcester
Barrett & Randall,	"
Bemis Edward,	"
Bigelow & Billings,	"
BROWN J. K. 246 Main,	"
Fisher A. H.	"
Hall Frank B.	"
Haven O. C.	"
Moody N.	"
Rist G. L.	"
Schwartz David,	"
Shea Thomas J.	"
Smyth Brothers & Co (wholesale),	"
Vail R. T.	"
Whittemore & Goddard,	"
Hallet Nathan, Yarmouth Port, Yarmouth	
Jenkins Elisha,	South Yarmouth, "
Larkin John,	" "
Parker Elisha.	" "

Boot and Shoe Findings, Tools, &c.

Damon Martin W (patterns).	Abington
Union Patent Knife & Needle Co.,	
G. A. Beal, treasurer,	"
Lewis George H.	East Abington,
Griffin O. P. & Co. (shoe lace),	Attleboro'
HEALD & SONS, (pegging and trimming jacks, see pages 796, 797),	
	Barre
	Brimfield
Varney Charles (tools), East Brimfield. "	
Carter Williams E.	Burlington
Shed S. S.	"
REED FRANKLIN (tools and machinery, see page 793)	Canton

DRAYTON CHARLES,	Danvers
NEWHALL BENJ. E.	"
KEEN SAML. & CO., (machinery),	
Joppa Village,	East Bridgewater
	Fall River
FRENCH J. B. & SON, 26 No. Main,	"
Annisquam.	Gloucester
Jewett Wm. H. (heel and toe irons),	"
Hastings G. W. (black ball),	Grafton
PACKARD SUMNER (pegging awls and shaves, see page 762) New England Village,	"
	Haverhill
Newcomb John D. (tools & findings),	"
Pettengill D. A. (patterns),	"
Ricard Hubert (tools and dies),	"
Smiley W. & Son (tools and findings),	"
	Hingham
Wilder E. F. (kits) South Hingham	"
	Holliston
STETSON & TALBOT (tacks and nails, see page 782)	"
Willis George,	Hubbardston
Busfield John G.	Hudson
Davidson F. A.	"
DAWES F. S. (see page 761)	"
Farnsworth & Watkins (awls hafts & shaves)	"
MILLAY P. E. (lasts and shoe-nails, see page 761)	"
Bacheller J. R.	Lynn
Breed T. N.	"
Collins & Delnow,	"
Coyle John (cutters & dies,)	"
FARRAR G. H. (tools, blacking, &c., see page 706) Union, cor. Washington,	"
Farnsworth E. M. (manufs. supplies)	"
Foster & Whitten, (awls & needles,)	"
Graves J. W. (patterns),	"
Hutchinson W. Henry,	"
MARSHALL J. OTIS, (die blocks & cutting boards, see page 750), rear 13 Broad,	"
MARTIN E. L. P. 54 Munroe, (see page 706),	"
Myrick Isaac, (dealer),	"
Parrott B. F.	"
Phillips O. (needles of all kinds),	"
Rose Wm. A. (manufacturer of irons),	"
Teel Eben S. (manufacturer of irons),	"
TRIPP S. D. (machinery, cutters, dies, &c., see page 750), 13 Broad,	"
	Mansfield
Fulton Robert (knives and peg awls),	"
MOOREHOUSE JOHN (shoe tools), see page 733)	"
Moran & Sons (shoe tools),	"
Moran & Robinson (knives),	"
	West Mansfield, "
Estabrook Edward C.	Marlboro'
Cummings S. A. (knives),	Middleton
Buxton J. L. (peg cutters, &c.),	Milford
Claflin E. C. (thread),	"
Crispin Nail & Tack Co.	"
Goodrich S. P. (kits),	"
Howe Jarvis & Co. (boot trees),	"
Hussey R. C. (patent cutting boards),	"
Littlefield J. W. (kits),	"
Mann E. & Howard (crimp screws),	"
Young J. A. (machine pegging awls),	"
Jennings J. J. jr. (tools),	Natick
Cobb Tyler (tools),	North Bridgewater
HATHAWAY C. L. & SONS, (blacking, &c., see page 799),	"
O'NEILL WM. H. (awls, see p. 769),	"
PACKARD J. W. (needles, &c., see page 769),	"

POPE T.W. (blacking, &c., see
  page 769)   North Bridgewater
Smith J. A. (leather string manufac-
  turer),   "
Snell E. S. & Co. (tools),   "
Snell & Atherton (tools),   "
TUCK S. V. (shoe knives, &c., see
  page 770),   "
WEBSTER W. (shoe knives, &c.,
  see page 769),   "
WASHBURN ELISHA (blacking,
  &c., see page 792),   "
Whittemore D. (pegging machines), "
Johnson A. E. (patent shoe shaves), Oxford
Pierce Geo. C. (cork soles), Peabody
Bassett Daniel H.   Pittsfield
Finney Harrison (kits),   Plymouth
Packard E. & Co. (ink),   Quincy
Reed C. T.   "
Pratt J. W. & Co. (shoe strings), Randolph
Pratt W. E. (shoe strings),
Thayer Royal & Son (all kinds of
  leather pieces),   E. Randolph, "
Whitcomb Jacob (shoe strings), " "
White Oramel,   "   "
Harrington Dexter (shaves), Southbridge
Harrington Theodore (shoe knives), "
Richards Stephen, agt. (knives),   "
Cutter, McIntosh, & Co.   Springfield
Rickardson B. F. (benches), Stoneham
LINFIELD M. & SON (lasts, see
  page 728),   Stoughton
Mann J. B. (knives & tools),   "
Southworth & Stevens (varnish
  and stain),   "
Townsend W. F.   Taunton
Stowell J.   Wakefield
Woodward J. F. & Co. (awls), "
Daniels George W. (punches and
  eyelet sets),   Waltham
Spaulding Cyrus (dealer),   Webster
Crane J. & Son (tools),   Weymouth
Allen Asa M. (shoe nails), Union, Worcester
Brannan B. (shoe strings),   "
Cushman & Thompson (dealers), "
Howe A. M. (cutting dies, &c.), "
MAWHINNEY SAMUEL (lasts, see
  page 783),   "
Pease L. J. & Co. (machinery), "
PORTER SAMUEL, Union st.
  (see page 781),   "
Richards C. J. (patterns),   "
Robinson H. P. (heel & toe irons), "
Rogers, Southgate & Co. (dealers), "
TOUGAS & DUPREY, 9 Cypress,
  (cutters and dies, see page 781), "

Boot and Shoe Finishers.

Tribou William, N. Abington, Abington
Churchill A. S. Joppa, E. Bridgewater
Churchill Geo. Campello, No. Bridgewater
Scribner Perry,   Haverhill
Bicknell J. Q., E. Weymouth, Weymouth
Rogers J. W.   "   "
Martin Thomas, S. Weymouth, "

Boot and Shoe Heelers.

Mayburry F. E. & J. O.   Haverhill
Annis & Vincent,   Lynn
Bailey Geo. M.   "
Baynton Benju. P.   "
Brooks A. W.   "
Burrows & Wedgewood,   "
Carew Wm E.   "
Carr A. S.   "
Chamberlain B. F.   "
Chapman Hiram,   "
Churchill G. F. & Co.   "

Coffin John G.   Lynn
Crossman George A.   "
Danforth, Ward, & Co.   "
Fuller A. H.
Howard F. P.   "
Howard J. E.   "
Kimball C. A.   "
Knowles A. M.   "
Lockwood J. C.
Moulton G. W.
Murphy & Shepherd,
Neally—
Nichols, Dixon, & Ballard,
Nichols Geo. A.
Nichols Horace B.
Oliver Charles D.
Pierce James M.   "
Preble W. H. & H.   "
Rogers Robert S.   "
Rogers T. G.   "
Smith & Vincent,   "
Stone Bros.
VELLA J. F., Willow st. (see
  page 712)   "
Wacey David & Co.   "
Widger Sam'l A.   "
Stevens & Carkin,   Marblehead
Hussey Simeon, East Saugus, Saugus
Lockwood J. C.

Boot and Shoe Machinery.

RICHARDSON GEO. H. (see
  page 771)   Athol Depot, Athol
Varney Charles (pegging-machines),
  East Brimfield,   Brimfield
Reed Franklin.   Canton
KEEN SAMUEL & CO.,
  Joppa Village,   East Bridgewater
Curtis Timothy A.   East Brookfield
Knox David,   Lynn
TRIPP S. D. (see page 759),
  13 Broad,   "
Howe Jarvis & Co.   Milford
Littlefield J. W.

Boot and Shoe Makers.

(See Boot and Shoe Manufacturers, also
    Boot and Shoe Dealers.)

Power R. B.   Abington
Beal F.   East Abington, "
Noyes Cephas D. (boots), N. Abington, "
Witherell James H. So.   "
Shattuck William, South Acton, Acton
Wyman O. C.   West   "
Mauter John, jr. Long Plain, Acushnet
Dean Job,   Adams
Randall D. M.
Roland Frank,
Easton James,   North Adams, "
Field Austin,   "   ":
McKay & Co.   "   "
Nelson Reuben E.   "   "
Radlo L.   "   "
Ball Alfred L.   Agawam
Bailey Thomas, Feeding Hills, "
Rowbotham William,   Amesbury
Sargent L. C.   "
Frye A. M.   West Amesbury, "
Pearson Luther,   "   "
Townsend M. B.   "   "   "
Newell William,   Amherst
JOHNSON JAMES,   Andover
Hill Howard W.   Arlington
Stiegel John,
Merriam J.   Ashburnham
Sawyer Edward,   "
Stearns Charles,   "

ers — continued.

Ashby	Dollard John,	Cambridgeport, Cambridge
"	Duris Daniel.	" "
Ashfield	Hilliard S D.	" "
Ashland	Hutchinson C.	
Athol	Learned Grant.	
"	McLeod Wm. G.	"
Athol Depot, "	Panmann Frederic,	
" "	Powers J. E.	"
Attleborough	Richardson James,	"
"	Sawyer William L.	"
Attleborough, "	Sheehan Patrick,	"
" "	Bass Jona. H.	East Cambridge, "
" "	Brown J.	" "
" "	Green John,	" "
Auburn	Grimm George,	" "
"	Marston J. H.	
"	Martin J.	
Barnstable	Kessehl Frederick,	"
Barre	Kay James W.	"
Beck-t	Smith H.	" "
" "	Clarke William.	North Cambridge, "
Bedford	Clausen Peter N.	" "
Belchertown	Heffernan Joseph,	" "
Bellingham	Hyde Thomas,	Canton
h Bellingham, "	Mabbot John,	"
Belmont	Sullivan Cornelius S.	
Barkley	Blaisdell Isaac,	Carlisle
"	Cobb L.	North Carver, Carver
Bernardston	Dunham John,	" "
"	Peck Charles,	Charlemont
"	Rogers Cephas,	"
Beverly	Taylor S.	
"	Barr Alexander,	Charlestown
"	Chaplin Oliver,	"
"	Condon Richard,	"
"	Connolly Cornelius,	"
"	Caughlin John S.	"
"	Dowd James,	"
"	Evans D. J.	"
"	Fitzpatrick J.	"
Billerica	Foster Charles,	::
Blackstone	Frye Levi,	"
"	Gross Andrew,	"
Blandford	Kearney John T.	"
Boxford	Mackay John,	"
"	McCurdy John,	"
"	McPhee William	"
Bradford	Murphy J.	"
"	Murray J. C.	"
Braintree	O'Hearn John,	"
Brewster	O'Meary Stephen,	
"	O'Meary J.	"
"	Quill M. H.	"
Bridgewater	Regan Cornelius,	
Brighton	Renno C.	"
"	Savage J.	
"	Schwartz Jacob L.	
"	Smith Joseph N.	
"	Sweetser Daniel.	
Brimfield	Wallace John H.	
"	Bailey E.	Chatham
Brookfield	Crosby Abijah,	"
Brookline	Hammond William,	"
"	Shaw John,	
"	Spalding A. F.	Chelmsford
Buckland	Green William P.	North Chelmsford, "
"	Whidden A. G.	" "
Cambridge	Ayers Oliver.	Chelsea
"	Dammerall Thomas;	"
"	Donaghy James,	"
"	Dyke William,	"
"	Gurney Reuben,	
"	LANGLEY ASAPH,	Winnissimmet st."
"	Leonard George M.	"
nbridgeport, "	Leslie Duncan,	"
" "	Martin Henry,	
" "	McLane B. J.	"
" "	Morse B. F.	"

Parkinson John, Chelsea
Powers Edward, "
Tewksbury S. H. "
Wilson Caleb S. "
Brien Thomas, Cheshire
Mansfield Hollis, "
Allen Charles, Chester
Chadwick J. "
Rhoades Thos. C., W. Chesterfield, "
Beals W. P. Chicopee
Donovan D. Chicopee Falls,
Lathe G. W. Clinton
Bates Philander, Cohasset
Beal Thomas, "
Souther John, "
Howard H. A. Coleraine
Davis George B. Concord
Hastings Jonas, "
Pierce Cyrus, "
Smith Martin, Conway
Thayer Edward C. Cummington
Burbank Joseph, Dalton
Newell B. F. "
Bryant Fred, North Dana, Dana
Tucker James H. Dartmouth
Raymond Edward F., N. Dartmouth, "
Swift Sylvanus, South " "
Patch Abraham jr. Danvers
Parry Albert, Danversport, "
Wiggin Andrew, Dedham
Barnaby Timothy, East Dedham, "
Williamson Martin, West " "
Gay Joel A. South " "
Horgan Jeremiah, " " "
Munn Philo, Deerfield
Griggor Dorley E. East Dennis, Dennis
Davis Solomon F. West " "
Howes H. E. " " "
Shute Daniel, South " "
Pidge Benj. Dighton
Ramelow Geo. No. Dighton, "
Gorman Patrick, Dorchester
Hart Kuran, "
Kelly Thos. "
Lary Richard, "
McGrath T. T. "
Willis Edward, "
Gauderer Geo. Harrison Square, "
Leonard S. W. " " "
Bird Stephen, Mattapan, "
Christmas Thos., Milton, " "
French Henry, " "
Wendemuth E. R. " "
Giavin John, Neponset, "
Mathews W. H. " "
Kelley Daniel, Douglas
Allen David E. Dover
Demeritt John, "
Coburn Horatio G. "
Stickney Nathaniel, Dracut
Whitcomb Lowell, Dunstable
Crocker George P. Duxbury
Stetson Andrew, "
Brackett William, "
Knowles William, Eastham
Colgan James, "
Gillen James, Easthampton
Goldenblum R. "
Friday G. "
King J. R. & Co. N. Easton, Easton
Mackey James N. "
Stuart Samuel S. Edgartown
Kline Mark, N. Egremont, Egremont
Makeley Wm. " "
Polinatier Geo. H., So. " "
Cutting David, Enfield
Howes Lewis, "

Thrasher Charles, Enfield
Turner Oren, Erving
Andrews William H. Essex
Cook Moses, "
Goldsmith Edward K. "
Carver David, Fairhaven
Jenney Dexter, "
McCarthy D. "
Stetson J. "
Weed Stephen, "
Adams J. W. Fall River
Babcock Alden, "
Brightman N. "
Brownell George C. "
Connell Thomas, "
Dawson W. M.
Duckworth Richard, "
Fletcher James, "
Haggerty Timothy, "
Hicks George A. "
Houghton William M. "
Kelly Jeremiah H. "
Leary J. R. "
Lewis Nathaniel, "
McDonough T.
McGraw F. "
Mc Hugh James, "
McKeown James, "
McNulty John, "
Rash John, "
Rockett John, "
Smith Thomas B. (also clog), "
Sullivan M. E. "
Walter John; "
Whiting Lewis, "
Wildes J. A. "
Edwards Watson, Falmouth
Green Ansel, "
McLane Albert C. "
Wicks John, "
Bowker Francis, Fitchburg
Farnsworth Leonard, "
Parkhurst S. "
Betts A. & Son, West Fitchburg, "
Billings Warren, Foxborough
Boyden Warren, "
Hughes David, "
Spofford Wm. "
Stitt James, "
Smith Norman, Framingham
Masterson Peter, S. Framingham, "
Newton G. H. "
Burrill E. Saxonville, "
Puffer Elijah, "
Biggs George, Franklin
Fisher L. L. "
Briggs Sylvester & Son, Freetown
Blodgett F. Gardner
Caswell A. W. "
Blair Lucian, South Gardner, "
Cheney Lorenzo, " " "
Perley Charles, Georgetown
Stocker Charles M. "
Roberts Holland F. "
Bray Albert A. Gill
Egan Patrick, Gloucester
Freeman James, "
Grant John B. "
Green Maurice, "
Hayden Luther,
Joyce Thomas, "
Monnter Robert,
South Geo. L. "
Sweet John, "
Thurston Samuel S. "
Bartoll Thomas R. E. Gloucester, "
Blinn Charles, " "
Richardson Edw. H. " "

Boot and Shoe Makers — continued.

Hunt Lowell,	Goshen
BOSWORTH SYLVANUS,	Grafton
Kellogg Walter B.	Granby
Beers Andrew, West Granville,	Granville
Smith E. " " "	
Fay Dexter,	Great Barrington
Carey Lockwood,	Housatonic. "
Edward G. D.	Greenfield
Forbes J. M. & Co.	"
Grostick Frederick,	"
Kean Edward,	"
Kelley G. S.	Greenwich
Vaughan S. R.	"
Lord Cyrus, Greenwich Village,	"
Harnden Albert,	Groton
Balch Jonathan,	Groveland
Lyon Charles P.	Halifax
Whitaker Schuyler,	Hancock
Bates Joshua,	Hanover
Munroe Hiram,	"
Beal George P.	Hanson
Soper Jeremiah,	"
Whitford David,	"
Foster Isaac & Sons, So. Hanson,	"
Burgess Joseph,	Hardwick
Jerome Joseph,	"
Robinson Charles,	"
Simpson Nathaniel,	"
Houghton Samuel W.	Harvard
Taylor Zopher,	"
Willard Robert,	"
Willard Russell, Still River,	"
Hall John N.	Harwich
Underwood Sidney B.	"
Small P. N. Harwichport,	"
Childs Henry,	Hatfield
Hinchey John,	Haverhill
Strange Pierce,	"
Winn J. W.	"
Crosby Daniel, Charlemont,	Hawley
Baker Harvey, West Hawley,	"
Barber S. W.	Heath
Elmer Orris O.	"
Marsh William F.	"
Cushing William C.	Hingham
Dyer Solomon L.	"
Fee Peter,	"
Hudson Edwin H.	"
Burbank Anthony,	Hinsdale
Picard Albert,	"
Burnett John,	Holden
Newell H. P.	"
Fairbanks Daniel,	Holliston
White O.	"
Butler Joseph,	"
Corser C. A.	Holyoke
Lander P.	"
Sackett Loren,	"
Welch James,	"
McGill C.	Hopkinton
Johnson David L.	Hubbardston
Woods F. N.	Huntington
Clapp P. C.	Hyde Park
Murray David,	"
Ellis Geo. W.	Ipswich
Johnston William,	"
Bradford George B.	Kingston
Richardson E. P.	"
Grant Sylvester.	Lakeville
Tinkham Horatio,	"
Bunting G. F.	Lancaster
Humphrey Reuben,	Lanesborough
Homan James,	"
Binns Nathan,	Lawrence
Clay H. T.	"
Corwell John,	"
Fenton J.	"

Gray John H.	Lawrence
Matthews Job,	"
Pearson James,	"
Reynolds Thos.	"
Rollins & Clark,	"
Tenney E.	"
Tyler F.	"
Alger Edmund,	Lee
Berry Thomas,	"
Farrell Thomas,	"
Heebner Edmund,	"
Hopkins Anson,	"
Johnson Isaac W.	"
Gay Wm. O.	Leicester
Bourn Alphonso,	Lenox
Cone & Bonin,	"
Wheeler Asahel, Lenox Furnace,	"
Bruce Isaac T.	Leominster
Chute Wm. G., N. Leominster,	"
Cutter C. B.	Leverett
Duren Warren,	Lexington
Ham Sampson,	"
Nash Oran, East Lexington,	"
Edwards Elijah,	Lincoln
Burnham D. D.	Littleton
Mitchell Lyman,	"
Bailey Manasseh,	Lowell
Berry Chas. R.	"
Brady & Smith,	"
Butler S. B.	"
Butterworth John,	"
Cooney W. J.	"
Dalton Michael,	"
Daly Z. S.	"
Farrell P.	"
Farwell J. R.	"
Flanders & Keith	"
Griffin J. W	"
Helson Geo	"
Hovey W.	"
Kent James,	"
King John,	"
King Stephen,	"
Leavitt W. B.	"
Loker W. N.	"
McCarty J.	"
McDERMOTT JAMES, 78 Middlesex,	"
McElholm Wm.	"
McKissock R.	"
McLees Thos.	"
McWiggin D.	"
Melvin B. F.	"
Moore J. N.	"
Quinn Patrick,	"
Strickland R.	"
Taylor D. B.	"
Tinker L.	"
White Ralph,	Ludlow
Barry John,	Lynn
Bradley & Harrington (machine),	"
Brown Charles,	"
Brickett E. S.	"
Burrows Egbert,	"
Byrnes John,	"
Cain J. R.	"
Colby H.	"
Dunbar E. H.	"
Farnum Benj. (machine),	"
Homan John,	"
Kane James R.	"
McDermott James,	"
Mellen Christian,	"
Morley John,	"
Nichols Joseph H.	"
Norton William (machine),	"
Parrott Geo.	"
Peabody Osgood,	"
Perry Geo. W.	"

Renton John A. Lynn
Sanborn B. F. & J. R. (machine), "
Sexton Thomas, "
Stevens John H. "
STILES J. G., at Almshouse, "
Story A. S. (machine), "
Thompson William H. "
Track John, "
VELLA JOSEPH F. (machine, see
   page 712), Willow st. "
Walsh John, "
Willey Daniel H. "
Hayward John, Lynfield Centre, Lynnfield
Cox Samuel W. Malden
Hill Charles, "
Mann & Woods, "
Randall J. P. "
Burns John, Mansfield
Drake James H. "
Pratt & French, "
Webb John, "
Brown C. K. Marblehead
Engles Joseph, "
Orne Wm. H. "
Tirrell Charles, "
WARREN WM. W. 153 Washington, "
Sherman Eli, Marion
Sherman Humphrey, "
HOLLIS DAVID, Marlborough
Baker Thomas, Marshfield
Sylvester Gideon, "
Hall Tilden, East Marshfield, "
Garnars Walter T. Mattapoisett
Kinney Jirey, "
Carey J. F. Medfield
Wiswell Lowell, "
Childs Aaron, Medford
Jacobs & Cushing, "
Mitchell Henry, "
Pitman Jasper, West Medford, "
O'Gara Thomas, Medway
Burditt E. E. Melrose
Gilson L. "
Howe F. D. "
Newhall George, "
Quigley James, Mendon
Butler Eliphalet, Methuen
Gage Lewis, "
Keith Justin E. Middleborough
Luippold John M. "
Whitcomb E. F. Middlefield
McIntire E. A. Middleton
Bradish L. P. Milford
Curran J. F. "
Darling R. L. "
Colburn F. A. "
Clifford John, Millbury
Gerry Elbridge, "
Goddard N. & Son, "
Foley Thomas, Milton
Wiley George, Monroe
Maguire J. C. Monson
Pittee William, "
Wright Frank, "
Brewer N. C. "
Payne J. F. Montague
Eno Ezekiel, "
Tyrrel Lewis, Monterey
Tyrrel Winfield S. "
Bennett Wm. H. Nantucket
Gray John, "
Haggerty George, "
Hart Wm. C. "
Hussey Edward, "
Jones Lemuel, "
Lewis Simeon L. "
Lovell Charles, "
Sweet J. N. V. "

Thompson R. Nantucket
SIMONDS F. P. Natick
Watson O. H. "
Flagg Isaac, Wellesley, Needham
Adams Eben C. New Bedford
Barnum S. J. "
Brown Jacob, "
Burbank S. M.
Cairns & West,
Chace Benj. M. "
Cunha De Joseph, "
Davis Benjamin, "
Davis James, "
Drinkwine John, "
Dunbar Wm. A. "
Dunlop Henry, "
Ellis R. L.
Freeman Henry B. ..
Freeman John C. "
Garland Barney, "
Graham J. T. "
Harrington Jeremiah, "
Hicks E. "
Howard J. & Brother, "
Janell Charles, "
Killigrew Daniel, "
Kirschbaum Jacob, "
Lucas Willis,
Marshall Michael, ..
Monroe Augustus W.
Muntzenberg Charles, "
Peed Thomas J, "
Pierce J. N. "
Pollock John, "
Putz Gustave, "
Rashburn Jacob, "
Schlasier C. R. "
Sears John P. "
Shay John, "
Silvisa John, "
Stell Frank, "
Thacher Wm. R. "
Thayer Charles H. "
Tower John, "
Wing John, "
YOUNG & ELDER, 60 Union, "
Thompson Sumner, New Braintree
Rogers Asa, Newbury
Armitage George, Newburyport
Batchelder D. T. "
Choate Elisha, "
Chaney Patrick, "
Currier Thomas, "
Freeman S. "
Knight Moses C. "
Lloyd Amos P. ..
Pettingill B. F. "
Reed Waterman, "
Whipple E. T. "
Hamilton Brothers, New Marlborough
Haynes Patrick, Mill River, "
Hudner James, "
Stratton Royal A. New Salem
Shaw Jaines, North Prescott, "
Mero John, Auburndale, Newton
Sadler Thos. N. Lower Falls, "
Shaw John, Newton Centre, "
Keefe Thomas, Newton Corner, "
Latta J. G. "
Leonard M. C. Newtonville, "
Jewell B. Upper Falls, "
Johnson Dexter F. "
Flagg Wm. West Newton, "
Anderson James, Northampton
Hixon Gilbert, "
Colgan T. Florence, "
Pond P. P. "
Daboll E. P. Northborough

Boot and Shoe Makers — continued.

Hunt Stephen H.	Northborongh
Knowlton J. M.	"
CUSHMAN N. & CO.,	No. Bridgewater
Davis Benj. P.	"
Manchester I.	"
Reynolds Joseph,	"
Brown David, Whitinsville,	Northbridge
Carr Samuel H.	"
Warren George R.	North Brookfield
Boole John,	North Chelsea
Pierce John P.	"
Billings Wm. C.	Northfield
Morgan Dwight,	"
Wilbur Horace,	Oakham
Goddard Abner.	Orange
Hills James M.	"
Morton Moses,	"
Wheeler Gardner,	"
Rogers Lincoln,	Orleans
Vose George,	"
Sparrow Alphonso, East Orleans,	"
Cornwell Chester R.	Otis
Elmer George,	"
Burrill L.	Oxford
Campbell William A.	"
Hervey J. F.	"
Gerald George,	Palmer
Eager F. M.	"
Hitchcock C.	"
Bishop Benj.	Peabody
Fallon James,	"
Meacom E.	"
Walker Franklin,	"
Thayer William,	Paxton
Chapman Samuel H.	Pepperell
Shattuck Putnam,	"
Hymes Claudius A.	Petersham
Hager George,	Phillipston
Brown John,	Pittsfield
Cummings Frank,	"
Fairbank W. J.	"
Fairfield David,	"
Nichols Isidore,	"
Pediger & Kuhl,	"
Wood John P.	"
Young Samuel,	"
Peasler Theodore, West Pittsfield,	"
Clark Levi,	Plainfield
Winslow William,	"
Fuller J. C.	Plymouth
Perry Sewall,	"
Fuller Ephraim,	Plympton
Holmes Ira S.	"
Bull William F.	Princeton
Loring L.	"
Haynes N.	Provincetown
Hennessey Wm.	"
Smith Freeman, jr.	"
Sumner Joshua,	"
Terry George H.	"
Joyce Perez,	Quincy
Gardner John	"
Nightingale Nathaniel,	"
Parker James,	"
Williams John,	"
Snow Wm. O.	Raynham
Bassett E.	Reading
Fenton Larkin,	Rehoboth
Leonard Joseph F.	"
Buchan Stephen,	Richmond
Woodruff Gilbert,	"
Bearse Gershom,	Rochester
Sherman Nehemiah,	"
Davis William G.	Rockport
Drown John O.	"
Hartley John, jr.	"
Mills R. P.	"

Neal Alfred,		Royalston
Clark Lyman, South Royalston,		"
Thomas Charles,		Rowe
Leonard C. W.		Russell
Baker Abel,		Rutland
Barker Reuben,		"
Hatch William D.		"
Stone Joel,		"
Stone John,		"
Barnes Joseph,		Salem
Bartlett Henry S.		"
Beston James,		"
Bott Thomas,		"
Collins Thomas,		"
Cross C. B.		"
Dodge Wm. M.		"
Drew Harrison,		"
Friend Joel,		"
Gallagher Wm.		"
Goodhue R. W.		"
Hay J. A.		"
Henderson Samuel,		"
Howard D. R.		"
Kimball A. M.		"
Law George D.		"
Low A. T.		"
Martin & Cunningham,		"
McLaughlin & Gormley,		"
Netter Martin,		"
O'Connell Timothy,		"
Pepper J. S.		"
Ramsdell P. A.		"
Rice Sylvester,		"
Rounds D. W.		"
Rundlett A.		"
Shatswell M.		"
Tirrell Z.		"
Tolman Silas,		"
Waterhouse I. A.		"
Lee Benj. Amesbury,		Salisbury
Ronan Thomas,		Sandisfield
White Edwin, Montville,		"
Heath D. New Boston,		"
Fisher L. D.		Sandwich
Russell Henry W.		Savoy
Sturtevant Robert,		"
Tubbs Henry J.		"
Pool James,		Scituate
Hewins Albert,		Sharon
Rosever George,		Sheffield
Phelps Joel A. Ashley Falls,		"
		Shelburne
Bates George W., Shelburne Falls,		"
Bardwell A. & Son,	"	"
Bullard Henry W.		Sherborn
Brownson H.		Shirley
Cowdry E.		"
Crandall Joel,		Shutesbury
Rogers Cyrus,		"
White Isaac,		"
Buffum Caleb,		Somerset
Hale Corey,		"
Pierce Frederick J.		"
Mayhew T. T.		Somerville
Chapman Sardis,		Southampton
Newton Lyman, 2d,		Southborough
Wheeler Henry S.		"
Magraunis Francis,		South Hadley
Gaylord John, South Hadley Falls,		"
Ellins Lincoln,		South Scituate
Pendleton R. C.		Southwick
Bartlett F. W.		Springfield
Barnard G. M.		"
Burke J.		"
Butterfield O. F.		"
Buchanan John,		"
Carman Samuel,		"
Chaltry Charles,		"

Colton Chauncy,   Springfield
Dew William,   "
During J. P.   "
Dunbar T. J.   "
Frost L. C.   "
Frost W.   "
Hill C. H.   "
Polk George,   "
Porter L. T.   "
Powers W. H.   "
Schafer A. F.   "
Squires M.   "
Stuchert & Bro.   "
Stewart Austin,   "
Swallow Henry,   "
Evans N.   Indian Orchard,   "
Willard I. H.   Sterling
Miller Lewis M.   Stockbridge
Lane Jabez,   Curtisville,   "
Goldthwaite W. H.   Stoneham
Rowe H.   Stoughton
Collins George W.   Stow
Costello A.   Fiskdale,   Sturbridge
Mason Charles D.   "
Garfield J. W.   Sudbury
Horr R. R.   South Sudbury,   "
Jones Wm. P.   "
Beaman Ira,   Sunderland
Harris N. M.   Swampscott
Haskell Charles W.   "
Tweed Frederick A.   "
Baker Henry A.   Swansea
Chace James T.   "
Slade Rufus S.   "
Betz Henry,   Taunton
Callaghan Patrick,   "
Carr John,   "
Churchill Geo. L.   "
Clark Samuel C.   "
Codding M.   "
Edgar Robert,   "
Field S.   "
Griffin Patrick,   "
Hautke Henry,   "
Horen Edward,   "
Johnson Almon,   "
Keirnan B.   "
Keyes Samuel,   "
Leach H. D.   "
Lent James,   "
Lincoln Marshall,   "
McShane Cornelius,   "
Moran Thomas,   "
Porter B. B.   "
Rounds A. B.   "
Shurtleff S. A.   "
Swinerton John P.   "
Tinkham Peter,   "
Townsend W. F.   "
Valentine Edward,   "
Whitley Aquila F.   "
Hinds Cornelius,   Templeton
Maynard Horace,   "
Winch James O.   "
Davis O. G.   Baldwinville,   "
Maynard Orin,   "
Maynard H.   Otter River,   "
Chadwick Thomas, West Tisbury,   Tisbury
Luce Timothy,   "
Branscomb Stephen, Holmes's Hole.   "
Hodges John,   "
Harger David,   Tolland
Pratt F. H.   "
Lawrence Americus,   Townsend
Bandlett G. W., West Townsend,   "
Elliott John,   "
Hopkins Isaac,   Truro

Hopkins Reuben R.   Truro
Collins James,   North Truro,   "
Tyrrel Jared,   Tyringham
Bull Anthony,   Upton
Harrington Henry,   "
Corbett T.   Uxbridge
Davis E.   "
Merrill Greeley,   Wakefield
Wood Richard,   "
McGinnis John,   Walpole
Brewer C. D.   Wales
Gouley Joseph,   "
Shaw E. D.   "
Vizard T.   "
Baker G. F.   Waltham
Ballard & Caughey,   "
Bemis Royal,   "
Guinan William,   "
Sherman P.   "
Warren Isaac,   "
Barnard E.   "
Gilbert Simeon   Ware
Gould Wm. D.   "
McBride T.   "
Hinckley Alpheus,   Wareham
Mooney M. C.   "
Capen L. C.   "
Jennings Chas.   Warren
Albee Abner,   Warwick
Conant James A.   "
Fisher Henry,   "
Cobar Frederick,   Washington
Simmons Joseph W.   "
Nicholson Thomas,   Watertown
Weston Charles,   Wayland
Gelineau N.   Webster
Hasler John,   "
Fish A. B.   Wellfleet
Hall Lot,   "
Holbrook Isaac B. (wooden sole),   "
Houghton Charles A.   Wendell
Aldrich Henry A.   Westborough
Eaton Wm. J.   "
Chamberlain Joshua,   West Boylston
Burrell J. D.   West Bridgewater
Jennings Wm. H.   Cochesset,   "
Vosmus Joseph,   "
Deihl John P.   Westfield
Hide Wm. B.   "
Olds Enoch,   "
Pendleton Lyman,   "
Snow & Terry,   "
Wright J. A.   "
Moore Henry,   Westford
Fenno Reuben,   West Hampton
Foskett John,   Westminster
Holden Jonah L.   "
Bailey Stephen,   West Newbury
Batchelder Samuel,   "
Brock Daniel,   "
Brown Eben,   "
Brown Moses,   "
Brown Stephen,   "
Odiorne J. L.   "
Coburn John,   Weston
Carr Thomas D.   Westport
Macomber Ezra,   "
Macomber Varnum, Westport Point,   "
Winslow Ezra,   Central Village,   "
Jordan Chauncey,   West Roxbury
Jordan R. C.   "
BUCHANAN JOHN, Jamaica Plain,   "
Follmer Casper,   "
Hooper Isaac D.   "
Kalb Peter C.   "
Vogel L.   "
Leonard Lewis,   West Springfield, Mittencague,   "

Boot and Shoe Makers — continued.

Gorham George,	West Stockbridge
Kinnane Joseph,	"
Winchell Charles L.	"
Gove S.	Weymouth
White Dorick,	"
Pratt & Bailey,	East Weymouth, "
Clark Edwin R.,	South Weymouth, "
Derby Edward C.	" "
Richards Charles,	" "
Graves Selah,	Whately
Flowers Jonas S.	Wilbraham
Firmin Francis B.,	S. Wilbraham, "
Rider George,	"
Rockwood G. A.	" "
Rice Channcy,	Williamsburg
Rice Elisha,	"
Rice Royal,	"
Noyes L.	Williamstown
Roberts George,	"
Welch Richard,	"
Bassett Lemuel,	South Williamstown, "
Dickinson William,	" "
Gowing Charles M.	Wilmington
Gowing Daniel,	"
Bouche Arthur,	Winchendon
Pollard Wm.	"
David S. H.	Winchester
Palmer George H.	"
Cathcart Oliver I.	Windsor
Stetson Judson,	East Windsor, "
Dollard Morris,	Woburn
Gorham P. & Son,	"
McCay James,	"
Mulheran Edward,	"
Parker N.	"
Shannon Christopher,	"
Wyman William R.	"
Hanson Mark,	East Woburn, "
Totman William,	" "
Bundy D. H.	Worcester
Buxton William,	"
Coburn Austin S.	"
Dahlman H.	"
Davis S. W.	"
Eaton Frederick,	"
Eldt Henry (French),	"
Fairbanks A. L.	"
Fisher J.	"
Gibson John,	"
Latham John,	"
Martell H.	"
Schwartz David,	"
Sullivan M. M.	"
Thompson S. B.	"
Wade Wm.	"
Gleason Horace,	Worthington
Larama Euclid,	"
Huckle John,	Wrentham
Rawson Otis,	"
Grush Nathan W.	Yarmouth
Gorham Benjamin,	Yarmouth Port, "
Hallet Nathan,	" "
Hamblin Joshua,	" "
Park James,	" "
Snow Hervey,	" "
Homer Isaiah,	South Yarmouth, "
Jenkins Elisha,	" "

Boot & Shoe Manufacturers.

(See also Makers; also Dealers.)

Cobb & Thompson,	Abington
Curtis & Co.	"
Cushing G. P.	"
Cushing Sylvanus,	"
Cushing W. W.	"
Dunham Henry, jr.	"

FAXON L. & CO.		Abington
Floyd Ira,		"
Hunt Henry,		"
Hunt, Semonin, & Co.		"
Lond Charles S.		"
Nash B. L.		"
Nash B. T.		"
Nash J. L.		"
Noyes S. C.		"
Osgood Gilman,		"
Pratt Henry J.		..
Richards Randall, jr.		
Shaw Jacob,		"
Thaxter Samuel B.		"
Vaughn J. Atherton (shoes),		"
Vaughan Geo. D.		"
Whitmarsh Albert,		
Whitmarsh James,		"
Whitmarsh Joshua,		
Bigelow J. F.	East Abington,	"
Blanchard Daniel,	"	..
Clapp George B.	"	..
Curtis Abner,	"	"
Curtis Leander,	"	"
Curtis Joshua,	"	"
Dill C. H.	"	"
Dill C. H. 2d,	"	"
Dill Joseph,	"	"
French J. E.	"	"
Jenkins & Tirrell,	"	"
LANE C. H.	"	"
Lane Jenkins & Sons,	"	"
Locke & Maguire,	"	"
Perry William G.	"	"
Poole Nathl.	"	"
Reed S., jr.	"	"
Shaw H. M.	"	"
SHAW MELVIN,	"	"
Shaw S. B.	"	"
Studley & Turner,	"	"
Torrey C. W.	"	"
Whiting Leonard	"	
Arnold M. N.	North Abington,	"
Bates & Beals,	"	"
Chamberlain Albert, (buffalo over-		
shoes),	North Abington,	"
Cleverly Joseph,	"	"
Grose D. & Co.	"	"
Wales C. M.	"	"
Wales Webster S.	"	"
Alden Amos.	South Abington,	"
Allen & Soule,	"	"
BLAKE S. (boots),	"	"
Burrage & Reed,	"	"
Morey Chas. S.	"	"
Noyes E. M. & Son,	"	"
Reed Nahum & Sons,	"	"
Tillson Isaiah & Son,	"	"
Fletcher John & Sons,		Acton
Cady Brothers,	N. Adams,	Adams
Millard & Whitman,	"	"
Sampson Calvin T. (shoes),	"	"
Snyder & Haskins,	"	"
Clarkson J. T.		Amesbury
TRUE ALFRED M. (see page 800),		"
Watson Oliver,		Amherst
Adams C. M. & Co.		Ashland
Balcom & Blake,		"
Cole Geo. B.		"
Leland Albert,		"
Newhall H. & Co.		"
Seaver & Sons,		"
Tilton Chas. H.		"
Wheelock Wm.		"
Jones & Baker (boots),		Athol
Lewis John S. (ladies'),		"
Lindsley, Shaw, & Co.		"
Proctor & Albee (boots),		..

Athol
Kendall O. & Son (boots), Athol Depot, "
Lee Charles M. (shoes), " "
Lee M. L. & Co. (boots), " "
Lord F. G. & C. L. & Co. " "
RICE JOHN W. (boots), Barre
Rice J. Allen, "
Chamberlin P. W. Bedford
Fairbanks W. & C., Caryville, Bellingham
Hastings Ruthven, Berlin
Bickford, Klennett, & Stetson, "
Baker Joseph H. Beverly
Baker & Woodbury, "
Bickery J. F. "
Bowdoin Porter D. "
Burnham A. P. "
Butman C. H. & Co. "
Caldwell Edward J. & Co. "
Clark P. E. & Co. "
Cole, Wood, & Co. "
Creesy & Wallis, "
Cross John H. "
Fisk Shadrack, "
Foster Daniel, 2d, "
Foster Edwin & Co. "
Foster Ezra O. "
Foster Ezra S. "
Foster Israel, "
Friend Char'es, "
Hammond Philip, "
Hill Benjamin B. "
Hitchings Josiah T. "
Kimball Joel, "
Larcom Rufus, "
Larcom & Galloup, "
Lefavonr David & Son, "
Lefavour I. & C. P. "
Lefavour John & Co. "
Lefavour Thomas & Co. "
Lunt Hervey, "
Marsters & Walker, "
Norwood Seth & Co. "
Ober William, "
Perry & Preston, "
Porter Francis E. & Co. "
Roundy George, "
Smith John G. "
Smith W. A. "
Stanley Andrew, "
Thissell David, "
Vickary Joseph F. "
Wallis Joseph F. "
Webb Philip S. "
Woodbury Francis W. "
Woodbury Geo A. "
Williams Augustus, Beverly Farms, "
Haynes Samuel B. & Co. Bolton
Hale John, Boxford
Hale Isaac, "
Howe Edward, "
Arnold B. F. & Son, Braintree
Loring & Searle, "
Penniman Elijah, "
Richards Lewis, "
Shaw F. & Co. (boots), "
Vinton Thomas B. (boots), "
Arnold Joseph A. S. Braintree, "
Bradford S. S. " "
Daggett Brothers (boots), " "
Holbrook, Hobart, & Porter, " "
Holbrook Moses D. " "
Kimball J. B. & Co. " "
White & Thayer, " "
Twichell E. & Co. Brookfield
Fales Charles, "
Montague J. S. "
Twichell Henry M. "
Warren L. & N. East Brookfield, "

Morse C. E. & Co. Charlton
Southwick E. S., Charlton Depot, "
Parker A. G. & Son, Chicopee
Avary Ephraim, Clinton
Fletcher & Hitchcock, "
Stacy & Davis, Coleraine
Andrews Winthrop, Danvers
Boardman I. P. "
Boardman N. H. "
Butler J. C. & Co.
Gould Charles H.
Goodale James,
Hyde, Hutchins, & Co.
Martin & Bryant,
Noyes Francis, "
Noyes W. H. & Co. "
Patch Abraham, Jr. "
Perley Frederick, "
Pope I. P. ..
Prentice Henry, ..
Preston & Blake, "
Putnam I. H. "
Putnam Joel & Co. "
Sawyer J. M. "
Sillers Malcolm, "
Trask Elbridge, ..
Wells Moses, "
White & Brother, "
Martin George B. Danvers Centre, "
Mudge E. & A. & Co. " " "
Wells Moses, " " "
Corning Phineas, Danvers Port, "
Allen J. S. East Bridgewater
EDSON FRANKLIN, "
Keith R. C. (shoes), "
Vinton William, " "
Bates Irving & Co. " Joppa, "
Bryant Seth, " "
Edson Henry, " "
Kingman E. & E. " "
REED G. WILSON, " "
Shaw S. & Son, (shoes), "
Soule J. W. " "
BRETT GEORGE (ladies'), North Easton,
Gilmore A. A. & Co., North Easton, " Easton
Hayward F. W. " "
King J. B. & Co. (men's boots), North Easton, "
Lynch John A. (shoes), " "
Newton Palmer & Co., South Easton, "
Packard I & E. " "
Packard N. R. " "
Thayer L. M. " "
Gardner Frederick P. Essex
Lowe David, jr. "
Dickinson E. M. & Co. Fitchburg
Prentice F. S., South Framingham, Framingham
Hammond J. D. Saxonville, "
Freeman James M. Franklin
Briggs Sylvester & Son, Freetown
Carleton Geo. H. Georgetown
Chaplin George W. "
Chaplin Henry P. "
Coker John P. "
Giles James B. ..
Hale Alfred, "
Harriman William B. "
Little & Moulton, "
Lovering J. A. & Son, "
Merrill John M. & Co., "
Noyes A. B. & Co. "
Spofford & Noyes, "
Tenney George J. & Son, "
Tyler Charles E. "
Jewett James S. Annisquam, Gloucester
Allen & Flagg, Grafton

Boot and Shoe Manufacturers — continued.

Axtell S. J. & Co.	Grafton
Forbush & Brown,	"
Greenwood H. C.	"
SLOCOMB J. W. & SON,	"
Warren H. S.	"
Wood C. C.	"
Allen J. H. N. E. Village,	"
Nelson Jasper S. (ladies'), "	"
Curtis Edwin T.	Groveland
Hovey Rufus A.	"
Huntress A. J.	"
Ladd Nathaniel E.	"
Page Paul,	"
Page Rufus H.	"
Stickney Charles & Co.	"
Stickney Niles T.	"
Celley J. C.	Hadley
Lundergan John,	"
Damon Rector,	Hanover
Killian & Turner,	"
Studley Joseph H.	"
Morse Marcus, West Scituate,	"
Foster Isaac, South Hanson,	Hanson
Robinson J. R.	Hardwick
Whitney J. M.	Harvard
Cape Cod Boot & Shoe Manuf. Co.	Harwich
Balcom Bros.	Haverhill
Bartlett C. H. & Co.	"
Bartlett Luther,	"
Bennett R. P.	"
Blaisdell R. W.	"
Blaisdell & Jaques,	"
BLANCHARD CHAS., 118 Merrimac, (see page 791)	
Boynton H. W.	"
Bradley S. P.	"
Brickett & Smith,	"
Carleton & Co.	"
Carr J. H. East Haverhill,	"
CHASE C. W. & CO., 14 Merrimac,	"
Chase C. T.	"
Chase J. E.	"
Chase & Laubham,	"
Chase & Tilton,	"
Chase Wm. M.	"
Cluff D. B.	"
Coffin Charles,	"
Corning G. & J. C.	"
Currier S. M.	"
DARLING B. F., 7½ Water,	"
Davis, Bros.	"
Davis G. L. & Co.	"
Davis H. P.	"
Davis John,	"
Day George W.	"
Day W. F.	"
Doten & Chase,	"
Dresser T. N.	"
Elliot S. & G.	"
Farnsworth J. H.	"
Farrar Brothers,	"
Farrington A. J.	"
Finney L. A.	"
Fitts & Spaulding,	"
Fitts & Stover,	"
Flanders D. D.	"
Forbush C. W.	"
Foss Henry G.	"
FOSS & ORDWAY, 172 Merrimac,	"
Foster D. B. & Co.	"
Gage J. A.	"
Gage Stephen H.	"
Gage John E.	"
Gardner J. & Sons,	"
George G. R.	"
Gilpatrick Henry C.	"
Gooding L.	"

Goodrich & Porter,	Haverhill
Goodrich & Fitts,	"
Greene G. A.	"
Griffin Brothers,	"
Ham George,	"
Harriman Daniel,	"
Haynes Phineas, Ayer's Village,	"
Herring A. H.	"
Hersey Caleb.	"
Hewes Wm. H. & Co.	"
Hobson J. H.	"
Hodgdon Bros.	"
How Moses,	"
HOW & TIBBETTS, Washington blk.	"
Hoyt H. & Co.	"
Hoyt Tasker,	"
Hubbard O. S.	"
Huntington Bros.	"
Jaques J. T.	"
Johnson L. &. Co.	"
Kelly A. S. & Co.	"
Kelly & Blaisdell,	"
Kendrick John & Co.	"
KIMBALL ALBERT L., 54 Merrimac,	"
Kimball Bros.	"
Kimball Wm. B.	"
Kimball & Greeley,	"
Ladd G. W.	"
Lamprey Wm. B.	"
Lancaster A. R.	"
Leighton & Gage,	"
Long W. N.	"
Marble J. H.	"
Maynard S. D.	"
McLain Chas. O.	"
McDuffie A.	"
Merrill Albert,	"
Merrill Alvah,	"
Merrill J. F.	"
Mitchell, Moulton, & Duncan,	"
Mitchell S. K. & Co.	"
Mitchell & Johnson,	"
Morse Charles F. & Co.	"
Nichols George H.	"
Nichols J. B. & Co.	"
Offutt Charles W.	"
Ordway Warren,	"
Osgood C. W.	"
Palmer & Cook,	"
Pearl P. E.	"
Perley William S.	"
Peaslee W. I.	"
Pilling John,	"
Poor & Wheeler,	"
Poor J. M. & Co.	"
Potter & Jaques,	"
Prescott S. F. & Davis,	"
Prescott S. P.	"
Reed A. L.	"
Richardson John B. & Co.	"
Richardson & Brown,	"
Ridgway Joseph,	"
Robinson J. H.	"
Russ & Noyes,	"
Sanger Ira O.	"
Sawyer E. A.	"
Sawyer S. C.	"
Shattuck L. P. jr.	"
Sleeper G. L.	"
Sleeper J. N.	"
Sleeper & Hall,	"
Smith Calvin,	"
Swett J. B. & Son,	"
Tappan John,	"
Tibbetts E.	"
TILTON A. J. 168 Merrimac,	"
Tilton E. G.	
Tilton W. W.	

Vittum Jos. W.	Haverhill
Webster Calvin A.	"
Wentworth John N.	"
West & Co.	"
Whittier L. & Co.	"
Wightman H. M.	"
Winchell Brothers,	"
Hutchins & Cloudman (boots),	Hingham
Hollis John A.	"
Stoddard William D.	"
Wilder Martin,	"
WHITMAN, WHITCOMB, & CO.	
(boots) South Hingham,	"
Ballou D. T.	Holliston
Batchelder B. F.	"
Batchelder John,	"
Batchelder William S.	"
Daniels G. T. & A. C.	"
Draper W. H.	"
Harriman & Leland,	"
Heath C. D.	"
Hopkins W. H. & Co.	"
Johnson Peter R.	"
Leland Alden,	"
Paddleford F. O.	"
Stone F. A.	"
Wiley Amos A.	"
Claflin, Coburn, & Co. (boots),	Hopkinton
Coburn A. &. Co.	"
Crooks & Co. (boots),	"
Gorham J. L. & Co.	"
Rising, Thompson, & Co. (boots),	"
Bowker L. H. & Co.	Hayden row,
Phipps W. H. & Co.	"
Kemp Amasa,	Woodville,
Bowker & Balcom,	Hubbardston
Morse & Pollard,	"
BRIGHAM F. & CO.	Hudson
GAY & RAND.	"
HOUGHTON GEORGE,	"
Jefts & Smith,	"
Stowe, Bills, & Co,	"
STRATTON GEORGE,	"
TROWBRIDGE W. F.	"
Johnson John A. (ladies),	Ipswich
TOZER WILLIAM H.	"
Wait N. R.	"
Wellington & Perkins,	"
Dean Henry A. & Co.	Lakeville
Shumway Geo. A.	Lancaster
Vogel & Behrman,	Lawrence
Shaw & Kendall,	Leominster
Haws Manson D.	"
Adams E. H. & Co.	Lowell
Humphrey Archibald H.	Lunenburg
Reynolds Joseph,	"
Abbott & Breed,	Lynn
Aborn C. H. & Co.	"
Allen Daniel W.	"
Attwill Gustavus,	"
Attwill I. M.	"
Bacheller Samuel,	"
Bacheller Thomas W.	"
BAILEY HENRY H. & CO.	"
Bancroft & Purinton	"
Bartlett Charles J.	"
Bates Bradford,	"
Beckford Eben,	"
Beede Geo. F. & Co.	"
Beede & Tebbetts,	"
Berry, Field, & Co.	"
Berry Leander S.	"
Berry & Beede,	"
Black & Merrill,	"
Boyce Samuel,	"
Boynton W. H.	"
Breed Amos F.	"
Breed Geo. R.	"
Breed Nathan,	Lynn
Breed W. F., Dole, & Co.	"
Brewer Thomas E.	"
Brown Charles,	
Brown & Brother,	
Brown, Fry, & Co.	
Bubier Edward T.	
Bubier Samuel M.	
Buffum & Moore,	
Buffum & Shelton,	
Caldwell Daniel A.	
Chadwell Harris O.	
Chase Charles W.	"
Chase D. F. & Brother,	
Chase James B.	
Chase Phillip A. & Co	"
Chase Wm. A.	
Clapp A. W. & Co.	
Cobb A. C.	
Coffin Charles F.	
Cutcheon F. M.	
Davis Joseph & Co.	"
Donk Benj. F. 2d,	"
Dore Benjamin F.	"
Dougherty John,	
Downing George W.	"
Driver S. P. & Bros.	"
Dupar B. & Co.	"
Emerton Jeremiah,	"
Frazier Lyman B.	
Gale Samuel, jr.	"
Gale William H.	"
Graves & Co.	"
Graves James & Co.	"
Grover James J.	"
Hanley Patrick,	"
Harrington Isaac M.	"
Haskell J. D. & Co.	"
Hawkes & Holmes,	"
Hawley George A.	"
Hay Joseph F.	"
Hazeltine Joseph W.	"
Herrick George W.	"
Hill Lebbeus,	"
Hill Parsons C.	"
Hollis H. H. & Co.	"
Hollis Samuel J.	"
Hilton C. S.	"
Holt & Hallowell,	"
Horgan & Donovan,	"
Hunt E. S. & G. M.	"
Ingalls C. B.	
Ingalls Jerome,	"
Ingalls & Burrill,	"
Ireson S. S. & Co.	"
Jones Edwin T. (ladies' and misses'),	"
Johnson Edwin H.	"
Johnson J. B. & Sons,	"
Keene George W. & Sons,	"
Knight T. B.	
Law George W.	"
Law Henry,	"
Law J. W.	
Lewis Albert,	"
Lewis & Collyer,	"
Lewis Charles W.	"
Locke Francis T.	"
Lord Chas. B.	"
Lorendo F. G.	"
Lovering C.	
Mahon John & Son,	
Mansfield & Pierce,	
Massey George W.	"
McAloon Thos. & Bro.	"
Medbury Edwin J.	"
Morgan Norris,	
Morgan Wm. F.	
Morse S. Q.	

Boot and Shoe Manufacturers — continued.

Morse & Flagg,	Lynn
Moulton Daniel,	"
Mower F. B.	"
Mower & Brother,	"
Mudge Nathan A.	"
Neal J. W. & Co.	"
Newhall Charles W.	"
Newhall G. G.	"
Newhall & Wellington,	"
Newhall Harrison,	"
Newhall Joseph P.	"
Newhall Lucius P.	"
Newhall Lucian,	"
Newhall Perry,	"
Newhall William P.	"
Newhall Warren,	"
Nichols & Ingalls,	"
Nourse John & Sons,	"
Oliver Benjamin F.	"
Oliver Stephen, Jr. & Co.	"
Oliver & Smith,	"
Patch Edwin,	"
Pearson Oliver G.	"
Pecker Charles D. (ladies' & misses')	"
Pecker George,	"
Pedrick Thomas,	"
Pillsbury Brothers,	"
Phelan James,	"
Phillips & Estes,	"
Pike & Walsh,	"
Pope Theodore,	"
Preble A. M. & J. H.	"
Porter William,	"
Pratt M. C. (C. F. Coffin),	"
Reynolds George,	"
Rhodes Sylvester,	"
Richardson Stephen N.	"
Richardson T. P. & Son,	"
Riley James,	"
SAMUELS JAMES, (Compo, see	"
page 791), 1 May st.	"
Sanborn & Johnson,	"
Sanborn & Parsons,	"
Saunderson Brothers,	"
Shaw B. F.	"
Shaw John 2d,	"
Sherry Patrick P.	"
SLOAN MARTIN B. 7 Mt. Vernon,	"
Smith Nathan & Co.	"
Smith & Co.	"
Spinney Benjamin F.	"
Spinney C. E. & Son,	"
Spinney George,	"
Spinney Gustavus N.	"
Spinney John B.	"
Spinney William F.	"
Spinney William N.	"
Sprague Benjamin,	"
Stacey Thomas & Co. (slippers),	"
Stearns Charles, B.	"
Stevens John H.	"
Story Allen,	"
Sutherland I. G.	"
Swain & Fuller,	"
Sweetser C. S.	"
Sweetser J. A.	"
Swett Lewis G. & Co.	"
Taber Charles A.	"
TAYLOR DAVID, 1 Taylor's Build-	
ing,	"
Tebbetts Chas. B.	"
Trask Charles H.	"
Valpey H. R & Co.	"
VELLA JOSEPH F. Willow st. (see	"
page 712)	"
Varney Brothers,	"
Vennard & Osgood,	"

Vittum C. S.	Lynn
Walden E. & Co.	"
Webster Eben W.	"
Wells E. C.	
Wells William,	
Wentworth Eli,	
Wooldredge John & Co.	
Calley B. F.	East Saugus, "
Calley J. B. & Son, " " "
Hall Harmon & Co. " " "
Hitchings Albert, " " "
Johnson R. A. " " "
Newhall A Clarke, " " "
Newhall Chas. W. & Co. " "
Newhall Dennis S. " " "
Oliver Benjamin, " " "
Oliver George, " " "
Putnam John, " " "
Raddin Nelson, " " "
Raddin & Newhall, " " "
Whittredge William A. & Co.	
Lynnfield Centre,	Lynnfield
Locke Francis T.	Manchester
ARMSTRONG THOMAS H. (see	
page 785),	Marblehead
Bailey James S.	"
Ballard Daniel,	"
Bartlett E. V. & Co.	"
Bassett T. L.	"
Bessom Philip, jr.	"
Boynton W H.	"
Brown Jonathan,	"
Bryer Alex. W.	"
Carroll S. E.	"
Cole Samuel H.	"
Crowell S. E.	"
Davis & Tucker,	"
Denning Bros,	"
Doak Michael J. & Co.	"
Gale Ambrose,	"
GLOVER NATHANIEL (childrens'),	"
Graves S. H.	"
Harris Joseph & Sons,	"
Hooper John P.	"
Hooper Wm. L.	"
Lefavour Henry A.	"
Lefavour Joshua P.	"
Lefavour Robert H.	"
Lefavour Rufus,	"
Lefavour T B.	"
Lefavour William C.	"
LeMaster George, jr.	"
Litchman & Bartlett,	"
Martin Henry A.	"
Merritt Thomas H.	"
Munroe F. W.	"
Orne & Merritt,	"
Peach John C.	"
Phillips Richard,	"
Phillips Thomas,	"
Pitman R. G.	"
Prentiss Caleb 3d,	"
Proctor John,	"
Proctor Thomas H.	"
Quiner John, jr.	"
Reynolds Michael H.	"
Reynolds William,	"
Shepard & Co.	"
Snow William H.	"
Sparhawk Samuel,	"
Spinney Thomas L.	"
Stevens William, jr.	"
Tucker Chadwell, jr.	"
Tucker James O.	"
Ware John,	"
Wilkins John H.	"
Woodfin James B.	"
Woodfin Thomas R.	"

BOYD, COREY, & CO. Marlborough
Boyd J. & Brigham, "
BRIGHAM A. S. "
Chase, Merritt, & Blanchard, "
Clapp & Billings, "
Coolidge T. A. "
Costello John F. & Co. "
Curtis John E. "
DADMAN & CUTTING, "
Davis Charles F. "
FELTON & CHIPMAN, "
Felton S. A. & Brothers, "
FRYE JOHN A. "
HOLLIS DAVID (custom), "
HOWE ABEL, "
Howe Frank A. "
HOWE L. A. & CO. "
HOWE GEO. W. "
Longley E. F. "
Maynard Geo. H. agent, "
Morse F. W. & G. H. "
Murphy D. F. "
O'Connell John, "
RUSSELL HENRY O. "
Stone Albert & Co. "
Partridge C. & Co. Medway
WHITNEY CHAS. E. "
Bullard J. N. W. Medway, "
Daniels L. S. " "
Daniels Willard, " "
Hunt & Partridge, " "
Partridge D. A. & W. S. " "
Pierce L. " "
Pond & Woodard, " "
Smith John S. " "
Emerson & Barrett, Melrose
Emerson & Co. "
Newhall George, "
Albee Enos T. Mendon
Comstock William H. "
George N. R. & J. A. "
Chase S. D. & Son, Methuen
Clark E. M. & Co. "
Currier Daniel & Co. "
Gutterson & Harris, "
Rollins & Saunders, "
Tenney & Co. "
Woodbury B. H. "
White A. J. "
Kingman Calvin D. Middleborough
Jenney & Marchant, "
Leonard & Burrows, "
Perkins & Burrows, "
Leach Geo. M., East Middleborough, "
Averhill E. P. & Co. Middleton
Hutchinson Wm. H. "
Merriam F. P. & Co. "
Alden & Harrington (boots, Milford
Ball H. T. "
Bragg Willard, "
Blake Geo. B. & Co. (fine boots), "
Chapin D. G. "
Claflin & Thayer, "
Clement, Colburn, & Co. "
Cochrane & Thayer, "
Daniels John P. (boots), "
Godfrey C. B. & Co. "
Hayward Bainbridge, "
Johnson, Wood, & Co. "
Libby Lee, "
Mann Elbridge & Son, "
Mayhew A. C. & Co. "
O'Brien Hugh, "
Sumner A. J. "
Thayer Otis, "
Underwood, Sons, & Fisher, "
Thurber Ziinri, "
Walker Samuel & Co. "

Bragg A. F. Braggville, Milford
Wood A. & Sons, W. Millbury, Millbury
Hart Wm. C. Nantucket
Bont Russell S. Natick
Black Joseph, "
Curry & Favour, "
Hammond James N. "
Hanchett Franklin, "
Felch C. H. "
Hayes Richard (shoes), "
Hanchett Wm. T. "
Howe D C. "
Johnson C. E. & Co. "
Mead Albert (shoes), "
Pebbles, Woodman, & Co. (shoes), "
Perry Calvin H. "
Saunders E. B. agent, "
Travis A. F. "
Travis C. B. "
Travis E. P. "
Walcott E. & Co. "
Walcott J. B. "
Washburn Dexter, "
Washburn Edmund (shoes), "
Wilson J. O. "
Felch J. F. & Co. Cochituate, "
Hoffman F. " "
Hathaway & Soule, New Bedford
South Shore Boot & Shoe Co. "
Rogers Justin O. Newbury
Batchelder E. K. Newburyport
DODGE & DANFORTH, "
Lunt Paul, "
Pike J. D. & Co. "
Rowe Jacob T. "
Tappan S. B. & Co. "
TIBBETTS E. F. 17 Middle, (see
page 723) "
McIntire J. H. Northborough
Keith A. & A. B. & Co., North-
bridge Centre, Northbridge
Baxendale John V. North Bridgewater
Brett Pliny (boots), "
Chesman Noah & Co. "
Cross Henry, "
Eldred Davis R. "
Ford C. R. "
French & Packard (boots), "
GURNEY G. H. (shoes and Con-
gress boots), "
HERROD SAMUEL (shoes), "
Hollis J. L. (Congress boots), "
Holmes C. F. (boots), "
Holmes & Southworth, "
Howard D. S. & W. A. "
Howard David (boots), "
Howard F. O. "
Howard D. & E. P. "
Johnson Nahum, "
Jones F. & Co. (shoes), "
Keith Horace G. "
Leach D. H. "
Leach Lucius (shoes), "
Leach Marcus (shoes), "
Leach P. S. "
MARSHALL H. T. (see page 769), "
Orr & Sears (shoes), "
Packard N. R. "
Packard N R., 2d, "
Packard Washburn, "
Parks Henry, "
Porter Lewis (boots), "
Porter & Packard, (shoes), "
Reynolds E. H. "
Stoddard R. A. (shoes), "
Thayer F. A. & H. B. "
Thayer E. L. "
White L. B. "

Boot and Shoe Manufacturers — continued.

North Bridgewater

Wild & Robinson, (shoes), "
Bryant Horace (shoes), Campello, "
Copeland P. & N. & Co. (shoes), " "
Emerson John O. " "
Keith A. & A. B. & Co. " "
Keith C. P. " "
Keith Martin L. " "
Keith Willard, (shoes), " "
Kingman G. J. (shoes), " "
Peterson Lewis, " "
REYNOLDS HOWARD W. " "
Reynolds Marcus V. " "
Snell Wm. (shoes), " "
Stevens George, " "
WALKER J. H. (shoes), " "
Howard N. C., Northwest Bridgewater, "

North Brookfield

BATCHELLER A. & E. D. "
BATCHELLER E. & A. H. & Co. "
Cunningham J. A. "
EDMANDS, DUNCAN, & HURLBUT, "
Howe P. K. "
Olmstead L. "
Richardson & Knight, "
Smith Edmund, "
Woodis & Crawford, "

Abbott Samuel E. North Reading
Breed Samuel P. "
Dooley Lawrence, "
Nichols Warren, "
Nichols W. W. "

Corbin L. B. & Co., (shoes), Oxford
Daniels Seth & Co. " "
Davis M. & B. " "
Davis & Williams, " "
Harwood E. E. " "
Nichols, Stowe, & Co. " "
Thurston Wm. H. " "

Bigelow B. E. & Son, Paxton
Partridge John & Son, "

Dane Francis & Co. Peabody
Farwell C. C. & Co. "
FISK A. R. "
Fuller Edward, "
Hardy & Osborn (shoes), "
Morrison Joseph, "
Phillips Oscar, "
Raddin Amos K. "
Southwick Caleb T. " "

Chapman Samuel H. Pepperell
Shattuck Putnam, "
Leighton Albert, East Pepperell, "
Shattuck D. Brainard, "

Goddard Emery, Petersham
Hymes C. A. "
West Lorenzo, "

Churchill John, Plymouth
Lannan Nathaniel C. "
Morey William, jr. " "
Bass E. W. H. "

Curtis William (boots), Quincy
Curtis T. & Co. " "
Hardwick Henry (boots), "
Maxim James E. "
Murdy H. "
Penniman James T. & Co. "
Whicher J. D. & Co. (boots), "
Whiting James B. "
Willett George, "
Newcomb Everett D., Quincy Point, "
Newcomb Jesse P. " "
Newcomb John A. " "
Newcomb Winslow M. " "
Belcher John W. "
Bracken Andrew, Randolph
Capen Samuel A. "

Clark Danforth, Randolph
Clark Hugh, "
Clark M. & Co. (boots), "
French C. B. & Son, "
Hayes William, "
Heal A. N. "
Holbrook & French, "
Howard Charles H. "
Howard Daniel, "
Howard, French, & Co. (boots), "
Howard & Wood, "
Kane Edward, "
Leach O. H. "
Lynch Thomas, "
McCarty Charles, "
Mann Elisha, jr. (boots), "
Moran Thomas, "
Niles & Thayer (shoes), "
Pendergrass O. "
Reynolds & Brothers, "
Smith Adoniram, "
Strong Alexander & Co. "
Thayer H. L. "
Whitcomb A. W. "
Bates W. L. East Randolph, "
Belcher C. H. " "
Bigelow Nelson, " "
Chandler Roscoe, " "
French Calvin, " "
Hayden Frank (boots), " "
Holbrook E. A. " "
Holbrook E. E. " "
Newcomb H. & Co. " "
Paine Benjamin, " "
Paine G. W. " "
Paine L. W. " "
Paine Royal, " "
Thayer E. W. & Co. " "
Thayer, Holbrook, & Co. " "
Vining S. A. " "
Whitcomb L. & Son " "
Whitcomb & Paine, " "
White T. & E. (shoes), " "
Wile L. F. & Co. " "
Faxon B. W. South Randolph, "
Faxon Daniel & Son, " "
White & Sprague (sewed), " "
Gilmore Cassander & Son, Raynham
Snow William O. "
Foster & Perkins, Reading
Holden Clinton B. & Brothers, "
Bancroft James A. "
Bancroft John H. "
Burrill John, "
Parker Jerome, "
Parker Stillman E. "
Richardson George A. (doll), "
Sweetser T. H. "
Weston Clifford P. (doll), "
Weston David F. "
Foster William C. Rowley
Henderson Daniel S. "
Prime D. N. & Sons, "
Todd John F. "
Todd Nathan, "

Salem

ANDERSON & REYNOLDS, (children's compo, see page 770), "
Larabee Somers, "
Lewis George B. "
McCurdy Thomas G. "
McKean William, "
Punchard J. P. "
Salem Boot & Shoe Co. "
Very Perley, "
Burpee John, Amesbury, Salisbury
Mellen Henry, Montville, Sandisfield
White J. " "

Bruce Geo. W. Saugus Centre, Saugus
Hitchings Chas. S. " "
Hitchings W. F. " "
Walton & Wilson, " "
    Scituate
Bailey J. W. & G. W., N. Scituate, "
Litchfield M. S. & Z, H. " "
Newcomb Henry, " "
Newcomb William, " "
Baker P. H. Sharon
Bullard S. W. "
Godfrey J. W. "
Hewins Albert, "
Hixon A. G. & C. D. "
Middleton J. S. "
Windship Charles, "
Dowse N. & Son (shoes), "
Bullard J. & J. W. Sherborn
Coolidge Lowell, "
Brownson H. Shirley
Fales Leander, Shrewsbury
Stetson Henry, Shutesbury
Gibbs Joseph & E. A. Somerset
Slade Levi, "
Washburn Horatio L. "
Hartt John & Co. Southborough
Newton & Hartt, "
Ford N. S. South Scituate
Curtis Brothers & Co. West Scituate, "
Buffum F. S. " "
Stoddard H. A. " "
Stowell Edward, " "
Willcutt Dexter M. " "
BULLARD AND BOYDEN, Spencer
Bush John L. (boots), "
Drury D. A. &. Co. "
Green Josiah & Co. (boots), "
Jones E. & Co. (boots), "
Kent & Bacon (boots), "
Prouty D. & Co. (boots), "
Prouty I. & Co. (boots), "
Watson R. S. & Co. "
Cutler, McIntosh, & Co. Springfield
Elmer & Smith (shoes), "
Henbesch Paul, "
Hixon, Birnie, & Shaw, "
Battles W. J. & Co. "
Bryant S. A. Stoneham
BRYANT & FOLEY, "
Dike C. C. "
Dike G. W. "
Drew & Buswell, "
Duncklee & Danforth, "
Emerson Charles, "
Emerson R. W. "
Green A. R. "
Hanscom Orrin, "
Hay Cyrus, "
HILL F. S. & CO. "
Hill John & Co. "
Hill & Rowe, "
Mawhinney H. H. & Co. "
Poore Henry, "
Richardson & Critchett, "
Rounds J. G. & Co. "
Sweetser Vernon (shoes), "
Trowbridge G. W. "
Usher Wm. R. & Co. "
Wyeth Hollis N. "
Belcher A. & G. W. Stoughton
Belcher L. & Son, "
Capen F. & Co. "
Delano Ellis & Co. "
Ellis & Gay, "
Fitzpatrick J. & H. "
French Daniel, "
Goldthwaite Joseph, "
Guild & Upham, "

Hawes G. W. Stoughton
Hill James, "
Kinsley Bradford, "
Morton N. & Co.
Packard Francis,
Parker & Wales,
Pettee S. G. "
Reynolds & Crane,
Savels Samuel & Son,
Swan J. & Co.
Blanchard D. H. & H., E. Stoughton, "
Littlefield Charles, " "
Littlefield Darius, " "
Littlefield & May, " "
Littlefield E. W. & G. W. & Co. " "
Noyes C. L. " "
Smith Charles, " "
Tucker E. & Son, " "
Allen C. N. Sturbridge
Morse A. C. "
Draper & Skerry, Fiskdale, "
Howard L. C. Sutton
King Nathaniel G. "
Lamb Frank T. Templeton
Tingley Henry (moccasins), Tewksbury
Bailey, Sanders, & Co. Topsfield
Boardman T. G. "
Herrick Charles & Co. "
Stiles Frederick, "
Towne Joseph, "
Fay W. B. (boots), Upton
Batchelor D. W. (boots), West Upton, "
Aborn John G. Wakefield
Evans J. M. "
Evans L. B. "
EMERSON'S THOMAS SONS (shoes), "
Hawkes Adam, "
Sweetser A. N. & A. G. "
Walton E. H. "
Bosworth H. B. Warren
Moore Cutler (shoes), "
Ramsdell & Tripp, (boots), "
Albee Abner, Warwick
Albee & Hastings, "
Hastings Charles F. "
Bent Wm. & J. M. (shoes), Cochituate, Wayland
Bryant Thomas, " " "
Dudley E. H. " " "
Dudley L. " " "
Hammond Wm. " " "
Hawes & Davis, " " "
Loker A. D. " " "
Lyon O. T. & Son, " " "
Ward & Spofford, " " "
Brown Chas E. " Webster
Bugbee H. E. " "
Coroin B. A. & Son, " "
Humphrey Robert, " "
Tourtelott James D. "
Merrill Arthur L. (shoes), Wenham
Brigham G. B. Westborough
Forbes George, "
Griggs C. B. "
Kimball J. B. & Co. "
Newton Otis & Son, "
Hastings N. & Co. West Boylston
Howe Geo. F. & Co. "
Hastings Lyman & Co., Oakdale. "
Copeland & Hartwell, West Bridgewater
Edson & Caldwell, "
Howard & Washburn, "
Leach Allen, "
Copeland P. & N. & Co., Campello, "
Alger & Perkins, Cochesett, "
Ring Joseph, "
TISDALE EDWARD, " "
Hayward Franklin W., South Easton, "

Boot and Shoe Manufacturers — continued.

Brown H.	West Brookfield
Cumner, Mansfield, & Co.	"
Falls John M., Sons, & Co.	"
FULLAM LEMUEL,	"
Garish, Thompson, & Co.	"
Shumway E. & Son,	"
Smith & Dane,	"
Lewis B. F.	Westfield
Bailey S. Waldo,	West Newbury
Durgin James & Son,	"
Durgin Samuel,	"
Hosum & Davis,	"
Moseley C. C.	"
Wood E. G.	"
Coburn Abijah,	Weston
Hastings F.	"
Chapin & Thayer,	Weymouth
Cook Samuel,	"
Hall Albion (boots),	"
Hart John,	"
Hunt A. N. & Co.	"
Hunt C. P. & Co.	"
Hunt R. A. (boots),	"
Hunt Henry,	"
Loud Cyrus,	"
Nash A. P. (boots),	"
Nash George & Co. (boots),	"
Nash S. W. & E.	"
Richards Elias (boots),	"
Robinson B. F. (boots),	"
SMITH D. & CO.	"
Sterling D. L. & A. H. (boots),	"
White D. & Co.	"
Bicknell H. F.,	East Weymouth,
Burrell G.	"
Canterbury N. D.	"
Clapp James H & Co.	"
DIZER M C. & CO. (boots),	"
Farren Wm. D. (boots),	"
French Asa T. & Co.	"
Hobart Elijah,	"
HOLBROOK A. & CO.	"
McKay Bros. & Tirrell,	"
Nash Cottington,	"
Randall Otis H.	"
Randall Quincy,	"
RAYMOND ALVAH,	"
Reed Isaac,	"
Rogers J. W.	"
Totman J. & Son,	"
Bates Elnathan,	North Weymouth,
BEALS AUGUSTUS (slippers),	"
Bicknell & Holbrook,	"
Dyer Warren,	"
French & Stoddard,	"
Moulton Andrew R.	"
Newton Henry,	"
Pratt George H.	"
TORREY ALEXIS & CO.	"
TORREY JAS. & CO.	"
Blanchard W. & C.,	South Weymouth,
Curtis & Howe,	"
Dyer William,	"
Fogg Charles S.	"
Fogg, Houghton, & Coolidge (boots),	"
Lindsley, Shaw, & Co.	"
Loud Cyrus,	"
Reed Josiah & Co.	"
Shaw Nathaniel & Co.	"
Tirrell A. & Co.	"
Tirrell Albert 2d,	"
Tirrell C. & P. H. & Co.	"
Torrey & Loud,	"
Vining & Randall,	"
White Jairus & Son,	"
Swain Charles W.	Wilmington
Adams D.	Woburn

Bancroft A.	Woburn
BURKE & MUNDAY, Main St.	"
Cragin F. J.	"
Gorham & Holmes,	"
Wyman Elijah, 2d,	"
Taylor & Cook,	"
Tidd John & Sons,	"
Gorham P. W. & Son, East Woburn,	"
Hanson M. A.	"
Hyde N. S.	"
Tidd Luke R.	"
Totman Wm. & Co.	"
Nichols, Winn, & Co., North Woburn,	"
Andrews S. C.	Worcester
Bay State Shoe & Leather Co.	"
Carey I. H.	"
Childs E. N.	"
Fay H. B. & Co.	"
Fitch C. H. & Co.	"
French Hiram,	"
Gould Albert,	"
Heywood S. R. & Co.	"
Houghton C. C.	"
Hubbard H. B.	"
Jenks H. B. & Co.	"
Manning David,	"
Muzzy E. A. & Co.	"
Newton C.	"
Peirce Thomas,	"
Rawson D. G. & Co.	"
Smith M.	"
Smyth Brothers & Co.	"
Stark E. H. & Co.	"
Stone, Walker, & Co.	"
Stowe L. & Co.	"
Walker J. & Co.	"
Walker J. H. & G. M.	"
Wesson J. E.	"
Wesson Rufus, jr. (shoes),	"
Wilson Dexter,	"
Aldrich Artemus & Son,	Wrentham
Fisher Henry K.	"

Boot and Shoe Stock Manuf.

(Soles, Heels, and Stiffenings.)

Dunham Worthy C. (heels), North Abington,	Abington
Gilbert L. W. (heels),	Amherst
Parmenter Charles (heels),	"
PATENT RUBBER HEEL STIFFENING CO.	Chelsea
Howe William A. (fillings),	Dover
Dinsmore Sumner,	Grafton
Hall A. J.	"
Ayer R. G.	Haverhill
Bradley & Simonds (heels),	"
BRAGG J. F., 8 Fleet st.	"
Burgess Wm.	"
Burnham & Cheney,	"
Buswell B. P.	"
Chase M. E.	"
Cheeny Fred P.	"
Currier A.	"
Currier W. W.	"
Ellsworth J. N. & Co.	"
Fifield Sumner (heels),	"
Fitts & Noyes,	"
Ford Charles T.	"
Ford H. K.	"
Fuller John S.	"
Haddock Edward,	"
Haines John W.	"
Herrick & Co.	"
Jones Abijah,	"
Jordan Wm. E. & Co.	"
Lord H. A.	"
Mace William,	"
Meadowcraft William,	"

Morse C. C.   Haverhill
Morse Charles E.   "
Newton Thomas F.   "
Noyes T.   "
OTIS O. B. 7½ Water,   "
Pettingill Rufus S.   "
Pike Warren,   "
Stuart Samuel,   "
Thing J. R. & Co.   "
Tilton R. H.   "
Tilton W. W.   "
Twombly Ira F. (heels),   "
Webster & Co.   "
White Robert,   "
Warren Charles W. (heels),   Leicester
Alley T. N.   Lynn
Attwill Theodore (soles),   "
Attwill William A. (soles),   "
Batchelder George H.   "
Batcheller George F.   "
Bessom & Ward (soles),   "
Boyce James P.   "
Boyle Edward, jr.,   "
Boynton D. S.   "
Brackett Joseph,   "
Burgess William,   "
Connor Stephen,   "
Emerson D. & C. K. (heels),   "
Estes Charles E.   "
Farnsworth E. M. (paper soles),   "
George & Bro. (soles),   "
Gloyd D. N. & Co. (heels, taps, &c.),   "
Green C. E. L. & Co. (straw and
  leather board),   "
Hay John F.   "
HILL A. C. (soles), 46 Exchange,   "
Hussey George W.   "
Jackson Pickmore,   "
Johnson, Hood, & Co.   "
Johnson P. & Son,   "
Lewis A. & Co. (heels),   "
Knowlton S. B. (heels),   "
Libbey Jeremiah L.   "
Marble James F.   "
Mullen A. E. (roundings),   "
Mullen Charles H.   "
Mullen J. E. (soles),   "
Newhall Eustis,   "
Newhall Perry (and sole leather),   "
Oliver Edwin H.   "
Pevear & Macomber,   "
Pierce & Ellis,   "
Prime S. L.   "
Proctor & Ingalls (soles),   "
Sargent T. C.   "
Sumner J. S.   "
Taber Charles A.   "
Towns Q. A. (heels),   "
Brown W. A.   Marblehead
McClearn F. S.   "
Spinney & Ramsdell,   "
Greene G. M.   Milford
                            North Bridgewater
KEITH & PACKARD (counters),   "
                              Northborough
Bartlett & Johnson (stiffenings),   "
Miles S. J.   "   "
Barnard Frederick F.   Oxford
Gates B.   "
Southwick Samuel (heeling),   "
Cassidy Michael,   Peabody
Goldthwait E. P.   "
Flint E. S. & Co.   "
Osborn Jonathan E.   "
Collier J. H.   Salem
Cass John,   "
Cusack Patrick,   "
Gwinn James S.   "

Powers John,   Salem
Prendergast Michael,   "
Rice Andrew J. jun. & Co. (heels),   "
Simmons J. H.   "
Stone & Prescott,   "
Brown & Oliver,   East Saugus, Saugus
Burrill Geo. (stiffenings),   "   "
Lockwood H. C. (heels),   "   "
CROSBY S. L.   Stoneham
                               Stoughton
Phinney S. C. & J. G. (counters).   "
Swift Orville (heels),   West Brookfield
Burrell J. W. (heels), East W. Weymouth
EARL D. C. (heels),   "   "
SIMONDS N. J.   Woburn

Boot and Shoe Stitchers and Fitters.

Powers William,   N. Abington, Abington
Blodgett Henry S.   Haverhill
Burbank P. E.   "
Hines E. M.   "
Osgood O. F.   "
Webster Calvin,   "
Batcheller John A.   Lynn
Blaisdell William B.   "
Bradford Daniel.   "
Brookhouse Nathaniel W.   "
Chipperfield J. C.   "
Collins A. L.   "
Cowles C.   "
Fawcett Amos,   "
Fuller Sylvester,   "
Hale E. A.   "
Hersey C. W. & Co.   "
Hussey Isaac W.   "
Mansfield H. W. & Co.   "
Moulton C. F.   "
Nichols F. W. & Co.   "
Pray C. E.   "
Packard Isaac H.   "
Scribner & Smith,   "
Turner Charles,   "
Wentworth Jeremiah,   "
Childs W. C.   Natick
Fairn J. L.   "
Parker J. H.   "
Blanchard C. F.   North Bridgewater
Churchill V.   "
Gilbert C. H. H.   "
Howard Charles,   "
Keith Edwin,   Campello, "
Sidelinger Z. H.   Quincy Point, Quincy
Stanwood William H.   Salem
Collins Isaac,   E. Saugus, Saugus
Hitchings Charles I.   "   "
Mansfield H. W.   "   "
Rivers Charles,   "   "
Lond L. H.   Weymouth
Wallace W. S.   "
Sweet & Cleverly,   North   "

Boot Top Gilders.

Blunt M. A.   Milford
Nash A. Prescott,   Weymouth

Boring Machines.

Richardson Nathan,   Gloucester
                               Sturbridge
SNELL MANUFACTURING Co.
  E. L. Bates, agent, (see page 763),
                               Fiskdale, "

Botanic Medicines.

(See also Patent Medicines.)

Bailey Kendall, jr.   Charlestown
Cummings Henry,   "

Botanic Medicines — continued.

Aldrich J. M.	Fall River
Brown P. S.	"
Chace J. E. & Son,	"
Priest M. L.	Haverhill
Dows Amos W.	Lowell
Kelsey Hugh	"
Thompson M. E.	"
Greenleaf C. Mrs.	Lynn
Knowles Daniel.	New Bedford
SWEET JOB, (see page 712), Kemp-	
ton cor. Summer,	"

Bottlers.

Kay James,	Fall River
Sowle Resolved,	"
Winn & Parker,	Gloucester
HEALD M. C. (see p. 714), 114 South	
Common,	Lynn
Gould & Cummings,	Newburyport
Bigelow E.	Springfield
BROOKS F. A.- (see page 778), 50	
No. Main,	"
Hall R. & Son,	"
Tripp William C.	Taunton

Bowling Alleys.

Pierce A. T. (patent),	Fairhaven
CARPENTER JOHN S. 72 So. Main,	
	Fall River
Cline Daniel,	Haverhill
Batty Samuel,	New Bedford
Hofford Stephen,	"
Sylvia Frank,	"
Holmes John F.	Plymouth
Reed Allen,	Provincetown
Rogers Otis,	Quincy

Box Board Manufacturer.

GOSS CHARLES H. (see page 769),
East Bridgewater

Box Makers.

(*See also Paper Boxes.*)

Chase Hyslop,	Abington
Cushing David, East Abington,	"
Keith A. W. North	"
Chase David, (packing),	Acushnet
Cushman Emery,	"
Lumbard John,	"
Staples Daniel R. (cheese),	Adams
Chilson Jacob B. North Adams,	"
Bangs & Hawes, North Amherst,	Amherst
Eldredge George L. (pill),	Ashfield
Metcalf Alvah (boot and bonnet),	Ashland
Stratton Reuben & Son,	Athol
Rice & Meacham. (shoe, &c.), Athol	
Depot	"
Dennis Dexter,	Barre
Rice Leonard,	"
Metcalf.Frank, Caryville,	Bellingham
Kimball & Sawyer. (shoe),	Boxford
	Boylston
Ray Tertullus (shoe), Boylston Centre,	"
MONATIQUOT STEAM MILLS,	
H. Gardner, proprietor (see page	
768), Weymouth,	Braintree
Pratt Z. (box boards),	Bridgewater
Draper John W. E. Brimfield,	Brimfield
Twitchell Geo. L. & Co.	Brookfield
Blood A. O. E. Brookfield,	"
MITCHELL L. D. (cigar, tobacco,	
small, fancy and packing), (see	
page 714), Broadway, Cambridge-	
port,	Cambridge
PAGE GEORGE G. &. Co. (packing	
and cigar), Hampshire st., Cam-	
bridgeport,	"

	Cambridge
Pearson John A. (paper), Cam-	
bridgeport,	"
Simpson W. E. & B. Cambridgeport,	"
Buttrick N.	Carlisle
Cole Harrison G. N. Carver,	Carver
	Charlton
Putnam & Brothers (cloth and shoe),	"
Peak John C.	Chelsea
Chilson Jacob B. N. Adams, Clarksburg	
Dooley Peter,	"
Call Bros. (butter),	Coleraine
Pierce, Morris, & Son (butter),	"
Stevens N. S. (silk packing), Cummington	
Bragdon J. & N. (shoe, soap, and	
candle). Danvers Port, Danvers	
Ross Josiah & Co.	"
Curtis Hiram.	Dorchester
Delano Elisha (soap and spice),	
West Duxbury,	Duxbury
	East Bridgewater
GOSS CHARLES H. (see page 769),	"
Rowand Benjamin (shooks), Fall River	
POND VIRGIL S. (packing), Foxborough	
Hill Lewis W. (boot),	Franklin
Hubbard Sabin, (boot and bonnet),	"
Folsom I. P. (shoe),	Georgetown
Bailey Stephen P., Greenwich Vil-	
lage,	Greenwich
Whitmarsh Benj. A. (packing), Hancock
Damon Thomas (shoe),	Hanover
Cushing Geo. & Theo. (shoe, &c.), Hanson
Robinson Jos. R. (boot),	Hardwick
Southworth Constant (packing),	Harvard
Fletcher E. E. & Brother (shoe),	Harvard
Green John N. B.	Haverhill
Pearsons Martha,	"
HERSEY EDMUND (fig, strawberry,	
and salt),	Hingham
HERSEY SAMUEL (fancy),	"
King Thomas,	"
Lane Leavitt,	"
Lewis James S.	"
Broad Ira (cloth),	Holden
Payson & Cutler,	Holliston
Phipps M. C.	Hopkinton
Howe Abel (boot, &c.),	Hubbardston
Tripp Brothers (shoe),	Hudson
Richmond E. (shoe),	Lakeville
Sargent L. D.	Lawrence
FISH WILLIAM T. (paper boxes), Lee
Converse George,	Leicester
Gould Amos A. (packing),	"
Sprague Asahel,	"
Moore Dexter (tobacco),	Leverett
Brooks A. L. Mechanics' Mills, Lowell
Davis Asahel (plain and fancy wood),	
Mechanics Mills,	"
Norcross & Saunders, agents,	"
ALLEN & BOYDEN (paper, see page	
760), 9 Broad street,	Lynn
Buffum James N.	"
Straw Eleazer,	"
	Marblehead
Roberts Otis W. (wood and paper),	"
Emerson Edwin R.	Marlborough
MANNING JOSEPH,	"
Patch Timothy B.	"
Hatch Chas. R., W. Marshfield, Marshfield
Hatch D. P. & J. F.	"
Magoun & Holmes,	"
BARSTOW N. H. & H. (pine, see	
page 727),	Mattapoisett
Nelson Thomas (mahogany),	"
Hill Lewis W. West Medway, Medway
Newton Benj. F.	"
Taft Sullivan H. (dry goods),	Mendon
Wilcox Samuel G. (boot),	"

MORSE E. P. (wood and paper), Methuen
Patterson D. H. (hat and shoe),   "
HARLOW I. H. & CO. (wood, see
  page 768),   Middleborough
Davis I. N. & Co.   Milford
Jones A. A.   "
Moore & Trumbull,   Monson
Smith Francis B.   Nantucket
Howard & Wheeler,   Natick
Woods O. & Co.   "
    New Bedford
Coffin Frederic,   (pasteboard),   "
Wood Tilson,   (candle),   "
Thurlow Wm.   (paper),   Newbury
    New Marlborough
Sisson H. D. (cheese), Mill River,   "
Bartlett W. A. 2d (shoe),   Northborough
    North Bridgewater
Continental Box Co. (strawberry),   "
Keith A. W.   (packing),   "
Vittum & Bennett, (packing),   "
Bryant George (shoe),   North Brookfield
Southworth Chas. "
Parker H. B. (tobacco),   Northfield
Lincoln Moses (wooden),   Norton
    Oakham
Haskins Erskine (cheese), Cold Brook, "
Parker Daniel M. (boot),   "
Putnam H. C. & Co. (shoe),   Oxford
Putnam & Brother (cloth),   "
Grover Z.   North Oxford,   "
Clark A. F.   Peabody
Oldham John 2d,   Pembroke
West James H.   "
Hatch Geo. F. North Pembroke,   "
Shepard N. T.   "
Green A. A. (chair),   Philipston
Lamb Jason (boot and chair),   "
Gardner Jeremiah   (butter),   Plainfield
Tirrell Jeremiah,   "   "
BARNES E. & J. C. (see page 717),
  Water st.,   Plymouth
Bonney James S.   (shoe),   Plympton
Ellis J. C. & H. K. (shoe and rivet),"
Barrows H.   North Dana,   Prescott
Belcher E. & G.   Randolph
Leonard & Lyons,   "
Walton Joseph (cigar),   Salem
Ames William H. (hat boxes, wood
  and paper),   Salisbury
Royce Newton W. (cheese),
  Montville,   Sandisfield
Smith A. D. (cheese), Montville,   "
Whitney E. A.   "   "   "   "
Bronson Wm. B.   New Boston,   "
Deming Amos & Mark (packing), Savoy
Clemence J. M. & L. D., Globe Vil-
  lage,   Southbridge
    South Hadley
Congdon B. South Hadley Falls,   "
Howe Ebenezer,   Spencer
Livermore Winthrop,   "
Smith M. & Son,   Stow
Snell T. (paper),   Starbridge
NEWCOMB W. L. & CO. (packing,
  see page 728),   Taunton
SPROAT JAMES H.   "
Richmond Eleazer, East Taunton,   "
Williams N. S.   "   "
Lamb Jason (packing),   Templeton
Lamb Justin,   "   "
Stone William,   Otter River,   "
Brinley & James,   Tyngsborough
Upton John G.   "
Fisk Evon   (boot and bonnet),   Upton
Wool Arba T.   "
Marby H. P.   (packing),   Wales
Brackett Charles A. (paper),   Waltham

Buttrick Francis,   Waltham
Bass William H. (boot),   Warwick
Drury George B. (packing), West Hampton
Loud Francis & Son,   "
Fairbanks Corning,   Westborough
Ensign Brothers (cigar),   Westfield
Loomis Wm. R. (packing, &c.),   "
Tewksbury J. G. (paper), West Newbury
Sisson Alden T. (wooden and
  shooks),   Westport
Loud Reuben & Sons, South
  Weymouth,   Weymouth
Sherman E. & C., S. Weymouth,   "
Fessenden Warren,   Woburn
Greenwood Curtis,   "
Buker Charles & Co.   Worcester
KEYES I. N. (see p. 720), 24 Central, "

Brackets.

Sherwin Levi & Son,   Fitchburg
RICE, GRIFFIN, & CO.   Worcester

Brass and Copper Founders.

HUNTER JAMES & SON, (see page
  770),   N. Adams,   Adams
Lazell, Perkins, & Co. . .   Bridgewater
Litchfield W.   Charlestown
Ames Manufacturing Co.   Chicopee
GAYLORD MANUF. CO. (see
  page 773),   "
Peverly Robert H.   Chelsea
Winslow John,   Fairhaven
BUSH WM. R. (see page 755), 27
  No. Main,   Fall River
HARDY WILLIAM A. & CO. (see
  page 802), 2 Laurel,   Fitchburg
Putnam Machine Co.   "
MUNSON J. M. (see page 716), Greenfield
Byrom James,   Lawrence
Wilder H. H. & Co.   Lowell
Field Benjamin,   Nantucket
Cragie Andrew,   New Bedford
Giffard & Allen.   "
de Rochemont G. W. & C. H., Newburyport
    Pittsfield
CLARY & RUSSELL (see page 720) "
SALEM BRASS FOUNDRY, Ira
  Choate, agent, Elm, corner Derby
  (see page 745),   Salem
Waters A. S.   "
Emory P. P. & Co.   Springfield
E. STEBBINS MANUF. CO. (see
  page 780),   "
Trefethen D. A.   Taunton
    Williamsburg
Hayden, Gere, & Co., Haydenville,   "
Chapin Jason,   Worcester
Wells & Rice,   "
WHEELER W. A., 42 Thomas (see
  page 792),   "

Brass Finishers.

Sargent, Earles, & Co.   Fitchburg
Barker & Co.   Lawrence
REED & HALLOWELL, Mechanics'
  Mills,   Lowell
CHOATE & PERKINS, 194 Derby
  (see page 747),   Salem
SALEM BRASS FOUNDRY, Ira
  Choate, Agent, Elm, cor. Derby
  (see page 745),   "
Avery & Co.   Springfield
Curtis George & Co.   "
Morgan H. & J.   "
Babbitt F. S.   Taunton

Brass and Malleable Iron Castings.

GAYLORD MANUF. CO. (see page 773),   Chicopee

Brewers.

French Walter,	Boxford
	Cambridge
Moore John M. & Co., E. Cambridge,	"
Kent John O.	Charlestown
Winn & Parker,	Gloucester
Blood Albert,	Lawrence
Dolliver T. H.	"
Gearin & Howard,	"
Heald Wm. E.	"
Giles George,	Newburyport
Gimlich & White,	Pittsfield
Shaw Joseph,	Salem
WINN S. B., Front, cor. Washington,	"
Shaw J. & Co.,	Springfield
Woodard Henry,	Tyringham
Riedl J. & Son,	Worcester

Brick Makers.

Cudworth H. P.	Adams
Hall Charles O.	North Adams,	"
Howard R. H.	Amherst
Whitney Austin,	Ashburnham
Smith Adin,	Athol Depot,	Athol
Burnham John F.	Beverly
Trask William T.	"
Hooper Mitchell & Co.	Bridgewater
Blodgett Calvin, Palmer Depot,	Brimfield
Hyde Samuel,	Brookfield
Moulton Jesse,	East Brookfield,	"
	Buckland
Toby & Comstock, Shelburne Falls,	"
Cofran Samuel M.	Cambridge
McCrane & Nagle,	"
Sands John L.	"
Sands John N.	"
Bay State Brick Co.	N. Cambridge,	"
Ferson Charles H.	Chelsea
McClellan Charles & Son,	Chicopee
Hartis Nathaniel,	Boston,	Chilmark
Griswold Joseph,	Coleraine
Day George H.	Danvers Port, Danvers
Elliott Henry,	"	"
Gray J. & Son,	"	"
Low Samuel,	"	"
Walcott William H.	"	"
Chandler Martin S.	Duxbury
Thompson Seth & Co.	East Bridgewater
Clark Theodore,	East Hampton
Haas Michael,	"
Rich Martin,	"
Pomeroy George & Son,	"
HAWKINS & KILHAM (dealers),	
Slade's Wharf (see page 718), Fall River	
SHOVE C. & CO. (dealer), 40 Davol,	"
Goodrich Edwin &.	Fitchburg
Hinds A., jr.	South Gardner, Gardner
Collins ——,	Great Barrington
Couch, Brewer, & Bently,	"
McClure Manley,	Greenfield
Hawley F. A.	Hadley
Richmond J. C.	Still River, Harvard
Allair Anthony, jr.	Hatfield
Sargent Robert,	Haverhill
Smiley Frank,	"
Tilton John O.	"
Goodrich Charles W.	Hinsdale
Bosworth Lewis P.	Holyoke
Richards E. T.	"
Tyler Abraham,	Hudson
Burbank Aaron,	Lancaster

Burbank Levi B.	Lancaster
Merrill J. T. & Co.	South Lee, Lee
Osborn Leonard,	Leominster
Maiden John, Springfield, Longmeadow	
Newhall Wm. M.	Lynn
Edminster Warren, South Malden, Malden	
Stimpson Stephen,	"
Bay State Brick Company,	Medford
Clark Elbridge, East Medway, Medway	
Clark John,	"	"
Thrasher Geo. B.	"	"
	Montague
Goss R. L. & C. W., Montague City,	"
	Needham
Wood Henry's Son & Co., Wellesley,	"
Doyle Cornelius,	Newbury
Doyle Charles,	Newburyport
Smith David,	"
Crowle P. Mrs.	New Salem
Day Samuel,	Northampton
Nutting Porter,	"
Howe Alonzo B.	Northborough
McClure John (pressed), North Chelsea	
Sarsfield Patrick,	"
Waite William A.	"
Lawrence Wm. T.	Pepperell
Hinds Cephas,	Petersham
Noble Norman,	Pittsfield
Barker J. & Brothers, West Pittsfield,	"
Clark S. W.	Plainfield
Hedge Barnabas,	Plymouth
National Brick Co. B. Draper, agt. Rehoboth	
Stocker Frederick, East Saugus, Saugus	
	Shelburne
Andrews B. Allen, Shelburne Falls,	"
Gerrish James,	Shirley
Shattuck William G.	"
	Somerville
Dana James, North Somerville,	"
Fiske Benjamin,	"	"
Fiske Mark,	"	"
Foster George A.	"	"
Gray James,	"	"
Hadley Benjamin,	"	"
Holt Chauncey,	"	"
Jaques Wm.	"	"
Littlefield Samuel,	"	"
Sanborn Joseph,	"	"
Smith J. W.	"	"
Tufts Brick Co.,	"	"
Washburn David,	"	"
Wyatt Geo. W.	"	"
Pomeroy George,	Southampton
Ball & Holman, Cordaville, Southborough	
Dresser & Brown,	Southbridge
Potter & Dresser,	"
Talbot Thomas,	Globe Village,	"
	South Hadley
Britton Royal, South Hadley Falls,	"
Richards E. T.	"
Jacobs Edward, W. Scituate, S. Scituate	
ALLIS W. H.	Springfield
King Henry & Son,	"
Leary John,	"
Madden John,	"
Morse Moses,	"
Talbot Thomas, Globe Village, Sturbridge	
Moulton C. N.	Fiskdale,	"
Godfrey John D.	Taunton
Hart John W. & Co.	"
Johnson Wm. T. & Co.	"
Johnson & Macomber,	"
Staples A. B.	"
Staples Silas L.	"
Taunton Brick Co. A. H. Williams, supt.	"
Wheeler Dexter B.	"
Williams A. H.	"

WILLIAMS J. R. (fire of all kinds)   Taunton
(see page 715),   "
Dyer H. N.   Otter River, Templeton
Evans Samuel D.   Townsend
Needham William L.   Wales
Lawton William B.   Ware
Sheldon W. C. & Co.   "
Cook Calvin B.   Williamstown
Lindley John,   "
Chamberlain S   Winchendon
Whitney B. D.   "
Bliss H. jr.   Worcester
Denny A. B.   "
Hobbs George,   "
Hooper Frank,   "

Bridge Builders.

Solid Lever Bridge Co.   Chelsea
Sawtell J. A.   Lowell
Briggs A. D. & Co.   Springfield
HAWKINS, HERTHEL, & BUR-
RALL, 88 Main (see page 781),   "

Britannia Ware Manufacturers.

Draper F. & Co. (glass trimmings,
East Cambridge,   Cambridge
Eldridge & Co.   Taunton
Porter Britannia and Plate Co.   "
REED & BARTON (see page 758),   "

Brokers.

CONROY DANIEL, 20 Union,   Fall River
EASTON & MILNE (money and
cotton), 14 North Main,   "
REMINGTON CLINTON V. S.
(cotton and cotton goods), 43
Pocasset, cor Main,   "
Slade John P.   "
Childs H. S. (real estate),   Greenfield
Dearborn G. F.   Lowell
RICHARDSON L. B. & CO. (money
and merchandise), 108 Central,   "
Codd James,   Nantucket
Burt E. N.   New Bedford
BURT SAMUEL P. (stock and com-
mission, 43 N. Water,   "
COOK SAMUEL H. 37 N. Water,   "
Cunningham John (pawn),   "
Furber G. W. (pawn),   "
Howland & Co. (pawn),   "
TAYLOR WILLIAM H. 37 N. Water, "
Newburyport
Greenleaf George (real estate & stock), "
Greenleaf Rufus L. (real estate
and stock),   "
Clarke John (money),   Northampton
Dawson L. A. (money and note),   "
Parsons E. (money, note, and real
estate),   "
PECK A. PERRY (real estate),   "
Harlow Nathaniel E. (fish),   Plymouth
Hathaway Benjamin (commercial),   "
Nelson William H. (fish),   "
ARCHER WILLIAM (stock, real
estate and insurance), 34 Front
and 18 Washington,   Salem
Nichols Charles S. (stock and insur-
ance),   "
Pierce N. (stock),   "
Burt Augustine (real estate),   Springfield
Clark Henry (real estate),   "
DAVIS L. L. 10 Fort block (machine-
ry),   "
Jordan Josiah,   "
Kingsbury Geo. & Co. (real estate),   "
RICE, FULLER, & CO. (real estate),
State cor. Main,   "

Smith Henry (pawn),   Springfield
Fletcher & Norton,   Westfield
Sutton & Wheeler (stock),   Worcester
Rice & Whiting (stock &c.),   "

Bronze Metal (patent.)

NEW BEDFORD COPPER CO.,
William H. Mathews, treas. (see
page 757),   New Bedford

Bronze Metal Sheathing.

NEW BEDFORD COPPER CO. (see
page 757),   New Bedford

Broom Manufacturers.

Amherst
Ingraham Austin, North Amherst,   "
Smith Lyman,   "
PACKARD & BURRILL (rattan),
East Cambridge,   Cambridge
Cook Charles, 2d,   Hadley
Cook Horace,   "
Edson F.   "
Reynolds Thomas,   "
Smith Charles,   "
West H. C.   "
Cook Chester,   North Hadley,   "
Lawrence Hubbard,   "   "
Smith Henry E.   "   "
Smith S. S.   "   "
Smith Thaddeus,   "   "
Bowen George S.   New Bedford
Graves John B.   Northampton
Graves Martin B.   "
Smith R.   "
Hancock Society of Shakers, Ira R.
Lawson, agent, West Pittsfield, Pittsfield
WHITELEY JOHN (see page 793),
Shirley Village,   Shirley

Brown Stone Manufacturers.

LYONS WM. J., Medford St. (see
page 735),   Charlestown

Brush Manufacturers.

Burton, Fellows, & Co.   East
Cambridge,   Cambridge
PACKARD & BURRILL,
East Cambridge,   "
Sheriff & Co.   Dedham
New England Tube Brush Co., Daniel
Stillwell, agent,   Fall River
STAFFORD JOHN H. (see page 742),
266 Essex,   Lawrence
Merrimac Brush Co.   Newburyport
PIERCE CHARLES M. jr. (dealer),
119 No. Water,   New Bedford
FLORENCE MANUFACTURING
COMPANY (toilet brushes), Geo.
A. Burr, treas., Florence, Northampton
COTSWOLD BRUSH CO. (wool
duster and fancy wool mats), T. S.
Mann, Trens., Florence,   "
THAYER ELLIS,   Worcester

Brush Wood Manufacturers.

Wheeler James S.   Warwick

Bucket Manufacturers.

(See Wooden Ware.)

Builders' Materials.

(See also Lime and Cement.)

PERKINS NOBLE M. Stebbins
Block,   Chelsea
Robinson J. D.   Neponset,   Dorchester

Builders' Materials — continued.

Conant P. D. | Fall River
HAWKINS & KILHAM, Slade's
　Wharf (see page 718), | "
SHOVE C. & CO. 40 Davol, | "
BLODGETT & BARRETT, | Hyde Park
BREED S. N. & Co. 83 Broad, | Lynn
MARTIN E. L. P. (see page 708),
　54 Munroe, | "
Paine S. S. & Brother, | New Bedford
Pierce Chas. M. jr., 119 No. Water, | "

Builders and Contractors.

(*See Carpenters; also Masons.*)

Building Movers.

Cammett Cyrus, | Amesbury
| Cambridge
Mellen Jas. & Co. Cambridgeport, | "
McElroy F. G. 　East Cambridge, | "
Richards David, | Charlestown
Richards S. | "
Alden John, | Fairhaven
Darling H. N. | Fall River
Thurston J. E. & Co. | "
Gordon Phineas, | Haverhill
Barker Chas. W. | Lynn
Barker James S. | "
Beede V. M. | "
Clark D. D. | "
Hammond Martin, | Natick
Page John H. | Newburyport
Higgins Willard, | Orleans
Johnson B. H. | Palmer
Trask Moses, | Peabody
Edwards J. D. | Salem
Holman Lyman, | "
Walker Otis, | Taunton
Packard C. S. | Waltham
Tubbs Charles, | West Springfield

Bung Manufs.

BACHELDER A. & CO. (manuf. of
　bungs, taps, and vents, see adv.
　page 789), Mt. Vernon, n, Broad-
　way, | Lowell
Peckham Perry M. | Fall River

Bunting Manufacturers.

U. S. Bunting Co., D. W. C. Farring-
　ton, agent, | Lowell

Burglar Alarm.

WOLTERS H. J. (see page 747),
　30 Mill, | Salem

Burning Brands and Seal Presses Manuf.

Hill Benjamin B. | Springfield

Burr Picker Manuf. (*Improved.*)

SARGENT CHARLES G. (see page
　749), Graniteville, | Westford

Butchers.

Blanchard Brothers, | Abington
Cushing Davis, 　East Abington, | "
Studley Reuben, 　 " 　 " | "
Bates Nahum, 　 South 　 " | "
Gardner George, 　South Acton, | Acton
Tuttles, Jones, & Wetherbee, " | "
Hundley Aaron C. 　West Acton, | "
Locke Henry, | Arlington
Allen C. S. | Ashby
Esterbrook W. | "
Bronson Chandler, | Ashfield
Noyes & Robinson, | Ashland

Swift Gustavus F. | Barnstable
Crocker M. M. 　Hyannis, | "
Graves E. & H. | Becket
Boynton John T. | Bedford
Brown Moses F. | "
Lawrence E. H. | Berlin
Baker Ebenezer, | Billerica
Hall & Rankin, | Blackstone
Bradstreet J. E. | Blandford
Cuiver John, | "
Cleveland Wm. P. | Boxford
Andrews J. T. | Boylston
Brigham P. M. | "
Thorndike Wm. | Bradford
French Samuel S. | Braintree
Hollis David N. | "
Hollis & Mann, | "
Sampson Josephus, | "
Baker Francis, | Brewster
Howard Marcellus G. | Bridgewater
Howard O. G. | "
Swift Martin, | "
Wilbar I. S. | "
Boynton P. P. (beef, wholesale), | Brighton
Brooks Timothy, 　 " | "
Dana B. S. 　 " | "
Gungenheizer A. 　 " | "
Jackson N. & S. 　 " | "
Lane J. S W. 　 " | "
Larned Samuel S. 　 " | "
Pierce Brothers, 　 " | "
Saunders & Hartwell, " | "
Zoller Christopher, 　 " | "
Zoller Geo. C. 　 " | "
Zoller Henry, 　 " | "
Zoller John, 　 " | "
Curtis & Boynton, 　(hog, wholesale), | "
Brown Simon (mutton and veal), " | "
Brown & Rogers, 　 " 　 " | "
Dupee John, 　 " 　 " | "
Dyer I. T. 　 " 　 " | "
Dyer & Frost, 　 " 　 " | "
Hollis Bros. 　 " 　 " | "
Hollis T. Quincy, 　 " 　 " | "
Hubbard John, 　 " 　 " | "
Pierce J. M. 　 " 　 " | "
Spaulding Pliny F. | Brimfield
Drake Dexter, | Bucklaud
Squire John P. & Co. (hog, whole-
　sale), 　E. Cambridge, | Cambridge
Mead A. & W., 　N. 　 " | "
Atwood Samuel M. | Chatham
Perham D. C. | Chelmsford
Perham P. P. | "
Upham C. | "
Stevens & Keefe, | Chester
Baker Edward, | Chesterfield
Witherell & Shaw, | "
Bourne Richard, | Cohasset
Bourne & Nickerson, | "
Thayer William F. | "
Johnson George, Shattuckville, | Coleraine
Reynolds & Derby, | Concord
Bigelow Samuel, | Conway
Orcutt E. F. | "
Richards Francis O. | Cummington
Burton John, | Dalton
Blackmer & Doane, | Dana
Trask Alfred, | Danvers
Howes David, | Dennis
Howes Zebina, jr., | "
Jones Nelson, | Douglas
Loring W. H. | "
Smith James, | "
Jones E. & A. F. 　East Douglas, | "
Chase Ira. M. | Dracut
Gage Daniel, | "
Luman Patrick, | "

Plummer John A.	Dracut
Whitney George T.	"
Whitney Rufus B.	"
Bradford George,	Duxbury
Pratt Bryant C.	"
Ward Benjamin,	East Bridgewater
Avery W. H.	East Hampton
Ludden A. S.	"
Ludden E.	"
Goward E. T. North Easton,	Easton
Goward J. F.	"
Norton John W.	Edgartown
Pease George W.	"
Harwood B. F.	Enfield
Randall J. Q.	"
Low William,	"
Story Charles A.	Essex
Story Epes S.	"
Millet Joseph,	Fairhaven
Howard Charles F.	"
Crapo Phineas,	Fall River
Grinnell George,	"
Anthony D. M.	"
Bagshaw Henry,	"
Buffinton E. P.	"
Davis A. J. & Bro.	"
Davis James,	"
Cahoon B. C.	Falmouth
Hatch James H.	"
Clark S.	Florida
Pike James,	"
Darling M. C.	Franklin
Johnson Daniel L.	Freetown
Pickering Paul R.	Georgetown
Poor Prescott A.	"
Miller M. B.	Granville
Day William H. & Co. Great Barrington
Fields Richard,	"
OWEN EUCLID,	Greenfield
Woodward H. G.	"
Tenney John,	Groveland
Dane George E. F.	Hamilton
Dane Lewis,	"
Dane Luther,	"
Porter Charles,	"
Paige John,	Hardwick
Powers Lysander,	"
Wesson E. L. B.	"
Farwell John,	Harvard
Whitney S. F.	"
Holmes & Weeks,	Harwich
Dickinson G. W.	Hatfield
Barnes Harmon,	Hawley
Litchfield & Trowbridge,	Hingham
Marsh Josiah L.	"
Ripley Henry & Son,	"
Cheney James E.	Holden
McFarland C.	Hopkinton
Phipps Waldo (wholesale),	"
Wood Frank, Woodville,	"
Morse Lyman,	Hubbardstown
Gowdy Martin S.	Huntington
Adams George T. & F. C.	Kingston
Canedy William,	Lakeville
Robinson A. J.	"
Rice A. J.	Lancaster
Wood Edgar P.	Lanesborough
Wood Manton A.	"
King A. P. B.	Lawrence
Valpey D. S. A.	"
Bullard J. & Co.	"
Chapman S.	Lee
Greeney R. B.	"
O'Connor John,	"
Wilder & Osborn,	Leominster
Wood Leonard, N. Leominster,	"
Holgman John E.	Lexington
Carpenter Dwight N.	Leyden

Clark Emery,	Littleton
Hager A. P.	"
Green Daniel,	Ludlow
McGregor Nelson,	"
PATCH & BAKER, (beef, wholesale,	
see page 717,) Summer st.	Lynn
Lovell I. & S. C.	Mansfield
Gibbs Charles M.	Mattapoisett
Curtis Bradford,	Medfield
Hevins William P.	"
Cook S. Warren	Mendon
Blood Cyrus,	Methuen
Pierce Darius,	
Skinner George,	Milton
Towns Augustus J.	
Mann & King,	Monson
Newton Edward P.	
Fay B.	Montague
King S. R.	
Hildreth H. T.	Natick
Morse Granville,	
Bacon H. Upper Falls,	Newton
Bowers Henry,	Needham
McIntosh C. & F.	"
Mills John F.	
Wing John A.	
Connell D. & J.	New Bedford
Howard A. N.	
Salisbury ——,	
Boyden A.	New Braintree
Whipple J. C.	
Woods G. D.	Newbury
Adams Brothers,	New Marlboro'
Adams & Waugh, Mill River,	
Bathrick Warren Whitin's,	Northbridge
Gale W.	Northborough
Stockwell M.	"
Winters S.	North Bridgewater
Cuthbertson John,	North Chelsea
Proctor John H.	
Lyman Albert K.	Northfield
Upton Alanson A.	North Reading
Upton Charles,	
Upton John R.	
Lane C. D. & O. H.	Norton
Bullard Sanford,	Oakham
Bacon S. S.	Orange
Carpenter George,	"
Dodge & Co.	"
Phinney Royal,	
Snow Charles H.	Orleans
Gould Franklin, South Orleans,	
Coggshall A. J.	Oxford
Shumway J.	"
Whiting & Campbell,	
Lawrence Wilson,	Palmer
Harrington Silas D.	Paxton
Emerson Robert,	Peabody
Thomas J. B.	
Blood David W.	Pepperell
Hart George A.	
Blodgett L. W.	Petersham
Stowell F. A.	"
Fuller M. D.	Phillipston
Ayers P. J.	Pittsfield
Gleason Monroe,	"
Hadsell J. H. & Co.	"
Read F. F. & Bro.	"
Whiting William C.	Plainfield
Arnold Chas.	Quincy
Baxter D. W.	"
Cook Jonathan,	"
Nightingale T. J.	"
Cain Reuben,	Raynham
Rowley E. S.	Richmond
Wheeler J. F. & H.	"
Earl Nathan H.	Rehoboth

11

Butchers — continued.

Pierce Luther,	Rehoboth
Hicks William A.	Rowe
Titcomb Albert,	Rowley
Titcomb Calvin R.	"
Hobbs John G.	Rutland
Holden Moses G.	"
Morrill Orvill, Montville,	Sandisfield
Tilden John L.	Sandwich
Gibbs Wm. R. West Sandwich,	"
Swift Noble P.	"
Nightingale Isaac,	Scituate
Otis Job P.	"
Boynton W. B.	Shirley
Warren Augustus Q.	Shrewsbury
Warren Henry E.	"
Wellington William,	"
Forbes John H.	Shutesbury
NORTH, MERIAM, & CO. (hogs,	
wholesale, see page 699),	Somerville
Webster Samuel,	Somerset
Marble M. M. & Co.	Southbridge
Chamberlin S. & A. M., Globe Village,	"
Goldthwaite & Spooner, So. Hadley Falls	
Seehanck & Carey,	" " "
Corthell John E.	South Scituate
Corthell Joseph W.	"
Wilder Charles,	"
Legate F. W.	Southwick
Loomis B. B.	"
Phelps William,	"
Newhall Joseph,	Sterling
Sawyer Luke,	"
Smith Benjamin, Assabet,	Stow
Stranger Milo, Fiskdale,	Sturbridge
Cutter & Rogers, S. Sudbury,	Sudbury
Brimblecomb John B.	Swampscott
Woodfin William C.	"
Chace Rufus M.	Swansea
Alger William H.	Taunton
Goward Lewis L.	"
Lincoln Amos N.	"
Lincoln J. W. & B. E.	"
Peck & Horton,	"
Pierce E. B.	"
Pratt E. A.	"
White Wm. L. & Co.	"
Withnarth L. J. & Bro.	"
Butler Chas. B.	Tisbury
Gould Ariel H.	Tolland
Manday William,	"
Paine Daniel,	Truro
Steadman Martin V. B.	Tyringham
Houghton Nathan S.	Upton
Jourdain Benjamin A.	"
Williams C.	Wales
Barnes H.	Wareham
Seagers Joseph C.	Washington
Taylor Justin,	Wellfleet
Witherell Whitfield, S. Wellfleet,	"
Warner Horace,	West Boylston
Cutting John S. Oakdale,	"
	West Bridgewater
Simmons David R. Cochesett,	"
Paige E. D.	West Brookfield
Egleston & Co.	Westfield
Owen & Sackett,	"
Davis A. L.	Westford
Day J. E.	"
Pettis E. E.	West Hampton
White & Carter,	Westminster
Barker Nathan, jr.	Weston
Coburn Edward,	"
Brownell J. B.	Westport
Chace George,	"
Davis Zebedee,	"
Lawlor E. P.	"
Cornell James, Central Village,	"

Colburn John D.	West Roxbury
Mason George B.	
Williams Joseph W.	"
Thomas Benj. P., N. Weymouth, Weymouth	
Thomas E. H.	"
Raymond A., S. Weymouth,	"
Martin Josiah,	"
Doane, Miller, & Co.	Winchendon
Raymond M. D.	"
Graves Rufus,	Whately
Bullan Myron,	Williamsburg
Gleason & Bisbee,	"
Knowlton Phineas,	Wilbraham
Chaffee Reuben, S. Wilbraham,	"
Walker George N.,	"
Jennings ——,	Williamstown
Sanford ——,	"
Buck N. E.	Wilmington
Buck Otis,	"
Buck Silas,	"
Carter Jonathan,	"
Carter J. L.	"
Eames George T.	"
Eames Horatio N.	"
Eames L. C.	"
Eames N. B.	"
Eames Warren,	"
Gowing William E.	"
Mulligan George,	"
Pearson George A.	"
Pearson Porter,	"
Sheldon Henry,	"
Patch Cyrus,	Winchester
Richardson J. W.	"
Michael, Nehemiah,	Windsor
Clark Henry (wholesale),	Worcester
Prentice J. H. (wholesale),	"
Kilbourn Alfred,	Worthington
Fairfield George R.	Wrentham
HOLMES R. E., Yarmouthport,	Yarmouth

Butt and Hinge Manuf.

Arms and Bardwell Manuf. Co.,
  J. C. Arms, agt.   Northampton
Strong A. F. (spring butt),   "

Butter and Cheese Dealers.

CHACE, ALLEN, & SLADE, 16
  and 18 Bedford,   Fall River

Button-Hole Maker.

(*Machine.*)

FOSS FRANKLIN, Munroe st.   Lynn

Button Manufacturers.

Evans D. & Co. (military and fancy
  gilt),   Attleborough
Robinson Willard (pantaloons),   "
Draper W. O. & Co. (ladies' dress),
  North Attleborough,
National Button Co., S. G. Knight,
  agent,   Easthampton
Butler Enoch (pearl),   Haverhill
Gates Davis & Co.   Leominster
Morse G. & Co.   "
Somers Winter D.   "
                           Medway
Blake James P. (steel), Rockville, "
FLORENCE MANUFACTURING
  CO.,   Florence, Northampton
Critchlow Alfred P. (ivory), Leeds, "
Goldthwait M. & Son,   Springfield
Newell Brothers,   "
Rhodes M. M. (tufting),   Taunton
Hill Hiram G.   Williamsburg
Spellman Onslow G.   "
Wade W. W.   Winchester

Cabinet Locks Manuf.

GAYLORD MANUFACTURING
CO. (see page 773),   Chicopee

Cabinet Makers.

(See also Furniture Manufacturers.)

Willey C. B.	Abington
Stetson Sanford,	Adams
Chase David,	Acushnet
Marsh M. M.	Amherst
Young Brothers,	"
Henry Terrence,	Andover
	Ashburnham
Jeffs C. A. & Co. (extension tables),	"
Puffer R. & Co., Ashburnham Depot,	"
Kendall James,	Ashby
Mann Horace, Athol Depot,	Athol
Fisher E. D.	Barnstable
Frost John H.	Hyannis, "
Spooner Timothy H.	Barre
Cole Weeden,	Beverly
Jaquith Andrew,	"
Patten Thomas,	Billerica
Prophett William,	Bridgewater
Parker P.	Brimfield
Koch John,	Brookline
Perry L. M.	"
Thompson J.	"
Robeart John O.	Cambridge
Bicknell Joseph G., Cambridgeport,	"
Collamore T.	" "
Grant & Mann,	" "
Hogan J. J.	" "
Schnabel & Mastling,	" "
Badger & Batchelder, E. Cambridge,	"
Holmes F. M. & Co.	Charlestown
Robinson John P. & Co.	"
Wemyss & Co.	"
Foy William & Son,	Chester
Hosley Dexter P.	Chicopee
Bemis F. E.	Concord
FARRAR WILLARD T.	"
Foote E. C.	Conway
Pew George W.	Danvers
Glover & Jones,	Dorchester
Hatchinson Brothers,	"
Cain M. W.	Milton, "
Clapp John J.	" "
Davenport James,	" "
Hill Oliver & Son,	" "
Martin Thomas (extension tables),	" "
Kenney Zelotes,	" "
Norcross William,	" "
Watson Walter S. (extension tables),	" "
Bowen Joseph,	Douglas
First John, Charles River Village.	Dover
Fent Francis,	Edgartown
Senford Stephen, N. Egremont,	Egremont
Baldwin Irwin D. W., S.	"
Tinkham Samuel,	Enfield
Gifford Jesse,	Fairhaven
Borden, Almy, & Co.	Fall River
Douglas Charles,	"
Westgate, Baldwin, & Co.	"
Westgate J. C.	"
Gifford Henry T.	Falmouth
Page Enoch,	Fitchburg
Child Otis,	Framingham
Kendall John,	"
Every Benjamin,	Gloucester
Langsdorff Frederick,	Great Barrington
Stye & Hood,	"
Jordan John T.	Greenwich
Landon Augustus H.	Hancock
Spooner Harmon C.	Hardwick
Fairbanks Jonathan,	Harvard
Harris William D.	Haverhill
Hobart S. L.	Hingham
Hudson Augustus L.	"
Leavitt A. L.	"
Ripley & Newhall,	"
Pond Nelson,	Holliston
Judd Solomon,	Huntington
Clarke Daniel,	Ipswich
Cushman Edwin,	Kingston
Cook Francis R.	Lawrence
Bassett Joseph,	Lee
GOODRICH R.	"
McDonald Alfred,	South Lee, "
Crosby Ephraim,	Lowell
CROSBY FURNITURE CO., D. S.	
Kimball, treas. Mechanics' Mills,	"
Hill H. E.	"
TROWBRIDGE & KIMBALL, Wamesit Steam Mills (see page 738),	"
Crosman J. H.	Lynn
Parker John H.	"
Taylor William,	Malden
Peabody John C.	Manchester
Wheaton William E.	"
Devereux Ralph,	Marblehead
Kent J. C.	Marion
Nelson Thomas,	Mattapoisett
Welker C.	Medfield
Wood Daniel,	Medway
Fairbanks L.	Milford
Ward Jonas,	Millbury
Glover Oliver, 2d,	Milton
White A. O.	Monson
Dike J. & Sons,	Montague
Richardson George F. & Co.	"
Adams James,	Natick
Dantsizen C.	New Bedford
Knight W. H.	"
Rolfe Eben,	Newburyport
Collins George,	"
Collins William,	"
Burrell Owen,	New Salem
Everett D. W.	Northampton
Calder H. M., Florence,	"
Copeland G. M.	North Bridgewater
Burrill Alfred,	North Brookfield
Whittredge William A.	North Reading
Carlton C. R.	Oxford
RAYMOND CHARLES, 35 Middle, (see page 766),	Plymouth
Wilson John B.	"
Dyer Charles P.	Provincetown
Kimball Charles H.	Quincy
Houghton Ralph,	Randolph
Bancroft Wendall,	Reading
Batchelder Alden,	"
Beard Henry,	"
Creesy Daniel,	"
Dinsmore & Gronard,	"
Harnden Sylvester & Son,	"
Kingman Francis,	"
Manning Charles,	"
Miller Frederic,	"
Phillips William M.	"
Richardson David G.	"
Temple & Bancroft,	"
Gouldrich George,	Richmond
Keith A. & E.	Rowe
Estabrook John,	Rutland
Wells John B.	"
Brown B.	Salem
Anderson L. J.	"
Fellows Israel,	"
Haskell, Lougee, & Co.	"
Locke N. C.	"
Raymond, Low, & Co.	"
Taft Russell H.	"

Cabinet Makers — continued.
Very Nathaniel, jr. Salem
Wallis Joseph, "
Crane Wm. F., Montville, Sandisfield
Allyne Samuel H. Sandwich
Pope John W. "
Campbell Wm. Somerville
Crooker Henry N. Shrewsbury
Dyer Samuel, "
Williams Samuel, Southbridge
Lyndes H. A. & J. M. Spencer
Belcher Daniel E. Springfield
Ellis Amos, "
Fisher, Buckhaus, & Knappe, "
Russell J. M. "
Brinton Edward C. Stockbridge
Withington P. M. Stoughton
Taylor Sewall B. Sudbury
Bourne & Brooks, Templeton
Greenwood Thomas T. "
Jones J. A. "
Fosters & Cole, . Tewksbury
Carpenter Edwin, Uxbridge
Bellis Matthew H. Waltham
Eldridge William E. Watertown
Spalding & Eddy, Webster
Tomblin John L. West Brookfield
Reese M. West Stockbridge
Norton J. D. & Son, West Hampton
Weymouth
Graves Samuel, No. Weymouth, "
Smith Sumner, Whately
Ingraham H. H.. Williamstown
Blos Wm. C. Worcester
CHOLLAR JOHN D, 198 Main,
(see page 783), "
Goodell J. M. "
Reeby R. M. "
Fuller George, Wrentham

Cabinet Organs.
Newburyport
CHENEY JAMES W., 14 State, "

Calcined and Farmers' Plaster.
BARNES E. & J. C., Water street
(see page 717), Plymouth

Calendering & Singeing Cocks.
JONES WILLIAM, 56 Park
(see page 794), Chelsea

Calenders & Mangles Manufs.
KILBURN, LINCOLN, & CO.
(see page 756), Fall River

Calico Printers' Rollers.
NEW BEDFORD COPPER CO. (see
page 757), New Bedford
CROCKER BROTHERS & CO. (see
page 756), Taunton

Calico Printing Machinery.
RICE, BARTON, & FALES MANU-
FACTURING CO. Worcester

Caliper and Divider Manufac-
turers.
SOUTHWICK & HASTINGS, .
7 Cypress, Worcester

Calkers and Gravers.
(*See also Shipwrights and Calkers.*)
TERRY J. C., Rodman's wharf, Fall River
Davis William, Fairhaven
Davis William H. "
Caswell Geo. & Co. Gloucester

Glass Frank, Kingston
Sampson Constant, "
Sampson Hiram, "
Cannon George, New Bedford
Drew James, "
Gage Benjamin, "
Randall David E. .
Stowell Daniel, "
Stowell F. S. "
Delano Otis, Newburyport
Flanders Enoch, "
Nason D. "
Beatly John W. Provincetown
Mott S. & J. & Co. "
Mott James M. Wellfleet
Cook E. P. "

Candle Mould Manufacturer.
Ditson Samuel J. Charlestown

Capstans, Windlasses, &c.
(*See Ships Wheels, &c.*)

Car Head Lining Manuf.
Husband Chas. & Co. Taunton
Holt George, Worcester

Car Manufacturers.
KEITH ISAAC & SONS, W. Sand-
wich, Sandwich
WASON MANUF. CO. Springfield
Bradley Osgood, Worcester

Car Wheel Manufacturers.
WASON MANUF. CO. Springfield
WASHBURN IRON CO. Edward
L. Davis treas., (see p. 784), Worcester

Card & Card Clothing Manufs.
ASHWORTH ROBERT (see page
721), Davol, Fall River
FALL RIVER CARD CLOTHING
MANUF., Jas. Newton, (see
page 722), "
Fitchburg Card Co. (card clothing), Fitchburg
Fuller Geo. A. (machine), Lawrence
WARREN & ROBINSON, Broad-
way, cor. Methuen, "
Leicester
BISCO & DENNY (machine card), "
HOLMAN WM. F. (hand card), "
MURDOCK J. & J. (machine card), "
SARGENT & BRO. (hand card), "
Sprague & Eddy (hand card), "
UPHAM GEORGE (hand card), "
Waite E. C. & L. M. & Co. (machine
card), "
Watson L. S. & Co. (hand card), "
WHITE A. & SON (machine card), "
WHITTEMORE W. & J. (machine
card), "
WOODCOCK J. & L. & CO. (ma-
chine card), "
Woodcock, Knight, & Co. "
HOWE & GOODHUE (cards for flax,
hemp, manilla, cotton, &c., see
page 740), 92 Market, Lowell
KITSON RICHARD, Worthen, cor.
Dutton (see page 737), "
LOWELL CARD Co. Jeremiah Clark,
agent, (see page 742), 96 Middle, "
Hampden Card Co. Springfield
Stetson Everett P. (machine card), Walpole
Uxbridge Card Co. Uxbridge
Worcester
EARLE T. K. & Co. (see page 788),
Grafton st. "

Howard Brothers, Worcester
SARGENT CARD CLOTHING CO.
(machine cards, see last white
page), Southbridge st. "

Carding Mills.

(*See Wool Carders; also Cloth Dressing.*)

Cards.

(*Enamelled Paper.*)

Tapley Geo. W. (manuf.), Springfield

Card Screen Manufacturers.

TROWBRIDGE & KIMBALL,
Wamesit Steam Mills, (see page
738), Lowell

Card-Setting Machine Manuf.

Kent Samuel W. Worcester
Prouty A. B. "

Carpenters and Builders.

Cobb John F. Abington
Faunce Elijah, "
Lyon John P. "
Nash William, "
Wade Henry, East Abington, "
Singleton Richard, North Abington, "
Smith Joseph, 2d " "
Bonney Charles, South Abington, "
Bonney Gladden, " "
Healy Oliver G. " "
Fletcher Cyrus, South Acton, Acton
Stevens Levi W., West Acton, "
Burton J. A. Adams
Crandall Hiram T. "
Marsh Charles, "
Simmons Philo, "
Baldwin Hiram, North Adams, "
Brown William N. " "
Jaquith Leonard, " "
Judd Albert R. " "
Judd Rusell B. " "
Morton Ranson, " "
PEIRCE HENRY, " "
Walker Alfred, " "
Bailey John W. Amesbury
Bartlett Joseph, "
Blaisdell Joseph, "
Foot Hiram, "
Wiggin James E. "
Haskins Henry E. Amherst
Haskins John H. "
Howland W. S. "
Lesley C. W. "
McCloud M. L. "
White & Church, "
Haskins James E., North Amherst, "
Smith Elisha S. " "
Abbott George L. Andover
Chickering William, "
Jenkins William S. "
Wilson Horace, "
Barton Jarves, Arlington
Chase James M. "
Storer Edward, "
Bennett Abram, Ashburnham
Fairbanks E. H. "
Sabin Lucius, "
Wellington Augustus, "
Wellington Luke, Ashby
Adams George H. "
Brewster Richard R. Ashland
Winchester R. H. "
Davenport J. A. "
Doane F. C. Athol
Oliver J. "

Dexter Joseph L. Athol Depot, Athol "
Haskins Henry, " "
Parminter H. " "
Whitney Gilbert H. " "
Woodward Charles, " "
Bates Jesse B. Attleborough
Pierce Alfred, "
Pierce Jonathan, "
Crocker Daniel, Barnstable
Crocker Samuel S. "
Hinckley John, "
Hinckley Lothrop, "
Lewis Charles, "
Lothrop Ansel D. "
Marston Warren, "
Matthews Russell, "
Nye James M. "
Crosley James, Centreville, "
Bearce C. C. Cotuit, "
Crocker John C. Hyannis, "
Linnell Uriah G. " "
Hinckley Gustavus, " "
Burgess Moses, West Barnstable, "
Bassett Henry, Barre
Carruth Arza, "
Giffin L. "
Hawes Daniel, "
Holland Merrill, "
Osgood Charles, "
Osgood Joseph, "
Spooner Timothy J. "
Jennings Wm. Austin, Becket
Cutler Amos B. Bedford
Lane Oliver J. "
Jackson Edwin M. Belchertown
Hatch Lemuel, Belmont
Hatch Simon D. "
Higgins Albert, "
Hastings S. H. Berlin
Sawyer J. E. "
Gaines Benjamin, Bernardston
Hale J. V. "
Hills S. Russell, "
Smith Horace, "
Tyler George W. "
Brewer Jacob, Beverly
Butman George, "
Gallup Augustus, "
Goodhue Adoniram, "
Hale Henry, "
Larcom Benjamin "
Meacom John, "
Morgan John E. "
Ober John, "
Ober Joseph E. "
Prince Warren, "
Remmonds Robert, "
Wallace Daniel, "
Webber William, "
Woodbury Augustus, "
Woodbury T. "
Floyd Daniel, Billerica
Shed T. R. "
Stone Jones, "
Salter J. J. North Billerica, "
Reed & Bachelor, Millville, Blackstone
Shepard E. W. Blandford
Burnham Reuben, Bolton
Hurlbart James D. "
Pollard Otis, "
Pollard Stephen C. "
Read J. Everett, Boxborough
Veazie D. T. "
Ayers Samuel N. Boxford
Carlton James, "
Shaw Elmer, Boylston Centre, Boylston
Carleton George, Bradford

Carpenters and Builders — continued.

Carleton J. P.	
Gage Waren,	Bradford
Longfellow Nathan,	"
Berry Horatio A.	"
Hobart Charles W.	Braintree
Rogers Zenas,	"
Hayward John, S. Braintree,	"
Penniman William R. "	"
GARDNER HENRY, P. O. address	
Weymouth, (see page 768)	"
Crocker Thomas,	Brewster
Crocker Watson,	
Foster Benjamin,	"
Freeman William,	"
Hopkins George C.	"
Hopkins Moses,	"
Jenkins A.	"
Seabury David,	"
Small Cornelius,	"
Small Joshua G.	"
Cutter William,	Bridgewater
Keith Ambrose,	"
Keith Solomon,	"
Campbell John,	Brighton
McCausland John,	"
Needham Alfred,	"
Wadleigh J. C.	"
Harvey James, jr.	Brimfield
Bowen William,	Brookfield
Cheney J. P.	"
Clapp C. C.	"
Ward A.	"
Putney R. O. East Brookfield,	
Beals Samuel,	Brookline
Delano Oliver B.	"
Davis William,	"
Haines C. L.	"
Jones C. W.	"
Long J. D.	"
Lyford Nathaniel,	"
Melcher W. K.	"
	Buckland
Frost J. B. & Co. Shelburne Falls,	"
Anderson J.	Cambridge
Black & French,	"
Danforth C.	"
Hall & Frazier,	"
Hatfield S.	"
Hayes L. S.	"
Huckins Thomas S.	"
Norris & Richardson,	"
Parsons A. B.	"
Perkins Levi,	"
Saunders Samuel,	"
Stevens Abel, jr.	"
Trow F. R.	"
Trow M. F.	"
Wilson John,	"
Withey Simon B.	"
Bailey Isaac W., Cambridgeport,	"
Blodgett & Rhodes, "	"
Crawford A. "	"
Clark Simon P. "	"
Harlow Thos. E. "	"
Hancock & Greely, "	"
Keenan J. H. "	"
Kelley J. & J. "	"
NORRIS & RICHARDSON, "	
Luke William H. "	"
Rivers Isaac H. "	"
Sparrow James H. "	"
Stevens Albert, "	"
Waddell J. "	"
LORING & SEELYE, East Cambridge	"
McCLOSKEY HUGH, "	
Curtis Charles, North Cambridge,	"
Webster T. B. " "	"

	Cambridge
Stiles Stephen, North Cambridge,	"
Blackman William,	Canton
Bright Samuel,	"
Fuller James W.	"
Sevcuy J. E.	"
Meserve Samuel W.	"
Duren Isaac F.	Carlisle
Green Thomas J.	"
Southworth Thomas,	Carver
Parsons C. D. North Carver,	"
Harlow Benjamin, South "	"
Williams John T.	Charlemont
Brown Amos,	Charlestown
Cass John,	"
Currier & Hatch,	"
Flanagan Samuel,	"
Hall William E.	"
Harmon Benjamin,	"
Hutchings Sincere,	"
Jones Jesse U.	"
Kelso J. G.	"
Laighton Mark,	"
Maynard James B.	"
Meserve John B.	"
Norris E. J.	"
Patterson William,	"
Perkins J. L.	"
Prescott S. T.	"
Savage W. F.	"
Shattuck N.	"
Simonds & Lord,	"
Snow J.	"
Starbird George M.	"
Tucker D. S.	"
Wellington C. W.	"
Wilson Jeremy,	"
Wilson J. B.	"
Wyman Earle,	"
Edwards David W.	Chatham
Young Prince, West Chatham,	"
Green Alonzo G.	Chelmsford
Larcom Jonathan,	"
Swett Edmund, Middlesex Village,	"
Davis A. A. North Chelmsford,	"
Howard Calvin, " "	"
Batchelder J. S.	Chelsea
Batchelder & Meserve,	"
Burnham & Lord,	"
Buzzell Joshua,	"
Cheever William,	"
Clark George W.	"
Corey T. S.	"
Curry Ephraim H.	"
Downs Samuel W.	"
Grant Washington,	"
Lawrence Parker,	"
Lawrence Prescott,	"
Pratt William,	"
Robbins & Hartford,	"
Rogers Andrew,	"
Soule James M.	"
Stone Benjamin F.	"
Storer C. F. & Co.	"
Severance Charles,	"
Tarr Benj. F.	"
Tenney & Wilkinson,	"
Wells Ivory,	"
White William H.	"
Wilkinson John H.	"
Brown Henry J.	Chesterfield
Brown Werden R.	Cheshire
Foster Daniel B.	"
Merry Charles W.	"
Bingham Horace,	Chicopee
Danks Lyman,	"
Porter Abram,	"
White Alfred,	"

Chicopee
Oaks James,	Chicopee Falls,	"
Sherman Nathaniel,	"	"	"
Warner N. P.	"	"	"
Vincent Moses C.	Chilmark
Worthy Henry, North Adams, Clarksburg
Belyea Samuel,	Clinton
Sawyer Peter,	"
Sawyer Wm.	"
Stone O.	"
Welch O. H.	"
Fox Philip,	Cohasset
Rich Zaccheus,	"
Tiden W. A. W.	"
Miller T.	Coleraine
Buttrick Frank,	Concord
George Joseph P.	"
Hobson Moses,	"
Hosmer N. S.	"
Wetherbee E. Cummings,	"
Hitchcock O. C.	Conway
Peabody George O.	"
Sherwin Thomas S.	"
Tillson Edmund W.	Cummington
Aldrich A. D.	Dalton
Phelps E. N.	"
Thompson Thomas D.	"
Wilner Thomas S.	"
Oakes Samuel L.	Dana
Couch Francis A.	Danvers
Berry Allen,	"
Cressey Enoch T.	"
Patterson James,	"
Eveleth Aaron,	Danvers Port,	"
Eveleth Francis,	"	"
Kelly James,	"	"
Whittier George,	"	"
Sisson Christopher G.	Dartmouth
Sisson Isaac,	"
Wood Humphrey,	"
Snell Thomas, North Dartmouth,	"
Tripp Benjamin T.	"	"
Crapo Isaac,	South Dartmouth,	"
Davis Samuel M.	"	"
Marden Charles,	Dedham
Waters Joseph,	"
Wilson Sumner	"
Gaffrey Peter,	East Dedham,	"
Withington W.	"	"
Thayer Tyler,	South Dedham,	"
Cooley Lewis A., South Deerfield, Deerfield
Hubbard Frederick,	"	"
Stewart James L.	"	"
Hall Isaiah D.	Dennis
Matthews Edmund,	"
Downs Barnabas S.	East Dennis,	"
Alexander H. G.	South	"	"
Hinckley Almon G.	West	"	"
Matthews Wm. G.	"	"	"
Sturgess Benjamin C.	"	"	"
Phillips David,	Dighton
Pierce Isaac,	"
Gay E. R.	North Dighton	"
Waldron Edward,	"	"
Waldron Henry,	"	"
Davenport Hartford,	Dorchester
Lapham Robert M.	"
McKechnie Edward,	"
Willcut & Grant,	"
Ballard & Ewell,	Harrison Square,	"
Crosby & Walker,	"	"
Glover A. H.	"	"
Merrill Edward, Jr.	"	"
Studley & Nichols,	"	"
Williams J. M. & J. D.	"	"
Burt J. H. & Co.	Mattapan,	"
Pope James, Jr.	Milton,	"
Blanchard Hiram,	Neponset,	"
Bowker Benj. C.,	Neponset,	Dorchester
Howe Albion K.	Dover
Paine Barnabas,	"
Durkey Erastus,	Dudley
Weston James M.	Duxbury
Bonney Charles H.	East Bridgewater
Fuller Ezra T.	"
Lasell Caleb,	"
Smith Sylvanus,	Orleans,	Eastham
Bosworth E. R.	East Hampton
Pomeroy F. H.	"
Pomeroy J. Thomas & Son,	"
Spear D. C.	"
Keith F. G.	North Easton,	Easton
Randall S. A.	"	"
Smith Lorenzo,	"	"
Donaldson Joseph,	Edgartown
Dunham Edward R.	"
Hobart Caleb,	"
Lewis Ellis,	"
Pease Freeman,	"
Pent William,	"
Ripley C.	"
Worth Charles,	"
Brown Ransom, North Egremont, Egremont
Doty Sanford,	"	"
Doty Seeley,	"	"
Dunn Henry,	"	"
Potter Charles,	"	"
Reasoner James,	"	"
Stillman Frederick,	"	"
Hull Abel,	South Egremont,	"
Patterson Luther H.	"	"
Schutt Charles, Jr.	"	"
Schutt Ira,	"	"
Butler E. E.	Enfield
Jones Ira,	"
Latham Joseph,	"
Choate Francis,	Essex
Cogswell Henry C.	"
Perkins P. P.	"
Proctor Joseph, Jr.	"
Story George M.	"
Alden John,	Fairhaven
Alden John F.	"
Pierce Frederick,	"
Savory Aaron,	"
Stetson Henry,	"
Tripp & Bourne,	"
Borden Melvin,	Fall River
Brownell W. W.	"
Covel Benjamin,	"
Coyle John,	"
Douglas Charles,	"
Earle J. M. & T. B.	"
Freeborn T. D.	"
Grinnell David,	"
Grinnell James,	"
MARBLE CHARLES C.	3 Winter,	"
Marble & Darling,	"
Millard & Porter,	"
Miller Lorenzo T.	"
Miller Southard H.	"
Pierce Edward M.	"
PIERCE JAMES F.	West Bank,	"
Shay Daniel,	"
Simmons Aaron,	"
Snow James,	"
Southworth Spaulding,	"
Vickery & Francis,	"
Robinson Henry,	Falmouth
Jenkins Henry W., East Falmouth,	"
Barker Lorenzo,	Fitchburg
Carter & McFarland,	"
Davis John E.	"
Fuller Benjamin F.	"
Goodwin William,	"
Kinsman George H.	"

Carpenters and Builders — continued.

Marshall Benjamin F.	Fitchburg
Morse & Hudson,	"
Parkhurst & Aldrich,	"
Starkey Calvin,	"
Wilson Arnold,	"
Angell W. W.	Foxborough
Carpenter Jos. W.	"
Drake Asa,	"
Fales Abner,	"
Jones E. F.	"
Lane Warren,	"
Leonard Edward,	"
Leonard William,	"
Lindley William,	"
Hemenway Adam,	Framingham
Hemenway Dexter,	"
Hemenway Elbra,	"
Rice Phineas G.	"
Haynes Nathan,	Saxonville, "
Moulton Charles,	"
Hemenway Josiah, South Framingham,	"
Pratt Metcalf, " " "	
Rice E. E. " " "	
Ballou B.	Franklin
CORSON H. W. (see page 753),	"
Hubbard Sabin,	"
Metcalf E. L. & O. F.	"
Marble John W.	Freetown
Pierce Allen,	"
Hodgman L.	Gardner
Mason B. S.	"
Holt Silas, South Gardner,	"
Clark Samuel F.	Georgetown
Plumer J. T.	"
Phillips Simon C.	Gill
Clough Moses H.	Gloucester
Dennis & Griffin,	"
Garland Orlando,	"
Griffin Bennett,	"
Hodgkins William,	"
Honors Brothers,	"
Hoyt E. C.	"
WATSON D. S.	"
Whidden John H.	"
Winchester Wm. M.	"
Blake John M. East Gloucester,	"
Packard Freeborn W.	Goshen
Clisbie Calvin	Grafton
Fletcher Noah,	"
Cusick Thomas,	"
Taft Reuben,	"
Fuller George, N. E. Village,	"
Harrington W. " "	"
Dickinson Calvin, jr.	Granby
Preston Dexter,	"
Preston J. L.	"
Warren Eli,	"
Gorham & Hayes,	Great Barrington
Luddington Edward,	"
Nettleton Lucius,	"
Patterson J.	"
Bryant Wm. Housatonic,	"
Van Alstyne Wm. "	"
CARL J. L.	Greenfield
Embury Henry C.	"
Hawkes Frederick,	"
Newton James & Sons,	"
Stratton ——,	"
Thorn Joseph,	"
Traver Philip,	"
Blood Luther,	Groton
Lewis George W.	"
Whiting & Son,	"
Childs D. Groton Junction	"
Fletcher Joel E. "	"
Lapham Morey, "	"
Spaulding Benjamin M. "	"

Hardy Abner,	Groveland
Hardy Charles,	"
Hardy Charles N.	"
Henry William H.	"
Knox Eli,	"
Knox Hiram,	"
Merrill Burton E.	"
Shaw Charles A.   South Groveland,   "
Marsh J. D.	Hadley
Marsh J. W.	"
Nash Lucius,	"
Ware Lauriston,	"
Porter Benjamin,	Hamilton
De Lano Jay G.	Hancock
Studley George,	Hanover
Turner Samuel N.	"
Loring Joseph S.	Hanson
Josselyn Benj. W.   S. Hanson,   "
Ramsdell Samuel D.   "   "
Earle Apollos	Hardwick
Newland Franklin,	"
Richardson Henry H.	"
Hosmer Samuel,	Harvard
Sawyer Jabez,	"
Baker Austin,	Harwich
Baker Cyrus,	"
Haymer John,	"
Moody James,	"
Paine L. H.	"
Smith Freeman,	"
Freeman Sanford, Harwich Port,	"
Hopkins E.   "   "   "
Tripp R. Gideon, South Harwich,	"
Batchellor & Dinsmore,	Hatfield
Richmond A. M.	"
Bishop E. P.	Haverhill
Chesley A. L.	"
Cane F. C.	"
Felch D. M.	"
French M. E.	"
Gage Alfred,	"
Hall & Wason,	"
Heath William D.	"
Hurd Orrin,	"
Littlefield J. M.	"
Longfellow Nathan,	"
Merrill J. M.	"
Mills Benj. Ayer's Village,	"
Nesmith James M.	"
Osgood Jacob,	"
Roberts Stephen,	"
Shapleigh Charles,	"
Hannum George A.	Heath
McGee H.	"
Sprague Joseph G.	Hingham
Bailey S. G. & Son,	"
Cushing Allyne,	"
Foster William,	"
Nelson William J.	"
Pearce John W.	"
Ripley Justin, jr.	"
Sprague Timothy,	"
Beals James S. So. Hingham,	"
Cushing Alonzo,	"
Cushing Isaac H. "	"
Ewell Walter,	"
Bragne Lewis P.	Hinsdale
Contruy Joseph,	"
Day Alvin,	"
Hamblen David,	"
Gleason W. L.	Holden
Hubbard Samuel D.	"
Hubbard Simon,	"
Knowlton Daniel,	"
Parmenter Elijah,	"
Butterworth T. D.	Holland
Robbins Wm. A.	"
Sanger Samuel A.	Holliston

Crowley Thomas, Holyoke
Donahue Jerry, "
Hand M. T. "
Joslyn H. C. "
Taft & Moody, "
Thorpe C. L. "
Wiggins & Flagg, "
Willard Asa, "
Archibald Charles, "
Blake Richard, "
Pond Caleb, "
Rollins E. N. Woodville, Hopkinton
Austin Charles, Hubbardston
Falis Joseph S. "
Fletcher Georrge W. Hudson
Hurlbut John, "
Russell Nathan, "
Strong Joseph, "
Tower Henry, "
Witt George D. "
Knight Edward G. Hull
Tower John W. "
Rust George B. Huntington
Sheldon Wellington, "
Angell David, Hyde Park
Blazo W. A. "
Chadbourn J. Perry, "
Fogg L. S. "
Haskell Besturo B. "
Higgins David, "
Hinckley I. Young, "
NEAL A. B. & CO. (see page 765), "
Pierce George, "
Russell L. H. "
Swift T. P. "
THOMPSON & RUSSELL, "
Willard & Hilton, "
Williams R. "
Williams J. M. & J. D. "
Canney S. A. Ipswich
Hodgkins D. A. "
Nourse Daniel P. "
Russell & Archer, "
Russell Foster, "
Smith W. H. "
Bartlett Cornelius A. Kingston
Bartlett Walter S. "
Delano David, "
Faunce Albert, "
Faunce George, "
Hammond Asa, "
Holmes Joseph, "
Holmes Stephen, "
Ripley Lewis, "
Ripley Samuel E. "
Simmons Henry, "
Waterman E. E. "
Briggs Joseph H. Lakeville
Nye Loren, "
Sampson Sylvanus W. "
Shaw Jairus H. "
Southworth Warren H. "
Estey Arba, Lancaster
Gardener Powell P. "
Somers Augustus B. Lanesborough
Beal Geo. P. "
Clement & Creesy, Lawrence
Couch Henry J. "
Currier A. A. "
Eaton J. W. "
Emerson C. T. "
Flanders F. & B. K. "
Floyd Thos. W. "
Flanders & Severance, "
Joplin A. L. "
Knowles & Noyes, "
Lord S. S. "
Merriam J. Frank, "

Perkins Moses, Lawrence
Reed W. B. & Co. "
Sanborn Lyman J. "
Sanborn George, "
Trueworthy C. H. & A. J. "
Winkley A. "
Withington Henry, "
Woodbury Lorenzo, "
Broderick James, Lee
Gibbons Geo. "
Millard Spencer, "
Stone William A. "
Bowen James, South Lee, "
Baker Leonard, Leicester
Earle Ira, "
Knowles Edward, "
Norcross Brothers, "
Loomis Ensign, Lenox
Loomis George, "
Smith Wm. S. "
Washburn Wm. I. "
Carpenter Franklin, Lenox Furnace, "
Capell Custis, Lexington
Locke William, "
Tuttle David A. "
Stetson G. W. Leyden
Fletcher J. W. Littleton
Law Cyrus, "
Robbins N. B. "
Tuttle N. E. "
Waters John S. Longmeadow
Corning B. F. E. Longmeadow, "
Barclay Cyrus P. Lowell
Bennett James W. "
Bennett John C. "
Berry T. D. "
Brown M. C. "
Chamberlin Joseph, "
Davis Bartlett, "
Dow John D. "
Emery A. H. "
Farnham G. B. "
Foster Jesse, "
Fowler George L. "
Furnald N. G. "
Gardner A. B. "
Grant Hugh G. "
Haseltine Geo. W. "
Harmon M. "
Holt Daniel, "
Hood A. K. "
Horton John F. "
Howe H. C. & J. F. "
Howe H. F. "
Howe James M. "
Howe Lorenzo G. "
Leonard George, "
Libby I. H. "
Mardin Joseph, "
Merrill & Calef, "
Page G. W. "
Peabody John T. "
PETTINGILL JOHN, "
Pitt John, "
Proctor S. N. "
Richards Luther, "
Sawtell Josiah A. "
Shedd Geo. W. "
Shaw J. M. "
Snell Orlando, "
Stearns E. "
Sylvester G. B. "
Wiley S. F. "
Wiggin William H. "
Wilson F. S. & F. T. "
Hyatt George W. Lunenburg
Jewett George A. "
Marshall Silas, "

Carpenters and Builders — continued.

Allen Walter B.	Lynn
Andrews Samuel H.	"
Boynton Benj. S.	"
Brierly Joseph,	"
Brown Ira P.	"
Campbell & Simpson,	"
Hall J. H.	"
Huntington C. H. N.	"
Hussey S. B.	"
Hyde Daniel,	"
Jewett Charles W.	"
Jones J.	"
Kelly Frank G.	"
Lee Nehemiah,	"
Mace & Swain,	"
McAllister Benj. R.	"
Merrill Samuel B.	"
Pease Edward,	"
Searles W. H.	"
Snow & Chapman,	"
Southworth James N.	"
Tewksbury James W.	"
Todd Nelson,	"
Trefethen B. B.	"
Weeks R. L,	"
Worthen C. H.	"
Badger Geo. W.	Malden
Clark Jonathan,	"
Eames John N.	"
Hunnewell N. M.	"
Morcombe Fred T.	"
McAllister George H.	"
Newhall Nathan,	"
Fuller & Hemmenway,	Maplewood, "
Kimball Lafayette,	"
Friend Daniel W.	Manchester
Goldsmith Abram,	"
Phillips & Kelham,	"
Cobb S. C.	Mansfield
Cobb Willard,	"
Harding A. C.	"
Penney Alvin,	"
Codding S. C.	"
Bowden Thomas & Son,	Marblehead
Goodwin H. R.	"
Hathaway Bedjamin G.	"
Martin Samuel,	"
Martin John S.	"
Sanborn N. B.	"
Traill Benj. G.	"
Allen Silas B.	Marion
Blankinship Warren,	"
Briggs William,	"
Braley Elijah,	"
Handy Augustus,	"
Berry Robert,	Marlborough
Black & French,	"
Brown & Rogers,	"
Holyoke Edward,	"
How Elbridge,	"
Kirby Philip,	"
Maynard L. G.	"
Kent Warren,	Marshfield
Sprague Edward,	"
Oakman Israel,	W. Marshfield, "
Boodry Dennis S.	Mattapoisett
Eaton S. K.	"
Hiller Jonathan,	"
Hiller Prince,	"
Purrington George,	"
Bullard Hinsdale F.	Medfield
Jacobs Charles S.	Medford
JOHNSON BROTHERS (see page 718)	"
Pierce James,	"
PINKHAM RICHARD G.	"
Thomas Wm. B.	"

Daniels T. M.	E. Medway, Medway
Force Samuel,	" "
Brooks J. W.	W. Medway, "
Davis & Ross,	" "
Partridge Sewall,	" "
Ross R. P.	" "
Atwood & Stantial,	Melrose
Whowell John & Co.	"
WOODWARD DAVID R.	"
Davenport J. L.	Mendon
Metcalf William T.	"
Taft S. C.	"
Taylor William,	Methuen
Towne Jesse A.	"
Haskins Franklin,	Middleborough
Reed Sylvanus W.	"
Sears Ivory H.	"
Sherman Joshua,	"
Sparrow James P.	"
Tinkham Lorenzo,	"
White Wm. B.	N. Middleborough, "
Eaton Lewis,	" "
Eaton Oliver,	" "
Eaton William,	" "
Phelps W. A. & H. D.	Middleton
Albee E. A.	Milford
Bergin James,	"
EDDY & BRITTON,	"
Fisher M.	"
Taft Amos,	"
Whitney Otis,	"
Lapham Charles,	Millbury
Sherman Daniel A.	"
Tucker John A.	Milton
Burt John H. & Co.	Mattapan, "
Higgins David,	Fairmount, "
Hitchcock John,	Monson
Newell Austin,	"
Orcutt John,	"
Warriner Ethan,	"
Gilbert George,	Montague
Moore Alpheus,	"
Pratt R. D.	"
Babbit N. T.	Montague City, "
Gifford Charles,	Monterey
Kinne James,	"
Thompson Sardis,	"
Woodin Frank,	"
Patterson Luther H.	Mount Washington
Perkins Geo. U.	Nahant
Wilson George W.	"
Easton Edward F.	Nantucket
Fisher & Bodfish,	"
Folger Eben R.	"
Gibbs James H.	"
Hallett Isaac,	"
Hallett Wm. M.	"
Hussey Andrew,	"
Robinson Charles H.	"
Toby Albert,	"
Woodward Samuel,	"
Cook Moses,	Natick
Bates J. jr.	"
Johnson G. W.	"
Morse Willard,	"
Mosman Judson,	"
Smith Nathaniel,	"
Caswell Asa,	South Natick, "
Phillips Thomas,	" "
Pray Henry,	" "
Coulter John S. jr.	Needham
Kingsbury George O.	"
Morton & Locke,	"
Pickering Oliver,	"
Fuller Hezekiah,	Grantville, "
Phillips Freeman,	" "
Clarke William L.	Wellesley, "
Winsor Whitman S.	" "

Carpenter Erastus C. New Ashford
Baker Lorenzo, New Bedford
Baker & Bosworth, "
Bates William, 2d, "
Bliss Moses H. "
Bosworth William, "
Brown Benj. C. "
Brownell C. H. "
Chadwick, Allen, & Co. "
Chase Joseph, "
Clark Ezra, "
Clarke E. P. "
Cushing John K. "
Davis Joseph (sailors' chests), "
DOULL JAMES, Front, cor. School, "
De Wolfe Charles, "
Enos M. (sailors' chests), "
Flynn & Bowen, "
Foster J. M. "
Foster E. L. "
Gifford William, "
Green Alfred, "
Hammond Caleb, "
Hammond & Weaver, "
Haskins O. & J. C. "
Hathaway Lewis, "
Kirby William A. "
Leach Chas. H. "
Look John W. "
Perry George W. "
Sears H. G. O. "
Sears Marshall G. "
Silver Manuel E. (sailors' chests), "
Sturtevant & Sherman, "
Tripp Washington, "
Tripp & Maxfield, "
Walker Henry, "
Walker William, "
Williams John (sailors' chests) "
Williston Alanson, "
Cooley G. New Braintree
Green Schuyler, "
Lincoln J. N. "
Knapp Anthony, Newbury
Adams & Noyes, Newburyport
Allen Jeremiah, "
Bailey John & Son, "
Batchelder Thomas L. "
Batchelder William, "
Brown Charles S. "
Cooper James M. "
Currier & Thurlow, "
Dockham Joseph H. "
Dodge Greenleaf, "
Dodge William S. "
Evans J. W. "
Gerrish, Lamprey, & Evans, "
Green George L. "
Hale Charles H. "
Haskell George W. "
Morrill & Morse, "
Page John H. "
Plummer Wm. H. P. "
Wheeler George, New Marlborough
Cook James, Southfield, "
Coolidge N. B. New Salem
Eaton Porter J. "
King Emery S. N. Prescott, "
Heustis Benj. Auburndale, Newton
Wight James H. " "
Jordan Allen, Lower Falls, "
Spring George, " "
Ellis Stephen, Newton Centre, "
Garey O. C. " "
Walker Timothy, " "
Holmes Stephen, Newton Corner, "
Leavitt W. P. " "
Pingree Brothers, " "

Whipple Orrin, Newton Corner, Newton
Hurd & Wilson, Newtonville, "
Flint S. " "
Waterman M. T. " "
Keyes G. W. Upper Falls, "
Bailey Luther, West Newton, "
Lucas M. & O. F. " "
Lucas R. M. " "
Abell Asahel, Northampton
Bosworth G. S. & Co. "
Breck Moses, "
Crosier & Harlow, "
Crouch Charles S. "
Currier Bros. & Smith, "
Jewett Joseph, "
Jewett & Everett, "
Stetson C. J. "
Strong E. W. "
Elbridge Amos, Florence, "
Squires Asa, " "
Hodgson H. M. North Andover
Holt Peter, "
Holt Samuel F. "
Rea Aaron G. jr. "
Summers Abram jr. "
Newton R. W. Northborough
Randlett Nathaniel, "
Ware William, "
Hagar S. D. Northbridge
Beal John F. North Bridgewater
Foye & Holmes, "
Snow Barnabas, "
Thayer Jarvis, Campello, "
Fullam William, North Brookfield
Hebard J. F. "
Prouty Benjamin, "
Rice A. "
Stoddard Dexter, "
Thompson Henry, "
Adams James E. North Chelsea
Stowers Daniel W. "
Maynard Caleb, Northfield
Stearns Albert D. "
Stearns Charles H. "
Swan Calvin T. "
Batchelder Henry, North Reading
Batchelder Josiah, "
Broad Nathaniel W. "
Campbell Warren A. "
Eames John, "
Holt Solon O. "
Hodges Leonard, Norton
Hunt Henry, "
Barr Sumner, Oakham
Bullard Dwight, "
Harrington Austin, "
Holden Amory, "
Barber Charles W. Orange
Davis Prentiss, "
Derby John, "
Howe Lewis R. "
Johnson W. & A. J. "
Gould Joseph K. Orleans
Mayo Ira, "
Crittenden Alanson, Otis
Latham Watson, "
Fuller Charles, Oxford
Joslin Esek, "
Stockwell L. "
Newton Amos P. North Oxford
Burleigh Albert, Palmer
Johnson B. H. "
Bond L. W. Bondsville, "
Canterbury Asa G. " "
Brown William, jr. Paxton
Parkhurst M. B. "
Beckett J. Peabody
Carr T. W. "

Carpenters and Builders— continued.

Chute & Parsons,	Peabody
Clark & Giddings,	"
Folsom Charles C.	"
Grant John S.	"
Hills Benj. M.	"
Parsons Samuel S.	"
Richardson Charles H.	"
Spalding Levi,	"
Pike Philander,	Pelham
Whitman T. T.	Pembroke
Ford James. 2d, North Pembroke,	"
Ford Barnabas,	"
Randall Nathaniel K. "	"
Howland David O. South Hanson,	"
Carter Sumner,	Pepperell
Chapman Elias,	"
Dow Daniel F.	"
Miller Jacob,	"
Tucker Samuel E.	"
Bottom Austin,	Peru
Bottom S. M.	"
Stowell Franklin,	"
Carter Hosea, jr.	Petersham
Mann Lot,	"
Prichard R. S.	"
Prouty George,	"
Prouty Ira,	"
Doane Francis E.	Phillipston
Gould Samuel N.	"
Searles Harrison H.	"
Ballou Dexter M.	Pittsfield
Burbank Abraham,	"
Chapman E. J.	"
Chapman Timothy,	"
Lawless Daniel,	"
Manyan A. B. & D. C.	"
Newcastle Peter,	"
Richardson Henry H.	"
Sanders Daniel J.	"
Strong John K.	"
Tottingham Anson,	"
Ward Zadock A.	"
Werden E.	"
Wellison George W.	"
Butler Dudley E., West Pittsfield	
Whitmarsh J. S.	Plainfield
Barnes Nathaniel C.	Plymouth
Barnes Nathaniel F.	"
Barnes William B.	"
Barnes William E.	"
Bartlett Thomas B.	"
Bates Comfort,	"
Bradford Caleb C.	"
Churchill Amasa,	"
Churchill William,	"
Diman James,	"
Diman Thomas,	"
Drew Winslow,	"
Eddy Lewis,	"
Harlow Ivory L.	"
Holmes William S.	"
Pope William W.	"
Rider Daniel,	"
Rider Joseph,	"
Weston Henry,	"
Weston William,	"
Whitton Charles,	"
Hoxie Edward, Chiltonville,	"
Langford John, South Plymouth,	"
Peterson Chas. H. "	"
Holmes George W.	Plympton
Sherman George W.	"
Vaughan D. K.	Prescott
White Ellis,	"
Chapman Nathan,	Provincetown
Cobb James,	"
Dyer Joshua,	"

Hedge William H.	Provincetown
Hill George,	"
Holwny Samuel A.	"
Knowles R.	
Lavender Wm. R.	
Rich Zaccheus,	"
Ryder James N.	"
Snow Josiah,	"
Snow Reuben,	"
Sparks Reuben G.	"
Small Alfred, North Truro,	"
Bailey & Baxter,	Quincy
Brackett Chas. C.	"
Litchfield Amos M.	"
Newcomb Richard,	
Parker William, jr.	
Pratt Henry G.	
Alden Morrison M.	Randolph
Alden Winslow,	"
Belcher Charles,	"
Belcher Linus,	"
Moulton Eben,	"
Peterson L. R.	"
Porter Ira,	"
Prescott Aaron,	"
Whiting T. W. E. Randolph,	"
Dean Pythagoras,	Raynham
King Benjamin,	"
King Edward,	"
Wilbur William F.	"
Bancroft Wendell,	Reading
Frost Charles,	"
Safford Edward,	"
Bliss George B.	Rehoboth
Bliss George E.	"
Wheaton Cyrus M.	"
Sherman Augustus T.	Rochester
West Benjamin H.	"
Bailey Levi,	Rockport
Choate Alfred B.	"
Choate John N.	"
Choate Paul,	"
Clark Albert,	"
Dade George W.	"
Knowlton Daniel W.	"
Parsons Benjamin, jr.	"
Pool Ebenezer,	"
Savage Jesse,	"
Rice Stanford,	Rowe
Todd Solomon,	"
Bailey Edward,	Rowley
Bailey Frederick,	"
Jewett Mark R.	"
Moody Luther,	"
Rundlett Oliver A.	"
Batchelder Isaac,	Royalston
Chase Chauncy,	"
King John,	"
Walker Joseph,	"
Miles Joseph,	Rutland
Moulton M. & Hiram V.	"
Stone David M.	"
Brown G. A. & C. A.	Salem
Brown J. M.	"
Bruce & Balcom,	"
Carleton J. F.	"
Cnrk George C.	"
Copeland E. M.	"
Danforth E. F.	"
Day Albert,	"
Dennis Devereux,	"
Easson & Saul,	"
Edwards John S.	"
Fairfield James, jr.	
FAXON & LOCKE, 72 Washington	
(see page 746),	"
Fuller E. P,	"
Gifford T. J. & Co.	"

Goldthwait & Day,	Salem	Sawyer Franklin A.	Shrewsbury
Gorman Thomas,	"	Tillson Zebina,	Shutesbury
Haley Shillaber,	"	Davis Leander P.	Somerset
Hammond William C.	"	Dean Asa,	"
Harris D. M.	"	Marble George A.	"
Hill Ira,	"	Wood Benjamin W.	"
Honeycomb Thomas P.	"	Brazillain J. M.	Somerville
Honeycomb W. H.	"	Randall Benjamin.	"
Hood David B.	"	Robinson J. O.	"
Hutchings A.	"	Sanborn David A. jr.	"
Locke N. C.	"	Snow F. D. & D. H.	"
Lord J. B.	"	Trefren Geo. W.	"
Lovejoy John,	"	Robinson John,	East Somerville, "
McIntire William E.	"	Brazillian James,	North " "
Moulton & Gardner,	"	Hyde Curtis,	Southborough
Ober Andrew,	"	Prentiss Benjamin F.	"
Perkins E. B.	"	Walker Lorenzo,	"
Richardson F. A.	"	Cutler Leonard,	Southbridge
Roberts Joseph W.	"	Chamberlain D. M.	"
Russell & Lord,	"	Stedman Wm. C.	Globe Village, "
Smith James A.	"	Phetteplace Edward,	"
Stiles Dean,	"	Burnett Jonathan,	South Hadley
Towle Abraham,	"	Judd Hervey,	"
Upton George L.	"	Stacy William,	"
Upton M. T.	"	White Charles F.	"
Walker P. D.	"	Turner David W.	South Scituate
Woodbury Ezra,	"	Turner Samuel,	"
Gale Foster,	Amesbury, Salisbury	Curtis Frederick,	West Scituate, "
Godsoe Benjamin,	" "	Aldrich Bennett,	Southwick
Judkins John M.	" "	Putney Alonzo,	"
Page Newell,	" "	Saunders William,	"
Moody Gardner S.,	East Salisbury, "	Barns Samuel,	Spencer
Pike Charles,	" "	Howland Pardon,	"
Balch Henry,	Sandisfield	Livermore Lorenzo,	"
Calkins Joseph,	Montville, "	Sanderson Tilson J.	"
Ingham Edward,	" "	Stone, Tower, & Co.	"
Parsons Joseph W.	" "	Temple Alonzo,	"
Richardson Levi J.	" "	Wedge Alex.	"
Gladding Brothers,	New Boston, "	Barton Eldredge,	Springfield
Bassett William W.	Sandwich	Brooks & Eaton,	"
Hall Joseph,	"	Currier & Richards,	"
Howland Gustavus,	"	Hitchcock Josiah,	"
Crowell Hiram,	West Sandwich, "	Hitchcock William,	"
Farnsworth J. W.,	Cliftondale, Saugus	Hogan & O'Keefe,	"
Mugridge & Farnham,	East Saugus, "	Hubbard & Hendrick,	"
Flye John,	Saugus Centre, "	Joyce, Burnham, & Co.	"
Parker A.	" "	King J. A.	"
Thomas J. W.	" "	Lathrop Belia,	"
Waldron Gilbert,	" "	Marvin & Prescott,	"
Horton Samuel T.	Savoy	Moulton C. C.	"
Maynard Eben L.	"	Page & Scripture,	"
Polly Harvey,	"	Scott & Merritt,	"
Cole & Coleman,	Scituate	SHATTUCK E. W., Taylor st.	"
Hayes Oliver P.	North Scituate, "	Shaw C. L.	"
Lee George C.	" "	Smith George	"
Merritt H. & A.	" "	Swan D. L.	"
Bowen Arnold M.	Seekonk	Vose & Brother,	"
Short Samuel,	"	Ross Taylor,	Sterling
Hitchcock William H.	Sharon	Grant Daniel R.	Stoneham
Tucker George,	"	Hersam Orrin,	"
Crippen W. W.	Sheffield	Richardson B. F.	"
Stillman David,	"	Brock Stephen,	Stoughton
Wright Gordon,	"	Clapp Samuel,	"
Ashley John,	Ashley Falls, "	Curtis S. W.	"
Balman Gurdon J.	" "	Gay Edwin,	"
Chapin Ansel,	" "	Holmes Albert,	"
Chapin Edward F.	" "	Hawes Elisha,	No. Stoughton, "
Turner John,	" "	Lawrence John W.	Stow
Newhall N. O.	Shelburne	Hebard Adrian,	Sturbridge
FROST J. B. & Co.,	Shelburne Falls, "	Phetteplace M.	Fiskdale, "
Richmond & Dole,	" "	Jones Samuel A.	Sudbury
Tillvert & Co.	" "	Puffer James J.	"
Lowse Charles D.	Sherborn	Harriman J. K.	Assabet, "
Foulding Eleazer	"	Bowen Arthur,	S. Sudbury, "
Lawrence O. F.	Shirley Village, Shirley	Darling Benjamin C.	Sunderland
Sawtell William,	" "	Chapman John,	Swampscott
Cutler Aaron G.	Shrewsbury	Emmons Ivory,	"
Green William A.	"	Davis Edwin,	Swansea

Carpenters and Builders — continued.

Gardner Chas. W.   Swansea
Hale William B.   "
Wood William H.   "
Ashley Noah,   Taunton
Atwood Walter H.
Bassett James T.   "
Baylies Charles,   "
Briggs J. W.   "
Burt William A.   "
Crapo N. N.   "
Cummings C. H.   "
Ellis Calvin T.   "
Lane J.   "
Macomber Philip A.   "
Manter, L. A.   "
Myrick ———   "
Pierce Samuel P.   "
Pinkerton & Barnaby,   "
Round A. S.   "
Russell William S.   "
Sandford E. R.   "
Seaver Samuel,   "
Seekill Joshua,   "
Sherman Zaccheus,   "
Tripp & Walker,   "
Waldron David A.   "
White H. G. O.   "
Wilbur J. W. L. & Brother,   "
Bancroft D. C.   Weir, "
Walker B.   "
Macomber E. jr.   Myrick's, "
Cutting Charles,   Templeton
Dudley Abel S.   "
Dudley J. F.   "
White Artemas,   "
Bronsden Lysander B.,   Baldwinville, "
Fuller Augustus,   " "
Fuller B. F.   " "
Willis A. S.   " "
Jennison Geo. W.   E. Templeton, "
Wheeler Jesse B.   Otter River, "
Brown Benj. F.   Tisbury
Cottle Edward,   "
Howland John W.   "
Harsell R. L.   "
Chase John G.   West Tisbury, "
Weeks Hervey,   " "
Marshall Samuel C.   Tolland
Foster Jacob,   Topsfield
Potter J. H.   "
Boutell Calvin,   Townsend
Morse Amos,   "
Whitcomb Jefferson,   "
Smith Samuel H. jr.   Truro
Small Abram C.   North Truro, "
Garfield George W.   Tyringham
Steadman Nathan,   "
Thomson Albert,   "
Videtto Charles,   "
Webster Orson,   "
Brown Caleb,   Upton
Fisk Evan,   "
Hall Nahum B.   "
Messenger David A.   "
Wood David C.   "
Brown E. K.   Uxbridge
Brown Willis,   "
Slater A. P.   "
Packard George,   Wakefield
Perkins Andrew,   "
Purrington John,   "
Wiley Adam,   "
Baker Luther,   Wales
Crawford O.   "
Lyon I. H.   "
Lyon I. M.   "
Vinton C. L.   "

Hartshorn Asa,   Walpole
Hartshorn Horace B.   "
Hartshorn Willard,   "
Bishop Wm. K.   South Walpole, "
Beal J. D.   Waltham
Bemis C. W.   "
Gilbert John,   "
Taylor George D.   "
Wetherbee Andrew,   "
Bassett Henry,   Ware
Clifford William,   "
Fairbanks Lorenzo,   "
Hilton Leander,   "
Howe John,   "
Nye Andrew S.   Wareham
Nye Thomas S.   "
Weston Abisha B.   "
Wing George F.   "
Bishop William,   Warren
Drury W.   "
Earle Benjamin,   "
Shepard William A.   "
Bonney S. S.   West Warren, "
Barber Edwin D.   Warwick
Taylor William R.   "
Berry & Moody,   Watertown
Norcross & Blaisdell,   "
Pierce George,   "
Sanger Joseph,   "
Weeks William,   "
Gorey Allen W.   Webster
Hall Caleb S.   "
Kibbee Vernon,   "
Hickman James,   Wellfleet
Landerkin Isaac W.   "
Newcomb Joshua,   "
Rich Anthony,   "
Sparrow Zoheth,   "
Dodge Rufus A.   Wenham
Dodge Simeon,   "
Morgan William B.   "
Porter William E.   "
Faulkner & Bullard,   Westborough
Hathaway B. C.   "
Hartwell George C.   "
Hodgdon J. R.   "
McKendry G. A.   "
Smith H. C.   "
Cutler Oliver B.   West Boylston
Holt Russell,   "
May John,   Oakdale, "
    West Bridgewater
Hayward & Mitchell,   "
Wilbur George,   "
Howard Friend,   Cochesett, "
Leonard Jacob,   "
Allen S. F.   West Brookfield
Livermore S. A.   "
Richards & Conway,   "
Bush Henry F.   Westfield
Cowles Enos,   "
Cowles Newell,   "
Gracea Antonio J.   "
Green George,   "
Jeffers Daniel W.   "
JOHNSON ELI, Jr.   "
Latham & Green,   "
Norton & Atkins,   "
Towne & Dickinson,   "
Drew George,   Westford
Fletcher C. L.   "
Sweetser Lorenzo,   "
Wright K. A.   "
Drury George B.   Westhampton
Jewett A. G.   "
Knight John M.   "
Loud F. & Son,   "
Torrey E. P.   "

Barrell J. Benson,   Westminster
Gibbs George W.   "
Whitney Augustine,   "
Carr George W.   West Newbury
Noyes Samuel C.   "
Poor Isaac,   "
Stevens L. D.   "
Titcomb Ichabod,   "
Watson Joseph,   "
Patch Samuel, jr.   Weston
Sisson John H.   Westport
Cornell John A.   Central Village, "
Allen John,   S. Westport,   "
Spear George A.   West Roxbury
Wason James W.   "
Adams E. W.,   Jamaica Plain, "
Armstrong Benj.   "   "
Day A. G.   "   "
Heath Stephen,   "   "
Kendall James,   "   "
Lincoln Paul,   "   "
SHAW J. J.   "   "
Shaw J. P.   "   "
Simpson James,   "   "
Walker Gideon,   "   "
Clark Edson,   West Springfield
Clark John G.   West Stockbridge
Olds Henry,   "
Reed Charles,   "
Turner Elisha M.   "
Van Horn Grove P.   "
Woodruff Franklin,   "
Bailey Jeremiah,   Weymouth
Baker Ashford,   "
Baker George S.   "
Penniman W. R.   "
Sherman Alex.   "
Bates Daniel,   East Weymouth, "
Daymour Rice,   "   "   "
Simmons Charles,   "   "   "
Turner Waldo,   "   "   "
Bicknell William,   North "   "
Bicknell & White,   "   "   "
Brown John F.   "   "   "
Eells Benjamin,   South "   "
Hobart & Sanbury,   "   "   "
Marlow Peter W.   "   "   "
Wade David N.   "   "   "
Wilcox Luther S.   Whately
Barnes ——,   Wilbraham
Jones Norman,   "
Calkins Alanson,   Collins Depot, "
Ely William,   "   "
Keyes Elias,   "   "
Haskell D. M.   "   "
Tupper Edwin L.   "   "
Scripter Hiram,   S. Wilbraham, "
West John R.   "   "
Kingsley E. G. & E. D.   Williamsburg
Morton & Woodard,   "
Vining Herman K.   "
Curtiss H. B.   Williamstown
Bryant William,   Wilmington
Eames John N.   "
Buttrick A. Warren,   Winchendon
Lyons Timothy F.   "
Raymond & Foristall,   "
Dupee C. H.   "
Fletcher Asa,   Winchester
Hatch Horace,   "
Shattuck Joseph,   "
Morgan F. W.   Windsor
Thompson Horace,   "
Pierce H. G.   East Windsor,   "
Belcher Dallas,   Winthrop
Belcher Warren,   "
Floyd W. Frank,   "
Griffin Sidney H.   "

Sawyer John L.   Winthrop
Corbett & DeLoreia,   Woburn
Kimball G. W.   "
Perham L. W.   "
WHITCHER JACOB C.   "
Willoughby E. K.   "
Wood Abner,   "
Bigelow G. C. & A. E.   Worcester
Chaffin Willard,   "
Dennis & Lee,   "
Eddy H. W.   "
Fish James R.   "
French J. C.   "
Fuller E. R.   "
Gates L. N.   "
Holbrook S.   "
Howe Leander,   "
Jefts Frederick,   "
Lamb Edward,   "
Lyon Edward,   "
Maynard M. W.   "
Palmer H. & A.   "
Partridge Brothers,   "
Peck C. H.   "
Pike S. E.   "
Raymond Tilly,   "
Rice E. K.   "
Sibley William,   "
Upham Freeman,   "
Ward W.   "
Woodworth J. S.   "
Draper David M.   Wrentham
Arnold James,   Sheldonville,   "
Matthews Asa E.   Yarmouth
Berry Albert,   S. Yarmouth,   "
Sears J. K. & B.   "   "
White Bartlett,   "   "
Bassett Henry,   Yarmouth Port, "

Carpenters' Tools.

BLAISDELL A. H. & CO. (gauges, see page 745),   Newton Corner

Carpet Dealers.

Carter A. J.   Charlestown
Kelso George R.   "
Merrill & Morrison,   Chelsea
Brimhall E. & Co.   Clinton
Buffinton & Waring,   Fall River
Nichols L. & Co.   "
Page Bilson,   "
Sprague L. & Co.   Fitchburg
Pattillo Alex.   Gloucester
Root T. D. & Co.,   Greenfield
Brooks Brothers,   Haverhill
Dexter A. J.   Lawrence
Butters & Kendall,   "
Stearns A. W. & Co.   "
Adams, North, & Co.   Lowell
Benner B. C. & M. A.   "
PATCH E. B. & CO. 1 & 2 Commercial square,   "
WELCH JACOB & CO. 1 Sagamore Hotel,
Harris M. & Co.   Lynn
Judson, Sawtelle, & Co.   Milford
Leavens Albert,   "
Little William (heirs),   New Bedford
Waite Benjamin H.   "
Waterman N.   "
Sweetser E S.   Newburyport
Stoddard & Kellogg,   Northampton
ROBINSON H. W. & CO., N. Bridgewater
Fenn & Carter,   Pittsfield
Platt S. H.   "
Burbank S. M. jr.   Plymouth
Snow C. B.   Provincetown
Downing, Archer, & Co.   Salem

Carpet Dealers — continued.
Goldthwait Willard & Co.   Salem
Pulsifer N.   "
Bryant Caleb & Son,   Taunton
Reed Edgar H.   "
Spear F. A. & Co.   Ware
Shumway Wm. T.   Webster
READ M. H.   Weymouth
Burnard, Sumner, & Co.   Worcester
Jenkins J. H. & Co.   "
Finlay, Lawson, & Kennedy,   "

Carpet Manufacturers.

Boston Flax Mills (hemp),   Braintree
BIGELOW CARPET CO (Brussels
   and Wilton), H. N. Bigelow and
   C. L. Swan, sup'ts.   Clinton
                                Dedham
Talbot E. F. (oil cloth), S. Dedham, "
DANVERS CARPET CO.   Danvers
Lowell Manuf. Co., Samuel Fay,
   agent,   Lowell
Naylor George,   "
Earley Robert W.   New Bedford
Pulsifer Nath. (painted),   Salem
Smith Lawrence A. (oil cloth), Truro

Carpet Lining Manufacturer.

LEWIS WILLARD,   Walpole

Carpet Slipper Manuf.

AMERICAN CARPET SLIPPER
   WORKS, M. Wesson, proprie-
   tor,   Springfield
Springfield Carpet Slipper Works,
   Elmer & Smith,   "

Carpet Sweeper Manuf.

Purrington George jr.   Mattapoisett

Carriage Axles.

KINSLEY IRON AND MACHINE
   CO., Frank M. Ames, agent
   (see page 730),   Canton
DALZELL D & SONS (see page
   799),   South Egremont,   Egremont

Carriage, Coach, and Sleigh Manufacturers.

*(See, also Wagon Makers; also Wheel-
   wrights.)*

Brown Bela,   Abington
Lean W. M.   "
Peirce M. B.   "
Cobbett Lewis,   East Abington,   "
Terrill Wm. H.   Acushnet
Bowen Daniel & Son,   Adams
Edmunds Joseph,   "
Alford & Cronk,   North Adams, "
Whipple & Nelson,   "   "
Barnes Harlow D.   Agawam
Sykes O. S.   "
Edgerton Marcus,   Feeding Hills, "
Smith Geo. W.   Alford
Bailey D. & C. W.   Amesbury
BRIGGS RICHARD F. (see page 754), "
CARR & ALLEN (see page 721),   "
Clark Seth jr. & Co.   "
Gale & Morrill,   "
HUME & MORRILL (see page 752), "
Huntington J. D.   "
Huntington & Ellis,   "
PARRY FELIX D. (see page 753), "
Patten Chas. W.   "
PATTEN ROBERT O. (see page 729), "
Chase Wm.   South Amesbury, "
Colby Wm. H.   "   "

                                Amesbury
                     South Amesbury, "
Gunnison Wm.   "   "   "
Sargent J. Warren,   "   "   "
Sargent Willis P.   "   "   "
Sawyer E. A.   "   "   "
Sawyer Thos. C.   "   "   "
Tuckwell S. S.   "   "   "
York George W.   "   "   "
Adams George,   West   "   "
Clement Geo. (bodies), "   "   "
Clement J. M. (bodies), "   "   "
Clement M. G.   "   "   "
Clough Geo. F.   "   "   "
Hall John,   "   "   "
Jones Isaac,   "   "   "
Judkins & Goodwin,   "   "   "
Little & Lancaster,   "   "   "
Loud L. C.   "   "   "
Nichols Alfred (bodies), "   "   "
Nichols Ichabod S.   "   "   "
Noyes C. H.   "   "   "
PATTEN THOMAS B. "   "   "   "
Pease Samuel C.   "   "   "
Sargent Edwin,   "   "   "
Sargent O. H.   "   "   "
Johnson E. L.   Amherst
Farnum Joseph,   Andover
Poor William,   "
Bucknam Samuel C.   Arlington
Hitchcock Geo. L.   Ashby
Cheney Dexter,   Athol
Hale Seth F.   "
Fish W. W. & H. L. Athol Depot, "
Bailey Enoch,   Attleborough
Ferguson Joseph,   "
Stanley John,   N. Attleborough, "
Crocker B. F. & C. C., Hyannis, Barnstable
Loring Chauncy,   Barre
Rice Charles H.   "
Wilkins Henry (wheels and spokes), "
Burnett L. A. & Co.   Belchertown
Cowles T. & S. D.   "
Dickinson F. M. & Co.   "
Leach Maynard,   "
Packard Joel & Co.   "
Blake Nelson,   Bernardston
Cushing John T.   Beverly
De Wolfe George H.   "
Fuller M. & O. W.   Blackstone
Edwards S. F.   Bolton
Sawyer James B.,   W. Boxford, Boxford
Peabody William,   Bradford
South Thomas,   Weymouth,   Braintree
Anderson C. G.   S. Braintree   "
Mansfield Warren, (also cars), "
   South Braintree,   "
Snow Zoeth, Jr.   Brewster
Wild Moses,   "
Dawley Charles C.   Brimfield
Rice Alfred,   Brookfield
Hunt Thomas G.   Brookline
Quinlan Michael W.   "
Chapman Francis L.   Cambridge
HURD AMOS D. (see page 735),   "
   Palmer St.   "
JONES ANDREW J.   "
Martin W. H.   Cambridgeport, "
Davis Solomon A., East Cambridge. "
Blackburn T. (bodies), No. Cambridge, "
Henderson Bros.   "   "   "
Henderson J. A.   "   "   "
Ivers Francis,   "
WEBB T. C. & Co.   "   "   "
   (see page 657),   "   "   "
Harris Almon,   Charlemont
Whitman Charles P.   "
Bryant John,   Charlestown

Morey & Robinson, Charlestown
Phipps John S. "
Willard Albert C. Charlton
Gilmore William H. Chicopee
Wood Lewis, "
Keyes & Thurston, Clinton
Winchester Bros. Coleraine
Smith Julius M. Concord
Holcomb John S. Conway
Amsden D. R. Dana
Brown Amos. Danvers
Hood Wm. H. "
Peart Wm. B. "
Waldron E. T., Dauvers Port, "
Gifford John J. Dartmouth
Cowen Abram B., No. Dartmouth, "
Flagg William H. Dedham
Billings Ira, So. Deerfield, Deerfield
Billings J. E. & Co. "
Ockington John H. " "
Bennette Edmund B. Dorchester
Brown B. F. "
Merriam George O. "
Brooks Lawrence, Dunstable
Harding Prince H., Orleans, Eastham
Clark O. N. Easthampton
DALZELL DAVID & SONS (see
   page 799), S. Egremont, Egremont
Simmons Robert M. Fairhaven
Chase James M. Fall River
Eames Asa, "
Robinson John H. "
Burgess Josiah, Falmouth
Hewins Lewellyn R. "
Fessenden Charles, Fitchburg
FROST S. GILMAN (see page 766), "
Sheldon J. P. "
Stoddard Charles B. "
Young William H. Foxborough
                        Framingham
Trowbridge George, So. Framingham, "
Betnis Henry, Franklin
Stewart R. B. "
Sawin Levi C. & Co. Gardner
Friend Samuel K. Jr. Gloucester
Jackson Wm. R. "
Burtis & Brothers, Great Barrington
Couch Rensselaer L. "
Sabin G. W. & Co. Housatonic, "
Whitmore & Pixley "
Moore & Withey, Greenfield
                        Greenwich
Jourdan John H., Greenwich Village, "
Eells Robert, Hanover
Turner Thomas, "
Cobb Fred. A. Hardwick
Bean Ira G. Haverhill
Brown John G. "
Greaves T. & Co. "
McGregor Daniel, "
Pethybridge Wm. H. "
Stickney J. I. "
Whittier A. "
Whiton Beja H. & Co. Hingham
Waters Samuel, South Hingham, "
Clark Chester & Son, Hinsdale
Winn Moses, Holden
Carpenter John, Holland
Webber G. L. !
Hunter Daniel K. Holyoke
Newton E. A. & Brother, "
Shelley Edwin D. "
Osgood Isaac, Hubbardston
Whittier R. B. & A. J. Hyde Park
Eldridge E. D. Kingston
Washburn Salmon, Lakeville
Dewey Wm. B. Lanesborough
Lloyd Samuel P. "

Gale & Ames, Lawrence
Lathrop E. & Co. "
Stowell Joseph, "
Couch H. S. Lee
Hinckley Bradford & Co. "
Couch Frederick M. East Lee, "
Swett & Durant (repairing), Leominster
Hobart Colburn, Leverett
Convers Samuel, Lowell
Eaton J. B. "
Furbish & Sanborn, "
GREEN AMOS, rear 200 Dutton, "
Hill Bros. "
Jenkins Joel, "
Lee John T. "
SAWYER A. C. 163 Middlesex, "
Skillings D. G. "
Swett Wm. L. "
Kimball Thomas, Lynn
Montrose Robert, "
Ploof & Dennis, "
Proctor Wm. H. "
Sawver J. A. J. "
                        Lynnfield
Simonds George W., Lynnfield Centre, "
Keen Wm. B. Malden
Hunne James, "
Damon F. N., East Marshfield, Marshfield
Cushman, Baker, & Co. Medfield
Moore H. F. Medford
Symmes Alexander S. "
Smith C. A. "
TEEL E. & CO. Main St. "
Corliss Varnum, Methuen
Waddell A. K. "
Pickens Philo H. Middleborough
Rockwood D. B. Milford
Woods E. "
Harrington J. E. Millbury
Parker Sumner R. "
Chapman & Strangman. Milton
CLAPP AVERY & SONS, Montague
Brownell Geo. L. New Bedford
Brownell, Ashley, & Co. "
COLE H. G. O., 44 Third (see page
   760), "
Forbes & Sears, "
HALE PATENT WASHER CO.
   Charles H. Gifford, agent and
   treas. (see p. 759), 82 Elm, "
Shaw Franklin, "
White Wm. G. "
Johnson C. D. New Braintree
Davis Charles S. Newburyport
Syms Edward, "
                        New Marlborough
White Alfred, Mill River, "
Curry R. Newton Corner, Newton
Davis R B. & Co. Northampton
Phelps George S. "
Pittsinger Wm. Florence, "
Lamb E. R. & W. B. North Andover
Flagg Webster M (sleighs), Northborough
Richardson S. S. "
                        Northbridge
Bachelor William H., Whitinsville
Bradford & Crocker, North Bridgewater
Mason A. H. (repairer), "
Tribou L. E. "
Reed Sumner, North Brookfield
Stearns Geo. "
Crawford Wm. S. Oakham
Ramsey John (sleighs), Orange
Loomis & Page, Palmer
Dole & Osgood, Peabody
PIKE & WHIPPLE (express wagons,
   see page 748), "
Bonney J. Dean, Pembroke

12

Carriage Manufacturers — continued.

	Pembroke
Damon Bailey D., West Duxbury,	"
Lawrence Sumner P.	Pepperell
Bosworth George,	Petersham
Goddard Daniel,	"
Hapgood Chauncey	"
Bowker George,	Phillipston
Clapp Jason & Son,	Pittsfield
Dunham Ebenezer,	"
Van Valkenburg George,	"
Whitcher J. H.	Plainfield
Ellis James,	Plymouth
Hatch & Blackmer,	"
Ryder Ezekiel,	"
Tirrell Sons,	Quincy
Loring John,	Randolph
Makepeace Sylvanus,	Raynham
Barney Alfred R.	Rehoboth
Bliss George E. W.	"
Hicks Nathan E.	"
Nelson Hosea E.	Rowe
Snow Fayette,	"
Rundlett Oliver A.	Rowley
Whittier Moses T.	"
Estabrook Taylor,	Rutland
Fletcher David W.	"
Smith David F.	"
Adams P. F.	Salem
Andrews Gilman,	"
Batchelder Joseph & Co.	"
Davidson M. & Co.	"
Lations J. P.	"
Loring E. D.	"
Roome George,	"
Stocker John W.	"
Bailey D. & C. W., Amesbury,	Salisbury
Morrill Edwin,	"
Cheswell & Boardman,	"
Clark Seth, jr. & Co.	"
Dennett & Clark,	"
Felch E. S.	"
Jeming Samuel J., Montville,	Sandisfield
Hunt W m. H., New Boston,	"
Pratt Geo. F.	"
Stevens D. W.	"
Cheesebro' Albert W.	Savoy
Thompson Geo., East Sheffield,	Sheffield
Powers R. M., Shelburne Falls,	Shelburne
Ware Vorastus,	Sherborn
King O. N.	Shirley
Whitney Charles S.	Shrewsbury
Johnson Levi,	Shutesbury
Clapp Otis,	Southampton
Bachelor James,	Southbridge
Judd E. B.	South Hadley
Basutt Joseph,	Springfield
Hood John,	"
Loomis J. & W.	"
Rogers J. H.	"
Smith David & Co.	"
Graham William,	Stoughton
Talbot J. jr.	"
Edgell O. A.	Stoneham
Haynes H. & Son,	Sturbridge
Arnold E. South Sudbury,	Sudbury
Wellington Benjamin S.	Swansea
Hace Thomas C.	"
Eddy Ira W.	"
Dunn Chas. A.	Taunton
Hault James,	"
ECK & WHITE, Weir St.,	"
Read Nathan,	"
Sweeting Ambrose P.	"
Jones Abijah,	Templeton
Maynard & Fiske,	"
Ellis E. T.	Uxbridge
Anderson W. H. & Bro.	Waltham

Crosby Charles,	Waltham
Wood William,	"
Barnes Bros.	Ware
Winslow George E.	"
Barrows H. W.	Wareham
Wilder A. A.	Warren
Kettell Samuel S.	Washington
Cameron & Ross,	Watertown
Amos Ebenezer,	Webster
Brigham F. A. (sleighs),	Westborough
Blake Wm. M.	"
Bryant A. S.	"
Carter Nehemiah,	"
Cloyes Gardner,	"
Fairbanks J. H.	"
Forbes & Fisher,	"
O'Brien John,	"
Williams & Bacon,	"
Fowler Chas. C.	Westfield
Gamache F. D.	"
Griggs Seth D.	"
Hartwell Leander,	Westminster
Sawyer Sandford,	"
Merrill Moses B.	West Newbury
Chace Elbridge,	Westport
Thompson Jeremiah T.	"
White Holder,	"
Brownell C. H. Central Village,	"
	West Roxbury
Bradley Geo. I., Jamaica Plain,	"
Shorey Wm. B.	"
Clark Edson, Ashleyville, W. Springfield	
	West Stockbridge
Caswell Wm., Housatonic,	"
Scribner Smith, State Line,	"
Bodge Ellis, East Weymouth, Weymouth	
Boles C. South "	"
Harding J. "	"
Bardwell William E.	Williamsburgh
Ely Henry L.	Williamstown
Parker Joseph H.	Woburn
Atchison G. T.	Worcester
Blood O. & Son,	"
McLeod Alex.	"
TOLMAN A. & CO., 18 Exchange,	"
Whiting W. C.	"
Allen Silas,	Wrentham
Grant Chas. A. Sheldonville,	"
Thacher Watson,	Yarmouth
Thacher & Taylor, Yarmouth Port,	"
White Rufus, South Yarmouth,	"

Carriage and Saddlery Hardware.

(See also Hardware.)

MUNSON J. M. (for children's carriages, see page 716),   Greenfield
HALE PATENT WASHER CO.,
   Charles H. Gifford, agent and treas.
   (see page 759), 32 Elm,   New Bedford
Lee & Baker,   Springfield
Walker Appleton,   Worcester
Wallace S. & Co.

Carriage Repositories.

KING FRANK D.   Bridgewater
   Cambridge
Henderson Robert (second hand),   "
Ward W. A.   Cambridgeport,
WEBB T. C. & Co., (see page 637),
   North Cambridge,   "
Sawyer T. C.   Lowell
Holmes Ethan,   Milford
HALE PATENT WASHER CO.,
   Chas. H. Gifford, agent and treas.,
   (see page 759), 32 Elm,   New Bedford
Dodge Dana & Son,   Newburyport

TROFATTER J. H.   101 Boston,   Salem
Robbins Thos. A.   "
Dewhurst G. C.   Worcester
Richmond A. K.   "
TOWER C. D., 51 Union, (see p. 724),   "

Carriage Smiths.

(See also Blacksmiths.)
Fortin J. D.   Amesbury
Langley True T.   "
Colby Amos,   West Amesbury,   "
England John J.   "   "   "
Osgood Enoch,   "   "   "
Palmer Chas. H.   "   "   "
Stevens H. G. & H. W.   "   "
South Thomas,   Weymouth,   Braintree
HURD AMOS D. (see page 735),
Palmer st.,   Cambridge
JONES ANDREW J., Church,
corner Palmer,   "
WEBB T. C. & Co., (see page 657),
North Cambridge,   "
Louer John,   Charlestown
Wright J F.   Dedham
Daniels John,   Harrison sq.   Dorchester
Terry Isaac,   Fairhaven
McGregor Daniel,   Haverhill
Kingman E. A.   Mansfield
Rockwood D. B.   Milford
Woods Edward,   "
Brownell, Ashley, & Co.   New Bedford
Linton Joseph B. & Co.   "
Skiff S. B. & Co.   "
Tripp James M.   "
Tyler A. D. & Sons,   North Bridgewater
Andrews Gilman,   Salem
Peirson Geo. H.   "
Shoules Chas. J.   "
Weir Daniel P.   "
Read Geo. B.   Springfield
Tibbitts Joseph,   Stoneham
Pye C. & J.   Stoughton
Coe Jerome W.   Taunton
PECK & WHITE, 19 Weir,   "
Pollard C. P.   Woburn
Corbett H. M.   Worcester
Melaven M.   "
Quinn Michael,   "

Carriage Spokes, Hubs, Shafts, Rims, Wheels, &c.

Locke & Jewell,   Amesbury
FOSTER & HOWE (wheels), West
Amesbury,   "
Sargent Elmer P. (supplies), West
Amesbury,   "
Forbes George & Co. (wheels), East
Brookfield,   Brookfield
    Cheshire
Lloyd & Jenks (oak and ash fellies),   "
Whitmore & Pixley (hubs, &c.),
Housatonic,   Great Barrington
Tower Edward J. (fellies),   Lanesborough
    Middlefield
Blush Wm. D. (shafts and fellies),   "
True Samuel (hubs),   Salisbury
    Southbridge
Plimpton W. P. & Co. (spokes),   "
Giffard George H.   Westport
Fitch & Winn (spokes),   Worcester
Peabody B. I. (wheels),   "
Reed C. G. & Co. (wheels),   "

Carriage Top Dressing.

HATHAWAY C. L. & SONS (see
page 799),   North Bridgewater
Stoddard N. W.   "

Carriage Trimmers.

Ames E. J. & M.   Barre
Davis S. A.   Cambridge
Rowe D. K.   "
Blaisdell Albert,   Charlestown
Dickson Joseph,   "
Walsh John M.   Weymouth,   Braintree
Blake John B.   Fall River
    Fitchburg
FROST S. GILMAN (see page 766),   "
LOVELL HORACE & CO., Harwich
Port,   Harwich
Butman S. L.   Lowell
SAWYER AARON C., 161 Middlesex,   "
Hollis James A.   Lynn
Plumstead M. & Son,   "
Nason Charles,   Milford
Smith O. G.   "
Wiswall E.   Natick
    New Bedford
LEVERETT WILLIAM, 51 Elm,   "
Fuller George,   West Newton,   Newton
Gilman T. F.   Newton Corner,   "
Tuttle H. A.   Salem
Whitney R. S.   "
LOVELL HORACE,   Sandwich
Hill C. R.   Stoughton
Coe Jerome W.   Taunton
Kellogg Thomas,   "
Macfarland William,   "
PECK & WHITE,   "
Patien Thomas,   Watertown
Turbell E. G.   "
Johnson Waldo,   Webster
    West Roxbury
Williams & Croeker,   Jamaica Plain,   "
    Worcester
TOWER C. D. 51 Union, (see p. 724),   "

Carriage Trimmings.

    Amesbury
Goodwin & Sargent, W. Amesbury,   "
Poyen John S.   "   "

Carriage Washers.

HALE PATENT WASHER CO.
Charles H. Gifford, agent and treas.
(see page 759), 32 Elm,   New Bedford

Cartridge Manufacturers.

HALL & HUBBARD, Park, cor.
Willow (see page 778),   Springfiel

Carvers.

Lees A.   Charlestown
Sherwin Levi & Son,   Fitchburg
Elwell Samuel 3d,   Gloucester
PURRINGTON HENRY J. (see page
754),   Mattapoisett
Brown Andrew,   Newburyport
Wilson J. W. & A.   "
Gardner J. A.   Springfield

Cask and Keg Manuf.

(See also Coopers.)
    Mattapoisett
BARSTOW N. H. & H. (see page 727),   "
Coffin William S.   Newburyport

Cement Drain Pipe Manufs.

PEIRCE CHARLES M. Jr. 119 No.
Water.   New Bedford
Wilcox J. P.   Springfield

Cement Manufacturers.

Morse S. R. (pearl),   Athol
STARKEY L. T. (see page 713), Attleboro'

Cement Manufacturers — continued.

Cambridge
Nudd Jacob (elastic), Campridgeport, "
Danforth Chas. H. (channel),   Lynn
Leach Albert & Son,   "
SAMUELS JAMES (see p. 791), May, "

Chair Finisher.

Brick Alfred H.   Gardner

Chair Machinery Manufs.

HEALD STEPHEN & SONS,
(boring machines, rounders, &c.,
see pages 796 and 797),   Barre
FITCHBURG MACHINE CO. (Jas.
L. Chapman), Summer st.   Fitchburg
Nichols & Adams, Otter River, Templeton
Young Albert F.   "   "
Whitney Baxter D.   Winchendon

Chair Manufacturers.

WINCHESTER C. & G. C. Ashburnham
Flint E. S. & Co., Ashburnham Depot, "
Pratt Brothers,   "   "
Wetherbee B. E. (camp stools), "   "
Whitney John,   "   "
Whitney Wilbur F.   "   "
White A. & Co.   Chelsea
Rankin Noah & Co.   Erving
Davis Alonzo,   Fitchburg
Heywood W. Chair Co., G. E.
Towne, treasurer,   "
Derby Philander,   Gardner
Eaton & Dunn,   "
Heywood Brothers & Co.   "
Knowlton A. & H. C.   "
Wright E. & Co.   "
Bent S. & Bros.   So. Gardner, "
Conant Bros. & Co.   "   "
Greenwood C. S. & Co.   "   "
GREENWOOD THOS. (see page
779),   So. Gardner, "   "
Pierce Sylvester K.   "   "
Traverse E. C & O. A.   "   "
WRIGHT & MOORE (see p. 775), "   "
Brown M.   Hubbardston
Heald T. S.   "
Johnson Andrew J.   Manchester
Dike Augustus,   Montague
KILBURN L. & Co., (L. E. Holmes
and Richard French, see p. 778); Orange
Mixter Orlando,   Phillipstou
Parker Joel D. & J. D. (frames),   "
Brown Wm. H., E. Princeton, Princeton
Stewart Brothers,   "
Whitney George, S. Royalston, Royalston
Crane William F., New Boston, Sandisfield
Hotchkiss & Gladding,   "   "
Alvord & Franklin,   Shelburne
Burpee Edward,   Sterling
Burpee Henry W.   "
Fitch James W.   "
Partridge H. & J. W.   Templeton
Leland H.   Baldwinville, "
Sawyer, Thompson, & Perley, "   "
Smith S. W.   "   "
Fales Joel G. & Co., E. Templeton, "
Hodge A. S. & Co.   "   "
Parker, Sawyer, & Co.   "   "
Sawyer Brothers,   "   "
Litch Geo. H.   Otter River, "
Coolidge F. S.   Westminster
Clark, Nichols, & Co.   "
Lombard & Noyes,   "
Merriam Jonas,   "
Merriam, Holden, & Co.   "
Smith George,   "

Westminster
Wyman Franklin, Wachusett Village, "
Waitt E. W. (folding),   Worcester

Chair Material Manufacturers.

Warren Levi,   So. Gardner,   Gardner
Wright M. & Co.   "   "

Chair Tools, Bits, &c.

Ellsworth Geo. F., So. Gardner, Gardner

Chalk and Crayon Manufs.

Parmenter & Walker,   Waltham

Chamber Furniture Manufs.

KILBURN L. & CO (see p. 778), Orange

Channel Cement Manuf.

SAMUELS JAMES, 1 May street
(see page 791),   Lynn

Charcoal Burners and Dealers.

Cambridge
Chaffee & Cummings, E. Cambridge, "
McCarty Jeremiah,   Charlestown
Alden Samuel G.   East Bridgewater
Egremont
Patterson David C., No. Egremont, "
Barnes Ira & Sons, So. Egremont, "
Benjamin J. M. & Geo. C.   "
Church Ephraim,   "   "
Goodale Henry S.   "   "
Weaver Henry P.   "   "
Whitbeck Orrin C.   "   "
Hughes John,   Mount Washington
Scutt Charles,   "
Spurr Isaac,   "
Weaver H. P. & W. H.   "
Whitbeck O. C.   "
Miles Fred. (Copake Iron Works, N.Y.), "
Wright Wm.   "   "
Purrington George,   Mattapoisett
Randall Lewis,   "
Cook S. R.   Springfield

Charts.

Sherman C. R. & Co.   New Bedford
Whipple Henry,   Salem

Cheese Manufacturers.

Barre Central Cheese Factory, John
T. Ellsworth, agent,   Barre
Barre Cheese Factory, Addison H.
Holland, agent,   Barre Plains, "
Boyce E.   Blandford
Bucklin Andrew J.   Cheshire
Card William M.   "
Lincoln Seneca L.   "
Lincoln Shubael W.   "
Peticler P.   "
Williams & Brown,   "
Hancock Cheese Factory,   Hancock
Hardwick
Hardwick Centre Cheese Factory, "
Hardwick Union Factory,   "
Mandell Joel D.   "
Walker James H.   "
Wood Luther D. & Co.   Lanesborough
New Braintree Cheese Manufactur-
ing Co.   New Braintree
Coy Hill Cheese Co.   Warren
Warren Cheese Co.   "
Worcester County Cheese Co.   "
Westborough Milk Co.   Westborough
Milk Producers' Ass'n (butter),   "
Lewis W. K. & Bros.   West Brookfield
West Brookfield Cheese Co.   "

Wilbraham
Wilbraham Cheese Manufacturing Co. "

Cheese Presses.

(See also Agricultural Implements Manufs.)
HEALD STEPHEN & SONS (see
pages 796 and 797),   Barre

Chemical Works.

Bowman, Grant, & Co. (saleratus),
Cambridgeport,   Cambridge
THAYER HENRY & CO. (medicinal
extracts and chemicals), 405 Main
street,   Cambridgeport,   "
Boston Chemical Works, East Cam-
bridge,   "
Chaffee & Cummings (pyroligneous),
East Cambridge,   "
Stowell John (manuf.),   Charlestown
Meldrum Robert,   Lowell
Taylor & Barker,   "
Cochrane Alexander & Co.   Malden
Salem Laboratory Co.   Salem
STAPLES & PHILLIPS (blue vitriol,
see page 759),   Taunton
Newton Chemical Co.   Waltham
        Woburn
Merrimac Chemical Co., N. Woburn,

Children's Carriage Hardware.

MUNSON J. M. (see page 716), Greenfield

Children's Carriages.

Dexter D.   Amherst
Haywood C. E., South Amherst,   "
Haywood Chandler,   "   "
Wood B. F. (sleds),   Arlington
Bullard Franklin (sleds),   Buckland
Shipman J. D.   Goshen
        Granville
Noble & Cooley, Granville Corners, "
Field Charles R.   Greenfield
Ring George S.   Huntington
Whitney F. A.   Leominster
Kelley F. P.   Lynn
Barker & Jones (toy wagons, carts,
&c.),   Montville,   Sandisville
Chapin Albert T.   South Hadley
        Springfield
WARNER R. W., 57 1-2 Main st.
(see page 779),   "
Baker Willard, Baldwinville, Templeton
Johnson Chester N., East Templeton, "
Cole Wm. (sleds), Kingville, Worthington

Chimney Caps.

PETTINGELL JOHN (iron), Mechanics Mills,   Lowell

Chisel Manufacturers.

BUCK BROTHERS (see page 761),
        Millbury and Worcester
Whiting A. L. & Co.   Worcester

Chocolate Manufacturers.

BAKER W. & CO. (Henry L. Pierce),
Milton Lower Mills,   Dorchester
Preston John, Harrison square,   "
Webb Josiah & Son,   Milton

Chopping-Knife Manufs.

        Winchendon
KETCHUM & LOUD (see page 770), "

Chronometers.

Kelley James S.   New Bedford
Munroe James (manufacturer),   "

KUHL WILLIAM, 42 Market sq.   New Bedford
(maker),   "

Chuck Manufacturer.
(Lathe.)
FAY L. D., 7 Cypress st. (see page
783),   Worcester

Cider.

SMITH CHARLES, 61 Lime st. (see
page 752),   Newburyport

Cider Refineries.

Adams ——,   Chelmsford
La Croix J.   East Medway
Veber George,   Charlemont
Cushing F. E., East Holliston, Holliston
Whiting Harrison,   "   "
Eames Edward A.   Hopkinton
        Quincy
FURNALD & BROOK (champagne). "
Weld Farm, Jamaica Plain, W. Roxbury

Cigar Dealers.

(See also Tobacconists.)
Haswell Amos K., Long Plain, Acushnet
Haswell Stephen S.   "   "
Getman M.   North Adams,   Adams
Briggs Crawford C.   Attleborough
Spear C. J. W.   "
Jacques Franklin, W. Boxford, Boxford
McDermott James,   Chicopee
McLean Frank A.   "
Witherell & Engram,   Chesterfield
Bliss Linus,   Dover
Toogood L. O.   East Hampton
Robinson John S.   Edgartown
ANTHONY WILLIAM A., 10 and
12 South Main street,   Fall River
Holmes Charles A.   "
Joel Brothers,   Fitchburg
Sherwin George,   "
Jones George N.,   Gloucester
Gorham E. L.   Great Barrington
Bliss W. B.   Greenfield
Howard Franklin,   Hanover
Wixon Freeman R. West Harwich, Harwich
Hosmer E. E. & Co.   Lawrence
Allen Henry H.   "
Burns D.   "
Loring & Loomis,   "
Currier J. W.   Lowell
Emerson D. G.   "
FLYNN M. X. 10 Merrimac (see
page 742),   "
Flood Peter H.   "
McDONOUGH JOHN R., 73 Charles, "
Mort James W.   "
Patrick Samuel C.   "
Weeks S.   "
Downs Simon T.   Lynn
Clapp George H.   "
Shaw Albert,   "
Stevens F. E. &. Co.   "
Kinney Jirey, jr.   Mattapoisett
Winston O. (wholesale),   "
Hale W. B., jr.   Milford
Cunha Joseph,   New Bedford
Francis John,   "
Haswell S. S. & Co.   "
Richards W. D.   "
Gatb C. N.   Northampton
Strecker E. & Co.   "
Brewer L.   North Brookfield
DeLand B. K.   "
Sargent S. B.   "

Cigar Dealers — continued.

Collins Gamaliel, Thorndike,	Palmer
Goodrich William H.	Pittsfield
Merrill Samuel B., Montville, Sandisfield	
Butler J. M.	
Case H. O.	Springfield
Frost & Merrick,	"
Margerum H. J.	"
Mort Mary E. Mrs.	"
Upton J. W. D.	"
Porter J. P.	"
Gray Warton H.	Swampscott
Wright John G. & Co.	Taunton
Bradley H.	"
Crowell B. D.	Tisbury
Wright Jason B.	"
Brackett E. J.	Waltham
Platt J. H.	"
Thompson J. P.	Webster
Mather C. H.	Whately
Smith N. F.	Williamstown

Badger John B.	
Fuller Charles,	Milton
Cunha Joseph,	Monson
Francis John,	New Bedford
Haswell S. S. & Co.	"
Oesting Chas. A. W.	"
Tilden Niles,	"
Atkinson Davis,	Newburyport
Baldwin William B.	New Marlboro'
Barber Hubert,	"
Walter George,	"
Rice George F.	Northborough
Wait Henry,	North Chelsea
Thayer & Dodge,	Palmer
Bates Elizur,	Pittsfield
Ende Emil,	"
Mead E. B.	"
Reardon W. E.	"
Streeter Theron L.	"
Ward S. C.	"
Bolin Chas. P.	"
Braley Lorenzo D.,	Quincy
Battis & Brown, 30 Front,	Richmond
Chapple John D.	Salem
Rowell Frederick, jr.	"
Semons Wm. C.	"
Skinner R.	"
Skinner S. S. & Co.	"
Smith & Helt,	"
Tabour William,	"
Fuller J. S., Montville,	Sandisfield
Sweetser Bros., Cliftondale,	Saugus
Raddin F. J. & J. A.	"
Trull Silas S.	"
Hascall James,	Shrewsbury
Acker John, So. Hadley Falls,	So. Hadley
Brower Wm. H., "	"
Hoffman J. G.	"
Walker Peter,	"
Granger S. L & O. A.	Southwick
Welcome & Rising,	"
Webb H. E.	"
CASE H. O., 259 Main,	Springfield
Whitcomb Joseph,	"
Wright Wm. H.	"
Han Michael,	Taunton
Leo Joseph,	"
Wright John G. & Co.	"
American Whip Co., Henry J.	
Bush, President,	Westfield
Allen C. S. & P. R.	"
Chester John B.	"
Harrison & Carpenter,	"
Kneil Thomas, agent,	"
Lane & Batty,	"
McMain Thomas F.	
Root J. W.	
Thayer, Waterman, & Beckman,	"
Tyron Samuel,	"
WHITNEY, LANE, & CO.	"
Worthington M.	"
Allman John,	Worcester
Armbruster A. P.	"
BRADFORD GEORGE, 66 Austin,	"
Forehand W.	"
Feltman C. B.	Worcester
Gray William I.	"
Rawson O. F.	"
Shattuck M. E. & Co.	
Welkel H. T. Mrs.	

Cigar Manufacturers.

Getman Michael, North Adams,	Adams
Huck Herman,	Agawam
Cushman E. P.	Amherst
Bridgman Lyman,	Belchertown
Cook Lucius,	Bernardstown
Lane George W.	"
Newton Horatio H.	Bolton
Aaron Moss, Cambridgeport,	Cambridge
Aberle Jacob,	"
Barnett Abraham,	"
Busnach Michael S.	"
Clark B. P. & Co.	"
Dailey Charles B.	"
Howlett Wm.	"
LeFrancis Peter,	"
LeFrancis Thomas,	"
Phillips J. S.	"
Russell E. T.	"
Witham Thomas,	"
Hammond Nathl. O., East Cambridge,	"
Junio Joseph,	Charlestown
Junio M.	"
Klous Isaac,	"
Nelson Abraham,	"
Everdean Joseph B.	Chelsea
Huntington Thomas,	"
Jones William,	"
Slade S. & G. F.	"
Taylor A.	"
Bliss Linus,	Dover
Judkins Wm. M.	East Bridgewater
Holmes Charles A.	Fall River
Wadington Samuel,	"
Bush E. S. & Co.	Fitchburg
Joel Brothers,	"
Sherwin George,	"
Bateman L. K.	Georgetown
Masury T. B.	"
Jones George N.	Gloucester
Lindberg A. F.	"
Overbeck J. C.	"
Perry & Spooner,	Hardwick
Elmer John B.	Heath
Perkins Henry F.	Kingston
Allen Henry H.	Lawrence
Loring & Loomis,	"
Cahill Chas. S.	Lowell
Patrick S. C.	"
Smith Wm. D.	"
Swan George,	Ludlow
Copp E. O.	Lynn
Stevens F. E. & Co.	"
Hale W. B. jr.	Medford
Pond W. A.	"

Cisterns, Tanks, &c.

(See also Coopers.)

PETTINGELL JOHN (wood), Mechanics' Mills,	Lowell
Codin William S.	Newburyport

Civil Engineers and Surveyors.

Hersey Isaac, Abington
HOWLAND CHAS. W. "
Corthell W. P. South Abington, "
Tuttle W. D. Acton
Richmond David, Adams
Granger Wm. P. North Adams, "
Ellis Wm. F. & Son, Ashland
Allen Samuel, Belchertown
Barbour W. S., Cambridgeport, Cambridge
Chase J. G. " "
Mason William A. " "
Ames T. Edward, Charlestown
Ball Horace W. "
Buchanan Roberdean, "
DOANE T. & J. 21 City sq. (see p. 666), "
Thissell J. Clinton
Raymond George, Fitchburg
Low David W. Gloucester
Webber J. S. "
Deland William N. Great Barrington
Loop Augustine B. "
Taylor Charles J. "
Field Alfred R. Greenfield
Fletcher Frank A. Groton Junction
Smith Joseph, Hanson
Gurney E. B. K. South Hanson, "
Spofford N. (surveyor), Haverhill
Seymour C. W. Hingham
Bradford Allen S. Kingston
Gray Edward, "
Barker James L. Lawrence
Littlefield C. H. "
FISH WILLIAM T. Lee
Kendall Henry D. Lenox
Lyman Josiah, "
Baker R. W. Lowell
Osgood William F. "
Ellis George A. Marlborough
Briggs George A. New Bedford
Dexter S. S. Orange
Woodward Hiram, "
Murdock George A. Pittsfield
Beal Eleazer, Randolph
Frost Brothers, Somerville
PUTNAM C. A. Salem
CRAIG GEO. A. Spencer
Bettes Stockwell, Springfield
Briggs A. D. & Co. "
Butler Wm. H. "
HARRIS D. S. "
Sommer Ernest J. "
Barney Charles E. Taunton
Talbot Charles, "
Curtis Joseph H. Waltham
Holmes Thomas, West Bridgewater
Howard Albert, "
Howard James, "
Root L. F. "
Ellis Bethuel, Westfield
Ball Phineas, Winchendon
Buttrick E. C. Worcester
Gould & Burbank, "
Low Gorham P. Jr. "

Claim Agents.

SAYLES FRANKLIN O. Center st. Adams
BINNEY WM. C. "
Brimlecom Charles, Amesbury
OSBORNE WM. H. Barre
Winslow B. F. East Bridgewater
Stearns Daniel, Fall River
Low David W. Fitchburg
Jayner Herbert C. Gloucester
Davis & DeWolf, Great Barrington
Reed S. H. Greenfield
Prescott Abel, Groton Junction
Gurney E. B. K., South Hanson, Hanson

JOSLIN JAS. T. Hudson
Turbox John K. Lawrence
BLAISDELL C. R., 3 Canal block, Central, Lowell
Frye John F. "
Mason Walter N. Natick
Borden A. New Bedford
CUSHMAN A. S. 117 Union, "
Gerrish Jos G. Newburyport
PERKINS JONAS R., North Bridgewater
Cheney Damon E. Orange
Allen James G. Palmer
EMERSON CHAS. N. Pittsfield
Wood Edgar M. "
Damon D. E. Plymouth
Osgood J. B. F. Salem
Porter John W. "

Field Samuel T., Shelburne Falls, Shelburne
DONNELLY HUGH, "
HOLMES J. W. Springfield
Tifft L. A. "
BROWN JAMES, Taunton
REED CHAS. A. "
Gillett & Stevens, Westfield
Rand A. P. "
Whitney Milton B. "
Leonard & Lewis, "
PIERCE L. W. Winchendon
Abbott & Estabrook, Worcester
Haskins D. W. "
Rice H. C. "

Clay Beds.

Sheffield China Clay Co., E. Sheffield; Sheffield "

Clergymen.

ABBREVIATIONS. — B. signifies Baptist; C.B., Calvinist Baptist; Ch., Christian; C. T., Congregational Trinitarian; C. U. Congregational Unitarian; E., Episcopal; F. B., Freewill Baptist; M., Methodist; M. E., Methodist Episcopal; N. J., New Jerusalem; Pres., Presbyterian; R. C., Roman Catholic; S. A., Second Advent; Swed., Swedenborgian; Uv., Universalist.

Abbe F. R. (C. T.), Abington
Hamlin Isaac S. (B), "
Marsden James (Uv.), "
Pettee Joseph (Swed.), "
Roach A. L. (R. C.), "
Dodge Benj. A. (C. T.). N. Abington, "
Ober Wm. (C. T.), So. Abington, "
Wilson J. E. (B.), "
Coleman George W. (C. T.), Acton
Jackson Wm. C. (C. T.), S. Acton, "
Davis Edwin (Uv.), West Acton, "
Davy Wm. K. (B.), "
Cobb Asahel (C. T.), Acushnet
Tripp Frederick (Ch.), "
Wooding George W. (M. E.), Long Plain, "
Holt Kilburn (C. B.), "
Briggs William A. (B.), Adams
Jessup Lewis (C. T.), "
Smith W. L. (M. E.), "
Gladden Washington (C. T.), N. Adams, "
Hodge D. Munson (Uv.), " "
Lynch Charles (R. C.), " "
Meeker W. F. (M. E.), " "
Sanford Miles (B.), " "
Colesworthy Geo. (B.) Agawam
Perry Ralph (C. T.), "
Merrill N. (M. E.), Feeding Hills, "
Sylvester C. S. (C. T.), "
Bacon Wm. F. (C. T.), Amesbury
Baker Joel (F. B.), "
Brady John (R. C.), "

Clergymen — continued.

Eaton W. H. (B.),   Amesbury
Estes D. G. (E.),   "
Tompkins F. P. (M. E.).   "
Gregory Lewis (C.T.), W. Amesbury,   "
Kling Henry,   "   "
Potter W. F. (C. U.).   "
Hickok Laurens P. (C. T.),   Amherst
Jenkins J. L. (C. T.),   "
Kingman D. (C. T.),   "
Leland J. H. M. (C. T.),   "
Lothrop Charles D. (C. T.),   "
Parker S. P. (E.),   "
Scott Nelson (C. T.),   "
Seelye J. H. (C. T.),   "
Seelye L. C. (C. T.),   "
Stearns Wm. A. (C. T.),   "
Tower Francis E. (B.),   "
Tyler Wm. S. (C. T.),   "
Herrick W. D. (C. T.), North Amherst,   "
Lee John (M. E.),   "   "
Richardson M. L. (C. T.), South "   "
Lane James P. (C. T.),   Andover
Litchfield D. C. (B.),   "
Merrill James H. (C. T.),   "
Smith Charles (C. T.),   "
Green Henry S. (C. T.), Ballard Vale,   "
Cady Daniel R. (C. T.),   Arlington
Harris Amos (B.),   "
Keyes J. W. (Uv.),   "
Salter Charles C. (C. U.),   "
Stevens M. A. (C. T.),   Ashburnham
Wilkie Walter (M. E.),   "
Wight Dan. jr. (C. U.), N. Ashburnham   "
Parker Horace (C. T.),   "
Shaw ———— (C. U.),   Ashby
Green Lewis (E.),   "
Jencks E. N. (B.),   Ashfield
Woodbury Webster (C. T.),   "
Mansfield G. W. (M. E.),   "
Potter George B. (B.),   Ashland
Burton W. S. (C. U.),   "
Cutler Temple (C. T.),   Athol Depot,   Athol
Harlow W. T. (M. E.),   "   "
Stoddard D. H. (B.),   "   "
Anderson A. (M. E.),   Attleborough
Pleoubet F. N. (C. T.),   "
Cooper George (B.),   N. Attleboro',   "
Pierce J. D. (Uv.),   "
Weston Thomas (C. U.),   Barnstable
Morse G. H. (C. T.), Centreville,   "
Chase S. B. (M. E.),   Cotuit,   "
Goodhue Henry A. (C. T.), West Barn-
   stable,   "
Pope R. S. (Uv.),   Hyannis,   "
Evans W. H. (B.),   "   "
Strong J. D. (C. T.),   "   "
Beach J. B. (C. U.),   Barre
George T. (M. E.),   "
Smith Edwin (C. T.),   "
Danay J. J. (C. T.),   Becket
Hill E. S. (B.),   "
Hartwell John (C. T.), Becket Centre,   "
Blake Henry B. (C. T.),   Belchertown
Curtis Moses (B.),   "
Donovan D. (B.),   "
Vinton Charles (M. E.),   "
Woodworth Wm. W. (C. T.),   "
Smith Amos (C. U.),   "
Turner J. W. (C. T.),   Belmont
Roberts James A. (C. T.),   Berkley
Houghton William A. (C. T.),   Berlin
Barber Stillman (C. U.),   Bernardston
Bailies Andrew (M.),   "
Merrill A. T. (C. T.),   "
White Edwin (Uv.),   "
Bailey J. C. (M. E.),   Beverly
Cookson Ferdinand M. (E.),   "

Foster Joseph C. (B.).   Beverly
Kimball John C. (C. U.),   "
Lamphiar O. T. (C. T.),   "
Van Norden Chas. (C. T.),   "
Rich Alonzo B. (C. T.),   "
Titus Eugene H. (C. T.),   "
Lathrop J. W. (B.), Beverly Farms,   "
Whitney G. W. (Uv.),   "
Cleaveland J. P. (C. T.),   Billerica
Hussey C. C. (C. U.),   "
Edwards J. E. (C. T.),   Blackstone
Porter E. W. (F. B.),   "
Rumney George (E.),   "
Townsend George W. (B.),   "
Browne E. C. L. (C. U.),   Bolton
Holbrook Amos (C. T.),   Boxborough
Coggin William S. (C. T.),   Boxford
Gammell Sereno D. (C. T.),   "
Park Calvin S. (C. T.), W. Boxford,   "
Bigelow Andrew (C. T.), Boylston
   Centre,   Boylston
Campbell Geo. W. (C. T.),   Bradford
Kingsbury John D. (C. T.),   "
Storrs R. S. (G. T.),   Braintree
Reed J. B. (B.),   Brewster
Dexter George (U.),   "
Hosmer G. H. (C. U.),   Bridgewater
McGuire M. T. (R. C.),   "
Walker H. D. (C. T.),   "
Warland Wm. (E.),   "
Wright ———— (Swed.),   "
Duncan A. G. (C. T.), Scotland,   "
McDaniels S. W. (C. U.),   Brighton
Holbrook C. A. (E.),   "
Keyes J. W. (Uv.),   "
Packard David T. (C. T.),   "
Hyde Chas. M. (C. T.),   Brimfield
Coit Joshua (C. T.),   Brookfield
Newell Chas. H. (M. E.),   "
Russell D. Allen (C. U.),   "
Perry Philander (B.), East Brookfield,   "
Finotti Joseph M. (R. C.),   Brookline
Hedge Frederick H. (C. U.),   "
Lamson William (B.),   "
Miles Henry A. (E.),   "
Silver Abiel (Swed.),   "
Tomkins Elliott D. (E.),   "
Wharton Wm. C. (E.),   "
Lord Charles (C. T.),   Buckland
Merrifield C. N. (M.),   "
Moore E. J. (M. E.), Shelburne Falls,   "
Hudson Alfred S. (C. T.),   Burlington
Anable Courtland W. (B.),   Cambridge
Briggs G. W. (C. U.),   "
Dougherty M. P. (R. C.),   "
Hoppin Nicholas (E.),   "
McKensie Alexander (C. T.),   "
Newell William (C. U.),   "
Peabody Andrew P. (C. U.),   "
Bulfinch Stephen G. (C. U.), E. Cam-
   bridge,   "
Bowles Benj. F. (Uv.),   "   "
Collyer I. J. P. (M. E.),   "   "
Donahue J. W. (R. C.),   "   "
Maguire Frank (Uv.),   "   "
Timlow H. R. (C. T.),   "   "
Croswell Andrew (E.), N. Cambridge,   "
Apsey W. S. (B.),   "   "
Merrill Abraham D. (M. E.),   "   "
Mears David O. (C. T.),   "   "
Marsters John M. (C. U.),   "   "
Wightman J. C. (B.),   "   "
Abbott E. (C. T.), Cambridgeport,   "
Chase Edwin B. (E.),   "   "
Howe William (B.),   "   "
Mason Summer R. (B.),   "   "
Scully Thomas R. (R. C.),   "   "
Stevens A. W. (C. U.),   "   "

Osgood Joseph (C. U.),   Cohasset
Fitts Calvin R. (C. T.),   "
Smith Charles B. (C. T.),   "
Daniels —— (C. B.),   Coleraine
Sanderson Alonzo (M. E.),   "
Strong Lewis (C. T.),   "
Williams J. E. (C. T.)   Concord
Reynolds Gimdall (C. U.),   "
Thompson Wm. A. (C. T.),   Conway
Townsend J. J. (B.),   "
Feltch Joseph H. (Ch.),   Cummington
Baldwin Joseph B. (C. T.), West
   Cummington,   "
Rodgers H. M. (Cong.),   Dalton
Wade R. T. (M. E.),   "
Janes ——,   Dana
Evans —— (E.),   Danvers
Le Long H. C. (Uv.),   "
Rice C. B. (C. T.), Danvers Centre, "
Holbrook Chas. F. (B.), Danvers Port, "
Chadwick N. S. (Ch.),   Dartmouth
Hawes Elnathan (Ch.), N. Dartmouth, "
Mosher Benjamin (Ch.),   " "
Matthews George (B.), S. Dartmouth, "
Wilson John. (C. T.),   " "
Babcock Samuel B. (E.),   Dedham
Brennan John (R. C.),   "
Edwards Jonathan (C. T.),   "
Jordan J. W. P. (M. E.), East Dedham, "
Bixby J. P. (Cong.), South "
Fairbanks George (B.),   " " "
Hill George (Uv.),   " " "
Burgess Isaac J. (B.), West   " "
Gifford Elisha (Uv.),   " " "
Crawford Robert (C. T.),   Deerfiel.
Hosmer George H. (C. U.),   "
Cadwell —— (M. E.), S. Deerfield, "
Jagger E. L. (C. T.),   " "
Burgess A. P. (M.), East Dennis Dennis
Tarlton —— (Cong.), South " "
Macomber Geo. S. (M.), West " "
Dawes Ebenezer (C. T.),   Dighton
Kelso Isaac (C. U.),   "
Smith Henry M.   "
Bates O. H. (M. E.), North Dighton, "
Brailey Martin (B.),   " "
Horton —— (B.),   " "
Manning Lucius W. (B.),   " "
Thomas S. Thomas (M. E.), " "
O'Keefe D. A. (R. C.),   Douglas
Briggs William T. (C.), E. Douglas, "
Silverthorne W. (M. E.),   " "
Hall Nathaniel (C. U.),   Dorchester
Hinckley F. (C. U.),   "
McNulty Thomas R. (R. C.),   '
Means James H. (C. T.),
Mills William H. (E.),
Mumford Thomas J. (C. U.),
Rowe Charles E. (B.),
Bemis Nathaniel, (M. E.), Milton, "
Tenney Michael (C. T.)   " "
Ayers W. M. (M. E.), Neponset, "
Barrows B. W. (B.),   " "
Carter Clark (C. T.)   " "
Catlin H. D. (C. U.),   " "
Battell E. Allen (B.),   Dover
Norton Thomas S. (C. T.),   "
Paine J. C. (C. T.),   Dracut
Patten Moses (C. T.),   "
Baker Jacob (Uv.),   Dudley
Lamount Wm. F. (M. E.),   "
Pratt Henry (C. T.),   "
Coggshall Samuel W. (M. E.), Duxbury
Moore Josiah (C. U.),   "
Tisdale William R. (W. M.),   "
Hall Edwin D. (M. E.), W. Duxbury, "
Aldrich J. K. (C. T.), East Bridgewater
Sheffield J. F. (M. E.),   "

Clergymen — continued.
Williams F. C. (C. U.), East Bridgewater
Paine T. O. (Swed.), Joppa, "
Fish John (M. E.), Eastham
Colton A. M. (C. T.), East Hampton
Johnson Charles T. (M. E.), "
Seeley S. T. (C. T.), "

Easton
Withington G. G. (C. U.), N. Easton, "
Chaffin W. L. (C. U.), " "
Husted J. B. (M. E.), " "

Egremont
Ashton — (M. E.), North Egremont, "
Bestor Foranda (B.), " "
Hazen Timothy A. (C. T.), South " "
Phelps Winthrop H. (C. T.), " "
Ewing Edward C. (C. T.), Enfield
Lee John W. (M. E.), "
Bassett E. B. (C. T.), Erving
Bacon James M. (C. T.), Essex
De Normandie C. Y. (C. U.), Fairhaven
Thomas J. W. (S. A.), "
Upham F. (M. E.), "
Walker A. S. (Cong.), "
Adams William W. (C. T.), Fall River
Butler S. Wright (Ch.), "
Duncan John (B.), "
Haughwout P. B. (B.), "
Hyde Wm. P. (M. E.), "
King J. D. (M. E.), "
Kyle Joshua R. (Pres.), "
Murphy Edward (R. C.), "
Thurston E. (C. T.), "
Wagner Francis J. (M. E.), "
Young Joshua (C. U.), "
Burgess Ebenezer (C. T.), Falmouth
Carlton — (E.), "
Kimball James P. (C. T.), "
Seabury Edwin (C. T.), E. Falmouth, "
Wheeler Azariah B. (M. E.), " "
Brigham David (C. T.), Waquoit, "
Crehore Joseph (Uv.), Fitchburg
Emerson Alfred (C. T.), "
Foley C. M. (R. C.), "
Harding Charles R. (M. E.), "
Hatch William H. (M. E.), "
Jenks Henry F. (C. U.), "
Jones Henry L. (E.), "
McIntire Farrington (Swed.), "
Spring Leverett W. (C. T.), "
Trask George (C. T.), "
Davis Jacob (B.), Florida
Tefft E. W. (S. A.), "
Dickinson N. S. (C. T.), Foxborough
Merrick J. M. (C. U.), "
Jones G. G. (E.), Framingham
Savage M. J. (C. T.), "
Spaulding H. J. (C. U.), "
Train Arthur S. (B.), "
Filmer T. T. (B.), S. Framingham, "
Fish Linus (M. E.), Saxonville, "
Hill Geo. E. (C. T.), " "
Eddy Richard (Uv.), Franklin
Holman J. W. (B.), "
Keene Luther (C. T.), "
Thayer Wm. M. (C. T.), "
Merrill — (C. T.), South Franklin, "
Boynton Francis (C. U.), Freetown
Williams A. A. (Ch.), "
Chase John P. (Ch.), E. Freetown, "
Tyler John, "
Belden Wm. (C. T.), Gardner
Burnett Joseph (B.), "
Closson Harrison (Uv.), "
Beecher Charles (C. T.), Georgetown
Burtt J. M. (B.), "
Marsh D. D. (C. T.), "
Baylies Andrew (M. E.), Gill

Potter E. S. (C. T.), Gill
Acquaron L. (R. C.), Gloucester
Capen E. H. (Uv.), "
Emerson F. F. (B.), "
Reid James D. (E.), "
Smith J. C. (M. E.), "
Thacher I. C. (C. T.), "
Benton Frederic A. (Uv.), Annisquam, "
Gannett J. H. (B.), East Gloucester, "
Wood Wm. C. (C. T.), Lanesville, "
Hall A. J. (M. E.), Riverdale, "
Walker Townsend (C. T.), Goshen
Scanlin Wm. G. (C. U.), Grafton
Windsor John H. (C. T.), "
Stevens N. F. (M. E.), N. E. Village, "
Jones J. D. E. (B.), " "
Bates A. J. (C. T.), Saundersville, "
Cushman John P. (C. T.), Granby
McLean A. (B.), Granville Cor., Granville
Grekis A. (C. T.), E. Granville, "
Gale W. (C. T.), W. " "
Grace C. F. (R. C.), Great Barrington
Olmstead Henry (E.), "
Scudder Evert (C. T.), "
Walsworth L. W. (M. E.), "
Penneman — (E.), Van Deusenville, "
Crane D. M. (B.), Greenfield
Finch Peter V. (E.), "
Lee Samuel H. (C. T.), "
Loomis A. G. (C. T.), "
Moors John F. (C. U.), "
Robinson H. L. (R. C.), "
Schwartz Augustus (Lutheran), "
Tucker Samuel (M. E.), "
Blodgett E. P. (C. T.), Greenwich
Ayer Oliver (B.), Groton
Folsom Geo. M. (C. U.), "
Chick J. M. (B.), Groton Junction, "
Donovan J. D. (B.), " "
Nightingale Crawford (C. U.), " "
Phillips Daniel (C. T.), "
Hinckley Henry (B.), Groveland
Noon Samuel H. (M. E.), "
Ayers Roland (C. T.), Hadley
Booth H. S. (M. E.), "
Dwight E. S. (C. T.), "
Beaman W. H. (C. T.), N. Hadley, "
Fobes Wm. A. (C. T.), Halifax
French Samuel F. (C. T.), Hamilton
Aiken James (C. T.), Hanover
Cutler Samuel (E.), "
Freeman Joseph (C. T.), "
Reed Andrew (B.), "
Miller Henry H. F. (B.), Hanson
Southworth Benjamin (C. U.), "
Tupper Martyn (C. T.), Hardwick
Wells David (C. T.), "
Fox J. M. (C. U.), Harvard
Pratt Geo. H. (C. T.), "

Harwich
Snow Solomon P. (M. E.), E. Harwich, "
Perry M. (M. E.), N. " "
Hammond — (M. E.), S. " "
Lothrop Joseph (Free), W. " "
Ela Walter, Harwich Port, "
Bray William L. (C. T.), Hatfield
Allen E. W. (C. T.), Haverhill
Barrows Homer (C. T.), "
Bradley C. A. (Uv.), Ayer's Village, "
Damon Calvin, (Uv.), "
Dunn A. (B.), East Haverhill, "
Garland J. (C. T.), "
Kelley George W. (C. T.), "
Mariner J. C. (F. B.), "
McDonald John T. (R. C.), "
Munger T. T. (C. T.), "
Padelford P. J. (B.), "
Plummer Henry (F. B.), "

Seeley R. H. (C. T.), Haverhill
Smith E. A. (M. E.), "
Thrall S. C. (E.), "
Miller Robert (C. T.), Hawley
Seymour Henry (C. T.), "
Samuel Robert (C. T.), West Hawley, "
Cutler Brainard B. (C. T.), Heath
Lord John H. (M. E.), "
Scott Ephraim (M. E.), "
Hanaford P. A. Mrs. (Uv.), Hingham
Fuller George E. (M. E.), "
Jones Henry W. "
Lincoln Calvin (C. U.), "
Richardson Joseph (C. U.), "
Tilson J. (B.), "
Dewhurst Eli (B.), "
Flint Ephraim (C. T.), Hinsdale
Griffin —— (R. C.), Holden
Paine Wm. P. (C. T.), "
Bliss Daniel (C. T.), Holland
Carpenter John (M. E.), "
Best E. S. (M. E.), Holliston
Hartley Benj. (E.), "
Holmes Geo. W. "
Savage William H. (C. T.), "
Bigelow L. B. (M. E.), Holyoke
Fish J. L. A. (B.), "
Frankell M. (German Cong.), "
Harkins P. (R. C.), "
Peet —— (E.), "
Trask J. B. (C. T.), "
Miller Simeon (C. T.), Ireland, "
Barry Thomas (R. C.), Hopkinton
Hambleton W. J. (M. E.), "
Green E. R. (B.), Woodville, "
Fay H. C. (C. T.), Hubbardston
Vinton P. M. (M. E.), "
Gay H. A. (B.), Hudson
Heywood William S. (C. U.), "
Jackson Samuel (M. E.), "
Dibble Lorenzo (M. E.), Hull
Bisbee John H. (C. T.), Huntington
Goddard Edward (B.), "
Collins W. H. (E.), Hyde Park
Davis P. B. (C. T.), "
Hamilton William H. (C. U.), "
Ventres W. H. S. (B.), "
Whittiker N. T. (M. E.), "
Gifford Benj. R. (E.), Ipswich
Morong Thos. (C. T.), "
Pearson Wm. H. (C. T.), "
Richardson A. M. (C. T.), "
Wagner Jesse (M. E.), "
Peckham Joseph (C. T.), Kingston
Phipps J. H. (C. U.), "
Merriman Titus H. (B.), "
Ward James W. (C. U.), Lakeville
Brown Theophilus (M. E.), "
Barrows Elijah W. (Ch.), "
Bartol George A. (C. U.), Lancaster
Leavitt George R. (C. T.), "
Whitney Quincy (Uv.), "
Mills William C. (E.), Lanesborough
Newman Charles (Pres.), "
Savage —— (M. E.), "
Bosworth Geo. W. (C. B.), Lawrence
Cooke H. A. (C. B.), "
Dougherty M. J. (R. C.), "
Dunning C. U. (M. E.), "
Chaddock E. G. (F. B.), "
Fisher Caleb E. (C. T.), "
Edge Lewis M. (R. C.), "
Gallagher M. F. (R. C.), "
Harris Charles C. (E.), "
Hogg John (Pres.), "
Knowles D. C. (M. E.), "
Moore J. B. (C. U.), "
Packard George (E.), "

Park William E. (C. T.), Lawrence
Snow W. F. (C. T.), "
Weaver G. S. (Uv.), "
Brennan J. H. (R. C.), Lee
Gale Nahum (C. T.), "
Hall William (M. E.), "
Morgan H. A. (B.), "
Oliver Cyrus (M. E.), "
Winslow William C. (E.), "
Battles Albert (Shaker), South Lee, "
Bradley Chas. F. (C. T.), " "
Causey L. P. (M. E.), Leicester
Coolidge A. H. (C. T.), "
Finley Everett (C. U.), "
Nelson John (C. T.), "
Hannaford C. H. (M. E.), Cherry Valley, "
Cook N. B. (B.), Clappville, "
Field Justin (E.), Lenox
Smith George M. (C. T.), "
Batt W. J. (C. T.), Leominster
Horton Edward A. (C. U.), "
McCurdy C. L. (M. E.), "
Russell —— (B.), "
Jones N. B. (B.), Leverett
Watson John (C. T.), "
Porter —— (C. T.), Lexington
Wescott Henry (C. U.), "
Stowe Wm. T. (Uv.), E. Lexington, "
Clark John M. (M. E.), Leyden
White E. (Uv.), "
Richardson Henry J. (C. T.), Lincoln
Frost C. L. (B.), Littleton
Loomis Elihu (C. T.), "
Vorse A. B. (C. U.), "
Harding John W. (C. T.), Longmeadow
Judd T. O. (B.), "
Ober Benjamin (C. T.), E. Longmeadow, "
Adams John G. (Uv.), Lowell
Blanchard Amos (C. T.), "
Crudden Peter (R. C.), "
Edson Theodore (E.), "
Foster E. B. (C. T.), "
Grimell Charles E. (C. U.), "
Hanks S. W. (C. T.), "
High William C. (M. E.), "
Hutchings Charles L. (E.), "
James Horace (C. T.), "
Jones S. F. (M. E.), "
Morehouse D. A. (F. B.), "
Morse F. R. (B.), "
O'Brien John (R. C.), "
Romana Anthony (R. C.), "
Stanton Wm. E. (C. B.), "
Street Owen (C. T.), "
Twiss James J. (Uv.), "
Whittaker George (M. E.), "
Whittier E. A. (B.), "
Wood Horatio (Free Chapel), "
Davis Elnathan (C. T.), Lunenburg
Locke John L. (M. E.), "
Allen Ralph W. (M. E.), Lynn
Attwill B. W. (E.), "
Barnes J. W. F. (M. E.), "
Biddle Charles W. (Uv.), "
Currier A. H. (C. T.), "
Farrar J. P. (B.), "
Goss John A. (Ch.), "
Holmes John S. (B.), "
Homes F. (C. T.), "
Medbury Nicholas, "
Morris Franklin G. (M. E.), "
Strain Patrick (R. C.), "
Sweetser Samuel B. (M. E.), "
Whiton James M. (C. T.), "
Stewart Samuel B. (C. U.), "
Vassar Thomas E. (B.), "
Wood Pliny (M. E.), "
Wright N. E. (Uv.), "

Clergymen — continued.

Boardman M. B. (Pres.), Lynnfield
Centre,   Lynnfield
Hood Jacob (Pres.),   "   "
Greenwood Thos. J. (Uv.),   Malden
Hamilton A. O. (M. E.),   "
Hooper E. P.   "
Huntington H. Howard (E.),   "
Lawrence Robert F. (C. T.),   "
Powers James F. (Uv.),   "
Reed Charles Edward (C. T.),   "
Ryan Geo. W. (R. C.),   "
Warren Geo. F. (B.),   "
Sargent A. D. (M. E.),   "
Smith Berton (M. E.),   "
Williams — (B.),   "
Tenney Francis B. (C. T.),   Manchester
Grover Thomas (Friends),   "
Hordon Chas. (Swed.),   "
Ide Jacob B., jr. (C. T.),   "
Lewis Welcome (B.),   "
Townsend Paul (M.),   "
Allen Benjamin R. (C. T.),   Marblehead
Buxton Wm. B. (Univ.),   "
Lawrence Edw. A. (C. T.),   "
Mudge Z. A. (M. E.),   "
Patch George W. (B.),   "
Woodbridge Wm. R. (Epis.),   "
Aldrich S. T. (Uv.),   Marlborough
Anthony George N. (C. T.),   "
Conlin John (R. C.),   "
Colburn W. W. (M. E.),   "
Deming M. R. (B.),   "
DeNormandie E. (C. U.),   "
Cobb Leander (C. T.),   Marion
Griffin Daniel J. (M. E.),   "
Smith George L. (Swed.),   "
Tozer William (E.),   "
Vose Henry C. (Uv.),   "
Alden Ebenezer (C. T.),   Marshfield
Cromack — (M. E.),   "
Davis Jacob (B.),   "
Leonard George (C. U.),   "
Williams Francis F. (C. T.),   "
Faunce William (Ch.),   Mattapoisett
Manwell B. F. (C. T.),   "
Carr A. W. (B.),   Medfield
Wiggins James H. (C. U.),   "
Davis Benj. H. (Uv.),   Medford
Hooker Edward P. (C. T.),   "
Hurd J. (B.),   "
Leroy Chas. H. (E.),   "
McCollom James T. (C. T.),   "
Towne E. C. (C. U.),   "
Waite Daniel (M. E.),   "
Sanford David (C. T.),   Medway
Cooley Benjamin F. (E.), E. Medway, "
Roberts Robert (C. T.),   "   "
Ide Jacob (C. T.),   West Medway, "
Brooks Samuel (B.),   "   "
Knowlton Stephen (C. T.),   "   "
Ray W. P. (M. E.),   "   "
Bale Albert G. (C. T.),   Melrose
Barnes William S. (Uv.),   "
Richmond J. B. (E.),   "
Stratton F. K. (M. E.),   "
Dwight — (M. E.),   Mendon
Linsley D. P. (C. U.),   "
Bradley C. S. (Uv.),   Methuen
Eastman L. L. (M. E.),   "
Grassie T. G. (C. T.),   "
Hersey Quincy (B.),   "
Holman J. B. (M. E.),   "
Williams N. M. (B.),   "
Ladd S. G. (C. T.),   Middleboro'
Ryder F. (M. E.),   "
Sawyer Rufus M. (C. T.),   "
Hutchinson Wm. (B.), N. Middleboro', "

Edwards S. G. (C. T.), N. Middleboro' Middleboro.
Pierce Charles M. (C. T.),   "   "
Rockwood Joseph M. (B.),   Middlefield
Hubbard James M. (C. T.),   Middleton
Carr S. J. (B.),   Milford
Crowell Loranus (M. E.),   "
Cuddihy Patrick (R. C.),   "
Demarest G L. (Uv.),   "
McIlvaine C. E. (E.),   "
Kendall S. C. (C. T.),   "
McDermott John (R. C.),   "
Ballou Adin (Prac. Ch.), Hopedale, "
Fowler Stacy (C. T.),   Millbury
Garrette E. Y. (C. T.),   "
Powers J. J. (R. C.),   "
Skinner C. A (B.),   "
Morison John H. (C. U.),   Milton
Teele Albert K. (C. T.),   "
Howard R. H. (M. E.),   Monson
Rossy — (R. C.),   "
Sumner Charles B. (C. T.),   "
Cronyn David (C. U.),   Montague
Norton E. (C. T.),   "
Clark James A. (C. T.),   Monterey
Hamlin — (M. E.),   Nahant
Bronson J. (B.),   Nantucket
Crawford James E. (B.),   "
Dawes Thomas (C. U.),   "
Hosmer Samuel D. (C. T.),   "
Starr William H (M. E.),   "
Jenkins W. M. (F. B.),   Natick
Leonard W. G. (M. E.),   "
Parker Addison (B.),   "
Welch John B. (R. C.),   "
Alger Horatio (C. U.), South Natick, "
Sargent George W. (C.),   "   "
Greene William B. (C. T.),   Needham
Williams C. H. (C. T.), Grantville, "
Phipps G. G. (C. T.),   Wellesley, "
Savage John (M. E.),   New Ashford
Batchelor B. S. (Ch.),   New Bedford
Batchelor M. (S. A.),   "
Bates Lewis B. (M. E.),   "
Coe Isaac H. (Ch.),   "
Craig Austin (Ch.),   "
Davis Thomas A. (colored, Zion Ch.), "
Dennison T. R. (city missionary), "
Fox Samuel (Seamen's Bethel),   "
Howe Moses G.   "
Jackson Wm. (colored, B.),   "
Knowlton Isaac C. (Uv.),   "
McMahon L. S. (R. C.),   "
Morgan John R. V. (colored M. E.), "
Moulton T. C. (Ch.),   "
Mulchahey James (E.),   "
Paine Bernard (C. T.),   "
Potter Wm. J. (C. U.),   "
Quint Alonzo H. (C. T.),   "
Thomas Moses G. (city miss.),   "
Valentine Theodore (B.),   "
Wagner Francis J. (M. E.),   "
Winn D. D. (M. E.),   "
Gurney J. H (C. T.),   New Braintree
Guy Joshua N. (C. T.),   Newbury
Mears James F. (M. E.),   "
Withington Leonard (C. T.),   "
Borden Thomas (Uv.),   Newburyport
Burnham Edwin (B.),   "
Campbell Randolph (C. T.)   "
Chapin John (M. E.),   "
Chapman George T. (E.),   "
Cole Jonathan (Uv.),   "
Cunningham Cyrus (Advent.),   "
Fiske Daniel T. (C. T.),   "
Hooker E. W. (C. T.),   "
Lennon Henry (R. C.),   "
May Joseph (Uv.),   "

Newburyport
McGinley William A. (C. T.),
McManus Charles (R. C.), "
Pike Daniel P. (Ch.), "
Spaulding Samuel J. (C. T.), "
Thurston John R. (C. T.), "
Tracy Thomas (Uv.), "
White J. Crocker (E.), "
Wright M. E. (M. E.), "
New Marlborough
Wickson Cyrus W. (M. E.), Hartsville, "
Crother James (Ch), Southfield, " .
Olds Henry S. (M. E.), New Salem
Trask J. N. (C. U.), "
Eastman David (C T.), "
Adams O. W., North Prescott, "
Cutler Calvin, Auburndale, Newton
Lummis Henry (M. E.), Newtonville, "
Clark J. B. (C. T.), " "
Eastman C. L. (M. E.), " " .
Worcester J. (Swed.), " " .
Furber D. L. (C. T.), Newton Centre, "
Stearns O. S. (B.), " "
Rogers C. S. (M. E.), Newton Corner, "
Steenstra P. H. (E.), " "
Tucker J. jr. (B.), " "
Wellman J. W. (C. T.), " "
Young E. J. (C. U.), " "
Coolidge J. W. (M. E.), Lower Falls, "
Putnam R. F. (E.), " "
True C. K. (M. E.), Upper Falls, "
Richards W. C. (B.), " "
Patrick H. J. (C. T.), West Newton "
Tiffany Francis (C. U.), " "
Hall Gordon (C. T.), Northampton
Hunt George (B.), "
Jenkins William L. (C. U.), "
Leavitt William S. (C. T.), "
Mansfield J. H. (M. E), "
Moyce P. V. (R. C.), "
Marshall Royal (E.), "
Burleigh Charles C. (Free Cong.) "
Florence, "
Cobb Elisha G. (C. L.), " "
Day John S. (M. E.), North Andover
Hamilton B. F. (C. T.), "
Vinal Charles C. (C. U.), "
Allen Joseph (C. U.), Northborough
Lamson D. F. (B.), "
Myrick H. L. (C. U.), "
Sanborn G. E. (C. T.), "
Willard M. Harding (C. T.), Northbridge
Adams R. G. (M. E.), Whitinsville, "
Clark Lewis F. (C. T.), "
Howson John (M. E.), North Bridgewater
McNuhy Thomas B. (R. C.), "
Stevens H. A. (C. T.), "
Wood Charles W. (C. T.), Campello, "
Beecher W. H. (C. T.), North Brookfield
Bent G. R. (M. E.), "
De Bevoise G. H. (C. T.), "
Dodge J. (C. T.), "
Smith H. M. (R. C.), "
Bessom —— (C. T.), North Chelsea
Senter J. Herbert (C. U.), "
Clark T. J. (C. T.), Northfield
Noyes Charles (C. U.), "
Ashley A. W. (B.), North Reading
Jones Thomas N. (C. T.), "
Coburn Washington L. (C. B.), Norton
Potter D. S. C. M. (C. U.), "
Halliday J. C. (C. T.), Oakham
Baker H. H. (Uv.), Orange
Foster A. B. (C. T.), "
Garmon John H. (C. T.), N. Orange, "
Hooper William H. (Uv.), " "
Gavitt Franklin (M. E.), Orleans
Poland James W. (B.), "

Orleans
Willis J. H. (Uv.), East Orleans, "
Wright John E. M. (Pres.), " "
Hall Thomas A. (C. T.), Otis
Jones Henry M. (B.), "
Austin Samuel J. (C. T.), Oxford
Brooks William H. (E.), "
Cushman I. S. (M. E.), "
Davenport J. E. (Uv.), "
Quan James (R. C.), "
Shedd William (B.), North Oxford, "
Vaill Joseph (C. T.), Palmer
Fullerton B. M. (C. T.), "
Haynes E. M. (B.), "
Bond William B. (C. T.), Thorndike, "
Shepardson —— (B.), Three Rivers, "
Phipps William (C. T.), Paxton
Galvin Edward I. (C. ..), Peabody
Hanson C. V. (B.), "
Hervey A. B. (Uv.), "
Knowles J. K. (M. E.), "
Noon John (M. E.), Pelham
Doggett T. P. (C. U.), Pembroke
Fletcher E. S. (M. E.), "
Babbidge Charles (C. U.), Pepperell
Barney —— (M.), "
Blake S. L. (C. T.), "
Jewett John C. B. (C. T.), "
Goddard Daniel F. (C. U.), Petersham
Shepardson John (B.), "
Stowell A. (C. T.), "
White Lyman (C. T.), Phillipston
Burdick Charles T. (M. E.), Pittsfield
Cummins John (R. C.), "
Purcell Edward H. (R. C.), "
Richards William C. (B.), "
Simmons J. J. (German Cong.), "
Strong Edward (C. T.), "
Todd John (C. T.), "
Watson D. S. (B.), "
Wells Edward L. (E.), "
Wentworth Erastus (M. E.), "
Damon Thos. (Shaker), W. Pittsfield, "
Clark Solomon (C. T.), Plainfield
Bremner David (C. T.), Plymouth
Brown —— (Adv.), "
Martin Harry H. (M.), "
Moody R. B. (B.), "
Fuller Alex. T. (C. T.), Chiltonville, "
Miller Wallace T. " "
Woodbury Samuel (C. T.), " "
Bancroft D. (C. T.), Prescott
Jones N. B. (B.), North Prescott, "
Cole J. Wesley (M. E.), Princeton
Leader Shadrack (M. E.), Provincetown
Davis —— (Uv.), "
McReading Charles S. (M. E.), "
Bisby Herman (Uv.), Quincy
Channing G. G. (C. U.) (Sailors' Snug Harbor), "
Frignglietti F. (R. C.), "
Hall James E. (C. T.), "
McClary H.
Stone D. J. (B.), "
Sullivan J. F. (R. C.), "
Wells John D. (C. U.), "
Laberee John C. (C. T.), Randolph
Denver W. J. J. (R. C.), "
Pryor John H. (B.), "
Russell E. East Randolph, "
Edson Ambler (C. B.), Raynham
Fiske Frederick H. (C. T.), "
Reed Frederick A. (C. T.), "
Barrows William H. (C. T.), Reading
Crawley Thomas W. (B.), "
Willcox William H. (C. T.), "
Coombs John (B.), Rehoboth
Johnson T. N. (C. T.), "

Clergymen—continued.

Sanford C. S. (M. E.),	Rehoboth
Coon Alfred (M. E.),	Richmond
Niel Henry (C. T.),	"
Cushing James R. (C. T.),	Rochester
Sweet Hiram (M.),	"
Acquaron L. (R. C.),	"
Ames Jarvis A. (M. E.),	Rockport
Vibbert George H. (Uv.),	"
Holmes —— (B.),	"
Bicknell William A. (C. U.),	Rowe
Wilmarth J. C. (B.),	"
Lyford Edward T. (B.),	Rowley
Pike John (C. T.),	"
Brooks Charles (B.),	Royalston
Bullard Ebenezer W. (C. T.),	"
Medbury J. H. (B.),	"
Cummings Henry (C. T.),	Russell
Atwood E. S. (C. T.),	Rutland
Batchelor George (O. U.),	Salem
Beane Samuel C. (C. U.),	"
Chase S. Freeman (M. E.),	"
Delahunty John (R. C.),	"
Elder Hugh (C. T.),	"
Emerson Brown (C. T.),	"
Felt J. B. (C. T.),	"
Gray John J. (R. C.),	"
Halley William (R. C.),	"
Hewes James T.	"
Jewett George B. (C. T.),	"
Johnson Samuel, jr. (C. U.),	"
Jordan Leonard G. (N. J.),	"
Kidder Joseph (E.),	"
Mills R. C. (B.),	"
Palmer C. R. (C. T.),	"
Pratt S. Hartwell (B.),	"
Russell John L. (C. U.),	"
Spaulding Willard (Uv.),	"
Very Jones (C. U.),	"
Wendell Rufus (S. A.),	"
Willson E. B. (C. U.),	"
Jameson Ephraim O. (C. T.),	Salisbury
Morton Albert G. (Ch.),	"
Sawyer Benjamin (C. T.),	"
Currier James (M. E.),	E. Salisbury, "
Gill O. H.	Amesbury, "
Safford H. G. (B.),	" "
Bradbury —— (C. T.),	Sandisfield
Teeple George (S. A.),	"
Maine R. H. (B.),	Montville, "
Bertolff Peter (R. C.),	Sandwich
Brown Thomas W. (C. U.)	"
Johnson Wilbur (Pres.),	"
Young Charles (M. E.),	"
Marsh Joseph (M.),	Pocasset, "
Whilden S. F. (M. E.),	W. Sandwich "
Blanchard William J. (S. A.),	Savoy
Deming Amos (B.),	"
McCulloch Eusebius (S. A.),	"
Pease David (B.),	Saugus Centre, Saugus
Greenwood T. J. (Uv.),	" "
Bassett J. F. (M. E.),	Cliftondale, "
Wood Pliny (M. E.),	East Saugus, "
Newell F. C. (M. E.),	Scituate
Conant Thomas (B.),	North Scituate, "
Kelton William (B.),	" "
Sessions A. J. (C. T.),	" "
Rhodes Amasa M. (Uv.),	Seekonk
Bryant S. I. (C. T.),	Sharon
Edwards B. A. (B.),	"
Stacy G. W. (C. T.),	"
Sabier D'Dubois (C. T.),	Sheffield
Towasend G. D. (M. E.),	"
Wright C. (M. E.),	Ashley Falls, "
Billings R. S. (C. T.),	Shelburne
Boyd P. S.	Shelburne Falls, "
Goodhue J. A. (B.),	" "
Moore E. J. (M. E.),	" "

	Shelburne
	Shelburne Falls, "
Stevenson V. B. (Uv.),	" "
Brown William (C. U.),	Sherborn
Dowse Edmund (C. T.),	"
Chandler Seth (C. U.),	"
Robbins E. (B.),	Shirley
Dutton A. I. (C. T.),	Shirley Village, "
Dyer E. Porter (C. T.),	Shrewsbury
Hascall Jefferson (M. E.),	"
Peterson John (M. E.),	"
Lentell J. V. (B.),	Shutesbury
Vaill William H. (C. T.),	"
Perry C. A. (M. E.),	Lock's Village, "
Carroll S. C. (M. E.),	Somerset
Clark Nelson (C. T.),	"
Haley J. W. (C. B.),	"
Hyde Edward T. (M. E.),	"
Tingley T. C. (B.),	"
Durell J. W. (E.),	Somerville
Page H. P. (E.),	"
Sweet John D. (B.),	"
Eastman L. R. jr. (C. T.),	E. Somerville, "
Miller J. J. (B.),	" "
Russ B. K. (Uv.),	" "
Virgin —— (C. T.)	" "
Barber H. H. (C. U.)	N. Somerville, "
Smith B. A. (C. T.),	Southampton
Colby John, "	Southborough
Hobbs S. L. (C. T.),	"
Watson W. H.	"
Wingate Charles (E.),	"
Barret A. M. (R. C.),	Southbridge
Braman —— (M. E.),	"
Bronson B. F. (B.),	"
Flint F. C. (Uv.),	"
Palmer E. B. (C. T.),	"
Dodge A. M. (Union),	Globe Village, "
Greene John B. (C. T.),	South Hadley
Morrill A. K. (M.),	S. Hadley Falls, "
Fisher George E. (C. T.),	"
Knight Richard (C. T.),	"
Fish Wm. H. (C. U.),	South Scituate
Perry W. A. (Uv.),	"
Dearborn D. A. (B.),	Southwick
Woodbury J. J. (M.),	"
Cruickshanks James, (C. T.),	Spencer
George N. D. (M. E.),	"
Peters Albert (R. C.),	"
Bailey G. W. (M. E.),	Springfield
Buckingham S. G. (C. T.),	"
Cone Luther H. (C. T.),	"
Galligher M. P. (R. C.),	"
Greene R. G. (C. T.),	"
Harrison Samuel (C. T.),	"
Hills Charles D. (M. E.),	"
Humphreys Charles S. (C. U.),	"
Ide George B. (B.),	"
McKnight George H. (E.),	"
Merrill Charles A. (M. E.),	"
Nye H. R. (Uv.),	"
Parsons Henry M. (C. T.),	"
Potter A. K. (B.),	"
Rice William (M. E.),	"
Roy Samuel (M. E.),	"
Scott Joseph (M. E.),	"
Trafton Mark (C. T.),	"
Haley P. (R. C.),	Indian Orchard, "
Cheever Samuel (B.),	Sterling
Nickerson A. S. (C. U.),	"
Allen Henry F. (E.),	Stockbridge
Eggleston Nathl. H. (C. T.),	"
Lawrence Amos (C. T.),	"
Dole George T. (C. T.),	Curtisville, "
Byington Swift (C. T.),	Stoneham
Fairchild E. B. (B.),	"
Parkhurst M. M. (M. E.),	"
Skinner Geo. W. (Ch.),	"

Chambreo A. St. John (Uv.), Stoughton
Paige A. W. (M. E.), "
Wilson Thomas (C. T.), "
Smith Charles M. (B.), E. Stoughton, "
Ball Wm. R. (M. E), No. Stoughton, "
Fuller R. W. (C. T.), Stow
DeForest J. E. (M. E.), Assabet, "
Caldwell Augustine (M. E.), Rock
  Bottom, "
Edes S. (C. U.), Sturbridge
Farrar J. P. (B.), "
Richardson M. (Pres.), "
Chapman George A. (M. E.), Sudbury
Patterson —— (C. T.), "
Peck David (C. i.), Sunderland
Fuller Willard (F. B.), Sutton
Lyman George (C. T.), "
Burbank J. P. (B.), Whitinsville, "
Spear Samuel S. (E.), Wilkinsonville, "
Abbott T. J. (M. E.) Swampscott
Dale H. U. (Ch.), "
Thompson John (C. T.), "
Ware F. W. (C. U.), "
Heaton George (E.), Swansea
Osborne J. W. (Ch.), "
Baskwell John A. (C. B.), North
  Swansea, "
Blake Mortimer (C. T.), Taunton
Berns M. J. (R. C.), "
Cobb R. H. (city mission), "
Conger E. L. (Uv.), "
Dunham Isaac (Union Cong.), "
Emery J. C. (Ch.), "
Maltby Erastus (C. T.), "
Miles George D. (E.), "
Pollard Andrew (B.), "
Quinn Francis (R. C.), "
Richmond T. T. (C. T.), "
Robinson Henry (M. E.), "
Rogers Robert C. (E.), "
Shahan Thomas H. (R. C.), "
Titus Charles H. (M. E.), "
Webber Charles H. (F. B.), "
Reed Frederick A. (C. T.), E. Taunton, "
Ward James (Cong.), "
Adams Edwin G. (C. U.), Templeton
Bushnell Gerard (Uv.), "
Sabin Lewis (C. T.), "
Orr William (R. C.), Otter River, "
Fletcher Clifton (B.), Tewksbury
Telman Richard (C. T.), "
Dixon Samuel (M. E.), Tisbury
Edson Edward (M. E.), "
Marshall H. B. (B.), "
Stephens Daniel W. (Uv.), "
Thomas S. A. (B.), "
Sturtevant Wm. H. (C. T.), West
  Tisbury, "
Ford George (C. T.), Tolland
Bridge William D. (M. E.), Topsfield
McLoud Auson (C. T.), "
Howard A. K. (M. E.), Townsend
Williams George S. (C. T.), "
Upham —— (B.), West Townsend, "
Gill Jason (M. E.), Truro
Noble Edward W. (C. T.), "
Sayer E. L. (M. E.), "
Stokes Charles (Ch.), N. Truro, "
Todd William G. (C. U.), Tyngsborough
Phippin George (B.), Tyringham
Lamdon —— (M. E.), South Lee, "
Ball George S. (C. U.), Upton
Dyer S. G. (C. T.), "
Burr Rushton D. (C. U.), Uxbridge
Barber Joseph (B.), "
Pison Thomas C. (C. T.), "
O'Keefe D. A. (R. C.), "
Society of Friends, "

Atkins Daniel (M. E.), Wakefield
Bliss Charles R. (C. T.), "
Hayward Wm. W. (Uv.), "
Scully Thomas (R. C.), "
Wilmarth James W. (B.), "
Hughes George (M. E.), Wales
Partridge Lyman (B.), "
Smith Wm. B. (C. U.), Walpole
Thurber Edward G. (C. T.), "
Bacon A. M. (B.), Waltham
Chapin Daniel E. (M. E.), "
Fales T. F. (E.), "
Flagg S. B. (C. U.), "
Flood Bernard (R. C.), "
Smith Benton (Uv.), "
Strong E. E. (C. T.), "
Worcester Benjamin (Swed.), "
Eaton G. F. (M. E.), Ware
Hudson John W. (C. U.), "
Moran Wm. (R. C.), "
Perkins A. E. P. (C. T.), "
Tuttle W. G. (C. T.), "
Carter Chas. F. (M. E.), Wareham
Cleary T. C. (C. T.), "
Austin S. J. (C. T.), Warren
Moore John H. (Uv.), "
Treadwell Thos. B. (M. E.), "
Sames A. H. (C. T.), West Warren, "
Bissell —— (C. T.), Warwick
Shepardson L. F. (B.), "
Willard —— (C. U.), "
Brown Jesse (M. E.), Washington
Bell James M. (C. T.), Watertown
McCarthy John (R. C.), "
Richardson Daniel (M. E.), "
Stubbert Wm. F. (B.), "
Weiss John (C. U.), "
Drake Ellis R. (C. T.), Wayland
Frost Leonard P. (M. E.), "
Robins Samuel D. (C. M.), "
Bean D. M. (C. T.), Webster
Hamilton A. C. (M. E.), "
Quan James (R. C.), "
Reding C. W. (B.), "
Nasou Charles (W. M.), Wellfleet
Fairley Samuel (C. T.), "
Brigham Willard (C. T.), S. Wellfleet, "
Piper C. W. (C. T.), Wendell
Gorham Abner D. (B.), Wenham
Jocelyn William (C. T.), "
Dean Artemas (C. T.), Westborough
Flanders Charles W. (B.), "
Nottage Wm. A. (M. E.), "
Litch J. L. (2d Adv.), "
Bromley Edwin C. (B.), West Boylston
Fitts James H. (C. T.), "
Murdock Wm. (C. T.), "
Judd Burtis (M. E.), Oakdale, "
Forman Jacob G. (C. U.), W. Bridgewater
Pasco Cephas (B.), "
Mather James (M. E.), Cochesett, "
Dunham Samuel (C. T.), West Brookfield
Marcy I. (M. E.), "
Chapin Martin C. (M. E.), Westfield
Hopkins Henry (C. T.), "
Jennings John J. (B.), "
Mansfield —— (M. E.), "
Miglionico —— (R. C.), "
Richardson E. H. (C. T.), "
Abbott E. (C. U.), Westford
Hodgman E. R. (C. T.), "
Luce L. (C. T.), "
Woodruff Henry D. (C. T.), "
Young George H. (C. U.), "
Allender Thomas (C. T.), West Hampton
Johnson R. G. (B.), Westminster
Proctor George (Uv.), "
Rich A. J. (C. T.), "

Clergymen — continued.

Barrett L. G. (B.),
Sears E. H. (C. U),   Weston
Sutherland George (M. E.),   "
Dean Gardner (B.),   "
Leonard H. L. (C. T.),   Westport
Parris J. R.   "
Snow Elder (B.),   "
Tripp Gideon W. (B.), Central Village,   "
Hubbell W. S. (C. T.),   West Roxbury
Miller H. F. H. (Union),   "
Babcock W. R. (E.), Jamaica Plain,   "
Gordon A. J. (B.),   "
Perkins F. B. (C. C.),   "
Bishop —— (M. E.),   "
Thompson J. W. (C. U.),   "   "
                                  West Springfield
Grout —— (C. T.), Mittineague,   "
Clark P. K. (C. T.),   "
Coons Alfred (M. E.),   West Stockbridge
Pomeroy Samuel (B.),   "
Pennell L. (C. T.), West Stockbridge
Centre,   "
Brown Olympia Miss (Uv.),   Weymouth
Cole Gideon (B.),   "
Ellsworth A. A. (C. T.),   "
Street —— (E.).   "
Morrison Wm. V. (M. E.), East Wey-
mouth,   "   "
Waldron Daniel W. (C. T.), "   "
Emery J. (C. T.), North Weymouth,   "
Rockwood S. L. (C. T.), "   "
Hayes S. H. (C. T.), South   "   "
Terry J. P. (C. T.),   "   "   "
Lane John B. (C. T.),   Whately
Brannagin —— (M. E.),   Wilbraham
Cooke Edward (M. E.),   "
Fisk Franklin (M. E.),   "
Furber Franklin (M. E.),   "
Howard —— (C. T.),   "
Howe A. S. (M. E.),   "
Hurcult Jona. (M. E.),   "
Jagger William S (M. E.),   "
Read Wm. (B.), South Wilbraham,
Toulman W. B. (M. E.), "   "
Pomfret William J. (C. T.),   Williamsburg
Bascom John (C. T.),   Williamstown
Durfee Calvin (C. T.),   "
Fitch George W. (M. E.),   "
Hopkins Mark (C. T.),   "
Perry Arthur L (C. T.),   "
Tatlock John (C. T.),   "
Wells E. P. (C. C.),   "
Tolman Samuel H. (C. T.),   Wilmington
Foster D. (C. T.),   Winchendon
Hitchcock Milan H. (C. T.),   "
Marvin Abijah P. (C. T.),   "
Pentecost William (M. E.),   "
Wheeler Charles (C. U.),   Winchendon
Bronson S. J. (B.),   Winchester
Metcalf Richard (C. U.),   "
Robinson R. T. (C. T.),   "
Holman Sydney (Pres.),   Windsor
Dadman John W. (M. E.),   Winthrop
Dunham Howard C. (M. E.),   "
Short John (M. E.),   "
Barnes William (C. U.),   Woburn
Dennen S. R. (C. T.),   "
Lansing John F. (M. E.),   "
Mayo Wm. (Swed.),   "
Porter G. W. (E.),   "
Qualey John (R. C.),   "
Townley H. C. (B.),   "
Wheeler M. G. (C. T.), North Woburn,   "
Blaisdell F. (Ch.),   Worcester
Bowles B. F. (Uv.),   "
Carroll A. (M. E.),   "
Cheever H. T. (C. T.),   "

Cutler E. (C. T.)   Worcester
Huntington Wm. R. (E.),   "
Mansfield J. H. (M. E.),   "
Peck J. O. (M. E.),   "
Pervear H. K. (B.),   "
Power William (R. C.),   "
Power J. J. (R. C.),   "
Richardson Merrill (C. T.),   "
O'Reilley P. T. (R. C.),   "
Shippen R. R. (C. U.),   "
Smith C. N. (M. E.),   "
Stratton R. B. (C. T.),   "
Sweetser S. (C. T.)   "
Virgin E. W. (M. E.),   "
Walker Allen (colored M. E.),   "
Weston D. (B.),   "
Chase B. F. (M. E.), New Worcester,   "
Morgan D. S (C. T.),   Worthington
Gordon Wm. (M. E.), S. Worthington,   "
Allen N. G. (E.),   Wrentham
Tompkins William R. (C. T.),   "
Dwight John (C. T.), N. Wrentham,   "
Rounds Daniel B.,   "   "
Boomer J. C. (B.), S. Yarmouth, Yarmouth
Bowdish L. (M. E.),   "   "
Cady Lawton (M. E.), Yarmouth Port,   "
Eaton Joshua T. (Swed.),   "
Lincoln Varnum (Uv.),   "   "
Perry J. P. (Swed.),   "   "

Cloaks and Mantillas.

Gifford Perry,   Fall River
Sherrer, Rice, & Co.   "
Pattillo Alex.   Gloucester
Flanders & Co.   Haverhill
Russell S. P. Mrs.   "
                                   Lowell
ABBOTT & EAMES, 132 Merrimac,   "
White M. C. (manuf.),   New Bedford
Baker Semantha,   Pittsfield
Wood & Garlick,   "
Curtis Charles,   Taunton
Hudson M. T. Mrs.   Worcester

Clocks.

(*See also Jewelry, Watches, &c.*)
Williams & Hatch,   North Attleborough
WRUCK F. A., 195 Essex (see page
748);   Salem

Clothes Cleaners.

Browning Willis,   Lynn
Choate Ezekiel W.   "
Flinn Frank M.   "
Fowler Edward.   "
Greenige Geo. W.   "
Harvey Jeremiah P.   "
Adams Stephen,   Plymouth

Clothes Wringers, Manufs.

                                   Waltham
Eureka Clothes Wringer Manuf. Co., "

Clothing.

(*See also Tailors.*)
Estes & Whiting, E. Abington,   Abington
Wilde Chas. M.   Long Plain,   Acushnet
Smith George W.   Adams
BRIGGS & BOLAND,   N. Adams, "
Fibel H. & Co.   "   "
Goldstone & Gastlick,   "   "
Holbrook & Bates,   "   "
Martin William,   "   "
Brown S. J. & Co.   Amesbury
Baker & Lapham,   Amherst
Pease Oliver & Co.   "
Dean John H.   Andover

Logue Daniel,	Andover
West J. N.	Ashland
Woodbury S. F.	"
Bixby William, Athol Depot,	Athol
Everett A. M.	Attleborough
Devlin Daniel, N. Attleborough,	"
Miller George,	Barnstable
Hallett A. C. Hyannis,	"
Orcutt F. V.	"
Barnes Wright,	Barre
Bridgman E. R.	Becket
Burnham Charles L.	Belchertown
Woodbury Henry,	Beverly.
Knowles & Freeman,	"
Shifeldt Isaac,	Brewster
Crane J. E.	Brookline
Howes Phineas,	Bridgewater
Rogers J. H. & Co.	"
	Brookfield
	Buckland
Strong & Ferary, Shelburne Falls,	"
Bartlett William B.	Cambridge
Burbank, Smith, & Co., Camb'dgeport,	"
DOYLE JOSEPH, 361 Main (second	
hand), Cambridgeport,	"
Fuller C. C. W. & Co. "	"
Levy Abraham, "	"
Roaf Robert N. "	"
PETTINGELL & SAWYER (oil, see	
page 762), E. Cambridge,	"
Grant Charles H.	Canton
Leavitt Joseph,	
Klous E. J.	Charlestown
Klous Louis,	"
Levy S. (second hand),	"
Packman Bowman,	"
Reinstein Oscar,	"
Spear James E. & Co.	"
Howard Edward,	Chatham
Currier James M.	Chelsea
Little Omar,	"
Pike J. J.	"
Bickford D. P. & Co.	Chicopee
Buckingham & Co.	"
Hitchcock & Hosley,	"
Hall & Tyler, Chicopee Falls,	"
Field C. W. & Son,	Clinton
Frazer & Fairbanks,	"
McQuaid T. A. & S.	"
Russell G. A.	"
Stewart R. S.	Coleraine
Tuttle Frank,	Concord
Lovell D. W.	"
Orcutt N. F.	Cummington
Richards D. L.	"
Greenwood M. East Dedham,	Dana
Norris S. M. "	Dedham
Jones A. F.	"
Rogers Wales,	Douglas
Allen S. B.	East Bridgewater
Strong W. V. Joppa,	"
Munroe J. H.	East Hampton
Osborn Samuel, jr.	Edgartown
Boyd Joel,	"
Howes Charles,	Essex
Williams T. D. & Co.	"
Ashley William H.	Fairhaven
Brennan M. W.	Fall River
Bromberg Bros.	"
Davol John jr.	"
Frank Charles,	"
Gibbs R. S. & Co.	"
McKenney Felix,	"
McKevitt Hugh,	"
Parkinson John T. (second-hand).	"
Riley Thomas,	"
Taylor & Co.	"
Wilbur & Gray,	"
Davis E. H.	"
	Falmouth

Carleton M. & Co.	Fitchburg
Cross Daniel,	"
Farnsworth L. B.	"
Goodrich Henry A.	"
Kittredge & Saxton,	"
Manning Joseph E.	"
Butterworth George H.	Foxborough
Nichols E. O.	"
Thompson B. Saxonville,	Framingham
Wood Levi W.	Gardner
Osgood Stephen,	Georgetown
Plumer Samuel,	"
Barrett C. P.	Gloucester
Bennett & Marr,	"
CARTER. J. F. (oil, see page 749),	"
Lawrence R. G.	"
Parkhurst E. A.	"
Rogers Charles H.	
Stacy E. F.	
Tappan J. S.	"
Jackson Daniel, Lanesville,	"
Cohen Brothers, Great Barrington	
Hubbell Andrew L.	"
Bailey Loren N.	Greenfield
Cohn Marcus,	"
Seward & Willard,	"
Tenney J. C. Groton Junction,	Groton
Curtis Henry J.	Hanover
Stetson I. G. & Co.	"
Brett Charles E.	Harwich
Weeks & Small, So. Harwich,	"
Chase Erastus & Co. West Harwich,	"
Butrick & Paul,	Haverhill
Kerrigan A. P. J.	"
Taylors Three	"
Wheeler J. S.	"
Todd John,	Hingham
Fiske George B. & Co.	Holliston
Whiting E. F.	"
Adler D.	Holyoke
Johnson, Luddington, & Co.	"
Miller & Co.	"
MITCHELL BROS.	"
Claflin Arthur M.	Hopkinton
Minturn W. E.	"
Hutchins & Co.	Hudson
Ring Sanford B.	"
Wheeler Nathan H.	"
Luce & Ingersoll,	Hyde Park
Baker S. N. jr.	Ipswich
Jordan Robert,	"
Fuller Frank, (manuf.),	Kingston
Atkinson J. B.	Lawrence
Bedell & Foster,	"
Bicknell Jas. jr.	"
Conlin Bros.	"
Dodge Marcus S.	"
Fairfield James M. & Co.	"
Fuller A. & Co.	"
Hills George W.	"
Hall D. S. & Co.,	"
Hodgman & Bartlett,	"
Levy Solomon,	"
Moore W. H.	"
Savage & Flood,	"
Simons A. & Co.	"
Spalding William R.	"
Weil Louis & Co.	"
Barnes John S. E.	Lee
Lyman & Chaffee,	"
Nelser M. & Co.	"
Thurston & Wheelock,	Leominster
Bowers A. E.	Lowell
Cushing Geo. S.	"
Fox Warren & Co.	"
French Abram & Co.	"
Gage & Jewell,	"
Green Geo. W. (manuf.),	"

Clothing — continued.

Grover & Harvey,　　　　Lowell
Haberstad H.　　　　　"
Hirshfield Herman,　　　"
Huse H. E.　　　　　"
Kileski H.　　　　　"
Putnam Addison,　　　　"
Richardson A. B. & Co.　　"
Ritchie J P.　　　　　"
Warren A. R.　　　　"
Wheeler Joseph A.　　　"
White Josiah,　　　　"
Woodward A. G.　　　　"
Worcester L. (manuf.),　　"
Badger D. N. jr.　　　　Lynn
Bray G. & Son,　　　　"
Butman M.　　　　　"
Chase James & Co.　　　"
Chase Moses,　　　　"
Cross Alfred & Co.　　　"
Currier B. H. & Co.　　　"
Harney & Seaverns,　　　"
Union Store 676, Moses Chase, agent,　"
Valpey Samuel B.　　　"
Graves Samuel, jr.　　　Marblehead
Selman Benjamin,　　　"
Hutchins E. E.　　　Marlborough
Roafe & Stocker,　　　"
Witherbee Nahum,　　　"
Sparrow J. Augustine,　Middleborough
Toole Michael,　　　　"
Aylward R. Mrs. (boy's),　　Milford
Barker & Whiting,　　　"
Brown C. D.　　　　"
Harris B. E.　　　　"
Fox & Beatly,　　　　"
Lewis Bros.　　　　"
Walker Frederick,　　　"
CATHCART CHARLES S.　Nantucket
Hallett John W.　　　　"
Edgerton L. R.　　　　Natick
Flynn W. J. & Co.　　　"
Edwards W.　　South Natick.
BARNETT JOHN, 104 Union, New Bedford
DeWolf A. J. (second-hand),　"
Doane, Swift, & Co.　　　"
Dootson John,　　　　"
Geils Garrett (second-hand),　"
Gifford N. T. & Co.　　　"
Goldsmith Gustavus,　　"
Harrington J. (second-hand),　"
Kelley Mirriam　　　"
Lucas A. E.　　　　"
Matthews Martha, (second-hand),　"
Openshaw Mary, (second-hand),　"
Packard E.　　　　"
Pedro J. H.　　　　"
Perry Francis T.　　　"
Pope, Richardson, & Co. (seamen's),　"
Roberts Joseph,　　　"
Sanders William,　　　"
Slocum Peleg & Co. (seamen's),　"
Swift Moses C.　　　"
Sylvia A. L.　　　　"
Tabor, Read, & Co.　　　"
Thomas Antoine (seamen's),　"
TUCKER HENRY R. 39 & 41 No.
　Water,　　　　"
Tucker William jr. (seamen's),　"
Ward R. C.　　　　"
Weaver E. & Co. (children's),　"
Wing J. & W. R. & Co.　　"
Williams F. D. & Co.　　"
Wordell Allen (seamen's),　"
Ballou C. N.　　　Newburyport
Ballou J. W.　　　　"
Dennett H. N.　　　　"
Griffiths Rufus S.　　　"

Hart J. S.　　　　Newburyport
Lunt Henry & Co.　　　"
Quinn Thomas (second-hand),　"
Smith F. W. & Co.　　　"
Toppin C. C.　　　　"
Welch Richard,　　　"
Jackson Wm. W.　Lower Falls, Newton
Clark Merritt,　　　Northampton
Cohn S. & M.　　　"
Draper J. L.　　　　"
French & Abbott,　　　"
Smith & Prindle,　　　"
Chesboro George L.　　Northborough
Montague R.　　　　"
Brett H. A.　　North Bridgewater
Bryant G. E. & H. L.　　"
Howard & Caldwell,　　"
Bartlett A. W.　　North Brookfield
TUCKER L.　　　　"
Ballou Warren S.　　　Orange
Dodge F. G.　　　　"
CUMMINGS JOSEPH H.　Orleans
Young Jonathan,　　　"
Shaw J. P.　　　　Palmer
Bott S. R.　　　　Peabody
Parker H. A. & Co. East Village, Pepperel
Saunders Amos J. Pepperell Centre,　"
Cohen & Wolf,　　　Pittsfield
Davis, Taylor, & Kelly,　"
Newman Isaac,　　　"
Atwood William 2d,　　Plymouth
Peterson Lewis & Son,　"
ADAMS WILLIAM,　Provincetown
Nickerson James H.　　"
Small J. F.　　　　"
Lombard J. W.　　　Quincy
Hoffman L.　　　　Randolph
Fletcher Franklin,　　Reading
Stickney J. E.　　　Rockport
Ashton William B.　　Salem
Bennett Abraham,　　"
Carpenter David P.　　"
Griffen E. & J. S.　　"
Jones G. & Co.　　　"
McCarn Daniel,　　　"
McKey John,　　　"
Norris C. H.　　　"
Palmer William H.　　"
Peck F. S.　　　　"
Quinn & Kelly,　　　"
Saroni E. Mrs. (children's),　"
Savory Wm. T.　　　Salisbury
Boyd C. A.　　Amesbury,　"
Livingston Herman,　　"
Merrill J. H.　　　Sandisfield
Taylor & Castle,　　　"
Moore J.　　New Boston,　"
Parsons & Wilcox,　　"
Drew George P.　　　Sandwich
Burgess C. S.　　　"
Miller John Q.　　　"
Murray John,　　　"
Sherman T. C.　　　"
Reed William,　　　Savoy
Foster John H. Shelburne Falls, Shelburne
Green E. T.　　　　"
Sherwin A.　　　　"
Sanderson W. L.　　　Shirley
Chace Joseph & Co.　　Somerset
Simmons George W.　　"
Comstock & Perry,　　Southbridge
Edwards & Co.　　　"
Granger S. E. & Bro.　Southwick
Baldwin J. A.　　　Springfield
Beebe J,　　　　"
Brigham D. H. & Co.　　"
Culver W. R.　　　"
Haynes T. L. & Co.　　"

Keyes Henry & Co. Springfield
Miller, Allin, & Co. "
Packard Sidney, "
Heath J. B. & Co. Stoneham
Phipps Nathan, "
Rowe Henry, "
Wentworth Jennings, "
Gay Hiram, Stoughton
Bates, Haynes, & Co. Fiskdale. Sturbridge
Potter Benjamin, Swampscott
COLBY SAMUEL (see front colored page), 11 Union Blk. Taunton
Fox & Fisher, "
Giles Cubit (second-hand), "
Grant Charles H. "
Harris Wm. H. "
Holt Benjamin R. "
Norris Henry (second-hand), "
Simmons E. S. "
Steele & Baker, "
Crocker R. W. Tisbury
Thomas S. A. Holmes's Hole, "
Cram David, Townsend
Dix William, "
Osgood Charles, "
Wheeler L. C. Uxbridge
Webster R. G. Wales
Appell Adolph, Waltham
Bamber Asher, "
Delany James, "
Frye C. G. "
Guild Virgil, Ware
Judd A. & Co. "
Lawton J. R. "
Howard Benj. F. Wareham
Runnells Levi A. "
Wetherbee S. & J. Warren
Rogers A. B. Watertown
Rawson James M. Webster
Higgins Allen, Wellfleet
Rich Snow, "
Tobey J. F. "
Whorf & Higgins, "
Burnap H. A. & Co. Westborough
Goddard L. M. "
Blair E. H. West Brookfield
Foote W. H. & Co. Westfield
Morrissey Richard, "
Shurtleff George & Co. "
WESTON, LEWIS, & CO. "
Sabins C. H. West Stockbridge
READ M. H. Weymouth
Williams Charles S. "
Lout Henry, East Weymouth, "
Rosenfeld Edward, South " "
Wright Eleazer S. " " "
Thayer C. L. Whately
Carruth J. A. Winchendon
Raymond Silas, "
Hammond J. W. Woburn
Allis P. (boys), Worcester
Bigelow & Longley, "
Cheney R. Mrs. "
Davis A. & J. E. "
Doherty Hugh, "
Eames D. H. "
Estabrook & Herrick, "
Hollander G. "
Lewisson Louis, "
Perry & Paul, "
Ware A. P. & Co. "
Ware & Pratt (boys), "

Cloths and Woolen Goods.

COLBY SAMUEL (also clothing of all kinds, see front colored page), Taunton
Rawson Orville, Fall River

Coal and Wood.

(See also Wood and Bark.)

Nash J. I. Abington
Reed A. N. & Co. North Abington
Rand Edward A. North Adams, Adams
Westcott W. S. Amherst
Cornell John, Andover
PEIRCE J. WINSLOW, Arlington
Morse Ezra, Ashland
Tilton & Pike, "
Hooper Q. A. Attleborough
Smith Ebenezer, Barnstable
Hallet Lot, Hyannis, "
Hinckley Marshall, "
Hartshorn Edward, Berlin
Girdler John, Beverly
PICKETT JOHN, "
Aldrich C. B. Blackstone
Stetson A. Warren, Weymouth, Braintree
Knowles & Freeman, Brewster
Lincoln Warren & Co. "
Tufts Washington, Brookfield
Twitchell J. L. & Co. "
Bartlett D. C. Shelburne Falls, Buckland
Hubbard Appleton, Cambridge
Richardson William T. "
Baldwin & Co Cambridgeport, "
Packard & Shaw, " "
Holmes & Rugg, " "
Lawson William, " "
Lerned Thomas P. " "
Luke & Bent, " "
Smith Martin L. " "
Brooks Wm. C. & Co. E. Cambridge, "
Wellington Brothers, " "
Wyman William, " "
Barry Charles J. Charlestown
Barry Jotham & Co. "
Bruce E. L. & Co. "
Carleton A. "
Dix A. H. "
Fall S. H. "
Keyes Edmund, "
Knight S. & E. "
Murdock, Stearns, & Co. "
Nason R. & Co. "
Oakman & Eldredge, "
Perkins & Goodwin, "
Stockman C. W. "
Wellington A. H. "
Williams S. & G. "
Atwood Sears, Chatham
Nickerson Zenas, jr. "
Taylor Christopher, "
Taylor George, "
Campbell Jeremiah, Chelsea
Chelsea Fuel Co., Daniel Sampson, "
Evans Samuel H. & Son, "
Hardin James M. & Co. "
Nagel George, "
Perkins J. H. "
Tinkom G. H. & Co. "
Town & Co. "
Abbe A. B. Chicopee
Bemis Robert E. "
Johnson Allen, "
Morton M. Chicopee Falls, "
Jewell Henry, Clinton
Tower Abraham H. jr. Cohasset
Hudson B. N. Concord
Fisher Amory, Dedham
Hall Nathan, Dennis
Kelley Doane, Dennisport, "
Kelley & Sears, East Dennis, "
Studley Coleman, West " "
Cobb George & Son, Dighton
Whitmarsh Charles E. "

Coal and Wood — continued.

Robinson J. D　Neponset,　Dorchester
Heath S. W. & Co.　　　　Douglas
Jones A. F.　　　　　　　"
Loring John S.　　　　　Duxbury
Alden Samuel G.　·　East Bridgewater
Hobart John,　　　　　　"
Janes J. E. (wood),　East Hampton
Mayher J.　　　　　　　"
Darrow Ira,　　　　　Edgartown
Ripley T. P.　　　　　　"
FISH ROLAND,　　　　Fairhaven.
Batt Richard W.　　·　Fall River
BOWEN J. A. (coal. wholesale and　·
　retail, for family and steam pur-
　poses),　Morgan's wharf,　"
BROWN DANIEL & SON (see ·
　page 729), foot Central,　　"
COOK V. & CO., Central, cor. Pond,　"
COOK WM. M., foot Ferry st.,　　"
HAWKINS & KILHAM, (see page
　718), Slade's wharf,　　　"
Kingsley George F.　　　　"
SHOVE CLARK & Co., 40 Davol,　"
Slade John P.　　　　　　"
Fairbank Charles L. & Co,　Fitchburg
Garfield & Proctor,　　　　"
Whittemore Chas. S.　Framingham
Russegue A. A.　　　Franklin
Davis M. R. & Co.　　Freetown
Osgood Ezra,　　　　Gardner
Folsom Joseph P.　　Georgetown
Bennett & Reed,　　Gloucester
Friend Samuel K. & Co.　　"
Herrick & Cook,　　·　·　"
Porter E.　　　　　　"
Story & Boynton,　　·　　"
Wallace & Tarr,　　　　"
Wonson H. S.　　E. Gloucester,　"
Wonson Wm. C.　　　"　　"
Norton S. & Co.　　Great Barrington
Arms George A. & Co.　Greenfield
Balch Thomas H.　　Groveland
Bosworth Martin,　　·　Halifax
Church & Sylvester,　　Hanover
Kelly Ahira,　　　　Harwich
Kelley H. jr. & Co. Harwich Port,　"
Weeks & Small, ·South Harwich,　"
Hardy J. C. & Co.　　　Haverhill
SARGENT & HOLDEN (see page
　714), Steamboat wharf,　　"
Smiley Charles,　　　　"
Bassett Daniel,　　　Hingham
Marsh Caleb B.　　　"
Gallott Lambert,　　Holliston
Hawes Josiah,　　　"
Judd W. A.　　　Holyoke
MARTIN W. L. (see page 724),　·
Claflin C. W.　　　Hopkinton
Phipps William G.　　　"
NEWTON & WILKINS,　　Hudson
Wilkins Henry,　　　　"
BLODGETT & BARRETT,　Hyde Park
McAVOY & CO. Readville,　"
Brown Wm. G.　　　Ipswich
Dodge Richard T.　　"
Andrews O. & Co.　　Lawrence
Brown C. A.　　　　"
Call & True,　　　　"
Reed Rufus & Co.　　"
Runals & Hayden,　　"
Sanborn & Tucker,　　"
Dresser & Co.　　　"
Root Henry J.　　　Lee
Longley Luther,　　Lenox
Bennett & Rodliff,　Leominster
Brown Hiram,　　　Lowell
Durant & Simons,　　"

HILL E. A. (all kinds wood), 337
　Middlesex,　　　　Lowell
Horne D. W.　　　　"
Keys John.　　　　"
Kittredge Wm.　　　"
LEONARD A. W. (wood, see page
　739), Jackson, n. the Round House,　"
Livingston W. E.　　　"
McGuirk P.　　　　"
Breed Henry,　　　　Lynn
Breed Wm. N.　　　"
EDMANDS E. P. (see page 716),　　··
　Summer street,　　　··
Hopner & Whipple,
Lamper & Brothers,　　　"
Newhall Brothers,
Thing & Rowe,
Ramsdell Oliver,
Newhall Wm. M.　　West Lynn,　"
Jacobs Hale,　　　　Malden
Rhoades Chas. H.　　　"
Dixie Benjamin D.　　Marblehead
Gregory Joseph,　　　"
Humphreys & Twisden,　"
Pitman George E.　　　"
Fay C. L.　　　　Marlborough
SMITH S. & A.　　　"
Sparrow William E.　Mattapoisett
Curtis & Co.　　　Medfield
Angier Luther,　　　Medford
Cushing Pyam,　　　"
Joyce Oakman,　　　"
Mann Chas. W., West Medway, Medway
Marston Daniel G.　　"　　"
Smith John,　　　　Melrose
Le Barron John,　　Middleboro
Crosby & Putnam,　　Milford
Field & Bailey,　　　"
Eddy Justus,　　　Millbury
Todd & Gannett,　　Milton
Adams F. E. & Sons,　Nantucket
McCleave Joseph, ·　　"
Perry Edward W. & Co.　"
Skinner William H. (wood),　"
Robinson & Jones,　　Natick
Bird Charles,　South Natick,　"
Johnson Welcome J.　Nabant
Rice Charles, jr. Newton Lower
　Falls,　　　　Needham
Bird Charles,　South Natick,
Baxter N. G.　　　New Ashford
Delano Richard M.　New Bedford
Hart Samuel (wood).　　"
Haskell Edward P. (coal),　"
Hathaway B. F.
Howland B. Franklin,　　"
Macy P. S.　　　　"
Morse F. H.　　　　"
Perkins A. N.　　　"
Perry Ellis,　　　　"
Perry J. H. & Co.　　"
Robbins A. (granular fuel),　"
Ryder Benjamin,
Springer Andrew R.　　"
Brown Newman,　·　Newburyport
Coffin Amos,　　　"
Littlefield Hiram,　　"
Brackett A.　Newton Corner,　Newton
Bourne G. L. & C. B.　Auburndale,　"
Trowbridge & Hill,　Newton Centre,　"
Jones A. H.　　Lower Falls,　"
Rice Chas,　　　　"
Sanger D. C.　　West Newton,　"
McIntire Lewis,　　Northampton
Williams Joseph C.　　"
FLORENCE MERCANTILE CO.,
　H. K. Parsons agt.,　Florence,　"
Moore L. B.　　　"　　"

Bartlett F. D.
Hayward D.   Northborough
Packard Ellis,   North Bridgewater
FOSS N. J.   Campello,   "
Ayres William R.   North Brookfield
Mayo Joseph C.
Smith Thomas,   Orleans
Snow Aaron,   "
Rich Reuben,   "
Squier & Wood,   Oxford
Potter, Batchelder, & Co.   Palmer
Guild Gerry & Co.   Peabody
Root & Burns,   Pittsfield
SPRAGUE, LAWTON, & CO. (coal),   "
Cobb F. B.   Plymouth
Atwood John, jr. & Co.   Provincetown
BOWLEY J. E. & G.   "
COOK H. & S. & CO.   "
Freeman & Hilliard,   "
NICKERSON R. E. & A. & CO.   "
SMALL E. E.   "
UNION WHARF CO.   "
Adams Eben & Son, Quincy Point, Quincy
Adams Owen,   "   "
Lee R. L. (granular fuel),   "   "
Thayer Daniel W., E. Randolph, Randolph
Boyce Robert M.   Reading
Parker Henry F.   "
Davis John, 2d,   "
Goff Zenas H.   Rehoboth
Lane Leverett,   Rockport
Marshall Lafayette,   "
Tarr D. T. & Co.   "
Marchant Wm.   Pigeon Cove,   "
BROOKS AUGUSTUS T. (coal),
117 Derby,   Salem
Clark Joseph,   "
Dodge J. L.   "
Fairfield James,   "
Grover John,   "
HATCH L. B. 113 Derby,   "
MANNING R. C. & CO. 189 Derby,   "
PHILLIPS W. P. Phillips' wharf, and
  Central cor. Essex (see page 746), "
PICKERING WM. jr. 17 Peabody,   "
Sanborn G. & F. T.   "
Smith L. A.   "
Wiggin & Clark,   "
Fowler Everett (coal), Amesbury,   Salisbury
Kingsbury Henry & Co.   "   "
Allen William P.   "
Bartlett D. C., Shelburne Falls, Shelburne
Davis David P.   Scituate
Wyatt George,   Somerset
Olney D. K. & Co.
Abbey Abner B.   Southbridge
Banks J. H. & Son,   Springfield
BEMIS, PHILLIPS, & CO.   "
Chapin A. W.   "
GRAY HENRY & SONS, 86 Main,   "
Mills Isaac,   "
Church T. L. & J. H.   "
Padelford D.   Taunton
STAPLES & PHILLIPS, 27 West
  Water (see page 759)   "
Stephens Charles E.   "
Smith David,   Holmes's Hole,   Tisbury
Dyer Samuel,   Truro
Hopkins Smith R.   North Truro,   "
Knowlton William,   "
Macomber J. M.   Upton
Taft & Spencer,   Uxbridge
Ahern Geo. W.   "
Coombs S. G. B.   Wakefield
CLARK F. F.   "
Larned A. H.   Waltham
Parmenter J. W. & Co.   "

Warren J. L.   "
Holden D.   Waltham
                                      Ware
GURNEY ANSEL S. (see page 774),   Wareham
Bosworth John,   "
Brigham F.   Warren
Fairbanks A.   "
Gilkey Royal & Co.
Goddard Joel,   Watertown
Central Trading Co.   Webster
Baker N. M. & Co.   Wellfleet
Newcomb, Kemp, & Co.   "
Southern Wharf Co.   "
Smith T. A.   "
Crowell George & Co.   Westborough
Blood L. B. & Co.   West Brookfield
Loud Joseph & Co.   Westfield
Tirrell Albert,   South Weymouth, Weymouth
Honey J.   "
Beals & Bowker,   Williamstown
Wood Geo. H. & Co.   Winchendon
Morse F. H. & Co.   "
LITTLEFIELD J. E. & SONS,   Winchester
McDonald Joseph B.   Woburn
Fuller Rufus,   "
Jourdan W. H.   Worcester
Santon J. & Co.   "
Strong & Rogers,   "
Wellington T. W. & Co.   "
Loring Hiram, So. Yarmouth, Yarmouth
Crocker & Matthews, Yarmouth Port, "

Coal Ash Sifters.

Harris Samuel (patent),   Springfield

Coal by the Cargo.

STAPLES & PHILLIPS, 27 West
  Water (see page 759),   Taunton

Coffee and Spice Mills.

Hathaway Jos. R.   Fall River
Weaver Geo. P.   Lawrence
Bayrd Edward,   Lynn
Berry N. & Sons,   "
Butman Joseph,   "
Davis & Hatch,   New Bedford
Hill & Ross,   Newburyport
Newhall H. B.   East Saugus, Saugus
Freeman M.   Springfield
Fowler George,   "
CHAMBERLAIN & BAKER, Union
  cor. Exchange (see page 786), Worcester
Todd J. & Co.   "

Coffin and Casket Manufs.

LOCKHART WILLIAM L. Bridge
  st., cor. Third (see page 731),
                  East Cambridge, Cambridge

Coffin Ware-rooms.

Wiley C. B.   Abington
Holbrook O. B.   East Abington,   "
Adams Jasper H.   North Adams, Adams
Isbell Cyrus P.   "
Abbott Hernion,   Andover
Clapp Samuel,   Athol
Mann Horace,   Athol Depot,   "
Spooner Timothy H.   Barre
Prophett William,   Bridgewater
Devens Thos., Cambridgeport, Cambridge
Hadley A. A.,   E. Cambridge,   "
LOCKHART WILLIAM L., Bridge
  st., cor. Third (see page 731),
                  East Cambridge,   "
Shepard Asa,   Canton
Bryant John,   Charlestown
Coburn E. N.   "
Perry John L.   "

Coffin Ware-rooms — continued.
Reade John,   Charlestown
Brimhall E. & Co.   Clinton
French Daniel,   Joppa, East Bridgewater
Westgate, Baldwin, & Co.   Fall River
Willis Sydney D. & Co.   Fitchburg
Whittemore P. B.   Foxborough
Ellery Benjamin,   Gloucester
Proctor Charles,   "
Chamberlin & Whitmore,   Greenfield
Cummings J. H.   Haverhill
Fowler O. R.   "
Harris William D.   "
Bemis C. W.   Holliston
Chase William,   Hudson
Bassett Joseph,   Lee
GOODRICH R.   "
Goodrich A. W.   "
Taylor George H.   Lawrence
BROOKS J. W. 19 Prescott,   Leominster
Gordon & Currier,   Lowell
Hanover T.   "
Crosman J. H.   "
Orcutt C. N.   Lynn
Bliss N. P. & Co.   Marblehead
Fay Hiram W.   Marlborough
Soule Geo.   Middleboro'
Bergin James,   Milford
Fairbanks L.   "
Smith F. B.   Nantucket
Folger Reuben G. & Frederick,   "
Adams James,   Natick
COGGESHALL & CO. 20, 22 &
  26 William (see page 734), New Bedford
Wilson Benjamin G.   "
Copp Charles,   Newburyport
Safford S. H. & Co.   "
Howard, Clark, & Co., North Bridgewater
Loomis J. S.   Palmer
PARKER C. E.   Pittsfield
RAYMOND CHARLES, 35 Middle,
  (see page 766),   Plymouth
Knowles R.   Provincetown
Kimball Charles H.   Quincy
Allen & Spring,   Salem
Buffum C. S.   "
Williams Samuel,   Southbridge
Bourke & Skehen,   Springfield
Pomeroy & Fiske,   "
Washburn E. G.   "
Brinton Edward C.   Stockbridge
Withington P. M.   Stoughton
Gaffney John,   Taunton
Washburn P. T. & H. S.   "
Carpenter Edwin,   Uxbridge
Goodnow William,   Waltham
Hilton L.   Ware
Sly A. T.   Webster
Spalding & Eddy,   "
Sparrow R. C. & Z.   Wellfleet
Lambson Clinton K.   Westfield
Haymon & Rice, E. Weymouth, Weymouth
Allen L. H.   Woburn
Hildreth George G.   Worcester
McConville F. A.   "
Sessions George & Son,   "

Coffin Trimmings Manufs.

Stanley & Staples,   Attleborough
Wilmarth Wm. D.   "
Howard Geo. H.   S. Braintree, Braintree
Cabot F. W.   Mansfield
    Taunton
RHODES M. M. (tacks), Porter st.,

Collar Manufacturers.

(*See also Paper Collars.*)
Baird Geo. K. (paper),   Lee

Nonpareil Collar Co.   Springfield
Ray & Taylor,   "

Collecting Attorney.

HILL E. L.   Waltham

Color Manufacturers.

FARRAR G. H. (Union cor. Washington (red stain and carmine, see page 706),   Lynn

Comb Manufacturers.

Harris Sydney & Sons,   Clinton
Blodgett & Phillips,   Leominster
COLBURN JONAS & SON (fancy back combs, scoops, spoons, &c., for druggists)
COOK BROTHERS (combs and imitation jet jewelry),   "
Derby & Whitcomb (back, side, and dressing),   "
Joslin C. L. (fancy, back and side),   "
LOOK HERVEY D. & CO. (fancy and ornamental back combs).   "
MORSE G. & CO. (back and side,)   "
Niles Joseph (fancy and dressing),   "
Palmer W. L.   "
Prescott Emerson (fancy and long),   "
Tilton & Look (combs and imitation rubber goods),   "
True D. E. & Co.   "
UNION COMB CO. (raw horn, dressing and fancy),   "
Wetherbee & Barnard (combs and eye glasses),   "
Drake Alfred (machine wool),   Lowell
Sugden John (wire),   "
Carr, Brown, & Co.   Newburyport
Hildreth M. & Co.   Northborough
Parker, Staples, & Co.   "
PATTON W. (magic comb).   Springfield
Carleton & Marshall,   West Newbury
CHASE H. G. O. & T. M.   "
Emery C. H.   "
Emery Lucien H.   "
Noyes S. C. & Co.   "

Comforter Manufacturer.

Fiske William,   Lowell

Commercial Colleges.

UNION MERCANTILE SCHOOL,
  H. T. Wheeler, Principal, 101
  Winnisimmet st.   Chelsea
Holmes's Commercial College, Fall River
Fitchburg Commercial Institute, Fitchburg
McCoy & Moore,   Lowell
Boynton S. P.   Lynn
MIDDLEBORO' COMMERCIAL
  COLLEGE, J. B. Hambly, Middleboro'
Carter's Commercial College, Pittsfield
Holmes's Commercial College,   Taunton
Howes B. G.   Worcester

Commissioners.

(*For full list of Commissioners, see page 99.*)
BINNEY W. C. (N. H., R. I., Cal.),   Amesbury
FISHER M. M.   Medway
PECK A. PERRY (Me.),   Northampton
PERKINS J. R. (Me.).   No. Bridgewater
EMERSON C. M. (N. Y., Me.)   Pittsfield
PIERCE LAFAYETTE W.   Winchendon

Commission Merchants.

(*See also Merchants.*)
Whipple & Ward,   Amherst
Howe A. & G. H.   Brighton

FISH ROLAND, Fairhaven
BROWN DANIEL & SON (see
p.ge 729), ft. Central st. Fall River
GREENE & SON, 12 Pleasant, "
Kingsley George F. "
CHACE, ALLEN, & SLADE, 16
and 18 Bedford, "
REMINGTON CLINTON V. S.
Pocasset cor. Main, "
Slade John P. "
Crowell Elisha, Gloucester
Stetson James A. "
Dodd, Turr, & Co. East Gloucester, "
Bartlett T. B. & Co. Haverhill
Kimball A. R. (boots and shoes), "
Bonney Milton & Co. Lawrence
Coan W. B. & A. "
PATCH E. B. & CO. 1 and 2 Com.
mercial sq. Lowell
WAITE A. L. & CO., Dutton opp.
Mechanic's Mills, "
Johnson William A. Lunenburg
Allen G. & Son, New-Bedford
Baker Benjamin, "
Bartlett I. H. & Sons, "
Baylies J. B. "
Baylies & Cannon, "
Bourne Edward, "
BOURNE GEORGE A., 27 No. Water, "
Greene David R. & Co. "
Haskell Edward P. (coal), "
Howland James H. "
Nye S. G. (provisions), "
Perry J. H. & Co. "
Ricketson Joseph, 2d, "
Robinson W. A. & Co. "
Taber, Gordon, & Co, "
Wady John G. "
White Jonathan P. & Co. "
Watkins J. B. "
Wing J. & W. R. "
Wordell Alden, "
Sumner, Swasey, & Currier, Newburyport
ARCHER WILLIAM, 34 Front and
18 Washington, Salem
GOODHUE WILLIAM P., 44 Derby, "
PHILLIPS W. P., Phillips' Wharf
and Central, cor. Essex (see page
745), "
Colby W. A. Springfield
Hamilton R. J. (oil), "
King, Norton, & Ladd, "
Lane & Smith, "
Palmer Samuel & Co. "
Babbitt George H. jr.
King William, Taunton
Seekell John & Son, "
STAPLES & PHILLIPS, 27 West
Water (see page 759), "
WATSON & FAIRBANK (flour and
grain), Ware
Edmunds J. E. Webster
ALDRICH C. D., Trumbull sq., Worcester
Chamberlain H. H. & Co. (wool), "
Clark & Houghton, "
Clark & Newton (wool), "
Cheney & Farley, "
Dexter & Curtis, "
Fish F. W. & Co. "
Harrington R. "
Holbrook W. D. & Co. "
Hoppin G. S. & Co. "
Hopion, Cole, & Co. "
Hyatt & Hubbs (wool), "
King P. D. "
Spurr E. & Co. "
Staples S. E. "
WESTON O. H., 5 Sargent's Blk. "

Compo Shoe Manuf.

SAMUELS JAMES (see page 791), Lynn

Composition Nails.

NEW BEDFORD COPPER CO.
(cast), (see page 757), New Bedford

Conductors.

NEWTON E. & C., Union (see
page 731), Worcester

Confectioners.

Clark B. P. & Co. Cambridge-
port, Cambridge
Reuter Gustave, East Cambridge, "
Sawtell B. W. Charlestown
FISH ISAAC H. (see page 735),
Neponset, Dorchester
Bray Bros. Lowell
PAGE DUDLEY L. 1 Middle, "
WRIGHT A. D. & CO. 8 Appleton
Block, "
Rhodes William W. Lynn
Hawes Levi. New Bedford
Menage Henry G. & Co. "
Washburn & Grover, North Bridgewater
PEIRCE JOSEPH H. 13 Main, Peabody
Pepper George W. "
Needham J. S. Salem
Roberts E. F. & J. W. "
Simon's, "
Tibbetts R. S. "
Turell B. F. & Co. "
Wise G. H. Mrs. "
Cowles A. F. Springfield
Saunderson George E. Sudbury
BLISS A. L. & CO., 65 Main (see
page 758), Taunton
Kreis John G. Waltham
Webster D. G., East Weymouth, Weymouth
Hooker F. G. Worcester

Confectionery and Fruit.

Easton Carroll W. Adams
Adams W. C. North Adams, "
IVES H. B. "
Manchester William, "
Hinckley H. Amesbury
Pike Geo. F. Andover
Swift Jonathan, "
Hardin N. H. Attleboro'
Spear C. J. W. "
Choate Geo. P. & Alfred P. Beverly
Masury George, "
Newton George B. Bolton
Hayward C. F. Bridgewater
Schoregge Henry, Brookline
Belcher Chas. F. Cambridge
McElroy William, "
Alden Thomas, Cambridgeport, "
Tower Geo. W. "
Clark B. P. & Co. (manuf.), "
Blake Chas. H. "
Longley Benj. A. "
Moore Clark, "
Smith James, "
Tandy Jane, "
Leaver O. A. "
Reuter Gustave (manuf.), E.Cambridge, "
Smith Charles, "
Finnegan P. W. Canton
Abbott Emma Mrs. & Co. Charlestown
Beynon Wm. C. "
Bliss & Perry, "
Boardman Benj. S. "
Hale Alfred, "
Litchfield John S. "

Confectionery and Fruit — continued.

Paxton James & Bro.   Charlestown
Sawtell B. W. (manuf.),   "
Sawtell R. Mrs.   "
Whittemore Alfred,   "
Wilson C. G.   "
Bruce John,   Chelsea
Caswell Jane B.   "
Chase Chas. M & Co.   "
Clinkard Henry R.   "
Richardson Mary C.   "
Wilson Ezra,   "
Benoit & Chabot,   Chicopee
Blackmer William L.   "
Downing Hiram,   "
Jacobs Simeon A.   "
Gilbert H. W.   Chicopee Falls,   "
Watson T. P.   "
Kuch Elizabeth Mrs.   Dedham
Fish Isaac H.   Neponset,   Dorchester
Russell Stillman,   Douglas
Stroug R. E.   East Hampton
Tuckerman Benjamin C.   Edgartown
Allen Chas. H. & Son,   Fairhaven
Adams & Campbell,   Fall River
ANTHONY WILLIAM A. 10 and 12
   So. Main,   "
Biltcliffe Fergus,   "
Burgess William,   "
Coggshall C. H.   "
Colman William,   "
Downsbury Isabella,   "
Fennelly William E.   "
Godley James,   "
Hathaway James B.   "
Kenney & Ellsbree,   "
McKevitt James T.   "
Noros L. J.   "
Nowell George W.   "
Thacker Thomas,   "
Cook Thomas J.   Fitchburg
EMORY S. P. 145 Main,   "
Jackson J. H. & Co.   "
Whitney E. D.   "
Bragg Alex. E.   Freetown
Campbell Charles H.   Gloucester
Jones Geo. N.   "
Millward B. F.   "
Young Wm. H.   "
Allerton Wm.   East Gloucester,   "
Coller D. F.   Greenfield
Tyler Major H.   Great Barrington
Clark John B.   "
Savage George G.   "
Bean C. G.   Haverhill
Dawley Wm.   "
Goodspeed Charles E.   "
Harlow J. M.   "
Kempton & Co.   "
Rogers F. D. Mrs.   "
Sheldon S. H.   "
Shute John P.   "
HERSEY SAMUEL,   Hingham
Mayetts Edward,   "
Perry Seth W.   "
Kinney Francis E.   Holland
Baker John R.   Holyoke
Brierly W.   "
Tefa E. T.   "
Terrell Lewis L.   "
Wedge & Ward,   "
Whittemore P. B.   Hyde Park
Lang James Mrs.   Ipswich
Lang Mary Mrs.   "
Watts J. W.   "
Willcomb William,   "
Akers Geo. G.   Lawrence
BEAL HENRY, Essex n. Broadway,   "

Bingham H. F.   Lawrence
Herriman Stephen,   "
Hutchins E. H.   "
Martyn D. W. &. Co.
Watkins Geo. B.
Webster Abel,   "
Backus P.   Lenox
Billings Samuel D.   Lowell
Gilbert M. Mrs.   "
Hall E. W.   "
Heald John,   "
Hildreth S. F.   "
Johnson A. E.   "
Marshall McLane,   "
Mason R. E.   "
Nichols & Hutchins,   "
PAGE D. L. 1 Middle and 89 Merrimac,   "
Walker C. H.   "
Worthen B. D.   "
WRIGHT A. D. & CO. 3 Appleton
   Block,   "
Blanchard John E.   Lynn
Clapp Geo. H.   "
Downs Simon T.   "
Goldthwaite H. A. Mrs.   "
Hould Herbert,   "
Larkin Arthur W.   "
McDermott John,   "
Millett D. K.   "
Richmond Wm. B.   "
Rhodes William W. (manufacturer,),   "
Shaw Albert,   "
Stone Frank E.   "
Toppan & Co.   "
Vickary Otis,   "
Caldwell & Vaughan,   Malden
Chapin Frank B.   "
Knight Wm. M.   Marblehead
Rogers F. E.   "
Wellman Jacob,   "
Kinney Jirey, jr.   Mattapoisett
Bond Dudley,   Medford
Tripp Benj. F.   Middleborough
Hunt L. &. Co.   Milford
Willis Edwin,   "
Hooper L. A.   Nantucket
Hussey O. F.   "
Cummings F. E.   Natick
Andrews Christopher,   New Bedford
Arnet Robert,   "
Brannan R. H.   "
Brook Chas. A.   "
Bates A. E. Mrs.   "
Bourne Edward,   "
Cobb C.   "
Carter M. Miss,   "
Duffy James,   "
Hawes Levi, (wholesale),   "
Lang Anthony,   "
Menage Henry G. & Co. (manuf.),   "
Parker Frederick,   "
Parkinson Robert,   "
Read Philip,   "
Tilden & Co.   "
Scott J. W.   "
Smith John,   "
Rice A. J.   "
Brown William,   Newburyport
Dresser E. G.   "
Stevens Geo. H.   "
Hyde H. N.,   Newton Corner,   Newton
Keyes J. C.   West Newton,   "
Thomason Ellen,   Upper Falls,   "
Prouty Benjamin,   Northampton
Strong E.   "
Hunt & Wilder,   North Bridgewater
Washburn & Grover,   "
Wires M. D.   North Brookfield

Bird Charles. jr. North Chelsea
Tenney F. M. Orange
Sparrow Joel, Orleans
Fox & Holbrook, Palmer
Holman C. F. "
Hyde Milton, . Peabody
PEIRCE JOSEPH H., 13 Main, "
Reed David N. "
Roche E. E. "
Tibbetts J. H. "
Booth E. A. Pittsfield
Millard Ansel E. "
PHELPS & CROSSMAN, 43 North, "
Smith Joseph H. "
Churchill Benjamin; Plymouth
Lucas S. "
Olney Z. "
Atkins Joseph, 2d, Provincetown
Brown Reuben F. "
Kilburn Edward J. "
Young James, "
Hodges Wm. A. Quincy
French Ansel, Randolph
Eaton Robert C. Rockport
Story Henry L. "
Tufts Joseph, "
Chandler & Co. Salem
Chapple John, "
DeCosta Emanuel, "
Estes G. W. jr. "
Merrill F. A. "
Moulton Wm. "
Needham J. S. "
Nourse E. "
Roberts E. F. & J. W. "
Rogers S. F. "
Simon's, "
Sadler J. D. "
Sweet H. S. "
Tibbetts R. S. "
Wise George H. Mrs. "
Marden Moses, Amesbury, Salisbury
Prevaux John, " "
Pellett H. E. Southbridge
Barr E. C. Springfield
Bliss & Co. "
Brown S. C. "
Clegg William L. "
Cogswell J. W. "
Collins William M. "
Colman P. B. "
Cowles A. F. (manuf.), "
Dickenson J. W. "
Gunn & Merrill, "
Kibbe Brothers & Co. "
LaBarron W. W. "
Lyon C. T. "
Pierce H. A. "
Quimby H. A. "
Sweetland & Fisher, "
Sweetland & Loomis, "
Caird F. S. Stoneham
Sanderson George E., (manuf.), Sudbury
Sanderson T. J. "
Harding George W. Swampscott
Porter J. P. "
BLISS A. L. & CO., 65 Main, (see
page 758), Taunton
Clary P. "
Congdon Wm. W. "
Cushman E. "
Fisher A. B. Mrs. "
Lothrop Cyrus H. "
QUIGLEY BERNARD, Weir, "
Richmond C. E. "
Sears J. B. "
Dexter Elisha, Holmes's Hole, Tisbury
Keith J. B. " "

Butler A. jr. Wakefield
Field I. Waltham
Fisher Joseph, "
Kreis John G. (manuf,) "
Merriam A. H. "
Wright J. B. "
Holden George C. Ware
White & McMahon, "
Briggs Ebenezer, Wareham
Adams T. C. "
Bassett Wash. E. Wareham, "
Wade Charles, Webster
Higgins John G. Wellfleet
Farrar Milton, Westfield
Lewis L. M. "
Miller E. S. & Co. "
St. John Myron, "
Swiatlund E. S. "
Whipple Charles F. "
West Roxbury
Hankey Joseph, Jamaica Plain, "
Avery E. A., Mittineague, W. Springfield
Hunt Richard B., West Stockbridge
Webster D. G. (manuf.), East
Weymouth, Weymouth
Leach Clinton C. Wilbraham
Allen S. E. Winchendon
Adkins C. S. Woburn
Thompson S. F. "
Bliss A. S. Worcester
Bruce Jos. "
Cutsing D. "
Gates D. C. "
Hillyer George, "
Hooker F. G. (manuf.), "
Hubbard C. K. "
Hutchinson A. & Son, "
Lilley A. J. "
Marrs Augustus, "
Newcomb A. "
Rawson D. J. "
Smith Ansel, "
Shepard Chas. "
Taft, Bliss, & Rice, "
Tyler & Gale, "

Contractors.

Barnes Eleazer, Dorchester
Draper & Vaughan, "

Contractors for Building.

PEIRCE HENRY, North Adams, Adams
Holyoke
BASSETT JOEL L., (see page 761), "

Conveyances.

Howland F. P. Abington
Corthell Wm. P., South Abington, "
Hart A. Orlando, Charlestown
Hart J. S. "
Shedd A. B. "
Billings H. W. Conway
Chamberlain Joseph, East Bridgewater
Keith Thomas, "
Winslow B. F. Fall River
Low David W. Gloucester
Bicknell Quincy, Hingham
Seymour Charles W. "
Whitney Edmund C. Marlborough
Coolidge Oliver B. Lynn
Holmes B. H. Plymouth
Rand Asa P. Westfield
Ellis Bethuel, Winchendon

Coopers.

Lawrence Ralph, Acton
Robbins Francis (kegs), "
Dole Joseph, S. Acton, "

Coopers — continued.

Fletcher Daniel,	South Acton,	Acton
Gilmore William,	W. Acton,	"
Bigelow Horace,		Berlin
Guellow Charles P.		Bernardston
Goodwin Robert,		Beverly
Wheeler James K.		Bolton
Wheeler Samuel,		"
Hastings James, Boylston Centre,		Boylston
Trowbridge Silas,		Buckland
Gerry J.	Cambridgeport,	Cambridge
Proctor Benj. F.		"
Bay State Barrel Co. East Cambridge,		"
Wilkins George,		Carlisle
Blood & Seaver,		Charlestown
Fisher John,		"
Johnson Lewis,		"
Lund Frederick,		"
Neiss David L. & Co.		"
Saunders G. W. & W. A.		"
Tyler Philip,		"
Dean & Martin,		Cheshire
Brown Thomas J.		Cohasset
Compton Charles,		"
Creed James,		"
Phinney James,		"
Chamberlain Amasa,		Dana
Waters George,		Dighton
Woodward James,		Dunstable
Winsor Seth,		Duxbury
Keniston Samuel,		Edgartown
Burnham William,		Essex
McAdams James,		Fall River
Bearse Christopher G.		Falmouth
Clark, Jenney, & Co.		Fairhaven
Pease John C.		"
Terry Benj.		"
Harrold Joseph,		Franklin
Everdean John J.		Gloucester
Marlin Joseph,		"
Tuck Azor H.		"
Crane Samuel R.	E. Gloucester,	"
Holcombe E.		Granville
Cooley James M.	E. Granville,	"
Perry Seth,		Hanover
Doane Ambrose N.		Harwich
Mercarther O. S.		"
Small Z. H. (cranberry barrels),		"
Turner Stephen,		"
Tuttle John,		"
Woodhouse William,		"
Fletcher Nathan,		Haverhill
Goodell Alvin,		Holland
Williams Ruel A.		"
Ashley Josiah R.		Lakeville
Farmer Charles,		"
Potter Alex.		Lancaster
Kelty James F.		Lawrence
Hutchinson James,	New Lenox,	Lenox
Hutchinson Orin,	"	"
White Asa,		Lincoln
Tuttle John P.		Littleton
Powers Wm. 95 Lowell,		Lowell
Aiken Warren,		Mattapoisett
BARSTOW N. H. & H. (kegs, see		
page 727),		"
Bolles Prince,		"
Richardson Simeon,		Medfield
Markham Ira,		Monterey
Elkins John,		Nantucket
Fisher Amaziah,		"
Carter Burton,		New Ashford
Adams Nathaniel,		New Bedford
Allen & Whitney,		"
Baker & McCulloch,		"
Churchill Sylvanus,		"
Ellis Caleb L. & Son,		"
Holmes Atwood,		"

Howland & Cogswell,		New Bedford
Luce Thomas,		"
Luscomb Richard,		"
Luscomb Ziba B.		
Myrick Alexander G.		
Norton William J.		
Parker Charles,		
Peck & Adams,		"
PEIRCE JOHN W. 99 So. Water (see		
page 757),		"
PEIRCE LLOYD N. 190 So. Water,		"
(see page 728),		
Randall Rufus,		
Walsh Maurice,		
Whitney Amasa,		"
Coffin William S.		Newburyport
Fitz Geo.		"
Goodwin Thomas C.		"
Pettingell J. S.		"
Pettingell Samuel,		"
		New Marlborough
Gilson William B.	Southfield,	"
Keyes Denison,	Mill River,	"
Page William,	Newtonville,	Newton
Higgins Daniel,		Orleans
Butterfield David,		Pepperell
Shattuck E. Cummings,		"
Stickney Walter B.,	East Pepperell,	"
Tarbell T. F.,	"	"
Whitney Joseph H.		Phillipston
Thayer Kingman,		Plainfield
Thayer Ormon,		"
Churchill Heman,		Plymouth
Harlow Abner H.		"
Holbrook Gideon,		"
D'Wolf George,		Provincetown
Macool Adam,		"
Warren D.		Quincy
Bradley Wm. H. jr. & J. W.		Rockport
Battis John,		Salem
Brady Thomas,		"
Felt & Phippen,		"
Florence Thomas T.		"
Getchell Benj. W.		"
Rowell Edward (kegs),		"
Richardson George F.		Sandisfield
Richardson Moses,		"
Calkins J.,	Montville,	"
Huxton J. M.	"	"
Burr Raymond H.		Seekonk
Booth E.		Southwick
Granger A.		"
Risley Caleb,		"
White Cyrus jr.		Springfield
Swasey S. S.		Swansea
Harlow I. H.		Taunton
Swenzen Charles,		Tolland
Swenzen Frederic,		"
ADAMS A. M. (kit),		Townsend
Adams Daniel,		"
Fessenden B. & A. D.		"
Fessenden Walter & Son,		"
Larkin E. A.		"
Spaulding Jonas, jr. (kit), Townsend		
Harbor,		"
Barrett A. & N. E. West Townsend,		"
Coburn E. H. F.	"	"
Evans Hosea,	"	"
Hodgman Rodney,		Tyringham
Stearie Hastings,		Upton
Fisk Evan,		"
Ryder Wm. W.		Wareham
Barker Isaiah,		Wellfleet
Newcomb Reuben,		"
Fletcher E.		Westford
Graves Levi,		Westminster
Wood B. F.		"
Carpenter J. W.		West Stockbridge

Howland William P., Westport Point, " Westport
Adams A. M. East Weymouth, Weymouth
Crafts Noah, Whately
Bushnell Asa, Wilbraham
Cole Porter R. Williamstown
Weston A. A. Windsor
Baker Frederick P. South Yarmouth, " Yarmouth

Coopers' Flags.

PEIRCE LLOYD N., 190. So. Water,
(see page 728), New Bedford

Cop Tube Manufacturer.

Wood James (paper), Fall River

Copper and Yellow Metal Bolts.

NEW BEDFORD COPPER CO. (see page 757), New Bedford

Copper Founders.

Lazell, Perkins, & Co. Bridgewater
REVERE COPPER CO. " Canton & Winthrop

Copper Manufacturers.

Lazell, Perkins, & Co. Bridgewater
NEW BEDFORD COPPER Co. (sheet, bolt, &c., see page 757), New Bedford
CROCKER BROS. & CO., Court, near City Square (sheet, bolt, &c., see page 758), Taunton
REVERE COPPER CO. Winthrop

Copper Paint.

(See also Paint Manufacturers; also Paints, Oils, &c.)
Tarr & Wonson, E. Gloucester, Gloucester

Coppersmiths.

Allen Samuel H. Charlestown
Hayward L. H. "
Reed William G. Chelsea
Spade William, "
Bush Charles H. Fall River
BUSH WILLIAM R., 27 1-2 No. Main (see page 755), "
Gardner John, "
WILDER S. & CO. (pumps, see page 767), Holliston
Wilder H. H. & Co. Lowell
Cragie Audrew, New Bedford
Gifford & Allen, "
Waters A. S. Salem
Emery P. P. & Co. Springfield
Mahar James T. Taunton
Chick & Wilmarth, "

Copper Stamp, Stencil, and Block Cutters.

Parsons & Gibby, Lowell
Preston John, "

Copying Press Manufs.

WHITCOMB C. & CO., Exchange, cor. Cypress, Worcester

Cordage Manufacturers.

(See also Twine and Line Makers.)
LAWTON & ESTES (see page 734), Fall River
Lindsey W. & N. & Co. (dealers), "
Corliss Benjamin H. "
Hingham Cordage Co. Gloucester
Wall N. & Son (small), Hingham

CLARK JEREMIAH, 96 Middle, (see page 738), Lowell
New Bedford
NEW BEDFORD CORDAGE CO. "
Juckman Moses B. Newburyport
Lunt Paul G. "
Pearson A. & Co. "
Plymouth Cordage Co. Plymouth
Boynton E. Rockport
Chisholm Joseph, Salem

Cordials, Sirups, and Extracts.

PLUMSTEAD DAVID C., 11 & 13 Winnisimmet, Chelsea

Cork Manufacturers.

Springfield Cork Manuf. Co. Springfield

Corn and Cob Cracker Manufs.

(See also Agricultural Implement Manuf.)
HEALD STEPHEN & SONS (superior shell hardened, see pages 796 and 797), Barre

Corn C ke Manufacturer.

MANNING WILLIAM (see page 739), Broadway, cor. School, Lowell

Corn Shellers.

(See also Agricultural Implement Manuf.)
HEALD STEPHEN & SONS (see pages 796 and 797), Barre

Corrugated Iron.

AMERICAN CORRUGATED IRON CO., Geo. Dwight, Jr., Treas. (see page 780), Springfield

Corset Bindings, Webbings, &c.

STEVENS J. TYLER & CO., successors to N. Richardson & Co. (see page 801), West Warren, Warren

Corset Jeans.

ROCKPORT STEAM COTTON MILLS, John H. Higgins, agt. (see page 798), Rockport

Corsets.

(See also Hoop Skirts.)
Odessa Skirt Co. (manuf.), Gloucester
Chace George W. New Bedford
STOEHR C. (see page 762), 53 North st., Pittsfield
Follette L. B. Salem
Thompson R. F. Taunton
Jackson C. H. West Brookfield
Hayden H. Miss, Worcester
Worcester Skirt Co. "

Cotton and Wool Wadding Manufacturer.

Bacon John H., office 1 Union st. Boston, manufactory at Winchester

Cotton and Wool Waste.

King J. M. Athol Depot, Athol
Millers River Manuf. Co., Geo. T. Johnson, agt., Athol Depot, "
Pine Dale Woolen Co. " "
Smith Abner, " "
Smith, Leonard, & Co. " "
MATOON & BLAISDELL (see page 773), Chicopee
Wallace Rodney, Fitchburg
Ray F. B. Franklin

Cotton and Wool Waste — continued.

Ray J. P. & J. G.　　　Franklin
Porter & Winslow,　　　Freetown
Thorpe John,　　　"
Briggs R. & Co.　　　Millbury
Gates Bros. & Co.　　　Oxford
PIERCE H. L. 25 Westminster, Taunton
Arms William S.　　　Springfield
Howard Brothers,　　　"
Olmsted John,　　　"
Simmons Joseph H. (cotton).　　Westfield
BUELL S. K. (see page 781), 18
　Foster,　　　Worcester

Cotton Banding and Rope Manufacturer.

Holden James,　　　Fall River

Cotton Batting Manufacturers.

Bailey C. & Son,　North Adams, Adams
Andrews R. R.　　　"　　　"
King J. M.,　　Athol Depot,　Athol
　　　　　Fall-River
LAWTON & ESTES (see page 734),
Stone A. J.　　　*　Hudson
WOOD WILLIAM E.　　Mansfield
Eaton Edward,　　　Medway
Wilson E. C. & Co.　　　"
Swan Brothers,　　　Mendon
Leavitt J. H.　　　Norton
Gates Brothers,　　　Oxford
　　　　　Pepperell
Parker Henry A. & Co., E. Pepperell, "
Chilton Batting Company,　　Plymouth
OLD COLONY BATTING CO.,　　"
Keith & Bumstead,　　　"
Welch H. H.　　　Princeton
LEWIS WILLARD (and carpet lin-
　ing),　　　Walpole
Tidd J. S.,　　West Warren,　Warren
Olmstead John & Co.　　　Westfield
Taylor & Chapin,　　　"
Westport Manufacturing Co.　Westport

Cotton Brokers.

EASTON A. D., 14 No. Main,　Fall River

Cotton Cloth Manufacturers.

(*See also Manufacturing Co's in Index;
also Print Works.*)

Adams Bros. & Co.　　　Adams
Jenks Elisha (print cloth),　　"
Plunkett & Wheeler (sheetings),　"
Andrews Reuben R. (satinett warps),
　North Adams,　　　"
Arnold Harvey & Co. (Arnold's
　Prints), North Adams,　　"
Arnold Oliver & Co. (printing cloths),
　North Adams,　　　"
Arnolds & Ray (printing cloths),
　North Adams,　　　"
Freeman W. W. & Co. (prints and
　printing cloths), North Adams, "
　　　　　Ashburnham
Naukeag Mills, George Blackburn
　& Co., proprietors (sheetings),　"
Fisher W. A. & Co., Athol Depot, Athol
Foster S. & W.　　　Attleborough
Hebron Manuf. Co. (sheetings),　"
Knight B. B. & R.　　　"
MECHANICS' MILLS (shirtings),　"
Smith C. W. & J. E. (sheetings),
　Worcester,　　　"
Smith C. W. & J. E. (4-4 sheetings), Auburn
Smithville,　　　Barre
Brookfield Manufacturing Co. (blue
　denims), W. G. Fay, agent, East
　Brookfield,　　　Brookfield
Aldrich A. J. (flannels),　　Blackstone

BLACKSTONE MANUFACTURING
　CO., (sheetings and print cloths), H.
　C. KIMBALL, agent.　　Blackstone
Learmont A. (denims, &c.), North
　Blackstone,　　　"
Clinton Co. (ginghams),　　Boylston
Neponset Cotton Factory (printing
　cloths),　　　Canton
CHICOPEE MANUF. CO. (sheet-
　ings, shirtings, &c.), E. Blake,
　agent, Chicopee Falls,　　Chicopee
DWIGHT MANUF. CO. (sheetings,
　shirtings, and drills), G. H. Nye,
　agent,　　　"
LANCASTER MILLS (ginghams),
　Franklin Forbes, agent.　　Clinton
LANCASTER QUILT CO., G. P.
　Whitman, agent,　　　"
Griswoldville Manuf. Co. (print
　goods),　　　Coleraine
Shattuck & Whitton (sheetings),　"
Smith Damon & Co. (flannel),　Concord
Westport Manufacturing Co., Wm.
　B. Trafford, agent, North Dart-
　mouth,　　　Dartmouth
Smithfield Manuf. Co., Readville, Dedham
AMERICAN LINEN CO. (print
　cloths), 82,512 spindles,　Fall River
AMERICAN PRINT WORKS, print
　180,000 yards daily.　　　"
ANNAWAN MANUFACTORY,
　(printing cloths), 9,984 spindles,　"
DAVOL MILLS (fine sheetings),
　13,312 spindles,　　　"
Durfee Mills (print cloths),　　"
Fall River Manufactory (printing
　cloths),　　　"
Fall River Print Works (printing
　cloths),　　　"
Granite Mills (printing cloths),　"
MASSASOIT STEAM MILL CO.
　(printing cloths), 14,448 spindles,　"
MECHANICS' MILL (print cloths),
　53,742 spindles,　　　"
MERCHANTS' MANUFACTURING
　CO. (print cloths), 53,424 spindles,　"
METACOMET MILLS (printing
　cloths), 23,808 spindles,　　"
MOUNT HOPE MILL (fine goods),
　9,024 spindles,　　　"
POCASSET MANUF. CO. (sheetings
　and printing cloths), 34,248 spin-
　dles,　　　"
Robeson Mills (print cloths),　　"
TECUMSEH MILLS (print goods),　"
TROY COTTON AND WOOLEN
　MANUFACTORY (printing cloths),
　38,786 spindles,　　　"
Union Mill Company (print cloths),　"
Watuppa Cotton Mill (printing cloths), "
Ellis Oliver, agent (duck),　Fitchburg
Sherwin Levi (sheetings),　　"
Ray James P. & Joseph G.　Franklin
Pratt C. L. & Co. (sheetings),　Grafton
Fisher E. & Son (sheetings), Far-
　numsville,　　　"
Morse Alfred (shirtings), Farnums-
　ville,　　　"
Grafton Mills (print cloths and sheet-
　ings), N. E. Village,　　"
SAUNDERS COTTON MILLS (shirt-
　ings and print cloths), Saundersville, "
Morse Alfred (sheetings and
　shirtings),　　　Holden
Walker & Wright (shirtings),　"
HAMPDEN MILLS (all kinds of
　colored cotton goods), John E.
　Chase, agent,　　　Holyoke

Lyman Mills (shirtings and umbrella cloth), Jones S. Davis, agent, Holyoke
Smithfield Manuf. Co., Rendville, Hyde Park
Wilder Charles L. (sheetings), Lancaster
ATLANTIC COTTON MILLS (sheetings and shirtings), Jos. P. Battles, agent, Lawrence
EVERETT MILLS (tickings, ginghams, stripes, and lastings), J. R. Perry, agent, "
Lawrence Duck Company (cotton duck), Isaac Hayden, agent, "
PACIFIC MILLS (prints), Wm. L. Chapin, agent, Canal st. "
Pemberton Co. (cotton cassimeres, flannels, ticks, stripes, &c.), Fred. E. Clarke, agent, "
WASHINGTON MILLS (cambrics), W. H. Salisbury, agent, Canal st. "
Appleton Co. Lowell
BOOTT COTTON MILLS (sheetings, drillings, and print cloths), A. G. Cumnock, agent, "
Hamilton Manuf. Co., O. H. Moulton, agent, "
LAWRENCE MANUF. CO. (sheetings, shirtings, and hosiery), Wm. F. Salmon, agent, "
Lowell Manuf. Company (carpets and worsted goods), Sam'l Fay, agent, "
Mass. Cotton Mills (sheetings, shirtings, &c.), Homer Bartlett, treas. "
Mather John & Co. (bocking) "
Merrimack Manufacturing Company, (prints), John C. Palfrey, supt. "
SUFFOLK MANUF. CO. (drillings and sheetings), Thomas S. Shaw, agent, "
TREMONT MILLS (sheetings, shirtings and flannels), Chas. F. Battles, agent, "
Ludlow Manufacturing Co. (sheetings), Ludlow
Manchaug Company (print cloths, J. M. Cunliff, agt. Manchaug, Mansfield
Methuen Co. (sheetings, cotton flannels, &c.), Methuen
NEMASKET COTTON MILLS, Brown & Sherman (yarn and wicking, see page 863) Middleboro'
Brierly James (print cloths), Millbury
Cordis Mills (denims, stripes, and tickings), "
Emerson & Brierly (print cloths), "
Millbury Cotton Mill (print cloths), "
Wheeler Cotton Mills (sheetings), "
WAMSUTTA MILLS (shirtings, jeans, &c.), Thomas Bennett, jr., agent, New Bedford
Bartlet Steam Mills (sheetings and shirtings), John Balch, agt. Newburyport
James Steam Mill (sheetings and shirtings), Wm. C. Balch, agent, "
Ocean Steam Mills (print cloths and sheetings), K. S. Lesley, agent, "
Peabody Mills (print cloths and sheetings), J. Smith, agent, "
Newton Mills (print cloths), D. L. Jewell, agent, Upper Falls, Newton
Robertson W. H. (ginghams), Northampton
Greenville Manuf. Company (sheetings and drills), A. L. Williston, resident agent, Florence, "
Chapin Caleb T. (sheetings), Northborough
Whitin Charles P. (sheetings), Whitinsville, Northbridge

Whitin J. F. (fine sheetings, Northbridge Whitinsville, "
Linwood Mill (shirtings), Whitinsville, "
Whitin Paul (sheetings and shirtings, Whitinsville, "
Rhodes & Wilmarth (sheetings), North Oxford, Oxford
Thorndike Company (shirtings, print cloths, denims, ticks, &c.), Palmer
Boston Duck Company (duck, sheetings, and ticks), Bondsville, "
Van Sickler Martin (sheetings), Pittsfield
PLYMOUTH WOOLLEN AND COTTON CO. (duck), Plymouth
Jenkins Brothers & Co., Plympton
Orleans Manuf. Co. (print cloths), N. G. Guild, agent, Rehoboth
ROCKPORT STEAM COTTON MILLS (jeans and duck), J. H. Higgins, agent (see page 798), Rockport
NAUMKEAG STEAM COTTON COMPANY (shirtings, sheetings, jeans, cotton flannels, &c.), Edmund Dwight, treas. Salem
Mann G. R. & Wm. R. (duck), Sharon
Phœnix Cotton Company (sheetings), Nathaniel B. Tobey, agt. Shirley
Edgarton Mills (sheetings), Munson & Edgarton, proprietors, Shirley Village, "
Holbrook L. & Co. (4-4 sheetings), Shirley Village, "
Central Mills Co. (sheetings), Southbridge
Columbian Manuf. Company, "
Dresser Manuf. Company (sheetings), "
Glasgow Co. (gingham), South Hadley Springfield
INDIAN ORCHARD MILLS, C. J. Goodwin, agent, Indian Orchard, "
Sturbridge Cotton Mills (print cloth), Fiskdale, Sturbridge
Sutton Manuf. Co. (print cloths), Sutton
Manchaug Company (print cloths), J. M. Cunliff, agent, Manchaug, "
Taunton
Dean C. & M. Co., R. S Dean, agent, "
Eagle Cotton Company, F. B. Dean, "
HODGES ALEXANDER, Alexander H. Champion, agent, "
Hopewell Cotton Mills, Charles Albro, "
WHITTENTON MANUF. CO. (cottonades, striped shirtings, apron checks, corset jeans, and drillings), Chesbrough Lewis R. Oakland, "
THORNDIKE COMPANY (shirtings, ticks, &c.), Geo. T. Hill, agt. Thorndike
Whitin James F. (fine sheetings), North Uxbridge, Uxbridge
Boston Manuf. Co. (shirting and sheeting), Waltham
OTIS COMPANY (denims and hosiery), S. J. Wetherll, agent, Ware
WARREN COTTON MILLS (sheetings and denims), A. F. Howard, agent, West Warren, Warren
Slater Samuel & Sons (finished cottons), Webster
BEAMAN MANUFACTURING CO. (drillings and counterpanes), Edward Howe, agent, West Boylston
Holbrook Eli W. (sheetings), "
Harris L. M. & Co. (sheetings and drills), Oakdale. "
Agawam Canal Co. (sheetings and jeans), Wm. Melcher, agent, Mittineague, West Springfield
Hayden Manufacturing Co. (shirtings), Williamsburg

Cotton Cloth Manufacturers — continued.
Walley Stephen (print cloth), Williamstown
WILLIAMSTOWN MANUF. CO.
(print cloths), S. Southworth, agt. "
Winchendon
White Nelson D. & Co. (4-4 sheetings), "
Curtis Albert (sheetings, &c.), Worcester

Cotton-Dealers.

EASTON A. D. 14 N. Main, Fall River
REMINGTON CLINTON V. S.
Main cor. Pocasset, "

Cotton Drills.

ROCKPORT STEAM COTTON
MILLS, John H. Higgins, agent
(see page 798), Rockport

Cotton-Gin Manufacturers.

Bates, Hyde, & Co. Bridgewater
Carver Joseph E. "
Southern Cotton-Gin Co. "
E. Carver Co., East-Bridgewater, "

Cotton Lacing Manufs.

(*For Boots, Shoes, Corsets, &c.*)

Mansfield G. H. & Co. Canton
Jenkins, Brother, & Co., S. Carver, Carver

Cotton Machinery Manufs.

(*See also Machinists, &c.*)

MARVEL, DAVOL, & CO. Fall River
DRAPER GEORGE & SON (patent
improvements, see page 753), Hopedale
KITSON RICHARD (see page 737),
Worthen n. Dutton, Lowell
LANE DAVID, Fletcher, cor. Cush-
ing (see page 738), "
Pettee Otis & Co., Upper Falls, Newton
WHITIN JOHN C. (see page 754),
Whitinsville; Northbridge
MASON WM. (builder of every vari-
ety of cotton machinery, locomo-
tives, machinists' tools, &c.; see
page 736), Taunton
Dean Cotton & Machine Co. "
SARGENT CHARLES G. (see page
743), Graniteville, Westford

Cotton Openers and Cleaners.

GERRY GEO. & SON, (see page
771), 6 Mill st. Athol Depot, Athol
KITSON RICHARD (see page 737),
Worthen, near Dutton, Lowell
LANE DAVID, (see page 738),
Fletcher, cor. Cushing, "

Cotton Tape and Webbing Manufacturers.

Witter H. M. (tape), Auburn
STEVENS J. TYLER & CO., suc-
cessors to Nathan Richardson &
Co. (see page 801), West Warren,
Warren
Hamilton C. W. & Co. Worcester
Smith Wm. A. "
Washburn L. K. & Co. (narrow), "

Cotton Thread and Twine Manufacturers.

Lanesville Manufacturing Company
(thread), Attleborough
MORSE E. J. W. & CO. (sea island
cotton thread and harness twine,
see page 749), South Easton, Easton
Southborough
Cordaville Mills (twine), Cordaville, "

CHACE BENJ. A. (spool & skein
threads and yarns, see page
756), North Dighton, Dighton
Williston Mills Co. Jas. Sutherland
agent, Easthampton
PRATT AMOS (thread, see page
707), Easton
Chace Augustus, Fall River
LAWTON & ESTES (twines, wicks,
warps &c., see page 734), "
McCOWAN D. & CO. (druggists' and
other, see page 711), Annawan st. "
NIANTIC THREAD CO., J. E.
Hills, treas.,
Fisher E. & Son (twines, wicks,
warps, &c.) Farnumsville, Grafton
HADLEY CO. (spool cotton), J. S.
Davis, agt. Holyoke
Merrick Thread Co. "
Newcomb Thomas (thread), Kingston
Lawrence Duck Company (twine),
Isaac Hayden, agent, Lawrence
Glace Thread Manuf Co. Mansfield
Medway
Wilson E. C. & Co. (bonnet, spool,
sewing, and shoe), "
Mason & Walker (thread), Rockville, "
Warner & Dart (twine), Oxford
SAMOSET MILLS (thread), E. Rus-
sel, treas. Plymouth
Central Mills Co. (twine), Southbridge
Pleasant Valley Mills, Sutton
Westport Manuf. Co. (twine), Westport
WARREN THREAD CO. (spool,
see page 716), Prescott st. Worcester

Cotton Warp Manufacturers.

Adams & Clark, Adams
Plunkett & Wheeler (satinet), "
RENFREW MANUFG. CO., Jas.
Renfrew, jr., agt. "
Johnson Sylvander, North Adams, "
Blackstone
Blue & Worrell, North Blackstone, "
Tucker & Cook, "
Tucker R. & Co. Conway
CHACE BENJ. A. (thread, see page
756), North Dighton, Dighton
LINCOLN L. & Co. (see page 724),
North Dighton, "
WILLISTON MILLS CO. (varns
and thread), James Sutherland,
agent, East Hampton
LAWTON & ESTES (see page
734), Fall River
Ellis Oliver, agent, Fitchburg
Pitts Hiram W. "
Fisher E. & Son, Farnumsville, Grafton
Great Barrington
Monument Mills, John M. Seeley,
treas. and agent, Housatonic, "
Wawbeek Mills, John M. Seeley,
treas. Housatonic, "
HOLYOKE WARP MILLS, James
G. Smith, agent, Holyoke
Whitaker Brothers, Huntington
Rhodes John (satinet), Millbury
Warner & Dart, (carpet), Oxford
HUGUENOT MANUF. CO. North
Oxford, "
Barker J. & Bro. Pittsfield
Peck Jabez L. "
Plympton
Jenkins, Brother, & Co. (carpet), "
Southbridge
Hamilton Woollen Co. Globe Village, "
Knowles L. J. Warren

Westport Manuf. Co. (carpet), Westport
Graves, Lamb, & Lymon, Williamsburg
Daniels J. M. Northville, Worcester

Cotton Yarn Manufacturers.

Daggett H. M., Attleboro' Falls, Attleboro'
Clinton Co. Boylston
Fuller & Bigelow, Clinton
CHACE B. A. (see page 756), North Dighton,
LINCOLN L. & CO. (see page 724), North Dighton, Dighton
Norfolk Mills, Harrison sq. Dorchester
WILLISTON MILLS, James Sutherland, agent, Easthampton
LAWTON & ESTES (see page 734), Fall River
Wawbeek Mills, John M. Seeley, treas. Housatonic, Great Barrington
Bigelow E. & Co. Holden
HOLYOKE WARP MILLS, James G. Smith, agent, Holyoke
Sayles J. M. West Mansfield, Mansfield
BROWN & SHERMAN (cotton yarns and wicking (see page 803), Middleborough
Wilson E. C. & Co. Medway
Dean James M. "
Clapp S. & A. E. Walpole
Jenks E. C. & Co. South Walpole, "
Dean James M, Wrentham
Wilmarth Joseph, "

Counsellors.
(See Lawyers.)

Country Stores,
Where is kept a general assortment of Dry Goods, Groceries, Agricultural Implements, Hardware, &c. Those dealing in only one kind of goods will be found under their appropriate heading.

Faxon B. E. Abington
Loud Alden S. "
Whitmarsh Z. N. "
Curtis Abner, East Abington, "
Rosenfeld N. "
Torrey D. & E. P. " "
Ford James, North Abington, "
Gigson & Greenwood, " "
Sprague Elbridge, " "
Bates Henry A., South Abington, "
Cook Randall & Son, " "
Dyer N. N. " "
Jenkins & Holbrook, " "
Perry Daniel, jr. " "
Reed Geo. W. " "
Cochran David, Acushnet
Davis John R. "
Lewis Richard & Son, Long Plain, "
Howland Alexander, " "
Jones Daniel, Acton
Wetherbee D James, "
TUFTLES, JONES, & WETHERBEE, South Acton,
Robinson Charles, West Acton, "
Shepard W. C. & O. " "
Anthony, Burlingame, & Co. Adams
Avery H. C. "
Cassidel & Walling, "
Green Wm. B. "
Jenks Elisha, "
Tanner S. J. & Co. "
Andrews Reuben R. North Adams, "
Brayton S. W. & Co. " "
Carmody & Cook, " "
Ellis & Field, " "

Freeman W. W. & Co. North Adams, Adams
Gallup & Smith, " "
Johnson Sylvander, " "
Manchester Wm. "
Smith Henry L. " "
Thayer Leonard D. " "
Smith & Bixby, " "
Spear John W. "
Witherell G. W. & Co. " "
Bodurtha Stephen H. Agawam
Freeland & Wright, Feeding Hills, "
Gaylord Ezra G. " "
Prindle & Landon, Alford
Briggs J. W. "
Higgins John, Amesbury Mills, Amesbury
Cleary John & Son, West Amesbury, "
Pike James D. " "
Atkinson B. F. South Amesbury, "
Rowell Charles E. " "
Conkey W. Amherst
Cutler W. & G. "
Hastings James, "
Kellogg William, "
Palmer & Bangs, "
Howard & Brown, North Amherst, "
Freeman W. H " "
Smith & Field, " "
Dickinson W. South Amherst, "
Abbott Albert, Andover
Abbott H. W. "
Beard H. P. & Co. "
Harding John, "
Holt & Higgins, "
Bird Bros. Ballard Vale, "
Haynes F. G. & Co. " "
Morrison John, " "
Vanness Henry, Ashburnham
Whitney & Greenwood, "
WINCHESTER C. & G. C. "
Green Charles O. Ashby
Whitney L. E. "
Bronson A. E. Ashfield
Cook Moses, "
Crafts A. W. "
Hall Franklin, South Ashfield, "
Ward & Ranney, " "
Coburn & Enslin, Ashland
Pease D. A. "
Wiggins S. W. "
Yeaton Homer, "
Fay Brothers, Athol
Lee & Stevens, "
Tyler P. C. & C. H. Athol Depot, "
Carpenter S. W. & Co. Attleborough
Hebron Manuf. Co. Hebronville, "
Knapp & Holmes, No. Attleborough, "
Lawrence J. E. Auburn
Ward P. M. & Co. "
Conant Chauncy, Barnstable
Howland G. B. & Co. West Barnstable, "
Howland S. N. " "
Parker Frederick, "
Parker J. W. B. & Co. "
Parker S. & Son, "
Crosby & Lewis, Centreville, "
Kelley F. G. "
Coleman John, Cotuit, "
Nickerson Daniel, "
Phinney Elijah, " "
Nickerson Leander, Cotuit Port, "
Chase & Baker, Hyannis, "
Chase L. F. Mrs. " "
Copeland R. B. " "
Hallett Gorham, " "
Hallett Hartson, " "
Thacher & Crowell, " "
Marston William, Marston's Mills, "

Country Stores — continued.

Crocker Israel,	Osterville,	Barnstable
Hinckley Geo. H.	"	"
Shattuck Elam B.		"
Smith Samuel & Son,		Barre
Woods, Harding, & Co.		"
Holbrook John W.	Smithville,	"
Ames Zephaniah,		"
Bidwell, Wheeler, & Co.		Becket
Geer Wm. M.		"
Corey Charles A.		"
Stiles Thomas,		Bedford
Bridgman E. R.		"
Bridgman F. B. & E. S.		Belchertown
Filer George,		"
Green T. R. & Co.		"
Longley S. W.		"
Town Nelson,		"
Thayer R. F.		"
Lawrence S. J. North Bellingham,		Bellingham
Adams Aaron A.		"
Cudworth Samuel H.		Belmont
Fletcher Philip H.		Berkley
Hastings R. S.		"
Cook Lucius W.		Berlin
Stratton Alfred M.		Bernardston
Slate Hollis B.		"
Temple George W.		"
Wright L. B.		"
Herrick S. D.		Beverly
Smith Eben,		"
Symms R. W.		"
Wales Abiel,		"
Perry & Haskell,	Beverly Farms,	"
Hathaway S. F.	North Beverly.	"
Hill S. S.		Billerica
Floyd W. L.	North Billerica,	"
Baker, Benson, & Co.		Blackstone
Boylan Lawrence,		"
Maher & Cosgrave,		"
Staples & Gough,		"
Wheelock & Mason,		"
Cole Wm. A.	Millville,	"
Welch A.	North Blackstone,	"
Robinson H. P.		Blandford
Shepard L. B. & Son,		"
Lloyd S. E. & Son,	North Blandford,	"
Tirrell & Brothers,	"	"
Moore Ezra S.		Bolton
Newton George B.		"
Gage Roscoe W.		Boxford
Walker William R.		Boylston
Kendall Horace, Boylston Centre,		"
Proctor Bros.		Braintree
Hollis S. W.		"
McEwan Wm.	East Braintree,	"
Scholey Thomas,	"	"
Holbrook P. D. & Co.	S. Braintree,	"
WHITE H. M.	"	"
Bates & Bowditch, Weymouth,		"
Foster Joseph,		"
Howes Samuel T.		Brewster
Knowles & Freeman,		"
Lincoln Warren & Co.		"
Robbins & Everett,		"
Ryder Eben F.		"
Winslow B. B. & Co.		"
Myrick Nathaniel,	S. Brewster,	"
Crane Joshua E.		Bridgewater
Crocker T. W.		"
Hobart Caleb,		"
ALLEN W. C.,	Washington st.,	Brighton
Baxter & Sanborn,		"
Brown James T.		Brimfield
Hitchcock Geo. M,		"
Rice William,	East Brimfield,	"
Ainsworth J. L.		Brookfield
Crosby & Davis,		"

Marcy F. N.		Brookfield
Rogers J. H. & Co.		"
Vizard & Mulcahy,		"
Adams Lucy A.	East Brookfield,	"
Donne L. & Co.	"	"
Warren L. & N.	"	"
Harris E. H.		"
Carley R. W.	Shelburne Falls,	Buckland
Newell Brothers,	"	"
Strong & Ferary,	"	"
Bennett Charles W.		Burlington
Cutler Silas,		"
Bent E. & N.		Canton
Billings Leonard & L. L.		"
Briggs Avery S.		"
Capen E.		"
Fuller D. & Bro.		"
Fuller E. O. & H.		"
Tucker A. E.		"
Tucker Robert,		"
Carter Bros.		Carlisle
Ellis M. & Co.	S. Carver,	Carver
Rider Charles,	"	"
Avery A. L.		Charlemont
Hawks J. D.		"
Peck Charles,		"
Tyler A. L.		"
Fiske & Cummins,		Charlton
Brown Amos,		"
Thayer E. C. & E. H.	Charlton City,	"
Ramsdell Wm. H.	" Depot,	"
Sampson Almon,	"	"
Atwood Levi,		Chatham
Buck Lorenzo D.		"
Eldredge Joshua,		"
Harding Freeman,		"
Freeman Benjamin T.		"
Howes Daniel.		"
Kent George N.		
Ryder Christopher,		
Steel Ephraim P.		
Taylor Washington,		"
Parkhurst S. S.		Chelmsford
Bennett J. S.	N. Chelmsford,	"
Wright S. T.	"	"
Woodward H. W.	"	"
Gerrish Thos. M.	South "	"
Perry John N.	West "	"
BOWEN HENRY C.		Cheshire
Brown & Tanner,		"
Cole J. R. & Bro.		"
Dean James B. & Son,		"
Jenks Homer H.		"
Keefe & Bro.		"
White & Ely,		"
Witherell & Engram,		Chesterfield
Tirrell Orrin,	West Chesterfield,	"
Oakes, Bragg, & Co.		Chicopee
Bray Geo. W.		"
Munn Eugene,		Chicopee Falls, "
Taylor & Gilbert,	"	"
Manter Wm. C.		Chilmark
Mayhew Ephraim,		"
Mayhew Oliver,		"
Vincent Matthew,		"
		Clarksburg
Thayer D. & L. D.,	North Adams,	"
Breckenridge I. F.	"	"
Bailey Waterman.		Cohasset
Beal Caleb & Sons,		"
Brown Ezra,		"
Elms E. E.		"
Gross Chas. A.		
Merriam Calvin,		
Nichols Caleb F.		
Pratt Howard,		
Stetson M. B. & Co.		"
Willard Charles H.		

Beal Welcome & Co., North Cohasset,   Cohasset
Beal Z. L. & Co.   "   "
Curtis O. B.   Coleraine
Bell P.   "
Griswoldville Manuf. Co.   "
Shattuck C. W. & Son,   "
Stacy & Davis,   "
Derby Edward.   "
Walcott & Holden,   Concord
Campbell W. C.   "
Andrews Hezekiah,   Conway
Hassell G. P. & Co.   "
Tucker R. M.   "
Lovell D. W.   "
Orcutt L. J.   Cummington
Orcutt N. F.   "
Caswell Albert M., West Cummington,   "
Carson Paper Co.   "
Clark E. & Son,   Dalton
Mitchell Elisha,   "
Brown & Balcom,   "
Johnson Joel,   Dana
Richard D. L.   "
Merriam N. P.,   North Dana,   "
Richards D. & Son,   Danvers Centre, Danvers
Perley A. P. & Co.   "
Prentiss Henry,   "
Warren A. W.   "
Slocum James H.   Danvers Port,   "
Barker Abner P.,   North Dartmouth,   Dartmouth
Reed & Turner,   "   "
Vickery Wm. C.   "   "
Whalen Hiram,   "   "
Potter E. F.   South Dartmouth,   "
Sherman J.   "   "
Boyden & Norris,   E. Dedham, Dedham
Cussier L.   "   "
Bigelow L. Waldo,   South Dedham,   "
Baker L. G.   West   "   "
Ware Edwin,   Deerfield
Harris W. M.   South Deerfield,   "
Lyman & Edwards,   "   "
Sammis D. L.   "   "
Tilton C. B.   "   "
Howes Chapman,   Dennis
Howes James S.   "
Kelley & Sears,   East Dennis,   "
Whelden Andrew,   South Dennis,   "
Crowell Uriah H.   West Dennis,   "
Crowell Zadock,   "
Andrews E. F.   Dighton
Cobb Geo. W. & Son,   "
Phillips William W.   "
Pitts Charles F.   "
Whitmarsh Charles E.   "
Almy Edward & Son, North Dighton,   "
Dunbar George,   "
Kendrick John,   Dorchester
Southworth & Hayden, Port Norfolk,   "
Heath S. W. & Co.   "
Kendall W. H.   Douglas
Putnam James,   "
Jones A. F.   "
Bliss Linus,   E. Douglas,   "
Wilson James H.   Dover
Marshall & Butterfield,   Dracut
Piper & Emery,   "
Barnes Moses, jr.   "
Davis William L.   Dudley
Prout Stephen,   Webster,   "
Folles H. J.   "
Ford Nathl. & Sons,   Dunstable
Chandler Charles H. & Co.   Duxbury
Protective Union, Div. 654,   "
Sampson George F.   "
Soule Harvey,   "
Freeman Winfield S., West Duxbury,   "
14

Conant John A. Mrs.   East Bridgewater
Nutter L. N. & E. W.   "
Shaw Samuel D.   "
Whiting John B.   "
Churchill L. & W. K.   Joppa,   "
Richard Luther W.   "   "
Higgins Beniah G.   Eastham
Knowles Elijah E.   "
Horton I. H.   North Eastham,   "
Chapman & Parsons,   East Hampton
Hathaway G. H.   "
Putnam F. H. & Co.   "
Wells John H.   "
Kimball J. T.   Easton
Drake Joel S.   "
AMES OLIVER & SONS, N. Easton,   "
Strout B & S. B.   N.   "   "
Copeland George,   S.   "   "
Drake George R.   S.   "   "
Bradley Wm.   Edgartown
Dillingham John,   "
Norton Richard,   "
Pease Timothy,   "
Robinson John S.   "
Smith Holmes W.   "

Dewey Seymour B., North Egremont,   Egremont
Joyner N. & Son,   "
Benjamin Calvin W., South Egremont,   "
Shattuck Frederick W.   "   "
Crosby J. M.   Enfield
Haskell Ira D.   "
Walker G. E.   "
Woods J. E. & Co.   "
Rankin Noah,   "
Stratton T. B. & Co.   Erving
Burnham Aaron,   "
Burnham D. B.   Essex
Burnham Geo. W.   "
Burnham Ira F.   "
Cogswell George W.   "
Richardson J. M.   "
Lawrence Thos. H.   Falmouth
Davis Joshua W.   East Falmouth,   "
Tobey George A.   "   "
Union Store No. 226,   "   "
Nye F. G.   North Falmouth,   "
Boyce Gilbert R.   West   "   "
Union Store No. 646,   "   "
Davis & Eldredge,   Woods' Hole,   "
Baldwin Wm. jr., W. Fitchburg, Fitchburg
Phelps Hiram G.   Florida
Smith P. W. & A.   "
Carroll E.   "
Kingsbury J. A.   Foxborough
Bean Cyrus,   "
Childs & Eaton,   Framingham
Trowbridge Geo. A.   "
Warren Edwin H.   "
Barber C. H.   South Framingham,   "
Crosby Seth,   "   "
Howe Willard,   "   "
Fuller L. F.   Saxonville,   "
Bruce & Turner,   "   "
Nye Caleb T.   Franklin
Peabody John W.   "
Bush C. Webster,   Freetown
Conant Francis,   Gardner
Howe N. B.   "
Wood A. S.   "
Stevens & Greenwood, South Gardner,   "
Whitemore & Son,   "   "
Boynton Wm. & Son,   Georgetown
Wheeler Wm. S.   "
Wilson Rockwell B.   "
Hale Otis F.   Gill
Dudley M.   Lanesville,   Gloucester
Godfrey John B.   Goshen

Country Stores — continued.

Falkner & Co.   Grafton
Harrington & Nichols,   "
Munyan W. L.   "
Fisher E. & Son,   Fairnumsville,   "
Morse Alfred,   "   "
Goodrich L. J. & Co.   N. E. Village,   "
Smith A. J. & Co.   "   "
Fowler C. & F.   Saundersville,   "
Chapin Philo,   Granby
Brown R. S.,   East Granville,   Granville
Gibbons J. M.,   Granville Corners,   "
Shepard L. W.   West Granville,   "
Durant Benjamin F.   Great Barrington
Hollister Egbert,   "
Lester & Co.   "
McLean Edwin M.   "
Sanford J. F. & F. T.   "
Siggins & Co.   "
Raymond Isaac,   Housatonic,   "
Selkirt William,   "
VAN DEUSEN NEWTON,   "
Van Densen W. J.   "
Dresser Julius,   Van Deusenville,   "
Dickinson George R.   Greenwich
Brown & Root,   Greenwich Village,   "
Thayer Brothers,   "   "
Bancroft George W.   Groton
Gerrish Charles,   "
Shattuck Walter,   "
Shattuck Milo H.   "
Stevens T. K.   "
Stuart G. W. & Co.   Groton Junction,   "
Robbins & Ames,   "   "
Wheeler, Brown, & Co.   "   "
Greenough Thomas,   Groveland
Hardy George,   "
Hunt Ira,   "
Savary Frank,   "
Griffin Mark,   South Groveland,   "
Parker Charles S.   "   "
Parker Peter,   "   "
Parker W. H. & E. P.   "   "
Porter Wm. P.   Hadley
Cooley S. F.   North Hadley,   "
Smith Thaddeus & Co.   "   "
Drew James T.   Halifax
Inglee Edwin,   "
Poole Caleb, jr. & Bros.   "
Hoyt David M.   Hamilton
Hubbard George W.   "
Norton Frank & Co.   "
Lapham Wm. H.   Hancock
Smith Hiram S.   "
Bates J. B. & Co.   Hanover
Brooks John S., agent Union Store,   "
Curtis Henry J.   "
Curtis Robert S.   "
Killam Robert W.   "
Magoun H. B.   "
Stetson Isaac G. & Co.   "
Bowker Andrew,   Hanson
Drew Cyrus & Son,   "
Howland Albert B.   "
Bowker G. T.   South Hanson,   "
Drayton John,   "
Knight Albert E.   Hardwick
Harny John,   Gilbertville,   "
Hitchcock Chas. F.   "   "
Day John B.   Harvard
Wheeler T. B.   "
Ellis Nathan,   Harwich
Kelly Oliver,   "
Nickerson Obed.   "
Robbins Nathaniel,   "
Smith R. & L. F.   "
Rogers W. S.   East Harwich,   "
Crowell Sheldon, North Harwich,   "

Bassett Ozias,   North Harwich,   Harwich
Robbins Freeman C.   "   "
Sears Elijah B.   "   "
Young Mulford,   "   "
Clark Elisha,   Harwich Port,   "
Doane Valentine,   "   "
Eldredge Z. D.   "   "
Nickerson & Baker,   "   "
Small Einlous,   "   "
Eldridge William M.,   South Harwich,   "
Weeks & Small,   "   "
Chase Erastus & Co.   West Harwich,   "
Nickerson Henry,   "   "
Fitch Bros. & Doane,   Hatfield
Wells & Bardwell,   "
Burnham C. H., Ayer's Village,   Haverhill
Ayer Monroe,   "   "
Scott Edwin,   Hawley
Benjamin Stephen,   W. Hawley,   "
Fuller Clark,   "   "
McGee Horace,   Heath
Burr F. & Co.   Hingham
Burr M. H. & J.   "
Corthell E. C. & E. L.   "
Fearing William,   "
Hersey George, jr. & Co.   "
Hersey Isaac,   "
Jacobs D. & Co.   "
TROWBRIDGE ROSWELL,   "
Whiton Royal,   "
Cushing Alonzo,   South Hingham,   "
Lane Josiah,   "   "
Wilder D. & J.   "   "
Beal Z. C.   North Cohasset,   "
Bowen, Converse, & Co.   Hinsdale
Shaw George D. & Co.   "
Taylor Amory E.   "
Armington S. K.   Holden
Merrick & Son,   "
Parker Charles F.   "
Colburn E. W.   Holliston
Whiting E. F.   "
Daniels Timothy,   "
Hartshorn Dennis,   Braggville,   "
Sweet A. A. & Co.   Hopkinton
Willard & Pillsbury,   "
Phipps Benjamin,   Hayden Row,   "
Gibson & Comey Bros., Woodville,   "
Smith John,   "   "
Morse William H.   Hubbardston
Woodward Lyman,   "
Holden W. P. & Son,   Hudson
Brown Josiah W.   "
Peters & Derby,   "
Tarbell Alden A.   "
Wood Solon,   "
Connell Martin,   Huntington
Munson E. G. & H. W.   "
Pease Edward,   "
Coggswell E. & Son,   Ipswich
Damon Curtis,   "
Jewett I. K.   "
Burges & Bafley,   Kingston
Cobb Philander,   "
Hunt & Sampson,   "
Robbins C. I. & E. F.   "
Fletcher Philip H.   Berkley,   Lakeville
Fairbanks Charles H.   Lancaster
Howard Daniel M.   "
Wilder Solon,   "
Lanesborough Iron Co.   Lanesborough
Fuller William A.   "
Wood L. D.   "
Page & Harding,   "
Boland Peter,   Lee
Bosworth Edward,   "
Cormick & Purcell,   "
Garfield Harrison,   "

Hitchcock & Bradley,	Lee
Langdon Edward A.	"
Sparks A. C.	"
Taylor William,	"
Bristol Alvin L.	East Lee, "
Hamblin William P.	" "
Hart E. M. & Co.	" "
Kellogg LeRoy S.	South Lee "
MERRILL J. T. & CO.	" "
THURSTON L. D.	Leicester
White William B.	"
Bottomly Jerome,	Cherry Valley, "
O'Brien T. J.	" "
Draper D. F.	Clappville, "
Jones & Graham,	" "
Heermance H. S.	Lenox
Wright Samuel C.	"
Lenox Iron Works,	Lenox Furnace, "
Dewey Chauncey E.	New Lenox, "
GOSS & HARTHAN,	Leominster
Chase F. C. & Co.	"
Wilder & Hills,	"
Fiske Joseph A.,	North Leominster, "
Howe William F.	" "
Field B. M.	Leverett
Field E. P.	"
Chittenden Otis,	North Leverett, "
Butters Charles A.	Lexington
Childs Augustus,	"
Holbrook & Wellington,	"
Saville Leonard A.	"
Darling U. T.	Leyden
Chapin James L.	Lincoln
Chase Geo. W.	Littleton
Conant Brothers,	"
Sawyer A. W. & Co.	"
Noble Lester,	Longmeadow
Billings Prescott,	East Longmeadow "
Russell Cortez F.	Ludlow
Ro't Hezekiah & Sons,	Ludlow
Smith Eli M.	"
Putnam Daniel,	Lunenburg
Putney G. H.	Lynnfield
Russell L. H.,	Lynnfield Centre, "
Allen Geo. F.	Manchester
Crafts Walter V.	"
Lee John E.	"
Little John,	"
Story L. W.	"
Rogerson & Hodges,	Mansfield
Delano Charles H.	Marion
Hadley A. J.	"
Hall S. W.	"
Mendall Jonathan,	"
Swift M. H.	"
Holman & Clapp,	Marlborough
Howe Lewis A.	"
Morse Henry,	"
MORSE & BIGELOW,	"
Quirk & Brewin,	"
Stewart & Moore,	"
Baker George M.	Marshfield
Crossly H. T. & Son,	"
Hall Warren,	"
Joyce David T.	"
Hall Elisha W.,	East Marshfield, "
Tilden Charles L.	"
Tilden William M.	" "
Weatherbee Geo. H. jr.	" "
Conant Mary T.	North Marshfield, "
LeBaron Lemuel,	Mattapoisett
Menhell Abby J.	"
Snow A. W.	"
Snow Harvey	"
Barney Thomas L.	Medfield
Fiske Isaac,	"
Chace B. S.	Medway
Kimball Wales,	"

Mason H. E. & Co.	Medway
Tyler E. H.	Rockville, "
Daniels Milton, East Medway,	"
Tuttle J. W.	"
Clark L. & E.	West Medway, "
Coombs James,	"
Ware & Hill,	" "
Aldrich Henry A.	Mendon
Carleton Guy,	Methuen
Dodge & Fulton,	"
Gale A. L.	"
Sawyer George W.	"
Peirce Peter H. & Co.	Middleborough
Washburn Philander,	"
Eddy J. M.	East Middleborough, "
White & Hooper,	N. Middleborough, "
Union Store,	So. Middleborough, "
Smith Israel,	Rock, "
Carver & Atwood,	"
Church S. U. & Brothers,	Middlefield
Holden H.	"
Smith Matthew,	"
Averill E. P. & Co.	Middleton
Merriam William A.	"
Wilkins Henry A.	"
Bancroft H. L. & Co.	Millbury
Emerson J.	"
Hall S. D. & Son,	"
Goulding Ephraim,	West Millbury, "
Babcock J. W.	Milton
Gordon David W.	"
Tarbox G. W.	"
Chapin Brothers,	Monson
Newton John,	"
Norcross Albert,	"
Towne E. E.	"
Learned James,	Montague
Learned J. H. & C. H.	"
Wright & Chenery,	"
Higley, Langdon, & Co.	Monterey
Langdon Wilbur,	"
Mansir Oscar L.	"
Johnson Franklin E.	Nahant
Johnson Welcome W.	"
Cathcart Ariel,	Nantucket
Cathcart Wm. C.	"
Colesworthy Henry,	"
Eldredge, Davis, & Kenney,	"
Eldridge K. & Co.	"
Fitzgerald N.	"
Luce Charles,	"
Avery George,	Needham
Parker O. C.	"
Smiley David,	Grantville, "
Tufts George K.	New Braintree
Pearson Henry E.	Newbury
Caldwell John,	Newburyport
Wright S. W. & Co.	New Marlborough
Starks J. R.	Hartsville, "
Baldwin William R.	Southfield "
Walter, Baldwin, & Co.	"
Stannard Dyer,	Mill River, "
Wolfe J. S.	" "
Haskell F. A.	New Salem
Bullard C. A.	North New Salem, "
Kellogg F. D. & E. N.	Millington, "
Wiley Moses, North Prescott,	"
Billings Albert,	Upper Falls, Newton
Trowbridge A.	Newton Centre, "
Clark Wm. & Co.	Northampton
Ross E. S.	Leeds, "
Cutler H. F.	Florence, "
FLORENCE MERCANTILE CO., H.	
K. Parsons, agt.	Florence, "
Parsons Isaac S. & Co.	"
Barnes P. W.	North Andover
Carleton Amos D.	"
CHENEY A. P.	

Country Stores — continued.

PRESCOTT ABBOTT,   North Andover
Stevens Warren,   "
Stone John & Co.   Northborough
Wadsworth John,   "
Wood Samuel, jr. & Co.   "
Pettee S.   Northbridge
Smith L. F.   "
Batchelor Charles O.,   N. Centre, "
Dudley P. W. & Co,   Whitinsville, "
Taft Peter M.   "   "
Whitin N. D.   "   "
Cobb David,   North Bridgewater
Hayward Daniel,   "
Sprague Chandler,   "
Packard George A.   North-West
   Bridgewater,   "
Keith Z. C.   Campello,   "
Clark Timothy P.   North Brookfield
Lincoln & May,   "
Poland & Stoddard,   "
SMITH AUGUSTUS,   "
Union Store No. 99, C. Duncan,
   agent,   "
Belding E. E.   Northfield
Fay W. L.   "
Osgood Charles,   "
Walker S. Y.   "
Penno Joseph H.   North Chelsea
Damon Alonzo F.   North Reading
Eaton James L.   "
Mutual Union,   "
Whitcomb Jared P.   "
Bates Horatio,   Norton
Boyland Thomas E.   "
Dean Lewis,   Oakham
Prouty Alanson,   "
Woodard & Davis,   Cold Brook, "
Addy & Goddard,   Orange
Penney H. C. & Co.   "
Whipple & Parker,   "
Johnson Nathan L.,   North Orange, "
Mayo Caleb   "   "
Shipman Reuben & Co.   Orleans
CUMMINGS JOSEPH H.   "
Higgins Abner,   "
Hurd Davis,   "
Nickerson George,   "
Rogers Prince,   "
Smith Thomas,   "
Sparrow Joel,   "
Young Jonathan,   "
Crosby Solomon, East Orleans,   "
Higgins Lot,   "
Higgins Nathan,   South Orleans, "
Snerick John,   "   "
Hull Lloyd,   Otis
Horton Samuel H,   "
Sandler Clark,   East Otis, "
Merriam A. E. & Co.   Oxford
Ela James C.   "
Howe William E. & Co.   "
Bartlett E.   North Oxford, "
Bailey L. E.   "   "
Daley A. W.   "   "
Smith S. S. & Co.   "   "
Case W. W.   Palmer
Nichols, French, & Tinkham,   "
Law James B.   "
Murdock & Brothers, Bond's Village, "
Murdock Elijah G.   Thorndike, "
Packard W. N.   "
Bliss Frank,   Three Rivers, "
Park Nathaniel & Co.   Paxton
Hinton Mynett E.   Pelham
Hall Jerald,   "
Protective Union 355, Isaac Jen-
   nings, agent,   Pembroke

Poole Andrew F., East Pembroke,   Pembroke
Arnold Francis P., North Pembroke,   "
Blackman Allen,   "   "
Holmes Samuel,   "   "
Bryant William H. H., South Hanson, "
Protective Union, Israel Thrasher,   "
Barrett Benjamin F.   Pepperell
Locke True T.   "
Saunders Amos,   "
Simpson L. C.   "
Loring John,   "
Parker H. A. & Co.,   East Pepperell, "
Tarbell T. F. jr.   "   "
Bowen W. S. & S. S.   Peru
Tolman J. & Co.   Petersham
Wetherell & Mudge,   "
Mixter Orlando,   Phillipston
Pike S. E.   "
Curtis & Evans,   Pittsfield
Morey & Hand,   "
Norton H. L.   "
West John C. & Brother,   "
Pomeroy's L. Sons,   "
Barker J. & Brothers, W. Pittsfield, "
Stearnsville Manuf. Co.,   "   "
Bartlett Ansel,   Plainfield
Campbell Leonard,   "
Bosworth J. P.   Plymouth
Morton Alvin G.   "
TURNER EZEKIEL C.   "
Wadsworth Wait,   "
Bartlett George F.,   Chiltonville, "
Bramhall George,   "   "
Battles Caleb,   "
Clark William,   South Plymouth, "
Hovey Josiah C.   "   "
Parker Zaccheus,   Plympton
Crosett Liberty,   Prescott
Hunt N. & Co.   North Prescott, "
Thomas E. A.   "   "
Davis John C.   Princeton
Gregory D. H. & Co.   "
Union Store,   East Princeton, "
Atwood John, jr. & Co.   Provincetown
BOWLY J. E. & G.   "
Chase Frank,   "
Conwell David,   "
Cook E. & F. K.   "
COOK H. & S. & Co.   "
Cook Stephen,   "
Cowing H. W.   "
Freeman Francis M.   "
Freeman & Hilliard,   "
Lewis Joshua,   "
Lewis Bangs A. & Co.   "
MAYO ISAAC F.   "
NICKERSON R. E. & A. & Co.   "
Paine J. & L. N.   "
Rich S. & J.   "
Rogers Manuel,   "
Ryder Reuben,   "
SMALL E. E.   "
UNION WHARF CO.   "
Abercrombie Wyman,   Quincy
Baxter Geo. L. & Co.   "
Blake A. F. & J. N.   "
Clapp Elbridge,   "
Hall & Lane,   "
Hammond Charles,   "
LOCKE GEORGE H.   "
Whitney & Nash,   "
Wood John A.   "
Crane L. L.   Quincy Point, "
Newcomb S. F.   "   "
Morton Cyrus, jr.   Randolph
Prescott G. H. & C.   "
Lincoln & Sylvester,   E. Randolph, "

Packard H. H., East Randolph, Randolph
King Theodore, Raynham
Lincoln Edward H. "
Makepeace Sylvanus, "
Robinson Samuel W. "
Washburn Chauncey G. "
Foot Jonathan, Reading
Black Johnson, Rehoboth
Leonard Joseph F. "
Norton Edward H. "
Peck Philip W. "
Pierce Lloyd B. "
Marvel John C. & Son, "
Peck Cyril G. jr., North Rehoboth, "
Castle E. C. Richmond
Richmond Mercantile Co. "
Cushman Jesse M. Rochester
Leonard Theodore W. "
Sherman John W. "
Story A. W. Pigeon Cove, Rockport
Amidon E. E. "
Boynton Henry, Rowe
Boynton John, Rowley
Kimball George, "
Prime D. N. & Sons, "
Todd J. Scott, "
Bartlett H. C. Royalston
Murdock B. B. & Co. S. Royalston, "
Newton C. H. & Co. " "
Rich Benjamin W. " "
Gibbs J. W. & Co. Russell
Root S. F. "
Davis Alonzo, Rutland
Putnam Charles H. "
Welch Guilford, North Rutland, "
Pierce Charles, West " "
Salisbury
Keniston F. & Co., Salisbury Point, "
Fifield A. L. " "
Kingsbury Henry & Co. " "
Morrill Ezra, " "
Purrington J. A. " "
Taylor & Castle, Sandisfield
Morrill J. H., Montville, "
Moore J. New Boston, "
Parson & Wilcox, " "
Burgess Charles H. Sandwich
ELLIS H. G. O. "
Holway Alvah, "
LAPHAM WILLIAM F. "
Blackington Charles A., Monument, "
Swift Abram, " "
Bourne Charles, North Sandwich, "
Ellis Rufus, " "
Collins Virgil B., South Sandwich, "
Crocker Heman C. " "
Crowell Paul, West Sandwich, "
Crowell Hiram, " "
Swift Levi, " "
Raymond Asa, Pocasset, "
Saugus Centre, Saugus
Lawrence J. D. & Co. "
Wyman Charles E. "
Union Store, Division 604, Savoy
Reed William A. & Son, "
Wing Branan, "
Allen William P. Scituate
Ford Daniel & Co. "
Smith J. Hill, "
Turner E. A. "
Brown Benj. jr. North Scituate, "
Litchfield M. S. & Z. H. " "
Severns & Cushing, " "
Vinal Dexter, " "
Charles Asa, Seekonk
Luther Gardner, "
Wheeler Dexter, "
Drake Nelson, Sharon

Long John F. Sharon
Pettee D. Webster, "
Turner Calvin, "
Field Joel H. Sheffield
Huckins John L. "
Little Lucius, "
Strong Tillinghast B. Ashley Falls, "
Leroy A. " "
Thurston Henry C. "
Rood & Taft, East Sheffield. "
Thayer Joel, Shelburne Falls, Shelburne
Clark Charles A. Sherborn
Clark George "
Ballou S. J. Shirley
Boynton W. B. "
Longley J. P. "
Gardner J. & Co. Shirley Village, "
Boutell Samuel B. Shrewsbury
Green Charles O. "
Harrington Eli, "
Howe Samuel Q. "
Brown & Broad, Shutesbury
Chase Leonard & Co. Somerset
Bell Edwin, Southampton
Judd A. G. "
Lyman G. "
Newton L. W. Cordaville, Southborough
Wright Brothers, " "
Alden Wm. E., Globe Village, Southbridge
Thayer Solomon, " "
Chamberlin George, South Hadley
Montague Elliot, "
Taylor John P. & Co. "
Smith Hiram, jr. South Hadley Falls, "
Wright Ira B. & Co. " " "
Fogg Ebenezer T. South Scituate
Ford Henry, "
Little Melvin, "
Tolman Thomas & Son, "
Torrey George H. "
Granger S. L. & O. A. Southwick
Shurtleff Carmi & Co. "
Bemis Lorenzo, Spencer
Grout J. N. & Co. "
Pope Joseph, "
Wilson Winthrop, "
Prouty T. A. & Co. "
Kimberly J. & Co. Springfield
HARRINGTON & McLEAN,
Indian Orchard, "
Sanborn Brothers, Sterling
Smith J. S. "
Fitts Julius, West Sterling, "
Custis Chauncey, Stockbridge
Plumb H. L. & Co. "
Seymour Egbert, "
Burrall Henry M. Curtisville, "
Jones Abner, "
Strong & Wentworth, Glendale, "
Belcher O. Stoughton
Drake & Tenney, "
Flint & Savels, "
Southworth Bros. "
Swan W. R. "
Wales Nathaniel, "
Blanchard Nathan, East Stoughton, "
Littlefield Isaac, "
Gill Henry M. North " "
Fletcher John L. Stow
Mossman & Co. Assabet, "
Gleason Alfred D. Rock Bottom, "
Murdock Charles, "
Chamberlain Alvan, Sturbridge
Chamberlain J. N. jr. "
Corey Frank "
Bates, Haynes, & Co. Fiskdale, "
Taft A. D. " "
Upham William H. " "

Country Stores — continued.

Burbeck & Willis,	Sudbury
Hunt J. S.	"
Hunt E. & Son,	South Sudbury, "
Eames A. A. & Co.	Assabet, "
Haynes Brothers	" "
Dunlap Samuel,	Sunderland
Holbrook Wilder S.	"
Woodbury Luther,	Wilkinsville, "
Hill William R.	" "
Waters Samuel N.	West Sutton, "
Abbott William,	Manchaug, "
Thompson G. E.	" "
Johnson Pliny F.	South Sutton, "
Chace Joseph F.	Swansea
Chace Elijah P.	"
Gray Samuel,	"
Luther Joseph G.	"
Mason Daniel,	"
Marvel Bennanuel,	"
Wood Henry O.	"
Albro B. D. & E. F.	Taunton
Chase & Spencer,	"
JACKSON & WILLIAMS, 43 & 45 City sq.	"
Farnham H. L.	"
Pratt & Thomas,	"
Sanders George B.	East Taunton, "
Taylor William E.	Myricks, "
Walker Allen C.	" "
MANN G. A. & A. F.	Westville, "
Dudley & Blodgett,	Templeton
Jones Julius A.	"
Sargeant Fitch L.	East Templeton, "
Rodiman W. S.	Baldwinville, "
Sawyer, Thompson, & Perley,	"
Leland F.	Otter River, "
Warner & Kirchner,	" "
Frost Aaron,	Tewksbury
Preston H. E.	"
	Tisbury
Bradley Thomas & Son, Holmes's Hole, "
Coffin R. W.	" "
Crocker Wendal,	" "
Crowell Benjamin D.	" "
Robinson John F.	" "
Taber James M.	" "
Weeks Charles,	" "
Gorham Job H.	West Tisbury, "
Mayhew Nathan,	" "
Rotch William J.	" "
Union Store, Joseph B. Nickerson, agent,	West Tisbury, "
Snow William,	Tolland
Adams Benjamin P.	Topsfield
Kimball W. E. & Son,	"
Dix William, Townsend Centre, Townsend
Osgood Charles,	" "
Taylor Wm. P.	" "
Emery Charles,	Townsend Harbor, "
Manning Charles & Co., W. Townsend, "
Shattuck E. A.	" "
Cole Joseph S.	Truro
Dyer Samuel,	"
Knowles Joshua,	"
Lombard E. P. & Son,	"
Paine A. & Co.	"
Rich Isaac,	"
Rich Josiah F.	"
Whorf Joseph,	"
Small Francis,	North Truro, "
Thompson John G.	" "
Littlehale J. H. D.	Tyngsborough
Webster Urson,	Tyringham
Cobbett A.	Upton
Forbush Horace & Co.	"
Holbrook Benjamin F.	"
Stoddard Hartford,	"

Fairbanks Charles,	Uxbridge
Mason & O'Keefe,	"
Scott & Murdock,	"
Thompson H. & E. F.	"
Chase Horatio C.	North Uxbridge, "
Sweet & Hayward,	" "
Barker Jacob,	Wales
Parker D. F.	"
Billings H. T. & Co.	Walpole
Craig E. C. & Co.	"
Hammond J. C. & Co.	"
Johnson George W.	E. Walpole, "
Boyden Jere.	South " "
Wilmarth & Boyden,	" " "
Hitchcock C.	Ware
Mongrain R. C. & Co.	"
Sanford Addison,	"
Snow & Puffer,	"
Bodfish P. N.	Wareham
Fearing F. H.	"
Gibb's Alvin,	"
Howard B. F.	"
Robinson M. & S. T.	"
Thompson E. N.	"
Gale & Humphrey,	East Wareham, "
Sanford George,	" "
Keyes William,	South " "
Fuller John S.	West " "
Allen Reuben,	Warren
Blair & Keyes,	"
Davis E.	"
Fairbanks & Newton,	"
Shepard D. W. & Co.	"
Lombard & Burroughs, West Warren, "
Atherton Arlon S.	Warwick
Goldsbury Forrest,	"
Howard C. L.	Wayland
Atwood Daniel C.	Cochituate, "
Loker John L.	" "
Moore Joseph M.	" "
McQuaid T. & P.	Webster
Pratt W. H.	"
Wood D. & H.	"
Atwood Harding,	Wellfleet
Baker N. M. & Co.	"
Freeman Timothy A.	"
HIGGINS J. R. & CO.	"
Higgins P. W.	"
Newcomb, Kemp, & Co.	"
Wiley F. A. & Co.	"
Forbes Joseph,	Wendell
Putnam Danforth,	"
Putnam John,	"
Fowler W. W.	Wenham
Griggs S. M. & Co.	Westborough
Sawyer & Walker,	West Boylston
Waite & Co.	"
Waite J. E. & Co.	Oakdale, "
Whiting Alfred N.	"
Baker & Williams,	West Bridgewater
Perkins Charles,	Cochesett, "
Blair E. H.	West Brookfield
Gleason A. C. & J. S.	"
Cutler J. E.	"
Fowler & Killam,	Westfield
Loomis Henry,	"
Snow & Hibbard,	"
Fletcher John B.	"
Fletcher Sherman D.	"
Wilcox Samuel,	"
Wright & Co.	Graniteville, Westford
Chapman Anson,	West Hampton
Judd Fred. H.	"
Kendall & Cheney,	Westminster
Eames & Giles,	"
Wyman Franklin, Wachusett Village, "
Chase Enoch D.	West Newbury
Bailey Daniel D.	"

Noyes & Whittier, West Newbury
Cutting George W. & Son, Weston
Anthony & Macomber, Westport
Westport Manuf. Co. "
Winchester & White, "
Brownell E. P. & Son, Central Village, "
Cory A. H. Westport Point, "
Macomber R. & Son, " "
Merrick & Haysington, West Springfield
Burgess J. L. & Son, Mittineague, "
Geer & Ames, " "
Bostwick & Tanner, West Stockbridge
Edwards William H. "
Kniffin Brothers, "
Shaw Nathan, . "
Tanner F. W. "
Arnold G. & Son, State Line, "
CHURCH SILAS L. " "
Radcliff & Allen, Weymouth
Tirrell E. G. "
Bicknell Bros. East Weymouth, "
Burrell Samuel, " "
Loud Henry, " "
Pratt Nathan, " "
Rogers N. C. " "
Shaw Benjamin F. " "
Bartlett J. W. North Weymouth, "
Blanchard Solon, " "
N. E. P. Union 136, " "
Nash Wm. G. South Weymouth, "
Stowell Noah jr. " "
Crafts Albert W. Whately
Thayer Caleb L. "
Leech C. C. Wilbraham
Pickering S. F. "
Wright R. R. & Son, "
Fuller Henry S. Collins Depot, "
Gates E. B. " "
Converse & Co. South Wilbraham, "
Hendrick H. H. " "
Spellman S. Clark, " "
Spellman Wm. P. " "
Carter T. M. Williamsburg
James L. D. & Brother, "
Wait C. D. "
Thayer W. E. "
Warner L. H. "
Smith & Fay, Haydenville, "
Cole Harvey T. Williamstown
Cole P. R. "
Mather Benjamin F. "
Mather Charles H. "
Mather S. T. "
Morey William, "
Sherman Eber, "
Whipple J. H. "
Ames Joseph A. Wilmington
Ames William, "
Nichols Samuel B. "
Parker C. C. Winchendon
Smith A. B. "
Whitney Amasa, "
Whittemore Wm. H. "
Bicknell L. E. "
Shaw F. E. Windsor
Erwin Samuel P. East Windsor, "
Johnson & Long, Winthrop
Magee Edward, "
TAY C. & CO. (see page 766), Woburn
Thompson A. E. & Co. "
NICHOLS & LINSCOTT, N. Woburn, "
Thompson A. & E. E. "
Brewster E. H. & Son, Worthington
Cole Horace & Son, "
Hoppin C. A. Webster Sq. "
Cook Daniel A. & Co. Worcester
Stone C. & Son, Wrentham
Andrews Nathl., N. Wrentham, "

North Wrentham, Wrentham
Bachelder E. M. " "
Trowbridge Henry, " "
Rhodes Edward T., Plainville, . "
Baker Braddock, S. Yarmouth, Yarmouth
Farris Russell D. " "
Matthews Freeman, " "
Crowell Freeman H., W. Yarmouth, "
Crowell Isaiah, " "
Baker Sylvester, Jr. & Co. Yarmouth
  Port, " "
Crocker Dan. B. & Co. Yarmouth Port, "
Knowles James, " "
Payne Dexter E. " "

Cracker Bakers.

MILLER BROTHERS (see page
  718), Great Barrington

Crayon Manufacturers.

Parmenter & Walker, Waltham

Crockery, China, Glass, and Earthen Ware.

Carpenter N. D., N. Adams, Adams
Urann & Keyes, "
Welles Henry N. "
Thorpe & Osgood, Athol Depot, Athol
STARKEY L. T. (see page 718), Attleboro'
Herrick Samuel D. Beverly
Symmes R. W. "
Hunting & Co. Brookline
Russell M. "
Newell Bros., Shelburne Falls, Buckland
Bates Geo. W. Cambridge
Graves Geo., Jr. "
Holmes & Davis, "
Oxford & Brigham, "
Russell Amos, "
Robinson John, Cambridgeport, "
Gage Benjamin W. Charlestown
Moore Wm. B. & Son, "
KNOX BENJ. H. & CO., 45 & 47
  Park st., Chelsea
Merrill & Morrison, "
SAUNDERS & LOGAN, 67 Park
  st. (see page 712), "
Chase C. H Clinton
McQuaid T. A. & Co. "
Tyler & White, "
Wilder W. G. & Co. "
Harwood J. Danvers
NEWHALL BENJAMIN E. "
Weeks Henry W. Dedham
Flint J. D. & Co. Fall River
Hathaway & Deane, "
Nichols L. & Co. "
Wilcox D. T. "
Wood H. S. "
Guy T. F. Fitchburg
Lewis & Sawtell, "
Sprague L. & Co. "
Mayo J., Jr. Gloucester
Procter Charles, "
Rogers C. H. "
Story Cyrus, "
ROBBINS HENRY T. Great Barrington
Pierce George, Jr. Greenfield
Appleton John A., Jr. Haverhill
Kimball & Gould, "
Gassett Brothers, Holliston
Crafts R. P. Holyoke
Doyle & Finn, "
HIGGINS DENNIS, "
Munsell & Sears, "
Tuttle & Moore, "
Morse W. H. & Co. Hopkinton
Woodward D. P. & Co. "

Crockery, China, etc.—continued.
Abrams L. H. & Co. (lamps, &c.), Lawrence
Howe & Co. "
Woodman Chas. S. & Co. "
Clough Ira A. Lowell
French & Puffer, "
MEHAN JOHN & BROTHER, 24
 Prescott, "
NASH J. W. & CO., 105 Central,
 (see page 739), "
Gordon E. H. Lynn
OSBORNE E. W. & CO., Market sq. "
WELCH JACOB & CO., 1 Sagamore
 Hotel, "
Hathaway Stephen, Marblehead
LeMaster George, "
WEEKS & SMITH, Marlborough
BAILEY CHARLES H. Nantucket
ALLEN & BLISS, 121 Union, New Bedford
Bennett Samuel, "
Purrington & Brown, "
Taylor Henry J. "
Bassett N. G. Newburyport
Foster N. & T. "
Moulton Joseph, "
White J. M. Newton Centre, Newton
Arnold W. F. & Co. Northampton
Morton & Hayden, "
Skilton Otis A. "
Curtis S. G. & B. E. North Bridgewater
Hayward Ambrose, "
Reed Thomas, "
Guy & Brothers, Peabody
Grant & Davis, Pittsfield
Henry Harvey, "
Harlow & Barnes, Plymouth
TURNER E. C. "
Snow C. B. Provincetown
SMALL REUBEN C. "
Burrill J. F. Quincy
FURNALD N. B. "
Story Austin W. Rockport
Wheeler D. A. "
Bowditch Wm. A. & Co. Salem
Glazier Ezra & Son, "
Guy & Bros. "
Simonds S. C. & E. A. "
Fifield Benj. E., Amesbury, Salisbury
Burgess Chas. H. Sandwich
Hamilton, Lincoln, & Co. Springfield
Hill William, "
Hoard N. S. Taunton
Reed Edgar H. "
Washburne E. E. "
West L. B. & Co. "
Padelford D. Weir, "
Hitchcock C. Ware
Sandford A. "
Wetherbee S. & J. Warren
NOURSE & BARNARD, Watertown
Pratt Wm. H. Webster
Wood D. & H. "
Gould Wm. R. Westboro'
Morse G. W. & Co. "
Gibbs J. W. & CO. Westfield
TAY C. & CO., Main (see page
 766), Woburn
Brown Albert S. Worcester
Black, Sawyer, & Co. "

Croquet Equipments.

Parker Bowdoin S. & Co. Greenfield
HADLEY & ROBEY, Rock. cor.
 Cushing, Lowell
Locke N. C. Salem

Crucible Manufacturers.

PHŒNIX MANUF. CO. Charles H.
 Atwood, agt., West Water st. (see
 page 726), Taunton
Taunton Crucible Co. "

Cultivators.

(See Agricultural Implements.)

Curled Hair Manufacturers.

(For Upholsterers.)

English Wm. G. Salem
Manning, Glover, & Co. Walpole

Curriers.

(See also Tanners and Curriers.)

West S. O. East Brookfield, Brookfield
 Cambridge
Downing Theodore, Cambridgeport, "
Fisher Ferdinand, "
Kuebler M. "
Muller Wm. "
Guild Chester & Sons, Charlestown
Lane George, "
Mann Alexander, "
McGinness Michael, "
Sears William, "
Davidson Walter, Chelsea
Farwell H. B. & Co. "
Follis John, "
Stone James, "
Chase Edmund, Fall River
Peirce Joseph, 2d, Fitchburg
Bigelow A. M. & Co. Grafton
Bigelow E. B. "
Dodge L. W. & Son, "
Estabrook Geo. W. "
McKenzie J. W. "
Moulton B. K. "
Stratton Oscar, "
Burget John, Great Barrington
Butters F. jr. Haverhill
Morrill J. B. & Co. "
EASTON D. M. & F. A. Hyde Park
Grout John M. Leicester
Mitchell P. East Lexington, Lexington
Cook E. G. Lowell
Ingham John, "
Cruse Solomon, Malden
Fisher H. & J. S. "
Walsh Michael H. "
Whittemore Geo. South Malden, "
Mayhew A. C. & Co. Milford
Fenton R. O. Monson
Tobey C. C. "
Wade Job, New Bedford
Morey H. A. Northampton
CLARK SAMUEL, North Brookfield
Rogers James R. "
Merriam William, Palmer
Adams Horace, Peabody
Brooks & Messer, "
Brown & Caller, "
Chandler S. C. "
Cook M. "
Fernald Luther & Co. "
Giddings Joshua, "
Jacobs Joseph, jr. "
Lord John A. "
Lord William N. "
McClure E. M. "
Osborn C. W. & Bro. "
Osborn F. jr. & Co. "
Pinder & Winchester, "
Plummer Hiram, "
Poor Joseph S. "
Poor L. & F. H. "
Porter Andrew, "

Proctor E. Thomas,   Peabody
Richardson & Coolidge,   "
Sanger Augustus H.   "
Sanger A. H. jr.   "
Southwick S. A.   "
Steele John,   "
Steward & Bacon,   "
Semonds R. S. D.   "
Wheeler A. F   "
Gigeeler William,   Quincy
Whiting Joseph W.   "
Andrews Gilman A.   Salem.
Bott James,   "
Bott Wm.   "
Braden James,   "
Conroy James H.   "
Conway J. H.   "
Culliton John,   "
Dalton Joseph A.   "
Derby George F.   "
Driscolls & Looney,   "
Dugan James,   "
Eagan & McGrath,   "
Egan Martin,   "
Evans A. A. & Sons,   "
Fanning James,   "
Frye Daniel & Co.   "
Gibney John,   "
Harrington Charles & Co.   "
Harrington L. B.   "
Haskell Daniel C.   "
Hill & Brown,   "
Horton & Crocker,   "
Huse John,   "
Madigan & Brennan,   "
Martin Wm. P.   "
McCarty M.   "
Muhlig Robert,   "
Perkins Joseph S.   "
Pitman Benj. jr.   "
Pitman George,   "
Pitman S. jr.   "
Pratt Elisha,   "
Putnam Jacob & Co.   "
Riley James,   "
Robson Matthew,   "
Sanborn James A.   "
Shaw & Bruce,   "
Snow & Redmond,   "
Simpson James B.   "
Treadwell Nathaniel R.   "
Varney W., D., & S.   "
Walden Joseph S.   "
Weston Charles & Sons,   "
Williams U. R,   "
Campbell H. C. & Co.   Stoneham
Cotton J. R.   Stoughton
Trott Samuel S.   "
Byron John T.   West Roxbury
Byron Joseph,   "
Dolan Charles,   "
Leach Ezra,   Weymouth
Morand Frank,   Westfield
Payne Sylvanus,   Winthrop
Colegate Wm. A.   Woburn
Cummings E. & Co.   "
Furbush J. R   "
KINNEY, GALLAGHER, & CO.   "
LINNELL & CUMMINGS,   "
Maxwell John,   "
Trowan & Wildgery,   "
Cummings J. O. & Co., N. Woburn,   "
Fox Warren,   "
Munroe Harris,   "
Richardson Clark T.   "
Skinner James & Co.   "
Putnam J. R.   "
Warren Samuel,   Worcester

Curriers' Grease.

         Cambridge
Cooper Charles & Son, Cambridgeport, "
Cooper Wm. & Son,   "

Curriers' Tools and Tables.

Grant Joshua B.   Salem
         Woburn
COFFIN T. T. . Horn Pond Station, "
Keyes Franklin,   "

Curtain Cord Manufacturers.

SILVER LAKE MANUF. CO., Newtonville

Curtain Fixture Manufs.

Marden C. W.   Chelsea
Putnam S. S. & Co. Neponset, Dorchester

Cutlery Grinder.

         Shelburne
Thompson John, Shelburne Falls, "

Cutlery Manufacturers.

(See also Edge Tools; also Knife Manuf.)
Taylor L. B. & Co.   Chicopee
JOHN RUSSELL MANUF. CO.
   (table cutlery and butcher knives),
   E. M. Chapman, agent,   Greenfield
MOORHOUSE WILLIAM,
   South Foxborough,   Foxborough
MOORHOUSE JOHN (see page
   732),   Mansfield
         Pepperell
Burkinshaw Aaron (pocket knives). "
Lothrop H. A. & Co.   Sharon
Dewsnap E. L., Shelburne Falls. Shelburne
LAMSON & GOODNOW MFG. CO.
   (manufacturers of every descrip-
   tion of pearl, ivory, horn, and
   wood-handle table cutlery: butch-
   er, cook, and shoe knives, and
   pocket cutlery; also at Windsor,
   Vermont, Lamson's patent wood
   and iron scythe snaths). Office
   and warehouse, 53 Beekman st.,
   N. Y.   Joseph W. Gardner,
   agent,   Shelburne Falls, "
Rose Jacob,   Springfield
Lee Samuel,   Taunton

Cutters and Dies.

Curtis T. A.   East Brookfield
Ricard Hubert,   Haverhill
Sheldon Elbridge,   "
DAWES F. S. (see page 781),   Hudson
Coyle John,   Lynn
TRIPP SETH D. 13 Broad (see
   page 750),   "
Draper & Woodbury,   Marlborough
Ladd N. D.   Sturbridge
Howe A. M.   Worcester
TOUGAS & DUPREY, 9 Cypress
   (see page 781),   "

Cyanuret of Potassium.

DAVIS HENRY V. (see page 729),
   40 No. Water,   New Bedford

Daguerreotypists.

(See Photographers, &c.)

Daguerreotype Case Manuf.

         Northampton
FLORENCE MANUF. CO., Florence, "

Decalcomanie.

NICKERSON GEORGE Y. 84 William,   New Bedford

Deck Plugs and Wedges.

Peckham Perry M.   Fall River

Dentists.

Bourne S. E.   Abington
Ring F.   "
DOSHAM & MIETT, East Abington,   "
Howland Samuel F.   Adams
Brown Wm. F.   North Adams, "
Davenport Ammon F.   "   "
Brown A. T.   Amesbury
Collins Hiram,   "
Perkins J. A.   "
Leach Benjamin F.   Amherst
Vincent J. J.   "
Blake Josiah S.   Andover
Williams & Humphrey,   Athol
Hemenway J.   Athol Depot,   "
Smith Horace C.   "   "
Martin Alfred,   Attleborough
Chapman J. W., Hyannis,   Barnstable
Howland A. A.   Barre
Hosmer Thomas B.   Bedford
Griswold Malcom,   Blandford
Bigelow W. H.   Bolton
Rowe H. D.   Brewster
Wasburn Christian,   Bridgewater
Washburn Nahum,   "
Grover J. M.   "
Allen Wilkes,   Brookfield
Andrews Robert R.   Cambridge
Bullock Charles,   Cambridgeport, "
Simonds James L.   "
White Edward Y.   "   "
Capen G. F.   Canton
Chamberlain George,   "
Coghlan John   Charlestown
Daigneau D. P.   "
Page Edward,   "
Phipps William S.   "
Webber James H.   "
White D. S.   "
Atwood Joseph,   Chatham
Taylor Sylvanus R.   "
Brown J. A.   Chelsea
Willard Alexander T.   "
Porter Jesse,   Chicopee
Fisk J.   Clinton
Ingalls & Bigelow,   "
Clarke Rodolphus,   "
Lindsey M. L.   Conway
Houghton Chilon,   Dana
Hazeltine William, S. Dedham, Danvers
Robbins Nathaniel L., Dennis Port, Dennis
Bradley John C.   Duxbury
Gilmore Charles,   East Bridgewater
Parsons Chas. E.   East Hampton
Sanderson H. L.   "
Angell Avery F.   Fall River
Borden S. M.   "
Fairbanks Geo. O.   "
Kendall James A.   "
Williams & Stebbins,   "
Ward Ezekiel G.   Falmouth
Ball W.   Fitchburg
Blood Thomas S.   "
Gill E. B.   "
Palmer Thomas,   "
Downs Charles,   Foxborough
Carter J. W.   Framingham
Cowles Henry,   Saxonville,   "
Metcalf W. W.   "
Stetson J. T.   Franklin
Greene C. R.   "
Dennett H. E.   Gardner
Dennett John P.   Gloucester
Swazey J. A.   "

Brackett E. F.   Grafton
BURGHARDT JOHN M. (see page
  724),   Great Barrington
Rice Arthur M.   "
Rice Willard W.   "
Beals Joseph,   Greenfield
Day Edward,   "
Leonard & Morgan.   "
Brown J. D.   Groton Junction, Groton
Hinds William H. H.   "   "
Downer Nathaniel,   Hanover
Rowe H. D.   Harwich
Taylor S. H.   "
Robbins Nathaniel, West Harwich,   "
Elliott Samuel H.   "
Howard Alvah,   Haverhill
Russell W. W.   "
Riley J.   "
Sellers William W.   "
Stevens F. J.   "
Daly & Rolfe,   Hingham
Hayes J. A.   Holliston
Murliess D.   Holyoke
Taylor L. C.   "
White O. C.   "
Bigelow W. H.   Hopkinton
Leslie L. N.   Hudson
Greenwood Edward.   "
PERKINS J. HENRY,   Huntington
Wells J. B.   Hyde Park
Leach Chas. W.,   Middleboro', Ipswich
Kendrick H. C.   Lakeville
Howland A. W.   Lancaster
Austin Joseph,   Lawrence
Kidder James H.   "
Lord J. F.   "
Porter David T.   "
Riggs W. E.   "
Way Lucius E.   "
Leslie L. N.   Lee
Smith Henry W.   Leominster
Boston D. I.   Leverett
Bryant A. M.   Lowell
Gerry G. A.   "
Gladwin S. F.   "
Johnson A. T.   "
Lawrence Ambrose & G. W.   "
Lawrence Samuel,   "
Vinall G. A. W.   "
Ward S. L. & W. G., & A. W. Burnham, "
Aspinwall C. L.   Lynn
Blethen A. C.   "
Crosby F. K.   "
Percival Benjamin,   "
Thompson E. J.   "
Trow J. M.   "
Marston C. E.   Malden
Perry F. D.   Mansfield
Clements T. W.   Marblehead
Chamberlin W. C.   Marlborough
Judd Orville W.   "
Dorr Richard H.   Marion
Henry Stephen,   Marshfield
Bolles Charles E.   Mattapoisett
Sanborn W. A.   Medford
Plumb Luke A.   Melrose
Leach C. W.   Middleborough
Cock A. A. & G. L.   Milford
Dickinson Gideon,   "
Cook S. W.   Millbury
Littlefield John,   Milton
Heath Charles E.   Monterey
Coffin Alexander G.   Nantucket
Hussey David G.   "
Jenks Arthur E.   "
Carter J. W.   Natick
Shurtleff A. J.   "
Channing William H.   New Bedford

Davis C. G.   New Bedford
McLeod E. V.   "
Mara James C.   "
STETSON EDWARD, 24 Purchase,   "
Taber George A.   "
TOBEY A. H., 166 Union,   "
Ward D. P.   "
Ward E. G.   "
Brown J. M.   Newburyport
Goddard C. W.   "
Kelley E. G.   "
Noyes William H.   "
Dow G. F., Newton Corner,   Newton
Bascom H. S.   Northampton
Davenport J. N.   "
Jones William H.   "
Meekins Thomas W.   "
North W. A.   "
Rust Lewis,   "
Brown R. D., Florence,   "
Packard J. W.   North Bridgewater
Puffer L. W.   "
Whitney George R.   "
Woodbury George E.   "
Whitman E. F.   North Chelsea
Bartlett H. P.   North Brookfield
Martin S. P.   "
Shepherdson Charles W.   Northfield
Felt John C.   Orange
Cook S. W.   Oxford
Newton William,   "
Cowan A. B.   Palmer
Dudley A. M.   Peabody
Farrar John N.   Pepperell
Davenport E. S.   Pittsfield
Gamwell James,   "
Gulliver William L.   "
Hall Clark R.   "
Leavitt Joseph,   "
Shumway Thomas D.   Plymouth
Howe Oscar,   Princeton
Atkins E. N.   Provincetown
Shortle Henry,   "
French C. S.   Quincy
Gilbert John H.   "
Leach Dwight W.   Randolph
Woodbury G. E., E. Randolph,   "
Mansfield W. J.   Reading
Manning Joseph,   Rockport
Batchelder J. H.   Salem
Bates W. M.   "
Bowdoin W. L.   "
Chapman & Swasey,   "
Currier George H.   "
Dudley A. S.   "
Fisk Joseph E.   "
Peach P. H.   "
Walwork Thomas,   "
Collins Hiram, Amesbury,   Salisbury
Brown A. T.   "
Perkins J. A.   "
Stevens J. H.   "
Russell E. M., Shelburne Falls,   Sandwich
Weber & Cole,   Shelburne
Calvin A. W.   "
McGregory John,   Southbridge
Lester William,   "
Ames N. E.   South Hadley
Anderson J. J.   Springfield
Collins W. E.   "
Derby P. H.   "
Dwire J. N.   "
Hathout G. S.   "
Hathout J. S.   "
Le Gro David,   "
Morgan Newton,   "
Perkins Cyrus,   "
Searle P.   "

Durkee T. G.   Stoneham
Tenney A. W.   "
Blake Edmund,   Stoughton
Buck Edgar,   Sturbridge
Parsons Charles E.   Sunderland
Chase William B.   Swampscott
DICKERMAN D. S. & J. Q., 74
   Weir (see page 717),   Taunton
Paige Onlus S.   "
Thompson Julius,   "
Utley James,   "
Battles Albert,   "
White Joel,   Tyringham
Magoon C. H.   Uxbridge
Papineau A.   Wakefield
Poole A. D.   Waltham
Reed G. S.   "
Sherman & Son,   "
Starbuck E. P.   "
Gould J. B.   Ware
Holden Daniel,   "
Miner D. W.   "
Yale Joseph C.   "
Horne C. F.   Watertown
Huckins D. T.   "
Joslin E. L.   Webster
Smith D. D.   "
Wyer George T.   Wellfleet
Henry S. G.   Westborough
Clapp Horatio W.   Westfield
GOODRICH EDWARD M.   "
Miller Henry M.   "
Nye A. O.   Weymouth
Cross Cyrus,   Wilbraham
Duncan Samuel,   Williamstown
Young ——,   "
White ——,   Wilmington
Foskett & Loveland,   Winchendon
Clough John,   Woburn
Lang Cyrus T.   "
Bishop Henry F.   Worcester
Boutelle D. K.   "
Childs J. A.   "
Cook & Barton,   "
Dickey A. O.   "
Gould J. W.   "
Green & Jenks,   "
Estabrook C. W.   "
Harris & Adams,   "
Moules Charles R.   "
Nettleton E. B.   "
Pevey Bros.   "
Snow W. N.   "
Tourtelott & Fuller,   "
BRIGHAM H. Q.   Yarmouth Port,   Yarmouth

Dentists' Materials and Instruments.

Williams Wm. M.   Springfield

Designers and Draughtsmen.

DALZELL DAVID, Jr. (see page 799), S. Egremont,   Egremont
Kimball John C.   S. Egremont,   "

Diary and Memorandum Manufacturers.

REMICK JOHN & SON, Cambridgeport,   Cambridge
Wood & Dresser, Cambridgeport,   "

Die Sinkers and Letter Cutters.

(See also Stencil Cutters.)

New York Tap & Die Co., N. Harwich,   Harwich

Die Sinkers etc., — continued.
TIMME E. A. (see page 801), 279
Main,   Worcester
Wilson C. W.   "

Distillers.

Porter H. & Co. (rye gin),   Agawam
Goodall Leon, Cambridgeport, Cambridge
Trull Ezra & Co.   Charlestown
Lawrence Daniel & Sons,   Medford
Caldwell A. & G. J.   Newburyport
Bush, Nelson, & Co. (rye gin), Westfield

Doors, Sashes, and Blinds.

(See also Planing Mills; also Moulding Mills.)

Fletcher Cyrus, South Acton,   Acton
BAKER JAMES, (see page 723),
State st., North Adams,   Adams
SNY ER & PATTISON (see page
728), Brooklyn st., North Adams,   "
Bangs & Hawes, North Amherst, Amherst
Ellis Edwin,   Athol
Humphrey J. F.   "
Amsden Washington H.   "
Cheney James M.   Athol Depot,   "
WAKEFIELD & GODDARD,   "
Rice Leonard,   Barre
Hapgood & Cartwright,   Berlin
MONATIQUOT STEAM MILLS,
H. Gardner, propr. (see page 768),
Weymouth,   Braintree
Hopkins Moses,   Brewster
Richmond J. A. & Co.   Buckland
             Cambridge
Osborn Dalphon, Cambridgeport,   "
Snow F. D. & L. H.   "   "
Fisher Samuel,   Canton
Waterman F.   Charlestown
SHATTUCK & FARWELL, (see page
767),   Clinton
Washburn William B. & Co.   Erving
Connant Prelet D.   Fall River
BECKWITH ALVAH A. & CO., (see
page 720),   Fitchburg
FITCHBURG LUMBER CO., (see
page 767)   "
GRIFFIN BENNETT,   Gloucester
Allen David G.   "
Wilson J. & Co.   Greenfield
Hunt & Carroll,   Haverhill
Hunt & Gould.   "
NOYES JAMES & CO., 50 Merrimac,
(see page 801),   "
Hannum George A.   Heath
Wiggin & Flagg,   Holyoke
Briggs & Allyn (blinds),   Lawrence
Favor Bros.   "
Williams Cyrus,   "
Favor N. B. & Son,   Lowell
KELLEY WM. (also painter and gla-
zier). Mechanics' Mills,   "
Peabody J. G.   "
Place Isaac,   "
Pratt M. C.   "
Harris Philo.   Ludlow
BAIRD WILLIAM & SON, (see page
728), 110 So. Common,   Lynn
Bay State Milling & Machine Co.   "
PROCTOR CHARLES E. (maker),
Beach st.   "
Taft Sullivan H.   Mendon
Albee, Eldredge, & Co.   Milford
Morse, & Woods,   "
             Millbury
ARMSBY & MORSE, (see page 768), "
         New Bedford
DOULL JAMES, Front. cor. School,   "

Foster J. M.   New Bedford
Mosher & Brownell,   "
Sturtevant & Sherman,   "
Blake & Noyes,   Newburyport
Burrill & Brown,   "
Creasey Joseph B.   "
Whipple O. Newton Corner,   Newton
Brewster C. H.   Northampton
Clark Isaac R. (dealer),   "
Soule Oakes S.   North Bridgewater
Parker H. B.   Northfield
Wakefield, Lovejoy, & Co.   Orange
Tucker Samuel E.   Pepperell
Booth C. H. & W. A.   Pittsfield
Brown George,   "
Harrington Henry (dealer),   "
Warner Charles H.   "
Worden E. & C.   "
Brown Nathaniel (dealer),   Plymouth
Hardy T. jr.   Salem
Gifford T. J. & Co.   "
Newall Joseph,   "
Phelps Wm. jr. & Co.   "
RICHMOND J. A. & CO. (see page
724), Shelburne Falls,   Shelburne
           Southbridge
Clemence J. M. & L. D., Globe Village, "
Howard & Gaylord,   South Hadley
Stone, Tower, & Co.   Spencer
Walker T. M. & Co.   Springfield
Warner David,   "
NEWCOMB W. L. & CO. (see page
728),   Taunton
CROWELL EZRA, 37 West Water,   "
Bronsden L. B.   Templeton
Jenkins Foster H.   Tisbury
Comstock Metcalf, West Upton,   Upton
Marsh Zenas,   Ware
SANGER N. C. (see page 772), Watertown
Kittredge B. L. & Co.   Westfield
Stow M. V.   "
BURRELL WATERMAN T.   Weymouth
Daymon & Rice, E. Weymouth,   "
MONATIQUOT STEAM MILLS,
Henry Gardner, Agent, (see page
768), Weymouth Landing, Weymouth
Harrington & Hayford,   Worcester
RICE, GRIFFIN, & CO.   "
ROSS & McGREGOR, 1 Central, (see
page 786),   "
Stevens D. & C. P.   "

Door Stop Manufacturer.

Smart D. C. (India rubber), Cambridgeport,   Cambridge

Drain and Sewer Tubing.

Pierce Bradford S.   New Bedford
PEIRCE CHARLES M. Jr., 119 No.
Water,   "
Wilcox J. P. & Co.   Springfield
Peirce Simeon E.   Taunton

Drain Pipe and Tile Manufs.

Edmunds & Co.   Charlestown
Day & Collins, Neponset, Dorchester
Houghton Irving R. (sole tile), Greenfield
Welch A.   South Malden.   Malden
PEIRCE CHARLES M. jr., 119 No.
Water,   New Bedford
Pierce Bradford S.   "
McIntire Lewis,   Northampton
FLINT SIMEON, 221 Derby,   Salem
           Worcester
NEWTON E. & C. (see page 731),
Union St.   "
TUCKER N. G. 23 Pleasant (dealer,
see page 786),

Dressmakers.

(See also Milliners.)

Turner & Knowles,	Abington
Shaw Mary N. Miss, East Abington,	"
Beal Harriet Mrs.	"
Boddry Mary Miss, South Abington,	"
Alger Frank Mrs.	"
Healey Susan H. Mrs.	"
West John Mrs.	"
Jones Lucy Mrs. North Adams,	Adams
Rathburn & Waitt,	"
Davidge G. K. Mrs.	Amherst
Bateman Eliza Mrs.	Andover
Drown N. M.	Attleborough
Walsh M. Miss, No. Attleboro',	"
Gilman Mary A.	Braintree
French Madison Mrs. So. Braintree,	"
Hayden Sarah W.	Bridgewater
Edgecomb Hollis Mrs.	Brighton
Merritt Maria Mrs.	Brookline
Soule E. H. Miss,	"
West Mrs.	"
Draper C. W. Miss,	Cambridge
Fowler H. M. Miss,	"
Hanscom O. J. Miss,	"
Estes N. G. Miss, Cambridgeport,	"
Nelson R. Miss,	"
Kenrick J. A. Miss,	Canton
Barker Augusta A.	Charlestown
Bixby R. P. Mrs.	"
Bliss H. M.	"
Chapman Priscilla,	"
Coffey John Mrs.	"
Cole Eliza J.	"
Crosby L. A. Mrs.	"
Daggett A. Mrs.	"
Davis A. D. Miss	"
Downing A. E. Mrs.	"
Eccles Julia,	"
Evre Harriet,	"
Field Nancy.	"
Fiske M. E. Mrs.	"
Frost O. Mrs.	"
Hackett R. F. Mrs.	"
Handy Lydia M.	"
Hoffman J. Mrs.	"
Johnson Ellen,	"
Lahmore Wm. Mrs.	"
Nagle Maurice Mrs.	"
Pierce Adaline S.	"
Pagne Susan C.	"
Prouty Sarah A.	"
Sargent Mary S. Mrs.	"
Smart Hannah E.	"
Stanley L. Mrs.	"
Stratton T. W. Mrs.	"
Sweetser H. B.	"
Tower R. jr. Mrs.	"
Trundy Anna L.	"
Waite Lydia A.	"
Webb N. P. Mrs.	"
Whitehead Mary,	"
Williston Margaret,	"
Lovett Mary E.	"
Morse Harriet L. Mrs.	Chelsea
Sargent E. Mrs.	"
Snow Harriet N.	"
Thompson Ruth A.	"
White E. A. Mrs.	"
Phillips & Godfrey,	Cheshire
Severence, J. F. Mrs.	Chicopee
Thompson E. M.	"
Harper E. P. Miss,	Dedham
Briggs Jane,	Dighton
Waters Eliza Miss,	"
Baxter C. A. Miss,	Dorchester
Light Ellen E. Neponset,	"

Bradshaw E. M. Miss,	Dorchester
Sargent Susan Mrs.	Neponset, "
Johnson Lucy A.	"
Trow Ada K.	East Bridgewater
Bishop P. Mrs.	East Hampton
Grout J. Mrs.	"
Owen Carrie C.	"
Smith & Clark Misses,	"
Hallenbeck Martha A.	North Egremont
Jenney Helen Miss,	Fairhaven
Stevens Geo. Mrs.	"
Baker E. M. Mrs.	Fall River
Barnaby Sarah,	"
Cleveland H. M. Mrs.	"
Clifford Eleanor	..
Crapo M. C. Mrs.	
Gould A. F.	
Gifford Betsey Miss,	
Greene M. E. Mrs.	
McCann Catharine,	
Olney A. I. Miss,	
Poole M. A. & M. E.	
Shaw & Blake Misses,	
Robbins Annie E. Miss,	
Walsh Sarah A. Mrs.	
Wolfendale Elizabeth Mrs.	"
Wrightington C. P. Miss,	"
Young E. M. Mrs.	"
Baldwin Sarah A.	Fitchburg
Osborn & Works Misses,	"
Burke S. B. Mrs.	Foxborough
Park Abbie Mrs.	"
Smith Anna C.	"
McDonald Isabella,	Gloucester
Battles Lucretia.	"
Burnham Martha,	"
Hazel S.	"
Bristol Levi Mrs.	Great Barrington
Steele Eveline A.	"
Wheeler L. D. A.	"
Fryer M. A. & J. B.	"
Tyler Hattie Miss,	Greenfield
Wilson J. A. Mrs.	"
Weeks Lydia M.	Harwich
Goodell Lucy M.	Haverhill
Stickney M. F. Miss,	"
Granger H. A. Mrs.	Holyoke
Prickett H. P.	"
Keyes Mary J.	Hudson
Burgess Betsey Mrs.	Kingston
Cushman S. A.	"
Joyce Sarah Mrs.	"
Anderson M. S. Mrs.	Lawrence
Armitage M. & M. J.	"
Breen Margaret,	"
Burbank Lucia A. R.	"
Butterfield Anna,	"
Cole L. C. Miss	"
Crosby Catharine,	"
Doyle J. Mrs.	"
Drewry Alice,	"
Durrell Hattie E.	"
Durrell Sarah M.	"
Dyer Armenta A.	"
Frost N. F.	..
Greely E. G. Miss,	"
Johnston Mary Miss,	"
Keleher Joanna,	"
Lawrence A. W.	"
Moore Emma.	"
Nealey A. J. Mrs.	"
Paige Mary L.	"
Pray Lavinia C.	"
Prescott & Veazie,	"
Priest C. M.	"
Ranno S. G.	"
Reynolds J. H. Mrs.	"

nued.

	Gulliver E. C.	
Lawrence	Hart Mary A.	Lynn
"	Hawkes Sarah S.	"
"	Henderson A. M. Mrs.	
"	Hoyt Jane,	
"	Jackson M. H. Mrs.	
"	Johnson M. O.	
"	Leavitt Mary Mrs.	
"	Lord Alma P.	
"	Marsh Susan S.	
Lenox	McKenzie E. J. Miss,	
Leominster	Merrill P. M.	
"	Neal Mary H.	
"	Norwood Ann F.	
Lowell	Nutter E. A.	
"	Peaslee Lucy S.	
"	Phillips E. S. Mrs.	"
"	Pierce E. Mrs.	"
"	Plummer K. B. M.	"
"	Richardson C. L.	
"	Rodman S. A.	
"	Rogers L. Mrs.	
"	Rollins S. M. Miss,	
"	Russell J. Miss,	
"	Sanborn W. J. Mrs.	
"	Starratt Lizzie,	
"	Shankland A. Mrs.	
"	Tobey Lizzie,	
"	Wentworth A. L. Mrs.	"
"	Coolidge S. J. Mrs.	Marlborough
"	O'Hanoran J. Mrs.	Medford
"	Richardson A. Mrs.	"
"	Briggs C. A. Mrs.	Middleborough
"	Chubbuck F. E.	"
"	Folsom M. J.	"
"	Fisher H. M. Mrs.	"
"	Olds C. Mrs.	Milford
"	Spencer M. E. Mrs.	"
"	Tyler M. Miss,	"
"	Greyrold E. J. Mrs.	Natick
"	Parlin Flora,	"
"	Bosworth H. W. Mrs.	New Bedford
"	Bosworth Jennie Miss,	"
"	Bradford C. C. Mrs.	"
"	Brightman A. E. Mrs.	
"	Carpenter M. W. & Co.	
"	Coleman Betsey R. Mrs.	
"	Cook Abbie W. Mrs.	
"	Dillingham Caroline C. Mrs.	
"	Gradehos Annie C.	"
"	Martin Joanna Mrs.	
"	Oliver Abbie Mrs.	
"	Raymond Mary Mrs.	
"	Sherman J. C. Mrs.	
"	Simmons Phebe A. Mrs.	"
"	Spencer Ellen Mrs.	"
"	Tucker Lydia E. Mrs.	"
"	Wagner Mary R. Mrs.	"
Lynn	Weeks M. A. Mrs,	"
"	Reed M. T. Mrs.	Newburyport
"	Ricker Abbie,	"
"	Brigham H. Mrs.	Northampton
"	Burnham J.	"
"	Ferry & Dickinson,	"
"	Tinker M. A.	"
"	Andrews M. E.	North Bridgewater
"	Foye E. A. Mrs.	"
"	Parish P. W. Mrs.	"
"	Washburn & Pierce,	"
"	Stearns Irene,	Orange
"	Thatcher L. E.	"
"	Graves S. A. Miss,	Palmer
"	Whitman Susan Mrs.	"
"	Baker Semantha,	Pittsfield
"	Gage M. & E. H.	"
"	Hatch Rosa M.	"
"	Shillingford H. W.	
"	Thomas Alice Mrs.	

Plymouth | Caswell Barney Mrs. | Taunton
" | Cooper Elizabeth E. | "
" | Fisher Ann D. Mrs.
" | Greene E. Mrs.
" | Lowell — Miss,
" | Morey Abby C.
" | O'Brien Ellen,
Quincy | Raymond A. F. Mrs.
" | Rogers Jerusha H.
" | Shedd N. W. Mrs.
" | Watts Emma Mrs. | "
" | Cushing S. J. | Wakefield
Salem | Wood Ellen, | "
" | Merriam H. E. Miss, | Waltham
" | Raymond C. A. Mrs. | Ware
" | Strickland A. F. Mrs. | "
" | Benson Hannah, | Wareham
" | Churchill A. C. Mrs. | "
" | Howard Martha, | "
" | Hinckley Sarah, | "
" | Hill J. A. Mrs. | Webster
" | Stockwell A. Mrs. | "
" | Hudson M. T. Mrs. | Westborough
" | Shaw Rosa Mrs., Cochesett, W. Bridgewater
" | Bruce O. & Co. | Westfield
" | Douglas G. H. | "
" | Ely George Mrs. | "
" | Holcomb B. L.
" | | West Roxbury
" | Bell A. R. Mrs., Jamaica Plain, | "
" | Paul Harriet E. | " | "
" | Shaw Lucy M. | West Stockbridge
" | Clapp Eleanor Mrs. | Weymouth
" | Bodge Sophia Miss, East Weymouth, | "
" | Terrell Elizabeth Mrs. | "
" | Clapp Selinda Mrs. | South | " | "
" | Humble Lydia Mrs. | " | " | "
" | Lewis Edward Mrs. | " | " | "
" | Jewett & Hale Misses, | Winchendon
" | Gleason L. H. Mrs. | Woburn
Ilen, | Webster Hannah B. Miss, | "
" | Weymouth Mary L. Mrs. | "
" | Adams A. A. | Worcester
" | Barnes P. A. Miss, | "
" | Campbell M. J. Mrs. | "
" | Childs A. E. | ..
" | Cheney R. Mrs.
" | Cook A. F.
" | Cutting N. H.
" | Gale J. Mrs.
" | Goodnow C. E. | "
" | Green H. S.
" | Heal L. E. Mrs. | "
" | Hudson M. T. Mrs.
" | Kimball J. W.
" | Larned C. E. Miss, | "
" | Ryan V. | "
" | Willis Carrie, | "
" | Taylor A. C. Miss,

Salisbury | **Drills.**
Somerville | | New Bedford
Southbridge | Morse Twist Drill & Machine Co. | "
Springfield | STACY E. S. & CO., Harrison
" | ave. (see page 784), | Springfield

Worth- | **Drugs and Medicines.**
" | (See also Apothecaries; also Dye Stuffs,
" | Drugs, &c.)
" | Remington Robert K. | Fall River
" | HOWLAND & LOWELL, | Greenfield
" | HALL JOHN T. | Plymouth
" | White J. C. & Co. | Worcester

Stoughton | **Drum Makers.**
" | | Granville
" | Noble & Cooley, Granville Corners, | "

Dry Goods.

(See also Country Stores; also Hosiery; also Laces, Embroideries, &c.)

Faxon A. W. & Co.　　　Abington
Whitmarsh Z. N.　　　　"
Rice J. A. & C. L., East Abington,　"
Rosenfeld Nathan,　　　"　　"
Howard G. B. & Co., South Abington, "
Pearson Geo. H.　　　　"　　"
Reed Geo. A.　　　　　　"　　"
Shepard W. C. & O.　West Acton, Acton
TUTTLES, JONES, & WETHER-
　　BEE,　　　S. Acton,　"
Terry Nancy,　　　　　Acushnet
Wilde Charles M.　Long Plain,　"
Dean D. J.　　　　　　Adams
Cronin Catherine,　North Adams,　"
Montgomery & Arnold,　　"　　"
Smith & Gaylord,　　　"　　"
Urann & Keyes,　　　　"　　"
Briggs J. W.　　　　　Amesbury
Chase Amos F.　　　　"
Childs E. A.　　　　　"
Ingoldsby John,　　　　"
Prichard J. B. W.　　　"
Pray S. E. & Co.　West Amesbury,　"
Allen M. A.　　　　　Amherst
Morrison John,　Ballardvale,　Andover
Anderson, Howes, & Co.　Arlington
Fowle Frederick E.
Savage Thomas W.　Athol Depot,　Athol
Thorpe & Thomas,　　　"　　"
Aishberg Julius,　　　　"　　"
Haskell F. R.　　　　　"　　"
Parmenter J. S. & F. C.　　"　　"
Thorpe & Osgood,　　　"　　"
COOPER JOHN,　　　Attleborough
Barden T. A.　North Attleborough, "
Knapp & Holmes,　　　"　　"
Hopkins E. S.　　　　Belchertown
Endicott Robert R.　　　Beverly
Morse John L.
Cann B. M.　　　　　Billerica
Randall S. M., South Braintree, Braintree
Rosenfeld Nathan,　　"　　"
Knowles & Freeman,　　Brewster
Robbins Isaiah,
Baxter & Sanborn,　　　Brighton
Lancy & Hollis,
Defrees G. T.
Klingman Martin,　　　Brookline
Read John & Co.
Saunders F. E.　　　　Cambridge
Bates John S.　Cambridgeport,　"
Bemmink & Ellis,　　　"　　"
Hyde Dana W.　　　　"　　"
Donnelly J. S. H.　East Cambridge,　"
Griffin D. C.　　　　"　　"
Hovey H. N. Jr. & Co.　"　　"
Sneach George,　　　　"　　"
Wheeler A. & Son,　　　"　　"
Barrett Edwin J.　　　Charlestown
Brintnall & Maynard,　　"
Chandler H. H.　　　　"
Fish William W.　　　　"
Flowers E. T.　　　　　"
Gammans & Chandler,　　"
Hill N. E.　　　　　　"
Moody E. T.　　　　　"
Murray William,　　　　"
Nichols M. E.　　　　　"
Shedd Chandler & Co.　　"
Temple I. B. F.　　　　"
Whitten & Coombs,　　　"
Hallett S. Eldridge,　　"
Elliott Benjamin F.　　Chatham
Harris Charles G.　　　Chelsea

Kaufman L. & J.　　　Chelsea
Newell Benjamin V.　　"
Oliver Thomas H.　　　"
RICHARDSON A. B., 188 & 190
　　Broadway
Williams H. N.　　　　"
Merrick Charles H.　　Chicopee
Rockwood J. T.　　　　"
Wool J. B.　　　　　　"
Davidson & Hosmer　　Clinton
Greeley H. C.　　　　"
Jenkins E. B. & Co.　　"
Richman & Wiesman,
Smith & Walker,　　　"
Wooster G. B.　　　　"
Brown John, jr.　　　Concord
Perkins Daniel,
PHILLIPS & SAMPSON,　Conway
Perley A. P. & Co.　　Danvers
Rayner & Howard,
Warren A. W.　Danvers Port,　"
Danforth C. B.　　　Dedham
Field Ferdinand C.　　"
Boyden & Norris,　East Dedham,　"
Greenhood M.　　　　"
Bigelow L. Waldo,　South Dedham,　"
Farrington D. B.　　　"　　"
Gay Ellis,　　　West Dedham,　"
Baxter Jane,　South Dennis, Dennis
Nickerson Susan H.　West Dennis,　"
Blackman E.　　　　Dorchester
Murphy E. C.,　Harrison square,　"
Esty Charles H.,　Hyde Park,　"
Savil Susan Mrs.　Neponset,　"
Kendall H.　　Milton,　　"
Littlefield M. W.　　　"　　"
Nutter I. N. & E. W.　East Bridgewater
Rosenfeld G.
Allen S. P.　　Joppa Village,　"
Lamble R. M. & J. E.　East Hampton
Baylies Frederick,　　Edgartown
Coffin J. W.
Holley T. R.
Burnham George W.　　Essex
Wilcox A. P.　　　　Fairhaven
Almy Charles,　　　Fall River
Allen & Hathaway,　　"
Andrews Thomas,　　"
Buffinton & Waring,
Chace James B.
Chace O. D.
Collins John E. & Co.　　"
Crowley Daniel,　　　"
Dean Charles H.
Dunmore Thomas jr.
Ferguson M. J. Mrs.
Gifford Perry,
Graham Catharine,
Harrington P. P.
Harris A. Mrs.
Howarth Brothers,
Marvel John B.
Mason William H.　　"
McDonough John F.
McDonough Mary,
Murray L. Mrs.
O'Connell Michael,
Ogden Henry,
Riley Thomas,
Rodman & Sargent,　　"
Sanders E. Miss,
Sherer, Rice, & Co.　　"
Smith Irain,
Strassman Charles,
Strassman Henry,
White Dennis,
Wolfendale Elizabeth,
Woodward & Gammons,　"

Davis Elihu H. — Falmouth
Brown Luther J. — Fitchburg
Carpenter Daniel M. — "
Corey D. A. — "
Macy E. R. & Co. — "
Moore Lizzie, — "
Sherman Andrew B. — "
Sprague L. & Co. — "
Stiles James F. — "
Lowe Joseph G. — Foxborough
Ryder & Crocker, — "
Wheeler T. H. Mrs. — Framingham
Danforth A. H. — Saxonville, "
Webster G. W. Mrs. — "
Brown Mathew, — Franklin
Stewart Charles W. — "
Bragg Alexander E. — Freetown
Morse Edward R. — Gardner
Baker C. G. — Georgetown
Allen Frederick, — Gloucester
Andrews & Marston, — "
Calef John C. & Co. — "
Lancaster T. Sewell, — "
Mansfield James & Sons, — "
Patillo Alex. — "
Procter John, — "
Sanford H. G. — "
White Fannie S. — "
Williamson & Pettigrew, — "
Bachman & Hepp, — Great Barrington
Durant B. F. — "
VAN DEUSEN NEWTON, Housatonic, "
Brown Franklin, — Greenfield
Browning & Co. — "
Eddy Geo. S. — "
Root Theodore D. & Co. — "
Sammis & Field, — "
Simonds D. A. & Co. — Groton Junction, Groton
STUART GEO. W. & CO. " — "
Bates John B. — Hanover
Brett Charles E. — Harwich
Knight Harriet J. Mrs. — Hardwick
Brooks Brothers, — Haverhill
Flanders & Co. — "
Folsom & Hurd, — "
Hastings & Co. — "
Jacobs F. W. — "
McKenney F. S. & Co. — "
Rhodes C. N. — "
Corthell H. R. — Hingham
Gates John D. — "
LINCOLN GEORGE. — "
Atkins S. H. & Co. — Holyoke
Barnes Henry, — "
Bateson John, — "
Bowden James, — "
Bowler John, — "
Brown C. J. & Son, — "
Higginbottom Allen, — "
King S. — "
Manning Honora, — "
Onger Abram. — "
Orrell E. A. Mrs. — "
Potvin Gilbert, — "
Sharon John B. & Bros. — "
Shumway Austin L. — "
Tuttle O. S. — "
Goldsbury Forest, — Hudson
Elliot Margaret, — Hyde Park
Williams Amanda Miss, — "
Clothey John F. & Co. — Ipswich
Cogswell E. & Son, — "
Damon Curtis, — "
Lord Asa, — "
Willcomb F. — "
Bailey George H. — Lawrence

Berry & Greenwood, — Lawrence
Butters & Kendall, — "
Campbell & Taylor, — "
Clark Francis C. — "
Copps, Lenfest, & Co. — "
Cross R. M. & Co. — "
Cuddy Thomas, — "
Davis William W. — "
Gould Edward, — "
Green Sarah, — "
Hanson James W. — "
Hart Rufus, — "
Keleher Joanna, — "
Leyland Thomas, — "
Linn Hugh M. — "
Linn John, — "
Lowe Harriet, — "
McKay Edward, — "
Merrill A. W. — "
Phillips H. H. — "
Riddell Sarah S. — "
Sharpe Andrew & Co. — "
Smith John, — "
Stearns A. W. & Co. — "
Truell Byron & Co. — "
Turner Melzer A. — "
Walker S. T. Mrs. & Co. — "
Watson E. — "
Wefers Bernard, — "
Whittier R. R. & A. C. — "
Wolger James G. — "
Wright W. H. & Co. — "
Levy Mary L. — Lee
Taylor G. W. — Lexington
ABBOTT & EAMES, — Lowell
Anderson O. D. & Co. — "
Brennan Michael & Co. — "
Brown Joseph S. — "
Collins Benjamin F. & Co. — "
Cook & Taylor, — "
Dick Peter, — "
Drew H. C. — "
Drew, Taft, & Welch, — "
Folsom J. P. — "
Gage James U. — "
Harris William G. & Co. — "
Hilton H. W. & Co. — "
Hosford H. & Co. — "
Keyes & Tucker, — "
Marin & Hight, — "
Montferand & Laiselle, — "
Shaw James W. B. — "
Spaulding G. L. & Co. — "
Taylor Joseph, — "
Anthony J. — Lynn
Bacheller Jonathan Mrs. — "
Ballard Martha, — "
Chase Blaney, — "
Chase William & Co. — "
Chase William B. — "
Duggan Ellen, — "
Frothingham B. H. — "
Gallagher Thomas, — "
Greene, Bacheller, & Poole, — "
Ham A. J. & C. F. — "
Hawkes Charlotte M. — "
Lesboa Elizabeth B. — "
Ricker Frank & Co. — "
Spalding R. A. & Co. — "
Spinney & Richardson, — "
Stimson S. S. B. Mrs. — "
Tolman G. B. — "
Trull John, jr. — "
Weinberg S. J. & Co. — "
Harris William G. & Co. — Malden
Harford Enoch L. — "
Newhall Henry A. — "
Holt Sarah Miss, — South Malden, "

15

Dry Goods — continued.

Swett Simeon T.	Manchester
Hardon N. H.	Mansfield
Passom Robert H. jr.	Marblehead
Chamberlain George,	"
Clothey John F. & Co.	"
Marden Richmond F.	"
Thayer & Osgood,	"
Tucker T. W.	"
Harrison Thomas,	Marlborough
Roche M.	"
Smith Benjamin F. & Co.	"
Wilson & Howe,	"
Le Baron Lemuel,	Mattapoisett
Taylor Henry,	"
Coburn Jonas & Co.	Medford
Woolley Daniel B.	"
Crosby Tully, jr.	Melrose
Leonard H. A.	"
Alden A. G.	Middleborough
Roddick & McJennett,	"
Foss Edward S.	"
Gilbert S. M.	Milford
Hale George W.	"
Leavens Albert,	"
O'Leary John,	"
Simonds & Knowlton,	"
Smith J. H. & Co.	"
Temple A. & Co.	"
Beal Margaret Miss,	Milton
Brooks C. S.	Nantucket
CATHCART CHARLES S.	"
Keene Francis B.	"
Macy Harriet,	"
Manter Priscilla C.	"
McCoy John,	"
Mitchell Francis,	"
Paddock Eunice B.	"
Paddock Susan,	"
Riddell C. C. Mrs.	"
Thompson James,	"
Bowker Ira E.	Natick
Cleland John,	"
Pope George S. & Co.	"
Woodbury P. F.	"
Clark I. B., South Natick,	"
Randall R. H.	"
Currier —— Mrs. Wellesley,	Needham
Bennett Mary B. Mrs.	New Bedford
Bennet Robert G.	"
Bessey Asa B.	"
Brownell Oliver G.	"
Buckminster & Macy (wholesale & retail),	"
Chandler Charles,	"
Corney C. M.	"
Delano Stephen,	"
Dootson John,	"
Eddy George M. & Co.	"
Eddy Job A. T.	"
Fisher James & Co.	"
Gifford George D.	"
Hadley & Allen,	"
Haskell Edward,	"
Howard Jacob & Brother (linens),	"
Irish E. A.	"
Kempton Thomas C.	"
King Joseph,	"
Martin Thomas,	"
Mitchell John L.	"
Pedro Joseph H.	"
Pond Frederick L.	"
Soule William T.	"
Tallman Charles S.	"
Tucker William, jr. (wholesale),	"
Waite Benjamin H.	"
Whitcomb O. B. & Co.	"
Whiting E. B.	"

Wilde W. S. & Brother,	New Bedford
Winslow H. & Co.	"
Woodman William O.	"
Altar S. J. Mrs.	Newburyport
Bassett Ann P.	"
Bassett S. E.	"
Bunting John,	
Caldwell John,	
Davidson & Pingree,	
Emery Josiah,	
Fearing F. F.	
Frothingham J. A. jr.	"
Frothingham Martha A.	"
Hesseltine Charles,	"
Johnson W. H.	
Lake N. B.	
Lane A. B.	
Levy & Co.	
O'Connell T.	
Perry Mary E.	"
Plummer Charles E.	"
Plummer Henry C.	"
Plumer Richard,	
Poor George E.	
Bacon G. W. & Co., Newton Corner, Newton
Colburn W. H. Upper Falls,	"
Wheeler Loring,	"
Jackson Wm. W. Lower "	"
Spaulding S. C. Newton Centre,	"
Mead John,	West Newton,	"
Lloyd M. A. Miss,	"
Bennett O. K.	Northampton
Fair R. I.	"
Field L. H.	"
Lincoln A. J. & Co.	"
PHILLIPS & SAMPSON,	"
Putvin Gilbert,	
Stoddard & Kellogg,	"
Wakefield & Southwick,	"
Grew J. L. (fancy),   North Bridgewater
Jones, Lovell, & Sanford,	"
ROBINSON H. W. & Co., "	
Hastings George,	Northfield
Rogerson John R.	Norton
Bridge Thomas E.	Orange
Fisher A. J.	"
Chapman Reuben & Co.	Orleans
CUMMINGS JOSEPH H.	"
Hopkins A. R. Mrs. East Orleans,	"
Sigourney George W.	Oxford
Cross W. W.	Palmer
Morrison Mary E.	Peabody
Simpson L. C.	Pepperell
Baxton & Shillingford,	Pittsfield
Cole T. E. & Co. (trimmings),	"
England & Brothers,	"
Friend E. & G.	
Jones J. M. & Son,	"
Malley William,	"
Morey & Hand,	"
Norton H. L.	"
Wood & Garlic,	"
Burbank S. M. jr.	Plymouth
Harlow J. H. & Co.	"
Strong B. O.	"
Turner E. C.	"
Cowan J. H. Mrs.	Provincetown
Crowell Mary E.	"
Jones B. E.	"
Mills Delia A.	
Nickerson Charles,	
Nickerson E. & M.	
Rosenfield M.	
Snow Jane, Mrs.	
Smith Amasa,	"
Lombard J. W.	Quincy
McLellan James A.	"
Morton C. jr.	Randolph

Rosenfield N.   Randolph
Fletcher Franklin,   Reading
Frost Jonathan,   "
Reid James & Co.   "
Ruggles Emily,   "
Brooks Reuben,   Rockport
Brooks Samuel H.   "
Clark Andrew F.   "
Harris Sarah,   "
Babson M. M. Miss,   Pigeon Cove,   "
Archer, Downing, & Co.   Salem
Bigelow W. K. & Co.   "
Black P. W. & Co.   "
Bray Ann R. Miss,   "
Cousins J. H. & Co.   "
Daniels G. P. & W. K.   "
Dix Asa C.   "
Gavett Wm. R.   "
Hill W. & R.   "
Ide E. R.   "
Pond James S.   "
Shatswell J. A.   "
Shepard J. B. & S. D.   "
Shillaber S.   "
Tuttle F. W.   "
Webber W. G. & C.   "
Wiggin & Weeks,   "
Beede L. M. & Co.,   Amesbury, Salisbury
Foye M. A.   "   "
Locke S. E.   "   "
Osgood Edwin W.   "   "
Patten S. L. & S. H.   "   "
Reed Eunice,   "   "
Burgess Chas. H.   Sandwich
Jones Joshua,   "
                Saugus
Townsend E. P. Miss, Saugus Centre, "
Carley R. W.,   Shelburne Falls, Shelburne
Labaree Brothers,   "   "
Packard Luther M.   "   "
Strong C. A.   "   "
Bartlett Mary,   Somerset
Marble Joseph,   "
Foster E. K.   Somerville
Comstock & Perry,   Southbridge
Oakes J. J.   "
Edwards & Co.   "
Hanson & Hyde,   Globe Village,   "
McKinstrey J. O.   "   "
Carter & Cooley,   Springfield
Chapin & Bushnell,   "
Colby John,   "
Cook William & Co.   "
Covell & Crowell,   "
Currier, Hodskins, & A. G. Lord,   "
Forbes & Smith,   "
Hall L. J.   "
Hallock L. E. & Co.   "
McKnight, Norton, & Hawley,   "
Strain John,   "
Tinkham & Co.   "
Bolger P. J.   Indian Orchard,   "
Crowell M. F.   "   "
Bartlett Perley,   Sterling
Curtis Jesse,   Stoneham
Heath James M.   "
Mitchell & Nickles,   "
Hersey Otis,   Stoughton
Brackett William D. jr.   Swampscott
Bodfish Wm.   Taunton
Chase & Spencer,   "
Dean P. Evarts,   "
Flinn John,   "
Godfrey Charles,   "
Grimes F. J.   "
Gorham Willard,   "
Hartwell G. H. & Co.   "
Hathaway E.   "

Higgins L. B. & Co.   Taunton
Luscomb J. E.   "
MARK & BLISS, Atheneum build-
   ing, Broadway,
Sanders George B.
Skinner N. H. & Co.
Southgate Samuel,   "
Chapin M. W.   Uxbridge
Hudson S.   "
Sweet & Haywood,   "
Cate J. M. Mrs.   Wakefield
Mansfield E. & H. A.   "
Martin William,   "
Baker O. W.   Waltham
Bigelow George & Son,   "
Clark, Maynard, & Co.   "
Ross M. J. Mrs.   "
Stone C. J.   "
Wood Wm.   "
Kennedy J.   Ware
Parker E. E.   "
Spear F. A. & Co.   "
Storrs J. H.   "
NOURSE & BARNARD,   Watertown
Otis Brothers,   "
Lamb Bros.   Webster
Pratt W. H.   "
Shumway Wm. T.   "
HIGGINS J. R. & CO.   Wellfleet
Higgins P. W.   "
Holbrook Lucy P.   "
Tobey J. F.   "
Gould W. R.   Westboro'
Homan & Child,   "
Brace O. & Co.   Westfield
Douglas George H.   "
Fowler & Noble,   "
Gillett Darwin L.   "
Holcomb B. L.   "
Loomis Henry,   "
Snow & Hibbards,   "
Wales James L.   West Newbury
Austin Grace H.   West Roxbury
McNALLY JOHN,   Jamaica Plain, "
Pingree Wm. J.   "
READ M. H.   Weymouth
Rice C. A.   "
Williams Charles S.   "
Loud Henry,   East Weymouth, "
Bartlett J. W.   No.   "   "
Rosenfeld Edward, S.   "   "
Wright C. A.   "   "
Pickering S. F.   Wilbraham
Sherman A. B.   Winchendon
Lee George W.   Winchester
McIntyre James,   "
Abbot A. A.   Woburn
Smith Charles A.
Woodbury William,   "
Barnard, Sumner, & Co.   Worcester
Clark H. O. & Co.   "
Clarke J. H. & Co.   "
Cummings J. W.
Dayton H. H.
Denny E. & Co.
Finlay, Lawson, & Kennedy,   "
Jenkins J. H. & Co.   "
Law H. D.
Peters J. L. & Co.   "
Sheldon Horace,
Thompson A. Y. & Co.
Ward A. H.
Wheeler G. E. B.
Wilcox S. J. & Co.
George & Bowen,   Wrentham
             Yarmouth
Kelley Daniel D.   South Yarmouth, "
Baker S. jr. & Co.   Yarmouth Port, "

Duck.

Corliss Benjamin H.   Gloucester.
Boynton Eleazer,   Rockport
ROCKPORT STEAM COTTON
  MILLS, John H. Higgins, agent,
  (see page 798),   "

Dusters.

COTSWOLD BRUSH CO. (fancy
  wool dusters), T. S. Mann, agt,
  Florence,   Northampton

Dye Stuffs, Drugs, &c.

Remington Robert K.   Fall River
Barton Henry & Co.   Lawrence
Talbot C. P. & Co.   Lowell
Taylor W. P.   "
Gerry Eldridge,   Lynnfield
     Pittsfield
WHELDEN C. M. & CO. 65 North,   "
Howe G. S. & A. J.   Worcester
Marble Jerome & Co.   "

Dyers.

Schouler Wm. (dyeing and printing),
  South Acton,   Acton
McKay Henry,   North Adams,   Adams
Pease Harlow,   Alford
Barr Thomas & Co.   Arlington
Locke William H. & Co.   "
WOLFENDEN ROBERT (bleacher
  and dyer of cotton and woolen
  yarns, braids, &c.), East Attle-
  borough,   Attleborough
Canton Dye House, J. A. White,   Canton
Cooper Edward J.   Charlestown
Boston Dye House, H. C. Ray,   Chelsea
CHELSEA DYE HOUSE, Williams
  St., Stephen Sibley, proprietor,
  (see page 727),   "
Jamieson Alex. Mrs.   Fall River
Small Samuel, jr., South Harwich, Harwich
Stuart W. & Co.   Lawrence
Trees John   "
Chambers C.   Lowell
Clifford Weare,   "
Crowther C. H.   "
LOWELL BLEACHERY, T. P. Apple-
  ton, agent,   "
Pickens John,   "
Bacheller Hartson A.   Lynn
Ireson N. H. P., agent,   "
Lewando A.   "
Roles Samuel, jr.   "
Barrett & Brother,   Malden
Hutchinson A. & Son, Rockville, Medway
Coleman Edward J.   Fairmount, Milton
Carroll William,   Northampton
Kaiser Frederick W.   "
Williston & Arms,   "
Reed Gottlieb,   Newburyport
Krumweide Charles,   Pittsfield
WHELDEN C. M. & Co., 65 North,   "
Roles Samuel, jr.   Salem
Thompson C. & F. J.   "
Sanger Joseph E. (straw goods), Sherborn
     Somerville
Middlesex Bleachery and Dye Works, "
Broadhurst Thomas & Son,   Springfield
Harmon Israel & Co,   "
King C. H.   "
Satough John,   Taunton
Aldrich Otis,   Upton
Gray Smith,   Walpole
Lewando A. (French),   Watertown
Tosford William H.   Williamstown
Adams Edward,   Worcester

Starkie John,   Worcester
Worcester Bleach & Dye Works,   "

Earthenware Manufacturers.
(See Potteries.)

Eating Houses.
(See also Oysters and Refreshments.)

Morrison E. G.   Amesbury
Fisk & Polley,   Amherst
Simmons G. H.   "
Pittt S. B.   Athol Depot,   Athol
Anderson David,   Barnstable
Baker H. H.   Hyannis,
Hallett J. S.   "   "
Sturgis Russell,   "   "
Hanscom S. C.   Brighton
JOHNSON W. H. Washington st.,   "
Larkin P. K.   "
Carter Frank,   Cambridge
Kent James B.   "
Leuchte Bernard,   "
Moore N. H.   "
Uhrig Joseph,   Cambridgeport,   "
Abrahams Frederick, E. Cambridge,   "
Martin John. A.   "   "
Hennessey John C.   "   "
McCormick B. J.   "   "
Clement & Wilcox, North Cambridge, "
Gerry F. A.   "   "
Whittemore H. W.   "   "
Daly H.   Charlestown
Jordan William J.   "
Sawyer S. F.   "
Brown J. E. & Co.   Chelsea
Lewis Fred. T.   "
Putnam John P.   "
Watson T. P.   Chicopee Falls,   Chicopee
Carter L. H.   Clinton
Johnson James N.   "
Curran Alexander,   Fall River
Godley James,   "
Nye J. T.   "
Thurston Vernon,   "
Wilbur Darius,   "
Battles & Porter,   Fitchburg
Derby Gilbert H.   "
EMORY S. P., ladies' & gent's,
  145 Main,   "
Hayward E. T.   "
Martin Willard,   "
Davis & Co.   Gloucester
Herrick & Laroque,   "
Remby John,   "
Sawyer Chas.   "
Woodman A. J. & Co.   "
Day George G., Groton Junction, Groton
Leavens James L.   "   "
Kempton J.   Haverhill
Kempton & Co.   "
Smith H. A.   "
Tilton & Wasson,   "
Willett & Devnell,   "
King Charles V. B.   Hudson
POPE DANIEL,   "
Drew J. D.   Lawrence
Gurly O. P.   "
Mudgett Thomas Mrs.   "
Popplewell John,   "
Thissell D. V.   "
Dowd J. & R. J.   East Lee,   Lee
Plunkett Thomas,   Leominster
Howard's Hotel,   Lowell
Richardson George,   "
Smith Wm. H.   "
Thompson & Hardy,   "
Blanchard J. E.   Lynn
Brown & Bryant,   "

Earl John S.　　　　　　　　　Lynn
Foss Ivory H.　　　　　　　　　"
Foss Robert,　　　　　　　　　"
Granger John B.　　　　　　　　"
Hatch Charles R.　　　　　　　　"
Hoyt J. M. & Bro.　　　　　　　"
Leavitt Joseph E.　　　　　　　"
McMinus Thos.　　　　　　　　"
MARTIN E. L. P., 9 Washington
　st. (see page 706),　　　　　　　"
MORRIS C. P, & CO., Union cor.
　Willow,　　　　　　　　　　"
Reed Henry D.　　　　　　　　"
Reynolds A. T.　　　　　　　　"
Sargent L. C.　　　　　　　　"
Sawtell Stephen H.　　　　　　"
Gassett & Flagg,　　　　Marlborough
Mero J. Henry,　　　　　　　　"
Richard Louis,　　　　　　　　"
Curry & Welch,　　　　　　Malden
Rich J. E.　　　　　　　　　　"
Lillbridge B. D.　　　　　Marblehead
Simson David,　　　　　　Medford
Doane D. W, Mrs.　　　　　Melrose
Lawrence H. B.　　　　　　　　"
Dean Wm. L.　　　　　Middleborough
Lane Charles,　　　　　　　Milford
Norris B. S.　　　　　　　　　"
Adams S. G.　　　　　　New Bedford
Allen N.　　　　　　　　　　"
Cook John L.　　　　　　　　　"
Dana Frank R.　　　　　　　　"
Dana Charles A.　　　　　　　"
Fish William G.　　　　　　　"
France John,　　　　　　　　　"
Hathaway P. S.　　　　　　　"
Hicks Samuel,　　　　　　　　"
Jennings Thomas G.　　　　　　"
Lewis M.　　　　　　　　　　"
Parker Charles,　　　　　　　"
Richards G.　　　　　　　　　"
Spence Henry,　　　　　　　　"
Stevens L. D.　　　　　　　　"
Thacher John,　　　　　　　　"
Thurston Peleg R.　　　　　　"
Widdoes Levi,　　　　　　　　"
Danforth J. I. & C. H.　　　Newburyport
Dickson Jacob F.　　　　　　　"
Dyer & Son,　　　　　　　　　"
Harrower Robert,　　　　　　　"
Swasey Charles K.　　　　　　"
Fulton Wm. H.　　　　　Northampton
Merrill L. D.　　　　　　　　"
MORTON LEVI,　　　　　　　　"
Parker M. C.　　　　　　　　　"
Robbins Henry J.　　　　　　　"
Washburn & Grover,　　North Bridgewater
Brewer & Deane,　　　North Brookfield
　　　　　　　　　　　　Pittsfield
PHELPS & CROSSMAN; 43 North, "
Richards Charles,　　　　　Orange
Gross S. S.　　　　　　Provincetown
Shaw S. B.　　　　　　　Randolph
Abbot John H.　　　　　　　Salem
Beckford A. N.　　　　　　　"
Clynes F. H.　　　　　　　　"
Covell Thos. N.　　　　　　　"
Davenport J. K.　　　　　　　"
Doherty John,　　　　　　　"
Holbrook J.　　　　　　　　"
Kezar Charles H.　　　　　　"
Rogers S. F.　　　　　　　　"
Smith Edward P.　　　　　　"
Tibbetts R. S.　　　　　　　"
Welch Patrick,　　　　　　　"
Morrill J. F.　　　　　　　　"
Crocker James W.　　　　Salisbury
Donovan C.　　　　　　　Sandwich

McCormic T. J.　　　　　　Somerville
Turner E. M.　　　　　　Southbridge
Barney C. E.　　　　　　Springfield
Barr E. C.　　　　　　　　　"
Curtis & Gunn,
Gilmore D. O.
Heffernon C. Mrs.
Johnson Norman C.
Johnson & Ashley,
Lennehan & Fitzgerald,
Manchester Charles N.　　　　　"
Sleeper M. D.
Smith J.
Thomas T.
White & Foote,
Wright S. E.　　　　　　　　"
CHURCHILL A. K., Franklin st. Stoneham
Simpson James,　　　　　　　"
Field L. E.　　　　　　　Taunton
QUIGLEY BERNARD,　　Weirs, "
Wilber S. & Brother,　　　　　"
Woodward William P.　　　　"
Goodwin Alfred,　　　　　Wakefield
Field Isaac,　　　　　　Waltham
Wood Paschal,　　　　　　　"
Adams T. C.　　　　　　Wareham
Briggs E.　　　　　　　　　"
Hart Edward,　　　　　　Webster
Smith J.　　　　　　　　　"
Higgins & Rodolph,　　　Wellfleet
Clegg William,　　　　Weymouth
Carter A. H.　　　　　Worcester
Fuller C. A.　　　　　　　　"
Hauff Jacob,
Kennen E. L.
Kibbe J. H.　　　　　　　　"
King L. D.　　　　　　　　"
Leathers E. G. & Co.
Lilley A. J.　　　　　　　　"
Newell N. F.　　　　　　　"
Peck E. D. Mrs.　　　　　　"
Perry S. D. & Co.　　　　　"
PLAISTED SIMON M., 91½ Main, "
Smith E. D.
Spaulding & Knowlton,
Stratton Samuel,
Thurston F. F. & Co.　　　　"
Taft, Bliss, & Rice,
Webster B. & Co.
Whitcomb Leonard,　　　　　"
Williams & Spurr,　　　　　"
Witt & Bennett,　　　　　　"

Eave Troughs and Gutters.

STEARNS A. T. (see page 695),
　Port Norfolk,　　　　　Dorchester
Drake A. S.　　　　　　　Milford
Child, Russell, & Hall,　Springfield
BANGS A. & CO., Foster st.,
　(see page 721),　　　　Worcester
NEWTON E. & C., Union st. (see
　page 731),

Edge Tool Manufacturers.

(See also Tools; also Cutlery; also Knife
　　　　Manufacturers.)

Lawrence John,　　　　　　Alford
Hobbs J. C. (machine knives), Arlington
Wood Wm. T. (ice tools),　　　　"
　　　　　　　　　　　　Bernardston
Haynes James M. (plane irons),　"
HANKEY A. & CO. (knives, rag
　cutters, &c. (see page 775), Chappville
Douglas Axe Manufacturing Co.,
　East Douglas,　　　　　Douglas

Edge Tool Manufacturers — continued.

SIMONDS MANUFACTUR-
ING CO. (machine knives
of every description, (see
page 658), Fitchburg
Whitman & Miles Manufac-
turing Co. (mowing machine
knives, &c. West Fitchburg, "
Lockwood L. Gardner
Ellsworth G. F. South Gardner, "
Bowers Darius, (pruning shears), Harvard
Jacobs Joseph & Son, (hatchet),
South Hingham, Hingham
DAWES F. S. (shaves, see page
761), Hudson
LOVEJOY DANIEL. Cushing, cor.
Rock st. (see page 744), Lowell
Fulton Robert (knives), Mansfield
MOORHOUSE JOHN (see page 782), "
Moran & Sons. West Mansfield, "
Murphy J. & R. (oyster knives), "
Frost & Horn (rag-cutters), Medfield
Cummings S. A. (shoe knives), Middleton
BUCK BROTHERS (chisels, gouges,
&c., see page 761), Millbury
Hathaway B. D. (carpenters' and
coopers' tools), New Bedford
Dean Henry N. "
Harrington Sam'l (shaves), New Braintree
Potter Leonard (axes). New Marlborough
WEBSTER W. (shoe knives, see
page 769), North Bridgewater
TUCK S. V. (see page 770), "
Bliss R. (shaves and knives), N. Brookfield
Jones A. W. (axes, &c.), Peabody
Jones T. J. (curriers' shovels), "
Holway Seth W., N Sandwich, Sandwich
Handy F. D. & Brother, Pocasset, "
Shelburne
LAMSON & GOODNOW MANUF.
CO. (table cutlery), Shelburne Falls, "
Ladd N. D. (leather cutters), Sturbridge
Elliott Henry. Taunton
Crossman A. W. & Son (chisels),
West Warren, "
Thayer W. E. (chopping and butcher Warren
knives), Williamsburg
Babbitt A. J. (axes), Savoy, Windsor
BUCK BROTHERS (chisels and
gouges, see page 761), Worcester
Whiting A. L. & Co. (plane irons), "

Egg Beaters.

Fitchburg
Monroe Bros. (one-minute egg beaters), "

Elastic Goods Manufacturers.

Boston Elastic Fabric Co., North Chelsea
Williston & Arms Manufacturing
Co., Northampton

Electric Washing Fluid.

STEVENS CHAS. R. & CO., 15
Brown's wf. (see page 752), Newburyport

Electro Platers.

(*See Silver Platers.*)

Electrotypers.

Bowles Samuel & Co. Springfield
Van Vlack Charles, "

Elevators.

Thayer, Sargeant, & Co., Northampton

Embroidery Stamping.

Leland Thomas, "
Moxley P. C. Miss, Lowell
GRISWOLD B. L., 112 Essex, Salem

Emery Grinders.

Washington Emery Mills, Ashland
Chester Iron Co. Chester
Northampton Emery Wheel Co.,
Florence, Northampton
HAWES & BLISS (manufacturers,
see page 725), West Stockbridge

Emery and Crocus Cloth and Sticks.

Stedman Perley, Braintree
Sibley F. K., Auburndale, Newton

Emigrant Agents.

CONROY DANIEL, 20 Union, Fall River
McDonough John F. "
READE LAWRENCE, 72 Main,
(see page 782), Milford
Ryan P. J. Springfield
Smith John, Taunton

Enamelled Cloth Manufs.

Husband Charles & Co., Taunton
Taunton Oil Cloth Co., Thompson
Newbury, agent and treasurer, "

Engine and Hand Lathes.

PERKINS F. S., Mechanics' Mills, Lowell

Engine Hose Manufacturers.

Gates Josiah & Sons, Lowell
Willis William H. New Bedford
Graton & Knight, Worcester

Engineer. (*Mechanical.*)

Sawyer Sylvanus, Fitchburg

Engravers.

Mumler Andrew C. Charlestown
Carpenter Fred. W. Foxborough
Almy James T. New Bedford
Phelps Ebenezer, Northampton
Bradley, Milton, & Co., Springfield
Chubbuck Thomas, "
Lutz J. C. & Co. "
Martin F. W. "
Morse James H. (jewelry), Westfield
Fairchild Lewis, Worcester
Leland H. F. "
Rice Calvin L. "
TIMME E. A. (see page 803), 279 Main, "
WHITTEMORE W. C. (wood), 197
Main (see page 782), "
Wilson C. W. "

Envelope Advertising.

Lowell
DAVIS ASAHEL, Mechanics' Mills, "

Envelope Manufacturers.

Morgan E. & Co. Springfield
Springfield Envelope Co. "
Hill, Devoe, & Co. Worcester
Whitcomb G. Henry & Co. "

Essences.

(*Manufacturers.*)

CONROY DANIEL, 20 Union, Fall River
Curtis S. B. & G. E., North Bridgewater

Express Wagons.

Davis S. A., East Cambridge, Cambridge
Andrews Gilman, Salem
Peabody
PIKE & WHIPPLE (see page 748), "

Chick Rowena Miss, Chelsea
Colby S. J. "
Comer E. H. Miss, "
Hooker Emma Miss,
McCullough E. Mrs. "
Owen Charles W. "
Perley A. R. Mrs. "
RICHARDSON A. R., 188 Broadway, "
Strauss Fanny Mrs. "
Polley S. J. "
PHILLIPS & SAMPSON, Conway
Phelps Timothy, Dedham
FRAZAR GEORGE L., Washington,
 cor. Harvard, Dorchester
Murphy E. C. "
Thielberg H. "
Littlefield M. W. Milton, "
Almy Charles, Fall River
Baker A. S.
Bennett William H. "
Bigelow Franklin,
Bowditch Emily,
Hawkins Amasa,
Lincoln & Kelley,
Milne J. Osborn, "
Noros L. J. "
Nowell George W. "
Smith C. H. "
WHITAKER J. W., Ferry, cor. Canal, "
Collins Ada, Fitchburg
Davis Hannah L. "
Dunn E. B. & W. A. "
King & Berwin, "
Stiles James F.
Tyler O. S. & Co. "
Moulton M. L. Miss, Framingham
Wheeler T. H. Mrs. "
Eames H. E. Mrs. Franklin
Andrews & Marston, Gloucester
Burns Joseph J. "
Collins Ada, "
Coolidge Charles E. "
Emanuel S. H. & Co. "
Perley M. V. B. "
PROCTER BROS. 121 Front st. "
ROGERS JOHN S. E. Low's Block, "
Tibbets Robert A. "
Ward F. M. "
Story Augustus E., E. Gloucester, "
Eldridge Rinaldo, Harwich
Snow David, Harwich Port, "
Bartlett J. C. Haverhill
Collins E. G. "
Dresser E. R. & Co. "
Kimball & Gould,
Paty S. B.
Rhodes C. N.
Simpson L. J. "
Hunt J. L. Hingham
Bateson John, Holyoke
Gilbert J. F. "
Gilmore C. R. "
Orrell Eliza A.
Austin P. L. Miss, Hyde Park
Cobb C. H. & Co. "
Williams A. Miss, "
Price William,
Tyler D. M. Ipswich
Willcomb William, "
Beals Sampson, Lawrence
Bisbee C. D. "
Booth Mary, "
Durrell S. M.
Ellis & Snow,
Gorwaiz George,
Gould Edward,
Graham Lydia W.
Hale George C.

Fancy Goods — continued.

Leyland Thomas,	Lawrence
Linn John,	"
Lowe M.	"
Moulton J. C.	"
Poor G. W.	"
Robinson Nellie R.	"
Sayward A. Miss,	"
Sibley & White,	"
Walker William G.	"
Watson Elizabeth,	"
Wiggin C. S. Mrs.	"
Young M. E. Mrs.	"
Levy Mary L.	Lee
Joy L. W. Mrs.	"
Parker A. J.	Leominster
Adams M. W. Mrs.	"
Barnard C. C.	Lowell
Bartlett H. J.	"
Bartelle Caroline A.	"
Bemis M. L. Mrs.	"
Bennett M. B.	"
Carney Honora Mrs.	"
Croxford L. J. Mrs.	"
Fruhauf Jacob & Co.	"
Gee Mrs.	"
Griffin S. P.	"
Hobbs Ruth A.	"
Hutchins Elvira R.	"
LELAND WILLIAM, 250 Gorham,	"
Marcy L.	"
MAYNARD C. I. W., 76 Merrimac,	"
McGill James,	"
McGoveren Frances,	"
McKanna Mary,	"
Montferand & Loiselle,	"
Morrill Hannah A.	"
Ogelbie N. J. Mrs.	"
Page Martha,	"
Robinson B. & Co.	"
Robinson C. S.	"
Sanborn Olive W.	"
Sargent S. A.	"
Scott C. M.	"
Shedd G. W. jr.	"
Skinner A. C.	"
Smith F.	"
Smith M. J.	"
Taylor Joseph,	"
Wright Andrew C.	"
Anthony Joseph,	Lynn
Austin L. M. Miss,	"
Ball S. A. Mrs.	"
Buffum S. E.	"
Clapp Geo. H.	"
Dickason Edward A.	"
Dobson J. S. Mrs.	"
Duggen Ellen Mrs.	"
Frothingham B. H.	"
Gurley L. J. Mrs.	"
Hood M. C. & Co.	"
Hoyt W. S.	"
McConnell James,	"
Meader E. V.	"
Stanley C. S.	"
Trafton H. L. Miss,	"
Upham S. J. Mrs.	"
WEBSTER W. T. 8 Exchange,	"
Newhall W. J.	"
Cloon Wm. F.	Malden
Shattuck Geo. W.	Marblehead
Wellman Jacob,	"
Chase Anna,	Medford
Collins J. H.	Milford
READE LAWRENCE, 72 Main, (see page 782)	"
White A. & J.	"
Aiken H. A.	"
	Millbury

Chase Wm. H. Mrs.	Nantucket
Coggeshall N.	"
Fisher E. H. jr.	"
Jaggar Charles H.	"
McCoy John,	"
Ray Geo. C.	"
Bates A. E. Mrs.	New Bedford
Bisbee A. A. & Co.	"
Cable N. M.	"
Case E. C. Miss,	"
Comey C. M.	"
Cottle H. B. Mrs.	"
Davis Maria E.	"
Dexter & Haskins,	"
Fisher E. H. jr.	"
Fisher James & Co.	"
Harlow Mary W. Mrs.	"
Haskell Edward,	"
Hopkins John,	"
Hunt Josiah,	"
Hutchinson S.	"
Irish E. A.	"
Jackson Brothers,	"
Munson H. W.	"
Nooning Wm. B.	"
Paul J. T.	"
Taber Abby P. Miss,	"
Tallman Charles S.	"
Tilden & Co.	"
Todd Henry,	"
Bassett Ann P.	Newburyport
Currier M. E.	"
Gorwaiz John,	"
Hale L. C. Mrs.	"
Haynes Andrew J.	"
Hervey & Co.	"
Hutchins Sarah L.	"
Johnson H. G. jr.	"
Johnson S. H.	"
Johnson Wm. A.	"
Lane Abbie B.	"
Morss William B.	"
O'Connel Timothy,	"
Peabody C. W.	"
Sanderson Mary A.	"
Teel Mary J.	"
Pierce F. L. Mrs.	Newtonville, Newton
Bixby C. C.	North Bridgewater
Clapp B. R.	"
Goldthwaite E.	"
Jones Lovell, & Sanford,	"
Reed Thomas,	"
Thomas H. O.	"
EDDY L. A.	North Brookfield
Wires M. D.	
PHILLIPS & SAMPSON,	Northampton
Sparrow Joel,	Orleans
Davis E. L.	Palmer
Hyde Mary J. Mrs.	Peabody
Morrison Mary E.	"
Roome George,	"
Malley William,	Pittsfield
Millard Ansel E.	"
Cole F. E. & Co.	"
STOEHR C. (see page 762), 53 North,	"
HALL JOHN T.	Plymouth
Kilburn Edward J.	Provincetown
Putman A. L.	"
Snow C. B.	"
Young James,	"
McLelian J. A.	Quincy
Nash James E.	Randolph
Porter F.	"
Reid James & Co.	Reading
Ruggles Emily,	"
Babson Mary M. Pigeon Cove,	Rockport
Bush Mary A.	Salem
Dresser A.	"

Peabody John P. Salem
Pillsbury S. H. "
Pitman James W. "
Plumer R. Mrs. "
Shattswell J. A. "
Stone Lydia, "
Story J. A. & Co. "
Coffin S. E. Mrs. Amesbury, Salisbury
Osgood M. C. " "
POPE FREDERIC S. Sandwich
Trull J. jr. Cliftondale, Saugus
Hawkes C. M. East Saugus, "
Bryant Chas F. Sharon
Kimball Anna Mrs. Somerville
Edlefson C. E. North Somerville, "
Bussell W. C. East Somerville, "
BARNES W. C. Southbridge
Kimball H. A. "
King J. A. "
Cowles & Bliss, Springfield
Gardner J. A. "
Jennison & Kendall, Mesdames, "
Kendall A. C. "
Kinsman W. D. "
Leavits, Gillespie, & Gilmore, "
Malley M. W. "
McFarland & Niebuhr, "
Montague Wm. H. "
Paquette Henry, "
PATTON WILLIAM, "
Sterr Jacob, "
Vining W. D. "
Wallach, Schwab, & Zinsser, "
WILCOX O. W. 187 Main, "
Mitchell & Nickles, Stoneham
Whittier E. T. "
DARLING H. W. Stoughton
Taunton
BLISS A. L. & CO. 65 Main (see
page 758), "
Hathaway E. "
Southgate Samuel, "
Tinkham S. M. & Sons, "
WASHBURN GEORGE W., West-
minster, cor. Washington (see
page 757), "
Whitney & Forbush, "
Wilbur & Co. "
Woodward & Son, "
Bond & Noble, "
Coussens M. H. Mrs. Waltham
Sawyer Henry C. "
Waltham Skirt Co, William A. Adams,
agent, "
Woolley George, "
MURDOCK CHAS. C. Wareham
Bryant & Co. Watertown
Lane George, "
NOURSE & BARNARD, "
Jacobs C. E. Webster
Higgins & Rodolph, Wellfleet
NOURSE, WHITE, & CO. (see page
799), Westboro'
Holcomb & Avery, Westfield
Hull John Mrs. "
Phelps S. M. Mrs. "
West Roxbury
Chase R. H. Mrs. Jamaica Plain, "
Crowe R. H. Mitteneague, West Springfield
Libby Alvah, "
Dewhurst William, Woburn
Brigham E. L. & Co. Worcester
Davis E. T. "
Dayton H. H. "
Eaton C. B. "
Forbes W. E. & Co. "
Fraquer G. "
Gross, Strauss, & Co. "

Lee H. O. Worcester
Sanford E. H. & Co. "
Smith Rufus L. "
Sutton E. "
Weinberg H. "
Witt S. H. Mrs. "
Harris R. H. Yarmouthport, Yarmouth

Fan Mills.
(See Agricultural Implements.)

Faucet Manufacturers.
Taylor L. B. & Co. Chicopee
E. STEBBINS MANUF. CO. Taylor
st. (see page 780), Springfield
Huntley George R. Taunton
Loud C. A. Winchendon

Feed-Cutter Manufacturers.
(See Agricultural Implements.)

Felloes Manufacturers.
(See also Carriage Spokes, &c.)
Lloyd & Jenks, Cheshire
Tower E. J. Lanesborough

Felt Manufacturers.
Lowell
LOWELL FELTING MILLS, Wm.
H. Thompson, prop., Pawtucket st. "
Bacon John H. office 1 Union, Boston,
manuf. at Winchester
ELLIOTT FELTING MILLS, Frank-
lin City, Wrentham

Fertilizers.
(See also Bone Dust; also Guano; also
Plaster Mills.)
Westcott William S. Amherst
Hargraves Manuf. Co. Fall River
Pond H. E. (patent), Franklin
Paine S. S. & Bro. New Bedford
Littlefield Hiram, Newburyport
McIntire Lewis, Northampton
WALTON TIMOTHY, Foot of Ord
(see page 748), Salem
Olney D. K. Southbridge
STAPLES & PHILLIPS, 27 West
Water (see page 759), Taunton
Weymouth
Bradley Wm. L., North Weymouth, "

File Manufacturers.
Whipple File and Steel Manuf. Co.
Ballard Vale, Andover
CULLEY ELI (see page 763), Fitchburg
Lamb George, Lawrence
ASHWORTH S. & CO. (files and
rasps), 2 Fletcher, n. Dutton, Lowell
HISCOX A. J. (all kinds of files and
rasps, see page 741), 132 Middlesex, "
HILL BROS. (see page 729), Taunton
WEBSTER JOSEPH, Court st. (see
page 758), "
HISCOX A. J. (see page 741),
10 Central, Worcester
WORCESTER FILE WORKS, Wm.
Hart, prop., Junction (see page
783), "

Fire Arms.
(See also Guns and Sporting Apparatus.)
Stevens J. & Co., Chicopee Falls, Chicopee
Brown Charles S. Newburyport
Dickinson E. L. (pistols), Springfield
SMITH & WESSON (revolving), "
WESSON FIRE ARMS CO. (breech-
loading shot guns), "

Fire Arms — continued.

Allen Ethan & Co. Worcester

WESSON FRANK, Manchester st. "
(rifles and pistols, see page 786),

Fire-Brick Manufacturer.

WILLIAMS J. R. (see page 715),
Weir Village, Taunton

Fire-Brick and Stove Linings.

Davis & Chaddock, office 127 Water,
(Boston), Chelsea

Somerset Potters'-Works, Somerset

PRESBREY STOVE LINING CO.
Wm. B. Presbrey, agent (see page
730), Taunton

STAPLES & PHILLIPS (also clay
for foundries, see page 759), 27
West Water, "

TAUNTON STOVE LINING CO. A.
W. Parker, agent and treas. (see
page 758), "

Fire-Sand.

BLAKE ZEBINA, West Water st.
(see page 758), Taunton

Fish Bait.

DODD A. W. & CO. (clam and
porgie, see page 731), Gloucester
Tarr & Brother, "

Fish Dealers.

Hammon E. B.
Randall J. B. Adams
Hogan M. "
Nichols R. A. North Adams, "
Gulloud G. B. "
Findley John, Amherst
Merrill Sylvester, Andover
Attleborough
Tufts Wm. C., North Attleborough,
Andrews Richard H. "
BURNHAM AUSTIN, Beverly
Fisk Elbridge, "
Smith Amos, "
Atherton William, "
Atwood Freeman, Boxford
Cahoon E. Brewster
Robbins Seth, "
Seabury David, "
Crosby B. H. "
Slack Geo. A. Brookline
Atkins & Chilson, "
Brown B. A. Cambridge
Millan & Snow, "
Buxton C. B. & Co., Cambridgeport, "
Weston Chas. H. "
Witherell Freeman C. " "
Dale Thomas J. East Cambridge, "
Dickerman Enos, "
Dunn V. M. Canton
Boardman Thomas C. Charlestown
Holbrook J. G. "
Brackett E. C. "
Cutler Henry, "
Hardy B. "
Hunt Geo. L. & Co. "
Marsh Eli C. "
Starks R. C. & H. C. "
Stockwell E. C. "
Tallon N. "
Eldredge & Stetson, "
Tripp J. H. & Co. Chatham
Hopkins Joshua, "
Hunt James, Chelsea
Riley Matthew, "
Stubbs & Brown, "

Brown Joseph S. Chicopee
Plaisted, Gardner, & Hunt, Clinton
Wishart William, "
Wood B. "
Bates John, Cohasset
Prouty A. F. (fresh), "
Snow Ephraim, "
Studley W. W. (fresh), "
Tower Abraham H. "
Tower A. H. jr. & Co. "
Rhodes, D. B., S. Dedham, Dedham
Dennis
Baker Joseph K. & Co., Dennis Port, "
Kelley & Sears, East Dennis, "
Baker David H. West Dennis, "
Burgess Anthony, " "
Small & Crowell, " "
Brown H. W. & Co. Dorchester
Cook & Hastings, Milton, "
Ryder J. E. Neponset, "
Cole Joshua (fresh), Eastham
Higgins B. G. "
Smith Philip, "
Smith Lewis, Orleans, "
Derby W. P. (fresh), East Hampton
Bradley William, Edgartown
Fuller Andrew B. "
Smith Holmes W. "
Hayden & Negus, Fall River
Mayhew T. H. & Co. "
Fish Hervey, Falmouth
Holmes Ezekiel, Fitchburg
Knowlton & Witham, "
Russell Francis, "
Thompson I. & Co. "
Chaffile T. J. (fresh), Georgetown
Hardy Stephen S. " "
Jewett James, " "
Longfellow Henry W. " "
Adams Geo. W. & Co. Gloucester
Ansell Wm. E. (commission), "
Babson David C. & H. jr. "
Barrett John, "
DODD A. W. & CO. (fresh, see page
731), "
Elweil George, jr. "
Field James, "
Gerring & Douglass, "
Gloucester & Boston Salt Fish Co. "
Maddocks B. & Co. "
New England Fish Co., A. W. Bray,
agent, "
Oakes William H. "
Parrott W. M. & Co. "
Parsons Isaac, "
Rust Moses, "
Sayward Epes, jr. & Co. "
Stockbridge S. & Co. (fresh), "
Tarr & Brother, "
Dennis Geo. & Co. E. Gloucester, "
DODD, TARR, & CO. (see
page 732), "
Garland George, "
Low Alfred & Co. "
Story Amos A. " "
Walen & Wonson. " "
Wonson Wm. H. & Son,
(smoked halibut), " "
Berry Lorenzo, Lanesville, "
Field Richard, Great Barrington
DAMON D. N. Greenfield
Stevens S. B. Groton
Kirk F. H. Groton Junction, "
Ruggles Elbridge (fresh), Hardwick
Small Shadrack, Harwich
Batchelder O. T. Haverhill
Davis D. M. & J. "
Stephenson John, Hingham

Spring C. (fresh), Hingham
Joslin G. M. Hopkinton
MARTIN W. L. (see page 724), Holyoke
Bennett Freeman R. Hudson
Mentzer Edward C. "
Tuck J. W. Hyde Park
Pezzy Thomas, (lobsters), Kingston
Ransom Harvey & Sons, "
Washburn Asa W. "
Washburn Francis, "
Watson Nathan B. (fresh), "
Wilder Joel (fresh), Lancaster
Small Cyrus, Lawrence
Small Lyman, "
Wiggin G. P. "
Wiley W. A. "
Chapman Samuel S. Lee
Hanover Patrick, Cherry Valley, Leicester
Walker F. C. Leominster
Smith Charles M. (fresh), Lexington
Cotton Neal, Lowell
Dow Albert F. "
Hight R. S. "
Hill James E. "
Knights J. H. "
Moxley H. C. "
Randlett M. B. "
Sargent E. D. & Son, "
Ackerman T. R. Lynn
Marsh & Leavitt, "
MACE WILLIAM H., Union, c. Pearl, "
Nickerson Thomas, "
Stevens D. W. "
Tarbox G. O. "
Brackett Z. H. Malden
McLean Philip, "
Pratt & French, Mansfield
Dean C. C. "
Latham S. B. Marion
MANSFIELD W. D. Marlborough
Baker Samuel C. Marshfield
Barlow Franklin (fresh), Mattapoisett
Barlow Gideon B. "
Maker Seth R. Medfield
Lewis F. Medford
Smith Sewall, West Medway, Medway
Leeds & Jones, Melrose
Cushing Josiah C. Middleborough
Haven W. P. Milford
Sheldon T. J. "
Johnson Charles W. (fresh), Nahant
Johnson J. Bishop, "
Burgess Watson, Nantucket
Beekman John, "
Cartwright Alexander, "
Davis, Elbridge, & Kenney, "
Dunham George F. "
Eldredge K. & Co. "
Nickerson & Emery, "
Johnson H. S. "
Bartlett-A. Natick
Bartlett Bowen S. New Bedford
Bassett William A. (fresh), "
Baker & Smith (dry and pickled), "
Clark & Bartlett, "
Cook William H. "
Crowell Charles P. "
Harwood & Leonard, "
Luce Ambrose E. "
Mason Humphrey S. "
Sisson Joseph L. "
Smith J. R. (dry and pickled), "
Thomas & Watson, "
Whitton Levi, "
Adams Simon A. (fresh), Newbury
Colby William T. "
Bamford Joseph A. Newburyport
Dennis Amos, "

Hale C. W. & Co. Newburyport
Harris Samuel, "
Howard J. T. "
Sargent & Norton, "
Whitten John, "
Woodbury S. "
New Marlborough
Adams & Waugh, Mill River, "
Blanchard M. L., Newton Corner, Newton
Hamilton E. North Bridgewater.
Maynard D. W. (fresh), Northborough
Lincoln Thomas (fresh), Norton
Sargent S. Brigham, North Brookfield
Ellis William A. (fresh), Oxford
Thayer A. Palmer
Kimball J. H. Peabody
Wood Addison, Pepperell
Lowden Thomas L. Pittsfield
Nickerson Francis, "
Rickard Samuel, Plymouth
Atkins John jr. & Co. (fresh, dry, and pickled), Provincetown
Brown Joseph (fresh), "
Cook James 2d (fresh), "
Higgins A. (fresh), "
SMALL R. C. (fresh, dry, and pickled), "
Young John (fresh, dry, and pickled), "
Clough William H. Salem
Cook George T. "
Derby-Wharf Co. "
Floyd S. P. "
Monarch Ebenezer, "
Paige I. W. & Co. "
Parsons J. M. "
Townes L. J. "
West B. A. (dry), "
Bonney E. H. Scituate
Gardner Enoch C. "
Lewis & Sparrow, Somerville
Clifford E. B., No. Somerville, "
Hersey John W. South Hadley Falls
Granger Brothers, Southwick
Daniels W. H. & Co. Springfield
Granger T. M. "
Ives & Quimby, "
Lillibridge & Batchelder, "
Robertson George W. "
Smith S. L. "
Scott H. "
Webber J. W. & Co. "
Cooley Lucian, Indian Orchard, "
Reed S. D. Sterling
Tweed Samuel, Stoneham
Prior Paron H. Stoughton
Stranger Milo, Sturbridge
Hadley Thomas, Swampscott
Honors John, "
Stanley, Seger, & Co. "
Baker Alfred, Taunton
Doane Francis, "
Field L. E. "
Reed Robert S. "
Townsend J. S. & Brother, "
Dias John H. Holmes's Hole, Tisbury
Gill Abijah, "
Watkins Samuel, Tyringham
Young A. J. Upton
Linnell Nathan, Wakefield
Newton Stephen L. Waltham
McCarroll T. Ware
Sturtevant E. R. "
Nightingale Ellis, Wareham
Searis & Barnes, Webster
Atkins Henry, Wellfleet
Swett James (mackerel), "
Tarr Caleb, Westboro'
Luce Francis N. West Boylston
Connor Jeremiah, West Newbury

Fish Dealers — continued.

Gowen Ezekiel,	West Newbury
Mayhew Thos. W., Westport Pt. Westport	
Moore James,	Weston
Fallon F. Jamaica Plain, W. Roxbury	
Thayer W. G.	Weymouth
Adams W. R. & E. A.	Woburn
Young James A.	
Newcomb A. S.	Worcester
O'GRADY WM. & SON, 295 Main,	"
Remington & Co.	"
Stubbs Charles,	"

Fish Oils.

DODD, TARR, & CO. see page 732,
   East Gloucester.   Gloucester
DODD A. W. & CO. (see page 731),   "

Fisheries.

Crowell David,	Beverly
Foster Daniel 1st,	"
Foster Geo. B.	"
Lovett William B.	"
Ober Samuel,	"
PICKETT JOHN,	"
Smith Francis A.	"
Stone James,	"
Eldredge & Stetson,	Chatham
Tripp J. H. & Co.	"
Cole Joshua,	Eastham
Higgins Beulah G.	"
Smith Philip,	"
Smith Lewis, Orleans,	"
Babson David C. & H. jr.	Gloucester
Brown Brothers,	"
Burnham Edward E. & Co.	"
Clark John J.	"
Clark & Somes,	"
DODD A. W. & CO. (see page 731),	"
Dennis & Ayer,	"
Friend George,	"
Friend Charles & Co.	"
Friend Joseph,	"
Friend Lemuel & Co.	"
Friend William H.	"
Gale John H.	"
Garland George,	"
Harvey John T. (fresh),	"
Lane Samuel & Bro.	"
Low David & Co.	"
Low John & Son,	"
Maddocks B. & Co.	"
Mansfield J. & Sons,	"
McKENZIE WM., Duncan n. Rogers,	"
New England Fish Co., A. W. Bray,	
agent,	"
Parkhurst David,	"
Parrott W. M. & Co.	"
Perkins Dean,	"
Perkins George & Son,	"
Perkins John & Co.	"
Pettingell & Cunningham,	"
PEW JOHN & SON, 83 Spring,	"
Poole Solomon,	"
Procter Joseph O.	"
Rowe & Jordan,	"
Saunders, Huntington, & Co.	"
Sayward Daniel,	"
Sayward Epes Jr. & Co.	"
Shute & Merchant (curers),	"
Smith & Gott,	"
Smith & Oakes,	"
Stanwood & Leighton,	"
Steele Wm. H.	"
Steele George,	"
Stockbridge S. & Co.	"
Tarr & Brother,	"
Tarr Daniel B.	"

Terrell, Parrott, & Co.	Gloucester
Wonson Wm. H. & Son,	"
Griffin Gustavus & Son, Annisquam,	"
Dennis Geo. & Co. E. Gloucester,	"
LODD, TARR, & CO. (wholesale	
and retail dealers in dry and	
pickled fish, see page 732),	
E. Gloucester,	"
Gerring & Douglass,	" "
Haskell Samuel, jr.	" "
Low A. & Co.	" "
McKenzie & Knowlton,	" "
Nelson & Day,	" "
Norwood George & Son,	" "
Parsons Wm. 2d, & Co.	" "
Walen & Wonson,	" "
Wonson John F. & Co.	" "
WONSON WM. C. (in-	
spector)	" "
Andrews Joseph L. & Sons, Lanesville, "	
Doane Valentine, Harwich Port, Harwich	
Nickerson & Baker,	"
Weeks & Small, South Harwich,	"
Nye Atkinson,	Hingham
Whiton Peter L.	"
Delano B. & Son,	Kingston
Holmes Edward,	"
Brown Samuel H.	Marblehead
Goodwin & Colley,	"
Hooper John P.	"
Hooper Joseph,	"
Knight Wm. R.	"
Pitman George E.	"
Pitman Henry F.	"
Quiner Wm.	"
Burrill E.	Newburyport
Goodwin W. jr.	"
Hale D. & I.	"
Thurlow B. F.	"
Atwood Jesse R.	Plymouth
Barnes Corban,	"
Brewster Isaac,	"
Churchill John D.	"
Finney Clark,	"
Finney E. C.	"
Harlow Nathaniel E.	
Leonard Nathaniel W.	
Morton A. G.	
Morton James,	
Nelson Wm H.	"
Perkins Gideon,	"
Robbins Augustus,	"
Whiting Henry,	"
Atwood John, jr. & Co.	Provincetown
BOWLY J. E. & G.	"
Conwell David,	"
COOK CHARLES A.	"
Cook E. & E. K.	"
COOK H. & S. & Co.	"
Cook Jesse, jr.	"
Cook Stephen,	"
Freeman Francis M.	"
Freeman & Hilliard,	"
Garland & Doggett,	"
Gifford Isaiah,	"
Lewis Bangs A. & Co.	"
Lewis Thomas,	"
MAYO ISAAC F.	"
NICKERSON R. E. & A. & Co.	"
Nickerson Seth, 2d,	"
Nickerson S. T. & L. M.	
PAINE ARTEMAS,	
Paine J. & L. N.	
Rich S. & J.	
SMALL E. E.	
SMALL REUBEN C.	
SMITH DAVID,	
UNION WHARF CO	"

Bradley Wm. H. jr. & J. W.   Rockport
Gott Addison & Co.   "
Hodgkins Charles (fresh)   "
Low, Brainard, & Co.   "
Parsons & Hodgkins,   "
Pool John,   "
Tarr, Judson, & Co.   "
Tarr & Thurston,   "
Tarr Stephen N.   "
Story, Larvey, & Co.   Pigeon Cove,   "
Derby Wharf Co.   Salem
Central Wharf Co.   Wellfleet
Commercial Wharf Co.   "
South Wharf Co.   "
Swett James,   "

Fishermen's Outfits.

Gloucester
CARTER JOHN F. (see page 749),   "
McKENZIE WM., Duncan, 'n. Rogers,   "
PEW JOHN & SON, 83 Spring,   "
Stacy & Co.   "
WONSON WM. C., East Gloucester,   "
TURNER E. C.   Plymouth

Fishing-Pole Manufacturer.
Mallory Simeon,   Russell

Fishing Tackle.
Burnham L. A. & Brother,   Gloucester
Howkhill Peleg,   New Bedford

Flag and Curb Stone.
PEIRCE CHARLES M. jr. 119 No.
Water,   New Bedford
BLAKE ZEBINA, (see page 758) West
Water,   Taunton

Flannels.
ROCKPORT STEAM COTTON MILLS,
John H. Higgins, agent (see page 798),
Rockport

Flavoring Extracts Manufs.
Colton John W.   Westfield

Flax Mills.
Smith & Dove Manuf. Co. Peter
Smith, agent,   Andover
Boston Flax Mills, E. Braintree, Braintree

Flyer Manufactories.
HALL RICHARD & CO. Canal,
east of Union (see page 749), Lawrence
HEAVEN JESSE, Canal, east of
Union,   "
LAWRENCE FLIER & SPINDLE
Works, (Henry P. Chandler, supt.
Canal, east of Union),   "

Flocks.
Medway Flock Co.
Medway
Worcester
BUELL S. K. 18 Foster (see page 781), "

Florists.
(See Nurserymen.)

Flour and Grain.
(See also Country Stores.)

Reed A. N. & Co. N. Abington, Abington
Butler S. P. (wholesale), N. Adams, Adams
Hodge William D.   "
Westcott Wm. S.   "
Fowle Samuel A.   (grain),   Amherst
Peirce J. Winslow (grain),   Arlington
Green Charles O,   "
Carpenter L. Z. & P. M.   Ashby
Attleborough

Thayer O. S.   Attleborough
Bacon Ebenezer,   Barnstable
CHASE HEMAN B.   Hyannis,   "
Shattuck Henry J.   "
Hobart L. W.,   Weymouth,   Barre
Brown Charles O.   Braintree
Twichell George L. & Co.   Brimfield
Walker F. & Co.,   E. Brookfield,   "
Brookfield
Buckland
Frost J. B. & Co.   Shelburne Falls, "
Cambridge
Davis & Bates,   Cambridgeport,   "
Luke Elijah H.   "   "
Hondley, Wheeler, & Co. East Cam-
bridge,   "   "
Train Edmund,   "   "
Perkins Alvin,   "
Melvin & Co. (grain and meal), Charlestown
Tufts N. jr.   "
Aldrich & Wallin,   Charlton
Atkins Zenas,   Chatham
Nickerson Franklin,   "
Ryder Isaiah,   "
Taylor George,   "
Knight E. H.   "
SLADE D. & L. (see page 718), 196 Chelsea
Broadway,   "
Warren Brothers,   "
Cone Geo.   Chester
Keefe T.   "
Brimhall E. & Co.   Clinton
Jewell H. & Co.   "
Moody & Day,   "
Hudson B. N.   Concord
Richards D.   Danvers
Fisher Amory,   Dedham
Bissett, Young, & Co. Readville,   "
Baker H. B.   South Dedham,   "
Hall Nathan,   Dennis
Kelley D. N.   South Dennis,   "
Underwood M. S.   "   "   "
Burgess Anthony,   West   "   "
Robinson N. T.   Dorchester
Robinson Asa,   Neponset,   "
Prior Allen & Co.   "
Hunting Amos,   East Bridgewater
Ordway Geo. N.   "
Knowles N. P.   Eastham
Cowles & Webster,   East Hampton
Thayer J. T.   "
Fisher Daniel,   Edgartown
Fisher Lorenzo,   "
Brayton D. A.   Fall River
BROWN D. & SON, ft. Central,
(see page 729),   "
HAWKINS & KILHAM, Slade's
Wharf (see page 718),   "
Kingsley George F.   "
Lindsey W. & N.   "
Massasoit Flour Mills, Chase, Na-
son, & Durfee,   "
Carleton Ira & Co.   Fitchburg
Cushing J. & Co.   "
Ferson D. D. & Co.   "
Johnson Daniel L.   Freetown
Phillips James M.   "
Bush C. W.   Gardner
Glazier Charles E.   "
Tenney Moses & Son,   Georgetown
Burnham Hardy,   Gloucester
Cook George H. & Co.   "
Phillips N. H. & Co. (wholesale),   "
Allerton Wm. East Gloucester,   "
Hulburt H. S.   Great Barrington
Lewis & Chapin,   "
Shattuck S. L.   Greenfield
Greenwich
Parker Daniel, Greenwich Village,   "

Flour and Grain — continued.

	Groton
Prescott Abel & Co., Groton Junction,	"
Rolfe Henry C.	"
Church & Sylvester,	Hanover
Knapp & Talbot,	"
Howland Calvin L.	Hanson
Perry & Spooner,	Hardwick
Batchelder John,	Harvard
Baker Joseph O., Harwich Port,	Harwich
Roberts O. H.	Haverhill
WHITON BELA,	Hingham
Judd W. A.	Holyoke
Prentiss E. W. & Co.	"
Wiggin & Flagg,	"
Morse W. H. & C. H.	Hopkinton
Woodward D. P. & Co.	"
NEWTON & WILKINS,	Hudson
Wilkins Henry,	"
CONNOR BARNEY,	Hyde Park
McAVOY & CO. Readville,	"
Haskins Cephas,	Lakeville
Carter D. A.	Lancaster
Hubbard Enoch, jr.	Lanesborough
Page & Harding,	"
Bonney M. & Co.	Lawrence
Butman Henry N. & Co.	"
Churchill J. E. & C.	"
Davis & Taylor,	"
Dennett H.	"
Edson & Richards,	"
Mosher Chas. E.	"
Prince H. B.	"
Dresser & Co.	Lee
Taylor William,	"
Page, Kidder, & Co.	Lowell
Stiles, Rogers, & Co.	"
WAITE A. L. & CO., Dutton n.	
Fletcher,	"
Wood Samuel N.	"
Breed & Co.	Lynn
Lamper & Brothers,	"
OSBORNE E. W. & CO., Market sq.	"
Holden L. D.	Malden
Dunham H. C.	"
Lewis J. G.	"
Sweet Elbridge, West Mansfield,	Mansfield
Graves Joseph, 4th,	Marblehead
Hatch Charles T.	Marshfield
Balch A. B.	Medfield
Green George B. & Son,	Medford
Prentiss E. J.	Milford
Wilber Davis,	"
Batcheller Amos,	Millbury
Gannett Samuel,	Milton
Bangs S. W. & Co.	Montague
Mansir Oscar S.	Monterey
Johnson Welcome W.	Nahant
Adams Freeman E. & Sons,	Nantucket
Cartwright Alexander,	"
McCleave Joseph,	"
Perry Edward W. & Co.	"
Kilborn Alexander, Wellesley,	Needham
Baylies & Cannon,	New Bedford
DENISON J. H. & CO. 42 South	
Water (see page 731),	"
Ely Edward M.	"
Kelley Amasa & Co.	"
Kirk John,	"
Lawrence Cyrus T.	"
Macomber Brothers,	"
Macomber Geo. B.	"
MORSE CLINTON, 151 Kempton,	"
New Bedford Flour Mills,	"
Rapson James,	"
TUCKER & CUMMINGS, 66	
and 68 William,	"
Wilbur Alfred G.	"

Knight J. B. & E. (grain),	Newbury
Balch John H.	Newburyport
Bayley R. & Sons,	"
Hale D. & I.	"
Knight Bros.	
Mooney A. W. & Co.	
Richardson Pottle,	"
Sumner, Swasey, & Currier,	"
	New Marlboro'
Alexander A. H., Mill River,	"
Brackett A. Newton Corner,	Newton
Whipple Orrin,	"
Clark S. D. & Co.	Northampton
McIntire Lewis,	"
Thayer, Sargeant, & Co.	"
Williams Joseph C.	
Moore L. B. Florence,	"
Bartlett F. D.	Northborough
Stockwell M.	"
Stone J. & Co.	"
Wood S. jr. & Co.	
Packard Ellis,	North Bridgewater
THOMPSON & PACKARD,	"
FOSS NELSON J. Campello,	"
Prescot Frank H.	North Chelsea
Webster Henry (grain),	Northfield
WHITNEY, LORD, & CO. (see	
page 776),	Orange
Arey James H.	Orleans
Chapman R. & Co.	"
Snow Aaron, East Orleans,	"
Smith Rufus,	Otis
Pease William E. & Co.	Oxford
Nichols, French, & Tinkham,	Palmer
Comins William,	Paxton
Guy & Brothers,	Peabody
Howard Eben S.	"
Hutchinson B. F.	"
Moulton John G.	
Osborn H. M.	"
Blake Gilman, East Pepperell,	Pepperell
Ames William A.	"
Cole & Powell,	Pittsfield
Moran M.	"
Rathbun J. S. & Co.	"
Weller J. C.	"
Adams Geo. W. West Pittsfield,	"
Hancock Society of Shakers, Ira R.	
Lawson, trustee, West Pittsfield,	"
Cobb F. B.	Plymouth
Pratt L. & Co.	"
Taylor Charles K.	Plympton
Gregory D. H. & Co.	Princeton
Atwood Joseph S.	Provincetown
Ryder Benjamin,	"
SMALL REUBEN C.	"
SMALL E. E.	"
Smith John,	"
Loud Joseph & Co.	Quincy
Jones Gilbert T.	Randolph
Eames E. W.	Rockport
Kingsley Frank,	Rowe
Knowlton Joseph,	"
BECKFORD & DODGE, 13 Front,	
Union Wharf, and Grove,	Salem
Bowker Brothers,	"
BROOKS AUGUSTUS T., 117 Derby,	"
Hanson J. V. & J.	"
Jones J. S. & Co.	"
Ropes Charles A.	"
Kingsbury Henry & Co., Salisbury Point	
Phelps Newton, Montville,	Sandisfield
HARTWELL GEORGE,	Sandwich
Cole & Jenkins,	Scituate
	Shelburne
FROST J. B. & CO., Shelburne Falls,	"
Kilburn C. A.	Shirley
Reed & Thrasher,	Somerset

Hale & Warner,   Southampton
Edwards William & Son (wholesale),   Southbridge
Boyle & Gilbert,   Southwick
Granger Brothers,
Capin James,   Spencer
Snow Cheney,   "
Bangs John,   Springfield
Birnie Brothers,   "
Bigelow & Adams (wholesale),   "
McNALLY J. R., 254 Main,   "
Parker & Foster,   "
Pebbles & Matoon,   "
Sibley & Rathbun,   "
Wilder & Puffer,   "
Worthy J. L.,   "
Waldo H. R.,   Stoughton
Wheaton & Carpenter,   "
Briggs C. A. & Co.   Taunton
Church H. W. & Co.   "
Church & Allyn,   "
Dean H. A. & Co.   "
GALLIGAN OWEN & CO. 55 and 57 West Water,   "
JACKSON & WILLIAMS, 43 and 45 City Square,   "
Paull J. & Co.   Weirs,
Green Julius A.   Templeton
Fisher Daniel, West Tisbury, Tisbury
ADAMS A. M.   Townsend
Warren B. F.   West Townsend,   "
Wilson John W.   Tyringham
Wood Arba T.   Upton
Perkins, Coffin, & Co.   Waltham
WATSON & FAIRBANK,   Ware
GURNEY ANSEL S., (see page 774),   Wareham
Fairbanks A.
Atherton A. S.   Warren
Delose Calvin W.   Warwick
Perkins, Coffin, & Co.   Watertown
Edmunds John E.   "
Shumway Oscar,   Webster
Daniels Timothy A.   "
Davenport A.   Wellfleet
Whitney C.   Westborough
Cowee R. G. & Co.   West Boylston
Crowell Geo. & Co.   West Brookfield
Blood Lemuel B.   Westfield
Griswold & Stebbins,   "
Strickland Francis G.   "
Yeamans Roland,   "
Heywood & Burbeck,   Westford
Chapman Anson,   West Hampton
Judd F. H.   "
Strong Franklin,   "
Merriam Caleb S.   Westminster
Gilford Henry,   Westport
Binney J. & Co.   Weymouth
Lond Joseph & Co.   "
Wells Charles & Co.   "
Wait S. K.   Whately
Town Charles S.   Williamsburg
Beals & Bowker,   Williamstown
Whitney Amasa,   Winchendon
Wood Geo H.   "
Ellis Alexander,   "
TAY C. & CO., Main st. (see p. 766),   Woburn
Aldrich & Co.   Worcester
Cheney & Farley,   "
Dexter & Curtis,   "
Clark & Houghton,   "
Farley Bros.   "
Gay D.   "
GODDARD D. B. (wholesale and retail), 284 Main,   "
Harrington F.   "
Holbrook Wm. D. & Co.   "

Holden Howard,   Worcester
Holden P.   "
Hoppin Geo. S. & Co.   "
King P. D.   "
Maynard W. H. & Co.   "
Rogers G. W.   "
Spalding E. K.   "
Spurr E. & Co.   "
Loring Hiram, South Yarmouth, Yarmouth
Crocker & Baker,   Yarmouth Port,   "
Loring William D.,   "   "

Flouring Mills.
(See also Grist Mills.)

Hodge M. D. & W., North Adams, Adams
Brayton D. A.   Fall River
BROWN D. & SON (see page 729), foot Central,   "
Massasoit Flour Mills,   "
Carleton Ira & Co.   Fitchburg
Lawrence Flouring Mill, Davis & Taylor, Amos W. Giles, agent, Lawrence
   New Bedford
EUREKA MILLS, J. H. Denison & Co. (see page 731), 42 South Water,   "
New Bedford Flour Mills,   "
Wahconah Mills, Cole & Powell, Pittsfield
Hancock Society of Shakers, Ira R. Lawson, Trustee, West Pittsfield,   "
Bangs John,   Springfield
Fisher Daniel, West Tisbury, Tisbury
   West Springfield
Worthy Justin L., Agawam Mills,
Kniffin & Sons,   West Stockbridge
Moffatt L. & Co.   "
Platt, Barnes, & Co.   Housatonic,   "

Flue Broom Manufacturers.
BUSH WILLIAM R. 27 No. Main, (see page 755),   Fall River

Forges.
KINSLEY LYMAN & CO., (see page 714), Cambridgeport, Cambridge
KINSLEY IRON & MACHINE CO., Frank M. Ames, agent, (see page 730),   Canton
Dearborn, Robinson, & Co., Harrison Square,   Dorchester
Lazell, Perkins, & Co.   Bridgewater
Talcott N. W.   Springfield

Forks.
(See Agricultural Implements.)

Frame Makers.
(See Looking Glass and Picture Frames.)

Free Stone Workers.
LYONS WILLIAM J., Medford, foot of Cook (see page 735), Charlestown

Fresco Painter.
NIXON T. J., Court st. (see page 728),   Taunton

Fruit Dealers.
(See also Confectionery.)

IVES H. B., Main st. North Adams, Adams
Eldridge Samuel,   Fairhaven
Keith Joseph,   Fall River
McKevitt T. James,   "
Blatchford Wm. H.   Gloucester
Campbell John,   "
Stevens Elias,   "
Akers Geo. G.   Lawrence
Bailey James R.   "

Fruit Dealers — continued.
BEAL HENRY, Essex near Broad-
   way,   Lawrence
Hosmer E. E. & Co.   "
Cheney Chas. W.   Lowell
Cheney E.   "
Collins J. T.   "
Eaton D. A.   "
FLYNN M. X., 10 Merrimack (see
   page 742),   "
Morse & Turner,   "
Newton Chas. N.   "
Newton C. E.   "
Page Chas. R.   "
Reilly B.   "
Jenkins C. S.   Nantucket
Bourne E.   (wholesale),   New Bedford
Damon Samuel H.   "
Scott J. W.   "
Gardner & Estes.   "
Roberts E. F. & J. W.   Salem
Merrill S. A.   "
Read J. F.   "
Dill Dexter,   Springfield
Gunn & Merrill,   "
BURBANK BROTHERS & CO.
  (wholesale), 1 Allen court,   Worcester
Fawcett E. A.   "
Warfield A. J. & Co.   "

Fuel (Granular).
Robbins A.   New Bedford
Hall W. M. & Son,   Worcester

Fur Dealers.
(*See also Hats, Caps, and Furs.*)
Webb Brothers   (manuf.),   Arlington
Bascom Wm.   (manuf.),   Lowell
Barnes C. C. & Co.   "

Furnace Grate Bar.
SMITH STERRY,   Salem

Furnaces and Ranges.
(*See also Stoves and Tinsmiths.*)
                Cambridge
GRIFFIN GEORGE H., N. Cambridge, "
DIGHTON FURNACE CO., Geo. F.
  Gavitt, treas, Boston office 96 & 98
  North (see page 733),
        North Dighton, Dighton
JONES WILLIAM, Dorchester
  Ave., cor. Commercial,   Dorchester
Cook, Grew, & Ashton,   Fall River
Flint J. D. & Co.   "
Wilcox D. T.   "
Bishop L. A. & Co.   Lawrence
Ricker O. A.   "
Costello T. & Co.   Lowell
Mack Sewall G.   "
NASH J. W. & CO., 105 Central
  (see page 789),
          New Bedford
Parker Warren W. (sheet iron),   "
Tripp S. A.   "
Wood, Brightman, & Co.   "
Jordan J. W.   Worcester
WHEELER W. A., 42 Thomas,
  (see page 792),   "

Furniture Dealers.
(*See also Cabinet Makers; also Furniture
Manufacturers.*)
Marsh M. M.   Amherst
Young Brothers,   "
Abbott J. A.   Andover
Houry Terrence,   "

Conant Chauncey,   Barnstable
Hallett R. F.   Hyannis,   "
Prophett William,   Bridgewater
Kernan James,   Cambridge
Whitney & Brackett,   "
Bates George W. (second hand),
  Cambridgeport,
Fatal John J. (second hand),
  Cambridgeport,
Holmes & Davis,   Cambridgeport,   "
Oxford & Brigham,   "
Russell Amos (second hand),   "
Bangs M. & Co.   E. Cambridge,   "
Graves Geo. jr.   "
Woodward James H. (second hand),
         North Cambridge,   "
Berry George W. & Co.   Charlestown
Brown Sumner,   "
Carter A. J.   "
Chamberlain T. Mrs.   "
Kelso George R.   "
Perkins D. B.   "
Robinson T. S. G. & Co.   "
Merrill & Morrison,   Chelsea
Reed Edward F.   "
SAUNDERS & LOGAN, 67 Park
  (see page 712),   "
Hosley D. P. & Co.   Chicopee
Brimhall E. & Co.   Clinton
Moody & Day,   "
Baker, Cheney & Co.   Dedham
French Daniel, Joppa, East Bridgewater
Bullock Geo. A.   East Hampton
Borden, Almy, & Co.   Fall River
Harriman & Mellen,   "
McNulty John,   "
Newell C. P.   "
Westgate, Baldwin, & Co.
Lane Patrick,   "
Morse Marcellus J.   Fitchburg
Willis Sidney D. & Co.   "
Hodges & Messenger,   Foxborough
Brick Alfred H.   Gardner
Pierce S. K.   South Gardner,   "
Browne Geo. W.   Gloucester
Dolliver Edward S. L. & Son,   "
Proctor Charles,   "
Chamberlin & Whitmore,   Greenfield
Smith R. & L. F.   Harwich
Smith Gilbert,   "
                Haverhill
LE BOSQUET J. H. & CO. 18½ Main, "
Randall J. P. & Son,
Crafts Roswell P. & Son,   Holyoke
Loring Bros.   "
Bates E. A.   Hopkinton
Knibbs J. H.   Hyde Park
MANN J. H.   Ipswich
Willcomb Frederick,   "
Howe M. N.   Lawrence
Howe & Co.   "
Jewett F. S. & Co.   "
Pedrick & Closson,   "
Pillsbury Joshua, jr.   "
Davison H. C.   Leominster
Adams, North, & Co.   Lowell
Banner M. A. & Co.   "
MEHAN JOHN & BROTHER, 24
  Prescott,   "
Nichols Jacob,   "
Offutt & Fairgrieve,   "
PATCH E. B. & CO. 1 and 2 Com-
  mercial sq.   "
Puffer & Bradley,   "
Ray Wm. E.   "
Austin David & Co.   Lynn
Bean John H.   "
Graves Philip H.   Malden
STIMSON ALDIN M. Main st.   Medford
Soule George,   Middleborough
Harris H. & Co.   Milford
Judson, Sawtell, & Co.   "
Coffin James M.   Nantucket
Folger R. G. & F. W.   "

Cleland John, Natick
Woodbury P. F. "
Randall R. H. South Natick, "
Bassett N. G. Newburyport
Ireland & Trefethen, "
Safford S. H. & Co. "
Stockman M. & Co. (second-hand), "
DeWolf A. J. New Bedford
Drury Warren, "
Geils Garrett. "
Knights William, "
MAXFIELD CALEB, "
Openshaw Mary (second-hand), "
Parsons L. J. "
Warner J. A. "
Smith Silas M. & Co. Northampton
Howard, Clark, & Co. North Bridgewater
Burrill Alfred, North Brookfield
FRENCH BROTHERS & CO. Orange
Loomis J. S. Palmer
Trask T. Peabody
PARKER C. E. (also undertaker), Pittsfield
WHIPPLE S. T. & CO. (undertakers and furniture dealers),21 North st, "
Brown J. P. Plymouth
Dyer Chas P. Provincetown
Arey Joseph jr. Quincy
FURNALD N. B. "
Currier & Millett, Salem
Fellows Israel, "
Glazier Ezra & Son, "
Haskell, Lougee, & Co. "
Henderson & Thurston, "
Hynes Patrick J. "
May Calvin W. "
Wallis Joseph, "
Cummings James, Amesbury, Salisbury
Fifield Benj. E. "
Allyne Samuel H. Sandwich
Pope John W. "
Swan H. S., Shelburne Falls, Shelburne
Williams Samuel, Southbridge
FISHER, BUCKHAUSE, & KNAPPE, Union Block, Main, Springfield
Maxfield & Kellogg, "
Spiller & Aiken, "
Driuton Edward C. "
Withington P. M. Stockbridge
Foster John M. Stoughton
Hoard N. S. Taunton
Jones T. E. W. "
Seckell John & Son, "
Washburn Edward E. "
Bourn & Brooks, Templeton
Hankerson & Bean, Waltham
Goodnow William, "
CONEY H. M. & CO. Ware
Soule Silas T. Wareham
Shepard D. W. & Co. Warren
Bent Luther & Co. Watertown
Davis S. H. Webster
Spalding & Eddy, "
Griggs S. M. & Co. Westborough
Lambson C. R. Westfield
Sloan Rufus A. Weymouth
Raymond Silas, Winchendon
Marcy J. Woburn
Oxford C. W. & Co. "
Pollock G. W. "
Brondueut James, Worcester
CHOLLAR JOHN D. 198 Main (see page 783), "
Lawrence Joseph B. & Co. "
Maynard D. B. "
Putman Bros. "

Furniture Manufacturers.

(See also Chair Manufacturers: also Furniture Dealers: also Cabinet Makers.)

Chase David, Acushnet
Adams Jasper H. North Adams, Adams
Isbell Cyrus P. "
Miller Brothers, Athol
Morse Laban & Son (towel-racks), "
Partridge Edward E. (pine furniture), "
Athol Depot, "
Pierce Joseph, Athol Depot, "
Rice James M. "
Allen, Leavitt, & Co. Beverly

16

Buckley & Co. Beverly
FOSS & INGALLS (see page 714), Cambridge
Austin George M. Cambridgeport,
Hixon Edward & Co. "
Hogan, Follansbee, & Co. (walnut chamber), Cambridgeport, "
Braman, Shaw, & Co. East Cambridge, "
Daniels Brothers & Co. "
Ellis John A. & Co. "
Gehlowsky Ferdinand, "
Gilman H. D. & Co. (tables), "
Beal & Hooper, Charlestown
Berry G. W. & Co. "
Brown Sumner (pine), "
Holmes F. M. & Co. "
Waterman A. & Co. (extension and centre tables), "
Winslow Seth & Co. (chamber), "
BAKER, CHENEY, & CO. Dedham
Everett Willard & Co. South Dedham, "
BAUCH AUGUSTUS (willow, see page 764), Bowdoin st. Dorchester
EDDY DARIUS & SON (library steps, see page 666), Harrison-sq. "
Glover & Jones, "
Hall Oliver & Son, "
Slve & Hood, Great Barrington
Whitmore & Pixley (folding), Housatonic, "
Hobart S. L. (cabinet), Hingham
Ripley & Newhall, "
BLODGETT & BISHOP (see page 717), Leominster
Davis H. G. "
PRATT GEORGE L. (see page 766), "
Merriam, Hall, & Co. N. Leominster, "
Crosby Ephraim, Lowell
CROSBY FURNITURE CO., D. S. Kimball, treas. (cabinet) Mechanics' Mills. "
TROWBRIDGE & KIMBALL, Wamesit Steam Mills (cabinet, see page 736), "
Woodbury, Gray, & Co. Lynn
Allen S. P. Manchester
Crombie & Morgan, "
Decker William, "
Dodge Cyrus, "
Jewett Alfred W. "
Kelham & Fitz, "
Leach, Annable, & Co. "
Lee Charles, (bedsteads), "
Rust & Marshall, "
Wheaton William E. "
Nelson Thomas, Mattapoisett
Small Brothers, Melrose
Glover Oliver, 2d, Milton
RICHARDSON GEO. F. & CO. Montague
MAXFIELD CALEB, New Bedford
Collins George, (extension tables), Newburyport
Collins William, "
Smallwood E. A., Newton Corner, Newton
Howard, Clark, & Co. North Bridgewater
Morse John N. (cabinet), Oakham
Bliss & Farnsworth, Orange
KILBURN L. & CO. (see page 778), "
Bill & Taylor, North Orange, "
Peirce & Stowell, "
Porter & Spear, Otis
WHIPPLE S. T. & CO. Pittsfield
Wilson J. B. "
Crane Wm. F. Montville, Plymouth
Swan H. S. Shelburne Falls, Sandisfield
Dickinson E. W. & Co. Shelburne
Washburn Edward E. Springfield
Taunton
Bourne & Brooks, East Templeton, Templeton
Greenwood Thomas T. "
Tyringham Shakers, Tyringham
Reed Reuben G. (what-nots and brackets), West Boylston
Lambson Clinton K. Westfield
Norton J. D. & Son, West Hampton
Shattuck William G. (school), Weston
Slater Geo., Jamaica Plain, West Roxbury
Daymon & Rice, E. Weymouth, Weymouth
Smith Sumner, Whately
Ingraham Henry H. Williamstown

Furniture Repairing.

Baker S. H.　　　　　　　　Charlestown
Douglass Charles,　　　　　　Fall River
Woodworth Albert A.,　North Bridgewater
RAYMOND CHARLES, 35 Middle st.
　(see page 796),　　　　　　Plymouth
Dawson James,　　　　　　　　Lynn
Calder H. M.　Florence,　　Northampton
Anderson L. J.　　　　　　　Salem
Smith Peleg W.　　　　　　　"
Lemou Gideon L.　　　　　　Westfield

Fuse Manufacturer.

Manning E. D. (blasting),　　　Medford

Galvanizers.

CROCKER BROS. & CO., Court st.
　(see page 756),　　　　　　Taunton

Garden Trellises.

NOURSE, WHITE, & CO. (see page
799)　　　　　　　　　Westborough

Garden Vegetables.

SMITH CHARLES, 61 Lime, (see
page 752),　　　　　　Newburyport

Garment Supporters.

SOUTHWICK & HASTINGS, 7 Cypress,　　　　　　　　　Worcester

Gas and Steam Pipe and Fit-
tings.

Walworth J. J.　　　　　Cambridgeport
SMITH H. W., Park, cor. School, Chelsea
　　　　　　　　　　　Dighton
DIGHTON FURNACE CO., Geo. F.
　Gavitt, treas., Boston office 96 and
　98 North (see page 733), N. Dighton,　"
Manchester George L.　　East Hampton
BUSH WILLIAM R. 27 North Main
　(see page 755),　　　　　Fall River
Wolfendale William,　　　　　"
HUBBARD A. W., Newton's lane
　(see page 767),　　　　　Fitchburg
Haughton & Bingham,　　　Lawrence
Sargent B. E.　　　　　　　"
Lenord & Durant,　　　　　Lee
Barker Horace R. & Co.　　　Lowell
Field George W.　　　　　　"
PROCTOR JOSEPH W. 29 Fletcher,　"
REED & HALLOWELL,　　　"
DEXTER THOMAS F., R. R. ave. cor.
　Washington,　　　　　　Lynn
　　　　　　　　　　New Bedford
SHERMAN & GIFFORD, 24 William,　"
Wood, Brightman, & Co.　　　"
Appleton J. H. & Co.　　　Springfield
Elwell E. M.　　　　　　　"
WITHERELL STEPHEN B.　　Ware
Slater George, Jamaica Plain, W. Roxbury
Barrett, Washburn, & Co.　　Worcester
Colbath J. & Co.　　　　　　"

Gas and Water Pipe Manufs.

DIGHTON FURNACE CO. Geo. F.
　　　　　　　　　　　Dighton
　Gavitt, treas. Boston office, 96 and
　98 North (see page 733), N. Dighton　"
　　　　　　　　　　　Taunton
TAUNTON IRON WORKS CO. Geo.
　M. Woodward, agent (see page 732),　"

Gas Fitters and Fixtures.

Adams John P.　　　　　　Cambridge
Dickson R. W.　Cambridgeport,　"
Stafford J. S.　　　　　　　"
Bailey & Gilman,　　　　Charlestown
Titus Franklin A.　　　　　"
JONES WILLIAM (see page 794), 56
　Park,　　　　　　　　Chelsea
H. W. SMITH, Park cor. School,　"
DIGHTON FURNACE CO. (see page
　733), North Dighton,　　　Dighton
Barker H. R. & Co.　　　　Fitchburg
HUBBARD A. W., Newton's lane (see
　page 767),　　　　　　　"

Sleeper D. A　　　　　　　Haverhill
PROCTOR JOS. W.　29 Fletcher,　Lowell
Sheldon Henry,　　　　　　"
HAUGHTON & BINGHAM, 195 Essex
　(see page 746),　　　　　Lawrence
Hague & Booth,　　　　　　"
Sargent B. E.　　　　　　　"
DEXTER THOMAS F., R. R. ave. cor.
　Washington,　　　　　　Lynn
Russell H.　　　　　　　Malden
Wilber N. D.　　　　　Middleborough
　　　　　　　　　　New Bedford
ALLEN & BLISS (fixtures), 121 Union,　"
Mahar James T.　　　　　　"
SHERMAN & GIFFORD, 24 William,　"
Taylor Henry J. (fixtures),　　"
Wood, Brightman, & Co.　　　"
Ingraham L. P.　　　　Newburyport
Sargent C. R.　　　　　　　"
Clark & Fox.　Newton Centre,　Newton
HUMPHREY & ALMON, W. Newton,　"
Wilber N. D.　　　　North Bridgewater
Lord Daniel jr.　　　　　　Peabody
　　　　　　　　　　Pittsfield
RICE, ROBBINS, & CO. West st.,　"
Staten Daniel F.　　　　　Salem
Staten E. H.　　　　　　　"
Sullivan C.　　　　　　Somerville
Archer A. S.　　　　　Springfield
Avery & Co.　　　　　　　"
Stevens W. H.　　　　　　"
TAUNTON GAS LIGHT CO.　Taunton
WETHERELL STEPHEN B.　　Ware
Gunn John,　　　　　　Webster
　　　　　　　　West Roxbury
White & Mayo, Jamaica Plain,　"
Barrett, Washburn, & Co.　　Worcester
Colbath J. & Co.　　　　　　"

Gas Heating Improvements.

JONES WILLIAM, 56 Park, (see page
794),　　　　　　　　　Chelsea

Gas Machine Manufacturers.

SPRINGFILD GAS MACHINE CO.
　Henry Cooley, treas. (portable, see
　page 770),　　　　　　Springfield
Woods, Wilcox, & Co. (portable),　"

Gas, Steam, and Water Fit-
tings.

CHOATE & PERKINS, 194 Derby (see
　page 747),　　　　　　　Salem

Gasometer Manufacturers.

　　　　　　　　　　Cambridge
Walter Charles B.　Cambridgeport,　"

Gauge Manufacturers.

BLAISDELL A. H. & CO. (see page
　745), Newton Corner,　　　Newton

Gaugers.

Case Allen,　　　　　New Bedford
Delano Abraham,　　　　　"

Gear Manufacturers.

Williams John,　　　　　Worcester
Winslow S. C. & S.　　　　"

Gearing and Shafting.

HEALD STEPHEN & SONS (see
　page 796 and 797),　　　　Barre

Gents' Furnishing Goods.

Craig Edward,　　　　　　Adams
BRIGGS & BOLAND, N. Adams,　"
Fisher C. B.　　　　　　　"
Martin Wm.　　　　　　　"
Brown S. J. & Co.　　　Amesbury
Greene M. E.　　　　　　"
Stockman M. jr.　　　　　"
Dean John H.　　　　　Andover
Hill S. W. Mrs. (neck-tie manuf.), Arlington
Everett Albert M.　　　Attleborough
Orcutt F. V. & Co.　　　　Barre
Burnham Charles L.　　　Beverly

ridge & Murphy, Charlestown
icks J. T. "
aud John W. "
near James E. "
homas John C. "
olton Mary Mrs. Chelsea
LDREIVE ROBERT, 73 Winnisimmet, "
ike John J. "
itchcock & Hasley, Chicopee
arshley Samuel W. "
ield F. C. Dedham
rong W. V. East Hampton
shley Wm. H. Fall River
romberg Bros. "
avot John, jr. "
rank Charles, "
ibbs R. S. & Co. "
aylor & Co. "
'ilbur & Gray, "
llen A. D. Foxborough
arrett C. P. Gloucester
ennett & Marr, "
awrence R. C. "
oodsell Henry T. Great Barrington
ubbell Andrew L. "
ond George, Greenfield
eward & Willard, "
oung A. Haverhill
atlin A. M. Hopkinton
inturn W. E. "
iske George B. Holliston
dler David, Holyoke
ller & Co. "
ITCHELL BROTHERS, "
ice & Ingersoll, Hyde Park
oore Wm. H. Lawrence
avage & Flood, "
ox Warren & Co. Lowell
ODGMAN B. 30 Central, "
ederer B. & Co. "
nith George, "
awyer Norris, Lynn
arker & Whiting, Milford
ox & Beatty, "
itchell, Jones, & Co. "
hayer & Houghton, "
ATHCART CHAS. S. Nantucket
 New Bedford
ARNETT JOHN, 102 and 104 Union, "
rownell Charles W. "
annon E. S. & Co. "
ook William & Co. "
ovell & Hathaway, "
avenport Cornelius, "
avis L. D. "
ilford N. T. & Co. "
ucas Allen, "
ucas A. E. "
ackard E.* "
erry E. S. "
vift Moses C. "
anders William, "
illiams T. D. & Co. "
ark Merritt, Northampton
raper J. L. "
rench & Abbott, "
ingsley D. & Son, "
ameny E. A. "
illou Warren S. Orange
haw J. P. Palmer
ott S. R. Peabody
ask Thomas, "
avis, Taylor, & Kelley, Pittsfield
eves & Wallace, "
DAMS WILLIAM, Provincetown
ooter S. C. Reading
alsof George S. Salem
own S. J. & Co. Salisbury
vingston Herman, "
urgess C. S. Sandwich
ller John Q. "
igham D. H. & Co. Spencer
OMINS & CLARK, "
anton John W. Springfield
euth J. B. Stoneham
rown & Jenney, Taunton
OLBY SAMUEL, (see front colored
page), 11 Union block, "
oster & Barnard, "

Grant Charles H.
Steele & Baker, Taunton
Thomas S. A. "
Wheeler L. S. Tisbury
Guild V. Uxbridge
Judd A. & Co. Ware
Lawton J. R. "
Rawson James M. "
Sabin Charles H. Webster
READ M. H. West Stockbridge
Clapp F. A. Weymouth
Cooley W. F. Worcester
Davis A. & J. E. "
Eames D. H. "
Eldred & Liscomb, "
Estabrook & Herrick, "
Geer George, "
Hollander G. "
Howland J. P. jr. "
Kendall & McClennen, "
Lewisson Louis, "
Mecorney Wm. "
Perry & Paul, "
Walker Asa, "
Ware A. P. & Co. "
Wiggin & Pike, "

German Silver Ware Manufs.

REED & BARTON (see page 758), Taunton

Gilders.

(See Looking-Glass and Picture-Frames).

Glass Cutter and Stainer.

COOK J. M. (see page 714), 131 to 141
Congress, Boston

Glass Ware Manufacturers.

Boston Silver Glass Co. Cambridge-
port, Cambridge
BAY STATE GLASS CO., E. W. Bet-
tinson agent, E. Cambridge, "
McElroy H. H. (homœopathic), East
Cambridge, "
New England Glass Co., E. Cambridge, "
Opal Glass Co., A. M. Farley, East
Cambridge, "
Massachusetts Glass Co. Charlestown
Page & Harding (window glass),
Berkshire, Lanesborough
LENOX PLATE GLASS CO., An-
drew T. Servin, agent, Lenox Fur-
nace, Lenox
New Bedford Glass Co., George How-
land, jr., president, New Bedford
Boston & Sandwich Glass Co. Sandwich
Cape Cod Glass Company, "
Union Glass Company, John P. Greg-
ory, agent, Somerville

Glass Sand Dealers.

Gordon George W., Russell C. Brown,
agent, Cheshire

Glaziers.

(See Painters, House and Sign.)

Glaziers' Points Manufactur-
ers.

 Dighton
DIGHTON TACK CO. (see page 715),
PLYMOUTH TACK & RIVET
WORKS, S. Loring, proprietor
(see page 713), Plymouth
Wood N. & Co. "
FIELD A. & SONS (see page 719), Taunton
RHODES M. M. Porter st. "

Glove Manufacturers.

Barrows William, Amherst
Draper & Sumner (woolen), Canton
Bamford Charles, Ipswich
Birch John. "
Burrows & Hunt, "
Glover John S. "
White Brothers & Kilburn, Lowell

Glove Restorers.

Reed J. T. & Co. Charlestown

Glue Manufacturers.

Gay W. H. & Co., So. Dedham,   Dedham
Butman M. C.   Lynn
NEWHALL JONATHAN M.   "
  27 Myrtle,   "
Brown Thomas,   Marblehead
Collins F. A.   Lower Falls,   Newton
Brown William H.   Peabody
Essex Glue Co. (Upton & Walker),   "
UPTON GEORGE.   "
ANDERSON JOHN M. (see page
  770),   Salem Turnpike,   Salem
Rich & Letnan,   Salem
Rowe John. jr. & Co.   Woburn
Baeder & Adamson,   E. Woburn,   "

Glue Substitute.

Windward James,   Fall River

Gold Chain Manufacturers.

Arthur, Rumrill, & Co.   Springfield
Shumway R. G.   "

Gold Pen Manufacturers.

HASKINS BROTHERS (see front
  colored page),   Shutesbury
Packard C. N.   Springfield

Grain Dealers.

(See Flour and Grain.)

Grain Elevators.

Green George B. and Son,   Medford
Thayer, Sergeant, & Co.   Northampton

Granite Quarriers.

(See also Stone Quarriers.)

Beatie John.
Beatie William,   Fall River
Harrison Barney,   "
Harrison William,   "
Lyon & Blanchard,   Fitchburg
Wheeler S. A. & Son,   "
Andrews Stephen P.   Gloucester
Barker H. & Bro.   Lanesville,
Butman John,   "
Corliss Daniel G. & Co.   Milton
Flynt William N. & Co.   Monson
PLUMMER GRANITE CO. (see
  page 754),   Northbridge
Abercrombie Joel, Florence, Northampton
Badger Brothers,   Quincy
Barker H. & Brothers,   "
Barker E. & Son,   "
BELL BROS. & CO. (see page 763),   "
Bouck Michael,   "
Frederick & Field,   "
French H. & Son,   "
Garrity James,   "
Granite Railway Company,   "
Hardwick Charles H. & Co.   "
McDonell Patrick,   "
Mead, Sargent, & Co.   "
Mitchell Charles R.   "
Mitchell George H.   "
Owens John & Co.   "
Quincy Granite Co., F. J. Fuller, agent, "
Redoute Luke,   "
Rogers O. T. & Co.   "
Smith Brothers,   "
Whitin & Chase,   "
WILLIAMS, SPELMAN, & CO. (see
  page 768),   "
Wilson Francis & Charles,   "
Weston, Fernald, & Co.   Rockport
Rockport Granite Company,   "
Stepp, Balfou, & Co.   Pigeon Cove, "
Kings Ezra & Co.   "
Reynolds James,   "
Fletcher Samuel,   Graniteville, Westford
Palmer Benjamin,   "
Hand David,   "
Hand William,   "

Granite Works.

Mt Auburn Granite Works, Knox &
  Augier,   Cambridge

DAVIS DANIEL C., Marginal st.
  (see page 714),   Chelsea
BLETHEN TRUE G., foot of Pleasant st. (see page 791),   Lynn
MANN A. G. Southbridge st.   Worcester

Grindstones.

POLLARD C. F., 6 Washington,
  (see page 766),   Lynn

Grist Mills.

(See also Flouring Mills.)

Beals N. A. jr.   East Abington, Abington
Reed A. S. & Co.   North   "
Robbins Francis,   "
Wetherbee Daniel,   Acton
Faulkner W. E.   South Acton,   "
Morse George P. & Co.   Acushnet
Spooner N. S. (estate),   "
Allen Darwin W.   Adams
Blackinton & Sherman,   N. Adams,   "
Chilson Jacob B.   "
Hodge M. D. & A. W.   "   "
Farrar Eugene,   Agawam
Sikes O. S.   "
Leonard Rufus.   Feeding Hills,   "
Pease Henry,   Alford
Stoddard Augustus R.   "
Amherst Mill Company,   Amherst
Gaylord & Holly,   "
Puffer Stephen P.   North Amherst, "
Fowle Samuel A.   Arlington
Barrett George H.   Ashburnham
Jefts C. A. & Co.   "
Gross Elijah,   Ashburnham Depot,   "
Davis John,   Ashby
Howes Z. & Son,   S. Ashfield, Ashfield
Cutler S. N. & Son,   Ashland
Kelley James,   Athol
Lord Ethan,   Athol Depot,   "
Adams John, jr.   Attleborough
Dunn M. M.   Auburn
Hinckley Nathaniel,   Barnstable
Jones Heman,   "
Hinckley Heman,   Centreville,   "
Lambert Leonard, Marston's Mills,   "
Conant Charles,   Barre
Knight Luke L.   "
Haywood Seth P.   Barre Plains,   "
Ballou Monroe E.   Becket
Ashby William M.   Bedford
Beaman J. L.   Belchertown
Dorman Asahel,   "
Rich R. P.   "
Barr Seneca,   Bellingham
Drake J. M. & A. B.,   N. Bellingham, "
Felton H. O.   Berlin
Wheeler Willard M.   "
Slate C. J.   Bernardston
Dodge Aaron,   Beverly
Chase ——   Billerica
Patten A. H.   "
Richardson John O.   "
                               Blackstone
Kelley J. & W. A.,   North Blackstone, "
Sawyer John F.   Bolton
Wolcott Freeman,   "
Andrews Dean,   Boxford
Day J. T.   "
Hayward Augustus,   "
Porter J. J.   "
Glazier John,   Boylston
Banister Eli B., Boylston Centre,   "
Ray Tertulius,   "   "   "
Hobart L. W.   Weymouth,   Braintree
Eldridge Jesse,   Brewster
Nickerson Warren,   "
Bryant Lewis,   Bridgewater
Brown Charles O.   Brimfield
Morgan Thomas J.   "
Draper John W.   East Brimfield,   "
Fosket Rufus,   Parksville,   "
Burbank Charles,   Warren,   "
Rice Frank,   Brookfield
Twichell George L. & Co.   "
Walker F. & Co.   E. Brookfield.   "
Hartwell William,   Buckland
Taylor Horace F.   "
Taylor R. S. & J. B., Buckland Centre, "

Reed Edward, Burlington
Cutter E. W., Cambridgeport, Cambridge
Shepard J. S. Canton
Adams Charles E. "
At ood Bartlet S. Carlisle
Perkins Alvin, Carver
Cole H. G. North Carver, "
Cushman Stephen. South " "
Marcy A. H. Charlemont
Melvin W. T. & Co. Charlestown
Tufts N. jr "
Aldrich & Wallin, Charlton City, Charlton
Jones Julius, Charlton Depot, "
Walker Otis, " City, "
Chelmsford Mill Co. Chelmsford
Russell Abbott, "
Dodge J. S. North Chelmsford, "
Ingraham n, Northrop, & Co. Cheshire
Nickerson Edwin F. "
Thomas O. Chester
Bisbee & Damon, . Chesterfield
Adams & Sprague, West Chesterfield
Stevens Lafayette, Worthington, "
Crittenden A. N. Willimansett, Chicopee
Boyton H. C. Chicopee Falls, "
Gaylord & Co. " "
Manter William C. Chilmark
Chilson Velorous, N. Adams, Clarksburg
Clark & Smith, Coleraine
Nelson Willard, "
Smith Brothers, "
Sutton L. South Halifax, "
Angier M. W. Concord
Barrett Samuel, "
Damon, Smith, & Co. "
Moulton James, "
Sprague John, Conway
Bradley Brothers, Cummington
Lovell Jacob, "
Whitmarsh Ephraim, "
Putnam Otis F. Danvers
Hansqu J. V. & J., Danvers Port, "
Ober J. L. " "
Richards Daniel, " "
Cummings Wm. H. Dartmouth
Howland Elihu, "
Turner Elbridge G., New Bedford, "
Terry —— North Dartmouth, "
Cummings Benj. T. " "
Smalley Mulford, South Dartmouth, "
Barrows Thomas, East Dedham, Dedham
Childs Robert, Deerfield
Porter Brothers, "
Felton A. South Deerfield, "
Goddard D. A. " "
Crowell Freeman, West Dennis, Dennis
Crowell Leonard, " "
Howes Obed, " "
Sears Benj. Dennis Port, "
Kelley Jos. B. " "
Cape Cod Steam Mill Co. " "
Simmons Wm. H. (estate), Dighton
Baker John A., North Dighton, "
Robinson Asa, Neponset, Dorchester
Brown A. F. East Douglas, . Douglas
Carlton Isaac C. Dracut
Varnum Nathaniel, "
Gleason & Wells, Southbridge, Dudley
Stevens Henry H. Webster, "
Swallow Daniel. Dunstable
Woodward James, "
Prior Allen & Co. Duxbury
Doane Rowland, · Eastham
Knowles N. P. "
Cowles & Webster, East Hampton
Drake Lincoln. Easton
Dean T. H. & J. O., South Easton, "
Chadwick William, Edgartown
Egremont
Van Bramer John E. North Egremont, ".
Benjamin Joseph A. South Egremont, "
Minot Manufacturing Co. Enfield
Swift River Manuf. Co. "
Essex Mill Co. Essex
Brayton David A. Fall River
BROWN D. & SON (see page 729), "
foot Central-st. "
Clark Barnabas. "
Massasoit Mills, "
Holmes Bartlett, Falmouth

Robinson Joshua C., E. Falmouth. Falmouth
Swift Silas, West Falmouth, "
Carleton Ira & Co. Fitchburg
Cushing J. & Co. "
Tower Dennis, Florida
McEvoy J. D. Foxborough
Wilmarth Kinsley, "
Wilson John D. Freetown
Winslow Thomas G. "
Lawrence David, East Freetown, "
Bush C. W. Gardner
Tenney Moses & Son, Georgetown
Arms John, Gill
Roberts Osias, "
Holmes & Wood, Turner's Falls, "
Brown & Wheeler, Riverdale, Gloucester
Burnham Grover, West Gloucester, "
Foote A., New-England Village, Grafton
Saunders A. Saundersville, "
Aldrich C. C. & Son, Granby
Clark Israel Mrs. "
Granville
Dickinson B. C., Granville Corners, "
Davis Calvin, Great Barrington
Hatch Billy, "
Kellogg C. T. (custom grist and feed
mill). "
Nash E. Q. Greenfield
Greenwich
Parker Daniel, Greenwich Village, "
Balch Francis, G. Junction, Groton
Hardy Charles N. Groveland
Nutting J. H. Hadley
Granger L. N. North Hadley, "
Bosworth Martin, Halifax
Monroe Ethan, East Bridgewater, Hanson
Ames Sampson, Hardwick
Watkins George F. "
Batchelder John, Harvard
Sparrow Zedda, Harwich
Burgess Seth, Harwich Port, "
Rogers Richard H. N. Harwich, "
Ryder Freeman, " "
Taylor Eben, South Harwich, "
Fitch Brothers & Porter, Hatfield
Robie Cyrus E. Haverhill
Vincent Willis, West Hawley, Hawley
Coats Charles P. Heath
WHITON BELA, Hingham
Bingham Silas, Hinsdale
Bottum Whitefield R. "
Parish Elisha H. "
Harris & Co. Holden
Butterworth T. D. Holland
Gordon Frank, "
Marcy George L. "
Pond Caleb, Hopkinton
Wood A. W. Woodville, "
Brigham O. S. Hubbardston
Hale J. Otis, "
Brigham Rufus H. Hudson
Tarbell A. A. "
Hutchins Parley, Huntington
Whipple & Stauton, "
McAVOY & CO. Readville, Hyde Park
Lord Daniel, Ipswich
Holmes Alexander, Kingston
Newcomb Thomas, "
Hinds Sumner. Lakeville
Richmond Eleazer, "
Carter D. A. Lancaster
Phelps B. S. "
Hubbard Enoch, . Lanesborough
Davis & Taylor, Lawrence
Webster H K. & Co. "
Gibbs Nathan, East Lee, Lee
Ingram Adin, " "
Pixley Isaac H. South Lee, "
Dutton H. Leicester
Draper D. F. Clappville, "
Merrell Wm. M., Lenox Furnace, - Lenox
Stratton Martin W. & Joel A., Leominster
Wright C. W. & Co., N. Leominster, "
Felton L. G. Leverett
Wood Ira, "
Felton Albert, North Leverett, "
Coolidge Charles, Leyden
Dennison A. J. "
Keet Roswell S. "
Blaisdell ——, Lincoln

Grist Mills — continued.

Harrington George F.	Lincoln
Rhoades ——,	"
Warren Luther S.	Littleton
	Longmeadow
Burdatha Henry, East Longmeadow,	"
Stiles, Rogers, & Co.	Lowell
Wood S. N.	"
Eaton J. S.	Ludlow
Fuller Warren D.	"
Houghton Albert,	Lunenburg
Butman Joseph,	Lynn
Lamper & Brothers,	"
Newhall H. B.	"
Quint Wilson,	Malden
Fisher Daniel,	Mansfield
Moran & Sons, West Mansfield,	"
Sweet Eldridge,	"
Dean & Parlow,	Marion
Holmes & Sparrow, Mattapoisett,	"
MANNING JOSEPH,	Marlborough
Dunham Henry C.	Marshfield
Hatch Samuel,	"
Little William F. & S., E. Marshfield,	"
Lewis Charles,	"
Hatch Samuel, North "	"
Bolles Solomon E.	Mattapoisett
Tinkham Abraham,	"
Town Mills,	"
Chenery Reuben,	Medfield
Kingsbury George W.	"
Green George B. & Son,	Medford
Jencks & Crooks,	Medway
Gay William, Rockville,	"
Partridge Elijah, E. Medway,	"
Hill Cyrus, West "	"
Belcher & Durfee,	Middleborough
Washburn Philander,	"
Chapman Nathan,	Milford
Gaskill Richard G.	"
Wilber Davis,	"
Hastings Cornelius,	Millbury
Lombard C. & W. W. Millbury,	"
Gannett Samuel,	Milton
Conant Seneca F.	Monson
Risley H. H.	"
Whiton J. L.	"
Langdon Homer,	Monterey
Axtell H. K.	Montgomery
Chase E. A.	Nantucket
Morse Daniel,	Natick
Roys Lester,	New Ashford
Pepper Henry A.	New Braintree
Knight J. B & E.	Newbury
Knight & Rolfe,	"
Pearson Toppan,	"
Hoxie John A.	Newburyport
Mooney A. W. & Co.	"
	New Marlborough
Alexander A. H. Mill River,	"
Keyes Dorence,	"
Allen & Rood, Hartsville,	"
Moore Lyman E. Millington,	New Salem
Brackett Albert, Newton Corner,	Newton
Ellis Charles, Upper Falls,	"
Clark Silas D. & Co.	Northampton
Thayer, Sargeant, & Co.	"
Nonotuck Silk Co., Samuel L. Hill, agent, Florence,	"
Ball Joseph,	Northborough
Bartlett William A. 2d,	"
Smith Jairus W.	"
Wixon E. R.	"
Marsh E.	Northbridge
Whitin Charles P. Whitinsville,	"
Packard Ellis,	North Bridgewater
French Merritt, North-west Bridge-water	"
Bridger George,	Northfield
Stratton Albert,	"
Webster Arad,	"
Slade D. & I.	North Chelsea
Eames Joseph,	North Reading
Jeffrey Elisha,	"
Braman Isaac T.	Norton
Lincoln Eddy,	"
Smith Nathan,	"
Bothwell Cheney,	Oakham
WHITNEY, LORD, & Co. (see page 770,)	
	Orange
Higgins Benjamin,	Orleans
Baker Obadiah, East Orleans,	"
Nickerson Zebina H. "	"
Gates Brothers,	Oxford
Rich Ebenezer D.	"
Blanchard A. V. & Co.	Palmer
Thorndike Co., Thorndike,	"
Wright ——, Three Rivers,	"
Conins William,	Paxton
Harrington William,	"
Gray Horace,	Pelham
Chandler & Bourne,	Pembroke
Oldham John 2d,	"
Blake Gilman,	"
Mention George A.	Pepperell
Cook Nathaniel,	Petersham
Hapgood Lyman W.	"
Green A. A.	Phillipston
Stewart Jacob,	Pittsfield
Osceola River Mills, George W. Adams, W. Pittsfield,	"
Nash James A.	Plainfield
BARNES E. & J. C. (see page 717,) Water st.	Plymouth
Cobb F. B.	"
Clark Wm, South Plymouth,	"
Taylor Wm. & C. K.	Plympton
Roper Samuel,	Princeton
Smith Flavel W.	"
Lord J. & Co.	Quincy
Baker Samuel,	Rehoboth
Perry Otis,	"
Thurber John,	"
Leonard Theodore W.	Rochester
Rounseville Alden, jr.	"
Carpenter Elijah,	Rowe
Dummer Nathaniel N.	Rowley
Coombs E. S.	Russell
Codding Frederick W ; West Rutland,	Rutland
BECKFORD & DODGE, Union Wharf, and Grove,	Salem
Hanson J. V. & J.	"
Clark Lewis, New Boston,	Sandisfield
Eldridge C. F.	Sandwich
Newhall H. B. East Saugus,	Saugus
Bourne John W.	Savoy
Maynard Albert M.	"
Clapp Thomas,	Scituate
Cole & Jenkins,	"
Gannett Freeman, North Scituate.	"
Burr Raymond H.	Seekonk
Kent Samuel,	"
Martin Calvin,	"
Leonard E. & Co.	Sharon
Manvel & Curtis,	Sheffield
Bailey Jeremiah J. Ashley Falls,	"
Taft Wm. I. East Sheffield,	"
Smead Solomon,	Shelburne
FROST J. B. & CO. Shelburne Falls,	"
Holbrook Jonathan,	Sherborn
Leland James H.	"
Kilburn C. A.	Shirley
Kilburn Jonathan,	"
Doane Orrin,	Shrewsbury
Fay William,	"
Wyman Oliver B.	"
Felton Charles,	Shutesbury
Reed & Thrasher,	Somerset
Stimpson & Co.	Southampton
Nichols Hiram,	Southborough
Rice Willard B.	"
Sawin Moses,	"
Walker F. W.	"
Williams Caleb S.	"
Gleason & Weld, Globe Village,	Southbridge
Smith Byron,	South Hadley
Jacobs B. W. Scituate,	South Scituate
Boyle & Gilbert,	Southwick
Capen James,	Spencer
Snow Cheney,	"
Bangs John,	Springfield
CRAWFORD & DEARNLEY,	"
Harper Edward,	Sterling
Stone John E.	"
Nichols Luke W. West Sterling,	"
Curtis Stephen C., Curtisville,	Stockbridge
Yale Allen,	"
Capen H. M.	Stoughton

Delany James, Stow
Smith Micah & Son, "
Wight George, Sturbridge
Gerry E. A. "
Willis J. P. Sudbury
Whitmore D. D. Sunderland
Coogan Michael, Sutton
Kinney Sumner, "
Stockwell John P. "
Warning Mills, Swansea
Wood Nathan M. "
Briggs C. A. & Co. Taunton
PHŒNIX MANUFACTURING CO.
(see page 725), "
King J. S. East Taunton, "
Pierce Alvin W. " "
Everett Chas. Otter River, Templeton
Trull Nathaniel, Tewksbury
Look Hannah, West Tisbury, Tisbury
Luce George, "
Marshall Alonzo & Son, Tolland
Perkins John P. Topsfield
Towne B. B. "
Adams A. M., Townsend Cen. Townsend
Spaulding Jonas, " Harbor, "
House Manuel, Truro
Upton John G. Tyngsborough
Tyringham Shakers, Tyringham
Fisk Luther, Upton
Holbrook N. W. "
Wood Arba T. "
Lackey Warren, Uxbridge
Marcy H. P. & Co. Wales
Fisher William H. Walpole
Morse Francis, East Walpole, "
Billings Daniel, Ware
Blackmer A. L. "
Snow R. C. & B. C. "
Dean George, Warren
Gould J. B. "
Barlow & Leonard, West Warren, "
Conant Josiah, Warwick
Jillson Henry H. "
Perkins, Coffin, & Co. Watertown
Grout William C. Wayland
Rice George A. "
Slater Samuel & Sons, Webster
Stevens H. H. "
Baker Freeman, Wellfleet
Higgins Thomas, "
Putnam Danforth, Wendell Depot, Wendell
Fairbanks & Fitch, Westborough
Fisher G. W. E. "
Sandra Frank, "
Cowee R. G. & Co. West Boylston
Ames O. & Sons, West Bridgewater
Alger Leonard W. Cochesett, "
Lewis R. K. & Co, West Brookfield
Griswold & Stebbins, Westfield
Bush, Nelson, & Co. "
Strickland Frank, "
Yeamans Roland, "
Heywood & Burbeck, Westford
Strong Franklin, West Hampton
Merriam Caleb S. Westminster
Cutting Marshall, Weston
Craw Charles N. Westport
Sisson Alden T. "
Church William, Central Village, Westport
West Springfield
Worthy J. L. & Co. Mitteneague, "
West Stockbridge
Platt, Barnes, & Co. Housatonic, "
Loud Joseph & Co. Weymouth
Wells Charles & Co. Whately
Wilbraham
Thompson Augustus A., S. Wilbraham, "
Adams & Sprague, Williamsburg
Green Albert C. Williamstown
Town Charles, "
Harden Henry, Wilmington
Wentworth Samuel, "
Beals & Bowker, Winchendon
Windsor
Allen Josiah & Sons, W. Cummington, "
Kendall Joseph R. Woburn
Richardson S. Son, North Woburn, "
Clark Dexter, Worcester
Hoppin Geo. S. & Co. "

Patch W. Whipple, Worcester
Stevens Lafayette, Worthington
Adams Benjamin F., W. Worthington, "
Fisher Lewis, jr. Wrentham
Fisher Luther, "
Grant John E. "
Hamblin Seth H. Yarmouth
Hafford William, South Yarmouth, "
Matthews Braddock, " "
Baxter's Mill, West " "
Chase Enoch E. " "
Hallett Lothrop, Yarmouth Port, "

Grocers (Wholesale).

Brown D. & Son, Fall River
CHACE, ALLEN, & SLADE, 16 and
18 Bedford, "
Hawkins & Brother, "
HAWKINS & KILHAM, Slade's whf.
(see page 71s) "
Kingsley George F. "
Lindsey W. & N. & Co. "
Pettey, Lawton, & Co. "
Buttrick Co. Lowell
Hall I. D. & Co. New Bedford
Barrows J. N. "
Knowles J. P. 2d, "
Nye S. G. "
Potter W. F. & Co. "
Shaw & Brother, "
Bayley R. & Son, Newburyport
Downing & Sturtevant, Springfield
Pynchon & Lee, "
West, Stone, & Co. "
Harrington L. Worcester
Learned L. M. "
Taft S. & Son, "

Grocers (Retail).

(See also Country Stores)

Dunham C. L. Abington
Reed Wm. H. "
Soule D. "
Beal John W. East Abington, "
French Joseph, "
Moore William, "
Poole Franklin & Co. "
Union Co. "
Culver George, North Abington, "
Noyes & Harding, South Abington, "
Tarbell Edwin, South Acton, Acton
Sayles C. F. "
Baldwin F. W. North Adams, "
Butler & Co. "
Brolley Daniel, "
Cummings John, "
Darling Moses B. "
Goodrich & Linsley, "
Smith Dexter, " "
Burnham, Siles, & Co. Amesbury
Cammett Gustavus, "
Evans C. W. & Co. "
Gallagher A. J. "
Hunting W. F. M. "
North John & Co. "
Stedman F. F. "
Swett William, '
Amesbury and Salisbury Mutual Benefit Society, Thomas Haigh, agt.,
Amesbury Mills, "
Burt H. & Co. Amherst
Holland S. & Co. "
Winslow, Piper, & Co. "
Puller Reuben G. North Amherst, "
Barnes & Lewis, Andover
Chapman E. "
Merrill Sylvester, "
Lancaster Thomas, Ballardvale, "
Morrison John, "
Cutter George H. Arlington
Hadley William F. "
Rowe Matthew, "
Russell Thomas H. "
Ellis William P. Ashburnham
Fay Brothers, Athol
Lee & Stevens, "
Fay Sereno E. Athol Depot, "

Grocers—continued.

Moulton & Cheeney, Athol Depot, Athol
Packard J. F. " "
Sears C. M. " "
Carpenter L. Z. & P. M. Attleborough
Monroe Charles, "
Follett N. B. & Co., Attleborough Falls, "
Barden J. G. & Co. N. Attleborough, "
Briggs & Hall, " "
Day J. S. South Attleborough, "
Hallett Lot, Hyannis, Barnstable
Hinckley W. L. " "
RICE JOHN W. Barre
Smith Samuel & Son, . "
Mann W. C. Caryville, Dellingham
Carter S. R. Berlin
Fuller S. M. "
Maynard G. W. "
BURNHAM AUSTIN, Beverly
Davenport & Pierce, "
Endicott Robert R. "
Foster George B. "
Hughes Ferdinand D. "
Lummus & Moulton, "
N. E. P. Union, 354, "
PICKETT JOHN, "
Plaisted William D. "
Porter Jeremiah, agent, "
Prince Asa, "
Symonds S. B. . "
Wallis Caleb, "
West Luther, "
Whipple Robert, "
Woodbury Horace P. . "
Day I. S. West Beach, "
Perry & Haskell, " "
Richardson F. E. Billerica
Easty Lott, North Billerica, "
Bates & Comstock, Blackstone
Parker A. B. "
Smith Thomas T. Millville "
Atwood A. H. Bradford
Perry B. G. "
WHITE H. M., South Braintree, Braintree
Winslow B. B. Brewster
Adams William H. Bridgewater
Hathaway William B. "
Keith L. M. "
Kingman W. B. "
Allen W. C. Brighton
Everett W. P. "
Harding F. & Co. "
Hunt Thomas & Co. "
Kendall Salina, "
Mackin Chas. "
Wethern Thomas, "
Vizard & Mulcahy, Brookfield
Hogan Edward, Brookline
Coolidge & Brother, "
Guild J. Anson, "
Hunting & Co. "
Russell Marshall, "
Seamans James M. & Co. "
Robbins M. C. Cambridge
Seavey Theodore B. "
Wood & Hall, "
Wyeth James H. "
Barton C. E. Cambridgeport, "
Booth Thomas, " "
Boyden B. F. " "
Bridge S. G. " "
Casey Richard, " "
Chadbourne C. H. " "
Dobbyn Margaret, " "
Farrell & Mullin, " "
Fyfe Charles E. " "
Goodnow Geo. W. " "
Hannum L. M. " "
Hatch & Arkerson, " "
Holmes J. A. & Co. " "
Houghton Henry M. " "
Hovey J. Dana, " "
Howard M. E. Mrs. " "
Ireland & Smith, " "
James Samuel, " "
King Benjamin, " "
Lyons John S. " "
Marsden James, " "
McCann Eliza Mrs. " "
McGinley John, " . "

Cambridge
Messer D. E. & Bro. Cambridgeport, "
Montgomery Andrew, " "
Nixon William, " "
Ricker Veasey P. " "
Ryder S. N. " "
Sargent Otis W. " "
Sargent & Verity, " "
Titus C. H. & Co. " "
Waite John B. " "
Blake Edwin H. East Cambridge, "
Campbell Hugh, " "
Connors Thomas, " "
Doloff & Harrington, " "
Fahy John L. " "
Flanagan Matthew, " "
Gurvan Terrence, " "
Hendley, Wheeler, & Co. " "
Hovey H. N. " "
Hughes Alexander, " "
Meagher Stephen, " "
Moor J. C. " "
O'Neil John, " "
People's Union Association, " "
Raybold W. T. " "
Robinson Charles, " "
Sexton Patrick, " "
Shea Timothy, " "
Shields Fardy, " "
Shields James, " "
Stevens George P. " "
Steward Alonzo & Son, " "
Train Edmund, " "
Bradford A. W. North Cambridge, "
Durgin James, " "
Smith A. R. " "
Billings L. & L. L. Canton
Brett Rufus, Carver
Ransom B. "
Shaw D. A. "
Adams John Q. Charlestown
Baker Wm. H. & Co. "
Barker Charles A. "
Barry John, "
Bettinson Richard B. "
Bingham L. R. "
Blazo Joseph, "
Bray James E. "
Brooks & Storer, "
Burgess Edward B. "
Burnes Lawrence, "
Burr Henry T. "
Charlestown Workingmen's Co-oper-
ative Association, "
Charlestown Workingmen's Trading
Association, "
Churchill J. C. "
Clark Thomas F. "
Coffey Patrick F. "
Corey & Goodwin, "
Darling & Brown, "
Dineen Ellen, "
Downer F. E. "
Downing Learnerd, "
Dunnigan John, "
Dunn V. M. "
Fillebrowne S. L. "
Flanagan Patrick, "
Flanagan William, "
Flynn John, "
Fox David B. "
Fuller O. G. "
Gallagher David, "
Ginn James F. "
Gline Bradford E. "
Gordon G. W. "
Hall B. R. "
Hall Moses B. "
Harrington Michael, "
Harris Wm. H. "
Hatch John F. "
Hathon Leonard B. "
Hathon Otis L. "
Hayes John Mrs. "
Henshaw Peter, "
Hill S. Prentiss & Co. "
Keane John, "
Kevill Patrick, "
Lovering G. H. & H. "
Mahoney Wm. H. "

Martin Ann,	Charlestown
McMahon Thomas,	"
McKenna M.	"
Moore James,	"
Morris Frank,	"
Mullett & Bradbury,	"
Nason Richard,	"
O'Brien William,	"
O'Connor Michael,	"
O'Neill Michael,	"
Pensleo & King,	"
Percy E. D.	"
Pingree Charles B.	"
Powers Bridget,	"
Quinlan Patrick,	"
Rea J. & Son,	"
Reed J. W.	"
Reed, Sawin, & Co.	"
Ronan Patrick,	"
Sanborn & Priest,	"
Scannell David,	"
Sharkey H.	"
South Isaiah & Co.	"
Stevens Jesse,	"
Stickney Lyman,	"
Sullivan P.	"
Swallow A. N.	"
Warren Daniel,	"
Wells F. A.	"
Wiley & Binford,	"
Dunne Samuel,	Chatham
Eldridge Joshua,	"
Hitchings William,	"
Jones Joseph D.	"
Nickerson Ziba,	"
SMALL ISRAEL N.	"
Smith Brothers,	"
Gerish T. M. S. Chelmsford.	Chelmsford
Ward Patrick R. N. Chelmsford,	"
Alden John,	Chelsea
Alger Edmund,	"
Butts John W.	"
Carter & Marett,	"
Cannon Hugh,	"
Chapin N. F.	"
Chelsea Workingmen's Co-operative Association,	"
Clapp & Smith,	"
Connor Cornelius,	"
Cook David P.	"
Cook Charles E.	"
CUTTING HENRY, Cedar, c. Malden,	"
Dean George W.	"
Dinnon James,	"
Donahoe Philip,	"
Drew & Parmenter,	"
Dyer Benj. A.	"
Eaton George W.	"
Farnum Thomas P.	"
Fuller Gurdon E.	"
Gilgun Thomas,	"
Greeley Thomas H.	"
Hagan Patrick,	"
Haneford Charles,	"
Keenan Edward,	"
Marr & Burke,	"
McCann Hugh,	"
McMullen Richard.	"
Mitchell Thomas,	"
Morrill George E.	"
Munroe John,	"
Munroe W. & C.	"
Murray Alice,	"
Newhall Cheever,	"
Nichols Charles,	"
Nicholson Patrick,	"
Ramsdell Henry,	"
Sanderson Henry W.	"
Shimunins Robert,	"
Taylor & Jolley,	"
Trainor Peter,	"
Tuttle & Spalter,	"
Vahey Thomas,	"
Wentworth & Bacon,	"
Bullens C. A.	Chicopee
BULLENS ISAAC & SONS,	"
Carter & Spaulding,	"
Devine Thomas & Son,	"
Dixon John,	"
Kimball Elijah P.	"
Lanckton & Pond,	Chicopee
McKeag John,	"
Wood N. R.	"
Boyd & Houghton, Chicopee Falls,	"
Brigham & Banister,	Clinton
Chase C. H.	"
Haskell W. H.	"
McQuaid T. A. & Co.	"
White David A.	"
Wilder W. G. & Co.	"
Derby Edward,	Concord
Buttrick & Pratt,	"
Walcott & Holden,	"
Cross F. L.	Danvers
Fisk —,	"
Flint Richard,	"
Prentiss Henry,	"
Mudge A. H.	Danvers Centre, "
Perley A. P. & Co.	" "
Putnam F. W.	" "
Warren A. W.	Danvers Port, "
Briggs Jerome B.	Dartmouth
Baker & Mann,	Dedham
Farrington G. M.	"
Lealand C. H. & Co.	"
Boyden & Norris,	East Dedham, "
Finn R. M.	" "
Sullivan Patrick O.	" "
Tapley W. T.	" "
Tracy Andrew,	" "
Webb Moses E.	South Dedham "
Wheelock E. jr.	" "
Soule Francis, jr.	West Dedham, "
Gay Theodore,	" "
Greeley —,	"
Arms Charles,	South Deerfield, Deerfield
Baker R. & J.	South Dennis, Dennis
Andrews E. F.	Dighton
Cobb G. W. & Son,	"
Phillips Wm.	"
Whitmarsh Charles E.	"
Baker Stephen,	Dorchester
GLEASON R. & SONS,	"
Hewins J. F. & Co.	"
Payson Thomas,	"
UPHAM J. H. & CO.	"
Whorf Jonathan,	"
Farrington F. & Co.	"
Foster Ira,	"
Parks H. jr.	Harrison sq. "
RUSSELL THOMAS,	Mattapan, "
Stevenson Charles E.	" "
Furness & Twombly,	Milton, "
Hall Joseph E.	" "
Karle John,	" "
Talbot J. C.	" "
Dolan Michael,	Naponset, "
Harding & Wilbur,	" "
Preston Edward,	" "
Warren John,	" "
Southworth & Hayden,	Port Norfolk, "
Everett George D.	Dover
Brewster Charles,	Duxbury
Sears Frank,	"
Chandler Chas. H. & Co., W. Duxbury,	"
Ballou, A. M.	East Bridgewater
Hunting Amos,	" "
Keith M. M.	" "
Ordway George N.	" "
Cobb H. K.	North Eastham, Eastham
Strout S. B.	North Easton, Easton
Johnson G. M. & Co.	East Hampton
Chapman & Parsons,	"
Langdon C. W.	"
Strangford Alexander,	"
Polmatier George H.	South Egremont, Egremont
Jones J. S.	Enfield
Burnham Aaron,	Essex
Burnham Lewis,	"
Cogswell Geo. W.	"
Richardson J. M.	"
Allen Rufus,	Fairhaven
Fairhaven Union Store, Noah Stoddard, agent,	"
Fuller F. M.	"
Nye Alfred,	"
Swift Seth S. & Co.	"
Taber Joseph B.	"
Andrews E. & R. H.	Fall River

Grocers — continued.

Arnold L. L.	Fall River
Ashley Job B.	"
Barney George W.	"
Bence Thomas,	"
Bliss Wm. B.	"
Briggs B. F.	"
Brownell & Cobb,	"
Butler James,	"
Callahan Dennis,	"
Caraghar Philip,	"
Carey Job S.	"
Carr John A.	"
Carroll & Butler,	"
Chace A. C.	"
Chace, Allen, & Slade	"
Church & Howland,	"
Clarkson George,	"
Connelly John,	"
CONROY DANIEL, 20 Union,	"
Covel Alphonso S.	"
Cuttle John,	"
Davis Jason,	"
Dean G. T.	"
Dodge & Seers,	"
Durass R.	"
Dyer David,	"
Egan John,	"
Egan Owen,	"
Fall River Co-op. Ass'n. J. Frost, agt.	"
FALL RIVER, UNION STORE, F. Y. Kearnan, agt.	"
Flynn D.	"
Flynn William,	"
Ford L. B.	"
Fuller & Brother,	"
Gifford S. B.	"
Greene C. S.	"
Harrington James T.	"
Harrington P. P.	"
Harrington Timothy,	"
Hathaway Oliver H. & Sons,	"
Hathaway & Deane,	"
Hill F. K.	"
Horton Garrett & Son,	"
Howe Patrick,	"
Johnson Peter S.	"
Keavy James,	"
Kelley Jeremiah,	"
Kelley & O'Neil,	"
Kennedy & Flynn,	"
Larkin Thomas,	"
Law Herbert,	"
Leary Patrick R.	"
Liberty Patrick,	"
Lingane David,	"
Lingane Richard,	"
Lyng Wright,	"
Maxam E. B.	"
Mahoney John,	"
Manchester Clark S.	"
Marble Wm. P. & Co.	"
Matthews Henry,	"
McDonald Edward,	"
McDermott Andrew,	"
McDonald P. J.	"
McDonough Michael,	"
McHugh John,	"
Monks William,	"
Morrow & Quigley,	"
Murphy Edward,	"
Murphy James,	"
Murphy J. F. & Co.	"
Murphy & Son,	"
Negus Robert & Co.	"
Newman Robert,	"
Nickerson Benjamin,	"
O'Hearne Robert,	"
O'Neil Jeremiah,	"
Pettey, Lawton, & Co.	"
Powers John,	"
Priestley Emanuel,	"
Pugh Richard,	"
Quinn James,	"
Read W. A. & Brother,	"
Regan Philip,	"
Regan Timothy,	"
Sanders J. Mrs.	"
Short Thomas,	"
Simpson & Fielding,	"

Smithies Robert,	Fall River
Stretton Thomas,	"
Sullivan Jeremiah,	"
Synan William,	"
Thompson Robert,	"
Thorley & Campbell,	"
Thornton Edward,	"
Wade & Pettey,	"
Waite Levitt,	"
Walsh Philip,	"
Waterhouse Wright,	"
WILBUR B. & BROTHER, 24 Elm,	"
Lawrence Meltiah,	Falmouth
Lawrence William C.	"
Baldwin Joseph,	Fitchburg
Brewster S. & Son,	"
Caldwell Thomas C.	"
Chamberlain Bros.	"
Choate E. N. & H. M.	"
Cleaves Francis E.	"
Fitchburg Co-operative Store,	"
Guy T. F.	"
Hatch Henry A.	"
Lewis & Sawtell,	"
Pero James,	"
Spaulding Josiah,	"
Streeter Daniel R. & Co.	"
Upham & Burr,	"
Wright John K.	"
Nelson L. L.	Florida
Carroll E.	Foxborough
Godfrey H. S.	"
Hixon & Fales,	"
Hodges & Messinger,	"
McEvoy J. D.	"
Brackett William,	Framingham
Kendall E. F.	"
Leslie Thomas, Saxonville,	"
Stone & Bill,	"
Putnam T. H.	Franklin
Rockwood William,	"
Stewart & Chapman,	"
Dean George H.	Freetown
Johnson Daniel L.	"
Phillips James M.	"
Drury L. M. & Co.	Gardner
Gardner Co-operative Association,	"
Berry J. O. & Co.	Georgetown
Hoyt John,	"
Lambert & Bailey,	"
Perley Gilman,	"
Allen J. D.	Gloucester
Boardman Samuel O.	"
Brown D. A.	"
Burnham L. A. & Brother,	"
Centre A. J.	"
Dolliver Brothers,	"
Elwell George,	"
Elwell Henry,	"
Firth Robert,	"
Friend Chas. & Co.	"
Friend George,	"
Gallagher Chas. H.	"
Goodnow & Reed,	"
Haskell B. & Sons,	"
Herrick Calvin C.	"
Hicks John S.	"
King A. C.	"
McKENZIE WILLIAM, Duncan n. Rogers,	"
Mansfield J. & Sons,	"
Marston Samuel,	"
Munsey William,	"
Parkhurst Charles,	"
Parkhurst David,	"
Parkhurst George,	"
Parsons John L.	"
Perkins & Foster,	"
PEW JOHN & SON, 83 Spring,	"
Plummer David,	"
Rogers Charles,	"
Rowe & Jordan,	"
Saunders, Huntington, & Co.	"
Sayward Daniel,	"
Sayward Epes, Jr. & Co.	"
Smith & Gott,	"
Steele George,	"
Wells Aaron D.	"
Winter Addison,	"
Winter Fitz W.	"

Wonson John W., Gloucester	Doyle & Finn, Holyoke
Davis John D., Annisquam, "	Ely Joseph & Son, "
Andrews J. L. & Sons, Lanesville, "	HIGGINS DENNIS, "
Berry Lorenzo, " "	Launahan J., "
Duley Michael, " "	Loomis & Pomeroy, "
Justin J. K., " "	Lynch Michael, "
Dodd, Tarr, & Co. East Gloucester, "	Manning Patrick, "
Low Alfred & Co. " "	Munsell & Sears, "
Wonson J. Warren, " "	O'Donnell John, "
WONSON WM. C. " "	O'Donnell V. J. "
Wonson J. F. jr. & Co. " "	Richards & Thayer, "
Richardson Jasper, West Gloucester, "	Thompson David, "
Babson John L. Riverdale, "	Tuttle & Moore, "
Newton B. Grafton	Welch M. "
Union Store, N. E. Village, "	Crafts Chester, Ireland, "
Barnes Edward, Great Barrington	Davis Charles, Hubbardston
Burget & Kilborn, "	Pope Joseph, Hull
Siggins & Co. "	Crocker & Lewis, Hyde Park
Smith Stephen E. "	Bonney W. A. "
Burk Michael, Greenfield	Fairbairn Wm. U. "
Cascoigne J. T. "	Follett Lorenzo, "
Coombs J. A. "	Gunnison Geo. W. "
Hall Thomas V. "	Lawson J. D. & T. "
Henry & Lucy, "	Thompson Robert, "
KELLOGG B. & SON, "	Conlon P. S. Readville, "
Nutting & Keith, "	O'Connell Daniel, "
Shattuck S. L. "	Wright Richard, " "
Wise Wm. M. "	Condon Thos. E. Ipswich
Blood Edmund, West Groton, Groton	Hills A. S. "
Harlow Wm. H. & Co. Groton Junction, "	Jewett Nathan, "
STUART GEO. W. & Co. " "	Lord Asa, "
Shipman William S. Hadley	Willcomb F. "
Howland Calvin L. Hanson	Haskins Cephas, Lakeville
Drayton John South Hanson, "	Wood Luther D. Lanesborough
Cobb & Moran, Hardwick	Andrews O. & Co. Lawrence
Harvey John, "	Andrews Wm. H. "
Perry & Spooner, "	Brady James, "
Clark Elisha, Harwich	Buxton W. T. "
Freeman Warren, "	Carley Patrick, "
Underwood Wm. H. "	Carney Michael & Bro. "
Kelley Shubaël B. Harwich Port, "	Carr Daniel jr. & Co. "
Chase W. W. West Harwich, "	COAN W. B. & A. 268 Essex, "
Allen A. M. Haverhill	Corporation Supply Store, P. Richard-
Bartlett T. B. & Co. "	son, agt. "
Bowley Edwin & Co. "	Currier J. Merrill, "
Crockett F. S. & Co. "	Decker & Andrews, "
Fox Bros. "	Devlin Edward, "
Greene Moses H. "	Dowd Margaret Mrs. "
Greenough Eben, "	Downe Henry A. "
Hill C. H. & Son, "	Eastman & Buell, "
Hoyt B. "	Edson & Richards, "
Jaques W. T. "	Fleming John M. "
Kimball Benj. "	Gadin Ambrose, "
Moody Brothers, "	Geran John, "
Ray Harvey "	Gorgin S. "
Regan Robert, "	Goodenow Jesse, "
Roberts O. H. "	Goodwin Michael, "
Roche J. M. & Co. "	Griffin Thomas, "
Snay John, "	Grimes & Co. "
Stearns & White, "	Hally Edward, "
Stickney George H. "	Harris & Foster, "
Taylor T. J. "	Hart & Lawler, "
Tewksbury J. B. "	Higgins Patrick, "
Webster C. A. & Co. "	HOLIHAN PETER, 389 Common, "
West Elisha S. "	Hogle H. A. & S. "
Withum & Poor, "	Hoyt & Cushman, "
Dunn Geo. East Haverhill, "	Jackman, Kimball, & Co.
Nichols John B. " "	Jordan A. S. & Co.
Sawyer William, " "	Kelcher Cornelius, "
Cain David, Hingham	Kennedy Thomas, "
Easterbrook Samuel, "	Lamprey A. A. & Co. "
Gardner Calvin, "	Lazell H. R. & Co. "
Hunt C. S. "	Leary Dennis, "
Thayer A. E. "	Manahan M. & H. D.
Cushing Alonzo, South Hingham, "	McGowan & Cushing,
Bowles Henry A. Hinsdale	Merrill M. P. & Son, "
Day & Nash, "	Meserve Wm. S.
Shaw Geo. D. & Co. "	Morache Joseph. jr.
Fisk Lovett, Holliston	Morrissey Edward, "
Gassett Brothers, "	Morse William, "
Metcalf S. "	MUTUAL BENEFIT STORE, P. Holi-
Parmenter A. J. "	han, agt. 389 Common, "
Morse W. H. & C. H. Hopkinton	Nevill John, "
Woodward D. P. & Co. "	O'Donnell P. "
Brown Brothers, Holyoke	O'Sullivan D. C. "
Crafts Roswell P. & Son. "	O'Sullivan Martin, "
Connor M. J. "	Payson H. "
Curren T. L. "	Perkins Nathan, "
Dillon Thomas, "	Phelen K. C. "
Downs James, "	Pierce Edwin W. "

Grocers — continued.

Pike & Pettengill,	Lawrence
Quirk & Corrigan,	"
RAFFERTY HUGH (see page 741),	"
Russell & Smith,	"
Shattuck J. jr. & Co.	"
Smith Chas. & Son.	"
Thomas, Dawson, & Co.	"
Webster Alvan H.	"
Boland Peter,	Lee
Ferry James W.	"
Moore E. A.	"
Nolan Michael,	"
Owen Patrick,	"
Reardon Daniel,	"
Putney Geo. F. Clappville,	Leicester
Wright Samuel C.	Lenox
Bancroft Selwin,	Lowell
Barnard Chas. H.	"
Bergeron Louis,	"
Blair E. R.	"
Blake Patrick,	"
Bohonan & Fletcher,	"
Burrows Valentine,	"
Buttrick & Co.	"
Callahan Charles,	"
Callahan Daniel,	"
Carolin T.	"
Chalmers James B.	"
Chamberlain Joseph A.	"
Chandler F. H. & Co.	"
Cheney & Hartwell,	"
Churchill S. W.	"
Clement E. A.	"
Clough Walter S.	"
Collins James,	"
Colwell Philip,	"
Conway Bernard,	"
Cosgrove John,	"
Coulson Samuel.	"
Courtney P. & J.	"
Dempsey Patrick,	"
Devine Patrick J.	"
Dexter S. K.	"
Donahoe James,	"
Duff John,	"
Escott William,	"
Eaton Job S.	"
Emerson Luther,	"
Farley Owen,	"
Finnegan M.	"
Fuller Jason,	"
Garrigan Thomas J.	"
Gibson Brothers,	"
Gove David & Co.	"
Greenwood Bros.	"
Hall C. & A. P.	"
Hemenway Marshall,	"
Higgins Edson S.	"
Hdar M.	"
Ingham W. A.	"
Jepson John C.	"
Jones Charles M.	"
Keyes Patrick,	"
Riley Lawrence,	"
Riley Roger,	"
Knowles Thomas,	"
Knowles & Holland,	"
Knox & Woodward,	"
Lee Michael Mrs.	"
Lehany James,	"
Leonard John,	"
Lennon John,	"
Lynch Jeremiah,	"
Lynch John,	"
Maguire Thomas,	"
Manning Daniel,	"
Marley Daniel,	"
Marren James,	"
Mathews & Lake,	"
McAloon William,	"
McCABE JAMES, 1 Whipple,	"
McCann John,	"
McCarty Michael,	"
McGuirk P.	"
McNabb Bros.	"
McQuaid Ellen,	"
McSorley Alexander,	"
Mollahan P. & F.	"

Mooney Christopher,	Lowell
Moran John F.	"
Morse Charles H.	"
Nichols & Fletcher,	"
O'Neill Bernard,	"
Orange & Rogers,	"
Owens James,	"
Pearson J. & J. M.	"
Persons R.	"
Puffer Asahel D. & Co.	"
Putnam J. D.	"
Richardson John B.	"
Richardson Sumner,	"
Riley Bernard,	"
Riley John,	"
Riley John 2d,	"
Runals Robert K.	"
Russell Cyrus K.	"
Russell S. S.	"
Russell & Blakslee,	"
Russell & Lane,	"
Smith Peter S.	"
Spencer T. S.	"
Springer James F. & Co.	"
Stickney & Spofford,	"
Streeter H. W.	"
Washburn & Pearl,	"
Wheeler Albert,	"
Whitehead Darius,	"
Whittemore & Blanchard,	"
Worthen E. B. & Co.	"
Wright A. C.	"
Young Felix,	"
Ambler S. C.	Lynn
BACHELLER HENRY B., 70 Lewis,	"
Bacheller John N. H.	"
Bacheller J. P.	"
Bates Thomas S.	"
Bayrd Edward,	"
Breed Joseph W.	"
Breed Sylvester B.	"
Carter Joseph S. agt.	"
Chamberlain & Co.	"
Chesley & Brock,	"
Childs Isaac,	"
Coburn George S.	"
Currier Joseph R.	"
Division 717,	"
Doyle L. P.	"
Farmer Patrick,	"
Franklin Grocery Co.	"
Gove E. B. T.	"
Hall William A.	"
Hollowell Samuel J.	"
Harlow A. J.	"
Hawkes Wm. R.	"
Holder Edward A.	"
Honors Arthur G.	"
Hussey G. B. & Co.	"
Lane Benjamin jr.	"
Lannan Dennis,	"
Lynn Grocery Co.	"
Marsh G. W.	"
Marsh J. E. F.	"
McMillen John,	"
McMillen R.	"
Merrill & Staples,	"
Mudge Samuel,	"
M. B. Association, J. Martin, agt.	"
Murphy Timothy,	"
Newhall William P.	"
Noyes A. P.	"
OSBORNE E. W. & CO. Market sq.	"
Paige & Carswell,	"
Parker G. E.	"
Payne & Miles,	"
Philpot Robert,	"
Proctor & Hurd,	"
Putnam Eugene A.	"
Putnam F. M.	"
Ramsdell Oliver,	"
Richardson Edward,	"
Sanderson J. A.	"
Shepherd John,	"
Skinner J. B. & Son,	"
Southworth George W.	"
Swain Thomas L.	"
Tarbox James M.	"
Tarbox Joseph E.	"
Thurston Wilder S.	"

Tilton Wm. H.   Lynn
Union Grocery Co.   "
Usher & Co.   "
Vickary Joseph, jr.   "
Cook Robert D.   Malden
Hammond Wm. S.   "
Hill Bros.   "
Houdlette P. F. & Sons,   "
Kaalback T. M.   "
Shepard Brothers,   "
Simons George L.   "
Shackford John,   E. Malden, "
Emmons Daniel,   South " "
Lane T. D.   "
Oakes U.   "
Hunting Wm. H.   Maplewood, "
Bessom W. C.   Mansfield
Lovell I. & S. C.   "
Read R. J.   "
Briggs E.   West Mansfield, "
Perry Albert,   " "
Allen Ambrose,   Marblehead
Allen A. jr.   "
Bartlett Nicholas,   "
Brown Benjamin F.   "
Burridge Robert,   "
Day Benjamin,   "
Blint David,   "
Gale Samuel,   "
Gilley William,   "
Glover John,   "
Graves, Joseph 4th,   "
Graves Samuel,   "
Green Joseph G.   "
Hanson Thomas D. jr.   "
Hathaway Stephen,   "
Harris Richard T.   "
HASKELL JOHN H.   "
Hidden Samuel B.   "
Hooper A. & F. T.   "
Hooper Benj. G.   "
Knight Azar O.   "
Knight George,   "
Knight George 2d,   "
Knight William R.   "
LeMaster George,   "
Levett Benjamin,   "
Lindsey Nathaniel B.   "
Martin Samuel C.   "
Mason Isaac W.   "
Nutting William,   "
Paine Henry,   "
Paine William B. jr.   "
Peach Stephen B.   "
Pitman John,   "
Rhoades A. S.   "
Trasher John,   "
Childs & Cunningham,   Marlborough
Edwards F. D.   "
Estabrook E. C.   "
Johnston John,   "
LATTINWELL LOUIS,   "
Lowe William,   "
Quirk & Brewin,   "
WEEKS & SMITH,   "
Atsatt John T.   Mattapoisett
Keith Charles,   "
Luce Thomas,   "
Mendull John Mrs.   "
Snow Allen W.   "
Snow Harvey,   "
Snow L. & M.   "
Callender D. B.   Medford
Citizens' Union Store,   "
Coleman W.   "
Hutchings Amos,   "
Jaquith Henry H.   "
Sampson Geo. H.   "
Frederick Wm. C., West Medford, "
Hyde James,   "
Whitney George W.   Medway
Adams J. L.   W. Medway, "
Worthen Bros.   " "
Bugbee & Barrett,   Melrose
Hayward C. H. & Co.   "
Singer John,   "
Wells William H.   "
Whitney Hiram,   "
Ballou Sumner,   Mendon
Carleton Gay,   Methuen

Gale & Frederick   Methuen
Sawyer George W.   "
Thomas Ira,   Middleborough
Cushing Matthew H.   "
Pickens George,   "
Thompson I. W.   "
Tinkham Geo. C.   "
Waterman George,   "
Wood Wm. B.   "
Averill E. P. & Co.   Middleton
Wilkins H. A.   "
Chapin C. F.   Milford
Fiske H. B. & Co.   "
Goodrich H. A.   "
Hodgkin C.   "
Howard William,   "
Howard & Pierce,   "
Hunt & Scott,   "
Jenks H. R.   "
Madden & Keys,   "
Navin Smith,   "
O'Neil Michael,   "
Taft F. A.   "
Walpole Edward,   "
Gibson H. O.   Hopedale, "
Bramanville Union,   Millbury
Millbury Protective Union,   "
Durell John,   Milton
Tarbox George W.   "
Maun & King,   Monson
Clapp George A.   Montague
Barrett Samuel,   Nantucket
Cathcart William C.   "
Calder Timothy W.   "
Coffin Obed G.   "
Davis, Eldredge, & Kenney,   "
Eldredge H. & Co.   "
Fitzgerald Nathaniel,   "
Hosier John H.   "
Hussey Oliver,   "
Keane P.   "
Macy Joseph B.   "
Nickerson Franklin,   "
Olin John W.   "
Parker E. H.   "
Russell William M.   "
Union Store, C. H. Bailey, Agent, "
Adams J. G.   Natick
Atwood Sidney,   "
Clark Edward,   "
Hathaway G. C.   "
Kiley & Burns,   "
Natick Protective Union,   "
Parker S. N.   "
West O. W.   "
Bartlett & Perry, South Natick, "
Smith G. & Co.   "
Tuck A. R.   "
Fuller F. W.   Wellesley,   Needham
Acushnet Co-operative store, New Bedford
Adams Z. L.   "
Allen Abraham A.   "
Bates Lot B.   "
Beetle C. H.   "
Booth George D.   "
Bonney Josiah S.   "
Braley J. W.   "
Briggs B. W.   "
Brock & Gifford,   "
Brownell & Wheaton,   "
Burgess D.   "
Central Union Association,   "
Chappell William H.   "
Childs James E.   "
Clare John,   "
Cook David,   "
Covell Jonathan,   "
COTA & SMITH, Middle, cor. Cedar, "
Cummings Solomon,   "
Doty William P.   "
Dwight James E.   "
Dyer Charles W.   "
Dyer George L.   "
Fisher & Lowe,   "
Francis Isaac,   "
Gallagher John,   "
Gardner T. A.   "
Gifford Fred. S.   "
Holcomb Henry,   "
Holcomb Roland,   "

Grocers — continued.

Howland Joseph,   New Bedford
Independent Union Store, S. Bennet,
  agent,   "
Jenney & Case,   "
Jordan Patrick,   "
King Annie L.   "
King George,   "
Kirby Nicholas,   "
Knowles J. P. 2d (ship),   "
Knowles Thomas & Co.   "
Lawrence Cyrus T.   "
Lawrence Edward P.   "
Lawrence Paul,   "
Lawton James M. & Son,   "
Lawton Russell S.   "
Lawton William B.   "
Lovell Jonathan,   "
Lowe John,   "
Lucas H. K. W.   "
Lucas & Barrows,   "
Luscomb Robert,   "
Macomber George B.   "
Manley John A.   "
Mason Humphrey S.   "
McFarlin S. W.   "
Milliken E. & Son,   "
Moore Samuel C.   "
MORSE CLINTON, 151 Kempton,   "
Morse F. & Co.   "
New Bedford Co-operative Work-
  ing Men's Association, Thomas
  Castle, agent,   "
Notter John,   "
Nye S. G.   "
Parker William G.   "
Patterson S. T.   "
Pease James H.   "
Peirce James, 2d,   "
Perry & Wood,   "
Reynolds Wike,   "
Rice Simeon,   "
Shaw & Brother,   "
Sherman Isaac C.   "
Sherman J. B.   "
Snow Sylvester,   "
Sparrow H. A.   "
Stanton A. G. & Co.   "
Stewart W. H.   "
Sturtevant Zachariah,   "
Taber, Gordon, & Co.   "
Taber James T.   "
Terry Job M.   "
Tillinghast H. C.   "
Tripp Thomas B.   "
TUCKER & CUMMINGS, 66 & 68
  William,   "
Washington Co-operative Association, "
Wheaton & Brownell,   "
Whitney J. W. C.   "
Winslow Holmes,   "
Wood & Brownell,   "
Wood Zenas,   "
Wordell & Ashley,   "
Young P. A. & Co.   "
Little Isaac W.   Newbury
Adams Rufus,   Newburyport
Adams Washington,   "
Batchelder E. K.   "
Bayley R. & Son,   "
Blumpey P. H.   "
Bowlen Caldwell,   "
Brookings P. B.   "
Brown Jenness,   "
Caldwell John,   "
Chase James M.   "
Clement Isaac C.   "
Currier Edwin,   "
Currier Richard,   "
Cusick William C.   "
Emery Josiah,   "
Fenimore Charles H.   "
Fowler Moses H.   "
French Curtis,   "
Goodwin Daniel A.   "
Goodwin M.   "
Greenleaf D. D.   "
Griffith Thomas,   "
Grinder John L.   "
Heury Patrick,   "

Hunt George W.   Newburyport
Huse R. C. & Co.   "
Ilsley Stephen,   "
Ireland Nathaniel jr.   "
Janvrin John,   "
Johnson H. G. O.   "
Knight Daniel H. jr.   "
Lane Abner,   "
Little I. W.   "
Martin Patrick,   "
McKay William,   "
Merrill P. A.   "
Moynihan Patrick T.   "
Pearson William,   "
Pettingill Cutting,   "
Pettingill Moses, jr.   "
Pingry Daniel A.   "
Plummer William C.   "
Plumer & Balch,   "
Poor Isaac,   "
Prescott H. G.   "
Quill John,   "
Quinn Timothy,   "
Richardson Pottle,   "
Riley John,   "
Roberts Parker,   "
Ross Lorenzo D.   "
Ross M. M.   "
Rowe Alonzo H.   "
Sargent Elbridge A.   "
Stacy N.   "
Stickney & Goodwin,   "
Stover George,   "
Sumner, Swazey, & Currier,   "
Thurlow William,   "
Tilton Albert,   "
Tilton Daniel G.   "
Toppan H. P.   "
Webster George E.   "
Winn Jeremiah,   "
Young James,   "
Plummer Albert,   Auburndale, Newton
Dimond & Weatherbee, Lower Falls, "
Hyde C. H. & Co.   "   "
Trowbridge J.   Newton Centre, "
White J. M.   "   "
Cole H. B. & Co.   Newton Corner, "
Dow & Stevens,   "   "
Warner John & Co.   "   "
Lovett J. B.   Newtonville, "
Stanwood E. P.   "   "
Fanning H. W.   Upper Falls,   "
Howe John W.   "   "
Houghton B. F.   West Newton, "
Robinson F. & G.   "   "
Stone L. P.   "   "
Clark & Parsons,   Northampton
Dewey & Loomis,   "
Edwards Oscar,   "
Fidd & Sawin,   "
Hillman, Ferris, & Co.   "
Jepson & Sampson,   "
Kingsley Charles B.   "
Knowlton & Newton,   "
Morton & Hayden,   "
Parsons S. C.   "
Rust Theodore & Son,   "
Smith Rodolphus,   "
Stockwell & Spaulding,   "
Towne & Bartlett,   "
Wright A. & Co.   "
Bartlett F. D.   Northborough
Stockwell M.   "
                          Northbridge
Fuller Wm. B., Northbridge Centre, "
Welch James,   Whitinsville, "
Carr J. L.   North Bridgewater
Cobb David,   "
Cobb Lyman E.   "
Curtis S. B. & G. E.   "
Gilmore John,   "
Hayward Ambrose,   "
Hayward Daniel,   "
Owens John,   "
Ripley Samuel B.   "
Southworth & Noyes,   "
Tilden John,   "
THOMPSON & PACKARD,   "
Whipple J. J. & Co.   "
Alden Lucas W.   Campello,   "

h Bridgewater	Blake A. F. & J. N.	Quincy
lo, "	Ditson Charles N.	"
North Chelsea	Gray H. W.	"
"	LOCKE GEO. H.	"
Northfield	Wilson G. F.	"
Norton	Briggs Levi,	Randolph
"	Donahoe Edward,	"
"	Johnson R. B.	"
"	Jones Gilbert T.	"
Orange	Page I. D.	"
"	Prescott G. H. & C.	"
"	Sweeney Rachel J.	"
Orleans	Tolman N. A.	"
"	Turner R. W. & Co.	"
"	Baker S.	East Randolph, "
Palmer	Lincoln & Sylvester, "	"
"	Packard H. H.	" "
"	Vining S. A.	" "
Peabody	Faxon Daniel, South "	"
"	West Thomas, agt. "	"
"	Atkinson G. W.	Reading
"	Nichols & Turner,	"
"	Pratt Thomas,	"
"	Savage E. D.	"
"	Boynton David P.	Rockport
"	Bradley Wm. H. jr. & J. W.	"
"	Fears Isaac P.	"
"	Gott Addison & Co.	"
"	Hoyt John,	"
"	Lane Albert W.	"
Pittsfield	Low Brainard & Co.	"
"	Millet Eben & Co.	"
"	Parsons & Hodgkins,	"
"	Patch Wm. H.	"
"	Rockport Granite Co.	"
"	Rowe Francis,	"
"	Tarr David Mrs.	"
"	Tarr D. T. & Co.	"
"	Tarr Francis, jr. & Bro.	"
"	Tarr & Thurston,	"
"	Wheeler Daniel A.	"
"	Pierce Alpheus C.	Pigeon Cove, "
"	Story Austin W.	" "
"	Union Store, 667, "	"
"	Barton William C.	Salem
"	Bicknell S. F.	"
Plymouth	Brooks Luke jr.	"
"	Brooks N. H.	"
"	Brown Joseph A.	"
"	Brown Lawrence,	"
"	Buckley J. J.	"
"	Calef John,	"
"	Carey Thomas B.	"
"	Chamberlain & Harris,	"
"	Chandler John,	"
"	Clark J. W.	"
"	Collins Edward A.	"
"	Emerson Nathan,	"
"	Foster Isaac F.	"
"	Foster Joseph S.	"
"	Friend F.	"
"	Fullam John,	"
"	Glidden J. H.	"
"	GOODHUE WILLIAM P. (wholesale	
"	and retail), 41 Derby,	"
"	Guy & Bros.	"
"	Gwinn & Maguire,	"
"	Hale James F.	"
Plympton	Hall & Co.	"
"	Ham & Hobbs,	"
"	Harris I. P.	"
lle, "	Hartnett Patrick,	"
Provincetown	Hodgkins G. L.	"
"	Janes John,	"
"	Lavers Richard,	"
"	Lindsey & Durgin,	"
"	Luscomb Henry,	"
"	Maguire Bernard,	"
"	Mahoney David,	"
"	Mann James B.	"
"	Millett J. Henry,	"
"	Moynahan Daniel,	"
"	Nichols David A.	"
"	Noyes Enoch K. & Co.	"
"	O'Donnell William,	"
"	Pickering Benjamin P.	"
"	Plummer Moses J.	"
"	Prime James M.	"
"	Redmond Miles,	"
"	Reeves William,	"

Grocers — continued.

Reynolds Moses C. & Co.
Ropes Timothy,   Salem
Ryan James,   "
Sheridan Francis,   "
Shreve Samuel V.   "
Spiller Richard O.   "
Stodder & Co.   "
Symonds B. R.   "
Symonds Joseph,   "
Symonds Thomas,   "
Trask James,   "
Very Samuel A.   "
Ward James L.   "
Webber I. J.   "
Webster, Wells, & Co.   "
White Franklin,   "
White & McCarty,   "
Beede L. M. & Co.   "
Brown Leonard,   Salisbury
Cammett Jona.   "
Fowler Everett,   "
Fuller Chas.   "
Gunnison Isaac,   "
Osgood Edwin W.   "
Allen W. & Son,   Amesbury,
Carruthers J. O.   "
French G. W.   "
Chapin E. S.   East Salisbury,
Keniston F. & Co.   Salisbury Point,
Purinton J. A.   "
Hobson Wm.   Sandwich
Burgess C. H.   "
ELLIS H. G. O.   "
HARTWELL GEORGE,   "
LAPHAM WM. F.   "
Union Store,   "
Raddin Hiram A.   Cliftondale,   Saugus
Lawrence J. D. & Co.   Saugus Centre,   "
Sparr Geo. G.   "
Whitehead Joseph,   "
Wyman Chas. E.   "
Cobb Warren,   East Sharon,
  Sharon
Goodnough & Sears,   Shelburne Falls,   Shelburne
Greene & Co.   "   "
NEWELL BROS.   "   "
Streeter J. D.   "   "
Wood E. W.   "   "
Wood Theodore,   "   "
Brown Seth W.   "
Cornell & Marble,   Somerset
Davis Nathan S.   "
Hood George B.   "
Marble Wm. H.   "
Read Benjamin T.   "
Bullard Charles H.   Somerville
Edson N. W. & C. F.   "
Edson & Wheeler,   "
Long William,   "
Mongan Charles A.   "
O'Brien J. & Co.   "
O'Leary Arthur,   "
Randall Benjamin A.   "
BENSON & SHERMAN, E. Somerville,
Roberts Brothers,   "
Littlefield Samuel,   N. Somerville,
Temple Thomas G.   "
Carpenter P. H. & Co.   Southbridge
Morse Brothers,   "
Potter Thomas & Co.   "
Davis Otis,   Globe Village,
Gleason James & Co.   "
Kelley Patrick,   "
Thayer Solomon,   "
Bly Erastus,   "
Bumstead A.   Springfield
Call C. A.   "
Camp Alonzo,   "
Casey Michael,   "
Cate N.   "
Colby C. H.   "
Cooley & Hayes,   "
Cornell T. W.   "
Couch & Miller,   "
Craig & Hazen,   "
Cutler Luther,   "
Davison H. J.   "
Dwight E.   "
Field Charles P.   "

Gowdy H. C.
Haskell G. S. & Co.   Springfield
Herrick N. J.   "
Hollister E. E.   "
Houghton F. T. & Co.   "
Houston, Smith, & Co.   "
Hudson Charles T.   "
Hudson George,   "
Jenks L. F.   "
Joy & Chandler,   "
King H. E.   "
Lyman H.   "
Marsh J. S. & Co.   "
McCarty James,   "
Niles A. F. & H. L.   "
Pember & Jenks,   "
PINNEY W. H. & Co.   "
Pomeroy W. H.   "
Quinby A. B.   "
Remington & Chapman,   "
Waire E. H.   "
Warriner Brothers,   "
Wood H. M.   "
Woolson C. A.   "
Winter L. S. & J. K.   "
Eaton C. J.   Indian Orchard,
Kelley Matthew,   "
Rivers & Desotel,   "
Hunt Chas. A.   Sterling
Sanborn Brothers,   "
Arnold A. W.   Stoneham
Bruce N. F.   "
Chase Brothers,   "
Ford Horace,   "
Holmes John,   "
Hill Aaron,   "
RICE W. D. Main st.   "
Stevens & Clements,   "
Walker W. F.   "
Wheaton & Carpenter,   "
Crane O. B.   East Stoughton,
  Stoughton
Wade Lorenzo & Son,   "
Ingalls & Foster,   Swampscott
McElroy & Ladd,   "
Stimpson & Mott,   "
Baker & Evans,   Taunton
Barrows & Williams,   "
Blake J. E. & L. A.   "
Blandin Edgar,   "
Bosworth William,   "
Brady & Coyle,   "
Brady & Callaghan,   "
Briggs C. A. & Co.   "
Burt B. L. & Co.   "
Chace & Spencer,   "
Church H. W. & Co.   "
Church & Allyn,   "
Cleary Patrick,   "
Congdon W. W.   "
Dean H. A. & Co.   "
Dorgan John,   "
Farnham H. L.   "
GALLIGAN OWEN & CO. 55 and 57
  West Water,   "
HARLOW O. JR. 58 City Square,   "
JACKSON & WILLIAMS, 43 and 45
  City Square,   "
Johnson & Macomber,   "
Knapp Z. jr.   "
Leonard George J.   "
Lothrop H. B.   "
Paull J. & Co.   "
Perkins David D.   "
Pratt & Thomas,   "
Pray Evander,   "
Protective Union, S. S. King, agt.   "
Reed William & Co.   "
Staples B. F.   "
Walker Brothers,   "
Washburn & White,   "
White, Child, & Co.   "
Woods Job N.   "
Woodward E.   "
Leach Isaac W.   East Taunton,
Sanders George B.   "
Washburn C. G.   "
Albro B. D. & G. F.   Hopewell,
Baker Charles F. & Co.   "
Taylor Benjamin B.   Myricks,
Walker Allen C.   "

MANN G. A. & A. F. Westville, Taunton
Butler & Norton, Tisbury
Holmes & Brothers, "
Audsley Richard, Uxbridge
Whitmore H. & Co. "
Brown Charles B. Wakefield
Co-operative Association, "
Eaton Everett W. "
Hayward W. L. "
Mansfield E. & Son, "
Eaton I. F. Greenwood, "
Fisk E. B. Wales
Clark William W. & Son, Waltham
Dalzell Samuel, "
Eddy S. S. & Co. "
Foster M. S. & Son, "
Glidden J. & Son, "
Hurt O. A. & Co. "
Hayward Frank D. "
Irish Cornelius, "
Pope Daniel E. "
Priest J. H. & Son, "
Wadsworth John & Co. "
KEEFE J. & CO. Ware
Sibley & Robinson, "
Snow & Puffer, "
Sturtevant E. R. "
Bartlett L. H. Wareham
Beese Lothrop A. "
Spear H. M. Washington
Berry Charles H. Watertown
Burnes J. "
Gleason S. S. "
Jackson W. & Son, "
Northrup & Wilcox, "
Noyes Samuel & Co. "
Parkhurst J. M. "
Sparrow Seth E. "
Stowell H. C. "
Alton & Shumway, Webster
Gillis J. J. "
Central Trading Co. Wellfleet
Daniels Timothy A. "
HIGGINS J. R. & Co. "
Higgins Reuben, 2d "
Swett John, "
Wendell
Putnam Danforth, Wendell Depot,
Boynton Reuben, Westborough
Homan & Child, "
Morse G. W. & Co. "
Rice C. P. & Co. "
Smith J. A. "
Union Protective, "
Whitney & Day, "
Rabidieu N. West Boylston
Hawks Lyman, West Brookfield
Birge Sidney, Westfield
Fowler & Noble, "
Gibbs J. W. & E. O. "
Loomis Henry, "
Loomis Merwin, "
Morrissey Richard, "
Parks & Clark, "
Piumb D. H. "
Snow & Rising, "
Gifford Henry H. Westport
Macomber Charles H. "
Cornell Robert S. South Westport, "
Lawrence Andrew, "
Blake J. J. West Roxbury
Blakemore Wm. B. & Co. "
Keith William S. "
Blackburn J. Jamaica Plain, "
Brown Daniel A. "
Bullock Kingsley, "
James George & Co. "
Leonard J. M. "
Marshall Cyrus M. "
Norcross & Myrick, "
Seaver Robert, "
Phelan Henry, "
Shaw Nathan, West Springfield
West Stockbridge
Barnes Seth A. Housatonic;
CHURCH SILAS L., State Line.
Boney Joshua & Co. Weymouth
Chipman E. K. "
Lane Peter, "
Pratt M. K. & Co. "
Willis & Worster, "

Dyer Joseph, S. Weymouth, Weymouth
Orcutt J R. " "
Rockwood S. A. & Co. " "
Reed Isaac, East Weymouth, "
Rogers N. C. " "
Lesure Samuel, Whately
Graves Elam, Williamsburg
Larkin Pierce, "
Coan Andrew J. Williamstown
Bryant & Co. Winchendon
Dodge George K. "
Dunn Isaac J. "
Cilley L. G. Winchester
Sanderson E. "
Stanton H. K. "
Connolly J. H. Woburn
Hayward A. S. "
Poole, Mann, & Co. "
Salmon & McDonald, "
Smith Rufus, "
Stearns, Brown, & Co. "
TAY C. & CO., Main st. (see page 766), "
Knapp J. G. East Woburn, "
Ballard J. S. & Co. Worcester
Brigham & Wadsworth, "
Brown & Marshall, "
Cady, Hendrick, & Co. "
Crosby S. B. "
Curtis S. "
Div. 42, N. E. P. Union, "
Eaton A. M. "
Eldridge & Cogswell, "
Emery J. R. & H. P. "
Foley Jeremiah, "
Grout J. D. "
Hanlon & McGrath, "
Harrington Loammi, "
Hawes & Emery, "
Hillman & Coombs, "
Hobbs & Winn, "
Holden & Brother, "
Holman A. R. "
Hoppin C. A. "
Houlihan D. M. "
Howe & Hackett, "
Kirby Charles, "
Ladd Vernon A. "
Lane Brothers, "
Lewis Joseph, "
Martin J. H. "
McManus B. "
Mechanics' Union, "
Miller & Laing "
O'Connor D. M. "
O'Sullivan C. "
Parker Charles G. "
Pease Wm. E. & Co. "
Penniman & Harrington, "
Phetteplace W. E. "
Putnam C. P. "
Putnam Darius, "
Putnam Sibley, "
Shepard R. R. & Co. "
Smith E. T. & Co. "
Sprague W. W. "
Stearns Brothers, "
Swazey & Rawson, "
Swett William O. & Co. "
Taft S. & Son, "
Trainer & Carroll, "
Whiting C. H. "
Willey J. J. "
Worcester Cöoperative Asso'n, "
Yeaton J. C. "
Cheever John P. Plainville, Wrentham.
Thatcher Samuel, Yarmouth.
Baker Laban jr., South Yarmouth, "
Chase William, "
Wing & Akin, "
Perry Jabez, West Yarmouth, "
Hallett N. T. Yarmouth Port, "
Payne E. Dexter, "
Taylor Thacher, " "

Ground Bone.

WALTON T., foot of Ord, (see page 748), Salem.

17

Guano Manufactories.

Pacific Guano Co.   Falmouth
                           Fall River
Brightman L. & Sons (Menhaden fish),   "
Fall River Oil & Guano Co., (Menha-
den fish), Job T. Wilson, treas.   "

Gum-Copal Manufacturers.
(See also Varnish Manufacturers)

Whipple Stephen & Bro.   Salem

Gunpowder Manufacturers.
(See Powder Manufacturers.)

Guns and Sporting Apparatus.
(See also Fire Arms.)

RICHARDSON L. B. & CO. 108 Central,   Lowell
Sedgewick & Brandon,   Pittsfield
WESSON FIRE ARMS CO. (breech-
loading shot guns),   Springfield

Gun, Rifle, and Pistol Manufs.

Boyd Francis,   Hyde Park
Allen Ethan & Co.   Worcester
WESSON FRANK, 2 Manchester
(see page 786),   "

Gunsmiths.
(See also Fire Arms.)

Hogan John B.   North Adams,   Adams
Hall N. C.   Blandford
Babcock M.   Charlestown
Pratt Alvan,   Concord
Faunce Zenas,   Duxbury
Davis N. R. & Co. Assonett, Freetown
Grant W. N.   Greenfield
Sawyer & Dennison,   Haverhill
McAllister Benjamin,   Lawrence
FROST J. W. & CO. 308 Common,   "
Richardson & Cutter,   Lowell
Butterfield Levi,   Lynn
Lawrence William,   Milford
Eggers Selmar,   New Bedford
Sherman William R.   "
Sisson Daniel W.   "
Sargent C. E.   Newburyport
Hannum & Avery,   Northampton
Dunham George F.   Plymouth
Woods John A.   Provincetown
Fuller J. S.   Montville, Sandisfield
Perry Horatio D. & Son,   Salem
Hemenway Levi J.   Shrewsbury
Gifford J. H.   Springfield
Smith M.   "
Diemar Richard,   Taunton
Taft E.   Westford
Hunt S. A.   Williamstown
Cummings Charles A.   Worcester
Johnson I.   "

Gutters and Conductors.

Hopkins Franklin, jr.   Charlestown
STEARNS ALBERT T. (see page
695),   Port Norfolk,   Dorchester
BANGS ANSON & CO. Foster, near
Cypress (see page 721),   Worcester
NEWTON E. & C. Union, near Ex-
change (see page 731),   "

Hair Dressers.
(See also Hair Workers.)

Jones William,   Abington
Hobson R.   East Abington,   "
Osborn Moses,   "
Butler J. H.   South Abington, "
Lewis Levi,   Adams
Church Erastus D. North Adams,   "
Jackson S.   "
Lattime B. H.   Amesbury
Davidge J. D.   Amherst
Fisk Edwin J.   "
Higgins George,   Andover
Smith William,   "
Sands George M.   Arlington

Hartshorn E. P.   Ashfield
Fay Levi B.   Athol
Crumley W. E.   Attleborough
Macdonald William A.   "
Macker George, North Attleborough, "
Pierce Joseph E.   Hyannis, Barnstable
Jones Samuel,   Barre
Kimball Fred. P.   "
DeFrece Jacob H.   Beverly
Thomas George W.   "
Burns William F.   Blackstone
Jones George B.   "
Reiser William H.   Bridgewater
Hilton T. B.   Brighton
Pond E. G.   "
Mideros A.   Brookfield
Hilton Thomas,   Brookline
Keiser Peter,   "
Lenox J. M.   "
Bushnach Henry,   Cambridge
Haddow James L.   "
McCoy T. S.   "
Sewall William,   "
Burr L.   Cambridgeport,   "
Crowd E. S.   "
Greco L. C.   "
Howard Peter M.   "
Pike George S.   "
Sharper George W.   "
Smith James A. L.   "
Smith Louis F.   "
Stanton & Wentworth,   "
Steer John,   "
West Henry,   "
West John E.   "
Benson Henry J. H., East Cambridge, "
Brum Antonio E.   "
Peterson Henry,   "
Silva I. T.   "
Silva T. J.   "
Stanton Richard F.   "
Waller J. A.   Canton
Beal E. & A. H.   Charlestown
Biddle Robert S.   "
Bixby Charles P.   "
Bobrosky F.   "
Coll Rafael,   "
Dewire John,   "
Green Frances A. (ladies).   "
Greenman O. A.   "
Hawkins J. P. & P. E.   "
Howard John,   "
Jennings & Hart,   "
Lemos M. E.   "
McCrea J. B.   "
Parker Pardon, P. C.   "
Powell Charles,   "
Redder & Morrison,   "
Smith S. P.   "
Thomas John A.   "
Vasconsellos J. M.   "
Chadwick Elvin,   Chelsea
Christopher & Custalon,   "
Curtis William D.   "
Eddix Jared C.   "
McKinnon Miles,   "
Mainjoy Charles,   "
Lewis Joseph,   Cheshire
Damon Sylvanus C.   Chesterfield
Blackmer J. K.   Chicopee
Planter F. L.   Chicopee Falls,   "
Carr Frank E.   Clinton
Foss I. W.   Concord
Simas B. A.   Danvers
Brown M. L. Mrs.   Dedham
Goodwin F. A.   "
Gethro Alex.   East Dedham,   "
Patten Frank A.   South Dedham, "
Pond E. W.   "
                           Dorchester
CAMM ISAAC G., Glover's Corner, "
Herman Charles,   Milton,   "
Korb Henry,   "
Capalja Antonio,   "
Dean Frank,   Neponset,   "
Johnson G. W.   "
Johnston Samuel,   "
Paul Brothers,   Douglas
Chandler Harvey,   East Bridgewater
Murphy Patrick,   N. Easton,   Easton

Robinson John T.	Edgartown
Lauder E. W.	Essex
Maynard W. C.	East Hampton
Jackson Edward,	Fairhaven
Cavalier D. J. & E. L.	Fall River
Crowley James C.	"
De Caro Frank,	"
Dyer Joseph X.	"
Dyer & Co.	"
Haggerty Patrick,	"
McKenney Felix, jr.	"
Moncada H.	"
Page Barton,	"
Spencer N. P.	"
Rabbit Willard N.	Fitchburg
Gerry Hattie R.	"
Howard Peter B.	"
Robinson Amory,	"
Williams & Avery,	"
Falvey Jeremiah,	Foxborough
Ladd Fred. L.	"
	Framingham
Sackett A. N.	South Framingham,
Wrinley Samuel,	Franklin
Lewe Peter B.	Gardner
Rickson Newell,	"
Pompelis C. G.	Georgetown
Goldthwait Philip H.	Gloucester
Ingersoll Chas M.	"
Lane George E.	"
Leonard Josiah E.	"
Lloyd Joseph D.	"
Marston Warren,	"
Morrill Geo. W.	"
Nute H.	"
Powers W. H.	"
Ingersoll John H.	East Gloucester,
Du Bois Alfred,	Great Barrington
Myslinski Frank J.	"
Adams George H.	Greenfield
Avery E. J.	"
Miller Frederick,	"
Jaquith David,	Groton Centre, Groton
Reed Samuel,	" Junction, "
Lewis Moses,	" " "
Cobb Edmond M.	No. Harwich, Harwich
Cranshaw Robert,	Haverhill
Cranshaw James W.	"
Knights Chas.	"
Scott Thomas,	"
Clary George C.	Hingham
Rickheit Conrad,	"
Potter Chas. Wm.	Hinsdale
Clark D H.	Holliston
Tyler Sylvester,	"
Avery A G.	Holyoke
Gilmor John R.	"
Stamps Geo. W.	"
Meisen Philip,	Hopkinton
Phelps E. F.	Hudson
JENNISON L. W.	"
Day W. H.	Huntington
Hacuber Ernest,	Hyde Park
Steamburg T. W.	"
Barton N. R.	Ipswich
Holland Charles,	"
Avilla M. J.	Lawrence
Bennett & Moore,	"
Clinton E. N.	"
Cunha & Thomas,	"
Kelly P. J.	"
Medina John J.	"
Nunes John,	"
Picaneo Manuel C.	"
Redford Wm.	"
Thomas Robt. jr.	"
Thompson J. G.	"
Wheelock Major,	"
Wood Thomas,	"
Woollsdale Geo. H.	"
Crispell I.	Lee
Lobasch Earnest,	"
Montgomery Wm.	"
Oliver Joseph,	"
Carter Henry J.	East Lee,
Liues J. Wallace,	Leominster
Aruda Frank D.	Lowell
Barth Daniel W.	"
Benson S. W.	"
Bonner L. H.	"
Bowman M.	Lowell
Brooks W. F.	"
Brown Jonus E.	"
Burton A. P.	"
Clifford Charles T.	"
Hapgood Harry,	"
Lewis W.	"
Libby Alexander H.	"
Manuel James,	"
McEnroe L. S.	"
Pike A. J.	"
Powers William M.	"
Proctor H. B.	"
Richardson G. M.	"
Tuttle Augustus,	"
Welch Edward,	"
White F. J.	"
Bessom Bros.	Lynn
Bowker Daniel C.	"
Cook Philip B.	"
Edge P. J.	"
Harris A. L. Miss (ladies').	"
Hill H. A.	"
Hutchinson Joseph,	"
Jarvis Wm. H.	"
Jenness Charles B.	"
Johnson Horace,	"
Lewis Wm. H.	"
McManus H.	"
Nelson Isaac T.	"
Norris Joseph H.	"
Syms R. S.	"
Towne John S.	"
West Ottoway,	"
Cobb H. A. & F.	Mansfield
Curry & Welsh,	Malden
Foss A. W.	"
Shiloh William H.	"
Stanley Edwin P.	Manchester
Bessom Philip C.	Marblehead
Fountaine Edward A.	"
Hathaway Daniel R.	"
Jackson Thomas W.	Marion
Berry Joseph C.	Marlborough
Cuthbert Geo. M.	"
King Augustus,	"
Malley Thomas,	"
Mitchell Henry,	Medford
Peak H. M.	"
Noss N. P.	Medway
Annis Joel N.	Melrose
Sprague Samuel,	"
Bond J. S.	Methuen
Cavalier Daniel J.	Middleborough
Sylvester Solomon H.	"
Dyer Joseph,	Milford
Gloucester J. H.	"
Lowther Geo. W.	"
Stallad J. J.	Millbury
Crawford James E.	Nantucket
Ross James, jr.	"
Clark A. F.	Natick
Gaudig E.	"
Loker C. P.	"
Davis Jacob,	South Natick
Aler William,	New Bedford
Ashley Daniel C.	"
Berry William,	"
Castello Marcellus,	"
Jourdain A. G.	"
Mitchell B M. Mrs.	"
Mitchell G. H.	"
Perkins C. M.	"
Piper & Johnson,	"
Scarborough Henry A.	"
Scott J. M.	"
Temple Lewis,	"
Thomas James,	"
Viereck Louis,	"
Webster George W.	"
Wilson James G.	"
Woods William H.	"
Barth Henry,	Newburyport
Hodge James,	"
Osborn J.	"
Sanders William P.	"
Walsh Peter,	"
Whiting Daniel B.	"
Williamson Isaac,	"
Young J. C. H.	"

Hair Dressers — continued.

Smith John, Lower Falls, Newton
Fayes A. J. Newton Corner, "
Williams Alfred, West Newton, "
Manger C. E. Northampton
Prouty E. F. "
Nichols Charles, Northborough
Barden W. H. North Bridgewater
Buckley D. J. "
Jacobs W. H. "
Taylor Clary, "
Donne J. M. North Brookfield
Lewis John, "
Maxwell C. "
Schneider William, Orange
Jones Henry, Palmer
Cone Geo. E. Peabody
HEYLINGBERG J. J. (see page 749),
   Warren National Bank Building, "
Deyo Elizabeth, Pittsfield
Fowler Henry G. "
Gardner William, "
Gilliard John E. "
Johnson Levi J. "
Waldschmidt Michael, "
Frink C. H. Plymouth
Holmes W. S. "
Maddox Stephen, "
Revaleon A. S. "
Whiting Joseph B. "
Mayo Joseph, Provincetown
Fluker Francis F. "
Pimentel Manuel, "
Emerson Thomas G. Quincy
Layton R. M. "
Phillips Joseph A. "
Adams John, Randolph
Freeman John E. "
Black Rhodes, East Randolph, "
Parker Clarkson, Reading
Gordon Samuel, Rockport
Babcock C. Mrs. (ladies'), Salem
Daniels & Bates, "
Full J. F. "
Fowler James W. "
Nichols James W. "
Osborn J. B. "
Putnam C. R. "
Rowe J. S. "
Saul James B. "
Savage A. C. "
Walker David A. "
Williams Andrew A. "
Felch S. A. Amesbury, Salisbury
Quimby James, "
Ellis Stephen G. F. Sandwich
Young Russell, "
Edge Philip J. East Saugus, Saugus
Thieme Lewis, Shelburne Falls, Shelburne
Seibert Philip, "
Nevis Emanuel, Somerville
Badger I. A. Southbridge
Adams J. B. Springfield
Adams, Thiemann, & Adams, "
Curry & Erb, "
Greene Brothers, "
Hall G. W. "
Hobson William O. "
James Henry, "
King David, "
Montague W. D. "
Queen George, "
Scottron S. N. "
Rathbun Frank H. Stockbridge
Locke Samuel S. Stoughton
Whiting Lemuel G. "
Moore E. Stoneham
Wentworth Jennings, "
Jackson William, Fiskdale Sturbridge
Sawyer J. M. Assabet, Sudbury
Wilson Henry W. Swampscott
Dobson John M. Taunton
BOWMAN A. E. MISS (ladies), "
BOWMAN SAMUEL, H. "
Bush J. Stanley, "
Ellis David P. "
McCormick Edward, "
Moore Charles H. "
Morris John, "
Rogers E. E. "

Willis E. Taunton
Woodward William P. "
O'Brien Richard J. Tyringham
Atwood Thomas, Wakefield
Tyler George L. "
Armstrong William, Waltham
Davis Joseph, "
Finegan Michael, "
Foster E. Ware
Winter W. M. "
Turner William M. Wareham
Fayes M. P. Watertown
Lenox John, "
Peeler & Whitney, "
Dailey J. C. Webster
Moore George, "
Higgins John G. Wellfleet
Krumsick George, Westborough
Renslow Lucius, Westfield
Mallory G. H. "
Snider O. "
West Roxbury
Albrecht Nicholas, Jamaica Plain, "
Murray B. E. "
Smith John F. Weymouth
Goodwin B. F. East Weymouth, "
Snyder William, " " "
Cleverly Alonzo, North "
Talbot Benjamin, Winchendon
Price J. W. Winchester
Barrett A. B. Woburn
Staggles William E. "
Webber Daniel M. "
Arial Isaac, Worcester
Barker B. C. "
Clark James, "
Clough Francis A. "
Gimby Edward, "
Geary W. H. H. "
Hecktor R. A. "
Jankins & Clark, "
Klein John, "
Kohl Joseph, "
McNorton & Walker, "
Miller George E. "
Palmer J. A. "
Walker Allen, "
Walker Gilbert, "
Weeber Jacob, "
Wright Richard, "

Hair Dye Manufacturers.

Morill Jason E. Holyoke
HUTCHINS H. & SON, Springfield

Hair Work, Wigs, &c.

McCrea J. B. (wigs), Charlestown
Adams George H. Greenfield
Medina John J. Lawrence
Medina E. J, Lowell
Raymond Daniel, "
Jourdain A. G. Mrs. New Bedford
Mitchell Bell M. "
Prouty E. F. Northampton
Babcock C. Mrs. (ladies), Salem
Putnam C. R. Mrs. "
Montague W. H. Springfield
Bowman J. Mrs. Worcester
Gilliard H. Mrs. (ladies'), "

Hair for Plastering.

BARNES E. & J. C. (see page 717),
   Water st. Plymouth
Griffin James & Co. Salem
Kent E. T. Cliftondale, Saugus

Halters (Braided Rope).

Le Baron E. H. Mattapoisett

Hames Manufacturers.

Tarbell William & Son, Brimfield
Smith Peter E. Haverhill
Blanchard Hame Co. Palmer

Hammer Manufacturers.

Norton T. S. & Co. Holyoke

Handle Manufacturers.

Hall R. George, North Adams, Adams
Amherst Mill Co. E. D. Fitts, agt. Amherst

Bisbee Orin & Son (broom),   Chesterfield
Persons & Healey (saw and plane
  handles), West Chesterfield,   "
Olds Fayette L. (saw and plain han-
  dles), West Chesterfield,   "
Brown Samuel (broom),   Cummington
Crosby N. B. (brush),   "
Harlow Charles (broom),   "
Lovell Jacob (plane),   "
Narramore H. L. "
MILLER'S FALLS MANUF. CO.,
  (adjustable, for awls, files, chisels,
  &c., see page 721),   Greenfield
Parker B. S. & Co. (tool),   "
Kittle Allen (paint brush),   Hancock
Eldridge Thomas,   Hawley
Crittenden Charles, . Charlemont,   "
Scott Elijah (broom & brush), "   "
Colby Charles (broom and brush),
  West Hawley,   "
Hunt & Larkin,   West Hawley,   "
Miller John,   "   "
Turner A. F. (broom and brush),
  West Hawley,   "
Vincent Willis (broom and brush),
  West Hawley,   "

           Newburyport
Noyes William, jr. (file and chisel),   "
Perry James H. & Charles (chisel
  and mallet),   Rehoboth
Amidon H. & Co. (broom),   Rowe
Kendrick H. A.   "
Smith Charles, 2d (saw and plane),
  South Worthington,.   Worthington
Parish Oliver (fork), W. Worthington, "

Hand Stamps.

Hill B. B. (seal stamps and
  presses),   Springfield
Medlicot A. D. (elastic),   "

Hardware and Cutlery.

(See also Cutlery Manufs.; also Iron and
    Steel.)

Twitchell Chas. S.,   W. Acton,   Acton
Burlingame & Darbys, N. Adams, Adams
Clark & Olds,   "
Wilkinson & Mole,   "
Winslow, Piper, & Co.   Amherst
Shattuck Ralph W. & Co.   Arlington
Bemis & Frost,   Athol
Sprague Lucius K.,   Athol Depot,   "
           Attleboro'
FESSENDEN HENRY, N. Attleboro',   "
Crocker B. F. & Co., Hyannis, Barnstable
Herrick S. D.   Beverly
Smith Eben,   "
Semmes R. W.   "
WHITE H. M., South Braintree, Braintree
Fairbanks J. H.   Bridgewater
Hobart Caleb,   "
Estes L. P.   Cambridge
Moore Charles,   "
Nutting J. D.   "
Palmer John,   "
Place George G.   "
Chamberlain D. U., Cambridgeport,   "
Towne & Fuller,   "
Price James M.,   E. Cambridge,   "
Capen E.   Canton
Hunt Lewis,   Charlestown
Plummer & Shattuck,   "
Harding Andrew,   "
HIGGINS SAMUEL,   Chatham
Fisher C. R. & Co.   "
PERKINS NOBLE M., Stebbins'   Chelsea
  Block, Broadway,   "
Slade Charles,   "
MULLENS ISAAC & SONS,   Chicopee

Bowman Charles,   Clinton
Bates Samuel,   Cohasset
DAYTON CHARLES,   Danvers
NEWHALL BENJAMIN E.   "
Lealand C. H. & Co.   Dedham
Thacher Benjamin, West Dennis, Dennis
Balcom Isaac S., East Douglas, Douglas
Mayher J.   East Hampton
Bradley William,   Edgartown
Fuller F. M.   Fairhaven
Conant P. D.   Fall River
Stillwell Daniel,   "
Westgate J. F.   "
Willard & Mason,   "
Fairbanks J. H.   Fitchburg
Litch & Sawtell,   "
Parkhurst Boardman,   "
Wright, Woodward, & Co.   "
Hodges & Messenger,   Foxborough
Bean Cyrus,   Framingham
Saville George,   Gloucester
Story Cyrus,   "
Brewer J. & Son,   Great Barrington
Norton S. & Co.   "
Allen's. S. Sons,   Greenfield
Arms George A. & Co.   "
Kelley H. jr. & Co.   Harwich
APPLETON J. A. JR.   Haverhill
Fellows C. H. & Co.   "
Hanscom M. W. & W. A.   "
Clement James F.   Hingham
Cushing David, 2d,   "
Pond G. N.   Holliston
Farrington & Burditt,   Holyoke
Snow Gustavus,   "
Woodbury George S.   Hopkinton
Tucker Samuel P.   Hudson
Bryant & Newcomb,   Hyde Park
Kimball W. A. & Co.   Lawrence
Mason C. R. & Co.   "
Quackenbush Peter,   Lee
Adams Charles E.   Lowell
Chase, Sargent, & Shattuck,   "
Fielding & Bartlett,   "
Rogers Jacob & Co.   "
Breed Joseph, 2d,   Lynn
Breed T. N.   "
Floyd William H.   "
Hutchinson W. Henry,   "
Lapham George H. & Co.   "
MARTIN E. E. P., 54 Munroe (see
  page 706),   "
Myrick N. H.   "
Peck L. H.   "
Cloon William F.   Marblehead
Prime Stephen T.   "
Colson Owen D.   Mattapoisett
Doane George H.   Middleborough
Bartlett & Heywood,   Milford
Bowers & Jenks,   "
Hosier William,   Nantucket
Macy George W.   "
Morse J. W.   Natick
Parlin W. D.   "
Almy John E.   New Bedford
Howland Peleg,   "
SULLINGS & KINGMAN, 123 Union,   "
Swift & Allen,   "
Vincent Ambrose,   "
Bassett N. G.   Newburyport
Lord T. H. & A. W.   "
Noyes David C.   "
Woodworth D. T.   "
Howes A.   Newton Corner,   Newton
Skilton Otis A.   Northampton
Todd William H.   "
Hunt John,   North Bridgewater
Southward & Noyes,   "

Hardware and Cutlery— continued.

Bliss & Pepper, North Brookfield
NEWCOMB T. S. & SON, Orleans
Brown Ebenezer, Palmer
Newman & Symonds, Peabody
Burkinshaw Aaron, Pepperell
Campbell & Francis, Pittsfield
Dutton & Peirson, "
Harlow & Barnes, Plymouth
TURNER E. C. "
Dyer Charles P. Provincetown
Holmes Hiram, "
Small J. F. "
Whitney & Nash, Quincy
Lane A. W. Rockport
Patch W. H. "
Thurston William H. "
Adams, Richardson, & Co. Salem
Hale Henry, "
Odell Charles, "
Ropes Timothy, "
Williston S. S. "
Allen W. & Son, Amesbury, Salisbury
Fifield B. E. " "
Lothrop H. A. & Co. Sharon
NEWELL BROTHERS, Shelburne
Falls. Shelburne
Merrifield John A. Somerville
Cummings & Williams, Southbridge
Lewis E. P. Globe Village, "
Bemis S. Augustus, Springfield
Blackstone C. J. "
Brewer James D. "
FOOT HOMER & CO. "
Graves Geo. A. "
Hill Aaron, Stoneham
Taunton
CROWELL EZRA, 37 West Water, "
NEWCOMB W. L. & CO. (see page
728), "
Washburn Edward E. "
Washburn Isaac, "
Sanders George B. East Taunton, "
Taft Charles A. Uxbridge
Wing Charles, "
Bill Charles H. Waltham
CONEY H. M. & CO. Ware
Howes Alfred, Watertown
Spaulding Cyrus, Webster
ATWOOD SIMEON & CO. Wellfleet
Montague & Hemenway, Westborough
Fletcher & Norton, Westfield
Radcliff & Allen, Weymouth
TUCK LORENZO, S. Weymouth, "
Mather B. F. Williamstown
Whipple J. H. "
Thompson L. jr. Woburn
Foster C. & Co. (importers), Worcester
Kinnicutt & Co, "
Miller Henry W. "
White & Conant, "
Farris Russell D., S. Yarmouth, Yarmouth

Hardware for Children's Carriages.

MUNSON J. M. (see page 716), Greenfield

Hardware Manufacturers.

Nutting J. D., Cambridgeport. Cambridge
REED FRANKLIN (see page 793), Canton
GAYLORD MANUF. Co. (see page
773). Chicopee
Taylor L. B. & Co. "
MILLER'S FALLS MANUF. CO.
(bit-braces, tool-holders, and drill-
chucks, see page 721), Greenfield
MUNSON J. M. (hardware for chil-
dren's carriages, see page 716), "

Noyes Baxter B. (children's carriage
hardware), Greenfield
THOMPSON MANUF. Co. (chisels,
iron gate and bit stock, see page
770),
BUCK BROTHERS (chisels, gouges,
&c., see page 761), Millbury
Arms & Burdwell Manuf. Co. (strap
and T hinges), Northampton
LAMSON & GOODNOW MANUF.
CO. (cutlery), Shelburne Falls
Shepardson H. S. & Co. (bit-braces), "
Bemis & Call, Springfield
English B. C. "
BUCK BROTHERS (chisels, &c.,
see page 761), Worcester

Harness Frame Manuf.

Putnam Jason, Worcester

Harness Makers.

(See also Trunks, &c.)

Brewster H. O. E. Abington, Abington
Calkins J. H. N. " "
Capen Wm. H. jr. S. " "
Meany T. " " "
Ball Warren, South Acton, Acton
Richmond Daniel C. & Son, Adams
Clark Earl, North Adams, "
Dowlin Marshall R. "
Currier Sawyer, W. Amesbury, Amesbury
Gould Daniel, " "
Nichols Rufus K. " "
Hutchinson C. E. Amherst
Whitney E. "
Burtt Henry, Andover
Mayer Charles, "
Clark Wm. L. & Co. Arlington
Everett Asa C. Ashby
Coleman Loring E. Ashfield
Winchester J. H. Ashland
Barber Harding R. Athol Depot, Athol
Crosby A. R. Attleborough
Ferguson Joseph, N. Attleborough, "
Holmes Wm. D. Barnstable
Gardner Andrew B. Centreville, "
Bassett J. A. Hyannis, "
Crocker R. W. jr. " "
Ames E. J. & M. Barre
White Jonathan S. & Co. "
Cutler Frederick A. Bedford
Chisholm John, "
Hoyt Richard H. Bernardston
Snow William, "
Hawes Gilbert T. Beverly
Whittier James, "
Gragg W. F. Billerica
Thompson E. Blackstone
Morse John, Bradford
Walsh John M. Weymouth, Braintree
Rogers Abner, Brewster
Gibbs J. W. Bridgewater
Bradley John B. Brighton
Colety P. H. "
Fiske J. "
Brown Henry F. Brimfield
Gates John, "
Quinlan M. W. Brookline
Campbell Edward, Cambridge
Fox Geo. J. "
Lincoln Edward M. "
Munroe N. W. "
Hancock Belcher, Cambridgeport, "
McAulay A. " "
Morris J. & H. " "
Howe D. K. E. Cambridge, "

Wells C. B. & Co.	Hancock
Prouty Joseph E.	Hanson
Perry William A.	Hardwick
LOVELL HORACE & CO.,	Harwich
Port,	Harwich
Gould W. A.	Haverhill
Littlefield E. L.	"
Peters Daniel,	"
Savory Robert,	"
Sawyer Amos,	"
Cushing Henry,	Hingham
Hersey David A.	"
Burbank Anthony,	Hinsdale
Dyke B. jr.	Holden
Jones H. E.	Holliston
Gould J. & G. B.	"
MARTIN WOODBURY L. (see page	
724),	Holyoke
Shaw Bently,	"
King James H.	Hopkinton
Savage James,	Hubbardston
Hall Charles E.	Hudson
Underwood E. C.	"
Arnold Henry,	Huntington
BOSTON HARNESS CO., J. Dooley	
& Co.	Hyde Park
Barker & Porter,	Ipswich
Stetson Joseph,	Kingston
Lathrop E. & Co.	Lawrence
Gale & Ames,	"
Nicholson Michael W.	"
Peters John,	"
Stowell Joseph & Co.	"
Wyatt L. B.	"
Harlbut & Turner,	Lee
Webster Wells E. South Lee,	"
Bangs David E.	Lenox
Spencer Edmund,	"
Barry Wm.	Leominster
Ellick Wm. C.	"
Lawrence Lyman,	Lexington
Robinson G. F.	"
Smith H. N.	Littleton
Allen J. G.	Lowell
Brabook Joseph A.	"
Butman Samuel L.	"
Hatch G. S. & Co.	"
SAWYER AARON C. 161 and 163	
Middlesex,	"
Sullivan J.	"
Willett Albert,	"
Barnes Samuel H.	Lynn
Hollis J. A.	"
Jennings Thomas D.	"
Plumstead Matthew,	"
Dodge Temple,	Malden
Wilson Andrew,	Mansfield
Jandrue Lewis E.	Marlborough
Barnard C. D.	Marshfield
LeBaron E. H. (halters),	Mattapoisett
Richardson H. F. A.	Medfield
Hartshorn A. P.	Medford
Nichols George,	"
Langtry Joseph,	Melrose
Lynde O. J. & W. O.	"
Boyden Lewis,	Mendon
Corliss Varnum,	Methuen
Shiverick William,	Middleborough
Wing William H.	"
Cushman Smith,	Milford
Lilley John N.	"
Nason Charles,	"
Hodgman F. K.	Millbury
Sumner B. C.	"
Clapp George W.	Milton
Smith Benjamin D.	Monson
Payne Samuel B.	Montague
Childs B. R.	Nantucket

Harness Makers — continued.

Jenks George W.
L'Hommedieu Wm. C.   Nantucket
Bispham Thomas,   "
Blake George E.   Natick
Allen & Brownell,   "
Barrett Francis J.   New Bedford
Brownell Geo. L.   "
Gifford B. F.   "
Kittredge B. R.   "
Marr William J.   "
Willis William H.   "
Coffin Joseph,   Newbury
Allen Ira H.   Newburyport
Jones Sewall,   "
Walton Joseph H.   "
White A.   Mill River, New Marlboro'
Foster George B., N. Prescott, New Salem
Fuller George,   West Newton, Newton
Jenkins E. C.   Lower Falls, "
Glennan T. F.   Newton Corner, "
Welch W.   " "
Hancock Ebenezer,   Northampton
Hubbard Wallace,   "
Eustis A.   "
Smith & Harkins,   "
McDonald & Haniford,   North Andover
Linton F. W., Whitinsville, Northbridge
Bird L. T.   North Bridgewater
Flagg Wm. H.   "
Rogers R. S.   "
Calvert & Pepper,   North Brookfield
Pineo Henry D.   North Chelsea
Pierce George F.   Norton
Hastings Charles W.   Orange
Hastings Ira,   "
Nickerson Winsor,   Orleans
Norton George J.   Otis
Brown Benjamin F.   Oxford
Snow Lawson,   "
Waite John,   Palmer
Crane J. F.   Three Rivers, "
Wilder Alonzo,   Thorndike, "
Cheever Samuel,   Peabody
Mower & Davis,   "
Simonds Edward,   "
Whitman Charles H.   Pembroke
Mace William P.   Pepperell
Clark William P.   Petersham
Chapman Lorenzo,   Pittsfield
Cullen Patrick,   "
Fairfield David & Brother,   "
Gerst & Smith,   "
Bartlett Edward,   Plymouth
Hathaway Edward,   "
Jackson Wm. H.   "
Ball Micah R.   Princeton
Lowe Ralph (collars and blankets), Quincy
Jones George J.   "
Tirrell Sons,   "
Cartwright Walter,   Randolph
Fowkes Geo. W.   "
Carleton Noyes,   Reading
Herrick Dwight,   Russell
Coombs Frederick,   Salem
Cunningham John,   "
Dayton Isaac,   "
Osgood Benj. H. & Son,   "
Tuttle Hiram A.   "
Tuttle John,   "
Watson Fenton,   "
Whitney R. S.   "
Foss Edwin,   Amesbury, Salisbury
Rothe W. L.   "
Fosdick Robbins, New Boston, Sandisfield
LOVELL HORACE,   Sandwich
Lovejoy V. R.   "
Howard Roland S.   N. Sandwich, "

Mendell David P., N. Sandwich, Sandwich
Blanchard Thomas,   Scituate
Thurber Hiram A.   Seekonk
Wheeler Dexter,   "
Henton Thomas, Ashley Falls, Sheffield
Wilder Joseph H. (also saddler),
   Shelburne Falls, Shelburne
Morgan C. C.   Shirley
Livingston James,   Shrewsbury
White John N.   Somerville
Carpenter C. T.   Southbridge
Comings John,   Globe Village, "
Hitchcock Elam,   Southampton
Burnham Geo. W.   South Hadley
Horgan Timothy J.   South Reading
Phipps John,   "
Marchalt Frank X.   Spencer
Cummings Josiah,   Springfield
Hewitt J. R.   "
Ilsley N. jr.   "
Payne William,   "
Russell Geo. B.   "
Russell John K.   "
Wellman, Frost, & Co.   "
White & Coolidge,   "
Wilkinson W. H. & Co.   "
Pratt Josiah R.   Sterling
Hosfinyer Simon,   Stockbridge
Baldwin M. B.   Stoneham
Haniford R.   "
May Bradford R.   Stoughton
May Ira,   East Stoughton, "
Taylor Francis C.   Assabet, Stow
Carpenter Charles,   Sturbridge
Haynes H. & Son,   "
Perry W. W.   "
Wood Alpheus,   Swansea
Hack Nathan E.   Taunton
Kellogg Thomas,   "
Packer James B.   "
Pierce J. W.   "
Whitters Edward,   "
Damon Urias,   Templeton
Chamberlin John F.   "
Chamberlin Moses,   "
Norton Leavitt T.   Tisbury
Cochran Silas,   Topsfield
Eaton Boardman, W. Townsend, Townsend
Barrett J. O.   Townsend Centre, "
Kent James C.   Upton
Kent Oliver S.   "
Wims Patrick,   Uxbridge
Rudge Wm.   Wales
Fuller Geo.   South Walpole, Walpole
Crosby Charles,   Waltham
Barlean Philip,   "
Kingsbury Joseph,   "
French Harrison,   Ware
Kurtz William,   "
Pratt E. H.   "
Crocker Walton M.   Wareham
Loring William G.   "
Pond P. & Son,   Warren
Patten Thomas,   Watertown
TARBELL E. G.   "
Carpenter Charles,   Webster
Dyke A.   "
Arnaud Raymond C.   Wellfleet
Cross & Stanley,   Wenham
Hobbs Henry,   "
Bacon Daniel,   Westborough
Felton L. S.   West Boylston
Adams Charles,   West Brookfield
Fairbanks Dwight,   "
Herrick Aaron,   Westfield
HOLCOMB WALTER C. (see page 727),   "
Young Charles A.   "

Joslin Milton,　　　　　Westminster
Farnham Jacob,　　　West Newbury
Manning B. W.,　　　　　　"
Ordway Rufus,　　　　　　"
Jones Thomas B.　　　　　Weston
Tripp Weston F.　　　　Westport
Bestwick A., Jamaica Plain, West Roxbury
Williams J. C.　"　　　　"
　　　　　　West Stockbridge
GALE FELLOWS, (see page 711),　"
Walsh John M.　　　　Weymouth
Damon I. B.　East Weymouth,　"
Hunnewell J.　South　　"　　"
Urquhart John,　　"　　"　　"
Stearnes Henry,　　　Williamsburg
Williams Whitney L.
Mole Thomas,　　　　Williamstown
Reagan Daniel J.
Weatherhead & Sinclair,　Winchendon
Berry E. G.　　　　　　Wobura
Haynes A. V.　　　　　　"
Parker Samuel P.　　　　　"
Thompson C. R.　North Woburn,　"
Allen Willard E.　　　　Worcester
Brown Daniel,　　　　　　"
Hastings L. A.　　　　　　"
Hutchinson B. E.　　　　　"
OLIVER HENRY C. 319 Main,　"
Rafferty P. W.　　　　　　"
Taylor C. W.　　　　　　"
TOWER C. D. 51 Union (see page 724),　"
Walker A. (dealer),　　　　"
Tinker Arba J.　　　　Worthington
Dart Gustavus F.　　　Wrentham
Hallet A. F.　South Yarmouth, Yarmouth
Hallet Benj.　Yarmouth Port,　"
Lovell Eldridge,　　　　　"

Harness Twine.

CLARK JEREMIAH, 96 Middle (loom,
　see page 738),　　　　　Lowell
MORSE E. J. W. & CO. (Sea Island
　Cotton, all numbers, see page 749),
　　　　　　South Easton

Harrows.

(See Agricultural Implements.)

Hat Manufacturers.

National Hat Co.　S. Braintree,　Braintree
PETTINGELL & SAWYER (see
　page 762),　　　East Cambridge
Phelps Timothy,　　　　Dedham
Ayer Brothers (wool),　　Haverhill
Butters & Rust (wool),　　"
Crowell C. W. & Co., Ayer's Village,　"
Houston John A.　　"　　"
O'Sullivan Bros. (wool),　Lawrence
Stratton T. S. & Co. (felt),　"
Hines C. G. (silk),　　　Lowell
Adams J. Q. (silk),
Bowen & Emerson (wool),　Methuen
Hawley A. A. (wool),　　"
Ingalls Charles & Son (wool),　"
Jackman W. H. & Co. (wool),　"
Messer M. & Son,　　　　"
Tenney C. H. (wool),　　"
Titcomb & Gleason (wool),　"
Mitchell Jones, & Co. (silk),　Milford
Fay G. P. (wool),　　　Natick
Covell J. L.　　　　New Bedford
　　　　　　Newburyport
Bayley Hat Co., A. L. Bayley, agent,
Essex Hat Manufacturing Co.　"
Porter Edward F.　　　　"
Moody B. D. (oiled),　　Newton Corner

Cowan William K.　　　Pittsfield
Dodge & Sloan,　　　　　"
Driscoll Cornelius,　　　Salem
　　　　　　Walpole
Gill Ira & Sons, (hat body formers),　"
Davis James S.　　　　Warren
Barker S. D.　　　　Worcester
Hacker M.　　　　　　"
Henville W. W.　　　　"
Maybaum Charles,　　　　"

Hats and Bonnets (Felt).

Bowkers S H. (felt for ladies'), Worcester
WILLIAMSON M. W. & CO. 5 Cen-
　tral Exchange,　　　　"

Hats, Caps, and Furs.

(See also Hat Manufacturers.)

Smith Geo. W.　　　　Adams
Crieg E.　　　　　　"
Munn Charles,　North Adams,　"
Spear John W.　"　"　　"
Pease Oliver,　　　・Amherst
　　　　　　Attleborough
Devlin Daniel, North Attleborough,　"
Pierce C. A.　　　　Blackstone
　　　　　　Cambridge
Maynard Eben W., Cambridgeport,　"
Bridge & Murphy,　　Charlestown
Rand John W.　　　　"
Thomas John C.　　　　"
Pike J. J. & Co.　　　Chelsea
Wiggin A. & Co.　　　Dedham
Pierce Amos T.　　　Fairhaven
Williams T. D. & Co.　　"
Ashley W. H.　　　Fall River
Davoll John, jr.　　　　"
Gibbs R. S. & Co.　　　"
Read Nathan & Co.　・　"
Wilbur & Gray,　　　　"
Emory Charles A.　　Fitchburg
Goodrich Henry A.　　　"
Spencer Edward H.　　　"
Barrett Charles P.　　Gloucester
Bennett & Marr,　　　　"
Parkhurst E. A.　　　　"
Holmes Horace,　Great Barrington
Hubble A. L.　　　　　"
Bailey L. M.　　　Greenfield
Seward & Willard,　　　"
Brett Charles E.　　　Harwich
Lancaster Thomas,　　Haverhill
Sleeper D. A.　　　　"
Wheeler J. S.　　　　"
Whiton E. L.　　　　Hingham
Johnson, Ludington, & Co.　Holyoke
Miller & Co.　　　　　"
MITCHELL BROTHERS,　　"
Goodrich J. B.　　　Hudson
Baker S. N. jr.　　　Ipswich
French Charles B.　　Lawrence
Fuller Augustus,　　　"
Hodgman & Bartlett,　　"
Barnes J. S. E.　　　Lee
Lyman & Chaffee,　　　"
Brazer Wm. P.　　　Lowell
Hines C. G. (silk hats),　　"
HODGMAN B. 30 Central,　"
Huse H. E.　　　　"
Lederer B. & Co.　　　"
Mansfield Samuel,　　Lynn
Torrey Mark A.　　　"
Mann William,　　　Malden
Hartwell George F. & Co.　Middleboro'
Mitchell, Jones, & Co.　Milford
CATHCART CHARLES S.　Nantucket
Brownell Charles W.　New Bedford

Hats, Caps, and Furs — continued.

Cannon E. S. & Co.	New Bedford
Covell & Hathaway,	"
Davenport Cornelius,	"
Gifford N. T. & Co.	"
Lucas Allen,	"
Pedro Joseph H.	"
Swift M. C.	"
Taber, Read. & Co	"
Geary George W. & Son,	Newburyport
Horton Daniel,	"
Piper J. E. & Co.	"
Deming Riley,	Northampton
Draper J. L.	"
Moody J. F.	"
Ramsay E. A.	"
Shepard George,	"
Brett H. A.	North Bridgewater
Bryant G. E. & H. L.	"
Howard & Caldwell,	"
Scott Walter,	"
Ballou W. S.	Orange
Shaw J. P.	Palmer
Dodge & Sloan,	Pittsfield
Fabricius George,	"
Platt Comfort B. jr.	"
Atwood William, 2d,	Plymouth
Peterson Lewis & Son,	"
Nickerson James H.	Provincetown
Small J. F.	"
Lombard J. W.	Quincy
Eeed C. T.	"
Flecker Franklin,	Reading
Hood Ass.	Salem
Kimball William,	"
Maynes William,	"
Nourse Aaron,	"
Osborne Stephen,	"
Chipman Samuel,	Sandwich
Drew George P.	"
Miller John Q.	"
BOWEN A.	Shelburne
Green E. T. Shelburne Falls.	"
Avery S. W.	Springfield
Brigham D. H. & Co.	"
Clark Walter S. & Co.	"
Lee & Williams,	"
Sanderson & Son,	"
Trafton John W.	"
	Taunton
COLBY SAMUEL, 11 Union Block,	
Oak Hall, (see front colored page),	"
Cowhy M. F.	"
Grant C. H.	"
Holt B. R.	"
Perry Henry C.	"
Washburn & Elliott, (furs),	"
Waite James M.	Templeton
Peck Charles,	Waltham
Gould Virgil,	Ware
Kennedy J.	"
Lawton J. R.	"
Hartshorn G.	Webster
Newell P. W.	"
Tobey J. F.	Wellfleet
Sabin C. H.	West Stockbridge
BEAD M. H.	Weymouth
Williams Chas. S.	"
Mather C. H.	Williamstown
Fairbanks C. P. Mrs. (furs),	Winchendon
Cooley W. E.	Worcester
Clapp F. A.	"
Eldred & Liscomb,	"
Geer George.	"
Howland J. P. jr.	"
Kendall & McClennen,	"
Kettell John P.	"
Larkin John, S. Yarmouth, Yarmouth	

Hay Cutters.

(See also Agricultural Implement Manufs.)

HEALD S. & SONS (see pages 796 and 797),	Barre
Coes L. & A. G. (knives),	Worcester
Rice Geo. F.	"

Hay Dealers.

Barry Charles J.	Charlestown
Perkins & Goodwin,	"
HAWKINS & KILHAM, Slade's wharf (see page 718),	Fall River
SHOVE C. & CO. 40 Davol,	"
Porter E.	Gloucester
Sargent & Holden,	Haverhill
McAVOY & CO., Readville,	Hyde Park
Chesley Thomas J.	Lawrence
Churchill J. E. & C.	"
Prince Henry B.	"
Breed S. Oliver,	Lynn
EDMANDS E. P., Summer st. (see page 716),	"
Estes Isaac H.	"
Lake & Starbird,	"
Thing & Rowe,	"
Sawin A. K. P.	New Bedford
Watkins J. B.	"
Wood E. T.	Northampton
Chase Wm. & Co.	Salem
HATCH L. B. 113 Derby,	"
MANNING R. C. & CO. 189 Derby,	"
Wiggin & Clark,	"
PICKERING WM., JR., 17 Peabody,	"
Binney Joshua & Co.	Weymouth
Gay D.	Worcester

Hay Spreaders.

(See also Agricultural Implement Manufs.)

HEALD S. & SONS (see pages 796 and 797),	Barre

Heat Regulators.

Pomeroy Daniel,	Orange

Hermetically Sealed Goods.

Boston Fruit Preserving Co.	Cambridgeport
HODGES & BROTHER,	Medway
Hall A. B. & Co. (pickles, &c.),	Worcester

Hides and Leather.

(See also Leather; also Tanners; also Curriers.)

Peirce Joseph, 2d,	Fitchburg
Burget John,	Great Barrington
Lawrence S. R.	Palmer
Lowrey Frederick N. South Lee,	Lee
Lamb William H.	Wendell
West Strong, South Wilbraham,	Wilbraham

Hides, Tallow, and Calf Skins.

BROWN WILLARD A., 88 Market,	Lowell
PATCH & BAKER, Summer st. (hides and tallow, see page 717), West Lynn,	Lynn

Hinge Manuf.

Gilmore E. W. & Co. (and washers and butts), North Easton,	Easton

Hoes.

(See Agricultural Implements.)

Hollow Ware Manufs.

(See also Iron Founders; also Store Manuf's.)

DIGHTON FURNACE CO., Geo. F. Gavitt, treas. Boston office 96 and 98 North (see page 733), North Dighton, Dighton
SOMERSET CO-OPERATIVE FOUNDRY CO. Somerset
TAUNTON IRON WORKS CO. George M. Woodward, agent (see page 732), Taunton
UNION FURNACE CO., Wright & Leeds (see page 719), "

Hook and Eye Manufacturers.

RICHARDS, CODDING, & CO. North Attleborough, Attleborough

Hoop Skirt Material Manufs.

Fuller & Bigelow, Clinton
RHODES M. M. Porter st. Taunton
STEVENS J. TYLER & CO. successors to N. Richardson & Co. (see page 801), West Warren, Warren

Hoop Skirts.

(See also Corsets.)

Byam Mary Mrs. Amesbury
Parminter Charles O. Amherst
Adams E. jr. Attleborough
Bay State Skirt Co. Clinton
Davis Hattie Miss, Fall River
Milne J. Osborn, "
Ryder Charles Mrs. Fitchburg
Odessa Skirt Co. Gloucester
White H. J. Mrs. Haverhill
Clark James, Lawrence
Hanson Jas. W. "
Mitchell A. "
Moulton S. H. "
Truesdell Henry, "
Blood Sarah A. Mrs. Lowell
Cheney William Mrs. "
Wools E. A. "
Wood Louisa E. Marlborough
Barney Thomas L. Medfield
Wheeler O. S. Milford
Chace George W. (manuf.) New Bedford
Arms & Bardwell Manfacturing Co. Northampton
Tinker M. A. "
STOEHR C. 53 North (see page 762), Pittsfield
Follette L. B. Salem
Porter M. A. "
Middlesex Skirt Manufactory, Shirley
Ferre C. D. & Co. Springfield
Thompson R. F. Taunton
Prince J. O. Walpole
Waltham Skirt Factory, Wm. A. Adams, Agent, Main st. Waltham
Raud, Lewis, & Rand (manuf.), Westfield
Pierce L. L. Worcester
Worcester Skirt Co. "

Hop Dealers.

WORCESTER M. A., 6 Bridge (see page 783), Worcester

Horse Dealers.

Hunt Benjamin L. Abington
Hunt Seth, "
KING FRANK D. Bridgewater
Tinkham O. G. North Bridgewater, "
Benson William, Fairhaven.
Shaw Emerson, Quincy

Horse Rakes.

KNIFFEN MOWING MACHINE CO. 12 Central, Worcester

Horse Shoe Manufacturers.

GOSNOLD MILLS, Jas. D. Thompson, agent and treas.,134 Ray (see page 727), New Bedford

Horse Shoers.

(See also Blacksmiths.)

White Charles, Brighton
Bolger & Shehan, . Cambridge
Felt I. G. East Cambridge, "
Lehan D. H. "
Smith Thomas, Cambridgeport, "
Brewster Frank & Co. Charlestown
Hogan Patrick, "
Strand T. D. "
DENNING PHILIP A. 56 Hawthorn, Chelsea
Hagerty John, Dorchester
Lawton George, Fairhaven
Terry Isaac, "
Field Henry, Fall River
Osborn W. & J. M. "
Packard W. H. "
Stevens Joseph, Lowell
Brownell, Ashley, & Co. New Bedford
Lee & Tripp, "
Smith & Roach, "
TAYLOR AMASA, Provincetown
Clark James, Salem
Harding David, "
McGlue Peter, "
Wilkins Charles, "
Burke Patrick, Springfield
Dasutt Joseph, "
Hood John, "
Sheery Patrick, "
Carey Daniel, Taunton
Conafy & McDonald, "
Goff T. P. "
Morse Jason, "
McDonnell Patrick, Watertown
Higgins N. C. Wellfleet
Bruce Brairard T., Jamaica Plain, West Roxbury
Jordan A. P. Worcester
O'Leary & Bro. "
Wellington H. B. "
Woodcock I. "

Hose Manufacturers.

(See Engine-Hose.)

Hosiery and Glove Dealers.

(See Gent's Furnishing Goods; also Dry Goods.)

Hosiery, Shirts, and Drawers Manufacturers.

Robbins & Everett, Brewster
Turner F. B. (fancy knit jackets), Brookline
Canton Woolen Mills, "
Neponset Hosiery Mills, (cotton and wool hosiery), Geo. R. Chandon, prop., South Canton, Canton
Sheldon George T. (cotton and woolen), North Chelmsford, Chelmsford
Chicopee Falls Hosiery Co. Chicopee Falls
Bamford Charles, Ipswich
Birch John, "
Dayton G. M. "
Glover J. S. (fancy hosiery), "
Burrows & Hunt (also head nets), "

Hosiery, Shirts, Drawers — continued.
Lawrence Manuf. Co. Lowell
CRANE & WATERS (also yarns
and zephyr worsteds), Millbury
Thompson James (hosiery and
mittens), Nantucket
Beless James & Son, Needham
Beless Thomas, "
Hall Chas. S. "
Hatch J. B. & Co. "
Lee Mark & John, "
Dudley Hosiery Co. Lower Falls, Newton
Wilson Jabez, Salem
Dalby Mills, Watertown

Hotels.

Abington
Centre Abington Hotel, H. Ferris, "
East Abington Hotel, Jacob Shaw,
2d, East Abington, "
Monument House, John E. Cutter, Acton
Railroad House, Levi Dow, South "
Greylock House, William G. Farns-
worth, Adams
BERKSHIRE HOUSE, Albert E.
Richmond, Main st. North Adams; "
Wilson House. Streeter & Rogers,
N. Adams, "
Amesbury
American House, Charles Tuttle, "
Amherst House. F. Kingman, Amherst
Union House, T. T. Sisson, "
Elm House, S. G. Bean, Andover
Mansion House, Charles Carter, "
Arlington House, W. H. Whitte-
more, Arlington
High Street House, Geo. Russell, "
Central House, W. R. Adams, Ashburnham
Cross Hotel, Lemuel Cross, Ashfield
Pleasant St. House, O. A. Wilcox, Ashland
SUMMIT HOUSE, Athol
PEQUOIG HOUSE, Adolphus
Bangs, Athol Depot. "
Hodges House, G. C. Hodges, Attleborough
RICHARDSON HOUSE, Chas.
Becker, North Attleborough, "
Barnstable
Globe Hotel, W. & E. H. Eldredge, "
Crosby's Hotel, Gorham Crosby, Cen-
treville, "
Sautuit House, James H. Coleman,
Cotuit, "
White House, E. C. White, Hyannis, "
Massasoit House, John F. Brooks, Barre
Naquag House, Cheney Hamilton, "
Bedford House, Wm. A. Putnam, Bedford
Belcher House, W. C. Owen, Belchertown
Union House, R. A. White, "
Draper's Hotel, Draper Bros. Berlin
Bernardston
New Eng. House, Henry C. Denham, "
Green J. W. Billerica
Blackstone
Lincoln House, E. Ormsbee & Co. "
Morey W. A., Millville, "
Union House, A. A. Wheelock, "
Boies E. W. Blandford
Hull Hotel, North Blandford, "
Bradford
Lafayette House, David C. Knowles, "
Ocean House, Benj. Fessenden, Brewster
Hyland House, W. G. Hull, Bridgewater
Brighton
BRIGHTON HOTEL, J. T. Wilson,
CATTLE FAIR HOTEL, T. H.
Brodrick, "
EASTERN MARKET HOTEL,
Dodavah Scates, "

Nagle Eugene, Brighton
Charles River Hotel, S. R. Perkins,
Brighton Corner, "
Brimfield Hotel, Amos Munroe, Brimfield
Wattawannuck House, Wm. Moulton,
East Brookfield, "
Franklin House, Arial Woodward,
Shelburne Falls, Buckland
Broadway House, J. C. Martain, Cam-
bridgeport, "
Union House, D. Stone, Cambridgeport, "
Fresh Pond House, O. C. Derby, "
Flanders Exchange, F. M. Flanders,
East Cambridge, "
Mansion House, W. Gavin, East Cam-
bridge, "
CAMBRIDGE MARKET HOTEL, F.
Locke, North Cambridge, "
Massapoag House, A. Richards, Canton
Ponkapoag House, DeForest Lewis, "
Charlemont
Franklin House, David A. Dalrymple, "
National House, J. Walker, Charlestown
Waverley House, Daniel Chamberlin, "
Nauset House, Isaiah Harding, Chatham
North Chelmsford Hotel, A. Waldo,
North Chelmsford. Chelmsford
City Hotel. J. Sweetzer, Chelsea
Continental Hotel, J. W. Hoffman, "
Trotier's Hotel, P. A. Trotier, Cheshire
Laselle. W. H. Chester
Chesterfield
Hayden's Hotel, Edson Hayden, "
Cabot House, Wm. H. Dickinson, Chicopee
Chicopee House, Everett M. Belden, "
Chapin House, A. P. Chapin, Chico-
pee Falls, "
Clinton House, F. M. Crossman, Clinton
Smith's Hotel, T. M. Smith, Cohasset
Coleraine House, O. M. Gaines, Coleraine
Middlesex Hotel, Marshall Davis, Concord
Conway Hotel, Wm. H. Orcutt, Conway
Cummington
Union House, Edmund M. Hunt, "
Eagle Hotel, John Chamberlin, Dalton
North Dana House, E. W. Shaw, North
Dana, Dana
Phoenix Hotel. J. D. Howe, Dedham
RE-UNION HOTEL, A. Klemm, "
Deerfield
Pocomtuck House, Charles O. Phillips, "
Bloody Brook House, A. Stetson, South
Deerfield, "
Sugar Loaf Mountain House, Granville
Wardwell, South Deerfield, "
Baker E. S. West Dennis, Dennis
Thayer Warren S. Milton, Dorchester
Neponset House, Nathan Holbrook, "
Nauset House, A. M. Horton, North
Eastham, Eastham
Easthampton
Mount Eyrie House, Mount Nonotuck, "
Union House. G. M. Fillebrown, "
Norton House, J. R. Norton, Edgartown
Ocean House, Damon Y. Norton, "
North Egremont Hotel, Elias Winchell,
North Egremont, Egremont
Mount Everett House, John Miller, "
South Egremont, "
Swift River House, A. M. Howard, Enfield
Erving House, A. Wall, Erving
Union Hotel. James Davis, Fairhaven
City Hotel, William B. Niles, Fall River
Mount Hope House, S. Hooper, "
National House, David Hurley, "
Wilbur House, Darius Wilbur, "
Union House, Falmouth
Hewins Wm. Wood's Hole, "

Waquoit House, Ichabod Childs, Waquoit, Falmouth
AMERICAN HOUSE, Joseph Waterhouse (see page 798), Fitchburg
Fitchburg Hotel, Wm. F. Day, "
Hoosac Tunnel House, Coolyard & Towers, Florida
Jencks & Rice, "
Cocasset House, T. E. Hancock, Foxboro'
Parker Orra, Framingham
Twitchell S. F. South Framingham, "
Franklin
FRANKLIN HOUSE, M. H. Johnson, "
STOCKWELL NELSON, South Gardner, Gardner
Pentucket House, Jos. Perry, Georgetown
American House, Peter Grant, Gloucester
Atlantic House, W. W. Sherburne, "
Pavilion Hotel (summer boarding), Allen Knowlton, "
Union House, George W. Floyd, "
WEBSTER HOUSE, Nathaniel Webster "
Highland House, Joseph Hawks, Goshen
Farnumsville Hotel, J. G. Nichols, Farnumsville, Grafton
Hathorn C. "
Quinsigamond House, N. E. Village, "
Union House, S. Crosby, East Granville, Granville
Moore's Hotel, G. E. Moore, Granville Corners, "
Exchange Hotel, H. H. Parsons, West Granville, "
Great Barrington
American House, A. Bright, "
Berkshire House, Elizabeth Pixley, "
Collins House, "
Ford Enos, Van Deusenville, "
Miller House, the Misses Holcomb, "
Union House, O. J. Brusie, "
American House, S. Simons, Greenfield
Mansion House, H. B. Stevens & Sons, "
Reed's Hotel, C. N. Reed, "
UNION HOUSE, John Cogan, "
Barrel Nelson D. Greenwich
Hay R. Greenwich Village, "
Central House, J. N. Hoar, Groton
Needham House, J. B. Spencer, Groton Junction, "
ROSS HOUSE, H. P. ROSS, Groton Junction, "
Shattuck C. H. Groton Junction, "
Thayer S. H. Hadley
Chebacco House, J. Whipple 2d, Hamilton
Hamilton House, Frederick B. Moore, "
Hanover House, Franklin Howard, Hanover
Hardwick House, A. C. Record, Hardwick
Harvard House, F. A. Willard, Harvard
Central House, E. Baker, Harwich
Atlantic House, E. Hopkins, Harwich Port, "
Hatfield House, L. S. Bliss, Hatfield
Haverhill
AMERICAN HOUSE, James Dewhirst, "
Eagle House, William Brown, "
Old Colony House, Hingham
DREW'S HOTEL, PHINEAS DREW, "
Hinsdale House, Mrs. C. Bottum, Hinsdale
RAILROAD HOUSE, Watson C. Livermore, "
Eagleville Hotel, E. F. Witt, Holden
Holyoke House, J. H. Ross, Holyoke
Sannosett House, M. E. Green, "
Craft's Hotel, Chester Crafts, Ireland, "
Winthrop House, J. Fuller & Sons, Holliston
Taft's Hotel, S. Taft, Hopkinton
Crystal House, S. B. Beaman, Hubbardston

Star Hotel, S. K. Savage, Hubbardston
Mansion House, Marshall Wood, Hudson
Beach House, J. & W. Beal, Hull
Mansion House, A. Vining, "
Nantasket House, Webster Hersey, "
Oregon House, Daniel Robbins, "
Rockland House, N. Ripley, "
White Head House, Pool & Lane, "
Parks House, John Parks, Huntington
Hyde Park
EVERETT HOUSE, O. C. Coffin, "
Agawam House, J. B. Eagan, Ipswich
EASTERN INTERNATIONAL HOUSE, Mrs. Mary D. Smith, "
Patuxet House, Josiah Cushman, Kingston
Sampson House, H. G. Carpenter, Lakeville
Lancaster House, J. Moore, Lancaster
North Lancaster House, C. Fairbanks, "
American House, John D. Hall, Lanesboro'
Lanesborough House, Chas. P. Munson, "
Lawrence
Commercial House, A. R. Ingham, "
ESSEX HOUSE, Geo. E. Ordway, prop., Essex st. "
FRANKLIN HOUSE, T. W. HUSE, Broadway, near the Depot, "
Jefferson House, Geo. Judd, "
LAWRENCE HOTEL, C. C. DEARBORN & SON, 255 to 259 Oak, "
Webster House, E. L. Webster, "
Strickland House, Watson Strickland, East Lee, Lee
Center Hotel, S. G. Mitchell, "
Morgan House, Edwin Morgan, "
SOUTH LEE HOTEL, J. T. Merrill & Co., South Lee, "
Union House, James Camwill, Clappville, Leicester
Wheeler S. S. "
Union House, J. S. Ryder, Cherry Valley, "
Curtis Hotel, Wm. O. Curtis, Lenox
Adair Charles, Lexington
Hancock House, C. H. Brown, "
Brown George D. Littleton
American House, Charles Going, Lowell
Central Hotel, G. W. Mark, "
City Hotel, Alden Lawrence, "
211 Middlesex, "
HOWARD HOUSE, Allen Waldo, "
Lafayette House, Thos. Heathwood, "
Merrimac House, H. Emery, "
Montgomery House, John Cusack, "
WASHINGTON HOUSE, B. Thurston, Central, cor. Church, "
Wamesit House, S. T. Dresser, "
Central House, Andrew Derby, Lunenburg
CENTRAL HOUSE, E. L. P. Martin, 9 Washington (see page 706), Lynn
Columbian House, Chas. F. Clark, "
Railroad House, James Hudson, "
Sagamore House, Wm. C. Thompson, "
Lynn Hotel, Moody Dow, West Lynn, "
Lynnfield Hotel, Chas. H. Poole, Lynnfield
Pratt's Hotel, John Pratt, Malden
Manchester Hotel, A. Peabody, Manchester
Pratt House, A. H. Townsend, Mansfield
Marblehead
Forsyth House, George W. Forsyth, "
Bay View House, J. S. Luce, Marion
Marion House, T. C. Miles, "
Gates House, M. Page, Marlborough
Marlboro' Hotel, W. H. Leighton, "
Webster House, Calvin Estes, Marshfield
Seaside House, Mattapoisett
Medford House, A. J. Emerson, Medford
Medway
Quinobequin House, C. A. Hayward, "

Hotels — continued.

Adams House, David Adams, Mendon
Mendon Hotel, Alvin T. Staples, "
                                     Methuen
Exchange Hotel, Silas K. Batchelder, "
Methuen House, J. R. Jones, "
                            Middleborough
NEMASKET HOTEL, P. E. Penniman, "
Mansion House, Lewis Fisher, Milford
Quinshapaug House, "
Millbury Hotel, C. A. Tourtelot, Millbury
Clark's Hotel, Wm. H. Clark, Milton
Monson Hotel, H. H. Parks, Monson
Lake House, Freeman Hager, Grout's
  Corner, Montague
Wildes' Hotel, A. F. Wildes, "
Tryon's Hotel, Albert Tryon, Monterey
Hood Cottage, Charles S. Pitman, Nahant
Village Hotel, Albert Whitney, "
Ocean House, R. H. Cook, Nantucket
Bailey Goin, South Natick, Natick
Lake Shore House, "
Summer Street House, W. G. Leonard, "
Mallery V. B. New Ashford
GERMAN HOTEL, Geo. Langguth,
  4 Hall's ct., near William, New Bedford
MANSION HOUSE, Louis Bontell, 87
  Union (see page 759),
Mariners' Home, Harrison G. Nye, "
Parker House, Bullock & Brownell, "
Sampson House, John Gawith, "
Sheridan House, John L. Cook, "
St. James Hotel, S. S. Manchester, "
New Braintree Temperance House,
  David Witherell, New Braintree
Plum Island Hotel, Smith Bros., Newbury
                      Newburyport
American House, Daniel Hamblet, "
Eagle House, J. W. Sliney, "
Essex House, Wm. B. Wentworth, "
La Fontaine House, S. B. Noyes, "
MERRIMAC HOUSE, Moses S. Little, "
New England House, Geo. Bushey, "
Ocean House, B. F. Atkinson, "
Wright House, N. Tuttle, New Marlboro'
Rogers' Hotel, W. Rogers, Mill River, "
New Salem House, E. Haskins, New Salem
Millington House, Millington, "
North New Salem House, Moses Her-
  rick, North New Salem, "
Cate S. Lower Falls, Newton
Nonantum House, Newton Corner, "
Cashman A. H., West Newton, "
Florence Hotel, E. L. Abercrombie,
  Florence, Northampton
Gold Wing House, S. R. Mathewson, "
Mansion House, C. F. Simonds, "
Prospect House, on Mt. Holyoke,
  John H. French, "
ROUND HILL WATER CURE AND
  HOTEL, Hatfield Halsted, M.D. "
Springdale Home for Invalids, E. E.
  Denniston, M.D. "
Warner House, C. F. Simonds, "
                      Northborough
Assabet House, Daniel C. Paige, "
North Bridgewater Hotel, Washburn
  & Grover, North Bridgewater
Atlantic Hotel, G. W. Luke, North Chelsea
Cove House, G. Wilkinson, "
Dale House, A. W. Emerson, "
Gurney's Hotel, William Gurney, "
Neptune House, J. Nason, "
Ocean House, Tarleton & West, "
Pavilion, J. O. Young, "
Robinson Crusoe House, Aaron W.
  Emerson, "
Rockaway, A. L. Armor, "

Northfield Hotel, T. B. Mattoon, Northfield
Mansion House, John H. Short, Norton
Bemis James C. Oakham
Franklin House, A. P. Putnam, Orange
Higgins House, James Chandler, Orleans
Otis Hotel, Rufus Smith, Otis
East Otis Hotel, Henry Jackson, East "
Alexander House, B. F. Sibley, Oxford
Antique House, E. B. Shaw, Palmer
Bullock Samuel J. Three Rivers, "
Nassowanno House, J. W. Weeks
  & Co. "
Palmer House, N. B. Royce, "
Summit House, Wm. W. Dodd, Paxton
Naumkeag House, H. W. Moore, Peabody
SIMONDS WASHINGTON, Peabody
  square, "
Prescott House, Charles F. Gilson,
  East Pepperell, Pepperell
AMERICAN HOUSE, C. Quacken-
  bush, Pittsfield
BURBANK HOUSE, A. Burbank, "
Farmer's Hotel, J. M. Anthony, "
Parker House, W. C. Fuller, "
Clifford House, A. & N. C. Hoxie, Plymouth
Davie House, Mrs. L. A. Bramhall, "
Manomet House. H. B. Holmes,
  South Plymouth, "
Samoset House, James S. Parker, "
Winslow House, David Seavey, "
Mountain House, S. B. Beaman, Princeton
Prospect House, I. F. Thompson, "
Wachusett House, P. A. Beaman, "
Pilgrim House, E. Hallett, Provincetown
Great Hill House, J. Mears, Quincy
Hancock House, John T. Willey, "
New Squantum House, T. Saunders, "
Old Squantum House, Reed Bros. "
Railroad House, Mrs. J. A. Durgan, "
Willard House, John McGowan, "
                      Randolph
Howard House, Chas. Easterbrooks, "
Railroad Exchange, J. Dooley jr. "
Sheridan House, Geo. Doe, Rockport
Pigeon Cove House, Mrs. E. S.
  Robinson, Pigeon Cove, "
Eagle House, Edward Smith, Rowley
Russell House, Lewis Herrick, Russell
ESSEX HOUSE, J. S. Leavitt,
  176 Essex, Salem
Montville House, Seth Seymour,
  Montville, Sandisfield
Hunt's Hotel, Charles H. Hunt,
  New Boston, "
Central House, Z. F. Chadwick, Sandwich
Harper's Hotel, Wm. H. Harper, "
West Sandwich House, M. Scott,
  West Sandwich, "
Ballard House, John G. Elder, East
  Saugus, Saugus
Green Mountain House, Calvin
  Bowker, Savoy
South Shore House, Mrs. Mary A.
  Torrey, Scituate
Glades House, —— Miller, Cohasset, "
Cobb's Tavern, Warren Cobb, Sharon
Lake House, Mrs. James Capen, "
Berkshire Soda Springs House,
  Chas. E. Botsford, Sheffield
Miller Stephen R. "
Ashley Falls Hotel, Wm. S. Ferris,
  Ashley Falls, "
East Sheffield, Mrs. Wm. M. Peck,
  East Sheffield, "
Franklin House, E. Woodward,
  Shelburne Falls, Shelburne
Shelburne Falls House, Cole &
  Lampman, Shelburne Falls, "

Davis Henry, Shirley
Washington House, J. G. Reed, Shutesbury
Mount Mineral Springs, C. A. Perry,
  Lock's Village, "
Sownunset House, W. W. Moore, Somerset
Willow Bridge House, Benj. Doughty,
  North Somerville, Somerville
Graves Lewis W. Southampton
Edwards House, M. Morse, Southbridge
  South Hadley
Smith's Hotel, Nelson Smith & Son, "
Hadley Falls Hotel, C. C. Barrett,
  South Hadley Falls, "
Half-Way House, Oliver Kimball,
  West Scituate, South Scituate
  Southwick
Southwick Hotel, Martin Taylor, "
Exchange Hotel, Brigham Sibley, Spencer
Watson House, J. S. Burgess, "
ALLIS HOUSE, S. R. Coburn, Springfield
Carlton House, A. Hanrahan, "
COOLEY'S HOTEL, J. M. Cooley, "
Exchange Hotel, E. Adams & Co. "
GRUENDLER'S HOTEL, Gruendler
  Brothers, "
HAMPDEN HOUSE, J. B. Frasier, "
Haynes Hotel, Curtis & Bowman, "
Massasoit House, M. & E. S. Chapin, "
Meagher P. "
Nayasset House, J. S. Robinson, "
Pynchon House, N. H. Chandler, "
Rockingham House, Aaron Nason, "
Sanford St. House, Bailey & Terrill, "
Springfield House, Augustus Sheppert, "
Union House, Leander Hall, "
United States Hotel, G. Burbach, "
Indian Orchard Hotel, C. C. Dodge,
  Indian Orchard, "
Sulphur Springs Hotel, Samuel
  Pease, Indian Orchard, "
Central Hotel, Lucien J. Priest, Sterling
Stockbridge House, Hiram Heaton,
  jr. (summer), Stockbridge
Central House, C. B. Melvin, Stoneham
Chemung House, I. F. Tower, Stoughton
DRAKE LEONARD, "
Briggs Hotel, Ezekiel Briggs, East "
Glendale House, James Boyd, Stow
Holden George T. C. Assabet, "
  Sturbridge
Central Hotel, Farmer Southwick, "
Fiskdale House, James Parker,
  Fiskdale. "
Annawan House, M. L. Rogers, Swampscott
Lincoln House, S. H. Wardwell, "
Little Annawan, Wm. B. Blany, "
Ocean House, E. N. Wardwell, "
Village House, Wm. H. Fletcher, "
Case Joseph, Swansea Village, Swansea
Graham Henry, North Swansea, "
Athenaeum Hotel, G. A. White jr. Taunton
Britanniaville Hotel, Allen Frazier, "
CITY HOTEL, A. L. Bliss, "
Exchange Hotel, Thomas P. Goff, "
Westminster Hotel, H. N. White, "
Grove Hotel, S. B. Upham, Templeton
Baldwinsville Hotel, Baldwinsville, "
Otter-River House, J. G. Goldsmith,
  Otter River, "
Mansion House, Leander West, Tisbury
Parkinson John, Topsfield
Topsfield House, Alphonso Munday, "
  Townsend
Adams Henry J. Townsend Harbor, "
Davis Thomas, West Townsend, "
Clark Horace M., Townsend Centre, "
Railroad House, John E. Terrell, "
Batchelor Daniel W. West Upton, Upton

Wacantuck House, S. T. Lovett, Uxbridge
Central House, S. R. Cook, Waltham
Prospect House, William H. Scott, "
Ware Hotel, J. B. Gould, Ware
Hartwell Hotel, Osgood & Son, "
  Wareham
Thompson's Hotel, David Thompson, "
  Warren
WARREN HOTEL, C. S. Hitchcock, "
  Warwick
Warwick House, Forrest Goldsbury, "
Spring Hotel, S. L. Batcheldor, Watertown
Pequod House, T. H. Simpson, Wayland
Joslin House, H. I. Joslin, Webster
Sheldon House, J. R. Johnson, "
  Wellfleet
Holbrook's Hotel, Henry A. Holbrook, "
Thayer J. A. Westborough
Westborough Hotel, Thomas Tucker, "
Valley Hotel, A. Harper, West Boylston
Oakdale House, J. S. Cutting, Oak-
  dale, "
Smith N. M. West Brookfield
Wickaboag House, J. W. Wood, "
Foster House, Mrs. N. S. Foster, Westfield
Hampden House, S. Birge, "
Railroad House, J. G. Buschmann, "
Westfield House, I. S. Wood, "
Woronoco House, Jas. S. Pickard, "
Union House, Westford
Westminster Hotel, Ferdinand Dick-
  inson, Westminster
Adams House, A. G. Smith, West Newbury
Fremont House, Thos. L. Tyler, "
Union Hotel, West Roxbury
Agawam House, Theo. Demond, Mit-
  tineague, West Springfield
Eagle Hotel, H. Bartholomew, "
West Springfield House, John Bannon, "
  West Stockbridge
American House, Lewis E. Rogers, "
STATE LINE, Silas L. Church,
  State Line, "
West Stockbridge House, J. C. Hare, "
Weymouth Hotel, A. B, Wales, Weymouth
Mansion House, H. D. Blanchard, So.
  Weymouth, "
Williamsburg Hotel, J. Hayden
  & Son, Williamsburg
Haydenvilla Hotel, Byron Loomis,
  Haydenville, "
Mansion House, A. G. Bailey, Williamstown
  Winchendon
American House, J. H. Fairbanks, "
Taft's Hotel, O. A. Taft, Winthrop
Central House, Frank Wetherbee, Woburn
Bay State House, Geo. Thrall, Worcester
Exchange Hotel, R. Lamb, "
Farmer's Hotel, J. G. Witherbee, "
Swan's Hotel, E. Swan, "
Waldo House, R. N. & L. B. Start. "
  Worthington
Bartlett's Hotel, Jacob M. Bartlett, "
Worthington Star Hotel, Emory
  H. Bruce,
SEARS HOUSE, R. E. HOLMES,
  Yarmouthport, Yarmouth

House Furnishing Goods.

(See also Hardware; also Wooden Ware.)

Moore Wm. B. & Son, Charlestown
KNOX BENJ. H. & CO., 45 and
  47 Park, Chelsea
NEWHALL BENJAMIN E. Danvers
Haynes George & Son, Milton, Dorchester
BAIRD OTIS, Neponset, "
Flint J. D. & Co. Fall River

House Furnishing Goods — continued.
Nichols L. & Co.   Fall River
ROBBINS HENRY T.   Great Barrington
APPLETON JOHN A. Jr.   Haverhill
Stark C. C.   Hyde Park
NASH J. W. & CO., 105 Central
   (see page 739),   Lowell
WELCH JACOB & CO., 1 Sagamore
   Hotel,   Lynn
Harris Moses & Co.   Milford
Judson, Sawtelle, & Co.   "
                             New Bedford
ALLEN & BLISS, 121 Union,   "
Bennett Samuel,   "
Lewis Nathan,   "
SULLINGS & KINGMAN, 123 Union, "
Taylor H. J.   "
Dutton & Pearson,   Pittsfield
Grant & Davis,   "
Hoard N. S.   Taunton
Washburn Edward E.   "

Husk Manufacturers.
Porter Brothers,   Deerfield

Hydraulic Presses.
Cook, Rymes, & Co.   Charlestown
KILBURN, LINCOLN, & CO. (see
   page 756),   Fall River

Ice Cream.
SMITH CHARLES, 61 Lime (see
   page 752),   Newburyport

Ice Crushers.
Richardson Mill Co.   .   Gloucester

Ice Dealers.
Noyes Lorenzo D.   Abington
Collins C. H.   East Abington,   "
Orr John,   North Adams,   Adams
Willey G. W.   Athol Depot,   Athol
Raymond Benjamin C.   Beverly
Prescott Wm. G., East Braintree, Braintree
Pratt Z.   No. Middleboro', Bridgewater
Eames H. H. & Son,   Cambridge
Chase & Horn,   Cambridgeport,   "
Boston Ice Co.   E. Cambridge,   "
Dean Oliver,   Canton
Boston Ice Co.   Charlestown
Gage Addison & Co.   "
Hittinger Jacob,   "
Tudor Co.   "
Putnam Otis,   Danvers
Fisher Amory,   Dedham
King & Nason,   Dorchester
Jenkins Merritt,   East Bridgewater
Stephens & Eldredge,   Fairhaven
COOK & DURFEE, No. Main,
   cor. Central (see page 757),   Fall River
Watuppa Ice Co., W. H. Gray, agt.   "
Young William,   "
Eames E., S. Framingham, Framingham
Day Abraham,   Gloucester
Williams S. E. & Co.   "
WEBSTER NATHANIEL,   "
Story Chas., jr. East Gloucester,   "
Jourdan G. F.   Grafton
Whitney George,   Hingham
Leland G. T.   Holliston
Rice S.   Hudson
Tripp Bros.   "
Holmes John F.   Kingston
Barker Chas. W.   Lawrence
McFarlin A.   "
McFarlin W. & L.   Lowell
Barker & Co.   Lynn
Porter B. F. & Co.   "

Wyer Albert,   Lynn
Brigham John W.   Marlborough
Howes Marshall,   Mattapoisett
Stimpson & Emerson (wholesale), Melrose
Bullard J. P.   Milford
Hall Asa,   Millbury
Burgess R. E.   Nantucket
Messenger J. B.   Natick
Ashley & Terry (wholesale), New Bedford
Hawes Simeon,   "
Howland Warren (wholesale),   "
Rodman B.   "
SMITH CHARLES, 61 Lime (see
   page 752),   Newburyport
Woods Charles W.   "
Cleveland Walter F.   North Bridgewater
Bancroft Sidney C.   Peabody
Beede I. S.   "
Guilds Gerry & Co.   Pittsfield
ROOT & BURNS,   "
Eaton Jacob F.   ..   Quincy
Prescott W. G.   "
Clark Josiah,   Randolph
Manning J. J.   Rockport
Haskell George,   Salem
Julyn C. R.   "
Pray R. & Son, Amesbury,   Salisbury
Stiles M. O.   "   "
Pope C. E. & E. T.   Sandwich
Springfield Ice Co.   Springfield
Taber J. D.   Stoughton
Williams Julius,   Taunton
Dyer Samuel,   Truro
Howard Brothers,   Waltham
Howard Brothers,   Watertown
Higgins Justus,   Wellfleet
Rich Mulford,   "
Goodale Aaron,   West Boylston
Tisdale Mace,   West Bridgewater
Hull Hiram,   Westfield
Lovell Solomon, N. Weymouth, Weymouth
Smith E. W.   S.   "   "
Walker & Sweetser,   Worcester
Arey Thomas,   Yarmouth Port
Hallett Nathan, .   "

Ice Tool Manufacturers.
                                  Cambridge
Cutter J. Harris & Co. N. Cambridge, "
PETTINGILL JOSEPH R. Brighton
   at. (see page 709),.   "
Cook, Rymes, & Co.   .   Charlestown

India Rubber Goods.
(See Rubber Goods.)

Ink Manufacturers.
Morrill Geo. & Co. (printers'), South
   Dedham,   Dedham
Leonard T. (writing),   Grafton
Bonney William E.   Hanover
Lummis T. J. (boot and shoe),   Lynn
Billings J. T. & Co. (mauve),   Lowell
POPE T. W. (boot and shoe, see
   page 769),   North Bridgewater
WASHBURN ELISHA (boot
   and shoe, see page 792),   "
Packard E. & Co. (boot and shoe,) Quincy
Union Paper Co.   Springfield
DUNBAR S. O. & SON (see page
   761),   Taunton

Ink Stands, Stamps, &c.
                                  Cambridge
Hudson Thomas S.   E. Cambridge,   "

Inspectors.
Howlett E. J. (milk),   Cambridge

Case Allen (oil), New Bedford
Holbrook Gideon (fish), Plymouth
Rust Geo. P. (fish), Salem

Instrument Makers.

Ritchie E. S. &. Sons (philosophical), Brookline
Pool H. M. (mathematical), Easton
Kelley James S. (nautical), New Bedford
Sherman C. R. & Co. "   "

Insurance Agents.

HOWLAND F. P. (fire and life) Abington
Pierce Henry B. (life), "
Cutter John E. Acton
Wetherbee J. K. W. South Acton, "
HUTCHINS I. (Berkshire Life), West Acton,
UPTON DANIEL, Adams
Porter Wm. P. (fire and life), N, Adams, '
Tinker A. M. (fire), "
Whitaker Ezra D. "   "
Briggs & Stone, Amesbury
Adams J. S. & C. Amherst
Allen G. W. (life), "
Cook W. S. "
Leland J. M. H. "
Humphrey Henry M. Athol
HUNT H. B. Athol Depot, "
BASSETT C. C. (Berkshire Life), "   "
STARKEY L. T. (see page 713), Attleboro'
Rice Henry, North Attleborough, "
Lothrop Ansel D. Barnstable
Washburn John P. "
BATES S. E. (Berkshire Life), Barre
Elliott A. N. "
Rice David, "
Wadsworth Joseph D. "
Wheeler Augustus, "
Woods Edwin, "
Bidwell Henry A. Becket
PRENTISS N. A. (Berkshire Life), "
Longley S. W. Belchertown
PORTER SAMUEL, Beverly
PUTNAM A. A. Blackstone
Tatlock William, "
Frasier Jos. R. (fire), Braintree
Kingman B W. S. Braintree, "
Kingman Philip D. Bridgewater
Trowbridge S. W. (fire and life), Brighton
SEVER, FRANCIS, & CO. Harvard sq., Cambridge
BIRD & WHITTEMORE, 433 Main, Cambridgeport, "
BUCKLEY DANIEL A. 433 Main, Cambridgeport, "
Sawyer J. S. Cambridgeport, "
Webber John H. "
Hastings, Kinsley, & Co. E. Cambridge, "
Mansfield Wm. Canton
Saunders G. W. "
Wood R. C. "
Abbott William, Charlestown
Benn J. C. "
Bradford Duncan, "
Brown Benjamin F. "
Kendall Isaac B. "
Miller William H. "
Shedd A. B. "
Slack D. E. "
Gerrish William, "
Gould Jesse & Son, Chelsea
Merriam E. L. "
MERRIAM OTIS, 5 Gerrish Block, (see page 714), "
RUGG ERASTUS, 101 Winnisimmet, "
Van Horn G. W. Chicopee Falls, Chicopee
Holcomb E. V. B. "

Dame John T. Clinton
Stevens Charles G. "
Tapley George, Danvers
Tapley D. J. "
Ames William, 2d, Dedham
Guild Francis, "
Hildreth Henry O. "
Sumner Myrick E. "
Baker H. B. South Dedham, "
Capen Thomas W. Dorchester
Hall Oliver, "
Bispham E. J. Milton,
Blanchard H. W. Neponset, "
TEMPLE THOS. F. "
Chamberlain Joseph (fire), E. Bridgewater
Keith B. W. (fire), "
Mitchell George T. (life), "
OSBORNE WM. H. (fire), "
Wheeler Geo. A. (life), "
Reed Charles. H. "
Carlisle Geo. M. Easton
EASTON & MILNE, 14 N. Main, Fall River
Eddy Morton, "
GREENE WM. S. 14 Pleasant, "
REMINGTON HALE (fire, life, & accident), Main, cor. Pocasset, "
Slade John P. "
Winslow B. F. "
Warren Edward, (life), "
Currier & Whitney, Fitchburg
Childs S. A. "
Daniel George T. "
Hildreth L. H. "
Piper J. L. & H. F. "
Walker William S. (life), "
Carpenter J. E. Foxborough
Smith Isaac (life & life), "
Thomas Wm. A. (fire & life), "
Adams C. S. Framingham
Esty C. C. "
Hastings Wm. "
Bill B. J. Saxonville, "
Cleaves Levi, Gloucester
Stacy Samuel A. "
Faulkner Winthrop, Grafton
Joyner H. C. Great Barrington
Seeley Isaac, "
WOODWORTH E. P. (Berkshire Life), "
Buddington H. A. Greenfield
Childs H. S. "
DAVIS & DEWOLF (fire and life), "
Eliot Wm. "
Lyons S. J. "
MATTOON & WILLIAMS, (fire), "
Brock J. C. Groton Junction, Groton
BOYNTON DAVID, Haverhill
CAVERLY & FRANKLE 4 Exchange "
GOODELL WALTER, 5 Chase block, "
Kittredge Alfred, "
Seymour Charles W. Hingham
Adams Wm. Hinsdale
Fiske Geo. B. (fire and life), Holliston.
Johnson R. B. "
UNDERWOOD PORTER, " Holyoke
Woolcott C. B. (life), "
Fitch J. A. Hopkinton
Meserve C. "
Woodbury A. H. "
JOSLIN JAMES T. Hudson
Rawson Geo. S. "
Bradbury S. A. Hyde Park
Esty W. F. "
Davis Enoch T. Readville, "
Ambrose N. Lawrence
Bourne B. T. "
Chadwick Alonzo C. (fire and life), "
Currier E. B. "
Edwards John, "

18

Insurance Agents — continued.

Joplin & Bugbee,   Lawrence
Mack A. E.   "
NORWOOD JOHN K. 130 Essex
  and 1 Pemberton (general insurance),   "
ROLLINS CHARLES E. 145 Essex,   "
STANNARD J. H. over Bay State
  National Bank, general insurance),   "
Swan D. S. & Son,   "
PEASE A. H. (Berkshire Life),   Lee
Denny J. A.   Leicester
Waterman A. J. (fire),   Lenox
Carter Chauncey W.   Leominster
Merriam Charles H.   "
COOK JAMES, 49 Central,   Lowell
DAVIS JOHN, 55 Central,   "
Davis Joseph B. & Son,   "
Devlyn John S.   "
Elliott Geo. M.   "
Folsom Jeremiah S.   "
Hunt Geo. F.   "
HUNT & ELLIOTT (Berkshire Life),   "
Litchfield G. A.   "
MERRILL JOSHUA, 37 Merrimac,   "
NORCROSS N. W. 4 Barrister's Hall,   "
OLIVER ANDREW Jr. 11 Barrister's
  Hall,   "
Page I. Henry,   "
RIPLEY GEORGE, 10 Middle,   "
SHERMAN EDWARD F. 27 Central,   "
Stickney S. W.   "
Walker George W.   "
Wheeler F. W.   "
YORK EDWARD L., Mass. State
  agent for Security Life Insurance
  Co., N. Y., 11 Barrister's Hall,   "
Batcheller E. Q.   Lynn
BUBIER JOHN H. 91 Market,   "
Gray John E.   "
Hill Newell,   "
Hilton John,   "
Hoag G. C.   "
Johnson Wm. F.   "
Kimball Chas. E.   "
Meader Valentine,   "
Newhall W. F.   "
Oliver James,   "
Sargeant Geo. D.   "
Silsbee & Pickford,   "
Thompson Waldo,   "
                                      Malden
MERRILL CHARLES (life and fire),   "
Gentlee Thomas P.   Manchester
Sawyer Charles,   Mansfield
Shepard S.   "
Colman Benjamin,   Marblehead
Trefry Samuel,   "
ALDRICH S. N.   Marlborough
Ellis George A.   "
Warren W. M.   "
WHITNEY E. C.   "
Hamant Charles,   Medfield
Angier Luther,   Medford
Farwell Luther,   "
Hall J. P.   "
HAYES BENJ. F.   "
Sparrell John,   "
FISHER M. M.   Medway
Collins T. C. (life),   Middleboro'
BEALS J. E. (Berkshire Life),   "
Cook L. H.   Milford
Holbrook Leander,   "
PARKER GEORGE G. (see page
  783), 2 Washington block,   "
READE LAWRENCE, 72 Main (see
  page 782),   "
Barney Wm. M.   Nantucket
Macy George W.   "

Mitchell William B.   Nantucket
Swain Joseph B.   "
Whitney Andrew,   "
Hollis E. P.   Natick
NUTT WILLIAM,   "
Shattuck J. N. (life),   "
Smith Nathaniel,   "
Almy Charles,   New Bedford
COOK SAMUEL H. (life, marine,
  and accident), 37 No. Water,   "
GILMAN F. L. (fire, life, and accident,
  43 No. Water,   "
Grinnell Lawrence,   "
James Thomas M.   "
TAYLOR Wm. H. (life, fire, and
  marine), 37 No. Water,   "
TILLINGHAST JOSEPH S. (fire),
  44 No. Water,   "
Turner Chas. W.   "
Van Campen Hiram,   "
Webb Hiram,   "
Carter B. F.   Newburyport
Griffith Thomas,   "
Pearson John L.   "
Sawyer Albert P. (life),   "
Bacon Geo. W., Newton Corner,   Newton
Holman Edward,   "   "
Brigham C.   Auburndale,
Allen H. F.   Newtonville,
Davis Seth,   West Newton,
Mead John,   "
Wheeling Loring, Upper Falls,   "
Allen & Pratt,   Northampton
Kirkland Henry,   "
PECK A. PERRY,   "
Pray & Edwards,   "
Lyman Luke (life),   "
Haywood S. A.   North Bridgewater
PERKINS & WINSHIP,   "
Puffer L. W.   "
De Land Luther P.   North Brookfield
Haskell Wm. J.   "
Skery Samuel H.   "
Pease Wm. E.   Oxford
Allen & Gardner (fire and life),   Palmer
Blair Joseph H. (life and fire),   "
Pool Fitch,   Peabody
DUNHAM J. N. & CO. (life, fire,
  &c.),   Pittsfield
Hart F. W. (life),   "
HOWE SAMUEL E. (life, fire, &c.),   "
Lamberson S. L. (life),   "
Mann C. S.   "
SANDYS E. F.   "
TAYLOR E. R. (Berkshire Mutual
  Life Insurance Co., see page 710),   "
VAN WART IRVING, Jr., Root's
  block (see page 712),   "
Danforth Wm. S.   Plymouth
HALL JOHN T.   "
Gifford James,   Provincetown
Gifford S. S.   "
Greene David (life and fire),   Quincy
Spear Horace B.   "
Alden Hiram C.   Randolph
Belcher J. White,   "
Hawes S. E.   "
Mann Seth, 2d,   "
Turner R. W.   "
Adams John,   East Randolph,   "
ARCHER WILLIAM, 34 Front and
  18 Washington sts.   Salem
Brown Henry A.   "
Derby John H. (life, fire, &c.),   "
Johnson Thomas H.   "
Mackintire S. A.   "
Nichols Charles S.   "
Northey William,   "

HALL CHARLES B. (fire), Sandwich
Benedict L. B. Sheffield
Dutcher Henry, "
Bowen A . Shelburne Falls, Shelburne
Duffin H. M. " "
Field Z. W. " "
Hayes G. B. " "
Dresser Sylvester, Southbridge
Botham F. W. "
Stone Emerson, Spencer
Burt Augustine & Co. Springfield
Chapin & Lee, "
Cooledge Augustus (life), "
DONNELLY HUGH, "
Fish W. L. (Continental Life, of N.Y.), "
Geer & Winslow, "
Gilmore H. G. (travellers'), "
Hall John A. (life), "
Hill Geo. J. (Phœnix Life, of Hartford), "
HOLMES J. W., 1 Union block, "
Johnson James L. (Continental Life, of Hartford, Conn.), "
Ladd R. E. & C. R. "
Lee M. C. "
Miller Henry D. (life), "
Moseley H. E. " "
Porter J. M & Co. "
Pynchon & Marsh, "
RICE & FULLER & CO., State, cor. Main, "
Sedgwick J. S. "
TIFFT L. A. "
WARRINER S. C. (fire), "
WATERMAN & BOWE (Mutual Life, of New York), "
DUNHAM HENRY J. Stockbridge
Curtis Jesse, Stoneham
Farrar Amasa, "
Gerry Ira, "
Paul S. & A. Stoughton
Hill Philip E. Taunton
Kelley Jeremiah, "
Muenscher William, "
Pratt Hiram A. "
Rhodes & Mitchell, "
Stone James L. "
Washburn Isaac, "
Williams S. A. "
Deane Francis, Uxbridge
Hobbs George W. "
French Daniel, Waltham
Johnson B. B. "
Smith S. W. "
Sprague Wm. G. "
Viles Daniel F. "
FENN GEO. C. (life, accident, &c.), Ware
Lane Otis, "
CLEARY T. C. (life), "
Hayden Joseph P. "
Lincoln Wm. & Co. Wareham
Brown F. D. Warren
Joslin H. I. Webster
Stockwell J. H. "
HIGGINS J. R. Wellfleet
Fletcher Wm. O. Westfield
Fuller Henry, "
Gillett & Stevens, "
Leonard Norman T. (fire), "
Rand Asa P. (general), "
Whitney Milton B. "
West Roxbury
Phillips George J., Jamaica Plain, "
Foye John O. Weymouth
Beals E. S., North Weymouth, "
Pierce L. W. (life and fire), Winchendon
Horton Sparrow (fire and life), Woburn
Porter B. T. H. "
Barbour L. R. jr. Worcester

Barbour Wm. C. Worcester
Beach H. jr. "
Burnham Louis W. "
Carpenter J. P. "
DENNY WM. S. & Co. (fire), 237 Main, "
Estabrook & Smith, "
Goodwin Wm. S. (life), "
Hayden F. M. "
Howland E. P. (fire), "
Howland S. A. (fire, life, &c.), "
Knox J. B. "
Nichols J. "
Parker A. M. "
POND O N. & CO., 8 Front Street Exchange, "
Parks L. C. "
Putnam Chas. L. (fire), "
Putnam John J. (life), "
Russell E. H. "
Scofield J. M. (life), "
Streeter Leonard, " "
Washburn John D. (fire), "
Whipple Franklin (life and accident), "
Williams Hartley (N. E. Mutual Life), "

Intelligence Offices.

Dalton P. R. Mrs. Charlestown
Smith Thomas B. Fall River
Fletcher Horatio, Lowell
Morgan Ebenezer, "
Winton John Mrs. "
Merrill P. M. Miss, Lynn
Bermingham C. Salem
Byrne Anna Mrs. "
Farnsworth E. S. Springfield
Ryan P. J. "
Giles Abby Taunton
BROWNE E. J. MRS., 236 Main, Worcester
Cowdin M. H. "
Elliott G. "
Rogers H. S. "
Sweeney T. "

Iron and Steel·

(See also Hardware and Cutlery.)

Willard & Mason, Fall River
Treat James A. & Co. Lawrence
Butcher John, Lowell
PEIRCE JOHN W. (hoop iron, see page 757), 99 So. Water, New Bedford
Watkins William, "
Brown Ebenezer, Palmer
Dutton & Peirson, Pittsfield
Shelburne
NEWELL BROS. Shelburne Falls, "
BEMIS, PHILLIPS, & CO. Springfield
FOOT HOMER & CO., Main c: State, "
STAPLES & PHILLIPS (pig, see page 759), 27 West Water, Taunton
Washburn Edward E. "
Foster C. & Co. Worcester
Pratt & Inman, "

Iron Builders.

Springfield
THE AMERICAN CORRUGATED IRON CO., Geo. Dwight, jr., treas. Goodrich block, (see page 780), "

Iron Fences and Railings.

(See also Iron Manufacturers, etc.)

HEALD S. & SONS (see pages 796 and 797), Barre
ROLLSTONE MACHINE WORKS, (see page 709), Fitchburg
Mack Sewall G. Lowell

Iron Fences, Railings —continued.
FOUNDRY & MACHINE CO., H.
S. Fairbanks, treas. and agent,
(see page 692),   Taunton
WHEELER W. A. (see page 702),
42 Thomas,   Worcester

Iron Founders.

(See also Iron Manufacturers; also Stoves.)

Champney Jonas C.   Adams
HUNTER JAMES & SON, (see
   page 770), North Adams,   "
WHEELER DELIVERANCE, Otis
   J. Hodge, agent (see page 786),
   North Adams,   "
Houghton D. W. (castings), Athol
   Depot,   Athol
HEALD STEPHEN & SONS (cast-
   ings of all kinds, see pages 796
   and 797),   Barre
Bent George W.   Hyannis,   Barnstable
LAZELL, PERKINS, & CO.   Bridgewater
Perkins Henry,   "
Moulton Jesse,   E. Brookfield, Brookfield
    Cambridge
Allen & Endicott,   Cambridgeport,   "
Broadway Iron Foundry, H. M. Bird,
   propr. Cambridgeport,   "
KINSLEY LYMAN & CO. Hamp-
   shire st. (see page 714), Cam-
   bridgeport,   "
Metropolitan Iron Foundry, Tobey
   & Co.   Cambridgeport,   "
Shawmut Iron Works,   "   "
Tobey Curtis,   "   "
KINSLEY IRON & MACHINE CO.
   (see page 730),   Canton
REED FRANKLIN (small machine
   castings, see page 793),   "
Pratt M. & Co.   North Carver,   Carver
Ellis M. & Co.   South   "   "
Codding & Osgood,   Charlestown
Chelmsford Foundry Co. N. Chelms-
   ford,   Chelmsford
Bisbee, Endicott, & Co.   Chelsea
Magee Furnace Co.   "
Bryant Royal & Bros., W. Chester-
   field,   Chesterfield
Belcher & Taylor Agricultural Tool
   Co.   Chicopee Falls,   Chicopee
Palmer G. M.   Clinton
Thomas A. L.   Coleraine
Moxam A. W.   Shattuckville,   "
Brown Charles P.   Cummington
    Dedham
Draper E. D. & Co.   West Dedham,   "
CODDING J. D. & CO. (see page
   760), North Dighton,   Dighton
DIGHTON FURNACE CO. Geo. F.
   Gavitt, treas. Boston office, 96 and
   98 North (see page 733),   North
   Dighton,   "
Dean & Perry,   East Bridgewater
BELCHER DANIEL (malleable iron,
   see page 711),   Easton
DRAKE LINCOLN (small castings,
   see page 712),   "
BOSTON AND FAIRHAVEN IRON
   WORKS, B. F. Leonard, ag't. Fairhaven
Fall River Foundry Co.   Fall River
Fall River Furnace Co.   "
FALL RIVER IRON WORKS CO.
   Richard Borden, agent,   "
KILBURN, LINCOLN, & CO. (see
   page 756),   "
Heywood, Wilson, & Co.   Fitchburg
Daniels Bros.   Foxborough

Felt & Co.   Greenfield
WOODS, PRESCOTT, & CO. Groton
   Junction,   Groton
Taylor Franklin,   Hancock
Whitaker Sylvanus,   "
Barstow Edwin W.   Hanover
Curtis George,   "
Howard Chas. & Co.   Hingham
Thomas William,   "
Watkins Marcus M.   Hinsdale
HOLYOKE MACHINE CO.   Holyoke
Cobb & Drew,   Kingston
Lanesborough Iron Co.   Lanesborough
Baker, Josselyn, & Co. (fine cast-
   ings),   Lawrence
Davis Edmund & Son,   "
Merrimac Iron Foundry, E. Joslyn,
   agent,   "
McLaughlin John,   Lee
TANNER EDWARD P. agent (see
   page 713),   "
Cote & Nichols,   Lowell
LOWELL MACHINE SHOP, A.
   Moody, supt. Dutton,   "
Walker & Barber,   Lynn
CHILSON GARDNER (see inside
   front cover),   Mansfield
Le Baron J. B.   Middleborough
Howe Jarvis & Co.   Milford
HOPEDALE FURNACE CO. Wm.
   F. Draper, treas. (see page 753),
   Hopedale,   "
Martin John,   Millbury
Grinnell Jos. G.   New Bedford
Bird & Greene,   "
Russell Albert,   Newburyport
    New Marlborough
Sheldon Gilbert L.   Hartsville,   "
Pettee Otis & Co. Upper Falls,   Newton
Clapp Wm. R.   Northampton
Hayden Foundry and Machine Co.   "
Davis & Furber,   North Andover
WHITIN JOHN C. (see page 754,),
   Whitinsville,   Northbridge
Norton Furnace Co.   Norton
Hunt, Waite, & Flint,   Orange
Squier & Wood,   Palmer
BROWN FREDERICK A. cor. Fenn
   and Second (see page 738),   Pittsfield
CLARY & RUSSELL, (see page 708),   "
Plymouth Iron Foundry, Wm. R.
   Drew, treas.   Plymouth
Richmond Iron Works,   Richmond
Salem Foundry and Machine shop, Salem
SMITH STERRY, E. Gardner, cor.
   S. Prospect,   "
Smith John R.   "
    Sandwich
Manomet Iron Works, N. Sandwich,   "
Blackwell & Burr (hollow-ware),
   Pocasset,   "
Mount Hope Iron Co., J. M. Leonard,
   agent and treasurer,   Somerset
Somerset Co-operative Iron Foundry, "
BRADFORD WM. R.   Somerville
HAWKINS R. F. (see page 781), Springfield
Trask Eliphalet,   "
Wasson manuf. Co.   "
Wright & Emerson,   "
    Stockbridge
BURGHARDT & BRO. Curtisville,   "
Potter W. R.   Taunton
FOUNDRY AND MACHINE CO.
   H. S. Fairbanks, agt. and treas.   "
LEONARD L. M., Wales st. near
   the depot (see page 726),   "
PERKINS SAMPSON & CO. (see
   page 729),   West Water,   "

Taunton
TAUNTON IRON WORKS CO. Geo.
M. Woodward, agent (see p. 732),   "

Isinglass.

MANNING & CO., J. J. Manning,
  agent (pure American Isinglass,
  see page 715),   Rockport
Manning J. J. & W. N.   "
Rockport Isinglass Co. Newell Giles,
  treas.

Japan Manufacturers.
(See *Varnish Manufacturers*.)

Japanners.

Boston Stamping & Manufacturing
  Co.   Cambridgeport,   Cambridge
Dean John & Co. Webster sq.   Worcester

Jet Goods Manufacturers.

Blackinton-V. H. (belt buckles,
  clasps, &c.)   Attleborough

Jewelry, Watches, and Plate.

Noyes Isaiah,   Abington
Darling M. A.   East Abington,   "
Studley W. B.   "   "
Davis John R.   Acushnet
Hurd L. F.   Adams
Barnes L. M. & Co. North Adams,   "
Hinman C. W.   "   "
Munn Charles,   "   "
White Luther W.   "   "
Carter John H.   Amesbury
Collins Hiram,   "
Kenfield C. S.   Amherst
Lavake T. W.   "   "
Brown John J.   Andover
WHITING J. E., Main, cor. Elm sq.   "
TINGLEY T. C. JR.   Arlington
Goddard George S.   Ashland
Rickey George W.   Athol
Bliss & Cook,   Athol Depot,   "
Folsom A. B.   "   "
CHASE H. W. (chasing),   Attleborough
White Wm. C. (chasing), N. Attleboro', "
Munroe John,   Barnstable
Cummings Daniel,   Barre
Arnold Levi,   Belchertown
Hill John B.   Beverly
Pierce C. A.   Blackstone
Keyes Rufus,   Boxborough
Hewett E. A.   Bridgewater
Greenleaf Mark H.   Brighton
Bailey G. A.   Brookfield
Cheney Alfred A.   Brookline
Hunnewell James A.   Cambridge
Huntington James,   "
Balch M. P.   Cambridgeport,   "
Gibbs Benj. W.   "   "
Bryant F. S.   East Cambridge,   "
Josselyn Aaron,   "   "
Farrington J. C.   Canton
Abbott C. P.   Charlestown
Leonard Nathaniel,   "
Morrill Enoch,   "
Porter Alonzo,   "
Stone Jasper,   "
Stratton M. E.   "
Ulmar J. B.   "
Addison Charles J. W.   Chelsea
White George W. & Co.   "
Judd D. B.   Chester
Stackpole J. & Son,   Chicopee
Greene Gilbert,   Clinton
Collier Asa,   Concord
Wing L. C. & Co.   "

Jewelry, Watches, Plate — continued.

Townsend Harvey,   Conway
Savage Daniel,   Danvers
Gudd George A.   Dedham
Hawes William K., South Dedham,   "
                                         Deerfield
Billings Lathrop, South Deerfield,   "
Potter J. Henry,   East Bridgewater
Chapman C. H.   East Hampton
Koehe Robert,   North Easton,   Easton
Lewis William S.   Edgartown
Pease Francis jr.   "
Aruzeu Neils,   Fall River
Carr Frank B.   "
Gifford C. E.   "
Lincoln & Kelley,   "
Macomber F. W.   "
Shove Stephen,   "
Conn Reuben R.   Fitchburg
Fairbanks J. H.   "
Whitney Edwin A.   "
Wilbur & Tyler,   "
Howe William H.   Franklin
Graham Henry L. South Gardner, Gardner
Hale Daniel.   Georgetown
Burns Joseph J.   Gloucester
Lane D. H.   "
Tibbets Robert A.   "
Hale C. A.   Grafton
Perry Isaac G.   Great Barringtou
Prindle & Tobey,   "
Forbes & Foster,   Greenfield
Hollister Joseph H.   "
Colburn A. F.   Groton Junction, Groton
Hovey H. C.   "   "
Morgan Luther,   Hamilton
De Lano Amos W.   Hancock
Eldridge Rinaldo,   Harwich
Freeman Warren,   "
Dole H. L. & Co.   Haverhill
Harris William,   "
Kimball & Gould,   "
Morse H. M.   "
Margetts T.   Hingham
Tower Reuben,   South Hingham,   "
Wilder Ezra,   "   "
Rust & Wilder,   Hinsdale
Rice Albert,   Holliston
Taber Luther A.   Holyoke
Cain Ansel,   "
Brown O. L.   Hopkinton
Tyler D. M.   Ipswich
Barrett Humphrey,   Lancaster
Huntoon Lemuel jr.   Lawrence
Baldwin W. E.   "
Knowles David,   "
Marston H. W.   "
Monar Humphrey,   "
WHITCOMB I. A. 93 Essex (see
    page 793),   "
Whitford Newell,   "
Levy Mary L.   Lee
Lyman & Chaffee,   "
Prevear Edward,   Leominster
Pike Ozin,   Leverett
Hallett Milo G.   Lowell
CARTER E. B. 83 Central,   "
Josselyn Charles R.   "
Ordway H. M.   "
Raynes J. & Co.   "
RICHARDSON L. B. & CO. 108
    Central,   "
Sanborn Amos & Co.   "
Wilkins Henry,   "
Williams G. T.   "
Bushby S. R.   Lynn
Carruthers John,   "
Clarke Edwin N.   "

Frothingham B. H.   Lynn
Hobbs William E.   "
Howe George,   "
Jewett Augustine,   "
Moore George H.   "
Olin J. G.   "
Robinson James G.   "
Homer C. C.   Malden
Homan Samuel,   Marblehead
Shattuck George W.   "
Brigham L. S.   Marlborough
Graves Charles H.   "
Hewett S. Myron,   "
Le Baron A. S.   Mattapoisett
Gibbs Joseph N.   Medford
Fuller A. M. B. West Medway. Medway
Carpenter Charles H.   Middleborough
Tinkham Foster,   "
Eldridge R. C.   Milford
Goodspeed P. P.   "
Wilcox C. W.   "
Aiken Henry A.   Millbury.
Worcester E. C.   Milton
Grout George E.   Monson
Coggeshall N.   Nantucket
SWAIN SAMUEL,   "
Tobey Benj. G.   "
Wood Wm. W.   "
Rutherford J. H.   Natick
Almy James T.   New Bedford
Brownell A. P.   "
Childs Sylvester,   "
Dexter & Haskins,   "
Fales James jr.   "
Hurll Charles W.   "
Jordan Stephen D.   "
Kelley James S.   "
Kelley William L.   "
Munroe James,   "
Otheman B. jr.   "
Paddack Geo. R.   "
Shephard Nathaniel,   "
Wilbor Alfred G.   "
Warner W. W.   New Braintree
Ballou E. F.   Newburyport
Carter J. H. & Co.   "
Drown Chas. L.   "
Drown John B.   "
Foster N. & T.   "
KUHL WILLIAM, 42 Market sq.   "
Moulton Joseph,   "
Osgood Alfred,   "
Pearson J. G.   "
Macomber A. J. Newton Corner, Newton
Cook B. E. & Son,   Northampton
Davison D. F. (repairer),   "
Fowle John H.   "
Hannum John,   "
Fay Horace,   Northborough
Hildreth M. & Co. (shell jewelry),   "
Spaulding D. S.   "
Gurney L. F.   North Bridgewater
Hewett Herman,   "
Studley Luther,   "
EDDY L. A.   North Brookfield
Horton James A.   Orange
Brooks E. S.   Palmer
Smith A. H.   Paxton
Burnell Lyman G.   Pittsfield
Childs C. C. & Co.   "
Root Washington M.   "
Scott John B.   "
Walker Wm. M.   "
Atwood Edward W.   Plymouth
Gooding Benj B.   "
PUTNAM A. L.   Provincetown
Holden John O.   Quincy
. ash James E.   Randolph

Thayer L. F.   Randolph
BEARD W. E.   Reading
Manning W. N.   Rockport
Appleton George B.   Salem
Fogg Julian A. & Co.   "
Kehew Wm. H.   "
Lawson Charles,   "
Low Daniel.   "
Luscomb J. G.   "
Mackintire John,   "
Nickerson Asa W.   "
Sampson Charles,   "
Smith E. A. & D. T.   "
Smith & Chamberlain,   "
WRUCK F. A. (see page 743), 195   "
Essex,   "
Osgood M. C.   Salisbury
Rowell John,   "
Carter John H.   Amesbury,   "
Collins Hiram,   "   "
Kelley Allen,   Sandwich
Wright H. M.   "
Bissell E. M.   Shelburne Falls, Shelburne
BARNES WM. C.   Southbridge
King J. A.   "
Phelps L.   "
BLISS E. M.   Spencer
Bailey S. E. & Graves,   Springfield
Buckland F. H. & Co.   "
Chandler A. C.   "
Gallupe E. A.   "
Kirkham Wm. Jr.   "
Parker, Underwood, & Stickney,   "
Porter & Prince,   "
Robinson M. F.   "
Shaw C. R.   "
Smith Henry,   "
Stearns W. R. (repairer),   "
Stowe L. S.   "
Whipple E. A.   "
Hunt John D.   Sterling
Heath Theodore,   Curtisville, Stockbridge
Gibbs Geo. H.   Stoneham
Darling H. W.   Stoughton
Barnard Lorenzo O.   Taunton
Briggs & Presbrey,   "
Pitts Albert,   "
Standish E. E.   "
Tisdale E. D.   "
Elijah West,   Tisbury
McKenzie S. S.   Topsfield
Blood Walter,   Townsend
Bettis Buel G.   Tyringham
Barton A.   Uxbridge
Cheney C. H. R.   Wakefield
Reed L. H.   "
Warren & Starbuck,   Waltham
Whitford George H.   "
Sagendorph P. H.   Ware
Sherman Nicholas J.   Wareham
Harwood Lucian,   Warren
Rogers William,   Watertown
Hinds John F.   Webster
Wood Moses,   Westborough
GROVER FRANCIS A.   Westfield
Kirst F.   "
Morse James H.   West Hampton
Davenport Thomas C.   West Hampton
                         West Roxbury
Fairbanks E. H., Jamaica Plain,   "
Tenfant A. F.   Weymouth
Harlow George, South Weymouth,   "
Wilder James H., So. Hingham,   "
Hunt S. A.   Williamstown
ABBOTT SOLON & CO.   Winchendon
Hodge Frank B.   Woburn
                                      Worcester
BLAKE & ROBINSON, 213 Main,   "

Buck D. A. A.   Worcester
Burbank A. I.   "
Fenno Wm. D.   "
Goddard Benj.   "
Harrington & Bullens,   "
Johnson L.   "
Lamb T. M.   "
Story S. N.   "
Weixler J. P. jr.   "
Kenney W. F., S. Yarmouth,   Yarmouth
Harris R. H.,   Yarmouth Port,   "

Jewelry Manufacturers.

Bates & Bacon,   Attleborough
Blackinton W. & Co.   "
CHASE H. W. (chasing),   "
BUSHEE A. & CO. see page 761),   "
Day, Bliss, & Dean,   "
Freeman & Co.   "
Hayward & Briggs,   "
Mason H. & Co.   "
Peckham J. R. (rubber),   "
Richards Geo. & Co.   "
Savory J. B. (chains),   "
Smith D. H.   "
Streeter Brothers,   "
Sturdy Brothers,   "
Sturdy William A.   "
Blackinton R. & Co.   Attleborough
   Falls,   "
Blackinton V. H. (jet goods), "   "
FRENCH G. W., Attleborough Falls,   "
STURDY J. F.   "   "
BARROWS H. F. & CO., North Attle-
   borough,   "
CODDING, SMITH, & CO., North At-
   tleborough,   "
Draper O. M.   N. Attleborough,   "
Draper, Pate, & Bailey,   "   "
Draper W. O. & Co.   "   "
Everett Dennis (and eye protectors), N.
   Attleborough,   "
Ginnado S. S. & Co., N. Attleborough, "
Guild S. S.   "
Guild & Hall,   "   "
Kingman E. Y. & Co.   "   "
Morse Brothers,   "   "
Pratt B. F.   "   "
RICHARDS, CODDING, & CO., Office,
   200 Broadway, N. Y., North Attle-
   borough,   "
RICHARDS IRA & CO., Office 200
   Broadway, N. Y., N. Attleborough, "
Richards J. J. & J. M.   "
Richardson Stephen & Co.   "   "
Soithes H. S. & Co.   "   "
WHITNEY & RICE, Office 179 Broad-
   way N. Y., North Attleborough,   "
Witherell S. A.   "
Attleborough City Jewelry Co., South
   Attleborough,   "
Doran John,   South Attleborough, "
Robinson Wm. H.   "   "
Sadler & Stanley,   "   "
White & Shaw,   "   "
Foote E. N. & Co., New England Vil-
   lage,   Grafton
Sanborn Amos & Co.   Lowell
Capron & Co. (imitation rubber), Mansfield
KINGMAN & HODGES (imitation
   rubber),   "
MERRITT & DRAPER,   "
Fogg Julian A. & Co.   Salem
Mackintire J.   "
Smith & Chamberlain,   "
BACON JOS. T.,   Plainville, Wrentham
SCHOFIELD BROTHERS, "   "
Witherell S. A.   "   "

Jig Sawing.

KNOWLTON GEO. K. & CO. (see page 751), 13 Union, Lynn
MARSHALL J. OTIS, rear 13 Broad, "
(see page 750),

Jointing and Matching Machines.

HEALD S. & SONS (flooring board, and hand and stave matchers, and shingle jointers, see pages 796 and 797), Barre

Junk Dealers.

Leonard Thomas, East Cambridge, Cambridge
Emery Daniel C. "
Henshaw Peter, Charlestown
Quinn Patrick, "
Taber Nathaniel, Fairhaven
Flint J. D. & Co. Fall River
Bateman C. A. Fitchburg
Mention William H. "
Patch Lyman, "
Simonds Joseph F. "
Williams J. F. "
Hersey Loring & Co. Gloucester
Mayo J. jr. "
Bishop N. A. Lawrence
Reed & Berry, "
Wellman John R. "
DODGE LUKE C. (see page 741), 55 Dutton, Lowell
Hapgood Ephraim, "
Langley S. & W. "
Nugent Michael, "
Ready J. L. "
Baker Benjamin, New Bedford
Bartlett H. "
BROWNELL WILLIAM O. 10, 12 & 14 Front, "
Cook Wm. H. "
Carroll John, "
Diver John, "
Drury Warren, "
Haley Michael, "
Jordan William, "
Keen Ebenezer S. "
McCullough John, "
Thacher A. D. "
Whitney Levi, "
Flanders A. S. "
Stanley John C. Newburyport
Stockman Moses & Co. "
Dunbar C. A. North Bridgewater
Robbins Alex. Plymouth
Burch James. Provincetown
Hainum Charles A. "
Higgins Aquilla, "
Burrill J. F. "
Crafts George, Quincy
Eaton J. D. & J. W. Salem
Dickinson & Mayo. "
HAMMOND S. T. & CO. Springfield
Stratton George, "
PIERCE H. L. 25 Westminster, Taunton
Pierce O. B. & A. W. "
Larrett Jonas, Wellfleet
Worcester
BUELL S. K. 18 Foster (see page 781), "
Buxton Edward, "
Holdsworth T. D. & Co. "
WEBSTER C. C. 44 Union (see page 720), "
WILDER CHARLES, agent, 30 Union, (see page 783), "

Jute Bagging Manufacturers.

Bengal Jute Factory, Salem
India Manuf. Co. "

Kaolin.

BLAKE ZEBINA (see page 758), West Water, Taunton

Keg Manufacturers.

(See also Coopers.)

Robbins Francis, Acton
Dennis Dexter (powder), Barre
Coffin Wm. S. Newburyport
Bradford Samuel (nail), Plymouth
Battis John, Salem
Brady Thomas, "
Felt & Phippen, "
Florance T. T. "
Rowell Edward, Webb's whf. "
SPROAT JAMES H. Taunton

Kitchen Furnishing Goods.

EDDY D. & SON (Refrigerators, see page 666). Harrison sq. Dorchester
NASH J. W. & CO. 105 Central, Lowell
(see page 739),
TUCK LORENZO, So. Weymouth, Weymouth

Knife Manufacturers.

(See also Cutlery; also Boot and Shoe Findings; also Edge Tools.)

REED FRANKLIN (shoe, see page 793), Canton
SIMONDS MANUF. CO. (see page 658), West Fitchburg, Fitchburg
MOORHOUSE WM. Foxboro
HANKEY A. & CO. (trimming, veneer, &c., see page 775), Leicester
Clappville,
LOVEJOY DANIEL (manufacturer of paper mill engine bars and plates; also planing machine, and all other pattern knives, see page 744), Cushing, cor. Rock st. Lowell
Fulton Robert (all kinds), Mansfield
MOORHOUSE JOHN (see page 732), "
Murphy J. & R. (oyster), "
Moran & Sons, West Mansfield
North Bridgewater
TUCK S. V. (shoe, see page 779),
WEBSTER W. (shoe, see page 769), "
Lothrop H. A. & Co. Sharon
Harrington Theodore (shoe), Southbridge
Crossman A. W. & Son (drawing), Warren
W. Warren,

Knife and Scissors Sharpeners

SOUTHWICK & HASTINGS, Worcester

Knitted-Goods Manuf.

(See also Hosiery.)

Morrison A. & Sons, Braintree
Robbins & Everett, Brewster
Long Frederick, Fitchburg
Burrows & Hunt (nets, clouds, nubias), Ipswich

Knitting Machine Agents.

CARTER N. C. (agt. "Lamb"), 103 Merrimack, Lowell
Lee H. C. Springfield

Knitting Machine Manufs.

Chicopee Falls
LAMB KNITTING MACHINE
MANUF. CO. (see page 773),   "
Winchendon
Goodspeed & Wyman (Hinkley),   "

Knitting Machines. (Loom Harness.)

Lawrence
SLADDIN & LORD, Page's building, Methuen st. (see page 746),   "

Label Manufacturers.

STAR LABEL CO. F. G. Sargent,
(ready strung, see page 743),
Graniteville,   Westford

Laces, Embroideries, &c.

(See also Dry Goods ; also Fancy Goods.)

Bartlett Helen J.   Lowell
MAYNARD C. I. W. 76 Merrimack,   "
Skinner A. C.   "
Smith Francis,   "
Storer N. W.   "
Malley William,   Pittsfield
Aborn H. E. & Co.   Salem
Gross, Strauss, & Co.   Worcester

Lace Leather Manufacturers.

Tiffany Brothers,   Attleborough
Coupe Wm. & Co. So. Attleborough,   "

Ladder Manufacturers.

Werden E. (step ladder),   Pittsfield
Somerville
Bishop H. R. & Co. E. Somerville,   "

Ladies' Furnishing Goods.

Harrington John &:Co.   Amesbury
Perley M. V. B.   Gloucester
Foster F. H.   Ipswich
Hanson Jas. W.   Lawrence
Moulton S. H. & Co.   "
Poor Geo. W.   "
Tebbets G. H.   "
Conrad David,   Salem
Moulton N. H.   "
Moulton Wm. C. C.   "
WILLIS GEORGE E.   Stoneham
Dunlap R. C. Mrs.   Worcester

Lampblack.

Cutler Wm. 2d,   Amherst
Chase Ensign, North Harwich, Harwich
Gage Freeman,   "   "
Robbins Kimball,   "   "
Lowell
LIVINGSTON A. J. 164 Middlesex,   "

Lamp Wicking Manufacturers.

Fall River
LAWTON & ESTES (see page 784),   "

Lamps.

(See also Crockery, Glass, etc.)

VOTOW & MONTGOMERY,   Amherst
Fitchburg
TOLMAN WILLIAM G. 150 Main,   "
Thayer Lewis,   Worcester

Lapidaries.

Luther J. W. & Co.   Attleborough
Brooks & Day, North Attleborough,   "
Luther & Co.   "

Lard and Tallow Manufs.

Furbush Andrew,   Charlestown
Taylor Allison,   Taunton

Last Makers.

(See also Boot and Shoe Findings, &c.)

Giles J. H.   Abington
Frohock, Kilby, & Co.   Cambridgeport
KELLY EZRA, Fleet st.   Haverhill
Wadleigh Levi C.   "
Hudson
MILLAY PHILIP E. (see page 761),   "
Barnes John H.   Lynn
Goodwin A. T.   "
Goodwin & Brother,   "
Hitchings B.   "
Jackson John,   "
Lamphier Brothers,   "
Cox George P.   Malden
Jackson Thomas,   Marlborough
Sawyer & Richardson,   Milford
Ramsdell Brothers,   Natick
Sprague Chandler, (also boot trees
and forms),   North Bridgewater
Haskell A. & W.   North Brookfield
Brown & Stiles,   Peabody
Stoughton
LINFIELD M. & SON (see page 728),   "
Sherman E. & C. & Co., South
Weymouth,   Weymouth
MAWHINNEY SAMUEL, 56 Union
(see page 783),   Worcester
PORTER SAMUEL, Union st.   "
(see page 781),   "

Lathe Manufacturers.

(See also Machinists.)

GERRY GEORGE & SON (see page
771), 6 Mill st. Athol Depot, Athol
RICHARDSON GEO. H. (see page
771), Athol Depot,   "
Worcester
FAY L. D. 7 Cypress (see page 783),
N. Y. STEAM ENGINE CO., A.
B. Couch, Supt. (see page 785),   "

Laundries.

(See also Dye Houses ; also Bleacheries.)

Cambridgeport
Cambridge Laundry, L. Cox,   "
Rayner W. H.   Charlestown
Boston Laundry, H. C. Ray,   Chelsea
CHELSEA LAUNDRY, Stephen
Sibley proprietor, William st.
(see page 727),   "
Malden Laundry, —— Higgins,   Malden
Springfield
Springfield Laundry, M. A. Welch,   "
Giles Cubit,   Taunton
Wetherbee Warren,   Waltham
Kelly A. W.   Worcester

Lawyers.

Keith Jesse E.   Abington
Harris Jacob B. East Abington,   "
Bliss Henry J.   Adams
SAYLES FRANKLIN O., Centre st.   "
Porter Wm. P.   North Adams,   "
Preston & Brown,   "   "
Robinson James T.   "   "
Rockwell Jarvis,   "   "
Thayer & Potter,   "   "
Fitch Henry,   Alford
BINNEY WILLIAM C. (see
page 723),   Amesbury
Cate George W.   "

Lawyers — continued.

Conkey Ithamar F.   Amherst
Cooper J. S.   "
DICKINSON E. & A.   "
DICKINSON W. A.   "
Foster George W.   Andover
Hazen Nathan W.   "
Merrill Samuel,   "
POOR GEORGE H.   "
Carter Ira O.   Arlington
Parmenter Wm. E.   "
Bement Wait,   South Ashfield, Ashfield
Fay F. F.   . Athol
Field Charles,   Athol Depot,   "
Herr George W.   "   "
Daggett John,   Attleborough
Bowen Simeon,   N. Attleborough,   "
Day J. M.   Barnstable
Higgins Jonathan,   "
King Geo. A.   "
Marston George,   "
Brimblecom Charles,   Barre
Gorham J. Martin,   "
Dickinson Franklin,   Belchertown
Hurd Chas. H.   Belmont
Ware George W. jr.   "
Choate Frederick W.   Beverly
Whitman George H.   Billerica
BURGESS SILAS A.   Blackstone
JOHNSON T. S.   "
PUTNAM A. A.   "
Ducklee Mark F.   Braintree
Avrey Edward,   East Braintree,   "
French Asa,   South Braintree,   "
Langley N. A.   "   "
White N. L.   Weymouth,   "
COPELAND GEORGE,   Brewster
Kingman Hosea,   Bridgewater
Latham Williams,   "
Baldwin Henry,   Brighton
Bennett Joseph,   "
BRAMAN JOSEPH B.   "
Norton Michael,   "
Simpson W. H.   "
Sinclair Albert T.   "
WARREN W. F.   "
Warren W. W.   "
Weston ——,   "
Johnson G. W.   Brookfield
Hyde Dwight,   "
Aspinwall William,   Brookline
Dexter Wm. S.   "
Griggs George,   "
Homer George F.   "
Kingman Bradford,   "
Barker James H.   Cambridge
Bates J. E.   "
WHITNEY BENJAMIN W.
   Brattle sq.   "
Hammond J. W.,   East Cambridge,   "
MARRETT LORENZO,   "   "
McIntire Chas. J.   "   "
Tyler Joseph H.   "   "
Andrews Freeman B., Cambridgeport,   "
Edwards Abraham,   "   "
Engley William F.   "   "
HOLT JOSEPH G., 449 Main,
   Cambridgeport,   "
Ames Ellis,   Canton
Endicott Charles,   "
Noyes Samuel B.   "
Bailey A. J.   Charlestown
Bigelow George B.   "
Bodwell J. C. jr.   "
Bragg Henry W.   "
Brown J. H.   "
Butler John H.   "
Cotton Joseph H.   "

Dunton Charles D.   Charlestown
Hart J. S.   "
Hayward C. C.   "
Hildreth Chas. H.   "
Neal Geo. B.   "
O'Brien J. W.   "
Pettingill John W.   "
Robinson Charles, jr.   "
Stearns Wm. S.   "
Sweeney Charles E.   "
Walker Edwin G.   "
Warren G. Washington,   "
White Rufus A.   "
Williams Daniel,   "
Willson Samuel S.   "
BATES HAMLETT, Stebbins Block,
   Broadway,   Chelsea
Chamberlain Mellen,   "
Cheever Tracy P.   "
Gerrish Benj. J.   "
Morris Robert,   "
Richmond James N.   Cheshire
KNAPP GEORGE H.   Chicopee
LATHROP E. H.   "
ROBINSON GEORGE D.   "
BEMIS DANIEL H.   Clinton
Dame John T.   "
STEVENS CHARLES G.   "
Beal Solomon J.   Cohasset
Lincoln Martin,   "
Lothrop J. Q. A.   "
Pratt Aaron,   "
Tower Edward,   "
Brooks George M.   Concord
Heywood George,   "
Johnson N. L.   Dana
Andrews I. W.   Danvers
Hadley Horace L.   "
Cobb Jonathan,   Dedham
Colburn Waldo,   "
Ely Frederick D.   "
Draper Jno. W.   Dorchester
Safford Nathaniel F.   "
Scudder Henry A.   "
Clarke A. C.   Neponset,   "
Brown A. F.   Douglas
Kimball Joseph C.   Dracut
Varnum Atkinson C.   "
Stetson Samuel,   Duxbury
OSBORNE WM. H.   East Bridgewater
Bassett W. G.   East Hampton
Rotch Albert A.   Easton
White G.,   South Easton,   "
Mayhew Theodore G.   Edgartown
Pease Joseph T.   "
Battelle Hezekiah,   Fall River
BLAISDELL JOSIAH C., over P. O.   "
Boomer F. A.   "
BRAYTON & MORTON, Granite
   Block, Section G,   "
FORD JAMES,   "
Lapham Louis,   "
Lovatt Benjamin K.   "
Peirce William H.   "
Williams Eliab,   "
WOOD JONATHAN M., Granite
   Block, Section F,   "
     Falmouth
Wood Richard S.   East Falmouth,   "
BROWN & LORING,   Fitchburg
Haynes Stillman,   "
Mason Charles,   "
MERRIAM DAVID H.   "
Merriam William J.   "
NORCROSS AMASA,   3 Main,   "
WARE (T. K.) & SNOW (C. H. B.),   "
WOOD (Nathaniel) & TORREY
   (Geo. A.), 151 Main,   "

Woodbury James M.	Fitchburg	Lawrence
Brown N. P.	Florida	THOMPSON WILLIAM L., 120 Essex, "
Carpenter Jas. E.	Foxborough	White Nathaniel G. "
Adams C. S.	Framingham	Wright Wm. H. P. "
Esty C. C.	"	Branning John, Lee
Gordon Robert,	"	Cook Jonathan F. "
Heard F. F.	"	SHORES NORMAN W. "
Hurd T. C.	"	Wilcox Marshall, "
Davis Edmund,	Franklin	Bennett Charles F. Lenox
Hathaway Nicholas,	Freetown	Bishop Henry W. "
Jones J. P.	Georgetown	Post Thomas, "
SMITH BENJAMIN H.	Gloucester	Taft Henry W. "
Thompson Charles P.	"	Tucker George J. "
Tullar A.	"	Tucker Joseph, "
Slocum William F.	Grafton	Tucker Wm. S. "
Joyner Herbert C.	Great Barrington	Waterman Andrew J. "
Palmer Billings,	"	Carter Chauncey W. Leominster
Sumner & Dewey,	"	Merriam Chas. H. "
Aiken & Hopkins,	Greenfield	Cottrell Asa, Lexington
Bartlett George W.	"	Scott A. E. "
Brainerd Almon,	"	Hodges E. F. Lincoln
Conant Chester C.	"	Whitman Wm. D. L. "
DAVIS & DEWOLF,	"	Hartwell Shattuck, Littleton
Griswold Whiting,	"	Abbott Julian, Lowell
Lamb S. O.	"	Abbott James C. "
Lyman E. E.	"	Bent W. H. "
MATTOON & WILLIAMS,	"	BLAISDELL CHAS. R., 3 Canal
Bennett Josiah K.		Block, Central,
Gerrish James, Groton Junction,	Groton "	Boardman H. W.
SPAULDING JOHN,	"	Bonney Arthur P.
Safford Daniel E.	Hamilton	BROWN (Alpheus R.) & ALGER
Lapham C. P.	Hancock	(Edwin A.), 55 Central, "
Simmons Perez,	Hanover	Butler & Webster, "
Blunt William E.	Haverhill	Caverly Robert B. "
Carter Henry,	"	Corliss H. G. F. "
DUNCAN JAMES H.	"	Cowley & Allen, "
Hodges Thorndike D.	"	DAVIS JOHN, 49 Central, "
Jenness J. K.	"	Free John F. "
JONES J. P., Bridge St.,	"	Griffin Geo. A. "
JACOBS T. W. 89 Merrimac,	"	Hadley Samuel P. jr. "
Kittredge Alfred,	"	HOWE & GREENHALGE, 49 Central, "
MARSH JOHN J., 29 Water,	"	Keyes Joseph B. "
Merrill Henry N.	"	KIMBALL J. CHELLIS, 5 Barristers' Hall, "
NOYES C. J., 2 Sawyer's block,	"	Knowles John A. "
Thaxter David,	Hingham	Ladd Jonathan, "
Bullard Elias,	Holliston	Loughran James, "
Chapin E. W.	Holyoke	MARSHALL (J. N.) & VARNUM
PEARSONS WM. B. C.	"	(J. P.), 3 Barristers' Hall, "
UNDERWOOD PORTER,	"	McEvoy John F. "
Meserve Clement,	Hopkinton	Moore Albert M. "
WAKEFIELD L. H.	"	Reed John W. "
JOSLIN JAMES T.	Hudson	Rice D. Hall, "
Copeland A. M.	Huntington	Richardson D. S. & G. F. "
Estey W. F.	Hyde Park	Scott G. Clarence, "
Turner C. W.	"	Shepard Luther E. "
Haskell George,	Ipswich	Sherman Edward F. "
Sayward C. A.	"	STEVENS (Geo.) & ANDERSON
Beal Joseph S.	Kingston	(Wm. H.), 1 Barristers' Hall, "
Holmes Joseph A.	"	Swan & Woodman, "
Filley William T.	Lanesborough	SWEETSER (Theodore H.) & GARDNER (Wm. S.), "
BACON H. C., 153 Essex,	Lawrence	Webster Wm. P. "
Barker Jas. L.	"	WENTWORTH (Tappan) & JEWETT (Andrew F.), 170 Merrimack, "
Burley Elbridge T.	"	Williams & Williams, "
GILE W. FISK, 120 Essex,	"	Fabens William C. Lynn
HARMON NATHAN W., 1 Appleton,	"	HAWKES N. MORTIMER, 133 Market, "
Knox William S.	"	Howland Wm. "
Harlow Robert P.	"	Newhall Jas. R. "
Ibad G. E.	"	NEWHALL THOS. B. 91 Market, "
Newton Christopher G.	"	Peabody Dean, "
Parsons T. A.	"	Parsons Eben, "
POOR GEO. H., 1 Appleton,	"	Stickney Charles H. "
SANBORN ARETAS R. 120 Essex,	"	STICKNEY JEREMIAH C.
Sanborn J. C.	"	Central sq. "
Saunders D. & C.	"	
SHERMAN (E. J.) & TARBOX (J. K.)	"	
Stevens I.	"	
Stevens William,	"	
Stone Andrew C.	"	

Lawyers — continued.

Tirrell Minot, jr.	Lynn
BORDMAN BENJAMIN,	Malden
Howes L. W.	"
Pettengill —,	"
Kimball David B.	Manchester
Grover Thomas E.	Mansfield
Reed E. M.	"
Fabens Wm.	Marblehead
ALDRICH SAMUEL N.	Marlborough
BAKER J, MURRAY,	"
GALE WM. B.	"
JOHNSON EDWARD F.	"
Hamant Charles,	Medfield
Badger Almarin F.	Medford
Harlow Thomas S.	"
HAYES BENJ. F.	"
Perry B. E.	"
Russell Charles,	"
Lovering Warren,	Medway
Deans Charles H. West Medway,	"
Farnsworth William C.	Melrose
Rogers Wm. M.	Methuen
Robinson Everett,	Middleborough
Wood Wm. H.	"
Fales Henry E.	Milford
Holbrook Leander,	"
Kent T. G.	"
PARKER GEO. G. (see page 753),	
2 Washington block,	"
Scammell John S.	"
Staples H. B.	"
Hopkins John,	Millbury
Buck Robert H.	Milton
Churchill Chas. M. S.	"
Churchill Joseph M.	"
Pierce Edward L.	"
Thayer James B.	"
Fargo Alburn J.	Monterey
Gardner Edward M.	Nantucket
MACY ALFRED,	"
BACON (John W.) & SLEEPER	
(Geo. L.),	Natick
Cooney P. H.	"
Mason Walter N.	"
NUTT WILLIAM,	"
Barney Edwin L.	New Bedford
Bonney Chas. T.	"
Borden Alanson,	"
Bunker James M.	"
CLIFFORD CHAS. W. 35 No. Water,	"
Clifford John H.	"
Cobb Wendell H.	"
Crapo Wm. W.	"
CUSHMAN AUSTIN S. 117 Union,	"
ELIOT & STETSON,	"
Johnson William H.	"
MACKIE ADAM, 110 Union,	"
Pierce P. A.	"
Pitman Robert C.	"
Pitman & Borden,	"
Porter Francis L.	"
Prescott Oliver,	"
RAY ISAIAH C. 36½ No. Water,	"
Stone Joshua C.	"
Stone & Crapo,	"
Wilcox Lemuel T.	"
BINNEY & MORSE (see page 723),	
25 State,	Newburyport
Chapman Henry W.	"
Currier Wm. E.	"
GERRISH JOSEPH G. 19 State,	"
Johnson Harrison G.	"
Lamson Caleb,	"
Morse C. O.	"
Noyes Amos,	"
Pierce Nathaniel,	"
Pike John N.	"

Stone Eben T.	Newburyport
	New Marlborough
Turner Augustus, Southfield,	"
Abbott J. S.	Auburndale, Newton
Kimball J. R.	"
Davis Seth, West Newton,	"
ALLEN WM.	Northampton
CHILSON H. H.	"
Delano & Hammond,	"
Forbes Charles E.	"
Hinckley H. R.	"
Smith C. Edgar,	"
SPAULDING & BOIES,	"
Strickland Wm. P.	"
Bond Daniel W. Florence,	"
Clark Samuel,	Northborough
PERKINS JONAS R.	North Bridgewater
White J.	"
Beecher Robert,	North Brookfield
Richardson Ivory N.	North Chelsea
Chase R. D.	Orange
Doane John,	Orleans
Higgins Jonathan,	"
Allen & Gardner,	Palmer
Blair Joseph H.	"
Bancroft Sidney C.	Peabody
Holman George,	"
Perkins B. C.	"
Wiley H. O.	"
Lewis Samuel P.	Pepperell
Wallace Levi,	"
Bowerman & Swift,	Pittsfield
Dawes Henry L.	"
EMERSON CHAS. N., Berkshire	
Life Ins. block,	"
Gamwell Lorenzo H.	"
Lauckton Matthias R.	"
Page Phinehas L.	"
PINGREE & BARKER,	"
PLUNKETT WILLIAM R.	"
SHEPARDSON WESLEY L.	"
Wood Edgar M.	"
Damon Daniel E.	Plymouth
Davis Charles G.	"
Loud Jacob H.	"
Mason & Morton,	"
Russell John J.	"
Thomas William,	"
Whitman William H.	"
Hutchinson B. F.	Provincetown
Adams John Q.	Quincy
Morton William S.	"
Pratt E. Granville,	"
Tirrell J. E.	"
Jewell W. E.	Randolph
Bancroft Solon,	Reading
Judd Chauncey P.	"
Prescott A. A.	"
Wright Carroll D.	"
Woods H. N.	Rockport
ABBOTT A. A. 24 Washington,	Salem
Bancroft Sidney C.	"
Choate George F.	"
Cogswell William,	"
Devereux Geo. H.	"
ENDICOTT W. C. 256½ Essex,	"
Flint George Foster,	"
Gillis James A.	"
Goodell A. C.	"
Holden Nathaniel J.	"
Holman George,	"
Hunt Thos. F.	"
HUNTINGTON ASAHEL, Court	
House,	"
IVES (Stephen B. jr.), & LIN-	
COLN (Solomon, jr.), 27 Wash-	
ington,	"
Kimball Charles,	"

Kimball Charles A.	Salem	FOX WM. H.	Taunton
Kimball D. B.	"	FULLER W. E. 8 Hotel Building,	"
Kimball Edward P.	"	Pratt Horatio,	"
Lord George R.	"	Reed E Maltby,	"
Lord N J.	"	SANFORD JOHN E.	
Lord Otis P.	"	Townsend S. R.	
Mansfield M. B.	"	Williams H. & G. R.	"
Moulton Henry P.	"	Cady Stillman, Baldwinville, Templeton	
Northend Wm. D.	"	Bonney A. P.	Tewksbury
Osgood Charles S.	"	Holmes C. H.	Topsfield
Osgood J. B. F.	"	Poole Benjamin,	"
Perkins Jonathan C.	"	WORCESTER F. A.	Townsend
PERRY (J. W.) & ENDICOTT (W.		Hopkins Smith K. North Truro, Truro	
C.), 256½ Essex,	"	Deane Francis,	Uxbridge
Phillips Stephen H.	"	DEANE F. B.	"
Porter J. W.	"	Hobbs George W.	"
Rantoul Robert S.	"	Boswell James O.	Wakefield
Safford Daniel E.	"	EATON CHESTER W.	"
Sewall Charles,	"	Upton Edward A.	
STIMPSON THOMAS M. 194 Essex,	"	French Daniel,	Waltham
Story Augustus,	"	HILL EDWARD L. (gives *special*	
Upham Wm. P.	"	attention to the collection and	
Waters J. G.	"	adjustment of claims of all	
Webb Stephen P.	"	kinds), Central blk.	"
Wheatland George,	"	Rutter (Josiah) & Teel (J. O.),	"
Wheatland S. G.	"	Stone F. M.	"
Whittemore E. Stowell,	Sandwich	DAVIS H. C.	Ware
Davis A. B. Saugus Centre, Saugus		Richards Franklin D.	"
Davis Jerome, " "		Bates William,	Wareham
Phillips Geo. W. " "		Miller Seth,	"
Snow Harmon,	Savoy	Sproat James G.	"
Bradford James,	Sheffield	Bemis Charles,	Watertown
Field S. T. Shelburne Falls, Shelburne		Bemis Isaac V.	"
Maxwell A. " "		Child D. L.	Wayland
Puffer H. M.	"	Fuller Richard F.	"
Clough A. J. Groton Junction, Shirley		Stockwell John H.	Webster
Gerrish James, Shirley Village, "		Tingier Seymour A.	"
Lincoln C. S., Laurel st.	Somerville	Davis John W.	Wellfleet
Tufts Francis,	"	Biscoe Arthur G.	Westborough
BARTHOLOMEW A. J.	Southbridge	Harlow William,	West Boylston
Botham F. W.	"	Packard Austin,	West Bridgewater
	South Hadley	Bates William G.	Westfield
Dwight R. O., South Hadley Falls,	"	Fuller Henry,	"
HILL LUTHER,	Spencer	Gillett & Stevens,	"
Ashmun, Leonard, & Wells,	Springfield	Leonard & Lewis,	"
Brown T. M.	"	Whitney Milton B.	"
Beach & Sanders,	"	Abbott J. W. P.	Westford
Dewey T. M.	"	Spaulding Wm. C.	West Stockbridge
DONNELLY HUGH,	"	Bumpus Everett C.	Weymouth
Greene & Bosworth,	"	Humphrey James,	"
Hildreth R. B.	"	Langley Newell A.	"
McIntire James E.	"	Kilton John F. S. Weymouth,	"
Morris Edward,	"	Spellman S. C.	Wilbraham
MORRIS HENRY,	"	Danforth Keyes,	Williamstown
Morton James H.	"	Talmadge Henry T.	"
Rumrill James A.	"	Tatlock John,	"
SANDERS SIDNEY,	"	PIERCE LAFAYETTE W. Winchendon	
Seymour S. E.	"	WHITNEY GILES H. (see page 776), "	
Shurtleff Wm. S.	"	Custis C. P.	Winchester
Soule Augustus L.	"	Joy A. K. P.	"
Smith Wm. L.	"	Converse J. P.	Woburn
Stearns & Knowlton,	"	Converse P. L.	"
Stebbins J. M.	"	BACON & ALDRICH, Central Ex-	
WINCHESTER C. A.	"	change,	Worcester
DUNHAM HENRY J.	Stockbridge	BANCROFT JAMES H. 2 Central	
Norris True,	Stoneham	Exchange,	"
Stevens Wm. B.	"	Blackmer F. T.	"
Boardman H. J.	Stoughton	CHAPIN (Henry) & DADMUN (Ap-	
Whitney Edwin,	Stow	pleton), 1 P. O. block,	"
Hyde Benjamin D.	Sturbridge	Dana John A.	"
Thompson Charles,	Sudbury	Davis Isaac,	"
BENNETT (Edmund H.) & FUL-		Dewey & Goulding,	"
LER (Henry J.), 7 Hotel Build-		Dodge Thomas H.	"
ing,	Taunton	Goddard S. B. I.	"
BROWN (James) & REED (Chas.		Green James, jr.	"
A.), 3 Union Block,	"	Greenleaf Wm.	"
Cushman J. M.	"	Harding W. B.	"
Dean James H.	"	Haskins D. W.	"

Lawyers — continued.
Hill J. Henry,
Hoar George F.   Worcester
Holbrook Charles A.   "
McCafferty M. J.   "
Manning J. F.   "
Maxwell William B.   "
Mellen Edward,   "
MERRIAM DAVID H. 159 Main,   "
NELSON T. L. 1 Brinley Hall,   · · · "
Parker Henry L.   "
Potter B. W.   "
Rice H. C.   "
RICE W. W.   8 P. O. Building,   "
SMITH (H. O.) & TITUS (J. A.),
    1 Front st. Exchange,   "
STODDARD E. B. 98 Main,   "
SWAN GEORGE, 5 Flagg's block,   "
Thayer Adin,   "
Utley Samuel,   "
Verry George F.   "
Verry Horace B.   "
Wetherell John W.   "
Williams Hartley,   "
WILLIAMS W. A. 2 Central Ex-
    'change,   "
Woodward Geo. M.   "
Randall Charles J.   Wrentham
Warner Samuel,   "

Lead Manufacturers.

                                                   Salem
Forest River Lead Company (George
    C. Chase, agent),   "
SALEM LEAD CO., (white lead and
    lead pipe),   "

Lead Pencil Manufacturers.

(*See Pencil Manuf.*)

Lead Pipe Manufacturers.

SALEM LEAD CO., Francis Brown,
    treas., 28 P. O. building,   Salem

Leather Belting.

(*See also Belting.*)

Colcord Elihu W.   Lawrence
Foster E. E.   "
Page Edward & Co.   "
Gates Josiah & Sons,   Lowell
Stevens Solon,   "
Whiting & Co.   "
DRAPER GEORGE & SON (see
    page 753), Hopedale,   Milford
FOSTER E. E. 196 Derby,   Salem

Leather Board, Artificial.

Harvard Manuf. Co.   Harvard
Hayden W. B. & Co.   Lawrence
FLAX LEATHER CO. S. Natick, Natick
                                                  Sudbury
Rogers, Edwards, & Co. S. Sudbury,   "
                                                 Townsend
Townsend Leather Co., W. Townsend,   "

Leather Cutters.

Shaw H. G. & Co.   Chicopee
Merrill J. G. & Co.   Peabody

Leather Dealers and Manufacturers.

(*See also Hides and Leather ; also Tanners and Curriers.*)

Cushman J. R. & Son,   Amherst
Savage John,   Blackstone
Warren James J.   Brimfield
Twitchell E. & Co,   Brookfield

West S. O.   East Brookfield,   Brookfield
Richardson & Wilkinson, (card
    leather,),   Cheshire
Chase Edmund,   Fall River
Warren R. E.   Grafton
Burget John,   Great Barrington
Evans S. D. & Son,   Haverhill
Hodgkins A. S.   "
Hoyt Humphrey & Co.   "
Wentworth & Downing,   "
HUDSON TANNING CO,   Hudson
Brown Willard A.   Lowell
Boyce James P. (soles),   Lynn
Hay John F.   "
HILL A. C. (and soles), 46 Exchange,   "
Luscomb S. & Co. (soles and leather),   "
Mayhew A. C. & Co.   Milford
Sumner Jabez (morocco linings),   Milton
Donaghy Thos. E.   New Bedford
Slate & Baker,   Northampton
Merriam William,   Palmer
Flint E. S. & Co.   Peabody
Brown John,   Pittsfield
Ferguson Thomas B.   Salem
Hixion, Birne, Shaw,   Springfield
Perry Henry C.   Taunton
Cushman & Thompson,   Worcester
DEAN A. H. (remnants), 58 South-
    bridge,   "
Lazell N. (remnants),   "
Putman J. R.   "
Rogers, Southgate, & Co.   "
Warren J. J.   "
WESTON O. H.   Sargent's block,   "

Leather, Enamelled & Patent.

                                                 Leominster
Putnam & Phelps, North Leominster,   "
Hubbard & Blake,   Lowell
Stimpson J. C.   Salem
BACON JOHN & CO.   Woburn
Cummings John, jr. & Co.   "
Skinner James & Co.   "

Leather Loom Pickers.

KIMBALL MOSES F. 92 Market,
    (see page 741),   Lowell

Leather Manufacturers.

(*See Leather Dealers ; also Tanners and Curriers.*)

Libraries.

East Abington Library Association,
    East Abington,   Abington
Second Social Library,   Ashfield
Social Library,   Attleborough
Sturgis Library,   Barnstable
Barre Library,   Barre
Bedford Library Association,   Bedford
Cushman Library,   Bernardstown
Billerica Circulating,   Billerica
Town Library,   Bolton
Ladies',   Brewster
Merrick Public Library,   Brookfield
Arms Library,   Buckland
Burlington Town Library,   Burlington
SEVER, FRANCIS, & CO.   Cambridge
Carlton C. (circulating), Cambridge-
    port,   "
Dana Library,   Cambridgeport,   "
Public Library,   "
Hayward Fanny C. (circulating),   Chelsea
Orcutt Samuel,   "
Cheshire Library Association,   Cheshire
                                                 Chesterfield
Chesterfield Second Social Library,   "
Bigelow Library Association,   Clinton

Conway Social Library,   Conway
Dedham Library,   Dedham
Dighton Public Library,   Dighton
Deerfield Library Association,   Deerfield
                                           Edgartown
Edgartown Library Association,   "
Agricultural Library,   Enfield
Farmers Library,   Essex
Essex Circulating Library,   "
Fall River Public Library,   Fall River
                                           Gardner
Young Men's Christian Association,   "
South Gardner Library Association,   "
South Gardner,   "
                                           Georgetown
Agricultural and Social Library,   "
PROCTER'S POPULAR (circulat-
  ing), 121 Front,   Gloucester
Grafton Public Library,   Grafton
Greenfield Library Association,   Greenfield
Harvard Public Library,   Harvard
Hatfield Social Library,   Hatfield
                                           Hinsdale
Hinsdale Public Library Association,   "
Hubbardston Public Library,   Hubbardston
Hudson Public Library,   Hudson
Lancaster Town Library,   Lancaster
Franklin,   Lawrence
Lenox Library,   Lenox
City Library, City Hall,   Lowell
Edwards George C.   "
Mechanics' Library, Mechanics'
  Building,   "
YOUNG MEN'S CHRISTIAN ASSO-
  CIATION, Dr. George C. Osgood,
  librarian, Barristers' Hall,   "
Town Library,   Lunenburg
Merrell P. M.   Lynn
Lunt A. F. Mrs.   Malden
Tufts J. W.   Medford
Ray George C. (circulating),   "
Athenæum Library,   Nantucket
Free Public Library,   New Bedford
Taber Brothers,   "
Agricultural Library,   New Braintree
Northampton Public Library,   Northampton
Whitinsville Library,   Northbridge
                                           North Bridgewater
North Bridgewater Public Library,   "
Weeks F. E.   North Brookfield
Palmer Public Library,   Palmer
Pepperell Agricultural Library,   Pepperell
Agricultural Library,   Petersham
Phillips Public Library,   Phillipston
Pittsfield Library Association and
  Athenæum,   Pittsfield
Poten C. C.   Plymouth
Ellis Bartlett,   "
Agricultural Library,   Princeton
Ladies Circulating Library,   "
Follett Chas. A. (circulating),   Quincy
Rutland Public Library,   Rutland
Beckford Charles A.   Salem
Grindall S.   "
WHIPPLE G. M. & A. A. SMITH,   "
Hawkes C. M.,   East Saugus,   Saugus
Arms Library, Shelburne Falls,   Shelburne
Fay Library,   Southborough
Jackson Library,   Stockbridge
TAUNTON PUBLIC LIBRARY, Taunton
Social Town Library,   Tyngsborough
Wayland Public Library,   Wayland
Westfield Athenæum,   Westfield
Westford Agricultural Library,   Westford
Westford Town Library,   "
Town Library,   Weston
Pratt Nathan (circulating), East
  Weymouth,   Weymouth

Winchendon Public Library, Winchendon
Dorman J. A. Mrs.   Worcester
Free Public Library,   "

Library Steps.

EDDY DARIUS & SON, Harrison
  sq. (see page 666),   Dorchester

Lightning Rods.

Trask Thomas,   Peabody

Lime Burners.

Follett L. J. & Sons (marble lime), Adams
Winchell Homer,   Cheshire
GROSS & STALMANN,   Lee
Humphrey Edwin L.   Pittsfield
Nicholson & Thompson, West Stockbridge
Truesdell Marcus,   "

Lime, Cement, Sand, &c.

Burlingame & Darbys, N. Adams, Adams
Westcott Wm. S.   Amherst
Carpenter L. Z. & A. B.   Attleborough
Gooch J. G. & N. G.   Brighton
Brooks Wm. C. & Co.   Cambridge
Burrage, Shepherd, & Co., Cam-
  bridgeport,   "
Barry Charles J.   Charlestown
Barry Jotham & Co.   "
Oakman & Eldridge,   "
Perkins & Goodwin,   "
Williams S. & G.   "
HAWKINS & KILHAM, Slade's
  wharf (see page 7₁₂),   Fall River
SHOVE C. & CO., 48 Davol,   "
GRIFFIN BENNETT,   Gloucester
Swett & Co.   "
Sargent & Holden,   Haverhill
Stimpson E. E. & Son,   "
West I. R.   "
COGSWELL JOHN H.   Ipswich
Hodgkins Daniel L. (lime),   "
Brown C. A.   Lawrence
Reed R. & Co.   "
Breed S. Oliver,   Lynn
EDMANDS E. P., Summer st. (see
  page 716),   "
Crosby & Putnam,   Milford
Bigelow Charles,   Natick
DOULL JAMES, Front, corner
  School,   New Bedford
Paine S. S. & Brother,   "
Pierce Chas. M. jr.   "
Thurston & Colman,   Newburyport
McIntire Lewis,   Northampton
Soule O. S.   North Bridgewater
BARNES E. & J. C., Water st. (see
  page 717),   Plymouth
Jackson George H.   "
Choate John S.   Rockport
FLINT SIMEON, 221 Derby,   Salem
GOODHUE WM. P. 44 Derby,   "
Edwards Wm. & Son,   Southbridge
Bigelow & Adams,   Springfield
GRAY HENRY & SONS, 86 Main,   "
GURNEY ANSEL S. (see p. 774), Wareham
STAPLES & PHILLIPS (see page
  759), 27 West Water,   Taunton
Edwards J. E.   Webster
Jackson Isaac,   Weymouth
Earle & Turner,   Worcester

Line and Twine.

(See Twine and Line.)

Linen Goods Manufacturers.

Mansfield G. H. & Co. (braids),   Canton
AMERICAN LINEN CO.   Fall River
Stevens Linen Works,   Webster

Liniment.

SWEET JOB, Kempton, cor. Summer (see page 712),   New Bedford

Lining Metal.

WEBSTER C. C. 44 Union (see page 720),   Worcester
WILDER CHARLES, agent, 30 Union ("Babbitt's," see p. 783),   "

Lining Nail Manufacturer.

RHODES M. M., Porter st.   Taunton

Liquid Blueing.

Putnam Charles H.   Rutland

Liquor Dealers.

Wallace Daniel,   Ashland
Buckley J. East Cambridge, Cambridge
Burns Thos.   "   "
Harrington J. E.   "   "
Sullivan T.   "   "
Hurley Charles,   Cambridgeport,   "
McGlone Charles,   "   "
McPeck N.   "   "
Saunders Joseph B.   "   "
Wright S. T.   Chelmsford
Dyer Chas. W.   Chelsea
McGowan John,   "
Mehan & McLaughlin,   "
Stone Moses,   "
Judd B. D.   Chester
Layzell W. H.   "
Mead C. W.   Chicopee
Vining G. B. (wholesale),   "
Campbell J. & T.   Fall River
Crapo J. D.   "
Reynolds Peter,   "
Worden Daniel,   "
Everett James B.   Falmouth
Donnan Wm. B.   Georgetown
Blackliner L. E.   Greenwich
Robinson Joseph R.   Hardwick
Eames A. D.   Hopkinton
Breen Terrence,   Lawrence
Cary Lawrence,   "
Casey James,   "
COAN W. B. & A. 268 Essex,   "
Connell Chas.   "
Dewhirst R.   "
Dixon Thomas,   "
Farrell John,   "
Harmon F.   "
How Richard,   "
Lord John,   "
McDermott J. J.   "
RAFFERTY HUGH, 37 Broadway (wholesale and retail, see p. 741), "
Reed Wm.   "
SMITH ROBERT H., Common cor. Franklin (wholesale and retail), "
Turbitt Henry,   "
Armstrong James,   Lowell
Bradley Christopher,   "
Callahan John,   "
Comer & Dozers,   "
Cummisky Patrick   "
FLYNN M. X. 10 Merrimac (see page 742),   "
Hoar Michael,   "
Keyes Patrick,   "
LYNCH P. 41 Market,   "
McDONOUGH JOHN H. 73 Charles, "
McNabb Bros.   "
Medley & Gayton,   "
Butler Edward F.   Lynn
Dudley Thomas E.   "

Fellows Harry,   Lynn
Hennessey Patrick,   "
Kelley Thomas H.   "
Neil Edward,   "
Oliver George S.   "
Parker Edward,   "
Snow Norcross,   "
Stocker H. P.   "
Joyce David T.   Marshfield
Tolman Henry,   "
Harris Samuel H. jr.   Methuen
Tinkham George C.   Middleborough
Fitzgerald N.   Nantucket
Snow Thomas,   "
Simonds T. F.   Natick
BLAKE JAMES E. 64 N. Second, New Bedford
Dennis Henry,   "
Kinsman G. D.   "
Perry & Wood,   "
Steere V. S.   "
Tillinghast Chas. E.   "
Fenno Joseph H.   North Chelsea
Rawson Charles,   Oxford
Yeoman Charles,   "
Taft S. S. & Co.   North Oxford, "
Gilson Chas. F. East Pepperell, Pepperell
Andrews Collins,   Petersham
Hubbard & Co.   Pittsfield
Murphy & McEnny,   "
Rouse J. P.   "
Boynton John,   Rowley
Barton Wm. C.   Salem
Carey Hugh,   "
Eagan James B.   "
Gardner Thomas N.   "
Keefe Andrew,   "
Kiely Richard,   "
Lawrence Patrick H.   "
Littlefield E.   "
Maguire Bernard,   "
Remond John,   "
Robinson B. F.   "
Keenan James,   Sandwich
Richardson L. J. Montville, Sandisfield
Robinson C. H.   Southbridge
Allen E. L. (wholesale),   Springfield
Eastman Wm. D.   "
Gunn Wm. & Co. (wholesale),   "
Jennings John & Co. (wholesale), "
MADDEN JOHN, Sandford st.   "
Matthews Wm.   "
McCauley D.   "
McCulloch James,   "
O'Reilly James A.   "
Pierce Simon,   "
Robinson E. C. & Co.   "
Ryan Daniel (wholesale),   "
Warren D. D. (wholesale),   "
Watts W. B.   "
Webster Shelden (wholesale),   "
Nash James L. Indian Orchard, "
DRAKE LEONARD,   Stoughton
Allen A. C.   West Brookfield
Burnham R. L.   Westford
        West Stockbridge
Barnes & Lortz,   State Line, "
CHURCH SILAS L.   "   "
Baker Wm. jr.   Whately
Dorman & White,   Worcester
Foley J.   "
Hill J. S.   "

Lithographers.

Dubois H. W. & Co.   Fall River
Bradley Milton & Co.   Springfield
Chubbuck Thomas,   "
Lutz J. C. & Co.   "

Livery Stables.

(*See Stables.*)

Lobster Dealers.

Johnson & Young, Charlestown
Kendall N. J. "
Taylor H. E. & Co. "

Lock Manufacturers.

GAYLORD MANUF. CO., A. F.
Gaylord, treas. (see page 773), Chicopee
Yale & Winn Manufacturing Co.
Shelburne Falls, Shelburne

Locksmiths.

(*See also Bell-hangers.*)

HOYT B. J., also bell-hanger,
495 Main (see page 801), Cam-
bridgeport, Cambridge
McCarty John, E. Cambridge, "
Junio Jacob, Charlestown
Webster E. O. "
Webster Geo. H. "
Webster Francis F. Chelsea
Grant W. N. Greenfield
Daw Samuel, Lawrence
FROST J. W. & CO., 308 Common, "
McAllister B. "
Batchelder A. G. & Son, Lowell
Curtis T. H. "
Trumbel James W. "
Sherman Wm. R. New Bedford
Hannum & Avery, Northampton
Bagg Martin, Pittsfield
Perry Horatio B. Salem
Gifford J. H. Springfield
Abbott Z. (keyes), Winchester
Cummings C. A. Worcester

Locomotive Tire Manuf.

WASHBURN IRON CO. (see page
784), Worcester
Washburn Nathan & Co. "

Locomotive Works.

(*See also Machinists; also Steam-Engine
Builders.*)

MASON WILLIAM (builder of every
variety of locomotives, cotton machinery, machinists' tools, &c., see
page 730), Taunton
Taunton Locomotive Manufacturing Co., Parley A. Perrin, supt. "

Looking Glass and Picture-Frame Manufacturers.

MORGAN ALFRED, Brattle sq.
(see page 727), Cambridge
Myer C. E. & Co. Cambridgeport, "
Aarons & Co. East Cambridge, "
Herrick & Poulan, "
Charlestown
Titcomb & Bellamy (emblematic), "
WILSON WM. H., Park st. (see
page 720), Chelsea
Westgate Joseph C. Fall River
Gloucester
PROCTER BROTHERS, 121 Front, "
ROGERS J. S. E. Low's Block, "
Downing E. K. Lawrence
Ellis & Snow, "
Richard J. M. "
Gordon & Currier, Lowell
Kagg & Griffith, "

19

Ellis Leonard B. New Bedford
Pierce B. W. "
Brown Andrew, Newburyport
Clark G. W. "
Thurlow Frank, "
Beckford Chas. A. Salem
Grindall S. "
Locke N. C. "
Shaw X. H. & Son, "
Burnham A. V. Springfield
Eldridge & Hastings, "
Holcomb Brothers, "
Gilmore W. H. Taunton
Davis S. H. Webster
Westborough
NOURSE, WHITE, & CO. (picture), "
Cumings Chester, Worcester
Peck Angustus E. "

Loom Manufacturers.

DUCKWORTH & SONS (see page
713), Pittsfield
Knowles L. J. & Brother, Worcester
CROMPTON GEORGE, Green st.
(see page 787) "
GILBERT C. W., Union, cor.
Exchange. "
TAINTER DANIEL, "

Loom Harness Manuf.

SLADDIN & LORD, Page's building (see page 746), Lawrence

Loom Harness Knitting Machine Manuf.

SLADDIN & LORD, Page's building (Patent self-acting, see page.
746), Lawrence

Loom Harness Twine Manufacturer.

CLARK JEREMIAH, 96 Middle
(see page 738), Lowell

Loom Pickers.

KIMBALL MOSES F. 92 Market
(see page 741), Lowell

Loom Reed and Harness Manufacturers.

KENDALL CARLO M. Chicopee
Flint James jr. Chicopee Falls, "
Hubbard H. B. "
Gibbs William H. (reeds), Clinton
GOWDEY J. A. & SON (see
page 716), Fall River
KENDRICK J. & J. H., 42
and 44 Pocasset (see page 711), "
NEWTON JAMES (see page 722), "
Carver George (reed strip), Granby
Clegg Thomas, Lawrence
Yeaton E. & Co. (power loom harness), "
Brown D. C. Lowell
Harris Geo. W. "
Stevens Solon, Fletcher corner
Western ave. "
TILLEY & CLARK, Hampden st.
(see page 778), Springfield
Booth Mary Mrs. Worcester
Gray & Batcheller, "

Loom Temple Manufacturers.

Dutcher Temple Co., Hopedale, Milford

Low Water Reporter.

AMERICAN LOW WATER RE-
PORTER CO., Geo. Lunt,
treas. Newburyport

Lumber Dealers.

(See also Saw Mills.)

Reed A. S. & Co. N. Abington, Abington
Faulkner W. E. S. Acton, Acton
Twitchell Chas. S. W. " "
Hamlin Samuel B. Acushnet
Lund Jonathan P. "
BAKER JAMES (see page 729),
North Adams, Adams
Martin William, " "
Amherst
Amherst Mill Co., E. B. Fitts, agent, "
Foster Leonard, Burrageville, Ashburnham
Bartlett Ira, Ashby
Sprague John, South Ashfield, Ashfield
Williams Darius, "
Brewster E. R. Ashland
Rice & Meacham, Athol Depot, Athol
Sprague Caleb, " "
Hooper Q. A. Attleborough
Hinckley Josiah, Barnstable
Crocker B. F. & Co. Hyannis, "
Snow Samuel, " "
Brown M. V. B. Belchertown
Root Harrison, "
Wesson L. B. & G. B. "
Barnes G. H. Berlin
Ober J. T. & Co. Beverly
Roundy George, "
Richardson J. O. Billerica
Aldrich C. B. Blackstone
Osborn Eli, Blandford
Collester G. North Blandford, "
Forbush Jonathan, Bolton
Sawyer Joel, "
Sawyer John F. "
Walcott Freeman, "
Andrews Dean, Boxford
Hayward Augustus, "
Braintree
GARDNER HENRY (agent), P. O.
address Weymouth (see page 768), "
Lincoln Warren & Co. Brewster
Fuller G. & Son, Brighton
Gooch J. G. & N. G. "
Morgan Thomas J. Brimfield
Shaw Darius, "
TWITCHELL GEO. L. & CO. Brookfield
Buckland
Frost J. B. & Co. Shelburne Falls, "
Burrage, Shepherd, & Co. Cambridge-
port, Cambridge
Gale & Russell, Cambridgeport, "
TRIBOU WALTER S. " "
Blanchard W. S. & Co., E. Cambridge, "
Daniels & Co. " "
Flint & Hall, " "
Hastings Oliver, " "
Holt S. A. " "
Howland & Doughty, " "
Skillings D. N. & Co. " "
Savery William, Carver
Brooks John W. & Son, Charlestown
Clark & Smith, "
Fuller S. W. & Co. "
Hopkins Franklin, jr. "
Knight Joel & Co. "
Trickey & Jewett, "
Emery John, Chatham
Nickerson Caleb, "
Bangs S. & J. H. Chelsea

Buck T. H. & Co. Chelsea
Hall Brothers, "
Trussell Rufus & Co. "
Hawes William, "
Russell Abbot, Chelmsford
Bisbee Orin, Chesterfield
Edwards O. jr. "
Bingham Horace, Chicopee
Davis George H. Chilmark
Clarksburg
Chilson Jacob B. North Adams, "
Dooley Peter, "
Ketchum Eleazer, " "
FULLER E. S. Clinton
Tower A. H. jr. & Co. Cohasset
Hudson B. N. Concord
Cleveland Cyrus, Dalton
Cleveland Wm. "
Mitchell P. "
Smith A. & J. "
Smith D. C. & Sons, "
Hale Warren & Co. North Dana, Dana
Eveleth Aaron, Danvers Port, Danvers
Potter & Batchelder, " "
Putnam Calvin, " "
Hall Nathan, Dennis
Snow & Inman, Dennis Port, "
Simmons Henry M. Dighton
GRAY WILLIAM H. Neponset, Dorchester
Pope A. & Son, Harrison Square, "
Shephard C. A. & Frost, " "
Pratt & Co. Port Norfolk, "
STEARNS ALBERT T. (see page 695),
Port Norfolk, "
French Benj. Dunstable
Taylor Oliver, "
Harding P. S. Orleans, Eastham
East Hampton
BASSETT JOEL L. (see page 761), "
Fisher Jared, jr. Edgartown
Huxford James B. "
Cadwell A. J. Enfield
Ward Benjamin, "
Washburn Wm. B. & Co. Erving
Burnham Jacob, Essex
Fairhaven
FISH ROLAND (Southern pine), "
Borden Cook & Co. Fall River
COOK WILLIAM M., Danforth st. "
COOK V. & CO. Central, cor. Pond, "
Crane J. A. (agent), "
TERRY J. C. (ship), 62 Durfee, "
Lawrence T. H. Falmouth
Davis & Eldred, Wood's Hole, "
BECKWITH A. A. & CO. (see page
720), Fitchburg
FITCHBURG LUMBER CO. (see page
767), "
Kemp S. A. Florida
Tower Chester, "
Hastings Wm. Framingham
Metcalf E. L. & O. F. Franklin
Pierce & Wilson (box boards), Freetown
Chace & Gurney, East Freetown, "
Parker David, Gardner
Lovewell John, South Gardner, "
Whitney J. A. "
Wright M. & Co. " "
Tenney M. Georgetown
Holmes & Wood, Turner's Falls, Gill
Allen David G. Gloucester
Bennett & Reed, "
GRIFFIN BENNETT, "
Swett & Co. "
Story Amos A. East Gloucester, "
Dresser C. C. Goshen
Hawks Rodney, "
Sears Freeman, "

Stone Luther,' Goshen
Norton S. & Co. Great Barrington
Goss R. L. & D. W. Greenfield
Newton James & Sons, "
Bailey S. P. Greenwich Vil'ge, Greenwich
Emsworth & Inglee, Halifax
House James W. West Hanover, Hanover
Studley Joshua, "
Southworth Constant, Hardwick
Spooner Bros. "
Dickinson Samuel W. Harvard
Farwell John, "
Fletcher E. E. & Bro. "
Richmond J. C. "
Kelley H. jr. & Co. Harwich Port, Harwich
Kelley A. " "
Fitch Brothers & Porter, Hatfield
Sargent & Holden, Haverhill
Stimpson E. E. & Son, "
West I. R. "
Fuller Clark W. West Hawley, Hawley
Clement James F. Hingham
Cushing David 2d, "
Broad Ira, Holden
Howe George W. "
Kinney Elisha, Holland
Marcy U. P. "
Wallis W. A. "
Chase Edwin & Sons, Holyoke
Wiggin & Flagg, "
Brigham O. S. Hubbardston
Hale & Williams, "
Tilton Eben'r, "
Underwood H. "
Hyde Park
NEAL A. B. & CO. (hard wood and
other finished lumber, see page 765), "
THOMPSON & RUSSELL, "
LEACH B. F. (see page 765), Readville,"
COGSWELL JOHN H. Ipswich
Hodgkins Daniel L. "
Lawrence Lumber Co., Luther Ladd
agent, Lawrence
Plummer H. & Co. "
Prescott J. H. & Co. "
Bradley Geo. F. Lee
Beebe Levi, South Lee,
Dudley Luther, Leverett
Dudley Samuel, "
Dudley William E. "
Field Harrison, "
Moore Dexter, "
Stetson William B. "
Denison A. J. Leyden
Hartwell E. P. Littleton
Kimball William, "
Brooks A. L. Lowell
Davis & Melendy, "
Howes & Burnham, "
Norcross & Saunders (agents), "
WHITNEY H. & A. (see page 782),
Western ave. "
Adams D. F. & Co. Lynn
Breed Joseph, 2d, "
BREED S. N. & CO., 83 Broad, "
Buffum J. N. (packing boxes), "
Neal & Lee, "
Newhall Wm. M. "
Breed S. Oliver. "
Gourlee Thomas P. Manchester
Kitfield Thomas H. "
Potter Henry A. Marblehead
Holmes & Sparrow, Marion
Pardow C. H. & E. S. "
SMITH S. & A. Marlborough
Afsutt John T. Mattapoisett
BARSTOW N. H. & H. (see page
727), "

Bolles Solomon E. Mattapoisett
Dexter E. & Son, "
Ellis Jarvis, "
Holmes Josiah, jr., & Bro. (ship), "
Foster F. E. & Co. Medford
Mann Chas. W. W. Medway, Medway
MORSE E. P. Methuen
Patterson D. H. "
Chapin D. S. Milford
EDDY & BRITTON, "
Todd & Gannett, Milton
Lawrence C. & H. C. Montague
Goss R. L. & D. W. Montague City, "
Hadsell John K. Monterey
Wood Thos. "
Whitbeck O. C. Mount Washington
Perkins George W. Nahant
Macy John W. Nantucket
Bigelow Charles, Natick
Needham
Rice Charles, jr., Newton Lower Falls, "
Beard W. A., (hard pine), New Bedford
DOULL JAMES, front cor. School, "
GREENE & WOOD, Leonard's whf. "
Hathaway B. F. "
Ripley & Tripp, "
Topham Robert C. "
Pepper H. A. New Braintree
Pollard M. "
Pearson Benjamin, Newbury
Kimball Edward, Newburyport
Kimball, Perkins, & Co. "
Littlefield Hiram, "
Thurston & Coleman, "
Allen & Rood, Hartsville, New Marlborough
Sisson H. D. Mill River, "
Sisson Henry, " "
Wolfe J. I. " "
McAlpine James, Southfield, "
Eaton & Merriam, New Salem
Adams Samuel, North New Salem, "
BANISTER EDWIN, Northampton
Gibbs Dwight, "
NONOTUCK SILK CO. Florence, "
Shaw L. W. "
Bartlett Wm. A. 2d, Northborough
BATCHELLER A. & E. D. N. Brookfield
Fullam William, "
Hebard J. F. "
Stoddard Leonard, "
Soule Oakes S. North Bridgewater
Green Charles, Northfield
Batchelder Henry, North Reading
Campbell Warren A. "
Holt Solon O. "
Parker Daniel M. Cold Brook, Oakham
Bill & Taylor, Orange
Coolidge Henry & James, "
Davis Edwin, "
Graham Ephraim, "
Hunt & Blodgett, "
Kilburn Levi & Co. "
Putnam Frederick, "
WHITNEY, LORD, & CO. (see page
776), "
Newcomb Thomas S. Orleans
Carter Charles J. Otis
Haskell Volney W. "
Strickland Lyman J. "
Stockwell H. S. & J. W. Oxford
Comins William, Paxton
Clark Aaron F. Peabody
Carter Sumner, Pepperell
Powers Edward, Phillipston
Nash Brothers, Pittsfield
WADHAMS & SPRAGUE, "
Campbell Levi N. Plainfield
Streeter S. C. "

Lumber Dealers — continued.

Brown Nathaniel,   Plymouth
Jackson George H.   "
Robbins Leavitt,   "
Bonney James S.   Plympton
Davis Daniel, jr.   Princeton
Davis R., jr.   "
Howe Jotham,   "
Miles D. C. & Co.   "
Brooks & Lancy,   Provincetown
COOK H. & S. & CO.   "
Ryder Benjamin,   "
SMALL REUBEN C.   "
     Quincy
Adams Ebenezer & Son, Quincy Point, "
Cox Hubbard,   Reading
Haskell William C.   Rochester
King & Hathaway,   "
Rounseville Alden, jr.   "
Gott Levi S.   Rockport
Choate John S.   "
Amidon H. & Co.   Rowe
Ford James M.   "
Kendrick H. A.   "
Holman Seth N.   Royalston
Perkins & Goddard,   "
Whitney George,   "
Stone Joseph,   Rutland
Austin Eleazer,   Salem
Brown G. F. & S.   "
Buffum David,   "
Langmaid P. J.   "
PICKERING WM., jr., 17 Peabody,   "
Putnam Nathan,   "
Thayer O. & Co.   "
Boyd Newell,   Salisbury
Phelps Newton,   Montville, Sandisfield
Stratton Theo. A.   "   "
Sage Edwin,   New Boston, "
Deming A. & M.   Savoy
Mason E. L.   "
Damon Franklin,   Scituate
     Shelburne
FROST J. B. & Co.   Shelburne Falls, "
Streeter A. W.   "   "   "
White E. L.   South Groton, Shirley
Dudley Samuel F.   Shutesbury
Felton Charles,   "
Ober Henry,   "
Penna Asa,   Somerset
Clemence J. M. & L. D., Globe Village,   Southbridge
Gilbert Edwin,   Southwick
Granger Brothers,   "
Abbe A. B.   Springfield
Day, Jobson, & Chase,   "
Robinson, Marsh, & Co.   "
Smith & Martin,   "
Wells River Lumber Co.   "
Bates & Adams,   Fiskdale, Sturbridge
Hovey M. M.   Sutton
Stockwell H. S.   "
BLAKE ZEBINA, West Water (see page 758),   Taunton
STAPLES & PHILLIPS, 27 West Water (see page 759),   "
Wilbur J. W. L. & Brother,   "
WILLIAMS B. F., Weir st.   "
Williams N. S.   East Taunton, "
Williams A. K. & Co.   Weir,   "
Bourne & Brooks,   Templeton
Sawyer Geo. W.   "
Day Gilman,   Baldwinsville, "
Sawyer & Thompson,   "   "
Hodge A. S. & Co.   E. Templeton, "
Stone W. & E. W.   Otter River, "
Cottle Edward,   Tisbury
Smith David,   Holmes's Hole, "

Moore Bennett E.   Tolland
Marshall A. & Son,   "
Brinley & James,   Tyngsborough
Butterfield James P.   "
Moore L. B.   Tyringham
Comstock Metcalf,   Upton
Hall Thomas I.   "
Wood Arba T.   "
Morey H. P. & Co.   Wales
Bustrick Francis,   Waltham
Bosworth & Makepeace,   Warren
Drury Franklin,   "
Fairbanks Asahel,   "
Gilkey R. & Co.   Watertown
Goddard Joel,   Webster
Wiley N. Parker,   Wellfleet
Bemis Theodore,   Wendell
Leach Luke,   "
Smith T. A.   Westborough
Pierce Henry,   West Boylston
Ames Thomas,   West Bridgewater
Clark Joseph S.   Westfield
Kittredge B. L. & Co.   "
Smith Spencer F.   "
Lymon William E.   West Hampton
Clark, Nichols, & Co.   Westminster
Merriam, Holden, & Co.   "
Miles Daniel C.   "
Smith George,   "
Wyman Benj.   Wachusett, "
Macomber B. & Son,   Westport
Jackson Isaac,   Weymouth
Loud & Pratt,   "
Rhines J. C.   "
Cole P. R.   Williamstown
Holbrook ——,   "
Wyman S.   Winchendon
Sibley William,   "
LITTLEFIELD J. E. & SONS,   Woburn
WHITCHER JACOB O.   "
BAKER CHARLES & CO.   Worcester
CHAMBERLIN & CO., Grove st. (see page 781),   "
Crane E. B.,   "
Earle & Turner,   "
Gates John & Co.   "
TENNEY CHARLES A. & CO.   "
White W. & A.,   S. Yarmouth, Yarmouth
Sears J. K. & B.   "

Lumber Manufacturers.

LEACH B. F. (see page 765), Readville,   Hyde Park

Machine Brokers.

PEIRCE JOHN N. 25 Howe (see page 742),   Lowell
DAVIS L. L., 10 Fort Block,   Springfield
WILDER CHARLES, Agent, 30 Union (see page 783),   Worcester

Machine Button-Hole Maker.

FOSS FRANK,   Munroe st.   Lynn

Machine Card and Machine Card Clothing.

(See also Card and Card Clothing Manufs.)

NEWTON JAMES (see page 722),   Fall River
Fuller Geo. A.   Lawrence
WARREN & ROBINSON, Broadway, cor. Methuen st.   "
BISCO & DENNY,   Leicester
MURDOCK J. & J.   "
Smith & Waite,   "
HOWE & GOODHUE (see page 740), 92 Market,   Lowell

KITSON RICHARD, Worthen, near
  Dutton, (see page 737), Lowell
LOWELL CARD CO. J. Clark, agt.
  96 Middle (see page 742), "
Hampden Card Co., Sanford st. Springfield
Stetson E. P. Walpole
EARLE T. K. & CO. (see page 788),
  Grafton st. Worcester
Howard Brothers, "
SARGENT CARD CLOTHING CO.
  Junction (see last white page), "

Machine Castings, &c.

(See also Iron Founders.)

FALL RIVER IRON WORKS, Fall River
KILBURN, LINCOLN, & CO. (see
  page 756), "

Machine Knives.

SIMONDS MANUF. CO. (see page
  658), W. Fitchburg, Fitchburg

Machine Screws.

STACY E. S. & CO., Harrison Ave.
  (see page 784), Springfield
  Worcester
BAGLEY E. A. & CO., 12 Central, "
  Winter & Marcy, "

Machinery and Tools.

*(See also Machinists and Machinery Manu-
  facturers.)*

LAZELL, PERKINS, & CO. Bridgewater
DRAPER & WOODBURY (see page
  572), Marlboro'
DAVIS L. L. (broker), Springfield
Kimball C. W. (broker), "
FOUNDRY AND MACHINE CO.,
  H. S. Fairbanks, treas. (see page
  692), Taunton
WILDER CHARLES, agent (second
  hand, see page 783), Worcester

Machinists and Machinery Manufacturers.

(See also Steam Engine Builders.)

Kimball E. A. & Co. Abington
Young Jacob K., East Abington, "
Bates James A., South Abington, "
Allen Darwin W. Adams
Champney Jonas C. "
Barnes Merrick M. (repairer), N.
  Adams, "
HUNTER JAMES & SON (see page
  770), N. Adams, "
WHEELER DELIVERANCE, OTIS
  J. HODGE, Agent (see page 786),
  N. Adams, "
  Amesbury
Sargent J. B. & E. P., W. Amesbury, "
Dickinson Porter, Amherst
Olney Nathan, North Amherst, "
Loring John R. Andover
Hobbs Alfred, Arlington
ATHOL MACHINE CO. (see page
  800), Athol Depot, Athol
GERRY, GEORGE & SON (see page
  771), 6 Mill st. Athol Depot, "
RICHARDSON GEORGE H. (see
  page 771), Athol Depot "
Blakeley T. Attleborough
Stone W. M. "
Willcox & Barnett, "
HEALD STEPHEN & SONS (man-
  ufacturers, jobbers, and repairers,
  see pages 796 and 797), Barre

McElwain Oliver, Becket
Page Moses, Bedford
Cook E. B. (shingle machines), Bellingham
Raymond Benjamin, Beverly
Hill & Proctor, Billerica
Bates, Hyde, & Co. Bridgewater
LAZELL, PERKINS, & CO. "
Southern Cotton Gin Co. "
Hobbs M. & J., East Brookfield, Brookfield
  Buckland
Foster Gustavus, Shelburne Falls, "
Sprague Nelson, "
  Cambridge
Allen & Endicott, Cambridgeport, "
Bullock O. S. " "
KINSLEY LYMAN & CO. (see
  page 714), Cambridgeport, "
Whittemore Amos, "
Baker William A. & Co., E. Cambridge. "
Blanchard Thomas, Canton
Deane Walter P. "
Gib Bush Co. (rings and gib bush), "
KINSLEY IRON & MACHINE CO.
  (see page 730), "
REED FRANKLIN (boot, shoe, &c.
  see page 793), "
Cook, Rymes, & Co. Charlestown
Silver & Gay, Chelmsford
Bisbee, Endicott, & Co. Chelsea
  Chesterfield
Bryant R. & Bros. W. Chesterfield, "
Ames Manuf. Co. George Arms,
  agent, Chicopee
Stevens J. & Co. Chicopee Falls, "
Parker J. B. & Co. Clinton
Barber Bros. Coleraine
Phelps E. N. Dalton
Boynton George, Milton, Dorchester
Burgess Silas, East Bridgewater
E. Carver Co. "
KEEN SAMUEL & CO. Joppa Village, "
Dudley E. S. (jobbing), East Hampton
Wilson J. W. "
Dean T. H. & J. O., South Easton, Easton
  Fairhaven
BOSTON & FAIRHAVEN IRON
  WORKS, B. F. Leonard, agent, "
ASHWORTH ROBERT, Davol n.
  Central, (repairs sewing ma-
  chines, see page 721), Fall River
FALL RIVER IRON WORKS CO. "
Gifford & Houghton, "
Hawes Wm. M. & Co. "
KAY BROTHERS (spool and thread
  machinery, see page 725), "
KILBURN, LINCOLN, & CO.
  (see page 756). "
MARVEL, DAVOL, & CO. "
Thurston Abraham G. "
WHITMAN & EDDY (manuf. of
  the Patent Vertical Drill, see
  page 708). "
BARKER T. L. & CO. (see page
  772), Fitchburg
FITCHBURG MACHINE CO., S. C.
  Wright, pres. J. L. Chapman, sec.
  A Whitman, treas. Summer st.
  (see page 707), "
PUTNAM MACHINE CO., S. W.
  Putnam, pres. (see page 707). "
ROLLSTONE MACHINE WORKS,
  J. Goodrich, agent (see page 709), "
Thompson L. F. "
Tyrrell H. P. "
UNION MACHINE CO. "
Waymouth, A. D. & Co. "
Parker R. D. Florida
Patterson Charles S. "

Lowell
ROBINSON WM., Mechanics' Mills, "
SAWYER HAMILTON J., Mt.
Vernon, near Broadway, "
Stevens Benj. F.
Henderson H. A. (sand papering
machines), Lynn
Holbrook & Glazier, "
Holmes E. & Son, "
KIMBALL WM. H. & CO., 42 Wash. "
Knox George, "
Sawyer Leonard, · "
TRIPP S. D., 13 Broad (see page 750), "
Thompson John, Marblehead
DRAPER & WOODBURY (see
page 672), Marlborough
Exley & Parsons, "
Barstow Henry W. Mattapoisett
Medway Flock Co. Medway
PARTRIDGE ALLEN & SON, "
Clark A. & E., Rockville, "
Thayer A. P. (bonnet and hat press-
ing machinery), West Medway, "
West Prescott (jobbing), Milford
Dutcher Temple Co. (loom temples),
Hopedale, "
DRAPER GEO. & SON (see page
758), Hopedale, "
HOPEDALE FURNACE CO., Wm.
F. Draper, treas. (see page 758),
Hopedale, "
Hopedale Machine Co., Hopedale, "
Woodin Frank, Monterey
Howe Jarvis & Co. "
Littlefield J. W. "
Franklin & Brigham, Natick
Gifford John A. New Bedford
Union Boiler Co., James C. Brad-
ford, agent, "
Stamp Edward L. Newbury
Cheney George A. Newburyport
Curtis Francis, "
Moody H. T. "
Noyes William, jr. "
Sargent C. R. "
Abbot William, Mill River, New Marlboro'
Huntley Joseph W. " "
Huntley William, " "
Eaton, Moulton, & Co. (paper and
other machinery), Lower Falls, Newton
Prttee Otis & Co. (cotton machinery),
Upper Falls, "
Clapp Wm. R. Northampton
Herrick Webster, "
Davis & Furbur (woolen), North Andover
Noyes H. W. North Bridgewater
Snell E. S. & Co. "
Snell & Atherton, "
WHITIN JOHN C. (cotton machinery,
see page 754), Whitinsville, Northbridge
Hunt, Waite, & Flint, Orange
TURBINE WATER-WHEEL MANUF.
CO. (manuf. of Chase's patent excel-
sior turbine water-wheel, and circu-
lar saw-mill, see page 777), "
BLANCHARD A. V. & Co. (wood
bending), Palmer
Balcom, Jennings, & Co. Peabody
Blake Brothers, East Pepperell, Pepperell
Clark William, Pittsfield
CLARY & RUSSELL (see page 708), "
May & Chapel, ·
Coffin T. M. Plymouth
PLYMOUTH MILLS, J. Farris, agt.
(see page 722), "
Badger Brothers, Quincy
LITTLEFIELD BROTHERS (see
page 728), Randolph

Chapman Wm. H.   Salem
Freeman T. (gear cutting machine),   "
Goodell Zina, 16 Lafayette,   "
GRISWOLD E. L. (sewing machines),   "
  142 Essex,   "
NEWCOMB GEO. L., 18 Peabody,   "
PHILLIPS HENRY B. 194 and 196
  Derby,   "
Salem Foundry and Machine Shop,   "
Salem Machine Co. (steam engines),   "
Weston John W.   "
                                  Saugus
HOLLIDAY WM. S., Saugus Centre,   "
Parker James L., Shirley Village, Shirley
Anthony Edward,   Somerset
Dribs Charles,   "
Johnson Hiram,   • "
Mount Hope Iron Co.   "
Scott Wallace,   "
Harris Wilbur F.   South Hadley
Judd Thomas & Son,   "
Curtis George & Co.   Springfield
Dickinson Edward L.   "
English B. C. (light machinery),   "
Grimes & Ellison,   "
HARRIS D. L. 1 Charles st.   "
JOHNSON & RANDALL, 6 Lyman,   "
ROCHE BROS. (see page 780),   "
Russell & Day,   "
STACY E. S. & CO. (see page 784),   "
                            Stockbridge
BURGHARDT & CO. Curtisville,
Anderson C. A.   Fiskdale,   Sturbridge
Smith A. P.   "   "
Babbitt F. S.   Taunton
FOUNDRY AND MACHINE CO.
  H. S. Fairbanks, treas. and agent,
  (see page 692),   "
Huntley Geo. R.   "
MASON WILLIAM (builder of every
  variety of cotton machinery, ma-
  chinist tools, locomotives, &c. see
  page 736),   "
Potter William R.   "
Strange Elias W. & Co.   "
Wilkinson John F.   Templeton
Stimpson James,   Baldwinville,   "
Nichols & Adams,   Otter River,   "
Young Albert F.   "   "   "
Cassidy Michael,   Tyringham
Pennock Samuel,   Upton
Shaw Machine Co. W. Shaw, agent; Wales
Daniels George W. (tools),   Waltham
Hobbs George F.   "
Stark John & Co. (watch-makers'
  tools),   "
Sawyer Oliver,   Watertown
                        West Boylston
Murdock D. C. (warper stop-motions), "
Shipman George,   West Bridgewater
Washburn H. L. & Co.   (eyelet),   "
Avery D.   Westfield
Halladay & Griffin,   "
Sizer Emerson,   "
Wheeler Lyman,   "
Williams, Stowell, & Co.   "
SARGENT CHAS. G. (woolen ma-
  chinery, burring and combing ma-
  chines, and all kinds of cotton
  machinery, see page 743), Granite-
  ville,   Westford
Metcalf Eli,   West Hampton
Bowen H. D. (butter and cheese tri-
  ers),   Weston
Sibley Nathaniel L.   "
Brown Hayden,   West Newbury
Noyes S. N.   "
Merritt Washington,   Weymouth

Powers David, E. Weymouth, Weymouth
Smith Justin R.   Whately
Backus Q. S.   Winchendon
Folsom John G.   "
GOODSPEED & WYMAN (see page
  776),   "
Whitney Washington,   "
Whitney Baxter D.   "
Whitney Joel,   Winchester
Buel James,   Woburn
Butler Levi,   "
Cooper Levi W.   "
Emery E. R. (comb),   "
Parker, Holden, & Co. (leather board-
  ing and graining),   "
BALL R. & CO. 26 School,   Worcester
Blaisdell P.   "
Blake Bros.   "
Brown Wm. H.   "
Cleveland & Bassett (woolen),   "
CROMPTON GEO. (looms, see page
  787),   "
Curtis & Marble (woolen, &c.),   "
FAY L. D. 7 Cypress (see page 783),   "
GILBERT C. W. (looms),   Union,   "
Gooding John jr.   "
Goulding John,   "
Henshaw A. F.   "
JOHNSON & CO. (woolen),   Union,   "
Kent Samuel W. (card setting),   "
Knowles L. J. & Bro. (looms),   "
LATHE & MORSE (tools), Junction,   "
LEE H. A. 56 Union (moulding, &c.,
  see page 750),   "
Lombard N. A. & Co. (woolen),   "
Mathews I. D.   "
NEW YORK STEAM ENGINE CO.
  A. B. Couch, supt. (see page 785),   "
Pease L. J. & Co.   "
Perkins John S.   "
POND LUCIUS W., Union,
Prouty A. B. (card-setting),   "
RICE, BARTON, & FALES MACHINE
  & IRON CO. (paper, &c.),   "
RICE & WHITCOMB, 11 Cypress, (see
  page 784),   "
RICHARDSON, MERIAM, & CO.
  (wood working),   Junction,   "
Seaverns John L. (paper),   "
SOUTHWICK & HATHAWAY, 7
  Cypress,   "
TAINTER DANIEL (woolen), Union,   "
Thomas Iron Works,   "
UNION IRON WORKS, Rice &
  Whitcomb (see page 784),   "
Union Water Meter Co.   "
Wheeler J. S. & Co.   "
WHEELER WM. A. 42 Thomas (see
  page 792),   "
Whitcomb B.   1 Cypress,   "
WHITCOMB C. & CO. Exchange st.   "
Williams John (gearing),   "
Winslow S. C. & S. (gearing, &c.),   "
WITHERBY, RUGG, & RICHARD-
  SON (wood working, see page 788),   "
Wood, Light, & Co.   (tools),   "

Machinists' Tools Manufacturers.

GERRY GEO. & SON (see page 771),
Athol Depot,   Athol
Ames Manuf. Co.   Chicopee
Hawes William M. & Co.   Fall River
KILBURN, LINCOLN, & CO. (see
  page 756),   "
WHITMAN & EDDY (patent upright
  vertical drills, see page 708),   "

Machinists' Tools Manuf. — continued.
BARKER T. L. & CO.   Fitchburg
FITCHBURG MACHINE CO. (see
page 707),   "
PUTNAM MACHINE CO. (see page
707),   "
UNION MACHINE CO.   "
Eagle Ratchet Co.   Holliston
HOLYOKE MACHINE CO.   Holyoke
Kidder Charles L.   Lowell
LANE DAVID, Fletcher, c. Cushing
sts. (see page 738),   "
LOWELL MACHINE SHOP,   "
PERKINS F. S. Mechanics' Mills,   "
ROBINSON WM. Mechanics' Mills,   "
Hopedale Machine Co. Hopedale,   Milford
Millbury Machine Co.   Millbury
BLAISDELL A. H. & CO. (gauges
see page 745). Newton Corner,   Newton
MORSE TWIST DRILL & MACHINE
CO.   New Bedford
LITTLEFIELD BROTHERS (see p.
728),   Randolph
HARRIS D. L.   Springfield
STACY E. S. Harrison Avenue (see
page 784),   "
FOUNDRY & MACHINE CO. H. S.
Fairbanks, treas. and agent, (see
page 692),   Taunton
MASON WILLIAM (builder of every
variety of cotton machinery, Machin-
ist's tools, locomotives &c. see page
736),   "
          Worcester
LATHE & MORSE, Junction shop,   "
LEE H. A. 56 Union, (see page 750),   "
Blaisdell P.   "
FAY L. D. 7 Cypress (see page 783),   "
Houghton H. H.   "
NEW-YORK STEAM ENGINE
CO., A. B. Couch, supt. (see
page 785),   "
POND LUCIUS W., Union, cor. Ex-
change,   "
RICE & WHITCOMB (see page 784),
7 Cypress,   "
Smith Thomas E. & Co.   "
Thomas Iron Works,   "
Wheeler J. S. & Co.   "
WHITCOMB C. & CO. Exchange,
cor. Cypress,   "
Wood, Light, & Co.   "
Wood & Ballard,   "

Magic Oil.

RENNE WILLIAM (see p. 793), Pittsfield

Magnesia Manufacturer.

Fearing Franklin, S. Yarmouth, Yarmouth

Magneto-Electric Machines.

DAVIS ASAHEL (for medical purposes), Mechanics' Mills,   Lowell

Mail Bags.

GAYLORD MANUF. CO. (see page
773),   Chicopee

Malleable Iron Founders.

(*See also Iron Founders.*)
GAYLORD MANUF CO. A. F. Gay-
lord, treas. (see page 773),   Chicopee
Belcher Daniel,   Easton
ARCADE MALLEABLE IRON CO.
W. McFarland, agent,   Worcester

Manufacturers' Agents.

Norris, Howes, & Co.   Springfield

Manufacturers' Articles.

Kendall J.   Lowell
Talbot Charles P. & Co.   "

Manufacturers' Supplies.

Burlingame & Darby's, N. Adams, Adams
GOWDEY J. A. & SON (see page
716), 22 Second,   Fall River
Remington Robert K.   "
Barton Henry & Co.   Lawrence
Treat James A. & Co.   "
CLARK JEREMIAH, 96 Middle
(see page 738),   Lowell
HOWE & GOODHUE (see page 740),
99 and 92 Market,   "
Kendall Jonathan,   "
LOWELL CARD CO. (see page 742),
96 Middle,   "
Bassett Daniel H.   Pittsfield
COLT & POWER (see page 707),   "
DUCKWORTH & SONS (see p. 713),   "
Crompton & Dawson,   Worcester
PRATT SUMNER, 22 Front (see
page 783),   "

Manufacturing Companies.

(*In Miscellaneous Department, see Index.*)

Maps, Charts, &c., for Mariners.

WHIPPLE HENRY, 243 Essex,   Salem

Marble Quarriers.

Berkshire Marble Co.   Alford
Fitch Frederic & Son,   "
GROSS & HEEBNER,   Lee
New York Quarry,   "
Goodale Chester,   "
Housatonic Marble Co.   Sheffield
SHEFFIELD MARBLE CO. John
R. Briggs, treas. (see page 800),   "
Berkshire Marble Quarry,—Reynolds,
agent,   West Stockbridge
Freedley J. K. & M.   "

Marble Workers.

(*See also Stone Cutters.*)
Fitzgerald William H.   Abington
Fairbanks A. F.   South Abington,   "
Sprague Nelson,   Adams
Blanchard & Hosley, N. Adams,   "
Clark J. D. & Co.   "
Berkshire Marble Co.   Alford
Fitch F. & Son,   "
Milligan Gilbert,   "
Sperry Sanford,   "
Morrill J. W.   Amesbury
Clapp Oliver M.   Amherst
Lewis Enoch T.   Athol
Swan Baxter,   Barre
Frankland William,   Beverly
Savage P. R.   Brookline
Carew Thomas A.   Cambridge
Horgan John J.   "
McDonald Alexander,   "
McNamee John,   "
Clausen Morton,   Charlestown
LYONS WILLIAM J., Medford st.
(see page 735),   "
Scott John C.   Chelsea
          Chesterfield
Morey Andrew S. West Chesterfield,   "
Benjamin C. & Son,   Concord
Jenks James H.   West Dennis, Dennis
BASSETT JOEL L. (stone, see
page 761),   East Hampton

Sholes G. P. East Hampton
Smith Brothers, Fall River
Smith G. W. & Co. "
Hartwell & Reed, Fitchburg
Kennedy P. Gloucester
Woods & Swift, Greenfield
Blood & Spencer, Harvard
Brown & Weeks, Haverhill
Bowker Davis W. Kingston
Scott Learned, Lanesborough
Boldnc Magloire, Lawrence
Hackett Luther H. "
Leonard John, "
Sturgis Edwin, East Lee, Lee
Andrews William, Lee
Nichols David, Lowell
Winter & Smith, "
Witherell George F. "
Guild I. O. Lynn
Harlow William, Malden
Johnson Wm. & Co. South Malden, "
Cole J. Le Baron, Mattapoisett
King R. L. Milford
Norton M. Millbury
Robinson Charles H. Nantucket
Allen Joseph jr. & Co. New Bedford
Cole T. W. "
Taylor John, "
Davis & Littlefield, Newburyport
French David M. "
Poole George, New Salem
Kinney Bros. Northampton
NORTHAMPTON MONUMENTAL
   WORKS, Isaac H. Black (see page
   720), "
Lincoln Samuel R. Norton
Bryant Geo. W. & Co. North Bridgewater
Crosby Winthrop M. Orleans
Linnell Oliver N. South Orleans, "
Hungerford Milan, Pittsfield
Logan, Fuller, & Co. "
Mullanny Michael, "
PLYMOUTH MARBLE WORKS,
   Clark & Swift, proprietors, Plymouth
Churchill Isaiah, Plympton
McGrath P. Quincy
Thompson Zebulon H. Rochester
Lord A. & D. Salem
LONGLEY EDMUND, 157 Derby, "
Morgan Thomas, "
Nye Edwin B. Sandwich
Shelley James, Ashley Falls, Sheffield
   Sheffield
   Shelburne
Temple J. C. & Co., Shelburne Falls, "
Clapp Geo. H., Hanover, South Scituate
Cooley H. W. Springfield
Crabtree & Short, "
Lyons & Barrows, Stoughton
Griswold J. B. Sturbridge
Burt D. A. Taunton
JACKSON WILLIAM H. 38 Wier
   (see page 708), "
Leary Jeremiah, Waltham
White & McMahon, Ware
Sanford Henry D. Webster
Williams Joseph B. Westfield
Bristol Orson, West Stockbridge
Brown Nathan, "
Bristol Remiro, Housatonic, "
McGregory Joseph, Wilbraham
Peck Henry, Winchendon
Briggs Richard, Woburn
Pickering R. "
Kinney B. H. Worcester
Pratt Charles J. "
Tateum & Horgan, "
Fisher Jabez M. & Son, Yarmouth

Marine Railways.

TERRY J. C. Fall River
Burnham Brothers, Gloucester
Parkhurst & Allen, "
DODD, TARR, & CO., East Glouces-
   ter (see page 732), "
City Wharf Railway Co., Horace G.
   Howland, agent, New Bedford
Fish Island Wharf and Railway, Wm.
   P. Howland, agent, "
   Provincetown
CENTRAL WHARF RAILWAY, "
EASTERN MARINE, "
UNION-WHARF CO., "
Essex Marine Railway, Benjamin
   Webb, supt. Salem
Salem Marine Railway Co., D. C.
   Becket, supt. "

Marine Shells.

Gregory John, New Bedford
NICKERSON GEO. Y. 36 William, "

Marketmen.

(See also Provision Dealers; also Butchers.)
Clark Wm. L. Springfield
Greenleaf J. S. "
Holcomb Moses, "
Hunt A. G. "
Richards & Dumbleton, "

Masonic Regalia.

WRUCK F. A. 195 Essex (see page
   745), Salem

Masons.

Bennett Nathaniel, Abington
Faunce Ichabod, "
Faunce Quincy, "
McIntire Joseph B. "
Chandler George, Acton
Conant Francis, South Acton, "
Wilbur George S. Acushnet
Madden John, Adams
Waters Charles, "
Waters John, "
Waters William, "
Adams John T. North Adams, "
Benton Horace, "
Horton S. H. "
Rosenvelt George, "
Smith Samuel, "
Austin R. Agawam
Bailey T. Feeding Hills, "
Prindle Russell, Alford
Wagner Heman, "
Wagner Henry, "
Cooke Aaron, Amherst
Currier Charles, "
Currier Daniel, "
Atkins Geo. E. North Amherst, "
Bacon Henry J. Arlington
Bacon Jesse, "
Lawrence Jonas, Ashburnham
Bowditch Granville, Ashland
Ellenwood Daniel, Athol
Wetherbee Benjamin, "
Burroughs ——, Athol Depot, "
Foster Nathaniel, "
Hamilton James, Attleborough
Lawson J. H. "
Cobb Isaac, Barnstable
Chamberlin George R. Barre
Burnett Addison, Belchertown
Allen F. E. H. Bernardston
Allen Jonathan C. "
Cleaves & Grant, Beverly
Dodge Charles F. "

Dodge George,	Dorchester
Greenwood & Jenkins,	Hyde Park, "
Pierce F. L.	Neponset, "
Fobes Henry F.	" "
Willis William,	Douglas
Coburn Warner,	Dracut
Marshall Horatio C.	"
Woodard H. M.	"
Bennett James,	Dunstable
Nerthey Andrew,	Duxbury
Barstow Henry W.	West Duxbury, "
Whiting John M.	East Bridgewater
Whitman M.	"
Brett B. T.	Joppa, "
Fales Lyman,	East Hampton
Topliff William,	
Keith Geo. W.	North Easton, Easton
Manahan Hervey,	" "
Butler William W.	Edgartown
Huxford Benjamin,	"
Smith James,	"
Killmer John, North Egremont,	Egremont
Holmes John, South Egremont,	"
Downing Stillman,	Enfield
Burnham John H.	Essex
Preston David,	"
Guild William S.	Fairhaven
Sampson E. T.	"
Barney Theophilus,	Fall River
Davis William,	"
Earle L. S.	"
Horton Danforth,	"
Horton Hiram,	"
Horton Mason,	"
Luther Samuel M.	"
Manley William,	"
Records Tillinghast,	"
Westgate Jerome B.	"
Westgate Sylvanus & Brother,	"
Jenkins Braddock,	Falmouth
Weeks Daniel R.	"
Haskell Jonathan R.	Fitchburg
Wetherbee & Derby,	"
Fisher Albert, jr.	Foxborough
Swan Eben W.	Framingham
Cummings E. H., So. Framingham,	"
Colby J. L. P.	Georgetown
Perley Osmon,	"
Friend Elbridge,	Gloucester
Marshall Benjamin,	"
Blackmer Harrison,	Great Barrington
Briggs Alonzo,	"
Briggs Luther,	"
Deveny Daniel,	"
Deveny Patrick,	"
Micue Nelson,	Housatonic, "
Billings Henry,	Greenfield
Briggs Samuel,	"
Childs Marshall,	"
Day & Parks (stone),	"
Merriam Geo. P.	"
Swan Francis, Groton Junction,	Groton
Giddings James,	Hamilton
Patch Oliver,	"
Bates Thomas O.	Hanover
Everson Barnabas,	Hanson
Harris Seth L.	"
Howland Friend W. South Hanson,	"
Gleason Alexander,	Hardwick
Manley Benjamin,	"
Ellis Cyrus,	Harwich
Long Nathan,	"
Hersey Warren A.	Hingham
Humphrey Charles,	"
Humphrey William,	"
Ripley Levi,	"
Dewyre David,	Hinsdale
Dewyre William,	"

Holden	Cowing Leander,	Marion
Holliston	Lovell Austin,	"
Holyoke	Nye J. B. B.	"
"	Faunce David,	
Hopkinton	Mendall F.	
Hubbardston	Parlow George,	"
"	Vail William,	"
"	Frost W. S.	Marlborough
Ipswich	Richardson E. P.	"
"	Dorr Rufus,	Marshfield
"	Kinney J. & Bro.	Mattapoisett
"	Wilber Solomon L.	
Kingston	Bruce H. P.	Medfield
"	Ellis Franklin,	"
Lakeville	Abbe Patridge,	Medway
"	Johnson John,	"
Lancaster	Fales J E.	West Medway, "
"	Page Wm.	" " "
Lanesborough	Cushman Joseph,	Melrose
Lawrence	Ellison Samuel,	"
"	Nichols S. W. & Son,	"
"	Page Rufus L.	Methuen
"	Russ William,	"
"	Winn Nahum P.	"
"	Thompson M.	Middleborough
Lee	Vaughn Harrison,	"
"	Vaughn John G.	"
"	Washburn Solomon,	"
"	Flint Sylvanus,	Middleton
"	Bradford J. C.	Milford
"	Horton & Inman,	"
"	Taft David,	"
"	Taft John,	"
Leominster	Harrington D. B.	Millbury
Lenox	Gardner Anthony,	Milton
"	Gardner William,	"
Leverett	Nute Joshua,	"
Lexington	Wing Samuel A.	Monson
"	Blodget L. D.	Montague
Littleton	Clary Carver,	"
Lowell	Bentley Elisha W.	Monterey
"	Clark Benjamin,	Nantucket
"	Pool Noah,	"
"	Underwood Bros.	Natick
"	Bowers Walter,	Needham
"	Kingsbury Isaac,	"
"	Cook Bennett,	New Bedford
"	Cook & Delano,	"
"	Davis F. D.	"
"	Francis Ezra,	"
"	Gifford Chas. H.	"
"	Howland Paul 2d,	"
"	Howland William C.	"
"	Ingalls William,	"
"	Lee E. W.	"
"	Murphy Thomas,	"
"	Nelson George,	"
Lunenburg	Peirce B. S.	"
"	PIERCE CHAS. M. 75 Elm,	"
"	Peirce Martin,	"
"	Pierce Otis H.	"
"	Sawyer G. T.	"
Lynn	Taber Charles H.	"
"	Taber Gibbs,	"
"	Underwood John,	"
"	Vinal Frederick H.	"
"	Vincent Peter M.	"
"	Barnes E.	New Braintree
"	Thresher H.	"
Malden	Currier Albert,	Newburyport
"	Currier Nathaniel,	"
"	Currier Joseph H.	"
Manchester	Cutter Daniel H.	"
Mansfield	Greeley John A.	"
Marblehead	Kimball Moody,	"
"	Lunt Moody,	"
"	Lunt Thomas H.	"
"	Piper Henry L.	"

Masons — continued.

Tappan William H.	Newburyport
Leonard George, Mill River, New Marlboro'	
Holden H. L.	New Salem
Holden Stillman,	"
Whitaker Proctor,	"
Scribner E.	Auburndale. Newton
Pittes Joseph,	Lower Falls, "
Freeman Russell, Newton Corner,	"
Hunting Martin,	Upper Falls, "
Scott Charles,	" "
Cushman J. H.	West Newton, "
Clark Daniel R.	Northampton
Dickinson Samuel G.	"
Macomber Squire J.	"
Mayers Robert R.	"
Strong John F.	"
Wilcutt Daniel,	"
Wilcutt George,	"
Hammond H. L.	Florence, "
Irwin John,	" "
Eldridge Davis R.	North Bridgewater
Mason Charles,	"
Washburn & Co.	"
Fuller Charles E.	North Chelsea
Russ Daniel H.	"
Alexander George A.	Northfield
Moody Lucius,	"
Moody Mednd,	"
Smith Joseph A.	North Reading
Blanding Allen S.	Norton
Tucker Albert S.	"
Adams Austin,	Oakham
Richards Charles,	Orange
Marble William H.	Oxford
Shaw John,	Palmer
Shaw Samuel,	"
Bancroft Alpheus,	Peabody
Bancroft R. B. & Bro.	"
Davis Daniel R.	"
Goodridge Zachariah,	"
Larrabee Benj.	"
Larrabee Hersay,	"
Larrabee J. H.	"
Trask Samuel,	"
Adams Phineas G.	Pepperell
Bennett Jonathan,	"
Lakin Edmund,	"
Parker Allen S.	"
Mason Dwight,	Petersham
White Martin,	"
Baker George G.	Pittsfield
Dodge H.	"
Foot George,	"
Hubbard Luke,	"
Johnson John,	"
Lament James,	"
Dyer Albert,	Plainfield
Dyer Samuel,	"
Churchill Thomas,	Plymouth
Doten Prince,	"
Dunham Richard W.	"
Hoyt John F.	"
Macomber Warren S.	"
Robbins Edmund,	"
Wood Isaac L.	"
Anthony Joseph W.	Provincetown
Fuller James,	"
Hamlen Alexander,	"
Paine Elkanab,	"
Lyon J. D. F.	Randolph
Thayer John B.	"
Leonard Cyrus,	Raynham
Lee Samuel A.	Rehoboth
Miller Henry W.	"
Norton Chas. A.	"
Leach Lambert,	Richmond
Giles Thaddeus,	Rockport

Leonard David,	Rockport
Tarr William H.	"
Whittridge Joseph,	Pigeon Cove, "
Witham E. jr.	" "
Mallory Allen J.	Russell
Bowditch George,	Salem
Davis & Farmer,	"
Elliott Andrew,	"
Farmer & Harris,	"
FLINT SIMEON, 221 Derby,	"
Hayward Aaron,	"
Hayward Josiah,	"
Hurd Thomas,	"
Kehew William B.	"
Lawrence George,	"
Mansfield Ira,	"
Moulton Frederick,	"
Neal Jonathan,	"
Parsons J. H. & J. M.	"
Ricker Morrill,	"
Stone George,	..
Stone James,	..
Dearborn Jas. W., Saugus Centre, Saugus	
Mann Reuben,	Scituate
Turner Samuel,	"
Manville Reuben,	Sheffield
Hoag Murray & Sons, Ashley Falls, "
Carter Studson, Shelburne Falls, Shelburne
Coleman Josiah,	" "
Dodge Brothers,	" . "
Farnsworth A.	" "
McKnight James,	" "
Merrill George G.	" "
Wheeler Abner,	Shirley
Kittredge Lucius,	Shrewsbury
Pratt Edwin,	Shutesbury
Davis David B.	Somerset
Simmons David E.	"
Simmons Geo. W.	"
Simmons Oliver,	"
Clapp Stephen D. jr.	Southampton
Page J. A.	Southborough
Potter William B.	Southbridge
Potter Alden,	Globe Village, "
Whitford Daniel,	" "
Whitford George,	"
	South Hadley
Burnett Dexter, South Hadley Falls, "
Ingraham Warren,	" "
Roberts A. J.	" "
Ellmes Nathaniel,	South Scituate
Turner R. V. C.	"
Kent Calvin,	Spencer
Farrar B. F.	Springfield
Gilman, Henry,	"
Harrington Royal,	"
Hawkes Alpheus,	"
Hawkes John W.	"
Hill William B.	"
Houghton Marcus,	"
Howe Abel B.	"
Hunt John W.	"
Spooner Zephaniah,	"
Topliff Jonn,	"
Buttrick James,	Sterling
Wilder Josiah H.	"
Burnham Emri,	Stoughton
Fuller John,	Assabet, Sudbury
Norton & Rowell,	Swampscott
Rowell William,	"
Ruffinton Benjamin T.	Swansea
Buffinton Martin L.	"
Cook Abijah D.	"
Estabrooks William,	"
Ingalls Job M.	..
Kingsley James R.	..
Luther Jeremiah,	"
Shade Francis,	"

Bosworth Gardner L.   Taunton
Briggs Abraham,   "
Hale William M.   "
Peirce S. A.   Weir, "
Tinkham W.   "
Wolcott Theron R.   Tolland
Brown Obadiah S.   Truro
Woodard Henry,   Tyringham
Pulkinton Levi.   Upton
Adams Leonard,   Uxbridge
Rawson J. A.   "
Miller C.   Wales
Fuller Henry C.   Walpole
Gray L. D.   "
Morris Lucian,   Waltham
Olcott John,   "
Peabody John,   "
Hills Austin,   Ware
Root William A.   "
Griffith George T.   Wareham
Griffith William W.   "
Hatch Job,   "
Hamblin John W.   East Wareham,   "
French J. L.   Watertown
Baker Charles,   Warren
Baker Rufus,   "
Foster Elijah P.   Warwick
Jacobs Elias,   Webster
Jacobs Orson,   "
Brown John,   Wellfleet
Jordan William,   "
Caswell Eben P.   Wenham
Forbush B. F.   Westborough
Harrington Charles A.   "
Bigelow Joseph,   West Boylston
Harthan Ward B.   "
Howard Everett,   West Bridgewater
Dewey Jason,   Westfield
Gridley & Little,   "
Mallory Thomas,   "
Watkley Lucius B.   "
Weller William,   "
Kidder James O.   Westford
Clapp Horace F.   West Hampton
Kendall Ezekiel,   Westminster
Upton Charles,   "
Dow George C.   West Newbury
Esterbrook S.   "
Williams Moses,   "
Dyer Abraham,   Westport
Potter Perry G.,   Central Village,   "
Cain Stephen,   E. Weymouth, Weymouth
Everett Benjamin,   "
Eastes Eli,   South Weymouth,   "
Elder Walter,   "
Pierce H. E.   Whately
Colton Edward C.   Williamsburg
Knowlton Nathaniel,   Wilbraham
Bakly Joseph,   "
Mosely Willard jr.   Williamstown
Carrigan Frank,   "
Dunbar H. A.   Winchester
Nichols Stephen,   "
Pierce J. A.   "
Pierce Reuben,   Windsor
White Chas. S.   "
York Wm. S.   Woburn
Allen J. W.   "
Burgess Alvin T.   Worcester
Burgess Daniel S.   "
Cooke David W.   "
Fitch Calvin,   "
Lovell A. B.   "
Male Marshall,   "
Kimel William D.   "
Ross William,   "
Stearns J. E.   "
White & Walker,   "

Osgood George, West Worthington,   Worthington
Rathbun Henry A.   "
Baker Luther,   Wrentham
                                       Yarmouth

Mast and Spar Makers.

Caldwell Joseph,   Charlestown
Cushing John,   "
Hutchins Porterfield,   Fairhaven
Beetle Rudolphus,   "
JONES WILLIAM,   Gloucester
SOMES JOHN J.   "
Beetle William,   New Bedford
Kirby & Johnson,   "
Ryder & Smith,   "
Smith & Allen,   "
Lunt E. W.   Newburyport
Brown Nathaniel,   Plymouth
COLLINS ISAAC,   Provincetown
Vincent A. L.   Salem

Mast Hoop Manufacturers.

Noyes & Barker,   West Acton,   Acton
McKay William,   Newburyport

Mat Manufacturers.

Furfey James (sisal, manilla, and jute),
    Cambridgeport,   Cambridge
Green J. (door),   Lowell
McDonald John,   "
WHITELEY JOHN (see page 793),
    Shirley Village,   Shirley

Match Manufacturers.

Russell Eliakim T.   Ashburnham
Hapgood Lyman W. (splints), Athol Depot
Byam, Carlton, & Co.   Boxford
Pierce H. E.   Charlemont
Parmenter & Wheeler,   Erving
Messinger Austin,   Norton
REPEATING LIGHT CO.,
    (see page 781),   Springfield
Whitney Baxter D.   Winchendon

Mattresses.

CONEY H. M. & CO.   Ware

Meat and Vegetable Choppers.

                                         Athol
ATHOL MACHINE CO, L. S. Starrett,
    agent (see page 800),   Athol Depot, "
Derby & Foster,   Fitchburg
                                    Winchendon
KETCHAM & LOUD (see page 776),   "

Mechanics' Tools.

TABER JOHN M. 20 Elm
    (see page 760),   New Bedford

Medicines.

(See Apothecaries; also Botanic Medicines;
    also Druggists; also Patent Medicines.)

Melodeon Manufacturers.

(See also Musical Instruments.)

Whitney Jonas,   Fitchburg
CLISBÉE GEORGE,   Marlborough
Reynolds Philip,   North Bridgewater
Marston A. B.   Campello,
Pierce William,   Pittsfield
Merritt Washington,   Weymouth
Morse M. M.   Worcester
Taylor & Farley,   "

Melodeon and Organ Reed Manufacturers.

Hammond A. H.   Worcester
Ingalls & Abbott,   "
MUNROE ORGAN REED CO. 5 Her-
    mon (see page 717)   "

Merchants.

(*See also Commission ; also Country Stores.*)

Chase Benj. H.	Fairhaven
Church James I.	"
Damon & Judd,	"
Hitch Obed F.	"
Jenney Dexter,	"
Tripp George F.	"
Terry Isaiah F.	"
Wing George F.	"
Rogers George H.	Gloucester
Adams Freeman E.	Nantucket
Gardner Robert F.	"
Macy J. & P.	"
Macy Joseph B.	"
Adams Zenas L.	New Bedford
Allen Gideon & Son,	"
Barney George,	"
Bartlett I. H. & Sons,	"
Blackler William G.	"
Bourne Jonathan. jr.	"
BROWNELL WILLIAM O., 10, 12, & 14 Front,	"
Burt Samuel P.	"
Cleaveland A. L.	"
Crocker Oliver & George O.	"
Gifford Charles H.	"
Gifford Nathaniel T.	"
Gifford & Cummings,	"
Greene David R. & Co.	"
Grinnell Lawrence,	"
Gunnell Joseph,	"
Hadley Joseph B.	"
Hastings George,	"
Hathaway Francis S.	"
Hathaway Horatio,	"
Hathaway Thomas S.	"
Hathaway William, jr.	"
Hawes Chas. E.	"
Hicks John,	"
Hitch Charles & Son,	"
Homer George & Co.	"
Howland Edward W.	"
Howland G. jr.	"
Howland Isaac, jr. & Co.	"
Howland Matthew,	"
Howland James H.	"
Howland William P.	"
Hussey George, jr.	"
Jones Edward C.	"
Kempton David B.	"
Knowles Thomas & Co.	"
Knowles J. P. 2d,	"
Mandell Thomas,	"
Maxfield Edmund,	"
Merrill Edward,	"
Nye Thomas, jr.	"
Peirce Lorenzo,	"
Phillips William & Son,	"
Pierce Andrew G.	"
Plummer L. A.	"
Pope William G. E.	"
Potter Andrew H.	"
Randall Charles S.	"
Richmond George B.	"
Richmond Joshua,	"
Rodman Samuel,	"
Rotch William J.	"
Seabury Otis & E. W.	"
Smith William T.	"
Snow Loum & Son,	"
Swift & Allen,	"
Swift & Perry,	"
Taber, Gordon, & Co.	"
Taber, Read, & Co.	"
Thatcher A. D.	"
Thompson J. D.	"
Thornton John R.	"

Tucker Charles,	New Bedford
Tucker C. R. & Co.	"
Watkins William,	"
West Simeon N.	"
Wilcox Thomas,	"
Wing J. & W. R.	"
Wood Dennis (shipping),	"
Wood J. B. & Co.	"
Bayley R. & Son,	Newburyport
Boardman Isaac H.	"
Graves William,	"
Hale D. & I.	"
Lunt Charles,	"
Lunt Micajah,	"
Allen G. H.	Salem
Bertram J. H. M.	"
Bertram John,	"
Curwen James B.	"
Fabens Benjamin,	"
Fabens C. H.	"
Goodhue Wm. P.	"
Hanson J. H.	"
Hoffman Charles,	"
Hunt William & Co.	"
Miller Charles H.	"
Osgood John C.	"
PHILLIPS WILLARD P. (shipping), Phillips Wharf, and Central, cor. Essex (see page 745),	"
Pingree Thomas P.	"
Ropes Edward D.	"
Ropes George,	"
Shatswell Joseph,	"
Silsbee B. H.	"
Silsbee George Z.	"
Silsbee John H.	"
Stone B. W. & Bros.	"
Webb Wm. G.	"
West Benjamin A.	"
West Samuel,	"

Metal Refiner.

Packard A. B. (lead),	Quincy

Metals.

(*See also Iron and Steel.*)

DODGE L. C. (see page 741), 55 Dutton,	Lowell
Stanley J. C.	Newburyport
HAMMOND S. T. & CO.	Springfield
Towne & Co. (perforated),	Worcester

Microscopist.

BICKNELL EDWIN, 256½ Essex (see page 748),	Salem

Military Accoutrements.

(*See also Fire Arms.*)

GAYLORD MANUF. COMPANY (see page 773), A. F. Gaylord, treasurer,	Chicopee
Cummings Josiah,	Springfield

Military Bands.

Abington Brass Band,	Abington
Beals & Faxon's Quadrille Band,	"
Stetson & Cushing's "	"
Mechanics' Brass Band,	Amesbury
	East Bridgewater
Joppa Cornet Band, Joppa Village,	"
Lynn Brass Band,	Lynn
Hingham " "	Hingham
South Hingham Cornet Band, South Hingham,	"
Mattapoisett Brass Band,	Mattapoisett
Milford " "	Milford
North Bridgewater "	North Bridgewater
Porter's Quadrille Band,	"

ttsfield Cornet Band, Edwin J.
Maschke, leader, Pittsfield
ymouth Brass Band, E. W. Atwood, leader, Plymouth
pton's Quadrille Band, Salem
etson's Weymouth Band, So. Weymouth
aunton Military Band, Taunton
ellfleet, Geo. T. Wyer, leader, Wellfleet

Military Trimmings.

ARROWS H. F. & CO. (belts and
  hats), No. Attleborough, Attleborough
rr, Brown, & Co. (manuf.), Hingham.

Mill Gearing.

EALD & SONS (saw and grist
  mill, water wheel, and light and
  heavy gearing, see pages 796
  and 797), Barre
ANE DAVID, Fletcher, cor.
  Cushing (see page 738), Lowell
OVEJOY DANIEL (see page 744),
  Rock, cor. Cushing, "
OBINSON WM. & CO. Fletcher,
  cor. Dutton, "
HILLIPS H. B. 194 and 196
  Derby, Salem

Milliners and Millinery Goods.

See also Dress Makers; also Laces and
  Embroideries.)

unham A. Mrs. Abington
ash Benjamin L. "
ratt Henry J. Mrs. "
urner & Knowles, "
haw Mary L. Miss, East Abington, "
tudley Susan Mrs. "
atch Alice J. Miss North " "
harpe E. E. Mrs. South " "
hayer E. J. " "
arding & Croston, South Acton, Acton
all Ira Mrs. West " "
  Acushnet
isbee Jenny L. Mrs. Long Plain, "
abbett Alice M. Miss, Adams
reen M. A. "
acon Elizabeth Mrs. North Adams, "
oope J. A. " "
itchell Annie, " "
owell Abbie R. " "
outhwick E. jr. " "
irroughs T. Miss, Amesbury
iase Amos F. "
emont E. D. Miss, "
iley Mary A. "
iais H. D. Amherst
irrett E. J. Mrs. "
ili C. A. "
rickland & Graves Misses, "
iw Emily W. Andover
orrison E. & Co. "
attuck S. J. "
orrison John, Ballardvale, "
ade R. T. Arlington
iughton Mary V. Mrs. Ashland
oper C. E. Mrs. Attleborough
own N. M. Miss, "
eever A. C. Mrs., N. Attleborough, "
hitman Henry Mrs. " "
LTON E. E. & E. M. Athol
vage Thomas W. "
od J. E. Mrs. "
odell M. J. Athol Depot, "
okell F. K. " "
ockwell Otis J. Mrs. " "
iham S. P. Mrs. " "
ss E. P. Hyannis, Barnstable
inell Retta, " "

Egery E. S. Miss, Barre
Gilmore S. R. "
Partridge Lavina E. "
  Becket
Bartlett Edward S. Mrs., N. Becket, "
Bridgman E. S. Mrs. Belchertown
Hopkins E. S. Mrs. "
Bascom Lucinda P. Bernardston
Ellenwood F. M. Beverly
Lane C. Miss, "
Stevens E. M. "
Brown M. J. Mrs. Blackstone
Kenney Misses, "
Staples C. Addie Mrs. "
Stockbridge Harriet A. "
Randall S. M. South Braintree, Braintree
Bray H. H. Miss, Brewster
Crocker T. W. Bridgewater
Edgecomb Hollis Mrs. Brighton
Nichols Lucy A. Brookfield
Winkley F. J. Mrs. "
Merritt Maria Mrs. Brookline
West R. A. Mrs. "
  Buckland
Cragin S. E. Miss, Shelburne Falls, "
Gale H. A. Miss, Cambridge
Lord Mary A. "
Sands Harriet E. "
Sullivan Ellen F. "
Boyd F. L. Miss, Cambridgeport, "
Callender Sarah B. "
Hyde A. F. Miss, " "
McCaffrey C. & S. " "
Osgood Sarah, " "
White Hannah, " "
Turner George R. " "
Cox Lavina C. Mrs., East Cambridge, "
Scanlan Timothy Mrs. " "
Hayden G. W. Mrs. Canton
Kenrick S. C. "
Rider Chas. Mrs. South Carver, Carver
Ballard Eliza B. Charlemont
Chapin Ellen H. Miss, "
Boyd Esther, Charlestown
Hart J. H. Mrs. "
Hoare & Byrne, "
Howard Alice M. "
Huntress F. C. Mrs. "
Knight E. D. "
Morse S. Mrs. "
Parker J. S. Mrs. "
Perry John L. Mrs. "
Severy H. L. "
Brown Cordelia A. Miss, Chelsea
Remick William B. "
Ridlon J. H. Mrs. "
Phillips & Godfrey, Cheshire
Fay Charles Mrs. Chester
Hapgood Jennie E. Miss, "
Connor J. F. Chicopee
Fuller A. J. "
Reilly George Mrs. "
White C. Mrs. & Co. "
Russell H. M., Chicopee Falls, "
Deming & Laird Misses, Clinton
Eagleshum J. Mrs. "
Logan James Mrs. "
Ford Hattie G. Cohasset
Shaw B. M. Miss, Coleraine
Andrews H. Mrs. Conway
PHILLIPS & CONWAY, "
Oakes John E. Mrs. Dana
Keating C. A. Miss, Dedham
Ingalls Anna Miss, E. Dedham, "
Arms Obed S. Mrs., S. Deerfield, Deerfield
Fuller Mira, West Dennis, Dennis
Sanborn S. A. Miss, Milton, Dorchester
Light Ellen E. Neponset, "

Milliners and Millinery Goods — continued.

Spear E. M. Miss, Neponset, Dorchester	
Whitney Hattie Miss, E. Douglas, Douglas	
Vinal James B. Mrs. Duxbury	
Allen S. B., Joppa, East Bridgewater	
Keith Mary S Miss, "	
Snow N. S. Mrs. "	
Kingsley & Phillips, East Hampton	
Owell Jane, "	
Thrall Misses, "	
Crockett I. B. Mrs. North Easton, Easton	
Smith Etta Miss, " "	
Crawford Caroline, Edgartown	
Jernegan Almira, "	
Egremont	
Hollenbeck Martha A., N. Egremont, "	
Clark Emeline, Enfield	
Giddings Mary E. Essex	
Delano Nancy P. Miss, Fairhaven	
Sampson M. Mrs. "	
Baker A. S. Fall River	
Borden S T. "	
Chace James B. "	
Chace L. Mrs. "	
Cook H. B. Miss, "	
Davis Hattie, "	
Eddy & Ashley Misses, "	
Harris A. Mrs. "	
Hathaway O. H. Mrs. "	
Hawkins Amasa, "	
McAdams Louisa Miss, "	
Murray L. Mrs. "	
Nooning Timothy J. "	
Poole & Ross, "	
Reed & Pearce, "	
Sanders J. Miss, "	
Lawrence Lizzie, Falmouth	
Gilbert Ivar R. Fitchburg	
Jewell & Mayer, "	
Stiles James F. "	
Trees Thomas Mrs. "	
Worcester V. M. "	
Austin M. B. Foxborough	
Clapp T. Mrs. "	
Stewart Charles W. "	
Wheeler H. C. "	
Wheeler T. H. Mrs. Framingham	
Eames A. A. S. Framingham,	
Abbott Jane, Saxonville, "	
Webster G. W. " "	
Hobson Caroline A. Georgetown	
Coas & Douglass Misses, Gloucester	
Collins Ada, "	
Emanuel S. H. & Co. "	
Shaw Francis M. "	
Ward F. M. "	
Allen M. S. Grafton	
Eaton S. W. "	
Costa Ellen Miss, Great Barrington	
Fryer M. A. & J. B. "	
Smith H. Elizabeth Mrs. "	
Walker Phebe E. Miss, "	
Bigelow Mary P. Greenfield	
Taylor Rinaldo R. "	
Wunsch William, "	
STUART G. W. & CO., Groton Junc-	
tion, Groton	
Nutting W. C, Groton Junction, "	
Hardy Ellen Mrs. Groveland	
Thomas Christiana, South Hanson, Hanson	
Knight Harriet J. Mrs. Hardwick	
Atherton Oliver Mrs. Harvard	
Eldridge R. Harwich	
Ellis V. Miss, "	
Bryant C. & E. Haverhill	
Buswell N. S. Mrs. "	
Clay M. G. "	
Collins E. G. "	

Dresser E. R. & Co. Haverhill	
Gilbert J. F. "	
Kimball & Woodman, "	
Kimball M. J. Mrs.	
Porter C. P. Mrs.	
Soule M. A. & Co. "	
Crocker E. C. Mrs. Hingham	
Studley B. G. Mrs. "	
Whitehead Wm. Mrs.	
Roach M. J. Mrs. Hinsdale	
Barnes Henry, Holyoke	
Bateson John, "	
Booden J. Mrs. "	
Gibson J. P. "	
Gilbert J. F.	
Manning Honora,	
Nichols D. F. "	
Orrell E. A. Mrs. "	
Worswick Angelina & Amelia, "	
Archibald A. L. Mrs. Hopkinton	
Richer L. D. Mrs. "	
Jennison Sarah A. Hubbardston	
Goodrich I. B. Mrs. Hudson	
Sanborn E L. Miss, "	
White L. H. Mrs. "	
Otis E. B. Mrs. Huntingdon	
Price William, Hyde Park	
Lord A. P. Miss, Ipswich	
Newman Sarah A. Miss, "	
Burns Ebenezer, Kingston	
Anderson M. S. Lawrence	
Barnard Lydia H. "	
Brasill B. Miss, "	
Breen Margaret, "	
Brown J. H. Mrs. "	
Burns Wm. M. "	
Chatburn H. A. Miss, "	
Cockshott Alfred, "	
Davis Mary A. Miss, "	
Gould E. "	
Graham L. W. Mrs. "	
Hagar Westford, "	
Hall D. F. Mrs. "	
Ham Dorcas, "	
Higgins & Wentworth, "	
Lowe H. Mrs. "	
Lowe M. D. "	
McDonough —— Miss, "	
Moffit Caroline M. "	
Motherwell J. Mrs. "	
Prescott & Veazie, "	
Reynolds J. H. Mrs. "	
Sayward Abbie Miss, "	
Stevens F. A. Mrs. "	
Trees John, "	
Wadleigh J. C. "	
Wass E. S. Mrs. "	
Wefer Bernard, "	
Wentworth & Higgins, "	
Whiting N. T. "	
Bailey Laura, Lee	
Horsfall Mary A. "	
Kane Anna, "	
King L. A. Mrs. "	
Hutchinson S. G. Mrs. Leominster	
Joy L. W. Mrs. "	
Houghton Clara, Lexington	
Ambrose A. Lowell	
Blanchard A. M. "	
Carter E. B. Mrs. "	
Colburn A. A. Mrs. "	
Crowley Daniel, "	
Danforth & Gwinn, "	
Donovan M. A.	
Doris C. A. & M. A.	
Elliott J. C Mrs.	
Feslor N. S.	
Finn C. S. Mrs.	

Folsom C. B.	Lowell	Bisbee A. A. & Co.	New Bedford
Furbish & Horne,	"	Buckley L. S. Mrs.	"
Gage Ann Mrs.	"	Cable N. M. Mrs.	"
Hall M. A.		Case Mercy,	"
Helliwell & Thomason,	"	Church L. C. Mrs.	"
Horn Emma E.	"	Crocker A. H.	"
Huntley C. M.	"	Dimond A. Mrs.	"
Huntley Ellen J.	"	Ely & Jenney,	
Lord H. Mrs.	"	Fillebrown R. A. Mrs.	
McDonough K. J.	"	Fuller S. D. Mrs.	"
McGill James,	"	Harlow Mary W. Mrs.	"
Moses Stephen T.	"	Hawley & Pierce,	"
Robinson F. W.	"	Kelley H. C. Mrs.	"
Stevens Mary F.	"	Merrill M. E. Miss,	"
Talsey L.	"	Nonning Wm. B.	
Thompson B. T. Mrs.	"	Nye L. J. Mrs.	
Waldron Mary A.	"	Nye M. D. Miss,	"
White Mary A.	"	Packard L. H. Mrs.	"
Wilson A.	"	Pierce Maria A.	"
Barnes Mary,	Lynn	Pond E. F. Mrs.	"
Breed Harriet M.	"	Potter Cynthia,	"
Chesley & Caswell,	"	Adams & Noyes,	Newburyport
Cobb M S. Mrs.	"	Batchelder L. T. Mrs.	"
Dow A. L. Miss,	"	Coolidge S. A. Miss,	"
Gorman J. N. Miss,	"	De Jean L. A.	"
Gove M. J. Mrs.	"	Goodwin S. A. Mrs.	"
Jackson M. H. Mrs.	"	Hervey & Co.	"
Lancey Leland Mrs.	"	Hutchins S. L. Mrs.	"
Marshall L. M. Miss,	"	Moody Sarah Miss.	"
Radford John Mrs.	"	Richardson Sophia,	
Ross E. Mrs.	"	Sanderson Mary A.	"
Snow Hannah Miss,	"	Smith & Appleton,	
Woodley A. E. Mrs.	"		New Marlborough
Welch A. Miss,	"	Brigham M. A. Mill River,	"
Young C. A. Miss,	"	Hart Miss,	Newton Centre, Newton
Roman T. Miss,	Malden	Dowse L. D. Mrs., Newton Corner,	"
Kimball S. E. Mrs.	"	Hodgdon D. Mrs.	" "
Watts Susie M. Miss,	"	Scales H. E. Mrs.	"
Cox James Mrs. Malden Centre,	"	Quimby M. Mrs. West Newton,	"
Baker Mary A. Miss,	Manchester	Dickinson R. V.	Northampton
Hodges L. Mrs.	Mansfield	Fair R.	"
Glover Mary F.	Marblehead	Frary H. & S.	"
Grater & Bartlett,	"	Kingsley F. A. Mrs.	"
Hawkes E. S. Miss,	"	PHILLIPS & SAMPSON,	"
Hopkins M. B. Mrs.	"	Andrews M. E. Mrs. North Bridgewater	
Wittel Annie E. Miss,	Marion	Reynolds M. R.	"
Arnold S. H.	Marlborough	ROBINSON H. W. & CO.	"
Cotting C. W. Mrs.	"	Shedd Wm. M.	"
Hardy Ellen F. Miss,	"	Studley S. H.	"
Russell C. C. Miss,	"	Thomsa H. O.	"
Gannon E. W. Miss,	Mattapoisett	Claflin J. M. Mrs.	Northborough
Paine F. M. Mrs.	"	Howell A. Miss. Whitinsville, Northbridge	
Rowe L. A. Mrs.	Medfield	Dewing J. B. Mrs. North Brookfield	
Frye S. R. & Co.	Methuen	Meade M. C. Mrs.	"
Barrows S. F. Miss,	Middleborough	Doolittle K. Mrs.	Northfield
Briggs C. A. Mrs.	"	Kellogg C. C. Mrs.	Orange
Gardiner R. T. Mrs.	Milford		Orleans
Lyons M. S. Miss,	"	Hopkins Eldora Mrs. East Orleans,	
Manheim M.	"	Linnell Abbie J. Miss,	"
Smith A. M. & H. M. Misses,	"	Morey M. A. Mrs.	Oxford
Wells L. Mrs.	"	Sigourney M. Mrs.	
Haywood E. A.	Millbury	Cross W. W.	Palmer
Spring Lewis Mrs.	"	Whitman S. Mrs.	"
Beal Margaret Miss,	Milton	Abbott Elizabeth,	Paxton
Anderson J. R. Mrs.	Monson	Buxton Abby,	Peabody
Collins A. C. Mrs.	"	Beal M. A. Mrs. S. Hanson, Pembroke	
Clapp S. & E. Misses,	Montague	Bryant Mary M.	"
Rice L. G. & Co.	"	Simpson L. C. Mrs.	Pepperell
Bunker Sarah,	Nantucket	Chapman Mary A. Mrs.	Pittsfield
Coleman S. A.	"	Devanny Margaret E. Mrs.	"
Hussey M. A.	"	Fuller Margaret J.	"
Manter M. H.	"	Hayes M. & S. Misses,	"
Mitchell Francis,	"	Kendall Sarah W. & Frances,	"
Gilmore S. T.	Natick	Malley William,	"
Hoyt E. J. Miss,	"	Smith Electa T.	"
Newhall C. R. Mrs.	"	Graves T. Miss,	Plainfield
Allen B. Mrs. & Co.	New Bedford	Atwood M. B. Mrs.	Plymouth
Arnold & Tibbitts,	"	Olney O. P. Mrs.	"

20

Milliners and Millinery Goods — continued.
Washburn & Turner,   Plymouth
Rogers Annie,   Plympton
Cowan J. H. Mrs.   Provincetown
McKennan E. Mrs.   "
Mills Delia A.   "
O'Brien Walter,   "
Weston Sophia H.   "
Curtis Mary E. Mrs.   Quincy
French M. A. Miss,   "
Hussey Susan H. Miss,   "
Jenkins D. F.   "
Richardson E. H. Mrs.   "
Howard M. R. Mrs.   Randolph
Morton C. jr.   "
Wales E. Mrs.   E. Randolph,
Cushman Dorcas,   Rochester
Richardson A. M.   Rockport
Thurston Wm. E.   "
Connell & Harding,   Salem
Copeland C. M. Mrs.   "
Crane Mary E.   "
Davis James P.   "
Draper A. Mrs.   "
Dudley S. J.   "
Elwell Mary W.   "
Felt Mary W.   "
Foster Matilda L.   "
Fogg Martha L.   "
Goodell A.   "
Gray Elizabeth,   "
Gwinn Mary A.   "
Harris N. W. Mrs.   "
Peabody John P.   "
Reith & Co.   "
Robinson Lucy T.   "
Symonds P. Miss,   "
Temple S. C.   "
Walwork S. E. Mrs.   "
Wilson Mary B.   "
Woodward E. S.   "
Collins H. N. Miss, Amesbury, Salisbury
Foye M. A.,   "   "
LOCKE S. E. Miss,   "   "
Patten S. L. & S. H.   "   "
         Sandisfield
Daniels James L. Mrs. New Boston, "
Harper Mary E.   Sandwich
Ingraham Hattie L.   "
Nye & Newcomb,   "
Litchfield Mary,   Scituate
Harrub Matilda,   N. Scituate, "
French Martha,   Sheffield
Goodridge Nancy,   "
Strong Mary,   Ashley Falls, "
Cragin S. & E., Shelburne Falls, Shelburne
Lamson Diana,   "   "
Thayer Delia,   "   "
Catlin Lottie Mrs., Shirley Village, Shirley
Wheaton W. F. Mrs.   Somerset
Clark Samuel Mrs.   Southborough
Cleme ce A. Mrs.   Southbridge
Cutting A. E.   "
Foskett M. Miss,   "
Jenks Nancy Miss,   "
Claflin J. A.   Globe Village, "
Lyman Joseph A. Mrs.   South Hadley
Newell Eliza A. Miss,   "
Guy Alice Miss, South Hadley Falls, "
Dearborn D. A. Mrs.   Southwick
Granger S. L. Mrs.   "
Dunton H. P. Mrs.   Spencer
Baumgartin J. L.   Springfield
Coleman M. & B.   "
Fallon John,   "
Hull J. S. Mrs.   "
Judd & Currier Misses,   "
Pease Wm. N. Mrs.   "

Pierce William,   Springfield
Wallach, Schwab, & Zinsser,   "
WILCOX O. W. & CO. 187 Main,   "
Magee Mary E. Miss,   Stockbridge
Hammond D. M.   Stoneham
Whitehouse M. M.   "
WILLIS GEO. E.   "
Ames F. J. Mrs.   Stoughton
Wales N.   "
Day A. Mrs.   Fiskdale,   Sturbridge
Hooker J. Miss,   "   "
Maxwell M. J. Mrs.   Assabet, Sudbury
Riley F. W. Mrs.   "   "
Armstrong L. A. Miss,   Swampscott
Bodfish Wm. Mrs.   Taunton
Copeland Elisha,   "
Gould Harriet W.   "
Hall N. W. Mrs.   "
Hathaway E.   "
Lawton E. A. Mrs.   "
Mason J. F. Mrs.   "
McNamara C. Miss,   "
Morey Samuel C.   "
Pratt S. W. Mrs.   "
Ryder L. J. Mrs.   "
Russell Lydia B.   Tisbury
Worth Julia A.   Holmes's Hole, "
Pingree C. P. Miss,   Topsfield
Rice Marja,   Upton
Hudson Samuel,   Uxbridge
Sweet & Haywood,   "
Evans C. P.   Wakefield
Hardy M. J. Mrs.   "
Hoyt Jennie S.   "
Cowles R. Lizzie,   Wales
Dolan Kate Miss,   Waltham
Hayden Lizzie M. Mrs.   "
Knapp & Currier,   "
Macurdy J. W.   "
Wilson S. A.   "
Parker E. E.   Ware
Raymond C. A. Mrs.   "
Storrs J. H.   "
Weeks H. M.   "
Besse & Bumpus,   Wareham
Bowen Deborah,   "
Howard M. S.   "
Burgess Calvin Mrs. E. Wareham, "
Capen L. C. Mrs.   Warren
Keyes Sophronia C.   "
Bates E. M.   Webster
Carter E. P.   "
Foskett S.   "
Rogers H. Mrs.   "
Holbrook L. Augusta,   Wellfleet
Sparrow Mary A.   "
Bragg M. L. Mrs.   Westborough
Green L E. Miss,   "
Smith H. C. Miss,   "
Wheeler L. A. Mrs.   West Boylston
Leach R. E. Mrs.   "
         West Bridgewater
Perkins Agnes Mrs.   Cochesett,   "
Tomblin Mary Mrs.   West Brookfield
Holcomb & Avery,   Westfield
Phelps S. M. Mrs.   "
Davis Caroline S.   Westford
Avery E. A., Mittineague, West Springfield
Steward J. D.   "
Shaw Lucy M.   West Stockbridge
Webster Martha,   "
Woodville M. L.   "
Ambler E. C. Mrs.   Weymouth
Cowing Martha Mrs.   "
LaForest F. Mrs.   "
Rice C. A. Miss,   "
Richardson E. A. Mrs., E. Weymouth, "
Clark Sarah,   Williamsburg

Lawrence Mrs.   Williamstown
Penniman Sarah,   "
Smith Fannie,   "
Converse E. A. Mrs.   Winchendon
Fairbanks C. P. Mrs.   "
Jewett & Hale Misses,   "
McIntire James,   Winchester
Carleton C. J.   Woburn
Delton Lonisa M. Mrs.   "
Teare M. Mrs.   "
                                  Worcester
Browning J. E. & Co. (wholesale),   "
Jordan & Hayes,   "
Joslyn T. Miss,   "
Knowles A. L. Mrs.   "
Lee H. O.   "
Leigh J. N. Mrs.   "
Lesure L. Mrs.   "
Nichols S. & Co.   "
O'Brien & Sweeney,   "
Parker A. L. Miss,   "
Pelton E. H.   "
Phelps L. A. Miss,   "
Rand J. S.   "
Richardson H. B. Mrs.   "
Roche M.   "
Russell E. Mrs.   "
Sanford C. A.   "
Williams M. R. Mrs.   "
Chase Sarah, S. Yarmouth,   Yarmouth
Cottelle Hannah & Mary, Yarmouth
  Port,   "
Tobey Betsey S.   Yarmouth Port,   "

Milling Machines.

Union Vise Co. of Boston,   Hyde Park

Millwrights.

Davis Daniel,   Adams
Woodward O. C.   "
Hodge Amos,   North Adams,   "
Phillips Jerome,   "   "
Woodward Warner,   "   "
Richardson Lysander, Athol Depot, Athol
McElwain Oliver,   Becket
Gillis Daniel S.   Boxford
Packard Charles L.   "
Brown Werden R.   Cheshire
Bonney Lucius,   East Bridgewater
Phillips Wadsworth & Mark,   "
Washburn Isaac,   "
SHELDON FRANCIS & CO. (see page
  762),   Fitchburg
Seeley E.   Great Barrington
Turner Miller,   "
Stetson Thomas,   Hanson
Whiting John A.   "
Phillips Lot,   South Hanson,   "
Field William,   Harwich
Everett Horatio,   Hinsdale
Bassett Ansel,   Lee
Graves Milo A.   "
Moore Edward A.   "
Couch & Oakley,   East Lee,   "
Gardner James,   South Lee,   "
Gilman Joseph,   Lynn
Parlow E. S. & C. H.   Marion
TURBINE WATER WHEEL MANF.
  CO. (see page 777),   Orange
Burdon Moses,   Oxford
Humphrey W. H.   "
Bomer Caleb P.   Peabody
Dennison Isaac,   "
Friend & Annable,   "
Perkins James,   "
Whitney John,   "
Jones Edward D. G.   Pittsfield
Fairfield Samuel W.   Salem

Getchell Charles E.   Salem
Barton & Elbridge,   Springfield
Clark Harry,   Stockbridge
Burghardt & Co.   Curtisville,   "
Willis Aaron S., Baldwinville, Templeton
Needham William M.   Wales
Dean Allen,   Westfield
Fox Joel H.   "
Knapp Benjamin,   "
Starr Dudley,   "
Rees Martin,   West Stockbrige
French Abel B.   Housatonic,   "

Mineral Water & Beer Manufs.

Davis & Hallberg,   Chelsea
HEALD M. C. 114 S. Common (see
  page 714),   Lynn
WINN S. B. Front, cor. Wash.   Salem
BROOKS F. A. (see page 778), Springfield
Tripp William C.   Taunton
Taylor L. C.   Waltham
Hewett Geo. F.   Worcester

Model Makers.

                                  Randolph
LITTLEFIELD BROS. (see page 728), "
Piper E. J.   Springfield
Merritt Washington,   Weymouth

Molasses Gates.

Taylor L. B. & Co.   Chicopee

Monuments.

BLETHEN TRUE G. (see page 791),
  Long wharf, foot of Pleasant,   Lynn
NORTHAMPTON MONUMENTAL
  WORKS (see page 720),   Northampton
DELL BROS. & CO. (granite, see page
  768),   West Quincy,   Quincy
WILLIAMS, SPELLMAN, & CO.
  (granite, see page 768),   "
JACKSON WILLIAM H. 38 Weir
  (see page 708),   Taunton

Mop Manufacturer.

                              Shirley Village
WHITELEY JOHN (see page 793),   "

Morocco Manufacturers and Dealers.

(See also Leather.)

Whitney Austin & Co.   Ashburnham
Callahan O.   Charlestown
Craig Wm. M.   "
Hall G. S.   "
Lindsey I. & Son,   "
Merriam & Norton (bindings),   "
Perkins C. C.   "
Sewall Freeman C.   "
Sewall Moses B.   "
Swift Joseph,   "
Waitt Ashbel,   "
Bates A. A.   Danvers Port, Danvers
Pratt & Co.   "
                                  Dedham
Smith Lyman & Sons, South Dedham,
Winslow Bros.   "
Hoyt Humphrey & Co.   Haverhill
Kimball B. & B. M.   "
Merrill J. F. (dealer),   "
Clark Charles G. & Co.   Lynn
Clark H. & N.   "
Coffee R. M. & Co.   "
Drown R. W.   "
Hennessey J. & Co.   "
Kelley Wm. A. & Son,   "
Lennox P. & Co.   "

Morocco Dealers, etc., — continued.
Lummus & Manning,   Lynn
Martin Augustus B.   "
MOULTON JOHN T. & Co. 56 Mar-
  ket (see page 718),   "
Norris Moses & Son,   "
OLIVER ROBERT, 24 Washington
  (see page 725),   "
Pevear & Co.   "
Sherry Phillip & Co.   "
Shute & Faulkner,   "
SOUTHER J. JR. & CO. Harrison ct.
  (see page 705),   "
Tapley Phillip P.   "
Wentworth Jacob S.   "
Williams James,   "
Clark W. P.   Peabody
Clarke G. & A. B.   "
Gill Peter R.   "
Goodridge J. L.   "
Gray Geo. W.   "
Egan & Nowell,   "
Hammond J. H.   "
Ingraham James F.   "
Jacobs W. M. & Son,   "
Pemberton F. K. & Son,   "
Poole Joshua H.   "
Roberts David,   "
Tigh C. H.   "
Tyler Franklin,   "
Winchester & Blaney,   "
Woodbury Daniel & Co.   "
Arnold Michael P.   Salem
Hurd William,   Stoneham

Moulding Machines.

                                     Worcester
LEE H. A. (see page 750), 56 Union,   "
WITHERBY, RUGG, & RICHARD-
  SON (see page 788), 12 Central,   "

Moulding Mills.

(See also Sawing and Planing.)

Chilson Jacob B.   North Adams, Adams
BAKER JAMES (see page 729),
  North Adams,   "
SNYDER & PATTISON (see page
  728),   North Adams,   "
Brown Amos,   Charlestown
STEARNS ALBERT T. (see page 695),
  Port Norfolk,   Dorchester
Copeland S. W.   Fall River
                                Hyde Park
NEAL A. B. & CO. (see page 765),   "
Mosher & Brownell,   New Bedford
Parsons P. (also scrolling),   "
Smith L. W.   Northampton
RICHMOND J. A. & CO. (see page
  724),   Shelburne Falls, Shelburne
Viner F. J.   Springfield
NEWCOMB W. L. & CO. (see page
  728),   Taunton
BANGS A. & CO. (see p. 721), Worcester
KEYES I. N. 24 & 26 Central (see
  page 720),   "
RICE, GRIFFIN, & CO. Union,   "
Russ & Eddy,   Manchester st.   "

Moulding Sand.

BLAKE ZEBINA (see page 758),
  West Water,   Taunton
STAPLES & PHILLIPS (see page
  759), 27 West Water,   "

Mowing Machines.

(See also Agricultural Implements.)

Buckeye Mowing Machine Co., A. B.
Barnard, agent,   Fitchburg

Whitman & Miles Manuf. Co. A.
  Whitman, treas. W. Fitchburg, Fitchburg
Brown Alzirus (Union mowers), Worcester
KNIFFEN MOWING MACHINE CO.
  12 Central,   "
RICHARDSON A. P. &. Co. (buck-
  eye), 9 Central,   "

Mowing Machine Knives.

SIMONDS MANUFACTURING CO.
  (see page 658),   Fitchburg

Music and Musical Instrument
Dealers.

(See also Melodeons; also Piano Fortes.)

Barnes L. M. & Co. North Adams, Adams
Arnzen Neils,   Fall River
Collester O.   Fitchburg
Fuller Simeon,   "
Whitney Andrew,   "
                                 Gloucester
PROCTER BROTHERS, 121 Front,   "
Bassett William W.   Great Barrington
Bullard O. B.   Holliston
Rugg & Griffith,   Lowell
Simpson Andrew J. & Co.   "
Oliver C. F.   Lynn
WEBSTER W. T. 8 Exchange,   "
                                  Milford
READE L. 72 Main (see page 782),
Brownell A. P.   New Bedford
Church Charles L.   "
Hazeltine Charles,   "
Hopkins John,   "
Cheney J. W.   Newburyport
Clark, Kidder, & Co.   Northampton
Childs C. C. & Co.   Pittsfield
Clarke, Nichols, & Co.   "
Brooks D. B. & Brother,   Salem
WHIPPLE G. M. & A. A. Smith,   "
BARNES WILLIAM C.   Southbridge
King J. A.   "
Burt Augustine & Co.   Springfield
Burt Roderick,   "
Hoadly E. G. & Co.   "
Hutchins M. J. D.   "
Matthews J. W.   "
Spear W. & Co.   "
Whiting A.   "
Tinkham S. M. & Sons,   Taunton
Cutler G. K.   Ware
Phipps Charles,   "
KREBS CARL,   Webster
Morse James H.   Westfield
STEER & TURNER (church organs),
  see page 766),   "
Baker Geo. S.   Weymouth
Chandler Wm. E. & Co.   Worcester
Gorham C. L. & Co.   "
Fay & Richards,   "
Leland S. R. & Son,   "
Merrifield L.   "

Musical Instrument Manufs.

(See also Music and Musical Instruments).

HAMILL SAMUEL S. 91 Gore (church
  organs), East Cambridge,   Cambridge
STEVENS GEORGE (church organs),
  East Cambridge,   "
Marston A. B. (organs and melodeons),
  Campello,   North Bridgewater
Reynolds Philip,
STEER & TURNER (church organs,
  see page 766),   Westfield
Fiske Isaac (band), 10 Foster, Worcester

Music Bands.
(See Military Bands.)

Music Teachers.
(See Teachers of Music.)

Nail Cask Manufacturers.
Middleborough
HARLOW I. H. & CO. (see page 768), "

Nail Manufacturers.
(See also Tack, Brad, and Shoe Nails.)
Dighton Rolling Mill Co.,   Dighton
DIGHTON TACK CO. (finishing and
  shoe, see page 715),   "
Leonard N. & Son,   No. Dighton,   "
Kingman Nail Co.   Neponset, Dorchester
Putnam S. S. &. Co. (horse shoe),
  Neponset,   "
East Bridgewater Iron Co. East Bridgewater
                           Fall River
FALL RIVER IRON WORKS CO.,   "
STETSON & TALBOT (shoe, see
  page 782),   Holliston
Lisbon E. (horse and ox),   Lowell
Cobb & Drew,   Plymouth
PLYMOUTH TACK AND RIVET
  WORKS, Samuel Loring (see page
  713),   "
Robinson Iron Co.   "
                       Raynham
Williams Martin G. (clinch and boat), "
Burkinshaw George (horse),   Salem
Mt. Hope Iron Co., J. H. Leonard,
  agent and treas.   Somerset
Sylvester B. F. & Co.   Somerville
ANTHONY & CUSHMAN (see page
  722),   Taunton
FIELD A. & SONS (see page 719),
  22 Spring,   "
OLD COLONY IRON CO., C. Robin-
  son, agent,   "
CROCKER BROS. & CO. (copper and
  yellow metal, see page 756),   "
Rounds L. A. & Co.   "
TAUNTON TACK CO., T. J. Lothrop,
  agent and treas. (see page 720), 26
  Union,   "
Parker Mills,   Wareham
Kinney Lewis & Co. S. Wareham,   "
Wareham Nail Co.   "   "
Tisdale Nail Co. J. F. Sherman, agt.
  East Wareham,   "
Tremont Nail Co.   West Wareham,   "
Forge Village Horse Nail Co. (horse),
  Forge Village,   Westford
Weymouth Iron Co., N. Stetson, agent,
  East Weymouth,   Weymouth

Natural History Stores.
Vickary N.   Lynn
Gregory John,   New Bedford
NICKERSON GEORGE Y., 86 Wil-
  liam,   "

Nautical Instruments.
(See also Chronometers ; also Instruments.)
PUTNAM A. L.   Provincetown
Kelley James S.   New-Bedford
Sherman C. R. & Co.   "

Needle Cases.
Hopedale
COX FREDERICK S. (see page 766), "

Needle Manufacturers.
COX FREDERICK S. (and importer of
  sewing needles, see page 766), Hopedale

PHILLIPS O. 6 Washington (see page
  735),   Lynn
           North Bridgewater
PACKARD J. W. (see page 769),   "

Nets and Seines.
American Net and Twine Co., J. S.
  Shepard, agent,   Canton
Bay State Net & Twine Co.   Gloucester

Newspapers.
(See Contents.)

Notaries Public.
(For other Notaries see Contents.)

Sayles Franklin O.   Adams
Wilkinson E. S.,   No. Adams,   "
Wellington H. H., So. Adams,   "
Dickinson E.   Amherst
Poor George H.   Andover
Porter Samuel,   Beverly
Burgess Silas A.   Blackstone
Whitney Benj. W.   Cambridge
Holt Joseph G.   Cambridgeport,   "
Marrett L.   East Cambridge,   "
Bates Hamlet,   Chelsea
Lathrop E. H.   Chicopee
Stevens Chas. G.   Clinton
Drew Charles,   Fairhaven
Blaisdell Josiah C.   Fall River
Brayton John S.   "
Morton James M. jr.   "
Torrey Geo. A.   Fitchburg
Ware T. K.   "
Wood Nathaniel,   "
Smith Benj. H.   Gloucester
Allen Wm. H.   Greenfield
Davis Wendell T.   "
Marsh John J.   Haverhill
Underwood Porter,   Holyoke
Stuart Silas H.   Hudson
Gile W. Fisk,   Lawrence
Harmon N. W.   "
Poor George H.   "
Shores Norman W.   Lee
Alger Edwin A.   Lowell
Hawkes N. Mortimer,   Lynn
Stickney J. C.
Bordman B.   Malden
Whitney E. C.   Marlboro'
Hayes Benj. F.   Medford
Macy Alfred,   Nantucket
Clifford Charles W.   New Bedford
Cushman A. S.   "
Elliot Thomas D.   "
Ray Isaiah C.   "
Stetson Thomas M.   "
Peck A. Perry,   Northampton
Spaulding S. T.   "
Perkins Jonas R.   North Bridgewater
Adams Robert W.   Pittsfield
Barker James M.   "
Emerson Charles N.   "
Endicott Wm. C.   Salem
Hall Charles B.   Sandwich
Hill Luther,   Spencer
Harris F. H.   Springfield
Dunham Henry J.   Stockbridge
Fuller Wm. E.   Taunton
Reed Charles A.   "
Eaton Chester W.   Wakefield
Hyde William S.   Ware
Lane Otis,   "
Whitney Giles H.   Winchendon
Bent Charles M.   Worcester
Stoddard E. B.   "

Nurserymen, Seedsmen, and Florists.

(See also Seedsmen.)

Barnes T. & J. Abington
Acushnet
Macomber Cornelius, Long Plain, "
Paul James M. North Adams, Adams
Page A. F. Billerica
Jacobs Geo S. Bolton
Gage Edmund, Bradford
Hall William, "
Loring Samuel C. Weymouth. Braintree
Hooper Thomas (florist), Bridgewater
Abbott John H. Buckland
Packard R. L., Shelburne Falls, "
Becker Frank, Cambridge
Howe William (florist). "
Smith Edmund (florist), "
Wisland Bros. (florists), "
Becker Frank (florist), Cambridgeport, "
Chase J. C. " "
Davis & Bates, " "
Hovey & Co. " "
Vandine Henry, " "
White Geo. W., North Cambridge, "
Shaw F. W. Carver
Twiss Wm. Chester
Stone Eliphalet, Dedham
Lewis John A. Dighton
Marroth J. Dorchester
Norton Brothers, "
Wales William, "
Clement Asa, Dracut
Holden Isaac, "
Mitchell William, East Bridgewater
Bryant George, Joppa, "
Clark E. W. East Hampton
Janes J. E. "
Howard John R. Easton Centre, Easton
Slade J. Fall River
Wood Leonard, "
Wight & Judd, Hatfield
Chandler George F. Lancaster
Tyringham Society of Shakers (seedsmen), South Lee, Lee
Lyman William H. Leverett
Sheehan John (florist), Lynn
Marblehead
Gregory James J. H. (seedsman), "
Nye John B. B. Marion
Gage Geo. W. Methuen
Bradlee John D. Milton
Cutting Cicero, "
Davenport Lewis (florist), "
Senter L. W. "
Alley Elijah H. Nantucket
King Samuel, "
Thompson James, "
Needham
Cartwright James & Co. Wellesley, "
Keen Washington, New Bedford
PEIRCE WILLIAM, Elm cor. Cottage, "
Hyde George, Newton Corner, Newton
Garmard & Hunnewell, W. Newton, "
Tyler Orville, "
Howard S. W. S. North Bridgewater
Porter Joshua, North Brookfield
Hay Timothy, North Chelsea
Campbell Festus, Pittsfield
Hancock Society of Shakers (seedsmen), West Pittsfield, "
Lowe J. Benjamin, Petersham
WATSON B. M. (see page 795) Plymouth
Ably Laban, Raynham
Half John A. "
Hanson F. (florist), Salem
Putnam Francis (florist), "

Fish Silas, Sandwich
Stone Josiah G. Shrewsbury
Abbott A. Southbridge
Cheney Leonard, Globe Village, "
Brooks Nathaniel, South Scituate
Lyman E. M. Springfield
Miellez A. "
OLM BROTHERS, "
Sheehan J. "
Pitman Samuel C. Swampscott
Peckham Darius N. Swansea
Smith Shubal D. Tisbury
Lake Charles H. Topsfield
Shakers, H. Storo, agent, Tyringham
Tyler D. A. Warren
Billings Willard, West Bridgewater
Dow Sam. (green-house plants), Westfield
Bunce & Co. Westford
Waterhouse Joseph, Westminster
Ordway Moody, West Newbury
Thurlow Thomas C. "
Westport
Macomber Leonard, Central Village. "
Cutter George B. Weston
Cushing S. P. Weymouth
Foote Asahel, Williamstown
Paul James, "
Carter Sabra Miss (florist), Wilmington
Adams George A. Worcester
Drury Lyman, "
Grout Jonathan, "
Hadwin O. B. "
Arey Thomas, Yarmouth

Nuts and Washers.

(See Bolts, Nuts, and Washers.)

Oars and Blocks.

Elwell Samuel, 3d, Gloucester
Merchant S. jr. "

Oculists.

(See also Opticians.)

Loring H. Lowell
Makepeace F. A. Worcester

Odd Fellows' Regalia.

WRUCK F. A. 195 Essex (see page 748), Salem

Oil and Candle Manufs.

Hastings & Co. New Bedford
Homer George S. "
Leonard Charles H. "
Leonard Nehemiah & Co. "
LEONARD SAMUEL & SON, Leonard st. (see page 760), "
Robinson W. A. & Co. "
Ryder H. & Co. (also paraffine candles), "
Ryder W. & Co. "
Thayer Judd, & Co. (also paraffine candles), "
Wales & Co. (paraffine), "

Oil Casks.

PEIRCE JOHN W. 99 South Water (see page 757), New Bedford
PEIRCE LLOYD N. (see page 726), "

Oil Manufacturers and Dealers.

Cambridge
Lincoln William & Co., E. Cambridge, "
Mason, Whiting, & Co. Cambridgeport, "
Cary Oil Company (petroleum), Chelsea
Chelsea Oil Company (linseed), "
Curry Daniel (rosin), "

Marion Carbon Oil Co.   Fairhaven
       Fall River
Brightman L. & Sons (menhaden oil), "
Fall River Oil and Guano Co. (menha-
   den oil, Job T. Wilson, agent),   "
Hatfield L. (lubricating),   "
DODD A. W. & CO. (fish, see page
   731),   Gloucester
Maddocks B. & Co. (fish),   "
Pettingell & Cunningham (fish),   "
Gerring & Douglass, East Gloucester, "
Walen & Wonson, ..   "
Hadley William (petroleum),   Lynn
Marion Carbon Oil Co.   Marion
Mead J. S. (neats foot),   Milford
LEONARD SAMUEL & SON (see
   page 760),   New Bedford
Kelley E. & Son (watch oil),   "
New Bedford Oil Co., A. H. How-
   land, jr. treasurer,   "
Petroleum & Coal Oil Co., Weston
   Howland, treasurer,   "
Seneca Oil Co., Pierce & Hadley,   "
SISSON OTIS A. 26 Middle,   "
COLT & POWER (see page 707), Pittsfield
    Provincetown
Atwood Nathaniel E. (cod liver),   "
Cook James,   "
Small D. A. (currier's),   "
Griffin H. B.   Salem
Salem & South Danvers Oil Co.   "
SECCOMB OIL MANUFACTURING
   CO. (lubricating and currier's),   "
Shepard Samuel (currier's),   "
WALTON TIMOTHY, foot of Ord st.
   (neats foot, see page 748),   "
     Springfield
WORTHINGTON S. & CO. 123 Main, "
Taylor R. C., Quinsigamond, Worcester

Oil Refiners.

Empire Rock Oil Co., W. P. Handy,
   agent,   Fairhaven
Petroleum & Coal Oil Co., Weston
   Howland, treasurer,   New Bedford
Seneca Oil Co., Pierce & Hadley,   "

Oil Silk.

Pierce S. H. & Co.   Medford

Oiled Clothing Manufacturers.

PETTINGELL & SAWYER (see page
   762), East Cambridge,   Cambridge
CARTER J. F. (see page 749), Gloucester
Cook S. K.   "
    New Bedford
YOUNG & ELDER, 69 Union,   "
Moody B. D.   Newton Corner
Wheeler Howard,   Rockport

Oiled Hats.

PETTINGELL & SAWYER (see page
   762), East Cambridge,   Cambridge

Opticians.

Pease E. C.   Athol Depot
Prevear Edward,   Leominster
Pitman Benjamin,   New Bedford
Burbank S. D.   Springfield
Chapin David M.   "
Makepeace F. A.   Worcester
Stockwell I. H.   "
Weixler J. P. jr.   "

Organ Builders.

(See also Musical Instruments.)
HAMILL SAMUEL S. (church), 91.
Gore,   East Cambridge, Cambridge

STEVENS GEORGE (church), Fifth
   street, East Cambridge, Cambridge
CLISBEE GEORGE,   Marlborough
Holbrook E. L., East Medway, Medway
Johnson Wm. A.   Westfield
STEER & TURNER (see page 766), "

Organs (Cabinet).

Reynolds Philip,   North Bridgewater
Marston A. B.,   Campello,   "
Loring & Blake Organ Co.   Worcester
Taylor & Farley,   "

Organ-Pipe Manufacturers.

    Cambridge
Somerby & Paine, East Cambridge, "
Ware A. L. & M. A., E. Medway, Medway

Organ-Reed Manufacturers.

Levi Henry T.   Westfield
Hammond A. H.   Worcester
Ingalls & Abbott,   "
MUNROE ORGAN REED CO. 5
   Hermon (see page 717),   "

Oven Tile Manufacturer.

WILLIAMS J. R. (also fire brick,
   see page 715),   Taunton

Oysters and Refreshments.

(See also Eating Houses.)
Wood Ezra L.   Abington
Douglas William, East Abington, "
Hallet Harvey H.   "
Gilman George H., North Abington, "
Arnold A. J.   Adams
Easton Carroll W.   "
Adams W. C., North Adams,   "
Brolley James,   "
IVES H. B.   "
Rice Jesse H.   "
Terry W. T.   "
Murphy James, S. Amesbury, Amesbury
    Attleborough
Pierce Andrew, Attleboro' Falls,   "
Blackinton Wm., North Attleboro', "
Sherman Robert H.   "
Tufts William,   "
Tanzy P. C.   Barre
Witt Horace,   "
Luscomb John C.   Beverly
Rich Elisha P.   "
Daggett John C., S. Braintree, Braintree
French Charles A.   "
Bourne William N.   Bridgewater
Baderschnider A.   Brighton
JOHNSON W. H.   "
Stokes William H.   "
Whitney Aaron Mrs.   Brookline
Hammond John,   Canton
Brackett Brothers,   Charlestown
Cass Rufus,   "
Clark J. H.   "
Daly H.   "
Flynn D. M.   "
Hall Oliver W.   "
Ham J. M.   "
Jordan Wm. J.   "
McDonald J. W.   "
McNaught John,   "
Moore James,   "
Morse Charles S.   "
Polette Nicolini,   "
Sawyer S. F.   "
Steger William,   "
White W. F.   "
Witherell E. B.   "
Lewis Frederick T.   Chelsea

Oysters and Refreshments — continued.

Putnam John P.	Chelsea
Fisher John W.	Dedham
KLEMM A.	"
Morse Geo. E.	"
Woodward C. C.	East Bridgewater
Williams M. F., North Easton,	Easton
Allen Charles H. jr.	Fairhaven
Eldredge Samuel,	"
Carpenter William,	Fall River
Davidson John,	"
Durass E.	"
Fellows Matthew,	"
Godley James,	"
McCarty Thomas,	"
McGuire James,	"
Nee John,	"
Thurston Vernon,	"
Tootle Michael,	"
Wilbur Darius,	"
Foster W. H.	Foxborough
Heywood & Matthews,	Gardner
Morse C. W.	"
Millward Benjamin F.	Gloucester
Rogers J. S. & Brother,	"
Gorham E. L.	Great Barrington
Norton John,	"
Savage George G.	"
Gascoigne J. T.	Greenfield
Lamb Joseph H.	"
Upson A. A.	"
Webber L. P.	"
Baker John R.	Holyoke
Blanchard J. M.	"
Knight S. W.	"
Taylor James,	"
Terrell Lewis L.	"
SMITH MARY D. Mrs.	Ipswich
Drew J. D.	Lawrence
Gurdy O. P.	"
Hutchins Enoch H.	"
Joslyn E. A.	"
Keeney W. H.	"
Mudgett E. Mrs.	"
Sargent J. W.	"
Bliss Chauncy T.	Lee
Couch Charles M.	"
Counters O.	"
Jones Thomas,	"
Riordon Patrick H.	"
Backus Philip,	Lenox
Bray Brothers,	Lowell
Dow Joshua,	"
Emerald J. R.	"
Emery Henry,	"
Follansby N.	"
French A. B. & Co.	"
Hale Mary J.	"
Hall Luther B.	"
Ingalls O. W.	"
Johnson Andrew E.	"
McDONOUGH JOHN H. 73½ Charles,	"
Meserve Ebeo,	"
Page Abram,	"
Richardson Daniel L.	"
Richardson George,	"
Richardson Sullivan,	"
Smith William H.	"
Foss Robert,	Lynn
Hammond R. C.	"
Hitchings I. B.	"
Hoyt Brothers,	"
Laggon John,	"
Messick Robert,	"
MORRIS C. P. & CO., Union, cor. Willow,	"
Millett D. K.	"
Sargent L. C.	"

Sawtell S. H.	Lynn
Knight W. M.	Marblehead
Wellman Jacob,	"
FLINT WALTER M.	Marlborough
Hardman Patrick,	"
MANSFIELD W. D.	"
Lane Charles,	Milford
Nash A. E.	"
Norris B. S.	"
Willis Edwin,	"
Altenkirch Jacob,	New Bedford
Betz Thaddeus,	"
Egreton James,	"
Gunning William,	"
Kinsman Gideon D.	"
Reardon John,	"
Richards G.	"
Spence Henry,	"
Edwards L. B.	Northampton
MORTON LEVI,	"
Washburn T. R.	North Bridgewater
Washburn & Grover,	"
Bacon H. DeWitt,	Oxford
Gibson William,	"
Yeomans C.	"
Feeney John,	Palmer
Fox & Holbrook,	"
Nelson Lyman,	"
Reed D. N.	Peabody
Campbell Festus,	Pittsfield
Clary Morris,	"
McLane James C.	"
PHELPS & CROSSMAN, 43 North,	"
Rockwell J. P.	"
St. Mary Louis,	"
Webb John,	"
Willis F. B.	"
Barnes & Rickards,	Plymouth
Dodge James E.	"
Holbrook James S.	"
Brown Reuben F.	Provincetown
Gross S. S.	"
French Joseph T.	Quincy
Rogers Otis,	"
French Ansell,	Randolph
Shaw S. B.	"
Baker James,	Reading
Ruggles Ira W.	"
Eaton James S.	Rockport
Beckford Asa N.	Salem
Cook A.	"
Covell T. N.	"
Doherty John,	"
Estes G. W. jr.	"
Holbrook Joseph,	"
Lewis J. W.	"
Lyons Timothy,	"
Moses Aaron,	"
Newcomb D. B. & J.	"
Parshley Albert A.	"
Tibbetts R. S.	"
Rogers S. F.	"
Dennett A. H. Salisbury Point, Salisbury	
Keenan James,	Sandwich
Brown C. K.	Sheffield
Streeter J. B. Shelburne Falls, Shelburne	
Marcy John A.	Southbridge
Turner E. M.	"
Howe Aaron,	Springfield
Phillips W. D.	"
Pierce Lucian,	"
Walker H. A.	"
CHURCHILL A. K.	Stoneham
Phinney S. C. Jr.	Stoughton
Pierce William Mrs.	"
Tower I. P.	"
Baker F. A.	Swampscott
Galeucia William,	"

Bolton Ansel, Taunton
Guthrie Roger, "
Field L. E. "
Hove Thomas, "
McCormick Edward, "
Simms William, "
Townsend J. S. & Bro. "
Walton Richard, "
Wilbur S. & Bro. "
CARYL HENRY, Ware
Weeks J. M. Warren
Harts Edmund, Webster
Perry J. H. "
Smith J. "
Higgins & Rodolph, Wellfleet
Elwell Lewis L. Westborough
Gerry J. M. "
Trowbridge J. A. "
Allen Timothy O. Westfield
Batty James, "
Hayden Albert L. "
Hudson & Tinkham, "
Mallory S. W. "
Vandakin Henry, "
Wilkinson H. L. "
Jones H. C. West Stockbridge
Clapp Charles S. Weymouth
Thayer W. G. "
Lufkin James M. East Weymouth, "
Rickards C. South " "
Wilbraham
Leach C. C. North Wilbraham, "
Still O. R. Woburn

Oyster Dealers.

DAMON D. N. Greenfield
Ford & Stevens, Holyoke
MARTIN W. L. (see page 724), "
Chapman Samuel S. Lee
Bartlett Bourne S. New Bedford
Crowell Charles F. "
Sisson J. L. "
Clapp Edward, Northampton
Rowe & Congdon, "
Goodsell J. D. Pittsfield
PHELPS & CROSSMAN, "
Atwood J. K. Plymouth
Newcomb D. B. & J. Salem
Smead —, Shelburne Falls, Shelburne
Ames S. (wholesale), Springfield
Granger T. M. "
Ives & Quimby, "
Jennings C. L. "
Scott H. "
Webber J. W. & Co. (wholesale), "
Searls & Barnes, Webster
O'GRADY WILLIAM & SON
(wholesale), 295 Main, Worcester
Utley John W. (wholesale), "

Pail Ear Manufacturers.

Clark James H. Orange
HANCOCK O. Winchendon
KETCHUM & LOUD (see page 776), "

Pails, Tubs, &c.

(See Wooden Ware.)

Paint Can Manufacturer.

Parker Warren W. New Bedford

Paint Manufacturers.

PARMENTER M. D. (Colley's Elastic
Composition, see page 707), 175
Broadway, Chelsea
Hunt John W. Milton
Wood's H. Son & Co. Wellesley, Needham
Cook Thomas W. & Co. New Bedford

Gifford Oliver E. New Bedford
Humphrey, Kirby, & Co. "
Springfield
Hampden Paint & Chemical Co. "
Willard & Lane, . Taunton

Painters (Carriage).

Pierce William N. Abington
Cobbett C. F. East Abington, "
Bates Asa, South " "
Bowen D. & Son, Adams
Edmunds Joab, "
Smith Edwin, Alford
Smith George W. "
Smiley Francis, S. Amesbury, Amesbury
Cilley J. B. West Amesbury, "
Flanders M. C. "
Sargent M. B. " "
Higgins E. P. Andover
Clark William L. & Co. Arlington
Wilcox O. W. Ashland
Clapp Samuel, Athol
Gibbs Warren P. "
Fish W. W. & H. L. Athol Depot, "
Bailey Enoch, Attleborough
Ferguson Joseph, North Attleborough, "
Mellish John, Auburn
Cushing John T. jr. Beverly
Moore Hiram, "
Hartshorn J. Blackstone
Griffin Thomas, South Braintree, Braintree
Walsh John M. Weymouth, "
Braman J. G. & Co. Bridgewater
Fisk Jonas, Brighton
Given & Buskirk, . Cambridge
JONES A. J. Church, cor. Palmer, "
Belcher George W. Cambridgeport, "
Donnelly & Butler, East Cambridge, "
WEBB T. C. & CO. (see page 657),
North Cambridge, "
Wisewell Timothy, Canton
Breed Anderson P. Charlestown
Clark E. J. "
Coburn J. "
Coles A. W. "
Gannett H. C. "
Ham Ivory C. "
Bird Patrick H. Chelsea
Norris George, "
Morrison Victor, Cheshire
Moulton W. B. Chester
Manchester William, Chicopee
Leland & Brown, Clinton
Tower Samuel D. Cohasset
Smith Julius M. Concord
Bestwick F. L. . Dedham
Flagg G. A. "
Robbins John C. "
Johnson Wm. South Dedham, "
Baker Eustace, West " "
Cooper Thomas, Dorchester
Gilbert W. H. Mattapan, "
Tucker William, Milton, "
Cushman A. Neponset, "
Wentworth Clark, East Bridgewater
Brayton Israel, Fall River
Marsh Jacob B. Fitchburg
White Ivers, "
Young Wm. H. Foxborough
Millett William L. Gloucester
Almont Bernard, Great Barrington
Bazzell Varney, "
Jaqua Frank, "
Moulton John F. "
Carey Lockwood, Housatonic, "
Cummings Abram, " "
Lyon David, Greenfield
Greenwich
Jordan F. H. Greenwich Village, "

Painters — continued.

Fowler G. S.	Haverhill
Hersey David A.	Hingham
Sprague & Loring,	"
Clark Chester & Son,	Hinsdale
Whitney J. W.	Hubbardston
Underwood E. C.	Hudson
Fowler Eben,	Ipswich
Eldridge E. D.	Kingston
Beadle B. D.	Lawrence
Foster, Patterson, & Co.	"
Morgan Joseph H. & Co.	"
	Lexington
Holbrook John L.	E. Lexington, "
Freeman Samuel J.	Lowell
Lynch Alonzo K.	"
Raclcot Alphonso,	"
Kimball J. F.	Lynn
Nason James R.	"
Natting Thomas J.	"
Sawyer J. A. J.	"
Smith & Co.	"
Spinney H. N.	"
Giles James,	Marlborough
Bingham T. A.	Medfield
Thayer J. E.	Medway
Hanscom, Palmer, & Co.	Melrose
Boomer Benj. L.	Middleborough
Sparrow Jacob G.	"
Southworth Rodney E.	"
Young Wm. L.	Milford
Woods Edward,	"
Allen Albert,	Millbury
Chapman & Strangman,	Milton
Dexter Thomas D.	New Bedford
Snow Otis,	"
Chase W. P.	Newburyport
Fuller George,	West Newton, Newton
Heywood M. T.	Newtonville, "
Langtry R.	Newton Corner, "
Hamilton L. W.	Northampton
Jones John B.	North Bridgewater
Sargent Samuel A.	"
Tribou Lyman E.	"
Howe T. R.	North Brookfield
Crane John H.	Norton
Crawford William S.	Oakham
Hastings Minot,	Orange
Hildreth James E.	Otis
Bouney J. Dean,	Pembroke
Freeman & Litchfield, W. Duxbury, "
Merry Nelson,	Pittsfield
Jones Charles L.	Plymouth
Tirrell Sons,	Quincy
Campbell Wm.	Randolph
Stark A. H.	"
Barney Alfred R.	Rehoboth
Fletcher Stillman J.	Rutland
Andrews Gilman,	Salem
Burbank E. G. & E. A.	"
Burbank J. L.	"
Burbank T. F.	"
Davidson M. & Co.	"
Rhoades J. W.	"
Foster W. M. H.	Shelburne
McRae James,	Shirley
Plummer J. H.	Somerville
Dasutt Joseph,	Springfield
Fisk H. C.	"
Lamb A. A.	Stoughton
Hamant L.	Sturbridge
Gerrish Charles H.	Taunton
Kelley E. H.	"
Sweeting A. P.	"
Jones Abijah,	Templeton
Maynard & Fiske,	"
Taylor Frank,	Otter River, "
Savage Leander,	Uxbridge

Knight C. S. & Co.	Ware
Barrows H. W.	Wareham
Woodard H. L.	Webster
Bacon Daniel, jr.	Westborough
Harris Sidney,	"
HEWITSON JAMES,	
Parson Henry A.	Westfield
Smith Harrison F.	"
Jones Thomas B.	Weston
	West Roxbury
ALDEN AMASA, Jamaica Plain, "
Pratt Charles L.	"
	Weymouth
Marston Wm. G. South Weymouth, "
Brown Chester F.	Winchendon
Sawin J.	"
Connor Wm.	Woburn
Bernard G. H.	Worcester
Hubbard & Beaman,	"
Rice A. P.	"

Painters (Decorative).

BAIRD WILLIAM & SON (see page 728), 110 So. Common,   Lynn
FRAZIER I. & SON (see page 751), 340 Main,   "

Painters (Fresco).

NIXON T. J. (see page 728), Court street,   Taunton

Painters (House and Sign).

Davis W. H.	Abington
French Joseph F.	"
Willey James H.	"
Ford B. F.	East Abington, "
Gilson L. C. & Son,	"
Lincoln Samuel B., North "	
Brennan Charles, " "	
Harding James S., South "	
Jones T. G. F.	Acton
Jackson L. M.	South Acton, "
Jones Francis, " "	
Houghton Warren, West, "	
Sumner A. R. " "	
Pierce Alex. O.	Acushnet
Smith Daniel V.	"
Warren James,	"
Curr A.	North Adams, Adams
Childs Henry, "	
Darling Allen B. "	
Derling J. W. "	
Wilbur & Manchester, "	
De Witt Reuben,	Agawam
Kane Amos,	Alford
Smith Edwin,	"
Smith George W.	"
Dennett John,	Amesbury
Carrier J. M.	W. Amesbury, "
Jones William, "	
Graves Brothers,	Amherst
Stebbins J.	"
Thomas & Ingraham,	"
Willis F. E.	North Amherst, "
Abbot R. M.	Andover
Barnard E. H.	"
Clark Thomas,	"
Higgins Eben P.	"
Lawrence John,	Arlington
Tufts D. H.	"
Greenwood T.	Ashburnham
Morton Orrin,	"
Allen S. M.	Ashby
Burr Henry W.	"
Dadmun Henry J. & Son,	Ashland
Spooner John W.	"
Wilcox O. A.	Ashland
Carter Alba W.	Athol

Humphrey John F.	Athol
Smith ——,	"
Twitchell E. L.	Athol Depot, "
Hammond W. B.	Attleborough
Stearns & Nye,	"
Coswell H. W.	N. Attleborough, "
McLeod Hector,	"
Briggs Joseph M.	Barnstable
Whittemore Joseph,	"
Ryder Joshua,	Cotuit, "
Baker Obed,	Hyannis, "
Baker Sidney,	" "
Nye Hiram,	" "
Robbins Joseph,	Osterville, "
Howland Josiah B.	W. Barnstable, "
Howland J. P.	Barre
Howland J.	"
Morgan A.	"
Norcross Jarvis,	Becket
Davis Charles,	Belchertown
Moody Ansel,	"
Higgins Albert,	Belmont
Johnson George E.	Berlin
Boyle James E.	Bernardston
Ryther Dwight,	"
Slate Jonathan,	"
Foster Nathan H.	Beverly
Porter J. & J. V.	"
Barker J. M.	Billerica
Burrows Edward,	"
Keith Simon,	Blackstone
Cannon Frank,	Blandford
Blood Amos F.	Bolton
Robinson Wm. W.	"
Moore James,	Boxborough
Ball Aaron,	Boylston Centre, Boylston
Flagg Ward N.	"
Boardman Abraham,	Bradford
Lang Frank,	"
Penniman Josiah,	Braintree
Stoddard T. B.	So. Braintree, "
Thayer Joseph,	" "
Harding Theophilus,	Brewster
Whittemore C. D.	"
Alden James S.	Bridgewater
Braman J. G. & Co.	"
Daniels Wm. P.	Brighton
Dearborn Samuel,	"
Ellis Francis,	"
Fiske Jonas,	"
Tubbs J. O.	"
Holdredge William H.	Brimfield
Morgan John W.	"
Upham George H.	"
Denton Newton,	Brookfield
Knight John,	"
Baker Benj. F.	Brookline
Chace Reuben A.	"
Gibson Brothers,	"
Hand J. B.	"
Mahoney John,	"
Palmer C. L.	"
Richmond J. A. & Co.	Shelburne Falls,
	Buckland
Danforth Geo. O.	Cambridge
Dillingham & Cass,	"
Flaherty Michael,	"
Holt James L.	"
PALMER C. L.	"
Parsons A. B.	"
Stewart H. L.	"
Ankers J. L. P.	Cambridgepoit,
Bassett H. H.	"
Grimason Daniel,	"
Holmes P. B.	"
Little A. F.	"
Sawyer Chas. A.	"
Smith J. V.	"

SHELDON JAMES, 420 Main.	Cambridgeport, Cambridge
Stacy George W.	" "
Stevens J.	" "
Taylor Wm. A.	" "
Thayer J. H. & J. P.	" "
Wentworth Benj. L.	" "
Wilder J. C.	" "
FILLEBROWN SAMUEL, jr.	East Cambridge, "
Heffernan David,	" "
Jewett A. N.	" "
McIntire Eben,	" "
Tufts F. H.	" "
Claflin David D.	North Cambridge, "
JOHNSON H. H., North ave.	North Cambridge, "
Horton G. F. H.	Canton
Saunders G. W.	"
Heald E. S.	Carlisle
Streeter Moses,	Charlemout
Caldwell Joshua,	Charlestown
Clark E. J.	"
Clark Thomas S.	"
Crane John H.	"
Curry Wm.	"
Fish Benj. F.	"
Hunt E. C.	"
Magrath Thomas,	"
Mason Rufus & Son,	"
McMath & Weston,	"
Mears & Emmons,	"
Parker Edward,	"
Pope Mark,	"
Seavey Moses,	"
Tyler Geo. E.	"
Waldron H. G.	"
West Charles,	"
Partridge Elijah,	Charlton
Pratt Lyman,	Charlton City, "
Cahoon Benjamin S.	Chatham
Freeman Nathaniel,	"
Smith Heman M.	"
Holt Horace,	Chelmsford
Sargeant David M.	N. Chelmsford, "
Carr J. H.	Chelsea
Carroll & Graw,	"
Clark W. L. D.	"
Everden W. F.	"
Legg Wm. H,	"
Martin Samuel J.	"
Penniman Adna L.	"
Ricker & Hutchins,	"
Stone S. P.	"
Young Wm.	"
Collier Nathan E. S.	Chesterfield
Hammersley Jonathan B.	Chicopee
Williams C.	Chicopee Falls, "
Wilbur Wm.	Clarksburg
Bowen Lovain,	North Adams, "
Brewer E. W.	Clinton
Brown J. R.	"
Barker E. N.	Cohasset
Gove S. S.	"
Nott D. S.	"
Barrett Edward S.	Concord
Hawks A. C.	Conway
Newton Charles B.	Cummington
Stearns Lawrence,	Dalton
Newcomb Joseph W.	Dana
Smith Wm.	"
Barnett Thomas,	Danvers
Lawson Oswald,	"
Edwards John L.	Danvers Port. "
	Dartmouth
Rider Leonard W.,	North Dartmouth, "
Manley A.	South Dartmouth. "
Bates A. L.	Dedham

Painters — continued.

Flagg George A.	Dedham
Johnson William,	"
Mitchell Joseph,	"
Peppers Robert,	"
Robbins John C.	"
Weeks Luther C.	"
Dennen J. J.	East Dedham, "
Smith Henry,	" "
Dexter W. W.	South Dedham, "
Baker Eustis W.	West Dedham, "
White John K.	"
Whittemore Hiram,	Dennis
Baker Calvin,	North Dennis, "
Burgess J. N.	South Dennis, "
Crowell Sylvester W.	" "
Bird J. H.	Dorchester
Fowler George W.	"
Graham James B.	"
Howe J. W.	"
Lawler J. W.	"
Yendell George,	"
White John B	Harrison sq. "
Angell Moses E.	Hyde Park, "
Angell G. C.	" "
Noyes George W.	"
Curtis George C.	Mattapan, "
Tileston Samuel,	Milton, "
Dennison George D.	Neponset, "
Dennison G. W.	" "
Steer Thomas,	East Douglas, Douglas
Keith L. S.	"
Mann Daniel F.	Dover
Jacques Josiah,	Dunstable
Stevens Kimball A.	"
Weston Edward E.	"
Chandler Alden,	Duxbury
Hathaway Joshua W.	"
Sampson Alfred, jr.	"
Davenport John,	East Bridgewater
Grow Henry A.	"
Moehler Henry,	"
Nickerson Thomas P.	Eastham
Gould F. J.	East Hampton
Robinson E.	"
Smith E. R. (sign),	"
TOOGOOD L. O.	"
Martin Joseph,	North Easton, Easton
Perry & Macomber, South	" "
Fish & Smith,	Edgartown
Goff William C.	"
Beston Alvin,	Enfield
Newell Elijah,	"
Bartlett Daniel W.	Essex
Burnham Rufus,	"
Allen Charles H.	Fairhaven
Purrington & Taber,	"
Simmons Robert M.	"
Tripp Alexander,	"
Baylies & Macomber	Fall River
Brown Thomas,	"
Chace & Waite,	"
Hill George,	"
Hoar George E.	"
Huntsman Wm. V.	"
Peckham George W.	"
Pitman Samuel,	"
Urswirth Enoch,	"
Waite Andrew J.	"
Shiverick Watson,	Falmouth
Davis John W. East Falmouth,	"
Lewis W. T.	" "
Coleman Nathaniel, West Falmouth,	"
Coleman J. J.	Fitchburg
ESTABROOK J. D. & CO.	"
Foster Samuel (glazier),	"
Himes T. M.	"
Bliss Geo. W.	Florida

Brigham Joseph,	Foxborough
HOOTON & HALL,	"
Perry J. P. P.	"
Potter J.	"
Ballard George,	Framingham
Coe Frederick,	"
Graham George,	"
Stowell L. H.	"
Roberts W. G. South Framingham,	"
McCann Robert,	" "
Priestly Thomas,	Saxonville, "
Blake Seth jr.	Franklin
Robinson J. K.	"
Rogers J. H.	"
Pratt William,	Freetown
Ray Emery B.	"
Priest Willard,	Gardner
Whitney A. B.	"
Brown Lucian W. South Gardner,	"
Harnden W. A.	Georgetown
Rollins ——,	"
Brown S. O.	Gloucester
Cook & Pew,	"
Cook E. L.	"
Griffin, Bowker, & Co.	"
Stacey & Babson,	"
Cook Leonard, East Gloucester,	"
Tarr & Wonson,	"
Lane Albert, Lanesville,	"
Barrows E.	Grafton
Dalrymple John,	"
Jones J. C.	"
Cady H. K. N. E. Village,	"
Legate C. J.	" "
Thayer Fisher,	" "
Jaqua Frank,	Great Barrington
Ball Joseph C.	Greenfield
Mark George W.	"
Rice Edward J.	"
Balch Leonard,	Groveland
Dougherty A. H.	Hadley
Marsh Wm. H. North Hadley,	"
Thomas Horace,	Halifax
Bailey Melzar C.	Hanover
Corbin Frank,	"
Eels John P.	"
Hill Charles R.	Hanson
Roberts John C.	"
Bonney Elbridge P. S. Hanson.	"
Aiken Charles P.	Hardwick
Granger Daniel,	"
Cummings Charles H.	Harvard
Pollard Luke,	"
	Harwich
Crowell Sheldon K. Harwich Port,	"
Eldredge Seabury, So. Harwich,	"
Eldredge Wm. M. " "	"
Robbins Gustavus, " "	"
Dougherty Wm.	Hatfield
Batchelder B. L.	Haverhill
Butler W. H.	"
BUTTERS SILAS, 51 Water,	"
Stanton C. H.	"
Tracy A. G. & Co.	"
Coss David,	Hingham
Cross & Reed,	"
Eldredge J. C.	"
Hersey John P.	"
Sprague J. & S.	"
Bartlett Peter,	Hinsdale
Willis J.	"
Rogers J. W.	Holden
Fisk Abner,	Holliston
Jones Daniel,	"
Plimpton & Burroughs,	"
Barnes George J.	Holyoke
Clapp Robinson,	"
Harris N. A.	Hopkinton

Hemenway F.	Hopkinton
Traverse Moses,	"
Savage S. K.	Hubbardston
Loice Amory,	Hudson
L cke & Randall,	"
Thomas H. A.	"
Wood Charles,	"
Harmon N. O.	Huntington
Macey H. J.	"
Crittenden & Snow,	Hyde Park
Dawson William,	Ipswich
Low Jacob,	"
Newman Benjamin,	"
Bonney Geo. H.	Kingston
Bonney Wallace,	"
Corey Gustavus,	"
Barrows Elijah W.	Lakeville
Churchill Libeus,	"
Pickens Henry C.	"
Healey Henry H.	Lancaster
Safford Charles,	"
Robbins Thomas D.	Lanesborough
Baldwin Monroe,	Lawrence
Barnes Timothy P.	"
Beadle B. D.	"
BEAL HENRY, Essex near Broadway,	"
Brown S. F.	"
Damon H. P.	"
Edwards Franklin,	"
Foster, Patterson, & Co.	"
Kent Richard H.	"
Kerr Colin,	"
Low Thomas B.	"
Merrill Moses G.	"
Morgan Joseph H. & Co.	"
Paine Jacob,	"
Pierce Abner,	"
Watson P. T.	"
Wood William,	"
Harding & Lyons,	Lee
Cogswell John D.	Leicester
Babcock Ezra & Son,	Lenox
Hobart Colburn,	Leverett
Fiske F. R.	Lexington
Merriam James,	"
Reed Newell,	"
Smith W. H. 2d,	"
Brown Oliver, East Lexington,	"
Davis Charles L.	Littleton
Robbins A. W.	"
	Longmeadow
Phillips John, East Longmeadow,	"
Adams G. W.	Lowell
Barnes Horace B.	"
Bradford & Stevens,	"
Brown & Carter,	"
Burrill & Wirt,	"
Crooker A. F.	"
Donovan M.	"
Emerson Nathan,	"
Farson & Crooker,	"
Hayward Clark,	"
Kelly William & John,	"
Kittredge Abner,	"
Kittredge Jeduthan,	"
LIVINGSTON ALFRED J. 164 Middlesex,	"
Marble C. H.	"
Morrill N. W.	"
Munroe W. H.	"
Pascal George N.	"
Parks George,	"
Phelps W. P.	"
Quimby Alonzo P.	"
Quimby James B.	"
Sears William,	"
Webster Charles O.	"

Wiley E. J.	Lowell
Webster Joseph P.	Ludlow
Bailey Ezekiel G.	Lunenburg
Merrill Geo. H.	"
Thompson James H.	"
Armstead S. L.	Lynn
Ashton & Weeks,	"
BAIRD WM. & SON (see page 728), 110 So. Common,	"
Bartol John A.	"
Chase Jacob,	"
Chase Philip,	"
Copeland Edward F.	"
Fitzgerald Edward,	"
FRAZIER I. & SON (see page 751), 340 Main,	"
Hiller & Barrett,	"
Holt Hermon,	"
Holt John,	"
Jewett H. C.	"
Luscomb & Nourse,	"
Martin Gratin,	"
Rice & Huse,	"
Rowell & Wilson,	"
Smith & Co.	"
Sullivan Brothers,	"
Twombly John F.	"
Brown B. T. Lynnfield Centre, Lynnfield
Almeder F. J.	Malden
Baldwin James M.	"
Brown Samuel,	"
Handcock & Redman,	"
Hill Aaron G.	"
Cloutman P. D.	Marblehead
Franks C. W.	"
Meader M. K.	"
Wormstead Joseph,	"
Wing Jabez,	Marion
McOslin James,	Marlborough
Rogers Wm., North Marshfield,	Marshfield
Dexter James W.	Mattapoisett
Jones Ebenezer,	"
Bullard John E.	Medfield
Sanborn W.	"
Ware Charles H.	"
PALMER CHAS. L. Main st.	Medford
Wood T. D.	"
Fisk Melville,	Medway
Hanscom, Palmer, & Co.	Melrose
Paul Edward,	"
Remick William,	"
Robinson Henry,	"
Carlton & Richardson,	Methuen
Pierce Abner,	"
West Charles A.	"
Sparrow Hartley A.	Middleborough
Sparrow Jacob G.	"
Wood Frederick E.	"
Whitcomb Fred. E.	Middlefield
Albee, Eldridge, & Co.	Milford
Bane T. J.	"
Morse & Woods,	"
Ryan Wm.	Millbury
White J. T. & Son,	"
Chapman Moses C.	Milton
Chapman Rufus,	"
Calkins A. L.	Monson
Gates Erasmus,	"
Gates William H.	"
Newton Truman,	Montague
Sawin A. Grout's Corner,	"
Luscomb Wm.	Nahant
Coffin Wm. H.	Nantucket
Macy Alexander I.	"
Paddack H. & Co.	"
Smith Wm. P.	"
Drummond W.	Natick
Parlin Asher,	"

Painters — continued.

Holt Wm.	South Natick,	Natick
Wheeler Aaron,	"	"
Manning Alvarez.		Needham
Flagg Eben,	Wellesley,	"
Wisner Abbott,	Grantville,	"
Akin Francis T.		New Bedford
Babcock Spooner,		"
Bradford C. F.		"
Braley Charles H.		"
Caswell Wm. H.		"
DeWolfe James,		"
Dunbam & West,		"
Gifford O. E.		"
Hillman H.		"
Jenkins B. S.		"
Kempton & Covell,		"
Lawrence Ephraim, 2d,		"
Manchester A. P.		"
Maxfield Wm.		"
Parker Wm. C.		"
Potter Pardon,		"
Sanford Benjamin T.		"
Tyler George,		New Braintree
Wood Charles W.		Newbury
Allen C. H.		Newburyport
Blake & Noyes,		"
Burrill & Brown,		"
Creasey Joseph B.		"
Cutter Charles J.		"
Cutter E. P.		"
Hale Oliver,		"
Hamilton Thomas A.		"
Pearson Augustus,		"
Woods A. D.		"
Ford James,	Auburndale,	Newton
Hubbard & Burr,	"	"
Nicholson C.	Lower Falls,	"
Sears J. L.		"
Rolfe Wm. A.	Newton Centre,	"
Bryant & Hargrave,	Newton Corner,	"
Evans J. O.	"	"
Holman L. S.	"	"
Langtry Richard,	"	"
Heywood M. T.	Newtonville,	"
Almond David,	West Newton,	"
Hayford & Griggs,	"	"
Phillips C. S.	"	"
Brown & Williams,		Northampton
Clark Isaac R.		"
Prentiss Wm. C.		"
Smith & Jones,		"
Whitcomb D. B.		"
Wilson Joel,		"
Boynton G. F.		Florence, "
Gould Geo. W.		North Andover
Harrington L. M.		Northborough
Valentine Geo. G.		"
Farnham Geo.		North Bridgewater
Sharpe John M.		"
Richmond Lucius,		"
Sargent Geo. T.		"
Hoyt Calvin,		North Brookfield
Underwood Chas.		"
Carr John H.		North Chelsea
Jewett Sewell P.		"
Piper Wm. N.		Northfield
Nichols Wm. J.		North Reading
Crane John H.		Norton
Messinger James O.		"
Packard James,		Oakham
Prentice Gilbert L.		Orange
Ramsey Luther P.		"
Sanger L.		"
Martin John,		Orleans
Copp Frederick A.		Oxford
Darling O. M.		"
Snow Wm. C.		"

Foster J. B.		Palmer
Taylor Newell,		"
Boynton D. R.		Paxton
Howard Charles P.		"
Adams, West, & Co.		Peabody
Blaney John C.		"
Blaney Wm.		"
Whidden Henry L.		"
Bonney J. Dean,		Pembroke
Gardner B. T.		"
Jones E. Morton,		"
Jones S. L.		"
White B. Franklin,	N. Pembroke,	"
Hutchinson Charles,		Pepperell
Peabody Newton,	East Pepperell,	"
Holman Solomon O.		Petersham
Williams Harrison,		"
Bates Emory S.		Phillipston
Bowker Geo.		"
Holland John M. & Sons,		Pittsfield
Lyons & Ladd,		"
Holmes Ephraim,		Plymouth
Jones Charles L.		"
Savery W. T.		"
Tribble Wm. B.		"
		Plympton
Bonney Geo. H.	North Plympton,	"
Aldrich B. W.		Prescott
Fay John B.		Princeton
Harrington C.		"
Dyer Benjamin H.		Provincetown
Dyer Thomas W. & Co.		"
Joseph Francis,		"
Robbins F.		"
French Harvey J.		Quincy
Hayward J. T. & W. V.		"
Hersey John W.		"
Lewis Roger,		"
Sawtell A. S.		"
Brown John L.		Randolph
Platt G. C.		"
Ward Eugene T.		"
White James W.	East Randolph,	"
Belcher Joseph,	South "	"
Bancroft Wm. H.		Reading
Nichols & McIntire,		"
Harmon C.		Richmond
Harmon Wm.		"
Damon Charles H.		Rochester
Rogers Mason,		"
Choate A. & Co.		Rockport
Fisk J. W.		Rowe
Butman John T.		Rowley
Torrey Joseph,		"
Putnam Geo. S.		Rutland
Abbott Phillip,		Salem
Ames Edward B.		"
Austin Richard H.		"
Averill J. W.		"
Brown Charles E.		"
Brown R. L.		"
Calley Samuel,		"
Clark S. C.		"
Davis Charles H.		"
Felt J. G.		"
Foley Edward,		"
Henderson Daniel,		"
Mansfield B. S.		"
Mansfield Joseph,		"
Martin J. C.		"
Pousland George A.		"
Pulsifer D. & Co.		"
Pulsifer Charles H.		"
Pulsifer Joseph,		"
Pulsifer Nathaniel,		"
Rowell B.		"
Simonds W. H.		"
Skerry E. S.		"

Stedman & Glover,	Salem	Stone George W.	Swampscott
Swasey Joseph,	"	Gray William A.	Swansea
Tibbetts Henry H.	"		Taunton
Fowler Eben P.	Salisbury	CROWELL EZRA, 37 West Water,	"
Richardson George, Montville,	Sandisfield	Gerrish Charles H.	"
Stuart J.	"	French John T.	"
Spring William,	Sandwich	Hayman Wm.	"
Williams David, East Saugus,	Saugus	NIXON T. J., Court st. (and fresco,	
Bliss William,	Savoy	see page 728),	..
Bouve Sylvanus R.	Scituate	Nugent Pierse,	"
Hayward John,	"	Parker George S.	"
Hayward Ward L.	"	Stanley J. J. & Co.	"
Young Charles,	"	Watts & Brothers,	"
Young Edwin,	"	Wood Cornelius,	"
Smith John M.	Sheffield	Chase Henry,	Templeton
Smith Lyman A., East Sheffield,	"	Gray T. C.	"
Russell J. Shelburne Falls,	Shelburne	Upham Charles W.	"
Babcock Lowell,	Sherborn	Gray G. F. East Templeton,	"
Duross Charles,	"	Litch George, Otter River,	"
Priest R. M.	Shirley	Jenkins Foster H., Holmes's Hole,	Tisbury
Allen Augustus A.	Shrewsbury	Marshall S. C.	Tolland
Chamberlain Daniel S.	"	Hanson William H.	Topsfield
Hascall James,	"	Orne B. A.	"
Maynard Augustus F.	"	Gates Christopher,	Townsend
Morton Edward,	"	SHATTUCK JOB,	"
Smallidge Henry,	Shutesbury	Copp Sewell T.	Upton
Davis Baylies,	Somerset	Salisbury William,	"
Chase Edward B.	"	Arnold Alfred,	Uxbridge
Sanford Joseph T.	"	Bacon & Sweetzer,	Wakefield
Peckham Charles B.	"	Fairbanks Lewis,	"
Twombly J. Q.	Somerville	Hamblin William H.	"
Hollis J. H. North Somerville,	"	Winter Joseph E.	Wales
Barney G. F.	Southborough	Bacon & Bullard,	Walpole
Thompson Daniel H.	"	Blackburn William,	"
Woods Hamlet S.	"	Merrill B. F.	"
Clarke P. M.	Southbridge	Hutchinson E. M.	Waltham
Booth Jacob, Globe Village,	"	Wentworth B. W.	"
McKinstry James T. "	"	Whelon John H.	"
Hyde P. Lucius,	South Hadley	Knight C. S. & Co.	Ware
Preston Joseph S.	"	Marsh Zenas,	"
Preston & Moody, South Hadley Falls,	"	MURDOCK CHAS. C.	Wareham
Bates Daniel C.	Southampton	Perkins Josiah F.	"
Lawrence Thomas R.	South Scituate	Tower A. D.	Warren
Spring Henry,	Southwick	Sanger Joshua F.	Warwick
Spring Milo,	"	Abbott Charles V.	Washington
Corliss E. H.	Spencer	Barnard John,	Watertown
Morland William J.	"	Griswold A.	"
Clark Luther,	Springfield	Page John,	"
Hammersly H. W.	"	Russell Henry,	"
Hancox Albert,	"	Lee Cyrus,	Wayland
Helms E.	"	Sawin Joseph,	"
Hildreth J. C.	"	Barnes Leonard,	Webster
Hook George,	"	Dresser H. M.	"
Pierce L. L.	"	Wiley F. A. & Co.	Wellfleet
Rice & Bartlett,	"	Choate Jeremiah, jr.	Wenham
Ryan & Powell,	"	Harris Sidney,	Westborough
Tucker Henry M.	"	HEWITSON JAMES,	"
Walker T. M. & Co.	"	Stone John,	"
Wood Frank,	"	Smith George J. Oakdale,	West Boylston
Boynton John S.	Sterling	Copeland Albert,	West Bridgewater
Saurin E. F.	Stoneham	Edson Alanson S.	"
Capen Samuel, jr.	Stoughton	Howard Milo,	"
Howland Calvin,	"	Marcy William,	West Brookfield
JONES W. O.	"	Shaw George W.	"
Lamb A. A.	"	Campbell Andrew, 2d,	Westfield
Ingham James, East Stoughton,	"	Chauncey R.	"
Osgood J. P.	Stow	Cook Stephen B.	"
Day John, Fiskdale,	Sturbridge	Sartelle J. J. & Co.	"
Harrington Samuel, "	"	Hewes & Lay,	"
Garfield Calvin,	Sudbury	Smith Beebe & Co.	"
Abbott Ephraim, South Sudbury,	"	Barnett S.	Westford
Brannan Horace G.	Sunderland	Hildreth George,	"
Fish G. Dwight,	"	Hildreth G. M. L.	"
Bond Henry D.	Sutton	Prince T. T.	"
Hastings George,	"	Hill David W.	Westminster
Hewett V. G. Whitinsville,	"	Mayo William,	"
Collins William H.	Swampscott	Merriam, Holden, & Co.	"
Morris Charles A.	"	Wood James B.	"

Painters — continued.

Gregory Abijah, Weston
Brightman Rufus W., Westport Point, "
Dinin R. A. West Roxbury
ALDEN AMASA, Jamaica Plain, "
Burke Allen, " "
Drew Geo. G. " "
O'Brien D. " "
Peabody W. H. " "
PERRY H. A. (25 Scollay's build.,
  Boston, see p. 678), Jamaica Plain, "
Colton B. W. West Springfield
Woodward James, Mittineague, "
Bliss Robbins K. West Stockbridge
Bliss W. D. "
Olds George, "
BURRELL WATERMAN T. Weymouth
Burrell Brothers, East Weymouth, "
Peakes Joseph, " "
Cushing H. North Weymouth, "
Morrison J. " "
Hersey Wm. B., South Weymouth, "
Martin Edward, " "
May Wm. B. "
Crafts Leander F. Whately
Bloomer E. B. Wilbraham
Bruce William E. "
Cobb Albert S. "
Crocker Russell D. South Wilbraham, "
Crocker Wm. L. " "
Carr L. W. Williamsburg
Hayden F. A. "
Richardson E. W. "
Bryant Walter, Williamstown
Cox Albert, "
Dunton Wm. "
Brooks Wm. Winchendon
Newman C. W. "
Poland Hiram L. "
Poland Stephen, "
Brookings S. R. Winchester
Bruce L. A. "
Low W. W. "
Belcher George G. Winthrop
Twiss Daniel, "
Weston Washburn, "
Brigham S. T. Woburn
Miller & Gage, "
Smith Franklin (sign), "
Albee E. Worcester
Ballou Amasa, "
Bowker C. A. "
Bowen T. "
Clark G. H. "
Drury Marshall L. "
ESTABROOK J. D. & CO., 113 Main, "
Fitzgerald William, "
Flynn J. W. "
Franklin E. A. "
Hutchinson Gerry, "
Kenney J. "
Kinney J. "
Pollock James, "
Prouty Wm. D. (furniture), "
Rice Thomas C. "
ROSS & McGREGOR, 1 Central (see
  page 786), "
Smith Thomas H. & Co. "
Stevens A. (grainer), "
Carr Henry G. Worthington
Kilbourn Alfred, "
Percival Isaac, Ringville, "
Munroe Charles D. Wrentham
Taber Constant, "
Baker H. & L., S. Yarmouth, Yarmouth
Hallett Calvin, Yarmouth Port, "

Painters (Ornamental and Sign).

Elwell K. W. Gloucester
Leighton Geo. A. Lawrence
BAIRD WILLIAM & SON, 110 South
  Common (see page 728), Lynn
FRAZIER I. & SON, 340 Main (see
  page 751), "
Prentiss William C. Northampton
Drake James C. Springfield
McIntire Charles, "
Wiese Frederick (fresco), "
Wood Francis, "
BRENNAN GERALD, 23 Westminster, " Taunton
NIXON T. J. (and fresco, see page
  728), Court st. "
MURDOCK CHAS. C. (and scenic) Wareham
Revere Frederick, Worcester
Rice Dexter, "

Painters (Portrait and Landscape.)

Hurd & Ward, North Adams, Adams
Wilber W. C. (scenic), Bridgewater
Sharp William, Cambridge
Scott John W. A. Cambridgeport, "
Ruggles Lucy Miss, Hardwick
Gay W. Allan, Hingham
Chaffin Caroline, "
Hinckley Thomas H. (animals), Milton
Hollingsworth George, Mattapan, "
Hartshorn Newton T. Lowell
Howes S. P. "
Lawson T. B. "
Cass George N. Medfield
Cole Lyman E. Newburyport
Hotchkiss W. Northampton
Bickford N. N. Salem
Osgood Charles, "
Southward George, "
Jones B. F. Amesbury, Salisbury
Johnson Mary A. Westfield
Edwards Thomas, Worcester
Gladwin Geo. E. "
Willard W. "

Painters (Ship).

Pitman Samuel, Fall River
Blatchford Benj. F. & Co, Gloucester
Cook & Pew, "
Cook L. E. Gloucester, "
Tarr & Wonson, " "
Cobb David, Hingham
Braley Charles H. New Bedford
Kempton & Covell, "
Blake & Noyes, Newburyport
Burrill & Brown, "
Creasey Joseph B. "
Cutter E. P. "
Dyer Benj. H. Provincetown
Dyer Thos. W. & Co. "
Choate A. & Co. Rockport
Austin Richard H. Salem
Foley Edward, "
Martin J. C. "
Skerry Edward S. "
Tibbets Henry H. "

Paints, Oils, and Glass.

Burlingame & Darbys, North Adams, Adams
Pike James D. West Amesbury, Amesbury
Humphrey J. F. Athol
Wadsworth J. D. Barre

Hussey B. S.   Charlestown
Mason Rufus & Son,   "
Hammersley Jonathan B.   Chicopee
TOOGOOD L. O.   East Hampton
Hathaway Daniel K.   Fairhaven
Purrington & Tuber,   "
Tripp Alex.   "
Brown Thomas,   Fall River
Conant Peelet D.   "
Hoar George E.   "
Unsworth Enoch,   "
Waite Andrew J.   "
BECKWITH ALVAH A. & CO., Fitchburg
ESTABROOK J. D. & CO.   "
Griffin, Bowker, & Co.   Gloucester
Tarr & Wonson,   East Gloucester, "
Brewer John & Son,   Great Barrington
NOYES JAS. & CO. 50 Merrimac
   (see page 801),   Haverhill
Goodall & Fitch,   Holyoke
Barton Henry & Co.   Lawrence
Treat James A. & Co.,   "
Coburn Charles B. & Co.   Lowell
Fielding J. B. 99 Central,   "
Kendall Jonathan,   "
Kittredge A. L.   "
Buffum Jonathan,   Lynn
Chase Jacob,   "
Russell John P.   "
Long George K.   Nantucket
Cook Thomas W. & Co.   New Bedford
Gifford O. E.   "
Kempton & Covell,   "
Maude's & A. P.   "
Maxfield William,   "
Perry J. H. & Co.   "
Potter Pardon,   "
Blake & Noyes,   Newburyport
Creasey Joseph B.   "
Cutter E. P.   "
Clark Isaac R.   Northampton
Smith & Jones,   "
Hunt John,   North Bridgewater
Sharpe John M.   "
NEWCOMB T. S. & SON,   Orleans
Brown Ebenezer,   Palmer
Harrington Henry,   Pittsfield
Holland John M. & Son,   "
                                      Provincetown
NICKERSON B. E. & A. & CO.   "
FERNALD N. B.   "
Tarr D. T. & Co.   Quincy
Adams, Richardson, & Co.   Rockport
Felt J. G.   Salem
Puisifer E. B.   "
Stedman & Glover,   "
RICHMOND J. A. & CO. (see
   page 724).   Shelburne Falls, Shelburne
Py. cnun & Lee,   Springfield
Walker T. M. & Co.   "
Warner David,   "
WORTHINGTON S. & CO. 123 Main,   "
Crowell Ezra,   "
French J. T.   Taunton
NEWCOMB W. L. & CO., 6 Weir st.   "
   (see page 728),   "
Stanley J. J. & Co.   "
Washburn J.   "
Washburn Edward E.   "
Wood Cornelius,   "
CONEY H. M. & CO.   Ware
Knight C. S. & Co.   "
MURDOCK CHARLES C.   Wareham
Seabor E. N.   Webster
Dresser H. M.   "
Wiley F. A. & Co.   Wellfleet
FERRELL W. T.   Weymouth
Clark G. H.   Worcester

ESTABROOK J. D. & CO. 113 Main,   Worcester
Foster C. & Co.   "
Kinnicutt & Co.   "
Marble Jerome & Co.   "
White J. C. & Co.   "

Palm-Leaf Colorers.

SNOW J. F. & CO.   Barré

Palm-Leaf Importers.

HILLS L. M. & SONS (see page 775),   Amherst

Palm-Leaf Hat and Hood Manufacturers.

HILLS L. M. & SONS (hoods, see
   page 775),   Amherst
Casavant Daniel (also webs and
   braids),   Athol
Gage Emory,   "
Adams B. R.,   Athol Depot,   "
Brown, Bothwell, & Co.   Barre
Dennis Dexter (wood packing),   "
DESPER JASON (finisher),   "
Gorham Wm. O. (hoods),   "
SNOW J. F. & CO.   "
Woods & Wheelock (hoods),   "
Clark E. A.   Fitchburg
Farrar Gardner (splitter),   "
Streeter D. R. & Co. (dealers and
   splitters),   "
Clark A. & Son (hoods),   S. Framingham
Perrin D. C. & Co.   Malden

Paper and Paper Stock.

MATOON & BLAISDELL (see
   page 778),   Chicopee
Bateman C. A.   Fitchburg
Marble B. & Co.   "
Wallace Rodney,   "
DODGE LUKE C. 55 Dutton (see
   page 741),   Lowell
Briggs R. & Co.   Millbury
Eaton John D. & J. W.   Salem
Grindal S.   "
Weston P. R.   "
Columbia Paper Co.   Springfield
Dickinson & Mayo,   "
Hollister & Co.   "
Salsbury Henry,   "
Oinsted John,   "
BUELL S. K. 18 Foster (see page
   781),   Worcester

Paper-Bag Manufacturers.

Grindal S.   Salem
Hollingsworth & Whitney,   Watertown

Paper-Box Makers.
(See also Box Makers.)

                                      Cambridge
Pearson John A., Cambridgeport,   "
Fraprie G. W.   Fall River
POND VIRGIL S.   Foxborough
Pathe & Smith,   Haverhill
Whitney H. O. (shoe),   "
FISH WILLIAM T.   Lee
Carter Charles,   Leominster
Parke & Tay,   Lowell
Pease George W.   "
ALLEN & BOYDEN, all kinds, 9
   Broad st. (see page 750),   Lynn
Collins & Delnow,   "
Cushman Geo. H.   "
Potter & Main,   "
Sargent S. & Son,   "

21

Paper Box Makers — continued.

Roberts Otis W.	Marblehead
MORSE E. P,	Methuen
Barton John B.	Millbury
Coffin Frederick,	New Bedford
Thurlow William,	Newbury
Crofoot H. T.	Newburyport
Grant John W.	Salem
Elliott & Kimball,	Springfield
Seymour Bros.	"
TAYLOR O. C.	"
Snell T.	Sturbridge
Hathaway W. G.	Taunton
Brackett Chas. A.	Waltham
Tewksbury J. G.	West Newbury
Converse H.	Worcester
Union Paper Box Co.	"
Whitman G. Henry & Co.	"

Paper Collars.

(See also Collar Manufs.)

Reversible Collar Co. G. N. March, treas.	Cambridge
Baird Geo. K. (manuf.)	Lee

Paper Hangers.

Hunnewell F.	Cambridge
Batfum J. L.	Cambridgeport, "
Taylor William J.	"
Holm Charles,	Charlestown
Gluby Wm. H.	Chelsea
Howard Noah P.	"
Richardson Wm. H.	"
Spencer H. A.	"
LIVINGSTON A. J. 164 Middlesex,	Lowell
BAIRD WILLIAM & SON, 110 So. Common (see page 728),	"
FRAZIER I. & SON, 340 Main (see page 751),	Lynn
Ellenwood Geo. R.	New Bedford
Collins Norris,	Newton Corner
MURDOCK CHAS. C.	Wareham
Lanier S. M.	Worcester
Mowbray J. G.	"
Rawson E. T.	"
Rawson W.	"
Toppin E.	"

Paper Hangings.

Darling Allen B.,	N. Adams, Adams
Uranu & Keyes,	"
Everett A. M.	Attleboro'
Brintall & Osgood,	Charlestown
Palmer A. C.	"
Worcester James A. D.	"
Gibbs & Son (manuf.)	Chelsea
KNOX BENJ. H. & CO. 45 and 47 Park,	"
MERRIAM & PUTNAM, 88 Second, (manufacturers, see page 717),	Chicopee
Hammersley Jonathan B.	Chicopee
Weeks H. W.	Dedham
Brown Thomas,	Fall River
Hoar George E.	"
Page Bison,	"
Peckham Geo. W.	"
Unsworth Enoch,	"
Waitu Andrew J.	"
Cleaves Francis E.	Fitchburg
	Gloucester
PROCTER BROTHERS, 121 Front st.	"
ROGERS JOHN S. E., Low's block,	"
Allen's S. Sons,	Greenfield
Noyes James & Co.	"
Wilson J. & Co.	"
Kimball & Gould,	Haverhill

NOYES J. & CO. 50 Merrimac st. (see page 801),	Haverhill
Smiley James V.	"
LINCOLN GEO.	Hingham
Bryant & Newcomb,	Hyde Park
MANN J. H.	Ipswich
Dow John C. & Co.	Lawrence
Fielding & Fisk,	"
Fielding J. B.	Lowell
MERRILL JOSHUA & SON, 3r Merrimack,	"
Chase Jacob,	Lynn
Munroe James M. & Son,	"
OSBORN E. W. & CO. Market sq.	West Lynn, "
WELCH JACOB & CO. 1 Sagamore Hotel,	"
Hathaway Stephen,	Marblehead
Albee, Eldridge, & Co.	Milford
Morse & Woods,	"
	New Bedford
ALLEN & BLISS, 121 Union,	"
Purrington & Brown,	"
Taylor Henry J.	"
Longfellow John R.	Newburyport
Moulton N. A.	"
Evans J. O.	Newton Corner, Newton
Reed Thomas,	North Bridgewater
ROBINSON H. W. & CO.	"
Sharpe John M.	"
Fenn & Carter,	Pittsfield
Platt S. H.	"
Prince W. M.	"
Snow C. B.	Provincetown
FURNALD N. B.	Quincy
Brooks S. H.	Rockport
Ives Henry P.	Salem
Lowd Mark & Son,	"
Lyons Timothy,	"
Whipple G. M. & A. A. Smith,	"
RICHMOND J. A. & CO. (see page 724),	Shelburne Falls, Shelburne
Prince W. M. & Co.	Springfield
Warner David,	"
	Taunton
CROWELL EZRA, 37 West Water,	"
French J. T.	"
NEWCOMB W. L. & CO. 6 Weir st. (see page 728),	"
Stanley J. J. & Co.	"
Washburn Edward E.	"
MURDOCK CHAS. C.	Wareham
Wiley F. A. & Co.	Wellfleet
BURRELL WATERMAN T.	Weymouth
Brown Albert S.	Worcester
Clark, Sawyer, & Co.	"
Maynard D. B.	"
Newton A. H. & Co.	"

Paper Machinery Manufs.

TANNER EDWARD P. (see page 713),	Lee
Frost & Horne,	Medfield
Eaton, Moulton, & Co. Newton Lower Falls,	Newton
CLARY & RUSSELL (see page 708),	Pittsfield
RICE, BARTON, & FALES MANUF. CO. Union st.	Worcester
Senverns J. L.	"

Paper Manufacturers.

Brown L. L. & Co. James Osborne, supt.	Adams
RICHARDSON, UPTON, & CO. (ledger),	"
Whitman & Porter,	Agawam
Cushman J. R. & Son (board),	Amherst

Cushman Brothers (manilla), Amherst
Roberts R. & Co. (straw wrapping), "
Taylor Ebenezer M (wrapping),
  Athol Depot, Athol
Buckley, Dunton, & Co. Becket
Robinson George & Co. Belchertown
Thomas E. A. "
Hollingsworth & Whitney, South
  Braintree, Braintree
Hollingsworth Lyman, Bridgewater
PORTER, CROSS, & MESSER
  (tarred sheathing, see p. 690), Chelsea
MERRIAM & PUTNAM, 63 Sec-
  ond (paper hangings, see page 717),
Hollister Paper Manuf. Co. West
  Cummington, Cummington
Bartlett & Cutting (blank book), Dalton
Carson Paper Co. "
Crane Z. jr. (collar & flat), "
Crane & Co. (collar & bond), "
Weston Byron (writing), "
Ellis Isaac & Co. (pasteboard),
  South Dedham, Dedham
    Dighton
LINCOLN L. & CO. (see page 724),
  North Dighton, "
    Dorchester
Tileston & Hollingsworth, Mattapan, "
Hill Wm. & Son (roofing), Charles
  River Village, Dover
Ripley George & Co. Dracut
    Dudley
Southbridge Paper Co. Southbridge, "
Crocker, Burbank, & Co. (news,
  book, card, and colored), Fitchburg
Fitchburg Paper Co. "
Snow B. jr. & Co. "
Wheelwright G. W. & Son, "
Crocker D. P. West Fitchburg, "
Lyon Moses G. " "
Van Crumb J. & Snyder, Franklin
Taylor, Cook, & Co. (manilla), Granby
Comstock Perry Green (manilla),
  Housatonic, Great Barrington
OWEN PAPER CO., H. D. Cone,
  treas. (writing paper, see page
  791), Housatonic, "
Hollingsworth L. Groton
Keeney Hudson, Groton Junction, "
Ware River Paper Co. Hardwick
Bemis Paper Co. (manilla), Holyoke
FRANKLIN PAPER CO. (collar
  paper), J. H. Newton, treas. "
Hampden Paper Co. (collar and
  writing), J. C. Newton, treas. "
Holyoke Manilla Co. (manilla), Aaron
  Bragg jr. agent, "
HOLYOKE PAPER CO. (writing
  paper), O. H. Greenleaf, agent "
Mt. Tom Paper Co. (white and col'd
  tissue), C. L. Frink, agent, "
PARSONS PAPER CO. (writing and
  envelope paper), Joseph C. Parsons,
  agent, "
RIVERSIDE PAPER CO, (all kinds
  of fine paper), J. T. Prescott, treas. "
Valley Paper Co. (fine writing), D.
  M. Butterfield, agent, "
Whiting Paper Co. (writing), "
GREENLEAF & TAYLOR MANUF.
  CO. Huntington
Bacon J. A. (book and news), Lawrence
Hayden W. B. & Co. (leather board), "
Munroe James S. (roofing), "
Russell Paper Co. (book, cap, and
  legal), Wm. A. Russell, treas. "
Russell Wm. & Son (book, cap, and
  news), "

WILDER S. W. (news and book
  printing), Lawrence
Baird Prentiss C. (writing and collar), Lee
Benton Brothers (ledger), "
Bottomley John (colored), "
Blauvelt W. H. & Co. (manilla for
  wrapping, and twine), "
Garfield Harrison, (book and writing), "
May & Rogers (writing), "
Smith Paper Co. (writing and print-
  ing), Elizur Smith, pres. "
Chaffee & Hamblin (ledger), E. Lee, "
Linn G. W. & Co (printing), " "
HURLBUT PAPER CO. (writing),
  D. B. Fenn jr. agent, S. Lee, "
Davis John B. Leominster
Wheelwright Geo. W. & Son, North
  Leominster, "
Davis H. L. (dealer), Lowell
Richmond C. B. "
RIPLEY GEO. & CO. (manilla), 10
  Middle, "
Campbell T. & G. (wrapping), West
  Medway, Medway
    Middlefield
Buckley, West, & Co. Bancroft, "
Crane Luther, Middleton
    Milton
Tileston & Hollingsworth, Mattapan, "
O'Neil John & Son, Monterey
Longfellow Nathan, Newton Lower
  Falls, Needham
Newfield Paper Co. N. M. Horton,
  treasurer, Newburyport
Curriell John (straw-printing), Mill
  River, New Marlborough
Marlborough Paper Co. (fine papers),
  Mill River, "
Sheldon Geo. S. (manilla), Mill River, "
    Newton
Crebore L. & Co. (press), Lower Falls, "
Rice Charles, 2d (board), " "
Rice Thomas jr. (printing), " "
Newell Benj. (sheathing), Upper Falls, "
Clark Wm. & Co. (writing), Northampton
Delany & Watson, "
Loud Caleb & Son, "
Thomas J. B. (hangings, printing,
  &c.), Bondsville, Palmer
Clarke H. M. & Co. Pepperell
Davis S. S. "
Colt Thomas, Pittsfield
Chapin & Gould (writing), Russell
Williams Brothers, Shirley
Southbridge Paper Co. Southbridge
Bolton & Moody (wrapping), South Hadley
Cook & Taylor (manilla), "
CAREW MANUF CO. (writing), So.
  Hadley Falls, "
Hampshire Paper Co. (writing), So.
  Hadley Falls, "
Chapin & Gould, Springfield
Union Paper Co. "
Powers Paper Co. "
Hunter Paper Co. (manilla), J. Hun-
  ter jr. treas. Glendale, Stockbridge
Parker William T. Sudbury
Hollingsworth Lyman (hangings),
  Assabet, "
Smith Paper Co. Lee, Tyringham
Trimble John, Bay State Mill, "
Campbell T. & G. N. Wrentham, Walpole
Bird F. W. & Co. East Walpole, "
Ellis Isaac & Co. " "
Mitchell David, S. Wareham, Wareham
Wheelwright Geo. West Wareham, "
Hollingsworth & Whitney, Watertown
Horton & Stearns (wrapping), Westfield

Paper Manufacturers — continued.
Jessup & Laflin (ledger), Westfield
Taylor & Stiles (manilla), "
Delaney & Watson, West Hampton
Wyman & Crocker, Wachusett Village, Westminister
W. Springfield
AGAWAM PAPER CO. (writing), "
Geo. L. Wright, treas, Mittineague, "
Southworth Manuf. Co. (writing), H.
W. Southworth, agt. Mittineague, "
Comstock Perry Green, Housatonic, "
Wrentham
Campbell T. & G., North Wrentham, "

Paper-Mill Bars and Plates.

Clappville
HANKEY A. & CO. (see page 775), "
Dowd J. & R. J, East Lee, Lee
LOVEJOY DANIEL (see page 744),
Cushing, cor. Rock, Lowell

Paper Stock.

Fall River
LAWTON & ESTES (see page 734), "

Paper Warehouses.

Leathe W. M. & Co. Fitchburg
Ladd & Miller, Lowell
Farnsworth Edward M. Lynn
Grindal S. Salem
Columbia Paper Co. Springfield
GREENLEAF & TAYLOR MANUF.
CO. "
Hollister & Co. "
Salsbury Henry, "
Sanford & Co. "
Union Paper Co. "
Stone H. R. & Co. Worcester

Passenger and Exchange Agents.

Brennan M. W. Fall River
CONROY DANIEL, 20 Union, "
EASTON A. D. 14 North Main, "
McDonough John F. "
Dike Edward R. Lawrence
Fletcher Horatio, Lowell
Molloy Geo. "
Smith John, "
READE LAWRENCE, 72 Main (see
page 782), Milford
Kelley J. New Bedford
DAVENPORT & MASON (see page
724), Taunton
Smith John, "
Lincoln C. A. Worcester

Patent Agents.

Crane John E. Lowell
Pevey Geo. E. "
Davis & Co. New Bedford
Allen Frank (solicitor), Salem
WOLTERS H. J. 30 Mill (see page
747), "
CURTIS T. A. (solicitor), Springfield
Norris H. & Co. (agents for patent
goods), "
SANDERS SIDNEY, "
Arnold J G. Worcester
Dodge Thomas H. (solicitor), "

Patent Leather.

(See *Leather, Enamelled and Patent.*)

Patent Medicines.

(See also *Botanic Medicines.*)

McCarthy John (lightning oil),
North Adams, Adams

CHASE H. W. Attleborough
WHITE H. M. South Braintree, Braintree
Dinsmore J. P. Cambridgeport, Cambridge
Hardy F. D. "
Ellis D. C. F. Canton
Davis Aaron S. (manufr.), Chelsea
KENT CYRUS F. (see page 774) Chicopee
Gifford Perry, Fall River
Lynn N U. "
Ayer J. C. & Co. Lowell
Knapp C. F. "
Mowe George S. "
Richards, Morton, & Colburn, "
Knights E. R. & Co. Melrose
Poland J. W. "
Selee N. P. (hair restorative), "
New Bedford
BLAKE JAMES E. 64 No. Second, "
Bunker Elihu, "
Pease Peleg, "
Pease W. A. "
SWEET JOB (sprain liniment, see
page 712), Kempton cor. Summer, "
Kidder A. (cordial), Cliftondale, N. Chelsea
WOOD & ALLEN (see page 774), Palmer
Lamberson Samuel L. (homœ.), Pittsfield
RENNE WILLIAM (Renne's pain-
killing magic oil, see page 793), "
Flint & Goodthwait, Salem
Price C. H. & J. "
Pettingell J. M. Amesbury, Salisbury
HUTCHINS H. & SON (headache
pills) Springfield
WASHBURN GEORGE W. (Gorton's
Compound Balm of Gilead for ex-
ternal and internal use (see page
757), Westminister cor. Washington, Taunton
Waltham
Parmenter & Walker (Field's lotion), "

Patent-Right Dealers.

DRAPER GEORGE & SON (see page
753), Hopedale, Milford
Marsh & Luther, Worcester

Patent Rubber Heel Stiffeners.

AMERICAN HEEL STIFFENING
CO. Winnisimmet st. Chelsea

Pattern Makers.

Fogg J. A. Lawrence
Crane John E. Lowell
Flint Joseph K. "
HADLEY & ROBEY, Cushing cor.
Rock, "
Hills Eliphalet, "
Hood H. P. "
Murkland W. & J. W. "
WESTON Charles H., Arch st. "
Henderson H. A. Lynn
KNOWLTON GEO. K. & CO. (see
page 751), 13 Union, "
HOPEDALE FURNACE CO. (see
page 753), Hopedale, Milford
Ellis Nathan B. New Bedford
Andrews Hiram, Salem
CHURCHILL & RICHARDSON,
196 Derby (see page 747), "
Fairfield S. W. "
Grant J. C. "
PERKINS WM. A., 20 Peabody, "
Fairbanks Asa, Springfield
Marshall & Sweetland, "
Piper E. J. "
Miller Samuel, Taunton
Andrews Daniel F. Worcester
Brown Wm. H. "
Pollard, Wilder, & Co. "
Wheeler J. S. & Co. "

Pavers.

Stiles J. C. & Sons (concrete),   Cambridge
Woodfall, Curtis, & Co.   Lynn

Peat Manufacturers.

Boston Peat Fuel Co.   Lexington
Bryant A. W.   "
Western Massachusetts Peat Fuel Co.
    S. L. Allen, sec.   Pittsfield
Bailey Chas. E.,   North Scituate,   Scituate
Sizer Emerson,   Westfield

Peddler's Supplies.

Perry E. & Co.   Ashland

Pegging Machines.

Northampton Pegging Machine Co.
    D. C. Rogers, agent,   Northampton

Pencil Manufacturers.

Ball Lewis F.   Acton
Miles Marshall,   South Acton,   "
American Pencil Co. Sylvester Hay-
    ward, agent,   Concord
Northampton Indelible Pencil Co.
    Henry Roberts, treas.   Northampton

Pen-Holder Manufacturers.

Brown I. W.   Cummington
Gilbert C. J.   "
Stevens N. S.   "
Sears Anthony,   West Hawley,   Hawley

Pension Agents.

Peirce Wm. H.   Fall River
Winslow B. F.   "
Abbott F. E.   Worcester
Perry F. W.   "

Perforated Cards and Metals.

Towne & Co.   Worcester

Perfumery.

ESTES J. J.   East Abington,   Abington
FRAZAR GEORGE L ; Washington,
    cor. Harvard,   Dorchester
Barney G. T. & Co. South Malden, Malden
    New Bedford
Lovering A. G. & Co. (wholesale),   "

Periodical and News Depot.

*(See Booksellers ; also Newspapers, Periodi-
cals, &c. in Index.)*

Nash Sylvanus,   Abington
Douglas William E. East Abington,   "
Dyer S.,   South   "   "
Fuller William,   Adams
Dalrymple Orson,   North Adams,   "
Phillips Harlan L.   "   "
Haynes Alfred,   Amesbury
Spear M. N.   Amherst
Chandler J. H.   Andover
Richardson M. A. & Co.   Arlington
Gleason Jonathan,   Ashland
Whitaker Wm. W.   "
Thompson C. J.   Attleborough
Jones T. R., North Attleborough,   "
Kendall James H.   Beverly
Bourne William N.   Bridgewater
Greenleaf M. H.   Brighton
Grush John H.   Brookline
    Cambridge
Lull Frederick A. Cambridgeport,   "
McDuffie John.   "   "
Vining C. M. Mrs.   "   "
Noble N. K.   East Cambridge,   "
Ellis D. C. F.   Canton
Cumming Chas. A.   Charlestown
Evans A. B.   "
Jones John G.   "
Perkins Nathan G.   "
Peterson Geo. E.   "
Schraw Henry,   "
Blandford James,   "
Orcutt Samuel,   Chelsea
    "
Judd D. B.   Chester

Downing Hiram,   Chicopee
Ballard E.   Clinton
Burditt Thomas F.   "
Harris & Chace,   "
Morse Philander,   "
Bates Newcomb,   Cohasset
Davis Cummings E.   Concord
Whitcomb Henry L.   "
DRAYTON CHARLES,   Danvers
Allwright Alfred,   Dedham
Doherty Edward,   "
Phelps Timothy,   "
Gay Joel A.   South Dedham,   "
Hawes Wm. K.   "   "
Russell Stillman,   Douglas
Kennedy Robert B.   Duxbury
Bardwell J. H.   East Hampton
Robinson John S.   Edgartown
Burnham George F.   Essex
Buttrick J. T.   Fairhaven
Noros L. J.   Fall River
Pope I. P.   "
Dunn E. B. & W. A.   Fitchburg
Butterworth Geo. H.   Foxborough
Symmes Wm.   Framingham
Phillips Joseph R.   Freetown
Jewett Chas. E.   Georgetown
Tenney B. F.   "
Morgan Wm.   Great Barrington
Tyler S.   Greenfield
Hardy Ellen M.   Groveland
Lyon George F.   Halifax
Ramsdell Jacob L.   Hanover
Bean C. G.   Haverhill
Shedd A. S.   "
Smiley J. V.   "
Willet & Devnell,   "
Jernegan Wm. H.   Hingham
CADY JOHN (paper, envelopes, and
    varieties),   Hinsdale
Haskins Milo J.   "
Fiske Geo. B.   Holliston
Baker John R.   Holyoke
Downing E. J. Miss,   Hyde Park
Hancock Zenas,   Huntington
Bower Robert,   Lawrence
WHITCOMB I. A, 93 Essex, (see
    page 793).   "
Northrop L.   Lee
Gotham Anna Mrs.   Lowell
Libby Nelson F.   "
Mason R. E.   "
Morse & Turner,   "
Stanton A. D.   "
Winton John Mrs.   "
Green Otis H.   Lynn
Larkin Arthur W.   "
Munroe J. M. & Son,   "
Putnam James F.   "
WEBSTER W. T. 8 Exchange.
Pickett Charles,   Marlborough
Peak H. N.   Medford
Downing Herbert,   Melrose
Harris Samuel H. jr.   Methuen
Shaw J. B & J.   Middleborough
READE LAWRENCE, 72 Main (see
    page 782).   Milford
Nye F. W. K.   Milton
Pope Henry,   "
Johnson Franklin E.   Nahant
Hussey O. F.   Nantucket
Jenkins C. S.   "
Fairbanks J. B.   Natick
Bullard Amasa,   New Bedford
Hitch & Allen,   "
Parsons & Co.   "
Phinney Otis B.   "
Richardson J.   "
Shiverick George,   "
Todd Henry,   "
McCusker John,   Newburyport
Marsh Joseph.   Northampton
Low Charles H.   North Andover
White A. S.   Northborough
Copeland C. F.   North Bridgewater
Brewer L.   North Brookfield
Weeks F. E.   "
Sanford James M.   Oxford
Knox Cyrus,   Palmer
Exchange News Room,   Peabody

Periodical and News Depots.—continued.

PEIRCE JOSEPH H. 13 Main,　Peabody
Simpson L. C.　Pepperell
Cowan James,　Pepperell
Holland J. D.　Pittsfield
Millard Ansel E.
Smith John,　Plymouth
PUTNAM A. L.　Provincetown
Follett Chas. A.
Crossley William,　Quincy
Clark Henry,　Randolph
Chandler & Co.　Rockport
DeCosta Emanuel,　Salem
Grindal S.　"
Moody Lewis B.　"
Pendergast Patrick, Amesbury,　Salisbury
HALL CHAS. B.　Sandwich
POPE FRED S.　"
BARNES WM. C.　Southbridge
BLISS E. M.　Spencer
Jennings A. F.　Springfield
Powers Paper Co.　"
DRAKE LEONARD,　Stoughton
Porter J. P.　Swampscott
Fisher A. B. Mrs.　Taunton
Seaver Wm. P.　"
Brown Moses,　Tisbury
Kingman Samuel,　Wakefield
Thompson M. M.　Waltham
Cutler G. K.　Ware
Clark John B.　Webster
Carl L. W.　Wellfleet
Rich S. A.　South Wellfleet,　"
Eaton Wm. J.　Westborough
Kendrick O. P.　West Brookfield
Fletcher J. W.　Westford
Poole Silas, Jamaica Plain,　West Roxbury
Pratt M. K. & Co.　Weymouth
Metcalf J. H.　Williamsburg
Smith N. F.　Williamstown
Merrill E. S.　Winchendon
Brown George P.　Winchester
Atkins C. S.　Woburn
　　　"　Worcester
CHAMBERLAIN E. H. 113 Main,　"
Thompson S. & Co.　"

Pew and Pulpit Manufacturer.

Wentworth T. B.　Cambridgeport,　Cambridge
　　　"

Photographic Stock Manuf.

Dean John & Co.　Webster sq.　Worcester

Photographs, &c.

Chamberlin Arnold,　Abington
Thompson Elijah,　East Abington,　"
Smith & Rhodes,　South　"
Marsh Levi,　Adams
Bowen J. Lorenzo & Co. N. Adams,　"
Hurd & Ward,　"
Adams Frank,　Andover
Thompson W. C.　Amesbury
LOVELL J. L. 41 Phœnix row,　Amherst
Chamberlain E.　"
Gilman & Gardner,　Arlington
Moore George W.　Ashland
Knox Oliver C.　Athol
Gardner G. M.　Athol Depot,　"
Hine J. M.　Hyannis,　Barnstable
Burrell D. T.　Barre
Aylsworth ——,　Bridgewater
Pearson David J.　Brookfield
Danforth Chas. M.　Cambridgeport,　Cambridge
Warren Geo. K.　"
Low Frederick C.　East Cambridge,　"
Vose J. H.　Canton
Adams Elliot.　Charlestown
Freeman G. W.　"
Haley J. F.　"
Reed E. A.　"
Thayer Charles,　"
Venner Geo. W.　"
Keeler Thatcher W.　Chatham
BAXTER O. F. (porcelain), 138 Broadway,　Chelsea
Lawson Alvan F.　"
Knox Herbert,　Chicopee

Boynton J. J.　Clinton
Spellman L. P.　Cummington
King Theodore E.　Dorchester
Whipple Frank D.　Douglas
Smith E. R.　East Hampton
Williams M. T.,　North Easton,　Easton
Cornell Enoch C.　Edgartown
Shute Richard & Son,
Brownell A. C.　Fall River
Carlisle G. M.　"
Douglass O. F.　"
Gay Edwin F.　"
Warren Joseph W.　"
JUDKINS DAVID R. 115 Main, Fitchburg
Morse J. E.
Moulton Joseph C.　"
POND FRANK L.　Foxborough
Allen Warren P.　Gardner
Harriman Wm. H.　Georgetown
Elxvell Wm. A.　Gloucester
White Augustus A.　"
Woolfindale E.　"
Buell Oliver B.　Great Barrington
Clark Edwin H.　"
Bradford P.　Greenfield
Horton & Wise,　"
Hay Henry, Greenwich Village, Greenwich
Wright J. W.　Groton Junction,　Groton
Cahoon C. A.　Harwich
Fowler Edward P.　Haverhill
Robinson G. C.　"
Vickery D. B.　"
Hudson Wm. jr.　Hingham
Lane Wm.
Haskins F. W.　Holyoke
Frew Joseph,　"
Leavitt A. L.　Hopkinton
Lewis Russell B.　Hudson
Greenwood E. D.　Huntington
Jones Geo. H.　Ipswich
Fuller Truman (landscape),　Kingston
Williams Geo. S.　Lanesborough
Bean A. M.　Lawrence
Judkins L. D.　"
Lufkin M. H.　"
Massuere F.　"
Robie H. B.　"
Russell Frank & Co.　"
Yeaw Albion,　"
Cutting Chauncey P.　Lee
Pease J. L.　"
Allen Wm. T.　Leominster
Collins Ira A.　"
Parkhurst Charles S.　"
Brigham E. T.　"
Cross A. B. & G. W.　Lowell
Daly I. Selwyn,　"
Emerson M. W.　"
Gilchrest Geo. C.　"
Gilchrest Geo. E.　"
Moore H. N.　"
Newton E.　"
Sanborn F. P.　"
Sanborn N. C.　"
Shattuck Sewall,　"
Towle Simon,　"
Washburn J. M.　"
Appleton Wm. R.　Lynn
Bowers Wilder T.　"
Bashby & Hart,　"
Elwell Edward W.　"
Dill A. E.　"
Peabody Everett,　"
PHILLIPS T. N. 3 Ellis Building,　West Lynn,
Elliott John H.　Marblehead
Woodbridge J. S.　"
Marshall F. A.　Marlborough
Chandler Martin,　Marshfield
Graham Nelson C.　Middleborough
Hatch S. R.　Milford
Willis E. L.　"
Wires E. L.　"
Freeman Josiah,　Nantucket
Summerhaes William,　"
Adams S. F.　New Bedford
Andrews Fred W.　"
Howard E.　"
Jenney & Smith,　"
Knowles & Hillman,　"

Nye William B.	
Parlow G. F.	New Bedford
Taber Chas. & Co.	"
Taber Lemuel W.	"
Tallman & Negus,	"
Wood L. C. jr.	"
Chase E. B.	"
McIntosh H. P.	Newburyport
Mason Philip C.	"
Meinerth Carl,	"
Thompson W. C.	"
Biddle James E.	"
Ingraham Brothers,	Northampton
Knowlton Brothers,	"
Wade John F.	Northborough
Howard L. B.	North Bridgewater
Howard S. W. S.	"
Poole —.	Orange
Nickerson G. H.	"
Cross H. G.	Orleans
O'Neal James,	Palmer
Barnard J. S. West Duxbury,	Pembroke
Dewey Rodney H.	Pittsfield
SEAVER C. Jr.	"
Gifford Fred. H.	Provincetown
Smith Mark G.	"
Barnard Geo. A.	Quincy
King J. T.	Randolph
Bousley & Co.	Salem
Bowdoin David W.	"
Moulton Joshua W.	"
Perkins E. B.	"
Proctor G. K.	"
Taylor & Preston,	"
Walls G. S.	"
White John,	"
Currier & Jones, Amesbury,	Salisbury
Burton Charles,	Savoy
Patch Jonas K. Shelburne Falls,	Shelburne
Chamberlain J. N. jr.	Southbridge
Lamb C. F.	"
Taylor Dwight,	South Hadley
Alden Augustus E.	Springfield
Clapp & Prew,	"
Moore Bros.	"
Richardson W. P.	"
Spooner J. C. (artist studio),	"
Sweetser C. A.	"
Townsend A. C.	"
Warren R.	"
Savage Wm. H.	Stoneham
Battelle Willard,	Taunton
King H. B.	"
Read P. R.	"
Woodward William F.	"
Kidder Benjamin D.	Tisbury
Richardson C. F.	Wakefield
Perry Alexander,	Waltham
Day Edwin,	"
Goss Ezra L.	"
Aiken J. M.	Ware
Breckenridge G. L.	"
Kidder G. R.	Watertown
Bennet George,	Webster
Miller Cornelius,	"
Baker Lewis H.	Wellfleet
Collins Thomas P.	Westfield
	West Roxbury
Emmons A. C. Jamaica Plain,	"
Cook L. W.	Weymouth
Alger Israel F.	Winchendon
Howard A.	"
Greydon W. B.	Woburn
Wyman S. W.	"
Carter M. T.	Worcester
Claflin C. R. B.	"
Critchetson G. P.	"
Daniels A. F.	"
Fitton & Rice,	"
Lawrence Frank,	"
Leland E. J.	"
Reed H. J.	"

Physicians.

Dudley H. W.	Abington
Jameson Robert E. (homœopathic),	"
Ryan James C.	"
Winslow J. A. W. Mrs. East Abington,	"
Underwood J. M. "	"
Tanner N. B. North Abington,	"

Copeland H. F. South Abington,	Abington
Hastings B. F.	"
Cowdrey Harris,	Acton
Little Charles,	"
Hutchins Isaiah (ecl.), West Acton,	"
Burnham Josiah (botanic),	Acushnet
Briggs Seth N. (bot.),	Adams
Estes —,	"
Holmes Horace M.	"
Babbitt Nathan S. North Adams,	"
Boullais Eugene L.	"
Briggs S. N. (bot.), "	"
Clark J. M. "	"
Hawkes Elihu S.	"
Lawrence Geo. C. "	"
Millard H. J. "	"
Phillips Henry P.	"
Tylor Wm. A.	"
Van Rensselaer D. C. (hom.) "	"
Williams A. G.	"
Bell Cyrus, Feeding Hills,	Agawam
Huett G. S.	Alford
Dearborn H. S. (eclectic),	Amesbury
Douglass John A.	"
Leslie H. G.	"
Sharhawk Thomas,	"
Rogers,— West Amesbury	"
Seavey Oscar F. "	"
Belden R.	Amherst
Bigelow O. F.	"
Cate H. J. (hom.),	"
Dole John,,	"
Taylor Israel H.	"
Fish D. B. N., North Amherst	"
Temple Theron, "	"
Bradford —— (hom.),	Andover
Kimball W. H.	"
Tracy Stephen,	"
Harris Jonathan C.	Arlington
Hodgdon R. L.	"
Jewett A. (ecl.),	Ashburnham
Pierce C. L.	"
Wallace M. (bot.),	"
Whitmore Locke L., Burrageville,	"
Blood J. M.	Ashby
Fairbanks J. R.	"
Warren Joseph,	Ashfield
Pierce G. C.	Ashland
Rogers William E.	"
Wiggin J. M. (ecl.),	"
Davis Kendall,	Athol
Lynde J. P.	"
Oliver James	"
Whitman — (clair.),	"
Broocz F. R. (hom.), Athol Depot,	"
Cooledge & Jackson,	"
Bronson John R.	Attleborough
Sanford E. (hom.),	"
Solomon James M.	"
Foster James W. (hom.), North Attleborough,	"
Phelps & Howard, N. Attleborough,	"
Turner O. C. "	"
Smith John M.	Barnstable
Donne Geo. W. Hyannis,	"
Pitcher Samuel, jr (bot.),	"
George — (hom.), Cotuit Port,	"
Jenkins F. H. West Barnstable,	"
Bassett Aaron (ecl.),	Barré
Billings Lucius F.	"
Brown George,	"
Whitcomb Charles W.	"
Dill Daniel M.	Becket
Packard Geo. W. (ecl.),	"
Shaw Henry,	Bedford
Chapin William A.	Belchertown
Thompson Geo F.	"
Tobias J. J.	"
Hathaway S.	Berkley
Gott Lemuel,	Berlin
Bowker Charles,	Bernardston
Dwight William,	"
Boyden W. C.	Beverly
Haddock Charles,	"
Swasey O. F.	"
Torrey Augustus,	"
Torrey Samuel W.	"
Munroe Geo. H.	Billerica
Booth Robert,	Blackstone
Ballard George E.	"

Physicians — continued.

Edwards D. M.   Blackstone
Kimball W. M.   "
Southwick Moses D.   Millville,   "
Wilbur Thomas,   "   "
Bell N. S. (bot.),   Blandford
Warren D. (hom.), North Blandford, "
Davis Hall,   Bolton
Cogswell George,   Bradford
Cogswell William,   "
Dearing T. H.   Braintree
Torrey Noah,   South Braintree,   "
Gould S. H.   Brewster
Alden Samuel (hom.),   Bridgewater
Forbes Joseph B.   "   "
Lowe Lewis G. (hom.),   "
Millett Asa,   "
Sawyer Edward,   "
Braman C. B.   Brighton
Braman I. G.   "
Bridgeman M. F.   "
Fowler A. C.   "
Mason Agustus,   "
Chamberlin Geo. F.   Brimfield
Fife George S.   "
Bates H. T.   Brookfield
Fiske Daniel S.   "
Rood J. T.   "
Hodgkins D. W., East Brookfield, "
AMORY ROBERT,   Brookline
Francis T. E.   "
Lawrence William,   "
Salisbury Stephen,   "
Sanford E. W. (hom.),   "
Shurtleff Augustine,   "
Shurtleff Samuel A.   "
Wesselhoeft G. F. (hom.),   "
Trow Josiah,   Buckland
Coutri L. G.   Cambridge
Driver Stephen Wm.   "
Nichols J. T. G.   "
Stocker Alfred A.   "
Vaughan Charles E.   "
Walcott H. P.   "
Wyman Morrill,   "
Allen Charles H,   Cambridgeport, "
Appleton John,   "   "
Chase Hiram L. (hom.),   "   "
Chenery Elisha,   "   "
Clarke Augustus P.   "   "
Cogswell Edward R.   "   "
Gaylord Edson,   "   "
Goddard John T.   "   "
Holt Alfred F.   "   "
Lathe Leonora F.   "   "
Marcy Henry O.   "   "
Morse Calvin E.   "   "
Palmer J. K.   "   "
Webber A. Carter,   "   "
Wellington Wm. W   "   "
Wood F. A.   "   "
Wright W. E. (ecl.),   "   "
Barrett W. M.   East Cambridge, "
Farnsworth Chas. H. (hom.), "   "
Hooker Anson   "   "
Hooker Anson P.   "   "
Norris A. L.   "   "
Rexford Richard W.   "   "
Taylor John B.   "   "
Weston Edward H.   "   "
Fletcher W. K. (hom.), N. Cambridge, "
Morse James R.   "   "
Abbott Ezra,   Canton
Holmes A. R.   "
Perry Ira,   "
Marsh Austin,   Carlisle
Cornish Ellis H.,   North Carver, Carver
Temple Hiram,   Charlemont
Walker William D. (ecl.)   "
Bailey J. B. (hom.),   Charlestown
Bancroft Amos B.   "
Bemis J. W. (surgeon),   "
Bickford H. C.   "
Bond Wm. L.   "
Cheever John (bot.),   "
Crozier Thomas, jr.   "
Cushman Holmes,   "
Davis Samuel A.   "
Dearborn J. G.   "
Fuller Henry H.   "

Goddard E.   Charlestown
Herrick G. H. W.   "
Hurd Samuel H.   "
Mason Wm.   "
McDonald J. A. (hom.),   "
McLeod A.   "
Morris William B.   "
Neilson J. C. (hom.),   "
Pierce Levi,   "
Plumb Samuel, (magnetic),   "
Plumb Samuel Mrs. (clair.),   "
Richardson Amos H.(ecl.),   "
Rideout Mary M. (M. D.),   "
Stevens Thomas J.   "
Towne J. W.   "
Wetherbee Angie G. (M. D.),   "
Whiting John S.   "
York C. C.   "
Hauscom S.   Somerville,
Fay Charles M.   Charlton
Taft George H. (hom.),   "
NEWTON ADIN H.   Chatham
Simmons Marshall E.   "
Cochrane James B.   Chelsea
Cutler Wm. C. (hom.),   "
Dresser S. A. Mrs.   "
Forsyth James B.   "
Graves John W. (marine hospital), "
Johnson Daniel A. (hom.),   "
Lynam J. P.   "
Mitchell Jacob,   "
Otis George W.   "
Page Horatio N.   "
Poole Alexander,   "
Shackford C. H.   "
Somerby E. P. Mrs.   "
Walker Chas. H.   "
WHEELER & BEAN, 145 Broadway, "
Bartlett John C.   Chelmsford
Howard Levi,   "
Edwards Nathan B., N. Chelmsford, "
Brown Thomas A.   Cheshire
Phillips Henry T.   "
Lucas H. S.   Chester
De Wolf T. R.   "
Streeter Dwight W.   Chesterfield
Abell E. D.   Chicopee
Denison George W.   "
Hurley John F.   "
Jenness W. W. (hom.),   "
Shephard Ransom (ecl.),   "
Smith Wm. G.   "
Stickney P. L. B.   "
Alvord Samuel (hom.), Chicopee Falls, "
Sawin Wm. J.   "   "
Wilbur John R.   "   "
Brooks C. A. (hom.),   Clinton
Taft L. W. (ecl.),   "
Pratt Gustavus P.   Cohasset
Greene E. W.   Coleraine
Smith Horace,   "
Barrett Henry A.   Concord
Bartlett Josiah,   "
Reynolds Joseph,   "
Hamilton E. D.   Conway
Vining D. T. (hom.),   "
Joy Royal,   Cummington
Richards William,   "
Ferre Henry,   Dalton
Lindsey Daniel,   North Dana, Dana
Lindsey M. L.   "   "
Chase F. M.   Danvers
Grosvenor David A.   "
Whiting Lewis (hom.),   "
Hunt Ebenezer,   Danvers Port, "
Mason Francis W.   Dartmouth
Bartlett Francis D., South Dartmouth, "
Burgess E. P.   Dedham
Chase J. W.   "
Maynard J. P.   "
Southgate George A. (hom.),   "
Stimpson Jeremy,   "
Wight D. P.   "
Weare William,   East Dedham,   "
Cragin F. M. (hom.), South Dedham, "
Fogg D. S.   "
Porter Ransom M.   Deerfield
Eaton John M.   South Deerfield, "
Lord Wm. E. (bot.), E. Dennis, Dennis
Swift Alfred S.   "   "   "

Hulbert C. M.   S. Dennis,   Dennis
Talbot Charles,   Dighton
Aldrich E. B.   North Bighton,   "
AlexanderAndrew,   Dorchester
Cushing Benjamin,   "
Gilbert Daniel D.   "
Jarvis Edward,   "
Miller E. D.   "
Spooner John P. (hom.),   "
Stetman Chas. H.   "
Stedman C. Ellery,   "
Fidield Wm. C. B.   Harrison sq.   "
Greene James S.   "
Davis Charles H.   Milton,   "
Blanchard Henry D., Neponset,   "
Holbrook S. P.   E. Douglas,   Douglas
Taft B. F. (ecl.),   "
White D. P.   "
Lindsey E.   Dudley
Lindsey Silas F.
Pratt Calvin,   Duxbury
Wilde James,   "
Chaplin Daniel,   East Bridgewater
Harris C. W.   "
Orr Samuel A.   "
Atwood S. C. (clair.),   Eastham
Green F. G.   East Hampton
Smith F. Delap,   "
Deans Samuel (hom.);   Easton
Cogswell Geo. B.   North Easton,   "
Swan G. W. J. (hom.), "   "   "
Swan Caleb (hom.),   South "   "
Maberry Edwin,   Edgartown
Pierce John,   "
Beebe Richard,   N. Egremont,   Egremont
Millard Louisa (hom.),   "
FOSTER SIMEON A., South "
Kemp E. A.   Enfield
Hull Wm. H. (ecl.),   Essex
Lovering John D.   "
Aldrich J. M. (bot.),   Fall River
Angell A. F.   "
Bowen S. W.   "
Brown P. S.   "
Campfield J. A.   "
Clarke John L. (hom.),   "
Clift & Terry,   "
Dwelly Jerome,   "
Fiske Isaac (hom.),   "
Golding P. J. C. W.   "
Hartley James W.   "
HOOPER FOSTER, 94 North Main,   "
Kreis J. A.   "
Learned E. T.   "
Marissal Felix V.   "
Noyes Geo. H.   "
Smith Isaac, jr. (and surgeon),   "
WHITTAKER J. B., Ferry, cor. Canal,   "
Wilbur Amos C. (ecl.)   "
Everett J. B.   Falmouth
Tubbs J. B. (hom.,   "
Brigham Hubbard H. (ecl.),   Fitchburg
Brigham Sarah C. Mrs.   "
Boutelle Thomas R.   "
Colony George D.   "
Freeland J. C. (hom.),   "
Hitchcock Alfred,   "
Jewett George,   "
Jillson H. D. (ecl.),   "
Marshall Jonas A.   "
Miller Alfred,   "
Pettengill E. H.   "
Pillsbury E. L.   "
Pillsbury Levi,   "
Rice C. H.   "
Sidney A. W. (ecl.),   "
Whittier Daniel B. (hom.),   "
Williams B. B. (clair.),   "
Taft E. W. (bot.),   Florida
Dickerman Lemuel, (hom.),   Foxborough
Dickerman Wm. A. (hom.),   "
Hitchcock J. G. S.   "
Morse ___ Mrs. (clair.),   "
Smith Isaac (hom.),   "
RIPLEY W K.   "
Sumner H. G. Mrs. (clair.),   "
Adams Z. B.   Framingham
Howe G. M.   "
Hoyt Enos,   "
Johnson Otis O. (hom.),   "

Cowles Henry,   Saxonville,   Framingham
Hutchins John W., S. Framington.
King George,   Franklin
Nolen Wm. B.,   "
Bump Thomas,   Freetown
Campfield James H.   "
Braley Bradford, East Freetown,   "
Emerson J.   Gardner
Garland G. W.   "
Parker David,   "
Sawyer E. J.   "
Huse Ralph C.   Georgetown
Root R. B.   "
Spaulding E. F.   "
Bergengren W. .   Gloucester
Conant Thomas,   "
Davidson Herman E.   "
Dyer J. F.   "
Garland Albert S.   "
Garland Joseph,   "
Hildreth Charles H.   "
Eveleth Edward S., East Gloucester, "
Saunders Levi,   Lanesville,   "
Griggs Thomas T.   Grafton
Pierce Delano,   "
Rawson Levi,   Farnumsville,   "
Whittemore Thomas K.   "   "
Fulton D. M.   N. E. Village,   "
Smith C. B.   Granby
King C. B.   Granville
Johnson J. W.   East Granville, "
Camp Samuel   Great Barrington
Cass Jonathan,   "
Clark Mrs. (clair.),   "
Collins T. Clarkson,   "
Parks William H.   "
Van Deusen Harlow A. (hom.),   "
Niles John O.   Housatonic,   "
Pickett Noble B.   "
Giddings ___,   Van Deusenville, "
Deane A. C.   Greenfield
Fisk Charles L. (ecl),   "
Fisk Charles L. jr. (ecl.),   "
Harding W. F. (hom.),   "
Hovey Daniel,   "
Osgood J. W. D.   "
Severance William S. (ecl.),   "
Stone Mrs.   "
Ulrich F.   "
Walker A. C.   "
Wunsch Paulina,   "
Greenleaf John R. jr.   Greenwich
Smith Norman,   Groton
Spaulding Miles,   "
Stearns George,   "
Webster William A.   "
Willis E. (hom.),   "
McCollister J. Q. A., Groton Junction, "
Parsons J. C.   "   "
Smith Gibson,   Groveland
Spofford Jeremiah,   "
Spofford Morris,   "
Bonney Franklin,   Hadley
Morton Cyrus,   Halifax
Downes Nathaniel,   Hanover
French John O.   "
Howse Woodbridge R.   "
Whitmarsh Abby (spiritualist),   Hanson
Barker Bowen,   South Hanson,   "
Gleason ___   Hardwick
Orcutt Almon M.   "
Ruggles Moses Mrs. (hom.),   "
Dow John O.   Harvard
Holman E. A.   "
Dodge Franklin,   Harwich
Eldredge B. D.   "
Mansell George N.   "
Robbins A. O., West Harwich,   "
Stetson John,   "   "
Lewis Alonzo   Hatfield
Barker L. M.   Haverhill
Barker William R.   "
Chase I. E. (hom.),   "
Coggswell William,   "
Crowell John.   "
Drinkwater Sidney,   "
Drury D. Mrs.   "
Flint Kendall,   "
How James C.   "
Johnson O. H.   "

Physicians — continued.

Lovejoy O. S.   Haverhill
Moore J. O. (hom.),   "
Priest M. L. (bot.),   "
Sawyer B. A. (hom.),   "
Sawyer B. K. (hom.),   "
Stevens F. J.   "
Towle Samuel K.   "
Whittemore J. P.   "
Kenniston Timothy,   E. Haverhill,   "
Fernald Otis,   Ayers Village,   "
Temple Fred,   Heath
Edes R. T.   Hingham
Spalding H. S. (hom.),   "
Stephenson Ezra,   "
Harlow J. E.   South Hingham,   "
Frothingham ——   Hinsdale
Williams Elisha,   "
Ames Joseph,   Holden
Burnap S. G.   Holliston
Clarke Ellery C.   "
Lake Hiram (Thomp.),   "
Draper E. L.   Holyoke
Humeston L. F.   "
Long Lawson   "
O'CONNOR JAMES J.   "
Smith G. H.   "
Taylor F. L.   "
Tuttle L. M. (hom.),   "
Woods —— (hom.),   "
Pratt Jefferson,   Hopkinton
Scammell L L.   "
Warren George A.   "
Phelps Moses,   Hubbardston
Tenney J. M. (bot.),   "
Barnes C. W.   Hudson
Harriman J. L.   "
Longenecker J. H.   Huntington
Goddard Josiah H.   "
Gamwell Harlow,   Hyde Park
Biss William M.   "
Edwards Chas.   "
Everett Willard S.   "
Hayes C. C.   Ipswich
Flitner Isaac,   "
Franklin I. H.   "
Hurd Y. G.   "
Palmer Charles,   "
Chandler Ira (clairv.),   Kingston
Jones Henry N.   "
Woodman A. P.   "
Cummings R.   Lancaster
Stevens Joseph,   "
Thompson J. L. S.   "
Pratt Henry,   Lanesborough
Ames B. K.   Lawrence
Bjornberg Adolf (bot.),   "
Boynton Worcester E.   "
Brickett G. Frank,   "
Burleigh William H.   "
Carleton C. G.   "
Chamberlain C. N.   "
Chandler L.   "
Chase Henry M.   "
Dana David,   "
Fellows Charles M.   "
French A. J.   "
Garland George W.   "
Hill Mary J. (bot.),   "
Humphrey Daniel (hom.),   "
Kenney M. B. Mrs.   "
Kenney & Welch (eclectic),   "
Lamb W. D.   "
Lougee William H. (hom.),   "
McAllister John G.   "
Moulton B F.   "
Ordway Aaron,   "
Roberts Michael,   "
Sargent G. W.   "
Sargent Seneca,   "
Scruton A. F.   "
Seyfarth E.   "
Tewksbury Isaac,   "
Thompson L. S. Mrs. (Indian),   "
Young J. D. (eclectic)   "
Greene W. W. B. (hom.)   Lee
Holcomb Clifford C.   "
Leonard John M.   "
Stratton C. W.   "
Wright Eliphalet,   "

Flint Edward,   Leicester
Scribner J. P.   "
Warner G. O.   "
Rosenthal Gustavus (hom.), Clappville,   "
Brown Paul R.   Lenox
Deming William, jr.   "
Penniman J. W. (hom.),   "
Farrar David,   Leominster
Field C. C.   "
Pierce George W.   "
Wheeler Charles A. (eclectic),   "
Rice O.   Leverett
Currier Wm. J.   Lexington
Holmes Howland,   "
Coombs L. W.   Leyden
Chapin Henry C.   Lincoln
Robinson J. H.   Littleton
Chapman Thomas L.   Longmeadow
Markham Ralph P. (eclectic),   "
Beebe E. S. East Longmeadow,   "
Allen Nathan,   Lowell
Allyn Rachel H.   "
Avery F. S. Mrs.   "
Bancroft Kirk H.   "
Bass William,   "
Bannister Frank O.   "
Birmingham S. T.   "
Burnham Walter,   "
Buswell A.   "
Chandler Herman,   "
Chandler Lysander,   "
Chase Geo. F.   "
Coggin David,   "
Coly P. (Indian)   "
Day Thomas J.   "
Dickey Hanover,   "
Dows Amos W.   "
Dowse John,   "
Farrar Cyrus S.   "
Fellows Rufus.   "
Fox Lorenzo S.   "
Gage Daniel P.   "
Gilman John H.   "
Green John O.   "
Hall Mary A.   "
Harmon James M.   "
Holt Daniel (hom.),   "
Jackson William,   "
Jenness L. W. (bot.),   "
Jewett Jeremiah P.   "
Kidder Moses W.   "
Kimball Gilman,   "
Langlois J. E.   "
Leighton W. H.   "
Livingston Alfred,   "
Lovejoy D H.   "
Masta Joseph A. (eclectic),   "
Maxfield James G.   "
Melvin J. (bot.),   "
Moody J. D. (Indian),   "
OSGOOD GEORGE C. 14 Barrister's Hall   "
Packer & Thompson,   "
Parker M. G.   "
Parker Daniel (hom.),   "
Parker Hiram,   "
Pearson J. W.   "
Pillsbury Harlin,   "
Pinkham Geo. E.   "
Plunkett F. C.   "
Savory Chas. A.   "
Simpson Benjamin F   "
Smith J. H.   "
Smith P.   "
Spalding Joel,   "
Thompson M. E.   "
Wells David,   "
Whitmore Geo. H.   "
Willey John F.   "
Winn Daniel K.   "
Wright Mary P.   "
Lyman T. W.   Ludlow
Wood Robert (bot.),   "
Barber Charles I.   Lunenburg
Ahearne C. A.   Lynn
Ahlborn Henry C. (hom.),   "
Batchelder C. A. Mrs. (ecl.),   "
Breed B. B.   "
Breed M. E. Miss,   "
Butman E. T. (electrician),   "

Clark James (eclectic), Lynn
Cushing A. M. (hom.), "
Drew David F. "
Emerson John S. "
Flanders Martha J. Miss (hom.), "
Galloupe Isaac F. "
Goodell J. W. "
Green B. F. "
Kimball James H. "
Newhall Asa T. "
Newhall Edward, "
Nye James M. "
Perley Daniel, "
Perley Jos. G. "
Barker L. M. "
Pinkham Joseph G. "
Burpee John P. (hom.), Malden
Davis W. G. "
Ladd Nath'l G. "
Woods Leonard, "
Sawtelle George B. (hom.), "
Sullivan John L. jr. "
Wadsworth Peleg jr. "
Wakefield Jones F. South Malden, "
Woodman O. P. "
PRIEST GEORGE A. Manchester
Allen W. G. Mansfield
Perry W. F. (hom.), "
Foster E. H. (hom.), Marblehead
Gile Daniel, "
MORSE M. T. B. "
Whittemore H. H. F. "
Sturtevant Charles, Marion
Vose Henry C. (hom.), "
Barnes E. F. Marlborough
Chamberlain Nathan S. "
Knight William L. (hom.), "
Marsh C. D. "
Putnam Charles L. (ecl.), "
Rice Sarah A. "
Hagar Jos. E. Marshfield, Marshfield
Sparrow Wm. E. Mattapoisett
Sweat Wm. W. "
Taber Leander H. (ecl.), "
Richardson J. H. Medfield
Bemis Charles C. V. Medford
Dorr James C. "
Hedenburg James (hom.), "
Pearl Martin, "
Pillsbury H. H. "
Brown H. W. Medway
Monroe A. L. B. "
Gale Amory (hom.), E. Medway, "
Perry Charles H. "
Gale James (hom.), W. "
Abbott Benj. F. (ecl.), Melrose
Knights E. C. (ecl.) "
Parker Moses. "
Phinney Erastus O. (hom.), "
Smith J. Heber (hom.), "
Metcalf John G. Mendon
Woodbury Geo. E. (hom.) Methuen
Comstock Wm. W. Middleborough
Drake E. W. "
Jackson C. S. "
Sherman J. H. (hom.), "
Robinson Morrill, N. Middleborough, "
Starkweather Charles F. Middlefield
Phelps E. S. Middleton
Barnes John, Milford
Burnham Caleb "
Cummings Royal (bot.), "
Fay Allen C. "
Fay J. A. "
Flatley Thomas, "
Friedrich G. L. "
Herbert C. D. (hom,), "
Parker Wm. M. "
Russell Dwight, "
Warren Charles, "
Lincoln William H. Millbury
Spalding Leonard, "
Underwood F H. (hom.), "
Bowditch Edward, Milton
Holmes C. C. "
Ware Jonathan, "
Fuller George F, "
Smith Alvin, Monson
Bradford David, "
Cobb Anson (bot.), Montague

Deane E. A. Montague
Heath Charles E. Monterey
Fearing P. Elisha, Nantucket
Franklin Augustus (hom.), "
King John B. "
Beard George (ecl.), Natick
Bryant A. H. "
Gunter W. G. (hom.), "
Hoyt A. E. "
Lincoln George C. "
Wright J. H. "
Townsend G. J. South Natick, "
Noyes Josiah, Needham
White Eliza (bot.), New Ashford
Abbe Edward P. New Bedford
Birmingham S. T. "
Channing J. W. (ecl.), "
Chisholm Wm. R. "
Clark J. Laing, "
Clarke Henry B. (hom.), "
Cornish A. "
Davis Betsey Mrs, (clair.), "
Holmes A. R. "
Hooper Frederick H. "
Hough George T. "
Jennings J. Henry (surgeon), "
Johnson Henry, "
Leaming Philip S. (ecl.), "
Mackie Andrew, "
Mackie John H. "
Matthes G. Felix (hom.), "
Prescott Charles D. "
Sisson E. R. (hom.), "
Spare John, "
Spencer C. L. (oculist), "
Stearns George W. (hom.), "
Stickney Charles D. "
Swasey C. L. (port) "
Sweet George (bone-setter), "
SWEET JOB (bone-setter), Kempton,
   cor. Summer (see page 712), "
Sweet William N. (bone setter), "
Webster Helen W. "
Wilder Daniel (hom.), "
Wilson B. F. "
WINSLOW EDWARD D. 105 So. Water "
Martin S. P. New Braintree
Plumer Daniel T. Newbury
Root Martin, "
Atkinson B. C. Newburyport
Atkinson J. "
Cole John T. "
Cross Enoch, "
Cummings E. P. (hom.), "
Dickens Job T. (ecl.), "
Foss D. (hom.), "
Gale S. M. (hom.), "
Howe Francis A. "
Ingalls L. A. "
Pender Robert, "
Perkins Henry C. "
Rideout John A. "
Snow George W. "
Spofford R. S. "
Tilton James A. "
Young William, "
Pease Seth, Mill River, New Marlborough
Rising Julius A. "
Pierce George, New Salem
Kemp Alba E. N. Prescott, "
Perkins G. T. Lower Falls, Newton
Warren Edward, "
Robinson T. P. Newton Centre, "
Field H. N. Newton Corner, "
Palmer F. N. (hom.), "
Scales E. P (hom.), "
Stone L. R. "
Teulon W. F. (ecl.), "
Jones D. W. Newtonville, "
Small Eben, "
Taylor C. W. (hom.), "
Edgerly — West Newton, "
Whitney A. W. "
Northampton
Denniston Edward E. (hydro), "
Dunlap & Stoddard, "
Earle Pliny (supt. State Insane Asylum) "
Easterbrook R. P. "
Fisk & De Wolf, "
HALSTED HATFIELD (hydro.), "

Physicians — continued.

Harding Evans B. (hom.),   Northampton
Knowlton C. S.   "
Roberts O. O. (hom.),   "
THOMPSON AUSTIN W.   "
THOMPSON DANIEL.   "
TYLER J. B.   "
Gilfillan Thomas,   Florence,   "
Davis Q. O.   North Andover
Kittredge Joseph,   "
Barnes Henry,   Northborough
Jewett Henry A.   "
Johnson J. J.   "
Clark Rouse R.   Whitinsville,   Northbridge
Borden A. K.   North Bridgewater
Dean E. E. (hom.),   "
Donham B. E.   "
Freeman G. E   "
Kingman A. W.   "
Paine A. Elliot   "
Swan James C.   "
Wade E. R. (bot.),   "
Richards James F.   Campbello,   "
Martin S. P.   North Brookfield
Porter Joshua,   "
Tyler Warren,   "
Whitman E. F.   North Chelsea
Mead M. S.   Northfield
Stratton Elijah,   "
Davis W. E.   North Reading
Grosvenor David A. (bot.),   "
Rounds B. M. (hom.),   Norton
Andrews Robert,   Orange
Barton Edward,   "
Drury O. M.   "
Meacham Hiram A. (bot.)   "
Seabury B. F.   Orleans
Wilson Timothy,   "
Champlin H. C. (hom.).   Otis
Spelman Henry K.   "
Holman David,   Oxford
Lynn Charles,   "
Paine Samuel C.   "
Rawson Charles (bot.),   "
Higgins A. M. (ecl.),   Palmer
Holbrook Wm.   "
Manning Isaac (Indian)   "
Ruggles Silas,   Thorndike,   "
Thomas J. B.   "
Davis Amasa,   Three Rivers,   "
Kittredge F. G.   Peabody
Leavitt D. F.   "
Osborne George,   "
Osborne G. S.   "
Osgood Joseph,   Pembroke
Collamore Francis. N.   Pembroke,   "
Whitmarsh Abby Mrs.   South Hanson,   "
Fletcher Samuel W.   Pepperell
Howe J. S. N.   "
Stickney James M.   "
Brooks Frederick (hom.),   Petersham
Loring Lewis W.   "
ADAMS J. F. A.   3 South,   Pittsfield
Allen Almon N.   "
Bailey Charles W. (hom.),   "
Becker William,   "
Burdick Frank N.   "
CLOUGH WILLARD, M. D.   "
Eastman Henry   "
Mercer William M.   "
Mills Charles D.   "
Paddock Frank K.   "
Smith A. M.   "
WAITE & WENTWORTH (hom.),   "
   39 North,   "
Taylor G. H.   Plainfield
Bacheller John,   Plymouth
Gordon & Brewster   "
Hubbard Benjamin,   "
Jackson Alexander,   "
Oehme G. (hom.),   "
Warren Winslow,   "
Wood C. J.   Chiltonville,   "
Hammond Josiah S.   Plympton
West Joseph O.   Princeton
Baxter J. B.   Provincetown
Crocker John M.   "
Hough Henry C.   "
Newton Horatio G.   "

Paine S. A.   Provincetown
Stone Jeremiah,   "
Gilbert John H.   Quincy
Duggan William B.   "
Guillmette Chas. A.   "
Ogden W. M.   "
Pattee Wm. S.   "
Stetson James A.   "
Underwood Joseph (hom.),   "
Woodward E.   "
Alden Ebenezer,   Randolph
Allen Emory A. (bot.),   "
Babbitt W. M. (hom.),   "
Howard Frederick,   "
Wood T. E.   East Randolph,   "
Brown F. F.   Reading
Block Leonard,   "
Hannaford J. H. (hom.).   "
Willis William H.   "
Randall Geo. H.,   N. Rehoboth,   Rehoboth
Randall M. R.   "
Drowne Henry W.   Richmond
Reynolds S. M.   "
Haskell Joseph,   Rochester
Haskell Benjamin,   Rockport
Manning Joseph,   "
Sanborn John E.   "
Gould Humphrey,   Rowe
Proctor Charles,   Rowley
Adams Henry O.   Royalston
Hanks Horace F.   "
Slocum C. C. (hom.),   Rutland
Tripp Benj. H.   "
Cate S. M. (hom.),   Salem
Breed Mary E.   "
Bryant H. K.   "
Choate David,   "
Cox Benjamin,   "
Fitzgerald Edward,   "
Holbrook S. H. (Magnetic),   "
Johnson A. H.   "
Johnson Samuel,   "
Kemble Arthur,   "
Mack William,   "
Morrill Ezekiel (hom.),   "
Morse Nathan (hom.),   "
Neilson William,   "
Peirson E. B.   "
Perkins Geo. A.   "
Quimby Elisha (ecl.),   "
Quimby E. Hervey,   "
Quimby S. Foster,   "
Stone H. Osgood,   "
Stone James. Jr.   "
Wheatland H.   "
Worcester Samuel H.   "
Carswell Robert B. (ecl.),   Amesbury,   Salisbury
Benjamin ——   Sandisfield
Mellen Henry,   Montville,   "
Parsons Samuel C.,   New Boston,   "
Delano M. F.   Sandwich
Hannon D. B. (hom.),   "
Leonard Jonathan,   "
Runnells Audrew,   Monument,   "
Allen D. S.   East Saugus,   Saugus
Smith T. H.   Cliftondale,   "
La Francois Edward A.,   Saugus Centre,   "
Wheeler Ashley A.   Savoy
Thomas Francis,   Scituate
Newcomb George,   North Scituate,   "
Hammond John A. (hom.),   Seekonk
Bacon Amasa D.   Sharon
Dickson James N.   Sheffield
Kellogg S. R.   "
Peck Oliver,   "
Train Horace D. (hom.),   "
Scovile John,   Ashley Falls,   "
Duncan C. M.   Shelburne
Puffer C.   Shelburne Falls,   "
Severance C. E. (ecl.),   "   "
Taylor A. H.   "   "
Wilson Milo,   "   "
Blanchard Albert H. (hom.),   Sherborn
Dennett George W. (hom.),   "
Parker James O.   Shirley
Plympton A. A.   Shirley Village,   "
Brigham Franklin W.   Shrewsbury
Jewett Frederic A.   "
Shurtleff Frank A.   Somerset

Chapin Horace,	Somerville
Knight N. J.	"
Van De Sande F. G. (hom.),	"
Hemenway H. P. (hom.), E. Somerville,	"
Henderson J.	"
Bell Artemas,	Southampton
Robinson J. Henry,	Southborough
Chamberlain M. L.	Southbridge
Fontaine Isaac,	"
Hartwell Samuel,	"
Hartwell S. C.	"
West H. D. (ecl.),	"
Whitney Schuyler (hom.)	"
Curtis L. W. Globe Village,	"
Lester William,	South Hadley
Pearson Wm. (hom.), S. Hadley Falls,	"
Melony C. E. (bot.), " " "	"
Brownell N. P.	South Scituate
Greely —— (houn.) West Scituate,	"
Rockwell Joseph W.	Southwick
Hall J. M.	Spencer
Wheeler Edward M.	"
Ahern William,	Springfield
Allen Edmund C. (hom.)	"
Beach J. C.	"
Breck T. F.	"
Breck W. G. (surgeon),	"
Buck N. L.	"
Calkings M.	"
Chaffee C. C.	"
Church Jefferson,	"
Coleman C. F.	"
Collins H. A. (hom.),	"
Fitch Worham L.	"
Foster G. E.	"
Gardner Wm. W.	"
Holmes H. W.	"
Hooker John,	"
Jacobs C. A.	"
Jacobs Horace,	"
Jelly Geo. F,	"
Kelley J. Wesley, 28 E. State,	"
Kemp C. P.	"
Ladd E. P. (electropathist),	"
Lambert Albert,	"
Lucas John E.	"
McClean A. S.	"
Miller Wm. B.	"
Overand D. G.	"
Owen V. L.	"
Peabody Daniel,	"
Pomeroy S. F.	"
Rice A. R.	"
Smith David P.	"
Stebbins Geo. S.	"
Stickney H. G.	"
Swizey G. W. (hom.),	"
Vaille Henry R.	"
Wadsworth Mary L.	"
White Wm. H.	"
Winans Stephen (ecl.),	"
Barstow Noyes, Indian Orchard,	"
Content A. " "	"
Dewell C. E. (ecl.),	Sterling
Lord F. D.	"
Adams Lucius S.	Stockbridge
Miller L.	"
Warner Thomas J. (hom.), Glendale,	"
Brown Wm. S.	Stoneham
Cowdrey A. H.	"
Goodrich Horace,	"
Hodgdon Richard (hom.),	"
Stevens Wm. F.	"
Swan W. E. C. (hom.),	Stoughton
Tucker Simeon,	"
Gifford S. S. East Stoughton,	"
Livermore Abel C.	Stow
Corey Frank,	Sturbridge
Witter J.	"
Allen L. (hom.), Fiskdale,	"
Goodnough Levi, S. Sudbury,	Sudbury
Trow N. G.	Sunderland
Hall David,	Sutton
Stickney A. L.	"
CHASE WM. B.	Swampscott
Porter J. P. (bot.),	"
Wellington James L.	Swansea
Andrews J. S.	"
Barney Bildad,	Taunton
Barrows Geo. (hom.),	"
Baylies Alfred,	Taunton
CHACE JOHN B. 45 Broadway,	"
Cobb John E.	"
Hayward Joseph W. (hom.),	"
Howe Charles,	"
HUBBARD CHAS. T. 37 Broadway,	"
Hubbard H. B.	"
Hubbard Simeon P. (ecl.)	"
Jones Elijah U.	"
Manley Edwin,	"
Murphy Joseph,	"
Nichols J. D.	"
Paige Nomus.	"
PRESBREY SILAS D. Weir cor. Harrison,	"
RIPLEY W. K.	"
Sampson Ira,	"
Washburn A. W.	"
Wendell D. A.	"
Wood A.	"
Batchelder Joseph C.	Templeton
Gould J. B	"
Butler Winthrop, Holmes's Hole,	Tisbury
Johnson J. G. (ecl.),	"
Leach Wm. "	"
Cleveland Daniel A, West Tisbury,	"
Luce Wm. H.	"
Allen Justin,	Topsfield
Kidder Walter,	Townsend
Towns C. J.	"
Boynton R. B. West Townsend,	"
Dutton Charles.	Tyngsborough
Wilson John W. (hom.),	Tyringham
Ward Geo. W.	Upton
Wilmarth Jerome (hom.),	"
Bennet A. W.	Uxbridge
Macomber J. M. (hom.),	"
Robbins James W.	"
Wilcox C. A.	"
Jordan Charles,	Wakefield
Mausfield Joseph D.	"
Marsh L. E.	Wales
Smith J.	"
Stone Ebenezer,	Walpole
Stone Silas E.	"
Adams B. F. D.	Waltham
Forbes C. F.	"
Hunt Otis E.	"
Kittredge F. R. C.	"
Kittredge Theodore,	"
Page James A.	"
Warren R. S.	"
Willis John W.	"
Worcester Edward (hom.),	"
Miner D. W.	Ware
Richardson E. C.	"
Yale John,	"
Chubbuck L. Mrs. (hom.),	Wareham
Doggett Perez F.	"
Eaton E. R. (hom.),	"
Fearing Benjamin,	"
Sawyer Fred A.	"
Carpenter Nelson,	Warren
DeLand A. B.	"
Hastings J. W.	"
Sibley F. R. (hom.),	"
French Samuel P.	Warwick
Hosmer Alfred,	Watertown
Hucklus D. T.	"
Morse L. B.	"
RICHARDSON SAMUEL,	"
Bosworth F. A.	Webster
Brown F. D.	"
Burnett E. G.	"
Emerson Geo. W. (eclectic),	"
Smith Henry,	"
Stone T. N.	Wellfleet
Andrews Orin (hom.),	Wendell
Robinson John L.	Wenham
Albee Geo. S. (hom.),	Westborough
Curtis Wm.	"
Harvey E. B.	"
Hero J. H. (hydro.),	"
Rising Henry H.	"
Conant Josiah (eclectic),	West Boylston
Hammond L. H.	"
Lovell Ephraim,	"
Warren Geo. W.	"
Marshall H. B. Miss,	West Bridgewater
Swan James C. (hom.),	"

Physicians — continued.

Blodgett Julius, West Brookfield
Forbes George (hom.), "
Abbott Jehiel (hom.), "
Andrews George (eclectic), Westfield
Bell William O. "
Holland James, "
Mullen Frank (hom.), "
Robinson M. L. "
Sherman —— "
Tucker George G. "
Wright Luclus, "
Dow Darius A. (bot.), Westford
Webster W. A. (bot.) "
Orcutt Hervey, West Hampton
Streeter D. W. "
Shepard W. Henry H. Westminster
Warner Clinton, "
Ambrose David L. (eclectic), W. Newbury
Warren Oren, "
Willis Reuben, Weston
Kidder Luther D. "
Parris John B. (hom.), Westport
West Roxbury
Faulkner George, Jamaica Plain, "
Guild P. K. (hom.) "
Little J. Russell, "
Stedman J. "
Winkler J. A. "
Bartholomew H. (eclec.), West Springfield
Belden Herbert, "
Ufford E. G. "
Leavitt Wm. W. West Stockbridge
Fotsaith E. F. Weymouth
Warren E. L. "
Fay George W. East Weymouth, "
Tirrell N. Q. North " "
Howe Appleton, South " "
Tower C. C. " "
Harwood Myron, Whately
Foskitt Stebbins (ecl.), Wilbraham
Foster J. M. "
Ballard George T. South Wilbraham, "
Bottom Abiel (eclectic), "
Johnson E. M. Williamsburg
Trow William M. "
Duncan Samuel, Williamstown
Sabin Henry L. "
Smith Andrew M. "
Toothaker Samuel A. Wilmington
White ——, "
Brown M. L. Winchendon
Geddes Robert W. (eclectic), "
Godding Alvah, "
Russell W. S. "
Chapin Alonzo, Winchester
Trask Mary E. (hom.), "
Winsor Frederick, "
Ingalls Samuel, Winthrop
Soule Horace S. "
Drew S. W. Woburn
Grosvenor J. M. "
Hutchings G. H. "
Andrews John A. Worcester
Albee G. S. (hom.), "
Baker Mary G. "
Barnard F. (bot.), "
Bates G. A. "
Bates J. A. "
Bemis Merrick (hospital), "
Buxton H. W. "
Chamberlain W. R. (hom.), "
Clark Henry, "
Deland E. H. "
Flagg E. B. "
Flagg Samuel, "
Francis G. E. "
Gage Thomas H. "
Heywood Benj. F. "
Hobart Anson N. "
Hunt D. (hom.), "
Kelley J. Wesley, "
Kelley F. H. (eclectic), "
Knight W. A. "
Mansfield Charles, "
Martin Oramel, "
Mignault Peter B. "
Moore J. C. W. (hom.), "
Nichols L. B. (hom.), "
Park John G. "

Phillips E. G. "
Puffer Charles T. Worcester
Rice F. H. "
Rice J. M. "
Richards W. E. (hom.), "
Sargent Joseph, "
Spaulding R. "
Thayer H. R. (hom.), "
Towne Dean, "
Schofield D. "
Warner Emerson, "
Wood Albert, "
Woodward Rufus, "
Workman William, "
Coy Erastus C. Worthington
Atwood S. Wrentham
Blake Jacob (hom.), "
Dean A. Sumner, "
Yarmouth
Harris H. M. (hom.), South Yarmouth, "
Springer W. O. G. " " "
Pineo Peter, West " "
Shove Geo. Yarmouth Port, "

Piano-Forte-Action Manufs.

Cambridge
Seaverns George W., Cambridgeport, "
Stedman Vernal R. "

Piano-Forte-Case Manufs.

Lane Howard M. Leominster
Lockey J. P. "
Stone J. E. Wendell
Cowdery, Cobb, Nichols, & Co. Winchester

Piano-Forte Dealers.

(See also Musical Instruments.)

Arnzen Neils, Fall River
Whitney A. Fitchburg
Lane E. (also organs), Gloucester
Parsons T. "
Foote W. S. & Co. Lowell
Hedrick Geo. "
Oliver C. F. Lynn
Hazeltine Charles, New Bedford
White T. E. M. "
Carter B. F. (piano-fortes and melodeons). Newburyport
CHENEY J. W. (and melodeons),
14 State, "
Noyes George, "
Clarke, Nichols, & Co. Pittsfield
Follett O. "
Bray Ann R. Salem
Brooks D. B. & Brother, "
Fentiloss Manuel, "
Lang B. J. "
KREBS CARL, Webster
Stimpson & Co. Westfield
Chandler W. E. & Co. Worcester
Gorham C. L. & Co. "
Leland S. R. & Son, "
Merrifield L. "

Piano-Forte and Melodeon Leg Manufacturers.

Hale W. & Co. Dana
Stone J. E. Erving
STIMPSON & CO. Westfield

Piano-Forte and Melodeon Sharps.

TAYLOR HENRY & CO. Hudson

Piano-Forte Hardware.

Kennedy Charles E. Lowell

Piano-Forte Manufacturers.

(See also Melodeon Manufacturers; also Organ Builders.)

ALLEN & JEWETT, Leominster
ARLINGTON PIANO CO. "
Lockey J. P. "

Piano-Forte Sounding Board Manufacturers.

Brown A. B. Leominster

Piano-Forte Stool Manuf.

Cunningham T. & Co. Charlestown

Piano-Forte Tuners.

Hayward Edward P. Braintree
Keith Thomas, East Bridgewater
CHENEY JAS. W. Newburyport
Ingalls Wm H. Quincy
Merritt Washington, Weymouth
Merrifield L. Worcester
Sumner Wm. "

Pickles, Preserves, &c.

ANTHONY WILLIAM A., 10
and 12 South Main, Fall River

Picture Frame Manufacturers.

(See also Looking Glasses.)
Abbott J. A. Andover
Schwamb Charles. Arlington
MORGAN ALFRED, Brattle sq.
(see page 727), Cambridge
Belcher Geo. G. (dealer), Cambridge't, "
Sargent B. & B. F. Chelsea
WILSON WM. H. (see page 720),
Park st. "
Westgate J. C. Fall River
Bassett William W. Great Barrington
MANN J. H. Ipswich
Gordon & Currier, Lowell
Rugg & Griffith, "
Simpson A. J. & Co. "
Orcutt C. N. Lynn
White A. & J. Milford
Clark C. Alexander, New Bedford
Ellis Leonard B. "
Pierce B. W. "
Tenney F. M. Orange
RAYMOND CHAS., 35 Middle
(see page 766), Plymouth
FURNALD N. B. Quincy
Burnham A. V. Springfield
Campbell J. B. "
Lilard Geo. E. "
Holcomb Bros. "
Talbot G. W. "
French John T. Taunton
Gilmore William H. "
Stanley J. J. & Co. "
Baker G. S. Weymouth
Cumings Chester, ag't. Worcester
Gardner C. A. "

Pictures and Frames.

MORGAN ALFRED, Brattle sq.
(see page 727), Cambridge
WILSON WM. H., Park st. (see
page 720), Chelsea

Pills.

RENNE WILLIAM (Clough's Columbian, see page 793), Pittsfield

Pilots.

Maraspen Paul, Barnstable
Lothrop John, Hyannis
Dunham Thomas J. Edgartown
Fisher William B. "
Simpson William, "
Pease Charles, Fairhaven
Pease John C. "
Taber Joseph, "
Ransom Harvey, Kingston

Bowman Luther, Mattapoisett
Snow Martin,
Baker Arvin, Nantucket
Eldredge Heman, "
Brownell Frederick A. New Bedford
Cobb John Q. A. "
Hersell John. "
Manchester Ellery, "
Sherman Silas C. "
Chase Jacob B. Newburyport
Coloy Wm. T. "
Lunt Benjamin, "
Lunt William J. "
Pettingill Andrew H. "
Stevens Michael, "
Perkins Joseph, Salem
Perkins Joseph jr. "
Plummer John F. "
Williams Charles N. "
Wing Azariah E. Sandwich
Luce Hiram, Tisbury
Winslow Leander L. "
Harding John, Wareham
Robbins Darius E. "

Pistols.

WESSON FRANK, 2 Manchester
(see page 786), Worcester

Plaiting Machinery.

Sizer Emerson (globe), Westfield

Plane Manufacturers.

GREENFIELD TOOL COMPANY,
Alonzo Parker, Agent, Greenfield
Prescott Charles, Lowell
TABER JOHN M. 20 Elm (see
page 760), New Bedford
Taber Plane Co., W. G. Lamb
(Taber's patent), "
Merritt James, South Scituate
Tolman & Merritt, "
James H. L. (bench), Williamsburg
Smith Ezekiel, Worcester

Planing Knives.

HANKEY A. & CO. (every descrip-
tion, see page 775), Clappville
SIMONDS MANUF. CO. (see
page 658), West Fitchburg, Fitchburg
LOVEJOY DANIEL, Cushing,
cor. Rock (see page 744), Lowell
WITHERBY, RUGG, & RICHARD-
SON, 12 Central (see page 788), Worcester

Planing Machine Manufs.

Athol Depot, Athol
GERRY GEORGE & SON (Wood-
worth's, 6 Mill st. see page 771), "
HEALD STEPHEN & SONS
(superior Woodworth cylinder,
Daniels' and irregular planers,
see pages 799 and 796), Barre
PUTNAM MACHINE CO. Salmon
W. Putnam, treas. and agent (see
page 707), Fitchburg
ROLLSTONE MACHINE WORKS
(see page 709), "
ROBINSON WILLIAM, Mechanic's
Mills, Lowell
DAVIS ASAHEL (wood, four sizes),
Mechanic's Mills, "
Springfield
HARRIS D. L. & CO. 1 Charles, "
GOODSPEED & WYMAN (see
page 776), Winchendon
WITHERBY, RUGG, & RICHARD-
SON, 12 Central (see p. 788), Worcester

Planing Mills.

(See also Sawing and Planing.)

BAKER JAMES (see page 720),
         North Adams, Adams
Chilson Jacob B.   "   "
Dooley Peter,   "   "
Ketchum Eleazar,   "   "
SNYDER & PATTISON
  (see page 728),   "   "
Abbott Geo. L.   Andover
PAGE GEORGE G. & CO.,
  Hampshire st. Cambridgeport, Cambridge
Dean & Martin.   Cheshire
Childs Robert,   Deerfield
Felton A.   South Deerfield,   "
Goddard W.   "
               East Bridgewater
GOSS CHARLES H. (see page 769),   "
Fall River Planing Co.   Fall River
POND VIRGIL S.   Foxborough
                 Hyde Park
NEAL A. B. & CO. (see page 765),   "
Lawrence Lumber Co.   Lawrence
Sargent L. D.   "
                 Millbury
ARMSBY & MORSE (see page 763),   "
Ripley & Tripp,   New Bedford
Smith L. W.   Northampton
Wright I. S.   "
BUTLER J. H.   Pittsfield
                 Plymouth
BARNES E. & J. C. (see page 717),   "
Taft William I.   East Sheffield,   Sheffield
Cutler A. D.   Springfield
Day, Jobson, & Chase,   "
Capen Henry M.   Stoughton
NEWCOMB W. L. & CO. (see page
  728),   Taunton
BAKER CHARLES & CO.   Worcester
KEYES I. N. 24 Central (see page 720), "
Merrifield Wm. T.   "

Plaster Block Manufacturers.

(See Bonnet and Hat Block Manufs.)

Plaster Dealer.

GOODHUE WM. P. 44 Derby,   Salem

Plaster Mills.

DALZELL DAVID & SONS (see page
  799), South Egremont,   Egremont
                 Plymouth
BARNES E. & J. C. (calcined and
  farmers, see page 717), Water st.   "
Manvel & Curtis,   Sheffield
Olney D. K. & M. K.   Southbridge
CRAWFORD & DEARNLEY, Springfield
Cone Nathan,   West Stockbridge

Plastering Hair.

BARNES E. & J. C. Water st. (see
  page 717),   Plymouth

Plows.

(See also Agricultural Implement Manufs.)
HEALD STEPHEN & SONS (see
  pages 796 and 797),   Barre

Plugs, Bungs, and Tap Manuf.

BACHELDER A. & CO. Mt. Vernon
  (see page 739),   Lowell

Plumbers.

(See also Coppersmiths.)
MARSH J. J. North Adams,   Adams
Trask Israel,   Beverly
Mills William & Co.   Brookline

Baumiester Augustus,   Cambridge
Bates Edward jr.   Cambridgeport,   "
Hawkes Levi & Co.   "   "
Stevens John H.   "   "
Devens E. & Co.   East Cambridge, "
Greenleaf George W.   "   "
Allen S. H.   Charlestown
Campbell Alexander,   "
Denvir Robert F.   "
Ditson Samuel J.   "
Gaffney James,   "
Griffin & Moran,   "
Jenkins J. D.   "
Jones W. H.   "
Titus F. A.   "
Webster George H.   "
Wing Charles H.   "
Betton John,   Chelsea
Campbell Alex.   "
JONES WILLIAM, 56 Park (see page
  794),   "
Newhall Luther,   "
Reed William G.   "
SMITH HENRY W., Park, cor. School, "
Winn Brothers,   "
Duffee & Hartnett,   Dorchester
BUSH WM. R. (see page 755), Fall River
Thompson John J.   Haverhill
Tower Bros.   Holyoke
HAUGHTON & BINGHAM, 195 Essex
  (see page 746),   Lawrence
Costello T. & Co.   Lowell
Wilder H. H. & Co.   "
Craigie Andrew,   New Bedford
Gifford & Allen,   "
Wood, Brightman, & Co.   "
HUMPHREY & ALMON, West New-
  ton,   Newton
Currier S. F.   Newton Corner,   "
Eames, Sprague, & Co.   Northampton
Backus W. G.   Pittsfield
FEELEY JOHN, 31 North,
Goss F. P.   Salem
Hart W. H.   "
Waters A. S.   "
Bolton C. E.   Somerville
Sullivan C.   "
Goodhue Charles L.   Springfield
Handyside A.   "
Knight Asa M. & Son,   "
Rice C. B.   "
Chick & Wilmarth,   Taunton
Mahar James T.   "
WITHERELL STEPHEN B.   Ware
Gunn John,   Webster
             West Roxbury
McDonald Thomas, Jamaica Plain,   "
Greene & Jordan,   Worcester
Matthews & Chamberlin,   "
Shields & Moody,   "
Sutton George T.   "
TUCKER N. G. (see page 786), 23   "
  Pleasant,

Pocket-Book Manufacturers.

Titus John G. Cambridgeport, Cambridge
Arms Charles, South Deerfield, Deerfield
Eaton L. L.   "   "
Hamilton & Co.   "   "
Ruddock Eli,   "
Clark, Palmer, & Co.   Montague
Arms & Bardwell Manuf. Co. Northampton
Sparks H. H.   North Brookfield
Cutler William,   Salem

Pocket Labels.

STAR LABEL CO. F. G. Sargent
  (see page 743), Graniteville, Westford

Polish Manufacturer.

PACKARD W. HENRY (stove, see page 770),   Quincy

Pop-Corn Cake Manufacturers.

MANNING WILLIAM (see page 739), Broadway, cor. School,   Lowell
Swift Ezra J.   New Bedford

Portable Circular Saw Mill Manufacturers.

HEALD STEPHEN & SONS (with screw and lever set works, see pages 796 and 797),   Barre

Post Offices and Post Masters.

(See page 73.)

Pot Plant & Garden Trellises.

NOURSE, WHITE, & CO. (see page 826),   Westborough

Potteries.

(See also Stone Ware.)

Lawrence & Bodge,   Beverly
Robertson A. W. & H. C.   Chelsea
Reed Joseph W.   Peabody
Snow & Wight, West Sterling,   Sterling
Wright F. D. & Son,   Taunton

Powder Dealer.

Parker Jacob,   New Bedford

Powder-Can Maker.

Sawyer H. A.   Milford

Powder Keg Machinery.

HEALD STEPHEN & SONS (stave saws, chucks, hoop shavers, matchers, lock cutters, &c., see pages 796 and 797),   Barre

Powder Manufacturers.

Massachusetts Powder Works, Nath'l L. Pratt, agent, South Acton,   Acton
Tinker E. D. & Son, North Adams, Adams
Massachusetts Powder Works, Samuel Potter, agent,   Smithville,   Barre
Rockwell Theron,   Southwick

Print Block Maker.

PETTENGELL JOHN (all kinds wood work for manufs.) Mechanics' Mills,   Lowell

Print Cloths.

REMINGTON C. V. S. (broker) Pocasset, cor. Main,   Fall River

Print Works (Cloth).

(See also Cotton Cloth Manufacturers.)
    Adams
Arnold Harvey & Co., North Adams,   "
Freeman W. W. & Co.   "
BARR THOS. & CO.   Arlington
Locke Wm. H. & Co.   "
Schouler Robert.   "
AMERICAN PRINT WORKS, Jefferson Borden, agent (prints 180,000 yards daily),   Fall River
Bay State Print Works,   "
Mount Hope Mills,   "
PACIFIC MILLS, William C. Chapin, agent,   Lawrence
Merrimac Print Works, Henry Burroughs, supt.   Lowell
Mystic Print Works,   Medford

    Southbridge
Hamilton Woolen Co., Globe Village,   "
Southbridge Print Works,   "   "

Printers, Book and Job.

Smith J. S.,   East Abington,   Abington
Williams James H.   Adams
Angell & Mandeville,   N. Adams,   "
Robinson Jas. T. & Co.,   "   "
Orr S. K.   Amherst
Snow H.   "
STORRS & McCLOUD,   "
Jones Edward F.,   Athol Depot,   Athol
Waterman R. Wm.   "   "
Goss & Phinney,   Barnstable
Goddard J. Henry,   Barre
Welch, Bigelow, & Co. (books), Cambridge
Wilson John & Son,   "
Cox James,   Cambridgeport,   "
Fisher George, -   "
Houghton H. O. & Co.   "
LENFEST SOLOMON (see page 717),   East Cambridge,   "
DeCosta Wm. H.   Charlestown
Rand Caleb,   "
RICHARDS & WASON,   "
Wheildon W. W.   "
Butts I. R.   Chelsea
HOVEY BROTHERS, 138 Broadway,   "
Mason Henry & Sons,   "
Wheelock George V.   Chicopee
Coulter W. J.   Clinton
Tolman Benjamin,   Concord
Cox John, jr.   Dedham
Spencer G. W. & Co.   Douglas
Barstow Henry,   Duxbury
Burrell Jarvis D.   East Bridgewater
Vincent Charles M.   Edgartown
ALMY, MILNE, & CO.   Fall River
Dubois H. W. & Co. (lithograph),   "
Robertson W. S.   "
Webb Thomas,   "
Garfield & Stratton,   Fitchburg
Kellogg & Simonds,   "
Piper John J.   "
Thomas Wm. H.   Foxborough
Hudson C. T.   Framingham
Lombard & Rogers,   Franklin
Bushnell A. G.   Gardner
    Gloucester
PROCTER BROTHERS, 121 Front,   "
ROGERS JOHN S. E., Low's block,   "
Rogers Marcus H.   Great Barrington
Eastman S. S.   Greenfield
    Groton
TURNER JOHN H., Groton Junction,   "
Emery John W.   Harwich
Frothingham E. G.   Haverhill
Safford Eben H.   "
Woodward & Palmer,   "
Blossom & Easterbrook,   Hingham
Clark J. O.   Holliston
Wood Wm. W.   Hudson
Bower Robert,   Lawrence
MERRILL GEO. S. & CO., Essex, cor. Appleton,   "
Morrison A.   "
WADSWORTH BROS. 153 Essex,   "
Hill Wm. H. & Co.   Lee
ROYCE JOSIAH A.   "
Chase & Hildreth,   Lowell
Hildreth & Hunt,   "
KNAPP & MOREY (see index to adv.),   "
MARDEN & ROWELL, Museum building, Merrimac (see adv. index),   "
PENHALLOW B. H., Wyman's Exchange (see index to adv.),   "
Propeller Printing Office, -   "

22

Printers — continued.

Stone & Huse (also copperplate), Lowell
Bessom Charles F. Lynn
Gardiner F. W. (card), "
Kellogg Wm. W. "
Nichols Thomas P. "
Wood W. W. Marlborough
Pratt & Husty, Middleborough
Stacy George W. Milford
Stewart J. M. "
Newton George H. Monson
Russey & Robinson, Nantucket
Hemenway W. W. & Co. Natick
New Bedford
ANTHONY EDMUND & SONS, "
FESSENDEN & BAKER, "
Lindsey Benjamin, "
Hunt Albert F. Newburyport
Huse Wm. H. & Co. "
Stimson H. M., Newton Corner, Newton
Metcalf & Co. Northampton
Trumbull & Gere, "
FISK GORDON M. & CO. Palmer
HOWARD CHARLES D. Peabody
Allen Phinehas & Son (job), Pittsfield
Chickering & Axtell, "
Durkee James M. "
ANDREWS BROS. (see index to
adv.), Plymouth
AVERY W. W., bus. agt. "True Ply-
mouth Rock" (see page 718), "
Prescott Geo. W. Quincy
Holmes Elmer W. Randolph
CHAPMAN & PALFREY, 193 Essex,
Salem Register, Salem
Felt Chas. W. "
FOOTE & HORTON, 199 Essex, Sa-
lem Gazette, "
Goodwillie W. S. "
Hutchinson T. J. "
Pease George W. & Co. "
Swasey L. A. "
Currier W. H. B. Amesbury, Salisbury
Nickles John R. jr. Sandwich
Shelburne
Mirick George W., Shelburne Falls, "
Morse Wm. B. Southbridge
Bowles Samuel & Co. Springfield
Miller J. "
Tannatt J. F. & Co. "
TAYLOR L. H. (job), "
Union Printing Co. "
Hack C. A. & Son, Taunton
DAWES, WILBAR, & DAVOL, "
HALL J. W. D. "
Hastings Josiah, Waltham
Phinney George, "
Hathaway R. L. Ware
Pierce & Stevens, Westborough
Morey Thomas, West Brookfield
Buell Phineas L. Westfield
Nichols James, "
Easterbrook C. G. Weymouth
Pratt Nathan, East Weymouth, "
Ward Franklin W. Winchendon
Grey H. C. Woburn
Adams Asa B. Worcester
Fiske Edward R. & Son, "
Goddard & Nye, "
Snow E. H. & E. P. "
Smith J. F. "
Tyler & Seagrave, "
Churchill E. C., Yarmouth Port, Yarmouth
Robbins E. L. " "
Swift C. F. " "

Printing Press Manufacturers.

Houghton D. W. Athol Depot, Athol

Pittsfield
CLARY & RUSSELL (see page 708), "

Produce Dealers.

(*See also Country Stores; also Flour and Grain.*)

Symonds S. B. Beverly
RICKER W. A. & SONS, 14 Waver-
ley bldg. Charlestown
Dunham & Benson, Chelsea
Kerth Joseph, Fall River
CHACE, ALLEN, & SLADE, 16 and
18 Bedford, "
Bray Bros. Gloucester
Carter Sherman J. "
Rust Wm. P. "
Bonney M. & Co. Lawrence
Churchill J. E. & C. "
Clark W. P. "
Hancock Levi, Lowell
Jepson J. C. "
Litchfield, Edwards, & Co. "
Nichols G. N. & E. "
Reynolds Bernard, "
WAITE A. L. & CO. Dutton, opp. Me-
chanics Mills; and Waite, Hovey, &
Co., 3 Chatham st., Boston, "
LAKEMAN JOSEPH, Lynn
Waitt Wilbur F. Malden
Bourne Edward (commission), New Bedford
Damon Samuel H. "
Gardner & Estes, "
Humphrey J. L. "
Shaw & Brother, "
Hyde Milton, Peabody
Perkins P. D. "
Crosby George W. Salem
Nelson J. S. & Co. "
Read John F. "
Rend W. A. "
Briggs C. A. & Co. Taunton
Church H. W. & Co. "
Church & Allyn, "
KEEFE J. & CO. Ware
ALDRICH C. D., Trumbull sq., Worcester
BURBANK BROS. & CO., 1 Allen ct. "
Clark & Houghton, "
Fish F. W. & Co. "
Heslor J. & Co. "
Hopson, Cole, & Co. "
Staples Samuel E. "
Young, Norcross, & Co. "

Provision Dealers.

(*See also Grocers.*)

Blanchard Brothers, Abington
Cushing Davis, East Abington, "
Lucas A. B. "
Hill E. F. South Abington, "
Lincoln & Gould, "
Johnson & Baker, Adams
Leach John, "
Tower & Co. "
Baker Thomas, North Adams, "
Chace & Dumville, " "
Dyke E. A. & Co. " "
Hayden R. "
Loomis E. W. "
Smith Hiram, " "
Tower Brothers, " "
Burlingame Franklin, Amesbury
Cole Augustus K. "
Webster E. F. "
Crandall S. H. & Co. Amherst
Hall A. P. & Co. "
Kendrick & Smith, "
Flint J. H. Andover

VALPEY BROTHERS, Main cor. Central, Andover
Stark William D. Ballardvale, "
LOCKE HENRY, Arlington
Brown Jesse, Athol
Swan F. J. Athol Depot, "
Swan John, jr. (fresh), " "
Lane C. D. & O. H. Attleborough
Pettis & Adams, "
Conant Hiram, N. Attleborough, "
William Earl S. " "
Hamilton S. S. Barre
Paige F. B. "
Williams E. & Co. "
Graves Edward & Henry, Becket
Davenport & Pierce, Beverly
Lord Cyrus W. "
Southwick H. & E. "
Blanchard R. A. Blackstone
Whiting Jared, So. Braintree, Braintree
Fiske & Marshall, Brighton
Hildreth H. T. "
Nagle Eugene, "
Barnes & Aiken, Brookfield
Howe E. East Brookfield, "
Brown Brothers, Brookline
WETHERN T. A. "
Woodbury Wm. P. "
Bean Brothers, Cambridge
Brewer David, "
Brewer Thomas H. "
Burns Peter, "
Burns Timothy, "
Doyle J. A. "
Farmer J. P. jr. "
Rhoades Solomon, "
Wallace James P. jr. "
Boyson George, Cambridgeport, "
Brown Benjamin A. " "
Brown Wm. P. " "
Chandler Ebenezer M. " "
Connell Patrick, " "
Dodge & Adams, " "
Fuller S. D. & Co. " "
Gove Colvin, " "
Leavitt H. T. " "
Mallows James, " "
Munroe Charles H. " "
Penny Samuel S. " "
Plumer Joseph B. " "
Vining David W. " "
WARD ANDREW A.,
Main, c. Prospect, " "
Ward Samuel, " "
Welch H. T. " "
White J. D. " "
Aylevard Richard, East Cambridge, "
Butters & Co. " "
Fitzpatrick James, " "
Hartwell J. Edwin, " "
Hubbard Wm. " "
Plummer Warren, " "
Baldwin & Pillsbury, N. Cambridge, "
Bradford A. W. " "
Hartshorn F. N. Canton
Wentworth C. P. "
Charlestown
Adams Isaac, jr. (butter & cheese), "
Allen David, "
Bradford & Gary, "
Brooks Brothers, "
Carroll L. & Co. "
Cobb Oscar W. "
Colson J. V. & Co. (produce), "
Cotton J. B. "
Ellis L. G. "
Farnum J. M. "
Fillebrown S. L. "

Flanders C. & J. Charlestown
Flynn Daniel, "
Frost A. A. "
Frost & Winning, "
Gould N. J. "
Jordan Wm. & Brother, "
Libbey Caleb, "
Melvin J. A. & Co.
Monroe George S.
Nason Hiram I. "
Newton George, "
Patterson Samuel, "
Peaslee & King, "
Porter Samuel, "
Potter G. N. "
Pratt Charles S. "
RICKER W. A. & SONS, 14 Waverley
House, "
Stanwood W. & H. "
Thomas Hiram, "
Trumbull & Co. "
Walcott Eldridge, "
Wyatt J. M. "
SMALL ISRAEL N. Chatham
Broad F. W. Chelsea
Chapin N. F. "
Collins Patrick W. "
Cook Charles E. "
Forristall Sylvender, "
Gallison Wm. "
Hobbs M. W. "
Hopkins Joshua, "
Litchfield Wm. G. & Co. "
Perkins J. S. & Co. "
Sullivan Thomas, "
Sylvester Geo. W. "
Taylor & Balch, "
Wells Geo. W. & Son, "
Wentworth & Bacon, "
Whittier H. C. "
Whittier Mozart, "
Denison A. J. & Co. Chicopee
McClench Joseph U. "
Stoddard & Steadman, "
Newell H. S. Chicopee Falls, "
Taylor A. C. & Co. " "
Kittredge & May, Clinton
Warren & Co. "
Eaton Henry L. Danvers
Glidden Mark, "
Hale & Woodman, Danversport, "
Smith Jarvis E. Dedham
Holtham Henry, East Dedham, "
PIERCE WILLIAM H. " "
Asten J. C. Dorchester
Bird & Brothers, "
GLEASON B. & SONS, "
Park Horatio F. "
Clark L. C. Hyde Park, "
Heustis W. H. "
Cox Wm. H. Mattapan, "
Frost Thomas, Milton, "
Everett George, "
Hall Robert & Co. "
Dolan Michael, Neponset, "
Glover George, "
Harding & Wilbur, "
Mitchell Simeon, "
Moore & Dix, "
Park H. jr. Harrison Square, "
Whorf J. D. "
Ballou A. M. East Bridgewater
Woodward C. C. "
Avery W. H. & Son, East Hampton
Goward J. F. North Easton, Easton
Millett Joseph, Fairhaven
Snow Sumner D. "
Swift Seth S. & Co. "

Provision Dealers — continued.

Anthony D. M.	Fall River
Anthony John, 2d,	"
Bagshaw H.	"
Bean Horace N.	"
Buffinton E. P. & Co.	"
Burr J. W.	"
Carroll & Butler,	"
Chace Joseph H.	"
Connelly John,	"
Corson D. Wm.	"
Cuttle John,	"
Davis Albert J. & Brother,	"
Davis Jason,	"
Davis James,	"
Dean G. T.	"
Flynn Daniel,	"
Harrington James T.	"
Harrington P. P.	"
Hathaway Elisha D.	"
Hill Frederick K.	"
Jefferson Thomas,	"
Julian Charles,	"
Lewin Charles Y.	"
Lindsey W. & N. & Co.	"
Maxam E. B.	"
McDonald P. J.	"
Murphy Edward,	"
Murphy & Brothers,	"
O'Hearn Robert,	"
Pooley Edward,	"
Whitehead Edward,	"
Emory Wm. C.	Fitchburg
Emory & Lawrence,	"
Holmes Elias,	"
Howe Nicholas R.	"
Osborn Samuel, agent,	"
Smith & Wright,	"
Upton Warren C.	"
Stiles Lewis,	Framingham
Hardy Wm. H.	Saxonville, "
Heaton & Chilson,	Franklin
	Gardner
Heywood & Matthews, S. Gardner,	"
Lovell C. L.	"
Bray Brothers,	Gloucester
Carter Sherman J.	"
Cressey & Bray,	"
Haskell Benj. & Sons,	"
Phillips N. H. & Co. (wholesale),	"
Rust Wm. P.	"
Bray S. Benton,	E. Gloucester, "
Jourdan Benjamin,	Grafton
Day Wm. H. & Co.	Great Barrington
Clark J. A.	Greenfield
Coombs J. A.	"
OWEN EUCLID, Groton Junction, Groton	
Harlow & Reed,	"
Baker John W.	Harwich
Holmes & Weeks,	"
Bean G. E.	Haverhill
Bean & Coffin,	"
Bradstreet J. E.	"
Davis Geo. W.	"
Davis M. & G. G.	"
Davidson L. A.	"
Heath Charles,	"
Starrett J. W.	"
Stevens C. C.	"
Thornton Wm.	"
Veasey George J.	"
West I. R.	"
Stephenson John,	Hingham
Thayer Elihu,	"
Hoffman & Co.	Holliston
Gerry J. W.	Hopkinton
Moore J. B.	"
Allyn A. &. S. B. (fresh and salt), Holyoke	

Allyn James F. & Co. (fresh and salt),	Holyoke
Doyle James,	"
Gates S. & Sons,	"
Perkins L. & W.	"
Morse Lyman,	Hubbardston
Arnold Stedman,	Hudson
Brigham & Chase,	"
NEWTON & WILKINS,	"
Ham A. D. & Co.	Hyde Park
Baker William,	Ipswich
Green George H.	"
Dodge Manning,	"
Bailey James R.	[Lawrence
Callahan Richard,	"
Chandler H. F. & Co.	
Churchill John & Co.	
Coan & Chapman,	
Currier J. Merrill,	"
Eastman & Buell,	
Grimes & Co.	
Meservo Charles E.	
Murphy James,	
Osgood Timothy,	
Payson H.	
Penniman John B. & Co.	
Shetler Geo. E.	
Starrett & Tebbets,	
Sykes James,	"
Thomas, Dawson, & Co.	"
Wiggin C. S.	"
Bullard J. & Co.	Lee
Chapman Samuel S.	"
Cheeney Robert B.	"
O'Conner John,	"
Roper Bros.	Leominster
Wilder & Osborn,	"
Bailey Gardner,	Lowell
Benson Daniel,	"
Blood & Mitchell,	"
Bowman & Bailey,	"
Brierton Edward,	"
Bryant Daniel,	"
Burtt J. A. & Co.	"
Carll A. W.	"
Chase Ira M.	"
Corbett Michael,	"
Corner John,	"
Courtney William,	"
Cusack John,	"
Daly Zebedee S.	"
Dexter S. K.	"
Downing E. T.	"
Dozois J. B.	"
Eacott Matthew,	"
Eaton Worcester,	"
Farrell Henry,	"
Fleck Patrick,	"
Flynn John,	"
Giblin Martin,	"
Gilman A. H.	"
Gove & Kidder,	"
Gray Daniel S.	"
Green Andrew,	"
Grimes Andrew,	"
Heath & Steele,	"
Haviland & Bro.	"
Hunt E. S. (wholesale),	"
Kelley Simon,	"
Knox Sylvester,	"
Lappen Thomas,	"
Lord Oliver,	"
Lovejoy E.	"
Lynch Patrick,	"
Lynch Philip,	"
McAnulty Lawrence,	"
McCarou James,	"
McDermott J. & M.	"

Lowell	Dunham Chas. H.	Nantucket
"	Colburn H. B.	Natick
"	Parker S. N.	"
"	Adams Z. L.	New Bedford
"	Baylies & Cannon (ship),	"
"	Booth Charles W.	"
"	Braley Jasper W.	"
"	Briggs B. W.	"
"	Bryant & Peirce,	
"	Caswell Thomas,	
"	Clare John,	
"	Clark Lothrop,	
"	Cook Chas E.	"
"	COTA & SMITH, Middle cor. Cedar,	"
"	Davis Nicholas,	"
"	Dwight J. E.	"
"	Gallager John,	"
"	Gardner T. A.	
"	Gifford & Barker,	
"	Handy Nye,	
"	Holcomb Henry,	"
"	Holcomb Roland,	"
"	Kinglen James,	"
"	Luce A. E.	"
195 Middlesex, "	Luce William T.	"
Lynn	Mason Humphery S.	"
"	Macomber Geo. B.	"
"	Milliken E. & Son,	"
"	Mills James,	"
"	Morse F. & Co.	"
"	Notter John,	"
"	Perry S. S.	"
"	Perry & Wood,	"
"	Richardson-Joseph,	"
Malden	Scribner & Tripp,	
"	Sisson J. L. (poultry and game),	"
"	Snow Sylvester,	"
"	Stanton A. G. & Co.	"
Ialden Centre, "	Sturtevant Zachariah,	"
"	Taber James T.	"
Manchester	Tillinghast Chas. E.	"
Mansfield	Tripp Thomas B.	"
Marblehead	Viall E. H. agent,	"
"	Viall Wm. B.	"
"	Whenton & Brownell,	"
"	WORDELL W. W., Sixth c. Market sq.	"
"	York O. S.	"
"	Akerman Joseph,	Newburyport
"	Akerman Oliver M.	"
"	Adams C. E. & Co.	"
"	Adams John Quincy,	"
Marlborough	Cotman Wm. T.	"
"	Davis James,	"
"	Green Geo. W.	"
"	Greenough F. P.	"
"	Hennessey Thomas,	"
Medfield	Hurt George W.	"
"	Kimball C. W.	"
Medford	Knight John L. & Sons,	"
"	Marshall H. N.	
"	Pearson Chas. F.	
Melrose	Plummer & Newman,	"
"	Poor Benj. F.	
Middleborough	Richardson Pottle,	"
"	Titcomb Solomon,	"
Milford	Sherman & Co. Newton Centre, Newton	
"	Brackett W. H. Newton Corner, "	
"	Park Wm. H. jr. " "	
"	Hayes Hiram, Newtonville, "	
"	Fisher Edward, West Newton, "	
"	Hillman, Ferris, & Co. Northampton	
"	Knowlton & Newton, "	
"	Thayer & Moody, "	
Millbury	Warren & Graves, Florence, "	
"	Rea & Hill, North Andover	
"	Field Chas. C. North Bridgewater	
Milton	Severance L. F. & Co. "	
Nantucket	Tilden John, "	

Provision Dealers — continued.

Allen Lucas W. Campello, N. Bridgewater	
Baker Horace, " "	
Clark T. P.	North Brookfield
Stoddard & Lincoln,	"
Bacon S. S.	Orange
Murdock Ephraim,	"
Coggshall A. J.	Oxford
Whiting & Campbell,	"
Dodge Freeman,	Palmer
Basford P. R.	Peabody
Butman J. M.	"
Fairfield Joseph,	"
Patterson N. P. C.	"
Thomas C. A.	"
Blood Daniel jr.	Pepperell
Gleason Munroe,	Pittsfield
Hadsell J. H. & Co.	"
Read F. F. & Brother,	"
Chandler P. C. & Co.	Plymouth
Holmes A. & Co.	"
Holmes C. B. & Son,	"
Adams Marshall L.	Provincetown
Percival James W.	"
Rider Ephraim,	"
Ryder Thomas,	"
Ryder Thomas H.	"
Allen Samuel T.	Quincy
Blake A. F. & J.	"
Nightingale T. J.	"
Totman Gridley & Son,	"
Wilson Allen,	"
Dyer C. H.	Randolph
Hawes A. & E.	"
May John,	"
Ryan Wm. P.	"
Whiting Jared, E. Randolph,	"
Morton J. R.	Reading
Nichols & Turner,	"
Richardson L. G.	"
Bray John & Co.	Rockport
Patch Wm.	"
Allen William E.	Salem
Ballard B.	"
Brown Daniel S.	"
Brown J. H.	"
Carr & Putnam,	"
Crosby George W.	"
Daniels Stephen,	"
Emerson Daniel P.	"
Haley James F.	"
Jackson Eben,	"
Millett Joseph Henry,	"
Nash P. Warren,	"
O'Brien Martin.	"
Paige I. M. & Co.	"
Peabody George W. & Son,	"
Plander J. G.	"
Pickering Jackson H.	"
Roberts & Bigelow,	"
Roberts & Porter,	"
Sawyer & Tilton,	"
Staples Lewis E.	"
Stoddard & Murray,	"
Tuttle Henry G.	"
Upton Ezra,	"
Ward A. A.	"
Ward J. O.	"
Welch Wm. E.	"
Wheeler Benj. S.	"
Wiggin & Munroe,	"
Webster F. H. Salisbury Point, Salisbury	
Brown Ephraim, Amesbury,	"
Hill George,	" "
Woodman S. & Son,	" "
Atherton James H.	Sandwich
Marchant Warren,	"
Sherman U. F.	"

Tilden John L.	Sandwich
Bruce Christopher, Saugus Centre, Saugus	
Flye V. E. " "	
Gale E. H.,   Shelburne Falls,   Shelborn
Bullard C. H.	Somerville
STURTEVANT & CO.	"
BENSON & SHERMAN,	"
Johnson C. T.	"
Jackson & Penniman,	Southbridge
Marble M. M.	"
Gleason James & Co. Globe Village, "	
Capen A.	Spencer
Pierce C. W.	"
Allen A. W. & Co.	Springfield
Allen Thos. H. & Bro.	"
ARNOLD & LYON,	"
Bumstead A.	
Byrnes James A.	
Calkins & Alderman,	
Chaffee & Nye,	
Cooley & Hayes,	
Fuller Sanford,	
Granger F. M.	
Greenleaf J. S.	
Holbrook C. B.	
Medbery J. C.	"
Perkins & Co.	"
Perkins V. (wholesale),	"
PINNEY W. H. & CO.	"
Pomeroy W. H.	". "
RICE JOHN L. 48 Main,	"
Robinson Jefferson,	"
Smith A. C.	
Smith Geo. B. & Bro.	
Colwell Walter S., Indian Orchard, "	
Ford Horace,	Stoneham
SWEETSER & BUCK,	"
Tweed E.	"
White Wm. H. jr.	Stoughton
Woodfin & Brimblecom,	Swampscott
Brady & Coyle,	Taunton
Chase & Spencer,	"
HARLOW O. Jr. 58 City square,	"
Macomber & Carpenter,	". "
White A. & Co.	
White Wm. L. & Co.	
Wilmarth L. J. & Bro.	
Pratt & Thomas, Hopewell, "	
POLAND BROTHERS,	Wakefield
Wiley James M.	"
Cutter Brothers,	Waltham
Fiske H. N.	"
Savill S. O.	"
Wellington Brothers.	"
Cummings J. A.	Ware
Ruggles E. S.	"
SHELDON W. C.	"
Green & Bannister,	Warren
Allison J. S. & Co.	Watertown
Lyman Wm. H.	"
Mason H. P.	"
Dennis B. C.	Webster
Dudley Wm. A.	"
Esten L. L.	"
Kingsbury J. D. & Co.	"
Carl L. W.	Wellfleet
Higgins Lewis H.	"
Taylor Justin,	"
Boynton Reuben,	Westborough
Rice C. P. & Co.	"
Whitney & Day,	"
Paige Levi,	West Brookfield
Egleston & Co.	Westfield
Hudson & Tinkham,	"
Owen & Sackett,	"
Bartlett A., Jamaica Plain, West Roxbury	
Brown D. A. & Co. "	"
Keezer David, "	"

Locke Abel,   Jamaica Plain, W. Roxbury
Reed J. W.   "   "
Williams J. W.   "   "
Newcomb Geo. C.,   West Springfield
  Mittineague,   "
Bissell Benj. P. & Son,   West Stockbridge
Thayor W. G.   Weymouth
Willis & Worster,   "
Martin Isaac,   East Weymouth,   "
Waugh & Hall,   "   "
Bulfinch Henry,   Woburn
Hartwell & Reynolds,   "
Soles E. O.   "
Reed T. F.   North Woburn,   "
Brigham L. L. & Co.   Worcester
Dennis J. & Co.   "
Ellis & Flagg,   "
Fobes Hiram & Co.   "
Geiger George,   "
Hall E. P.   "
Hillman & Combs,   "
Maynard & Belcher,   "
McFarland A. J.   "
McManus & Kelley,   "
Monahan Thomas,   "
Morse & Smith,   "
Nye M. P.   "
Peasley & Hyde,   "
Pavey Edward P.   "
Pratt C. B. & Co.   "
Prentice Henry L. & Co.   "
Prentice J. E.   "
Smith E. T. & Co.   "
Stowell N. E.   "
Streeter J. P. & Bro.   "
Westcott J. F.   "
White Leonard,   "
Whittemore A. F. & Co.   "
HOLMES R. E. (wholesale and
  retail),   Yarmouth Port,   Tarmouth

Prussian Blue, Prussiate and Cyanuret of Potash.

DAVIS HENRY V. (see page 729),
  40 North Water,   New Bedford

Public Houses.

(See Hotels.)

Publishers.

(See also Booksellers.)

SEVER, FRANCIS, & CO.   Cambridge
PROCTER BROTHERS,   Gloucester
ROGERS JOHN S. E.   "
Bridgman & Childs, ..   Northampton
  Springfield
Bill, Gurdon, & Co. (subscription),   "
Bradley Milton & Co, (home amuse-
  ments),   "
Fisk D. E. & Co. (books),   "
Fuller F. S. & Co. (engravings),   "
Holland W. J.   "
Merriam G. & C. (book),   "
Robinson L. D. (engravings),   "

Pump and Block Makers.

Doane Hiram,   Beverly
Caswell Harvey,   Fairhaven
Hall Frank,   Fall River
SOMES JOHN J.   Gloucester
Davis William,   Hingham
Leavitt John & Son,   "
Griffin J. E. & Co.   Lowell
Luce William,   Mattapoisett
Bunker George F.   Nantucket
Gardner Timothy M.   "
Clarke Joseph,   New Bedford

Coggeshall & Co.   New Bedford
Swan W. D.   "
Swift T. W.   "
Taber Joseph,   "
Holmes George H.   Provincetown
Kennedy Andrew,   "
Adams Josiah,   Quincy
Burnham Newell,   Rockport
Donaldson Alexander,   Salem
  Stoughton
Tucker H. N. (jib and stay hanks),   "
Collins Benjamin,   Wellfleet

Pump Manufacturers.

Parker Oliver & Son (wood), North
  Adams,   Adams
National Pump Co. E. B. Fitz,
  agent,   Amherst
Fletcher A. F. & A. V.   Athol
  Cambridge
Ingalls John D.   Cambridgeport,   "
Howe Herman,   Carlisle
Billings Charles W. (wooden),
  South Deerfield,   Deerfield
COTTON J. P. (wood), Giovers'
  Corner,   Dorchester
EAST HAMPTON PUMP & EN-
  GINE CO. (steam pumps, see
  page 790),   East Hampton
  Fall River
BUSH W. R. (manuf. Cephydrion,
  or garden engine, see page 755),   "
ROLLSTONE MACHINE WORKS
  (see page 709),   Fitchburg
Wonson Wm. H. & Son,   Gloucester
WILDER S. & CO. copper, of all
  kinds (see page 767),   Holliston
Farnham Josiah W. (wooden),   Lawrence
Kenney Stephen,   "
Tainter Albert J. (chain),   Lee
Kelley & Brother,   Lynn
Tyler Kimball,   "
Pollard John (wood),   Malden
Pike George A.   Newburyport
Stickney Caleb,   "
Stockman H. & Son,   "
Todd & Brown,   "
Peabody Stephen,   Peabody
Wales Peter,   Randolph
Freeman P. W.   Spencer
Knight A. M. & Son,   Springfield
Rice C. B.   "
White H. G. O.   Taunton
KNOWLES & SIBLEY (steam,
  see page 789),   Warren
Sutton Geo. T.   Worcester
TUCKER N. G. 23 Pleasant (see
  page 786),   "

Pyrotechnists.

Wedger Benjamin, Harrison sq. Dorchester
Hunt Edward S.   Weymouth
Walker R. R.   "

Quarriers.

(See Granite Quarriers; also Marble
  Quarriers; also Stone Quarriers.)

Railroad Car Manufs.

(See Car Manufacturers.)

Railroad and Car Builders' Supplies.

Howard & Bros.   Springfield
Rand, Lewis, & Rand,   Westfield

Railroad Machinery.

FOUNDRY & MACHINE CO., H. S.
  Fairbanks, treas. and agent (see
  page 692),   Taunton

Railroad Splicings.

KINSLEY IRON & MACHINE CO.
Frank M. Ames, agt. (see page 730), Canton

Railroads.

(In Miscellaneous Department, see Index.)

Railway Iron.

WASHBURN IRON COMPANY
(see page 784), Worcester

Rake Manufacturers.

(See Agricultural Implements.)

Range Dealers.

DIGHTON FURNACE CO. Geo.
F. Gavitt, treas., Boston office
96 and 98 North, (see page 783),
North Dighton, Dighton

Rattan Workers.

Packard & Burrill (broom), East
Cambridge, Cambridge
AMERICAN RATTAN COMPANY,
Moses Wood, treas. (chair-cane
skirt-reeds, basket stocks, and ma-
terials for covering bottles; also
brooms), Water st. Fitchburg
Boston Rattan Works, Wakefield

Razor-Strop Makers.

Badger Benj. F. Charlestown
Emerson Charles, "
Emerson Joseph, "
Pomeroy Joseph E. Worcester
Torrey J. R. "

Real-Estate Agents.

(See also Brokers.)

Horr Geo. W. Athol Depot, Athol
BUCKLEY DANL. A. 433 Main st.
Cambridgeport, Cambridge
Fiske Chas. A. " "
Moore Clark, " "
Bradford Duncan, Charlestown
Cooper G. D. "
Dix & Simons, "
Flanagan Samuel, "
Hart J. S. "
Mason Rufus & Son, "
Phipps Benjamin, "
Potts James H. "
Raymond O. F, "
Robinson T. S. G. & Co. "
Gerrish William, Chelsea
MERRIAM OTIS, 5 Gerrish Block,
Broadway (see page 714), "
PRATT ALLEN, 139 Broadway, "
Rollins H. S. "
RUGG ERASTUS, 101 Winnisimmet, "
SAUNDERS & LOGAN, 67 Park st.
(see page 712), "
Soule J. M. "
Baker H. B. South Dedham, Dedham
Fall River
GREENE & SON, 12 and 14 Pleasant, "
Steele Wm. H. Gloucester
Buddington H. A. Greenfield
Kittredge Alfred, Haverhill
Seymour C. W. Hingham
Joplin & Bugbee, Lawrence
Harding Wm. H. Lee
Goward Francis & Z. Lowell
Hubbard Josiah, "
Manahan J. F. "
Morgan Ebenezer, "
Shepard L. H "

Wheelock A. C. Lowell
Williams H. L. "
Gray John E. Lynn
Ireson John J. "
Sargeant Geo. D. "
Silsbee & Pickford, "
Brown Wm. B. Marblehead
Conway John, jr. "
Cook L. H. Milford
New Bedford
BOURNE GEO. A. 27 No. Water, "
Collins Stephen, Newburyport
Clapp B. R. North Bridgewater
Francis James, Pittsfield
Faxon Henry H. Quincy
Beach T. D. Springfield
Burt Augustine & Co. "
Fitzgerald P. "
Gemmel R. J. "
Hill Geo. J. "
Kingsbury George O. "
RICE & FULLER, "
Babbitt George H. jr. Taunton
Rand Asa P. Westfield
Bartlett A. Jamaica Plain, West Roxbury
Allen C. F. Worcester
Eaton A. J. "
Ely L. A. & Co. "
Perry F. W. & Co. "
POND O. N. & CO. 8 Front st. ex-
change, "

Reed and Harness Manufs.

(See also Loom Reed and Harness.)

KENDALL C. M. Chicopee
Gibbs William H. Clinton
GOWDEY J. A. & SON (see page
716). Fall River
KENDRICK J. & J. H. 42 & 44
Pocasset (see page 711), "
NEWTON JAMES (see page 722), "
Nichols J. F. "
Weston & Place. Fitchburg
Whittaker Edmund, Holyoke
Clegg Thomas, Lawrence
Yeaton E. & Co. "
Brown Darius C. Lowell
Cleworth William & Son, "
Harris G. W. "
Stevens Solon. "
TILLEY & CLARK, Hampden st.
(see page 778), Springfield

Refreshment Rooms.

(See Eating Houses: also Oysters, &c,)

Refrigerator Manufs.

EDDY DARIUS & SON (see page
666), Harrison sq. Dorchester
Fletcher & Simpson, Lowell
Harrison Sylvester & Son, Reading

Renne's Magic Oil.

Pittsfield
RENNE WILLIAM (see page 758), "

Ribbon, Belt, and Fringe Manufacturer.

Wilkins Thomas, Dorchester

Rifles.

WESSON FRANK, 2 Manchester (see
page 786), Worcester

Riggers.

Akin John, Fairhaven
Butman Thomas, "
Hammond Wilson, "

Sawyer Robert, Fall River
Bowens & Esterbrook, Gloucester
Fisher Jacob, "
MERLET MOSES, "
Somes Geo. W. "
Witham Addison & Co. "
Peterson Ichabod, Kingston
Cannon & Curtis, New Bedford
Mathews John, "
Searell Chas. & Son, "
Pritchard J. B. & Co. Newburyport
Smith Peter, Plymouth
Bennett Stephen, Provincetown
Doane Curtis, "
Roberts David, "
Wilson Frederick, Salem

Rivet Manufacturers.

KINSLEY IRON AND MACHINE CO.
Frank M. Ames, agent (see page
730), Canton
Old Colony Rivet Co. Hall Brothers
& Co. Kingston
Cobb & Drew, Plymouth
PLYMOUTH TACK AND RIVET
WORKS, Samuel Loring, propr.
(see page 713), "
PLYMOUTH MILLS, J. Farris, agt. "
(see page 722),

Roll Coverers.

Bullard T. F. Chicopee
FOSTER GEO. H. (top, see page
754), Clinton
Nichols John F. Fall River
WITHERELL D. & O. B., shop Met-
acomet Mill, "
FOSTER EBEN E. Lawrence
Page Edward & Co. "
KIMBALL MOSES F. 92 Market,
(see page 741), Lowell
Crockett William E. Newburyport
FOSTER E. E. 196 Derby, Salem

Rolling Mills.

(See also Iron Manufacturers.)
Lazell, Perkins, & Co. Bridgewater
Cambridge
KINSLEY LYMAN & CO. (see page
714), Hampshire, Cambridgeport, "
KINSLEY IRON AND MACHINE CO.
(see page 730), Canton
Moseley Iron Building Works,
Readville, Dedham
Dighton Rolling Mill Co. Dighton
East Bridgewater Iron Co. E. Bridgewater
GOSNOLD MILLS (see page 727),
134 Ray, New Bedford
Barden Frederick, Upper Falls, Newton
Robinson Iron Co. Plymouth
OLD COLONY IRON CO. Taunton
WASHBURN IRON CO. (see page
784), Worcester

Roofing.

Wolcott Freeman, Bolton
Murray T. J. Brookline
Sawyer J. S. Cambridgeport
Pleadwell John, Charlestown
West Charles, "
Chapman & Sedon, Chelsea
Edwards John, "
PORTER. CROSS, & MESSER
(manuf. see page 690), "
Gunn H. N. & Co. Fall River
Haskell John, "
Dyer Henry B. Fitchburg
Mayo I. C. Gloucester

Horn Geo. W. Lawrence
Kittredge J. "
Lane F. T. "
Bennett J. W. Lowell
Goulding R. (slate and tin), "
Kittredge J. "
Gard John, Lynn
Purrington George, Mattapoisett
Eldridge J. T. Milford
Macy & Eldredge, "
Martin John, Orleans
Chipman Andrew M. Salem
Kittredge E. R. "
Pinnock Thomas, "
Cole Horatio (composition), Taunton
Rockwood & Nickerson, Worcester

Rope Manufacturers.

(See also Cordage Manufacturers; also
Twine and Line.)
Arkerson James, Brighton
Goss George P. Lynn
Pattee John H. North Chelsea
Lorimer Alexander, Worcester

Rubber Goods Manuf.

Tyer Henry G. Andover
Canton Elastic Fabric Co. Canton
Davidson Rubber Co., H. D. & R.
Lockwood, "
Boston Elastic Fabric Co. Chelsea
East Hampton Rubber Thread
Co. East Hampton
Glendale Elastic Fabric Co.
(cord, braid, &c.), "
Boston Rubber Shoe Co. Malden
Hale Alfred & Co. Milton
Frary O. Springfield

Saddle Makers.

(See Harness Makers.)

Saddlery Hardware.

(See Hardware; also Carriage Trimmings.)
Blanchard Hame Co. (hames), Palmer
Amalgam Metal Works, Springfield
Lee & Baker, "
Walker Appleton, Worcester
Wallace S. & Co. "

Safe Dealers.

Springfield
GRAY HENRY & SONS, 88 Main, "

Safe Manufacturers.

American Steam Fire Proof Safe
Co., Hopedale, Milford
Yale & Winn Manuf. Co., Shelburne
Falls, Shelburne
Howland J. A., agent (Wilder's) Worcester

Safety Fuse Manufacturers.

Boston Safety Fuse Co. Medford

Sail Makers.

Coffin J. W. Hyannis, Barnstable
Hallett F. "
Foster George B. Beverly
Kelley N. D. & Co. Dennis Port, Dennis
Beard E. D. Dighton
Mayhew Joseph M. Edgartown
Worth Edward, "
Hitch Obed F. & Bro. Fairhaven
Zuill William P. Fall River
Allen Daniel & Son, Gloucester
Burnham James F. "
Dennis & Colby, "

Sail Makers — *continued.*

Friend & Smith,   Gloucester
Fears Robert & Bro.   "
Prindall Charles,   "
Rowe Edward L.   "
Steele Isaac A. S.   "
Parsons Wm. 2d & Co., E. Gloucester,   "
Kelley N. D. & Co., W. Harwich, Harwich
Kelley Shubael B., Harwich Port,   "
Small Abner L.   "
Nye Henry,   Hingham
Gilbert Thomas,   Marblehead
Graves Philip E.   "
Coleman Thomas,   Nantucket
Schieffliu Theodore,   "
Almy Job,   New Bedford
Bonney J. S. & Son,   "
Chapman Alfred M.   "
CHAPMAN JOHN H., 122 North
    Second,   "
Hart Simpson,   "
Hitch Charles & Son,   "
Hitch Hardy,   "
Shurtleff J. R.   "
Currier Chas. O.   Newburyport
Davis William A.   "
Drew David,   "
Goodwin E. P.   Plymouth
Richmond John A.   "
Atkins Paul,   Provincetown
Bangs Solomon, jr.   "
Cook Lemuel 3d,   "
Dyer Chas. H.   "
Hannum Chas. A.   "
Lewis Geo. H. & Co.   "
Paine F. A. & Co.   "
Pettice Geo. W.   "
Whiton & Lincoln,   Quincy Point, Quincy
Parsons & Allen,   Rockport
Crandall John,   Salem
Lane Edward B.   "
Oakes Thomas,   "
Whipple John H.   "
Baker B. H.   Taunton
Peak John C. & Co.   Wellfleet
Rich S. B.   "
Lane Wm.   So. Wellfleet, "

Saloons.

FLINT WALTER M.   Marlborough
MANSFIELD W. D.   "

Salt Dealers.

PEW JOHN & SON,   Gloucester
Cartwright A.   Nantucket
Bowker Brothers,   Salem
Staples Samuel E.   Worcester

Salt Manufacturers.

Crocker Loring,   Barnstable
Eldredge Truman,   "
Chelsea Salt Co. Baker & Downs, Chelsea
Baxter Elijah,   West Dennis, Dennis
Eldridge Davis G.   Yarmouth

Sashes and Blinds.

(*See Doors, Sashes, &c.*)

Sausage Makers.

Furbush Andrew,   Charlestown

Saw Benches.

ROLLSTONE MACHINE WORKS
    (see page 769),   Fitchburg
GROSVENOR J. P., Mt. Vernon st.
    (adjustable circular, see p. 737), Lowell

Saw Manufacturers.

Griffiths, Welsh, & Co.   Arlington

Andrews M.   Bridgewater
Elwell E. M.   Springfield
GOODSPEED & WYMAN (stave
    saws, see page 770),   Winchendon
Henshaw & Co.   East Woburn, Woburn

Sawing and Planing Mills.

(*See also Moulding, also Planing Mills.*)

                                          Abington
Reed R. & T. & S., East Abington,   "
BAKER JAMES (see page 729), North
    Adams,   Adams
Wells O. & Son,   North Adams,   "
Witt & Alford,   "
Amherst Mill Co.   Amherst
Smith Elisha,   North Amherst,   "
Ober John T. & Co.   Beverly
Aldrich C. B.   Blackstone
MONATIQUOT   STEAM   MILLS,
    Henry Gardner propr. (see page
    768),   Weymouth,   Braintree
Priest John W.   Brighton
Hyde & Young,   Cambridge
Osborn Dalphon,   Cambridgeport,   "
PAGE GEORGE G. & CO. "   "
Calef & Son,   East Cambridge,   "
Woodbury & Co.   "
Brown Amos,   Charlestown
Hayward W. P. & Co.   "
Waterman Anthony,   "
Calef I. W. & Co.   Chelsea
Curtis Hiram,   Dorchester
Hutchinson Brothers,   "
STEARNS ALBERT T. (see page 695),
    Port Norfolk,   "
                                  East Bridgewater
GOSS CHARLES H. (see page 769),   "
DALZELL DAVID & SONS (see page
    799), South Egremont,   Egremont
Borden C. & Co.   Fall River
BECKWITH A. A. & CO. (see page
    720),   Fitchburg
FITCHBURG LUMBER CO. (see page
    767),   "
Metcalf E. L. & O. F.   Franklin
Wright M. & Co. South Gardner,   Gardner
Burnham Brothers,   Gloucester
Burnham Joseph B.   "
Gilmore Benjamin F.   Great Barrington
Berkshire Woolen Co. Asa C. Russell,
    agent,   "
Kilbourn Mark,   Greenfield
Goss R. L. & D. W.   "
Newton James & Sons,   "
Bottum Whitfield R.   Hinsdale
Payson & Cutler,   Holliston
Wiggin & Flagg,   Holyoke
                                        Hyde Park
NEAL A. B. & CO. (see page 765),   "
THOMPSON & RUSSELL,   "
Couch & Oakley,   East Lee,   Lee
Brooks A. L.   Lowell
Norcross & Sanders,   "
Pratt M. C. & Co.   "
WHITNEY H. & A.   Western avenue
    (see page 792),   "
Breed S. Oliver,   Lynn
Buffum James N.   "
KNOWLTON GEO. K. & CO. 13
    Union (see page 751),   "
MARSHALL J. OTIS (sweep, see
    page 750),   rear 13 Broad,   "
Potter & Main,   "
Roberts Otis W.   Marblehead
MANNING JOSEPH,   Marlborough
                                      Mattapoisett
BARSTOW N. H. & H. (see page 727), "
Davis I. N. & Co.   Milford

GREENE & WOOD, Leonard's wharf, New Bedford
Bailey John & Son, Newburyport
Kimball Edward, "
Pearson Alonzo, "
Sanger D. C.   West Newton, Newton
Whipple Orrin,   Newton Corner, "
Andrews T. S.   North Bridgewater
Copeland G. M. "
Packard Ellis, "
Putnam & Brothers, Oxford
Clark Aaron F. Peabody
Booth C. H. & W. A. Pittsfield
Buffum David, Salem
CHURCHILL & RICHARDSON, 195 Derby (circular and jig, see page 747), "
Gifford T. J. & Co. "
Cadieu & Co.   Amesbury, Salisbury
Morrill G. H. "
Chapin Henry B.   Ashley Falls, Sheffield
Babbitt F. S. Taunton
Dean Joshua, 2d, "
NEWCOMB W. L. & CO. (see page 728), "
SPROAT JAMES H. "
Woodward Lloyd M. "
Williams N. S.   East Taunton, "
White John B. North Uxbridge, Uxbridge
Snow R. C. & Co. Ware
SANGER N. C. (see page 772), Watertown
Newcomb Reuben, Wellfleet
Smith Spencer F. Westfield
Penniman W. R. Weymouth
Daymon & Rice,   E. Weymouth, "
BAKER CHARLES & CO. Worcester
KEYES I. N. (see page 720), 24 Central, "
RICE, GRIFFIN, & CO. "

Sawing and Planing Machine Manufacturers.

HEALD STEPHEN & SONS (Woodworth planer, see pages 796 and 797), Barre

Saw Mills.

(See also Shingle Mills.)

Robbins Francis, Acton
Faulkner W. E.   S. Acton, "
Ellis John, Acushnet
Hamlin Samuel B. "
Lund Jonathan P. "
Morse George P. & Co. "
Arnold Henry, Adams
Staples Daniel B. "
Chilson J. B.   North Adams, "
Dooley Peter, " "
Ketchum Eleazar, " "
King David B. " "
Farrar Eugene, Agawam
Sikes O. S. "
Pease Henry, Alford
Stoddard Augustus R. "
Amherst Mill Co. Amherst
Gaylord & Holley, "
Dickinson Leander M., North Amherst, "
Ward Isaac D. Ashburnham
Gross Elijah, Ashburnham Depot,. "
Foster Leonard, Burrageville, "
Hodges Brothers, " "
Russell Eliakim T. " "
Ward Alvin, " "
Bartlett Ira, Ashby
Davis John, "
Whitney J. C. "
Sprague & Gardner, Ashfield
Williams Darius, "

Ellenwood Austin, Athol
Ellis Edwin. "
Newton S. H. "
Dexter & Woods,   Athol Depot, "
Lord Ethan, " "
Mellen & Lamb, " "
Millers River Manuf. Co. " "
Pine Dale Woolen Co. " "
Pollard Brothers, " "
Rice James M. " "
Rice & Meacham, " "
Stratton Amos T. " "
Townsend Charles, " "
Adams John, jr. Attleborough
Dunn M. M. Auburn
Crocker Laban,   Cotuit, Barnstable
Allen J. A. Barre
Bassett Henry, "
Rice & Clark, "
Holden Alfred, "
Loring Nelson, "
Knight Luke L. "
Heywood Seth P.   Barre Plains, "
Lyman E. L. Becket
McElwain Oliver, "
Church & Green,   West Becket, "
Thomas Manna L. " "
Ashby William M. Bedford
Brown M. V. B. Belchertown
Bruce D. B. "
Elsbree B. B. "
Groves & Ferry, "
Pratt & Randall, "
Root Harrison, "
Shumway John R. "
Weston Jeremiah, "
Barnes George H. Berlin
Felton H. O. "
Wheeler W. M. "
Bagg R. & O. Bernardston
Hale Hartley, "
Newton James, "
Wright L. B. "
Patten Thomas, Billerica
Richardson J. O. "
Reed & Bacheler,   Millville, Blackstone
Kelley Moses,   North Blackstone, "
Nye L. R. Blandford
Harger Daniel, "
Phelps William, "
Heatley D. C.,   North Blandford, "
Forbush Jonathan, Bolton
Sawyer Joel, "
Sawyer John F. "
Walcott Freeman, "
Andrews Dean, Boxford
Brynn, Carleton, & Co. "
Hayward Augustus, "
Kimball & Sawyer, "
Lowe William, "
Day Joshua T.,   West Boxford, "
Porter Jonathan J. W. " "
Glazier John, Boylston
Ray Tertullus,   Boylston Centre. "
Pratt Z. Bridgewater
Baker Calvin, Brimfield
Brown Charles O. "
Morgan Thomas J. "
Draper J. W.,   East Brimfield, "
Powers Norman S.   Palmer, "
Fosket Rufus,   Parksville, "
Burbank Charles,   Warren, "
Rice Charles F. Brookfield
Twichell Geo. L. & Co. "
Walker F. & Co.,   East Brookfield, "
Ward Sumner J. Buckland
Reed Edward, Burlington
Fisher ——, Canton

Saw Mills — continued.

Adams Charles E.	Carlisle
Holmes Jacob,	Carver
Savery William (steam),	"
Vaughan Thomas,	"
Cole H. G. & Co. North Carver,	"
Cushman S., South Carver,	"
Baker Dennis W.	Charlemont
Bassett H. & Sons,	"
Grant Charles H.	"
Hart & Rice,	"
Hawks E. D. & Sons,	"
Hawks Edward C.	"
Negus Eliot A.	"
Negus & White,	"
Thayer Ruel C., East Charlemont,	"
Chelmsford Mill Co.	Chelmsford
Russell Abbott,	"
Dean & Martin,	Cheshire
Lloyd & Jenks,	"
Marsh Jonathan H.	"
Fay William,	Chester
Wright F. G.	"
Bisbee Orin & Son,	Chesterfield
Damon & Torrey,	"
Edwards & Baker,	"
Bryant P. & Sons, West Chesterfield,	"
Culver Horace,	"
Dooley Peter,   North Adams,   Clarksburg
Ketchum E. "	"
Fuller E. S.	Clinton
Dutton D. F.	Coleraine
Griswoldville Manuf. Co.	"
Nelson Willard,	"
Pierce Maurice,	"
Smith Brothers,	"
Wilson W. H. H.	"
Barrett S.	Concord
Bennett C. N.	Conway
Fay Wm. B.	"
Bradley Brothers,	Cummington
Brown Samuel W.	"
Guilford Wm. H.	"
Cleveland Cyrus,	Dalton
Cleveland G.	"
Cleveland Wm. K.	"
Mitchell Priestly,	"
Smith David C. & Sons,	"
Smith James & Amos,	"
Barrows Harrison,	Dana
Doubleday N. H.	"
Hale Warren & Co.	"
Putnam Otis F.	Danvers
Howland Elihu,	Dartmouth
Cummings Benj. T., N. Dartmouth,	"
Terry ——,	"
Childs Robert,	Deerfield
Porter Brothers,	"
Felton A., South Deerfield,	"
Goddard & Co.	"
Briggs Albert,	Dighton
Gooding George, North Dighton,	"
Brown A. F.	Douglas
Carleton Isaac C.	Dracut
Kingsbury J. D. & Co.	Dudley
Gleason & Welds, Southbridge,	"
Stevens H. H. Webster,	"
Cummings Dr. A.	Dunstable
Parkhurst George,	"
Swallow Daniel,	"
Woodward James,	"
Chandler C. H., West Duxbury, Duxbury
Keene Isaac,	"
Peterson Stephen,	"
Alden S. G.	East Bridgewater
E. Carver Co.	"
Shaw Samuel D.	"
BASSETT J. L. (see p. 761), E. Hampton

Pratt Amos,	Easton
Williams E. D.	"
Ames O., North Easton,	"
Howard Seba, South Easton,	"
Rood & Pixley, North Egremont, Egremont
Van Bramer John E. "	"
DALZELL, DAVID & SONS (see
page 799), South Egremont,	"
Lamson Ira,	"
Slater Samuel,	"
Cadwell A. J.	Enfield
Swift River Manufacturing Co.	"
Ward Benjamin,	"
Newton James,	Erving
Newton D. H.	"
Priest Calvin,	"
Stone J. E.	"
Washburn Wm. B. & Co.	"
Moore James, Grout's Corner,	"
Essex Mill Co.	Essex
Story Perkins,	"
Fall River Planing Co.	Fall River
Baker Wm.	Fitchburg
Putnam James P.	"
Kemp S. A.	Florida
Thatcher S. S.	"
Tower Chester,	"
Tower Dennis,	"
Tenney Moses & Son,	Georgetown
Arms John,	Gill
Holmes & Wood,	"
Janes Samuel,	"
Dresser Caleb C.	Goshen
Hawks Rodney,	"
Sears Freeman,	"
Stone Luther,	"
Pratt C. L. & Co.	Grafton
Dadmun S. N. E. Village,	"
Carver Wm.	Granby
Chapin D. D. & Sons,	"
Clark Israel Mrs.	"
Green H. A.	Granville
Stow Volney, East Granville,	"
Noble & Cooley, Granville Corner,	"
Clark Benjamin, West Granville,	"
Coe Ira,	"
Hall J.	"
Johnson James W. "	"
Berkshire Woollen Co.   Great Barrington
Comstock Hiram,	"
Ford Enos,	"
Gilmore Benjamin F.	"
Hatch Billey,	"
Kilbourn Mark,	"
Gage Simeon,	"
Goss R. L. & D. W.	Greenfield
Larabee Eben N.	"
Newton James & Sons,	"
	Greenwich
Parker Daniel, Greenwich Village,	"
Phelps L. W.   Groton Junction, Groton
Spaulding & Page, "	"
Hardy Charles N.	Groveland
Adams J. & Sons,	Hadley
Nutting J. H.	"
Granger L. N. North Hadley,	"
E. Carver Co.	Halifax
Jones H. H.	Hancock
Barstow Edwin,	Hanover
Wilder & Co.	"

Cushing Elijah, Hanson
Cushing Geo. & Bro. "
Hobart & Harding, South Hanson, "
Leavitt & Keene, " "
Monroe Ethan, E. Bridgewater, "
Gilbert Geo. H. & Co. Hardwick
Howard Geo. C. "
Presho & Frye, "
Southworth Constant, "
Spooner Brothers, "
Watkins Geo. F. "
Fletcher Edward E. & Brother, Harvard
Fitch Brothers, Hatfield
Fitch Brothers & Porter, "
Eldridge Thomas, Hawley
Scott Elijah, "
Crittenden Chas. Charlemont, "
Colby Charles, West Hawley, "
Hunt & Larkins, " "
Miller John, " "
Turner Alonzo, " "
Vincent Willis, " "
Fairbanks Henry, Heath
Hitchcock Dwight, "
Lamb G. W. "
Bottum Whitefield R. Hinsdale
Parish Elisha H. "
Tracy Charles E. & Brother, "
Broad Ira, Holden
Howe Nathan, "
Butterworth T. D. Holland
Gordon Frank, "
Marcy George, "
Pond Caleb, Hopkinton
Smith J. H. "
Wood A. W. Woodville, "
Brigham O. S. Hubbardston
Brown G. "
Brown M. "
Conant L. "
Hale & Williams, "
Heald T. S. "
Tilton Ebenezer, "
Brigham Rufus H. Hudson
Bruce Horatio, "
Little Benjamin, Huntington
Bradford Orrin W. Kingston
Chandler David, "
Prince & Bryant, "
Reed & Jones, "
Richmond Eleazer, Lakeville
Phelps B. S. Lancaster
Wilder C. L. "
Newton Sidney, Lanesborough
Page & Harding, "
McLaughlin John, Lee
Beebe Levi, South Lee, "
HURLBUT PAPER CO. " "
Dutton H. Leicester
Sargent Edward, "
Kent D. W. Cherry Valley, "
Clark Asa W. Chappville, "
Post Elda'd, Lenox
Johnson Billings, New Lenox, "
Miller Levi C. "
Stratton Martin W. & Joel A., Leominster
Wright C. W. & Co. "
Ball O. Leverett
Field Zebina, "
Field Harrison, "
Shaw F. G. "
Clarke Warren, North Leverett, "
Dudley Luther, " "
Folton Albert, " "
Moore Dexter, " "
Watson H. N. " "
Coolidge Charles, Leyden
Keet R. S. "

Denison A. J. Leyden
Hall H. W. "
Harrington George F. Lincoln
Warren Luther S. Littleton
Burdatha Henry, Longmeadow
Alden Orsemus, Ludlow
Fuller W. D. "
Harris Philo, "
Plumley Elijah, Collins Depot, "
Baker Wm. Lunenburg
Dickson Wm. "
Houghton Albert, "
Spaulding Wm. "
Buffum J. N. Lynn
Sweet Elbridge, W. Mansfield, Mansfield
Hagar W. & M. Marlborough
Manning Joseph, "
Parlow O. H. & E. S. Marion
Holmes & Sparrow, Mattapoisett, "
Chandler Simeon B. Marshfield
Dunham H. C. "
Packard Lemuel, "
Eames William, East Marshfield, "
Magoun & Holmes, North " "
Hatch Samuel, " " "
BARSTOW N. H. & H. (steam, see
  page 727), Mattapoisett
Bolles Solomon E. "
Cowan & Macomber, "
Dexter E. & Son, "
Ellis Jarvis, "
Tinkham Clark, "
Town Mills, "
Chenery Reuben, Medfield
Smith J. H. Medway
Fisher's Lewis Sons, East Medway, "
Partridge Timothy A., West " "
Ellis James H. Rockville, "
Inman N. Arnold, Mendon
Swan Bros. "
Taft S. "
HARLOW I. H. & CO. (steam, see Middleborough
  page 768), "
Brown & Sherman, "
Cox George, "
Rock Steam Mill, Rock, "
Blush Wm. D. Bancroft, Middlefield
Emerson & Flint, Middleton
Wilkins A. W. & E. W. "
Hull Elias, Millbury
Rice G. W. "
Hovey M. M. West Millbury, "
Greggs Salem, "
Hicks Albert A. Monroe
Stafford Emerson, "
Stafford Nathan, "
Tower Warren F. "
Whitcomb Stillman, "
Day E. A. Monson
Smith Melville, "
Warriner Andrew A. "
Whiton J. L. "
Goldsmith A. & D. Montague
Lawrence C. & H. C. "
Marsh E. H. "
Ripley Eben, "
Brewer Reuben R. Monterey
Hadsell John K. "
Langdon John H. "
Axtell H. K. Montgomery
Fowler Daniel & Co. "
Lamson Ira, Mount Washington
Miles Frederick, "
Scott Charles, "
Whitbeck Orrin C. "
Roy Lester, New Ashford
Pepper Henry A. New Braintree

Saw Mills — continued.

Pearson Benjamin,	Newbury
Brever John,	New Marlborough
McAlpine James,	Mill River, "
Sisson Henry,	" "
Chapin Albert,	" "
Allen & Rood,	Hartsville, "
Norton Henry,	Southfield, "
Canfield B.	" "
Chapin Frederick,	" "
Gilson Origen,	" "
	New Salem
Cleveland George W.,	Millington, "
Fory & Giles,	" "
Kilburn L. &. Co.,	Orange, "
Haskell Jacob,	N. New Salem, "
Stratton F. E.	" "
Day Samuel,	Northampton
NONATUCK SILK CO.,	Florence, "
Smith Jairus W.	Northampton
Walker J. B.	"
Davis & Furber,	North Andover
Bull Jas.	"
Bartlett W. A. 2d,	Northborough
Bush Wilder,	"
Smith Jairus,	"
Prentice Marvil,	Northbridge
Stone Wm.	Whitinsville, "
Whitin Charles P.	" "
Whitin John C.	" "
	North Bridgewater
Howard Welcome & Thomas,	"
Sprague Chandler,	"
	North Brookfield
BATCHELDER A. & E. D.	"
Stoddard Leonard,	"
Bridge George,	Northfield
Collar H. B.	"
Johnson Henry,	"
Murdock Henry,	"
Long D. & A.	"
Stewart C.	"
Eames Joseph & Co.	North Reading
Flint Abijah,	"
Jeffrey Elisha,	"
Lane A. D. & A.	Norton
Dane C. D. & O. H.	"
Lincoln Benjamin,	"
Lincoln Eddy,	"
Lincoln Seneca,	"
Willis Loren,	"
Dean David P.	Oakham
Parker Daniel M.,	Cold Brook, "
Bliss Milton,	Orange
Coolidge Henry & James,	"
Graham Ephraim C.	"
Merriam Chauncey,	"
Orcutt John,	"
WHITNEY, LORD, & CO. (see page 776),	"
Bill & Taylor,	North Orange, "
Carter Charles J.	Otis
Lyman & Chaffee,	"
Hunt Curtis,	East Otis, "
Hudson Joseph,	Oxford
Childs Benjamin,	"
Rich Ebenezer D.	"
Warner & Dart,	"
Bartlett E.	North Oxford, "
Blanchard A. V. & Co.	Palmer
Potter P. P. & Co.	Bondville, "
Comins William,	Paxton
Harrington Wm.	"
Hills, Westcott, & Co.	Pelham
Mitchell Andrew,	"
Chandler & Bourne,	Pembroke
Hatch George F.	North Pembroke, "
Oldham John 2d,	" "
Blake Gilman,	Pepperell
Kemp William,	"
Mention Geo. A.	"
Sartell Levi,	"
Brown Orrin,	Peru
Goldthwait Elias,	"
Jackson Marshall,	"
Watkins Zenas,	"
Cook Nathaniel,	Petersham
Crockett Benj. M.	"
Plympton George,	"
Shattuck Henry A.	"
Lamb Jason,	Phillipston
Powers Edward,	"
Howard Jesse,	Pittsfield
Pitt Charles,	"
Stewart Jacob,	"
Stearnsville Woolen Co. (Henry Stearns, agent), West Pittsfield,	"
Campbell S. N.	Plainfield
Cleveland William M.	"
King George W.	"
Scott Elijah,	"
Streeter S. C.	"
Whitmarsh Fordyce,	"
Willcutt William,	"
Andrews S. L.	Plympton
Bonney James S.	"
Ellis J. C. & H. H.	"
Hayward Martin,	"
Willis Edward,	"
Hills & Westcott, Amherst,	Prescott
Barrows Harrison, North Prescott,	"
Brown Foster,	" "
Davis Daniel, jr.	Princeton
Howe Jotham,	"
Miles D. C. & Co.	"
Smith Flavel W.	"
Wilder Mark,	East Princeton, "
Perry E. A.	Randolph
Hall Ellis B.	Raynham
Tracy John,	"
Wilbur Emery S.	"
Williams Martin G.	"
Harnden Sylvester & Son,	Reading
Martin Hiram,	Rehoboth
Perry Otis,	"
Richmond Iron Works,	Richmond
Ellis Thomas,	Rochester
Gifford Abraham,	"
King & Hathaway,	"
Rounseville Alden, jr.	"
Amidon Henry A.	Rowe
Hyde Rufus,	"
Kendrick H. A.	"
Dodge Phineas,	Rowley
Moore L. J.	Royalston
Partridge Maynard,	"
Whitney George,	South Royalston, "
Bishop Newman,	Russell
Goff C. H.	"
Miner Holmes,	"
Parks Vestus,	"
Wright Marvin,	"
Munroe James L.	Rutland
Reid Charles E.	"
Roper Samuel,	"
Homer & Bryant,	North Rutland, "
Ware Caleb A.	West "
Webster A. & Son,	Sandisfield
Crane Wm. F.	Montville, "
Downs A. B.	" "
Frost Wm. P.	"
Hawley Wm. H.	"
Langdon John H.	"
Seymour Seth,	"
Thompson Lester,	" "
Belden Henry,	New Boston, "

Brunson Wm. B.	New Boston,	Sandisfield
Hodgkins, Gladden, & Co.		"
Webster Rowland,	South Sandisfield,	"
		Sandwich
Cape Cod Glass Co.	N. Sandwich,	"
Deming Amos, jr. & Mark,		Savoy
Haskins Dennis,		"
Maynard Albert M.		"
Polly Harvey,		"
Sears Dennis,		"
Shaw Lorenzo (portable steam),		"
Smith John M.		"
Snow Harman,		"
Clapp Thomas,		Scituate
Morris Joseph,	North Scituate,	"
Burr Raymond H.		Seekonk
Kent Samuel,		"
Kent Virgil,		"
Curtis Ira,		Sheffield
Foot Bradford,		"
Manvill & Birch,		"
Peck Oliver,		"
Taft William I.	East Sheffield,	"
Fisk Wm. M.		Shelburne
Peck Abner,		"
Smead Soloman,	Shelburne Centre,	"
FROST J. B. & CO.	Shelburne Falls,	".
Streeter A. W.	"	"
Holbrook Jonathan,		Sherborn
Leland James H.		"
Burgess Asa,		Shirley
Kilburn C. A.		"
Kilburn Jonathan,		"
Doane Orrin,		Shrewsbury
Fay Wm.		"
Wyman Oliver B.		"
Baker John J.		Shutesbury
Dudley Samuel F.		"
Felton Charles,		"
Learnard Rufus,		"
Ober Henry,		"
Pratt E. L.		"
Reynolds John,		"
Stetson Wm. B.		"
Reynolds Thomas,	Lock's Village,	"
Stimpson & Co.		Southampton
Nichols Orin,		Southborough
Sawin Moses,		"
Dresser Chester,		Southbridge
Clemence J. M. & L. D.	Globe Vil.,	"
Merriam & Ballard,	"	"
Moody Pliny (estate),		South Hadley
Rush Brothers,		"
Congdon B.,	S. Hadley Falls,	"
Hatch Leonard,		South Scituate
Jacobs B. & B.		"
Merritt Joseph, 2d,		"
Torrey D. jr.		"
Turner John, 2d,		"
Gilbert Edwin,		Southwick
Hastings F. C.		"
Lamson F. D. W.		"
Bemis Joshua,		Spencer
Bemis T.		"
Howe Hiram,		"
MYRICK & SUGDEN,		"
Newhall Otis,		"
Stone, Tower, & Co.		"
Thompson Wm. L.		"
CRAWFORD & DEARNLEY,		Springfield
Bemis Solon L.		Sterling
Burpee H. W.		"
Richardson Wm. B.		"
Stone John E.		"
Pratt James A.	Pratt's Junction,	"
Nichols Luke W.	West Sterling,	"
Comstock & Sandford,		Stockbridge
Curtis Stephen C.,	Curtisville,	"
Yale Allen S.	Glendale,	Stockbridge
Smith Wm. H.		"
Southworth Jedediah,		Stoughton
Smith Micah & Son,		Stow
Allen Ethan,		Sturbridge
Phillips & Westgate,		"
Bares & Adams,	Fiskdale,	"
Wight George,	"	"
Gerry E. A.		Sudbury
Willis J. P.		"
Assabet Manufacturing Co.	Assabet,	"
Maynard Amory,	"	"
Delano J. L.		Sunderland
Whitmore D. D.		"
Kenney Sumner,		Sutton
Manchaug Co.		"
Shaw Salem J.		"
Stockwell H. S.		"
Wood Nathan M.		Swansea
Dean Joshua, 2d,		Taunton
Pierce A. W.		"
Williams A. K. & Co.		"
Bourne & Brooks,		Templeton
Bourne & Hadley,		"
Jones Abijah,		"
Leland Wm. E.		"
Partridge H. & J. W.		"
Sawyer Geo. W.		"
Day & Stone,	Baldwinville,	"
Sawyer & Thompson,	"	"
Hodge A. S. & Co.	E. Templeton,	"
Sawyer Brothers,		"
Nichols & Adams,	Otter River,	"
Stone William,	"	"
Burtt & Livingston,		Tewksbury
Trull Nathaniel,		"
Bently Wm. N.		Tolland
Marshall A. & Son,		"
Moore Bennett E.		"
Larkin Erastus,		"
Twining P. F.		"
Briuley & James,		Tyngsborough
Butterfield James P.		"
Upton J. G.		"
Garfield Elijah,		Tyringham
Shaker's Mill,		"
Steadman M. V. B.		"
Fisk Luther,		Upton
Grundy Z.		"
Holbrook Nahum W.		"
Taft P. P.		"
Wood Arba T.		"
Taft John S.		Uxbridge
Marcy H. P.		Wales
Peck Ira,		"
Shaw Daniel,		"
Tisdale J. P.		Walpole
Morey G. P.		"
Clark Truman,	South Walpole,	"
Blackmer A. L.		Ware
Holden D.		"
Miner & Yale,		"
Snow R. C. & Co.		"
Kenney Lewis,	South Wareham,	Wareham
Bosworth & Makepeace,		Warren
Fairbanks Asahel,		"
Sibley S. H.		"
Atwood Lyman,		Warwick
Bliss Joseph,		"
Conant Josiah,		"
Harris Martin,		"
Williams Melzar,		"
Brooker Isaac S. (steam),		Washington
Slater Samuel & Sons,		Webster
Stevens H. H.		"
Bemis Theodore,		Wendell
Fiske Stephen,		"
Leach Luke,		"

Saw Mills — continued.

Sinclair S. S.   Wendell
Dodge Henry,   Wenham
Fisher G. W. E.   Westborough
Giles J. B.   "
Parker Elisha,   "
Sandra Frank H.   "
Warner W. W.   West Boylston
Alger Cyrus,   West Bridgewater
Ames O. & Sons,   "
Pierce M.   West Brookfield
Tyler George F.   "
Fowler Frederick,   Westfield
Griswold & Stebbins,   "
Root Matthew,   "
Heywood & Burbeck,   Westford
Bridgman Lucas,   West Hampton
Burt Joel,   "
Loud C. N.   "
Lyman Wm. E.   "
Parsons Henry M.   "
Rhoades Leander L.   "
Clark, Nichols, & Co.   Westminster
Coolidge Frederick S.   "
Merriam, Holden, & Co.   "
Smith George,   "
Wyman Benj.   Wachusett Village,   "
Craw C. N.   Westport
Sisson Alden N.   "
Bartholomew Andrew,   West Springfield
Dewell James,   West Stockbridge
Freedley & Spencer,   "
French Abel C.   "
Gaston A. E.   "
Wilson John G.   "
Smith Chandler, heirs of, State Line,   "
Woodruff Russell,   "   "   "
Sanderson Eli W.   Whately
Sanderson Luther,   "
                                    Wilbraham
Beck Orlando.   South Wilbraham,   "
Stanton Sullivan W.   "   "   "
Adams & Sprague,   Williamsburg
Pageot Joseph,   "
Cole P. R.   Williamstown
Talmadge Edwin A.   "
Walley Stephen,   "
Brown Silas,   Wilmington
Harnden Henry,   "
Fairbanks Sidney,   Winchendon
Loud Edward, jr.   "
Murdock E. & Co.   "
Wyman S.   "
Clark O. R.   Winchester
Hopley John,   "
Cady Harvey,   Windsor
White J. L.   "
Pierce Reuben,   East Windsor, "
Torrey H. P.   "
Allen Josiah & Sons, West Cum-
  mington,   "
Coleman Ambrose,   "   "   "
Richardson Stephen & Sons, East
  Woburn,   "
Merrifield Wm. F.   Worcester
Sampson P. & Son,   Worthington
Stevens Aaron & Son,   "
Higgins J. S.   Ringville,   "
Higgins Lyman,   S. Worthington,   "
Adams Benj. F.   West   "   "
Parish Oliver,   "   "   "
Fisher Lewis jr.   Wrentham
Fisher Luther,   "
Mann Levi,   North Wrentham,   "
Ray F. B.   "
Grant John E.   West   "   "

Saw-Mill Manufacturers.

HODGE OTIS J. (see page 786), North
  Adams,   Adams
GERRY GEO. & SON (jack and
  bench, see p. 771), Athol Depot, Athol
HEALD STEPHEN & SONS (port-
  able circular mulay, sash, and jig-
  ger mills, bench saws, saw man-
  drels, saw set and up-setting
  tools, &c., see pages 796 and 797), Barre
Andrews M.   Bridgewater
Clapp Wm. R.   Northampton
Herrick Webster (portable circular
  saw-mills),   "
TURBINE WATER WHEEL CO.
  (circular saw-mills, see page
  777),   Orange
Nichols & Adams, Otter River, Templeton

Scale and Balance Manufs.

Stephenson L. & Co.   Hingham
Knowles John A. jr.   Lowell

Screen Manufacturers.

(For Cotton and Woolen Cards.)

TROWBRIDGE & KIMBALL (see
  page 738), Wamesit Steam Mills, Lowell

Screw Manufacturers.

HEALD STEPHEN & SONS (large
  jack, wagon, cider-press, factory
  cheese-press, and bench-screws,
  &c. (see pages 796 and 797),   Barre
American Bolt Co.   Lowell
Atherton Thomas & Co.   "
Peabody & Co.   "
SMITH S. C. (set and cap), Mt. Ver-
  non, near Lowell Gas Works,   "
International Screw Nail Co. Northampton
American Screw Co. (Br.),   Taunton
BAGLEY E. A. & Co. 12 Central, Worcester

Sculptors.

Carew T. A.   Cambridge
Dexter Henry,   Cambridgeport,   "
French David M.   Newburyport
Kinney B. H.   Worcester

Scythe and Scythe-Snath Manufacturers.

(See also Agricultural Implements.)

Harris Scythe Co. Milo Knicker-
  bocker, agent,   Ashley Falls, Sheffield

Scythe-Stone Manufacturers.

Guilford Wm. H.   Cummington
Orcutt L. J.   "
Stevens N. S.   "
Jordan Elijah,   East Windsor, Windsor

Seamen's Outfits.

TUCKER HENRY R.   39 and 41
  No. Water,   New Bedford

Seed Stores.

(See Agricultural Warehouses.)

Sewer Pipe (Hydraulic Cement).

FLINT SIMEON, 221 Derby,   Salem

Sewing Machine Cases.

Grover & Brother,   Cambridgeport

Sewing Machines.

Shaw B. East Abington, Abington
Barnes M. M. (Weed), N. Adams, Adams
BRIGGS & ROLAND (Singer's),
  North Adams, "
LAMB KNITTING MACHINE MANUF.
  CO. (Chicopee sewing machine, see
  page 773), Chicopee Falls, Chicopee
Carlisle G. M. Fall River
Deur Wm. N. T. "
Davis Epes, jr. Gloucester
Lane Eustace, "
Parsons T. "
Bassett William. Walton, Great Barrington
Fryer M. A. & J. B. (Grover & Baker), "
Nye Avis Mrs. "
Hooke Daniel, Haverhill
Gilbert J. F. (Weed), Holyoke
Watts James W. Ipswich
Grover & Baker Machine Co. Deborah
  Martin, agent, Lawrence
McKay Sewing Machine Co. (manufs.)
  Thos. Scott, agent, "
Newhall John F. "
Robinson & Cusack, "
Morgan Mary M. Miss, Lee
CARTER N. C. (agent Weed), 109
  Merrimack, Lowell
Dean Horace C. (agent), "
Stratton H. B. "
Holt J. S. Lynn
KIMBALL WM. H. & CO. (dealers),
  42 Washington, "
NICHOLS F. W. & CO., Vine, cor.
  South Common (see page 752), "
Sawyer N. (agent Howe), "
Scribner & Smith, "
The Singer Manuf. Co. (J. Bradford,
  agent), "
TRIPP S. D. (see page 750), 13 Broad, "
Weed Sewing Machine Co. G. W.
  Fowler & D. H. Burt, agents, "
Tucker T. W. Marblehead
Adams A. H. Milford
Bacon H. S. "
Bailey P. M. "
Rockwood C. E. Natick
Johnson S. H. Newburyport
Noyes George, "
Booth Emily Mrs. New Bedford
Eddy Job A. T. "
Mann Henry S. "
   Northampton
Bushman J. Mrs. (Wheeler & Wilson), "
Tinker W. A. "
FLORENCE SEWING MACHINE CO.
  Sidney S rong, treas. John M. Ward-
  well, agent, (see p. 705), Florence, "
Hamilton W. D. (dealer), N. Bridgewater
Whittemore D. (wax-thread), "
Johnson A. F. & Co. Orange
Singer's Sewing Machines, Eliza H.
  Gage, agent, Pittsfield
Baker Semantha Miss (Grover &
  Baker), "
Gregory J. (American button hole), "
Lamberson Samuel L. (Wheeler &
  Wilson), "
Lincoln J. B. "
Shaffer John D. (Singer's). "
LITTLEFIELD BROTHERS (repair-
  ers, see page 728), Randolph
GRISWOLD B. L. (also findings),
  142 Essex, Salem
Weston Samuel C. "
BROWN S. C. 80 Worthington, Springfield
Coburn F. C. (Etna), "
Ferre C. D. & Co. "

Griswold Ogden, Springfield
Lee & Williams, "
Otis S. G. "
Pierce William, "
COLBY SAMUEL (Singer, see front
  colored page), Taunton
Huntley George R. "
Potter Wm. K. "
Phipps Charles, Ware
Clark J. S. Webster
Folsom John G. Winchendon
GOODSPEED & WYMAN (Bartlett
  machines, see page 776), "
Culver A. L. Worcester
Howland J. A. "
Sawyer J. A. "
Shaffer & Marquand, "
Spaulding L. Q. "

Sewing-Machine Findings.

KIMBALL WM. H. & CO. 42 Washington, Lynn

Sewing-Machine Needles.

Spring C. & A. Hyde Park
PHILLIPS O. 6 Washington st. (see
  page 735), Lynn
FENN & DANIELS, W. Medway, Medway
Cushman H. S. Milford
Killey & Co. "
Prine N. (wax-thread), "
Laett Henry (wax-thread), N. Bridgewater
Howard Charles, "
Bingman L. A. "
PACKARD J. W. (see page 769), "
GRISWOLD B. L., 142 Essex, Salem
Stuart Silas, "
Stetson Bradford, Sterling
Worcester Needle Co. Uxbridge
   Worcester

Sewing-Silk Dealers.

GRISWOLD B. L., 142 Essex, Salem
Rankin & Judd, Springfield
Read W. P. "

Sewing-Silk Manufacturers.

SEAVEY, FOSTER, & BOWMAN
  (sewing-silk and machine twist,
  see page 694), Canton
FARWELL I. Jn. & CO. (all kinds
  silks and machine twist), Lower
  Falls, Newton
NONOTUCK SILK COMPANY,
  (sewing and machine twist, see
  page 705), Florence, Northampton
Warner Joseph (skein silk), "
Worcester Silk Co. Worcester

Shafting, Pulleys, &c.

HUNTER JAMES & SON (see page
  770), North Adams, Adams
HEALD STEPHEN & SONS (shafting,
  pulleys, and hangers of all descrip-
  tions, see pages 796 and 797), Barre
ROLLSTONE MACHINE WORKS
  (see page 709), Fitchburg
   Pittsfield
CLARY & RUSSELL (see page 708), "

Shear Blades.

LOVEJOY DANIEL, Rock, corner
  Cushing st. (see page 744), Lowell
Coes L. & A. G. Worcester
Toulmin John, "

Shears and Punching Presses.

   Worcester
RICE & WHITCOMB (see page 784), "

23

Sheathing for Ships.

NEW BEDFORD COPPER CO.,
  William H. Mathews, treas.
  (see page 757),   New Bedford
CROCKER BROTHERS & CO.
  Court, near City Square (also
  bolts and nails, see page 756), Taunton

Shingle Machines.

HEALD STEPHEN & SONS (see
  pages 796 and 797),   Barre
Cary Mordicai, East Brookfield, Brookfield

Shingle Mills.

(See also Saw Mills.)

Gurney D. B.   Abington
Reed A. S. & Co. North Abington, "
Ellis John,   Acushnet
Hamlin Samuel B.   "
Lund Jonathan P.   "
Morse George P. & Co.   "
Stoddard Augustus R.   Alford
Barrett A.   Ashby
Ashby William M.   Bedford
Bruce D. B.   Belchertown
Pratt & Randall,   "
Shumway J. R.   "
Weston Jeremiah,   "
Felton Henry O.   Berlin
Wright L. B.   Bernardston
Chase ——,   Billerica
Dayton Milo,   Blandford
Harger D.   "
Sawyer John F.   Bolton
Andrews Dean,   Boxford
Ray Tertullus, Boylston Centre, Boylston
Morgan Thomas J.   Brimfield
Draper J. W. East Brimfield, "
Fosket Rufus,   Parksville, "
Burbank Charles, Warren, "
Rice Bros.   Brookfield
Bent John,   Carver
Holmes Jacob,   "
Savery William (steam),   "
Cole H. G.   North Carver, "
Cushman Stephen, South " "
Howard David, E. Charlemont, Charlemont
Fitts Bradley,   Charlton
Call Charles,   Coleraine
Fay Wm. E.   Conway
Barrows Harrison,   Dana
          Dartmouth
Cummings Benj. T., North Dartmouth, "
Wallis John,   Douglas
Goulding Henry,   Dover
Kingsbury J. D. & Co.   Dudley
Cummings Doctor A. Dunstable
Keene Isaac, West Duxbury, Duxbury
Phillips & Co.   East Bridgewater
Pratt Amos,   Easton
Slater Samuel, S. Egremont, Egremont
Cadwell A. J.   Enfield
Swift River Manufacturing Co. "
Ward Benjamin,   "
POND VIRGIL S.   Foxborough
Wilmarth Kinsley,   "
Wilson John D.   Freetown
Gurney & Chace, East Freetown, "
Rounseville & Allen, " "
Tenny Moses & Son, Georgetown
Carver William,   Granby
Johnson J. W. E. Granville, Granville
Gilmore B. F.   Great Barrington
Barnes Elnathan,   "
Kilbourn Mark,   "
         Greenwich
Parker Daniel, Greenwich Village, "

E. Carver Co.   Halifax
  Porter Chipman, "
Barstow Edwin W.   Hanover
Wilder Cushing,   "
Monroe Ethan, E. Bridgewater, Hanson
Chandler D. C. South Hanson, "
Leavitt & Keene, " "
Perry E. Y. & Co., South Hanover, "
Howard Geo. C.   Hardwick
Presho & Frye,   "
Southworth Constant, "
Spooner Bros.   "
Broad Ira,   Holden
Bryant L.   "
Howe Nathan,   "
Butterworth T. D.   Holland
Gordon Frank,   "
Marcy G.   "
Brigham O. S.   Hubbardston
Conant L.   "
Hale & Williams,   "
Heald T. S.   "
Tilton E.   "
Searle Spencer,   Huntington
Bradford Orrin W.   Kingston
Chandler David,   "
Chandler Ira,   "
Prince & Bryant,   "
Davis Charles J.   Lakeville
Hinds Sumner,   "
Richmond Eleazer,   "
Westgate C. T.   "
Beebe Levi, South Lee, Lee
Ball O.   Leverett
Field Harrison,   "
Ripley Eben, North Leverett, "
Coolidge Charles,   Leyden
Hall H. W.   "
Carver Henry,   Ludlow
Fuller E. W.   "
Plumley Elijah, Collins Depot, "
Moran & Sons,   Mansfield
Parlow C. H. & E. S. Marion
Holmes & Sparrow, Mattapoisett, "
Chandler Simeon B. Marshfield
Dunham Henry C.   "
Eames Wm. East Marshfield, "
Bolles S. E.   Mattapoisett
Dexter E. & Son,   "
Cowan & Macomber,   "
Ellis Jarvis,   "
Tinkham Clark,   "
Taft Thomas,   Mendon
Ripley E.   Montague
Hadsell John K.   Monterey
Langdon John H.   "
Axtell H. K.   Montgomery
Dewey Josiah, New Ashford
Pepper H. A. New Braintree
      New Marlborough
Allen & Rood,   Hartsville
Chapin Albert, Mill River, "
Coolidge N. B.   New Salem
Crowle Joel,   "
       Northampton
BANISTER EDWIN, (dealer), "
Bartlett Wm, A. 2d, Northborough
Smith J. W.   "
Jeffrey Elisha, North Reading
Arnold George H.   Norton
Lincoln Eddy,   "
Lane A. D. & A.   "
Dean David R.   Oakham
Parker Daniel M. Cold Brook, "
Childs B. W.   Oxford
Harrington William, Paxton
Gold Miner,   Pelham
Chandler & Bourne, Pembroke

Mention George A.   Pepperell
Sartell Levi,   "
Powers Edward,   Phillipston
BARNES E. & J. C. (see page 717),
Water st.   Plymouth
Andrews S. L.   Plympton
Bonney J. S.   "
Hills & Westcott,   Amherst,   Prescott
Barrows H.   North Dana,   "
Davis Daniel, jr.   Princeton
Miles D. C. & Co.   "
Wilder Mark,   East Princeton,   "
Hall Ellis B.   Raynham
Tracy John,   "
Wilbur Emery S.   "
Wilbur Oliver S.   "
Baker Samuel,   Rehoboth
Guy Jabez K.   "
Martin Hiram W.   "
Perry Otis,   "
Place Thomas,   "
Gifford Abraham,   Rochester
King & Hathaway,   "
Rounseville Alden, jr.   "
Smellie Walter G.   "
Kendrick H. A.   Rowe
Dummer Nathl. N.   Rowley
Munroe James L.   Rutland
Reid Charles E.   "
Roper Samuel,   "
Homer & Briant,   North Rutland,   "
Ware Caleb A.   West   "   "
Webster R. A.   South Sandisfield
Clapp Thomas,   Scituate
Bailey H. & Co. North Scituate,   "
Burr Raymond H.   Seekonk
Taft William P.   E. Sheffield,   Sheffield
Peck Abner,   Shelburne
Smead S.   "
Richmond Deal,   Shelburne Falls,   "
Kilburn Jonathan,   Shirley
Ober Henry,   Shutesbury
Ober Joseph,   "
Pratt E. L.   "
Stetson Wm. B.   "
Hatch Leonard,   South Scituate
Gilbert E.   Southwick
Dewey E.   "
Hastings F. C.   "
Myrick & Sugden,   Spencer
Newhall Otis,   "
Snow C.   "
Bemis Solon L.   Sterling
Pratt James A.   Pratts Junction,   "
Allen Ethan,   Sturbridge
Wight George,   "
Bates & Adams,   Fiskdale,   "
Gerry E. A.   Sudbury
Burdon Ames,   Sutton
Hooker V. G.   "
Bourn & Brooks,   Templeton
Leland W. E.   "
Gifford Charles,   Tisbury
Rolfe H. C.   Townsend
Larkin E. A.   "
Fisk Luther,   Upton
Taft P. P.   "
Marcy H. P.   Wales
Peck Ira,   "
Shaw Daniel,   "
Warner W. W.   West Boylston
Alger Cyrus,   West Bridgewater
Eddy & Hayward,   "
Pierce M.   West Brookfield
Smith Geo.   Westminister
Sanderson Luther D.   Whately
     Wilbraham
Beebe, Hunt, & Stanton, S. Wilbraham

Chaffee Daniel, S. Wilbraham, Wilbraham
Cole Porter R.   Williamstown
Brown Silas,   Wilmington
Wentworth Samuel,   "

Ship Agents.
(See Passenger Agents.)

Ship Block Manufacturers.
(See Pump & Block Makers.)

Ship Builders.

Eldredge Oliver,   Chatham
Hall Isaac,   Cohasset
Mashow John,   S. Dartmouth,   Dartmouth
Shiverick Asa,   E. Dennis,   Dennis
Keene Nathl. P.   Duxbury
Paulding William,   "
Lewis George,   Edgartown
Burnham Aaron O.   Essex
Burnham Ebenezer,   "
Burnham Jeremiah,   "
Burnham Luke,   "
Burnham Oliver,   "
Burnham W. R. & Co.   "
Burnham & Story,   "
James & McKenzie,   "
Story Job,   "
Story Joseph & Co.   "
Blackler Wm. G.   Fairhaven
TERRY J. C., Rodman's wharf, Fall River
FRISBEE & STORY,   Gloucester
Parkhurst Charles,   "
Davis E. jr.   E. Gloucester,   "
Holmes Edward,   Kingston
Choate Edward W.   Ipswich
Choate Lewis,   "
Clark William,   Marion
Delano John,   "
Barstow N. H, & H.   Mattapoisett
Cannon Brothers,   "
Holmes Josiah, jr. & Bro.   "
Curtis James O.   Medford
Foster J. T.   "
Hayden & Cudworth,   "
Blackler W. G.   New Bedford
Chaney Ephraim,   "
Chase Abraham,   "
Damon Samuel & Co.   "
Edwards & Soule,   "
Howland John W.   "
Mashow John,   "
Atkinson & Fillmore,   Newburyport
Colby & Lunt,   "
Currier Charles H. & Co.   "
Currier John J.   "
Manson Eben,   "
McQuillon J. H. P.   "
WHITCOMB JOHN G.   Provincetown
Jones P. F.   Quincy Point,   Quincy
Thomas George H.   "
Brown Joshua,   Salem
Miller Edward F.   "
Burnham Cyrus,   Salisbury
Hardy S.   "
Keniston F. & Co., Salisbury Point,   "
Briggs James S., North Scituate, Scituate
Barstow & Waterman,   Hanover,   "
Davis David P.   Somerset
Cannon John C.   Tisbury

Ship Carpenters.
(See also Carpenters; also Ship Joiners.)

Brown George,   Fairhaven
Delano Moses,   "
Fish Reuben,   "
Lewis Samuel J.

Ship Carpenters — continued.
TERRY J. C., Rodman's whf., Fall River
Andrews H. N. & Co. Gloucester
Davis Bros. "
Parkhurst & Allen, "
Baker L. New Bedford
Bowen Wm. P. '
Bray Wm. "
Brown Benjamin C. "
Chaney Ephraim, "
Chase Abraham, "
Damon Samuel, "
Edwards & Soule, "
Howland John, "
Mashow John, "
Cox Wm. R. Plymouth
Kendrick Asa, "
COLLINS ISAAC, Provincetown
Hopkins Nathaniel, "
WHITCOMB JOHN G. "
Hamond Wm. C. Salem
Hopkins Giles, Wellfleet
Hopkins Hiram, "
Snow N. "

Ship Chandlers.

Carey J. B. Charlestown
Cobb G. W. & Son, Dighton
BROWN D. & SON (see page 729),
ft. Central st. Fall River
HAWKINS & KILHAM (see page
718), Slade's Wharf, "
Corliss Benj. H. Gloucester
Calder Timothy W. Nantucket
Davis, Eldredge, & Kenney, "
Eldredge K. & Co. "
Macy Joseph B. "
Baylies & Cannon, New Bedford
BROWNELL WILLIAM O. 10, 12,
and 14 Front, "
Kirby H. S. "
Knowles John P., 2d. "
Parker Wm. G. "
SULLINGS & KINGMAN, 123 Union, "
Swift & Allen, "
Taber, Gordon, & Co. "
Watkins William, "
Boardman W. D. Newburyport
Coker Stephen, "
Woodwell D. T. "
Atwood John, jr. & Co. Provincetown
BOWLEY J. E. & G. "
Conwell David, "
Cook E. & E. K. "
COOK H. & S. & CO. "
Cook Stephen, "
Freeman & Hilliard, "
Lewis B. A. & Co. "
MAYO ISAAC F. "
NICKERSON R. E. & A. & CO. "
Paine J. & L. N. "
Rich S. & J. "
SMALL E. E. "
UNION WHARF CO. "
Boynton Eleazer, Rockport
GOODHUE WM. P., 44 Derby st. Salem
Tucker H. N (jib-hanks), Stoughton
STAPLES & PHILLIPS, 27 W. Wa-
ter (see page 759), Taunton
Baker N. M. & Co. Wellfleet
Central Trading Co. "
HIGGINS J. R. & CO. "
Newcomb, Kemp, & Co. "

Ship Joiners.

(See also Ship Carpenters.)
Barstow Henry W. Mattapoisett
Baker Lorenzo, New Bedford

Brown Benjamin C. New Bedford
Damon Doane W. "
Hathaway Lewis, "
Look John, "
Bruce P. D. "
Evans Winthrop O. & Co. Newburyport
Sampson Wm. G. "
Hamond Wm C. Salem
Hood David B. "

Shippers of Ice.

COOK & DURFEE, N. Main, cor.
Central (see page 757), Fall River

Shipping Offices.

New Bedford
MAUCH HERMAN, 33½ S. Water, "
TUCKER HENRY R. 39 and 41
North Water, "
Griffin E. & J. S. Salem

Shipsmiths.

(See also Blacksmiths.)
Cole Luther, Fairhaven
Raymond & Webb, "
Babbitt Isaac, Fall River
Damon John, "
Hinkley Nathaniel, "
Voss Adolph & Brother, Gloucester
Harvey George, "
Drew Job W. Kingston
Washburn Martin, "
Barton James, New Bedford
Butts Peleg & Son, "
Dean & Driggs, "
Dean Henry N. "
Durfee James, "
Macy E. B. & P. "
Sawyer & Read, "
Snow James M. "
Adams Joseph C. Newburyport
Kenniston J. & J. R. "
Moody Henry T. "
Pettigrew Charles D. "
Raymond E. S. Plymouth
Shaw Ichabod, "
Hartford R. C. Provincetown
Small I. A. "
Snow A. D. "
TAYLOR AMASA, "
Ward & Alexander, "
Allen N. P. Salem
Nichols J. Henry, "
Nichols John, "
Grant M. W. Wellfleet

Ship Tank Builder.

Coffin Wm. S. (wood), Newburyport

Shipwrights and Calkers.

(See also Calkers and Gravers.)
Frisby & Story, Gloucester

Ships' Wheels.

Peckham P. M. Fall River
Leavitt A. L. Hingham
Pearson Alonzo, Newburyport
Holmes George H. Provincetown

Shirt Manufacturers.

*(See also Collar Manufacturers; also Gents'
Furnishing Goods; also Hosiery.)*
Braintree
Morrison A. & Sons (also drawers), "
PALMER H. A. (see page 794), Lynn
Edwards W. & E. (fancy flannel,
South Natick, Natick

Fewey H. S.   Springfield
Wilson W. H.   Worcester

Shirt, Drawer, and Stocking Boards.

TROWBRIDGE & KIMBALL, Wamesit Steam Mills (see page 738),   Lowell

Shoddy Manufacturers.

Wilcox & Co.,   Millville,   Blackstone
Ray F. B.   Franklin
Ray J. P. & J. G.   "
Wawbeek Mills (wool), Geo. Church,
 tress. Housatonic,   Great Barrington
McAllister William,   Lawrence
Kent D. W.,   Cherry Valley,   Leicester
Parsons Charles E.   Malden
Mansfield Woolen Co.   Mansfield
Eaton Edward,   Medway
                                   Newton
Cordingley W. S. & F., Lower Falls.   "
Newton D. A.,   Otter River,   Templeton
Keith J. C.   Uxbridge
Sayles & Taft,   "
LEWIS WILLARD,   Walpole
BUELL S. K. (see page 781),   Worcester
Ray F. B.   "
Ray Frank B.   N. Wrentham, Wrentham

Shoes.

(For every thing connected with this business, not printed here, see Boots and Shoes.)

Shoe Kit Manufacturer.

(See also Boot and Shoe Findings.)

PACKARD SUMNER (awls and shaves, see page 762), N. E. Vill. Grafton

Shoe Nail and Tack Manufs.

(See also Tack, Brad, and Shoe Nail Manufacturers: also Boot and Shoe Findings, &c.)

BRIGHAM, WHITMAN, & CO. (see page 712),   S. Abington,   Abington
DIGHTON TACK CO. (see page 715),   Dighton
STETSON & TALBOT (see page 732),   Holliston
MILLAY P. E. (see page 761),   Hudson
ANTHONY & CUSHMAN (see page 722),   Taunton
FIELD A. & SONS (see page 719), 22 Spring,   "
TAUNTON TACK CO., Thomas J. Lothrop, agent and treasurer, 26 Union (see page 720),   "

Shoe Thread.

MORSE E. J. W. & CO. (Sea Island cotton, bank and spool, see page 749),   South Easton,   Easton

Shoe Tips.

                                   New Bedford
Ripley Shoe Tip Co. (leather),   "

Shoe Tools.

(See Boot and Shoe Tools and Findings.)

Shook Manufacturers.

                                   Middleborough
HARLOW I. H. & CO. (see page 768).   "

Shoulder-brace Manuf.

CUTTER & WALKER, 48 Central,   Lowell

Shovel Manufacturers.

(See also Agricultural Implements.)

AMES OLIVER & SONS, North Easton,   Easton
                                   Middleborough
BROWN & SHERMAN (see p. 803),   "
Jones Thomas J.   Peabody
OLD COLONY IRON CO. Charles Robinson, agent,   Taunton

Shuttle Manufacturers.

(See also Bobbin Manufacturers.)

Blackinton W. & Sons,   Attleborough
Richardson O. P.   "
Coburn Shuttle Co.   Lowell
JAQUES JOHN S. & CO. Wamesit Power Co. (see page 747),   "
Litchfield & Co. (shuttle and shuttle iron manufs.)   Southbridge
Dudley D. T. & Son,   Sutton
Pollard, Wilder, & Co.   Worcester

Sieve Makers.

(See also Wire Workers.)

Bigelow Chauncey,   Springfield
Bryant R. & Bros. (rims), W. Chesterfield,   Chesterfield

Sifting Machines.

Harris Samuel (patent for all sifting purposes),   Springfield

Silk Goods Manufacturers.

Mansfield G. H. & Co. (braids),   Canton
NONOTUCK SILK CO. (sewing and twist), H. L. Hill, treas. (see page 705), Florence,   Northampton
Johnson Wm. (weaver),   Tewksbury
Skinner William,   Williamsburg
Smith W. A. (braids, &c.)   Worcester
Hamilton C. W. & Co. (braids, &c.),   "

Silver Burnisher.

Clark William, N. Attleboro' Attleborough

Silver-Plated Goods.

Folsom A. B.   Athol Depot, Athol
Ames Manufacturing Co. George Arms, agent,   Chicopee
                                   Chelsea
KNOX BENJ. H. & CO. 45 & 47 Park,   "
GLEASON ROSWELL & SONS, Dorchester
Smith E. A. & D. T.   Salem
Springfield Silver Plate Co.   Springfield
Porter Britannia & Plate Co.   Taunton
Eldridge & Co.   "
REED & BARTON (see page 758),   "

Silver Platers.

                                   Amesbury
Sargent Willis P.,   South Amesbury,   "
Short & Nerney (electro),   Attleborough
Barnes Lemuel,   Charlestown
MUNSON J. M. (see page 716),   Greenfield
PHELPS WM.   Mansfield
SCHOONMAKER D. Taylor st. Springfield
Warner J. N.   "
REED & BARTON (see page 758). Taunton
Fales Ablather,   E. Templeton, Templeton
Harwood E. A. & Co.   Worcester
Jennings H. J. (electro),   "

Silversmiths.

                                   Attleborough
Whiting Manuf. Co. N. Attleborough.   "
Sanborn Amos & Co.   Lowell
Pitman Benjamin,   New Bedford
Gard Thomas D.   Worcester

Silver Ware.

WRUCK F. A. 105 Essex (see page 748),   Salem

Skate Manufacturers.

Murphy J. & R.   Mansfield
Barney & Berry,   Springfield
Winslow S. C. & S.   Worcester

Skate Spur Manufacturers.

SOUTHWICK & HASTINGS,   Worcester

Skirt and Skirt Hoop Manufs.

(See Hoop Skirts.)

Slate Dealers.

Lunt Daniel,   Newbury
                                        Pittsfield
CLOUGH WILLARD (roofing slate),   "

Slaters.

(See also Roofing.)

Jenks Porter J.   South Adams,   Adams
Pease William,   "   "
Blevins John,   Cambridge
Howe Timothy,   East Cambridge,   "
Howe John & Brother,   Chelsea
Goulding Robert,   Lowell
Waugh John,   "
Raynor William,   Northampton
Fowler George & Co.   Salem
Pinnock Thomas,   "

Slipper Manufacturers.

                                        Weymouth
BEALS AUGUSTUS, N. Weymouth,   "
WESSON M.   Springfield

Smoked Halibut.

DODD, TARR, & CO. (see page 732),
    East Gloucester,   Gloucester

Snuff Manufacturers.

(See also Tobacconists.)

Larkin & Morrill,   Newbury
Sweetser Brothers,   Cliffondale, . Saugus
Bond C. M. jr.   "   "
Howlett John,   Saugus Centre,   "

Soap and Candle Manufs.

Chase John N.   North Adams,   Adams
Stiles Martin (candles),   "   "
Hildreth G. M.   Beverly
Day John A.   Bradford
Drake Francis, East Brookfield, Brookfield
                                        Cambridge
Brazier & Whittemore, Cambridgeport,   "
Cooper Charles & Son,   "   "
Cooper Wm. & Son,   "   "
Davis Curtis,   "   "
Davis T. M.   "   "
Jones C. L. & Co.   "   "
Kemp Lysander,   "   "
Reardon John & Sons,   "   "
Tobacco Soap Co.   "   "
THE AM. PEERLESS, Broadway,   "
Livermore N. & Son, East Cambridge,   "
Rand & Ryan,   Charlestown   "
Sargent & Co.   "
Kingsbury E. G. & Co.   Chelsea
NORRIS WM. H. Second st.   "
PARMENTER & LAWSON (Russian
    cleansing),   "
Perkins & Davis,   "
Sargent ——,   "
Holt H. M. & Co.   Dorchester
Dixon George S.   Enfield
ANTHONY J. S. & CO. (see page 755),
    57 Pleasant,   Fall River
Hargraves Manuf. Co.   "
Remington Joshua,   Fitchburg
Sabin & Cowdin,   "
Bacon Martin,   Framingham
Marchant & Shepherd,   Gloucester
Coombs Walter,   Greenfield
Pratt Isaac,   South Hanson,   Hanson
Beach & Wentworth,   Haverhill
Gleason S. B.   Holden
Evans Green,   Kingston

Beach L. & Son,   Lawrence
Cheeney R. B.   Lee
Horn Samuel & Co.   Lowell
McAloon A.   "
Putnam & Currier,   "
Walker Geo P.   "
Emery George E.   Lynn
Hanson Joseph,   "
Marsh G. E. & Co.   "
PALMER J. R.   Marlborough
WELCH S. A. & BRO.
Conant Winslow,   Marshfield
Hammond Wm.   Mattapoisett
Fletcher James,   Milford
Aldrich H. W.   Millbury
Gibbs Chas. H.   Nantucket
Stevens George W.   "
SISSON OTIS A. 26 Middle, New Bedford
Smith & Varley,   "
Whittemore Z.   "
Blake Frederic W. (soap powders), Newbury
Jaques B. H.   Newburyport
Jaques Joseph N.   "
Stanwood A. & Co.   "
Sawyer Amos,   Northampton
Rice Curtis,   Northborough
Merritt Geo.   North Bridgewater
Burbeck John C.   Peabody
Hildreth Paul,   "
Winchester Perez L.   "
Noble Wm. jr.   Pittsfield
Warren Stephen,   "
Bartlett William,   West Rutland, Rutland
Robertson Stratton W.   Salem
Little & Hurlburt,   Sheffield
Kenney A. & Co.   Southbridge
ARNOLD & LYON,   Springfield
Fisk L. I. & Co.   "
Foster Henry,   "
Sawyer J. A.   Stoughton
Smith & Drake,   "
Field H. & J.   Taunton
TAUNTON SOAP AND OIL CO.
    (soaps of all kinds). E. W. Cross-
    man, agent (see page 723),   "
Lalley John,   Upton
Meacham G. A.   Watertown
Alger Cyrus,   West Bridgewater
Sharon Edward,   Westminster
Thompson James (tallow chandler),
                       East Woburn,   Woburn
RUGG GEO. W. 33 Grafton,   Worcester

Soap-stone Manufacturers.

Groton Soap-stone Co. Daniel McCaine,
    agent,   Groton Centre, Groton

Soda-Water Manufacturers.

Patten M. B.   Charlestown
Kay James,   Fall River
Allen G. S.   "
Sowle Resolved,   "
Winn & Parker,   Gloucester
Heald Wm E.   Lawrence
Bartlett. Moody, & Co.   Lowell
HEALD M. C. 114 S. Common (see
    page 714),   Lynn
Wheaton & Brownell,   New Bedford
Billings J. & Co.   Pittsfield
BROOKS F. A. (see page 778), Springfield
Hewett G. F.   Worcester

Spar Makers.

(See also Mast Makers.)

JONES WILLIAM,   Gloucester
SOMES JOHN J.   "
COLLINS ISAAC,   Provincetown

Spectacle Manufacturers.

(See also Opticians.)

Vinton & Edmonds,   Lowell
Skerry H. F. & Son,   Salem
Cole Robert H. & Co.   Southbridge
Arumblown H. C. & Co.
Burbank . D.   Springfield
Chandler S. F.   Worcester

Spice Mills.

(See also Coffee and Spice Mills.)

Stickney & Poor, Charlestown
SLADE D. & L. (see page 718), 190 Broadway. Chelsea
CHAMBERLAIN & BAKER, Union, cor. Exchange (see page 786), Worcester

Spike Manufacturers.

NEW BEDFORD COPPER CO. (wrought, see page 757), New Bedford
OLD COLONY IRON CO., Chas. Robinson, agent, . Taunton

Spindle Manufacturers.

HALL RICHARD & CO. Canal, east of Union (see page 746), Lawrence
HEAVEN JESSE, Canal, east of Union, "
LAWRENCE FLIER AND SPINDLE WORKS; Henry P. Chandler, supt., Canal, East of Union, "

Spirit Levels.

Stevens J. & Co. Chicopee Falls, Chicopee

Spoke Manufacturers.

(See also Carriage Spokes.)

VAUGHN J. N. E. Brookfield, Brookfield
Archibald E. A. Methuen
Plimpton W. P. & Co. Southbridge
Fitch & Winn, Worcester

Spoke-shaves and Wrenches.

Bliss Renssalaer, North Brookfield

Spool Manufacturers.

(See Bobbins.)

Spool Cotton Manufs.

(See also Cotton Thread.)

NIANTIC THREAD CO. Fall River
HADLEY CO. Holyoke
WARREN THREAD CO. Grove st. (see page 716), Worcester

Spoons and Forks Manufs.

REED & BARTON (see p. 758), Taunton

Sprain Liniment.

SWEET JOB, Kempton, cor. Summer (see page 712), New Bedford

Spring Makers.

(See Carriage Springs.)

Spring-Bed Manufacturers.

Howe Tyler, Cambridge
Pettingill & Pear, Cambridgeport, "
American Spring-Bed Co, Springfield
Excelsior Spring-Bed Co., C. J. Leonard, agent, "
UNITED STATES SPRING-BED CO. Taylor st. "

Stables.

Folsom H. Abington
Whiting William H. "
Burrell Adney, East Abington, "
Nason W. P. " "
Shaw Jacob, 2d, " "
Wood George, " "
Bates E. R. North Abington, "
Shaw Jacob 2d, " "
Whitmarsh J. F. L. " "
Hersey Jason, South " "
Cutter John E. Acton
Dow Levi, South Acton, "
Hersom Thomas, Acushnet
Anthony E. & Co. Adams
Millimam A. J. "
Smith Henry D. "
Benton Hiram C. North Adams, "

Clark Earl, North Adams, Adams
Crandall Chas. E. (boarding), " "
Flagg James H. " "
Wilbur John, " "
Collins William, Amesbury
Cummings William, "
Gunnison Isaac, "
Rowell George, "
Tuttle Charles, "
Gowen Frank, Salisbury Point, "
Aldrich C. P. Amherst
Stebbins Wm. E. "
Whitney E. P. "
Curtin E. North Amherst, "
Bean S. G. (transient and sale), Andover
Burtt Henry. "
Carter Charles, "
Cornell John, "
Wardwell J. W. "
Currier W. C. Arlington
Foster George C. Ashburnham
Wetherbee Marshall, "
Clark John & Co. Ashland
Scott William A. & Son, "
Lee James M. Athol
BANGS ADOLPHUS, Athol Depot, "
Moore Chandler W. " "
Southland H. H. " "
CAPRON D. H. Attleborough
Edwards S. C. N. Attleborough, "
Eldridge W. & E. H. Barnstable
Holmes Oliver, "
Crosby G. Centreville, "
Hallet John, Hyannis, "
Hallet Lot, " "
Carter Porter, Barre
Smith & Holland, "
Corey Charles C. Bedford
Putnam William A. "
Owen W. C. Belchertown
Southwick P. B. Berlin
Batchelder Ezra, Beverly
Green J. W. Billerica
Taft Miles, Blackstone
Bacon E. O. "
Wheelock A. A. "
Penniman L. S. "
Robinson William W. Bolton
Hovey Orville D. Boxford
Kimball Jefferson, "
Morse Eben, Bradford
Woodsum Rufus, S. Braintree, Braintree
Howes S. T. Brewster
Hull Warren G. Bridgewater
Keith Thomas. "
KING FRANK D. "
Howe Albert, Brighton
Willis John D. "
Giffin & Livermore, Brookfield
Hallowell R. East Brookfield, "
Bowler Joshua, Brookline
Morse Eben, "
Parker Frank E. "
Fairbanks Joseph B. V. Cambridgeport, Cambridge
Pike James, " "
Pike J. S. " "
Stearns James, " "
Daly George E. " "
Hunting Henry E. " "
Smith Henry D. " "
Dailey William, East Cambridge, "
Daily U. J. " "
Buxton G. H. North Cambridge, "
Leonard George, Canton
Stratton David, "
Porter Joseph N. Charlemont
Bariaut & Shaw, Charlestown
Barnard John P. "
Chapman William H. "
Dearborn John B. "
Harris & Hollis, "
Maynard Bros. "
Moore & Rideout, "
Wiley William S. & Geo. O. "
Small Elisha, Chatham
Ward Charles. "
Holt George B. Chelmsford
Bartlett John W. Chelsea
Green James S. "

Stables — continued.

Lazzells W. H.
Belden Everett M.   Chester
Hatch Edward,   Chicopee
Wait Albert A.   "
Wait Alonzo,   "
Blake William,   Chicopee Falls, "
Morton Morris,   "
Howard G. F.   "
Laythe & Lyon,   Clinton
Smith T. M.   "
Denison George B.   Cohasset
Scott H. O. & Co.   Coleraine
Brown George,   "
Todd George W.   Concord
Pease Solomon & Henry,   "
Kimball E.   Conway
Shattuck Wesley W.   Dalton
Tapley John W.   North Dana, Dana
Davis Jos. T., So. Dartmouth, Dartmouth
Carroll Sanford,   Danvers
Kennedy & McClane,   Dedham
Hall Chas. O.   East Dedham, "
Twitchell C. P.   South   "
Stone S. J.   Deerfield
Ware John,   "
Warren William,   South Deerfield, "
Chapman Howes,   Dennis
Baker E. S.   West Dennis, "
Crowell Sears.   "
Whitmarsh Charles E.   Dighton
Dunbar George,   N. Dighton, "
Holden Franklin,   Dorchester
Wheelock A. P.   "
Goss Abel,   Harrison sq. "
Weeman M. F.   Mattapan, "
Brock & Crane,   Milton, "
Crane Henry,   "
Pratt Jefferson,   Neponset, "
Thayer E. T.   East Douglas, Douglas
Goodhue Carlos A.   Dracut
Sampson E. S.   Duxbury
Brewster Charles,   "
Sampson Eden,   "
Griffin Alfred,   East Bridgewater
Harding George W.   "
Waterman John,   "
Horton A. M.   Eastham
Alvord & Strong,   Easthampton
Knapp H. F.   "
Shaw & Jepson,   "
Bump Wm. E. jr.   North Easton, Easton
Fecto P. William,   "
White Sanford,   "
Pease John,   Edgartown
Wells E. G.   Enfield
Burnett H. F. & Co.   Erving
Lowe Edward,   Essex
Story George Washington,   "
Dunham R. A. & Co.   Fairhaven
Cole William,   Fall River
Dunmore & Blake,   "
KIRBY ELIHU, 36 Pleasant, "
Kirby Charles S.   "
Payne Job F.   "
Slocum Mark A.   Fall River
Hewins William,   Falmouth
Dadman & Co.   Fitchburg
Dole Samuel M. & Edward B.   "
Costello Wm.   Foxborough
Leach Emery,   "
Parker Orra,   Framingham
GLAZIER MARSHALL, Saxonville, "
Goodnow J. W.   "
Twitchell S.   South Framingham, "
De Witt H. S.   Franklin
Thayer B. Lyman,   "
Hathaway Samuel C.   Freetown
Johnson Daniel L.   "
Hill Edwin,   Gardner
Sawin L. C. & S.   "
Fairbanks A. E.   South Gardner, "
Kimball Nelson & Co.   Georgetown
Spofford & Adams,   "
Hilton David H.   Gloucester
James George,   "
Shaw Edward H.   "
WEBSTER NATHANIEL,   "
Colby Stuart H.   Annisquam, "
Griffin O. E.   "

Dennen Levi,   Lanesville, Gloucester
Vinton Silas,   Grafton
Fairbanks D. G.   N. E. Village, "
Gray Loring,   "
Brazer O.   Great Barrington
Tillotson G. D.   "
Burr E. W.   Greenfield
JOSLYN & KIMBALL,   "
Simons S.   "
Waite Lyman,   "
Wood Henry S.   "

Fletcher Charles H.   Groton Junction, Groton
Pemberton John.   "
Somers Richard F.   Groveland
Howard Franklin,   Hanover
Sherman William S.   "
White Joseph.   "
Jerome William,   Hanson
Torman Henry K.   Hardwick
Willard F. A.   Harvard
Young Simeon,   Harwich
Baker J. A.   Harwich Port, "
Clark Elisha,   "
Shumway H. & O. C.   Hatfield
Langley Thomas & Co.   Haverhill
Richards Wm. B.   "
Sawyer William,   E. Haverhill, "
Bailey Caleb,   Hingham
Bassett George,   "
Cushing George,   "
Wilder E.   "
Goodridge Charles W.   Hinsdale
Tuttle John M.   "
O'Connell Dennis D.   Holliston
Shippee J. D.   "
Prentess R. T. & Co.   Holyoke
Shea Michael,   "
Wellington Thomas H.   "
Hayden L. B.   Hopkinton
Morse James O.   "
Thayer S. F.   "
Coolidge E. J.   Woodville, "
Felton G. W.   "
Morse J. Q.   Hubbardston
Fairbank Omar,   Hudson
POPE DANIEL,   "
Parks & Laflewer,   Huntington
Adams H. C.   Hyde Park
COFFIN O. C.   "
Brown W. G.   Ipswich
Cushman Josiah,   Kingston
Foster Alexander B.   "
Harris Josiah,   Lancaster
Bailey M. A.   Lawrence
Brewster A. R.   "
Churchill A.   "
DEARBORN C. C. & SON, 259 Oak, "
Leavitt D. G.   "
Porter John W. & Co.   "
Stowell & Spalding,   "
Woodburn C. T.   "
Snow Marshall S.   Leicester
Canwell James,   Clappville, "
Upham Lyman,   Cherry Valley, "
Curtis W. O   Lenox
Pierce, Robbins, & Parker,   Leominster
Harrington Franklin M.   Lexington
Butters George,   Lowell
Cohant Julius E.   "
Going Charles,   "
Hadley John,   "
Leavitt Daniel G.   "
Morse H. O.   "
Norris George W.   "
Perry J. B.   "
Scott A. (sale),   "
Seaver J. C.   "
Derby Andrew,   Lunenburg
Brown & Pollard,   Lynn
Breed & Selman,   "
Bucknam T. J.   "
Dorr Moody,   "
Goldthwaite James W.   "
Harris Nathaniel S.   "
Ingalls Benjamin J. R.   "
Mower Amos E.   "
Thompson Edmund B.   "
Roundy Wm. R.   Lynnfield Centre, Lynnfield

Clark & Cutter,	Malden	White Lorenzo,	Whitinsville,	Northbridge
Jackson David F.	"	Smith George,	"	"
Pratt John W.	"	Bennett E. E.		North Bridgewater
Brown Andrew,	Manchester	Holmes George N.		"
Peabody Abijah,	"	Porter A. S.		"
Belcher C. W.	Mansfield	Rogers Harrison,		"
Cobb E. C. & A. W.	"	Tinkham O. G.		"
Wheeler George L.	"	Cole Charles,		Campello, "
Perkins Enoch A.	Marblehead	Bush Charles A.		North Brookfield
Lovell A. & Co.	Marion	Duncan James,		"
Brown & Brigham,	Marlborough	Fenno Henry A.		North Chelsea
Pattison Lawson B.	"	Short John H.		Norton
Onthank W. H.	"	Adams & Whitney,		Orange
Dunham Henry C.	Marshfield	Stone Seth J.		"
Hatch F. W.	"	Hurd Davis,		Orleans
Parker Alonzo B.	Medfield	Rosebrooks W. F.		Oxford
BLANCHARD SAMUEL & SON,		Page J.		Palmer
High st.	Medford	Shaw E. B.		"
Fuller Wm. H.	Medway	Weeks J. W.		"
Green Asa A.	"	Abbott Simon C.		Paxton
Adams John,	West Medway, "	Mower & Davis,		Peabody
Bancroft John,	" "	Williams Luther F.		Pepperell
White Wm.	" "	Tarbell Thomas F.,	E. Pepperell,	"
Anderson John L.	Melrose	Babcock Frederick G.		Pittsfield
Boardman Warren,	"	Bates W. G.		"
Adams David,	Mendon	Bridges James A.		"
Corliss Varnum,	Methuen	Chapman & Barden,		"
Low John,	"	Dolen Asahel,		"
Cole James. jr.	Middleborough	Nash Harvey L. (also sale),		"
Fuller Marcus,	"	Bartlett Stephen,		Plymouth
PENNIMAN P. E.	"	Chandler Albert C.		"
Vaughn S. H.	"	Churchill Fred. L.		"
Edwards Michael W.	Milford	Drew George A.		"
Hayes Martin,	"	Parker James S.		"
Underwood J. jr.	"	Stewart John,		"
Boardman A.	Millbury	Beaman P. A.		Princeton
Brown William,	"	Knowles John & Son,		Provincetown
Lovell W. F.	"	Nickerson & Jacobs,		"
Crossman Lemuel,	Milton	French Washington M.		Quincy
Carroll George O.	"	Hall John, jr.		"
Cushman Solomon F.	Monson	Prescott Abram,		"
Park H. H.	"	Cole Wm. jr.		Randolph
Wildes A. F.	Montague	Long John,		"
Hood Elbridge G.	Nahant	Leonard Richard A.		Raynham
Martin Charles W.	"	Litchfield Hiram,		Reading
Coffin Gardner,	Nantucket	Maynard William,		"
Hamblin Joseph,	"	Randall Stephen P.		Rockport
Morse Edward C.	"	Marchant Wm.	Pigeon Cove,	"
Clark A. J.	Natick	Boyden Augustus,		Rowley
Bailey Goin,	South Natick, "	Boynton John,		"
	Needham	Flint R. M.		Royalston
Eaton Geo. E. Newton Upper Falls,	"	LEAVITT J. S. rear Essex House,		Salem
McIntosh Wm. H.	"	Smith & Manning,		"
Allen William W.	New Bedford	Tuttle John,		"
Bailey & Perry,	"	Robbins Thomas A.		"
Bliss Samuel S.	"	Long William L.		Salisbury
Brownell Perry & Son,	"	Atkins T. F.		Sandwich
Brownell H. M. & Co.	"	BOYDEN WM. E.		"
Coffin W. H.	"	Howard Nathaniel,		"
Cook John S.	"	Torrey W S.		Scituate
Dwelly & Gifford,	"	Gannett Benjamin,		Sharon
Gifford David M,	"	Couillard H.,	Shelburne Falls,	Shelburne
Gray & Jones,	"	Terrett Charles W.		"
HATHAWAY JOHN M. 28 William,	"	Adams John,		Shirley
Sherman James H.	"	Plympton Henry A.		Shrewsbury
Sherman Wm. H.	"	Warren George H.		"
Wetherell D.	New Braintree	Hood Julius R.		Somerset
Boardman Greenleaf,	Newburyport	Simmons Bradford,		"
Dole Edward,	"	Wheaton William F.		"
LITTLE MOSES S., Merrimac House,	"	Sanborn Albert L.		Somerville
Lucy George,	"	Webster & White,		"
Ordway Charles H.	"	Cooper S. & Bro.	East Somerville,	"
Reinick John E.	"	O'Brien Patrick,		Southborough
Sargent H. P.	"	Bacon H. W.		Southbridge
	Newton	Keith W. J.	Globe Village,	"
Dudley E. C. & C. E. Newton Centre,	"	Chamberlain S.	" "	"
Settes & Ricker, " Corner,	"	Shepard A. H.	" "	"
Cate S. F. West Newton,	"	Judd Alfred,		South Hadley
Cate L. & Son, Lower Falls,	"	Kellogg & Judd,		"
Harrington Daniel, Newtonville,	"	Hatfield Horace,	S. Hadley Falls,	
Clark C. S. & Co.	Northampton	Eames Joshua,		Wakefield
Holley Jacob,	"	Bates Lorenzo,		South Scituate
Strong Ebenezer,	"	Kimball Oliver,	West Scituate,	"
Wood Ebenezer T. jr.	"	Gewan Joseph,		Spencer
Abercrombie Joel.	Florence, "	Tucker & Woodbury,		"
Graves Edwin & George,	" "	ALVORD E.		Springfield
Taylor L. C.	Leeds, "	Beckwith F.		"
McKone Edward,	North Andover	Briggs J. L.		"
Moore Lorenzo L.	Northborough	Collins William S.		"
Rice Charles A.	"	Donnelly Thomas,		"

Stables — continued.

Field M. D.	Springfield
Henry & Marsh,	"
Hosford A.	"
Patch E. H.	"
Richmond F. & J. M.	"
Robinson E. C.	"
Sexton & Nason,	"
Stickney C. R.	"
Talmadge S. J.	"
Wildes & Houston,	"
Fuller H. C.	Indian Orchard, "
Litchfield George A.	Sterling
Wight Abner S.	"
Darbe William,	Stockbridge
Berry Charles,	Stoneham
Leeds Joseph,	"
Powers W. H.	"
Atwood N. S.	Stoughton
Holmes John,	East Stoughton, "
Parker James,	Fiskdale, Sturbridge
Carter L.	Assabet, Sudbury
Harding James,	"
McDonough John,	Swampscott
Newhall & Knowlton,	"
Washburn John,	"
Hammond Isaac,	"
Harrub George & Co.	Taunton
Lane G.	"
Reilly A.	"
Read Joseph,	"
Wilde Samuel,	"
Seaver John H.	Templeton
Jackson & Brock,	East Templeton, "
Tamplin T. J.	Baldwinsville, "
Davis Charles W.	Otter River, "
Crocker R. W.	Holmes's Hole, Tisbury
Howland John W.	"
Norton Leavitt T.	"
Long Henry,	Topsfield
Davis Thomas,	West Townsend, Townsend
Warren Frank H.,	Townsend Centre, "
Clark Hiram,	Tyringham
Steadman Lawrence,	"
Ide Ira,	Upton
Wood Elijah B.	"
Newell C. S.	Uxbridge
Taylor John,	"
Fisk L. A.	Wales
Parker Luther,	Walpole
Hartshorn Charles H.	"
Pierce Mason,	"
Fuller James,	South Walpole, "
Cheney J. H.	Waltham
Davis R. H.	"
Kendall Levi J.	"
Ross Ansel,	Ware
Snow R. & Son,	"
Nickerson W. T.	Wareham
Hennessey Patrick,	"
Thompson David,	"
Peirce Nelson,	West Wareham, "
Hitchcock C. S.	Warren
Reed N. G.	West Warren, "
Albee Abner,	Warwick
Stockwell George B.	Watertown
Simpson L. B.	Wayland
Loker William,	Cochituate, "
Brown David A.	Webster
Day A. E.	"
Johnson J. R.	"
Joslin H. I.	"
Atwood Joshua,	Wellfleet
Hall Lot,	"
Holbrook Henry A.	"
Jacobs Thomas,	"
Bryant William H.	Wenham
Davis & Bullard,	Westborough
Thayer J. A.	"
Harper Augustus,	West Boylston
Rourke H. William,	West Bridgewater
Pratt Shepard L.	Cochesett, "
Gleason L.	West Brookfield
Rawson O. N.	"
Wood I. W.	"
Baber John C.	"
Grant C. W.	Westfield
Mallory Homer,	"
Moseley George,	"
Sackett & Cadwell,	"

Thomas Albert H.	Westfield
Cutler A. M.	Westminster
Bailey Wm. P.	West Newbury
Johnston Charles E.	"
Beckwith Henry, Jamaica Plain,	West Roxbury
Demond T., Mittineague,	West Springfield
Hare Joseph C.	West Stockbridge
Rogers L. E.	"
Cushing P. H.	Weymouth
Ford John,	"
White & Burrill,	"
Cushing M.	East Weymouth, "
Lovell James,	"
Raymond Enos D.	"
Pratt Elisha, North Weymouth,	"
Burrill Wm., South Weymouth,	"
Collins Levi,	"
Lathrop Frederic K., South Wilbraham,	Wilbraham
Loomis Luther & Son,	Williamsburgh
Shaw Henry W.	"
Williams Charles A. & Son,	"
Gavitt Marcus M.	Williamstown
Waterman J. M.	"
Morse J.	Winchendon
Whitcomb Henry,	"
Rand & Woods,	"
Winn A.	Winchester
Jones O. F.	Woburn
Porter T. J.	"
Bemis N. T. & Co.,	Worcester
Brown & Barnard,	"
Fairbrother Charles,	"
Harrington O. A.,	"
Howard Justin,	"
Howard S. T.,	"
Kendrick George P.,	"
Stockwell E. M.	"
Wheelock E. & Co.,	"
Farrington C. W.	Wrentham
Gilmore J. & W. K.	"
Ware Josiah, North Wrentham,	"
Hewes Freeman,	Yarmouth
Arey Thomas, Yarmouth Port,	"
Baker Frederick A., South Yarmouth,	"
Chubb David,	"

Stair Builders.

(See also Carpenters.)

French W. A.	Cambridge
Boyer Samuel, Cambridgeport,	"
Adams J. French, East Cambridge,	"
Page & Littlefield,	Charlestown
Blackmer Green,	Chelsea
Waldron J.	Fall River
Allen C. P.	Fitchburg
Sprague R. O., South Hingham,	Hingham
Fisher & Perkins,	Lawrence
Pratt Thomas,	Lowell
GORDON THOMAS, 13 Union (see page 751),	"
KNOWLTON GEORGE K. & Co., 13 Union (see page 751),	Lynn
MARSHALL J. OTIS, rear 13 Broad (see page 750),	"
Taylor Thomas,	"
Tewksbury J. W.	"
Margeeon John B.	Malden
Hussey R. C.	Milford
Morse Nathaniel,	Newburyport
Clark Ezra,	New Bedford
Parsons J. M.	Northampton
Churchill Bradford D.	Pittsfield
Brown George, jr.	Salem
FAXON & LOCKE, 72 Washington (see page 746),	"
Kendall Alvah,	"
Roburson O. G. & Brothers,	Somerville
Corbin A. O.	Springfield
Fitts L. L.	"
PARK G. H. & J. F. (see page 717), Franklin street,	Tauntou
Carter E. W.	Worcester
Stratton F. A.	"

Stamp and Stencil Cutters.

(See also Die Sinkers.)

APPLETON J. A. jr. 3 Water,	Haverhill
Clover William B.	Lowell

GROVER ARISTON, 134 Middlesex, Lowell
Haskell Job H.   "
Parsons & Gibbey,   "
Preston John,   "
Whitmore William,   "
Folger R. jr.   Milford
Meade George W.   Pittsfield
TIMME. E. A. (see page 801),
   279 Main,   Worcester

Starch Manufacturers.

Liversidge W. & T.   Milton

Stationary Engines.

FOUNDRY & MACHINE CO. H. S.
  Fairbanks treas. and agent (see page
  692),   Taunton

Stationers.

(See also Books and Stationery.)
REMICK JOHN & SON, Cambridge-
  port,   Cambridge
PROCTER BBOS. 121 Front,   Gloucester
ROGERS J. S. E., Low's Block,   "
                                 Lawrence
BEAL HENRY, Essex n. Broadway,   "
WEBSTER W. T. 8 Exchange,   Lynn
Bullard Amasa,   New Bedford
Munson H. W.   "
Todd Henry.   "
HALL JOHN T.   Plymouth
TURNER E. C.   "
Bradley M. & Co. (manuf),   Springfield
Morgan E & Co. (envelopes),   "
Burbank A. L.   Worcester
Gray Chas W.   "
Sanford W. H. & Son,   "
Whitney Edward,   "

Stave Knife Manufs.

LOVEJOY DANIEL, Rock cor. Cushing
  (see page 744),   Lowell

Stave Machinery Manufs.

Coffin Wm. S.   Newburyport
Kenney Lewis, S. Wareham,   Wareham

Stave Mills.

Brown D. B.   Cheshire
Dean & Martin,
                                Mattapoisett
BARSTOW N. H. & H. (see page 727), "
                                 Middleboro'
HARLOW I. H. & CO (see page 708),   "
New Bedford Stave Dressing Co.
  John W. Bryant, agt.   New Bedford
Union Stave Dressing Co.
  A. G. Hayes, agt.   "

Steam and Gas Pipe and Fittings.

(See also Gas and Steam Pipe.)
MARSH J. J.   North Adams,   Adams
DIGHTON FURNACE CO. Geo.
  F. Gavitt, treas. Boston Office,
  96 and 98 North St. (see page
  733),   North Dighton,   Dighton
                                  Fall River
Fall River Steam and Gas pipe Co.   "
Wolfendale Wm   "
HUBBARD A. W. (see page 767), Fitchburg
ROBBINS HENRY T.   Great Barrington
Tower Brothers,   Holyoke
HAUGHTON & BINGHAM, 195 Essex
  (see page 716),   Lawrence
Sargent B. L.   "
Barker Horace R. & Co.   Lowell
Cheever Joseph C.   Lynn
Kennedy John & Co.   "
RICE, ROBBINS, & CO.   Pittsfield
Ferguson Geo B.   Salem
Staten Daniel F.   "
Mateu E. H.   "
Appleton J. H. & Co.   Springfield
KEITHE BROS., (see page 780),   "
Gunn John,   Webster
BARRETT, WASHBURN, & CO.,
  6 Pearl,   Worcester

Colbath J. & Son,   Worcester
UNION WATER METER CO.
  (gongs and valves),   "
WHEELER W. A. (see page 792), 42
  Thomas,   "

Steam Boilers and Engines.

FOUNDRY AND MACHINE CO.
  H. S. Fairbanks, treas. and agent,
  (see page 692),   Taunton
The Washburn Steam Works,   Worcester
NEW YORK STEAM ENGINE CO.
  A. B. Couch, Supt. (see page 785)   "

Steam Engine Builders.

(See also Machinists ; also Boiler Makers.)
Allen & Endicott, Cambridgep't, Cambridge
Rawson & Hittinger,   "   "
Cook, Rymes & Co.   Charlestown
KILBURN, LINCOLN, & CO. (see
  page 756),   Fall River
Brown C. H. & Co.   Fitchburg
PUTNAM MACHINE CO., Salmon W.
  Putnam, president and agent, (see
  page 707),   "
Hoadley John C. & Co. (portable) Lawrence
Bugres Thomas F. & Co.   Lowell
LOWELL MACHINE SHOP (A.
  Moody, supt.)   "
CLARY & RUSSELL,
  (see page 708),   Pittsfield
NEWCOMB GEO. L. 18 Peabody,   Salem
Salem Machine Co. (Hick's Engine),   "
ROCHE BROS. (see page 780),   Springfield
MASON WM. (locomotives, see page
  780),   Taunton
FOUNDRY & MACHINE CO. H. S.
  Fairbanks, treas. and agent (see
  page 692),   "
                                  Worcester
NEW YORK STEAM ENGINE CO.
  A. B. Couch, supt. (see page 785),   "

Steam, Gas, and Water Fittings.

CHOATE & PERKINS, 194 Derby
  (see page 747),   Salem
                                   Lowell
PROCTOR JOSEPH W. 29 Fletcher,   "

Steam, Gas, and Water Pipe Manufs.

DIGHTON FURNACE CO   Geo. F.
  Gavitt, treas. Boston Office 96 and
  98 North (see page 733), North Dighton,   Dighton
TAUNTON IRON WORKS CO. Geo.
  M. Woodward, agent and treas. (see
  page 782),   Taunton

Steam Heating Apparatus.

RICE, ROBBINS, & CO.   Pittsfield
GRAY HENRY & SONS,   Springfield
HOWARD STEAM HEATING CO.
  88 Main (see page 751),   "
Smith H. B. & Co.   Westfield
Barrett, Washburn, & Co.   Worcester

Steam Packing Manufs.

Silver Lake Manufacturing Co. Newtonville
Wheelock Jerome (cylinder),   Worcester

Steam Press Brick Machine.

ALICE W. H, 1 Alice House,   Springfield

Steam Press Plates.

DOBBINS & CRAWFORD (see page
  737), Dutton, n. Mechanics' Mills, Lowell
WESTON C. H. Arch St.   "

Steam Pumps.

Robinson Boiler Works,   Clinton
                                East Hampton
EAST HAMPTON PUMP AND
  ENGINE COMPANY, J. W.
  Winslow, treas. (see page 790)   "

KNOWLES & SIBLEY (see page
  759),   Warren
The Washburn Steam Works,   Worcester
                      •

Steamers.

Nantucket & Cape Cod Steamboat Co.
  Joseph A. Starbuck, Clerk   Nantucket
                            New Bedford
New Bedford, Vineyard, & Nantucket
  Steamboat Co. A. G. Pierce, treas. "
New Bedford & New York Steam Pro-
  peller Co., Benj. Irish. agt., New Bedford
PROVINCETOWN & BOSTON, J. E.
  Bowley, agent,   Provincetown

Steamship Agent.

READE LAWRENCE, 72 Main, see
  page 782),   Milford

Steel Letter and Stamp Cutters.

                            Lowell
GROVER ARISTON, 134 Middlesex, "
                          Worcester
TIMME E. A. (see page 801), 279 Main, "

Steel Manufacturers.

Whipple File & Steel Manuf. Co, Ballardvale

Steering Wheels.

Richardson Nathan,   Gloucester

Stencil and Stamp Cutters.

(See Die Sinkers ; also Stamp and Stencil
  Cutters.)

Stereotype and Electrotype Foundry.

Welch, Bigelow, & Co. Riverside, Cambridge

Stone Cutters and Dealers.

(See also Marble Workers ; also Granite.)
Wetherbee Joseph, E. Abington, Abington
Gowell William,   North   "   "
Powers Enoch,   South   "   "
Reed Ebenezer,   "   "
Howard Samuel,   Ashburnham
Whitney Charles W.   "
McDonald & Mann,   Cambridge
Mount Auburn Granite Works, Knox
  & Angier,   "
Davis & Goodrich,   Cambridgeport, "
Parker Artemus,   "
Rowe Hugh,   "
Sanborn A. C. & Co.   E. Cambridge, "
Gilman J. F. & F. L.   Charlestown
LYONS WM. J. (freestone, see page
  735),   "
DAVIS DANIEL C. (granite, see page
  714),   Chelsea
Tribou D. W.   East Bridgewater
Bassett Albert,   Fall River
Beatie John & Brother, .   "
Ames Joel & Co.   Fitchburg
Bates Daniel,   "
Hale & Green,   "
Lyons & Blanchard,   "
Wheeler S. A. & Son,   "
Ballou Frederick,   Foxborough
Andrews Stephen P.   Gloucester
Harvey & Jones,   Annisquam, "
Jones, Sargent, & Co.   "
Keeffe D. & C. (paving),   "   "
Trumbull S. T. & Co.   "   "
Barker H. & Brothers,   Lanesville, "
Batmann John,   "
Webber & March, Groton Junction. Groton
Gage Asa,   Haverhill
Chandler Geo. W.   Lawrence
Leonard Daniel,   "
Wortnley P. C. V. (granite),   "
Runnels, Clough, & Co.   "
WRIGHT MERRILL S., Oliver P. Lowell
  Trask, agent, School, cor. Nashua,
  R. R. (see page 739),   "

BLETHEN TRUE G. (see page 791),
  Long wharf, foot Pleasant st. Lynn
Carroll R.   Milford
Littlefield A.   "
Drew Phineas (granite),   New Bedford
HATHAWAY A. (granite, see page
  759), 37 North Sixth,   "
Hathaway Elnathan (granite),   "
Davis & Littlefield,   Newburyport
Torrey Joseph,   "
PLUMMER GRANITE CO. (see
  page 754),   Northbridge
Morse William R.   Orange
Ward Leonard,   "
Brown John,   Peabody
Brown Samuel,   "
Lord Nathaniel,   '   "
Newhall Henry H.   "
Putnam & Newhall,   "
DELL BROS. & CO. (granite, see page
  768),   Quincy
Mitchell George H.   "
Vogel Adam & Son,   "
WILLIAMS, SPELMAN, & CO. (gran-
  ite. see page 768),   "
Preston, Fernald, & Co.   Rockport
Rockport Granite Co.   "
Clapp, Ballou, & Co.   Pigeon Cove, "
Eames Ezra & Co.   "
Edmunds James,   "   "   "
Butler J. S.   Salem
LONGLEY EDMUND (granite), 157
  Derby,   "
Lord A. & D.   "
Merritt J. H. (granite),   "
Dwelly A. S. & Co.   Springfield
HATHAWAY ANTHONY (granite),
  Myrick's (see page 759),   Taunton
Hathaway Horace,   "
Pierce Henry,   "
Blanchard D. J. N. Uxbridge, Uxbridge
Cummings Walton, Graniteville, Westford
FLETCHER SAMUEL " (granite), "
Palmer Benjamin,   "   "
Reed David,   "   "
Reed William,   "   "
Pratt & Vining, S. Weymouth, Weymouth
Peck Henry,   Winchendon
Plummer Charles E.   "
James Audrew,   Woburn
MANN A. G. Southbridge st. Worcester
PLUMMER GRANITE CO. (see page
  754),   "
WOODWARD DAVID M.   "

Stone Quarriers.

(See also Granite ; also Marble Quarriers.)
Manville Edward,   Great Barrington
Warner Levi,   "
Chapp H. W.   Greenfield
Dwelly A. S. (freestone), Longmeadow
Pierce Bradford,   New Bedford
Pierce Chas. M.   "
Rogers Abiathial,   "
Terry Benjamin,   "
Clark Daniel R.   Northampton
Burbank Abraham,   Pittsfield
Carver Calvin,   "
Merrill Ayre (gray stone),   "
Sykes Amos,   "
Billings C. F. (slate),   Quincy
BRIGGS JOHN R. (marble, see page
  800),   Sheffield
Merrill G. G. Shelburne Falls, Shelburne
Woodward Zopher,   "
Gilson Charles H.   Stockbridge
Goodrich & Co.   Glendale, "
Williams J. B.   Westfield

Stone-Ware Manufacturers.

(See also Potteries.)
Powers & Edmunds,   Charlestown
Somerset Potters Works,   Somerset
Purinton D. P.   "
Wright Franklin D. & Son,   Taunton
Norton F. B. & Co.   Worcester

Stove Boiler Bottoms.

CROCKER BROS. & CO. Court st.
  near City sq. (see page 753), Taunton

Stove Damper Manufacturers.

Nutting & Co. (slide damper),
Pomeroy D.,   Orange
Parker Alfred,   "

Stove Dealers and Tinsmiths.

(See also Furnaces and Ranges.)

Farrar J. P.   Abington
Littlefield J. P.   East Abington, "
Cloud H. H.   North   "
Holbrook Loring,   South   "
Twitchell Chas. S.   West Acton,   Acton
Wilbur James S.   Adams
DECKER ISAAC W.   N. Adams,   "
Goodrich, Cary, & Co.   "   "
Sheldon Son & Co.   "   "
Bartlett William D.   Amesbury
Ropes Joseph E.   West Amesbury,   "
Hitchcock W. H.   Amherst
Hunt Oliver D.   "
Barnett William,   Andover
Merrifield J. A.   Arlington
Shattuck R. W. & Co.   "
Lane Martin B.   Ashburnham
Perry E. & Co.   Ashland
BEMIS & FROST,   Athol
Bancroft C. O.   Athol Depot,   "
Ryder Chas. E.   Attleborough
FESSENDEN HENRY, N. Attle-
   borough,   "
Seabury D. M.   Barnstable
Lincoln Clark,   Centreville,   "
Cash A. G.   Hyannis,   "
Davis James F.   Barre
White Thomas,   "
Smith Clarkson,   North Becket,   Becket
Cole Lyman,   Bedford
Tyler Charles,   Bernardston
Hinkley William W.   Beverly
Lunt Benjamin S.   "
Baker, Benson, & Co.   Blackstone
Crocker Elisha, jr.   Brewster
Winslow B. B. & Co.   "
Fairbanks J. H.   Bridgewater
Rogers J. B.   "
Cross John,   Brighton
Warner Thomas,   Brookfield
Houghton J. F.   Brookline
Kenrick Brothers,   "
Carr Erwin S.   Cambridge
Estes I. P.   "
Hilton James M.   "
Moore Charles   "
Robbins J. M.   Cambridgeport,   "
Starbuck Jas. C.   "
Taylor Simeon,   "
Towne & Fuller,   "
Bailey Jacob L.   East Cambridge,   "
Monblo & Blanchard,   "
Place George W.   "   "
Price James M.   "
Pratt Chas. O. & Co.   "   "
GRIFFIN GEO. H., North ave., N.
   Cambridge,   "
Goodrich D. M.   Canton
Chapman Stephen L.   Charlemont
Cole Jackson,   Charlestown
Cooper & Burgess,   "
Deavir Robert F.   "
Ditson S. J.   "
Edmunds Geo. E.   "
Gaffney Thomas,   "
Gibson Griffin,   "
Hadley & Wright (milk cans),   "
Jenkins James D.   "
McLoud John,   "
Moore, W. B. & Son,   "
Perkins H. H.   "
Titus Franklin A.   "
Wing Charles H.   "
HAMILTON HARRISON,   Chatham
Rogers Sullivan,   "
Axton Lemuel L.   Chelsea
Kent Hathaway,   "
Newhall Luther,   "
Reed W. G. & Co.   "
Spade William,   "
Webber Gilbert T.   "

Bliss Wm. G.   "
Hill & Co.   Chicopee
Wallace George,   Chicopee Falls,   "
Bowman Charles,   Clinton
Green George L.,   "
Bates Samuel,   Cohasset
Marsh Philo,   Coleraine
Sanborn John C.   Concord
Rice Albert,   Conway
Ropes & Upton,   Danvers
Russell Charles,   Dedham
Keelan Michael,   E. Dedham,   "
Engles James,   South Dedham,   "
Tyler C. H.   South Deerfield,   Deerfield
Davis Geo. L.   West Dennis,   Dennis
Tolman C. P.   Dorchester
JONES WILLIAM, Dorchester ave.
   corner Commercial,   "
Smally N. F.   Harrison sq.   "
Tolman J. P.   "
Haynes George & Son,   Milton,   "
Tileston Charles,   "   "
BAIRD OTIS,   Neponset,   "
Field E. F.   "
Balcom I. S.   East Douglas,   Douglas
Clark Willard,   Duxbury
Johnson Willard,   East Bridgewater
Mayher J.   East Hampton
Sprague & Judd,   "
Spooner E. P.   North Easton,   Easton
Chadwick Wm. P. & Son,   Edgartown
Mayhew Charles,   "
Burnham Jonathan,   Essex
Taber Nathaniel S.   Fairhaven
Christmas T. J.   Fall River
Cook, Grew, & Ashton,   "
Flint J. D. & Co.   "
Johnson Thomas,   "
McCloskey C. J.   "
Nichols B. D. & Co.   "
Nichols L. & Co.   "
Nowell John P.   "
Wilcox D. T.   "
Fish Joseph F.   Falmouth
Starbuck Joseph B.   "
Dow & Starbuck,   Fitchburg
Litch & Sawtell,   "
Magee & Spear,   "
Patch Lyman,   "
Robbins George & Co.   "
Garside John,   Foxborough
Carr D. A.   Framingham
Frost J. B. & D. O.   Saxonville,   "
Cotton Daniel C.   Franklin
JORDAN A. H.   Gardner
Morse C. M.   Georgetown
Cooper Wm. T.   Gloucester
Harvey A. E.   "
Loring Francis M.   "
Mayo Israel C.   "
Mayo Josiah, jr.   "
Sanborn George,   "
Currier John J.   East Gloucester,   "
Holden Orren C.   "
Leland J. W.   Grafton
Patterson & Barnum,   Great Barrington
Wood & Olds,   "
Chase G. A.   Greenfield
Lester Edward,   "
Wiley Oren,   "
Reed Samuel,   Groton Junction,   Groton
Peterson & Co.   Hanover
Willard Alonzo,   Harvard
Rogers Sullivan W.   Harwich
Smalley Geo. D.   Harwich Port,   "
APPLETON JOHN A. Jr. 3 Water,   Haverhill
Currier W. A.   "
Duncan R. & J.   "
Le Bosquet Jos.   "
Loring E. & I. W.   Hingham
Stevens Henry T.   Hinsdale
Bassett Milo,   Holden
Pond George N.   Holliston
Buckley P. M.   Holyoke
Tower Brothers,   "
WING DANIEL B.   "
Woodbury Geo. S.   Hopkinton
Davis, Waite, & Co.   Hubbardston
Bradley G. O.   Hudson

Store Dealers — continued.

Lyman Samuel T.	Huntington
Dolan Thomas,	Hyde Park
Jones J. D.	"
Stark C. C.	"
Newman Mark,	Ipswich
Plouff Edward jr.	"
CLARK GEORGE H.	Kingston
Myrick Wm. H.	
Rowell Leander,	Lancaster
Baston J. F. & W. C.	Lawrence
Bishop Lemuel A.	"
Farnum & Robbins, 99 Essex,	"
Favor J. B.	"
HAUGHTON & BINGHAM, 195 Essex (see page 746),	"
Johnson Samuel,	"
Knowles A. H.	"
Martin D. M. & C. N.	"
Ricker O. A. & Co.	"
Smart Geo. B. & Co.	"
Vatter Henry,	"
Hinckley John W.	Lee
Phelps George H.	"
Atherton W. F.	Leominster
Fish Wm. T.	"
Goddard Alonzo,	Lexington
Costello Thomas & Co.	Lowell
Dustin Harlow,	"
Foote J, L. & Co.	"
Mack Sewall G.	"
Mead Mathias,	"
Mehan J. & Brother,	"
NASH J. W. & Co. 105 Central (see page 739),	"
Nichols Jacob.	"
Page James Y. & Co.	"
Smith Martin & Co.	"
Wier N. J. & Co.	"
Whitton Wm. T.	"
Wight Daniel W.	"
Gard John,	Lynn
Larrabee & Brother,	"
Larrabee J. R. & Co.	"
Paul Amasa, jr.	"
Russell John R.	"
Rust Samuel,	"
WELCH JACOB & CO. 1 Sagamore House,	"
Bailey George T.	Malden
Buntin George W.	"
Kimball Hervey Z.	"
Evans J. H.	Manchester
Wheeler George L.	Mansfield
Cole Benjamin,	Marblehead
Silver Harris,	"
Kelley Henry H.	Marion
Bradley & Brigham,	Marlborough
Miles Thomas M.	"
Colson Owen D.	Mattapoisett
Horsington Dennis,	Medfield
Parsons J. E.	Medford
Small John D.	"
Hodges Wm. B.	Medway
Cox Enoch.	Melrose
Homer E. B.	Methuen
Doane George H.	Middleborough
Bowers & Jenks,	Milford
Harris H. & Co.	"
Judson, Sawtelle, & Co.	"
Cunningham W. R.	Millbury
White Hamilton,	Monson
Clapp R. N.	Montague
Abbott Virgil S.	Monterey
Austin James,	Nantucket
Hussey John A.	"
Macy George Wendall,	"
Perry Joseph H.	"
Crofoot Edwin,	Natick

French Leander,	Natick
Morse J. W.	"
Almy John E.	New Bedford
Caswell John P.	"
Hatch George E.	"
Hayden Wm. G.	"
Lewis Nathan,	"
Parker Warren W.	"
SULLINGS & KINGMAN, 123 Union,	"
Tobey & Cogswell,	"
Tripp S. A.	"
Vincent Ambrose,	"
Wilson John C.	"
Wood, Brightman, & Co.	"
Chamberlin John,	Newburyport
Dodge Samuel,	"
Drown T. S.	"
Davis Abel H.	"
Frost J. D.	"
Jackman George L.	"
Sumner John,	"
Wells Wallace D.	"
Young Daniel,	"
Woodworth C. S.	New Marlborough
	Mill River, "
Sumner J. S.	Newton Corner, Newton
Gammons L. A.	Lower Falls, "
Cady Collin,	Upper Falls, "
Trowbridge J. E.	" "
Leavitt O. B.	Newtonville, "
HUMPHREY & ALMON, W. Newton, "
White J. M.	Newton Centre, "
Eames, Sprague, & Co.	Northampton
Boland & Prindle,	"
Lee & Hussey,	"
Hunt Frederick P.	Northborough
Hervey L. D.	North Bridgewater
Hunt John,	"
Stevens E. Z.	"
Graves Leonard,	North Brookfield
Gale James O.	Northfield
Washburn Enoch,	Orange
NEWCOMB T. S. & SONS,	Orleans
Chapman Reuben & Co.	"
Taylor Amos S.	Oxford
Nichols E. & Co.	Palmer
Whittier James O.	Peabody
Lawrence Sumner P.	Pepperell
Andrews Collins,	Petersham
Gates Charles,	"
Backus Wm. G.	Pittsfield
FEELEY JOHN, 31 North,	"
Foote James H.	"
Drew W. R.	Plymouth
Harlow & Barnes,	"
Whitten H. C.	"
Holmes Hiram,	Provincetown
Sparrow & Snow,	"
Weston W. H. H.	"
Fellows Ensign S.	Quincy
Pierce Charles F. & Co.	"
Baker & Thayer,	Randolph
LITTLEFIELD TRISTRAM,	Reading
Bartlett Joseph,	Rockport
Haskins Joseph T.	"
Chipman A. M.	Salem
Eaton J. D. & J. W.	"
Frothingham T. H. & Co.	"
Fuller Wm. P.	"
Mooney & Wadleigh,	"
Pease Samuel W.	"
Preston Jonathan, jr. (tinsmith),	"
Ropes John T.	"
Staten E. H. (gas),	"
Cummings James,	Amesbury, Salisbury
Pease Levi,	Montville, Sandisfield
Pratt Oscar,	New Boston, "
Burbank W. H. F.	Sandwich

Foster Josiah, Sandwich
Brown Horace, East Saugus, Saugus
Waterman Andrew J. Scituate
Andrus & Woodward, Sheffield
Strong George P. Ashley Falls, "
Ott P. Shelburne Falls, Shelburne
Mitchell G. F. & Co. " "
Warner A. A. Shirley Village, Shirley
Purinton John N. Shrewsbury
Manchester Abner, Somerset
Manchester Wm. A. "
Merrifield John A. Somerville
Cummings & Williams, Southbridge
Winter George L. "
Lewis E. P. Globe Village, "
South Hadley
Harris Wm. F. South Hadley Falls, "
AYERS C. S. Spencer
Abbe James, Springfield
Alexander John, "
Beach T. D, "
Clark·L. "
Clark S. "
Cushman E. J. & Co. "
Lewis L. S. "
Montague D. B. "
Spooner Wm. A. "
Wilcox W. L. & Co. "
Goss Frederic, Sterling
Van Dusen M. & J. M. Stockbridge
Lovejoy J. A. Stoneham
Clapp Timothy, Stoughton
Bacon J. L. Fiskdale, Sturbridge
Treadwell John H. Swampscott
Babbitt Jerome, Taunton
Briggs & Co. "
Brownell A. C. "
Hutchinson Wm. "
Padelford David, "
West L. B. & Co. "
Lord & Walker, Templeton
Smith William, "
Luce James L. Holmes's Hole, Tisbury
Burt F. C. Townsend
Baker Leonard P. Truro
Wing Charles, Uxbridge
Littlefield E. H. Wakefield
Littlefield S. F. "
Knapp W. B. Waltham
Stickney Rufus & Sons, "
Marsh Daniel C. Ware
MARSH P. C. & CO. "
WITHERELL STEPHEN B. "
Bent Isaac B. Wareham
Burbank Walter D. "
Stiles Wm. L. Watertown
Bates A. J. Webster
Spaulding Cyrus, "
ATWOOD SIMEON & CO. Wellfleet
Montague & Hemenway, Westborough
Sawyer Henry, West Boylston
Allen & Beales, West Brookfield
Gowdy C. H. & Co. Westfield
Knowles Benjamin W. "
Starr & Campbell, "
Tufts Eben, Westford
Clapp C., Jamaica Plain, West Roxbury
Russell Levi H. " "
White & Mayo, " "
Boughton Morgan L. West Stockbridge
Pratt S. W. Weymouth
Whitten George W., East Weymouth, "
TUCK LORENZO, South " "
Sharp E. & Co. Williamsburgh
Stebbins & Williams, "
Solomon Charles, Williamstown
Barber J. P. & Son, Winchendon
Bateman A. P. "

Gladstone R. G. Winchester
FIFIELD W. S. Woburn
Thompson L. jr. "
Willey Albert, "
Jordan J. W. Worcester
Loring Jos. F. "
Lucas Wm. & Son, "
Miller H. W. "
Murphy & Co. "
Oliver F. P. "
Phelps & Cooley, "
Reed Thomas H. "
Russell A. & Co. "
Russell I. D. "
Williams G. W. & Co. "
Yarmouth
Hall J. H. H. Yarmouthport, "
Hallett·Matthews C. " "
Farris R. D., South Yarmouth, "

Stove Lining Manufacturers.

(*See also Fire Brick Manufacturers.*)

TAUNTON STOVE LINING CO.,
A. W. Parker, agent and treas.
(see page 758). Taunton
PRESBREY STOVE LINING CO.
W. B. Presbrey, agent (see page 780),
WILLIAMS J. R. also oven tile and fire bricks (see page 715), W. Water, "

Stove Manufacturers.

(*See also Iron Founders.*)

Twitchell Chas. S. West Acton, Acton
Houghton D. W. (box and air-tight), Athol Depot, Athol
Ellis Matthias & Co. South Carver, Carver
HEALD S. & SONS (manufacturers of and dealers in large shop, box, and cylinder stoves, see pages 796 and 797), Barre
MAGEE FURNACE CO. (see front colored page), Chelsea
Bates Samuel, Cohasset
CODDING JAMES D. & CO. (see page 760), North Dighton, Dighton
DIGHTON FURNACE CO. George F. Gavitt, treas.; Boston office. 96 and 98 North (see page 733), N. Dighton, "
Fall River Foundry Co. Fall River
Cobb & Drew, Kingston
NASH J. W. & Co. 105 Central, (see page 739), Lowell
CHILSON GARDNER (see inside front cover), Mansfield
Norton Furnace Co. Norton
Plymouth Iron Foundry, Plymouth
SOMERSET CO-OPERATIVE FOUNDRY CO. William Homer, agent, Somerset
LEONARD LEMUEL M., Wales st. near the depot, (see page 726), Taunton
PERKINS SAMPSON & CO. (see page 729), West Water st. "
TAUNTON IRON WORKS CO. George M. Woodward, agent (see page 732), "
UNION FURNACE CO. Wright & Leeds (see page 719), "
LORD & WALKER (see page 772), Otter River, Templeton
Boston & Maine Foundry Co. Wakefield
Pratt, Miles, & Co. Watertown
Fobes Dwelley, West Bridgewater
Earle Stove Co. Worcester
WHEELER W. A. (see page 792), 42 Thomas, "

Stove Polish Manufacturers.

Canton

MORSE BROTHERS, (see page 764), "
PACKARD WILLIAM HENRY (see
page 770), Quincy
PHŒNIX MANUF. CO., C. R. Atwood, agent (see page 725), Taunton

Straw Goods Manufacturers.

(See also Bonnet Manufacturers.)

Hills L. M. & Son (Shaker hoods), Amherst
Attleborough
BARNES L. W. (bonnets and hats), "
Foster & Carpenter, "
Foxborough
Carpenter & Cook (bonnets and hats), "
Clark A. & Son (Shaker hoods), So.
Framingham, Framingham
Barber C. H. (hats and bonnets),
So. Framingham, "
Kennedy J. R. " "
Richardson A. (hats & bonnets),
So. Framingham, "
Richardson G. & Son (hats & bon-
nets), So. Framingham, "
Daniels & Hubbard, Franklin
GREENE HENRY M. "
Marvin & Gowen, "
Morse A. H. "
Morse H. S. "
Thayer Davis, jr. "
Slocum & Thompson, Holliston
Hale J. B. (palm leaf), Medfield
Curtis & Co. "
Harding & Bassett, Medway
Metcalf G. T. "
Bay State Straw Works, Albert Al-
den & Co. Middleborough
Mowry & Spaulding, Milford
Seaver & Co. "
Merrick & Fay, Monson
Squier & Bro. (Shaker hoods), "
ATLANTIC STRAW WORKS,
A. T. Mowry, agent, Nantucket
Benson & Nelson (bonnets), Upton
Knowlton Wm. & Sons (bonnets),
West Upton, "
Blood Charles E. Ware
Demond L. "
Bates, Parker, & Co. Westborough
Smalley Geo. N. "
Snow & Fellows, "
Wilbraham
Warren John B. South Wilbraham, "
George William E. Wrentham
Perry Harvey, North Wrentham, "
Guild Benj. H. Sheldonville, "

Stucco Workers.

Brooks Charles P. Charlestown
Titus Daniel, "
Blake Joseph P. Haverhill
Prescott D. Moody, Lowell
Delano Gustavus, New Bedford
Parsons J. H. & J. M. Salem

Sub-Marine Diver.

Baker Benjamin, New Bedford

Sugar Refinery.

Union Sugar Refinery, G. A. Jasper, supt., Front, bet. Third and
Union, Charlestown

Surgeons.

Chelsea
WHEELER & BEAN, 145 Broadway, "

Surgical Instruments.

CADWELL WM. P. S. (dealer),
49 Purchase st. New Bedford

Surveyors.

(See also Civil Engineers.)

Charlestown
DOANE T. & J. jr. (see page 666), "
LOW DAVID W., Low's blk. Gloucester
Webber John S. "
Hammond John Q. Lynn
PUTNAM CHAS. A. 251 Essex, Salem

Suspender Manufacturers.

(See also Shoulder Brace Manufacturers.)

Boston Elastic Fabric Co. North Chelsea
Nashewannuck Manuf. Co. Ed.
mund H. Sawyer, treas. East Hampton
Boardman H. W. & Co. Lowell
CUTTER & WALKER (Eureka), 48
Central, "
Watertown
Nonantum Co., F. S. Bellows, agent, "
Bay State Suspender Co. Worcester

Sword Manufacturers.

Ames Manufacturing Co. Chicopee

Table Manufacturers.

(See also Furniture.)

Drew, Jackson, & Co. Charlestown

Tack, Brad, and Shoe Nail Manufacturers.

(See also Nail Manufacturers.)

Gurney D. B. (also heel plates), Abington
BRIGHAM, WHITMAN, & CO.
(see page 712), South Abington, "
DIGHTON TACK CO. (see page
715), Dighton
LEONARD NATHANIEL & SON,
(shoe, see page 771), N. Dighton, "
Keith Z. jr. & Co. East Bridgewater
American Tack Co. Fairhaven
Perry E. Y. & Co. Hanover
Stetson Charles T. "
Waterman L. C. & Co. "
Cushing & Co. Hanson
Howland Luther, "
Perry E. Y. & Co. "
Bullen Thaddeus, Haverhill
STETSON & TALBOT (see page
782), Holliston
MILLAY P. E. (see page 761), Hudson
Reed Alphonso, Kingston
Reed P. C. "
Soule Henry, "
Stetson Kimball, West Kingston, "
Cobb & Drew, Plymouth
PLYMOUTH TACK & RIVET
WORKS, Samuel Loring, pro-
prietor (see page 713), "
Wood N. & Co. "
Caswell Wm. F. Raynham
King Geo. W. "
Rounds L. A. & Co. "
Sandwich Tack Co., Isaiah T. Jones,
agent, Sandwich
Sudbury
Howe J. C. & Co. South Sudbury, "
FIELD A. & SONS, 22 Spring (see
page 719), Taunton
ANTHONY & CUSHMAN (see page
722). "
RHODES M. M. (carpet and coffin), "

TAUNTON TACK CO., Thomas J.
Lothrop, agent and treas., 26 Union
(see page 720),   Taunton
Reed W. H. S. Weymouth, Weymouth

Tack Leatherers.

Dighton
DIGHTON TACK CO. (see page 715), "
Cobb & Drew,   Plymouth
PLYMOUTH TACK & RIVET
WORKS, Samuel Loring, proprietor
(see page 713),   "
ANTHONY & CUSHMAN, Mealnnic
st. (see page 722),   Taunton
Cushman & Coggeshall,   "
FIELD A. & SONS, 22 Spring (see page
719),
TAUNTON TACK CO., T. J. Lothrop,
agent and treas., 26 Union (see page
720),   "

Tack Plate Manufacturers.

LAZELL, PERKINS, & CO. Bridgewater
Dighton Rolling Mill Co.   Dighton
East Bridgewater Iron Co. E. Bridgewater
Plymouth
Robinson Iron Co. F. S. Russell, agent, "
OLD COLONY IRON CO., Charles
Robinson, agent,   Taunton

Tag Manufacturers.

Union Label Co.   Shirley
STAR LABEL CO., F. G. Sargent,
(ready strung, see page 743), Graniteville,   Westford

Tailors.

(See also Clothing.)

Agnew John,   Abington
Walsh Lawrence,   "
Daly Cornelius,   East Abington, "
Sproul John,   South   "
Tuttles, Jones, & Wetherbee, South
Acton,   Acton
Wilde Charles M. Long Plain, Acushnet
Morgan James,   Adams
BRIGGS & BOLAND, North Adams, "
Butler Charles B.   "   "
Day E. C.   "   "
Holbrook William & Co.   "   "
Rogge C. L.   "   "
Hume John,   Amesbury
Manley Michael,   "
Baker & Lapham,   Amherst
Foley E.   "
Pease Oliver & Co.   "
Williams & Deady,   "
Dean John H.   Andover
Logue Daniel,   "
Durnan Peter,   Arlington
Merritt W. S.   Ashfield
West J. N.   Ashland
Black George W.   Athol
Bannon C. W.   Athol Depot,   "
Talbot & Cutler,   "
BOYLE JOHN, N. Attleboro', Attleboro'
Edwards Samuel C.   "   "
Jones T. B.   "   "
Hallett Alex. C.   Hyannis,   Barnstable
Miller Geo. A.   "   "
Orcutt F. V.   Barre
Woods, Harding, & Co.   "
Higley Wm. E.   Becket
Gragg William H.   Belchertown
Bates E. D.   Blackstone
Mulgrew Michael,   "
Despeau Samuel,   Bolton
Leonard D. F., South Braintree, Braintree

Allen Joshua N.   Brewster
Howes Phineas,   Bridgewater
Baxter Daniel,   Brighton
Gerald E B.   Brookfield
Helfenstine A.   Brookline
Levi M.   "
Dalton Richard,   Cambridge
Hewlett A. Molyneaux,   "
Kimball Wm.   "
McCoy Wm.   "
Shea Dennis,   "
DOYLE JOSEPH, 361 Main, Cam-
bridgeport,   "
Fitzpatrick Patrick, Cambridgeport, "
Kimball J. Frank,   "   "
Mallen & Fitzpatrick,   "   "
Neligan & Son,   "   "
Brine Robert,   East Cambridge, "
Brine Wm.   "
Fitzpatrick Dennis,   "   "
Higgins James,   "   "
McGinnes Robert,   "   "
McKinley G. P.   "   "
Walker Samuel,   "   "
Evons L.   Canton
O'Dea M.   "
Niles Wm. E.   Charlemont
Alberty R. B.   Charlestown
Anderson John,   "
Bazin J. W.   "
Bigelow Charles,   "
Cahill Michael,   "
Denvir William,   "
DeWolf Lewis E.   "
Doherty Philip,   "
Foster Isaac S.   "
Hull Stephen,   "
Klous E. J.   "
McDonald & McKay,   "
Merrill & Gale,   "
Nelson Charles,   "
Sager Francis G.   "
Whiton James,   "
Wakefield William L.   Charlton
Bearse Reuben L.   Chatham
Howard Edward,   "
Carneil Henry,   Chelsea
Currier James M.   "
Harper Henry,   "
Menzies James,   "
OLDREIVE ROBERT, 73 Winnisim-
met,   "
Buckingham & Co.   Chicopee
Moffet B.   "
Barnes Marvin H. Chicopee Falls, "
Jerauld A. A.   Clinton
Johnson S. W.   "
St. John James,   Cohasset
Russell Geo A.   Coleraine
Stewart R. S.   Concord
Tuttle Frank,   "
Freeman T. M.   Conway
Warren Caleb S.   Dalton
Foster E. W.   North Dana,   Dana
Potter Leander,   Dartmouth
Gray John,   South Dartmouth, "
Hilles Conrad,   Dedham
Morse Oliver,   South Dedham, "
Pierce C. A. South Deerfield, Deerfield
Miller G. J.   Dennis Port,   Dennis
Whelden Andrew,   South Dennis, "
Crowell Diantus,   West   "
Cronin Daniel,   Neponset,   Dorchester
Hill J. D.   "
Wiswell Joseph,   Milton,   "
Kennedy Robt. B.   Duxbury
Landers Edmund,   "
Miller J. A.   East Hampton

24

Tailors — continued.

Preston Lucius,	East Hampton
Strong W. V.	"
Allen Samuel B., Joppa, East Bridgewater	
Schindler M. D. N. Easton,	Easton
Coffin Isaiah D.	Easton
Munroe J. H.	Edgartown
Crosby J. M.	"
Burnham Edward,	Enfield
Williams T. D. & Co.	Essex
Barnes Thomas,	Fairhaven
Bean Horace,	Fall River
Boone J. H.	"
Fay and Taylor,	"
Frank Charles,	"
Gibbs R. S. & Co.	"
Isherwood Henry,	"
Marsden J. & J.	"
McKevitt Hugh,	"
McQuilty Robert J.	"
Munroe John H.	"
Smith & Cameron,	"
Wilbur & Gray,	"
Cross Daniel,	"
Gibbs George L.	Fitchburg
Manning Joseph E.	"
Markham Daniel,	"
Allen A. D.	Foxborough
Davidson J. H.	Franklin
Alger J. L.	Gardner
Howe N. B.	"
Woods L. W.	"
Osgood Stephen,	Georgetown
Plumer Samuel,	"
Barrett Charles P.	Gloucester
Dann Joseph,	"
Elwell A. & Co.	"
Gardner Charles,	"
Lawrence R. C.	"
Stockwell Leander,	Grafton
Wood J. H.	"
Brabrook Wm. F.	New Eng. Vill. "
Bailey Alpheus H.	Great Barrington
Cohen Brothers,	"
McHugh C.	"
Silva Albert P.	"
Bailey Loren N.	Greenfield
Cohn M.	"
Keurah H. E.	"
Schuler Wm.	"
Seward & Willard,	"
Bartlett R. T.	Groton Junction, Groton
Riddle James M.	Hardwick
McCrumb John,	Harwich Port, Harwich
Evans Chas R.	Haverhill
Hayden J.	"
Kimball Gilbert,	"
Treab George,	"
Way Alonzo,	"
Webber S. R.	"
Woodcock F.	"
Jacobs Loring,	Hingham
Todd John,	"
Bristol A. Theodore,	Hinsdale
McGee Thomas J.	"
Fleming Wm.	Holden
Simonds J. F.	Holliston
Carroll Wm. D.	Holyoke
Johnson, Ludington, & Co.	"
Miller & Co.	"
MITCHELL BROTHERS,	"
O'Callahan Michael,	"
Bates E. A.	Hopkinton
Flynn John B.	Hubbardston
Hall Asa F.	Hudson
Wheeler N. H.	"
Tinker G. W.	Huntington
Tinker Wm. S.	"

Archibald Charles,	Ipswich
Jordan Robert,	"
Burns Ebenezer,	Kingston
Rockwell Charles R.	Lanesborough
Atkinson John B.	Lawrence
Bainbridge H. H.	"
Brown Joseph,	"
Conlin Brothers,	
Connell Charles jr.	
Connors Michael,	
Davis S. B. W.	
Dolan Bernard,	
Fairfield J. M. & Co.	"
Gordon John,	"
Kennedy T.	"
Riley Bros.	
Moore Wm. H.	
O'Neill T. F.	
Savage & Flood,	
Schaake Frederick W.	"
Davies Wm. L. jr.	Lee
Neiser M. & Co.	"
Newton A. H.	Leominster
Pollard G. A.	"
Taylor R. B.	Longmeadow
Barnes H. H.	Lowell
Bender Frederick,	"
Bennett Wm. S.	"
Birnbaum W. L.	"
Burbank & Winnek,	"
Cook H. P.	"
Costello Michael,	"
Chase, Sargent, & Shattuck,	"
Delaney T.	"
Doyle Moses,	"
Gilman Alfred,	"
Holland Michael,	"
Lancaster & Totman,	"
Leslie Edwin C.	"
Mead Patrick,	"
Murphy John,	"
Napolski F. X.	"
Nimms J.	"
O'Neal Hugh,	"
Quinn John,	"
Smith George,	"
Bowden Thomas R.	Lynn
Baxter F. W. & Co.	"
Chase James & Co.	"
Currier Geo. B.	"
Edwards Joseph, jr.	"
Flinn F. M.	"
Flinn Wm. J.	"
Foley Edward,	"
Janes Henry,	"
Nolan James,	"
O'Grady John,	"
Partridge Winfield S.	
Reilly William,	"
Roberts N. A. Mrs.	"
Smith Wm.	
Wilson C. W.	"
Buckley James B.	Malden
Tay Francis J.	"
Fox John,	Mansfield
Marrs John,	Marblehead
Sturtevant Perez,	Marion
Rock John,	Marlborough
Sullivan John,	"
Quirk Patrick,	"
Witherbee & Lewis,	"
Witherbee Nahum,	"
Paine Martin,	Marshfield
Hervey George C.	Medford
Boos George,	Medway
Cushing John, West Medway,	"
Cunnabel James H.	Mendon
Denny Timothy,	Methuen

Hartwell Geo. F. & Co.	Middleborough	Carberry Francis,		Pittsfield
Cain Wm.	Milford	Cohen & Wolf,		"
O'Callaghan P.	"	Crowley J. C.		"
Fox & Beatty,	"	Dainty Daniel.		
Thayer & Houghton,	"	Harrington Edward M.		
Walker Frederick,	"	Kirtland Wm. S. ·		
Taylor L. C.	Millbury	McIntire Charles,		
Bennett T. A. M.	"	Newman Isaac,		"
Bronson J. Warren,	Milton	Newman Joseph R.		"
Miller H. F.	"	Pagert J. M.		"
Whitney J. M.	Monson	Gleason John G.		Plymouth
Williams F. D.	Montague	Holmes B. H.		"
Colbert John,	"	Shiverick Frank A.		"
Allen Avery T.	Monterey	ADAMS WILLIAM,		Provincetown
Cobb Leander,	Nantucket	Nickerson James H.		"
Weston Wm. H.	"	Small J. F.		"
Deignan James,	Natick	Hails Richard,		Quincy
Edgerton L. R.	"	Holden John A.		"
Flynn W. J. & Co.	"	Lombard J. W.		"
Demeritt Wm. F.	"	Gifford P.		Randolph
Edwards William,	South Natick, "	McMullen Joseph,		"
Akin Eben, jr.	New Bedford	O'Brien John,		"
Allen Daniel B.	"	Whittemore George E.		"
Bach George,	"	Spooner S. C.		Reading
BARNETT JOHN, 102 and 104 Union,	"	Tarr J. Truman,		Rockport
Cook Wm. & Co.	"	Ballou John,		Rowe
Davis L. D.	"	Pomeroy Wm.		Russell
Doane, Swift, & Co.	"	Anderson John W.		Salem
Dwyer M.	"	Burbeck Wm. H.		"
Eddy George M. & Co.	"	Chamberlain Samuel,		"
Gifford N. T. & Co.	"	Cornelius A. G.		"
Govewater M.	"	Dease Lawrence.		"
Howland Daniel W.	"	Guilfoyle John F.		"
Perry E. S.	"	Lefavour T. H. & Co.		"
Platt William,	"	Mackenzie Roderick A.		"
Richmond Joshua,	"	Moore S.		"
Spooner Sylvester,	"	Perkins Daniel & Co.		"
Swift M. C.	"	Purbeck Wm. A.		"
Sylvester W. C.	"	Rice John,		"
Taber, Read, & Co.	"	Rooney Michael,		"
Veara Joseph,	"	Ryan Patrick,		"
Ward B. C.	"	Sibley Moses H.		"
Williams T. D. & Co.	"	Smith Edward,		"
Wing J. & W. R. & Co.	"	Vail Maurice,		"
Gould B.	New Braintree	Merrill James H.	Montville,	Sandisfield
Tidd S.	"	Pixley E.	"	"
Ballou C. N.	Newburyport	Miller John Q.		Sandwich
Ballou J. W.	"	Murray John,		"
Dennett H. N.	"	Green E. T.,	Shelburne Falls,	Shelburne
Dunn James,	"	Strong C. A.	"	
Hart James S.	"	Sanderson W. L.		Shirley
Knight & Pierce.	"	Campbell D.		Shrewsbury
Smith F. W. & Co.	"	Chase Joseph,		Somerset
Birdsman Barney,	New Marlborough	Sayle John A.		"
Harford Nicholas,	Mill River, "	Wagner M. W.		Southbridge
Smith Lizzie,	West Newton, Newton	Hickey Patrick,	Globe Village,	"
Carroll Wm. D.	Northampton	Kind & Butler,	"	"
Clark Merritt,	"			South Hadley
Cohn S. & M.	"	Patterson James S.,	So. Hadley Falls,	"
Kingsley Daniel & Son,	"	Granger S. L.		Southwick
Smith & Prindle,	"	Ingalls T. B.		Spencer
Paul Walter,	Northborough	Avery Henry,		Springfield
Dermott Stuart,	Whitinsville, Northbridge	Barber J. D.		"
Hollywood P. F.	North Bridgewater	Blodgett Brothers,		"
Howard & Caldwell,	"	Haynes T. L. & Co.		"
Scott Walter,	"	Kellogg D.		"
Tighe John,	"	King C. H.		"
Wilbour G. E.	"	Merrick & Huber,		··
TUCKER LYMAN,	North Brookfield	Miller Allen & Co.		"
Ballou Warren S.	Orange	Paine Charles,		··
Dodge F. G.	"	Ray Samuel C·		"
Staverts Walter,	Otis	Schober Charles,		"
Raymond T. W.	Oxford	Sweeney Wm.		"
Tolman Jonas,	North Oxford, "	McKenzie R.		Stoneham
Munger H. W.	Palmer	Northup S.		Stoughton
Wassum P. J.	"	Hayden Lott,		Sudbury
Ennis Edward,	Peabody	Brown & Jenney,		Taunton
Comerford Peter,	Petersham			

Tailors — continued.
COLBY SAMUEL, 11 Union block,
  (see front colored page),   Taunton
Foster & Barnard,   "
Green Thomas,   "
Harris Wm. H.   "
Heine F.   "
Knight & Howard,   "
O'Mahoney Wm. O.   "
Simmons E. S.   "
Skinner F. T.   "
Steele & Baker,   "
Davis P. S.   Templeton
Moran P.,   Otto River,   "
Watts J.   "   "
Andrews Samuel, Holmes's Hole, Tisbury
Anthony Abraham,   "   "
Parkinson John,   Topsfield
Cram David,   Townsend
Wheeler L. C.   Uxbridge
Cate John M.   Wakefield
Kline John P.   Wales
Early John,   Walpole
Silver J. W.   Waltham
McKinstry Wm.   Ware
Mulligan P.   "
Runnells Levi A.   Wareham
Wetherbee S. & J.   Warren
McMaster A.   Watertown
Rogers A. B.   "
Bullard Ethan,   Webster
Hethrington John jr.   "
Thompson Wm. W.   "
Higgins Allen,   Wellfleet
Rich Snow,   "
Whorf & Higgins,   "
Forbes Joseph,   Wendell
Burnap H. A. & Co.   Westboro'
Goddard L. M.   "
Rowley H.   West Brookfield
Foote W. H. & Co.   Westfield
Gehle Charles P.   "
Greene L. C.   "
Phelps C. H.   "
Snow & Thayer,   "
    West Roxbury
Henderson George,   Jamaica Plain,   "
BUCHANAN JOHN,   "   "
Bristol A. T.   West Stockbridge
Thorpe D. G.   "
Kitchen & Redwood,   Weymouth
READ M. H.   "
Merchant R. V.   East Weymouth,   "
Dembroeder A.   North Weymouth,   "
Winch L. J.   Williamsburgh
Austin Joseph,   Williamstown
Hindley George,   "
Carter Charles L.   Winchendon
Davis P. S.   "
Salisbury Wm.   Winchester
Crohan Patrick,   Woburn
Gage G. R. & Co.   "
GRANT A.   "
Teare P.   "
Tyler J. P.   "
Bigelow & Longley,   Worcester
Bradshaw T. C.   "
Brown W. & T.   "
Davis A. & J. E.   "
Doherty Hugh,   "
Eames D. H.   "
Elliott M. H.   "
Foley Maurice,   "
Garretty James,   "
Hollander G.   "
Kind Frederick,   "
Mecorney Wm.   "
Parker Samuel,   "

Perry & Paul,   Worcester
Smith Thomas F.   "
Strom T. H. & Co.   "
Sturtevant L. W.   "
Walbridge A.   "
Walker Asa,   "
Willard & Devereaux,   Yarmouth
Crowell Joseph,   South Yarmouth,   "
Hale Joseph,   Yarmouth Port,   "

Tallow Chandlers.

(See also Soap and Candles.)

RUGG GEO. W.   Grafton st.   Worcester

Tank Builders.

DOBBINS & CRAWFORD, Dutton,
  near Mechanics' Mills (see page
  737),   Lowell

Tanners and Curriers.

(See also Curriers; also Hides and Leather; also Morocco Dressers.)

Dean H. Nelson & Son,   Adams
Butler A. P. & Co.   North Adams,   "
WHITNEY AUSTIN & CO. Ashburnham
Sanderson L. C.   Ashfield
Lee, Davenport, & Williams,   Athol
Davenport Otis P.   "
Jones & Baker,   "
Tiffany Brothers,   Attleborough
Coupe Wm. & Co.   S. Attleborough,   "
Warren E. G. & J.   Auburn
Claflin & Co.   Becket
Bates David,   Blandford
Bates Francis,   North Blandford,   "
Loring & Searle,   Braintree
Higgins Asa,   Brewster
Browning John W.   Brimfield
Robinson S. A.   Brookline
Warren Wm.   "
Bailey S. B.   Buckland
Fisher F.   North Cambridge,   Cambridge
Kueller M.   "   "
Muller Wm.   "   "
Guild Chester & Sons,   Charlestown
Mason & Coles,   Cheshire
Richardson & Wilkinson,   "
Hopgood G. D.   Chester
Byrt & Bullens,   Chicopee
Clapp Wm. T.   Conway
Kaulback Geo. C.   "
Shaw Lorenzo,   Cummington
Fowler Samuel P., Danvers Port, Danvers
Hersey Samuel D.   "   "
Merrill Joseph,   "   "
Perry Joseph F.   "
Smith Lyman & Son,   S. Dedham,   Dedham
Smith Whiting,   "   "
Winslow Brothers,   "   "
    Deerfield
Billings Samuel D., South Deerfield,   "
Pratt Henry,   Dudley
Clark Edward,   Eastham
Connell Hugh,   "
Sherman Amos,   "
Shoals H. B.   East Hampton
Goodhue Francis,   Essex
Chase Edmund,   Fall River
Briggs Sylvester & Son,   Freetown
Hillard H. P.   Georgetown
Marks L. B.   West Granville, Granville
Kilburn Levi,   Great Barrington
Barton Lyman G.   Greenfield
Alley J. B. & Co., Groton Junction, Groton
Parker Nathaniel,   Groveland
Hancock Shakers' Tannery,   Hancock
Church Wm.   Hanover

Butters F.   Haverhill
Loring Alfred,   South Hingham,   Hingham
Knight Asher & Warren,   Hinsdale
Warren W. G. & Son,   Holden
Woodward J. F.   Hubbardston
HUDSON TANNING CO.   Hudson
Porter Seth & Son,   Huntington
                                  Leominster
Putnam & Phelps, North Leominster,   "
Empire Tanning Co.   Leverett
Mitchell Patrick,   Lexington
Crok E. G.   Lowell
Webster & Co.   Malden
Knight John, jr.   Manchester
Gibson William,   Medfield
Norfolk Tannery,   Medway
Greggs Salem,   West Millbury,   Millbury
Sumner Jabez,   Milton
Pond B. F.   Montague
New Bedford Tanning Co.   New Bedford
Davis Geo. C.   Northborough
Rogers James R.   North Brookfield
Davenport, Williams, & Co.   Orange
Brown & Celler,   Peabody
Chandler Samuel C.   "
Elliot Isaac B.   "
Elliot L. W.   "
Frost John,   "
Hardy Isaac, jr.   "
Harrington Chas. & Co.   "
Harris Samuel,   "
Hodgkins Joseph,   "
Jacobs Joseph, jr.   "
Munroe Isaac,   "
Nelson & Merrill,   "
Osborn Calvin P.   "
Osborn D. W.   "
Osborn C. W. & Bro.   "
Osborn Franklin jr. & Co.   "
Osborn Geo. P. & Co.   "
O'Shea Timothy,   "
Pierce William,   "
Pinder & Winchester,   "
Poor Henry C.   "
Poor Joseph,   "
Poor L. & G. H.   "
Proctor Thomas E.   "
Sanger A. H.   "
Smith Richard,   "
Smith Silas,   "
Southwick S. A.   "
Stevens John V.   "
Symonds Samuel, jr.   "
Torr Andrew,   "
Treadwell Nathaniel R.   "
Upton F. & Co.   "
Wilson Warren,   "
Sanderson P. Myron,   Phillipston
Coogan Owen,   Pittsfield
Paine & Garrity,   Quincy
Page John, jr.   "
Benton Steven R.   Richmond
Scott Thomas & Son,   Rowe
Hull E. B. & Co.   Boston,   Russell
Andrews Gilman A.   Salem
Braden James,   "
Carleton Edward F.   "
Carleton Henry W.   "
Conway John H.   "
Culliton John,   "
Dugan James,   "
Egan Martin,   "
Erin & McGrath,   "
Evans A. A. & Sons,   "
Frye Frederick A.   "
Frye Joseph S.   "
Gibney John,   "
Hadley George S.   "

Harrington Charles & Co.   Salem
Haskell Daniel C.   ·   "
Hill & Brown,   "
Kenney William,
Lord James & Son,   "
Madigan & Brennan,
Maloon William,
Morse L. B.   "
Muhlig Robert,
Nichols William F.
Osgood N. W.
Pope Eleazer & Son,   "
Pratt Elisha,   ◂   "
Putnam Jacob & Co.   "
Riley James,   "
Sanborn James A.   "
Snow & Redmond,
Stimson James C.   "
Turner Calvin,   "
Varney Henry,   "
Varney W. D. & S.
Weston Charles & Sons,
Wilkins John H.   "
Wilkins Albert,   "
Burt Orlo,   New Boston,   Sandisfield
Hull Albert,   "   "
Brown Leonard,   Sheffield
                                 Shelburne
Bardwell A. & Son, Shelburne Falls, "
Nelson & Rice,   Shrewsbury
Galpin J. A.   Southwick
Kellogg Lorenzo,   Westfield,   "
Proctor Edward & Son,   Spencer
Bailey Charles M. & Son,   Sterling
TIDD WILLIAM & CO.   Stoneham
Bennett Nelson,   Sturbridge
Allen L.   Fiskdale,   "
Sibley Israel P.   Templeton.
Luce & Sawyer. Holmes's Hole, Tisbury
Hull Albert & Co. New Boston, Tolland
Southwick J. F.   Uxbridge
Farrington Zeno,   Wales
Bosworth H. B.   Warren
Freeman D. C.   Wellfleet
Paige William,   West Brookfield
Rice Mathias & Son,   West Hampton
Ely Cotton, Ashleyville, West Springfield
Ely Homer,   "   "
Benton Stephen,   West Stockbridge
Graves & Lamb,   Williamsburg
Nelson & Rice,   Winchendon
Bachelder C.   Winchester
Johnson W.   "
Mosely A.   "
Nutter L.   "
Thompson A. 3d,   "
Pierce Reuben,   East Windsor, Windsor
Paine Sylvanus,   Winthrop
BACON JOHN & CO.   Woburn
BLAKE, HIGBEE, & CO.   "
Conn Horace & Co.
Cummings John jr. & Co.
Dever P. J.
Shepard A. N. & Co.
Thompson A. & Co.
Winn J. B. & Co.
Winn, Eaton, & Co. North Woburn,   "

Tap and Die Manufacturers.

NEW YORK TAP & DIE CO. (see
    page 686),   North Harwich, Harwich

Tape Weavers.

Williston & Arms Manufacturing
    Co.   Northampton
Richardson N. & Co.   Warren
Hamilton C. W. & Co.   Worcester
Washburn L. K. & Co.   "

Tassel Manufacturers.

Burr, Brown, & Co.   Hingham

Taxidermists.

Jillson Samuel,   Hudson
Vickary Nathaniel,   Lynn
Leighton W. H.   Marlborough
Sylvester S. H.   Middleborough
Sherman Isaac C.   New Bedford
Sedgwick & Brandon,   Pittsfield
Horsford B.   Springfield
Blood Charles L.   Taunton

Tea Dealers.

(See also Grocers.)

Biddle Bros.   Amesbury
Ar Chun Joseph,   Chelsea
Daley & Miller,   Fall River
Higgins E. S.   Lowell
Hughes John,   "
Humphrey Clark E.   "
Ryerson C. E.   "
    New Bedford
Haswell S. S. & Co. (wholesale),   "
TUCKER & CUMMINGS, 66 & 68
    William,   "
Wilde Samuel,   "
Hall Alvan,   Salem
Guy & Brothers,   "
Potter Jesse F.   "
Japan Tea Co. S. E. Goodyear, Springfield
Little J H. & Co.   "
Springfield Tea Co.   "
Sweetland, Crowell, & Co.   "
Bourke Brothers,   "
Holden A. & Co.   Worcester
Marden James,   "

Teachers.

(Principals of High, Grammar, and Private
Schools; and Male Assistants in the same.)
(See also Colleges, &c.; page 94.)

Richardson George L. (high),   Abington
McDonald J. W. (high), E. Abington,   "
Poole Jerome B. (high), North   "   "
Meserve Alonzo (high), So.   "   "
Spaulding W. W. (high),   Adams
Miner Anson D. (academy), N. Adams,   "
Blaisdell Albert P. (grammar), Amesbury
Lane D. N.   "   "
Wiggin Frank,   "   "
Warren H. P. (high), W. Amesbury,   "
Nash H. C. (institute),   Amherst
Parkhurst C. H. (high),   "
Goldsmith Wm. G. (high),   Andover
Sawin H. C. (grammar),   "
Norris J. O. (high),   Ashland
Bradford Geo. R. (grammar),   Arlington
Grover E. O. (grammar),   "
Bardwell C. (high),   Athol
Rice Gardner (high),   Attleborough
Rice Watson (grammar),   "
Daggett Cora Miss, North Attleboro',   "
Porter Burrill, jr.   "   "
Bassett Theodore F.   Barnstable
Russell Wm. H. (high),   "
Lovell Asa E.   Osterville,   "
Tappan E. (high),   Centreville,   "
Clark Stephen (high),   Barre
Davis Abbie (grammar),   Bedford
Terry N. M. (high),   Belchertown
Davies Eben H. (high),   Belmont
Mack David (boarding),   "
Burrows B. S.   Bernardston
Ward L. F.   "
Griffin D. N. (grammar),   Beverly
Griffin LeRoy F. (high),   "

Haskell Wm. (grammar),   Beverly
Tucker Samuel (high),   Billerica
Hill Melvin H. (high),   Blackstone
Phillips Sidney A. (high),   Bolton
Bisbee Annie M. (grammar),   Bradford
Fiske Martin,   "
Webster Mary E. (private),   "
Groce Byron (high),   Braintree
Faxon E. A. Miss (private),   East Braintree,   "
Baker Addie (grammar),   Brewster
Baker Olivia (primary),   "
Sears Julia A. (grammar),   "
Snow Amanda F. (grammar),   "
Boyden Albert G. (normal),   Bridgewater
Freeman T. (high),   "
Willard Horace M. (academy),   "
Brookings Elias (grammar),   Brimfield
Harrington Samuel (high),   Brookfield
Bentley D. H. (grammar),   Brookline
Daniels David H. (grammar),   "
Horr John E. (high),   "
Knapp A. M. (high),   "
Lannan T. E. (grammar),   "
Bradbury W. F. (high),   Cambridge
Gillet Joseph A. (high),   "
Kendall Joshua (private),   "
Orne John, jr. (high),   "
Williston L. B. (private),   "
Cogswell F. (grammar), E. Cambridge,   "
Fletcher R. H. (grammar),   "   "
Mansfield Daniel (grammar),   "   "
Wheeler D. B. (gram.), N. Cambridge,   "
Magoun A. B. (gram.), Cambridgeport,   "
Rice Mary E. Miss (private),   "   "
Roberts B. W. (grammar),   "   "
Smith A. C. (grammar),   "   "
Wood A. E. Miss (private),   "   "
Earle J. E. (grammar),   Canton
Messenger H. S. (grammar),   "
Miner H. B. (high),   "
Pratt E. T.   North Carver,   Carver
Adams John G. (high),   Charlestown.
Badger Catharine (female seminary),   "
BAXTER TRACY (elocution, see
    page 805),   "
Boynton Sarah F. (private),   "
Darling L. A. (young ladies' institute),   "
Eaton W. E. (grammar),   "
Emery Caleb (high),   "
Gage Alfred P. (grammar),   "
Griffin B. F. S. (grammar),   "
Littlefield Geo. T. (grammar),   "
Murdock Caleb (grammar),   "
Swan George (grammar),   "
Waldo Susan A. (private),   "
Hadley D. (grammar),   Chatham
Blake Mary G. F. (private),   Chelsea
Hoyt Elizabeth G. (girls' grammar),   "
Payson John P. (grammar),   "
Pitkin Q. C. (high),   "
Stickney Edward (grammar),   "
WHEELER H. T. (mercantile), 101
    Winnisimmet,   "
Martin Jane C.   Cheshire
Pierce L. M. (high),   Chicopee
Valentine Wm. (grammar),   "
Stickney Warren B.   "
Tilton Thurston W. (high),   Chilmark
Hunt Josiah H. (high),   Clinton
Buck William E. (high),   Cohasset
Neal Geo. W. (high),   Concord
Forbes S. C. (high),   Conway
Morley F. G. (high),   "
Bowen C. Miss (high),   Dalton
Long Julia (grammar),   Dennis
Thacher Mary B.   South Dennis,   "
Howard Virgil M. (high),   Deerfield

Slafter Carlos (high), Dedham
Baker Frances Miss (grammar), "
Westcott Wm. H. "
Alger Roland F., (gram.), S. Dedham, "
Kimball C. F. " East " "
Knight Wm. H., " West " "
COCHRANE S. M. Mrs. (prin. Young
Ladies' School), Codman Hill, Dorchester
Aldrich Asahel F. Douglas
King E. A. "
Lovetta Minnie L. "
Streeter R. (grammar), "
Trufant Isaiah (high), Dudley
Chandler George T. (grammar),
West Duxbury, Duxbury
Moore Josiah (acad.),
Faxon Geo. L. (high), East Bridgewater
Sandford Austin, " "
Chapin Miss (high), East Hampton
Henshaw M. "
Wright E. M. "
Adams W. B. (high), Edgartown
Decker Nancy Miss (select),
South Egremont, Egremont
Burnham Sally (private), Essex
Perkins Martha,
Hitch A. F (private), Fairhaven
Bronson George W. (grammar), Fall River
Cook Benjamin, "
Davis James (private), "
Gordon Wm. R. (grammar), "
Hall J. Milton, " "
Hicks Charles R. "
Jones Sarah K. (private), "
Leonard G. F. (high), "
Slade A. K. "
Tewksbury M. W. (supt. schools), "
Davis Job F. Falmouth
Whitnee A. H. (private), Fitchburg
Tower Alonzo D. (high), Florida
Johnson & Way Misses, Foxborough
Torrey Mary, "
Walker Leonard (private), "
Allard J. W. (high), Framingham
Johnson A. Miss (State normal), "
Butler Henry (high), Saxonville, "
Bryant M. A. Miss (grammar), Franklin
Osgood Lydia A. Miss, " "
Senter T. G. (academy). "
Briggs Chester W. (grammar), Freetown
Briggs Harriet L. " "
Bacon Geo. A. (high), Gardner
Fickett E. S. (high), Georgetown
Hodgkins Sarah T. (grammar), Gloucester
Morrill J. L. (boys), "
Parmenter Henry A. (grammar), "
Rice Stillman (high), "
Tucker C. S. (grammar), "
Woodbury Harmon (boys), "
Malley Edward (high), Grafton
Great Barrington
Clark Frances M. Mrs. (select), "
Pratt S. Parsons (institute), "
Rood & Turner Misses (select), "
Nash H. N. Miss, Greenfield
Stickney W. B. (high), "
Stone Almy (boarding), "
Dawley Helen C. Miss (select), Hancock
Knight John G. (high), Hanover
Thorndike J. Prince (acad.), "
Bonney Otis L. (grammar), Hanson
Alden Cornelia Miss (grammar), Hardwick
Manly Clara (grammar), "
Morroe Louise Miss, "
Sibley Leander, " "
Brown Lucius, Haverhill
Cummings Henry (grammar), "
Shores Joseph A. (high), " .

Bates De Wit C. (grammar), Hingham
Goodrich Hosea G. "
Soule N. T., South Hingham, "
Childs M. Mrs. (high), Hinsdale
Perry Nancy (high), Holden
Lyon Wm. B. (high), Holliston
Andrews Amos (grammar), Holyoke
Andrews Jennie, "
Baldwin W. R. (high), "
Bates Elia, "
Branscomb C. M. Miss, "
Collins L. P. "
Ives Ellen, "
Jackson E. P. (high), "
Whiting E. Miss, "
Hill B. M. (high), Hopkinton
Morse James H. Hubbardston
Fickett W. C. (high). Hudson
Adams Charles (grammar), Ipswich
Cowles John P. " "
Lefavour I. (high), "
Ross T. B. (grammar), "
Worcester Leigh R. (grammar), "
Ellis W. R. (private), Kingston
Wormelle Benjamin (high), "
Gilbert Alfred A. (private), Lanesborough
Brewster J. L. (grammar), Lawrence
Cole J. K. " "
Perkins Albert C. (high), "
Rice Abner (high), Lee
Childs E. Miss, South Lee, "
Van Deuren P. Miss, " "
Leicester
Sackett D. P. (military academy), "
Littlefield A. (high), Lenox
Milller J. D. (high), Leominster
Knight W. H. (high), Lexington
Peabody S. (grammar), "
Moulton Nancy L. (high). Lincoln
MORRILL CHARLES, Supt of Public Schools, Office City Government
Building, Lowell
Balch Perley (grammar), "
Bement Samuel, " "
Chase Charles A. " "
Chase C. C. (high), "
Chase Samuel A. (grammar), "
Dodge F. O. Mrs. (grammar), "
Du Quet Edward (languages), "
Folsom Mary L. (private), "
Galloupe D. P. (grammar), "
Heywood Amos B. "
Hovey Harriet C. Miss (private), "
McCoy James, "
Moore Elisha, "
Moore E. jr. (business college), "
Peabody Joseph (grammar), "
Bancroft E. B. (private), Lynn
Batchelder John (grammar), "
Boynton S. P. Miss (private), "
Chase Henry L. (grammar), "
Ellis L. L. (private), "
Freese J. W. (grammar), "
Hills Nathaniel (high), "
Johnson Edward (private), "
Lewis Sarah F. (grammar), "
Moore Henry "
Shedd & Vassar Misses, "
Shorey Martha H. (grammar), "
Daniels Charles A. (high), Malden
Manchester
Richardson Augusta (grammar), "
Sargent N. B. (high), "
Berry John H. " Mansfield
Alley M. A. Miss (grammar), Marblehead
Brackett J. B. " "
Graves M. E. Miss " "
Noyes Joseph H. (high), "

Teachers — continued.

Wason T. H.　　　　　　　Marlborough
Wensel A. H. (high),　　　　　"
Cummings Charles (high),　　Medford
Hayes J. D. (grammar),　　　"
Sawyer Rufus,　　　　　　　"
　　　　　　　　　　　　　Medway
Moses Vincent (high), West Medway, "
Leighton R. F.　　　　　Melrose
Taft Putnam W. "　　　Mendon
Thayer Alice A. (grammar),　　"
Williams Gustavus B. (high),　　"
Sargent S. G. (grammar),　　Methuen
　　　　　　　　　　Middleborough
HAMBLY J. B. (commercial),　　"
JENKS J. W. P. (acad.),　　　"
Hill F. A. (high),　　　　　Milford
Hale C. G. (high),　　　　　Millbury
Atwood W. B. (grammar),　　Milton
Crafts F. F.　　　　　　　"
Hunt S. D. (high),　　　　　"
Howard H. F. (grammar),　　"
Richardson C.　　"　　　"
Hammond Charles Rev. (acad.),　Monson
Ingraham E. Miss (high),　Montague
Johnson Pauline T. (primary),　Nahant
Jose Edwin H. (grammar),　　"
Baxter J. F.　　　　　Nantucket
Dame Loren L.　　　　　"
Hussey H. C. (grammar),　　"
Macy Alex. jr. "　　　　"
Mildram Frank B. "　　　"
Tower Gideon N. (high),　　Natick
Clarke J. B. (acad.),　　Needham
Clarke Jefferson (high),　　"
Robinson Geo. F. (high),　Wellesley, "
Dewey Caroline,　　　New Ashford
Stanton Levi W. (acad.),　　Newbury
Parsons B. F. (institute), New Marlborough
Foster F. F.　　　　New Salem
Woodbridge J. E. Auburndale, Newton
Cushing C. W.　　　"　　"
Allen N. T. (acad.), West Newton,　"
Bartlett E. D. Miss (gram.), Northampton
Cudworth Electa Miss,　　　"
Clark & Spaulding,　　　"
Dickinson Mary E. Miss,　　"
Frisbee E. S. Rev. (high),　　"
Haskell Charlotte C. Miss,　　"
Ladd Carrie K. Miss (high),　　"
Bond Mary (high),　　Florence,　"
Judd E. F. Miss,　　　　　"
Thompson —— (gram.),　North Andover
Smith Samuel C. (high),　　"
Davis J. B. (grammar),　Northborough
　　　　　　　　　　Northbridge
Coburn Geo. (high), Whitinsville,　"
Dewing Almira S. (gram.), North Chelsea
Hawkes M. B.　　"　　　"
Oliver Carrie E.　　"　　"
Pollard Martha E. (primary),　"
Metcalf C. C. Mrs. (seminary),　Norton
Huse Mary F. (private),　　Northfield
Eastman S. Mrs. (private),　Orange
Eldredge Esther Y. Mrs. (gram.), S.
　　　　　　　　　　　Orleans
Hammond C. John (high),　Oxford
Conant Everett W.　"　Paxton
Blood Lorenzo P. (academy),　Pepperell
Leonard W. T. (institute),　Petersham
Shepardson J.　　"　　　"
Carter Emerson F.　　Pittsfield
Hubbard Dwight,　　　"
Lamb Anna C.　　　　"
Richards Wm. C.　　　"
Sloan Martha,　　　　"
Spear Charles V. (principal Maple-
　wood Young Ladies' Institute),　"

Tolman Albert (high),　　Pittsfield
Adams Theodore P.　　Plymouth
Cornish Aaron H. (grammar),　"
Davie Emma.　　　　"
Loring Lucy M.
Bates G. D.　　　Chiltonville.
Holmes Angeline (gram.), S. Plymouth, "
Barrows Deborah D. (gram.),　Plympton
Cobb Julia W.　　　"
Loring Nancy S.　　　"
White Mary A　　"　　"
Burt Ansel O. (high),　Provincetown
Chase Moses (grammar),　"
Brown H. B. (grammar),　Quincy
Hillman B. T.　"　　"
Hobbs Lewis F.　"　　"
Travis Charles V. (high),　"
Webster Granville S. (grammar),　"
Deane V. H.　　　　Randolph
Thayer Wales B. (grammar),　"
West Thomas H.　　　"
Beal John V. (gram.), E. Randolph. "
Cole Cyrus (high),　　Reading
Rounseville Cornelia (acad.),　Rochester
Sparrow Susan (private),　"
Bradstreet Ezekiel (boys'),　Rockport
Parsons Jeannette (high),　"
Pool Sophia A.　"　　"
Smith Alfred L. (grammar)　Rowley
Brown Jacob F. (grammar),　Salem
Brown Charles B.　"　　"
Chisholm A. F. (private),　"
Davis Abner H. (high),　"
Eustis Nancy R. (private),　"
Fitz Mary A. (grammar),　"
Francis A. B. (French),　"
Gomes Anna (private),　"
Hayward Wm. P. (grammar),　"
Leavitt Wm. (navigation),　"
Richards W. W. (private),　"
Shepard Mary L. (grammar),　"
Taylor Matilda P. (private),　"
Tibbets Sarah H.　"　　"
Very Frances E.　"　　"
Very M. N.　　"　　"
Ward E. W.　　"　　"
Warren Levi F. (grammar),　"
Woodman Henry F.　"　"
Davis J. H.　　"　Salisbury
French Frederick (high),　"
Rogers J. Burton,　"　"
　　　　　　　　Sandisfield
Shepard Geo. A. (high), Montville, "
Sears Clara H. (academy),　Sandwich
Spring Wm. Clifton, "　"
　　　　　　　　Saugus
Hall Mary Miss (gram.) Cliftondale, "
Allen Amy F. (primary),　Scituate
Curtis M. E.　　　"
Ellins Ellen,　　　"
Litchfield Sarah T.　　"
Perry Mary O. (primary), N. Scituate, "
Rogers M. L. (high),　"　"
BILLINGS SANFORD W.　Sharon
Clark Clementine N. Miss (gram.),　"
　　　　　　　　Sheffield
Peck Mary A. (select), Ashley Falls, "
　　　　　　　　Shelburne
Hayes Florett Miss, Shelburne Falls, "
Buffinton Geo. B. (gram.),　Somerset
Baxter Geo. L. (high),　Somerville
Hunt S. C.　　(grammar),　"
Makechnie H. P.　"　　"
Marston ——,　　"　"
Pope C. G.　　"　　"
　　　　　　　　Southborough
Heath D. C., St. Mark's School,　"
Patterson G. H. (private),　"

Emery Edwin, (high), Southbridge
Hitchcock R. C. (grammar), South Hadley
Brown Henry B. (high), South Reading
Thompson D. G. (inst.), South Scituate
Egleston A. F. (grammar), Southwick
Chace ——, Spencer
Barrows Charles (grammar), Springfield
Bennett Grace (private), "
Burnett C. C. (institute), "
Gordon W. G. (private), "
Hoadley E. S. "
Howard Kate Miss (private), "
Foster E. F. (grammar), "
Fernald O. M. (high), "
Stebbins Milan C. " "
Stratton J. D. (grammar), "
Tracy M. M. (grammar), "
Willard Miss (private), "
Howe Alvah S. (private), Sterling
Bradley Geo. P. (high), Stockbridge
Canning E. W. B. (acad.) "
Hoffman Ferdinand, "
Reid Jared, jr. (boy's academy), "
Lowell Aaron (high), Stoneham
Marden Fanny Miss (gram.), Stoughton
White Wm. H. (high), "
Capin Rodney B. (gram.), E. Stough-
ton, "
Hitchcock Henry (private), Sturbridge
Hyde Sarah, " "
Shumway Kate (high), "
Porter P. C. (grammar), Swampscott
Swinerton John P. jr. (high), Taunton
Thayer Edwin (grammar), "
Wilson George C. " "
Lane H. F. (high), Templeton
Mitchell Moses (private), Tisbury
Tilton Thurston W. (gram.), "
Lovell Cyrus, West Tisbury, "
Clark Harmony (private), Tyringham
Northrup Laura, "
Hanson James (high), Uxbridge
Snow Benjamin T. Wakefield
Howard Albert (gram.), Ware
Walker Isaac (high), " "
Powers Erastus B. (high), Warehant
Stone O. B. " Warren
Kimball A. S. " Webster
Walker S. N. " Westborough
Dunbar Charles H. West Bridgewater
Westfield
Dickinson John W. (State normal), "
Greenough James C. (normal), "
Gibbs —— (high), "
Halladay J. H. (normal), "
Lloyd M. M. (grammar), "
Tuttle W. H. H. " "
Davis Albert E. Westford
Whitman M. "
Benton George (acad.), Westminster
Casey John (high), Weston
West Roxbury
Billings J. D. (gram.), Jamaica Plain, "
Forbush Leander P. (gram.), " "
Gregg James B. (high), " "
Howe E. W. " " "
Nutter Abner J. (grammar), " "
Smalley Daniel S. (private), " "
Willis Nathan E. (high), Weymouth
Fox E. B. (gram.), E. Weymouth, "
Shaw Geo. (high), N. " "
Ganwell F. B. " S. " "
Boothby Asa, Wilbraham
Cooke Edward, "
Hastings ——, "
Howe U. S. "
Lamb J. "
Robbins ——, "

Neil Miss (gram.), Williamstown
Smith Miss, (high), "
Russell F. W. " Winchendon
Patten D. D. " Winchester
Gardner Judith (primary), Winthrop
Green Winnie, "
Minor Albert J. (grammar), "
Hanson J. I. Woburn
Linscott A. R. "
Perkins George, "
Adams Geo. A. (young mens'), Worcester
Comins Edward I. (grammar), "
Foster C. C. " "
Fitz Samuel E. "
Howes B. G. (coml.), "
Hunt Addison A. (grammar), "
Huntington H. A. " "
Metcalf Caleb H. (highland), "
Parish Roswell (high), "
Peterson Ellis, " "
Souther Mary Miss (private), "
Wiggin Geo. W. (high), Wrentham
Yarmouth
Wing Daniel (gram.), S. Yarmouth, "
Cross Jos. W. jr. " Yarmouthport, "

Teachers of Music.

Noyes Henry, Abington
Wales S. R. Mrs. N. Abington, "
Gurney E. L. South Abington, "
Carter Mary Miss, N. Adams, Adams
Hinckley Abby L. Barnstable
Hayward Edward P. Braintree
Ingalls Wm. H. "
Kuessman August, Brookline
Loring Fannie L. "
Lopey Clara B. Miss, Canton
Harvey Alice Miss, Cambridge
Lincoln Nathan, "
Taylor Geo. M. "
White Helen Mrs. "
DeVilliers F. Madame, Cambridgeport, "
Hawkes Ellen E. Miss, " "
Munroe Henry P. " "
Ball Jennie Miss, E. Cambridge, "
Gilbert James L. " "
Putnam Henry H. " "
Rexford Lizzie M. Miss, " "
Arnold Augustus L. Charlestown
Anguera J. de, "
Ingraham C. A. "
Mulle E. "
Ricker M. S. Mrs. (piano), "
Rimback George, "
Zuchtmann Frederick, "
Capin Charles. Dedham
Thayer H. B. "
Keith E. W. East Bridgewater
Tripp H. Miss, Fairhaven
Bennett Hiram J. Fall River
Dean Lyman W. "
Dunning Josephine Miss, "
Fallowfield Wm. "
Peck Mary Miss, "
Robbins Charles H. "
Bascomb Ella Miss, Franklin
Day Preston, "
Lane Eustace, Gloucester
Loud Francis P. "
Parsons T· "
Wilson J. G. Greenfield
Baker Olive M. Miss, Harwich
Colby J. K. Haverhill
Cummings Helen B. "
Thaxter Ellen O. Miss, Hingham
Bullard O. B. Holliston
Jones S. P. "
Fosgate Charles O. Hudson

Teachers of Music — continued.

Killon M. A. M.	Lawrence
Massuere Winnie,	"
Richards John M.	"
Bradley Sarah,	Lee
Foote Warren S.	Lowell
Hamilton Mary H.	"
Hill Asa V.	"
Hutchinson Reuben,	"
Lennon Joseph G.	...
Morrison John F.	"
Stevens S. W.	"
Wheeler H. Mrs.	"
Willey Geo. F.	"
Bartol J. Mrs.	Lynn
Coffin Mary F.	"
Dearborn B. F. Miss,	"
Ellis Wm. C.	"
Keith C. N. R.	"
King Wm. S.	"
Knowlton S. B.	"
Roche T. D.	"
Weston Edward K.	"
Guiot Victor A.	Malden
Bates Mary J.	Mansfield
Cobb Pliny M.	"
Pickens Albert G.	Middleborough
Bacheller Warren,	Milford
Eldridge Lydia A.	"
Parker P. J. Mrs.	"
Wight Charles F.	"
Hussey O. F.	Nantucket
Aiken Nancy C.	New Bedford
Clark Elizabeth A.	"
Church Charles L.	"
Eaton Joseph, jr.	"
Kempton M.	"
Pierce H. P.	"
Thorup Andreas T.	"
White Charles A.	
	Newburyport
CHENEY JAMES W. 14 State,	"
Clarke Wm. H.	Northampton
Jones Henry (vocal),	"
Prince Kate E. Miss,	"
Shepard Julia Miss,	"
Faxon Wm. jr. (vocal), North Bridgewater	
Gurney J. V. (piano and organ),	"
Gurney Norton M. (organ),	"
Gurney Thomas J. (vocal),	"
Perkins S. C. (instrumental),	"
Dunham George H.	Pittsfield
Muschke Edwin J.	"
Clark Lizzie M.	Plymouth
Harlow Mary Mrs.	"
Russell Susan Miss,	"
Standish Sylvia Mrs.	"
Cook Eliza,	Provincetown
Kilburn Hattie,	"
Nickerson Rebecca,	"
Smith Lydia C.	"
Chisholm Martha H.	Salem
Comstock Celestia E.	"
Cutts Love P.	"
Emilio M.	"
Fenollosa Manuel,	"
Floyd Elizabeth E.	"
Honeycomb Sarah E.	"
Quimby A. M.	"
Safford Harriet M.	"
Upton Francis,	"
McLaughlin M. C.	Sandwich
Moon Norman L., Ashley Falls, Sheffield	
Clark Dwight,	Springfield
Coenen Louis,	"
Hoadly E. S.	"
Hutchins M. J. D.	"
Porter Byron,	"

Storrs Henry,	Springfield
Weibe Edward,	"
Whiting A.	"
Drake Frances Miss,	Stoughton
Meserve Maria Mrs.	"
Dunbar Joseph (vocal),	Taunton
Holmes F. A.	"
Humphrey C. R. Mrs.	"
Orth Jacob,	"
Ryan Wm. H.	"
Winch A. B.	"
Cummings E. S.	Ware
Richardson E. C. Mrs.	"
Ross J. Miss,	"
KREBS CARL,	Webster
Howard John E.	West Bridgewater
Fairchilds S. Miss,	Westfield
Gleason Margaret (piano and organ),	"
Lewis Ella Miss (piano),	"
Viner E. Miss, "	"
	West Roxbury
Rickley Marie Miss, Jamaica Plain,	"
Raymond R. F., E. Weymouth, Weymouth	
Bates Alpheus,	"
Loud Sarah E.	"
Blanchard H. A. Miss, N. Weymouth,	"
Ainsworth H. L.	Worcester
Allen B. D.	"
Allen A. S.	"
Bacon J. F.	"
Chaudter W. E.	"
Fiske Nellie,	"
Smith C. H.	"
Stearns C. C.	"
Sumner G. W.	"
Sumner M. J. Mrs.	"
Sumner William,	"

Teachers of Painting and Drawing.

Twombly J. H. Mrs.	Charlestown
Cole M. A. Miss, N. Scituate, Cohasset	
Raymond C. W. Mrs.	Gloucester
Magown S. B.	Lynn
Wright Helen M.	Lowell
Howland Fannie E. Miss,	Pittsfield
Merrill L. E. Miss,	Salem
Burrell Ambrose M.	Quincy
Cole M. A. Miss, N. Scituate, Scituate	
Gladwin G. E.	Worcester

Teachers of Penmanship.

Hartison Bertram,	Lowell
Rawson R. T.	"
MIDDLEBORO' COMMERCIAL COLLEGE,	Middleboro'
Brown Otis T.	Milford
Hayward L.	
Thompson Lyman H.	Monterey
Carter E. F.	Pittsfield
Potter W. W.	Springfield
Holmes F. A.	Taunton
Lamb Watson F. (acad.),	Wilbraham
Howes B. G.	Worcester

Teaming.

MARTIN W. L. (see page 724), Holyoke

Telegraph Office.

WESTERN UNION TELEGRAPH CO., Wm. P. Potter, manager, Fall River

Thimble Manufacturer.

Burbank S. D.   Springfield

Thread Manufacturers.

(*See also Cotton Thread Manufacturers.*)

CHACE B. A. (spool and skein), (see page 756), North Dighton, Dighton

PRATT AMOS (cotton, see p. 707), Easton
MORSE E. J. W. & CO. (Sea Island
  cotton, see p. 749), S. Easton, "
Connell Peter, Fall River
NIANTIC THREAD CO., J. E.
  Hills, treasurer, "
Wyoming Thread Co. "
HADLEY CO. (spool), Jones S. Davis,
  agent, Holyoke
Merrick Thread Co., T. Merrick, agt. "
  Lancaster
MANSFIELD P. R., S. Lancaster, "
Wilson E. C. & Co. (Sea-Island cot-
  ton), "
MASON & WALKER, Rockville, Medway
Blush Jerome P. Middlefield
SAMOSET MILLS, Plymouth
WARREN THREAD CO. (spool cot-
  ton and whip thread), Prescott st.
  (see page 716), Worcester

Ticket Agent.

READE LAWRENCE, 72 Main (Western and European, see page 782), Milford

Tile Manufacturers.

(See Brick Manufacturers.)

Tin Cylinder Manufacturer.

Peckham G. R. Worcester

Tin Plate and Sheet Iron Worker.

CLARK GEORGE H. Kingston

Tinned Wire Goods.

WOODS, SHERWOOD, & CO. Lowell

Tinsmiths.

(See Stove Dealers and Tinsmiths.)

Tin-ware Manufacturers.

(See also Stove Dealers and Tinsmiths.)
  Cambridge
Dover Stamping Co., Cambridgeport, "
White Cornelius, "
GRIFFIN GEO. H., North avenue,
  North Cambridge, "
Mitchell Porter, Greenfield
NASH J. W. & CO. 105 Central,
  (see page 739), Lowell
CLARK GEO. H. Kingston
Parker Warren W. New Bedford
Henry Harvey, Pittsfield
Dickinson & Mayo, Springfield
  Weymouth
TUCK LORENZO, South Weymouth, "
Smith & Murdock, Worcester

Tire Manufacturer.

Foster Walter K. (patent concave),
  Cambridgeport, Cambridge

Tobacco Dealers.

FULLER G. M. (leaf), Northampton
Forward J. M. & A. J. (leaf), Southwick

Tobacco Manufacturers.

Tudor Co. Charlestown

Tobacco Warehouses.

FULLER GEORGE M. Northampton
Graves & Tucker, "
Thayer, Waterman, & Beckman, Westfield
WHITNEY, LANE, & CO. "

Tobacconists.

(See also Cigars; also Snuff).

Cushman E. B., North Amherst, Amherst
Elliott G. H. Cambridge

Everdean Joseph B. Chelsea
Jones Wm. "
Taylor A. "
Abell J. L. Cummington
Holmes Charles A. Fall River
Abbott Wm. W. Lawrence
Foster C. R. "
Patrick S. C. Lowell
Meehan James, "
Mort James W. "
Napolski F. X. "
Weeks S. "
Oesting Charles A. W. New Bedford
FULLER G. M. Northampton
Battis & Brown, Salem
Chapple John D. "
Gardner Thomas N. "
Rowell Fred, jr. "
Skinner R. "
Skinner S. S. & Co. "
Semons Wm. C. "
Smith & Helt, "
Tabour Wm. "
CASE H. O. Springfield
Hosmer F. J. "
Mort Mary E. Mrs, "
Warner Frank G. "
Whitcomb Joseph, "
Gray Wanton H. Taunton

Tool Manufacturers.

(See also Edge Tools; also Machinists.)

Willcox & Barnett (jewellers),
  Attleboro' Falls, Attleboro'
PETTINGILL J. R. (ice tools), Cambridge
Hofer F. East Cambridge. "
MILLER'S FALLS MANUF. CO. (bit
  braces, wrenches, drill chucks, &c.,
  see page 721), Greenfield
Greenfield Bit and Stock Co. "
GREENFIELD TOOL CO. Alonzo
  Parker, agent, "
THOMPSON MANUF. CO (chisels,
  bit stocks, &c., see page 770), "
RUSSELL J. MANUF. CO. (knives), "
BRYANT A. & SON, 250 Lowell (picks,
  stone tools, &c.), Lawrence
Shepardson, H. S. & Co. Shelburne Falls
PARTRIDGE ALLEN & SON (pat.
  mallet), Medway
SNELL MANUF. CO. (augers, bits, &c.,
  see page 763), Fiskdale, Sturbridge
James H. L. (planes and moulding
  tools), Williamsburg
Thayer W. E. (screw-drivers), "
Elliott Henry, Taunton

Top Roller Coverers.

  Clinton
FOSTER GEORGE H. (see page 754), "
Nichols J. F. Fall River
WITHERELL D. & O. B., shop Meta-
  comet Mill, "
Russell & Houston, Holyoke
Page Edward, Lawrence
FOSTER E. E., Methuen, cor Frank-
  lin, "
Woodward John T. "
FOSTER E. E. 196 Derby, Salem

Torpedo Manufacturer.

Fay Henry H. Winthrop

Town Clerks.

(See page 79.)

Toy Manufacturers.

Noble & Cooley, Granville
Hersey Reuben, Hingham

Toy Manufacturers — continued.

HERSEY SAMUEL,   Hingham
Houghton & Edson,   Hudson
Union Manuf. Co.   Northampton
Barker & Jones (carts, sleds, hoops,
  &c.),   Montville,   Sandisfield
Chapin Albert T   South Hadley
Baker William, Baldwinsville, Templeton
Johnson C. N.,   East Templeton,   "
Cole William & Son (sleds), Ring-
  ville,   Worthington
Weeks Asahel (sleds), S. Worthington, "

Toy Stores.
(*See also Variety Stores.*)

Varnum C. T., East Cambridge, Cambridge
Jones J. G.   Charlestown
Ives Mary A. Mrs.   Chelsea
Nowell Geo. W.   Fall River
HERSEY SAMUEL,   Hingham
Clapp Geo. H.   Lynn
Kelley Warren,   "
McConnell James,   "
WEBSTER WM. T. 8 Exchange,   "
Borden C. T.   "
Hunt L. & Co.   Mansfield
Bates Ann E. Mrs.   Milford
Cobb Cephas,   New Bedford
Gregory John,   "
Hale L. C.   "
Haynes A. J.   Newburyport
Smith Joseph H.   "
Stevens Liberty,   Pittsfield
Skerry H. F. & Son,   "
Lyon C. T.   Salem
St. John Myron,   Springfield
Towle Olive C.   Westfield
Harrington F. W.   "
Merrill Enoch,   Worcester
Weixler Jacob P.   "

Transportation Agents.
(*See also Passenger Agents.*)

Cobb William,   Dighton
Whitmarsh Chas. E.   "
Taber, Gordon, & Co.   New Bedford
STAPLES & PHILLIPS (see page
  759),   Taunton
Munroe A. C.   Worcester

Trellises.

NOURSE, WHITE, & CO. (pot plant, Westboro'
  garden, and veranda, see page 826) "

Tripe Dealers.

Kay Nancy Mrs.   Fall River
Mead J. S.   Pittsfield
Taylor Addison,   Taunton

Trowell Manufacturer.

Bisbee Franklin,   Duxbury

Truckmen.

Butman James L.   Fairhaven
Ford William C.   "
Brown Andrew,   New Bedford
Brown, Helford, & Dudley,   "
Brown John,   "
Brownell John,   "
Corson Charles,   "
Corson Temple S.   "
Duff David,   "
Gammons George F. W.   "
Gifford Squire,   "
Gomley Alexander,   "
Greene Neil,   "
Hathaway Charles,   "

Hathaway Frederick A.   New Bedford
Leavitt Clark,   "
McFarlin Stephen,   "
Moulton Nathaniel,   "
Sawin A. K. P.   "
Snow George,   "
Thompson Samuel,   "
Tripp Francis,   "
Tripp Philip M.   "
Walker Charles,   "
Weaver Alfred,   "
Brooks A. R.   Salem
Dowst D. B.   "
Evans James G.   "
Full William L.   "
Gardner & Carter,   "
Hoyt Erastus,   "
Pitts Darling,   "
Pitts Nathaniel,   "
Smith Thomas,   "
Pratt & Heald,   Worcester

Trunk and Valise Manufs.
and Dealers.

Burrill John B.   Fall River
Coburn Charles,   "
Cragin H. H.   Holyoke
Allen J. C.   Lowell
Burgess E.   "
Knowles Bros.   "
Marriott John jr.   "
Molloy George,   "
Pierce & Washburn,   Middleborough
Kittredge B. R.   New Bedford
Waterman N.   "
Willis Wm. H.   "
Osgood B. H. & Son,   Salem
Cummings Josiah,   Springfield
COLBY SAMUEL, 11 Union blk.   Taunton
  (see front colored page),
Brown P.   Worcester

Trunk Wood Manufs.

Jones John H.   South Scituate
Pratt & Vinall,   "
Torrey David, jr.   "

Truss Makers.

CADWELL W. P. S. (dealer),
  49 Purchase,   New Bedford

Tubs, Pails, &c.
(*See Wooden Ware.*)

Turbine Water Wheels.

KILBURN, LINCOLN, & CO. (see
  page 756),   Fall River
TURBINE WATER WHEEL CO.,
  J. D. Chase & Sons (see page
  777),   Orange
Jordan John,   East Windsor, Windsor

Turners of Wood.
(*See also Bedstead Manufacturers.*)

Hills, Westcott, & Co.   Amherst
Morse Laban,   Athol
Jennings Willis T.   Becket
Hyde & Young,   Cambridgeport
Osborn D.   "
Scranton H. A. & O.   "
Copeland Chas. D.   Fall River
Copeland S. W.   "
POTTER R. N. & BROS., Davol st.   "
  (see page 756),
Hosmer H. J. & Co.   Fitchburg
Waymoth A. D. & Co.   "
Wright M. & Co.   So. Gardner, Gardner

Hyde Park
NEAL A. B. & CO. (see page 795), "
KNOWLTON GEO. K. & CO., 13
Union (see page 751), Lynn
MARSHALL J. OTIS (see page 750), "
Mayhew & Hayes, New Bedford
Parsons P. "
Collins George, Newburyport
Churchill Bradford D. Pittsfield
CHURCHILL & RICHARDSON,
190 Derby (see page 747), Salem
Clapp L. & A. "
Raymond, Low, & Co. "
Fitts L. L. Springfield
Babbitt F. S. Taunton
Murdock David C. West Boylston
Reed Reuben G. "
Culins Peter M. Westfield
Goodell J. M. Worcester

Twine and Line Manufs.

(See also Cordage; also Cotton Twine; also Rope Manufacturers.)

Slater L. Ashland
Boston Flax Mills, E. Braintree, Braintree
Shepard J. S., agent (seine and net
twine), Canton
East Hampton
Mansfield G. H. & Co. (fish lines), "
MORSE E. J. W. & CO. (Sea-island
cotton harness twine, see page 749),
South Easton, Easton
Hardy Alphonso M. Essex
Mears David, "
Mears Wm. H. "
Fall River
LAWTON & ESTES (see page 734), "
McCOWAN D. & CO., Annawan st.
(see page 711), "
Ray J. P. & J. G. Franklin
Lancaster
MANSFIELD P. R., S. Lancaster, "
Blauvelt W. H. & Co. (paper), Lee
CLARK JEREMIAH, 96 Middle
(loom harness, see page 738), Lowell
Hale B. S. & Son, Whipple's Mills, "
Deane George H. Ludlow
Taber Thomas, S. Malden, Malden
Holden Michael, Marblehead
Jackman Moses B. Newburyport
Silver Lake Manuf. Co. (chalk,
fish, and signal lines), Newtonville
Pattee John H. North Chelsea
Warner & Dart (cotton), Oxford
Parker Henry A. & Co. Pepperell
Diman Ezra, Plymouth
Irish C. B. "
Wilson David, "
Marvel John C. Rehoboth
Chisholm Joseph, Salem
Southborough
Cordaville Mills (twine), Cordaville, "
South Hadley
Aldrich Benjamin, South Hadley Falls, "
Spencer John, South Scituate
Stoughton
Southworth A. & Co. (harness twine), "
Hunter William, Tewksbury
Westport Manuf. Co. Westport

Umbrella Manufacturers.

Eastwood John (repairer), Fall River
TOLMAN WM. G., 150 Main, Fitchburg
Butler Enoch, Haverhill
Butler Wm. "
Ellis & Snow, Lawrence
Rugg & Griffith, Lowell
Cross Hugh, Lynn

Fitzgerald & Kelly, Salem
Lynch P. "
Servev Wm. T. "
Eldridge & Hastings, Springfield
Tittle Wm. (repairer), Taunton
Moore N. P. 207 Main, Worcester
r

Undertakers.

(See also Coffin Manufacturers.)

Holbrook O. M., East Abington, Abington
Pratt George W., North "
Holbrook Loring, South "
Fletcher Cyrus, South Acton, Acton
Stetson S. Adams
Adams Jasper H., North Adams, "
Isbell Cyrus P. "
Abbott Hermon, Andover
Hartwell John B. Arlington
Hartwell John H. "
Burr Robert, Ashby
Seaver Wm. Ashland
Lewis E. Athol
Stone J. G. Auburn
Conant Chauncey, Barnstable
Frost John H. Hyannis, "
Spalding Charles, Bedford
Spears John P. Belchertown
Hatch Lemuel, Belmont
Cushman A. R. Bernardston
Bowers Albert, Billerica
Osgood Samuel, "
Kimmens A. P. Bolton
Wetherbee Silas, Boxborough
Boylston
Wright Joseph M. Boylston Centre, "
Tenney William, Bradford
Gage Leander, Braintree
Thayer Jonathan, "
Crocker Elisha, jr. Brewster
Prophett William, Bridgewater
Pettengill T. S. Brookline
Marion A. P. Burlington
Devens Thomas, Cambridge
Wyeth Benjamin F. "
Hunt Samuel F. Cambridgeport, "
Litchfield Roland, jr. "
Pear John, "
Casey William, East Cambridge, "
Hadley A. A. "
LOCKHART WILLIAM L., Bridge,
cor. Third (see page 761), East
Cambridge, "
Shepherd Asa, Canton
Duren George F. Carlisle
Murdock Henry C. Carver
Vaughn Thomas, "
Cobb Thomas, North Carver, "
Hawks Myron, Charlemont
Bryant John, Charlestown
Coburn E. N. "
Denvir Patrick, "
Perry John L. "
Reade John, "
Nichols C. Charlton
Eldridge Gideon H. Chatham
Byam S. E. Chelmsford
Proctor Charles, "
Sheldon A. H. North Chelmsford, "
Pollard Dawson, West "
Haskell Thomas, Chelsea
Lynde James, "
Moon Thomas E. "
Noyes Henry, "
Stidley George, "
Bisbee Orin, Chesterfield
Hosley D. P. & Co. Chicopee
Vincent Moses C. Chilmark
Burdett Nathan, Clinton

Undertakers — continued.

Kent Isaac,	Cohasset
Rich Z.	"
Miller H. B.	Coleraine
FARRAR WILLARD T.	Concord
Flagg Joshua,	Dana
Mathews E. C.	North Dana, "
Chapman Howes,	Dennis
Burgess Isaac,	South Dennis, "
Bird Ebenezer,	Dorchester
Gleason S.	"
French Rufus,	Milton, "
Bowen Joseph,	Douglas
Kendrick Richard,	Dover
Proctor Zephonia P.	Dunstable
Chandler Charles H.	Duxbury
Weston Augustus,	"
Pomeroy Thomas J. & Son,	East Hampton
Pent Francis,	Edgartown
Moon William G.	Enfield
Powers Robert,	"
Gage Caleb S.	Essex
Borden, Almy, & Co.	Fall River
Masterson Thomas,	"
Westgate, Baldwin, & Co.	"
Davis Samuel P.	Falmouth
Hatch Harvey,	North Falmouth, "
Bourne Barnabas E.	Waquoit, . "
Cummings M. W.	Fitchburg
Bemis Henry,	Franklin
Alexander Easmon,	Gardner
Gould M. C.	"
Brocklebank David,	Georgetown
Thompson Otis,	"
Davis John,	Gloucester
Mason Eben E.	"
Gleason James,	Grafton
Langsdorff F.	Great Barrington
Slye & Hood, .	"
Trask Danforth,	Greenwich
Balch Thomas H.	Groveland
Richmond Andrew,	Halifax
Sturtevant Simeon,	"
Tibbetts John,	Hamilton
Damon Thomas,	Hanover
King George,	Hardwick
Eldridge Isaac G.	S. Harwich, Harwich
Cummings Joseph H.	Haverhill
Ripley & Newhall,	Hingham
Clark A. & Co.	Hinsdale
Bryant Lyman,	Holden
Bemis Cyrus W.	Holliston
Quint Nathaniel W.	Holyoke
Whittemore J.	Hopkinton
Ellithorp Levi P.	Hudson
Priest Silas,	"
Whittemore P. B.	Hyde Park
Clark Daniel,	Ipswich
Chandler Nathan,	Kingston
White Emory H.	Lancaster
Goodrich A. W.	Lawrence
Mahony John J.	"
Porter K. S.	"
Reynolds J. H.	"
Bassett Joseph,	Lee
GOODRICH R.	"
Kendall Oliver W.	Lexington
Flagg Henry,	Lincoln
Robbins N. B.	Littleton
Gordon & Currier,	Lowell
Burr Lyman,	Ludlow
Fuller Luther,	Lunenberg
Hadley Calvin,	"
Crossman John H.	Lynn
Orcutt Consider N.	"
Cobb E. C. & A. W.	Mansfield
Bliss N. P, & Co.	Marblehead
Stacy Wm. L.	"

Nelson Thomas,	Mattapoisett
Parker A. B.	Medfield
Woods Daniel,	Medway
Harding Theodore,	East Medway, "
Adams Stephen,	West " "
Morrison Daniel T.	Methuen
Soule George,	Middleborough
Fairbanks Leonard,	Milford
Bergin James,	"
Ryan William,	Millbury
Shepherd Henry V.	Milton
Richardson George B.	Montague
Doud Artemas,	Monterey
Johnson David,	Nahant
Sheffield Benjamin,	Nantucket
Burks A. W.	Natick
Perry E.	South Natick, "
Eaton George C.	Needham
Jenkins E. C.	Newton Lower Falls, "
Winch Moses,	Wellesley, "
Roy Lester,	New Ashford
COGGESHALL & CO. 20, 22,	
and 26 William (see page	
734),	New Bedford
Wilson Benj. G.	"
Crawford H. W.	New Braintree
Young Hiram,	Newbury
Copp Charles,	Newburyport
Donnell Geo. E.	"
Safford S. H. & Co.	"
Gammons J. E.	West Newton, Newton
Jenkins E. C.	Lower Falls, "
Phillips Wm.	Newton Corner, "
Smith Silas M. & Co.	Northampton
Burditt William,	Northborough
Howard, Clark, & Co.	North Bridgewater
Brewer Lysander,	North Brookfield
Burrill Alfred,	"
Pratt Joseph G.	North Chelsea
Wright Henry, 2d,	Northfield
Abbott Sumner S.	North Reading
Packard James,	Oakham
Bacon S. S.	Orange
Mayo Calvin,	"
Moore Nelson,	"
Temple Augustus,	"
Ward Willard,	No. Orange, "
Porter & Spear,	Otis
Carlton Chas. R.	Oxford
Harrington Silas D.	Paxton
Jones E. Morton,	Pembroke
Titus Moses,	Pepperell
Sawyer Elmer W.	Phillipston
PARKER C. E. (also furniture	
dealer),	Pittsfield
WHIPPLE S. T. & CO. (also	
furniture dealer), 21 North,	"
RAYMOND CHARLES, 35 Middle	
(see page 768),	Plymouth
Loring L.	Princeton
Knowles Robert,	Provincetown
Hall John,	Quincy
Kimball Chas. H.	"
Houghton Ralph,	Randolph
White Martin,	Raynham
Gleason Gilman C.	Reading
Pierce Lloyd B.	Rehoboth
Choate Caleb S.	Rockport
Stockwell Jerathmel,	Royalston
Woodbury George,	"
Baker Asa,	Rutland
Allen & Spring,	Salem
Buffum Charles S.	"
Buffum Geo. W.	"
Blake B. S.	Salisbury
Seymour Seth,	Montville, Sandisfield
Crane W. F.	New Boston, "
Allyne S. H.	Sandwich

Pope John W. Sandwich
Bliss William, Savoy
Hammond F. Scituate
Thomas Francis, "
Newcomb George, North Scituate, "
Leggett E. B. Shelburne Falls
Hartwell J. C. Shirley
Park William M. "
Maynard Augustus F. Shrewsbury
Forbes J. H. Shutesbury
Poull Nathan, "
Shove Joseph, Somerset
Randall Benjamin, Somerville
Hixon Edward, Southborough
Newton H. "
Marble Joel, Southbridge
Sparrell C. W. South Scituate
Moore Marcus A. Southwick
Lyndes H. A. & J. M. Spencer
Pomeroy & Fiske, Springfield
Washburn E. G. "
Patterson T. B. Stockbridge
Brinton Edward C. "
Withington P, M. Stoughton
Haynes M. Sturbridge
Lombard A. A. Sutton
Wheeler James, Swampscott
Gaffney John, Taunton
Gilmore William H. "
Washburn P. T. & H. S. "
Camberlin Moses, Templeton
Sawyer E. B. Baldwinsville, "
Preston H. E. Tewksbury
Peaks James D., Holmes's Hole, Tisbury
Seaver Thomas, Townsend
Waters J. J. West Townsend, "
Smith Samuel H. jr. Truro
Young Hiram O. Tyringham
Hunt John, Upton
Hilton Leander, Ware
Hastings Samuel, Warwick
Bullard Joseph, Wayland
Sly Amos T. Webster
Spalding Hiram, "
Sparrow R. O. & Z. Wellfleet
Bickford Joseph, Wenham
Robbins Chandler, Westborough
Leonard Elihu, West Bridgewater
Lambson Clinton K. Westfield
Day Amos, Westford
Nutting Asia, "
Snow Levi, "
Gibbs Geo. W. Westminster
Bradley Thomas, West Newbury
Dow Abram, "
Jones Theodore, Weston
White Holden, Westport
Curtis Samuel, Weymouth
Daymon & Rice, East Weymouth, "
Crafts Eli, Whately
Rice James A. Wilbraham
Ingraham H. H. Williamstown
Nichols Samuel B. Wilmington
Peck Henry, Winchendon
Sharon J. D. Winchester
Floyd John, Winthrop
Hildreth Geo. G. Worcester
McConville F. A. "
Sessions Geo. & Son, "
Drury Abel P. Worthington
Fuller George, Centre, Wrentham
Randall E. B. "
Mann Levi, North Wrentham, "
Pond J. E. South Wrentham, "
Hawes Amos C. Plainville, "
Vaughn D. S. "

Upholsterers.

Livermore & Thaxter, Brighton
Koch John, Brookline
Moore Albert H. "
Perry L. M. "
Thompson John, "
Graves George, jr. Cambridge
Harris Stephen S. "
Holmes & Davis, "
Holt J. A. "
Whitney & Brackett, "
Swett Lewis C. & Co., Cambridgeport, "
Baker S. H. Charlestown
Homer H. W. "
Johnson John L. "
Perkins D. B. "
Bosson Wm. Chelsea
Newell Hervey, "
PETTINGELL A. T. Dedham
Borden, Almy, & Co. Fall River
Newell C. P. "
Westgate, Baldwin, & Co. "
Fosgate M. C. Fitchburg
Harris W. D. Haverhill
Stowe A. F. "
Wyatt Charles, East Haverhill, "
Colby E. C. Holyoke
Loring Bros. "
Cook Francis R. Lawrence
Pillsbury J. jr. "
Offutt George & Son, Lowell
Ray William E. "
Attwill Jesse L. Lynn
Austin David, "
Bean, Johnson, & Co. "
Higgins T. B. Marblehead
Webster G. H. Medford
Knight William, New Bedford
MAXFIELD CALEB, "
Warner J. A. "
Lord T. H. & A. W. Newburyport
Swan Richard W. "
Wetherbee B. S., Newton Corner, Newton
Maker Henry, Newton Upper Falls, "
Smith Silas M. & Co. Northampton
Caldwell H. M. Florence, "
RAYMOND CHARLES, 35 Middle
(see page 766), Plymouth
Arey Joseph, jr. Quincy
FURNALD N. B. "
Collier Perry, Salem
Goldthwaite Willard & Co. "
Ide Edwin R. "
Mackie John, "
Rogers John W. "
Shepard Samuel, "
FISHER, BUCKHOUSE, & KNAPPE,
Union Block, Springfield
Maxfield & Kellogg, "
Gilmore William H. Taunton
Maxham L. M. "
Robbins C. "
Nourse B. R. & Co. Westborough
Gibbs Geo. W. "
Boman H. A. Westminster
Brown Wm. Worcester
Cary Phineas, "
CHOLLAR JOHN D. 198 Main (see
page 783), "
Eidt Jacob, "
Maynard D. B. "

Upholstery Goods Manuf.

Burr, Brown, & Co. Hingham

Valentines.

Whitney Manufacturing Co. Worcester

Variety Stores.

(See also Country Stores.)

Fairbanks C. W.   S. Abington, Abington
Carter Sarah Mrs.   Amesbury
Poyen Francetti,   West Amesbury,   "
Sargent J. W.   "   "   "
Thayer O. S.   Attleboro'
Thompson C. J.   "
Jones Thomas R.   North Attleboro',   "
Parsons Mrs.   Brighton
Gilbert Edward Mrs.   Brookline
Tandy Jane Mrs.
Cambridgeport,   Cambridge
Hunting Thos.   East Cambridge,   "
Kelley Margaret L.   "   "
Smith Charles,   "   "
Stoddard H. T.   "   "
Ellis D. C. F.   Canton
Wood Rufus C.
Burroughs Anna L.   Charlestown
Dickey Harriet,   "
Evans A. B.   "
Hunt Sarah,   "
McGowan Judith,   "
Perkins Nathan G.   "
Fanning Bernard,   Chelsea
Frisbie John Mrs.   "
Hartley F. N. Mrs.   "
Kendall Joanna,   "
Nunns Elizabeth,   "
Robertson M. Mrs.   "
Rogers Charlotte Mrs.   "
Saville John T.   "
Blackmer W. L.   Chicopee
Sullivan James,   "
Davis C. E.   Concord
Melvin James C. & Co.   "
Bradshaw Aaron,   Dorchester
Kendrick John,   Milton,   "
Keene James,   East Hampton
Barrows J. L.   Edgartown
Devine Catharine,   Fall River
Ford L. B.   "
Horton Geo.   "
McDonough John F.   "
McKenney Felix,   "
Rafferty Michael,   "
Smith Thomas B.   "
Tidmer John A.   "
Webb Thomas,   "
Jones John,   Gloucester
Wait John H.   "
Barrett Moses,   East Gloucester,   "
Brazer John W.   "   "
Douglas Jonathan,   "   "
Story Charles,   "   "
Duston John K.   Lanesville,   "
Haskell Henry C. L.,   W. Gloucester,   "
Barker Wm. T.   N. E. Village,   Grafton
Barnard John,   Hingham
Tower William,   S. Hingham,   "
Haskins Milo J.   Hinsdale
Baker John R.   Holyoke
Tefts E. F.   "
Plummer C. E.   Ipswich
Tibbetts M. J.   "
Brown J. P.   Lawrence
Burns Thomas,   "
Davis L. Mrs.   "
Graham Margaret,   "
Henderson Wm. S.   "
Holmes Joseph,   "
Horne Joseph,   "
Kennedy Stephen,   "
Leybourn Mary,   "
Logan Eliza,   "
Payson C.   "

Reardon Bros.   Lawrence
Stanley William,   "
Sykes John,   "
Williams Chas. S.   Lawrence
Alcott A. G. A.   Lowell
Bamford C. T.   "
Baxter O. P. Mrs.
Belleisle Oliver,
Berry Harriet Mrs.
Besse J. V.
Blake E. O.
Boyle Catharine,
Brewster John L.
Brown Alice,
Cavanaugh Thomas,
Chase A. W.
Clark Anna,   "
Clark Betsey,
Clark John H.
Collins Josiah T.
Cook William G.
Courtesmanches Peter,
Cowen Wm.   "
Crombie Wm.
Cummiskey James W.
Curtis Rose Mrs.
Devlin James,
Dooley Edward,
Dowling John,
Drury Thomas,   "
Eastman Daniel,   "
Eaton Daniel A.   "
Elliott Edmund,   "
Evans Wm.   "
Faunce A. B.   "
Fisher M. Mrs.   "
Follansby Ellen Mrs.
Ford Lydia N.
Glazier & Taylor,   "
Glidden N. A.   "
Gower Richard,   "
Grush Clara,   "
Hall John,   "
Herrick Edward S.   "
Higgins James,
Higgins William,   "
Hill E. W. Mrs.
Hinchcliffe Richard,   "
Hobbs Ruth,   "
Huntley John,   "
Kaley Michael,   "
Lamere A.   "
Lamere John,   "
LELAND WILLIAM, 250 Gorham,   "
Libbey N. F.
Livingston J. H.
Lynch Abbie S. Mrs.   "
Marble C. H.   "
Martin George L.   "
Martin Hannah,   "
Martin & Bryant,   "
Mayberry Eliza,
McBride B. F.
McCanney John,
McGuire Cornelius,
McLaughlin James,   "
McNamara Mrs.
Melvin Susan J.
Norris John,
Ogilvie Nancy J.
O'Grady John,
Page Martha,   "
Pussell James,   "
Rand M. A.   "
Reiley B.
Riley James E.
Rodcliffe Wm.
Ryan John,

Salls H. M Mrs. Lowell
Senior George Mrs. "
Shandley J. Mrs. "
Shaw Ruth S. "
Sheban E. "
Slavin Mary Mrs. "
Smith Kate, "
Sparks John, "
Stanton Charles P. "
Stevens A. "
Sugden Wm. "
Symonds Edward, "
Tierney Michael, "
Tolman J. C. "
VARNEY CHARLES L. 157 Middle-sex, "
Waite James, "
Welch J. "
Whelan Annie Mrs. "
Whiteside W. "
Whitty John, "
Wilby Benjamin, "
Wiley R. F. "
Wilkins M. F. "
Willoughby M. E. "
Wilson John, "
Wing J. T. "
Hall Richard H. Lynn
Kelley Warren, "
Preble M. A. & Co. "
Butman Thomas M. Malden
Ray Lydia Mrs. Maplewood,
Rabardy J. F. Manchester
Hordon N. H. Mansfield
MOWRY G. W. & C. H. "
Bartol Hannah, Marblehead
Court Charles, "
Symonds Henry O. "
Wilford George, "
Howe Sidney, Marlborough
Dudley Elijah, Millbury
Coggeshall Nathaniel, Nantucket
Bates Ann E. Miss, New Bedford
Buckley L. S. Mrs. "
Costa Joseph, "
De Wolfe A. J. Mrs. "
Drury Warren, "
Ferguson Charles F. (second-hand articles), "
Fuller S. D. Mrs. "
Gardner James T. "
Gardner Thomas A. "
Goodale Ada S. Mrs. "
Howland Lydia W. "
Howland E. Mrs. "
Johnson H. J. "
King Joseph F. "
Lewis F. "
Marshall Joseph T. "
Marshall R. P. "
Openshaw Mary Mrs. "
Paul Frank, "
Pease Peter, "
Tilden & Co. "
Waterman N. "
Wood Josiah, "
Blodgett Jesse G. Newburyport
Brown Charles F. S. "
Fegan James L. "
Haynes A. J. "
Henderson Joseph, agent, "
Jackman Thomas H. "
McCusker John, "
McKay William, "
Morton Reginald, "
Pearson W. M. "
Sullivan John D. "
Tappan Joseph & Co. "

25

Childs H. P. Mrs., Lower Falls, Newton
Clapp B. E. North Bridgewater
Higgins Abner, Orleans
Peirce Joseph H. Peabody
Ellis Bartlett, Plymouth
Hopkins Joshua F. Provincetown
Hopkins Rufus, "
Terry George H. "
Willard Harry, "
Young James, "
Briggs Charles, Randolph
Veazie B. G. "
Gleason L. E. Reading
Andrews Betsey F. Rockport
Boynton David P. "
Butman S. H. "
Elwell George, 2d, "
Gee James W. "
Harris Sarah Mrs. "
Haskins Moses Mrs. "
Story Henry L. "
Tufts Joseph, "
Witham George, "
Alton Carrie S. Salem
Berminghaun C. "
Byrne A. E. Mrs. "
Caraway S. C. "
Carlton J. "
Clark Sarah F. "
Currier Lydia, "
Gorman Margaret, "
Knight M. B. & M. "
Lemon Helen W. "
Minor A. H. "
O'Keefe Mary, "
Phillips George Mrs. "
Plummer R. "
Reid Mary A. "
Rhodes M. Louisa, "
Smith M. B. Miss, "
Stephenson Elizabeth, "
Stickney Joseph, "
Story Francis B. "
Symonds E. G. "
Teague William, "
Tibbetts Betsy, "
Wuhr L. W. "
Currier S. Salisbury
Dennett A. H. "
Clark C. W. "
Lyon C. T. Springfield
Sanderson W. "
Drake Leonard, "
Pierce William Mrs. Stoughton
Fisher A. B. Mrs. "
WASHBURN GEO. W., Westminster, Taunton
cor. Washington (see page 757), "
Woodward W. P. "
Cummings J. W. Ware
Hathaway P. M. Warren
Morgan E. C. "
Britton J. W. jr. Westborough
Burrell J. D. West Bridgewater
Sweetland E. S. Westfield
West Roxbury
Chase H. H. Mrs., Jamaica Plain, "
Allen Mark, Woburn
Parks F. Charles, North Woburn, "
Weixler Jacob P. Worcester
Young P. "

Varnish Manufacturers.

Porter J. & Co. Charlestown
Chard A. B. Chelsea
Miller Lyman, "
Page Samuel & Son (paraffine), "
PORTER, CROSS, & MESSER, (black, see page 690),

Varnish Manufacturers — continued.
BLANCHARD CHARLES (boot and
  shoe makers', see page 791), Haverhill
FARRAR G. H., Union, cor. Wash-
  ington (see page 706), Lynn
Shaw George H., Middleborough
POPE T. W. (for boots, see page
  789), North Bridgewater
Stoddard N. W. (carriage), "
WASHBURN ELISHA (for boots,
  see page 792), "
Whittemore D. (for boots), "
Southworth & Stevens (boot), Stoughton

Velocipede Manufacturers.
DALZELL D. & SONS (see page
  799), South Egremont, Egremont
Brownell George L., Third, corner
  Cannon, New Bedford

Veneers.
(See Mahogany.)

Veranda Trellises.
NOURSE, WHITE, & CO. (see
  page §26), Westborough

Vessels' Outfits.
DODD, TARR, & CO. (see page
  782), East Gloucester, Gloucester

Veterinary Surgeons.
Gilman Caleb, East Abington, Abington
Cutting J. M., South Braintree, Braintree
   Cambridge
Jennings Joseph H., Cambridgeport, "
Daily U. J., East Cambridge, "
Putnam Lewis, North Cambridge, "
Stocking John W. Charlestown
Gay Jarvis, South Dedham, Dedham
Wilton A. B., Harrison sq. Dorchester
Wood Robert, Lowell
Flagg Oren H. New Bedford
Thayer E. F., West Newton, Newton
Wood Ebenezer T. Northampton
Dolen Asahel, Pittsfield
Middleton Patrick, "
Saunders Robert J. Salem
Bracket Gilbert, Worcester
Fenniman J. "

Vinegar Manufacturers.
Fox David B. Charlestown
Stetson Nahum, Hanson
Damon Elijah, South Hanson, "
SMITH CHARLES, 61 Lime (see
  page 752), Newburyport
Goulding John A. Sherborn
Hodge William H. "
Holbrook Jonathan, "
Paul E. R. "
Salisbury James C. "
Whiting C. H. 81 Washington sq. Worcester

Vise Manufacturers.
New-England Vise Co., W. Acton, Acton
Union Vise Co. of Boston, Hyde Park
Backus Q. S. Winchendon

Wadding and Batting Manuf.
(See also Cotton Batting Manuf.)
King J. M. Athol Depot, Athol
Fiske William, Lowell
RIPLEY GEO. & CO. 10 Middle, "

Wagon Hubs, Shafts, Spokes, Wheels, &c.
(See Carriage Shafts, Spokes, and Hubs.)

Wagon Makers.
(See also Wheelwrights.)
Reed Abiah, East Abington, Abington
Sheldon J. W. Adams
Miller L. North Adams, "
Witherell E. J. " "
Dickinson Levi E., N. Amherst, Amherst
Creed Patrick, Cherry Valley, Leicester
Stone George, Palmer
Robinson George W. Pittsfield
Bailey Henry F. Springfield

Washers (carriage).
HALE PATENT WASHER CO.
  Chas. H. Gifford, agent and treas.
  32 Elm (see page 759), New Bedford

Washing Fluid Manuf.
STEVENS C. B. & CO. (electric, see
  page 752), Newburyport
Barber J. (Kent's), Worcester

Washing Machine Manuf.
Ford M. W. Chelsea
Wilder Samuel, Conway
Edmands C. H. Lynn

Watch Manufacturers.
(See also Jewelry, &c.)
CARTER E. B. 83 Central, Lowell
Tremont Watch Co. Melrose
Shepherd Nathaniel, New Bedford
Carter John H. & Co. Newburyport
KUHL WM. 42 Market sq. "
WRUCK F. A. 195 Essex (see page
  748), Salem
New York Watch Co. Springfield
Standish E. E. Taunton
AM. WATCH COMPANY, Waltham

Watch Materials Manuf.
Metzger Joseph (crystals), Cambridge
Buffinton F. (case springs), Milford

Watches and Jewelry.
(See also Jewelry, &c.)
PATTON WILLIAM, Springfield

Water-Cure Establishment.
Springdale, Edward E. Denniston,
  M. D. Northampton
ROUND HILL, HATFIELD HAL-
  STED, M. D. "

Water Power.
HOLYOKE WATER POWER CO.
  S. S. Chase, agent, Holyoke
Essex Company, Lawrence
Locks & Canals, props. of, D. C. C.
  Field, agent, Lowell
Wamesit Power Co. "

Water-Wheel Manufacturers.
HEALD STEPHEN & SONS (iron,
  Allen's patent improved turbine,
  &c. see pages 796 and 797), Barre
Sawyer Joel, Bolton
LAZELL, PERKINS, & CO. Bridgewater
SWAIN TURBINE CO. N. Chelms-
  ford, Chelmsford
   Chicopee
Ames Manufacturing Co. (turbine), "
KILBURN, LINCOLN, & CO. (see
  page 756), Fall River
SHELDON FRANCIS & CO. (see
  page 762), Fitchburg

Stevens G. C. & J. F., Groton Junction,   Groton
Holyoke Machine Co. (Reynold's patent turbine),   Holyoke
LOWELL MACHINE SHOP, A. Moory, supt. (turbine), Dutton,   Lowell
TURBINE WATER WHEEL MANUF. CO. J. D. Chase & Sons, agents (see page 777),   Orange
PLYMOUTH MILLS, J. Farris, agt. (see page 722),   Plymouth
PLYMOUTH TACK AND RIVET WORKS, Samuel Loring, proprietor (Leffel's double turbine, see page 713),   "
Williams, Stowell, & Co. (Bodine's jouval turbine water wheel),   Westfield
Houghton J. P.   Worcester
Munroe A. (turbine),   "
Upham J. W. (inverted turbine),   "

Weather-Vane Manufacturers.

Cushing & White,   Waltham
Washburn H. L. & Co.   West Bridgewater

Webbing Manufacturers.

Canton Elastic Fabric Co.   Canton
Boston Elastic Fabric Co.   No. Chelsea
Boardman H. W. & Co.   Lowell
                                   Northampton
Williston & Arms Manufacturing Co.   "
Nonantum Company (elastic), Watertown

Wharfingers.

Knight E. H.
Walen Michael,   Salem
                                         "

Wheel Manuf. and Stock.

(See also Carriages, Spokes, &c.)

Foster W. K.   Cambridgeport
                                       Amesbury
FOSTER & HOWE, West Amesbury,   "

Wheelwrights.

(See also Carriage Builders.)

Bates Asa,   South Abington, Abington
Smith Luke,   Acton
Brooks Amos,   South Acton,   "
Stevens L. W.   West   "
Terrill Wm. H.   Acushnet
Bennett Gustavus L.   Long Plain,   "
Spooner Walter R.   "
Johnson ————,   Amherst
Russell Emerson,   "
Preston Jonathan,   North Amherst,   "
Richardson W. H.   Ashburnham
Hitchcock Geo. L.   Ashby
Elmer Wm. H. & Son,   Ashfield
Adams Abijah,   Ashland
Taggart R. A.   "
Bucknam Saml. C.   Arlington
Dickson Albert L.   "
Briggs Darius,   Attleborough
Fuller N. F.   "
Hicks H. A. & Co.   "

                              Barnstable
Crocker B. F. & C. C.   Hyannis,   "
Weeks Hiram,   Osterville,   "
Crocker Erven,   West Barnstable,   "
Atwood Marshall,   Barre
Loring Chauncy,   "
Rice Henry,   "
McCarty Felix,   Becket
Bacon Isaac P.   Bedford
Brooks Silas,   "
Staples Henry,   "
Bishop Frank,   Belchertown
Hannum Elijah,   "

Knight R. A   Belmont
Keys John F.   Berlin
Weatherhead Albertus,   Bernardston
Blodgett O. M.   Billerica
Gatchell Jeremiah,   Blackstone
Smith H. L.   Blandford
Edward S. F.   Bolton
                                 Braintree
Anderson Chas. G., South Braintree, "
Wild Elisha,   "
Wilds Moses E.   Brewster
Snow Zoeth jr.   "
Darling Berjamin,   Bridgewater
Edson J. W.   "
Brennan John,   Brighton
Caldwell J. W.   "

                                 Brookfield
Forbes Geo. & Co.   East Brookfield. "
Barlow & Hamilton,   Brimfield
Blashfield William C.   "
Brown Daniel,   Cambridge
HURD AMOS D. (see page 735), Palmer st.   "
JONES A. J., Church, cor. Palmer,   "
Givens & Buskirk,   Cambridgeport, "
McCue James,   "
Pierce Joseph,   "
Thompson J. B.   "
Thwing James,   "
Waugh William A.   "
Davis S. A.   East Cambridge, "
Libbey Chas. W.   "
Munroe Enoch,   "
WEBB T. C. & Co. (see page 657), North Cambridge,   "
Talbot Peter,   Canton
Buskirk Charles V.   Charlestown
Dickson Oliver & Son,   "
Dinevan Cornelius,   "
Harrison John,   "
Hunnewell T. F.   "
Louer John,   "
McCarthy Philip,   "
Phipps John S.   "
Willard A. C.   Charlton
Eldredge Edmund N.   Chatham
Proctor Charles,   Chelmsford
Spalding Isaiah B.   "
Draper Wm. L., North Chelmsford,   "
Gibson F. M.   Chelsea
O'Donnell Patrick,   "
Uart John,   "
Gilmore Wm.   Chicopee
Wood Lewis,   "
Keith & Thurston,   "
Fenno John,   Clinton
Buck S.   Cohasset
Garfield George,   Coleraine
Howland John,   Concord
Brown Amos,   Conway
Hood W. H.   Danvers
Waldron Edward T., Danvers Port,   "
Flagg Wm. H.   "
Henihan Thomas,   Dedham
Trefry James,   East Dedham,   "
Perkins Alex.   South   "   "
Rogers John,   West   "   "
Thacher Joseph F. West Dennis, Dennis
Palmer John O.   Dighton
Palmer John W.   "
Walker Gilbert,   "
Waldron E. L.   North Dighton,   "
Bennett Edmund B.   Dorchester
Homer Reuben,   "
Upham Charles A.   "
Bird George H.   Mattapan,   "
Swan Wm. G.   Neponset,   "
Sweeting S. M.,   East Douglas, Douglas

Wheelwrights — continued.

Battell Rufus & Son,	Dover
Brooks Lawrence,	Dunstable
Wilson Frederick,	"
	Duxbury
Boynton Benjamin,	West Duxbury, "
Simmons Mason,	" "
Stetson Nelson,	" "
Jones John,	East Bridgewater
Trow Bartholomew,	"
Harding Prince S.	Orleans, Eastham
Hayward Albert,	Easton
Simpson Dexter,	South Easton, "
Kelley Joseph V.	Edgartown
Pease Rodolphus,	"
Pease Daniel,	"
Kelsey James, North Egremont, Egremont
Harwood Harlem,	Enfield
Gage Caleb S.	Essex
Simmons Robert M.	Fairhaven
Chace James,	Fall River
Thurston James E.	"
Burgess Josiah,	Falmouth
Hewins Lewellyn R.	"
West Benjamin W.	Fitchburg
Young Wm. H.	Foxborough
Hannegan N.	Framingham
Hastings O. F.	"
Horne Charles E.	"
Eames David, South Framingham,	"
Lombard Nathaniel, "	" .
Bemis Henry,	Franklin
Stewart R. B.	"
Clark James,	Freetown
Sawin Levi C. & Co.	Gardner
Boyes Robert,	Georgetown
Currier Joseph J.	"
Clark John H.	Gill
Atkinson John,	Gloucester
Friend Samuel K. jr.	"
Pullard C. E.	Grafton
Burtis & Bros.	Great Barrington
Sabin George W.	"
Trask Danforth,	Greenwich
Vaughn Nathan P., Greenwich Village, "
Eells Robert,	Hanover
Turner Thomas,	"
Clarke Thomas G.	Hanson
Whiting John A.	"
Crocker Luther,	South Hanson, "
Cobb Fred A.	Hardwick
Foster Emory B.	"
Copeland Fred.	Harvard
Robbins Benjamin F.	Harwich
Small Joshua,	"
Young Simeon,	"
Burgess Wm. B,	Harwichport, "
Nickerson Bangs	East Harwich, "
Whiton B. H. & Co.	Hingham
Clark Chester & Son,	Hinsdale
Winn Moses,	Holden
Webber George L.	Holland
Partridge J.	Holliston
Taylor Edward,	"
Cunningham N.	Hopkinton
Fairbanks Freeman,	Woodville, "
Moulton W. H.	Hudson
Eldridge David G.	Kingston
Washburn Salmon,	Lakeville
Stowe Moses,	Lancaster
Cochran W. N. & B.	Lawrence
Furnham Josiah W.	"
Couch F. M.	East Lee, Lee
Rivers & Langevin,	Leicester
Moore S. H	Leverett
Tucker Charles K.	Lexington
Ward E. P.	"
Brigham Wm., East Lexington,	"

Lapham Luther,	Littleton
Manning Otis,	"
Taylor Newton E.	Longmeadow
Taylor George, East Longmeadow, "
Garland N. & Co.	Lowell
GREEN AMOS, 200 Dutton,	"
Horn Eben,	"
Chapin Ashbel,	Ludlow
Wait William,	"
Cutts Richard A.	Lynn
Smith & Coulson,	"
Hawkes Adam,	Lynnfield
Harding Samuel, Lynnfield Centre,	"
Ayer John L.	Malden
Kingman Edward A.	Mansfield
Tobey J. A.	"
Goodwin Frank H.	Marblehead
Brigham W. E.	Marlborough
Hemenway E. W.	"
Damon F. N.	Marshfield
Taylor William,	"
Simmons Hewett, North Marshfield, "
Jenney A. M.	Mattapoisett
Snow Ephraim,	"
Tred Wm. B.	West Medway, Medway
Walker D. Henry,	Melrose
Ellis Timothy,	Mendon
Archibald & Waddell,	Methuen
Corliss Varnum,	"
Atwood Reel,	Middleborough
Snow Venus,	"
Vaughan Wm. H.	"
Waterman E. H.	"
Bradley J. F.	Milford
Pickering Silas,	"
Putman Maynard,	Millbury
Glover Warren, West Millbury, "
Chapman & Strangman,	Milton
Morris George F.	Monson
Wilson G. C.	"
Thomson Sardis,	Monterey
Woodin Frank,	"
Folger Reuben P.	Nantucket
Hatch Oliver,	"
Mitchell Thomas S,	"
Thurston Nathaniel,	"
Stearns Charles,	Natick
Mahar John, South Natick, "
Webber Henry,	Needham
Pulsifer John, Newton Lower Falls, "
Allen James, Wellesley, "
Corey Isaac,	New Bedford
Sherman Abraham,	"
Simmons Allen S.	"
Snow Otis,	"
Tripp Jeremiah,	"
Lincoln J. V.	New Braintree
Dorman Jesse,	Newburyport
Haynes Hamilton,	"
Sargent Tappan,	"
Syms Edward,	"
Putnam Tarrant,	New Salem
Pulsifer John, Lower Falls,	Newton
Mac Farlane C.	Newton Centre, "
Curry Robert,	Newton Corner, "
Keegan Patrick, West Newton,	"
Rand Willard,	"
Lamb E. R. & W. B.	North Andover
Bailey D. M.	Northborough
Eager Denna,	"
Batchelor W. H., Whitinsville, Northbridge
Reed Sumner,	North Brookfield
Stearns Geo.	"
Mason A. H.	North Bridgewater
Tribou L. E.	"
Fuller Daniel T.	North Chelsea
Somes Kiah B.	"
Howard Elbridge A.	North Reading

Briggs Charles H.	Norton
Capen William,	"
Thompson Barney, West Orange,	Orange
Rogers Samuel,	Orleans
Harris S.	Oxford
Trumbull A.	"
Stone G. N.	Palmer
Canterbury Asa G., Bonds Village,	"
Berry William,	Peabody
Dole & Osgood,	"
PIKE & WHIPPLE (see page 748),	"
Sylvan, n. Audover,	"
Bonney J. D.	Pembroke
Simmons Mason, East Pembroke,	"
Damon Bailey D. West Duxbury,	"
Durant John,	Pepperell
Durant John W.	"
Campbell Henry J.	Pittsfield
Merry H. N.	"
Robinson George W.	"
Foote Gilbert G. West Pittsfield,	"
Bruiev Jonas,	"
Ellis James,	Plymouth
Hatch & Blackmer,	"
Ryder Ezekiel,	"
Briggs Seneca Francis,	Plympton
White Ellis, North Prescott,	Prescott
Harrington Charles,	Princeton
Hall Thomas,	Quincy
McCunly Daniel,	"
Whitney Loring,	"
Loring John,	Randolph
Winship Silas M.	"
Shaw Samuel,	Raynham
White Charles,	"
Brown Samuel,	Reading
Houghton N. S.	"
Kingman Ambrose	"
Barney Alfred B.	Rehoboth
Bliss George E. W.	"
Hicks Nathan E.	"
Williams Caleb,	"
Sparrow Josiah,	Rochester
Swift Pelham E.	"
Webber Philip,	Rockport
Nelson Hosea E.	Rowe
Snow Fayette,	"
Whittier Moses T.	Rowley
Adams P. F.	Salem
Barker J. W.	"
Batchelder Joseph & Co.	"
H. yt Henry,	"
Ingham Edward,	Sandisfield
Calkins J. Montville,	"
Nye Lemuel B.	Sandwich
Dearborn W. H. E. Saugus,	Saugus
Cheesbro Albert W.	Savoy
Packard Isaac,	Scituate
Litchfield Isaac, North Scituate,	"
Merritt J. C.	"
Vinal Bailey,	"
Whitaker David F.	Seekonk
Winn Marcena C.	"
Crippen Francis B.	Sheffield
Sackett Nelson, East Sheffield,	"
Smith Lyman A.	"
Meacham Hiram, Ashley Falls,	"
Foster Wm. H., Shelburne Falls,	Shelburne
Whitman J.	"
Ware Vorestus,	Sherborn
Wing O. N. Shirley Village,	Shirley
Whitney Charles L.	Shrewsbury
Johnson Levi,	Shutesbury
Leland J.	Somerville
Fairbank Horace,	Southbridge
Estabrook Joseph,	South Hadley
Sessions H. P. South Hadley Falls,	"
Waters Samuel, West Scituate,	S. Scituate
Reed S. W.	Southwick
Hart Lewis,	Spencer
Roberts Andrew J.	"
Gerry Thomas L.	Sterling
Hinckley Luther T.	Stockbridge
Lincoln Henry,	"
Jones Abner D.	Curtisville, "
Talbot Jabez, jr.	Stoughton
Collins Bartlett, East Stoughton,	"
Brown Edwin,	Stow
McKernell James,	"
Hooker P. C. Fiskdale,	Sturbridge
Arnold E. South Sudbury,	Sudbury
Abbey G. F.	Sunderland
Shaw Salem J.	Sutton
Buffinton B. S.	Swansea
Bosworth Joseph,	Taunton
Mann C. A.	"
Paull James,	"
Jackson Charles W.	Templeton
Jones A.	"
Frost Aaron,	Tewksbury
	Tisbury
Adams Washington, W. Tisbury,	"
Clarke Samuel,	Topsfield
Herrick Benjamin,	"
Leach T. K.	"
Lewis Wm. H.	Townsend
Ellis E. T.	Uxbridge
Ohnenus Andrew,	Waltham
Winslow G. E.	Ware
Packard Leander L.	Wareham
Wilder A. A.	Warren
Tucker John,	Watertown
Rand George W.	Wayland
Ames Ebenezer,	Webster
Warren Wm. H.	"
Collins Benjamin,	Wellfleet
Hopkins Eddad A.	"
Sparrow R. C.	"
Johnson William,	Wendell
Clark Jason,	Wenham
Sibley W. H. & F.	Westborough
Keyes Artemus,	West Boylston
Smith Benjamin,	"
Howard Isaac,	West Bridgewater
Noble Jacob M.	Westfield
Griffin J.	Westford
Tuttle P.	"
Drury George B.	West Hampton
Dwinells Jacob G.	West Newbury
Merrill Moses B.	"
Smith Daniel,	Weston
Briggs Jeremiah,	Westport
Guild Abner,	West Roxbury
Bradley George I. Jamaica Plain,	"
Powers T.	"
Bliss Lyman,	West Stockbridge
Foskett George J.	"
Kinney Nathan,	"
Willis George,	Weymouth
Spear A. A. East Weymouth,	"
	Wilbraham
Adams Edward, South Wilbraham,	"
Beebe Marcus,	"
Town Edwin A.	Williamstown
Morrill Cadwalader,	Wilmington
Lynch James C.	Winchendon
Barrett Abel,	Woburn
Ames J. D. & Co.	Worcester
Barker J. G., Union st.	"
Haynes L. C.	"
Reed C. G. & Co., 54 Union,	"
Allen Silas, Centre,	Wrentham
Grant John F., West Wrentham,	"
Thacher Watson,	Yarmouth
Thacher & Taylor, Yarmouth Port,	"
White Rufus, South Yarmouth,	"

Whip-Lash Manufacturers.

Galpin J. A.   Southwick
Webb H. E.   "
Darling, Smith, & Co.   Westfield

Whip Manufacturers.

Darling Wm. Cambridgeport, Cambridge
Moor George L.   Montgomery
Moor O. A.   "
Russell Charles D.   Southampton
Tiffany L. C.   "
American Whip Company,   Westfield
Boynton & Brothers,   "
Campbell A.   "
Cooper Bruce,   "
Cowles & Atwater,   "
Darling, Smith, & Co.   "
Dickey L.   "
Dow Samuel,   "
Hadley Charles (whip-turner),   "
Henderson & Bailey,   "
King Gamaliel,   "
King Joseph & Son,   "
Knowles & Kellogg,   "
Phelps Edwin,   "
Phelps, Light, & Co.   "
Phelps Salmon M.   "
Pratt, Atwater, & Co.   "
Provin William,   "
Rand, Lewis, & Rand,   "
Russell Isaac N.   "
Russell Joseph H.   "
Shepard, Holcomb, & Cook,   "
Spencer Charles W.   "
Whipple C. M. & Co.   "
Kirby Geo. E. & Co.   Worcester

Whip Mountings.

Whipple James P.   Westfield

Whip Plaiting.

Brass W.   Westfield
Brooks Peter,   "

White-Lead Manufacturers.

(See also Paints, Oils, &c.)

Forest River Lead Co.   Salem
SALEM LEAD CO., Francis Brown,
  treas. 26 P. O. Building,   "

Whiting Manuf.

Stickney J. W. & Co.   Chelsea

Willow Furniture Manufac-
turer.

BAUCH AUGUSTUS, Bowdoin
  st. (see page 784),   Dorchester

Willow Ware Manufacturers.

BAUCH AUGUSTUS, Bowdoin
  st. (see page 764),   Dorchester
Gough F. W.   Hingham
Fleming George,   Sherborn
Fleming John,   "

Window Shades and Fixtures.

Carpenter & Eaton (wood),   Rowe
Wiese F.   Springfield

Wines (Native).

SMITH CHARLES, 61 Lime (see
  page 752),   Newburyport
Howard John B.   Lawrence
Dickenson J. W.   Springfield

Wire Cloth Manufacturers.

Clinton Wire Cloth Co. C. H. Waters,
  agent,   Clinton
Bigelow C.   Springfield

Wire Gauze Strainer Manuf.

WOODS, SHERWOOD, & CO. (and
  other fine wire goods), Bridge st. Lowell

Wire Heddles (patented).

Brown D. C.   Lowell

Wire Manufacturers.

Prentiss Geo. W.   Holyoke
Whitaker Edmund (flat wire),   "
Brown Darius C.   Lowell
Cady Geo. L.   "
Hale B. S. & Son (iron and copper), "
Lamb Horace,   Northampton
MYRICK & SUGDEN,   Spencer
Prouty Manuf. Co.   "
Cooper & Southworth (bonnet), Stoughton
WASHBURN & MOEN MANUF.
  CO. (see page 735),   Worcester

Wire Workers.

Allen L. H.   Amherst
Hildreth H. A.   Lowell
WOODS, SHERWOOD, & CO. Bridge, "
Dean Lewis (sieves, &c.),   Oakham
Lincoln & Ayres (sieves, &c.),   "
Bigelow C.   Springfield
Howe, Bigelow, & Co.   Worcester

Wood Acid and Iron Liquor
Manufacturers.

Wells Orson & Son,   N. Adams, Adams

Wood and Bark.

(See also Coal and Wood.)

Clark Henry,   Fall River
COOK VERNON & CO.   "
Freelove Leander,   "
Wheeler Leander,   "
Wordell G. R. & Co.   "
Wyatt George,   "
Bourne Francis W.   Hanson
Bourne William,   "
Brewster Philip,   So. Hanson, "
Bailey Alvah W.   Lowell
Brown Hiram,   "
Buckley Michael,   "
Carlton Caleb,   "
Clement D. W. (wood),   "
Henderson S. F. & Son,   "
HILL E. A. 341 Middlesex,   "
LEONARD A. W. Jackson, n. Round
  House (see page 739),   "
Richardson & Smith,   "
Riley Bernard,   "
Brown G. F. & S.   Salem
Clark Joseph,   "
HATCH L. B. 113 Derby,   "
MANNING R. C. & CO. 189 Derby,   "
PICKERING WILLIAM, Jr. 17
  Peabody,   "
Smith L. A.   "
LITTLEFIELD J. E. & SONS,   Woburn
Garfield & Parker,   Worcester
Hall W. M. & Sons,   "
Santon Joseph & Co.   "
Smith J. F. & Co.

Wood Dealers.

(See also Coal and Wood.)

Ashton J. W. (kindling),   Taunton
Burnham A. L.   "

Wood Mouldings.

(See also Moulding Mills.)

Glantz T. R. & Co.   Pittsfield
NEWCOMB W. L. & CO. (see page 728),   Taunton

Wood Pulp Manuf.

Pagenstroher Alberto, Centreville,   Stockbridge "

Wood Turners.

(See also Turners.)

Morse Laban,   Athol
Eldridge G. L.   Ashfield
Copeland S. W.   Fall River
POTTER R. N. & BROS. Davol st.
   (see page 755),   "
Leavitt John & Son,   Hingham
Aldrich Milton,   Lowell
Fuller Ensign C.   "
HADLEY & ROBEY, Cushing, cor. Rock,   "
Hills Eliphalet,   "
Crockett Bartlett D.   Lawrence
KNOWLTON GEO. K. & CO., 13 Union (see page 751),   Lynn
MARSHALL J. OTIS, rear 13 Broad (see page 750),   "
Mayhew & Hayes,   New Bedford
Booth C. H. & W. A.   Pittsfield
Carlisle George,   Rutland
Fernald & Priest,   Springfield

Wood Working Machinery.

(See also Machinists.)

GERRY GEO. & SON (see page 771). 6 Mill,   Athol Depot, Athol
RICHARDSON GEO. H. (see page 771),   Athol Depot, "
HEALD STEPHEN & SONS (planing jointing, and matching, wood turning lathes, bench saws all sizes, boring, tenoning, scroll-sawing machines, &c. see pages 796 and 797),   Barre
ROLLSTONE MACHINE WORKS (see page 709),   Fitchburg
Union Machine Co.   "
   Groton
Stevens G. C. & J. F., Groton Junction, "
Carey & Harris,   Lowell
DAVIS ASAHEL, Mechanics' "
GROSVENOR J. P., Mt. Vernon st. (see page 737),   "
Lawrence Benjamin,   "
ROBINSON WILLIAM, Mechanics' Mills,   "
BLANCHARD A. V. & CO. (machines for bending wood),   Palmer
PHILLIPS H. B. 194 & 196 Derby, Salem
BALL R. & CO. 26 School,   Worcester
FAY L. D. 7 Cypress (see page 783); "
LEE H. A. (see page 750). 56 Union, "
RICHARDSON, MERIAM, & CO., Junction,   "
Tainter E. C.   "
WETHERBY, RUGG, & RICHARDSON (see page 788),   "

Wooden Eaves Troughs.

Child, Russell, & Hall (patent), Springfield

Wooden Ware Dealers.

FESSENDEN HENRY, North Attleborough,   Attleborough
APPLETON J. A. Jr., 3 Water, Haverhill

BARNEY ALFRED,   Lowell
Kelley F. P.   Lynn
ALLEN & BLISS, 121 Union, New Bedford

Wooden Ware Manufacturers.

(See also Handle Manufacturers.)

Wood B. F.   Arlington
Carr & Wilder,   Ashby
Gardner Nelson,   Ashfield
Day F. B. & C. H. (turned), South Ashfield,   "
Guilford Henry,   "
Parker M. T.   "
Pierce John R. (pails). Athol Depot, Athol
Bartlett & Lloyd, N. Blandford, Blandford
Bryant R. & Bros. (sieve hoops), West Chesterfield,   Chesterfield
Warner & Co.   Concord
Washburn William B. & Co. (pails), Erving
Bancroft Amasa & Co. (pails and tubs),   Gardner
Sears Anthony (skewers), West Hawley,   Hawley
Barnes Lyman (buckets),   Hingham
Corthell Nelson,   "
Hersey Caleb S.   "
Hersey Cushing,   "
Hersey Jacob,   "
Hingham Wooden Ware Co.   "
Tower Leavitt (barrel covers),   "
Wilder C. & A. (buckets), S. Hingham, "
Hitchins Parley (bowls),   Huntington
Tyringham Society of Shakers (Albert Battles, trustee). South Lee,   Lee
BARNEY ALFRED, 247 Merrimac, Lowell
Caldwell & Miller (tubs),   Leominster
Graves S. S. (pails and tubs), North Leverett,   Leverett
Bay State Milling and Machine Co., Lynn
Johnson Henry (pails),   Northfield
WHITNEY, LORD, & CO. (pails, see page 776),   Orange
   Pittsfield
Hancock Society of Shakers, Augustus W. Williams, West Pittsfield, "
Perry J. H. & Co. (butter moulds), "
Pierce Horace & Son (pails),   Royalston
Raymond Sullivan,   "
Stockwell Edmund,   "
Farrar Solomon S. S. Royalston,   "
Royce N. W. (sap and butter tubs and pails), Montville,   Sandisfield
Stratton T. A. (maple turn keelers), Montville,   "
Aldrich H. & Co.   Winchendon
Beaman Wm. (pails and tubs),   "
HANCOCK OZRO (pail ears),   "
Loud C. A. (wood faucets),   "
MASON ORLANDO (tubs, pails, churns),   "
Murdock & Co.   "
MURDOCK E. & CO.   "
Murdock E. jr.   "
Sibley William (pails),   "
Weston Irvin E. (churns, &c.),   "
Woodcock & Sawyer (pails),   "
Pierce & Thurber. E. Windsor,   Windsor
Stevens A. & Son (sieve rims), Worthington

Wooden Ware Manufacturers' Materials.

Bancroft A. & CO.   Gardner
MURDOCK E. & CO.   Winchendon
Murdock E. jr.   "

Wool Burring and Washing Machinery.

SARGENT CHARLES G. (see page 743), Graniteville,   Westford

Wool Carders.

Shattuck Richard, North Adams,   Adams
Winslow Thomas G.   Freetown

Wool Dealers.

Clark & Brown,   . .   Milton
         Northampton
COTSWOLD BRUSH CO. (fancy),
   T. S. Mann, treas. Florence,   "
Blaney Stephen,   Peabody
Houston N. F. & Co.   "
SUTTON WILLIAM Jr., Main n.
   Grove,   "
Winchester & Blaney,   "
Colt Henry,   Pittsfield
Murray James J.   "
Murray Wm. H.   "
Billings Joseph H. & Co.   West Roxbury
          Worcester
BUELL S. K. 18 Foster (see page 781),
Chamberlin H. H. & Co.   "
Clark & Newton,   "
Follansbee J. M.   "
Hyatt & Hobbs,   "

Wool Dusters.

COTSWOLD BRUSH CO., Florence,   Northampton

Wool Pullers.

Butler A. P. & Co,   N. Adams,   Adams
Winslow Brothers,   S. Dedham,   Dedham
Freeman Charles,   Milton,   Dorchester
Blodgett & Brown,   Lynn
SUTTON WM. jr. Main,   Peabody
Clark Horace,   Watertown
Hollis John W.   "
Billings Joseph H. & Co.   West Roxbury

Wool Scouring and Murring.

Cordingly W. S. & F. Lower Falls, Newton

Wool Stock.

BUELL S. K. 18 Foster, (see page 781),   Worcester

Woolen Flock Manufacturers.

Medway Flock Co.   Medway

Woolen Goods Manufacturers.

(See also Carpet Manuf's; also Hosiery Manufs.; also Yarns, &c.)

SCHOULER WILLIAM (flannels), S. Acton,   Acton
BLACKINGTON P. & CO.   Adams
Blackington Sanford & Son (fancy cassimeres),   "
Phillips B. F. & Co. (fancy cassimeres and shawls),   "
Brayton S. W. & Co. (cassimeres), N. Adams,   "
Briggs Brothers (fancy cassimeres). N. Adams,   "
Glenn Mill (fancy cassimeres). N. Adams, "
North Adams Woolen Co. (fancy cassimeres), Geo. B. Perry, agt. North Adams,   "
Tyler & Bliss (fancy cassimeres), N. Adams,   "
Agawam Co. (satinet),   Agawam
         Amesbury
Amesbury Mills (fancy cassimeres),   "
SALISBURY MILLS (fancy cassimeres), M. D. F. Steere,   "

BALLARDVALE MILLS (fine flannels), J. P. Bradlee, agent, Ballardvale,   Andover
Marland Manufacturing Co. (fancy woolens and satinets), Nathan Frye, agent,   "
Davis, Fales, & Co. (doeskins and satinets),   Ashland
EAGLE MILLS (blankets and lap robes), Athol Depot,   Athol
Millers River Manufacturing Co (satinets and flannels), George T. Johnson, agent,   Athol Depot,   "
PINE DALE WOOLEN CO. (satinet), David Smith, agent. Athol Depot.   "
Dagget H. N. (worsted braids), Attleborough
Pond & Larned (satinet),   Auburn
DENNY EDWARD & CO. (flannels), Barre Plains,   Barre
Heywood Seth P. (cassimeres, &c.), Barre Plains,   "
Faulkner J. R. & Co. (flannels), North Billerica,   Billerica
Talbot C. P. & Co. (flannels), North Billerica,   "
       Blackstone
Ballou F. M. & Co. (fancy cassimeres), "
Evans, Seagrave, & Co. (fancy cassimeres),   "
Needham & Mason (fancy cassimeres),   "
Ballou E. S. (satinets), N. Blackstone,   "
Blackstone Woolen Co. (satinets), N. Blackstone,   "
Scott & Benson (satinets), N. Blackstone,   "
Morrison A. & Sons (hosiery, shirts, and drawers),   Braintree
Parks William R. (fancy cassimeres), Palmer,   Brimfield
Canton Woolen Mills (fancy woolen goods),   Canton
Draper R. (fancy hosiery, rubber linings, &c.),   "
Draper & Sumner (hoods, glove linings, &c.),   "
Townsend M. (fancy woolens),   "
Mansfield G. H. & Co. (silk, linen, and woolen braids),   "
Smith Benjamin (fancy),   "
Eagle Mills (cashmeretts, flannels, &c.), West Chelmsford,   Chelmsford
CHELSEA WOOLEN MILL (repellants), Williams Street, Stephen Sibley, proprietor (see page 727),   Chelsea
Valley Mills (satinets and wool cloth), Willimansett,   Chicopee
Briggs Brothers (cassimeres), Clarksburg
Damon, Smith, & Co. (flannels),   Concord
       Conway
Delebarre Edward (cassimeres, &c.),   "
Cordaville Mills (blankets), H. Wilson, agent,   Cordaville
Davis, Fales, & Co. (doeskins),   "
Birmingham Bros. (fancy cassimeres and satinets),   Dalton
Hawkins, West, & Co. (balmorals and blankets),   "
Kittridge C. J. & Co. (fancy cassimeres and satinets),   "
DANVERS CARPET CO.   Danvers
Winona Mills, West Danvers,   "
BARROWS THOMAS (cassimeres), East Dedham,   Dedham
MERCHANTS WOOLEN Co. East Dedham,   "
Merrimack Mills (cassimeres),   Dracut
Chase O. F. & Co.   Webster,   Dudley
Perry J. & Son,   "
Minot Manuf. Co (satinets),   Enfield
Swift River Manufacturing Co. (fancy cassimeres),   Fall River
WAMSUTTA STEAM MILLS (fancy cassimeres), Jesse Eddy & Son,   "
Mornakies Company (kerseys, satinets, &c.), J. C. Robinson, agent. Waquoit,   Falmouth
Pacific Factory (cassimeres), East   "
Crawford Mills (cassimeres), West Fitchburg,   Fitchburg

Fitchburg Woolen Mill (cassimeres and broadcloth-), "
Saxonville Mills (yarns, worsted yarns, and blankets). Saxonville, Framingham
Ray J. P. & J. G. (satinets), Franklin
Porter & Winslow, Freetown
Thorpe John, "
Aldrich C. C. & Son (satinets), Granby
Berkshire Woollen Company (cloths and cassimeres), Asa C. Russell, resident agent, Great Barrington
Greenfield Manufacturing Company (fine black doeskins), Theodore Leonard, agent, Greenfield
Hale E. J. M. & Co. (flannels), South Groveland, Groveland
Revere Mills (blankets), Hamilton
Hancock
Barker J. L. & G. W. (balmoral skirts), "
Jones H. H. (satinets, &c.) "
Taylor John, jr. (balmoral skirts), "
Gilbert George H. & Co. (flannels and balmorals), Hardwick
Birmingham Bros. (satinets), Hinsdale
Hinsdale F. W. & B'other (Moscow and castor beavers), "
Kittredge C. J. & A. (satinets), "
Plunkett Woolen Co. (union cloths and satinets), Wm. A. Taylor, treasurer, "
Chaffin R. H. & A. (satinets and frocking,) Holden
Howe & Jefferson (satinet), "
Stowell & Ward (satinet), "
Beebe Jared (doeskins), Holyoke
GERMANIA MILLS (beavers), Augustus Starsberg, agent, "
New-York Woolen Company (cassimeres), J. H. Spitzle, agent, "
Little & Stanton (flannels), Hampshire Woolen Mills, Huntington
Marseilles Quilt Company, "
Taylor Horace (satinet). "
HYDE-PARK WOOLEN CO. Chas. H. Allen, treasurer, Hyde Park
Ipswich Woolen Mills (yarns), Ipswich
ARLINGTON WOOLEN MILLS (worsted dress goods), J. W. Bailey, agent, Lawrence
EVERETT MILLS (fancy shirting flannels). J. R. Perry, agt., Union st. "
Lawrence Woolen Company, (woolen shawls,) Oliver H. Perry, agent, "
McAllister William, "
PACIFIC MILLS (delaines and other worsted goods), Wm. C. Chapin, agent, Canal, "
Pemberton Co. (shirtings, flannels, &c.). Fred E. Clark, agent, Canal, "
WASHINGTON MILLS (shawls, cloths, flannels, delaines, &c.), Canal, "
Mann & Marshall (satinets), Leicester
Stone & Bottomly (satinets), "
Cherry Valley Manufacturing Company (satinets), Cherry Valley, "
Hodges Samuel L. agent (tweeds and cassimeres), Cherry Valley, "
Kittredge H. G. & Co. (satinets), Cherry Valley, "
Smith G. N. & J. A. (fancy cassimeres), Cherry Valley, "
CLAPPVILLE MILLS (flannels), Clappville, "
CROCKER, PERRY, & CO. (cloths and fancy cassimeres), Leominster
Field Alden C. & Son (fulled cloth. flannels, &c.), Leverett
Belvidere Woolen Manufacturing Co. (flannels), Lowell
CHASE MILLS (fancy cassimeres), Lawrence, near Whipple's Mills, "
Faulkner L. W. & Son (flannels), "
Holt John (flannels), "
Livingston, Carter, & Co. (flannels), "
Merrimack Mills, E. Barrows, agent, "
MIDDLESEX CO. (piece goods and shawls), O. H. Perry, agent, "
Stott Charles (flannels), "
Stott Charles A. "
U. S. Bunting Company, "

Walker William & Co. "
Methuen Woolen Co. James Walton, agent, Methuen
Middleborough
STAR MILLS, Geo. Brayton, trea-. Middlefield
Blush Oliver (satinets and flannels), "
Church S. U. & Bros. (broadcloths), "
Atlanta Mills (cassimeres), Millbury
Coogan Michael (flocks grinding). "
Greenwood Mills (fancy cassimeres), "
Lapham M. & S. (cassimeres), "
Merriam & Simpson (satinets), "
Walling Nelson (fancy cassimeres), "
Hampden Cotton Manufacturing Co. (satinets). Monson
MONSON WOOLEN MANUFACTURING CO. (satinets), "
MONSON & BRIMFIELD MANUFACTURING CO. (satinets), "
Norcross Albert, "
Reynolds Joseph L. (satinets),* "
North Andover Mills (flannels), John Elliot, jr. agent, North Andover
Stevens N. & Sons, "
Sutton's Mills, Wm. Sutton, prop. "
Wood D. F. Northborough
Buffum M. & Son (doeskins), Oxford
Hodges George (flannels). "
HUGUENOT MANUF. CO. (fancy cassimeres), North Oxford, "
PARKS WILLIAM R. (fancy cassimeres), Palmer
Winona Mills, Train & Polloc, Brookdale, Peabody
Atwood T. G. Ashlar Mills, (balmorals and flannels), Pittsfield
Barker J. & Brothers (union cassimeres), "
Brown N. G. (balmoral skirts), "
Friend E. & G. (balmoral skirts). "
Jones John M. & Son (balmoral skirts), "
Peck J. L. (flannels), "
Pittsfield Woolen Co. (fancy cassimeres), W. F. Bacon, agent, "
Pomeroy's L. Sons (black union 6-4 cloths and satinets), "
PONTOOSUC WOOLEN MANUF. CO. (cassimeres, cloths, blankets, and balmoral skirts), T. Clapp, agt. "
Russell S. N. & C. L. (fancy cassimeres and balmoral skirts), "
Whittelsey Elihu B. "
Taconic Mills (union cassimeres), George Y. Learned, Treas. and resident agent," "
Stearnsville Woolen Co. Henry Stearns, agent (fancy cassimeres), West Pittsfield, "
Tillotson & Collins (fancy cassimeres), West Pittsfield, "
Streeter S. C. Plainfield
Plymouth
Plymouth Woolen Mills (flannels), "
Day Stephen P. (satinets), Rowe
Whitney George (cassimeres and doeskins), South Royalston, Royalston
PRANKER & CO. (flannels), Saugus Centre, Saugus
Nichols W. B. & Co. (satinets), Cordaville, Southboro'
Cordaville Mills (blankets), H. Willson. agent, Cordaville, "
Southbridge
Hamilton Woolen Co., Globe Village, "
Agawam Woolen Co. (satinets and flannels), South Hadley
Stony Brook Mill, L. H. Arnold, agent, "
Peel —— (satinets), Spencer
Upham Wm. (union cassimeres), "
Alden Caleb (doeskins), Springfield
King L. (cassimeres), Stockbridge
Goodrich, Fenn, & Co. (satinets), Glen. dale.
FRENCH & WARD (hoods, glove linings &c.), Stoughton
Southworth A. & Son, "
Gleason B. W. & Co. (flannels), Rock Bottom, Stow
Merriam & Ballad (satinets), Sturbridge

Woolen Goods Manufacturers—continued.

Assabet Manuf. (flannels, cassimeres, and blankets), Assabet, Sudbury
Fisher W. A. & Co. (satinets), Sutton
Otter River Co., D. A. Newton, agent (satinets), Otter River, Templeton
River Mills, Wm. Scott, Supt. (cassimeres), Otter River, "
Cleveland Henry (satinets), West Tisbury Tyngsborough
Butterfield James P. (cloth, &c.), "
Capron & Hayward (satinets), Uxbridge
Scott S. W. (satinets), "
Taft D. W. (fancy cassimeres), "
Uxbridge Woolen Manuf. Co. (fancy cassimeres), R. & J. Taft, "
Wheelock C. A. & S. M. (cassimeres), "
Dell Manuf. Co. (doeskins), Wales
Hegan Mills (doeskins), "
Shaw A. & E. D. (doeskins), "
Shaw Manuf. Co. (doeskins), "
Wales Mill, E. Shaw, agent, "
GILBERT GEO. H. MANUF. CO. (white silk warp, opera, moleskin, zephyr, shirting, shaker, Welch, silesian, gauze, French plaid, domett, flannels, ladies' sackings and repellents, ladies' and misses' balmoral skirts), Ware
STEVENS CHAS. A. (all-wool shaker and silk-warp flannels), "
WARREN WOOLEN CO., S. H. Sibley (fancy woolens), Warren
Ætna Mills (ladies' cloths, tweeds, and cassimeres), Watertown
Chase O. F. & Co. (cassimeres), Webster
Perry J. H. & Sons (cassimeres), "
Slater Samuel & Sons, "
SLATER WOOLEN CO. (doeskins, &c.), "
Abbot Worsted Co. (worsted yarns, &c.) Graniteville, Westford
West Boylston Manuf. Co. (blankets), Oakdale, West Boylston
Bardwell Seth & Son (flannels), Whately
Ellis Dwight L. Wilbraham
Lacowsic Woolen Co., S. Smith, Supt. South Wilbraham, "
Ravine Mills, L. E. Sage, agent, South Wilbraham, "
Scantic Manuf. Co. J. W. Leonard, agt. (doeskins), South Wilbraham, "
James H. L. (satinets), Williamsburg
Nash Thomas (flannels), "
Worcester
Adriatic Mills (fancy cassimeres), "
Bigelow & Barber (satinets), "
James Benjamin (fancy cassimeres), "
Messinger & Wright (fancy cassimeres), "
Reed & Davis (satinets), Tatnuck, "
Ashworth & Jones, Cherry Valley, "
Bottomly Joseph, "
Darling Cyrus (satinets), "
Hunt John A. (satinets), "
Thayer & Kimball, "
Curtis Albert (satinets), Webster sq. "
Elliot Feiting Co. (piano and table covers), Franklin city, Wrentham
Wrentham Manuf. Co.

Woolen Machinery.

GERRY GEORGE & SON (improved dusters, see page 771), 6 Mill, Athol Depot, Athol
MARVEL, DAVOL, & CO. Fall River
LANE DAVID (see page 738), Fletcher, cor. Cushing, Lowell
PEIRCE JOHN N. (also dealer in second hand looms, see page 742), 25 Howe, "
Davis & Furber, North Andover
Hunt, Waite, & Flint, Orange
SARGENT CHARLES G. (see page 743), Graniteville, Westford
Lombard N. A. & Co. Worcester
Cleveland & Bassett, "
CROMPTON GEORGE (looms, see page 767), Green st. "
Curtis & Marble, "
GILBERT C. W., Union st. "

JOHNSON & CO. Union st. Worcester
Knowles J. L. & Bro. (looms), "
PRATT SUMNER (see page 783), 22 Front, "
TAINTER DANIEL, Union st. "

Worsted Goods Manufs.

Winter Joseph, Braintree
Mansfield Geo. H. & Co. (cord), Canton Chelmsford
Baldwin Manuf. Co. (worsted yarn), Sutton Wm. Chelsea
Booth J. & Co. (yarn and braids), Fitchburg
Arlington Woolen Mills, J. W. Bailey, agent, Lawrence
EVERETT MILLS (real Earlstone ginghams), John R. Perry, agent, "
HEAVEN JESSE (braid), Canal, east of Union, "
Lawrence Braid Co. W. King & Son, "
LAWRENCE WORSTED CO. J. L. Chaplin, treas. (yarns and braids), "
ROBINSON SAMUEL & CO. (worsted yarns), "
WASHINGTON MILLS (plain and plaid poplins, Italian cloths, &c.), "
Wright Manuf. Co. (braid), A. S. Wright, agent, "
BRACKETT S. R. (worsted yarns), Whipple's Mills, Lowell
U. S. Bunting Company, D. W. C. Farringtou, agent, "
DUGDALE JAMES (yarns, alpaca braids, &c.), Wiley st. "
Abbot Worsted Co. (yarns), Graniteville, Westford
Worcester
Hamilton C. W. & Co. (bindings, &c.), "
Smith W. A. "
WRENTHAM MANUF. CO. (yarn), South Wrentham, Wrentham

Worsted Machinery.

LANE DAVID (see page 738), Fletcher, cor. Cushing, Lowell
ROBINSON WILLIAM & CO. Fletcher, cor. Dutton, "
SARGENT CHARLES G. (see page 743), Graniteville, Westford

Worsteds and Patterns.

Borden S. T. Mrs. Fall River
Eddy & Ashley Misses, "
McAdams Louisa Miss, "
Gove M. J. Mrs. Lynn
Case E. C. Miss, New Bedford
Cottle H. B. Miss, "
Hunt Josiah, "
Paul John Charles, "
Teel M. J. Newburyport
Malley William, Pittsfield
Holmes S. M. Plymouth
Ireson F. A. Salem
Shillaber S. "
Dean P. Evarts, Taunton
Southgate S. "
Wilbur & Co. "

Wrench Manufacturers.

(*See also Machinists.*)

Coes L. & A. G. Worcester

Wringing Machine Manuf.

Edmands Chas. H. Lynn
Huntley Geo. R. Taunton
EUREKA WRINGING MACHINE CO. T. J. Alexander, agent (see page 670), Waltham

Wrought Iron Pipe Manuf.

DIGHTON FURNACE CO. Geo. F. Gavitt, treas. (see page 733), North Dighton. Dighton
TAUNTON IRON WORKS CO. George M. Woodward, agent (see page 732), Taunton

Yankee Notions.

Bennett William H.   Fall River
Bigelow Franklin,   "
Blake E. O.   Lowell
Lapham Geo. H.   Lynn
Peck L. H.   "
English B. C.   Springfield
PATTON WM.   "

Yarns, Warps, &c.

(See also Cotton Yarns and Warps.)

Johnson Sylvander (cotton warps),
   North Adams,   Adams
Blackburn. George & Co. (cotton
   warps),   Ashburnham
Daggett H. M. (cotton),   Attleboro'
Boston Flax Mills,   Braintree
Morrison A. & Sons,   "
Morrison B. L. (woolen yarns),   "
Baldwin Co. (woolen yarn), North
   Chelmsford,   Chelmsford
Sheldon Geo. T. North Chelmsford.   "
Reed ——, (woolen yarn),   Clarksburg
Fuller & Bigelow (cotton yarns), &c. Clinton
Gloyd Noah L. (woolen yarn),   Cummington
Lovell D. W.   "   "
CHACE B. A. (cotton yarn, &c.),
   North Dighton (see page 756),   Dighton
LINCOLN L. & CO. (cotton yarns
   and warps), North Dighton (see
   page 724),   "
Curtis Thomas (cotton yarn and bat-
   ting), Harrison sq.   Dorchester
Perry David (woolen yarn), Webster, Dudley
WILLISTON MILLS, Jas. Suther-
   land, agent,   East Hampton
           Fall River
LAWTON & ESTES. (see page 734),   "
Saxonville Mills (woolen and wors-
   ted yarns,   Saxonville,   Framingham
Revere Woolen Mills (woolen).   Hamilton
Collier Eli (woolen yarn), Cherry
   Valley,   Leicester
ROBINSON SAMUEL & CO.   Lawrence
BRACKETT S. R. (worsted yarn),
   Whipple's Mills,   Lowell
Briggs Richard & Co. (yarns and
   lastings),   "
CLARK JEREMIAH, 96 Middle
   (see page 738),   "
DUGDALE JAMES (worsted yarns,
   alpaca braids, &c.), Wiley st.   "
Irish James & Co.   "
U. S. Bunting, D. W. C. Farrington,
   agent,   "

BROWN & SHERMAN (see page
   801),   Middleborough
           Millbury
CRANE & WATERS (woolen yarn),   "
Rhodes John (satinet warp),   "
Howard H. M. (woolen yarn),   Newbury
Morrison Leonard A. & Son (woolen
   yarn),   Byfield,   "
Peck Jabez L. (cotton warp),   Pittsfield
Southworth A. & Son (woolen),   Stoughton
           Walpole
Clark Henry S. (woolen), S. Walpole, "
Abbot Worsted Co. (worsted yarn)
   Graniteville,   Westford
WRENTHAM MANUF. CO. (wors-
   ted yarn), South Wrentham,   Wrentham

Yeast Cakes and Powders.

SLADE D. & L. 196 Broadway (see
   page 718),   Chelsea
Shattuck C. S. Mrs.   Lynn
Smith C. H. & Co.   "
WORCESTER M. A. 6 Bridge (dry
   hop, see page 783),   Worcester

Yellow Metal.

LAZELL, PERKINS, & CO.   Bridgewater
REVERE COPPER CO.   Canton
NEW BEDFORD COPPER CO.
   (also patent bronze metal, see page
   757)   New Bedford
CROCKER BROTHERS & CO.
   (sheathing, bolts, nails, &c. see
   page 756),   Taunton

Yellow Metal Bolts & Spikes.

NEW BEDFORD COPPER CO. (see
   page 757),   New Bedford

Zephyr Yarns.

LOWELL FELTING MILLS, Wm.
   H. Thompson, Proprietor,   Lowell

Zinc Manufacturers.

Edes Oliver,   Plymouth
Wood N. & Co.   "
CROCKER BROTHERS & CO.
   (sheet, nails, &c., see page 756),   Taunton

Zinc Paint Manufacturers.

CROCKER BROTHERS & CO. (see
   page 756), Court,   Taunton

DIRECTORY.---CAUTION.

THE DIRECTORY OFFICE,

No. 47 CONGRESS STREET, BOSTON.

ESTABLISHED IN 1846, BY GEORGE ADAMS.

Carried on from 1857 to 1865, by

ADAMS, SAMPSON, & CO.

Since 1865, continued by the same firm, under the style of

SAMPSON, DAVENPORT, & CO.

From this Office the

BOSTON DIRECTORY

has been issued annually for **TWENTY-TWO YEARS.**

THE PROVIDENCE (R. I.) DIRECTORY, NINE YEARS,
ALBANY (N. Y.) DIRECTORY, TWELVE YEARS,
TROY (N. Y.) DIRECTORY, ELEVEN YEARS.

Charlestown Directory, Roxbury Directory, Fall River Directory, Taunton Directory, Salem Directory, Lynn Directory, Lawrence Directory, Newburyport Directory, Lowell Directory, Manchester (N.H.) Directory, each biennially for from ten to twenty years.

THE NEW ENGLAND DIRECTORY

IN 1856, 1860, 1865, AND 1868,

THE NEW YORK STATE DIRECTORY.

IN 1859, 1864, AND 1867.

THE MASSACHUSETTS REGISTER AND BUSINESS DIRECTORY SINCE 1852,

THE MAINE REGISTER AND BUSINESS DIRECTORY,

AND THE RHODE ISLAND REGISTER AND DIRECTORY.

Besides the publication of Directories, a great deal of public business of a similar character has been done through this office ; some of it as follows : —

CENSUS OF BOSTON, 1850 ;
CENSUS OF BOSTON, MAY, 1855 ;
CENSUS OF BOSTON, JUNE, 1855 ;
CENSUS OF BOSTON & ROXBURY, 1865 ;
CENSUS OF VOTERS IN BOSTON IN 1857.
STATISTICS OF INDUSTRY IN BOSTON 1850.
STATISTICS OF INDUSTRY IN BOSTON AND ROXBURY, 1865.

The city has been canvassed twice annually for nineteen years for the Record of Births. An annual census of persons liable to enrolment in the State Militia has been taken some eighteen times, and a Census of School Children thirteen times.

S., D., & CO. can furnish, beside their own publications, nearly all other Directories published in the United States, and some from Foreign Countries.

DIRECTORY OFFICE,

SAMPSON, DAVENPORT, & CO.,

No. 47 CONGRESS STREET, BOSTON, MASS.

Account and Book Adjusters.

Holbrook Geo. 10 Traveller building
HUNTING GEO. F. 11 Bromfield
(see page 689)
Mair Geo. H. 27 Doane
Mair Thomas, 27 Doane

Acetic Acid Manuf.

FLICK GEO. F. 54 Hampden, near
Boston Lead Works (see page 805)

Actuary, Consulting.

Wright Elizur, 39 State, room 22

Adjuster of Complicated Accounts.

HUNTING GEO. F. 11 Bromfield
(see page 689)

Adjusters of Marine and Fire Losses.

Bradford & Folger, 56 State
Tyler John S. 28 State

Advertising Agents.

ADAMS THOMAS, 33 School
ALLEN & SHAILER, 199 Washington (see Index to advs.)
Automatic Electro Magnetic Advg.
Co., 50 School
Bryant A. L. & Co. 334 Washington
Cooley & Dauchy, 3 School
COOLIDGE GEO. 3 Milk
Dockham C. A. 96 Wash.
Dodd Horace. 23 Congress
Evans T. C. 106 Wash.
Lincoln A. F. & Co. 89 Court
Niles S. R., 1 Scollay's building
Pettingill S. M. & Co. 10 State
Propeller Adv. Agency, 21 Cornhill
Towne Arthur, 41 Kilby
Wilder E. W. 34 School

Agricultural Engineer.

SHEDD J. HERBERT, 7 Court sq.
room 38 (see page 668),

Agricultural Stores.

(See also Seed Stores.)

Ames Plow Co., Quincy Hall
Breck Jos. & Son, 51 North Market
Holbrook F. F. & Small, 10 South
Market
Hovey & Co. 53 North Market
Morse Plough Co. 13 Commercial
Parker, Gannett, & Osgood, 49 North
Market
Webster Bros. 19 Central
Whittemore, Belcher, & Co. 34 Merchants row

Air and Sub-Marine Pumps.

DENNETT & POTTLE, 71 Sudbury
(see page 691)

Albums.

DODGE, COLLIER, & PERKINS,
113 Wash. (see page 829)

Alcohol.

MILLS D. T. & CO. 13 Central
wharf
MILLS W. R. 46 India (see page
681)
PERKINS & SANDERSON, 96 and
98 Broad
DODGE JOHN T. & CO. 6 Custom-house st. (see page 834)

Ale, Porter, and Cider.

Ahlers Adolph, 7 Lindall
Benz Anthony, 1154 Wash.
Bixby S. C. 2 Congress sq.
Bonnie Louis, 2 Endicott
Boston Beer Co. D. H. Tully, treas.
19 Central whf. and Second, c. D
Brintnall N. Y. 138 Commercial
Burkhardt G. F. 3 Central
Cameron J. A. O. F. 20½ Howard
CARRUTH D. J. 63 Blackstone (see
page 677)
COBURN, LANG, & CO., manufacturers of soda and mineral water,
sarsaparilla, hop, and ginger beer;
also, dealers in Massey, Collins, &
Co.'s Philadelphia Ale and Porter,
and other ales; champagne cider,
lager beer, &c., for shipping and
family use. All orders promptly
attended to. 100 West Worcester
Street, Boston.
COMSTOCK, GOVE, & CO., manufacturers and dealers in syrup, soda,
and mineral water; porter, ale,
cider, and brown stout; lager beer,
draught ale, Scotch and English
Ales, 27 Merrimac and 30 Canal
Cook Isaac & Co. 25 Central
CUSHING J. H. 278 Commercial
(see page 697)
FAIRBANKS & BEARD, Howard
Athenæum (see page 803)
Ford J. 156 Federal
Ferguson Wm. 128 Essex
Flanigan Michael, 54 South
Flynn Michael, 1214 Tremont
Fracker Charles A. 1340 Tremont
Freeman Elizabeth, 1 Dover-st. place
Geary John, 318 Federal

Ale, Porter, and Cider — *continued.*
Gebordine Louis, 131 North
Greevey Michael, 1361 Tremont
Heil Edward, 85 Pynchon
Hennessy J. C. 252 Hanover
Kelley Thomas B. 1220 Tremont
Kelton J. P. 12 Chardon
Kent John O. 23 Haverhill
Lenzi F. 3 Central
McCaffrey Hugh, 1390 Tremont
McKnight John's Son, 20 Kilby
Mitchell Mary, 262 North
Moorhead William, 79 Essex
Mulligan Thomas, 1275 Tremont
Perkins Patrick, 16 Hawley
POTTER & FOSTER, 88 and 90 Kneeland, and 53 and 55 Utica (see page 683)
Riley Wm. 55 South
Robinson, Wilson, & Legalee, 102 Sudbury
Sauls Patrick, Elmwood, cor. Clay
Scripture & Parker, 31 Court sq.
Shmolz Jacob, Amory
Smith James M. & Co. 9 Court sq.
Smith Wm. J. & Bro. 12 Lindall
Speidel Leopold, Water, cor. Wash.
Stevens & Co. 51 Salem
Stowe S. F. & L. H. & Co. 155 Dudley (small beer)
Taylor J.'s Son, 117 Commercial
VAN NOSTRAND W. T. 118 Lincoln (see page 678)
Vincent & Hathaway, 1220 Wash.
Warren Timothy, 1703 Tremont

Ammonia Manuf.

PORTER, CROSS, & MESSER, 110 Milk (see page 690)

Anchors.

ATLANTIC WORKS, Chelsea, cor. Marion, E. B., office 114 State (manuf., see page 700)
BOSTON FORGE CO. J. Smith, treas. Maverick, E. B. (manuf., see page 698)
Lufkin Nathaniel, 136 Bremen, E. B.

Annunciators.

HUMPHREY BROS. & SMITH, 38 Old State House (see page 832)
FULLER SETH W. 25 Devonshire (see page 831)

Apothecaries.

*Those marked with a * are members of the* MASSACHUSETTS COLLEGE OF PHARMACY.

Adams A. L. 295 Meridian, E. B.
Allen William M. 1152 Tremont
*Almy Sylvester, Tremont, c. School
Appleton Geo. H. 271 Meridian, E. B.
Appleton Geo. J. 56 Phillips
Arnold C. R. 50 Causeway

Atkinson W. D. jr. 185 Tremont
*Babo Leopold, 12 Boylston
Batchelder S. F. 1179 Federal
Badger Wm. & Co. 1388 Tremont
Barrett & Co. 55 Green   [sea
Bartlett G. R., Bennington, cor. Chel-
Bartlett & Darling, 175 North
*Blasland Thomas, Broadway, cor. D
Boston Dispensary, Ash, cor. Bennet
*Boyden Ashel, Joy, cor. Myrtle
Brooks Geo. P., Fourth, cor. Federal
Brown Geo. T. 519 Tremont
*Brown Joseph T. 292 Wash.
Burleigh John A. 86 Hanover
Bushee J. A & Co. 21 Maverick sq.
*Campbell Isaac T. 241 Broadway
Canning Henry, 135 Cambridge
Caraway P. C. 149 Hampden
Carleton J. 494 Tremont
Chamberlain Edson C. 84 Trenton
Choate Henry A. under Revere House
Church F. T., Court, cor. Howard
Clock Frank B. 20 Cambridge
Cobb G. W., Meridian, cor. London
Colby J. R., Dearborn, cor. Eustis
Colby Moses D. 8 Maverick sq. E. B.
Colton G., Cambridge, c. N. Anderson
Colton James B. 766 Tremont
*Connor T. J., Broadway, cor. I
Cordwell Geo. B. 1856 Wash.
Cox Lucian A. 31 Blossom
Cutler Geo. E. Shawmut ave. c. Dale
Dalziel Charles, 96 Salem
Day C. H. & F. B. 285 Meridian
Dean Edward, 1179 Federal
Dodge L. G. 156 Endicott
Dows G. D. 525 Washington
Duard Franz, 787 Tremont
Dyer Joseph H. 238 Shawmut avenue
Eaton Charles L. 1233 Washington
FENELON BROS. 282 Broad
*Ferguson Dennis, 2 Broadway
Folger W. S. & Co. 723 Tremont
Foster Charles H. 194 Harrison ave.
*Fowle H. D. 71 Prince
Foy Frank E. 153 Broadway
Fraser Charles L. 110 Meridian, E. B.
*French Charles, 867 Hanover
Frothingham D. D. 131 Leverett
Gilman J. P. 171 North
*Gleeson J. A., Harr. ave. c. Harvard
*Gleeson M. H, Summer, c. High
*Gleeson T. J. 1608 Washington
Gordon R. K. & Co., Dudley, corner Warren
Graves & Newcomb, 95 Cambridge
Hammond T. D., Essex c. South
Hardy Wm. G. 671 Broadway
Harris Theodore S. 130 Tremont
*Henchman Daniel, 65 Cambridge
Henderson Bros. 1681 Washington
Henry Chas. F. under Norfolk House
Hollis J. O. 43 & 45 Salem
*Hollis Thomas, 23 Union

Howard Wm. P. 396 Hanover
Howe & Neilson, 364 Broadway
Holbert C. A. Causeway, c. Lowell
Hantoon H. P. 161 Cambridge
Ivers R. A. 206 Cambridge
Jenks T. L., Merrimac, c. Portland
Jenkins L. L. 119 Leverett
Jenkins Wm. E., Fourth, c. B.
Kane Thomas 722 Washington
*Kent Robert R. 7 Winthrop Block
Kidder Darius B. 12 Maverick square
Knight Henry T. 86 Merrimac
LAMBERTON J. F., Eustis, corner
  Dearborn
*Lincoln H. W., Charles, c. Chestnut
Little A. H. B. & Co. 111 Hudson
*Littlefield A., Beach, c. Lincoln
Lyon Charles H. jr. 21 Pleasant
McSheehy J. J. 334 North
*Melvin & Badger, 325 Washington
*METCALF THEO. & CO. 39 Tremont (see page 699)
Morris Patrick, Federal, c. Purchase
Nims O. F. 80 Cambridge
Noble S. J. 31 Carver, c. Eliot
Nowell W. F. 192 Merrimac
Noyes C. D. U. 192 Hanover
*O'Brien Jas. J., Hudson, c. Kneeland
O'Brien J. A. & Co. 140 Broad
Page W. W., Tramont, c. Pleasant
*Parker J. L., Tremont, c. Eliot
*Parmenter G. W. 270 Hanover
Pattee A. F. 165 Shawmut avenue
*Patten I. B. & Co. 27 Harrison ave.
Peabody N. C. (hom.) 56 Beach
Percival & French, 68 Washington
*Perry E. H. 745 Washington
Perry & Duncan, 33 Boylston
Pierce William C. 1153 Tremont
Powers John P. 1140 Tremont
Prescott B. T. & Son, 516 Tremont
Restieaux Thomas, 29 Tremont
Richmond Wm. B. 54 Church
*Ricker Geo. D. 178 Salem
Ricker O. P. & Co. 654 Washington
Russell Edward, 1079 Washington
Sampson Z. S. 32 Harrison avenue
Savell Chas. E. & Co. 4 Guild row
Sewall David J. 1257 Washington
*Sheppard S. A. D. & Co. 881 Wash.
Skinner Edw. M. 27 Tremont
*Smalley Elijah, 170 Harrison ave.
Smith Theo., Court, cor. Hanover
SNOW J. WALKER, Portland, cor.
  Merrimac
Souther E. 75 Green, cor. Lyman
Stebbins E. S. & Co. 1 & 2 Charlestown
Stone V. R. 251 North
Street Samuel B. 57 Causeway
Sullivan & Loty, 63 Tremont
Swett & Harding, 817 Washington
Tappan C. E. & Co. 649 Tremont
Thayer Eli, Salem, cor. Richmond

Thayer Walter B. 298 North
*Tompkins Orlando, 271 Washington
*Tower Levi, jr., 1523 Washington
Tower W. B. 147 Leverett
Tucker & Co. 62 Chambers
TUFTS J. W. & CO. 138 Hanover
  (see page 668)
Underwood C. G., Maverick square,
  corner Lewis
Warren George, 1805 Washington
*Warren Henry, Green, c. Leverett
Watson W. H. 3 North square
Wetherbee F. M. 425 Washington
Weymouth H. L. 516 Tremont
White Henry, Eliot square
White John, 38 Leverett
White J. F. 48 Sudbury
White J. H. agt. Kingston, c. Essex
White Robert, 165 Broad
Wilbor Alexander B. 166 Court
*Wilbor A. G. 547 Washington
Willson J. W. F. 479 Broadway
Wilson William J. 1336 Tremont
Wood Webster C. 823 Washington
Woodman D. S. 21 Central sq. E. B.
Woods B. O. 351 Federal
*Woods Samuel H. 5 Beacon
Woodward J. B. & Co. 160 Hanover
*Woodward W. E. 258 Dudley
*Wright Wm. R. West Cedar, corner
  Revere
Young P. Ambrose, 607 Washington

Archil.

MANCHESTER MANUF. CO. 54
  Kilby (also Cudbear, see page 699)

Architects.

Allen F. 61 State.
Barton S. M. 65 Studio Building
Billings H. & J. E. 33 School, room 62
Bradley Nathaniel J. 18 Pemberton
  square
Briggs Luther, 81 Wash. room 20
Brooks B. H. 15 Pemberton square
Bryant G. J. F. & L. P. Rogers, 17
  Pemberton square
Cabot E. C. 2 Pemberton square
Caldwell Edward G. 6 Studio building
Clark George R. 7 Studio building
Colburn T. E. 26 Studio building
Cummings & Sears, 9 Studio building
Dorr Morris, 31 Studio building
Dwight B. F. 149 Tremont
Emerson & Fehmer, 12 West
Esty Alex. R. 2 Change ave.
Faulkner H. Floyd, 7 Studio building
Fox John A. 149 Tremont
Frink A. 28 State and 22 Guild row
Fuller George F. 18 Pemberton sq.
Graves H. 15 Congress
Hall Henry P. 41 Tremont
Hall John R. 27 & 28 Old State
  House

Architects — continued.

Hartwell H. W. & A. E. Swasey, jr. 31 Pemberton square
Jepson S. 1806 Washington
Kirby C. K. 17 Pemberton square
Lee & Follen, 16 Pemberton square (landscape)
Lummus Wm. W. 40 State
Martin A. C. & W. P. P. Longfellow, 18 Pemberton sq. rooms 8 and 9
Meacham George F. 23 Congress
Merrill W. F. 39 Court
Moore Frederick H. 33 School, room 20
Newcomb L. & Son, 12 West
Odiorne & Wheeler, 32 Pemberton sq.
Parker Chas. Edwl. 8 Congress sq.
Preston J. 81 Washington, room 8
Preston Wm. G. 81 Wash. room 8
Rand J. H. 83 City Exchange
Richards & Park, 46 Court
Ropes Geo. jr. 32 Pemberton sq.
Ryder & Harris, 41 Tremont
Samuels Isaac B. 46 Court
Sayer Rheimunt, 13 Pemberton sq.
Silloway Thomas. W. 71 Green
Sleeper Charles F. 33 School, room 19
Smith O. F. 17 Pemberton square
Snell George 38 Studio building
Snell & Gregerson, 15 Studio building
Sparrell William, 9 State
Stevens John, 34 School
Sturgis J. H. & Charles Brigham, 50 Bromfield
SYLVESTER L. G. 256 Meridian (see page 805)
Thayer S. J. F. 39 Court
Towle John D. & Son, 33 Studio building, 110 Tremont
VARNEY W. H. Sumner, cor. People's Ferry ave. E. B. (naval)
Voelckers Theo. 80 Washington
Ware & Van Brunt, 2 Pemberton sq.
Washburn William, 7 Change ave.
Weissban L. 82 City Exchange
Weld Samuel B. 18 Pemberton sq.
Wilson H. M. 11 Bromfield
WOODCOCK S. S. 13 Exchange (see page 804)
Woodward Wm. E. 24 Tremont row

Artesian Wells.

PIERCE G. E. & E. R. 22 State and 26 Bremen (see page 833)

Art Gallery.

Schwabe L. B., Gallery of Fallen Heroes, 17 E. Canton

Artificial Limbs.

Jewett Leg Co. 33 Tremont
Palmer B. Frank, 81 Green
Randall G. W. 87 Causeway (arms)

Artists' Materials.

Crowell Bros. & Co. 92 Sudbury
FROST & ADAMS, 33 & 35 Cornhill (see page 673)
Hollis Lambert, 46 Temple Place
SPRINGER L. R. 351 Washington (see page 662)
Tobey M. B. 28 Temple Place (indelible ink)
Walker A. A. 322 Washington
Wheeler Ashael, 67 Water

Assayers and Refiners.

EHRHARDT, DUBELLE, & CO. 62 Congress (see page 689)
Guild S. F. 16 Devonshire

Astrologers.

Lister Thomas, 25 Lowell
Wright Madam, 260 Washington

Auctioneers.

Abrams Isaac, 712 Washington
Atwood George M. 81 Wash.
Bayley Dudley H. & Co. 91 Federal
Beck Gideon, 84 Federal
Brown Brothers, 9 State
Brown H. A. 39 State
Clark B. A. & Co. 186 Washington
Collamore H. L. & Co. 113 Court
Conway John, 81 Washington
COOK COLEMAN, 4 Maverick sq. E. B. (see page 693)
Cowing & Hatch, 45 Pearl
CUSHING BROS. 221 Wash.
Damon Charles E. 31 Washington
Dearborn & Co. Court House
Drury C. F. 106 Court
Farnham J. C. 31 State
Faunce Geo. B. 22 Guild row
Fitzpatrick Wm. H. & Co. 374 Wash.
Gridley & Co. 50 School
Hall Edward F. 29 Old State House
Harris Horatio & Co. 18 India
Harris & Phinney, 9 Central wharf
Hart Geo. L. & Co. 32 Congress
Hatch Samuel & Co. 3 Morton place
HENSHAW & BRO. 5 Merchants Exchange
Hichborn Geo. R. & Co. 1 Scollay's building
Hyde J. F. C. 2 Court square
Isburg & Rowland, 8 and 10 East
Jackson S. S. 15 Congress
Kyle W. S. & T. 10 State
Leonard & Co. 48 and 50 Bromfield
Lester John H. (shoes), 121 Pearl, and Real estate, 22 Old State House
Lynes E. G. 27 State
McGilvray D. F. & Co. 171 Tremont
McKey W. R. (agent) 2 Pearl-street House
Merriam W. H. & Co. 509 Wash.
NASON & METCALF, 96 Wash.
Nogler S. 275 Hanover

Osgood F. D. 113 Dudley
Osgood J. H. 65 Hawley
Patton & Ginn, 130 Commercial
Porter J. K. & Co. 5 Court
Porter J. L. 25 Kilby
Potter & Boyd, 95½ Washington
Power T. C. & Co. 15 School
Proctor & Hallett, 136 Broadway
Riddle Edward. 126 Union
SHERIDAN W. A. & CO. 7 Green
 (see page 807)
Spinney E. B. & Co. 15 Congress
Sprague Francis & Co. 11 Central
SWETT A. O. 81 Hanover
Thayer E. F. E. 11 Court
Thompson Newell A. & Co. 10 and 11
 Old State House
Tucker Nathaniel & Co. 52 Pearl
Tyler John. 18 India
Vose A. Dammers, 27 Guild Row
Walker A. R. 15 Central
Walker Samuel A. 15 Central
Whitmarsh J. F. L. 509 Washington

Auditor of Accounts.

Turner A. R. 30 Court

Awnings.

Bowen & Erickson, 18 N. Market
Crocker & Otis, 105 Commercial
Kingman & Robinson, 102 Commercial
Lamprell & Marble, 357 Commercial
Martin James & Son, 114 Commercial
VAUGHN J. J. 323 Washington (see
 page 681)
Yale R. M. & Co. 14 Commercial

Axes.

Amoskeag Axe Co. 70 Kilby
DOUGLAS AXE MANUF. CO., D.
 D. Dana, treas. 215 Federal (see
 page 688)

Axles.

ABBOTT & HOWARD. 11 Oliver
 (see front colored page)
BOSTON FORGE CO. Maverick,
 E. B. (manufs., see page 698)
Dodge, Gilbert, & Co. 37 Kilby
Kinsley Lyman, 25 Fulton
Linden Iron & Steel Co. 82 Federal

Bacon Works.

Knowles H. W. 510 Harrison ave.
Parsons & Wiggin, 470 Harrison ave.
Wright C. & Co., Fellows, cor. Hun-
 neman

Bags and Bagging.

Chase H. & L. 233 State
Jewell I. B. 91 Haverhill
Kimball Daniel, 106 Fulton
Stearns A. F. 52 Brattle
26

Bakers.

Allen John, 82 Brighton
Allman F. G. 57 Emerson
Amrhein A. 44 Oneida
AUSTIN C. F. & CO. 116 Comml.
 (ship, see page 660)
Bancroft John W. 41 South
Barry E. W. 267 Fourth
Bartlett A. G. 17 East Dedham, 869
 Albany. 164 Endicott, and 53 Pop-
 lar
Becker & Stoddard, Bennington, cor.
 Porter, and 80 Meridian, E. B.
Bemis O. 696 Washington
Bennighof A. & P. 1210 Tremont
Blaser John J. 71 Elliot
Blood Ai & Co. 75 Lincoln
Bond Timothy D. 12 Canal (crackers)
Boston Wheat & Bread Co. 1480
 Washington, Thos. J. Gargan, treas.
Boynton & Brown, 216 Friend
Breivogeil Daniel, 82 West Canton
Brewer & Fowle, 66 Commercial,
 and 148 Purchase
Brigham John A. 392 Shawmut ave.
Brigham Martin F. 1854 Washington
Brown Gilbert C. 53 Pleasant
Burke James, 94 Essex
Burke Richard, 116 Tyler
Callaghan Michael, 14 Central square,
 E. B.
Callahan Philip, S. Margin, cor. Gouch
Chater James, 883 Washington
Chater John. 132 Cambridge
Clarke A. W. & Co. rear Clifton pl.
Connell Austin H. 151 Hampden
Cusack Thos. 296 Sumner, E. B.
Darragh J. 1007 and 1360 Tremont
English Maurice, 1810 Washington
Field Simon C. 5 Bennington, E. B.
Fisher E. 144 Court
Flanders Robt. L. 14 Central sq. E. B.
Frost George, 24 Taber
Gaut Samuel N. 474 Washington
Gill John, E. corner Firth
Goodale Geo. W. 1038 Federal, W. V.
Gould Wm. E. 173 Harrison avenue
Hamblin & Balfour, 1136 Federal
Hawkins C. A. 133 W. Brookline
Hayden Richard, 222 Federal
Hewes J. F. 140 Prince
Heyl A. A. 181 Broadway
Hoernle John C. 6 Bennet
Howard E. L. & Co. 51 Causeway
Howard Samuel. 42 Myrtle
Howard Samuel P. 104 Cambridge
Hurter C. 49 Warrenton
Irving M. Mrs. 30½ Cambridge
James B. F. (crackers). r. 1842 Wash.
Karcher Jacob. Salem e. N. Bennet
Kiesele F. 184 Harrison avenue
Knight C. I. 10 Cross
Knower T. 130 Endicott
Kraft Albert, 153 Harrison avenue

Bakers — continued.

KRIEGEL GEORGE. 24 Chadwick, office 5 Dock square (for price of cocoanut cakes, see page 818)

Kurtz Geo. 79 Warrenton

Lambert John, 598 Harrison avenue

Litchfield & Fox, 61 Portland

Loud J. C. & E. A.. 39 Prince

Lowenbach Isaac, 2113 Washington

Maheux Lucien, 105 W. Canton

Martin F. 91 Warrenton and 42 Northampton

McArdle Henry, 16 East

McConihe Luther, 99 Prince

McDevitt Robert, 42 Broadway

McGill J. 194 E, corner Eighth

McKenzie Adelaide, 1 Cooper

McKenzie Daniel, 18 Chadwick

McLaughlin P. 105 Cross

McShane Henry, 192 North

Merello J. 1090 Washington

Millett Charles L. 90 West Cedar

Milligan Thomas, 22. Federal

Morlock Jacob. 22 Fleet

Morrill Helen H. 66 Maverick, E. B.

Morse A. 13, and 320 Broadway, and 102 Dorchester

Mullen Thomas, 65 Green

Murdock John & Son, 687 Fourth and 352 Dorchester

Murray Edward W. 338 Broadway

Newmarch H. J. Miss, 9 Bedford

O'Hanlon George, 542 Second

O'Neill John, 327 North

Ordway J. M. 294 Hanover, 68 Beach, and 39 Charter

Parmelee & Newell. 46 Chester Park

Perry Alvin, 183 Ruggles

Pike Jona. 51 Poplar

Poole W. H. 9 Leverett

Presby Geo. C. 338 Sumner and 75 Princeton   [793 Washington

Randall Wm. B. 134 Pleasant and Robbins B. 76 Leverett

Robertson Daniel, 18 Chadwick

Rowe Maria, 432 Commercial

Rugg M. F. 1534 Washington

Schlehuber Joseph. Heath place

Shields James, 81 Maverick, E. B.

Smith Nelson, rear 294 Hanover

Smith William & Co.. 100 Salem

Stackpole S. A. 120 Fourth

Stamm Lewis, 309 Fourth

Stephenson J. E. 31 High

Stone Eben, 399 Hanover

Taylor & Co. 857 Washington

Tierney Norah Miss, 41 Clarendon

Tuttle Thomas W. 72 Essex

Wakefield D. K. 71 Maverick

Walsh John, 118 Merrimac

Washburn G. W. C., Dearborn, c. Dudley

Welchlin Charles F. 1332 Tremont, and 57 W. Dedham

Weller J. 8 Hollis place

Wesner Matthias, 1116 Tremont

Whitcomb E. D. 1854 Washington

White E. 10 Blossom

Wood John F. 89 Princeton, E. B.

Wood P. K. 63 Billerica

Woodman E. M. 78 W. Cedar

Wyeth N. S. 73 Harrison avenue

Zielinger Charles, 289 Sumner, E. B.

Balances.

Fairbanks, Brown, & Co. 118 Milk

Howe Scale Co., L. I. Howe, agent, 131 Federal

Preston Wm. B. 20 Faneuil Hall sq.

Ballast.

Arseneaux F., Arch Wharf

Brown J. (agent), 188 Commercial

Caddigan J. J. agent. 248 Comm'l

Dunbar Peter, 70 Broad

Parker B. W. 252 Commercial

Simons Nicholas, 209 Commercial

Smith & Adams, 194 Commercial

Bank and Safe Locks.

(See Locks.)

Bankers.

Attwood Gilbert & Co. 14 Merchants Exchange

Ballou & Mifflin, 60 State

Baring Bos. & Co. 28 State

Blake Brothers & Co. 28 State

Bowles Brothers & Co. 76 State

Bolles Matthew & Co. 90 State

Brewster, Sweet, & Co. 40 State

Brown Brothers & Co. 4 State

Burnett, Drake, & Co. 88 State

Child Lewis, 29 Merchants row

Curtis Daniel Sargent, 4 State

Davis George P. 60 State

Day R. L. & Cobb, 31 Kilby & 16 Lindall

Dwight, Richardson, & Co. 28 State

Fogg Brothers & Bates, 20 Congress

Foote & Walker, 7 Congress

Fuller C. E. & Co. 2 State

Gilbert B. W. 18 State

Howe James Murray & Co., 92 State

Hubbard Brothers & Co. 31 State

Hunnewell H. H. & Sons. 13 Ex.

Kidder, Peabody, & Co. 40 State

Lawrence & Ryan, 10 Broad

Lee, Higginson, & Co. 40 State

Lee Thomas J. & Hill, 60 State

Page, Richardson. & Co. 70 State

PAPENDIEK, CHASE, & CO. 62 Congress

Parker & Cobb, 8 Devonshire

Putnam Charles A. 60 State

Spencer, Vila, & Co. 13 Congress

Stone & Downer, 28 State

Tower, Giddings, & Torrey, 74. State

Walley & Bates, 20 State

Warren Geo. W. & Co. 60 State
Way Samuel A. & Co. 43 State
Wellman W. A. 28 State (attorney)
Williams Jarvis & Son, 41 Kilby

Bark. (*Tanners'.*)
Burnham & Darrow, 636 Federal

Barometer Manuf.
SIEFERT CHAS. A. 70 Washington
(see page 686)

Barrel Manuf.
HILL & WRIGHT, 145 and 157
Sumner, E. B. (see page 813)

Barrels, Casks, and Bungs.
Brown David (second hand), Hampden, near Adams
LANG & DELANO, 2 India wharf
(see page 806)
Twitchell J. 21 Cove
VAN NOSTRAND W. T. (ale barrels) 118 Lincoln (see page 678)

Basket Makers.
Porter James & Co. 13 Marshall and
68 Haverhill
Wakefield Cyrus, 36 Canal

Baskets and Toys.
HARPER & CO. 44 Temple place
(Fayal)
PARTHEIMULLER F. 4 Lowell
place (see page 669)

Baths.
BLODGETT CYRUS, rear Marlboro' Hotel (vapor and Turkish,
see page 663)
Bruce Cyrus, Cragie's bridge
Holland Wm. A. 478 Washington
Lipman J. C. 83 Sudbury
Turkish Baths, 1427 Washington and
17 Essex

Bedding, Feathers, &c.
Allen A. H. 1 and 2 Dock square
BRABROOK E. H. 4 Union
Brooks W. P. B. 120 Blackstone, and
9 Marshall
Gray & Bail, 32 Union and 19 Friend
Haley, Morse, & Boyden. 407 Wash.
HALLETT JAMES H. & SONS,
17 Dock square (see page 702)
Haskell A. L. & Son, 124 Hanover
Holman John & Co. 60 Union and 47
Friend
Hopkins Charles, 39 Cornhill
INSTITUTION FOR THE BLIND
20 Bromfield (see page 667)
Kittredge F. O. (husks), 14 Canal
Manning, Glover, & Co. 102 Hanover
PARSONS & TORREY, 460 and
464 Washington (see page 693)
Putman John, 6 Beach
Sammet G. A. 130 Blackstone

WARE GEORGE W. & CO. 12
Cornhill (see page 679)
Wheeler A. W. & Co. 21 Union

Beds. (*See also Spring Beds.*)
BURR S. S. 49 Temple place (see
page 677)

Bedstead Manufacturer.
Comins George T. 173 Blackstone

Beer. (*Small or Root.*)
CUSHING J. H. 278 Commercial
(see page 697)
FAIRBANKS & BEARD, Howard
Athenæum building (see page 803)

Beer Apparatus.
Puffer A. D. 48 Portland

Bells.
Foster & Roby, 178 Commercial
Hooper H. N. & Co. 66 Causeway
NAYLOR & CO. 80 State

Bell Hangers.
Blood E. B. 144 Sumner, E. B.
Campbell Daniel E. 1197 Wash.
Crane A. B. 5 Beach
Fernald G. M. D. 460 Tremont
FULLER SETH W. 25 Devonshire
(see page 831)
Harrington Geo. E. 25 Province
Howe Napoleon B. 479 Tremont
HUMPHREY BROS. & SMITH,
38 Old State House (see page 832)
James George E. 199 Sumner, E. B.
Janes D. W. 783 Wash.
Rowe A. E. & Co. 5 Wash.
Trefry Geo. W. 1 Warren ave.

Bellows Manufacturer.
Garland James, 136 Lincoln

Belt and Leather Stuffing.
Noyes Person, 47 India

Belting.
(*See also Leather Belting.*)
AMERICAN TOOL AND MACHINE CO. 45 Kingston (see page
669)
BOSTON BELTING CO. 57 Sumner (see front colored page)
CLARK A. N. & CO. 31 Devonshire
(see page 807)
MAY & CO. 1 Broad (see inside
back cover)
PAGE E. F. & CO. 46 Congress (see
inside back cover)
PUTNAM G. D. & CO. 13 Central
(see page 807)
Wilson James W. & Co. 79 and 81
Haverhill (see page 680)

Bi-Carb. Soda.
Bowman, Grant, & Co. 168 State
Emmerton & Co. 13 and 15 Custom
House street

Bill Posters.

Donnelly John, 9 Wilson's lane
Kelly, Foley, & Co. 5 Williams court

Billiard Rooms.

Ariola Gio Batta. 36 Ferry
Bailey & Marshall. 114 Sudbury
Bonnie Louis, 2 Endicott
Brown O. C. 106 Union
Cheney John. 17 Brattle
Cobb Isaac, Tremont, opp. station
Daniels & Heath, 7 Green
Flack John. H. 1557 Wash.
Frost Thad. B. 115 Court
Garrigan James H. 55 Hanover
Goell Frank A. 139 Wash.
Hancock S. A. 101 Cambridge
Hess Charles, 7 Eliot
Homer Valentine, 1863 Wash.
Housman W. 484 Washington
Jones Gordon, 367 Washington
Lowd T. Quincy, 84 W. Springfield
McNeil Francis, 361 Hanover
Mitchell T. 109 Court
Muller Charles. 419 Wash.
Murphy John C. 1020 Wash.
Newhall L. C. 75 Court
Newman Charles, 6 Canal
Page George, 339 Broadway
Pindell Isaiah, 1144 Wash.
Porter L. W. 188 Tremont
Rice C. E. 57 Temple place
Sargent C. 91 Union
Roessle J. F. Boylston
Solomon H. B. 169 Hanover
Stoddard Geo. H. 8 Lindall
Stoehr Henry, 472 Wash.
Tobin W. A., Williams Hall [doin sq.
UNDERHILL L. M. & CO. 1 Bow-
Wakefield J. J. 145 Hanover
Walker Henry A. 1916 Washington
Whipple & Benton. 1155 Washington
Yeaton R. F. 69 West Concord

Billiard Table Makers.

Bailey A. W., Harrison ave. cor. Way
CAME J. E. & CO., sole manufacturers of Billiard Tables, with
Phelan's latest improved Standard
Combination Cushions; also agents
for Phelan's Standard Billiard Tables, for the New England States.
Proprietors and manufacturers of
the Patent Time and Price Billiard
Registers. Balls, cloths, cues, and
all articles connected with the business for sale. Balls turned and colored with dispatch. 114 Sudbury.
Heims Henry, 106 Sudbury
Schouller Peter & Son. 1049 Wash.

Birds and Cages.

Brewster C. G. 16 Tremont
Greenleaf & Anthony, 104 Court
Rice Geo. E. 52 Court

Blacking. (Boot and Shoe.)

Bassett & Whitcomb, 7 Bath
Brown B. F. & Co. 133 Fulton
Chadbourne & White, 134 Wash.
Collamore Wm. & Co. 26 N. Market
HATHAWAY C. L. & SONS, 56
Fulton, and 1 and 3 Ferry (manuf.
see page 826)
Mason's Challenge Blacking, George
Merrill, agt. 18 South Market
Reed Geo. H. & Co. 570 Commercial

Blacksmiths.

(See also Shipsmiths.)

ATLANTIC WORKS, Chelsea, cor.
Marion, E. B., office 114 State (see
page 700)
Barry J. 509 Second
Batterman J. 471 Harrison ave.
Blood & Judkins, 149 Beach
Bramhall Otis, 119 Congress
Brackett Andrew D. 582 Shawmut av.
Brock Wm. 2159 Washington
Brown O. G. 90 Travers
Burnham & Lowell, 84 Chardon
Buzzell John E. 18 King
Cahill Leander, Liverpool, E. B.
Callahan N. 25 Stillman
Cardinal H. 18 King
Carroll R. C., Second, n. Dorchester
Carroll Wm. 21 Lancaster
Chisholm Alex. 41 Bowker
Coleman P., Warren, n. Grove Hall
Connolley T., F. cor. Third
Cornish John, 12 People's Ferry ave.
Croft James T. 97 Beverly
Cunningham & Worthley, 633 Fourth
Davern Wm., Grove Hall avenue,
Densmore & Kennedy, 89 Travers
Denton J. W. 270 Cabot   [way
Dodd George H., Medford, n. Cause-
Dow Jonathan R. 9 Lime
Dowd D. & J. 55 Palmer
Dowd Thomas C. 80 Hampden
Durick & Mulcahy, 10 Swan
Eaton H. R. 1179 Tremont
Fall Henry, 277 Federal
FOSS A. S. 246 Sumner. E. B.
Freeman Moses H. 22 Andover
Gantage S. F. Charlestown
Geraghty Wm. 1517 Tremont
Goldie John, 69 W. Dedham
Graves J. & Co. 35 Haverhill
Gray Edward, 267 Causeway
Hall H. G. 155 Beach
Haberstroh M. 480 Tremont
Ham L. M. 158 Portland
Hartford B., Second, near E
HATHAWAY SAMUEL. Border,
near Central square, E. B.
Hewitt John, 26 Hampshire
Hill J. F. 113 Albany
Hooker David S. 123 and 127 Sumner
Jaquith & Buss, 118 Dover

Keefe Martin, 478 Harrison avenue
Keniston J. & J. R., Border, opp.
 Townsend's shipyard, E. B.
Lakin Sylvester, 398 Broad
Lally Patrick. 3 First
Lazell Wm. H. 6 Bumstead court
Lewis Joel W. 45 Richmond
Low Wm. H. 22 Harvard place
Mack N. 914 Shawmut avenue
Manning G. W. 29 Morton place
Mason Lewis, 159 Harrison avenue
McBarron J., Emerald, near Chapman
McBarron Bros. & Lucas, 664 Harrison avenue
McClosky D. A. 43 Sumner, E. B.
McCort J, & G. 33 Richmond
McGatigan Wm. 102 Charlestown
Meade William, 628 Harrison ave.
Mennig George, Parker, n. Longwood avenue
Moody & Burnett, 17 Bowker
Mountjoy Wm. 86 Porter, E. B.
Mullowney Michael, 8 N. Anderson
Murphy Patrick, 18 Suffolk
Newman A. W. 44 Eustis
O'Brien P. 833 Harrison avenue
Onderdonk M. C. 264 Broad
Perry & Bickford, 58 Beverly
Ray Richard, Granite, Boston wharf
Ray Robert, 293 Second
Richards David W. 501 Commercial
Riddle John A., Hampden, cor. Norfolk avenue
Roberts J. L. 63 Merrimac
Robinson A. E. 188 Second
Rouke James & Co. 135 Beach
Sawyer W. W. 65 Beverly
Scott John A. 42 Warren
Shafer & O'Connor, 99 Orleans, E. B.
Shepard William, Charlestown, cor. Beverly
Simpson D. S. 144 Beach
Smith & Lovett, 57 Devonshire
Stone William P. 179 First
Thomas John, 50 Eustis
Tuckerman W. I. 851 Federal
Twitchell & Libby, 45 Causeway
Ward Patrick, 126 Charlestown
Weekes Richard, Centre, near R. R.
Williams Patrick, 19 Lancaster
WILSON J. W. & CO. 79 and 81 Haverhill (see page 680)

Black Walnut Frames.

DODGE, COLLIER, & PERKINS, 113 Wash. (oval and square, see p. 829)

Blank Book Manufacturers.

Bennett B. F. & Co. 116 State
COLEMAN GEO. & CO. 116 Wash. (see page 825)
Cottrell Geo. W. 36 Cornhill

Cutter, Tower, & Co. 89 Devonshire
Darling Charles K. 15 Exchange
Gay Aaron R. & Co. 130 State
Gay Richard L. & Co. 63 Milk
Groom Thomas & Co. 82 State
Hallgreen H. J. & Co. 14 Exchange
HAMMETT J. L. 37 and 39 Brattle
Hooper, Lewis, & Co. 120 State
Humphrey B. F. 114 State
Little N. & Co. 49 Cornhill
Marsh H. F. Co. 17 Cornhill
McAdams William & Co. 18 Water
Merrick C. L. 27 Cornhill
NICHOLS & HALL, 43 Wash. (see page 804)
YERRINTON F. M. 56 Washington (small, see page 827)
Ward Samuel & Co. 8 State

Bleacheries.

LOWELL, S. G. SNELLING, 82 Milk
Middlesex, James Lee jr. 9 India

Blind and Sash Makers' Supplies.

WASHBURN B. D. 137 Congress

Blueing.

Brown B. F. & Co. 133 Fulton
Hartshorn Edward. 133 Water
Sawyer H. 20 North Market

Boarding Houses.

Adams Isaac, 504 and 510 Wash.
Anderson D. B. 56 Essex
Anderson John P. 4 Prince
Andrew Charles, 120 Harrison ave.
Bailey H. N. 155 Summer
Bailey L. A. Mrs. 20 Bulfinch
Bumbauer Jacob, 10 Avery
Barron A. F. Miss. 32 Indiana place
Barry John, 119 Charlestown
Bearse Stephen, 2 Arch place
Bennett T. 20 Moon
Berry John B. 14 Pitts
Berry Mary H. Miss, 16 Joy
Bitzer Louis, rear 25 Eliot
Blasser A. 121 Hampden
Bond C. D. 8 Lincoln
Boston J. 266 North
Bowman C. 24 Broadway
Brackett B. F. 46 Essex
Briggs Harriet Mrs. 740 Wash.
Brothers Kate Mrs. 91 Portland
Brown D. 13 Anderson
Brown H. 57 Richmond
Brown Solomon, 47 Clark
Bulger J. Mrs. 138 Purchase
Bunton A. F. Mrs. 20 Chardon
Burgess S. G. 39 Harrison avenue
Burrill L. 14 Lexington, E. B.
Cameron John, 104 Portland
Carr Alfred, 1 Hancock
Carruth R. 32 Albany

Boarding Houses — continued.

Chase Harriet, 665 Harrison avenue
Clark John, 9 South
Clark M. E. 178 W. Springfield
Cluner George Mrs. 93 Portland
Coffin A. Mrs. 58 Andover
Coffin James, 53 Leverett
Colburn H. 44 Cambridge
Cole Wm. Mrs. 9 Ashburton place
Colson W. A. Mrs. 37 Chester Park
Cook John H. 9 and 10 Crescent pl.
Cormier J. H. 384½ Hanover
Cummings C. B. Mrs. 6 Allston
Cunningham M. A. Mrs. 331 Hanover
Daggett M. 5 Harrison avenue
Daley Hannah Mrs. 68 Kingston
Danforth J. C. 62 Andover
Davidson C. 85 Border. E. B.
Davis Joseph, 830 Hanover
Dearborn L. 16 Ashland place
Deichart John J. 10 Essex
Dodge Samuel, 180 Broad
Doe Emma Mrs. 147 Cambridge
Dolan C. 368 Hanover
Dorgan M. E. Mrs. 14 Moon
Eaton Robert A. 16 Beach
Eccleston Thos. W. 91 Purchase
Evans J. E. 19 Eastern avenue
Farwell F. P. Mrs. 4 Montgomery pl.
Finnigan L. 37 Lowell
Fletcher S. A. 29 Meridian, E. B.
Fletcher S. A. Mrs. 3 Cambridge
Flynn Mary Mrs. 163 Summer
Frank William, 5 Fayette court
French A. 66 Leverett
French George T. 82 Portland
Gallagher James W. Mrs. 17 Pitts
Gleason John W. 55 Indiana place
Goodmanson Daniel B. Mrs. 268 Commercial
Griffin E. H. 331 Hanover
Halden Frank T. 18 Essex
Halpin John, 82 Portland
Hancock Hannah J. Mrs. 11 Crescent place
Hardy M. D. 14 Oliver place
Harris William A. Mrs. 111 Harrison avenue
Hawes Caroline A. 30 Leverett
Havey John Mrs. 471 Hanover
Hickey C. Mrs. 26 Minot
Hickie John, 14 Portland
Horton Myrick C. 1085 Wash.
Hughes Susan E. 60 Pleasant
Hussey James, 15 Montgomery pl.
Jackson G. A. 21 Battery
Jackson G. H. 17 Stillman
Jarvis William, 124 Purchase
Johnston Harriet, 76 to 80 Green
Kaler N. J. 26 Sumner, E. B.
Karcher F. 2 Ward
King James Mrs. 52 Prince
Kreglenski M. M. 3 Crescent place
Kyle Rosanna, 5 Province court

Lang J. L. 4 Lincoln
Lang Richard, 36 Boylston
Laninger F. 145 Dover
Leeds M. S. Mrs. 44 Harrison ave.
Lewis C. J. 451 Hanover
Lewis John, 18 Clark
Little Lucy, 1324 Tremont
Logan B. 2 Garden-court street
Lowe George, 28 Lancaster
Lyons M. A. 1333 Tremont
Mack E. J. Mrs. 7 and 9 Gouch
Marble Hannah B. 1597 Wash.
Martin J. 3 Lewis
Mattheson M. 13 Fleet
May Pamelia, 7 Allston
McAvoy Arthur, 42 Portland
McBride Hugh, 54 Cross
McCormick Raphael, 21 Albany
McCoy John, 336½ Commercial
McDonald John, 872 Hanover
Mears Susan A. 35 Pitts
Mereen E. J. 82 Sumner, E. B.
Miles L. 20 Kneeland
Mitchell Theodore, 28 Somerset
Molay Michael. 29 Albany
Monard L. 366 Hanover
Moore Henry A. 1679 Washington
Moynihan Ann Mrs. 13 Columbia
Mulloy John, rear 12 Gouch
Munday John, 846 Albany
Murray L. 75 Harrison avenue
Nicholson William, 388 Hanover
Nolan T. 277 Hanover
Noether A. 22 La Grange
Ogier M. Mrs. 148 Shawmut avenue
Olsen G. 89 Richmond
Otis William R. 5 Allston place
Packard Maria G. 2050 Wash.
Patten Anna A. Mrs. 21 Green
Phillips A. G. 21 North Russell
Pierce John S. 155 Court
Pierce S. S. Mrs. 148 Court
Pollard Isaac, 80 South Russell
Porter L. A. Mrs. 13 Essex
Pratt C. D. 63 and 65 Bedford
Preston R. M. Mrs. 13 Tyler
Prince L. A. Mrs. 116 Harrison ave.
Rand Thos. Mrs. 13 Montgomery pl.
Ray Catharine, 136 Purchase
Read C. T. 54 Chambers
Reinbold Frederick J., Dearborn, near Dudley
Ridley A. Mrs. 2033 Washington
Roberts D. S. Mrs. 12 Essex
Robertson Andrew, 228 North
Rodriquez Ralph, 422 Hanover
Ross Philip, 2 Winter place
Rogers Susan Mrs. 7 Crescent place
Russell H. 20 La Grange
Russell M. E. Mrs. 607 Fifth
Russell M. A. Mrs. 84 Friend
Ryan H. 276 Commercial
Sailors' Home, 99 Purchase
Sargent Julia, 18 Ashland place

Schwerer J. M. 21 Boylston square
Scruton Stephen, 15 Morton place
Sears Mary A. Mrs. 98 Pleasant
Seiferth F. H. G. 112 Pleasant
Severson W. 406 Commercial
Shaw E. jr. 147 Court
Skowhegan House, Mrs. Hill, 7 Pine
Smith Elizabeth M. Mrs. 5 Emerald
Snow L. G. 1618 Washington
Spear J. M. Mrs. 8 Newland (for children)
Spokesfield H. C. 1689 Washington
Stearns M. Mrs. 22 Bowdoin
Steele Henry, 30 Fleet
Steinkrauss Charles L. 100 Portland
Stone S. O. 4 Province court
Taylor Wm. 260 North
Towne C. F. 7 Rochester
Trask Hiram, 1171 Washington
Tulley Catharine, 1326 Tremont
Umbehend J. 24 Camden
Walsh William, 67 Lowell
Ward P. 27 Salem
Weaver M. 423 Commercial
Webster C. W. 175 Court
Weeber Caroline Mrs. 4 Mason
Wells Thomas M. 124 Harrison ave.
Wenige Herman, 5 Fayette court
Whalen Daniel, 12 North square
Whelan J. F. Mrs. 51 Tileston
White Nellie Mrs. 86 Portland
White J. Mrs. 2 Marginal
White Sarah A. Mrs. 12 & 22 Bulfinch
White Wm. F. 2 and 4 Bowdoin
Whiting L. Henry, 5 Lincoln
Wightman C. D. Mrs. r. 255 Hanover
Williams A. 336 North
Wilson John, 346 North
Woods J. 88 Portland
Young J. A. 379 Meridian, E. B.
Young William, 71 Chambers

Boats and Boat Builders.
Clinkard Henry R. 421 Commercial
Clinkard J. G. 421 Commercial
Cragin & Sheldon, 184 Broad
Davis Hiram A., Carleton's whf. E. B.
Horgan Thomas, Kelly's dock, E. B.
Howes & Pierce, 115 Sumner, E. B.
Leonard John S. 46 Long wharf
Macomber C. D. P., corner Sixth
Nash W. H. & Son, Harris wharf, 182 Broad
Norcross Wm. T. 297 Commercial
Pierce Brothers, Sixth, near P
Vallely Thomas, 95 Sumner, E. B.
Winsor & Bradlee, 13 Com'l wharf

Boiler Makers.
Allen & Endicott. 5 Liberty square
ATLANTIC WORKS, Chelsea, cor. Marion, E. B., office 114 State (see page 709) [mont
Campbell, Whittier, & Co. 1176 Tre-
Chubbuck S. E. & Son, 971 Tremont

Clogston T. S. & Co. 80 & 82 Sudbury
Hinkley & Williams' Works, 552 Harrison avenue
HODGE E. & CO. Liverpool, near Central square, E. B. (marine and stationary. see page 697)
Lally John, First, corner Granite
Loring Harrison, City Point
MAYNARD JAS. A., New, corner Maverick, E. B., (marine and stationary, see page 699) [North
McMurtrie Horace & Co. 83 and 85
OSBORN LOUIS, Marginal, opp. Cunard wharf, E. B. (see page 702)
SNOW WM. H. 14 Lewis, E. B. (marine and stationary)
Whiteley E. 59 Charlestown (Green House)

Bolt Makers.
HAWES & HERSEY, Second cor. E. (see page 693)

Bolting Cloths.
HOLMES & BLANCHARD, 9 & 11 Haverhill (see page 816)

Bolts, Nuts, and Washers.
MAY & CO. 1 Broad (see inside back cover)

Bonnet and Hat Bleachers.
Baker Nelson, 179 Washington
Claflin W. H. 166 Washington
Cutler James, jr. 22 Hanover
Fisher W. M. 10 Elm
King D. J. 429 Washington
Morse E. 1806 Washington
Morse E. jr. 1806 Washington
Pool Brothers, 16 Hanover
Storer & Co. 519 Washington
Taft S. 251 Washington
Thomas J. & Co. 19 Province
Thompson L. 544 Washington
Ware Frank T. rear 191 Washington

Bonnet Frame Manufacturers.
Adrienne Julio & Co. 586½ Wash.
Birch & Henderson, 19 Milk
Hodges F. F. 199 Washington
MORGAN C. & CO. 22 Winter
SCHUSTER LOLA MADAME, 19 Essex
Sheplie DeL. & Co. 156 Washington

Book Binder Manufacturers.
Covert & Co. 15 School

Bookbinders.
Abbott S. K. & Co. 13 Washington
Adams Benj. & Son, 27 Cornhill
Adams & White, 3 Washington
Bradley Benj. & Co. 57 Washington
Bradley Ira & Co 29 Washington
Brady Philip H. 149 Tremont
Carter George P. & Co. 76 Sudbury
Clark Orus, 11 Morton place

Bookbinders — continued.

Coleman George, 20 Water
COLMAN GEO. & CO. 116 Wash.
(see page 825)　[Sudbury
Fleming Edwin & Son, 70 and 82
Foster H. T. 103 Court
Goldsmith Seth, 11 Bromfield
Gorham Andrew, 130 State
Guardenier John, 90 Washington
Hersey Charles, 179 Washington
Humphrey B. F. 114 State
Le Cain W. H. 62 Congress
McAdams Hugh, 91 Washington
Merrick C. L. 27 Cornhill
Moore Alex. & Co. 21 Franklin
Noyes D. A. & Co. 34 Cornhill
Rand O. J. 79 Milk
Ripley Jos. W. 21 Cornhill
Roberts J. G. & Co. 24 Water
Russ William H. 15 Water
Sanborn & Fields, 30 Hanover
Seidensticker J. 55 Water
Terry Henry G. 62 Sudbury
Tyler Charles E. 73 Cornhill
Ulman William, 38 Summer
Woodward E. P. & Co. 19 Lindall

Bookbinders' Machinery.

Dean & Co. 11 Shoe and Leather
HOE R. & CO. 41 Foundry

Bookbinders' Stock and Tools.

Gane H. A. & Son, 50 Cornhill
Marshall, Son, & Haynes, 47 Cornhill

Book Lettering and Embossing.

Chase Wm. P. 49 Washington

Book Pager.

HATHAWAY ALFRED, 116
Washington (see page 827)

Booksellers and Publishers.

(*See also Periodicals.*)

Adams, Sampson, & Co. see Sampson,
Davenport, & Co.
Adams & Co. 25 Bromfield
Allen J. H. 203 Washington
Am. S. S. Union, 419 Washington
Am. Tract Society, 164 Tremont
Am. Unitarian Asso. 26 Chauncy
Backup John, 109 Dudley
Bartlett N. J. 62 and 64 Cornhill
Bennett B. F. & Co. 116 State
Bowles Leonard C. 26 Chauncy
Bradley Ira & Co. 20 Washington
Brady P. H. 149 Tremont
Brewer & Tileston, 131 Washington
Briggs Oliver L. & Co. 573 Wash.
Briggs & Co. 25 Kilby
Brooks D. B. & Bros. 55 Washington
Brown F. G. 3 Tremont row, room 8
Brown George B. & Co. 94 State
Brown H. A. & Co. 3 School

Burnham T. O. H. P. 68 School
Butler Brothers, 46 School
Campbell James, 18 Tremont
Carter H. H. & T. W. 25 Bromfield
CLAPP DAVID & SON, 334 Wash.
(see page 663)
CLAPP OTIS, 3 Beacon (homœopathic, see page 686)
Colesworthy Charles J. 57 Court
Colesworthy D. C. 66 Cornhill
Cong. S. S. & Pub. So. 13 Cornhill
COOLIDGE GEO. 3 Milk
Cottrell G. W. 36 Cornhill
Crocker & Brewster, 51 Washington
Crosby William, 117 Washington
Curran R. H. & Co. 48 Winter
Davis Robert S. & Co. 45 Wash.
Dennet Wm. H. 221 Washington
DeVries, Ibarra, & Co. 145 Tremont
(foreign)
Dockham & Co. 96 Washington
Donahoe Patrick, 19 Franklin
Dudley & Greenough, 8 Congress sq.
Dutton E. P. & Co. 135 Washington
EARLE JAMES H. 96 Washington
(see page 827)
Elliott, Thomes, & Talbot, 63 Congress
Ellsworth Oliver, 73 Cornhill
Fields, Osgood, & Co. 124 Tremont
Foltz J. Frank, 39 Maverick sq.
Fuller H. B. 14 Bromfield
Gill Edwin H. 233 Broadway
Gleason F. 40 Summer
Goss W. L. & Co. 68 Cornhill
Goss W. S. & Co. 37½ Cornhill
Gould & Lincoln, 59 Washington
Graves A. F. 20 Cornhill
Graves & Leavitt, agts. 19 Tremont r.
Hall Thomas, 19 Bromfield
Hall & Goss, 36 Old State House
Halliday W. H. & Co. 58 Cornhill
HAMMETT J. L. 37 and 39 Brattle
Hawks & Co. 26 Washington
Hill Wm. H. jr. & Co. 32 Cornhill
Hodges S. W. 14 Bromfield
Hoyt Henry, 9 Cornhill
Johnson, Frye, & Co. 22 Bromfield
Lee & Shepard, 149 Wash.
Littell & Gay, 30 Bromfield
Little, Brown, & Co. 110 Wash.
London Printing and Publishing Co.
C. F. Ware, agent, 121 Court
Loring A. K. 319 Wash.
Lothrop D. & Co. 38 Cornhill
Lovering Albert W. 233 Wash.
MAGEE JAS. P. agent, 5 Cornhill
Mason Brothers, 154 Tremont
Mass. Bible Depository, 15 Cornhill
McAdams W. 18 Water
Mendum J. P. 84 Wash.
Merrill R. I. 11 Morton place
METHODIST BOOK DEPOSITORY, 5 Cornhill
Moore A. & Co. 21 Franklin

National Art Association. 48 Winter
N. E. Branch Am. Tract Society, 104 Washington
N. E. NEWS CO. 41 Court
NICHOLS & HALL, 43 Wash. (see page 804)
Nichols & Noyes, 117 Wash.
Piper W. H. & Co. 133 Wash.
Pratt Brothers. 37 Cornhill
Remick B. J. 515 Washington
Roberts Brothers, 143 Wash.
Russell B. B. 55 Cornhill
SAMPSON, DAVENPORT, & CO. 47 Congress, publish the Boston Directory, New England Directory, New-York State Directory, Massachusetts Register and Directory ; also Directories for Albany, Troy, Providence, Charlestown, Lynn, Newburyport, Salem, Fall River, Manchester, Taunton, Lawrence, Lowell, and Gloucester. Directories for other parts of the United States, and foreign countries, for sale.
SARGENT M. H. 13 Cornhill
Scriptural Tract Repository, 19 Lindall [field
SEVER, FRANCIS, & CO. 21 Bromfield
SHAW & SANDFORD, 22 School (see page 808)
Shorey John L. 13 Washington
Soldiers & Sailors Pub. Co. 75 Court
SPENCER W. V. 203 Wash. (see page 670)
Sprague C. F. & Co. 32 Brattle
Stuart Alexander. 1838 Washington
Symonds, Chase, & Co. 11 Traveller building
Taggard & Thompson, 29 Cornhill
Tuethorn F. B. 21 Eliot (German)
TEUTHORN JULIUS, 518 Washington (German)
Tewksbury W. P. 482 Wash.
Tilton & Co. 161 Wash.
Tucker Gilman H. (agt. for C. Scribner & Co., N.Y.), 135 Wash.
Universalist Pub. House, 37 Cornhill
Urbino S. R. 14 Bromfield (foreign)
Usher James M. 21 and 27 Cornhill
Virgin Geo. A. (second hand) 21 Water
Virtue & Yorston, 50 Bromfield
Walker Samuel & Co. 3 Tremont row
Walker Thomas O. 3 West
White Wm. & Co. 158 Washington
Whittemore J. M. & Co. 114 Wash.
Wiggin & Lunt. 221 Washington
WILDE, BOWLER, & CO. 1 Cornhill
Williams A. & Co. 106 Washington
Williams N. M. 1203 Wash. (Cath.)
Winkley & Boyd, 662 Washington
Woolworth, Ainsworth, & Co. 117 Washington
Young Henry A. & Co. 24 Cornhill

Boot, Shoe, and Leather Dealers. (Wholesale.)

(See also Hides and Leather.)

Alden J. H. 122 Pearl
Alden T. R. & Co. 106 Sudbury
Allen & Soule, 84 Pearl
Anderson & Reynolds, 75 Pearl
Andrews & Co. 52 Elm
Avery E. 95 Pearl
Bachelor J. 119 Pearl
Bailey E. C. 72 Pearl
Ball H. A. 75 Pearl
Batchelder M. T. & Co. 52 Pearl
Batchelder W. S. 57 Hanover
Batcheller E. & A. H. & Co. 65 Pearl
Bates E. 57 Hanover
Bath John, 92 Federal
Battles W. J. & Co. 117 Pearl
Belcher A. & G. W. 94 Pearl
Belcher Luther & Son, 96 Pearl
Bent R. S. 9 Pearl
Berry, Field, & Co. 95 Pearl
Blake S. 38 Pearl
Blanchard D. H. 48 Hanover
Blanchard Ira, 4 Pearl
Blanchard L. 70 Pearl
Blanchard W. & C. 151 Pearl
Blanchard & French, 66 High
Boardman N. H. 44 Hanover
Bodenbrown Wm. & Co. 25 Milk
Bowker L. H. & Co. 93 Pearl
Bowser W. L. & Co. 60 and 62 Pearl
Boyd Joseph & Brigham, 75 Pearl
Boyd, Corey, & Co. 27 Pearl
Boyd Samuel & Co. 27 Pearl
Bradley J. W. 73 Pearl
Bragg Fowler 57 Hanover [Beach
Bray & Stewart, 29 Pearl and 65
BRETT GEORGE. 48 Hanover
Brigham F. & Co. 110 Pearl
Brigham J. W. 123 Pearl
Brooks & Lincoln, 140 Pearl
Brown Jonathan, jr. 44 Hanover
Brown & Goodwin, 137 Pearl
Bryant S. 1 Pearl
Buckman J. C. 145 Pearl
Burrage & Reed, 133 Pearl
Calley B. F. 48 Hanover
Calley J. B. & Son, 48 Hanover
Campbell B. F. & Co. 79 Pearl
Canterbury N. D. 30 Pearl
Chase, Merritt, & Blanchard, 20 Pearl
Chessman N. & Co. 76 Pearl
Claflin A. & Co. 90 Pearl
Claflin, Allen, & Co. 84 Pearl
Claflin, Coburn, & Co. 83 Pearl
Claflin Wm. & Co. 83 Pearl
Claflin & Thayer, 90 Pearl
Clapp A. W. & Co. 20 Federal
Clapp George B. 91 Pearl
Clapp Joseph, 73 Pearl
Clapp & Billings, 91 Pearl
Clark E. M. & Co. 40 Pearl

Boots, Shoes, &c. — continued.
Clark & Warren, 70 Federal
Clement. Colburn. & Co. 125 Pearl
Coburn A. & Co. 83 Pearl
Cochrane & Thayer, 81 Pearl
Coggin G. A. 48 Hanover
Cole. Wood. & Co. 15 Pearl
Conant A. P. & Co, 60 & 62 Pearl
Converse Franklin, 73 Pearl
Corning, Putnam, & Co. 54 Pearl
Cowing & Hatch, 45 & 47 Pearl
Cox C. & M. 42 Pearl
Crain, Heidenreich, & Seaverns, 53 & 55 Pearl
Cressy, Brackett, & Co. 32 Pearl
Crooks & Co. 83 Pearl
Cross D. K. & Co. 84 Pearl
Cummings D. 44 Hanover
Currier D. C. & Co. 81 Pearl
Currier J. C. & Co. 96 Pearl
Curtis Abner, 51 Pearl
Curtis Joshua. jr. 107 Pearl
Curtis T. & Co. 62 Milk
Daggett H. L. & Co. 101 & 103 Pearl
Damon Henry, 20 Milk
Damon, Thomas. & Lewis, 57 Hanover
Dane Francis & Co. 90 Milk
Dane J. F., Grinnell & Co. 69 Pearl
Davis C. C. 74 Pearl
Davis, Hovey, & Co. 28 Pearl
Dike Geo. W. 40 Pearl
Dike Lyman, 72 Pearl
Dill C. H. 2d, 97 Pearl
DIMICK J. C 28 Pearl
Dizer M. C. & Co. 75 Pearl
Doggett, Bassett, & Hills, 79 Pearl
Dore Benjamin, 59 Hanover
Downing Wm. 80 Pearl
Dunbar. Hobart, & Co. 105 Pearl
Dunham C. A. 72 Pearl
Durgin J. & Son, 70 Pearl
Durgin Samuel, 48 Hanover
Dyer William. 48 Hanover
Einstein Z.. Bros., & Co. 70 Pearl
Ellis C. D. 98 Pearl
Emerson R. W. 80 and 82 Pearl
Emerson & Barrett, 75 Pearl
Emerson & Co. 60 and 62 Pearl
Emerson's Thos. Sons, 51 Pearl
Emmons Nelson, 29 Pearl
Fairbanks Drury & Co. 81 Kilby
Farren W. D. 60 Pearl
Farwell C. C. 48 Hanover
Faxon B. E. & Co. 72 Pearl
Fay & Stone, 94 Pearl
Field, Thayer, & Whitcomb, 33 Pearl
Fisher Henry K 76 Pearl
Fitch Charles H. & Co. 72 Pearl
Fogg, Houghton. & Coolidge, 64 Pearl
Forbush C. W. & Co. 54 Pearl
Forness E. 57 Hanover
Foss John F. & Co. 58 Blackstone
Foster Daniel, 2 l, 1 Pearl St. House
Foster & Perkins, 48 Hanover

Frye C. L. 29 Pearl
Gage T. K. 131 Pearl
Gilmore A. A. & Co. 60 Pearl
Gilmore C. & Son. 80 and 82 Pearl
Gilmore Sanford, 33 Pearl
Godfrey C. B. & Co. 84 Pearl
Gorham J. L. & Co. 88 Pearl
Gould Charles H. 59 Hanover
Gould J. M. 107 Pearl
Hall & Blasland. 75 Pearl
HAPGOOD & CO. 56 Congress
Harris J. & Sons, 80 and 82 Pearl
Hartt J. & Co. 114 Pearl
Harvey A. B. & Co. 76 Pearl
Harwood D. & Co. 17 Pearl
Hatch J. W. 48 Hanover
Hayden. Guardenier, & Co. 88 Milk
Hayes C. E. & S. C. 72 Pearl
Hecht Bros. & Co. 44 Hanover
Henderson D. S. & Co. 90 Milk
Henry John J. 35 Pearl
Henry & Daniels. 76 Pearl
Herrick Charles & Co. 44 Hanover
Hersey S. Q. 44 Hanover
Hersey T. W. & L. P. 2 Pearl St. Ho.
Hill F. S. & Co. 118 Pearl
Hill John & Co. 86 Pearl
Hill & Rowe, 71 Pearl
Hitchcock John & David W. 66 Pearl
Hitchings O. M. 72 Pearl
Holbrook A. & Co. 37 Pearl
Holbrook, Hobart, & Porter, 72 Pearl
Holmes, Crandell, & Co. 25 Federal
Holton Frederick & Co 9 Pearl
Hook Aaron. 49 Federal
Hopkins W. H. 52 Milk
Hosmer & Winch Brothers, 47 Federal
Hosum & Davis, 48 Hanover
Houghton & Ames, 60 Pearl
Houghton & Bailey. 95 Pearl
Howard Daniel, 75 Pearl
Howe T. J. & Co. 40 Pearl
Howe & Dwight, 78 Milk
Hoyt & Tasker, 48 Hanover
Hoyt & Wheeler. 29 Pearl
Hunt A. N. & Co. 75 Pearl
Hunt David, 9 Pearl (rubber)
Hunt, Semonin, & Co. 122 Pearl
Hunt & Russell, 7 Federal
Hyde, Hutchinson. & Co. 74½ Milk
Ireson J. & Sons, 3 Pearl
Jackson, Richards. & Co. 125 Fed'l
Jaquith & Wales, 97 Pearl
Jefts & Smith, 76 Pearl
Johnson C. E. & Co. (brogans), 84 Pearl
Johnson Geo. 84 Pearl
Johnson, Wood, & Co. 87 Pearl
Jones Frederick & Co. 102 Pearl
Jones L. S. & Co. 87 Pearl
Jones Nahum & Co. 104 Pearl
Keith A. & A. B. & Co. 119 Pearl
Keith C. E. 100 Pearl
Keith M. L. 3 Pearl

Kimball Aaron, 34 Pearl
Kimball John & Son, 62 Sudbury
Kimball J. B. & Co. 107 Pearl
King J. B. & Co. 48 Hanover
Kingman E. & E. 5 Pearl
Kingsbury Brothers, 19 Federal
Kinsley Bradford, 44 Hanover
Knowlton C. E. 70 Pearl
Knowlton D. C. 70 Pearl
Lancaster Chas. B. 127 Pearl
Lane Jenkins & Sons, 61 Pearl
Lee Bros. 105 Pearl
Leeds Geo. J. 71 High
Leland Alden, 54 Pearl
Learnard W. H. 10 Marshall
Lester J. H. 121 Pearl
Lewis O. J. & Co. 95 Pearl.
Lindsley & Gibbs, 9 Federal
Litchman & Bartlett, 48 Hanover
Littlefield E. W. & G. W. W. 59
  Hanover
Littlefield F. H. 48 Hanover
Loring & Reynolds, 110 Pearl
Loring & Searl, 78 Pearl
Lynch John A. 48 Hanover
Mallard & Butler, 36 Pearl
Manny J. T., Goodwin & Co. 81 Pearl
MANSFIELD G. A. & CO. 36
  Faneuil Hall square (see page 704)
Mansfield & Pierce, 5 Pearl
Martin & Bryant, 13 Pearl
Mawhinney H. H. & Co. 5 Pearl
Mayhew A. C. & Co. 84 Pearl
McKey & Tirrell, 2 Pearl St. House
Melendy, Dexter, & Co. 59 & 61 Congress
Merriam F. P. & Co. 89 Pearl
Merrick W. W. 8 Pearl
Morton N. & Co. 47 Hanover
Mudge E. & A. & Co. 39 Pearl
Mullen, Phillips, & Co. 18 Pearl
Nash, French, & Co. 40 Pearl
Nash J. L. 87 Pearl
Nash S. W. & E. 40 Pearl
Newhall H. & Co. 39 Pearl
Newton & Hartt, 114 Pearl
Newell T. S. 48 Hanover
Nichols, Winn, & Co. 71 Kilby
Nute Lewis W. 55 Pearl
Oliver S. jr. & Co. 97 Pearl
Orne & Merritt, 57 Hanover
Otis George H. 95 Pearl
Page E. B. 53 N. Market
Page, Peel, & Moran. 107 Pearl
Parker Chas. F. & Co. 106 Pearl
Parker David & Co. 50 Pearl
Parker S. E. 122 Pearl
Parker & Wales, 48 Hanover
Parsons C S & Sons, 55 Pearl
Pebbles & Woodman, 45 Pearl
Pecker G 116 Pearl
Perry J & Co. 2 Pearl Street House
Perry W. G. 76 Pearl
Pettee S. G. 117 Pearl

Phillips E. P. & Co. 46 Pearl
Phipps Wm. H. & Co. 93 Pearl
Pike J. D. & Co. 72 Pearl
Poland Benj. 44 Hanover
Poland B. F. 44 Hanover
Pomeroy R. M. & Co. 65 Pearl
Pope Ira P. 59 Hanover
Porter F. E. & Co. 126 Pearl
Potter S. & W. N. 13 Pearl
Potter, White, & Bayley, 57 Pearl
Prentiss Henry, 48 Hanover
Prentiss T. M. 100 Pearl
Preston & Blake, 48 Hanover
Proctor John 2d, 48 Hanover
Putnam J. H. & Wheeler, 93 Pearl
Putnam W. E. & Co. 92 Pearl
Raddin, McGibbons, & Co. 37 Pearl
Raddin T. 37 Pearl
Rawson D. G. & Co. 98 Pearl
Reed I. 48 Hanover
Reed Samuel, jr. 51 Pearl
Reynolds H. W. 48 Hanover
Reynolds & Crane, 110 Pearl
Rhodes T. M. 54 Pearl
Rice & Hutchins, 95 Pearl
Richards A. S. & Co. 92 Pearl
Richardson, Knight, & Peabody, 5
  Pearl
Rising, Thompson, & Co. 96 Pearl
Roberts George E. 122 Pearl
Roberts H. L. & Co. 116 Pearl
Roberts, McNish, & Co. 122 Pearl
Robinson J. W. 29 Pearl
Robinson & Longley, 110 Pearl
Ruddock Thomas S 89 Pearl
Salem Boot and Shoe Co. 48 Hanover
Sanders M. M. & Co. 71 Pearl
Saunders Brother & Co. 124 Pearl
Sawyer J. M. 48 Hanover
Shaw Jefferson, 48 Hanover
Shaw S. & Son. 48 Hanover
Shaw T. V. & W. A. 34 Pearl
Shaw & Child. 21 Pearl
Slocomb J. W. & Son. 123 Pearl
Smith Adoniram, 48 Hanover
Smith Charles. 48 Hanover
Southwick C. T. 48 Hanover
Sparhawk S. 59 Hanover
Sprague & Walker, 25 Pearl
Steele John. 92 Pearl
Stern Louis & Bros. 116 Pearl
Stetson M. S. & Co. 38 Pearl
Stevens Wm. jr. 48 Hanover
Stickney C. & Co. 70 Pearl
Stone Albert. 24 Pearl
Stowe, Bills. & Co. 68 Pearl
Strong A. & Co. 97 Pearl
Studley & Turner, 48 Hanover
Swan J. & Co. 86 Pearl
Swanberg C. G. T 48 Hanover
Sweetser Samuel & Co. 48 Hanover
Swett L. G. & Co. 90 Milk
Taft & Coverly. 1 Pearl St. House
Tapley Amos P. & Co. 84 Milk

Boots, Shoes, &c. — continued.

Temple H. 57 Hanover
Tenney & Aldrich, 31 Pearl
Tenney & Co. 1 Pearl Street House
Thayer E. L. 93 Pearl
Thayer F. A. & H. B. 48 Hanover
Thayer & Brother, 14 Pearl
Thing & Norris, 13 Federal
Thurston & Hayes. 95 Pearl
Tirrell A. & Co. 151 Pearl
Torrey A. & Co. 123 Pearl
Torrey C. A. 69 Pearl
Torrey C. W. 48 Hanover
Torrey James & Co. 107 Pearl
Travis E. P. 48 Hanover
Trescott E. 56 Milk
Tucker E. & Son, 13 Pearl
Tucker James & Co. 113 Pearl
Tucker Nathaniel & Co. 52 Pearl
Tucker Wales & Co: 49 Pearl
Tyer Henry G. 86 Pearl
Underwood Sons & Fisher, 28 Pearl
Varney William H. 122 Pearl
Vaughan G. D. 118 Pearl
Vaughan Joseph & Co. 117 Pearl
Vella Joseph F. 48 Hanover
Vining & Randall, 44 Hanover
Vittum J. W. 48 Hanover
Walcott E. & Co. 75 Pearl
Walcott John B. 44 Hanover
Wales, Emmons, & Co, (rubber) 173 Pearl
Walker J. & Co. 53 Pearl
Walker J. H. & Co. 48 Hanover
Walker S. & Co. 79 Water & 9 Bath
Wallace W. & J. 41 and 43 Pearl
Walton & Wilson, 48 Hanover
Ward & Spalding, 28 Pearl
Ware P. jr. & Co. 169 Pearl
Warren C. C. 79 Pearl
Warren John D. & Co. 69 Pearl
Webb T. H. & Bro. 93 Pearl
Webster Charles W. 84 Pearl
Weels Moses, 48 Hanover
Weld, Bryant, & Co. 25 Pearl
Wentworth G. B. 15 Pearl
Wheeler James H. & Co. 89 Pearl
Wheeler W. H. 90 Milk
Whicher J. D. & Co. 139 Pearl
Whitcomb & Paine, 37 Hanover
White Brothers, 48 Hanover
White T. & E. 24 Pearl
White & Sprague, 48 Hanover
Whitman, Whitcomb, & Co. 118 Pearl
Whitney C. B. 110 Pearl
Whitney D. 96 High
Whitney E. 116 Pearl
Willis W. P. & Co. 54 Pearl
Wood E. F. & Co. 87 Pearl
Woodman B. P. & Co. 97 Pearl
Wooldredge J. & Co. 77 Pearl
Wright J. E. & Co. 1 Pearl Street House

Boots and Shoes. *(Retail.)*

Allen Wm. H. 91 Cambridge
Allen Wm. W. & Son, 32 Faneuil Hall square
Allen & Bent, 83 Meridian
Almy George W. 52 North Market
Appleton Chas. T. P. 139 Court
Baker Joseph, 140 Broadway
Barlow Edward, Lincoln, c. Essex
Barnard J. W. & Co. 171 Hanover
Bath David & Co. 539 Washington
Bath John, 537 Washington
Bell Theo. H. 153 Washington
Benari Joseph, 413 Washington
Billings E. G. 159 Court
Bodwell N. 3 Beacon
Bornstein M. I. 648 Washington
Boynton H. E. & Co. 101 Hanover
Burgess E. M. 27 Pleasant
Carleton Robert H. 269 Hanover
Carleton & Robinson, 165 Court
Carty J. D. & T. M. 1813 Wash.
COAN W. A. 31 Maverick square (custom, see page 691)
Colburn H. 40 Merchants row
Coburn J. H. 1427 Washington
Colby H. C. 61 Leverett
Collier Wm. 61 West Dedham
Collins M. L. 15 Central square, E. B.
Cone Arthur W. 839 Washington
Connell R. 140 Shawmut avenue
Connolly & Power, 10 School
Cotter Timothy. 157 Federal
Cronan W. J. 354 Hanover
Cummiskey Michael, 58 Merrimac
Currier John B. 1848 Washington
Curtis T. & Co. 62 Milk
Daly Thomas, 53 Fleet
Deule James, 156 Merrimac
Dennely & Co. 145 Cambridge
Doane & Rider, 204 Hanover
Doic Charles E. 272 Hanover
Donegan W. 105 North
Duffy P. J. 236 Hanover
Dyer Edward. 251 Hanover
Dyer J. & P. 269 Broadway
Edney Geo. P. 140 Cambridge
Eldridge & Co. 47 & 48 N. Market
Feyhl C. F. A. 1900 Washington
Fenner Chas. E. 1895 Washington
Fenner Wm. B. 1583 Washington
Field E. H. 3 Maverick sq. E. B.
Fillebrown William, 134 Court
Fisk A. J. 222 Commercial
Folsom F. 1837 Washington
Folsom & Co. 27 Essex
Fox J. 727 Washington
Fuller R. A. & Son, 116 Merrimac
Goldthwait D. E. 196 Hanover
Goodwin Reuban, 21 Meridian, E. B.
Graham M. H. 501 Washington
Griffin F. A. 53 Meridian
Harley Wm. 227 Hanover
Harris Joseph. 819 Washington

Hathaway F. E. Merch. row c. North
Heileman Wm. 125 Cambridge
Hill & Co. 106 Merrimac
Hobart Josiah, 347 Washington
Holton Lemuel, 79 Court
Holton Samuel S. 108 Hanover
Hook Aaron, 254 Hanover
Jesser Joseph, 894 Washington
Kemp Robert H. 794 Washington
Kempton Brothers, 136 Court
Knott R. & T. 37 Bromfield (ladies')
Lahin Daniel, 1146 Washington
Lamkin Guy, 10 Tremont row
Lamkin W. C. 1278 Tremont
Learnard W. H. 10 Marshall
Lee Thomas, 305 Broadway
Lincoln P. 8 Broadway
Litchfield Bros. 1829 Washington
Mahoney W. 1684 Washington
Malone M. 676 Washington
Mann H. M. 77 Hanover
MANSFIELD GEORGE A. & CO.
  36 Faneuil Hall sq. (see page 704)
Mansfield John & Son, 14 Tremont
  row
McAnulty Daniel, 63 Lincoln
McCarthy Patrick, 6 Chelsea, E. B.
McDermott James, 92 Merrimac
McElwain Thad. 1616 Washington
McLean Archibald, 84 Merrimac
McLean & Co. Broadway, corner D.
  and 110 Court
Mitchell Alex. 6 Kneeland
Mitchell John, 1059 Washington
Mitchell John A. 669 Washington
Monroe David B. 4 Maverick Sq.
Monroe Geo. R. 5 Meridian, E. B.
Morrow & Halloran, 11 Essex
Morse B. S. 261 Hanover
Moseley T. E. & Co. 293 Washington
Moulton D. 189 Broadway
Newcomb T. C. & C. F. 166 Hanover
Newell J. A. 28 & 30 Essex
Nickerson S. L. 339 Hanover
Nordenshiebl F. & Co. 757 Wash.
Oliver H. B. & Co. 22 Essex
Page Eben B. 53 North Market
Palmer E. B. & Co. 25 Guild row
Parker Wm. J. 326 Hanover
Pearson Geo. & Co. 142 Hanover
Pearson W. H. & Co. 311 Washington
Pevear C. B. 1883 Washington
Pevear James M. 340 Washington
Pevear Warren E. 1289 Washington
Peyser Joseph, 43 Cambridge
Pray John F. & Sons. 107 Washington
Regan John B. 20 Essex
Rogers John H. 1 & 3 Tremont
Rowe B. S. & Co. 10 Essex
Russell L. 205 Broadway
Schayer Bros. 43 Congress
Sherburne C. H. 20 Tremont (rubber
  repairing)
Sinnot Wm. 5 Fleet

Southworth Chas. 217 Hanover
Staniford Edwin, 298 Broadway
Stetson & Dunn, 158 Hanover
Stratton Chas. 85 Leverett
Thayer E. H. 56 Cambridge
Topham J. 151 Broadway
Travers ———, 48 Hanover
Tucker Eli, 3 Winthrop block, E. B.
Turner Chas. A. 364 Hanover
Turner Geo. E. 16 Essex
Tuttle H. H. & Co. 259 & 261 Wash.
Tyler Asa, 20 Tremont
Van Kuran Cornelius, 689 Wash.
Vining D. W. (boots), 20 Tremont
Wallace J. 18 Essex
Waterman & Co. 148 Hanover
Waters Abram, 77 Meridian
Weber Andrew, 1343 Tremont
Whittemore S. D. & Co. 212 Wash.
Whittredge & Bro. 807 Washington
Whittredge T. J. 228 Federal
Wiswell D. W. 222 Hanover
Wood Alex. 134 Hanover
Woodward Jas. & Son, 1283 Tremont
Wyman A. C. 120 Cambridge
Young J. B. 1386 Tremont

Boot and Shoe Blacking.

HAUTHAWAY C. L. & SONS, 56
  Fulton, and 1 & 3 Ferry (see page
  826)

Boot and Shoe Buckles.

AMERICAN STANDARD CO. 1
  Pearl (see page 810)
WOODMAN & CO. 1 Pearl (see
  page 810)

Boot and Shoe Dies and Cutters.

AMERICAN STANDARD CO. 1
  Pearl (see page 810)
DRAPER & WOODBURY, 86
  High (see page 672)
TAYLOR S. K. & CO. 145 South
  (see page 804)
WOODMAN & CO. 1 Pearl (see
  page 810)

Boot and Shoe Findings.

Alley J. B. & Co. 38 Pearl
Armstrong Wm. & Co. 39 Merchant's
  Row
Bacheller J. C. 85 Milk
Baxter L. 7 Union
Boston Shoe Stud and Button Co.
  Sumner Shaw, pres. 2 Pearl
Boyce W. S. & Sons, 6 Pearl St. Ho.
Breed Geo. F. 19 Pearl
Brooks & Young, 58 Pearl
Brown Gerry, 53 Congress
BUTLER E. K. 63 Pearl (see page
  668)
BUTTERFIELD WILLIAM. 26
  Pearl (see page 694)

Boot and Shoe Findings — continued.

Clapp Benj. & Co. 89 Pearl
COLBURN ISAAC & CO. 72 Milk (see page 657)
Cragin, Page, & Co. 104 Milk
Daggett H. L. & Co. 103 Pearl
Dwyer & Barrett, 27 High
Faxon, Elms, & Co. 27 Pearl
Foss John F. & Co. 58 Blackstone
Gilson & Walker, 117 North (lasts)
Goers Louis & Co. (inner soles and heels), 282 Commercial
Greenman Wm. G. & Co. 61 Hanover
HAUTHAWAY C. L. & SONS, 56 Fulton, and 1 & 3 Ferry (see page 826)
Haven & Wright, 26 Pearl
Henshaw Brothers & Co. 83 Milk
Holbrook H. J. 105 Milk
How Brothers & Co. 11 Pearl
Kitfield Henry & Son, 7 Bath
McLaughlin H. & Co. 107 Fulton (inner soles)
Merriam & Norton (machine shoe-binding), 12 Pearl
Nichols & Farnsworth, 63 Hanover
Noble & Brooks, 110 Milk
Pelton, Snell, & Co. 99 Milk
Phinney & Phillips, 85 Kilby
Pope Albert A. & Co. 47 Pearl
Rand H. C. & Co. 45 Merchant's row
Sears Isaac H. 7 Pearl
Sears & Warner, 61 Pearl
Seibert F. F. 5 Eliot
Simonds W. A. & Co. 687½ Washington, (cement)
Sweetland E. M. 2 Pearl St. House
Sweetser, Skilton, & Dole, 16 Pearl
Walker S. 682 Harrison ave. (webbings)
Weld, Bryant, & Co. 25 Pearl
Weld John, 506 Washington
Weymouth Adjustable Heel Co. office 93 Haverhill
Whall & Mansfield (linings), 101 Milk
Wilson & Merrill, 43 Pearl
Windram, McDonald, & Co. 71 Congress
WOODMAN & CO. 1 Pearl (see page 810)
Young C. H. 36 Pearl

Boot and Shoe Finishing.

Blaisdell C. 100 Pearl

Boot and Shoe Heel and Toe Irons.

COLBURN ISAAC & CO. 72 Milk (see page 657)
Crane A. O. 22 Beach (patent heels)
MANSFIELD GEORGE A. & CO. 36 Faneuil Hall Sq. (see p. 704)

Boot and Shoe Heelers.

Warner J. W. 2 Pearl St. House

Boot and Shoe Lacing Manufs.

Fletcher Manufacturing Co. S. G. Trippe, agent. 66 Kilby
Jenkins, Bro., & Co. 74 Water

Boot & Shoe Lasts & Trees.

AMERICAN STANDARD CO. 1 Pearl (see page 810)
Gilson & Walker, 117 North
WOODMAN & CO. 1 Pearl (see page 810)

Boot and Shoe Machines.

American Lasting and Pegging Machine Co. George H. Johnson, agt., 76 Sudbury
Arnold Edward, 53 Congress
Baldwin & Clark, 61 & 63 Haverhill
Blanchard & Lavers, 30 Pearl
Bray, Newell, & Co. 53 Haverhill
BUTTERFIELD WILLIAM, 26 Pearl (see page 694)
COLBURN ISAAC & CO. 72 Milk (see page 657)
DRAPER & WOODBURY, 86 High (cutters or dies, see page 672)
Hawkins L. D. 30 Pearl
Howe Jarvis, 30 Pearl
Keniston & Sawyer, 131 Congress
Noble & Brooks, 110 Milk
Robinson D. 2 Bath (McKay's heeling)
RYERSON E. & SON, Kemble, near Hampden (leather-splitting knives, see page 834)
Safford Joseph A. 61 & 63 Haverhill
STEVENS E. M. 13 Haverhill (see page 664)
VOGEL KASIMIR, 36 Chardon (button hole, see page 833)
Vrooman H. S. 46 Portland
Whittemore & Bean, 30 Pearl

Boot and Shoe Manufs. Goods.

BUTLER E. K. 68 Pearl (see page 668)
COLBURN ISAAC & CO. 72 Milk (see page 657)

Boot and Shoe Patterns.

AMERICAN STANDARD CO. Woodman & Co. factors, 1 Pearl (see page 810)
Hartford & Gallup, 30 Pearl
Henderson D. 40 Pearl
Silvester N. 36 Pearl
Whittemore E. W. 88 High
WOODMAN & CO. 1 Pearl (see page 810)

Boot and Shoe Styles.

AMERICAN STANDARD CO. 1 Pearl (see page 810)
WOODMAN & CO. 1 Pearl (see page 810)

Boot and Shoe Tips.
American Shoe Tip Co. 56 Pearl

Boot-Counter Makers.
CLATUR A. A. 132 Pearl
CUSHING E. J. 128 Pearl
Dunham E. R. 4 Blackstone
Harding T. rear 107 Fulton
Nichols O. & Co. 136 Pearl

Boot Crimper.
Boos Jacob, 15 Marshall

Boot Fitters.
Applequist I. F. 26½ Exchange
Farrow Wm. 150 Hanover
Kammler Bros. 18 Bedford
O'Brien M. 15 Marshall
West J. 106 Blackstone
West & Valois, 102 Union

Boot and Shoe Makers.
Abel Andrew, 315 Third
Acker Andrew, 333 Fourth
Adams Joseph K. 7 Pinckney
Adler J. 4 Bedford
Aglar N. H. 150 Fourth
Anderson H. M. 15 Hawley
Arnold Samuel V. 42 Elm
Ayers Geo. 1923 Washington
Bailey James, 112 Pleasant
Balcomb Wm. 127 West Brookline
Barker James, 139 Essex
Barry Geo. T. 14 Phillips
Barutio J. H. 1055 Tremont
Bates Asa, Broadway, near I
Bauer John N. 24 Carver
Bean John, 39 Merchants row
Beaty Wm. L. 369 Hanover
Becker E. 799 Washington
Bigelow Elisha, 121 Meridian
Blaney Daniel, 18 South Margin
Bodwell N. (ladies), 3 Beacon
Brasby Arthur, 5 Lincoln block
Broderick Jas., Havre, cor. Marion
Brown Benj. 82 Meridian, E.B.
Brown James B. 31 Maverick, E.B.
Brown Thomas, 38 Silver
Brown Thomas, 75 Purchase
Burchell Thomas, 13 Middlesex
Burke Robert, 50 Prince
Burke Wm. 170 Sumner, E.B.
Burns Wm. J. 76 Cross
Bush P. W. 610 Washington
Byrne Richard, 55 Warren
Cannon M. 163 Endicott
Cannon Peter, 89 Causeway
Cannovan Thomas, 89 Havre
Carlisle James, 14 Curve
Cavanagh C. J. 331 North
Chambers J. G. 109 Emerson
Clare Frederick. 24 Myrtle
Cleary Wm. 18 Newton place
Cliff Joseph, 175 Broad
COAN W. A. 31 Maverick sq. (custom, see page 691)

Coburn James F. jr. 174 Hanover
Commin Andrew, 24 Avery
Connell Richard, 140 Shawmut av.
Converse B. M. 215 Broadway
Cook Henry, 74 Friend
Cooper Charles C. 257 Meridian
Cosgrave James, 10 Prince
Cowan Thomas W. 201 Sumner
Coyle Michael, 218 Sumner
Cronin W. J. 354 Hanover
Deacy Timothy, 4 Stoddard
Dadman J. 132 Lincoln
Dailey James, 301 Broad
Daly Thomas, 53 Fleet
Deale James S. 156 Merrimac
Denny Daniel. 19 Lincoln
Desmond J. 446 Commercial
Devlin J., Bedford, cor. Kingston
Doherty Patrick, 120 Prince
Dolan John, 1442 Tremont
Dolan Michael, 1398 Tremont
Dolan Patrick, 25 Avery
Donnelly Dennis, 298 Federal
Donnelly Wm. 24 Grove
Dorcey James, 196 Federal
Dore Patrick, 55 Chambers
Dorr & Litcher, 35 Bromfield
Ecker Leopold, 74 Green
Eckert V. 15 Lincoln
Egan Nicholas, 1279 Tremont
Elliott Wm. R. 378 Chelsea, and Eutaw, cor. Brooks
Engel Peter, 7 Hotel Pelham
Evans Wm. 11 Monmouth
Fandel M. & T. 129 West Canton
Fenton Thomas, 81 C
Finn Cornelius, 100 Essex
Flanagan James, 98 Fourth
Flister F. L. 15 Morton place
Foley John, 24 Border
Foss John F. & Co. 58 Blackstone
Freeman Thomas, 52½ Charlestown
Friese H. 68 Yeoman
Friese Wm. 1142 Tremont
Gabel Henry, 10 Yeoman
Geary Owen, 403 Harrison avenue
Geib Jacob, 109 Eustis
Gill James, 141 Salem
Glenon Thomas, 16 Factory
Gorman Cornelius, 180 Merrimac
Gorman Peter, 1756 Washington
Goss A. J. 121 Chelsea
Green John, 6 Wash. sq. & 155 Broad
Griffin Thos. 52 Liverpool, E.B.
Gunning E. C. 97 Sudbury
Gurney Bennoni, 78 Brighton
Guthrie John, 464 Harrison ave.
Guttermuth Henry, 4 Bennet
Hagan C. W. 316 North
Haggerty Patrick, 80 Chapman
Haglan Charles, 233 North
Hall A. M. 2 Garden
Hamilton P. 35 Cross
Harper W. E. 216 Commercial

Boot and Shoe Makers — continued.

Hayden Arthur L. 20 Green
Hayden I. J. 39 Sudbury
Hayes Dennis, 451 Second
Hayes Wm. 137 Beach
Henry Wm. C. 130 Cabot
Hesz Andrew, 34 Hawley
Higgins Timothy, 52 Pitts
Hirsch Isadore, 2 Way
Hirsch Max, 30 LaGrange
Hirsh Moses, 58½ Warrenton
Hodgson M. 157 Eighth
Holderried Jacob, 81 Dorchester
Holman J. S. 198 Federal
Howe Edward, 463 Hanover
Hunter N. C. 8 North Russell
Hurley Jeremiah, 662 Federal
Hurley John, 257 Federal
Hurley M. 297 Federal
Hurst John, 188 D
Isenberg L. 68 Salem
Jenkins Wm. 3 Oak place
Jesser F. J. 804 Washington
Judge Bernard, 1398 Tremont
Kafer F. 1091 Tremont
Karcher C. 1148 Federal, W. V.
Karns M. 35 Harvard
Ketz Philip, 34 Northampton
Kinley H. 334 Commercial
Kingman James H. 121 Court
Kinlin Timothy, Elliot sq.
Kirchgesner M. 93 Carver
Knauber Frederic, 768 Tremont
Knott R. & T. 37 Bromfield (ladies)
Krebs A. 11 Friend
Kubasch H. 147 Harrison avenue
Lacount T. 66 Anderson
Lahm D. 1146 Washington
Lally & Hyde, 99 Union
Lambrecht Joseph, 68 Portland
Lanagan James, 50 South
Laule M. 474 Tremont
Leavitt I. 1166 Federal
Leear Henry, 1678 Washington
Leeds Henry, 313 Meridian
Leussler J. E. 134 Blackstone
Levy S. 112 Leverett
Lincoln Peter, 8 Broadway
Lonergan P. 16 Camden
Lynch Charles, 124 and 156 North
Lyons P. H. 9 Oneida
Lyons Wm. 13 Wharf
Mayhew Chas. 37 Faneuil Hall sq.
Mahoney Wm. 1684 Washington
Malone R. 18 Bedford
Manery James, 61 Emerson
Marchant John F. 150 Meridian, E.B.
Marquand Henry, 84 Princeton
Marshall John, 431 Commercial
Mathews W. H. 10½ Chapman
Matt Xavier, 24 Groton
Mayer Jacob, 27 Russell court
McBride John, 25 Travers
McBride John, jr. 19 Cross

McCarthy John, 200 Broad
McCarthy Patrick, 25 Prince
McCawley J. 27 North sq.
McDonnell M. 413 Harrison ave.
McGonagle Hugh, 69 Albany
McGrann Thomas, Everett, near Cottage, E.B.
McGullin Peter, 502 Commercial
McIntire Michael, 5 Shaving
McKeever John, 420 Commercial
McLaughlin B. 610 Harrison ave.
McLaughlin John, 172 Purchase
McLaughlin J. 205 Endicott
McNally D. 105 Leverett
McNamara George, 70 Prince
McNaught Alex. 2 Gooch
McNeil James, 59 Hampden
Meade Michael, 32 School
Mellen F. 337 Broadway
Merrill Wm. A. 787 Tremont
Miller Robert A. 34 Congress
Moore E. G. 91 Eliot
Morgan Michael, 458 Hanover
Murphy Jeremiah, 334 Federal
Murray David, 1777 Washington
Myers Frederick, 90 Salem
Newcomb C. J. 37 Salem
Newcomb Winslow M. 26½ Exchange
Newman Wm. 800 Shawmut ave.
Noble George C. 5 Winthrop, E.B.
Noether Jacob, 87 Pleasant
Noonan T. 29 High   [E.B.
Norwood Christopher, 295 Sumner,
Nowlen J. P. 24 E
O'Brien Felix, 144 Everett
O'Brien John, 64 Harrison avenue
O'Brien John, 5 Howard
Ochs F. J. 99 West Concord
Ochs George, Broadway, near I
O'Connor Daniel, 207 Congress
Odenwald G. A., Chestnut, bel. Chas.
O'Donnell Michael, 223 Endicott
Oelschleger A. 16 Brattle
Oechsle Frederick, r. 1301 Tremont
O'Keefe Edward, 377 Federal
O'Keefe John, 120 Purchase
Oliver W. S. 8 Lexington, E. B.
O'Mahony Dennis, 446 Second
O'Mara James, 49 Kingston
O'Neill Francis, 6 Lewis
O'Sullivan Daniel L. 390 Commercial
O'Sullivan M. 121 Second
Patterson T. 740 Federal
Peyser Joseph, 34 Cambridge
Pitman John, 11 Franklin avenue
Pitman Thomas P. 28 Brattle
Porter David, 61 Cross
Proctor J. 83 Sudbury
Proctor William 19 Water
Remmes Bernard, 13 East Castle
Ritter John, 50 Lenox
Robbins I. H. 7 Spring lane
Roche P. C. 27 Province
Rooney Peter, 22 Pleasant

Roth M. 648 Parker
Ruby J. G. 101 Canton
Rudolph Frederick, 24 Boylston
Rupert Geo. L. 80½ Joy
Salcicher Adam, 211 Ruggles
Schafer John, 1040 Tremont
Scannell Daniel. r. 240 Hanover
Schayer Vincence, 13 Water
Schlegel Charles. F. 199 Cambridge
Scholpp Louis, 99 West Concord
Schwartz Simon, 5 Yeoman
Seiferth Mary, 112 Pleasant
Shay J. R. 1880 Washington
Sigins J. A. 279 Meridian
Silva J. 24 Moon
Silva J. F. 23 Fleet
Small Frederick, 33 Bromfield
Smith A. 313 Sumner
Smith J. 788 Federal
Smith M. 8 City Hall avenue
Smith T. S. 11 Kingston
Snapp P. J. 67 Kingston
Snow E. S. 710 Washington
Sprague C. H. 132 Leverett
Stecher William, 33 Water
Stengel P. 350 Broadway
Stephenson C. 106 Water
Stetson H., Orleans, cor. Webster
Sullivan John, Bennington, c. Chelsea
Sutter Jos. Dorchester, near Eighth
Sutton B. 76 Leverett
Swain S. 527 Seventh
Tackaberry J. H. 49 Causeway
Thayer A. L. 28 Friend
Thompson R. C. 10 Blossom
Todtman Jacob, 35 Fleet
Tirrell Charles, 9 Beach
Townsend G. W. 168 Friend
Trow E. 95 Leverett
Waitt Jacob. 81 Cambridge
Walker R. R. 1 Lindall alley
Ward C. 131 Fourth
Watkins Henry, 37 Water
Weale S. M. 112 Sumner, E. B.
Weiler Joseph, 1164 Tremont
Weinsiin Robert. 1384 Tremont
Wendell Henry, 15 Marshall
Weimer John 11 Prentiss
West & Valois, 102 Union
Whalen P. 86 Richmond
Whelton D. 46 Causeway
Wilfert John N. 113 Eliot
Williams P. 75 Second
Wilson William, 28¼ School
Woods Patrick, 119 Hampden
Woodworth E. F. & Co. 2 City Hall
    avenue
Young B. 102 Dover
Yunker G. 321 E
Ziegler Peter, 38 Charles

Bowling Saloons.

Colburn William W. 375 Wash.
Dyer Charles H. Friend, c. Market

Heywood & Ramsay. 2 Chapman pl.
Leadworth Thomas H. 66 Portland
Murphy J. C. 1020 Washington

Box Manufacturers.
(See also Paper Boxes.)

Cushman H. W. 11 Shoe and Leather
Drisco P. C., Sweet, near Reed
Hall & Fuller, 101 Merrimac
McNUTT JOHN J. Novelty Wood
    Works, Wareham, cor. Malden (see
    page 818)
Smith Wm. P. 1220 Federal

Box Wood and Mahogany.
ROBERTS BROTHERS, 6 Frank-
    lin ave. (for engraving, see p. 806)

Bracket and Book Rack Manufacturers.
COSTELLO EDWARD J. 80 North
    (see page 805)
Gray C. H. & Co. 19 Harvard place
Leonard, Clark, & Co. 20 Beach
Rodgers & Burleigh, 11 Bowker
Strout C. W. & Co. 14 Charlestown

Brass Finishers.
CLARK WM. P. 9 Province court,
    (see page 704)
Curley & Lennon, 19 Spring lane
Foster & Roby, 178 & 180 Com'l
Grundy Joseph, 20 Hawley
LANGLEY, CARBEE, & CO. Bor-
    der, near Central square, E. B. (see
    page 696)
Loehr Henry, 1½ Pitts
MEAD & ADDY, 4 Chickering pl.
    (see page 795)
Murray, Burns & Fitzgerald, 6
    Charlestown
Puffer A. D. 48 Portland
Redfern W. C. 69 Haverhill
Scrannage, Bate & Co. 75 Portland
Stone Henry N. 132 Commercial
Strater Herman & Sons, 78 Sudbury
Summers & Hunt, 45 Water
UPHAM THOS. A. 17 Harvard pl.
    (see page 825)
Vannevar E. B. & Co. 58 Fulton
Vose W. S. 86 Utica

Brass Founders.
CODY EDWARD, 33 Hawkins (see
    page 694)
Connor Hugh, 135 Sumner, E. B.
CROWLEY J., furnishes all kinds of
    brass, copper, composition, lead,
    zinc, tin, German silver, and white
    metal castings, at the lowest cash
    prices, at the corner of Albany and
    Curve Streets. where all orders
    will be promptly attended to. Bab-
    bitt Metal made to order. All
    metals bought and sold.
Curley & Lennon. 19 Spring lane

Brass Founders — continued.

Foster & Roby, 178 & 180 Com'l
Grundy J. 20 Hawley
Hall John & Sons, 25 S. Margin
HILL ROWLAND, Carlton's wharf,
　E. B. (see page 725)
Hooper H. N. & Co. 66 Causeway
Ingols J. P. & Co. 113 A
Litchfield H. T., Sumner
Puffer A. D. 48 Portland
Robinson G. W. & Co. 85 Richmond
Scrannage, Bate & Co. 75 Portland
Stone H. N. 132 Commercial
Vannevar E. B. & Co. 58 Felton
Willis & Curley, Albany, cor. North-
　ampton

Brass Manufacturers.

Ansonia Brass & Battery Co. J. Pratt
　agent, 2 Pearl Street House
Benedict & Burnham Manuf. Co. 68
　Federal
BROWN & BROTHERS, MAY &
　CO. agents, 1 Broad, (see inside
　back cover)

Bread.

Boston Wheat & Bread Co. 1480
　Washington

Brewers.

Boston Beer Co. D. H. Tully, treas.
　19 Central wharf
Burkhardt Gottleib F., Parker
Coburn, Lang. & Co. 100 Worcester
Comstock, Gove, & Co. 27 Merrimac
　and 30 Canal
Cook Isaac & Co. 25 Central
East Boston Brewery, Conrad Decher,
　Marginal, near Simpson's dock
FAIRBANKS & BEARD, Howard
　Athenæum (see page 803)
Jutzi Christian, 37 Station
Kenney Niel, 1207 Tremont
Kent J. Oscar, 23 Haverhill
McCormick James, Ward
New England Beer Co. 278 Comml.
Norfolk Brewery, A Richardson, Ce-
　dar, near Pynchon
Pfaff Brothers, 1 Franklin
Pfaff H. & J., Pynchon. near Wash.
Richardson A. 2 Congress square
Roessle John, 401 Washington
ROGERS'S BREWERY, B. L.
　THOMPSON, Ruggles place (see
　page 830)　　　　　　　[Heath
RUETER & ALLEY, Parker, c. New
Souther Henry & Co., 528 Second
Suffolk Brewery, 43 and 45 Utica
Taylor J.'s Sons, 117 Commercial
Tremont Brewery Co., Castle, corner
　Suffolk
VAN NOSTRAND W. T., Eighth,
　cor. G (brewers' supplies, see page
　673)

Bricks.

Babbitt W. W. 22 State
Bay State Brick Co. 17 Pemberton
　square
Bly & Bryant, 22 State
Cargill Joseph, 14 Commercial
Claflin & Wellington, 20 Doane and
　240 Federal
Cofran Samuel M. 22 State
Cook, Jordan, & Morse, 1191 Wash.
Cox & Davenport, 81 Wash. room 24
Dana James, 14 Old State House
Davis & Chaddock (fire), 125 Water
Edmester W. 22 State
Ferson C. H. 22 State
Fisk Benjamin, 22 State
Fisk M. (face) 22 State
Hill S. S. 22 State
Holt Chauncy, 22 State
Hoxie T. W. & Co. 43 Long wharf
Hubbell Peter, 17 Pemberton sq.
Jacques William, 22 State
Littlefield Samuel, 22 State
MASS. BRICK CO. GEORGE W.
　COPELAND, treas. 12 Pemberton
　square
McAbee N. S. & Co. 52 First
McClure John, 22 State
New England Brick Co. 5 Lindall.
　D. B. Rich. general agent
Sands J. L. 22 State
Smith J. W. 22 State
Taylor S. P. & Co. 16 State
Tucker L. B. 22 State
Tufts Brick Manufg. Co. 16 Pember-
　ton square
Washburn David, 22 State

Brick Machines.

BLAKE GEO. F. & CO. 51 Chardon
　(see page 686)

Bridge and Wharf Builders.

Bixby & Cole, 22 State
Kenrick W. A. 22 State
Mayo W. G. 22 State
Solid Lever Bridge Co. 46 Congress

Britannia Ware Manuf.

Dover Stamping Co. 88 North
Dunham R. 63 Congress
Forbes & Fletcher, 54 Kilby and 55
　Sudbury
MOREY & SMITH, 49 Haverhill
　(see page 812)
Smith Thomas, jr. 65 Union

Brokers.

Cotton and Print Cloths.

Bacon Francis E. 54 State

Currency.

Kendrick & Elwell, 31 State

Custom House.

Stone & Downer, 28 State

Drug.

Carroll H. H. 127 State
Cushing, Porter, & Cades, 161 Milk
French C. E. 11 Central wharf
Mansfield Ira K. 34 India
Swain Paul M. 47 Broad

Flour.

French G. W. 14 Commercial
Greely Joseph, 188 State . .
Hammond Benjamin, 188 State

Hemp.

Sawyer Leonard, 19 India

Insurance.

Bonney Pelham, 27 State
Coffin G. W. 4 Merchants Exchange
Cowles, Brown, & Co. 39 State
Foster N. jr. & F. B. Cotton 103 State
Foster & Cole, 27 State
Goodwin Daniel, 81 Wash. room 34
Haven & Penhallow, 102 State
Hayes H. Y. 18 State
Holden, Allen, & Lord, 128 State
Holman E. 32 Congress
Holman R. W. 32 Congress
Lewis & Folger, 51 Commercial
Loring & Clark, 15 Kilby
Meigs & Co. 10 State
PEARSON F. W. 4 State
Reed T. F. 27 State
SEARS W. B. 40 State, room 2 (see front colored page)
Thompson & Reed, 48 State

Leather.

Claasen E. J. 127 Congress
Gore H. W. & Co. 153 Congress

Merchandise.

Alden & Edmands, 23 India
Anderson W. L. & A. 70 Friend
Austin Wm. R. 104 State
Bancher John F. (spirits), 125 Broad
Banks D. S. (tea), 16 Central
Barnes L. B. & Son (tea and tobacco), 15 India
Bates W. A. & Co. (hides and skins), 62 Kilby
Beede & Co. 7 Tremont row
Blanchard J. Henry (chemicals), 23 Central
Bogert & Lowell, 50 School
Briggs Jas. W. 11 Custom House st.
Briggs Frederick M. 4 Liberty sq.
Buckingham S. H. 26 Central
Cabot, Bowles, & Co. 31 Kilby
Canterbury & Co. 104 State
Carroll H. H. 127 State
Clark Charles, 70 Broad.
Clark Geo. A. 159 Milk
Cleaves N. P. (oil and spirits), 3 Central wharf
Crosby Josiah, 134 Commercial

Cunningham & Pratt, 6 Channing
Currier & Fowle, 239 State
Cushing, Porter, & Cades, 161 Milk
Darling C. B. (spirits). 129 State
Dickerman & Gregory, 6 Com'l.
Dickson John. 150 State
D'Wolf J. L. 24 Central
Ehrlich S. 502 Washington
Elliot H. F. 163 Blackstone
Emmons J. A. & Co. 19 India (sugar)
Fearing Lincoln, 164 State
Fiske Edward, 68 Congress
Fiske Josiah (spirits), 164 State.
Forbes E. A. 88 Friend
Freeman & Co. 50 Kilby (cotton)
French Chas. E. (drugs), 11 Central wharf
Frothingham & Backus, 230 State
Fuller & Co. 24 Central
Glover J. B. & Co. 30 Central
Greely J. L. 75 Court
Griffiths Barry, 200 Friend
Hall A. B. & Co. 144 State
Hall George T. & Co. 15 India
Hall, Williams, & Co. 6 Channing
Hartshorne J. F. & Son (teas), 19 Broad
Hayward Geo. P. & Co. 12 India (tea)
Hovey E. W. 3 Central wharf
Howard Benjamin's Sons, 26 Kilby
Irish Isaac. 198 State
Jewett D. E. 23 Central
Keeney B. J. 11 Central wharf
Lee & Co. 7 Tremont row
LEONARD JAMES A. 138 Broad (oils)
McElroy J. W. 24 Broad (tobacco)
McLellan Joseph W. 16 Central
McLellan Wm. H. 13 India
Morey Wm. C. & Co. (hides), 153 Congress
Morse S. Henry (spirit). 34 India
Neufeld Leopold (tobacco), 7 Central wharf
Penniman A. P. 24 Central
Perkins & Blanchard, 23 Central
Pickering Mark. 163 Blackstone
Prescott Harrison, 19 Kilby
Putnam E. & Co. 48 State (general)
Randall David & Co. 29 India
Reynolds E. B. 44 Kilby
Sawyer L. (hemp), 19 India
Scott Robert (cotton), 75 Kilby
Shattuck L. A. & Co. 5 Broad (metal.)
Silsbee & Fowler, 26 Broad
Southwick P. R. & Co. (hides), 210 Congress
Starbuck Walter, 110 Water
Stone J. W. (provisions). 15 Com'l.
Sumner Fred. A. 9 Merchants row
Swain Paul M. (drug), 47 Broad
Townsend T. B. & Co. 80 Court
Townsend & Co. 36 Central

420

MASSACHUSETTS DIRECTORY.

Brokers — continued.

Tuckerman G. & Co. 25 Kilby
Wainwright & Amory, 40 State
Warner B. F. (spirit), 5 Central whf.
Waters Wm. C. & Co. (tobacco), 13 India
Weld Aaron D. Sons, 193 State
Wetherill, Morey, & Co. 208 Congress (goat skins)
WHITEHOUSE C. H. 693 Washington (see page 828)
Williams R. & Son, 19 Central
Wing & Morse, 12 India
Winslow E. D. & Son, 12 India (teas)
Woodworth A. S. & Co. (teas), 38 Central

Metal.

Cutler E. P. 15 Kilby

Mortgage.

Apthorp, Hazard, & Co. 21 City Ex.
Coffin & Gray, 31 State, room 1
Dearborn S. O. 32 Congress
EVANS B. S. 31 State, rooms 14 & 15
FRENCH JAMES, 80 Washington (mortgages bought and sold)
LEICESTER GEO. V. 206 Tremont
Merrill J. 32 Congress
Richardson, C. E. 9 State
Thompson N. A. & Co. 10 & 11 Old State House
Warren A. B. 11 Merchants Ex.
WHITEHOUSE C. H. 693 Washington (see page 828)
Williams S. G. 13 Exchange

Note.

Ager Solomon, 93 Pearl
Alderman, Stewart, & Co. 4 Congress
Alexander J. L. 34 Congress
Brown B. & Sons, 56 State
Cowles, Brown, & Co. 39 State
Eastman J. S. 33 School
Eaton Benjamin A. 15 Congress
Fogg Bros. & Bates, 20 Congress
Lawrence George H. 50 Congress
Lawrence W. F. 50 Congress
Lothrop Cyms S. 4 Congress square
March J. S. & Co. 70 Milk
Miller George, 31 Exchange
Morse E. Rollins, 27 State
Nash & Cushing, 2 Bath
PAPENDIEK, CHASE, & CO. 62 Congress
Richardson C. E. 9 State.
Smith Edward M. & Co. 84 Water
Spofford Samuel W. 17 State
Taylor & Co. 20 State

Patent.

BENT, GOODNOW, & CO. 84 Washington

Pawn.

Alexander J. 18 Salem

Anderson W. L. & A. 70 Friend
Bonnie Louis, 173 Hanover
Bowman Henry, 6 Salem
Bugbee Gilbert D. 288 Hanover
Carbrey James, 209 Congress
Cassidy P. F. 120 Kneeland
Collat H. 103 Cambridge
Crombie Wm. G. 10 Brattle square
Cummings J. R. 108 Portland
Ehrlich N. 24 Salem
Ehrlich S. 502 Washington
Emery C. H. & Co. 15 Endicott
Feleh H. E. 4 Salem
Frank Isaac, 157 Cambridge
Heinemann B. 20 Brattle square
Henchey John, 146 Kneeland
Knopf Lewis, 49 Merrimac
Lamb L. 133 Dover
Langley Wm. 309 Hanover
Levengston J. 83 Cambridge
Levy A. 78 Cambridge
Lissner B. L. 24 Merrimac
Lissner Ephraim, 36 Merrimac
Lissner H. 20 Salem
Lovinski A. 12 Brattle square
Lowe James, 20 Merrimac
Myers A. 30 Merrimac
Nelson H. M. 118 Essex
Page M. S., Salem, cor. Endicott
Perkins A. P. 32 Merrimac
Phillips G. 40 Merrimac
Rich Seth, 11 Salem
Richards J. L. 7 Brattle square
Rogers Charles M. & Co. 23 Salem
Savage T. L. 5 Endicott
Warshauer Jacob, 624 Washington
Warshauer S. 343 Hanover

Real Estate.

Apthorp, Hazard, & Co. 21 City Ex.
Baker K. W. 9 Merchants row
Banfield J. S. 81 Washington
Barnes F. G. & Appleton, 18 City Ex.
Barnes & Carter, 5 Scollay's building
Bearse A. 22 State
Boswell J. O. 31 Exchange
Browne & Co. 23 Congress
Carr T. M. 31 Exchange
Carruthers W. F. 117 Hanover
Chamberline J. S. & Co. 66 State
Chapin J. L. & Co. 36 Washington
Clapp J. B. & Son, 63 Court
Cleland Wm. 84 Washington
Coffin & Gray, 31 State, room 1
Conley C. C. 23 Congress
Coverly S. 31 Exchange
Curtis J. F. 22 Congress
Davis Joseph C. & Co. 15 School
Davis J. & Co. 80 State
Edmunds C. 32 Congress
Eldredge James T. 23 Congress
Elliott & Co. 42 & 43 Old State Ho.
Farrington H. 18 Old State House
Fiske O. W. 32 Congress

MASSACHUSETTS REGISTER AND DIRECTORY, Published by Sampson, Davenport, & Co. (formerly Adams, Sampson, & Co.), 47 Congress St., Boston.

Flanders O. H. 81 Washington
Forbes William W. 31 Exchange
Foster D. W. 61 State
FRENCH J. 80 Washington (rents and dividends collected)
Fuller Samuel D. 26½ Exchange
GLEASON L. W. & CO. 102 Washington (special attention given to the sale of farms and residences)
Graves & Leavitt, 19 Tremont (rm. 8)
Hart G. L. & Co. 32 Congress
Hawkes T. B. 28 State
Holbrook S. P. 8 Kilby
Jackson F. H. 40 State
Jackson S. S. 15 Congress
Jaques S. (appraiser), 6 Tremont
Jeffries J. jr. 17 City Exchange
Jones Wm. 13 Exchange
Kingsley Gardner P. 33 Devonshire
Kyle W. S. & T. 10 State
LEICESTER GEO. V. 206 Tremont
Loring & Abbott, 89 Court
Maynard J. W. 9 State
Meacham George A. 40 Old State Ho.
McIntire Charles, 9 State
Moulton H. W. 4 State
Niles C. E. & Coe, 15 Congress
Norcross & Pattee, 31 Exchange
Norris & Jones, 18 Exchange
Peterson C. A. 31 Exchange
Porter J. K. & Co. 5 Court
Power T. C. & Co. 15 School
Priest D. H. & Co. 3 Tremont row
Read J. Stacy, 13 Tremont row
Rhodes L. S. 32 Congress
Rice Samuel, 9 State
Richardson B. & Co. 31 Washington
Shattuck Isaac, 31 Exchange
Skilton John, 18 Exchange
Smith Charles L. 1451 Washington
Spooner S. 106 Blackstone
Stears E. 31 Exchange
Stockbridge W. R. 49 Washington
Taylor & Co. 20 State
Thayer W. D. 18 Old State House
Thompson N. A. & Co. 10 & 11 Old State House
TOMBS & JOHNSTON, 255 Broadway
Veazie J. A. 76 State
Wainwright I. P. 18 State
Wakefield E. H. 81 Washington
Walker & Co. 23 Court
Ward H. B. 2 Court square
Warren A. B. 11 Merchants Ex.
Whitaker & Moore, 13 Traveller building
White C. H., School, cor. Wash.
WHITEHOUSE C. H. 693 Washington (see page 828)
Whittemore B. F. 29 City Exchange
Williams G. F. 48 State
Wilson Thomas, 7 Scollay's building

Ship.

Baker Brothers, 73 Commercial
Baker Freeman, 119 Commercial
Benner E. & Co. 1 Commercial wharf
Binney C. J. F. 164 State
Blanchard, Pousland, & Co. 140 Commercial
Bridge, Lord, & Co. 181 State
Browne & Wilde, 128 State
Bruce Benjamin, 156 State
Clark Geo. P. & Co. 233 State
Conant E. S. 21 Commercial
Cook Wm. & Co. 14 Commercial
Emery J. S. & Co. 154 State
Fitz Philip & Co. 111 Commercial
Frisbie W. J. 152 State
Frothingham N. F. 230 State
Hannum James W. 3 Commercial
Haskell T. H. 150 State
Hunter, Ryder, & Crawley, 1 Commercial wharf
Kilham, Loud, & Co. 21 Commercial
Lewis & Folger, 51 Commercial
Linnell John N. 9 Merchants row
Lovell C., Commercial wharf
Page, Richardson, & Co. 70 State
Parsons & Reed, 73 Commercial
Patton & Ginn, 130 Commercial
Ray & Walter, 168 State
Sturges R. C. 9 Merchants row
Thayer & Lincoln, 13 Commercial
Thayer & Peabody, 134 State
Torrey E. E. & Co. 127 Commercial
Upton H. P. 3 Commercial
Weltch Samuel & Co. 129 State

Specie.

Burnett, Drake, & Co. 88 State
Child Lewis, 29 Merchants row
Gooding Geo. H. 16 State
Hammett J. 37 State
Mann & Rhodes, 31 State
Pycott & Bennett, 8 State
Stone & Downer, 28 State
Worster & Babsen, 7 State

Stock and Exchange.

Adams J. H. 16 State
Arnold Charles, 30 City Exchange
Attwood Gilbert & Co. 14 Mer. ex.
Baker Charles, 28 State
Ballou & Mifflin, 60 State
Blake Brothers & Co. 28 State
Bolles Matthews & Co. 90 State
Brewer James P. 31 State
Brodhead D. D. 7 Doane
Brown Benj. & Sons, 56 State
Burnett, Drake, & Co. 88 State
Chandler A. F. 6 Congress
Clark & Jones, 76 State
Comins L. B. 22 Congress
Cutter J. A. B. 21 Central
Dalton S. F. 40 State
Davis F. A. 2 Change avenue
Davis George P. 60 State

Brokers — continued.

Davis James W. 2 Change avenue
Day R. L. & Cobb, 31 Kilby
Doane Geo. A. 2 Change avenue
Dodd Wm. 3 Congress square
Dupee, Beck, & Sayles, 102 State
Durant W. C. 28 State, room 9
Dwight, Richardson, & Co. 28 State
Farley J. P. 15 State
Farley Robert, 2 Change avenue
Farrington Horace, 18 Old State H.
Fay Wilson W. & Co. 31 State
Fisk Wm C. 92 State
Fiske F. S. 40 State
Fiske Joseph N. 76 State
Fuller C. E. & Co. 2 State
Gilbert B. W. 18 State
Gilbert Samuel, 14 Merchants Ex.
GILL C. H. 4 Faneuil Hall square
Gilley John E. M. 5 Devonshire
Gorham Francis, 15 Congress
Grant Fred. 6 Phœnix building
Hall & Brewster, 27 State
Hammatt James, 37 State
Hastings J. P. 10 Traveller building
Hawkes T. B. 10 Exchange
Hayward C. L. 1 P. O. avenue
Head & Perkins, 32 City Exchange
Heath C.   }
Heath C. H. } 2 Change avenue
Heath F. A. 2 Change avenue
HENSHAW & BROTHER, 5 Merchants Exchange
Howe Jas. Murray & Co. 92 State
Hubbard Bros. & Co. 31 State
Iles Wm A. 24 Central
Johnston T. A. 2 Change avenue
Keith Wm. W. 23 City Exchange
Lamson A. D. 66 State
Lee, Danforth, & Co. 48 State
Lee, Higginson, & Co. 40 State
Lee Thomas J. & Hill, 60 State
Lincoln Chas. D. 7 Phœnix building
Long Geo. W. & Co. 4 Phœnix buil.
Lothrop C. S. 3 and 4 Congress sq.
Mandell M. J. 10 Exchange
Marston Wm. S. 2 Change avenue
Martin Joseph G. 10 State
May Wm. B. 31 State
McNeal J. D. 36 Washington
Mead Samuel O. 2 Change avenue
Morse E. Rollins. 27 State
Morse S. jr. 22 Congress sq.
Parker & Cobb. 8 Devonshire
Perkins T. Henry, 30 City Exchange
Peters & Parkinson, 24 Congress sq.
Pickering H. W. 48 State
Pickering J. 40 State
Pratt R. M. 7 Union building
Pycott & Bennett, 8 State
Putnam Charles A. 60 State
Soley J. J. 13 Exchange
Spencer A. W. 13 Congress
Spencer, Vila, & Co. 13 Congress

Stevens, Amory, & Co. 39 State
Stowell John B. jr. 7 Phœnix build'g
Studley S. G. 22 Congress sq.
Taylor & Co. 20 State
Tenney & Reed 22 Congress sq.
Thompson W. L. 22 Congress
Tyler W. C. 28 State
Wainwright & Amory, 40 State
Walley & Bates, 20 State
Wetherbee John, 11 Phœnix building
Wheelock J. B. 2 Change avenue
Wilder Geo. E. 13 Phœnix building
Williams S. G. 13 Exchange
Worster & Babson, 7 State

Bronze Iron Goods.

Winn John A. & Co. 23 Exchange

Bronze Powders.

DONALD W. C. & CO. 12 Spring lane (see see page 836)

Bronze Statuary.

BIGELOW, KENNARD, & CO. 331 Wash. and 10 West

Bronzer and Electro Gilder.

Whiteley Henry, rear 20 Bedford

Broom Corn.

Seaverns A. 120 Milk

Broom Manufacturers.

INSTITUTION FOR THE BLIND, 20 and 22 Bromfield (see p. 687)
Packard, Burrill, & Co. (rattan), 33 Exchange
Smith E. P. & C. E. 120 Milk
Wotton C. W. & Co. 92 Broad

Brush Manufacturers.

Burton, Fellows, & Co. 21 Exchange
Canning John F. & Co. 88 Sudbury
Doane H. S. & Co. 80 Water
EASTHAM, HARVEY, & MORRIS, 15 Union
McLaughlin Francis, 28 Exchange
Packard, Burrill, & Co. 33 Exchange
REED GEORGE T. 179 Wash.
Sheriff & Co 22 Exchange
THOMPSON D. Jr. 20½ Elm (varnish brushes, see page 825)
White D. & Son. 27 Exchange
Whiting J. L. 8 Blackstone
Worcester & Austin, 86 Chardon

Builder of Churches.

SYLVESTER L. G. 256 Meridian. E.B. (see page 805)

Building Materials.

Ham Jos., Northampton, c. Albany
SHEPARD H. S. & CHESTER, Swett, foot of Northampton, and 10 Devonshire (see page 825)

NEW-ENGLAND DIRECTORY, Published by Sampson, Davenport, & Co. (formerly Adams. Sampson, & Co.)' 47 Congress street, Boston.

Building Movers.

Bird John Q. 22 State
Blair, Proctor, & Skinner, 502 Harrison avenue
Cavanagh W. R. & W. P. E. near railroad, S.B. and 22 State
Drinan M. 512 Harrison avenue

Bungs and Taps.

VAN NOSTRAND WM, T. 118 Lincoln (see page 678)

Burning Brands.

JACOBS GEORGE, 151 Washington (see page 662)
BARNES WM. H. 74 Wash. (see page 688)
Penney F. L. 8 Dock sq.

Burning Fluid.

Hebard B. F. & Son, 149 Broad
HOWE & FRENCH, 69 Blackstone (see page 674)
Kimball W. H. & Co. 5 T wharf
Masury A. C. & Co. 28 India
Mears Bros. & Co. 121 Water
MILLS W. R. 46 India (see p. 681)
Noyes Person, 47 India
PORTER JOHN & CO. 101 Water (see page 672)

Burr Millstones.

HOLMES & BLANCHARD, 9 and 11 Haverhill (see page 816)

Butt Hinge Manufacturers.

LOTHROP GEO. B. & CO. 30 Exchange (see page 663)

Button Dealers.

ALLEN EZRA & SON, 295 Washington (see page 696)
Bartlett, Swadkins, & Miller, 105 Devonshire
Boone, Cannell, & Co. 72 Summer and 23 Otis
Gillis W. K & Co. 237 Wash.
Glazier, Marean, & Co. 81 Summer
GRISWOLD D. C. & CO. 164 Devonshire
Maflyn, Mullen, & Elms, 68 and 70 Summer, cor. Otis
Mason & Tucker, 160 Devonshire
Morse & Browne, 24 Milk
Sibley, Cumner, & Co. 16 Otis

Button Hole Machines.

American Button-Hole, Over-Seaming, and Sewing Machine Co., R. S. Marston, agent, 288 Wash.
VOGEL KASIMIR, 36 Chardon (see page 833)

Cabinet Beds.

BURR S. S. 49 Temple place (see page 677)

Cabinet Makers.

Aldrich W. L. & Co. 19 Hanover pl.
ARMSTRONG GEO. 4 Faneuil Hall sq. (repairing, see page 803)
BARDWELL & McELWAIN, Border, n. Central square, E. B. (see page 807)
Blake Christopher, 100 North
ROSSOM & BORSH, 68 Albany, (see page 830)
Braman, Shaw, & Co. 27 Sudbury
Briggs Seth, 16 Chapman place
Brownell B. C. 32 Sudbury
Cady Wm. A. 723 Washington
Canning Alex. B. 105 Brighton
Carr Joseph, 69½ Union
COSTELLO EDWARD J. 80 North (see page 805)
Debock & Co. 48 Albany
Dexter N. S., Border, n. Central sq.
Drummond & Prichard, 815 Wash.
Dunham I. P. 87 Causeway
Durant J. 39 Kingston
Ellis John A. & Co. 2 Studio building
Gifford J. A. 109 Court
HALEY, MORSE, & BOYDEN, 407 Washington
Haskell Augustus, 86 Utica
Haven H. P. 59 Cambridge
Heintz J. 1124 Tremont
Hixon E. & Co. 172 Washington
Holmes F. M. & Co. 188 Hanover
Howard J. H. 90 Utica
Ivers S. 144 Blackstone
JELINEK CHARLES, 383 Federal (see page 684)
Kornilweiz J. 4 Mall
LITTLEHALE, DRAKE, & WILLETT, 94½ Utica & 139 South
Mann John H. 167 F
MANSON & PETERSON, Border, cor. Decatur, E. B. (see page 700)
Morton Jas. C. 84 Chapman
Rinn & Co. 20 Studio Building
Scales James, 1170 Washington
Shackford Edwin, 1476 Wash.
Shute Augustus P. rear 97 Border
Soyard C. J. 392 Tremont
Stephens Charles H. L. 1752 Wash.
Strout C. W. & Co. 14 Charlestown
Taylor H. R. 1908 Washington
Thwaites Wm. G. 85 Hudson
Toussaint W. 526 Washington
Watts Edward, 23 Harvard
Weafer Richard, 109 Cambridge
Weeks M. T. C. 107 Eustis
Wetherbee J. W. & Co. 164 Portland
White & Co. 60 Albany
Woodbury, Gray, & Co. 51 Hanover

Cabinet Organs.

Boston Organ Co., Wash. cor. Avery
Smith S. D. & H. W., Tremont, opp. Waltham